THE FAMILY, LAW & SOCIETY

Sixth edition

Baroness Hale of Richmond DBE, FBA, MA (Cantab)

Lord of Appeal in Ordinary
Visiting Professor, King's College London
Chancellor, University of Bristol
Visitor, Girton College, Cambridge

Judge David Pearl MA, LLM, PhD (Cantab)

Circuit Judge
President, Care Standards Tribunal
Honorary Professor, University of East Anglia
Bencher of Gray's Inn
Life Fellow, Fitzwilliam College, Cambridge

Elizabeth Cooke MA (Oxon), LLM (Reading)

Solicitor
Professor of Law, University of Reading
Law Commissioner

Daniel Monk LLB (Warwick), LLM (London)

Solicitor
Senior Lecturer in Law, Birkbeck College, University of London

OXFORD
UNIVERSITY PRESS
Great Clarendon Street, Oxford OX2 6DP

Oxford University Press is a department of the University of Oxford.
It furthers the University's objective of excellence in research, scholarship,
and education by publishing worldwide in

Oxford New York

Auckland Cape Town Dar es Salaam Hong Kong Karachi
Kuala Lumpur Madrid Melbourne Mexico City Nairobi
New Delhi Shanghai Taipei Toronto

With offices in

Argentina Austria Brazil Chile Czech Republic France Greece
Guatemala Hungary Italy Japan Poland Portugal Singapore
South Korea Switzerland Thailand Turkey Ukraine Vietnam

Oxford is a registered trade mark of Oxford University Press
in the UK and in certain other countries

Published in the United States
by Oxford University Press Inc., New York

First published 2009

British Library Cataloguing in Publication Data
Data available

Library of Congress Cataloging in Publication Data
Data available

Typeset by Newgen Imaging Systems (P) Ltd., Chennai, India
Printed in Great Britain
on acid-free paper by
Ashford Colour Press, Gosport, Hampshire

ISBN 978-0-19-920424-3

1 3 5 7 9 10 8 6 4 2

PREFACE

This book has always been good fun to write and we hope that it is also good fun to read. The idea is to introduce students of family law to all sorts of material which it may not have occurred to them might be relevant to the study of the law (although of course we have some cases and statutes too). Family law is a subject in which it is not enough just to know the law; it needs to be set into its social and economic context, and this is changing all the time. People run their intimate relationships very differently these days even from how they ran them in 1983 when the first edition of this book was published. The law struggles to know whether it should try to keep up with what people actually do or whether it should try to keep them in check. So the attempts to modernise divorce law in the 1990s failed but the movement to recognise same sex relationships in the 2000s has succeeded. Students need to know about and reflect upon the policy debates which continue to rage.

When we first wrote this book, David Pearl and I were experienced University Law teachers. Since then, I have been both a Law Commissioner and a Judge, and David has also become a Judge. Between us, we have learned a good deal about how the law is made and even more about how it is put into practice in the family courts. But we know less and less about law students and what will suit them best. So we were delighted when Elizabeth Cooke joined us for the fourth edition in 1996. Since then she has taken the lion's share of the responsibility for preparing each new edition and deserves the lion's share of the credit for the finished product (the blame of course is equally shared). We congratulate her on her appointment as a Law Commissioner and hope that her experience of working on the book will be as helpful to her as was my experience of working on the first edition when I was appointed a Commissioner in 1984. For this edition we are also delighted to welcome Daniel Monk who has taken on some of the most intricate chapters in this revision.

Like many law books which have gone through several editions, this one had become rather too large, its typeface rather too small, and its pages rather too full. It has been very substantially revised, rearranged and reduced for this edition. Our new publishers have also given it a new look. We think that it is all a great improvement and we hope that others do so too.

We should like to thank Laura Edwards, Laura Graham and Corinna Ferguson for their invaluable help with our research and, of course, our ever-growing families for their patience and understanding. We have tried to be up-to-date to 14 December 2007 when the typescript was delivered to the publishers.

11 March 2008 Brenda Hale

ACKNOWLEDGEMENTS

Grateful acknowledgement is made to all the authors and publishers of copyright material which appears in this book, and in particular to the following for permission to reprint material from the sources indicated:

Extracts from unreported case reports, Law Commission Reports, Consultation papers and Home Office reports and statistics are Crown copyright material and are reproduced under Class Licence Number C2006010631 with the permission of the Controller of OPSI and the Queen's Printer. Extracts from House of Lords case reports are Parliamentary copyright and are reproduced by permission of the Controller of HMSO on behalf of Parliament.

Advice Services Alliance for cartoon and extract from *Living Together Agreement*, from www.advicenow.org.uk/livingtogher, a campaign run by Advicenow Project and funded by the Ministry of Justice.

Michael Anderson for extract from M Anderson (ed.): *Sociology of the Family* (Penguin, 1980).

British Association for Adoption and Fostering (BAAF) for extracts from D Howe and J Feast: *Adoption, Search and Reunion* (BAAF, 2003) previously published by The Children's Society in 2000.

Cambridge University Press and the authors for extracts from P Laslett and R Wall: *Household and Family in Past Time* (Cambridge, 1972); from *Social Policy & Society*: Sacha Roseneil: 'Why we should Care about Friends: An Argument for Queering the Care Imaginary in Social Policy', 3 (4) *Social Policy & Society* 409 (2004); and from *International Journal of Law in Context*: John Haskey and Jane Lewis: 'Living-apart-together in Britain: context and meaning', 2 (1) *I J Law in Context* 37 (2006). The first estimates of the numbers Living Apart Together, and profiles of their demographic characteristics, were published in J Haskey: 'Living arrangements in contemporary Britain: having a partner who usually lives elsewhere and Living Apart Together', *Population Trends* 122, 35 (2005).

The Children's Rights Alliance for England for extract from *Report to the UN* (2007).

The Council of Europe for extract from *Konrad and others v Germany* (2006) ECHR Application No 35504/03 to the European Court of Human Rights, published at www.echr.coe.int/ECHR. The official reports are published by Carl Heymanns Verlag KG, Luxemburger Str. 449, D-50939 Cologne, Germany.

Gillian Douglas, Cardiff Law School, for extract from G Douglas, J Pearce, and H Woodward: *A Failure of Trust: Resolving Property Disputes on Cohabitation Breakdown* (Cardiff Law School, 2007).

Equality and Human Rights Commission for illustration from *The Gender Agenda* (Equal Opportunities Commission, 2007), copyright © Equal Opportunities Commission 2007.

European Communities for graphs from *Population Statistics 2004*, Eurostat, copyright © European Communities 2004, www.epp.eurostat.ec.europa.eu.

The Family Rights Group and Beth Neil for extract from *Family Rights Group Advice Sheet for Families* (2006), published at: www.frg.org.uk.

The Free Press, a Division of Simon & Schuster Adult Publishing Group, for extracts from Joseph Goldstein, Anna Freud and Albert J Solnit: *Beyond the Best Interests of the Child* (Collier Macmillan, 1973), copyright © 1973, 1979 by The Free Press. All rights reserved.

Hart Publishing Ltd for extracts from R Collier and S Sheldon: *Fragmenting Fatherhood; A Socio-Legal Study* (Hart, 2008); E Jackson: *Regulating Reproduction* (Hart, 2001); and H Reece: *Divorcing Responsibly* (Hart, 2003).

Pat Hudson and Robert Lee for extracts from P Hudson and W R Lee: 'Women's Work and the Family Economy in Historical Perspective' in P Hudson and W R Lee (eds): *Women's Work and the Family Economy in Historical Perspective* (Manchester University Press, 1990).

Incorporated Council of Law Reporting for extracts from the *Law Reports: Appeal Cases* (AC), *Chancery Division* (Ch) and *Family Court Reports, Family Division.*

The Independent for extract from R Deech: 'Marriage as a Short-Term Option', *The Independent*, 2.11.1990, copyright © The Independent 1990.

Jordan Publishing Ltd for extracts from *Family Law Reports;* extract from Bridge & H Swindells: *Adoption, The Modern Law* (Jordan, 2003); extracts from *Child and Family Law Quarterly*: R Bailey-Harris, G Davis, J Barron, and J Pearce: 'Settlement culture and the use of the "no order" principle under the Children Act 1989', 11 *CFLQ* 53 (1999); M Burton: 'Coherent and effective remedies for victims of domestic violence – time for an integrated domestic violence court?' 16 *CFLQ* 317 (2004); B Clarke: 'Should Greater Prominence be given to Pre-Nuptial Contracts in the Law of Ancillary Relief?', 16 *CFLQ* 399 (2004); S Cretney: 'The Family and the Law: Status or Contract?' 15 *CFLQ* 403 (2003); G Davis, J Pearce, R Bird, H Woodward and C Wallace: 'Ancillary Relief Outcomes' *CFLQ* 43 (2000); J Ginn & D Pearce: 'Can divorced women catch up in pension building?' 14 (2) *CFLQ* 157 (2002); J Herring & R Taylor: 'Relocating relocation', 18 *CFLQ* 517 (2006); N Lowe: 'The changing face of adoption – the gift/donation model versus the contract/services model', 9 *CFLQ* 371 (1997); V May & C Smart: 'Silence in Court? – hearing children in residence and contact disputes', 16 *CFLQ* 305 (2004); Kenneth McNorrie: 'Marriage is for Heterosexuals – May the Rest of Us Be Saved from It', 12 (4) *CFLQ* 363 (2000); D Quinton, A Rushton, C Dance and D Mayes: 'Contact with birth parents in adoption – a response to Ryburn', 10 *CFLQ* 349 (1998); M Ryburn: 'In whose best interests? – post adoption contact with the birth family', 10 *CFLQ* 536 (1998); C Smart: 'Objects of concern? – children and divorce', 11 *CFLQ* 365 (1999); M Smith: 'New stepfamilies – a descriptive study of a largely unseen group', 15 *CFLQ* 185 (2003); and N Wikely: 'Child Support Reform – throwing the baby out with the bath water', *CFLQ* (2008); and from *Family Law*: A Buchanan, J Hunt, H Brotherton and V Bream: 'Families in Conflict – perspectives of children and parents on the family court welfare service', *Family Law* 900 (2001); A Heath Jones: 'Divorce and the Reluctant Father', 10 *Family Law* 75 (1980): K O'Donovan: The Principles of Maintenance', 7 *Family Law* 229 (1978); V Reid: 'ADR Professional: ADR Update from the ASA Alliance', *Family Law* 1033 (2007); P Singer: 'Sexual Discrimination in Ancillary Relief',

Family Law 115 (2001); and C Sturge & D Glaser: 'Contact and Domestic Violence – the Experts' report', *Family Law* 615 (2000).

The Judicial Studies Board for extracts from *Handbook on Ethnic Minority Issues (1994) and Equal Treatment Bench Book* (2005).

New Clarion Press for extracts from G Hague and E Malos: *Domestic Violence: Action for Change* (New Clarion Press, 1993).

News International Syndication for extract from 'Till flossing his teeth do us part' by Jane Gordan, *The Times*, 19.02.1996, copyright © The Times 1996.

The Nuffield Foundation and the author for extracts from E Cooke, A Barlow and T Callus: *Community of Property: A Regime for England and Wales* (Nuffield, 2006).

Open University Press Publishing Company for extract from Valerie Walkerdine: 'Developmental psychology and the study of childhood' in *An Introduction to Childhood Studies* edited by Mary Jane Kehily (Open University Press, 2004).

Oxford University Press for extracts from E Cooke: 'Community of property, joint ownership and the family home' in M Dixon and G Griffiths (eds): *Contemporary Perspectives on Property, Equity and Trust Law* (OUP, 2007); G Davis, S Cretney, and J Collins: *Simple Quarrels* (Clarendon Press, 1994); I Ellman: 'Divorce in the United States' in S Katz, J Eekelaar and M Maclean (eds): *Cross Currents* (OUP, 2000); J Lewis: 'Family Policy in the post-War Period' in S Katz, J Eekelaar and M Maclean (eds): *Cross Currents* (OUP, 2000); Elizabeth F Emans: 'Just Monogamy' in Mary Lyndon Shanley (ed): *Just Marriage* (OUP, 2004); M L Shanley: 'Just Marriage: On the Public Importance of Private Unions' in Mary Lyndon Shanley (ed): *Just Marriage* (OUP, 2004); and F Olsen: 'Children's Rights: Some Feminist Approaches to the United Nations Convention on the Rights of the Child' in P Alston, S Parker and J Seymour (eds): *Children, Rights and the Law* (Clarendon Press, 1992); and from *International Journal of Law Policy and the Family*: J Burley & F Regan: 'The Fear, the Floodgates and the Reality', 16 *I J of Law Policy and the Family* (2002); and from *Oxford Journal of Legal Studies*: A Bainham: 'Men and Women Behaving Badly: Is Fault Dead in English Family Law?', 21 *OJLS* 219, (2001); and John Eekelaar: 'The Emergence of Children's Rights', 6 *OJLS* 161 (1986).

Palgrave Macmillan for extracts from D Gittins: *The Family in Question* (Macmillan 1993); and J Pahl: *Money and Marriage* (Macmillan 1989, 1990).

The Joseph Rowntree Foundation for extract from Bryan Rodgers and Jan Pryor: *Divorce and Separation: The Outcomes for Children* (Joseph Rowntree Foundation, 1998)

Reed Elsevier (UK) Ltd trading as LexisNexis Butterworths for extracts from *Family Court Reports* and from *New Law Journal*: D Burrows: 'A Brave New World', 157 *NLJ* 888 (2007).

Sage Publications Ltd and the authors for extracts from M Chamberlain: 'Brothers and sisters, uncles and aunts: a lateral perspective on Caribbean Families' in E B Silva and C Smart (eds): *The New Family?* (Sage, 1999); and from *Feminism & Psychology*: R Auchmuty: 'Same Sex Marriage Revived: Feminist Critique and Legal Strategy', 14 *Feminism and Psychology* 101 (2004).

Carol Smart for extracts from C Smart: *The Legal and Moral Ordering of Child Custody*

(University of Warwick, Dept of Sociology, 1990), republished as 'The legal and moral ordering of Child Custody, in 18 (4) *Journal of Law and Society* 485 (1991).

Sociological Research Online, University of Surrey for extracts from B Shipman and C Smart: 'It's Made a Huge Difference: Recognition, Rights and the Personal Significance of Civil Partnership' *Sociological Research Online* Vol 12 (1) (2007).

Springer and the authors for extracts from *Feminist Legal Studies*: Ralph Sandland: 'Feminism and the Gender Recognition Act 2004', 13 *FLS* 43 (2005); and Andrew Sharpe: 'Endless sex: the Gender Recognition Act 2004 and the persistence of a legal category', 5 *FLS* 57 (2007).

Sweet and Maxwell Ltd for extracts from *Criminal Law Review*: E Finch: 'Stalking the perfect stalking law', *Crim LR* 703 (2002); and from *European Human Rights Reports* (EHRR).

Taylor & Francis Books (UK) for extracts from H Barnet: *An Introduction to Feminist Jurisprudence* (Cavendish, 1998); R Lister: 'Income Maintenance for Families with Children', in R N Rapoport, M P Fogarty and R Rapoport (eds): *Families in Britain* (RKP, 1982); K O'Donovan and N Marshall: 'After Birth: Decisions about Becoming a Mother'; and C F Stychin: 'Family Friendly? Rights Responsibilities and Relationship Recognition' in A Diduck and K O'Donovan (eds): *Feminist Perspectives on Family Law* (Routledge Cavendish, 2006).

Taylor & Francis Informa UK Ltd - Journals via Copyright Clearance Center for extract from *Journal of Social Welfare Law*: M Richards: 'Post Divorce Arrangements for Children: A Psychological Perspective', 4(3) *JSWL* 133 (May, 1982).

Barbara Tizard for extracts from B Tizard: *Adoption: A Second Chance* (Open Books, 1977).

Wiley-Blackwell Publishing Ltd for extracts from A McFarlane: *Marriage and Love in England 1300-1840* (1986); J Packman with J Randall and N Jacques: *Who Needs Care? Social Work Decisions about Children* (1986); and J Packman: *The Child's Generation: Child Care Policy in Britain* (2e, 1981); extracts from *Law & Policy*: M McLean and J Eekelaar : 'The Significance of Marriage: Contrasts between White British and Ethnic Minority Groups in England', 27 *Law & Policy* 3 (2005) 381; and from *Modern Law* Review: L Ellison: 'Prosecuting Domestic Violence without Victim Participation', *MLR* 834 (2002); M King: 'Children's Rights as Communication: Reflections on Autopoetic Theory and the United Nations Convention', 57 *MLR* (1994) 385; and H Reece: 'The End of Domestic Violence', 69 (5) *MLR* (2006) 770.

John Wiley & Sons Ltd for extract from R Parker for the Department of Health, Social Services Inspectorate: *Adoption Now - Messages for Research* (J Wiley, 1999).

Women's National Commission for extract from *Unlocking the Secret: Women Open the Door on Domestic Violence, Findings from Consultations with Survivors* (Women's National Commission, 2003) from www.thewnc.org.uk.

Every effort has been made to trace and contact copyright holders prior to publication but this has not been possible in every case. If notified, the publisher will undertake to rectify any errors or omissions at the earliest opportunity.

TABLE OF CONTENTS

TABLE OF CASES

A

B

E

F

G

H

M

TABLE OF STATUTES

UK STATUTES

UK STATUTORY INSTRUMENTS

NATIONAL LEGISLATION

Australia

Austria

France

Ireland

New Zealand

Sweden

United States

INTERNATIONAL INSTRUMENTS

CODES OF PRACTICE

1

THE FAMILY AND THE LAW

In this chapter we ask, first, what is a family? The answer to this question is complex and, within our multi-ethnic and culturally diverse society, far from static. We then look at the way the law responds to the family. That, of course, is the theme of this book; here we consider how far legal recognition of the family corresponds to the sociological reality we have surveyed. We shall introduce the Human Rights Act 1998, and some of the provisions of the European Convention on Human Rights; the provisions of that Convention flavour much of what we say throughout the book.

1.1 DEFINITIONS OF 'FAMILY' AND 'HOUSEHOLD'

Traditionally, the word *family* refers to a group of persons related to each other by blood or marriage. The introduction of an additional word, such as 'immediate', suggests that the members of the family probably live together within a single household, and (although to a variable extent) pool their resources for the common well-being of the unit. However, many important questions are immediately raised by this series of assumptions. Is it necessary for the members of the family to be related in the manner described? Or is family based on the provision of care? Is it a prerequisite that there be a single household? Is it necessary for family members to pool resources?

For an example of a family that challenges some of these assumptions, see how Matthew Kavanagh describes his family in 'Rewriting the legal family beyond exclusivity to a care based standard' (2004):

> The immediate family in which I grew up began with two adults and their two biological sons. During my childhood, however, it included (at various times) two households, shared custody, lesbian mothers, heterosexual stepparents, a foster child, and three stepsiblings, all in the same town. I have ex-step-grandparents. A typical day when I was ten might have begun in the home of my mother or my father, who shared equal custody of my brother and me. If that day began at my mother's house, we would have risen early so that my mother, a teacher, could head to work across the river. My mother's female partner, Lisa, who was one of our three parents, would have driven my brother, me, and our foster brother to my father's house across town. There, because my father did not have to go to work until later, we would eat breakfast and board the bus to school. After school we would head back to my mother's house and stay with a neighbour until my mother or Lisa got home. If we were staying at my father's house that week, our foster brother (who lived with my mother) would be dropped off in the morning to join us for breakfast and, in the evening, my father would pick us up from my mother's after he got off work.
>
> Our family also included a community of adults on whom the children in the family could and did regularly rely for care, support, and guidance – who stood in various relationships to various children. Some were close family members who provided direct care, while others were more peripheral. Christmas in my family was always a joyous family occasion, with dinner table set for 20 or more – almost none of whom were blood relatives, but many of whom were close members of our family network.

Our family changed during my childhood – homes moved, stepparents and children were added and subtracted, and new adults came into our lives. It was not always easy in our family – there were difficult times and difficult relationships, as in any family. What remained stable, however, was the abundance of care provided to children by different adults – through interwoven, supportive connections. Mine was a family, built on changing relationships, that provided the children with an incredibly supportive and healthy environment in which to grow, learn, and become adults.

The following extract from the Judicial Studies Board, *Equal Treatment Bench Book* (2007, see: www.jsboard.co.uk) makes clear that we must not assume that the answer to the question 'What is a family?' is necessarily going to produce a simple and straightforward response.

1.2.3 Families and Diversity

Key points

- The family unit is the cornerstone of most communities: for many minority communities the family is a key source of personal identity which allows for differentiation from the majority.
- Differences in outlook amongst all families will exist in a diverse society: assumptions about the make up of the family unit have to be put aside . . .
- Our cultural outlook is based on our own knowledge and understanding: there is a fine line between relying on this and resorting to stereotypes which can lead to injustice . . .

No such thing as the 'average' family We do not have to think hard to understand that all families are unique. However, there are factors which lead to a shared understanding:

- socio-economic background, schooling and employment,
- racial and national identities,
- gender composition,
- religious framework,
- cultural outlook (e.g. secular or traditional).

The combination of all these variables contribute to people's understanding of what a 'family' is. The task of respecting the differences in lifestyle has to be understood from the starting point that for many of us the 'norm' is actually our understanding of the ethnic European White model of families. Statistics tell us that that 'norm' does not in fact exist. Families share tendencies but have idiosyncrasies as well.

QUESTION

Who do you consider to be your family? What do you think influences your view?

It is important to be clear about the difference in meaning between 'household' and 'family'.

A *household*, according to Stone, writing about the family in England from 1500 to 1800, consists of persons 'living under one roof'. In *The Family, Sex and Marriage in England 1500–1800* (1977), he says:

> The core of any household is clearly the family, namely members related by blood or marriage, usually the conjugal pair and their unmarried children, but sometimes including grandparents, the married children, or occasionally kin relatives. But most households also included non-kin inmates, sojourners, boarders or lodgers, occupying rooms vacated by children or kin, as well as indentured apprentices and resident servants, employed either for domestic work about the house or as an additional resident labour force for the fields or the shop.

Laslett and Wall, in their seminal work *Household and Family in Past Time,* published in 1972, define the two words 'household' and 'family' in the context of the historical demographic data which they collect and analyse:

> It must be strongly stressed that in this vocabulary the word *family* does not denote a complete coresident domestic group, though it may appear as an abbreviated title. The word *household* particularly indicates the fact of shared location, kinship and activity. Hence all solitaries have to be taken to be households, for they are living with themselves, and this is the case when they have servants with them, since servants are taken as household members....
>
> The expression *simple family* is used to cover what is variously described as the *nuclear family,* the *elementary family* or (not very logically, since spouses are not physiologically connected) the *biological family.* It consists of a married couple, or a married couple with offspring, or of a widowed person with offspring. The concept is of the conjugal link as the structural principle.... For a simple family to appear then, it is necessary for at least two individuals connected by that link or arising from that link to be coresident: *conjugal family unit* (CFU) is a preciser term employed to describe all possible groups so structured.
>
> No solitary can form a conjugal family unit and for such a group to subsist it is necessary for at least two immediate partners (spouses and/or offspring) to be present. More remotely connected persons, whose existence implies more than one conjugal link, do not constitute a conjugal family unit if they reside together with no one else except servants. Nor do brothers and sisters. Hence a widow with a child forms a conjugal family unit, but a widow with a grandchild does not, nor does an aunt with a nephew. Whenever a conjugal family unit is found on its own, it is always taken to be a household, just as solitaries are, and such a coresident domestic group is called a *simple family household....*
>
> An *extended family household* [or stem family] consists of a conjugal family unit with the addition of one or more relatives other than offspring, the whole group living together on its own or with servants. It is thus identical with the simple family household except for the additional item or items.
>
> *Multiple family households* comprise all forms of domestic group which include two or more conjugal family units connected by kinship or by marriage. The disposition of a secondary unit, that is of a constituent unit which does not contain the head of the whole household, is said to be UP if its conjugal link involves a generation earlier than that of the head, as for example when his father and mother live with him. Such a secondary unit can include offspring of the head's parents other than the head himself, that is his resident unmarried brothers or sisters, and the presence of such persons keeps this secondary unit in being if one or other of the head's parents dies. A secondary unit is disposed DOWN if, for example, a head's married son lives with him along with his wife and perhaps offspring, with similar implications about siblings and widowhood....
>
> If conjugal family units within households of the multiple kind are all disposed laterally, as when married brothers and/or sisters live together, the overall arrangement is the one often referred to as the 'fraternal joint family' by social anthropologists.

QUESTIONS

i. Is your family a simple family household, an extended family household or a multiple family household?

ii. What about your parents' or grandparents' families?

Social Trends 37 (2007) provides the following overview of the shifting composition of household structures:

> People live in a variety of household types over their lifetime. They may leave their parental home, form partnerships, marry and have children. They may also experience separation and divorce, lone-parenthood, and the formation of new partnerships, leading to new households and second families. Recent decades have seen marked changes in household patterns. The traditional family household of a married couple with a child or children is less common, while there has been an increase in lone-parent households. There has also been an increase in one-person households, suggesting that people are spending time living on their own before forming a relationship, after a relationship has broken down, or following the death of a spouse or partner.

Household Composition

There were 24.2 million households in Great Britain in spring 2006 (Table 2.1). The trend towards smaller household sizes has contributed to the number of households increasing faster than the population and hence an increased demand for housing. The number of households in Great Britain increased by 30 per cent between 1971 and 2006. The population of Great Britain increased

Table 2.1 Households:[1] by size

Great Britain					Percentages
	1971	1981	1991	2001[2]	2006[2]
One person	*18*	*22*	*27*	*29*	*29*
Two people	*32*	*32*	*34*	*35*	*36*
Three people	*19*	*17*	*16*	*16*	*16*
Four people	*17*	*18*	*16*	*14*	*13*
Five people	*8*	*7*	*5*	*5*	*4*
Six or more people	*6*	*4*	*2*	*2*	*2*
All households (=100%) (millions)	18.6	20.2	22.4	23.8	24.2
Average household size (number of people)	2.9	2.7	2.5	2.4	2.4

1 See Appendix, Part 2: Multi-sourced tables, Households, and Families.

2 Data are at spring for 2001 and Q2 for 2006. See Appendix, Part 4: Labour Force Survey.

Source: Census, Labour Force Survey, Office for National Statistics

by 8 per cent in the same period ... The average household size fell over this period from 2.9 to 2.4 people. Reasons for this decrease include more lone-parent families, smaller family sizes and an increase in one-person households, although the rise in one-person households has leveled off since 1991. As a proportion of all households, one-person households increased by 9 percentage points from 18 per cent to 27 per cent, but only by a further 2 percentage points between 1991 and 2006. Most of the increase in the proportion of one-person households since 1991 is a result of the rise in the number of people below state pension age living alone.

The proportion of households in Great Britain comprising a couple with dependent children fell from more than one-third in 1971 to less than one-quarter in 2006 (Table 2.2). The decrease was mostly among couples with one or two dependent children. Over the same period, the proportion of lone-parent households with dependent children more than doubled from 3 per cent of households in 1971, to 7 per cent of households in 2006.

Table 2.2 Households:[1] by type of household and family

Great Britain					Percentages
	1971	1981	1991	2001[2]	2006[2]
One person					
Under state pension age	*6*	*8*	*11*	*14*	*14*
Over state pension age	*12*	*14*	*16*	*15*	*14*
One family households					
Couple[3]					
No children	*27*	*26*	*28*	*29*	*28*
1–2 dependent children[4]	*26*	*25*	*20*	*19*	*18*
3 or more dependent children[4]	*9*	*6*	*5*	*4*	*4*
Non-dependent children only	*8*	*8*	*8*	*6*	*7*
Lone parent[3]					
Dependent children[4]	*3*	*5*	*6*	*7*	*7*
Non-dependent children only	*4*	*4*	*4*	*3*	*3*
Two or more unrelated adults	*4*	*5*	*3*	*3*	*3*
Multi-family households	*1*	*1*	*1*	*1*	*1*
All households (=100%) (millions)	18.6	20.2	22.4	23.8	24.2

1 See Appendix, Part 2: Multi-sourced tables, Households, and Families.
2 Data are at Q2 each year. See Appendix, Part 4: Labour Force Survey.
3 Other individuals who were not family members may also be included.
4 May also include non-dependent children.
Source: Census, Labour Force Survey, Office for National Statistics

There are differences in household size between the ethnic groups in Great Britain. Some ethnic groups tend to have larger families and are more likely to live in extended families. The 2001 Census showed that Indian, Pakistani and Bangladeshi households in Great Britain contained more people, on average, than households from other ethnic backgrounds (Figure 2.3).

Bangladeshi households were largest, with an average of 4.5 people per household, followed by Pakistani households (4.1) and Indian households (3.3). White Irish households were the smallest, with an average of 2.2 people per household and Black Caribbean and White British households both had an average of 2.3 people. Variations in the age profiles of the different ethnic groups contributed to differences in household size. White British, Black Caribbean and White Irish households have an older age structure than the other ethnic groups and more than three in ten households headed by these groups were one-person households.

Figure 2.3 Average household size: by ethnic group, 2001

Source: Census 2001, Office for National Statistics; Census 2001, General Register Office for Scotland

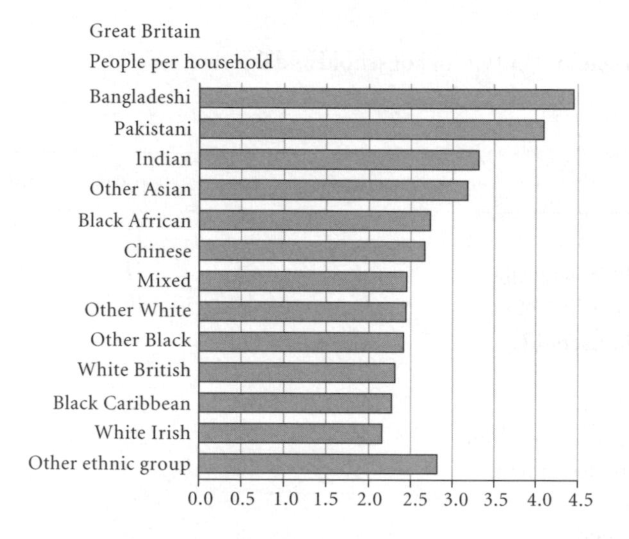

Table 2.2 is an analysis of households and family type, and is therefore directly relevant to housing policy and related issues. For other purposes it is necessary to understand the numbers of people in different types of households. Table 2.4 shows that more than two-thirds of people living in private households in Great Britain in spring 2006 lived in couple families. However, since 1971 the proportion of people living in the traditional family household of a couple with dependent children has fallen from more than one-half (52 per cent) to more than one-third (37 per cent) in spring 2006. Over the same period the proportion of people living in couple families with no children has increased from almost one-fifth (19 per cent) to one-quarter (25 per cent). This trend has been driven both by delayed childbearing among younger couples and an increase in the number of older couples whose children have left home. One in eight people lived in a lone-parent household in spring 2006 – three times the proportion in 1971.

The proportion of dependent children within different family types has changed over the last 35 years. In April to June (Q2) 2006, 76 per cent of children lived in a family unit headed by a couple, compared with 92 per cent in 1972 (Table 2.5). Since the early 1970s there has been a fall in the proportion of children living in families headed by a couple with three or more children, from 41 per cent in 1972 to 22 per cent in spring 2006. In contrast there was an increase in the proportion of children living in lone parent families, from 7 per cent in 1972 to 24 per cent in Q2 2006. Lone mothers head around nine out of ten lone-parent families.

Table 2.4 People in households:[1] by type of household and family

Great Britain					Percentages
	1971	1981	1991	2001[2]	2006[2]
One person	*6*	*8*	*11*	*12*	*12*
One family households					
Couple					
No children	*19*	*20*	*25*	*25*	*25*
Dependent children[3]	*52*	*47*	*53*	*39*	*37*
Non-dependent children only	*10*	*10*	*12*	*9*	*8*
Lone parent[4]	*4*	*6*	*9*	*12*	*12*
Other households	*9*	*9*	*4*	*4*	*5*
All people in private households (=100%) (millions)	53.4	53.9	54.1	56.4	57.1

1 See Appendix, Part 2: Multi-sourced tables, Households, and Families.
2 Data are at spring each year. See Appendix, Part 4: Labour Force Survey.
3 May also include non-dependent children.
4 Includes those with dependent children only, non-dependent children only, and those with both dependent and non-dependent children.

Source: Census, Labour Force Survey, Office for National Statistics

Table 2.5 Dependent children:[1] by family type

Great Britain					Percentages
	1972	1981	1997[2]	2001[2]	2006[2]
Couple families					
1 child	*16*	*18*	*17*	*17*	*18*
2 children	*35*	*41*	*37*	*37*	*36*
3 or more children	*41*	*29*	*25*	*24*	*22*
Lone mother families					
1 child	*2*	*3*	*6*	*6*	*7*
2 children	*2*	*4*	*7*	*8*	*9*
3 or more children	*2*	*3*	*6*	*6*	*6*
Lone father families					
1 child	..	*1*	*1*	*1*	*1*
2 or more children	*1*	*1*	*1*	*1*	*1*
All children[3]	*100*	*100*	*100*	*100*	*100*

1 See Appendix, Part 2: Multi-sourced tables, Households, and Families.
2 Data are at Q2 each year. See Appendix, Part 4: Labour Force Survey.
3 Excludes cases where the dependent child is a family unit, for example, a foster child.

Source: General Household Survey, Census, Labour Force Survey, Office for National Statistics

Among households with dependent children, those headed by someone from the Black ethnic group had the highest proportion of lone-parent families in Great Britain in 2001. About half of other Black and Black Caribbean households with dependent children were headed by a lone parent (52 and 48 per cent respectively), as were more than one-third of Black African households (36 per cent). Lone-parent families were less common among Indian households (10 per cent), Bangladeshi households (12 per cent), Pakistani households (13 per cent), Chinese households (15 per cent) and White British households with dependent children (22 per cent). Between 1991 and 2001, the proportion of lone-parent households with dependent children decreased among the Black Caribbean group (from 20 per cent to 18 per cent) and the Black African group (21 per cent to 17 per cent) (Figure 2.6). During the same period the proportion of Pakistani, Bangladeshi, Chinese and White lone-parent households with dependent children all increased to between 6 per cent and 9 per cent.

Figure 2.6 Lone-parent households with dependent children:[1] by ethnic group

Source: Census 2001, Office for National Statistics; Census 2001, General Register Office for Scotland

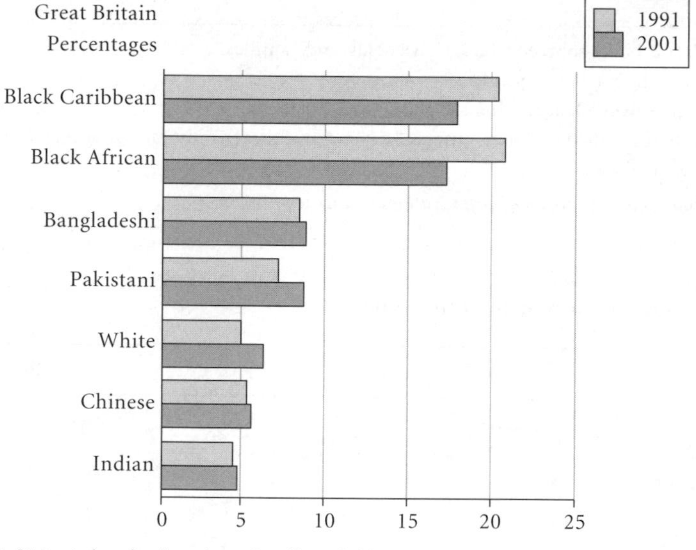

1 Living in 'one family and no others' households.
2 Of the households reference person, see Reference persons box above.

One of the most notable changes in household composition since 1971 has been the increase in one-person households. In 2005 there were 7 million people living alone in Great Britain compared with 3 million in 1971. This increase was most marked between 1971 and 1991 but has levelled off since 1991. In the mid-1980s and 1990s these households mainly comprised older women according to the General Household Survey. This was a reflection of there being fewer men than women in older age groups ... and, in particular, the tendency for women to outlive men. In 2005, 60 per cent of women aged 75 and over were living alone, much the same proportion as in 1986/87 (Figure 2.7). More recently there has been a tendency for people to live alone at younger ages. The largest increase over the past 20 years has been among those aged 25 to 44 years. The proportion of men in this age group who lived alone more than doubled between 1986/87 and 2005 from 7 per cent to 15 per cent and the proportion of women living alone also more than doubled from 4 per cent to 9 per cent.

Figure 2.7 People living alone: by sex and age[1]

Source: General Household Survey (Longitudinal), Office for National Statistics

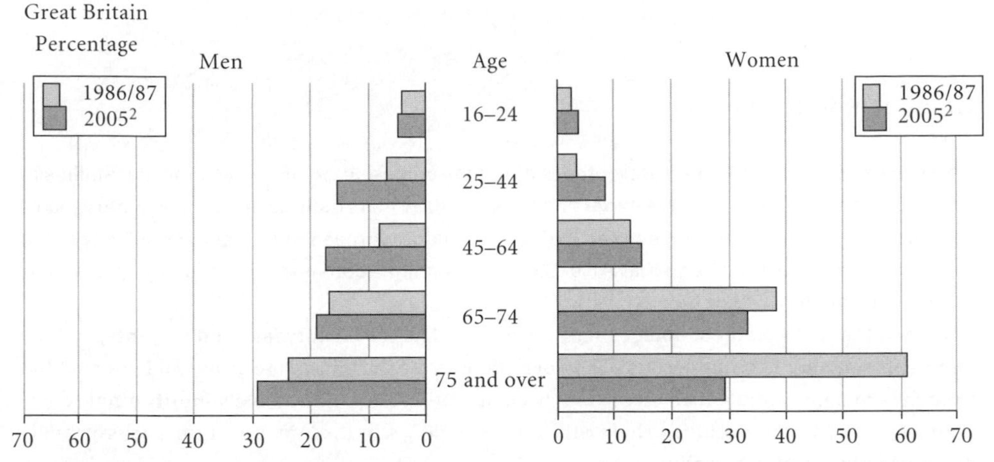

1 Data from 2001/02 onwards are weighted to compensate for nonresponse and to match known population distributions.
2 Data for 2005 includes last quarter of 2004/05 due to survey change from financial year to calendar year. See Appendix, Part 2: General Household survey.

Another notable change in family structure and relationships has been the increase in the number of adults who live with their parents (Table 2.8). Some adults remain at home while in education or because of economic necessity, such as difficulties entering the housing market. Others choose to continue living with their parents. Young men are more likely than young women to live with their parents. In Q2 2006, 58 per cent of men aged 20 to 24 in England lived with their parents compared with 39 per cent of women in the same age group. Between 1991 and 2006 the proportion of men and women in this age group who were living with their parents increased by 8 and 7 percentage points respectively. Over the same period the proportion of women aged 30 to 34 living with their parents decreased from 5 per cent to 3 per cent while the proportion of 30 to 34-year-old men living with their parents remained at around 8 per cent.

Table 2.8 Adults living with their parents: by sex and age[1]

England					Percentages
	1991	2001[2]	2002[2]	2005[2]	2006[2]
Men					
20–24	50	57	56	57	58
25–29	19	22	19	23	22
30–34	9	8	8	8	9
Women					
20–24	32	36	37	38	39
25–29	9	11	10	11	11
30–34	5	3	2	3	3

1 See Appendix, Part 2: Multi-sourced tables, Households, and Families.
2 Data are at spring for 2001, 2002, 2005 and Q2 for 2006. See Appendix, Part 4: Labour Force Survey.

Source: Survey of English Housing, Communities and Local Government; Labour Force Survey, Office for National Statistics

The following extract from an earlier edition of the Judicial Studies Board's *Handbook on Ethnic Minority Issues* (1995) suggests the need for a degree of caution in how we think about the statistics in Figures 2.3 and 2.6 above, when thinking about ethnic minority families:

Composition of Families

There are a number of common stereotypes about the composition of ethnic minority families in Britain, the accuracy of which it is important to ascertain. These include that ethnic minority families are larger in size than those of the indigenous majority; that South Asian families take the form of 'extended families'; and that Afro-Caribbean families consist typically of a single mother bringing up children on her own.

Despite the fact that these images may have some basis in reality, as rigid stereotypes they can be misleading and dangerous. They over-generalise certain tendencies, and conceal the existence of considerable diversity in family composition among Britain's minority ethnic communities. They also do nothing to help with understanding why there may be differences in family patterns between ethnic groups.

3.1 Family Size

By 'family size' is normally meant 'size of household'. Statistics for the size of households do in fact show some quite substantial differences between ethnic groups. . . .

It is important to bear in mind that when overall averages differ in this way, they tend to highlight – and thus perhaps exaggerate – the differences. Not only do averages of this kind conceal substantial variation within each group, but they conceal also a great deal of overlap in the distribution of family size between the groups. Thus 60% of Pakistani/Bangladeshi families, and 84% of Indian families, are of between 1 and 5 persons in size, the range that accounts for almost all of the white families.

On the other hand, the fact that 41% of Pakistani/Bangladeshi households include 6 persons or more, as compared with 2% in the white group, is clearly a very substantial difference. Further statistical breakdown shows that part of this difference can be attributed to the larger numbers of children in such households. The other part is explained by the much more frequent presence of more than two adults than in 'white' homes.

To some extent these differences may be explained by cultural factors, which include marriage and child-bearing practices, and the greater strength of obligations to elderly parents and other kin. The differences, however, should not be presumed to be due to cultural factors alone. Economic circumstances are also important, as are the age profiles of minority ethnic communities, which tend (especially within the Bangladeshi community) to be relatively youthful due to their immigration being more recent.

3.2 Extended Families

One of the cultural factors which explains the larger size of South Asian households in Britain is undoubtedly the greater significance of what is often referred to as the 'extended family'. This term, however, may refer to various features and can sometimes be misleading, and it is important to clarify the respects in which this applies to South Asian communities.

In the white British context, the 'extended family' usually means one of two things: a household which consists of three generations (i.e. including grandparents/grandchildren), or a wider network of relatives who are felt to belong to one another and cooperate in certain ways. Generally speaking, the former is usually viewed as a temporary arrangement when it occurs: a married child is waiting to be able to obtain a home of its own, or a widowed grandparent is taken in so that he or she does not have to live alone. The latter is most often observed and referred to at temporary gatherings such as weddings or funerals, though in some circles (e.g. established working-class or rural communities, or among Travellers) this network may be of much greater significance in people's social and economic lives.

In all these examples, however, it remains the case that the primary unit is seen as the 'nuclear family', and the 'extension' is relative to this nucleus which is in control of its own affairs. In the white British context, therefore, the 'extended family' is precisely what the word implies: an extension of a nuclear unit of parents and children which is assumed to be the appropriate and basic core.

At first sight, there may appear to be no difficulty about applying this term also to families from the Indian sub-continent, and to those from other parts of the world. For example, the term may be presumed to apply to their tendency to form larger households, due to the presence of a wider range of relatives than that of parent and child alone. Likewise, it may be applied to the commonly observed tendency for such families to maintain a greater degree of social contact than the white British, and to use family ties commonly as the basis for business partnerships as well.

Care needs to be taken, however, over whether this term (and the thinking behind it) captures the distinctive character of these cultural patterns, and whether it is in danger of misleading us as to why these patterns occur. The important point to appreciate, here, is that not all family systems operate on the same principles as the white British one, and that misunderstanding can arise by assuming this is so.

Unlike the white British family system, most Asian and African systems traditionally have not operated on the basis that there is a 'nuclear unit' of parents and children that should be autonomous and sovereign. Their view, on the contrary, has tended to be that the interests of individual parents and children should be seen as subordinate to the wider group of kin as a whole. The membership of this group is most commonly defined in terms of shared patrilineal descent (i.e. in the male line), although matrilineal descent is used in some areas, notably in parts of West Africa. This larger group will act corporately in dealing with a wide range of affairs – certainly most economic and property matters, and often marriage and domestic affairs as well.

In family systems of the above kind, the 'nuclear family' as a biologically related group is usually given some degree of recognition, and in most cases would co-reside. However, it would be a mistake to view the group as a whole as 'made up' of such units in terms of how it organises its affairs: such families are not 'extended' in the British sense, but function traditionally as enduring corporate units of persons related through the male (or in some cases female) line.

On the Indian sub-continent, this family pattern has generally been known as the 'joint-family' system. The term 'joint-family' refers to the common situation that, following the death of the father as head of the family, the sons jointly inherit and manage the family property, forming a single corporate kinship group together with their wives and children. In China, those sharing descent in the male line would similarly own and manage property corporately, the ethos of solidarity among patrilineal kin being especially strong due to belief in the spiritual powers of dead ancestors over the living.

Family systems of this kind are probably far older and certainly have been far more extensive across the world than the fragmented 'nuclear' British/European forms. Early urban civilisations were built upon them – but they tend to break down in the face of the more aggressive kinds of urbanisation and change in the modern era. For migrants, however, they often continue to provide a framework within which life can be organised, even if this may need to be modified and adapted to circumstances for which such traditional family patterns were not devised. Features such as corporate family enterprises, and 'arranged marriages', should therefore be expected to be maintained to some degree within migrant communities (perhaps even for several generations), and they need to be understood in terms of their original context and not solely as departures from their host country's norms.

If the term 'extended family' is used to refer to Asian and African families, therefore, it is important that the distinctive character of such family traditions is appreciated. This does not imply that such traditions will be always maintained: some people may not wish to do so anyway, whilst others in attempting to do so may find practical problems in their way. The effects of migration and of immigration controls can be very divisive for such families, and the small size of housing units in Britain also constrains the establishment of traditional corporate family groups.

Nonetheless, the higher degree of family cooperation (especially among the migrant generation) often found among Asian and African as compared with the white British population is witness to the strength of such cultural traditions. For example, a married son with his wife and children may readily continue to live under the same roof as his father, even in a relatively small home, as it is not traditionally the norm to move away on marriage as among white British families. On the other hand, some South Asian households recorded in the statistics as 'nuclear-family households' will be socially autonomous units as the term implies; but many may, despite their spatial separation, be extremely closely linked with other households in the traditional way. Localised settlement, and activities such as weekend visiting and use of the telephone, are examples of ways in which the physical obstacles to family unity can be overcome.

Mary Chamberlain, in 'Brothers and sisters, uncles and aunts: a lateral perspective on Caribbean Families' (1999), has collected some case studies, which powerfully illustrate the way the extended West Indian family works. Here is one family's experience:

Arianne was born in Trinidad in 1931, the eldest of five children as well as 'quite a lot of half-sisters', who originated in the first marriages of both her parents. Arianne's grandmother came from Venezuela, trading goods in Trinidad until eventually settling there. Arianne's father was born in Trinidad, of (African) Venezuelan parents, although her family was ethnically diverse, 'pure, pure [Amer]Indian.... we grow with them. On the father's side, we have Chinese... we have Assyrian... we're all kind of people in our family... oh, it was... colourful'.

Her mother, though born in Venezuela, was brought up in Trinidad (while *her* mother was travelling) by her elder siblings, in particular 'the eldest... [who] used to see after the smaller ones. So my mother stay here and she went to school here in Trinidad'. The parenting role of siblings in this family continued across the generations. Arianne grew up with her seven siblings, including two from her mother's first marriage, and a cousin, 'like sisters'. Her father died when Arianne was 15, and when she was 18 her mother; her aunt who was also her godmother, assumed the role of parent looking after Arianne, her brothers and sisters and by this time another nephew. The family was surrounded by aunts and uncles and, as with Maude's experience, the metaphor of family extended throughout the neighbourhood, from material support ('anything we give... this is for Mr Joe, this is for this body, this is [for those] less fortunate... there's so much in this giving... they have something, they will send something to give') to control.

> 'You hardly could have misbehaved really long ago, you know, because... family, and the neighbours... want to know what going on. Why you here? Who you know, what you know. If they see you talking to anybody that they know, well, let us say, a loose person, somebody whom, you know, bad to the parents... they would call you and tell you "Listen, you must not keep that person's company, because they would lead you astray".'

Moral and practical guidance in sexual matters was assumed to be the province of older women in the neighbourhood, 'I always have older people friend..., my mother hadn't any course to tell us anything, but she used to tell us...everything. ... What to do, what not to do, what we mustn't do, what to expect'. Arianne became pregnant when she was 20 and gave birth to her only child, Clarissa, in 1951. She did not marry Clarissa's father and although he supported Clarissa when he could, Arianne had to work to keep them both, moving from the country to a suburb of Port-of-Spain in order to do so. Arianne's siblings remained in Rio Claw. Although Arianne was not the oldest in the family (her half-siblings preceded her) she was the eldest girl and was 'always ... responsible for everybody...everyone turned to her...If they had problems...anything at all, it's "Auntie Ad would sort it out"'.

As a child Clarissa spent her holidays with her grandparents, who owned a cocoa plantation, and her aunts and uncles where 'all the children would be growing up together'. Her grandfather played the quatro in a Parang (traditional folk) band and 'we would go round with him as well, to all the houses...he liked all his grandchildren'. Clarissa describes her father as a 'lady's man'. It was not until she was in her teens that Clarissa discovered that she had eight other brothers and sisters and 'last year, I found I had another one'.

Clarissa was her mother's only child although, in addition to her siblings through her father, Clarissa also had a number of step-siblings, the children of the man with whom her mother eventually lived during Clarissa's adolescence. Prior to that, however, Arianne shared a household with another family in Lavantille, replicating here her 'siblings' left behind. It was there that Clarissa spent her formative years as a singleton child.

> '...we grew up together...we were never alone. We were either with Aunty Iris, as I call her, or Mum was there, and Mum would have the two girls, or Auntie Iris would be looking after us. ...They're in America at the moment. They're all married with their families in America...[we are] like sisters...we had people like Aunt Iris and friends who had their own families and who were...sort of like sisters...they were that close. ... It was like having aunties, really...you felt as part of the family. ... I was always treated like one of the family. ... I really had a lot of influences from the families. And basically, you know, had a lot of family life.'

Arianne's 'way of life' incorporated not only the creation of substitute families, but within that replicated the role of elder sister: 'my mother...was always being called upon to do something for everyone, and so I've had loads of aunts and uncles, by virtue of being friends of hers.... there have always been people around'.

Clarissa came to England to train as a nurse, and had a child by a Barbadian 'who turned out just like my father, really'. She did not marry him and, like her mother, found herself having to work and bring up a child alone, removed (like her mother) from broader family networks. It may have been that earlier childhood experience of co-parenting which inspired her own choice of childrearing pattern. Clarissa re-created a communal home, first with her aunt whom she describes as a:

> 'respectful aunt, not family aunt. She is someone I met when I first came over, one of my friends...because we're Trinidadians together, we all sort of cottoned on...so at the time when I got pregnant I stayed with her.'

And then with her daughter's childminder which was:

> 'extremely convenient. I didn't have to go anywhere, to take [my daughter] anywhere, I just leave and go to work and come back. And that seemed to work out well enough....[She] *was, to be honest, like another mother.* She really loved [my daughter]. [She] was the life and soul of her...she loved children.'

> Such a pattern may be seen as a variant of 'child shifting'..., although in the case of both Arianne and her mother, they remained present in the household. It may also be seen as an example of co-mothering, common in Latin America and now emerging as a recognized pattern in some Latin American regions, and African American communities in the USA. Three generations had migrated, Arianne's mother from Venezuela, Arianne from the country to the city, and Clarissa from Trinidad to England, and all adopted strategies which incorporated collaterals – blood or 'respectful' – in a coparenting role. 'I was', as Clarissa says, 'quite happy to bring [my daughter] up the way I was brought up'.

The equating of 'family' with 'households' is increasingly problematic when we consider the significant increase in one-person households, as it is highly unlikely that these people consider themselves not to have any family (see Figure 2.7 above). The Office for National Statistics comments that the increase suggests that, 'people are spending time living on their own *before* forming a relationship, *after* a relationship has broken down, or *following* the death of a spouse or partner' (see above at p. 4; emphasis added). This explanation may be true for many people, but defining these individuals in relation to the absence of a partner upholds 'the couple' as the social norm. Jill Reynolds and Margaret Wetherell in 'The Discursive Climate of Singleness: The Consequences for Women's Negotiation of a Single Identity' (2003) take up this idea:

> Those who lack 'rightness' help define what is 'right'. Some modes of living become accountable while others remain unexceptional and taken for granted. Our interest in women defined as single began with the commonplace observation that whereas married women or women in long-term partnerships with men are rarely asked to explain themselves, single women do seem to have to engage in a lot of explaining. Women in long-term relationships do not tend to be asked (in a concerned tone of voice), for example, 'how did you end up married?' Apology and confession are not the dominant discursive genres for these accounts. The single woman, in contrast, is expected to have an explanation for her 'condition', preferably a story of 'circumstances' and 'missed opportunities' or one that blames herself for being 'unable to hold on to her man' ... . Singleness is a troubled category (difficult to align oneself with) and yet, in a double bind, the positive and idealized interpretative resources that are available seem to make other aspects of women's lives and expectations pathological. Women are faced with a difficult set of dilemmas. On the one hand they can choose to construct singleness very positively through the repertoires of choice and independence and self-development and achievement and then it becomes difficult to talk about any move out of the category. On the other hand, women can talk unashamedly about their desire for a relationship and risk being constructed as deficient and 'desperate', and marked by their failure to already have a man. There seem to be few satisfactory ways out of these dilemmas given the contemporary politics of relationships.

The next two extracts draw on qualitative research that highlights ways of viewing single households, which are rendered 'invisible' by the statistics. The first focuses on friendship and the second on people 'living-apart-together'.

Sasha Roseneil, 'Why we should Care about Friends: An Argument for Queering the Care Imaginary in Social Policy' (2004).

> The particular version of modern friendship which emerged in the mid-twentieth century, which promoted the companionate intimate heterosexual couple as the primary arena of intimacy, and emphasized a new culture of mutual disclosure between husband and wife and the importance

of joint leisure activities, has recently started to be unsettled. ... As geographical mobility increases, as marriage rates drop and marriage takes place later, as divorce rates have soared over the past 30 years, as births outside marriage, and indeed outside any lasting heterosexual relationship, increase steeply, as the proportion of people living in single person households rises and the proportion of women not having children climbs, patterns of sociability – as well as the more widely discussed patterns of intimacy – are undergoing transformation. A smaller proportion of the population is living in the heterosexual nuclear family of idealized mid-twentieth century form, and fewer people are choosing or able to construct their relations of cathexis according to the symmetrical family, intimate couple model. ...

Against this backdrop, the findings of the 'Care, Friendship and Non-Conventional Partnership' project... add weight to the idea that friendship is an increasingly socially significant relationship. This research has investigated how the most 'individualized' in our society – people who do not live with a partner – construct their networks of intimacy, friendship, care and support. We wanted to find out who matters to people who are living outside conventional families, what they value about their personal relationships, how they care for those who matter to them, and how they care for themselves. We carried out in-depth interviews with 53 people aged between 25 and 60 in three locations – a former mining town that is relatively conventional in terms of gender and family relations; a small town in which alternative, middle-class, 'downshifted' lifestyles and sexual nonconformity are common; and a multi-ethnic innercity area characterized by a range of gender and family practices, a higher-than-average proportion of women in the labour force and a large number of single-person and noncouple households. We talked to men and women with and without children, of a diversity of ages, ethnic origins, occupations and sexual orientations, and with varying relationship statuses and living arrangements. This gave us detailed insights into the texture of people's emotional lives.

We found that, across a range of lifestyles and sexualities, friendship occupied a central place in the personal lives of our interviewees. Whether they were in a heterosexual couple relationship or not, the people we interviewed were turning to friends for emotional support. Jools, a heterosexual woman of 28 from a former mining town, spoke for many people when she said: 'I think a friendship is for life, but I don't think a partner is ... I'd marry my friends. They'd last longer'. There was a high degree of reliance on friends, as opposed to biological kin and sexual partners, particularly for the provision of care and support in everyday life, and friendship operated as a key value and site of ethical practice for many. Far from being isolated, solitary individuals who flit from one unfulfilling relationship to another, most of the people we interviewed were enmeshed in complex networks of intimacy and care, and had strong commitments and connections to others. In contrast to the mythology of the singleton in desperate search for a marriage partner – exemplified by Bridget Jones – very few showed any yearning to be part of a conventional couple or family. A great many, both of those with partners and of those without, were consciously placing less emphasis on the importance of the couple relationship. Instead, they were centring their lives on their friends. Of those with partners, almost all had *chosen* not to live together. Very few saw cohabitation as the inevitable and desirable next stage of their relationship....

Friends were an important part of everyday life in good times and bad. Most of the people we spoke to put considerable effort into building and maintaining friendships in the place where they lived. A good number had moved house, or had persuaded friends to move house, with the aim of creating local friendship networks that could offer reciprocal childcare and help in times of illness, as well as pleasurable sociability. It was friends far more than biological kin who offered support to those who suffered from emotional distress or mental health problems, and who were there to pick up the pieces when love relationships ended. Many of the people we interviewed were opening up their homes to people who were not part of their conventionally defined family. It was not just the twenty-somethings who spent much of their leisure time hanging out with friends at each other's homes or having people round to dinner, for parties and barbecues.

Friends were invited to stay during periods of homelessness, when out of work or when they were depressed or lonely.

What this research suggests is that social researchers have often failed to see the extent to which, often as a matter of preference, people are substituting the ties of friendship for those of blood, particularly in terms of everyday care and emotional support....

Attention to friendship can facilitate a useful reconceptualization of our notion of an adequate ethics of care. Friendship is a significantly different relationship from that of mothering, lacking controlling institutions and firm cultural expectations and conventions.... It is, as Aristotle stated, a relationship (at least ideally) between equals, based in mutuality and reciprocity, to which the partners come of their own free will, not out of need, and which requires a firm sense of the separateness of the parties. Or, as Andrew Sullivan puts it:

> Friendship is for those who do not want to be saved, for those whose appreciation of life is here and now and whose comfort in themselves is sufficient for them to want merely to share rather than to lose their identity. And they enter into friendship as an act of radical choice. Friendship, in this sense is the performance art of freedom. (1998: 212)

If we take friendship seriously we will have to confront the question of how care may be given and received by equals, without violating individual autonomy, without self-sacrifice and subservience, and maintaining the affection which constitutes the relationship....

Taking friendship seriously ... can offer those of us interested in a progressive agenda for a welfare society important discursive resources. Firstly, it provides an important counterpoint to the pessimistic tone which characterizes the work of sociologists such as Zygmunt Bauman and Robert Putnam, whose ideas have been taken up in a widespread public discourse about a supposed crisis in personal relationships and community. Such ideas feed into, and implicitly express, a patriarchal, conservative hankering after a lost golden age of stable families and seemingly more secure structures of care. A recognition of the value that people place on extra-familial relationships, and the care and support that they offer, also offers a challenge to the familialism that runs through the policies of New Labour (notwithstanding its commitment to diversity). From this we can start to map a policy agenda which moves beyond the rhetoric of 'supporting families' (Home Office, 1998), to consider how we can support, and recognize the importance of, friendship.

For instance, work-life balance policies are called for which are framed in terms of the range of important personal relationships and commitments within which people live their lives, rather than narrowly with reference to family responsibilities. Employment benefits should be redefined to extend bereavement leave to apply to all the people about whom an employee cares or with whom he or she shares a special relationship. More radically, it is time to explore an extension of the proposed legislation on civil partnerships for lesbian and gay couples to recognize any significant relationship – sexual or otherwise – and to open up fiscal benefits, inheritance and other 'next of kin' rights to those whose intimate lives do not map on to a policy framework which focuses on conjugal couples and families.

QUESTIONS

i. Would you ever describe your 'friends' as your 'family' or your 'family' as your 'friends'? How do you distinguish the two concepts?

ii. John Eekelaar in *Family Law and Personal Life* (2006) discusses the meaning of friendship in some depth and concludes:

> I seem to have reached a position which should be uncomfortable for any family lawyer. It seems to be that, if we discount the framework of marriage, and look only at the underlying relationship, if that relationship is one of full friendship, and only that, it is not one which of itself generates any legal entitlements

Why do think this conclusion should make a family lawyer uncomfortable?

John Haskey and Jane Lewis, 'Living-apart-together in Britain: context and meaning' (2006).

The first estimates in Britain of the numbers Living Apart Together, and the profiles of their demographic characteristics, were published in Haskey, J. (2005) Living arrangements in contemporary Britain: having a partner who usually lives elsewhere and Living Apart Together, *Population Trends*, 122, pp.35–46.

'Living-apart-together' (LAT) – having a regular partner but living in separate households – is now internationally recognised as a form of partnering .... While living-apart-together is hardly a new phenomenon – there are many famous historical cases, for example Simone de Beauvoir and Jean-Paul Sartre – it is only in the last decade that this form of partnering has been identified in the academic literature and begun to be investigated ...

As a form of partnering, LAT raises many questions: who is involved, why, and how does this practice relate to co-residential cohabitation and marriage? And what, if anything, does it infer about commitment in such partnerships? For demographers, LAT raises questions similar to those asked about cohabitation almost a generation ago: how common is it and how common might it become, will it become a new stage in partnering, leading to cohabitation or marriage, or will it become an alternative form? ... There are also more sociological questions about why people live-apart together and what they hope to get out of it. Does the practice of LAT constitute further evidence of growing 'individualism'? ... Is LAT a 'step' on the way to co-residence, or does it represent a different (and lesser) type of commitment? ... Cohabitation that is not co-residential would seem to offer even greater opportunities for exit. However, Levin and Trost (1999) were able to divide their sample into involuntary and voluntary LATs: those who would have liked to be co-resident but were prevented from so doing, usually by work or care responsibilities, and those who chose to live apart for a wide variety of reasons often to do with wishing not to repeat 'past mistakes', which raises issues of trust and avoidance of risk, as well as desire for independence or autonomy. Voluntary LATs may be more individualistic, ... but living-apart-together may take place at a number of different points in the life course, which makes it unlikely that the meaning of this form of partnership can be generalized. Certainly, the motives and understandings of elderly LATs are likely to be very different from those in their late teens and early twenties....

The fact that the transition between different kinds of partnerships is so fluid [see Figure 1] makes it tempting to argue that different forms of personal relationships can be treated the same. However, people living-apart-together do seem to have a strong sense of the way in which this particular form of relationship is perceived as different from co-resident partnerships. In 1980, a strong argument was made to the effect that cohabitants had chosen a partnership status different from marriage, which should not be regulated (Deech, 1980). In all probability this argument can be advanced with more power today in respect of LATs than cohabitants.

Our exploratory study leaves more questions for future research than it has answered. We need to know more about the socio-economic position of the LAT population. We need to know more about the effects of LAT among the young on subsequent patterns of partnership formation and

Figure 1 Diagram indicating possible transitions between different forms of partnership

Reproduced with permission from Haskey, J. and Lewis, J. (2006) Living-apart-together in Britain: context and meaning, *International Journal of Law in Context* 37, 2(1), pp. 37–48, Cambridge University Press.

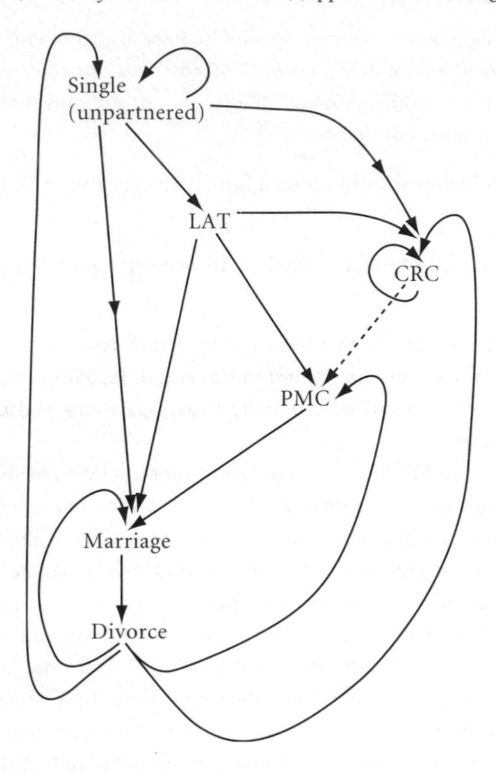

LAT–Living apart together
CRC–Co-residential cohabitation
PMC–Pre-marital cohabitation (assumed co-residential)

An arrow circling a given state indicates a continuation in that state (rather than a transition out of it)
Some reverse transitions are also possible: from CRC to unpartnered, from CRC to LAT, and from LAT to unpartnered
The dotted line denotes the difficulty in distinguishing CRC and PMC as two separate stages

on fertility, and as yet we know nothing about LAT in later life in the UK. We have tentatively concluded from our limited qualitative evidence that LAT represents a particular kind of sharing and is characterized more by caution and conservatism than radicalism and individualism, but we need to have more evidence on this score and also how easily those living-apart-together make transitions into other forms of relationship. On a practical level, the immediate possibilities for further research are somewhat limited, insofar as surveys which include questions on LAT need to be specifically devised and designed for the purpose. None of the current regular social surveys asks about LAT, and certainly no UK census has attempted to do so to date ... The development of these questions could mark a new era in trying to discern and measure the more complex living arrangements of modern citizens. For there is no doubt that the prevalence of LAT is by no means insignificant, and it is important that trends in it prevalence are estimated.

QUESTION

What do you think are the advantages and disadvantages to 'living-apart-together'?

The relative silence about friendship and 'living-apart-together' highlight an introductory matter which it is important to consider, namely the difference between *familial experience* and *familial ideology*.

One of the most dominant norms surrounding relationships in western societies is that of monogamy (we shall see in Chapter 4 that it is enshrined in the law relating to divorce). Laslett and Wall (1972), however, argue that although the nuclear monogamous family has a claim to universality, it has never possessed a normative and ideological force:

> There must be few behavioural institutions of which it can be said that ideology and experience are entirely congruent. No one would question that the English society of our day is correctly described as monogamous, because monogamous behaviour is nearly universal amongst a people whose belief in monogamy as a value is very widespread, and whose conduct is consistent with monogamy as the norm. It could be called the marital institution under which the English live, for no other distinct practice-with-belief exists alongside it as an alternative. Yet divorce is now quite frequent, scepticism about single spouse unions often encountered, and sexual intercourse outside marriage a commonplace. Indeed we know that children have been begotten illegitimately in appreciable numbers in England during the whole period for which figures can be recovered. . . .
>
> Departure from the monogamous ideal of behaviour, amongst English people nowadays, and perhaps amongst their ancestors, has been particularly conspicuous within the elite, and rejection of the beliefs associated with monogamy especially common with the intellectuals, the makers of opinions and of norms. Monogamy as an institution, then, has been underwritten by a general correspondence of ideology and experience, but is consistent with an appreciable degree of disharmony between the two. We do not find ourselves enquiring how much they could diverge before a practice ceased to be *the* institution, and became one amongst others, *an* institution. We do not easily contemplate a situation where plural institutions, or highly variable behaviour, exist in one society at one time in such matters as sexual behaviour and marriage.
>
> Yet if we turn to the question of how far any of the forms of the coresident domestic group, . . . could be called *the* institution, or *an* institution, of the societies where examples of them are found, this issue becomes inescapable. Glancing again at England as it is today, it seems safe enough to claim that the nuclear family, the simple family household, is *the* familial institution, and that again because experience of it, belief in it, willingness to obey its norms, are in fact all congruent with each other. The nuclear family, of course, complements the English institution of monogamy in a particular way. But it has, and has had for hundreds of years as far as we can yet see, a markedly better claim to universality in behaviour and experience than monogamous marriage with exclusively marital sexual intercourse. Yet the nuclear family never seems to have possessed the normative force, certainly not the ideological potential of monogamy, in England or indeed in Western culture.
>
> The hiatus, therefore, between familial experience and familial ideology is of a somewhat different character than that which divides the two in the matter of monogamy. The intellectuals and opinion makers who deal in the ideology of our world, have a tendency to deplore the circumstance that the complex family household is not sufficiently established as a norm in our society. Extended and even multiple households exist amongst us, but not in anything like enough numbers to ensure that the widowed and the elderly unmarried have a family to live in, or our children the emotional advantage of the presence of the extended kin in the households where they grow up.

Laslett and Wall's definition of monogamy may be contrasted with the following extract from Engels, *Origins of the Family, Private Property and the State* (1884):

> Sex love in the relation of husband and wife is and can become the rule only among the oppressed classes, that is, at the present day, among the proletariat, no matter whether this relationship is

officially sanctioned or not. But all the foundations of classical monogamy are removed. Here there is a complete absence of all property, for the safeguarding and inheritance of which monogamy and male domination were established. Therefore, there is no stimulus whatever here to assert male domination....

Moreover, since large-scale industry has transferred the woman from the house to the labour market and the factory, and makes her, often enough, the bread winner of the family, the last remnants of male domination in the proletarian home have lost all foundation – except, perhaps, for some of that brutality towards women which became firmly rooted with the establishment of monogamy. Thus, the proletarian family is no longer monogamian in the strict sense, even in cases of the most passionate love and strictest faithfulness of the two parties, and despite all spiritual and worldly benedictions which may have been received.

A further perspective on monogamy is provided by Elizabeth F. Emans in 'Just Monogamy?' (2004):

Like an 'unmannerly wedding guest', I want to invite the reader to pause amidst the whirlwind of marriage talk, to think about alternatives to monogamy. In particular I want to talk about multiparty relationships, or 'polyamory', as these relationships are called by some of their participants. ... When thinking of such relationships, most people think of polygamy, and more particularly, polygyny: one man married to multiple wives. I want to make two points about polygyny's worst-case scenario – which I take to be the coercion of underage girls into marriage and sexual relations. If the girls truly have not consented, or are incapable of consent, then the power of the state should be brought to bear on their persecutors ... second, polygamy, like monogamous marriage, also has a best-case scenario. One version of it is described in an article by Elizabeth Joseph, a Utah layer, who lived in a polygamous marriage of nine wives until the recent death of her husband. For Joseph, polygyny is a 'whole solution' to the problems of the modern woman trying to balance career and family. Joseph cherishes the fact that, when she goes off to her full-time job as an attorney, her daughter is cared for at home by one of the other wives whom the daughter adores. In this respect, the charge that polygyny is oppressive to woman is contingent; the validity of the charge depends on the individual relationship, just as in monogamous marriage....

Perhaps less familiar ... is the existence of an entirely different model of multiparty relationships called 'polyamory'. Polyamory is the practice of sustaining sexual, loving relationships among more than two, called 'ethical nonmonogamy' by some, polyamory is viewed by its adherents as an alternative to the frequent practice of promised monogamy accompanied by sexual 'cheating' behaviour.

Polyamorous relationships can involve just men, just women, or both men and women. The relationships' size and shape, and the types of bond among the individuals, are as varied as the people who form them. For instance, three women may form a closed group of exclusive partners; two men and a woman may share a household in which only the different-sex pairs have sex; three men and a woman may form a family in which the woman sleeps with only one of the men, and the men all sleep with each other and are open to outside sexual partners. These are only a tiny sample of the various forms of polyamorous relationships.

Polyamorists aspire to what I understand to be five core values, some of which they share with monogamists: (1) possessing oneself rather than trying to possess others; (2) self-knowledge, both about one's own desires for monogamy or nonmonogamy and as the basis for honest communication; (3) radical honesty, both about nonmonogamous practices and desires and about one's feelings and needs more generally; (4) consent between the parties to the rules and priorities of the relationship(s); and (5) privileging more sexual and loving experiences over other activities and emotions such as jealousy.

...[T]he existence of some number of people choosing to live polyamorous lives should prompt us all to think harder about this issue. It should prompt us to think about our own choices and about the ways that our norms and laws urge upon us one model rather than pressing us to make informed, affirmative choices about what might best suit our needs and desires. At the moment when same-sex couples rush to toward the altar, I suggest that we take this opportunity to question the desirability and justice of monogamy's law.

QUESTIONS

i. Polygamy is permitted in some cultures; for example, in classical Islamic law a man is permitted four wives; the husband inherits a large slice of his wife's property, but she does have rights of ownership and can inherit a share of the estate of her deceased father. Do you think that polygamy has anything to do with: (a) control of property; and (b) male domination?

ii. Do you think that a man with a job has a vested interest in the domination of his wife and children?

iii. Why do you think polyamory is not advocated more widely as a legitimate alternative lifestyle?

iv. Section 8(3) of the Immigration Act 1971 states that the provisions introduced under the Act for immigration control shall not apply to any person so long as he is a member of a mission, or 'a person who is a member of the family and forms part of the household of such a member'. Are the following exempt from control:

(a) the distant cousin of a Pakistani diplomat who has been looked after by this diplomat and his wife after the death of the parents;
(b) the fourth wife of a Yemeni diplomat who has been provided with separate accommodation by her husband in Yemen in accordance with Islamic law; and
(c) the young brother of an Indian diplomat who has equal rights with the diplomat in the joint property they have both inherited from their father?

The changed nature of the monogamous partnership is highlighted by Jane Lewis, in 'Family Policy in the post-War period' (2000):

In the European context, it has long been thought that family policy is something that the continental European countries (especially France) had and Britain did not. Not until the 1990s did government, first Conservative and then Labour, attempt to formulate a family policy. However...the absence of an explicit family policy does not mean that governments do not have one. This chapter begins with the assumptions underlying policies and seeks to show how the story of the development of family policy in Britain has been the movement away from a relatively firm and coherent set of (implicit) assumptions about what the family looks like and how it works. Only with the dawning realization as to the profound and rapid change in family patterns over the past twenty-five years and especially over the last decade has government put the family on the policy agenda.

> Not surprisingly, historically government has assumed the existence of a two-parent family, in which the husband and father's primary task is to earn and maintain and that of the wife and mother to care. This rendered the woman dependent on a male breadwinner, and women gained entitlements in respect of modern welfare policies chiefly as wives rather than as mothers. Indeed the early feminist literature on the post-war welfare state emphasized the extent to which social policies represented 'the state organisation of domestic life'. Certainly, the assumptions about female dependency were the same ones that made it possible for the vote to be confined to male 'heads of families' throughout the nineteenth century and part of the twentieth.
>
> However, the social reality is more complicated. Women's position in the modern welfare state is more complex than that of men, and has also undergone more change. Broadly speaking, the proportion in the labour market of women with children has increased dramatically, but the amount of unpaid domestic work (housework and caring work for young and old) carried out by men has changed very little. The mix of work (although not necessarily the kind of work) performed by women has changed much more than the mix of work performed by men. The sources of income for women have therefore also changed. During the twentieth century there was a major shift away from dependence on individual male relatives (especially husbands), and towards increased dependence on the labour market for married women and for single women without children, and dependence on the state for lone women with children. In the case of the latter, modern social welfare policies have permitted the transformation of traditional family forms and the formation of autonomous households by lone mothers, while at the same time attempting to enforce assumptions about men's obligation to maintain. Thus state policies have in practice often been Janus-faced in this respect.
>
> The nature of the relationship between the increase in women's employment, the development of state benefit programmes, and the increasing autonomy of women is a highly fraught subject. The position of the family as a mediating institution between the individual and the state has undergone huge change. The fundamental dilemma for government at the end of the twentieth century has become how far it can or should treat adult family members as independent individuals. In face of the increasing proportion of adult women in the workforce, should it completely abandon any notion of dependency inherent in the male breadwinner model? In face of changing family forms, with less marriage, later marriage, more cohabitation, and more lone motherhood, should it abandon the attempt to regulate family life via the law of husband and wife? If so, does this not mean that new measures are needed to secure the position of children? Family policy in the form of public *and* private law has never been entirely coherent in its treatment of family members at the level of either principles or practice. The trend in terms of the social reality has been towards greater 'individualization', although this does not mean that women have become fully individualized. In the closing years of the twentieth century the problem for government has become how far to recognize the changing social reality, the problem being that in taking steps to recognize it, the law may also promote it.

We shall be returning to this theme in Chapter 4. Before we look more generally at the law's response to the family, let us pause and ask whether the history of the family can have any relevance for lawyers in the first decade of the twenty-first century. In *Sociology of the Family* (1980) Michael Anderson asks the question whether family history can 'justify itself':

> ...It can do so above all by drawing out the implications of these changes for the kind of family life which is possible today and, above all, by demonstrating that old moralities and old behaviours cannot meet new situations and that, accordingly, present problems require new and not obsolete solutions.

Perhaps the most significant, and certainly analytically the most difficult of these changes have been in the family's relation to production. The peasant household was the focus of production with head and spouse organizing production using the household's own labour and exploiting and co-ordinating the contribution of all household members. Each class of individual had a clearly prescribed role and each member was dependent on the activities of all the others. In this situation there is a high degree of role interdependence both between spouses and between generations.... Not merely was production a joint activity but almost all consumption was either shared or was undertaken in some way or other on behalf of the household.

By contrast, under our kind of capitalist system of production, work for the mass of the population becomes directed by others who select and reward labour on an individualistic basis. One or more household member leaves the domestic arena and each is remunerated by outsiders on a basis which normally takes no account of his or her family situation. The wage received is the personal property of the individual, is dependent on the individual's own level of activity and achievement, and is paid to the individual in private leaving him or her to negotiate with the rest of the family over how and to what extent the money is to be distributed in order to satisfy their wants.

The contrast between the jointness of income generation in the peasant family and its individualistic basis under capitalism was, to a considerable extent, concealed under early capitalist production by the continued participation of all except the youngest family members in income-generating activities. Even after legislation had removed children from full time factory employment there remained within local communities significant opportunities for children to add to family resources through cash or goods in kind obtained in return for odd jobs done outside school hours. In addition, the substantial levels of labour input required to process food and other materials for domestic consumption, together with the significant amount of domestic productive activity for both home production and for the market, allowed those who remained in the domestic arena to contribute significantly to family resource generation processes. Thus, in as far as the husband earned income outside the home on behalf of the family, the children (and particularly the male children) sought odd jobs on behalf of the family, and the wife (aided by the female children) produced domestically on behalf of the family, all resources being pooled together, the role interdependence remained and there was little analytical difference between this situation and the peasant system where the husband and male children worked in the outfield producing in part marketable products to pay the rent, while wife and female children worked in the infield and the home on the production and reproduction of labour power. Of course, because wages were the private property of the individual there was no guarantee that wages were in fact pooled – as the harrowing descriptions of the wives of nineteenth-century factory workers trying to extract their husbands from public houses on pay day testify....

However, developments of the last fifty years have moved most families significantly away from this position. Children have become almost totally dependent. They leave the home daily for education which is oriented far more to their individual futures than to their current family roles and subsequently enter the labour force to receive pay much of which is again retained for their own use even in the very few years that now typically remain between starting work and marriage. In this way children have almost totally ceased to be part of an interdependent resource-generating system. Similarly, in as far as both spouses enter the labour force and each receives a private reward for labour (and particularly as in many dual career families where outside workers come in to perform most of the domestic work, which anyway can now if desired require a much smaller labour input), the work of the spouses can no longer so easily be seen as a co-operative productive activity or even as involving a complementary division of labour where each performs different but interrelated tasks on behalf of the family unit.... The ties between family members thus

> become based not on an interdependence rooted in cooperative productive activity essential for survival, but on personal interdependence oriented towards the joint attainment of essentially intrinsic 'projects' of highly diverse kinds.
>
> However, these aspirations are much more susceptible to change over time than are the basic survival objectives of pre-industrial European societies, and their interpersonal basis is much more fragile. ... Thus it is not surprising that wherever we see communities moving from family groups based on property and co-operative production, so we also see a decline in parental involvement in mate selection and, usually, a fall in the age of marriage and a rise in marital instability. ...
>
> Viewed in a historical perspective, therefore, there is in the contemporary capitalist world a marked lack of structural support for familial bonds. In addition, demographic changes have increased the emphasis on intrinsic functions of marriage through the reduction in the period of the family life cycle which is devoted to the bearing and rearing of small children. ...
>
> Equally importantly, the other main prop to traditional family morality – close community supervision – has also been undermined and, indeed, in a comparative perspective, family behaviour has become the most private and personal of all areas of behaviour, almost totally free from external supervision and control.

QUESTIONS

i. Does a possibly false view of family history in this country prevent us from accepting that families fall today and have always fallen into different types?

ii. Do you agree that personal behaviour is now 'almost totally free from external supervision and control'.

1.2 THE LAW'S RESPONSE TO THE FAMILY

The challenge for the law is to respond to the wide range of family patterns we see in society today. At times it has been difficult for legal systems to develop the necessary breadth of vision, and law has been used to both resist and acknowledge changes. Contrast, for example, section 28 of the Local Government Act 1988 (repealed in 2003), which outlawed support by local authorities for the 'acceptability of homosexuality as a pretended family relationship', and the Civil Partnership Act 2004, which treats same-sex couples in almost the identical way as married couples. Legal debates about the meaning of the family have, as we shall see, frequently focused on issues of sexuality: same-sex relationships, transsexuality and opposite-sex relations outside of marriage. The historian and sociologist Jeffrey Weeks in *Sexuality and its Discontents* (1985) argues that issues concerning sexuality frequently appear to occupy a 'front-line in the battle for the future of western society'. This explains, perhaps, why the meaning of the family is so hotly contested. Similarly, Elizabeth Silva and Carol Smart, in 'The "New" Practices and Policies of Family Life' (1999), note that conservative politicians and commentators see 'changes in family life as bringing social disorder in their wake'. And that:

> While there is a widespread consensus that society is undergoing a process of rapid and radical change, political rhetoric tends to claim that the family is an institution which must not change.

> The family is still supposed to stand outside and above economic restructuring, market forces and financial, legal, technological and political change, as a pillar of supposed stability.

Since the last edition of this book significant changes have occurred. The Gender Recognition Act 2004 and the Civil Partnership Act 2004 are particularly noteworthy, and we discuss them in more detail in Chapter 2. And in Chapter 6 we discuss the law and latest proposals relating to the rights of unmarried cohabitants. Here, however, we review the changing ways in which the courts have interpreted the concept of the family and the meaning of the word 'spouse' and, in particular, the impact of the incorporation into domestic law of the European Convention on Human Rights.

Our starting point is the cases in which the courts have had to decide whether or not two individuals have lived together 'as man and wife' or whether or not a given individual is a member of another's 'family', for the purpose of succession to tenancies under various statutory regimes. The law in this area provides an overview of changing understandings of the family; both judicial reluctance and willingness to acknowledge them; and, the relationship between statutory and judicial law making.

The Increase of Rent and Mortgage Interest (War Restrictions) Act 1915 extended succession rights to widows of tenants who died intestate or family members who had resided in the property as a family member for six months prior to the death of the tenant. In accordance with the provisions of this Act in *Gammans v Ekins* [1950] 2 KB 328, [1950] 2 All ER 140 the Court of Appeal refused to grant a man the right to succeed to the tenancy of his female partner, even though they had been living together for over twenty years and were regarded by their neighbours as husband and wife. Lord Justice Asquith commented that:

> If ... the relationship involves sexual relations, it seems to me anomalous that a person can acquire a 'status of irremovability' by having lived in sin, even if the liaison has been one protracted in time and conclusive in character. To say that two people masquerading, as these two were, as husband and wife – there being no children to complicate the picture – that they were members of the same family, seems to me an abuse of the English language.

Similarly, Lord Evershed MR observed that:

> [I]t may not be a bad thing that it is shown by this decision that in the Christian society in which we live one, at any rate, of the privileges which may be derived from marriage, is not equally enjoyed by those who are not married.

Twenty-five years later, however, in *Dyson Holdings Ltd v Fox* [1975] QB 503, [1975] 3 All ER 1030, CA the Court awarded the tenancy to a woman who had been living with the tenant, although again unmarried and with no children. Lord Denning MR commented that:

> [I]f the couple had a baby nineteen years ago which died when a few days old, or as a young child, the woman would be a 'member of the tenant's family', but if the baby had been still-born, or if the woman had had a miscarriage nineteen years ago, she would not be a member of his family. Yet for the last nineteen years they had lived together as man and wife. That seems to be a ridiculous distinction. So ridiculous, indeed, that it should be rejected by this court.

A more restrictive approach followed in *Carga Properties (formerly Joram Development) v Sherratt* [1979] 1 WLR 928, [1979] 2 All ER 1084 where the House of Lords refused to grant a tenancy to a

24-year-old man who was living in a non-sexual relationship with the tenant – a 75-year-old woman. Lord Diplock referred to the following extract from the judgment of Russell LJ in *Ross v Collins* [1964] 1 WLR 425, CA as the rationale for his decision:

> [Family] still requires, it seems to me, at least a broadly recognizable de facto familial nexus. This may be capable of being found and recognised as such by the ordinary man – where the link would be strictly familial had there been a marriage or where the link is through adoption of a minor, de jure or de facto, or where the link is 'step', or where the link is 'in-law' or by marriage. But two strangers cannot, it seems to me, ever establish artificially for the purposes of this section a familial nexus by acting as brothers or as sisters even if they call each other such and consider their relationship to be tantamount to that. Nor in my view, can an adult man and woman who establish a platonic relationship establish a familial nexus by acting as a devoted brother and sister or father and daughter would act, even if they address each other as such and even if they refer to each other as such and regard their association as tantamount to such. Nor in my view, would they indeed be recognised as familial links by the ordinary man.

Subsequently in *Harrogate Borough Council v Simpson* [1986] 2 FLR 91, [1986] Fam Law 359, the Court of Appeal held that a woman who lived in council accommodation with another woman, a secure tenant, and who shared a 'committed, monogamous, homosexual relationship' with her, was not a 'member of the tenant's family' within the meaning of section 113(1), (2) of the Housing Act 1985, and accordingly was not entitled to succeed to the tenancy on the death of the tenant (section 87 of the 1985 Act).

Following this case, the Housing Act 1988 redefined 'spouse' to include persons 'living as husband and wife'. This is the background to the decision of the House of Lords in *Fitzpatrick v Sterling Housing Association Ltd* [2001] 1 AC 27, [1999] 3 WLR 1113.

Waite LJ, in the Court of Appeal ([1998] Ch 304, [1997] 4 All ER 991) summarises the facts:

> The short but difficult question raised by this appeal is whether the surviving partner in a stable and permanent homosexual relationship can claim succession rights under the Rent Acts in respect of premises of which the deceased partner was a protected tenant. The facts are not in dispute. Mr John Thompson became the statutory tenant of a flat, No 75 Ravenscourt Road, London W6 (the flat), in 1972. The appellant, Mr Fitzpatrick, moved in to live with him there in 1976, and the two of them maintained from then onwards a close, loving and faithful homosexual relationship. Early in 1986 Mr Thompson suffered, as a result of a fall, head injuries which required surgery and then a stroke which left him a tetraplegic. From the summer of that year Mr Fitzpatrick nursed him at home, and dedicated himself to providing, with love and devotion, the constant care which he required. In 1994 Mr Thompson died.
>
> The landlords are a charity providing families and individuals with accommodation at affordable rents. ... Mr Fitzpatrick applied to take over the tenancy of the flat (which comprises four rooms plus kitchen and bathroom) but the landlords, though willing to rehouse him in smaller accommodation in another of their properties, were not prepared to agree.

The Rent Act 1977 provided that Fitzpatrick could succeed to the tenancy if he was, in relation to the tenant, (a) a spouse, (b) someone living with him or her as wife or husband, (c) a member of his or her family residing with him or her in the dwelling house at the time of and for a period of two years before his death. The Court of Appeal, by a majority, decided that Fitzpatrick fell within none of these three categories.

Waite LJ:

If endurance, stability, interdependence and devotion were the sole hallmarks of family membership, there could be no doubt about this case at all. Mr Fitzpatrick and Mr Thompson lived together for a longer period than many marriages endure these days. They were devoted and faithful, giving each other mutual help and support in a life which shared many of the highest qualities to be found in heterosexual attachments, married or unmarried....

The survey which I have undertaken in this judgment shows, however, that the law in England regarding succession to statutory tenancies is firmly rooted in the concept of the family as an entity bound together by ties of kinship (including adoptive status) or marriage. The only relaxation, first by court decision and then by statute, has been a willingness to treat heterosexual cohabitants as if they were husband and wife. That was a restrictive extension, offensive to social justice and tolerance because it excludes lesbians and gays. It is out of tune with modern acceptance of the need to avoid any discrimination on the ground of sexual orientation.... The question is: how is it to be put right?

Discrimination is not, unfortunately, the only arbitrary feature in this area of the law. Endemic within its system is a high risk of harsh or anomalous results – excluding from rights of succession many deserving instances of common households in which the survivor would have a strong moral case to succeed to the tenancy. Friends of long standing (widowers or spinsters for example) who share accommodation in old age without any sexual element in their relationship, but who often give and receive much the same kind of devoted care as we have admired in this case, are (and always have been) excluded. If succession rights are to be extended to couples of the same sex in a sexually based relationship, would it be right to continue to exclude friends? If friends are to be included, how is the stability and permanence of their household to be defined?

These questions have to be judged in the light of a further policy consideration – fairness to home-owners. Every enlargement of the class of potential successors to rent controlled tenancies involves a deeper invasion of rights of house-owners to possession of their own property. That there is a need to reconcile these competing social priorities is something on which it would be easy to find a broad consensus. The difficulty arises when it comes to finding ways and means. At that point opinions are bound to vary, and a political judgment may in the end become necessary. That is what makes the process of reconciliation a task better suited to the legislative function of Parliament than to the interpretative role of the courts.... As the law now stands, however, I feel bound, notwithstanding the respect and sympathy to which Mr Fitzpatrick is entitled, to dismiss the appeal.

Ward LJ (dissented):

Was the Appellant Living With the Original Tenant as his Wife or Husband?

[1] 'As' means 'in the manner of' and suggests how the couple functioned, not what they were. I agree with the test of Woolf J in *Crake v Supplementary Benefits Commission, Butterworth v Supplementary Benefits Commission* [1982] 1 All ER 498 at 502 which, so far as I can tell, was not referred to this court in *Harrogate BC v Simpson* (1984) 17 HLR 205. There being no dispute but that the appellant and the deceased were living together, it is 'necessary to go on and ascertain in so far as this is possible, the manner in which and why they (were) living together in the same household'. If asked, 'Why?', would not both they and also the heterosexual couple equally well reply, 'Because we love each other and are committed to devote comfort and support to each

other'? I can readily envisage that the immediate response to the question, 'How do you two live together?' may well be, 'As a gay couple'. But when the next question is asked, 'In what manner do you, a gay couple, live together?' would their answer be any different from that given by the heterosexual couple save only in the one respect that in their case their sexual relations are homosexual, not heterosexual? No distinction can sensibly be drawn between the two couples in terms of love, nurturing, fidelity, durability, emotional and economic interdependence – to name but some and no means all of the hallmarks of a relationship between a husband and his wife.

[2] With regard to the only distinguishing feature, sexual activity, that is a function of the relationship of a husband and his wife, a man and his mistress and it is a function of homosexual lovers. That the activity takes place between members of different sexes or of the same sex is a matter of form not function. Since the test I would apply is functionalistic, the formalistic difference can be ignored.

[3] It was Parliament's will in 1996 that public sector homosexual partners enjoyed protection from eviction, albeit only by use of guidelines issued to the local authority. Given that the broad intention of the 1977 Act is to protect against the loss of one's home, then conferring protection by extending para 2(2) to include the homosexual partnership is to provide the private sector tenants with security comparable to their public sector counterparts. Since the Glenda Jackson amendment was withdrawn in order not to exclude the homosexual couple but to extend protection to others, I consider I am more likely to reflect Parliament's will by finding for the appellant than by finding against him.

[4] I would say there is no essential difference between a homosexual and a heterosexual couple and accordingly I would find that the appellant had lived with the deceased tenant as his husband or wife.

Ward LJ also held that Fitzpatrick was a member of his partner's family and he concluded:

I have not reached this decision lightly. In truth, it has caused me a great deal of anxiety. I have worried that I have gone too far. If it is a matter for Parliament, and not for me, I hope Parliament will consider it soon. I have endeavoured to reflect public opinion as I see it but I am very conscious that public opinion on this topic is a continuum and it is not easy to see where the line is to be drawn. As Bingham MR said in *R v Ministry of Defence, ex p Smith* [1996] 1 All ER 257 at 263, [1996] QB 517 at 554: 'A belief which represented unquestioned orthodoxy in year X may have become questionable by year Y and unsustainable by year Z'.

I have come to a clear conclusion that *Harrogate BC v Simpson* was decided in year X; Waite and Roch LJJ, for reasons with which I could well have agreed, believe us to be in year Y whereas I have been persuaded that the discrimination would be thought by the broad mass of the people to be so unsustainable that this must by now be year Z. To conclude otherwise would be to stand like King Canute, ordering the tide to recede when the tide in favour of equality rolls relentlessly forward and shows no sign of ebbing. If I am to be criticised – and of course I will be – then I prefer to be criticised, on an issue like this, for being ahead of the times, rather than behind the times. My hope, to reflect the intent of this judgment, is that I am in step with the times. For my part, I would have allowed this appeal.

Fitzpatrick's claim was eventually successful. The House of Lords agreed with the Court of Appeal majority that the couple were not living as husband and wife, but followed the lead of the dissenting judgment of Ward LJ in holding, by a majority, that Fitzpatrick was a member of the tenant's family.

Lord Slynn of Hadley:

Given, on the basis of these earlier decisions that the word [family] is to be applied flexibly, and does not cover only legally binding relationships, it is necessary to ask what are its characteristics in this legislation and, to answer that question, to ask further what was Parliament's purpose. It seems to me that the intention in 1920 was that not just the legal wife but also the other members of the family unit occupying the property on the death of the tenant with him should qualify for the succession. The former did not need to prove a qualifying period; as a member of the tenant's family a two-year residence had to be shown. If more than one person qualified, then, if no agreement could be reached between them, the court decided who should succeed.

The hallmarks of the relationship were essentially that there should be a degree of mutual interdependence, of the sharing of lives, of caring and love, of commitment and support. In respect of legal relationships these are presumed, though evidently they are not always present, as the family law and criminal courts know only too well. In de facto relationships these are capable, if proved, of creating membership of the tenant's family. If, as I consider, this was the purpose of the legislation, the question is then who in 1994 or today (I draw no distinction between them) are capable in law of being members of the tenant's family. It is not who would have been so considered in 1920. In considering this question it is necessary to have regard to changes in attitude...

In *Barclays Bank plc v O'Brien* [1993] 4 All ER 417 at 431, [1994] 1 AC 180 at 198 Lord Browne-Wilkinson (with whom other members of the House agreed) said that in relation to the equity arising from undue influence in a loan transaction:

> 'But in my judgment the same principles are applicable to all other cases where there is an emotional relationship between cohabitees. The "tenderness" shown by the law to married women is not based on the marriage ceremony but reflects the underlying risk of one cohabitee exploiting the emotional involvement and trust of the other. Now that unmarried cohabitation, whether heterosexual or homosexual, is widespread in our society, the law should recognise this.'

In particular, if the 1988 amendment had not been made ('as his or her wife or husband') I would have no hesitation in holding today when, it appears, one-third of younger people live together unmarried, that where there is a stable, loving and caring relationship which is not intended to be merely temporary and where the couple live together broadly as they would if they were married, that each can be a member of the other's family for the purpose of the 1977 Act.

If, as I think, in the light of all the authorities this is the proper interpretation of the 1920 Act I hold that as a matter of law a same-sex partner of a deceased tenant can establish the necessary familial link....

It seems to be suggested that the result which I have so far indicated would be cataclysmic. In relation to this Act it is plainly not so. The onus on one person claiming that he or she was a member of the same-sex original tenant's family will involve that person establishing rather than merely asserting the necessary indicia of the relationship. A transient superficial relationship will not do even if it is intimate. Mere cohabitation by friends as a matter of convenience will not do. There is, in any event, a minimum residence qualification; the succession is limited to that of the original tenant. Far from being cataclysmic it is, as both the county court judge and the Court of Appeal appear to recognise, and as I consider, in accordance with contemporary notions of social justice. In other statutes, in other contexts, the same meaning may or may not be the right one. If a narrower meaning is required, so be it. It seems also to be suggested that such a result in this statute undermines the traditional (whether religious or social) concept of marriage and the family. It does nothing of the sort. It merely recognises that, for the purposes of this Act, two people of the same sex can be regarded as having established membership of a family, one of the most significant of human relationships which both gives benefits and imposes obligations.

It is plain on the findings of the county court judge that in this case, on the view of the law which I have accepted, on the facts the appellant succeeds as a member of Mr Thompson's family living with him at his death.

On that ground I would allow the appeal.

QUESTIONS

i. If Fitzpatrick's partner had died in 1960, what legal advice would you have given him?

ii. Suppose Mr Fitzpatrick and Mr Thompson's relationship had been an unhappy one; or suppose it had not been monogamous; or suppose Mr Fitzpatrick had not given up his job to look after his partner; would Mr Fitzpatrick's appeal have succeeded?

iii. Leslie J. Moran, in 'What's home got to do with it?' Kinship, Space and the Case of Family, Spouse and Civil Partnership in the UK' (2005), argues that judicial interpretation here is represented as continuity and that 'in *Fitzpatrick*, the House of Lords represents their radical support for same-sex couples as no change at all'. How do you think they achieve this?

iv. In what circumstances do you think couples who are 'living-apart-together' or close friends who cohabit should be considered to be 'family members'?

v. Stephen Cretney and Frances Reynolds in 'Limits of the Judicial Functions' (2000) query the judgment of the majority, in part, on the basis that:

> the defendant ... was not a Victorian rack-renting landlord but a Housing Association ... bound to comply with ministerial guidance on such matters as the allocation of housing accommodation between individuals ... this is emphatically not a question apt for decision by a judicial tribunal.

Do you agree that public housing issues should be dealt with only by Parliament?

In *Ghaidan v Mendoza* [2004] UKHL 30, [2004] 2 AC 557 the House of Lords returned to the question of same-sex relationships and tenancy rights – a major difference was that by then the Human Rights Act 1998 had come into effect and we turn to the impact of this now.

1.3 THE HUMAN RIGHTS PERSPECTIVE

Following the implementation of the Human Rights Act 1998, most of the European Convention on Human Rights is incorporated into our domestic law. The articles most frequently in the minds of family lawyers are Articles 8 and 12. (Article 12 concerns the right to marry, and we look at that in Chapter 2):

Article 8

1. Everyone has the right to respect for his private and family life, his home and his correspondence.

2. There shall be no interference by a public authority with the exercise of this right except such as is in accordance with the law and is necessary in a democratic society in the interests of national security, public safety or the economic well-being of the country, for the prevention of disorder or crime, for the protection of health or morals, or for the protection of the rights and freedoms of others.

This article was considered by the European Court of Human Rights in *Keegan v Ireland (family life: adoption)* (Application 16969/90) (1994) 18 EHRR 342, European Court of Human Rights.

Shortly after the birth of a child, the parents' relationship broke down and the child was placed for adoption by the mother, without the knowledge or consent of the father (the applicant). The Adoption Act 1952 permitted the adoption of a child born outside marriage without the consent of the natural father. The applicant applied to the Circuit Court and was appointed guardian and awarded custody of the child. The decision of the Circuit Court was upheld by the High Court, but on appeal the Supreme Court ruled that the wishes of the natural father should not be considered if the prospective adopters could achieve a quality of welfare which was to an important degree better. The case was remitted to the High Court. On the rehearing a consultant psychiatrist gave evidence that if the placement with the prospective adopters was disturbed after a period of over a year, the child was likely to suffer trauma and to have difficulty in forming relationships of trust.

An adoption order was subsequently made.

Judgment of the Court:

A. Applicability of Article 8

[42] The Government maintained that the sporadic and unstable relationship between the applicant and the mother had come to an end before the birth of the child and did not have the minimal levels of seriousness, depth and commitment to cross the threshold into family life within the meaning of Article 8. Moreover, there was no period during the life of the child in which a recognised family life involving her had been in existence. In their view neither a mere blood link nor a sincere and heartfelt desire for family life were enough to create it.

[43] For both the applicant and the Commission, on the other hand, his links with the child were sufficient to establish family life. They stressed that his daughter was the fruit of a planned decision taken in the context of a loving relationship.

[44] The Court recalls that the notion of the 'family' in this provision is not confined solely to marriage-based relationships and may encompass other *de facto* 'family' ties where the parties are living together outside of marriage. A child born out of such a relationship is *ipso iure* part of that 'family' unit from the moment of his birth and by the very fact of it. There thus exists between the child and his parents a bond amounting to family life even if at the time of his or her birth the parents are no longer cohabiting or if their relationship has then ended.

[45] In the present case, the relationship between the applicant and the child's mother lasted for two years during one of which they cohabited. Moreover, the conception of their child was the result of a deliberate decision and they had also planned to get married. Their relationship at this time had thus the hallmark of family life for the purposes of Article 8. The fact that it subsequently broke down does not alter this conclusion any more than it would for a couple who were lawfully married and in a similar situation. It follows that from the moment of the child's birth there existed between the applicant and his daughter a bond amounting to family life.

...

[50] According to the principles set out by the Court in its caselaw, where the existence of a family tie with a child has been established, the State must act in a manner calculated to enable that tie to be developed and legal safeguards must be created that render possible as from the moment of birth the child's integration in his family (see, mutatis mutandis, the *Marckx v Belgium* judgment of 13 June 1979, Series A no. 31, p. 15, para. 31...). In this context reference may be made to the principle laid down in Article 7 of the United Nations Convention on the Rights of the Child of 20 November 1989 that a child has, as far as possible, the right to be cared for by his or her parents. It is, moreover, appropriate to recall that the mutual enjoyment by parent and child of each other's company constitutes a fundamental element of family life even when the relationship between the parents has broken down.

[51] In the present case the obligations inherent in Article 8 are closely intertwined, bearing in mind the State's involvement in the adoption process. The fact that Irish law permitted the secret placement of the child for adoption without the applicant's knowledge or consent, leading to the bonding of the child with the proposed adopters and to the subsequent making of an adoption order, amounted to an interference with his right to respect for family life. Such interference is permissible only if the conditions set out in paragraph 2 of Article 8 are satisfied.

Held unanimously:

(i) that it was unnecessary to examine the Government's preliminary objection concerning the applicant's standing to complain on behalf of his daughter;
(ii) that the remainder of the Government's preliminary objections should be dismissed;
(iii) that Article 8 applied in the instant case and had been violated;
(iv) that Article 6(1) had been violated;
(v) that it was unnecessary to examine the applicant's complaint under Article 14.

Another decision on the unmarried family was *Kroon v Netherlands* (1994) 19 EHRR 263. Not surprisingly, the case law of the European Court of Human Rights has continued to explore and develop the meaning of 'family life'. It is has done so by looking at particular relationships (grandparents/grandchildren: *Price v UK* (1988) 55 DR 1988; siblings: *Moustaquim v Belgium* (1991) 13 EHRR 802), and their nature in individual cases; for example, not all unmarried fathers will have family life with their children. In *K and T v Finland* (Application 25702/94), [2001] 2 FLR 707, one of the many issues considered (we return to this case at p. 602) was the lawfulness of the removal of a newborn baby from her mother into emergency care, immediately after her birth; it was held that mother and baby had a family life, and that in this case their right had been interfered with:

[168]... the taking of a new-born baby into public care at the moment of its birth is an extremely harsh measure. There must be extraordinarily compelling reasons before a baby can be physically removed from the care of its mother, against her will, immediately after birth as a consequence of a procedure in which neither she nor her partner has been involved. The shock and disarray felt by even a perfectly healthy mother are easy to imagine. The court is not satisfied that such reasons have been shown to exist in the present case in relation to the child J.

K and J were both in hospital care at the time. The authorities had known about the forthcoming birth for months in advance and were well aware of K's mental problems, so that the situation was not an emergency in the sense of being unforeseen. The Government has not suggested that other possible ways of protecting the new-born baby J from the risk of physical harm from the mother were even considered. It is not for the court to take the place of the Finnish child welfare authorities and to speculate as to the best child care measures in the particular case. But when such a drastic measure for the mother, depriving her absolutely of her new-born child immediately on birth, was contemplated, it was incumbent on the competent national authorities to examine whether some less intrusive interference into family life, at such a critical point in the lives of the parents and child, was not possible.

The reasons relied on by the national authorities were relevant but, in the court's view, not sufficient to justify the serious intervention in the family life of the applicants. Even having regard to the national authorities' margin of appreciation, the Court considers that the making of the emergency care order in respect of J and the methods used in implementing that decision were disproportionate in their effects on the applicants' potential for enjoying a family life with their new-born child as from her birth. This being so, whilst there may have been a 'necessity' to take some precautionary measures to protect the child J, the interference in the applicants' family life entailed in the emergency care order made in respect of J cannot be regarded as having been 'necessary' in a democratic society.

QUESTIONS

i. Is the view of 'family life' developed by the European Court of Human Rights in *Keegan v Ireland*, *Kroon v Netherlands* and *K and T v Finland* different from your own understanding of what is meant by 'family life' and, if so, how does it differ?

ii. To what extent is the understanding of the House of Lords different from that of the European Court? (See p. 29 above.)

As is clear from the above extract from *K and T v Finland*, the court (and of course the courts in this country) must consider not only whether or not there is family life but also whether or not it has been interfered with contrary to Article 8 (2). (See *P, C and S v UK* [2002] All ER (D) 239 at p. 572.)

X, Y and Z v UK (Case No. 75/1995/581/667)
[1997] 2 FLR 892, European Court of Human Rights

The application was for a decision on whether or not the refusal to register X as the father of Z amounted to a violation of Article 8. The facts are summarised by the court as follows:

[12] The applicants are British citizens, resident in Manchester, England. The first applicant, 'X', was born in 1955 and works as a college lecturer. X is a female-to-male transsexual and will be referred to throughout this judgment using the male personal pronouns 'he', 'him' and 'his'. Since 1979 he has lived in a permanent and stable union with the second applicant, 'Y', a woman born in 1959. The third applicant, 'Z', was born in 1992 to the second applicant as a result of artificial insemination by donor ('AID'). Y has subsequently given birth to a second child by the same method.

[13] X was born with a female body. However, from the age of 4 he felt himself to be a sexual misfit and was drawn to 'masculine' roles of behaviour. This discrepancy caused him to suffer suicidal depression during adolescence. In 1975 he started to take hormone treatment and to live and work

as a man. In 1979 he began living with Y and later that year he underwent gender reassignment surgery, having been accepted for treatment after counselling and psychological testing.
[14] In 1990 X and Y applied through their general practitioner ('GP') for AID.... In November 1991 the hospital ethics committee agreed to provide treatment as requested by the applicants. They asked X to acknowledge himself to be the father of the child within the meaning of the Human Fertility and Embryology Act 1990.
[16] On 30 January 1992 Y was impregnated through AID treatment with sperm from an anonymous donor. X was present throughout the process. Z was born on 13 October 1992...
[18]...[F]ollowing Z's birth, X and Y attempted to register the child in their joint names as mother and father. However, X was not permitted to be registered as the child's father and that part of the register was left blank. Z was given X's surname in the register.
[19] In November 1995 X's existing job contract came to an end and he applied for approximately 30 posts. The only job offer which he received was from a university in Botswana. The conditions of service included accommodation and free education for the dependents of the employee. However, X decided not to accept the job when he was informed by a Botswanan official that only spouses and biological or adopted children would qualify as 'dependents'. He subsequently obtained another job in Manchester where he continues to work.

The Court had to consider whether or not the applicants shared a family life; and, if so, whether or not the registration rules amounted to a failure to respect their family life:

The Existence of 'Family Life'

[33] The applicants submitted that they had shared a 'family life' within the meaning of Art 8 since Z's birth. They emphasised that, according to the jurisprudence of the Commission and the Court, social reality, rather than formal legal status, was decisive. Thus, it was important to note that X had irrevocably changed many of his physical characteristics and provided financial and emotional support to Y and Z. To all appearances, the applicants lived as a traditional family.
[34] The Government did not accept that the concept of 'family life' applied to the relationships between X and Y or X and Z. They reasoned that X and Y had to be treated as two women living together, because X was still regarded as female under domestic law and a complete change of sex was not medically possible. Case-law of the Commission indicated that a 'family' could not be based on two unrelated persons of the same sex, including a lesbian couple... Nor could X be said to enjoy 'family life' with Z since he was not related to the child by blood, marriage or adoption.

At the hearing before the Court, Counsel for the Government accepted that if X and Y applied for and were granted a joint residence order in respect of Z, it would be difficult to maintain that there was no 'family life' for the purposes of Art 8.
[35] The Commission considered that the relationship between X and Y could not be equated with that of a lesbian couple, since X was living in society as a man, having undergone gender reassignment surgery. Aside from the fact that X was registered at birth as a woman and was therefore under a legal incapacity to marry Y or be registered as Z's father, the applicant's situation was indistinguishable from the traditional notion of 'family life'.
[36] The Court recalls that the notion of 'family life' in Art 8 is not confined solely to families based on marriage and may encompass other de facto relationships (see *Marckx v Belgium* (1979) 2 EHRR 330, § 31, *Keegan v Ireland* (1994) 18 EHRR 342, para (44) and *Kroon and Others v the Netherlands* (1994) 19 EHRR 263, § 30). When deciding whether a relationship can be said to amount to 'family

life', a number of factors may be relevant, including whether the couple live together, the length of their relationship and whether they have demonstrated their commitment to each other by having children together or by any other means (see, for example, the above-mentioned *Kroon and Others* judgment, loc cit).

[37] In the present case, the Court notes that X is a transsexual who has undergone gender reassignment surgery. He has lived with Y, to all appearances as her male partner, since 1979. The couple applied jointly for, and were granted, treatment by AID to allow Y to have a child. X was involved throughout that process and has acted as Z's 'father' in every respect since the birth... In these circumstances, the Court considers that de facto family ties link the three applicants.

It follows that Art 8 is applicable.

B. Compliance With Art 8

1. The Arguments as to the Applicable General Principles

[38] The applicants pointed out that the Court had recognised in *The Rees Case* [1987] 2 FLR 111, para 47, that the need for appropriate legal measures affecting transsexuals should be kept under review having regard in particular to scientific and societal developments. They maintained that there had been significant development since that decision: in particular, the European Parliament and the Parliamentary Assembly of the Council of Europe had called for comprehensive recognition of transsexual identity...; the European Court of Justice had decided that the dismissal of a transsexual for a reason related to gender reassignment amounted to discrimination contrary to Community Directive 76/207 (*P v S and Another (Sex Discrimination)* [1996] 2 FLR 347); and scientific research had been published which suggested that transsexuality was not merely a psychological disorder, but had a physiological basis in the structure of the brain... These developments made it appropriate for the Court to re-examine the principles underlying its decisions in the above-mentioned *Rees Case* and *Cossey v UK* [1991] 2 FLR 492, insofar as they had an impact on the present problem. The Court should now hold that the notion of respect for family and/or private life required States to recognise the present sexual identity of post-operative transsexuals for legal purposes, including parental rights.

However, they also emphasised that the issue in their case was very different from that in *Rees* and *Cossey,* since X was not seeking to amend his own birth certificate but rather to be named in Z's birth certificate as her father. They submitted that the margin of appreciation afforded to the respondent State should be narrower in such a case and the need for positive action to ensure respect much stronger, having regard to the interests of the child in having her social father recognised as such by law.

[39] The Government contended that Contracting States enjoyed a wide margin of appreciation in relation to the complex issues raised by transsexuality, in view of the lack of a uniform approach to the problem and the transitional state of the law. They denied that there had been any significant change in the scientific or legal position with regard to transsexuals: despite recent research, there still remained uncertainty as to the essential nature of the condition...

Like the applicants, they stressed that the present case was not merely concerned with transsexuality. Since it also raised difficult and novel questions relating to the treatment of children born by AID, the State should enjoy a very broad margin of appreciation.

[40] The Commission referred to a clear trend within the Contracting States towards the legal recognition of gender reassignment. It took the view that, in the case of a transsexual who had undergone reassignment surgery in the Contracting State and who lived there as part of a family

relationship, there had to be a presumption in favour of legal recognition of that relationship, the denial of which required special justification.

2. The Court's General Approach

[41] The Court reiterates that, although the essential object of Art 8 is to protect the individual against arbitrary interferences by the public authorities, there may in addition be positive obligations inherent in an effective respect for private or family life. The boundaries between the State's positive and negative obligations under this provision do not always lend themselves to precise definition; none the less, the applicable principles are similar. In both contexts, regard must be had to the fair balance that has to be struck between the competing interests of the individual and of the community a whole, and in both cases the State enjoys a certain margin of appreciation...

[42] The present case is distinguishable from the previous cases concerning transsexuals which have been brought before the Court..., because here the applicants' complaint is not that the domestic law makes no provision for the recognition of the transsexual's change of identity, but rather that it is not possible for such a person to be registered as the father of a child; indeed, it is for this reason that the Court is examining this case in relation to family, rather than private, life.

[43] It is true that the Court has held in the past that where the existence of a family tie with a child has been established, the State must act in a manner calculated to enable that tie to be developed and legal safeguards must be established that render possible, from the moment of birth or as soon as practicable thereafter, the child's integration in his ... However, hitherto in this context it has been called upon to consider only family ties existing between biological parents and their offspring. The present case raises different issues, since Z was conceived by AID and is not related, in the biological sense, to X, who is a transsexual.

[44] The Court observes that there is no common European standard with regard to the granting of parental rights to transsexuals. In addition, it has not been established before the Court that there exists any generally shared approach amongst the High Contracting Parties with regard to the manner in which the social relationship between a child conceived by AID and the person who performs the role of father should be reflected in law... Since the issues in the case, therefore, touch on areas where there is little common ground amongst the Member States of the Council of Europe and, generally speaking, the law appears to be in a transitional stage, the respondent State must be afforded a wide margin of appreciation...

3. Whether a Fair Balance Was Struck in the Instant Case

[47] First, the Court observes that the community as a whole has an interest in maintaining a coherent system of family law which places the best interests of the child at the forefront. In this respect, the Court notes that, whilst it has not been suggested that the amendment to the law sought by the applicants would be harmful to the interests of Z or of children conceived by AID in general, it is not clear that it would necessarily be to the advantage of such children.

In these circumstances, the Court considers that the State may justifiably be cautious in changing the law, since it is possible that the amendment sought might have undesirable or unforeseen ramifications for children in Z's position. Furthermore, such an amendment might have implications in other areas of family law. For example, the law might be open to criticism on the ground of inconsistency if a female-to-male transsexual were granted the possibility of becoming a 'father' in law while still being treated for other legal purposes as female and capable of contracting marriage to a man.

[48] Against these general interests, the Court must weigh the disadvantages suffered by the applicants as a result of the refusal to recognise X in law as Z's 'father'.

The applicants identify a number of legal consequences flowing from this lack of recognition. ...For example, they point to the fact that if X were to die intestate, Z would have no automatic right of inheritance. The Court notes, however, that the problem could be solved in practice if X were to make a will. No evidence has been adduced to show that X is the beneficiary of any transmissible tenancies of the type referred to; similarly, since Z is a British citizen by birth and can trace connection through her mother in immigration and nationality matters, she will not be disadvantaged in this respect by the lack of a legal relationship with X.

The Court considers, therefore, that these legal consequences would be unlikely to cause undue hardship given the facts of the present case.

[49] In addition, the applicants claimed that Z might suffer various social or developmental difficulties. Thus, it was argued that she would be caused distress on those occasions when it was necessary to produce her birth certificate.

In relation to the absence of X's name on the birth certificate, the Court notes, first, that unless X and Y choose to make such information public, neither the child nor any third party will know that this absence is a consequence of the fact that X was born female. It follows that the applicants are in a similar position to any other family where, for whatever reason, the person who performs the role of the child's 'father' is not registered as such. The Court does not find it established that any particular stigma still attaches to children or families in such circumstances.

Secondly, the Court recalls that in the UK a birth certificate is not in common use for administrative or identification purposes and that there are few occasions when it is necessary to produce a full length certificate.

[50] The applicants were also concerned, more generally, that Z's sense of personal identity and security within her family would be affected by the lack of legal recognition of X as father.

In this respect, the Court notes that X is not prevented in any way from acting as Z's father in the social sense. Thus, for example, he lives with her, providing emotional and financial support to her and Y, and he is free to describe himself to her and others as her 'father' and to give her his surname... Furthermore, together with Y, he could apply for a joint residence order in respect of Z, which would automatically confer on them full parental responsibility for her in English law...

[51] It is impossible to predict the extent to which the absence of a legal connection between X and Z will affect the latter's development. As previously mentioned, at the present time there is uncertainty with regard to how the interests of children in Z's position can best be protected... and the Court should not adopt or impose any single viewpoint.

[52] In conclusion, given that transsexuality raises complex scientific, legal, moral and social issues, in respect of which there is no generally shared approach among the Contracting States, the Court is of the opinion that Art 8 cannot, in this context, be taken to imply an obligation for the respondent State formally to recognise as the father of a child a person who is not the biological father. That being so, the fact that the law of the UK does not allow special legal recognition of the relationship between X and Z does not amount to a failure to respect family life within the meaning of that provision.

It follows that there has been no violation of Art 8 of the Convention.

QUESTIONS

i. The Gender Recognition Act 2004 now permits transsexuals to get married in the gender they are living (see Chapter 2). Do you think the arguments based on the margin of appreciation were justified?

ii. Do you think Z has a right to know about her biological parentage? Or about X's gender reassignment?

iii. Do you think that X should have been registered as Z's father? (Come back to this when you have read Chapter 9.)

Two further issues that the courts have had to consider are the relationship between Article 8 and Article 14, the latter of which guarantees that the rights set out in the Convention shall be secured 'without discrimination', and the duty of the courts under section 3 of the Human Rights Act 1998 to ensure that all legislation must be read and given effect to in a way which is compatible with the Convention rights.

Ghaidan v Mendoza
[2004] UKHL 30, [2004] 2 AC 557

The facts were as follows: Godin-Mendoza wished to succeed to the tenancy of his long-term male partner. While the decision in *Fitzpatrick* entitled him to an assured tenancy, as a member of his partner's 'family', he argued that he should be recognised as having lived with his partner 'as his wife or husband' and therefore be treated as his 'spouse' – a status that would entitle him to a more beneficial statutory tenancy. As the survivor of a homosexual couple he argued that he was being treated less favourably than a survivor of a heterosexual couple.

Lord Nicholls of Birkenhead:

[6] Mr Godin-Mendoza's claim is that this difference in treatment infringes Article 14 of the European Convention on Human Rights read in conjunction with Article 8. Article 8 does not require the state to provide security of tenure for members of a deceased tenant's family. Article 8 does not in terms give a right to be provided with a home: *Chapman v United Kingdom* (2001) 33 EHRR 399, 427, para 99. It does not 'guarantee the right to have one's housing problem solved by the authorities': *Marzari v Italy* (1999) 28 EHRR CD 175, 179. But if the state makes legislative provision it must not be discriminatory. The provision must not draw a distinction on grounds such as sex or sexual orientation without good reason....

[7] That is the first step in Mr Godin-Mendoza's claim. That step would not, of itself, improve Mr Godin-Mendoza's status in his flat. The second step in his claim is to pray in aid the court's duty under s 3 of the Human Rights Act 1998 to read and give effect to legislation in a way which is compliant with the Convention rights. Here, it is said, s 3 requires the court to read para 2 so that it embraces couples living together in a close and stable homosexual relationship as much as couples living together in a close and stable heterosexual relationship....

Discrimination

[9] ... Discrimination is an insidious practice. Discriminatory law undermines the rule of law because it is the antithesis of fairness. It brings the law into disrepute. It breeds resentment. It fosters an inequality of outlook which is demeaning alike to those unfairly benefited and those unfairly prejudiced. Of course all law, civil and criminal, has to draw distinctions. One type of conduct, or one factual situation, attracts one legal consequence, another type of conduct or situation attracts a different legal consequence. To be acceptable these distinctions should have a rational and fair basis. Like cases should be treated alike, unlike cases should not be treated alike. The circumstances which justify two cases being regarded as unlike, and therefore requiring or susceptible of different treatment, are infinite. In many circumstances opinions can differ on whether a suggested ground of distinction justifies a difference in legal treatment. But there

are certain grounds of factual difference which by common accord are not acceptable, without more, as a basis for different legal treatment. Differences of race or sex or religion are obvious examples. Sexual orientation is another. This has been clearly recognised by the European Court of Human Rights: see, for instance, *Fretté v France* (2003) 2 FLR 9, 23, para 32. Unless some good reason can be shown, differences such as these do not justify differences in treatment. Unless good reason exists, differences in legal treatment based on grounds such as these are properly stigmatised as discriminatory.

[10] ... Article 14 of the Convention does not confer a freestanding right of non-discrimination. It does not confer a right of non-discrimination in respect of all laws. Article 14 is more limited in its scope. It precludes discrimination in the 'enjoyment of the rights and freedoms set forth in this Convention'. The court at Strasbourg has said this means that, for Article 14 to be applicable, the facts at issue must 'fall within the ambit' of one or more of the Convention rights....

...

[12] ... It is common ground between all parties, and rightly so, that para 2 of Schedule 1 to the Rent Act 1977 is a provision which falls within the 'ambit' of the right to respect for a person's home guaranteed by Article 8. It is, in other words, common ground that Article 14 is engaged in the present case....

[13] In the present case para 2 of Schedule 1 to the Rent Act 1977 draws a dividing line between married couples and cohabiting heterosexual couples on the one hand and other members of the original tenant's family on the other hand. What is the rationale for this distinction? The rationale seems to be that, for the purposes of security of tenure, the survivor of such couples should be regarded as having a special claim to be treated in much the same way as the original tenant. The two of them made their home together in the house in question, and their security of tenure in the house should not depend upon which of them dies first.

...

[15] Miss Carss-Frisk QC submitted there is a relevant distinction between heterosexual partnerships and same-sex partnerships. The aim of the legislation is to provide protection for the traditional family. Same-sex partnerships cannot be equated with family in the traditional sense. Same-sex partners are unable to have children with each other, and there is a reduced likelihood of children being a part of such a household.

[16] My difficulty with this submission is that there is no reason for believing these factual differences between heterosexual and homosexual couples have any bearing on why succession rights have been conferred on heterosexual couples but not homosexual couples. Protection of the traditional family unit may well be an important and legitimate aim in certain contexts. In certain contexts this may be a cogent reason justifying differential treatment: see *Karner v Austria* [2003] 2 FLR 623, 630, para 40. But it is important to identify the element of the 'traditional family' which para 2, as it now stands, is seeking to protect. Marriage is not now a prerequisite to protection under para 2. The line drawn by Parliament is no longer drawn by reference to the status of marriage. Nor is parenthood, or the presence of children in the home, a precondition of security of tenure for the survivor of the original tenant. Nor is procreative potential a prerequisite. The survivor is protected even if, by reasons of age or otherwise, there was never any prospect of either member of the couple having a natural child.

[17] What remains, and it is all that remains, as the essential feature under para 2 is the cohabitation of a heterosexual couple. Security of tenure for the survivor of such a couple in the house where they live is, doubtless, an important and legitimate social aim. Such a couple share their lives and make their home together. Parliament may readily take the view that the survivor of them has a special claim to security of tenure even though they are unmarried. But the reason underlying this social policy, whereby the survivor of a cohabiting heterosexual couple has particular protection, is equally applicable to the survivor of a homosexual couple. A homosexual couple, as much as a heterosexual couple, share each other's life and make their home together. They have an equivalent relationship. There is no rational or fair ground for distinguishing the one

couple from the other in this context: see the discussion in *Fitzpatrick v Sterling Housing Association Ltd* [2001] 1 AC 27, 44.

[18] This being so, one looks in vain to find justification for the difference in treatment of homosexual and heterosexual couples. Such a difference in treatment can be justified only if it pursues a legitimate aim and there is a reasonable relationship of proportionality between the means employed and the aim sought to be realised. Here, the difference in treatment falls at the first hurdle: the absence of a legitimate aim. None has been suggested by the First Secretary of State, and none is apparent. ...

...

[20] ... I appreciate that the primary object of introducing the regime of assured tenancies and assured shorthold tenancies in 1988 was to increase the number of properties available for renting in the private sector. But this policy objective of the Housing Act 1988 can afford no justification for amending para 2 so as to include cohabiting heterosexual partners but not cohabiting homosexual partners. This policy objective of the Act provides no reason for, on the one hand, extending to unmarried cohabiting heterosexual partners the right to succeed to a statutory tenancy but, on the other hand, withholding that right from cohabiting homosexual partners. Paragraph 2 fails to attach sufficient importance to the Convention rights of cohabiting homosexual couples.

[21] Miss Carss-Frisk advanced a further argument, based on the decisions of the European Court of Human Rights in *Walden v Liechtenstein (Application no 33916/96)* and *Petrovic v Austria* (1998) 33 EHRR 307. ... In the *Petrovic* case the Applicant was refused a grant of parental leave allowance in 1989. At that time parental leave allowance was available only to mothers. The Applicant complained that this violated Article 14 taken together with Article 8. In dismissing the application the court noted that, as society moved towards a more equal sharing of responsibilities for the upbringing of children, contracting states have extended allowances such as parental leave to fathers. Austrian law had evolved in this way, eligibility for parental leave allowance being extended to fathers in 1990. The Austrian legislature was not to be criticised for having introduced progressive legislation in a gradual manner.

[22] Miss Carss-Frisk submitted that, similarly here, society's attitude to cohabiting homosexual couples has evolved considerably in recent years. It was only in July 2003 that the European Court of Human Rights in *Karner v Austria* [2003] 2 FLR 623 effectively overruled contrary decisions as already mentioned. The United Kingdom government responded speedily to the decision in *Karner's* case by including in two government Bills currently before Parliament, the Housing Bill and the Civil Partnership Bill, provisions which if enacted will have the effect of confirming on the face of legislation that the survivor of a cohabiting homosexual couple is to be treated in the same way as the survivor of a cohabiting homosexual couple for the purposes of para 2. The State should not be criticised for this gradual extension of the rights of cohabiting unmarried couples, first to heterosexual couples in 1988, and now more widely. The extension of para 2 to include homosexual couples would be at the expense of landlords, and in the interests of legal certainty this extension should be made prospectively by legislation and not retrospectively by judicial decision. Mr Wallwyn-James died more than two years before the decision in *Karner's* case.

[23] I am unable to accept this submission. Under the Human Rights Act 1998 the compatibility of legislation with the Convention rights falls to be assessed when the issue arises for determination, not as at the date when the legislation was enacted or came into force: *Wilson v First County Trust Ltd (No 2)* [2003] 3 WLR 568, 587, para 62. The cases of *Walden* and *Petrovic* concerned the margin of appreciation afforded to contracting states. In the present case the House is concerned with the interpretation and application of domestic legislation. In this context the domestic counterpart of a state's margin of appreciation is the discretionary area of judgment the court accords Parliament when reviewing legislation pursuant to its obligations under the

Human Rights Act 1998. I have already set out my reasons for holding that in the present case the distinction drawn in the legislation between the position of heterosexual couples and homosexual couples falls outside that discretionary area.
[24] In my view, therefore, Mr Godin-Mendoza makes good the first step in his argument: paragraph 2 of Schedule 1 to the Rent Act 1977, construed without reference to section 3 of the Human Rights Act, violates his Convention right under Article 14 taken together with Article 8.

Section 3 of the Human Rights Act 1998

[25] I turn next to the question whether s 3 of the Human Rights Act 1998 requires the court to depart from the interpretation of para 2 enunciated in *Fitzpatrick's* case.
[26] Section 3 is a key section in the Human Rights Act 1998. It is one of the primary means by which Convention rights are brought into the law of this country. Parliament has decreed that all legislation, existing and future, shall be interpreted in a particular way. All legislation must be read and given effect to in a way which is compatible with the Convention rights 'so far as it is possible to do so'. This is the intention of Parliament, expressed in s 3, and the courts must give effect to this intention.
[27] Unfortunately, in making this provision for the interpretation of legislation, s 3 itself is not free from ambiguity. Section 3 is open to more than one interpretation. The difficulty lies in the word 'possible'. Section 3(1), read in conjunction with s 3(2) and s 4, makes one matter clear: Parliament expressly envisaged that not all legislation would be capable of being made Convention-compliant by application of s 3. Sometimes it would be possible, sometimes not. What is not clear is the test to be applied in separating the sheep from the goats. What is the standard, or the criterion, by which 'possibility' is to be judged? A comprehensive answer to this question is proving elusive. The courts, including your Lordships' House, are still cautiously feeling their way forward as experience in the application of s 3 gradually accumulates.

...

[32] ... the mere fact the language under consideration is inconsistent with a Convention-compliant meaning does not of itself make a Convention-compliant interpretation under s 3 impossible. Section 3 enables language to be interpreted restrictively or expansively. But s 3 goes further than this. It is also apt to require a court to read in words which change the meaning of the enacted legislation, so as to make it Convention-compliant. In other words, the intention of Parliament in enacting s 3 was that, to an extent bounded only by what is 'possible', a court can modify the meaning, and hence the effect, of primary and secondary legislation.
[33] Parliament, however, cannot have intended that in the discharge of this extended interpretative function the courts should adopt a meaning inconsistent with a fundamental feature of legislation. That would be to cross the constitutional boundary s 3 seeks to demarcate and preserve.... There may be several ways of making a provision Convention-compliant, and the choice may involve issues calling for legislative deliberation.
[34] ... [T]hese features were present in *In re S (Minors) (Care Order: Implementation of Care Plan)* [2002] 2 AC 291. There the proposed 'starring system' was inconsistent in an important respect with the scheme of the Children Act 1989, and the proposed system had far-reaching practical ramifications for local authorities. ... In *Bellinger v Bellinger* [2003] 2 AC 467 recognition of Mrs Bellinger as female for the purposes of s 11(c) of the Matrimonial Causes Act 1973 would have had exceedingly wide ramifications, raising issues ill-suited for determination by the courts or court procedures.
[35] In some cases difficult problems may arise. No difficulty arises in the present case. Paragraph 2 of Schedule 1 to the Rent Act 1977 is unambiguous. But the social policy underlying

the 1988 extension of security of tenure under para 2 to the survivor of couples living together as husband and wife is equally applicable to the survivor of homosexual couples living together in a close and stable relationship. In this circumstance I see no reason to doubt that application of s 3 to para 2 has the effect that para 2 should be read and given effect to as though the survivor of such a homosexual couple were the surviving spouse of the original tenant. Reading para 2 in this way would have the result that cohabiting heterosexual couples and cohabiting heterosexual couples would be treated alike for the purposes of succession as a statutory tenant. This would eliminate the discriminatory effect of para 2 and would do so consistently with the social policy underlying para 2. The precise form of words read in for this purpose is of no significance. It is their substantive effect which matters.
[36] For these reasons I agree with the decision of the Court of Appeal. I would dismiss this appeal.

Baroness Hale of Richmond:
[130] It is not so very long ago in this country that people might be refused access to a so-called 'public' bar because of their sex or the colour of their skin; that a woman might automatically be paid three-quarters of what a man was paid for doing exactly the same job; that a landlady offering rooms to let might lawfully put a 'no blacks' notice in her window. We now realise that this was wrong. It was wrong because the sex or colour of the person was simply irrelevant to the choice which was being made; to whether he or she would be a fit and proper person to have a drink with others in a bar; to how well she might do the job; to how good a tenant or lodger he might be. It was wrong because it depended on stereotypical assumptions about what a woman or a black person might be like, assumptions which had nothing to do with the qualities of the individual involved; even if there were any reason to believe that more women than men made bad customers this was no justification for discriminating against all women. It was wrong because it was based on an irrelevant characteristic which the woman or the black did not choose and could do nothing about.
[131] When this country legislated to ban both race and sex discrimination, there were some who thought such matters trivial, but of course they were not trivial to the people concerned. Still less trivial are the rights and freedoms set out in the European Convention. The state's duty under Article 14, to secure that those rights and freedoms are enjoyed without discrimination based on such suspect grounds, is fundamental to the scheme of the Convention as a whole. It would be a poor human rights instrument indeed if it obliged the state to respect the homes or private lives of one group of people but not the homes or private lives of another.
[132] Such a guarantee of equal treatment is also essential to democracy. Democracy is founded on the principle that each individual has equal value. Treating some as automatically having less value than others not only causes pain and distress to that person but also violates his or her dignity as a human being. The essence of the Convention, as has often been said, is respect for human dignity and human freedom: see *Pretty v United Kingdom* (2002) 35 EHRR 1, 37, para 65. Second, such treatment is damaging to society as a whole. Wrongly to assume that some people have talent and others do not is a huge waste of human resources. It also damages social cohesion, creating not only an under-class, but an under-class with a rational grievance. Third, it is the reverse of the rational behaviour we now expect of government and the state. Power must not be exercised arbitrarily. If distinctions are to be drawn, particularly upon a group basis, it is an important discipline to look for a rational basis for those distinctions. Finally, it is a purpose of all human rights instruments to secure the protection of the essential rights of members of minority groups, even when they are unpopular with the majority. Democracy values everyone equally even if the majority does not.
[133] It is common ground that five questions arise in an Article 14 inquiry, based on the approach of Brooke LJ in *Wandsworth London Borough Council v Michalak* [2003] 1 WLR 617, 625, para 20, as

amplified in *R (Carson) v Secretary of State for Work and Pensions* [2002] EWHC 978 (Admin), para 52 and [2003] EWCA Civ 797, [2003] 3 All ER 577. The original four questions were:

(i) Do the facts fall within the ambit of one or more of the Convention rights?
(ii) Was there a difference in treatment in respect of that right between the complainant and others put forward for comparison?
(iii) Were those others in an analogous situation?
(iv) Was the difference in treatment objectively justifiable? ie, did it have a legitimate aim and bear a reasonable relationship of proportionality to that aim? ...

...

[135] It is common ground that one of the Convention rights is engaged here. Everyone has the right to respect for their home. This does not mean that the state – or anyone else – has to supply everyone with a home. Nor does it mean that the state has to grant everyone a secure right to live in their home. But if it does grant that right to some, it must not withhold it from others in the same or an analogous situation. It must grant that right equally, unless the difference in treatment can be objectively justified....

[136] It is also common ground that there is a difference in treatment in respect of that right between the respondent and the survivor of an opposite sex relationship. It is also common ground that sexual orientation is one of the grounds covered by Article 14 on which, like race and sex, a difference in treatment is particularly suspect. For the reasons given earlier, the grounds put forward to justify it require careful scrutiny....

...

[141] The relevant difference which has been urged upon us is that a heterosexual couple may have children together whereas a homosexual couple cannot. But this too cannot be a relevant difference in determining whether a relationship can be considered marriage-like for the purpose of the Rent Act. First, the capacity to bear or beget children has never been a prerequisite of a valid marriage in English law. Henry VIII would not otherwise have had the problems he did. Even the capacity to consummate the marriage only matters if one of the parties thinks it matters: if they are both content the marriage is valid. A marriage, let alone a relationship analogous to marriage, can exist without either the presence or the possibility of children from that relationship. Secondly, however, the presence of children is a relevant factor in deciding whether a relationship is marriage-like but if the couple are bringing up children together, it is unlikely to matter whether or not they are the biological children of both parties. Both married and unmarried couples, both homosexual and heterosexual, may bring up children together. One or both may have children from another relationship: this is not at all uncommon in lesbian relationships and the court may grant them a shared residence order so that they may share parental responsibility. A lesbian couple may have children by donor insemination who are brought up as the children of them both: it is not uncommon for each of them to bear a child in this way. A gay or lesbian couple may foster other people's children. When the relevant sections of the Adoption and Children Act 2002 are brought into force [note: they are now], they will be able to adopt: this means that they will indeed have a child together in the eyes of the law. Thirdly, however, there is absolutely no reason to think that the protection given by the Rent Act to the surviving partner's home was given for the sake of the couple's children. Statutes usually make it plain if they wish to protect minor children. These days, the succession is likely to take place after any children have grown up and left home. Children, whether adult or minor, who are still living in the home may succeed as members of the family under para 3 of the Schedule. It is the longstanding social and economic interdependence, which may or may not be the product of having brought up children together, that qualifies for the protection of the Act. In the days when the tenant was likely to be a man with a dependent wife, it was understandable that preference was given to the widow over anyone else in the family. But in 1980 that preference was

extended to widowers, whether or not they were dependent upon the deceased wife. In 1988 it was extended to the survivor of unmarried marriage-like relationships, again irrespective of sex or financial dependence.

[142] Homosexual couples can have exactly the same sort of interdependent couple relationship as heterosexuals can. Sexual 'orientation' defines the sort of person with whom one wishes to have sexual relations. It requires another person to express itself. Some people, whether heterosexual or homosexual, may be satisfied with casual or transient relationships. But most human beings eventually want more than that. They want love. And with love they often want not only the warmth but also the sense of belonging to one another which is the essence of being a couple. And many couples also come to want the stability and permanence which go with sharing a home and a life together, with or without the children who for many people go to make a family. In this, people of homosexual orientation are no different from people of heterosexual orientation.

[143] It follows that a homosexual couple whose relationship is marriage-like in the same ways that an unmarried heterosexual couple's relationship is marriage-like are indeed in an analogous situation. Any difference in treatment is based upon their sexual orientation. It requires an objective justification if it is to comply with Article 14. Whatever the scope for a 'discretionary area of judgment' in these cases may be, there has to be a legitimate aim before a difference in treatment can be justified. But what could be the legitimate aim of singling out heterosexual couples for more favourable treatment than homosexual couples? It cannot be the *protection* of the traditional family. The traditional family is not protected by granting it a benefit which is denied to people who cannot or will not become a traditional family. What is really meant by the 'protection' of the traditional family is the *encouragement* of people to form traditional families and the *discouragement* of people from forming others. There are many reasons why it might be legitimate to encourage people to marry and to discourage them from living together without marrying. These reasons might have justified the Act in stopping short at marriage. Once it went beyond marriage to unmarried relationships, the aim would have to be encouraging one sort of unmarried relationship and discouraging another. The Act does distinguish between unmarried but marriage-like relationships and more transient liaisons. It is easy to see how that might pursue a legitimate aim and easier still to see how it might justify singling out the survivor for preferential succession rights. But, as Buxton LJ [2003] Ch 380, 391, para 21, pointed out, it is difficult to see how heterosexuals will be encouraged to form and maintain such marriage-like relationships by the knowledge that the equivalent benefit is being denied to homosexuals. The distinction between heterosexual and homosexual couples might be aimed at discouraging homosexual relationships generally. But that cannot now be regarded as a legitimate aim. It is inconsistent with the right to respect for private life accorded to 'everyone', including homosexuals, by Article 8 since *Dudgeon v United Kingdom* (1981) 4 EHRR 149. If it is not legitimate to discourage homosexual relationships, it cannot be legitimate to discourage stable, committed, marriage-like homosexual relationships of the sort which qualify the survivor to succeed to the home. Society wants its intimate relationships, particularly but not only if there are children involved, to be stable, responsible and secure. It is the transient, irresponsible and insecure relationships which cause us so much concern.

[144] I have used the term 'marriage-like' to describe the sort of relationship which meets the statutory test of living together 'as husband and wife'. Once upon a time it might have been difficult to apply those words to a same sex relationship because both in law and in reality the roles of the husband and wife were so different and those differences were defined by their genders. That is no longer the case. The law now differentiates between husband and wife in only a very few and unimportant respects. Husbands and wives decide for themselves who will go out to work and who will do the homework and childcare. Mostly each does some of each. The roles are inter-changeable. There is thus no difficulty in applying the term 'marriage-like' to same-sex

relationships. With the greatest respect to my noble and learned friend, Lord Millett, I also see no difficulty in applying the term 'as husband and wife' to persons of the same sex living together in such a relationship. As Mr Sales, for the Secretary of State, said in argument, this is not even a marginal case. It is well within the bounds of what is possible under s 3(1) of the Human Rights Act 1998. If it is possible so to interpret the term in order to make it compliant with Convention rights, it is our duty under s 3(1) so to do.

QUESTIONS

i. Lord Millett dissented from the majority judgment on the basis that that the matter was one that should be left to Parliament. He observed that:

> [I]n support of their conclusion that the existing discrimination is incompatible with the Convention, there is a tendency in some of the speeches of the majority to refer to loving, stable and long-lasting homosexual relationships. It is left wholly unclear whether qualification for the successive tenancy is confined to couples enjoying such a relationship or, consistently with the legislative policy which Parliament has hitherto adopted, is dependent on status and not merit (para [100]).

Could you now give a legal definition of a spouse?

ii. Following the decision in *Ghaidan*, in *Nutting v Southern Housing Group Limited* [2004] EWHC 2982, [2004] All ER (D) 347 a man's claim to succeed to his deceased male partner's tenancy was rejected on the basis that he failed to satisfy the court that their relationship constituted a spousal relationship. The test applied by the Registrar and held to be 'entirely adequate' by Evans-Lombe J was as follows:

> (b) Is the relationship an emotional one of mutual lifetime commitment rather than simply one of convenience, friendship, companionship or the living together of lovers?
> (c) Is the relationship one which has been presented to the outside world openly and unequivocally so that society considers it to be of permanent intent – the words 'till death us do part' being apposite?

Do you think 'lifetime commitment' reflects popular understandings of marriage?

iii. Nicholas Bamforth comments in 'The Benefits of marriage in all but name?' (2007) that:

> In *Karner v Austria*, the Court stressed that 'differences based on sexual orientation require particularly serious reasons by way of justification' and that states had only a narrow margin of appreciation in this context. However, the Court also accepted, perhaps puzzlingly, that 'protection of the family in the traditional sense' was 'in principle, a weighty and legitimate reason which might justify a difference in treatment' in appropriate circumstances.

Can you think of any reasons why handicapping those who by nature or temperament are unable or unwilling to enter into heterosexual relationships serves to promote heterosexual family life?

iv. The Law Commission (2003) *Renting Homes* Cm 6018 has proposed that social landlords should have available to them a ground for seeking possession based on under-occupation (although this would not apply to spouse successors). Do you think private and public landlords should have the same rights?

v. Martin Davis and David Hughes argue in 'What's sex got to do with it? – the ever contentious issue of succession to tenancies' (2005) that:

> Unless the courts are willing to use the HRA to further extend protection to carers and close friends in relation to succession then discrimination has not been eliminated, merely refocused.

Do you agree?

vi. The Law Commission of Canada in *Beyond Conjugality: Recognizing and supporting close personal adult relationships* (2001) asks: 'Can we imagine a legislative regime that accomplishes its goals more effectively by relying less on whether people are living in particular kinds of relationships?' They recommended that:

> Governments should review all their laws and policies to consider whether legislative objectives could be better accomplished if individuals were entitled to choose which of their close personal relationships they want to be subject to particular laws or polices, if so legislation should be revised to permit self-designation of included relationships.

What do you think is the relevance of relationships in the context of the 'legislative objectives' of taxation, immigration and housing? How would the above recommendation require a change in the law in the UK?

In *Ghaidan* it was accepted that the right to respect for the home was an issue that was within the scope of Article 8. But the scope, or 'ambit', of Article 8 is not always so clear.

M v Secretary of State for Work and Pensions
[2006] UKHL 11, [2006] 2 AC 91

The claimant challenged the calculation of child support payments under the Child Support Act 1991, on the grounds that a parent who lived with a same-sex partner was not treated in the same way as a parent who lived with an opposite-sex partner. As a result of the Civil Partnership Act 2004 this is no longer the case. However, the majority of the House of Lords rejected her claim and the case demonstrates different approaches to the question of the ambit of Article 8.

Lord Bingham of Cornhill:

[5] ... I do not think the enhanced contribution required of Ms M impairs in any material way her family life with her children and former husband, or her family life with her children and her current partner, or her private life. No doubt Ms M has less money to spend than if she were required to contribute less ... But this does not impair the love, trust, confidence, mutual dependence and unconstrained social intercourse which are the essence of family life, nor does it invade the sphere of personal and sexual autonomy which are the essence of private life . . . .

[6] Even if the child support regime is, in the respect complained of, within the ambit of a Convention right, Ms M's complaint of discrimination is in my view anachronistic. By that I mean that she is applying the standards of today to criticise a regime which when it was established represented the accepted values of our society. ... [T]he Civil Partnership Act 2004, has established a new consensus and removed the feature of the old social security and child support

regimes of which Ms M complains. If such a regime were to be established today, Ms M could with good reason stigmatise the regime as unjustifiably discriminatory. But it is unrealistic to stigmatise as unjustifiably discriminatory a regime which, given the size of the overall task and the need to recruit the support of the public, could scarcely have been reformed sooner.

Lord Nicholls of Birkenhead:

[24] ... [T]he concept of family life in article 8 is an 'autonomous' Convention concept having the same meaning in all contracting states. According to the established Strasbourg jurisprudence that meaning does not embrace same-sex partners. Under the Strasbourg case law same-sex partners still do not fall within the scope of family life.

[25] This was reiterated by the ECtHR in *Mata Estevez v Spain* Reports of Judgments and Decisions 2001-VI, p 311. The court noted the growing tendency in a number of European states towards the legal and judicial recognition of stable de facto partnerships between homosexuals. The court considered that, despite this, there was still little common ground between the contracting states. This was an area where the contracting states 'still enjoy a wide margin of appreciation'. The court held that, accordingly, the applicant's relationship with his late partner 'does not fall within article 8 in so far as that provision protects the right to respect for family life'.

[26] ... By the reference to 'margin of appreciation' in this context I do not understand the court to be saying that each contracting state may decide for itself whether the relationship between same-sex couples constitutes family life within the Convention. If that were so, the effect would be that, as applied to same-sex-couples, family life in article 8 would have a different content from one contracting state to another. That would be surprising. Rather, the court was saying that, in the present state of Strasbourg jurisprudence, contracting states are not required by the Convention to accord to the relationship between same-sex couples the respect for family life guaranteed by article 8. For the time being the respect afforded to this relationship is a matter for contracting states.

[27] This means that, as Strasbourg jurisprudence currently stands, the relevant law of the United Kingdom is not subject to scrutiny by the ECtHR so far as its Convention-compatibility is challenged on the basis that the relationship between a same-sex couple constitutes family life within article 8. As confirmed in the *Mata Estevez* ruling, the ECtHR does not at present recognise that the Convention guarantee of respect for family life is applicable to this relationship.

Lord Walker of Gestingthorpe:

[85] All three members of the Court of Appeal rejected the argument that the method of calculation of Ms M's maintenance assessment under the 1991 Act and the Regulations fell within the ambit of the right to respect for the family relationship between Ms M and her two children by her marriage to her ex-husband. ... In my opinion they were right to do so. Ms M is of course entitled to respect for her continuing relationship with her children. But she is not complaining of being deprived of all contact with her children, or of being deprived of contact with them at her home where her same-sex partner lives. On the contrary, they spend part of the time with her at her home. She is complaining because she considers that she should be paying less towards their maintenance. As Neuberger LJ said, at para 99, her article 14 complaint has nothing to do with respect for her relationship with her children.

[86] Ms M's stronger argument (as regards family life) depends on her present relationship with her same-sex partner. Kennedy LJ held ... that *Mata Estevez* is still good law at Strasbourg, and that our domestic law has not moved further forward. Sedley and Neuberger LJJ held that domestic law has moved further forward, ... relying heavily on *Fitzpatrick v Sterling Housing Association Ltd* and *Ghaidan v Godin-Mendoza*.

[87] I do not go into their reasoning because I am content to assume that the unit consisting of Ms M, her new partner and (especially when living with them) their children by their former marriages should be regarded as a family for article 8 purposes. I would also accept that the complicated formulae employed by the 1991 Act and the Regulations are intended to strike a fair balance between the competing demands (on often limited financial resources) of the children (when living away from the new home) and the new household. To that extent the legislation is intended, in a general sort of way, to be a positive measure promoting family life (or, it might be more accurate to say, limiting the damage inevitably caused by the breakdown of relationships between couples who have had children). But I do not regard this as having more than a tenuous link with respect for family life. I do not consider that this way of putting Ms M's case brings it within the ambit of respect for family life under article 8.

Lord Mance:

[151] This appeal is concerned with a period in the years 2001 to 2002 commencing only just after the decision in *Mata Estevez v Spain* (para 132 above). The decisions in *Karner v Austria* 38 EHRR 528 and *Ghaidan v Godin-Mendoza*, which followed it domestically, were concerned with the right to respect for the home (paras 146 and 147 above). In the light of the Strasbourg court's decision in *Mata Estevez v Spain* and what your Lordships' House has previously stated regarding article 8(1)–cf para 136 above–the concept of 'family life' under article 8 cannot, I think, be regarded as having included same-sex relationships during the relevant period from 13 August 2001 to 18 February 2002.

[152] I have little doubt that the Strasbourg court would see the position now as having changed very considerably, and that, if such an issue were to come before it in respect of the position in 2006, Ms M's same-sex relationship could very well be regarded, in both Strasbourg and the United Kingdom, as involving family life for the purposes of article 8. But that is because there have been continuing changes in social attitudes and in the legislative picture across Europe.

Baroness Hale of Richmond (the only dissenting judgment):

[107] The child support scheme is clearly capable of affecting the enjoyment of the right to respect for the family life of the mother and father and their children. There is no doubt that family life was established between this mother, this father and their children. There is equally no doubt that the family life of the mother and her children did not come to an end when the parents separated and divorced. Most children whose parents do not live together do not see themselves as living in 'single parent families'. They see themselves as having two parents, indeed sometimes more than two, who happen not to be living in the same household....

[108] Does the operation of the child support scheme fall within the ambit of the mother's right to respect for her family life with her children? In my view, it clearly does. It is one aspect, among many others, of the state's support for family life.... There is a private law obligation upon every parent to support their children and a private law right of the parent looking after those children to receive that money for the benefit of the children (and sometimes there is an express private law right for the children to receive it directly). But there is also a public law obligation upon every parent to support their children, currently expressed in section 78(6) of the Social Security Administration Act 1992. The child support scheme is the state's way of enforcing both of these obligations – the obligation owed to the children and the obligation owed to the state to prevent the children becoming a charge on the state. Before the child support scheme was instituted, the private law obligation was enforced through the family courts, no doubt not as efficiently as the state would have liked, but then neither is the child support scheme conspicuous in its efficiency....

> ...
>
> [110] Test it this way. The private law of child maintenance used to discriminate *systematically* between mothers and fathers. There was power to order a father to pay maintenance to the mother for the benefit of the children when there was no power to order the mother to pay maintenance to the father. The enforcement of the obligation to maintain one's children was one of the ways in which the state respected and facilitated the family life of both parents and children. Had the system continued to discriminate between mothers and fathers, this would surely have been sufficient to engage article 14. ...
>
> ...
>
> [112] The European Court of Human Rights has not yet recognised that the relationship between two adult homosexuals amounts to family life. But then I know of no case in which it has recognised that the relationship between two unmarried adult heterosexuals amounts to family life. Family life has so far been confined to the relationships between married couples and between parents or other relatives and carers and their children. This includes the relationship between a same-sex parent and his children and between a same-sex couple and the children of their family. This mother and her partner were clearly enjoying their right to respect for the family life which they had with their children while those children were with them. And family life continues even when parents and children are apart. The assessment and enforcement of child support clearly affects that family life, whether for better or for worse.

QUESTIONS

i. How do the judges differ in their approach to 'the ambit question'?

ii. Do you think a same-sex relationship is now within the ambit of 'family life' under Article 8?

iii. To what extent do you think child support payments impact upon family life?

iv. How would you explain the very different results in *Ghaidan* and *M*?

The issue of discrimination against non-spousal relationships was considered more recently.

Burden and another v United Kingdom
(2006) App No 13378/05, [2006] All ER (D) 160

The applicants were unmarried sisters aged 88 and 81 respectively. They had lived together all their lives; for the last 30 years in a house built on land inherited from their parents. The house was owned in their joint names and was currently worth £875,000. Each sister, in addition to her joint share in the house, owned investments and other property worth over £150,000. They submitted that the value of the house had increased to the point that each sister's one-half share was worth more than the current exemption threshold for inheritance tax, and that the survivor might have to sell the house in order to pay the tax. They argued that they could properly be regarded as being in a similar situation to a married or same-sex couple who have entered into a Civil Partnership Act (who are exempt from inheritance tax on bequests to each other) and complained to the European Court of Human Rights under Article 1 of the First Protocol to the European Convention on Human Rights, taken in conjunction with Article 14.

Article 1 of Protocol No. 1:

Every natural or legal person is entitled to the peaceful enjoyment of his possessions. No one shall be deprived of his possessions except in the public interest and subject to the conditions provided for by law and by the general principles of international law.

The preceding provisions shall not, however, in any way impair the right of a State to enforce such laws as it deems necessary to control the use of property in accordance with the general interest or to secure the payment of taxes or other contributions or penalties.

The Court held as follows:

[53] Since the duty to pay tax on existing property falls within the scope of Article 1 of Protocol No. 1, Article 14 is applicable.

[54] It is for the national authorities to make the initial assessment, in the field of taxation, of the aims to be followed and the means to be used ... The State enjoys a wide margin of appreciation in this field, as is usual when it comes to general measures of economic or social strategy ... A government may often have to strike a balance between the need to raise revenue and the need to reflect other social objectives in its taxation policies. Because of their direct knowledge of their society and its needs, the national authorities are in principle better placed than the international judge to appreciate what is in the public interest on social or economic grounds. The Court will generally respect the legislature's policy choice in this field unless it is 'manifestly without reasonable foundation' ... and subject to the proviso that, in creating and implementing a scheme of taxation, the State must not discriminate between tax-payers in a manner which is inconsistent with Article 14 of the Convention.

...

[56] The applicants claim to be in a similar or analogous position to co-habiting married and civil partnership couples for the purposes of inheritance tax. The Government, however, argue that there is no true analogy because the applicants are connected by birth rather than by a decision to enter into a formal relationship recognised by law.

[57] The Court recalls that in *Shackell v UK* (dec.) no. 45851/99, while observing that there might well be an increased social acceptance of stable relationships outside the traditional relationship of marriage, it found that the situations of married and unmarried heterosexual cohabiting couples were not analogous for the purposes of survivors' benefits, citing the Commission's opinion in *Lindsay v UK* [(dec.) no. 11098/84], that '[m]arriage continues to be characterised by a corpus of rights and obligations which differentiate it markedly from the situation of a man and woman who co-habit.' Since the coming into force of the 2004 Act in the United Kingdom, a same-sex couple now also has the choice to enter into a legal relationship designed by Parliament to correspond almost exactly to marriage.

[58] It is true that the decisions in *Shackell* and *Lindsay* were made in the knowledge that a man and a woman outside the prohibited degrees of family relationship are generally free to choose whether or not to take on the 'corpus of rights and obligations' involved in marriage. The applicants, as sisters, do not have this choice, and indeed it goes to the heart of their complaint that, despite their decision to live together in an exclusive relationship for many years, English law does not accord a level of recognition to their co-habitation approaching that given to a married or civil partnership couple. The Court does not, however, have to decide if that lack of choice has any bearing on the question whether, for the purposes of inheritance tax, the applicants can be regarded as being in an analogous position to married and civil partnership couples, because, for the reasons set out below, it considers that, even assuming that the

applicants can be compared to such a couple, the difference in treatment is not inconsistent with Article 14.

[59] In this regard, the Court recalls its finding in *Shackell* that the difference of treatment for the purposes of the grant of social security benefits, between an unmarried applicant who had a long-term relationship with the deceased, and a widow in the same situation, was justified, marriage remaining an institution that was widely accepted as conferring a particular status on those who entered it. The Court decided in *Shackell*, therefore, that the promotion of marriage by way of the grant of limited benefits for surviving spouses could not be said to exceed the margin of appreciation afforded to the respondent State. In the present case, it accepts the Government's submission that the inheritance tax exemption for married and civil partnership couples likewise pursues a legitimate aim, namely to promote stable, committed heterosexual and homosexual relationships by providing the survivor with a measure of financial security after the death of the spouse or partner. The Convention explicitly protects the right to marry in Article 12, and the Court has held on many occasions that sexual orientation is a concept covered by Article 14 and that differences based on sexual orientation require particularly serious reasons by way of justification ... The State cannot be criticised for pursuing, through its taxation system, policies designed to promote marriage; nor can it be criticised for making available the fiscal advantages attendant on marriage to committed homosexual couples.

[60] In assessing whether the means used are proportionate to the aim pursued, and in particular whether it is objectively and reasonably justifiable to deny co-habiting siblings the inheritance tax exemption which is allowed to survivors of marriages and civil partnerships, the Court is mindful both of the legitimacy of the social policy aims underlying the exemption, and the wide margin of appreciation that applies in this field ... Any system of taxation, to be workable, has to use broad categorisations to distinguish between different groups of tax payers ... The implementation of any such scheme must, inevitably, create marginal situations and individual cases of apparent hardship or injustice, and it is primarily for the State to decide how best to strike the balance between raising revenue and pursuing social objectives. The legislature could have granted the inheritance tax concessions on a different basis: in particular, it could have abandoned the concept of marriage or civil partnership as the determinative factor and extended the concession to siblings or other family members who lived together, and/or based the concession on such criteria as the period of cohabitation, the closeness of the blood relationship, the age of the parties or the like. However, the central question under the Convention is not whether different criteria could have been chosen for the grant of an inheritance tax exemption, but whether the scheme actually chosen by the legislature, to treat differently for tax purposes those who were married or who were parties to a civil partnership from other persons living together, even in a long-term settled relationship, exceeded any acceptable margin of appreciation.

[61] In the circumstances of the case, the Court finds that the United Kingdom cannot be said to have exceeded the wide margin of appreciation afforded to it and that the difference of treatment for the purposes of the grant of inheritance tax exemptions was reasonably and objectively justified for the purposes of Article 14 of the Convention. There has accordingly been no violation of the Article, read in conjunction with Article 1 of Protocol No. 1 to the Convention, in the present case.

Joint Dissenting Opinion of Judges Bonello and Garlicki

...

[2] The majority seems to agree that there has been a marginal situation or an individual case 'of apparent hardship or injustice' (paragraph 60) in respect of the applicants. What

seems to us, however, to be missing in the majority's position is a full explanation as to why and how such injustice can be justified. A mere reference to the margin of appreciation is not enough....

The national legislature is, generally speaking, free to adopt any reasonable policy of inheritance tax exemptions. As long as the United Kingdom confined the exemptions to married couples, such categorisation might have been justified under Article 12 of the Convention. However, once the UK legislature decided to extend the exemption to permanently cohabiting same-sex couples, the problem left the specific sphere of Article 12. Thus, any further categorisation in the area of inheritance tax-exemptions has to satisfy general standards of reasonableness and non-arbitrariness resulting from Article 14. ... The problem of siblings living together permanently did not escape the attention of the UK legislators and an appropriate amendment was proposed by the House of Lords. It was, however, rejected in the House of Commons on the basis of widespread agreement that the Civil Partnership Bill 'is not the appropriate legislative base on which to deal with [the problem]' (see paragraph 19 of the judgment). Such an approach may have been correct from the perspective of parliamentary technique, but it could not absolve the legislature from providing an equitable solution to the problem at a later stage.

[3] The situation of permanently cohabiting siblings is in many respects – emotional as well as economical – not entirely different from the situation of other unions, particularly as regards old or very old people. The bonds of mutual affection form the ethical basis for such unions and the bonds of mutual dependency form the social basis for them. It is very important to protect such unions, like any other union of two persons, from financial disaster resulting from the death of one of the partners.

The national legislature may establish a very high threshold for such unions to be recognised under tax exemption laws; it may also provide for particular requirements to avoid fraud and abuse. But unless some compelling reasons can be shown, the legislature cannot simply ignore that such unions also exist.

The situation of permanently cohabiting siblings under the UK legislation has also been negatively affected by the fact that – being within the prohibited degrees of relationship – they cannot form a civil partnership. In other words, they have been deprived of the possibility of choice offered to other couples. That is why the present case cannot be determined by reference to the *Shackell* decision ... since the latter was based on the fact that the persons affected were generally free to choose whether or not to enter into a formal union.

[4] The injustice generally inherent in the UK approach appears particularly striking in the circumstances of this case. Both sisters have already attained a rather advanced age; they have been together for several decades and neither of them has children. It is obvious that the State will be able to collect its tax in full upon the death of the surviving applicant. But the State wants to do it twice: first upon the death of the first sister and later by imposing a new inheritance tax on what still remains of the estate. As we see it, this is scarcely compatible with Article 14 taken in conjunction with Article 1 of Protocol No. 1. It may also raise problems under Article 8 if the extent of her tax obligations compels the surviving sister to leave her house or otherwise sacrifice the lifestyle to which she has been accustomed.

Dissenting Opinion of Judge Pavlovschi

... In my opinion, the decisive element in the case before us is the nature of the property belonging to the applicants, and their personal attitude to it.

Had assets purchased by the applicants during their co-habitation been at stake, I would have had no difficulty in accepting the majority's approach and, moreover, I would have readily agreed that part of such shared assets, inherited by a surviving sibling, could and should be considered as taxable property. In the case before us, however, we are faced with a qualitatively different situation. The case concerns the applicants' family house, in which they have spent all their lives and which they built on land inherited from their late parents. This house is not simply a piece of property – this house is something with which they have a special emotional bond, this house is their home.

It strikes me as absolutely awful that, once one of the two sisters dies, the surviving sister's sufferings on account of her closest relative's death should be multiplied by the risk of losing her family home because she cannot afford to pay inheritance tax in respect of the deceased sister's share of it.

I find such a situation fundamentally unfair and unjust. It is impossible for me to agree with the majority that, as a matter of principle, such treatment can be considered reasonable and objectively justified. I am firmly convinced that in modern society there is no 'pressing need' to cause people all this additional suffering.

QUESTIONS

i. Do you agree with the decision of the majority or the dissenting judgments?

ii. Why do you think Article 8 was not raised? (See Baroness Hale's reference to the right to respect for the home at para 135 in *Ghaidan* above.)

iii. If the sisters were living in rented accomodation and the sister who was the legal tenant died first, would the other have been able to succeed to the tenancy?

iv. Why is a sibling relationship that is 'loving, stable and long lasting' not treated in the same way as a spousal relationship?

v. Go back to the quotes from the *Gammans* case in the judgments of Asquith LJ and Evershed MR (p. 25 above). The treatment of unmarried partners seems outdated now. Do you think family law students in the future will see the current limited recognition of friends, carers and siblings as equally outdated?

vi. In 'Shifting Familiarity' (2005) Alison Diduck questions the extent to which opening up the meaning of the family is just about equality and pluralism:

> If everyone can now be in a family, and if families are the foundation for a healthy society, then it becomes all too easy for 'can' to become 'should'. Family members have responsibilities, to each other and to society, and families as a unit have responsibilities, too. And so, familiarization might, intentionally of unintentionally, operate as an emotional and psychological corrective to individualization, and its eager embrace by law means that more and more of us will now bear the legal responsibilities of family membership that are an important social and economic part of that corrective'.

Do you think siblings and friends should ever be required to support each other financially? Or children for their elderly parents? Does the pursuit of individual rights risk neglecting broader collective social responsibilities?

BIBLIOGRAPHY

1.1 Definitions of 'family' and 'household'

We quoted from:

M. Chamberlain 'Brothers and sisters, uncles and aunts: a lateral perspective on Caribbean Families' in E.B. Silva and C. Smart (eds), *The New Family?* (1999) London, Sage Publications Ltd, 135–138.

J. Eekelaar in *Family Law and Personal Life* (2006) Oxford, OUP, 44.

E.F. Emans, 'Just Monogamy?' in *Just Marriage* (2004) Oxford, OUP, 75–79.

F. Engels, *Origins of the Family, Private Property and the State* (1884) New York, Lawrence and Wishart, 244.

J. Haskey and J. Lewis 'Living-apart-together in Britain: context and meaning' (2006) 2(1) *International Journal of Law in Context* 37, 37–38, 45–47.

Judicial Studies Board, *Equal Treatment Bench Book* (2007), para 1.2.3 available at http://www.jsboard.co.uk.

Judicial Studies Board, *Handbook on Ethnic Minority Issues* (1995) chapter 6, 3.1–3.2.

M.M. Kavanagh, 'Rewriting the legal family beyond exclusivity to a care based standard' (2004) 16 *Yale Journal of Law and Feminism* 83–143, 84.

P. Laslett and R. Wall, *Household and Family in Past Time* (1972) Cambridge, Cambridge University Press, 28–30, 63, 64.

J. Lewis, 'Family Policy in the post-War period' in S. Katz, J. Eekelaar and M. Maclean (eds) *Cross Currents* (2000) Oxford, OUP.

The Office for National Statistics *Social Trends No. 37* (2007) Chapter 2, 14–17.

J. Reynolds and M. Wetherell in 'The Discursive Climate of Singleness: The Consequences for Women's Negotiation of a Single Identity' (2003) 13 *Feminism & Psychology* 489–510, 490, 507.

S. Roseneil, 'Why we should Care about Friends: An Argument for Queering the Care Imaginary in Social Policy' (2004) 3:4 *Social Policy and Society* 409, 411–416.

L. Stone, *The Family, Sex, and Marriage in England 1500–1800* (1977) London, Weidenfeld and Nicholson, 26–27, 102–104.

Additional reading

M. Anderson (ed.), *Sociology of the Family* (1980) Harmondsworth, Penguin Books.

M. Anderson, *Approaches to the History of the Western Family (1500–1914)* (1980) London and Basingstoke, Macmillan.

R. Ballard, 'South Asian Families' in R.N. Rapoport, M. Fogarty and R. Rapoport (eds), *Families in Britain* (1982) London, Routledge.

J. Barrow, 'West Indian Families: An Insider's Perspective' in R.N. Rapoport, M. Fogarty and R. Rapoport (eds), *Families in Britain* (1982) London, Routledge.

R. Deech, 'The Case Against Legal Recognition of Cohabitation' (1980) 29 *International and Comparative Law Quarterly* 480.

G. Driver 'West Indian Families: An Anthropological Perspective' in R.N. Rapoport, M. Fogarty and R. Rapoport (eds), *Families in Britain* (1982) London, Routledge.

L. Fox Harding, *Family, State and Social Policy*, (1996) Basingstoke, Macmillan.

E.J. Leib, 'Friendship and the Law' (2007) 54 *University of California, Los Angeles Law Review* 631.
R. Oakley, 'Cypriot Families' in R.N. Rapoport, M. Fogarty and R. Rapoport (eds), *Families in Britain* (1982) London, Routledge.
S. Poulter, *English Law and Ethnic Minority Customs* (1986) London, Butterworths.
E. Shorter, *The Making of the Modern Family* (1975) New York, Basic Books; (1977) London, Fontana, p. 38.
J. Weeks, B. Heaphy and C. Donovan, *Same Sex Intimacies: Families of Choice and Other Life Experiments* (2001) London, Routledge.

1.2 The law's response to the family

We quoted from:

S. Cretney and F. Reynolds, 'The Limits of the Judicial Functions' (2000) 116 *Law Quarterly Review* 181, 184.
L.J. Moran, 'What's home got to do with it? Kinship, Space and the Case of Family, Spouse and Civil Partnership in the UK' (2005) 17:1 *Yale Journal of Law and Feminism* 267, 279.
E.B. Silva and C. Smart, 'The "New" Practices and Policies of Family Life' in E.B. Silva and C. Smart (eds), *The New Family?* (1999) London, Sage Publications Ltd, 2–4.
J. Weeks, *Sexuality and its Discontents* (1985) London, Routledge, 17.

Additional reading

K. Boele-Woelki, 'The Road Towards a European Family Law' (1997) *Electronic Journal of Comparative Law* 1.1 available at http://www.ejcl.org/11/art11-1.html.
J. Dewar, 'The normal chaos of family law' (1988) 61 *Modern Law Review* 467.
M.A. Glendon, *State, Law and Family* (1977) Amsterdam, North Holland.
A.L. James and M.P.M. Richards, 'Sociological perspectives, family policy, family law and children: Adult thinking and sociological tinkering' (1999) 21(1) *Journal of Social Welfare and Family Law* 23.
A. McGlynn, 'The Europeanisation of family law' (2001) 13(1) *Child and Family Law Quarterly* 35.

1.3 The human rights perspective

We quoted from:

N. Bamforth, 'The benefits of marriage in all but name? Same-sex couples and the Civil Partnership Act 2004' (2007) 19 *Child and Family Law Quarterly* 133, 144.
M. Davis and D. Hughes, 'What's sex got to do with it? – the ever contentious issue of succession to tenancies' [2005] *The Conveyancer and Property Lawyer* 318.
A. Diduck 'Shifting Familiarity' (2005) 58 *Current Legal Problems* 234, 237.
Law Commission of Canada, *Beyond Conjugality: Recognizing and supporting close personal adult relationships* (Ottawa: Law Commission of Canada, 2001), 29 and Recommendation 3 at 141 (see http://www.lcc.gc.ca).

Additional reading

C. Archbold, 'Family Law-Making and Human Rights in the United Kingdom' in Mavis Maclean (ed.), *Making Law for Families* (2000) Oxford, Hart Publishing.

A. Baker, 'The Enjoyment of Rights and Freedoms: A New Conception of the "Ambit" under Article 14 ECHR' (2006) 69 *Modern Law Review* 714.

B. Cossmann and B. Ryder, '"What is marriage-like like?" The irrelevance of conjugality' (2001) 18 *Canadian Journal of Family Law* 269.

G. Douglas, *An Introduction to Family Law* (2001) Oxford, OUP, 41–57.

D. Feldman, 'The Developing Scope of Article 8 of the European Convention on Human Rights' (1995) 1 *European Human Rights Law Review* 265.

H. Swindells, M. Kushner, A. Neaves, R. Skilbeck, *Family Law and the Human Rights Act 1998* (1998) Bristol, Jordans/Family Law.

R. Wintemute, '"Within the Ambit": How Big *Is* the "Gap" in Article 14 European Convention on Human Rights?' (2004) *European Human Rights Law Review* 366.

2

RELATIONSHIP RECOGNITION: MARRIAGE AND CIVIL PARTNERSHIP

In this chapter we turn from exploring different forms of family life, to focus on the two adult relationships that are recognised by law: marriage and civil partnership. After considering the statistical trends we explore some of the historical and current reasons why the state recognises these relationships. From figures and theories, we turn to qualitative research, to consider the reasons why people get marrie d or enter civil partnerships. Here we look at 'sham marriages' as an example of how the reasons can differ from the expectations of the state. We then look at the legal rules that determine whether a marriage (or civil partnership) is void or voidable, and here we consider the impact of the Gender Recognition Act 2004 and the distinction between 'arranged' and 'forced marriages'. In the final section we look at the differences between marriage and civil partnership, and in examining the issue of 'gay marriage' we return to consider the meaning of marriage.

2.1 THE FACTUAL BACKGROUND

The number of marriages in England and Wales has fallen to the lowest level since records began. *Social Trends 37* (2007) provides some background to this trend.

> Partnership formation patterns have changed since the early 1970s as the overall number of people marrying has decreased. Despite this, married couples are still the main type of partnership for men and women. In 2006 there were 17.1 million families in the UK and around seven in ten contained a married couple.
>
> In 1950, there were 408,000 marriages in the UK and the number grew during the mid- to late-1960s to reach a peak of 480,000 in 1972. This growth can be attributed to the large number of babies born in the immediate post-Second World War baby boom reaching childbearing age and getting married at younger ages than in more recent years. The annual number of marriages then declined, reaching 286,000 in 2001 (Figure 2.9). From 2001 the number of marriages increased each year to 311,000 in 2004, before falling to 283,700 (provisional) in the UK in 2005.
>
> The average age at which people get married for the first time has continued to rise. In 1971 the average age at first marriage was 25 for men and 23 for women in England and Wales. By 2005 this had increased to 32 for men and 29 for women. There has been a similar trend across Europe. Between 1970 and 2004 the average age at first marriage in the EU-25 increased from age 26 to 30 for men and age 23 to 28 for women. However, there were differences in age of first marriage between EU-25 member states. In 2004 the country with the youngest newly-weds was Lithuania, with an average age of 27 for men and 25 for women, while Sweden had the oldest, with an average age of 34 for men and 31 for women.
>
> In England and Wales in 2005, 160,000 civil marriage ceremonies (marriages performed by a government official rather than by a clergyman) took place and accounted for more than two-thirds (65 per cent) of all marriages. This proportion was 68 per cent in 2004. More than one-third of all marriages (88,700), representing over half of all civil marriages, took place in approved premises (as opposed to places of worship or registry offices), which are licensed by local authorities under the *Marriage Act 1994* for the solemnisation of civil marriages (for example hotels or stately homes). This was a large increase from 5 per cent of all marriages in 1996 (Figure 2.10).

Figure 2.9 Marriages and divorces

Source: Office for National Statistics; General Register Office for Scotland; Northern Ireland Statistics and Research Agency

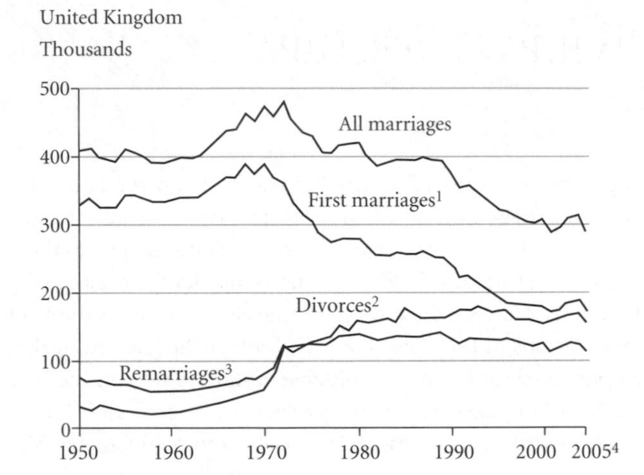

1 For both partners.
2 Includes annulments. Data for 1950 to 1970 for Great Britain only. Divorce was permitted in Northern Ireland from 1969.
3 For one or both partners.
4 Data for 2005 are provisional. Final figures are likely to be higher.

Figure 2.10 Marriages: by type of ceremony

Source: Office for National Statistics, 2004

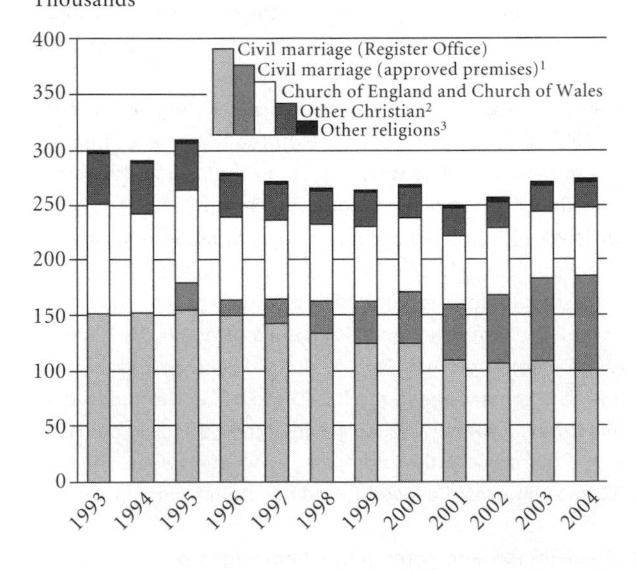

1 The *Marriage Act 1994* made provision for civil marriages to be solemnised in approved premises (with effect from 1 April 1995).
2 Includes Roman Catholic, Methodist, Congregationalist, Baptist, Calvinistic Methodist,
United Reformed Church.
3 Includes Jews, Muslims, Sikh and other unattached bodies.

Young Muslim adults were more likely to be married (22 per cent) than were young people from any other religious background. As with people from other religions, not all of these were living with their spouse. Christians and those with no religion were the least likely to be married – 3 per cent of 16 to 24 year olds in each group.

Percentage of 16 to 24 year olds who were married: by religion, April 2001, GB

Source: Office for National Statistics, 2004

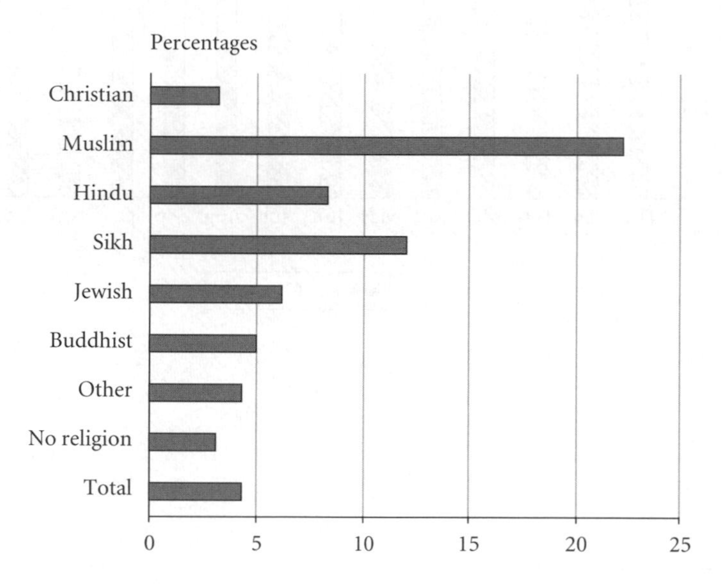

There were 18,059 civil partnerships formed in the UK between December 2005 and the end of December 2006. A total of 16,173 took place in England with 1,131 in Scotland, 627 in Wales and 128 in Northern Ireland ... More men than women formed civil partnerships. In 2006, 60 per cent of all civil partners were male compared with 66 per cent in December 2005. ... Male civil partners tended to be older than female civil partners. The average age at formation in the UK in 2006 was 47 for men and 44 for women compared with 54 and 46 in December 2005.

London was the most popular region within the UK in which to register a partnership between December 2005 and the end of 2006. A quarter of all civil partnerships took place in London, whereas the region accounts for only 12 per cent of the UK adult population. Areas in which the largest number of civil partnership formations took place were Greater Manchester Metropolitan County (734) Brighton and Hove Unitary Authority (689) and the London Borough of Westminster (602).

Up to the end of 2006, 10 per cent of men and 24 per cent of women forming a civil partnership in the UK had been in a previous marriage.

Civil partnerships

Source: Office for National Statistics, 2007

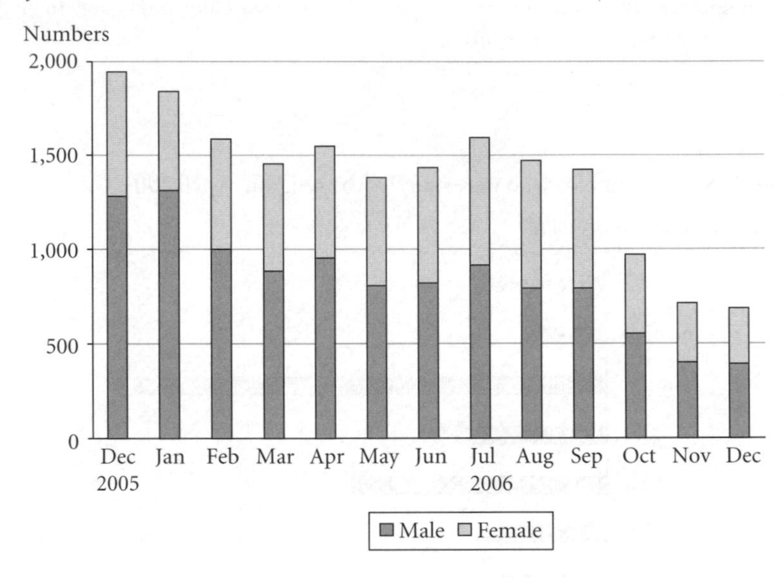

QUESTIONS

i. Why do you think the marriage rates have fallen?

ii. Why do you think the average age for entering a civil partnership is significantly older than that for marriage?

2.2 WHY DOES THE STATE RECOGNISE RELATIONSHIPS?

People who marry or enter a civil partnership are both protected and regulated by law; in other words, the status awards them both rights and responsibilities. The consequences are extensive and impact on almost all areas of law: tax, probate, property, adoption, evidence, tenancies, social security, immigration, to name but a few. (There is no simple statutory list of all the legal consequences but, in effect, this is now provided by the Civil Partnership Act 2004, as its aim was, as far as possible, to mirror the provisions relating to marriage.) We will examine some of the *consequences* in later chapters, but here we focus on the *reasons* for state recognition. One way to think about this is to ask 'what is a marriage, anyway?' The answer to this question is not as straightforward as might appear and in law the answers are often framed in the negative, as we shall see when we look at marriages that are deemed 'void', 'sham', 'forced' and 'gay'.

In the following list in 'The Autonomy Myth', Martha Albertson Fineman (2004) captures the interaction of religious, cultural, economic, moral and political factors that underlie the variety of potential meanings of marriage:

> ... [A] legal tie, a symbol of commitment, a privileged sexual affiliation, a relationship of hierarchy and subordination, a means of self-fulfilment, a social construct, a cultural phenomenon, a religious mandate, an economic relationship, the preferred unit for reproduction, a way to ensure against poverty and dependence on the state, a way out of the birth family, the realization of a romantic ideal, a natural or divine connection, a commitment to traditional notions of morality, a desired status that communicates one's sexual desirability to the world, or a purely contractual relationship in which each term is based on bargaining.

QUESTIONS

i. Which of the above definitions most closely reflects your own understanding of marriage?
ii. Can you identify legitimate public interests in relation to these different meanings of marriage?

While many of the above meanings can coexist within one jurisdiction, meanings can vary across time and in different societies.

C.C. Harris, in *The Family: an Introduction* (1979), expressed the problem in the following way: 'The inhabitants of Europe and America have an idea which they call marriage. People in other cultures have other ideas which are similar to, but not the same as, our ideas. Traditionally, the argument has been about how dissimilar the ideas have to get to force us to stop describing their ideas as "marriage".' E.R. Leach, in 'Polyandry, Inheritance, and the Definition of Marriage' (1955), argues that no definition can be found which applies to all institutions which ethnographers and anthropologists commonly refer to as marriage. Therefore he submits for consideration a definition based on a 'bundle of rights'. At least one part of the bundle must be present before the term 'marriage' can be used. The list, which according to Leach is not closed, is as follows:

> A. To establish the legal father of a woman's children.
> B. To establish a legal mother of a man's children.
> C. To give the husband a monopoly in the wife's sexuality.
> D. To give the wife a monopoly in the husband's sexuality.
> E. To give the husband partial or monopolistic rights to the wife's domestic and other labor services.
> F. To give the wife partial or monopolistic rights to the husband's labor services.
> G. To give the husband partial or total rights over property belonging or potentially accruing to the wife.
> H. To give the wife partial or total rights over property belonging or potentially accruing to the husband.
> I. To establish a joint fund of property – a partnership – for the benefit of the children of the marriage.
> J. To establish a socially significant 'relationship of affinity' between the husband and his wife's brothers.

In contrast with Leach, there are other scholars, of whom E. Kathleen Gough, in 'The Nayars and the Definition of Marriage' (1959), is representative, who argue that 'the status of children born to various types of union [is] critical for decisions as to which of these unions constitute marriage'. As a tentative definition that would have cross-cultural validity, and will fit the unusual cases such as that of the Nayar, Gough suggests: 'Marriage is a relationship established between a woman and one or more other persons which provides that a child born to the woman under circumstances not prohibited by the rules of the relationship, is accorded full birth-status rights common to normal members of his society or social stratum.' In a period before the British took control of India, Nayar women customarily had a small but not a fixed number of husbands. When a woman became pregnant, it was essential for one of those men to acknowledge probable paternity. The genitor, however, had no economic, social, legal or ritual rights, in nor obligations to, his children, once he had paid the fees of their births. Their guardianship, care and discipline were entirely the concern of their matrilineal kinsfolk.

In English law, marriage is defined as 'the voluntary union for life of one man and one woman, to the exclusion of all others' (*Hyde v Hyde and Woodmansee* [1866] LR1 P & D 130). Historically, while voluntary, the relationship, or union, was not one between equals. Blackstone in his *Commentaries on the Laws of England* (1765) noted that:

> By marriage, the husband and wife are one person in law: that is, the very being or legal existence of the woman is suspended during the marriage, or at least is incorporated and consolidated into that of the husband: under whose wing, protection, and *cover*, she performs every thing; and is therefore called in our law-french a *feme-covert, foemina viro co-operta*; is said to be *covert-baron*, or under the protection and influence of her husband, her *baron*, or lord; and her condition during her marriage is called her *coverture*. Upon this principle, of a union of person in husband and wife, depend almost all the legal rights, duties and disabilities, that either of them acquire by the marriage. . . .

Rosemary Auchmuty in 'Same-Sex Marriage Revived: Feminist Critique and Legal Strategy' (2004) argues that:

> Despite significant legal and social changes to the institution over the past 200 years, the radical critiques of marriage have remained remarkably consistent in their portrayal of the effects of its socially approved unequal dynamics of power on men and women. Marriage has been shown to endow men with a better lifestyle, greater freedom and more power, while it has the opposite effect on women, limiting, impoverishing, and rendering them vulnerable to abuses of power by their husbands. From Mary Wollstonecraft in 1792, who refused to marry because she would have had to surrender to her husband all her rights to her money, her children and her body, to Germaine Greer's exposure of 'The Middle-Class Myth of Love and Marriage' in *The Female Eunuch* (1970); from John Stuart Mill in the mid-19th century, who publicly renounced his rights as a husband when he married Harriet Taylor, to Lee Comer's bitter revelations in *Wedlocked Women* (1974); from Mona Caird's edited collection of a 10,000-strong correspondence to *The Times* on 'The Morality of Marriage' (1897) at the end of the 19th century, to the second-wave feminists' analyses of the gendered exploitation and abuse of late 20th-century marriage: 200 years of feminist agreement that marriage permits, even encourages, oppression makes the institution untouchable and irredeemable in the eyes of many women. . . .

It is clear that, so far as the law is concerned, one spouse no longer automatically predominates. However, the movement towards gender equality has by no means been a straightforward or swift process. Indeed it was not until the decision of the House of Lords in *R v R* [1992] 1 AC 599, [1991] All ER 481 that a husband could be found guilty of raping his wife. Moreover, formal legal equality can often mask the continuing impact and significance of gender inequalities. (We will look at this in the context of contemporary debates about property and children.)

Auchmuty (2004) goes on to remind us that one of the reasons why the laws relating to the position of women in marriage were reformed was to ensure the continuing support for the institution. She also compares the motives for these reforms with conservative arguments made in support of the introduction of civil partnerships.

> In the second half of the 19th century, too, Britain suffered a steady decline in the marriage rate, to the extent that, by the end of the century, a good quarter of the population would never marry. In a society premised on the centrality of marriage, especially for women, this was a calamity and sparked a volume of agonized debate in the journals of the day. The reasons for the decline were many and various, but one undoubted factor was the legal and social framework in which marriage took place, according to which a husband was completely responsible for his wife, children and household, while the wife was virtually without legal protection against any abuse of his power. If middle-class men baulked at the weight of duty and expense (for Victorian families were large and households expensive, while one could lead a comfortable bachelor life with only a housekeeper and a mistress), more and more women of the same class began to feel little inclination to enter an institution which enforced total dependence, especially as alternatives in the form of fulfilling careers were opening up in the second half of the century. The liberalization of the marriage laws in the same period was likewise due to many factors, but one was certainly a panic response to the marriage crisis. The divorce law of 1857, the Married Women's Property Acts of 1870 and 1882, the right granted to women in the Matrimonial Causes Act 1878 to separate from violent husbands and receive maintenance, custody of children and access provisions for divorced and separated mothers in the Infant Custody Acts of 1839 and 1873 – these changes were all in part motivated by Parliament's recognition that, without them, marriage was becoming an increasingly unattractive option for the educated classes. As a result of them, marriage received a huge boost in numbers and enjoyed increased popularity and prestige in the first half of the 20th century. The extension of marriage to same-sex couples would almost certainly have the same effect now.

The above account highlights the role of the state in supporting the institution of marriage. But within western societies personal relationships are increasingly perceived as a private issue, a 'life-style choice' and marriage as, 'just a piece of paper' or a private contract. In 'Just Marriage' (2004) Mary Lyndon Shanley responds to these claims by emphasising the continuing relevance of marriage and both the need and ability for it to be transformed:

> The contractual image has much to be said for it. It captures what Milton Regan, Jr., in *Alone Together* calls the 'external stance' toward marriage, which focuses on the ways in which marriage serves the interests of distinct individuals. Contract represents well the role that choice and negotiation play in any marriage. Drafting a marriage contract is a useful exercise for a couple because it encourages potential partners to asses their individual needs and sources of personal satisfaction, make their expectations explicit, and identify areas of both agreement and conflict. Legal notions of spousal unity and the sentimentalization of a woman's role as 'the angel in the house' have often served to undercut married women's agency and autonomy. The external stance provides an important antidote.
>
> Contract does less well in capturing what Regan calls the 'internal stance' toward marriage, which regards it from within the relationship and focuses on shared experience rather than lives lived in parallel association. The internal stance reflects the fact that when people marry they

become part of an entity that is not reducible to or identical with its individual components. Historically this concept of a marital entity distinct from either spouse was oppressive to women. ... Despite this dismal history, the notion that marriage creates an entity that is not reducible to the individual spouses captures a truth about significant human relationships and could be used to reshape social and economic institutions in desirable ways. This understanding of the marriage relationship as something distinct from the individuals could be used in the future not to subordinate women but to press for marriage partners' rights to social and economic supports that sustain family relationships and enable spouses to provide care to one another. Such a right to provide care to and receive care from a spouse is not the same as an individual's right to health care or social services. Nor does public protection and support for associational and affective ties need to be limited to marriage partners and parents and children. Rather, recognition of the inevitability of dependency and the importance of care giving should lead people to ask what other relationships deserve public support.

Marriage suggests, as contract does not, the role of committed relationships in shaping the self. The promise to love someone else, in a marriage or in a friendship or in a community, binds a person to act in ways that will fulfill that obligation. Contract also does not express the notion of unconditional commitment, both to the other person and to the relationship. Contract in lieu of marriage rests upon a notion of quid pro quo, in which each party offers something and agrees on the terms of any exchange as a rational bargainer. But the marriage commitment is unpredictable and open-ended, and the obligations it gives rise to cannot be fully stated in advance. What love attuned to the well-being of another may require is by its nature unpredictable.

With so much of our public discourse reducing individuals primarily to consumers in the market, it is especially important to insist on the social and relational sides of our lives. The contractual model for marriage that presents marriage, as Hendrik Hartog says in *Man and Wife in America*, as 'nothing more than a private choice and as a collection of private practices' is insufficient to the tasks of reconfiguring marriage. Marriage entails respect for individuals and for their relationships. It is a particularly striking instance of a practice founded on both individuality and 'a shared purpose that transcends the self' (Regan). If such a commitment is a valuable aspiration and one that our political community wants to facilitate, then we need to examine and remove impediments to such relationships. Those impediments are legion, especially among the poor. Removing them thus confronts us with a formidable agenda – reforms of the workplace, of welfare, and of care giving. But with notions of the public good and collective responsibility under constant assault, withdrawing the state from the pursuit of justice in marriage and family moves in the wrong direction. We need to insist instead that marriage and family law can and must be made to conform to the principles of justice that affirm the equality and equal liberty of all citizens.

QUESTIONS

i. Do you think marriage is 'just a private matter'?
ii. Is commitment a value that the law should support? If so, how?
iii. Do you think marriage has the same meaning for men and women?
iv. What reforms in the workplace and in welfare would support marriage?
v. Is 'supporting families' the same as 'privileging marriage'?

In recent years marriage has been opened to transsexuals by the Gender Recognition Act 2004 (see p. 74). Equally significant here is the Civil Partnership Act 2004. Jacquie Smith, the Deputy Minister for Women and Equality, introducing the second reading of the Civil Partnership Bill in the House of Commons, described it as creating:

> ... [A] parallel but different legal relationship that mirrors as fully as possible the rights and responsibilities enjoyed by those who can marry... . a historic step on what has been a long journey to respect and dignity for lesbians and gay men in Britain ... In creating a new legal relationship for same-sex couples, this Bill is a sign of the Government's commitment to social justice and equality ... (*Hansard*, HC, 12 October 2004, Col 174)

According to the historian Jeffrey Weeks, in 'Same-Sex Partnerships' (2004), 'What is new in same-sex unions is not so much the existence or affirmation of loving same-sex relationships, but their "coming out", and the claim to rights and full recognition that flow from them.' Stephen Cretney in *Same Sex Relationships* (2006) places the Act in a historical context, noting that the Act was enacted 100 years after Oscar Wilde was imprisoned for the 'love that dare not speak its name' and contrasts that trial with the words of Baroness Hale of Richmond in *Ghaidan v Godin-Mendoza* [2004] para 142 (see p. 44 above).

Weeks and Cretney see the Civil Partnership Act as part of a progressive trend that began with the decriminalisation of homosexuality in 1969. In this context it is worth noting that in the first edition of Bromley's pioneering textbook *Family Law* (1957), homosexuality is referred to under the heading 'Unnatural Offences' and as a form of 'aggravated adultery' (p. 129). The law has moved a long way. However, Didi Herman notes in 'The Politics of Law Reform: Lesbian and Gay Rights into the 1990s' (1993) that 'the extension of existing liberal categories to "new identities" [as in same-sex 'marriage'] not only "recognises", but regulates, contains, and constitutes them'. We have seen above how traditional constructions of marriage 'constituted' them as a patriarchal relationship. In 'Family Friendly? Rights, Responsibilities and Relationship Recognition' (2006), Carl Stychin locates the Civil Partnership Act within key elements of the political ideology of New Labour's 'Third Way'.

Rights and Responsibilities

> The theme of rights and responsibilities runs throughout the Act, the commentary that surrounds it and the parliamentary debates. The Act itself is characterised...as aiming to 'balance the responsibilities of caring for and maintaining a partner with a package of rights for example, in the area of inheritance' (DTI, 2003, *Responses to Civil Partnership*, Women and Equality Unit). This ideal of balance – between, for example, care and money – is prevalent in the explanatory material. The explicit logic is that one does not receive rights without the taking on of responsibilities. Moreover, the implicit assumption is that one will be less likely to take on responsibilities towards others (such as care) unless rights are accrued. We find here a very utilitarian notion of rights and responsibilities in which the two are almost quantifiable and measurable to achieve a perfect balance....

Family Values

The importance of the family is pivotal as the ideological basis for the legislation. In particular, the family is cited for its central role in producing responsible, active new citizens, and as providing a counterbalance to rugged individualism and atomisation. Furthermore, the family is largely indistinguishable from the importance of 'stable relationships', which have empirically *proven* benefits to individuals and to society as a whole. These familial relationships are assumed to take a particular form based on a couple dyad, with or without children, and with little sense of extended familial relationships or alternative living arrangements. Although cohabitation is not a requirement of civil registration, there is an implicit assumption that registration and cohabitation will probably go hand in hand.

The benefits of this mode of living – assumed to be facilitated and enhanced by the Act – are far-reaching and, it is claimed, empirically grounded. These advantages of stable couplehood flow both to individuals and to society as a whole:

> The availability of civil partnership status would encourage stable relationships, which are an important asset to the community as a whole. It would reduce the likelihood of relationship breakdown, which has a proven link to both physical and mental ill health. As the Government said in its 1998 consultation document *Supporting families,* 'Strong and stable families provide the best basis for raising children and for building strong and supportive communities'. Strengthening adult couple relationships not only benefits the couples themselves, but also other relatives they support and care for, and, in particular, their children as they grow up and become the couples, parents and carers of tomorrow.
>
> Stable relationships also benefit the economy. It is expected that civil partners would share their resources and support each other financially, reducing demand for support from the State and, overall, consuming fewer resources. Increased stability would help to reduce the burden on the State in terms of family breakdown, which cost the taxpayer an estimated £5 billion in 1999.
>
> (DTI, 2004, p 16, Final Regulatory Impact Assessment (RIA): Civil Partnership)

Thus, the stable couple form is good for the individual, for the couple, and for society as a whole (both socially and economically). Living outside of that form is inefficient and costly, and the breakdown of the relationship form is both unhealthy and socially expensive. As a consequence, long-term stable relationships become the socially preferred option for government.

Consensus Politics

[This] ... aspect of New Labour ideology is a desire for consensus within One Nation, in which acceptance of multiculturalism and tolerance of 'difference' (within limits) prevails. This message is omnipresent in the material surrounding the legislation. Lesbians and gay men become understood as another constituency that needs to be managed. This is 'their' law and it is part of the government's 'gay agenda'. The Act is aimed at social inclusion of *this* group and certainly not at rectifying injustices more broadly. This is one of the ways in which the British approach can be distinguished from the French 'solution' of the *Pacte Civil de Solidiarite* (PaCS). The PaCS can be ideologically situated firmly within the French conception of republicanism and universality. It is justified as a universal status to which all are equally entitled to participate on the basis of being members of the Republic. It is the antithesis of multiculturalism, which the French consistently describe as part of an 'Anglo-Saxon' mentality, which inevitably fragments social solidarity.

By contrast, within the United Kingdom, the Civil Partnership Act is explicitly and specifically designed for one group – lesbians and gays – who are (problematically) constructed as another element within the multicultural mosaic. There is no expectation that the needs of other constituencies – such as platonic home sharers – can be solved by this legislation. These other groups must wait their turn.

The Power of Law

The final aspect of Third Way ideology is faith in law itself, and a belief in micro-managerialism through law. It is assumed throughout the documentation that surrounds the legislation that the availability of the legal status – as well as the difficulty in dissolution procedures for relationships – will encourage long-term, stable relationships. In this regard, law is thought to be a discourse of considerable power in shaping relationship forms, *granting to* lesbians and gays the very ability to live according to its norms. As well, law is assumed to be central in shaping social attitudes and, in particular, in reforming homophobia and encouraging tolerance and social inclusion.

Finally, perhaps less obviously, there is a message within the Act, I would argue, that the encouragement of the rights and responsibilities of civil partnership through law will provide a disincentive for 'irresponsible' behaviour. In the context of New Labour politics, irresponsibility seems to include promiscuous sex, relationship breakdown at will, and the selfishness of living alone (or perhaps even living with friends and acquaintances). Thus, law is employed to achieve social policy ends that have been determined by government in advance based on empirical fact and science in order to help people to help themselves to lead richer lives.

QUESTION

Do you think Stychin's commentary applies equally to marriage?

2.3 WHY DO PEOPLE MARRY OR ENTER CIVIL PARTNERSHIPS?

In 'The Significance of Marriage: Contrasts between White British and Ethnic Minority Groups in England' (2005), Mavis Maclean and John Eekelaar looked at 'how people themselves think about their relationships'. Their research reveals that people marry for reasons that are often quite distinct from the claims made on behalf of marriage that are 'manifestations of idealizations of the institution, which reflect deeper ideological and/or religious positions'. They found that people married for three types of reasons:

- *pragmatic* (where marriage was entered only to fulfil some collateral, instrumental objective, and had no further significance for the respondent);

- *conventional* (where in marrying the respondent was following some prescriptive convention, usually religious or cultural, but often following parents' wishes); and
- *internal* (these reasons were of three kinds: *confirmation* (where the marriage symbolically confirmed that a stage in the relationship involving commitment had already been reached); *completion* (where the marriage itself provided the additional 'seal' completing the commitment); and *construction* (where the marriage provided the framework within which the relationship would be expected to develop, often reaching the stage of commitment on the birth of a child)).

Looking at the differences between ethnic minorities (EM) and white British (WB) communities, their research revealed strong conventional reasons for marrying amongst the former:

> *Being an Asian, although I was born in this country, still, to keep Mom and Dad happy, I keep their Asian values.* (Male, 36, Married, Asian British, Hindu) This respondent later referred to 'parent's law rather than government's law' as being significant. . . .
>
> One respondent combined this with religious prescription:
>
> *I am a practising Catholic. . . . my Dad told us to get married. . . .* (Female, 38, Married, Black African)
>
> Of course, such sentiments were not confined to the EM group. For example:
>
> *I fell in love I suppose; it was the right thing to do, there was no such thing as living together when I was 18. My parents would have frowned on anything else.* (Female, 40, Cohabitant after Divorce, white British) . . . .
>
> But there was a tendency among the WB group for respondents to appear to 'distance' themselves from the conventions they were following by characterizing themselves as 'traditional.' . . . Following a tradition suggests a lifestyle choice, freely entered, rather than being subject to prescriptions by reason of one's membership of a community that one may not have freely chosen.
>
> Interviewer:
>
> *Why marry and not carry on living together?*
>
> Respondent:
>
> *Because it was something that I've always believed in . . . . never thought of not doing it. Just a traditionalist really.* (Female, 30, Married, white British)
>
> It did not follow that EM respondents did not have pragmatic reasons for marrying . . . .
>
> Compare:
>
> Respondent:
>
> *My husband went to work in* [Middle Eastern country] *and the only way I could go out there was if we were married.* (Female, 39, Cohabiting after previous marriage ended in divorce, white British, speaking of first marriage) . . . .
>
> With:
>
> Respondent:
>
> *Inheritance tax . . . my husband saw the Panorama programme on TV last October. He got a real thing about this . . . . with owning the house and everything.* (Female, 39, Married, black British (Afro-Caribbean)) . . .
>
> This serious attitude to marriage also shows in the fact that, when looking at 'internal' reasons for marrying, we found that no member of the EM group fell into the 'Confirmation' category. That category refers to cases where marriage was seen entirely as a one-off event, a 'party' or 'celebration,' symbolically important to proclaim the parties' relationship, but not perceived as being of itself valuable.

As one WB respondent put it:

You just get out of the pool, get married, get back in the pool .... it's just a good day; a really good party. Just a day to remember. (Male, 33, Cohabitant, white British)

Such a view was not found in the EM group. In the 'Completion' category, marriage ... assumed a more personal nature, and provided in itself an added impetus for, or source of, further commitment. We found such perceptions in both the EM and WB sets.

It was personal, to show our commitment. (Male, 39, Married, white British)

Interviewer:

... did marriage make a difference?

Respondent:

Yea, it did – I still look at it as a long term commitment ... but again it made a difference to the way I felt about [wife] protecting-wise, but the actual relationship ... it didn't make a great deal of difference, but ... it is more my male role I imagine ... I jumped from being a boyfriend to a husband.

(Male, 32, Married, black British (Afro-Caribbean))

These cases all show marriage operating as an event which seals, or raises to a new level, a relationship that has been maturing over time.... In the final category, however, (the 'Construction' cases) the marriage operates more as a framework within which the partners work towards the deeper commitment ... :

Interviewer:

Why marry at all?

Respondent:

I don't know. I s'pose we just wanted to ... it was like a way of saying 'I want to be with you for ever' ... [but] when you're married, you've always got a get-out, not that you hope to divorce, but you're not bonded in the same way. The real commitment is having kids, not the marriage. Then you're connected to that person further. (Female, 38, Married, white British)

Interviewer:

So marriage itself isn't the commitment?

Respondent:

No, it's the children. (Female, 40, Married, white British)

Marriage played a more significant part for the EM than for the WB respondents. It did so in the following ways. Its members tended to cite stronger 'conventional' reasons for marrying, indicating a stronger sense of feeling bound by the prescriptions mandating that long-term relationships should only be undertaken within marriage. But, while being married certainly gave rise to a sense of responsibility, this was consistent with a recognition of a later and stronger source of obligation, which arose out of the development of the relationship itself, and in particular if a child was born. It was indeed a particular feature of the EM group that marriage could be used as a framework within which it was expected that the relationship would grow towards a new stage. Interestingly, though, it is this feature (what we call the 'Construction' category of marriages) that illustrates the extent of the common ground between most of our respondents, whether married or unmarried, and whether in the EM or WB set. This is that the relationship itself is seen as setting the demands to behavior. For many married people, and especially those in the EM set, the relationship is seen to be so closely integrated with the institution of marriage, that it is possible more easily to anchor responsibilities in that institution, perhaps making it easier to refer more openly to love as a driver of the relationship itself. ... People use marriage in different ways depending on the different perceptions they have about its place with regard to their personal relationships. These perceptions differ between cultures. It therefore seems too simple, and even futile, for policy makers to embark on general campaigns to promote marriage ... because their goals and understanding of marriage may be different from the way people use it.

QUESTIONS

i. How and why do you think the reasons for getting married have changed over the last 50 years?

ii. Do you think men and women marry for the same reasons?

In '"It's made a huge difference": Recognition Rights and the Personal Significance of Civil Partnership' (2007), Beccy Shipman and Carol Smart looked at why lesbians and gay men entered civil partnerships (CP) or held commitment ceremonies. They found that 'although the issue of legal rights was important ... the significance of entering into a CP was not driven purely by instrumental reasons, nor a preoccupation with equality'.

> Lobby groups who supported gay and lesbian rights and interests put forward competing messages with some proclaiming that a 'separate but different' system is progressive and better, some saying that only making heterosexual marriage open to same-sex couples will suffice, while others have argued that state recognition, particularly in the form of relationship regulation, de-radicalises and co-opts gay men and lesbians who will feel less inclined or able to forge new, more progressive ways of developing relationships outside the new system. But, in talking to same sex couples we found that a different set of issues emerged. ... they developed a stance in relation to this debate which was based on their everyday lived experiences.
>
> Jule: My neice said to me. ... I think she was six, and she said 'Why are you getting married? And I said 'Because we want to and we love each other.'
>
> Shona: Part of my drive, my main drive for doing this is because I want to and because I love Jean and it's a natural progression in our relationship. Another part of my drive is that I experienced the legal and technical and officialdom problems when my former partner died and I really resent the fact that just because we are same sex we can't have the same rights and things so that's kind of where my feeling behind the legal recognition comes from.
>
> Sally: Legitimising our relationship in everybody else's eyes [was] really for his [her son's] benefit as much as anything else. So that, you know, should I not be able to care for him or whatever there was some acknowledgement that Jude was his parent as well.
>
> Audrey: [M]aking [your mother] understand that this is serious, this is a serious commitment, this isn't something that is going to change, that I am now her daughter-in-law from our perspective ... She came up to us at the start of the wedding and said 'Oh here's my two daughters' as she came up to us, and I thought, 'It has worked; it's made a huge difference'.
>
> Kevin: It is mainly for the legal recognition that we are interested in it, because neither of us has a particularly good relationship with family. It is extremely irksome that we are not each other's next of kin. So that is really why we plan to have it, friends have done it, and the need to get some kind of legal recognition.
>
> Brenda: But for those of us who have waited a long, long time and for whom it is an issue around things like pensions and inheritance, it has got a quite different meaning. It is just a piece of legal equality that we will get as soon as it is there, ... Just briefly I think there will be hordes and hordes of old people storming the register offices and then it will all die away won't it and it will just get down to a normal routine like marriages are.
>
> Debbie: We were, we just wanted to make a public sort of statement to everybody, to all our friends and family and to celebrate our relationship really so. The legal side obviously is important to us with the house and everything and our rights and stuff but the ... just to make a declaration really that was just our main reason for the ceremony ...

One of the main motivations for the introduction of CP was to inculcate stability. . . . the point for many of our interviewees was that they were already in stable, committed relationships with shared obligations and mutual responsibilities. CP was seen as a means of protecting the relationship they had achieved, not as a kind of glue which would ensure that they stuck together in the future ... For some of the couples we interviewed, their most significant battles for recognition were not with the state or the law, rather they sought recognition from their families. This was not an issue in the public debate, and yet the desire to create firmer or better links with kin was of considerable importance at the everyday level. Quite simply, many couples wanted the kind of respect and acknowledgement given automatically to their heterosexual brothers and/or sisters who either married or made a commitment. Recognition allowed these couples to be treated as both 'adults' (i.e. becoming fully fledged citizens), but also as part of the family. . . . [Audrey] used the language of marriage and weddings when discussing their ceremony with family in order to impart the seriousness of the occasion and also to use concepts which would already be familiar and accepted by other family members. In this regard it may be that the established Churches' fears about the blurring of heterosexual and same-sex marriage are well founded since it seems likely that most people will slip into the familiar terminology of marriage. This is particularly likely to be the case because terms such as marriage or wedding (problematic as they may be in many ways) convey the idea that a couple love one another. CP by comparison merely suggests that people will find it legally convenient to exchange contracts safeguarding their interests. In other words CP conveys no sense of emotions, and this may be particularly significant when couples are keen for their families to recognise the emotional quality of their relationships. . . . It was clear that the older the individuals in a couple were the more likely it was that CP would be viewed as a straightforward legal contract which merely acknowledged what was already apparent from the longevity of their partnership. . . . For some couples an important component of CP (or a commitment ceremony) was the fact that it was a public statement. This did not mean that they felt they had to have lots of family and friends present because the 'public' could be a kind of virtual public rather than known people. In fact some were worried about the press turning up and turning their ceremony into a kind of spectacle. So being public did not have to mean a huge ceremony, but it did mean that a kind of civic recognition could be called upon. For others it was the huge wedding that was important because this was a literal and metaphorical statement about 'having arrived' and being acknowledged. For yet others it was just a straightforward shared celebration without political overtones.

QUESTION

What differences, if any, are there between the reasons why lesbians and gays enter civil partnerships and why opposite-sex couples get married?

While love is clearly a reason why many people marry or enter civil partnerships it is not a *legal* requirement (nor, similarly, is an intention to live together). This was confirmed in *Vervaeker v Smith* [1983] 1 AC 145, where the House of Lords upheld the validity of a marriage between a Belgian prostitute and a British subject, entered into to enable her to avoid being deported. Marriages such as this are often described as marriages of convenience or, less sympathetically, as 'sham marriages'.

Immigration law provisions have attempted to prevent these marriages from taking place by requiring registrars to report suspicions to the Home Office (Immigration and Asylum Act 2001, section 24). A stricter approach was introduced by section 19 of the Asylum and Immigration (Treatment of Claimants) Act 2004. Under this scheme, non-EEA nationals with limited leave to remain were required to show they have a fiancé visa, or obtain a certificate of approval from the Home Secretary (costing £135) before being married in a legally recognised ceremony in the UK. Moreover, the Home Office could refuse people the certificate to those with less than six months' valid leave-to-remain, effectively treating them as seeking to enter 'sham marriages'.

Following the introduction of these rules the number of suspicious marriage reports fell from 3,740 in 2004 to less than 300 by the end of May 2005, and the rules may have had an impact on the drop in marriage (see p. 58 above).

However, in *R (on the application of Baiai and another) v Secretary of State for the Home Department, R (on the application of Bigoku and another) v Secretary of State for the Home Department, R (on the application of Tilki) v Secretary of State for the Home Department* [2007] EWCA Civ 478, [2007] All ER (D) 397, the Court of Appeal held that the new rules violated Article 12 of the European Convention of Human Rights. Article 12 states that 'Men and women of marriageable age have the right to marry and to found a family, according to the national laws governing the exercise of this right'. Moreover, the fact that the rules did not apply at all to persons married by the Anglican Church was held to be discriminatory and incompatible with Article 14.

Buxton LJ:

[W]hilst immigration control is accepted to be a legitimate ground for interfering with the article 12 right, all that that does is to open the possibility of some limitations on the article 12 right. It does not mean that the state is free to choose whatsoever means of controlling immigration that it considers prudent or necessary, irrespective of the impact on article 12. ... it is difficult to see that interference with article 12 rights on grounds of immigration control could ever be justified in a case where the parties did indeed intend to live together as man and wife. ... the Secretary of State can only interfere with the exercise of article 12 rights in cases that involve, or very likely involve, sham marriages entered into with the object of improving the immigration status of one of the parties. To be proportionate, a scheme to achieve that end must either properly investigate individual cases, or at least show that it has come close to isolating cases that very likely fall into the target category. It must also show that the marriages targeted do indeed make substantial inroads into the enforcement of immigration control (paras 43, 5, 58).

As a result of this decision the rules relating to Certificate of Approval have been amended, see the Home Office website for details: http://www.ind.homeoffice.gov.uk/applying/generalcaseworking/coaformarriageorcivilpartnership.

The Home Office has been granted leave to appeal the decision in *Baiai* to the House of Lords (where it will be reported as: *R (on the application of Trzcinska and others) v Secretary of State for the Home Department*).

QUESTIONS

i. How do you think a registrar would spot a marriage of convenience?

ii. Do think the law should permit *any* interference with the right to marry on the basis of the parties reasons for marrying?

iii. Is there a moral difference between 'marrying for money' and marrying for immigration purposes?

iv. What factors do you think will determine the outcome of the appeal to the House of Lords?

While the purpose, definition and functions of marriage and civil partnerships are open to debate, what is clear is that our legal system is committed to establishing a rigid distinction between relationships that fall within or outside these institutions. It is thus important to know what, in a formal sense, is and is not a marriage/civil partnership; and the legal tool for that identification is the law of nullity.

2.4 WHO CAN MARRY, AND HOW NOT TO MARRY

Sections 11 and 12 of the Matrimonial Causes Act 1973 (as amended by the Gender Recognition Act 2004 and the Civil Partnership Act 2004) read as follows:

11. Grounds on Which a Marriage is Void

A marriage celebrated after 31st July 1971 shall be void on the following grounds only, that is to say –

(a) that it is not a valid marriage under the provisions of the Marriage Acts 1949 to 1986 (that is to say where –
  (i) the parties are within the prohibited degrees of relationship;
  (ii) either party is under the age of sixteen; or
  (iii) the parties have intermarried in disregard of certain requirements as to the formation of marriage);

(b) that at the time of the marriage either party was already lawfully married or a civil partner;

(c) that the parties are not respectively male and female;

(d) in the case of a polygamous marriage entered into outside England and Wales, that either party was at the time of the marriage domiciled in England and Wales.

For the purposes of paragraph (d) of this subsection a marriage is not polygamous if at its inception neither party has any spouse additional to the other.

12. Grounds on Which a Marriage is Voidable

A marriage celebrated after 31st July 1971 shall be voidable on the following grounds only, that is to say –

(a) that the marriage has not been consummated owing to the incapacity of either party to consummate it;

(b) that the marriage has not been consummated owing to the wilful refusal of the respondent to consummate it;
(c) that either party to the marriage did not validly consent to it, whether in consequence of duress, mistake, unsoundness of mind or otherwise;
(d) that at the time of the marriage either party, though capable of giving a valid consent, was suffering (whether continuously or intermittently) from mental disorder within the meaning of the Mental Health Act 1983 of such a kind or to such an extent as to be unfitted for marriage;
(e) that at the time of the marriage the respondent was suffering from venereal disease in a communicable form;
(f) that at the time of the marriage the respondent was pregnant by some person other than the petitioner.
(g) that an interim gender recognition certificate under the Gender Recognition Act 2004 has, after the time of the marriage, been issued to either party to the marriage;
(h) that the respondent is a person whose gender at the time of the marriage had become the acquired gender under the Gender Recognition Act 2004.

These provisions have been subject to extensive case law and raise a variety of issues. Here we focus on sections 11(a)(i), (c) and 12(b), (c), (h).

2.4.1 WHO CAN MARRY?

Section 11(c) states that a marriage will be void if 'the parties are not respectively male and female'. This requirement excludes same-sex couples from entering into a marriage, but note that section 3(1)(a) of the Civil Partnership Act 2004 'mirrors' this provision by excluding those 'not of the same sex' from entering a civil partnership. We discuss the heterosexual nature of marriage in paragraph 2.5. Here we discuss the implications of section 11(c) for transsexuals.

Until the enactment of the Gender Recognition Act 2004, transsexuals were prevented from marrying in their desired gender. In the leading case of *Corbett v Corbett (otherwise Ashley)* [1971] P 83, [1970] 2 All ER 33 Ormrod J defined a person's sex according to his birth and by a congruence of chromosomal, gonadal and genital factors. Disregarding the relevance of any sex change operation, Ormrod J held that:

> [S]ex is clearly an essential determinant of the relationship called marriage, because it is and always has been recognised as the union of man and woman. It is the institution on which the family is built, and of which the capacity for natural heterosexual intercourse is an essential element.

QUESTIONS

i. What does the exclusion of transsexuals tell us about purpose of marriage?
ii. Why is the Gender Recognition Act not called the Sex Change Recognition Act? (Come back to this question again after you have read the rest of this chapter.)

The decision in *Corbett* was upheld in a series of domestic cases. However in *Goodwin v UK* (Application 28957/95) [2002] All ER (D) 158 the European Court of Human Rights held that the margin of appreciation no longer extended to declining to give legal recognition to all cases of gender reassignment and found – unanimously – that the UK was in breach of Articles 8 (the right to respect for private life) and 12 (the right to marry).

> [A] serious interference with private life can arise where the state of domestic law conflicts with an important aspect of personal identity .... The stress and alienation arising from a discordance between the position in society assumed by a post-operative transsexual and the status imposed by law which refuses to recognise the change of gender cannot, in the Court's view, be regarded as a minor inconvenience arising from a formality. A conflict between social reality and law arises which places the transsexual in an anomalous position, in which he or she may experience feelings of vulnerability, humiliation and anxiety .... In this case, as in many others, the applicant's gender re-assignment was carried out by the national health service, which recognises the condition of gender dysphoria and provides, *inter alia*, re-assignment by surgery .... The Court is struck by the fact that nonetheless the gender re-assignment which is lawfully provided is not met with full recognition in law, ... The coherence of the administrative and legal practices within the domestic system must be regarded as an important factor in the assessment carried out under art 8 of the Convention.... It remains the case that there are no conclusive findings as to the cause of transsexualism and, in particular, whether it is wholly psychological or associated with physical differentiation in the brain. The expert evidence in the domestic case of *Bellinger v Bellinger* [2002] 1 All ER 311 was found to indicate a growing acceptance of findings of sexual differences in the brain that are determined pre-natally, though scientific proof for the theory was far from complete. The Court considers it more significant however that transsexualism has wide international recognition as a medical condition for which treatment is provided in order to afford relief .... While it also remains the case that a transsexual cannot acquire all the biological characteristics of the assigned sex (*Sheffield and Horsham v UK* (1998) 5 BHRC 83 at para 56), the Court notes that with increasingly sophisticated surgery and types of hormonal treatments, the principal unchanging biological aspect of gender identity is the chromosomal element. It is known however that chromosomal anomalies may arise naturally (for example, in cases of intersex conditions where the biological criteria at birth are not congruent) and in those cases, some persons have to be assigned to one sex or the other as seems most appropriate in the circumstances of the individual case. It is not apparent to the Court that the chromosomal element, amongst all the others, must inevitably take on decisive significance for the purposes of legal attribution of gender identity for transsexuals ... the very essence of the Convention is respect for human dignity and human freedom .... In the twenty first century the right of transsexuals to personal development and to physical and moral security in the full sense enjoyed by others in society cannot be regarded as a matter of controversy requiring the lapse of time to cast clearer light on the issues involved.

The need for statutory reform was confirmed in *Bellinger v Bellinger* [2003] UKHL 21; [2003] 2 All ER 593. But while the present law was held to be incompatible with Articles 8 and 12, the issue was considered, 'pre-eminently a matter for Parliament' (para 37).

QUESTION

Why do you think the House of Lords in *Bellinger* did not use its powers under section 3 of the Human Rights Act to interpret 'man and woman' in section 11(c) of the Matrimonial Causes Act to include post-operate transsexuals? Contrast this decision with that in *Ghaidan* (see p. 38).

Section 9(1) of the Gender Recognition Act 2004 states that: 'where a full gender recognition certificate is issued to a person, the person's gender becomes for all purposes the acquired gender (so that, if the acquired gender is the male gender, the person's sex becomes that of a man and, if it is the female gender, the person's sex becomes that of a woman)'. For a certificate to be granted a Gender Recognition Panel (comprised of lawyers and medical practitioners) must be satisfied that the applicant has or has had gender dysphoria, has lived in the acquired gender throughout the period of two years and intends to do so until death (section 3 (1); Schedule 1). (For information about the panel see: http://www.grp.gov.uk.)

Unlike legislation in other jurisdictions, the Act enables applicants to change their legal gender *without* genital reassignment surgery or proof of capacity for intercourse or compulsory sterilisation. In *Bellinger* Lord Nicholls held that:

> Much uncertainty surrounds the circumstances in which gender reassignment should be recognized for the purposes of marriage... Plainly, there must be some objective, publicly available criteria by which gender reassignment is to be assessed. If possible the criteria should be capable of being applied readily so as to produce a reasonably clear answer.... There must be an adequate degree of certainty (paras 39–42).

Ralph Sandland, however, in 'Feminism and the Gender Recognition Act 2004' (2005) describes the criteria established by the Act as, 'a transition from an economy of certainties to something altogether more fluid':

> It is misleading to say that the Gender Recognition Act (GRA) merely implements the decisions of the European Court in *Goodwin* and *I*. The European Court was not overly-prescriptive as to how its judgment should be implemented by the UK Government. And the GRA does in fact go further than strictly required by the European Court ... the GRA does not defer merely to medicalism in a broad sense, but specifically to the 'psy' discourses; psychiatry, psychology and psychoanalysis. It is the mind, not the body, which is the prime site for medicalised intervention in the scheme adopted by the Act. That which is hidden from view, clothed, namely sexual organs, etc, is, of itself, irrelevant. This means that the GRA is prepared to licence [*sic*], as female, persons with functioning male sexual organs and, as male, persons with functioning female sexual organs. ... The GRA is concerned with a public politics of the presentational, the proper appearance of the gendered body, which trades only in that which is on public display, the various signs and indicators of gender identity that figure the interaction of gendered individuals. That which is below the surface, here the body of the person in question, is deemed fully beyond the sphere of public regulation .... The consequence, then, of the radical public/private divide that the GRA constructs at this point is that, for the purposes of the governmentability of gender, the body, and its biology, does not exist .... It was, in a roundabout way, this aspect of the Government's proposals for recognition that so upset conservatives. Lord Tebbit, moving an amendment to the draft of the GRA as it passed through the House of Lords ... said:
>
>> 'I beg the Government to see the world as it is. There is something absurd in the proposition that the problems – I accept that they are real problems – of transsexual people require us to accept that while today the marriage of two people each bearing the chromosomes and the sexual organs of the same sex would be a same-sex marriage and therefore illegal, a piece of paper that declares one of those two people to be of the opposite sex would be permitted by this legislation to make it a legal marriage of opposite sexes' (House of Lords, Hansard, 3 February 2004, Col. 618).

> Although my perspective differs from that of Lord Tebbit, it has to be conceded that he has a point. The GRA is made from the same cloth from which was cut the Emperor's New Clothes. Lord Tebbit further pointed out that Government policy is not to allow same sex marriage, and yet the GRA allows two persons both of whom had given birth to children ('and I can think of no better test of whether a person is female than that' 3 Feb Column 618) to marry. Such a couple could also, under the terms of the GRA, both continue to produce further children following their marriage. It might be objected that an FTM transsexual who continued to engage in sexual activity as a female would not satisfy the criteria for recognition. In particular, it might be thought that such a person, even if suffering from gender dysphoria, could not be said to have 'lived in the acquired gender throughout the period of two years ending with the date on which the application is made', nor to 'intend to continue to live in the acquired gender until death'. But if the only evidence that he or she did and does not, respectively, is his or her sexual practices, then that is poor evidence, and demonstrates how a normative heterosexual perspective trips over its own assumptions .... In consequence, the Government, and the law, finds itself in the position of 'recognising' men with vaginas and women with penises, and indeed a whole range of gendered identities and individual morphologies. This is the nub of Lord Tebbit's objection. I find it an exciting prospect, for precisely the same reason: it undermines the neatness of the division between the sexes (although where Lord Tebbit sees biology I see ideology, or 'biology' as ideology).

To date the GRP has received 2,199 applications, 2,024 of which have received Gender Recognition Certificates – as surgery is not a requirement, no statistics are available on whether applicants have or have not had surgery.

QUESTIONS

i. Has the Gender Recognition Act 2004 achieved the certainty that Lord Nicholls called for in *Bellinger*?

ii. Homosexuality is no longer perceived as a medical condition or psychological disorder. Why is transsexuality?

iii. Germany, Denmark, Sweden and the Netherlands require transsexuals to be sterilised before they can be permitted to marry. What purpose do you think this serves?

2.4.2 WHOM CAN I MARRY?

Most people do not marry their kin. MacFarlane, in *Marriage and Love in England 1300–1840* (1986), provides historical background to the move from kinship marriages to what he refers to as 'free-floating' marriages:

> We may wonder when and how it originated. Is there any evidence in the period from the fifteenth to the nineteenth century of a transformation from the marriage system based on kinship rules, to the free-floating marriages based on psychology and economics which exist today? In answering the questions concerning the curious link between economics and demography raised by

Malthus and Wrigley, we need to pursue this further. A marriage system embedded in kinship is close to biological restraints: marriage for women will very often be at or near puberty. Marriages will not adjust sensitively to economic changes, since they are mainly determined by kinship. Nor will there be space for personal psychological pressures. Likes and dislikes, love and passion, have no formal place where the decision about whom to marry is encoded in the kinship structure...

...Essentially one may marry all except members of the nuclear family and all those, including uncles and aunts, nephews and nieces, in the ascending and descending generations. First cousin marriage is now, as it was from 1540, legal, if often disapproved of. At marriage the couple became 'one blood'. Thus a man was forbidden from marrying the same range of wife's kin as of his own blood relatives. For instance, he could not marry his wife's aunt even though she was not a blood relative. The prohibitions continued after the spouse's death. Hence marriage with a deceased wife's sister was forbidden.

In the three centuries before 1540 the prohibitions were wider. By the decision of the Fourth Lateran Council of 1215, impediments of consanguinity and affinity were set at the fourth degree, according to the canonical computation. Thus a person could not marry his own or his wife's third cousin, or any nearer relative. Furthermore, wide rules of spiritual affinity prevented those related by godparenthood from marrying. On the other hand, dispensations were easily available, for a price, from the Church. There was a very limited prohibition in early Anglo-Saxon England, then a widening of the ring of prohibited persons, and then a narrowing again, so that England in 1540 returned to the situation that had prevailed in the seventh century. The change at the Reformation was important, but it was neither unprecedented nor indicative of a shift from 'elementary' to 'complex' structures. Indeed, by allowing all to marry first and second cousins without dispensation, the Reformers, if anything, encouraged a move towards the possibility of an elementary system. It is difficult to see how preferential kin marriages can have been enormously attractive and common when the whole weight of the Church forbade them.

More important in assessing the presence of kinship pressures are the positive rules. To prevent estates going out of the family, or to consolidate social, political and other ties, most societies are organized so that strong pressures are put on the individual stating which kin he should marry. To find a person standing in the right kinship relationship is one of the central tasks of an elaborate kinship vocabulary, as well as of the 'marriage brokers' who exist in many societies.

QUESTION

What do you see as the advantages of a preferential kin system?

Under the current law, marriage and civil partnership between certain relatives are void (Marriage Acts 1949, section 1; Civil Partnership Act 2004, section 3 (2), Schedule 1 paragraph 1(1)). Sexual intercourse with these relatives is also a criminal offence (Sexual Offences Act 2003, section 64). Rather than set out the wording of these provisions, the following figure represents the prohibited degrees in diagram form. Note that the single lines refer to blood relationships only, while the double lines refer to relationships by blood or adoption, and that siblings includes half-bothers and sisters, but not stepbrothers and sisters.

Prohibited degrees of relationship

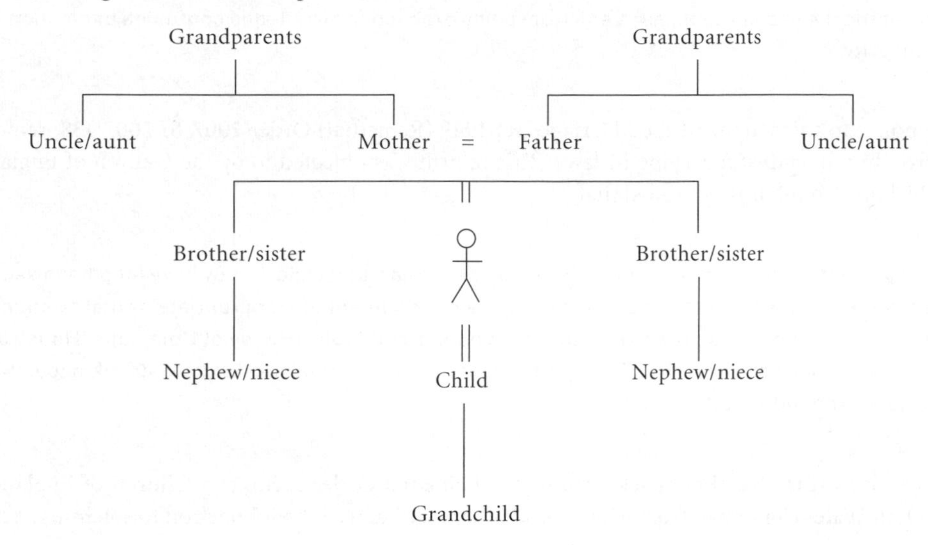

The surviving prohibitions based on affinity are not absolute but qualified (Marriage (Prohibited Degrees of Relationship) Act 1986, section 1, Schedule 1; Civil Partnership Act 2004, Schedule 1, paragraph 2(1)). Marriage (or entering a civil partnership) with anyone in the list below is prohibited unless both have reached the age of 21 and the younger has not at any time before reaching the age of 18 been a 'child of the family' in relation to the other:

- child of former civil partner;
- child of former spouse;
- former civil partner of grandparent;
- former civil partner of parent;
- former spouse of grandparent;
- former spouse of parent;
- grandchild of former civil partner;
- grandchild of former spouse.

Until recently, marriage (and civil partnership) between people who were children or parents by marriage (or 'in-laws') was only permissible if both the proposed partner's spouse and other parent were dead. In other words, a man could not marry his mother-in-law unless *both* his wife and his wife's father were dead. However, in *B and L v United Kingdom* (Application No 36546/02) [2006] 1 FLR 35 the European Court of Human Rights held that the ban was irrational, illogical and a violation of the right to marry, as guaranteed by Article 12 of the European Convention.

> The bar on the marriage between parents-in-law and children-in-law meant that B and L were unable to obtain legal and social recognition of their relationship. The fact that, hypothetically, the marriage could take place if both their former spouses died, did not remove that impairment. The same applied to the possibility of applying to Parliament as that was an exceptional and costly procedure, totally at the discretion of the legislative body and not subject to discernable rules or precedent. The Court observed that the bar on marriage, although pursuing a legitimate aim in protecting the integrity of the family, did not prevent such relationships occurring. Furthermore, since no incest, or other criminal law provisions prevented extra-marital relationships between

> parents-in-law and children-in-law, it could not be said that the ban on the applicants' marriage prevented the second applicant's son from being exposed to any alleged confusion or emotional insecurity.

In response to this judgment the Marriage Act 1949 (Remedial) Order 2007, SI 2007/438, removed the prohibition against marrying in-laws. This reform was objected to by the Church of England's Archbishops Council. They argued that:

> ... legal impediments to marriage between parent-in-law and child-in-law have long been seen as justified by the importance of preventing the development of inappropriate sexual relations (or rivalry) within the family and to protect the parent-child role. (House of Commons. House of Lords, Joint Committee on Human Rights Twenty-ninth report of session 2005–06 HL paper 248 HC 1647, Appendix 1 (b)).

As a result of this objection article 2(b) of the Remedial Order exempts a Church of England or Church in Wales clergyman from what would otherwise be his or her obligation to solemnise a marriage between those now permitted to marry.

QUESTIONS

i. What justification is there for retaining any bars based on affinity?
ii. Why should both parties to a marriage involving a step relationship have to be over 21 at the time of the marriage?
iii. Do you think the right of clergy to refuse to solemnise a marriage between 'in-laws' is justified?

Stephen Cretney (2006) questions why the rules apply to civil partnerships:

> Originally, no doubt, marriage with blood relatives was prohibited in part because of what could be presented as reasons of genetic prudence but also in part because of an atavistic revulsion to blurring different family roles – remember the Oedipus story. These genetic considerations can, however, have no applications to same sex relationships .... I am afraid it is difficult to avoid the suspicion that the main motive for simply copying the prohibited degrees of marriage into civil partnerships was so as to have some kind of rough and ready – perhaps one could even say 'crude' and 'arbitrary' – check on the use of civil partnerships as a means of tax minimization within the family.

The Law Commission, in their Report on *Nullity of Marriage* (1970), saw no need to change the law relating to consanguinity:

> 52. (a) In so far as the question is biological, the answer depends on an evaluation of scientific evidence. The marriage of uncle and niece, or nephew and aunt is permitted in some countries

and by some religions and it may well be that there is no such biological objection to these marriages as to justify legal prohibition. They may well be no more objectionable biologically than the marriage of a man with his grandparent's sister or of a woman with her grandparent's brother, which is not within the prohibited degrees.

(b) Nevertheless, the question raises social and moral problems, the answer to which must depend on public opinion. Would public opinion tolerate or object to marriages between uncle and niece or nephew and aunt and, if it objects to such unions, does it wish to extend the prohibition to great-uncle and great-niece and great-nephew and great-aunt? Many people would no doubt instinctively hold the view that such marriages are unnatural and wrong, just as they would view with revulsion a marriage between brother and sister, even if there were no biological reasons against such a union. There are some matters of conviction on which men hold strong feelings of right and wrong though they cannot place their fingers on any particular reason for this conviction. It may be that such unions would be generally regarded as just as wrong as a marriage between adopter and adopted child – a union which is clearly considered objectionable although there cannot be any biological ground for this.

QUESTIONS

i. What are the arguments, for and against, amending the law still further so as to *permit* marriages between uncle and niece or aunt and nephew and to *prohibit* marriages between first cousins?

ii. Do you think same-sex relations between relatives by affinity necessarily raise the same objections?

2.4.3 VOIDABLE MARRIAGES: SECTION 12(b) AND (c)

In *Singh v Singh* [1971] P 226, [1971] 2 All ER 828, CA the wife was aged seventeen and from an orthodox Sikh family. She went through a ceremony of marriage in a Register Office with a 21-year-old Sikh man. The marriage was arranged by her parents, and the bride had never seen the bridegroom before the actual ceremony of marriage. The plan was that there would be a religious ceremony of marriage and then the parties would commence living together. When the wife saw the husband at the Register Office, she did not like what she saw, and although she participated in the civil ceremony, she refused to go through with the religious ceremony or to live with the husband. She petitioned for a decree of nullity on two grounds, namely, duress and incapacity to consummate due to her invincible repugnance. Her petition was dismissed. Karminski LJ dealt with the issue of duress and continued:

> There is the alternative matter of repugnance. It is true that the wife never submitted herself to the physical embraces of the husband, because after the ceremony of marriage before the registrar it does not appear that she saw him again or went near him. Having taken the view which she did, that she did not want to be married to him, it is understandable that she did not want to have sexual intercourse with him; but that again seems to be a very long way from an invincible repugnance. True, as counsel for the wife argued, invincible repugnance can have a number of forms; and he reminded us of a decided case where the wife refused to undress when she went to bed so that the husband could not have intercourse with her. But here the wife abandoned the

idea of her marriage altogether, and there is nothing of a psychiatric or sexual aversion on her part which is in any way established. In my view that ground of nullity fails completely.

Appeal dismissed.

In *Kaur v Singh* [1972] 1 WLR 105, [1972] 1 All ER 292, the parties – both Sikhs – solemnised a civil ceremony of marriage which, in accordance with the custom of their community, was an arranged marriage. It was clearly understood by all that the civil ceremony would be followed by a religious ceremony, and that the parties would not cohabit prior to the religious ceremony. The husband failed to make arrangements for the religious ceremony, and the wife succeeded in obtaining a decree of nullity based on, section 12(b) of the Matrimonial Causes Act 1973, in that the husband's action (or inaction) amounted to wilful refusal to consummate the marriage.

QUESTIONS

i. In *Kaur v Singh*, if the husband had attempted to consummate the marriage, would the wife have had a valid excuse?

ii. When does 'I can't', mean 'I won't'?

iii. What is the point of keeping alive, even for a short time longer, a marriage such as the one contracted in the *Singh v Singh* litigation?

iv. It is clear that inability to consummate does not render the marriage void. Should it? If not, why not?

v. Why should 'mistake' render a marriage merely voidable rather than void?

vi. Should English law retain the concept of a voidable marriage in relation to section 12(a) and (b) of the Matrimonial Causes Act 1973?

In 2004 only 492 petitions for nullity were filed (Judicial Statistics 2004 (2005), Table 5.5). The Law Commission Report on *Nullity of Marriage* (1970) provides the following reasons for retaining nullity of a voidable marriage:

24. (a) It is not true to say that the difference between a nullity decree of a voidable marriage and a decree of divorce is a mere matter of form. It may be that the consequences of the two decrees are substantially similar, but the concepts giving rise to the two decrees are quite different: the decree of nullity recognises the existence of an impediment which prevents the marriage from initially becoming effective, while the decree of divorce records that some cause for terminating the marriage has arisen since the marriage. This distinction may be of little weight to the lawyer, but is a matter of essence in the jurisprudence of the Christian Church.

(b) The Church attaches considerable importance to consent as a pre-requisite to marriage. Consent to marriage includes consent to sexual relations and, hence, impotence can be regarded as having the effect of vitiating consent. Likewise, the grounds under section 9(1)(b), (c) and (d) of the Act of 1965 (mental disorder, epilepsy, pregnancy by another or venereal disease) can be considered to fall under the head of conditional consent [see now, section 12(d)(e)(f) Matrimonial Causes Act 1973] and are acceptable to the Church. Except with regard to wilful refusal to consummate, which the Church of England considers should cease to be a ground for nullity and be a ground for divorce, the Church is satisfied with the existing law of nullity. Therefore, so radical a change as is involved in the substitution of a decree of divorce for a decree of nullity in respect of matters which the Church regards as relevant to the formation of marriage and irrelevant to divorce, is likely to be unwelcome to the Church. It is also likely to be resented by people not necessarily belonging to the Church who associate a stigma with divorce and who would therefore prefer to see such matters as impotence and mental disorder, which are illnesses, remain grounds for annulling the marriage rather than causes for dissolving it.

(c) It may be that many people do not appreciate the distinction between divorce and nullity. They, presumably, would not oppose turning a nullity of a voidable marriage into a divorce. If, however, such a change is likely to cause offence to a substantial minority, then the proposal cannot be recommended unless some worthwhile advantage is to be gained from the change. The only advantage to be gained would be that one of the present voidable marriages (i.e., one voidable for wilful refusal to consummate), might be thought by some to fit in more 'neatly' among divorces than among nullities.

25. We are therefore, opposed to the abolition of the class of voidable marriages and think that it should be retained. But the effect of the decrees of nullity of a voidable marriage should be modified so as to make it clear that the marriage is to be treated in every respect as a valid marriage until it is annulled and as a nullity only from the date when it is annulled.

On wilful refusal, in particular, they said:

(a) Wilful refusal to consummate is in most cases the alternative allegation to impotence as it is often uncertain whether the respondent's failure to consummate is due to one cause or the other; the petitioner may not know whether the respondent refuses to consummate the marriage because he is unable to have sexual intercourse or because, though able to have sexual intercourse, he does not want to have it; in such cases the court must draw an inference from the evidence before it and it seems unreal that the relief granted to the petitioner – nullity or divorce – should depend in any given case on the court's view as to which of the two reasons prevented the consummation of the marriage.

(b) Failure to consummate, whether it be because the respondent is unable or because he is unwilling to have sexual intercourse, deprives the marriage of what is normally regarded as one of its essential purposes. Parties would think it strange that the nature of the relief should depend on the court's decision whether non-consummation was due to the respondent's inability or whether it was due to his unwillingness. From the parties' point of view the relevant fact would be that the marriage had never become a complete one. To tell them that, in the eyes of the law, failure to complete it due to one cause results in their marriage being annulled, whereas such failure due to another cause results in their marriage being dissolved, would seem to them to be a strange result.

QUESTIONS

i. What advantages, other than those mentioned by the Law Commission, can you see for retaining the concept of nullity in this context?

ii. Do you agree with the arguments referred to in the Law Commission Report generally?

iii. Are the two arguments in relation to wilful refusal sufficient reasons by themselves to justify the retention of the present state of the law?

In *Shame* (2007) Jasvinder Sanghera, who grew up in Derby in a South Asian family, describes what happened to her when she was fourteen years old:

> A few months after ... the subject of my marriage came up. I was in the living room doing my homework when she showed me a picture, ever so casually. 'What do you think of him?' she said. 'Do you think he's nice? He's the man you're going to marry.' I must have known this moment would come but I still felt as if I had been slapped. I didn't want to look at the picture, in my head I didn't want to go there, ... I tried to put it to the back of my mind and get on with my life, but every so often Mum would mention it. At first she was always light-hearted and jokey, but over the weeks she became more insistent. She kept saying I should be happy that she had found me such a good husband and that it was my duty to marry him. As the weeks went by I got more and more frightened. I kept thinking of my sisters and the bruises I'd seen on them; I remembered them sobbing as they told my parents how their husbands abused them; I remember my mum saying, 'This is how men are, it is your duty to look after him.' .... I felt as if my life were sliding out of my control. When I said, 'Mum, I want to finish school and go to university,' she just laughed.
>
> Even if I had been brave enough to tell a teacher, I didn't think they'd understand. [My sister] Robina stayed in India six months when she went to have her marriage and when she came back the teachers never even asked her where she'd been or why ... anyway I was ashamed to tell anyone that my mum was arranging my marriage while I was still at school. And I was afraid of what my family would do to me, and what the rest of the community would say about them if I did.

In order to escape being forced into the marriage Sanghera ran away from home and was disowned by her parents. Her sister who was terrified of her husband, but knew that her family would be dishonoured if she left him, committed suicide.

Section 12(c) of the Matrimonial Causes Act 1973 (see p. 74 above) is reinforced by the following international provisions. Article 16(2) of the Universal Declaration of Human Rights states that 'Marriage shall be entered into only with the free and full consent of the intending spouses', and Recommendation No 21 of the UN Committee on the Elimination of All Forms of Discrimination Against Women states that 'A woman's right to choose a spouse and enter freely into marriage is central to her life and her dignity and equality as a human being.'

Despite these pronouncements, the experience of Sanghera and her sister is not unusual and preventing forced marriages remains a serious challenge for the law.

NS v MI [2006]
EWHC 1646 (Fam), [2007] 1 FLR 444

The petitioner and the respondent husband were both only seventeen years old when they were married in Pakistan. The petitioner was born and brought up England and lived at home with her parents. The husband, who was born and always lived in Pakistan, was her first cousin and prior to their wedding they had never met. The petitioner was taken to Pakistan by her parents shortly after her sixteenth birthday. She was persuaded to go and relax after her exams and was promised by her family that they were not sending her to Pakistan to be married. However, shortly after she arrived her relatives started telling her that she would be staying until she was married. The petitioner's boyfriend arranged for his parents to visit her in Pakistan and ask for her hand in marriage. This caused a huge amount of tension in the family, given that the petitioner's parents had arranged her marriage to another person. The petitioner came under emotional pressure from her family, who blackmailed her by saying they would kill themselves if she did not marry the respondent. The petitioner's family told her the only way she would be returning to the UK would be if she married the respondent.

Munby J:

Arranged marriages are perfectly lawful. As I emphasised in *Re SA (Vulnerable Adult with Capacity: Marriage)* [2005] EWHC 2942 (Fam), [2006] 1 FLR 867, at para [26], such marriages are not, of course, in any way to be condemned. On the contrary, as Singer J said in *In re SK (An Adult) (Forced Marriage: Appropriate Relief)* [2004] EWHC 3202 (Fam), [2006] 1 WLR 81, at para [7], arranged marriages are to be supported as a conventional concept in many societies. And for that very reason they are, I emphasise, not merely to be supported but to be respected. Forced marriages, in contrast, are utterly unacceptable. I repeat what I said in *Re K, A local authority v N* [2005] EWHC 2956 (Fam) at para [85]: 'Forced marriage is a gross abuse of human rights. It is a form of domestic violence that dehumanises people by denying them their right to choose how to live their lives. It is an appalling practice'. As I said in *Singh v Entry Clearance Officer, New Delhi* [2004] EWCA Civ 1075, [2005] 1 FLR 308, at para [68]: 'forced marriages, whatever the social or cultural imperatives that may be said to justify what remains a distressingly widespread practice, are rightly considered to be as much beyond the pale as such barbarous practices as female genital mutilation and so-called "honour killings". No social or cultural imperative can extenuate and no pretended recourse to religious belief can possibly justify forced marriage.' Forced marriage is intolerable. It is an abomination. And, as I also said in *Re K* [2005], (at paras [87]-[88]), the court must bend all its powers to preventing it happening. The court must not hesitate to use every weapon in its protective arsenal if faced with what is, or appears to be, a case of forced marriage. The court must be alert to the possibility of forced marriage – something more prevalent than some would care to admit – and robust in its response to it. But we must always equally be careful not merely to distinguish been arranged marriage and forced marriage but also.... as I said in *Re K,* [2005] (at para [93]): 'We must guard against the risk of stereotyping. We must be careful to ensure that our understandable concern to protect vulnerable children (or, indeed, vulnerable young adults) does not lead us to interfere inappropriately – and if inappropriately then unjustly – with families merely because they cleave, as this family does, to mores, to cultural beliefs, more or less different from what is familiar to those who view life from a purely Euro-centric perspective' (paras 2–4, 37).

In relation to this case Munby J applied the test to establish duress established in *Hirani v Hirani* (1982) 4 FLR 232, CA:

The threats and pressure to which she was subjected ... were such as to destroy the reality of her consent. Her will was overborne. Her lips may have spoken, but not her mind. In my judgment she is not bound by the ceremony. She did not validly consent. She is entitled to the decree nisi of nullity which she seeks. I use the word 'her' because in this case, as in many such cases, the victim was a young woman. It must never be forgotten, however, that many victims are in fact young men. Just as forced marriage takes place in many communities, being as Singer J rightly emphasised in *In re SK (An Adult) (Forced Marriage: Appropriate Relief)* [2004] EWHC 3202 (Fam), [2006] 1 WLR 81, at para [6], 'by no means restricted to communities of one faith, or to communities in or from any one part of the world', it equally needs to be emphasised that forced marriage is not gender specific (paras 41, 42).

QUESTIONS

i. Is it necessary to have genuine feelings of attraction or affection for a marriage to be valid in English law?

ii. Is the marriage in this case 'forced', 'arranged', or a 'sham' or all three?

iii. Why do nullity cases such as *NS v MI* rarely come before the courts?

iv. In *Sheffield City Council v E and another* [2004] EWHC 2808 (Fam), [2005] All ER (D) 192 Munby J held that:

> The question of whether E has capacity to marry is quite distinct from the question of whether E is wise to marry .... We must be careful not to set the test of capacity to marry too high, lest it operate as an unfair, unnecessary and indeed discriminatory bar against the mentally disabled'

What factors should a court consider in order to determine whether an individual has the necessary capacity to marry?

In his judgment in *NS v SI* Munby J sets out the range of legal procedures and provisions available to courts to prevent 'forced marriages' occurring. These include injunctions under wardship jurisdiction (where the proposed bride is a child) and the comparable adult inherent jurisdiction to restrain the celebration of the marriage and to prevent both travel abroad and, where appropriate, repatriation. In addition a variety of other protective orders can be made to prevent further attempts at forced marriage or to protect the victim from the risk of victimisation or retaliation at the hands of her oppressors. Where preventative measures have failed:

> The primary remedy is, of course, a suit for nullity. I emphasise: a suit for nullity, not a suit for divorce. As Coleridge J said in *P v R (Forced Marriage: Annulment: Procedure)* [2003] 1 FLR 661 at paras [17]–[18]:
>
> > [17] ... there is a real stigma attached to a woman in the petitioner's situation if merely a divorce decree is pronounced and it is desirable from all points of view that where a genuine case of forced marriage exists the court should, where appropriate, grant a decree of nullity and as far as possible remove any stigma that would otherwise attach to the fact that a person in the petitioner's situation has been married. (Paras 9–10 NS case)

In August 1999 the Home Office Minister for Community Relations, Mike O'Brien MP, established a Working Group, chaired by Baroness Uddin of Bethnal Green and Lord Ahmed of Rotherham, to investigate the problem of forced marriage in England and Wales and to make proposals for tackling it effectively. The following extracts from their report, *A Choice by Right* (2000), give an indication of its scope and its message:

Forced Marriage in England and Wales

> The Working Group believes that forced marriage must be seen primarily as an issue of violence against women. It was clear from the consultations that it is women who most often live in fear and suffer violence as a result of forced marriage...

Most of the cases of forced marriage that the Working Group encountered involved young women, from teenagers to people in their early twenties. The Working Group heard of cases where girls under 16 years old were married abroad, despite not being legally capable of contracting a marriage in England and Wales. Many women forced into a marriage only sought help much later, when they had endured the relationship for several years. Family, social and economic pressures have all been cited as factors in a woman enduring an abusive relationship.

There is a spectrum of behaviours behind the term forced marriage, ranging from emotional pressure, exerted by close family members and the extended family, to the more extreme cases, which can involve threatening behaviour, abduction, imprisonment, physical violence, rape and in some cases murder. People spoke to the Working Group about 'loving manipulation' in the majority of cases, where parents genuinely felt that they were acting in their children and family's best interests.

'My parents said that I could go to University, but only if I agreed to marry a cousin from back home once I'd graduated.'

(*Young woman, Leeds*)

...

International Dimensions

Many of the cases brought to the Working Group's attention involved a spouse from overseas. A British national is either taken to live in their spouse's country (where they often have antecedents) or they are to act as a sponsor for their spouse's immigration to the UK.

Women described the fear that compelled them to support their spouse's immigration to the UK. Often family members had directly threatened them before their interview with an immigration officer. This fear prevented most women from putting on record that their marriage was forced.

Some women who had been brought to the UK for a forced marriage told the Working Group of the hardship they had suffered because of their unsound immigration status. Not being able to speak English and not having any family or friends to support them in the UK often added to these women's problems.

Some anecdotal evidence has been presented to the Working Group of cases where forced marriage has been deliberately used as part of a wider scheme to circumvent the immigration rules. These cases are not the norm. . . .

Cause and Effect

While it is important to have an understanding of the motivations that drive parents to force their children to marry, this does not mean we should accept justifications for denying the right to choose a marriage partner. Motivations are complex and highly personal. It is important not to oversimplify when thinking about motivations – there will often be deeper reasons, which are not understood. These are some of the key motivations that the Working Group has heard about:

- peer group or family pressure
- attempting to strengthen family links
- protecting perceived cultural and religious ideals (which can often be misguided or out of date)
- preventing 'unsuitable' relationships (e.g. outside ethnic, cultural, religious or caste group)
- family honour

- long-standing family commitments
- controlling female behaviour and sexuality.

The Working Group has found that perspectives on motivations vary significantly between the parents themselves, their children and others outside of the immediate relationship.

Parents who forced their children to marry often justified their behaviour as building stronger families and protecting cultural or religious traditions – they did not see anything wrong with their actions. Many people felt that parents believed they were upholding the cultural traditions of their home country, when in fact practices and values there had moved on. They described a fossilization of cultural values within some families who had migrated to the UK. ...

Whatever the motivations, the consequences of a forced marriage can be devastating to the whole family. The victims of forced marriage suffer terribly, but parents, siblings, and the wider family members suffer too. Young women forced into a marriage often become estranged from their families. The impact on the children of a forced marriage is often that they themselves become trapped in the cycle of abuse with serious long-term consequences.

Preventing Forced Marriage

The Working Group has found that challenging and changing people's attitudes is the key to preventing forced marriage.

There is a general lack of awareness and understanding of individual's rights – both legal and religious – relating to marriage. Young people, their parents and families need to be educated about these rights and a dialogue needs to be facilitated between young people and their elders about their different expectations. For such a dialogue to be meaningful it would need to ensure that both young people and their parents are empowered to talk openly and safely about their expectations.

The Working Group acknowledges the importance of the role of opinion formers in developing an understanding of the right to choose. This includes anyone who is able to influence values, attitudes and behaviours. Religious and community leaders are key opinion formers, but the definition also takes account of local and national politicians, leaders of community and women's groups and many others who can make a difference.

The Working Group has heard people talk of their disappointment with many of these opinion formers who have failed to speak out against forced marriage because it was seen as a 'taboo' subject. People who have spoken to the Working Group have an expectation that opinion formers will send a clear and consistent message about the unacceptability of forced marriage. It is hoped that following this report, opinion formers will be in a more robust position to lead and send a clear message about the unacceptability of forced marriage.

A crucial area of misunderstanding that needs to be addressed is the effect on a family of a forced marriage. The Working Group has found that one of the main motivations for parents forcing their children into marriages is the desire to strengthen families and protect their cultures. In fact, the opposite is often the outcome, with families breaking apart and children turning against their cultural background because of their experiences. People who spoke to the Working Group felt that an understanding of the consequences of forced marriage would help prevent it happening.

Since this report, a number of initiatives have taken place. In 2005 the Home Office and Foreign and Commonwealth Office established the Forced Marriage Unit (see www.fco.gov.uk/forcedmarriage). In 2005 over 250 cases of forced marriage were reported to the Unit. Some involved girls as young as thirteen and approximately 15 per cent of the cases involved young men. However, forced marriage is in many ways a hidden problem and many more cases exist that are not reported.

In September 2005, the Foreign and Commonwealth Office and the Home Office published a consultation paper, *Forced Marriage A Wrong not a Right* (http://www.fco.gov.uk/Files/kfile/forcedmarriageconsultation) which sought views on whether there should be a specific criminal offence of forced marriage. The paper summarised the arguments:

> Arguments against creating a specific criminal offence include:
>
> 1. the risk that the fear of their families being prosecuted may stop victims from asking for help;
> 2. the risk that parents may take children abroad, and marry them off or hold them there, at an earlier age to avoid increased risks of prosecution in Britain;
> 3. that there are already sufficient criminal offences and protective measures that can be used;
> 4. that if it were very difficult to mount a successful prosecution the new offence might be routinely flouted with impunity;
> 5. that a new offence would disproportionately impact on Black and Minority Ethnic communities and might be misinterpreted as an attack on those communities;
> 6. that families concerned may not feel implicated by such an offence because many may believe their children did consent to the marriage, even though that consent was obtained under duress;
> 7. that implementing a new offence would be expensive and the funds might be better spent on improving support for those at risk;
> 8. that increased risks of prosecution or threat of prosecution would make it harder for victims to reconcile with their families;
> 9. that increased involvement in criminal prosecutions could be harrowing for victims who wanted to move on; and –
> 10. that there are other better non-legislative means of working within communities to change views and tackle the abuse.
>
> Arguments for creating a specific offence include:
>
> 1. that primary legislation could change public opinion, and thus perception and practice;
> 2. that it could have a strong deterrent effect;
> 3. that it could empower young people with more tools to negotiate with their parents and in some cases with parents facing pressure from relatives;
> 4. that it could simplify and clarify matters for public sector employees tackling this issue; and –
> 5. that it would make it clearer what steps can be taken and easier to take action against perpetrators.

In 2006 The Forced Marriage (Civil Protection) Bill was introduced into the House of Lords as a private members bill. The Bill sought to create civil rather than criminal remedies. Its sponsor Lord Lester explained the change of focus:

> There is already plenty of criminal law to tackle murder, kidnapping, abduction, rape and all the other evil manifestations associated with forcing people into marriage against their will. Terrible things follow in some of these appalling cases. The problem with the criminal process is that, although there is plenty of existing criminal law, there is a criminal burden of proof and a criminal

> standard of proof; the court is a criminal court and is held in public, with police and a jury brought into play. It has not proved to be an effective way of tackling a major social problem.
>
> People who deal with these cases daily tell me that often the victim does not want to dishonour her family by having a public and punitive hearing. One of the great advantages of the family law approach is that the court can sit in private, sensitively and in a way that will, I hope, reconcile the victim with her or his family, while providing effective protection to put a stop to a course of conduct that may lead to real tragedy. It was originally my decision to move into the civil area, not because I thought that the Government could not be persuaded in any particular way but because I thought that it was the right approach. That approach was supported, not just by me – I am a white man, the least qualified person to make judgments of that kind – but by the Southall Black Sisters, a whole variety of women's organisations, including Asian women's organisations, and children's organizations .... I am not saying it would be inconceivable to have a new crime; other countries have done that. Although female genital mutilation is a crime, there has not been a single prosecution, for all kinds of reasons. This shows that the criminal process is not the best process, even though, with forced marriages and honour killings, one needs to have serious crimes for serious wrongs. (HL Deb 13 June 2007 c1756,7–8).

The campaign group Rights of Women supported the Bill and their response to the consultation addressed the concerns raised by some that a specific law about forced marriage is racist or stigmatises those communities where such human rights abuses occur:

> As a feminist organisation concerned with the protection and safety of women, Rights of Women strongly disagrees with the use of such concerns as a reason not to support the Forced Marriage Bill. As noted above, it is Rights of Women's position (and that of United Nations bodies) that forced marriage is a form of violence against women. According to international human rights law arguments, violence against women cannot be justified by culture, religion or ethnicity. To view forced marriage as an issue of race or ethnicity, culture or religion, masks the violence experienced by Black and Minority ethnic women (BME). Whilst Rights of Women does not subscribe to the rhetoric that forced marriage is an issue of community relations, race, ethnicity or religion, we do recognise that these may be factors in addressing forced marriage, presenting cultural barriers in terms of access to services, protection, support and legal justice. Thus many women, who have experienced forced marriage, have found it difficult to access assistance, support and protection, particularly from State bodies and institutions such as the police, social services, and the courts. It is therefore vital that women who have hitherto been marginalized from protection are able to apply for a remedy and access justice. The creation of a specific civil remedy for forced marriage is not about singling out certain communities, but rather is about redressing this historical marginalisation. It is about recognising that BME women who fear being forced into marriage are a specific group that have historically been marginalised or excluded from the legal process and who often face very real barriers in terms of accessing assistance.
>
> Rights of Women believes that arguments based on stigmatisation cannot be used to deny women justice. ...
>
> Further, we believe that criticisms of the Forced Marriage Bill based on stigmatisation of a particular community or religion, simply serves to perpetuate the myth that forced marriage occurs in only these communities/religions. This contradicts the evidence of both the Government, the police, statutory sector agencies and women's organisations, which have reported cases from Middle Eastern, African, Turkish, Kurdish, Chinese and other communities. (See: www.rightsofwomen.org.uk/pdfs/consultation/forced_marriage)

The Bill received wide cross-party support. In Grand Committee the Bill was completely rewritten by way of Government amendments and the Forced Marriage (Civil Protection) Act 2007 was passed in July 2007 and will come into force in October 2008. The Act inserts a new Part 4A in the Family Law Act 1996 (sections 63A-S), a move that reflects the view that forced marriage should be viewed within the wider legal framework around domestic violence (see p. 316 below). Under the Act the victim or a third party can apply to the High Court or county courts for an order to prohibit, restrict or require any conduct that protects a person from being forced into a marriage or from any attempt to be forced into a marriage. Powers of arrest can be attached to the orders and the conduct need not be directed against the victim. 'Force' is defined by the Act to include threats and other psychological means and the orders can relate to conduct outside the UK.

QUESTIONS

i. In the House of Lords debate Baroness Uddin argued that:

> I fear that a solitary Act may be a symbolic outlawing of forced marriage – a good thing – but, without sufficient practical and mainstream support such as economic emancipation and opportunities for education and training for women from specific minority communities, it will not be able to eradicate forced marriage. HL Deb 26 January 2007 cc 1324–5

What difference do you think the new law will make?

ii. How do you think registrars distinguish a 'forced marriage' from a 'marriage of convenience'.

iii. Should the time limit for nullity petitions be extended from the current time limit of three years?

iv. The original Bill contained provision for a claim for damages. However the Government removed them, Baroness Ashton arguing that in a case of forced marriage they were unsuitable 'as it could prolong adversarial contact between the victim and the respondent, often a close family member' (HL Deb 10 May 2007 c232GC). Do you think the option of damages should be available?

v. Do you think focusing on the issue of forced marriage risks stigmatising certain ethnic minority groups?

2.4.4 VOIDABLE MARRIAGES: SECTION 12(h)

This new ground for nullity, introduced by the Gender Recognition Act 2004, provides that where, at the time of the marriage, one party to the marriage did not know that the other was previously of another gender, the former may seek to annul the marriage.

In 'Endless sex: the Gender Recognition Act 2004 and the persistence of a legal category' (2007) Andrew Sharpe, discusses its rationale:

> In cases where transgender individuals have not disclosed their gender history prior to marriage legal anxiety has proved to be especially evident. ... in the English decision of *ST (formerly J) v J.* ([1998] 1 All E.R. 431), J, a female to male transgender man, who had been 'married' to a biological woman for seventeen years, but had been found to be female for the purposes of

marriage law, applied for ancillary relief under the Matrimonial Causes Act 1973. It was the merits of this application that both the trial judge and, on appeal, the Court of Appeal, had to determine. In dismissing the defendant's appeal, the Court of Appeal held that:

> [J] had committed a serious crime: he had deceived the plaintiff into the marriage ... His conduct at the time of the marriage, when judged by principles of public policy, brought down the scales overwhelmingly against the grant of relief.

In evaluating J's conduct in public policy terms, and in concluding that J's act of 'perjury' had crossed the threshold of seriousness, thereby invoking the principle of public policy and barring ancillary relief, the Court of Appeal noted that there was 'a present public interest in buttressing and protecting the institution of marriage'. Like the trial judge, Hollis J, the Court of Appeal took the view that the 'deception' perpetrated by J against S-T, one 'as profound a betrayal of trust as between two people as can be imagined' went to 'the heart of marriage' given that 'single sex unions remain proscribed as fundamentally abhorrent to [the] notion of marriage' ....

Turning to the other conduct-based ground for rendering a marriage voidable, namely, lack of consent due to duress or mistake, it might appear to cover the scenario envisaged by the Gender Recognition Act. In other words, and while duress is clearly inapplicable, a party to a marriage might claim that s/he did not consent to the marriage on account of the fact that s/he remained, at the time of the marriage, unaware of the other party's gender history. Yet, as Cretney, Masson and Bailey-Harris note, there are 'only two groups of case in which mistake has been held sufficient to vitiate consent to marriage' (2002, p. 61). These are 'mistake as to the person' (A marriage would be voidable on this basis if a party to the marriage thought the person they were marrying was someone else, such as, in circumstances of impersonation (see, for example, *Militante v Ogunwomoju* [1993] 2 FCR 355); and 'mistake as to the nature of the ceremony.' It is only the former that concerns us here. A crucial legal distinction that arises is one between mistake as to the person and mistake as to an attribute of the person. In the latter instance, the party lacking knowledge is presumed to consent. By way of example, if a party to the marriage enters the contract wrongly believing the other party 'to be a chaste virgin of good family and possessed of ample wealth the marriage will be unimpeachable' (Cretney, Masson and Bailey-Harris 2002, p. 61).

Thus it might be argued that non-disclosure of gender history provides a basis for claiming that a marriage was entered into under a fundamental mistake as to person. Yet, such a claim could only succeed if a transgender person's representation of gender at the time of a marriage could be said to be an impersonation. This possibility, always problematic in transgender contexts, is clearly foreclosed by the Gender Recognition Act. After conferral of a full Gender Recognition Certificate, no subsequent marriage can be objected to on the basis of a mistake as to person. For in order to entertain such a claim it would be necessary to conclude that a person, legally recognised as female by virtue of the Gender Recognition Act, is not female in some important sense, at the time of the marriage ceremony. When a male to female transgender woman, possessing a recognition certificate stating that she is female, stands before a man at a wedding ceremony and asserts that she is a woman, such a statement is unquestionably correct in law. It is precisely this fact, and therefore the inapplicability of the mistake ground in the Matrimonial Causes Act to the issue of non-disclosure of gender history that accounts for the legislative accretion to that Act contained within the Gender Recognition Act. Thus the Gender Recognition Act, through amending the Matrimonial Causes Act, effectively overcomes the difficulties associated with establishing mistake at common law. That is to say, in the context of gender history, the nature of the mistake made need not be one as to the person who is physically present at the ceremony. Rather, where there had previously been no basis at common law for concluding that there had been a mistake recognisable by law for the purposes of annulling a marriage, the law now recognises non-disclosure of attribute or circumstance as sufficient warrant. This is a remarkable departure from common law conceptualisations of the category of mistake.

QUESTION

Why do you think nullity, rather than divorce, is permitted by this provision?

2.5 CIVIL PARTNERSHIP – 'PARALLEL BUT DIFFERENT'

The key differences between marriage and civil partnership relate to either religion or sex.

Section 2(5) of the CPA states that 'no religious service is to be used while the civil partnership registrar is officiating at the signing of a civil partnership document', and section 6(2) provides that a civil partnership cannot take place in 'religious premises'. In this respect it is similar to a civil marriage in a register office. Stephen Cretney (2006) explains that this prohibition represents:

> part of the deal struck between Church and State way back in the nineteenth century – what today would be called a restrictive practice or cartel – the civil marriage is to be strictly secular: you are not even allowed to have Robbie William's *Angels* . . . .

The result is that lesbians and gays are denied the choice of a civil or a religious ceremony. Cretney suggests that 'this reflected the Government's concern to defuse opposition from the traditional Christian church to giving any formal statutory recognition to a relationship still regarded by some as sinful', but as he makes clear 'There are professedly Christian churches which are indeed willing to solemnize same sex marriages'.

Beccy Shipman and Carol Smart's (2007) research indicates that for some lesbians and gays religion is an important factor. For example, they quote one woman who stated that:

> I have been going to church since I was little and I have been brought up in the whole Christian marriage thing. Just because I am in a gay relationship, that did not change for me really. It is still important to me to get married in front of people and in front of God and in front of friends. And also my family have not been very supportive and my parents are both very strong Christians and I kind of wanted to make a statement to them: 'Look this church that I am going to is prepared to give me a ceremony and recognise my relationship, just because you do not does not mean that therefore it is kind of wrong'.

QUESTION

Why should the state not recognise religious same-sex ceremonies where religious bodies are willing to permit them?

During the parliamentary debates about civil partnership, critics of the Bill attempted to extend the benefits to heterosexual cohabitants and other non-conjugal family relationships.

Lisa Glennon in 'Displacing the conjugal family in legal policy – a progressive move?' (2005) comments that:

> The inclusion of family members was a tactic to disturb the passage of the legislation or, failing that, to make it easier to digest by displacing its central objective of extending the legal incidents of marriage to same-sex couples and, instead, making it about the value of care-giving responsibilities. Indeed, the amendment has been referred to as a 'fig leaf to disguise ... opposition to the Bill in total' .... As such, the distinct and express legal recognition of same-sex partnerships is a preferable reform option to the possible absorption of lesbian and gay relationships within de-sexualised legal categories, which can amount to little more than homophobic responses to the demands for legal development. Boyd and Young conclude that, in recognising relationships:
>
> > ... a focus on sex may well be unnecessary, except to the extent that it is needed to ensure the visibility of lesbian and gay lives, and that they are not erased in the very process of receiving recognition.

The attempts to derail the Act in this way failed. Nevertheless, one of the most commented features of the Act is the extent to which it 'de-sexualises' the relationship. In marriage, adultery is a fact which can be used to establish a ground for divorce (see p. 149), and non-consummation or the fact that a respondent has a venereal disease can be a ground for rendering a marriage voidable. None of these provisions apply to civil partnerships. Cretney (2006) asks:

> Are we not entitled to assume that a partner's sexual infidelity will be as abhorrent in the committed same sex relationship created under the Civil Partnership Act as it may be in the committed heterosexual relationship called marriage? Surely the draftsman could have provided a suitable form of words to cover the case? As it is the wronged civil partner who wants to terminate the relationship because his or her partner has been unfaithful will have to rely on the allegation that the other has 'behaved in such a way that the applicant cannot be expected to live' with him or her. So it is to be left to the judiciary to determine what level of sexual fidelity is appropriate to a same sex couple and what kind of conduct is inconsistent with that standard.... On what basis is the judge to make his determination? How far is civil partnership founded on the notion of sexual fidelity, or indeed on sexuality at all?

Kenneth McK Norrie answers some of these questions in 'Marriage is for Heterosexuals – May The Rest Of Us Be Saved From It' (2000) by arguing that it is important to acknowledge *differences* between heterosexuals and gays and lesbians.

> In opposite-sex relationships an extremely high premium is paid in most societies to sexual fidelity. The marriage laws of most legal systems are full of concepts designed to emphasise the importance of keeping sex within marriage: concepts such as adultery, child-illegitimacy, consummation, incest and impotency. And the reason is not hard to find. For the single most important difference between heterosexual activity and homosexual activity is that the former has the unique potential, and the latter has absolutely no potential, to create new human life. Child creation is of the utmost importance to society. But it should be remembered that these rules were not designed to ensure that children have a stable family upbringing – that is

a very late twentieth century notion. More important was the need for safe and secure property devolution. A man needs to know that the children who inherit his property are actually *his* children. A child needs to know that his or her father is not spreading his seed, and the child's inheritance, abroad. The very terminology of the law tells us this quite clearly if we care to look: adultery is the adulteration of the male blood line (so gay sex and oral sex never were – and cannot be – adultery). ... In other words, heterosexual activity outwith the family relationship is economically very risky and property claims from outwith the family disrupt both the family and, thereby, society itself. Child creation therefore needs to be controlled for the stability of society .... It is not the mean-spirited fear that one's partner is getting a modicum of physical pleasure outwith the relationship, for otherwise masturbation would be as much a ground for divorce as adultery, but the fear that one's partner may be creating children outwith the family.

None of these fears applies to same-sex relationships where, when there are children, both parties will nearly always be fully aware of where they came from – not through sex between the parties but often through hard-fought and traumatic legal and medical battles. This, I think, is the real reason why sexual fidelity plays a far less central role in same-sex than in opposite-sex relationships. It is not that gay men and lesbians are naturally more promiscuous than non-gay people, nor even that men are naturally more promiscuous than women. It is that gay sex has, in practical terms, far fewer social consequences. It is therefore far lower down in participants' scale of values than non-gay sex, which might involve not only physical pleasure but economic costs, which is, of course, high on anyone's scale of values. The end result of this is that fidelity for gay men and lesbians tends to be understood in a rather different way. It is more emotional and less physical in meaning than it is for non-gay people: but it is no less important for all that.

In 'Sex and the Civil Partnership Act: The Future of (Non) Conjugality?' (2006) Nicola Barker suggests that the sexual practice provisions relating to marriage reinforce the 'romantic mystique, drawing a boundary around sexual relationships as the "ideal"'. She then offers two interpretations for the silence about sex in the CPA:

First, that the only 'legitimate' sexual relationship is a heterosexual one ... therefore same-sex civil partnerships do not need to be sexual; conjugality being reserved for the pinnacle institution in the hierarchy of relationships: marriage. Alternatively, the absence of a specific conjugal requirement to civil partnerships, an institution otherwise almost identical to marriage, could indicate that the boundaries between sexual (primary, significant) and non-sexual (secondary, less significant) relationships are being challenged. There is no longer any significant legal difference (in terms of provisions) between sexual and non-sexual relationships for same-sex civil partners. However, while sexuality is absent, the C.P.A. is very clear, in its provisions and structure, about the level of commitment required (for example, in terms of the difficulty of dissolving a civil partnership), and therefore the statute assumes other aspects of conjugality to exist, particularly shared economic lives. Boyd and Young identify a switch from conjugality to economic interdependence as the marker, or boundary, of a relationship 'deserving' recognition in the Canadian context (2003, p. 770). This indicates that any move away from (sexual) conjugality will not be in itself either progressive or conservative, especially if the purpose of loosening the boundaries around sexual relationships is in order to encompass more relationships into 'the family' for the purposes of privatising care and dependency.

QUESTIONS

i. Do you think the distinctions relating to sexual practice are good or bad for lesbians and gays?
ii. Do you think the provisions relating to sexual practice in *marriage* are still necessary or relevant?
iii. If two male friends (who are not and have never been lovers) enter a civil partnership for purely financial/tax saving reasons is it a 'sham civil partnership'?

2.6 'GAY MARRIAGE'

Rosemary Auchmuty (2004) commented that 'Simply because they are different, registered partnerships are unlikely to be seen as truly 'equal' to marriage' (at 103). This view is the basis of the claim in *Wilkinson v Kitzinger* [2006] EWHC 2022 (Fam), [2007] 1 FLR 29. The case concerned a lesbian couple who had been *married* in accordance with the law of British Columbia, Canada. (Marriage is currently also open to lesbians and gays in the state of Massachusetts, the Netherlands and Spain). In accordance with sections 212–218 of the Civil Partnership Act 2004 the marriage was recognised under UK law, but only as a civil partnership. The claimants argued that it was:

> [5]... simply not acceptable to be asked to pretend that this marriage is a civil partnership. While marriage remains open to heterosexual couples only, offering the 'consolation prize' of a civil partnership to lesbians and gay men is offensive and demeaning. Marriage is our society's fundamental social institution for recognising the couple relationship and access to this institution is an equal rights issue. To deny some people access to marriage on the basis of their sexual orientation is fundamentally unjust, just as it would be to do so on the basis of their race, ethnicity, and nationality, religion, or political beliefs.
>
> ... I believe that the argument of 'separate but equal' is unacceptable because: (a) there should not be separate sets of laws for recognising different-sex and same-sex relationships; and (b) marriages and civil partnerships are clearly not equal. They are not equal symbolically, when it is marriage that is the key social institution, celebrated and recognised around the world; and they are not equal practically, when it is apparent that civil partnership is a lesser alternative, which will not be recognised around the world, or even across Europe. Even if the rights and benefits conferred by civil partnership are identical (at least in practical terms) to those conferred by marriage within Britain itself, this is not so beyond its boundaries.

Their application to have their marriage recognised as a marriage was rejected. Sir Mark Potter P held that there was no violation of Article 8, as their relationship did not fall within the ambit of family or private life:

> [88] The CPA is a measure which is not concerned with the privacy or family life of such couples as such. It was introduced and has effect as a measure to afford equivalent legal rights to same-sex partnerships as are available to opposite partners through marriage. By

withholding from same-sex partners the actual title and status of marriage, the Government declined to alter the deep-rooted and almost universal recognition of marriage as a relationship between a man and a woman, but without in any way interfering with or failing to recognise the right of same-sex couples to respect for their private or family life in the sense, or to the extent, that European jurisprudence regards them as requiring protection. Withholding of recognition of their married status does not criminalise, threaten, or prevent the observance by such couples of an intimate, private life in the same way as a married heterosexual couple and indeed provides them, as so far European jurisprudence does not dictate, with all the material legal rights, advantages (and disadvantages) of those enjoyed by married couples. Not only does English law recognise and not interfere with the right of such couples to live in a very close, loving, and monogamous relationship; it accords them also the benefits of marriage in all but name.

...

[107] Like the House of Lords in *M*, in relation to the statutory scheme there under consideration, I do not consider that the failure to recognise the status of the Petitioner and the First Respondent as being validly married amounts to any kind of intrusion upon their right to respect for their private life in the sense contemplated by the Convention. Neither has the personal or sexual autonomy of the Petitioner been invaded, nor has she been criminalised, threatened, or humiliated in anyway. So far as the matter is put on the basis of her *family* life, the Convention has yet to recognise a childless same-sex relationship as constituting family life. However, even if that were not so, the withholding of recognition of the relationship between the Petitioner and First Respondent does not impair the love, trust, mutual dependence and unconstrained social intercourse which are the essence of family life and the matter falls outside the ambit of arts 8 and 14 combined.

However, he held that there was a violation of Article 12, when considered in conjunction with Article 14:

[115] ... By reason of its very definition, it is the opposite sex component of marriage which is under scrutiny. It seems clear to me that the reality of the underlying position is that the different treatment is one based on sexual orientation. The question is whether it can withstand scrutiny and this depends on whether it has a legitimate aim and whether the means chosen to achieve that aim are appropriate and not disproportionate in their adverse impact.

In deciding that the aim was legitimate, Potter P referred to the decision of *Karner v Austria* and the reference in that case to the 'protection of the family in the traditional sense' discussed above at p. 45. He then continued:

[116] ... On the question of the proportionality of any discriminatory measure reflecting that aim, in this case the CPA, it is complained by the Petitioner that, in denying her and the First Respondent the name and formal status of marriage and 'downgrading' her Canadian marriage to the status of civil partnership, the impact of the measure upon her is one of hurt, humiliation, frustration and outrage. I can understand her feelings in that respect. At the same time, it is certainly not clear that those feelings are shared by a substantial number of same-sex couples content with the status of same-sex partnership.

[117] Regrettable as the adverse effects have been upon the Petitioner and those in her situation who share her feelings, they do not persuade me that, as a matter of legislative choice and

method, the provisions of the CPA represent an unjustifiable exercise in differentiation in the light of its aims.

[118] It is apparent that the majority of people, or at least of governments, not only in England but Europe-wide, regard marriage as an age-old institution, valued and valuable, respectable and respected, as a means not only of encouraging monogamy but also the procreation of children and their development and nurture in a family unit (or 'nuclear family') in which both maternal and paternal influences are available in respect of their nurture and upbringing.

[119] The belief that this form of relationship is the one which best encourages stability in a well regulated society is not a disreputable or outmoded notion based upon ideas of exclusivity, marginalisation, disapproval or discrimination against homosexuals or any other persons who by reason of their sexual orientation or for other reasons prefer to form a same-sex union.

[120] If marriage, is by longstanding definition and acceptance, a formal relationship between a man and a woman, primarily (though not exclusively) with the aim of producing and rearing children as I have described it, and if that is the institution contemplated and safeguarded by art 12, then to accord a same-sex relationship the title and status of marriage would be to fly in the face of the Convention as well as to fail to recognise physical reality.

[121] Abiding single sex relationships are in no way inferior, nor does English law suggest that they are by according them recognition under the name of civil partnership. By passage of the CPA, United Kingdom law has moved to recognise the rights of individuals who wish to make a same sex commitment to one another. Parliament has not called partnerships between persons of the same-sex marriage, not because they are considered inferior to the institution of marriage but because, as a matter of objective fact and common understanding, as well as under the present definition of marriage in English law, and by recognition in European jurisprudence, they are indeed different.

[122] The position is as follows. With a view (1) to according formal recognition to relationships between same sex couples which have all the features and characteristics of marriage save for the ability to procreate children, and (2) preserving and supporting the concept and institution of marriage as a union between persons of opposite sex or gender, Parliament has taken steps by enacting the CPA to accord to same-sex relationships effectively all the rights, responsibilities, benefits and advantages of civil marriage save the name, and thereby to remove the legal, social and economic disadvantages suffered by homosexuals who wish to join stable long-term relationships. To the extent that by reason of that distinction it discriminates against same-sex partners, such discrimination has a legitimate aim, is reasonable and proportionate, and falls within the margin of appreciation accorded to Convention States.

QUESTIONS

i. Do you think civil partnerships and marriage are 'equal symbolically'?

ii. Go back to *M v Secretary of State for Work and Pensions* on p. 46. Which approach to the ambit question does Potter P adopt?

iii. Do you agree with Potter P's reasoning in relation to Article 12 (the right to marry)?

iv. What is the relevance of procreation to marriage? Compare Potter P's judgment with that of Baroness Hale in *Ghaidan* at paras 141, 142 (see pp. 43, 44 above).

v. The Judicial Studies Board, *Equal Treatment Bench Book* (2007), (see: http://www.jsboard.co.uk) provides the following advice to judges:

> Some judicial office-holders may be concerned that to grant more judicial recognition of alternative family forms will undermine the institution of marriage. This, of course, depends on acceptance of the proposition that to promote the rights of one category of citizen necessarily undermines those of another. That argument would seem curious if applied to the rights of women versus men, or to the rights of a racial minority versus the majority. In promoting social stability, the courts are increasingly asked to recognize diversity. The one does not preclude the other.

Does preventing a same-sex couple from marrying protect or promote the traditional family? Has Potter P followed this advice?

vi. What is the difference between a gay marriage and a marriage between a man and a male-to-female transsexual (who has not had surgery)?

Contrast Potter P's judgment with that of Chief Justice Marshall of the Supreme Judicial Court of Massachusetts in the case below.

Hillary Goodridge & others v Department of Public Health & another (2003)

> Marriage is a vital social institution. The exclusive commitment of two individuals to each other nurtures love and mutual support; it brings stability to our society. For those who choose to marry, and for their children, marriage provides an abundance of legal, financial, and social benefits. In return it imposes weighty legal, financial, and social obligations. The question before us is whether, consistent with the Massachusetts Constitution, the Commonwealth may deny the protections, benefits, and obligations conferred by civil marriage to two individuals of the same sex who wish to marry. We conclude that it may not.
>
> We are mindful that our decision marks a change in the history of our marriage law. Many people hold deep-seated religious, moral, and ethical convictions that marriage should be limited to the union of one man and one woman, and that homosexual conduct is immoral. Many hold equally strong religious, moral, and ethical convictions that same-sex couples are entitled to be married, and that homosexual persons should be treated no differently than their heterosexual neighbors. Neither view answers the question before us. Our concern is with the Massachusetts Constitution as a charter of governance for every person properly within its reach. 'Our obligation is to define the liberty of all, not to mandate our own moral code.' *Lawrence v Texas*, 123 S.Ct. 2472, 2480 (2003).... For decades, indeed centuries, in much of this country (including Massachusetts) no lawful marriage was possible between white and black Americans. That long history availed not when the Supreme Court of California held in 1948 that a legislative prohibition against interracial marriage violated the due process and equality guarantees of the Fourteenth Amendment, *Perez v Sharp*, 32 Cal.2d 711, 728 (1948), or when, nineteen years later, the United States Supreme Court also held that a statutory bar to interracial marriage violated the Fourteenth Amendment, *Loving v Virginia*, 388 U.S. 1 (1967). As both *Perez* and *Loving* make clear, the right to marry means little if it does not include the right to marry the person of one's choice, subject to appropriate government restrictions in the interests of public health, safety, and welfare.... In this case, as in *Perez* and *Loving*, a statute deprives individuals of access to an institution of fundamental legal, personal, and social significance – the institution of marriage – because of a single trait: skin color in *Perez* and *Loving*, sexual orientation here.

As it did in *Perez* and *Loving*, history must yield to a more fully developed understanding of the invidious quality of the discrimination ....

The department posits three legislative rationales for prohibiting same-sex couples from marrying: (1) providing a 'favorable setting for procreation'; (2) ensuring the optimal setting for child rearing, which the department defines as 'a two-parent family with one parent of each sex'; and (3) preserving scarce State and private financial resources. We consider each in turn.

... The 'marriage is procreation' argument singles out the one unbridgeable difference between same-sex and opposite-sex couples, and transforms that difference into the essence of legal marriage.... In so doing, the State's action confers an official stamp of approval on the destructive stereotype that same-sex relationships are inherently unstable and inferior to opposite-sex relationships and are not worthy of respect.

... The department's first stated rationale, equating marriage with unassisted heterosexual procreation, shades imperceptibly into its second: that confining marriage to opposite-sex couples ensures that children are raised in the 'optimal' setting. Protecting the welfare of children is a paramount State policy. Restricting marriage to opposite-sex couples, however, cannot plausibly further this policy .... The department has offered no evidence that forbidding marriage to people of the same sex will increase the number of couples choosing to enter into opposite-sex marriages in order to have and raise children. There is thus no rational relationship between the marriage statute and the Commonwealth's proffered goal of protecting the 'optimal' child rearing unit. Moreover, the department readily concedes that people in same-sex couples may be 'excellent' parents. These couples (including four of the plaintiff couples) have children for the reasons others do – to love them, to care for them, to nurture them. But the task of child rearing for same-sex couples is made infinitely harder by their status as outliers to the marriage laws .... Excluding same-sex couples from civil marriage will not make children of opposite-sex marriages more secure, but it does prevent children of same-sex couples from enjoying the immeasurable advantages that flow from the assurance of 'a stable family structure in which children will be reared, educated, and socialized.'

The third rationale advanced by the department is that limiting marriage to opposite-sex couples furthers the Legislature's interest in conserving scarce State and private financial resources.... An absolute statutory ban on same-sex marriage bears no rational relationship to the goal of economy. First, the department's conclusory generalization – that same-sex couples are less financially dependent on each other than opposite-sex couples – ignores that many same-sex couples, such as many of the plaintiffs in this case, have children and other dependents (here, aged parents) in their care. The department does not contend, nor could it, that these dependents are less needy or deserving than the dependents of married couples. Second, Massachusetts marriage laws do not condition receipt of public and private financial benefits to married individuals on a demonstration of financial dependence on each other; the benefits are available to married couples regardless of whether they mingle their finances or actually depend on each other for support ....

The department ... argues that broadening civil marriage to include same-sex couples will trivialize or destroy the institution of marriage as it has historically been fashioned. Certainly our decision today marks a significant change in the definition of marriage as it has been inherited from the common law, and understood by many societies for centuries. But it does not disturb the fundamental value of marriage in our society.

Here, the plaintiffs seek only to be married, not to undermine the institution of civil marriage. They do not want marriage abolished. They do not attack the binary nature of marriage, the consanguinity provisions, or any of the other gate-keeping provisions of the marriage licensing law. Recognizing the right of an individual to marry a person of the same sex will not diminish the validity or dignity of opposite-sex marriage, any more than recognizing the right of an individual to marry a person of a different race devalues the marriage of a person who marries someone of her own race. If anything, extending civil marriage to same-sex couples reinforces the importance of marriage to individuals and communities. That same-sex couples are willing to embrace marriage's solemn obligations of exclusivity, mutual support, and commitment to one another is a testament to the enduring place of marriage in our laws and in the human spirit...

The marriage ban works a deep and scarring hardship on a very real segment of the community for no rational reason. The absence of any reasonable relationship between, on the one hand, an absolute disqualification of same-sex couples who wish to enter into civil marriage and, on the other, protection of public health, safety, or general welfare, suggests that the marriage restriction is rooted in persistent prejudices against persons who are (or who are believed to be) homosexual. 'The Constitution cannot control such prejudices but neither can it tolerate them. Private biases may be outside the reach of the law, but the law cannot, directly or indirectly, give them effect.' *Palmore v Sidoti*, 466 U.S. 429, 433 (1984) (construing Fourteenth Amendment). Limiting the protections, benefits, and obligations of civil marriage to opposite-sex couples violates the basic premises of individual liberty and equality under law protected by the Massachusetts Constitution.

QUESTIONS

i. Do you think enabling gays and lesbians to marry would help strengthen the institution or undermine it?

ii. In Massachusetts the option of a civil partnership does not exist. To what extent do you think that explains or justifies the different conclusions reached by Potter P in *Wilkinson* and Marshall CJ in *Goodridge*?

iii. In *Goodridge*, the court accepted that the right to marry may be 'subject to appropriate restrictions in the interests of public health, safety and welfare'. There are no such restrictions in the UK but some jurisdictions have required people to undertake an HIV test before they can be married. Do you think such restrictions violate the right to marry? Can you think of any other reasons for restricting entry to marriage?

iv. '... it would have been a great deal simpler and more straightforward to accord formal status of "marriage" to gay relationships' (Cretney, 2006). Do you agree? If not, why?

BIBLIOGRAPHY

2.1 The factual background

We quoted from:

Office for National Statistics, *Social Trends 37* (2007) 18–19.

2.2 Why does the state recognise relationships?

We quoted from:

M. Albertson Fineman, *The Autonomy Myth: A Theory of Dependency* (2004) New York/ London: The New Press, 99.

R. Auchmuty, 'Same-Sex Marriage Revived: Feminist Critique and Legal Strategy' (2004) 14 *Feminism and Psychology*, 101.

W. Blackstone, *Commentaries on the Laws of England* (1765) 17th edn by E. Christian et al. (1830) London, Tegg.

E.K. Gough, 'The Nayars and the Definition of Marriage' (1959) 89 *Journal of the Royal Anthropological Institute* 23.

C.C. Harris, *The Family: an Introduction* (1979) London, Allen & Unwin, 49.

D. Herman, 'The Politics of Law Reform: Lesbian and Gay Rights into the 1990s', in J. Bristow and A.R. Wilson (eds), *Activating Theory: Lesbian, Gay, Bisexual Politics* (1993) London, Lawrence & Wishart, 246, 250.

E.R. Leach, 'Polyandry, Inheritance, and the Definition of Marriage' (1955) *Man*, no. 199, 183.

M. Shanley, 'Just Marriage: On the Public Importance of Private Unions', in *Just Marriage* (2004) Oxford, OUP 26–28.

C.F. Stychin, 'Family Friendly? Rights, Responsibilities and Relationship Recognition', in *Feminist Perspectives on Family Law* (2006) London, Routledge Cavendish, 27–31.

J. Weeks, 'Same-Sex Partnerships (2004) 14 *Feminism and Psychology*, 158, 160.

Additional reading

S.B. Boyd, 'Family, Law and Sexuality: Feminist Engagements', (1999) 8 *Social and Legal Studies* 369.

E.M. Clive, 'Marriage: An Unnecessary Legal Concept' in J.M. Eekelaar and S.M. Katz (eds), *Marriage and Cohabitation in Contemporary Societies: Areas of Legal, Social and Ethical Change* (1980) Toronto, Butterworths.

B. Hale, 'Homosexual Rights' (2004) 16 *Child and Family Law Quarterly*, 125.

2.3 Why do people marry or enter civil partnerships?

We quoted from:

M. Maclean and J. Eekelaar, 'The Significance of Marriage: Contrasts between White British and Ethnic Minority Groups in England' (2005) 27(3) *Law and Policy*, 381.

B. Shipman and C. Smart. '"It's Made a Huge Difference": Recognition, Rights and the Personal Significance of Civil Partnership' (2007) 12(1) *Sociological Research OnLine*, available at http://www.socresonline.org.uk/12/1/contents.html.

2.4 Who can marry, and how not to marry

We quoted from:

Law Commission, *Report on Nullity of Marriage*, Law Com. No. 33 (1970) London, HMSO, paras 24, 25, 52.

A. MacFarlane, *Marriage and Love in England 1300–1840* (1986) Oxford, Basil Blackwell, 246.
R. Sandland, 'Feminism and the Gender Recognition Act 2004' (2005) 13 *Feminist Legal Studies*, 43, 44–45.
A. Sharpe, 'Endless sex: the Gender Recognition Act 2004 and the persistence of a legal category' (2007) 15 *Feminist Legal Studies* 57–84.
Working Group on Forced Marriage, *A Choice by Right* (2000) London, Home Office.

Additional reading

Cabinet Office, Women's Unit, *Living without fear: an integrated approach to tackling domestic violence* (1999).
Hutchinson, Hayward and Gupta, 'Forced Marriage Nullity Procedure in England and Wales' (2006) *International Family Law* 20.
S.N. Katz, 'State Regulation and Personal Autonomy in Marriage: How can I marry and whom can I marry?' in A. Bainham (ed.), (1996) *The International Survey of Family Law*, 487.
S. Monro, 'Transgender: destabilizing feminism?', in Stychin and Munro (eds.), *Sexuality and the Law* (2007) London, Routledge-Cavendish.
R. Probert, 'When are we married? Void, non-existent and presumed marriages' (2002) 22 *Legal Studies* 398.
M. Welstead, 'Who are my family?' in B. Atkin (ed.), *The International Survey of Family Law* (2007), Bristol, Family Law, 67.

2.5 Civil partnership – 'parallel but different'

We quoted from:

N. Barker, 'Sex and the Civil Partnership Act: The Future of (Non) Conjugality?' (2006) 14(2) *Feminist Legal Studies* 241.
S. Cretney, *Same Sex Relationships: From 'Odious Crime' to 'Gay Marriage'* (2006) Oxford, Oxford University Press, 24, 33, 36–37, 42.
L. Glennon, 'Displacing the conjugal family in legal policy – a progressive move?' (2005) 17 *Child and Family Law Quarterly* 141.
K.McK Norrie, 'Marriage is for Heterosexuals – May The Rest Of Us Be Saved From It' (2000) 12 *Child and Family Law Quarterly* 363.
B. Shipman and C. Smart, '"It's Made a Huge Difference": Recognition, Rights and the Personal Significance of Civil Partnership', (2007) 12(1) *Sociological Research OnLine*, available at http://www.socresonline.org.uk/12/1/contents.html.

Additional material

S. Boyd and C. Young, "From Same-Sex to No Sex'?: Trends Towards Recognition of (Same-Sex) Relationships in Canada' (2003) 3(1) *Seattle Journal of Social Justice*, 757–793.
M. Closen, R. Gamrath and D. Hopkins, 'Mandatory Premarital HIV Testing: Political Exploitation of the AIDS Epidemic' (1994) 69 *Tulane Law Review*, 71.
L. Crompton, 'Civil Partnerships Bill 2004: The Illusion of Equality' [2004] *Family Law* 888.

N. Fraser, 'Social justice in the Age of Identity Politics: Redistribution, Recognition, and Participation', in N. Fraser and A. Honneth (eds.), *Redistribution or Recognition? A Political-Philosophical Exchange*, (2003) London, Verso.

L. Glennon, 'Strategizing for the Future through the Civil Partnership Act' (2006) 33(2) *Journal of Law and Society*, 244.

E. Steiner, 'The spirit of the new French registered partnership law – promoting autonomy and pluralism or weakening marriage', (2000) 12 *Child and Family Law Quarterly* (2000), 1.

J. Summer and J. Chase, 'Civil Partnership's First Year' [2006] *Family Law* 1077.

2.6 'Gay Marriage'

We quoted from:

The Judicial Studies Board, *Equal Treatment Bench Book* (2007) para 7.1.5, available at http://www.jsboard.co.uk.

Additional material

N. Bamforth, 'The benefits of marriage in all but name'? Same-sex couples and the Civil Partnership Act 2004' (2007) 19 *Child and Family Law Quarterly*, 133.

3

MAKING ENDS MEET: FAMILY RESOURCES AND STATE SUPPORT

Living in a family, of whatever form, involves at least some degree of sharing, and usually some economic interdependence. In this chapter we look at some aspects of the way families, particularly couples, generate their income, and at the advantages and inequalities created by interdependence. We explain the support available in the form of welfare benefits for low income families, and of tax credits for a wider constituency. Finally we look at the family's property, asking why the law of England and Wales does not operate any form of community of property during marriage.

The concern of the lawyer in this area tends to be expressed most often in terms of a sensible allocation of the economic assets of the parties after the relationship has broken down. However, there can be no logical and realistic readjustment of these tangled affairs unless there is a clear understanding of the economic expectations of the parties during their relationship. Thus, the question 'what happens to property after divorce?' is closely interlinked with the question 'what were the economic arrangements of the husband and the wife when they were married?'; and a similar question must be asked in the context of a non-marital union. The storms of chapters 5 and 6 cannot be navigated unless we first sail the calmer waters of this chapter.

3.1 THE FAMILY'S INCOME

Tony Honoré was fully aware of the link which we have just made between the dynamic and subsisting marriage and what has been described as the 'pathology of family law', when he categorised marriage ideologically into three distinct groups – as a partnership, as a contract, and thirdly as an arrangement by which a husband assumes the role of provider. The following extract is taken from *The Quest for Security: Employees, Tenants, Wives* (1982):

> There are three main ways of viewing marriage. Some see it as a *partnership*. On a traditional view, it is a partnership, come what may, for life. In that case, after divorce the partnership notionally continues, and the wife is entitled to the support she would have received had the marriage not broken up, or at any rate to a standard of living which continues to be the equal of her husband's. ... More often, marriage is now seen as an equal partnership which lasts, like other partnerships, until it is dissolved. On that view there must on divorce be a fair division of the profits of the partnership, including property acquired during the marriage. ...
>
> Another conception of marriage is that of an *arrangement* (a collateral contract?) *by which a husband induces his wife to change her career.* Had it not been for the marriage she might, for example, have had good earning prospects. She gives these up to marry. On divorce she must now retrain, sometimes late in life, with diminished prospects. If so, her husband must compensate her by keeping her, during a transitional period, while she brings up the children, if she wants to, and redeploys. If, after a long time together, she has become emotionally attached to her status as a wife, her husband may also be required to compensate her for the wrench.
>
> Yet another conception views marriage not as a contract but *as an arrangement by which a husband assumes the role of providing for his wife's needs and those of their children.* This idea, more ancient and

> deeply rooted in genetics than the contractual ones, makes the husband to some extent the wife's insurer. If she is in need, it is to him, rather than the state, that she turns in the first instance. It is he who must see to her subsistence, and perhaps more, in ill-health, old age or disablement. It is only in this framework of anticipated security that childbearing and childrearing can flourish. But how far does the husband's responsibility extend? How far, in modern conditions does that of the state or community? [Emphasis added.]

QUESTIONS

i. To what extent are these categories relevant to cohabiting couples?
ii. To what extent are they relevant to civil partners?
iii. Can you think of other ways of describing the economic relationship between couples?

The evolution of family economics has had a profound effect on the nature of welfare benefits and also on the way we think about redistribution of assets after divorce.

Diana Gittins in *The Family in Question* (1993) describes how the ideology of a single male breadwinner per family developed during the nineteenth century:

> Although never an entirely secure institution, marriage in pre-industrial society had provided women with a reasonable means of economic survival involving both production and domestic work in and around the home, with a good chance of some minimal security in the event of widowhood. The growth of wage labour and the increasing separation of home from work put women more than ever before at the mercy of two increasingly unstable markets: the marriage market and the labour market. In both their position was weak, and economic survival was precarious whether a woman entered one or both.
>
> In other areas the response to mechanisation, de-skilling and proletarianisation was different. Sometimes machine breaking was an immediate response, as in the Luddite and Captain Swing riots...More often, men in skilled crafts or industries formed themselves into associations or unions. Their general purpose was to defend their members against further capitalist exploitation, mechanisation and wage cuts, and to protect themselves from cheap labour. Since most cheap labour was made up of women and children, the unions tended to contribute further to the already disadvantaged position of women. Until the second half of the nineteenth century, however, the majority of unions were made up of men from only the most skilled trades and crafts, and one of their main aims was to procure a 'family wage' – a single wage that was adequate to support a man and dependent wife and children on his work alone. This new emphasis on the father/husband as sole earner was a powerful factor in the development of modern notions of 'masculinity'. While the concept of a single male breadwinner had started with the rise of the middle classes in the late eighteenth century, this was the first time a sector of the working class – and a very small sector at that – did so.
>
> ...it is hard to know whether their argument for wanting to keep their wives and children out of the workforce was more a matter of conviction or a rationale for higher wages that they knew would appeal to middle-class ears. Whatever the rationale, the ideal of a family wage became increasingly important as an ideal of the organised trade union movement, and it was an ideal which coincided with the new middle-class ideology of women and children as dependants of the husband/father.

During the nineteenth century, however, the proportion of working-class families who could survive on the basis of the man's wage alone was very small. Nevertheless, the objective of a single male breadwinner per family was one of the most radical changes in family ideology of the modern era, and one that had dramatic effects on notions of fatherhood, masculinity, motherhood, femininity, family life and family policy, and still has. The ideal, then as now, was often very far removed from the reality, and the majority of working-class families in the nineteenth century still relied heavily on a household economy based on several wages. Working-class men and women, but women in particular, were therefore dependent on both wage labour in the labour market and a partner through the marriage market in order to survive economically. Both markets were insecure and in fact many individuals had to find extra economic support through children's or other kin's labour.

QUESTIONS

i. Do you feel that the campaign for a 'family wage' was one worth winning?

ii. Think of your grandparents and great-grandparents. Do, or did, their household economies fit into any of the descriptions provided by the previous extracts?

iii. What about your parents and contemporaries – have we moved on from the 'third stage' described above to an era where the economic demands upon the family, and in particular the cost of housing, mean that the 'family wage' is often an impossible ideal?

iv. You, our readers, are both men and women, and most of you expect to begin building a career in the near future. How do you feel about the 'family wage'?

Hudson and Lee, in *Women's Work and the Family Economy in Historical Perspective* (1990), describe the scale of married women's involvement in the formal labour market, which altered dramatically in the twentieth century:

...The post-1945 period in particular witnessed a rapid development in women's employment in advanced industrial economies despite the resurgence of a 'back to the kitchen ideology' in the 1970s fuelled by official concern about male unemployment. The abolition of the marriage bar in public-sector employment in Britain aided this trend. There were significant changes in a variety of areas, with women increasingly dominating such occupations as clerical work, retail sales, elementary teaching and nursing. The increasing importance of 'new industries' in the 1920s and 1930s, including rayon manufacture, light engineering, food processing, and white goods provided a boost for female employment in the formal sector, although on a regionally selective basis and with an emphasis on 'semi-skilled' and 'unskilled' work. Furthermore, the inter-war period generally was characterised by official restrictions on married women's employment as a reaction to male unemployment.

'New' female occupations in the service sector continued to expand after 1945, particularly in retailing, banking, public administration and other forms of clerical work. This trend was assisted by a variety of factors, including improved levels of female pay in certain sectors, shorter working hours, lower fertility, and the gradual provision of suitable, if still inadequate welfare support. ...Technological innovations in the production and conception of household consumer durables such as vacuum cleaners, cookers and electric irons were potentially a source of reduction of domestic burdens as they slowly percolated down the social scale, especially from the 1960s, but new higher standards of domestic cleanliness and decor put pressure on women to spend as much time as in the past on homemaking.

Despite growth in the employment of married women in the formal economy in the twentieth century, many of the factors which determined female labour force participation in the early stages of capitalist development continue to affect occupation choice, gender segregation and women's overall subordination in work. Married women frequently choose jobs which do not directly challenge the prevailing concept of a 'woman's proper place', and many people still 'view it unseemly and inappropriate for wives to work'. Women's occupational choices are clearly influenced by a variety of factors, both work and non-work related. The nature of the labour-market is important but persistently negative facets of women's employment, such as sex-typed jobs, low-ranking position and low comparative earnings, reflect the continued operation of more long-term and deep-seated factors. Married women are still not expected to express any dissatisfaction with their domestic status, so that a return to formal employment frequently has to be legitimised in a socially accepted fashion, with hours tailored to suit child care (for example, mothers' evening shifts in factories) and with earnings treated as 'pin money', or with work portrayed as an emergency measure. As important is the assertion that women have a different relationship to money and wages from men, a notion which has helped to cement the social construction of gender dependency.

Just as women's wage labour in the early phases of capitalist development was frequently an extension of home-based skills, so the general expansion of the service sector, particularly in the twentieth century, has tended to replicate a similar bond between the domestic and work environments. There has been an unprecedented expansion in nursing services since the nineteenth century, accompanied by the formation of professional nursing associations, but these have been based on women's 'traditional' role as carer. Moreover, gender segregation in the health sector as a whole has been associated with persistent low pay for nurses in comparison with other sections of the medical profession. Librarianship has also provided a fast-growing demand for low-paid, but educated, female recruits. Women librarians have frequently been employed because of their submissive attitudes or, as in Tsarist Russia, because of their function as 'guardians of traditional culture'. Even in the retail trades women have been employed not just because they were cheaper than men but because they had such positive virtues as 'politeness' and 'sobriety'. They could also function effectively in a 'world of women', linking women as workers with women as consumers.

In the long term, therefore, despite an unprecedented expansion in the employment of married women in the formal economy, many of the earlier facets of women's work have been retained, particularly in relation to economic marginalisation, pay discrimination, occupational segregation and trade union participation.

QUESTIONS

i. If you are a student, what is the ratio of women to men on your course? And in your family law group?

ii. About 8% of women solicitors work in family law, compared with about 4% of men (Bolton and Muzio, 2007). Why is there this imbalance?

Social Trends 37 (2007) provides a great deal of information about women's employment patterns.

Figure 4.4 Employment rates:[1] by sex

Source: Labour Force Survey, Office for National Statistics

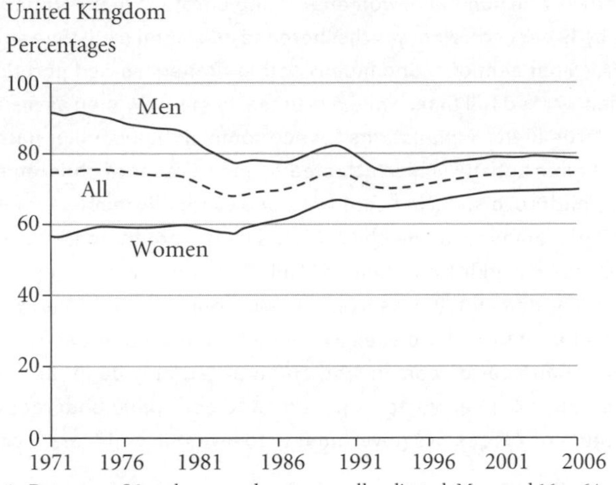

1 Data are at Q2 each year and are seasonally adjusted. Men aged 16 to 64, women aged 16 to 59. See Appendix, Part 4: Labour Force Survey.

Figure 4.2 Economic activity and inactivity status: by sex and age, 2006[1]

Source: Labour Force Survey, Office for National Statistics

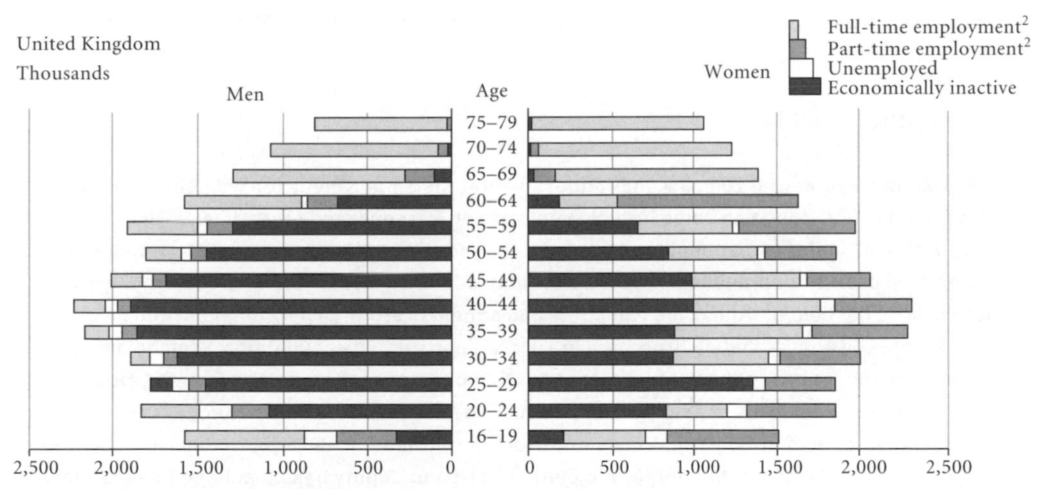

1 Data are at Q2 and are not seasonally adjusted. See Appendix, Part 4: Labour Force Survey.
2 The Labour Force Survey asks people to classify themselves as either full time or part time, based on their own perceptions.

Note the distinction between 'employment' and 'economic activity': economic activity is defined (*Social Trends 37*, p.43) as 'those aged 16 and over who are in employment or are unemployed.' And 'unemployment' means '... those aged 16 and over who are without a job, are available to start work in the next two weeks, who have been seeking a job in the last four weeks or are out of work and waiting to start a job already obtained in the next two weeks'.

Hilaire Barnett, in *Introduction to Feminist Jurisprudence* (1998) has this to say about women's employment patterns:

> In 1971, 44 per cent of women were 'economically active' (in either full time or part time employment); in 1994 53 per cent, and the figure projected for the year 2006 is 57 per cent. By contrast, between 1971 and 1994, the economic activity rate for men fell to 73 per cent, and is projected to

fall to 70 per cent by the year 2006. Of mothers with children between the ages of five and 10, in 1994, 20 per cent were working full time, 44 per cent part time, six per cent were unemployed and 30 per cent were 'inactive'. The number of women working part time in the United Kingdom between 1984 and 1994 rose by 19 per cent, whereas the increase in women's full time employment was only 12 per cent. In 1994, 45 per cent of economically active women worked part time, nearly twice as many men as women worked full time, while five times as many women as men worked part time.

Childcare looms large in the explanations for economic activity, full or part time, or inactivity, and a woman's economic activity is also affected by the number of children she has. Of women with three or more children, over 50 per cent were economically inactive in 1994, compared with less than one-third of women with one child. Moreover, where there is more than one child the mother is most likely to be working part time, if at all. The number of places in registered day nurseries in the United Kingdom in 1993 was over 120,000, compared with 1981 when there were less than 20,000. The number of total day places available for children under five in 1993 was close to one million. Given the number of women who could potentially be in the workforce, and compared with the position in China, women's poverty and economic underactivity is most clearly explained by the failure of successive governments to invest in childcare facilities.

Women's Earnings

Women remain lower paid than men in the United Kingdom according to the Government's statistics. In 1994, one-third of women earned £190 per week or less, compared with only 13 per cent of men. On the other hand, 75 per cent of men earned over £230 per week compared with only 50 per cent of women.

Occupational Data

Clerical and secretarial remains the highest source of employment for women, with nearly 80 per cent of active women being in such employment. Personal and protective services is second, with just under 65 per cent, sales only slightly lower. Under 50 per cent of women are in associated professional and technical employment, and 40 per cent in professional employment. Just over 30 per cent of women are managers and administrators; 20 per cent plant and machine operatives, and approximately 10 per cent are in craft and related occupations. Women outnumber men by four to one in the health sector and by two to one in the education sector. However, when it comes to seniority of employment position, the statistics reveal another picture.

In primary schools in England, Wales and Northern Ireland in 1991–92, women represented 81 per cent of all teachers, but only 57 per cent of head and deputy head teachers. In secondary schools, women represent 49 per cent of all teachers, but only 30 per cent are head and deputy head teachers. In the police force, where women have traditionally been under-represented, 13 per cent (or nearly 20,000) of police officers in the United Kingdom in 1994 were female. In 1994, of Chief Constables, Deputy Constables and Assistant Chief Constables of approximately 42 police forces, only six were women. There were nine Chief Superintendents, 36 Superintendents, 70 Chief Inspectors, 285 Inspectors, 1,330 Sergeants and 18,245 Constables. Among the officers of the armed forces in the United Kingdom in 1995, seven per cent were women.

Barnett's definition of 'economically active' is 'in full-time or part-time employment' and therefore it is to the first of the two tables from *Social Trends 37*, above (p. 109), that we have to look to compare her projections of economic activity rates for 2006 with the actual rates. Table 4.7 from *Social Trends 37* gives some more information about the spread of different types of employment for men and women; and table 4.18 looks at the prevalence of flexible working patterns for men and women.

Table 4.7 Employees: by sex and occupation, 2006[1]

United Kingdom			Percentages
	Men	Women	All
Managers and senior officials	19	11	15
Professional	14	12	13
Associate professional and technical	13	15	14
Administrative and secretarial	6	21	13
Skilled trades	15	1	8
Personal service	3	14	8
Sales and customer service	5	12	9
Process, plant and machine operatives	13	2	7
Elementary	13	12	12
All occupations	100	100	100

1 Data are at Q2 and are not seasonally adjusted. People aged 16 and over. See Appendix, Part 4: Labour Force Survey.

Source: Labour Force Survey, Office for National Statistics

Table 4.18 Employees with flexible working patterns[1], 2003[2]

United Kingdom			Percentages
	Males	Females	All employees
Full-time employees			
Flexible working hours	9.7	14.9	11.6
Annualised working hours	4.9	5.1	5.0
Four and a half day week	1.8	1.1	1.5
Term-time working	1.2	5.8	2.9
Nine day fortnight	0.4	0.3	0.3
Any flexible working pattern[3]	18.0	26.7	21.1
Part-time employees			
Flexible working hours	6.6	8.4	8.0
Annualised working hours	3.4	4.2	4.0
Term-time working	3.9	11.2	9.8
Job sharing	1.2	3.5	3.1
Any flexible working pattern[3]	16.9	26.7	24.8

1 Percentages are based on totals which exclude people who did not state whether or not they had a flexible working arrangement. Respondents could give more than one answer.

2 At spring. Data are not seasonally adjusted and have not been adjusted to take account of the Census 2001 results. See Appendix, Part 4: LFS reweighting.

3 Includes other categories of flexible working not separately identified.

Source: Labour Force Survey, Office for National Statistics

QUESTIONS

i. Is there gender segregation in the legal profession? Have a look at the statistics for women in the judiciary, at www.judiciary.gov.uk/keyfacts/statistics/women.htm. Note that women now represent the majority of salaried solicitors, but only a quarter of partners (Bolton and Muzio, 2007).

ii. How many reasons can you think of for the imbalance seen in those statistics?

From *The Gender Agenda*, Equal Opportunities Commission (2007)

As to women's earnings, Figures 5.3 and 5.6 in *Social Trends 37* tell an interesting story:

Figure 5.3 Median individual total income:[1] by sex and age, 2004/05

Source: Family Resources Survey, Department for Work and Pensions

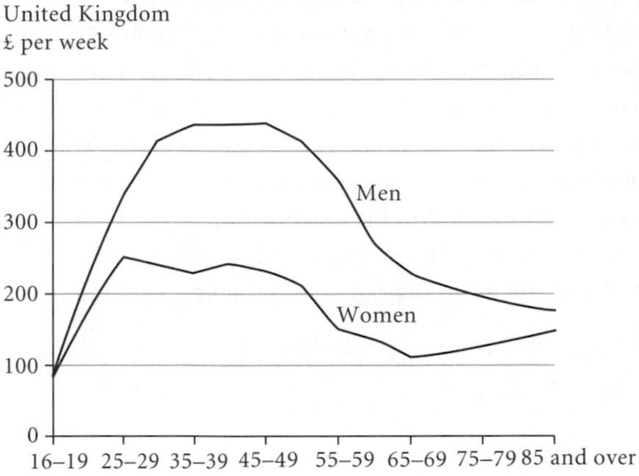

United Kingdom
£ per week

500
400
300
200
100
0

Men
Women

16–19 25–29 35–39 45–49 55–59 65–69 75–79 85 and over

1 See Appendix, Part 5: Individual income.

Figure 5.6 Pay gap between men's and women's median hourly earnings[1]

Source: Annual Survey of Hours and Earnings, Office for National Statistics

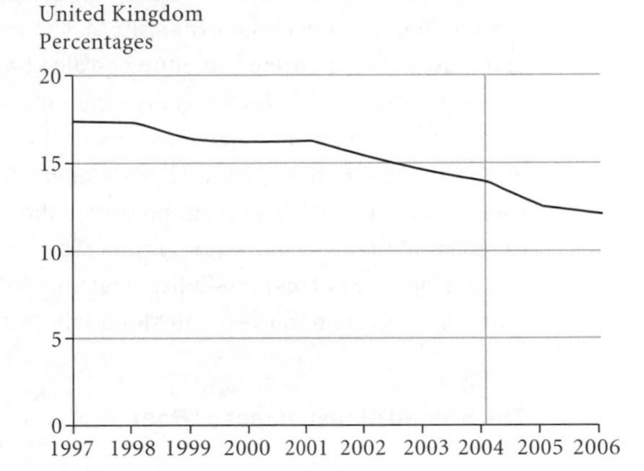

1 Full-time employees on adult rates at April each year, whose pay for the survey period was unaffected by absence. Excludes overtime.

2 Higher percentage includes supplementary information. See Appendix, Part 5: Earnings Surveys.

What do families, and particularly couples, do with their earnings? Distribution of family income between its members is a difficult research field. Notwithstanding the difficulties, Jan Pahl in *Money and Marriage* (1984, 1990) attempted a structure for the research she and others had conducted in this field:

Patterns of Allocation of Money

There is an infinite variety of different allocative systems within the great variety of types of households. ... In reality, the proposed typology represents points on a continuum of allocative systems, but previous research suggests that the typology has considerable validity both within Britain and in other parts of the world. Two criteria are central in distinguishing one system from another: these are, first, each individual's responsibility for expenditure between and within expenditure categories, and second, each individual's access to household funds, other than those for which he or she is responsible.

The Whole Wage System

In this system one partner, usually the wife, is responsible for managing all the finances of the household and is also responsible for all expenditure, except for the personal spending money of the other partner. The personal spending money of the other partner is either taken out by him before the pay packet is handed over, or is returned to him from collective funds. If both partners earn, both pay packets are administered by the partner who manages the money. Where a whole wage system is managed by a husband, his wife may have no personal spending money of her own and no access to household funds.

The Allowance System

In the most common form of this system the husband gives his wife a set amount, which she adds to her own earnings if she has any; she is responsible for paying for specific items of household expenditure. The rest of the money remains in the control of the husband and he pays for other specific items. Thus each partner has a sphere of responsibility in terms of household expenditure. If a wife does not earn she only has access to the 'housekeeping' allowance and, since this is allocated for household expenditure, she may feel that she has no personal spending money of her own: the same phenomenon can also be seen in the case of the whole wage system where the wife is responsible for all family expenditure but has no personal spending money. The allowance system has many variations, mainly because of the varying patterns of responsibility. At one extreme a wife may only be responsible for expenditure on food; at the other extreme she may be responsible for everything except the running of the car and the system may come close to resembling the whole wage system. The allowance system is also known as the 'wife's wage' and the 'spheres of responsibility' system, while the whole wage system is sometimes called the 'tipping up' system (Barrett and McIntosh 1982).

The Shared Management or Pooling System

The essential characteristic of this system is that both partners have access to all or almost all the household money and both have responsibility for management of the common pool and for expenditure out of that pool. The partners may take their personal spending money out of the pool. On the other hand one or both of them may retain a sum for personal spending; when this sum becomes substantial the system begins to acquire some characteristics of the independent management system....

The Independent Management System

The essential characteristic of this system is that both partners have an income and that neither has access to all the household funds. Each partner is responsible for specific items of expenditure, and though these responsibilities may change over time, the principle of keeping flows of money separate within the household is retained.

The Political Economy of the Household

Distinguishing different types of allocative system is, however, only a beginning. What are the variables which determine the allocative system adopted by any one couple at any one time? What are the implications for the couple as a whole, and for individuals, of adopting one system rather than another?

QUESTIONS

i. Are you impressed by the 'ideological' reasons given, or do you think that people simply drift into particular arrangements?

ii. Is it more or less likely that parties to a marriage or civil partnership who have been married or in a civil partnership before will opt for an independent management system?

iii. Is it more or less likely that cohabitants will opt for an independent management system? Would your answer differ depending upon whether those cohabitants are a man and a woman, two men, two women, friends, or siblings living together?

iv. To what extent might age be a factor in this sort of decision? (Think again about your grandparents or great-grandparents – ask them if you can. Might they have operated a 'whole wage' or an 'allowance system'?)

v. What system do you feel comfortable with?

We can see that while women are participating more and more in the employment market, they are not reaping the same rewards as men. The picture becomes more alarming when we look at women's working lifetimes. The Women's Unit of the Cabinet Office has carried out some research about this, and in particular about both the 'gender gap' and the 'mother gap'. The following is from the Cabinet Office's 'Briefing' (2000), summarising the research findings:

Women's Incomes Over the Lifetime

In spring 1999 the Cabinet Office Women's Unit commissioned a research report into women's incomes over their lifetimes. The research set out to examine the key features of women's incomes over their lifetimes, and to identify, and quantify, the factors behind men's and women's lifetime incomes, drawing on existing research and undertaking new analysis, constructing illustrative biographies.

For the first time this research quantifies those parts of the lifetime earnings gap of equally-skilled men and women due to being female (the gender gap) and to motherhood (the mother gap). The overwhelming conclusion is that the level of a woman's educational achievement has the biggest single impact on her likely lifetime's earnings, but the hours she works, how many children she has and when she has them, and whether she divorces all have significant impacts on her lifetime income.

For example:

- the mid-skilled childless woman is estimated to experience a lifetime gender earnings gap of £241,000. The mid-skilled mother of two experiences an additional earnings penalty (a mother gap) of £140,000;
- the low-skilled mother of two is estimated to earn around half a million pounds less than her low-skilled husband;
- women are likely to lose out financially as a result of divorce as they lose at least some access to the husband's income. For the mid-skilled mother of two the initial income loss of divorce is estimated to be £169,000 where the marriage is short (seven years) and £127,000 for a long marriage (17 years). Even with remarriage women can be net losers from divorce;
- low-skilled mothers of two lose 42% of their earnings-related pension (84% if they have four children) as a result of having children, while the mid-skilled lose 21% if they have two children (69% with four children);
- the low-skilled, never-married teenage mother of two children forgoes £300,000 in gross earnings, compared to what she is estimated to earn had she remained childless.

Background

It is nearly 30 years since the first anti-discrimination and equal pay legislation was introduced, and women's role in the economy has in many ways been transformed. But a number of key issues remain: women's and men's working lives continue to be very different as women are more likely to take time out of paid work to look after children; the pay gap is still an issue; and discrimination can still restrict women's opportunities. While we know quite a lot about income comparisons between individuals at particular moments in time, these do not tell us about the impact over women's lifetimes of the pattern and level of their earnings, the effect of the tax-benefit system and the importance to women's incomes of transfers within families.

Using a simulation model, the report estimates the lifetime incomes of women and men, examining closely the influence of differing educational attainment, the number and timing of children and other life events including early parenthood and divorce.

The findings relate to hypothetical individuals with given characteristics, not averages of all actual cases. A key characteristic is skill level, constructed at three levels:

- 'Mrs. Low-skill' who has no qualifications;
- 'Mrs. Mid-skill' who has qualifications at GCSE level; and
- 'Mrs. High-skill' who has a degree level qualification.

...

Summary of Findings

1. The Earnings Gap Between Men and Women

The earnings gap measures the difference in total gross earnings and therefore is based on both hourly pay rates and the number of hours worked.

The lifetime gap has a number of components which this study quantifies for the first time.

The Gender Earnings Gap

This represents the difference in lifetime earnings between equivalently-skilled childless women and men, at current rates of pay and patterns of work. Figure 1 shows estimates of this gap by education level. Mrs. Mid-skill is estimated to incur an earnings gap of £241,000 over her lifetime.

Around half of the gender earnings gap relates to the fact that married, childless women work fewer hours over their lifetimes than equivalent men; and around half is due to the hourly pay gap which exists between men and women.

Figure 1 Lifetime earnings of men, childless women and women with two children

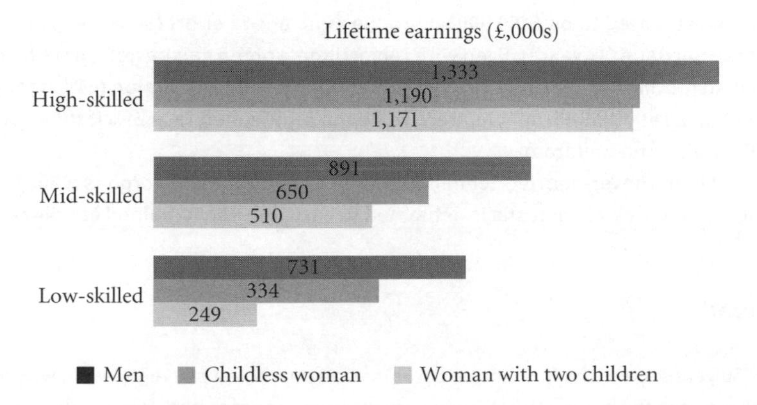

The size of the gender earnings gap varies by educational level. For Mrs. Low-skill and Mrs. Mid-skill the gender gap represents over a third (37%) of their lifetime earnings, compared to Mrs. High-skill who experiences a shortfall of around an eighth (12%). In absolute terms, the gap is largest for Mrs. Mid-skill (241,000) with Mrs. Low-skill experiencing a gender earnings gap of £197,000 and Mrs. High-skill of £143,000.

The Mother Gap

In addition to the gender earnings gap, women who have children experience a 'mother gap' which represents the difference in lifetime earnings between equivalently-educated women with and without children. For two children these figures are: Mrs. Low-skill, £285,000; Mrs. Mid-skill, £140,000; and Mrs. High-skill, £19,000. Although there is some impact, high-skilled mothers forgo much less income than low- or mid-skilled mothers as they largely retain their place in the employment market.

However, they may incur very high childcare costs. (Childcare costs were left outside the scope of this study, along with all other expenditures on children.)

For Mrs. Mid-skill and Mrs. High-skill, motherhood has a smaller impact than that of being a woman. For Mrs. Low-skill, on the other hand, the effect of becoming a mother exceeds the already large impact of gender on her lifetime earnings.

Delaying childbirth has a significant, positive impact on lifetime earnings. For example, it is estimated that if Mrs. Mid-skill starts her family at 24 and has two children she forgoes more than twice the earnings than if she started her family at age 30. Figure 2 illustrates how Mrs. Mid-skill's mother gap is made up at different ages of first birth.

The Parent Gap

The combined effect of both the gender and the mother gap can be thought of as the difference in lifetime earnings between the mother and father in a family. The parent gap is substantial

Figure 2 Breakdown of the mother gap for a mother of two children by age of mother at first birth: mid-skilled woman

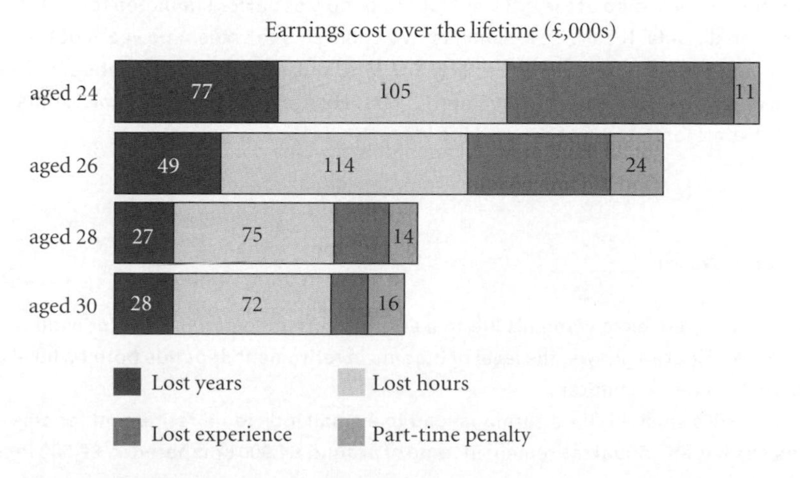

across the skills spectrum. Mrs. Low-skill with two children earns around half a million pounds less than her low-skilled husband. For Mrs. Mid-skill the equivalent figure is £380,000, and for Mrs. High-skill, £160,000.

However, the parent gap is much more significant for Mrs. Low-skill, whose husband has a lifetime earnings nearly double hers. Mrs. Mid-skill's husband has earnings 75% greater than her while Mrs. High-skill's husband has lifetime earnings just 14% higher.

Figure 3 Gross lifetime earnings

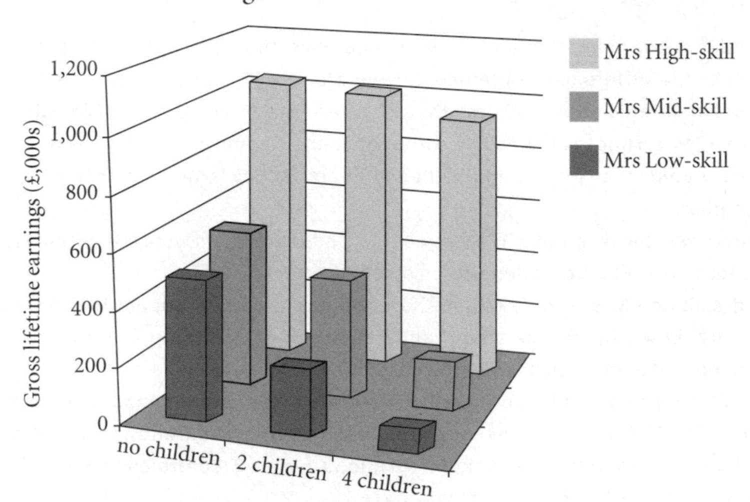

2. Women's Lifetime Earnings and Educational Attainment

The most important source of variation on women's lifetime earnings is the level of educational attainment. The impact of educational level on lifetime earnings is illustrated in Figure 3. Looking from front to back, this shows the dramatic difference between women of different educational levels whatever the number of children they have. Looking from left to right, it also shows that having children has a very different impact on women of different educational levels.

These differences are a consequence of the levels of earnings commanded by women at different educational levels, and of the different labour supply behavior simulated for women at different educational levels. If Mrs. Low-skill has two children she takes nine years out of the labour market and works part-time for a further 28 years. Mrs. Mid-skill is out of the labour market for just two years and works part-time for a further 12. Mrs. High-skill works part-time for just one year, working full-time for the rest of her working life.

...

6. Pension Provision

The notable differences in women's lifetime earnings are reflected in their individual income in retirement. As Figure 4 shows, the level of income in retirement depends both on level of education and the number of children.

Mrs. Low-skill's small lifetime earnings lead to a small individual retirement income – if she is childless she has an annual retirement income of around £4,900 compared to £9,600 for childless

Figure 4 Own net income in retirement

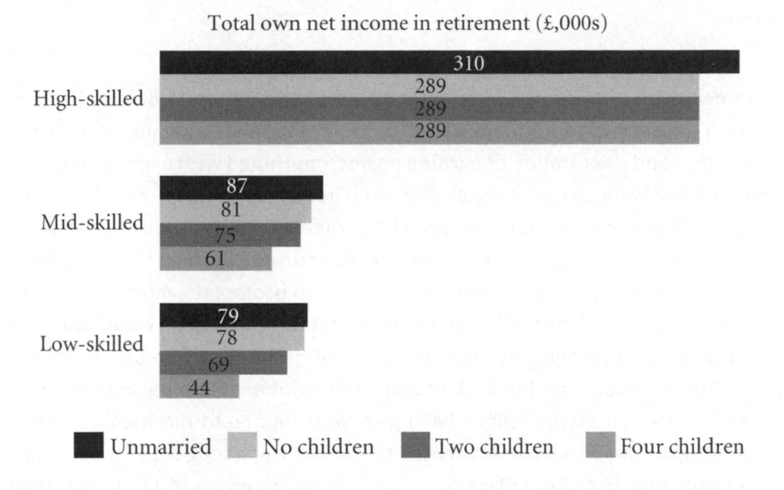

Mrs. Mid-skill and £20,700 for childless Mrs. High-skill. Mrs. Low-skill and Mrs. Mid-skill are assumed to be in SERPS, while Mrs. High-skill is in an occupational pension scheme. Low-skilled mothers lose 42% of their earnings-related pension if they have two children (84% if they have four). For Mrs. Mid-skill, comparable losses of pension are 21% if they have two children (69% with four). High-skilled mothers do not lose out at all.

The modelling of current trends builds up a picture of growing polarisation among women – in retirement as in working life. Thus, as differences between men's and some women's lifetime incomes have narrowed, the differences appear to be growing among women.

QUESTIONS

i. Do you find these statistics alarming?

ii. The statistics tell us what women lose through the 'mother gap'. What, economically, do they gain?

iii. Do men lose anything, economically, when their partners leave employment?

iv. What should be the impact of this information upon the financial consequences of divorce?

v. Should it have the same impact on civil partnership?

vi. But what about cohabitants?

3.2 STATE SUPPORT

What does the family do – where does it turn for help – when its own income is inadequate or non-existent? We have a 'welfare state', the role of which has always been debated but which nevertheless continues to provide a safety net. Some decades away from those origins we perhaps take it for granted and it is worth looking again at the thinking of the 1940s.

In her chapter on 'Income Maintenance for Families with Children', in *Families in Britain* (1982), Ruth Lister described the framework of the system of state support up until the reforms in the Social Security Act 1986:

> The basic framework for today's income maintenance provisions was laid down in the Beveridge Report of 1942. The Beveridge Plan envisaged a comprehensive 'scheme of social insurance against interruption and destruction of earning power' combined with a 'general system of children's allowances, sufficient to meet the subsistence needs' of children. Family allowances (for all children but the first) and contributory national insurance benefits (such as unemployment and widows' benefits) were introduced after the war. The Beveridge Plan also included the safety-net of a means-tested national assistance scheme designed to protect the minority who fell through the meshes of the insurance scheme. It was intended that this safety-net would wither away until it was catering for only a tiny minority. Instead, because of the failure to pay adequate national insurance benefits, as recommended by Beveridge, the numbers claiming means-tested assistance (renamed supplementary benefit in 1966) trebled from one to three million between 1948 and 1978. Further, governments have attempted to bolster up inadequate income maintenance provisions for both those in and out of work through the introduction of a range of means-tested benefits, which have been much criticised. A classic example was the introduction, in 1971, of Family Income Supplement for poor working families, as an alternative to fulfilling an election pledge to increase family allowances. The failure to pay high enough national insurance benefits and family allowances was one reason for the growing dependence on means-tested benefits. The other was the exclusion from the Beveridge Plan of people such as the congenitally disabled who could not meet the contribution conditions attached to the insurance benefits. During the 1970s a number of non-contributory benefits were, therefore, introduced to help the disabled and those at home to care for disabled relatives.
>
> The overall picture today is, thus, one of a confusing patchwork of contributory, non-contributory and means-tested benefits. Much of this patchwork has grown up in isolation from the other main element in our income maintenance provisions: the tax system. ... The system of personal tax allowances was supposed to ensure that 'there should be no income tax levied upon any income which is insufficient to provide the owner with what he requires for subsistence' (Royal Commission on the Taxation of Profits and Income, 1954). [However,] the personal tax allowances patently no longer perform this function. The value of the tax allowances has been so eroded since the war that people can now start to pay tax at incomes which are below the poverty line. ...
>
> The most recent development in income maintenance provision for families has been the introduction of the child benefit scheme. This represented the fusion of two hitherto separate strands of financial support for children: family allowances and child tax allowances.

The Social Security Act 1986 replaced the supplementary benefit with a system known as income support. Income support is now regulated by the Social Security and Contributions and Benefits Act 1992, and remains the source of financial support for those, such as lone parents, who are not available for work (the Jobseekers Act 1995 introduced the jobseekers allowance, replacing unemployment benefit, for those available for work). A claimant is entitled to income support if he or she is aged 16 or over and not working, or working less than 16 hours a week and on a very low income. No claim can be made if the claimant has capital of over £16,000, and his claim will be reduced on a sliding scale if he has £6,000 or more.

The rates payable from April 2007 are shown in the following table published by the Department of Work and Pensions:

Personal allowances for single people:	
aged 16–17	£35.65
or depending on their circumstances	£46.85
aged 18–24	£46.85
aged 25 or over	£59.15
Personal allowances for couples:	
both aged 18 or over	£92.80
where one or both partners are aged under 18,	
their personal allowance depends on their circumstances	
Personal allowances for lone parents:	
aged 16–17	£35.65
or depending on their circumstances	£46.80
aged 18 or over	£59.15
Personal allowances for dependent children:	
from birth to September following 20th birthday	£47.75
Premiums:	
Family	£16.43
Family (one lone parent rate for people with preserved rights)	£16.43
Disabled child	£46.69
Carer	£27.15
Severe disability – paid for each	£48.45
Pensioner	£88.90 (couple)
Enhanced pensioner – aged 75–79	£88.90 (couple)
Higher pensioner	£88.90 (couple)
Disability	£25.25 (single)
	£36.00 (couple)
Enhanced disability premium	£12.30 (single)
	£17.75 (couple)
	£18.76 (child)

People who receive income support are also entitled to housing benefit, which will pay their rent, or, subject to significant limitations, mortgage interest.

Note that payment is made to one adult for the whole family; and that the income of cohabitants is amalgamated: thus, although they have no common law duty to support each other, social security legislation assumes they are doing so. When does living together mean cohabitation? In *Kimber v Kimber* [2000] 1 FLR 383, his Honour Judge Tyrer approved the following list of factors to be considered in answering that question:

[1] membership of the same household;
[2] stability;
[3] financial support;

[4] sexual relationship;
[5] children; and
[6] public acknowledgement

The origins of that list are now quite obscure; it derives from a 1979 *Supplementary Benefits Handbook*. The factors were summarised, in a revised form, in *A Guide to Income Support* published by what was then the DSS in 2002.

One of the amendments consequential upon the Civil Partnership Act 2004 was to section 137(1) of the Social Security (Contributions and Benefits) Act 1992 which now reads:

> "'couple' means–
> (a) a man and woman who are married to each other and are members of the same household;
> (b) a man and woman who are not married to each other but are living together as husband and wife otherwise than in prescribed circumstances;
> (c) two people of the same sex who are civil partners of each other and are members of the same household; or
> (d) two people of the same sex who are not civil partners of each other but are living together as if they were civil partners otherwise than in prescribed circumstances."

QUESTIONS

i. Why is it necessary or appropriate to treat cohabitants as being obliged to support each other for the purposes of social security payments (and what would happen if they were not)?

ii. Why is the obligation to support limited to those who are living together? What about those who are living-apart-together (see John Haskey and Jane Lewis' research, chapter 1, p. 17)

Throughout the post-war period it has been accepted that resources should be targeted at families with children. From 1945, there was in existence a system of family allowances. The philosophy behind this scheme was that the state should not meet the whole cost of the needs of children. And under a child tax allowance scheme, tax payers could obtain exemption from a certain amount of their income from taxation for each dependent child. Child benefit was phased in as from 1977, and provides a merger of child tax allowances and family allowances. Child benefit is a universal, non-means tested and tax-free cash benefit for all children. The benefit was seen by politicians from all parties as a way 'to put cash into the hands of mothers and to give a measure of independence to mothers' (Patrick Jenkin MP on 9 February 1977, in a debate on the Child Benefit Scheme in the House of Commons). In the same debate, the then Minister, Mr Stan Orme MP, said:

> Child Benefit is non-means tested and non-taxable. The scheme has two big advantages over the present method of family support which relies on child tax allowances and family allowances. The child benefit will be paid to the mother, as it is typically the mother who is responsible for the

housekeeping in raising the children. This contrasts with the child tax allowances, which typically go to the father. Thus, income is transferred within the family from father to mother. Wage earners who earn under the tax threshold do not get the benefit of the child tax allowances, but they will get the child benefit.

QUESTIONS

i. Of the patterns of money management identified by Jan Pahl (see p. 113–114 above), which did Stan Orme have in mind here?

ii. It is still the rule that child benefit is paid to one carer of the relevant child, and that where there are several potential claimants the child's mother (including a step-mother) gets priority (Schedule 10 of the Social Security Contributions and Benefits Act 1992). Is this still appropriate? Is it contrary to Article 14 of the European Convention of Human Rights (see p. 38)?

In addition to child benefit, there has been a series of different sources of support for families with children where one or both parents are in work but earnings are inadequate. Earlier versions were known as Family Income Supplement and then Family Credit; since 1999 it has taken the form of tax credits. Nick Wikeley in *Child Support* (2006) explains:

The system of tax credits has undergone a dramatic transformation in recent years. 'True' tax credits in the sense of allowances against tax are a well established feature of the income tax system but are not relevant in this context. In October 1999 the existing family credit and disability working allowance, both in-work social security benefits for the low paid, were reconfigured and re-launched as WFTC [Working Families' Tax Credit] and DPTC [Disabled Person's Tax Credit] respectively. Although described as 'tax credits', both the eligibility criteria and the essential features of WFTC and DPTC remained the same as their predecessor, social security benefits. In April 2001 the government introduced a children's tax credit, a reduction of income tax, as a partial replacement for the abolished married couple's allowance. These were, however merely transitional measures as a more fundamental recasting took place under the Tax Credits Act 2002. WFTC, DPTC and the short-lived children's tax credit were swept away as part of these reforms. In their stead, since April 2003 the Inland Revenue (now HMRC) has been responsible for administering working tax credit and CTC [Child Tax Credit]. Working tax credit is a new-style tax credit, replacing the adult elements of WFTC and DPTC, which brings together the main credits and allowances paid to people in work on low incomes, irrespective of whether or not they have children. CTC is arguably more radical still, in that it replaces the children's tax credit and the child element of WFTC and DPTC, as well as the child-related allowances and additions that were previously paid with both means-tested and national insurance benefits. CTC is paid in addition to the universal child benefit and, unlike working tax credit, is available to middle-income groups as well as to the low-paid. (Words in square brackets added.)

Many of the families in receipt of welfare benefits are headed by a single parent. The growth in the number of lone-parent families in Great Britain is apparent from the following table from *Social Trends 37* (2007).

Table 2.2 Households:[1] by type of household and family

Great Britain					Percentages
	1971	1981	1991	2001[2]	2006[2]
One person					
Under state pension age	6	8	11	14	14
Over state pension age	12	14	16	15	14
One family households					
Couple[3]					
No children	27	26	28	29	28
1–2 dependent children[4]	26	25	20	19	18
3 or more dependent children[4]	9	6	5	4	4
Non-dependent children only	8	8	8	6	7
Lone parent[3]					
Dependent children[4]	3	5	6	7	7
Non-dependent children only	4	4	4	3	3
Two or more unrelated adults	4	5	3	3	3
Multi-family households	1	1	1	1	1
All households (=100%) (millions)	18.6	20.2	22.4	23.8	24.2

1 See Appendix, Part 2: Multi-sourced tables, Households, and Families.
2 Data are at Q2 each year. See Appendix, Part 4: Labour Force Survey.
3 Other individuals who were not family members may also be included.
4 May also include non-dependent children.

Source: Census, Labour Force Survey, Office for National Statistics

Thus in 2006 lone parents comprised 28% of all households in Great Britain with dependent children; in 1961, the figure was about 14%. Who are lone parents? The table on p. 125 comes from John Haskey's article, 'One-parent families and their dependant children in Great Britain', *Population Trends 91* (1998).

Two reports which are still of profound importance are Sir William Beveridge's report on *Social Insurance and Allied Services* (1942) and Sir Maurice Finer's *Report of the Committee on One-Parent Families* (1974).

Sir William Beveridge's report (1942) had this to say of the divorced and separated:

347. End of Marriage Otherwise Than by Widowhood

Divorce, legal separation, desertion and voluntary separation may cause needs similar to those caused by widowhood. They differ from widowhood in two respects: that they may occur

Figure 1 Percentage of families with dependent children headed by lone mothers (by marital status) and lone fathers, 1971–1996

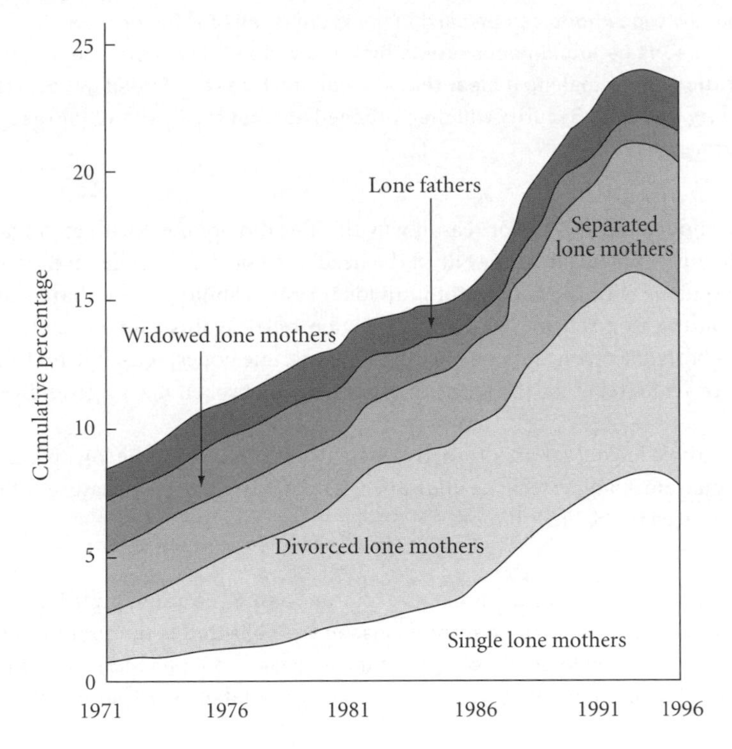

through the fault or with the consent of the wife, and that except where they occur through the fault of the wife they leave the husband's liability for maintenance unchanged. If they are regarded from the point of view of the husband, they may not appear to be insurable risks; a man cannot insure against events which occur only through his fault or with his consent, and if they occur through the fault or with the consent of the wife she should not have a claim to benefit. But from the point of view of the woman, loss of her maintenance as housewife without her consent and not through her fault is one of the risks of marriage against which she should be insured; she should not depend on assistance. Recognition of housewives as a distinct insurance class, performing necessary service not for pay, implies that, if the marriage ends otherwise than by widowhood, she is entitled to the same provision as for widowhood, unless the marriage maintenance has ended through her fault or voluntary action without just cause. That is to say, subject to the practical considerations mentioned in the note below she should get temporary separation benefit (on the same lines as widow's benefit), and guardian or training benefit where appropriate.

NOTE. – The principle that a married woman who without fault of her own loses the maintenance to which she is entitled from her husband should get benefit is clear. It is obvious, however, that except where the maintenance has ended through divorce or other form of legal separation establishing that the default is not that of the wife, considerable practical difficulties may arise in determining whether a claim to benefit, as distinct from assistance, has arisen. There will often be difficulty in determining responsibility for the break-up of the marriage. There will in cases of desertion be difficulty in establishing the fact or the permanence

> of desertion. There will in all cases be the problem of alternative remedies open to the wife. The point to which the principle of compensating a housewife for the loss of her maintenance otherwise than by widowhood can be carried in practice calls for further examination. It may for practical reasons be found necessary to limit the widow's insurance benefit to cases of formal separation, while making it clear that she can in all cases of need get assistance and that the Ministry of Social Security will then proceed against the husband for recoupment of its expenditure.

The proposal was not adopted. A major reason why the idea did not meet with approval, apart from the practical difficulties noted above, may lie in the need to reconcile the collective security involved in an insurance scheme with the concept of individual responsibility. In a welfare state, the moral virtue of contributing to a scheme which will provide relief against, for example, sickness and unemployment – both one's own and one's neighbour's – is, one hopes, self-evident. Contributing to a scheme which provides relief for the wives in other people's broken marriages, however, is not so easy to justify.

The Finer Committee looked for an alternative state benefit to resolve the lone parent's problems, and opted for a 'guaranteed maintenance allowance' (GMA). The ten main features of the proposed benefit are summarised in the Finer Report:

> (1) The allowance would normally, in the hands of the lone parent, be a substitute for maintenance payments; maintenance payments would be assessed and collected by the authority administering the allowance; they would be offset against the allowance paid and any excess paid to the mother; the need for lone mothers to go to court to sue for maintenance awards would be largely eliminated;
>
> (2) the level of the benefit would be fixed in relation to supplementary benefit payments, and, like them, would be reviewed regularly, so that, taken in conjunction with whatever family support was generally available (family allowances or tax credits) it would normally be sufficient to bring one-parent families off supplementary benefit even if they had no earnings;
>
> (3) all one-parent families would be eligible for the benefit, including motherless families;
>
> (4) the benefit would be non-contributory;
>
> (5) the benefit would consist of a child-care allowance for the adult and a separate allowance for each child;
>
> (6) the benefit would not be adjusted to the particular needs of individual families, except in so far as it would reflect the size of the family;
>
> (7) for lone parents who are working or have other income the benefit would be tapered, after an initial disregard, so that it fell by considerably less than the amount by which income increased;
>
> (8) the adult benefit would be extinguished by the time income reached about the level of average male earnings, but the child benefit would continue to be payable to all lone parents, whatever their income;
>
> (9) once awarded, benefit would be fixed at that level for three months at a time, without in the normal way being affected by changes in circumstances. There would thus normally be no need for changes, including the beginning of a cohabitation, to be reported, until a fresh claim to benefit was made. Taken in conjunction with subparagraph (6) above this should much reduce the need for detailed enquiries;
>
> (10) the benefit would be administered by post, on the lines of the family income supplements scheme.

QUESTION

i. The Finer proposals have not been adopted: besides the obvious economic reasons, why do you think the Conservative and the Labour parties, for their differing reasons, have both been slow to support the scheme?

The National Council for One-Parent Families reports in 2007 (on their website, www.oneparent-families.org.uk/):

> Nearly half (48 per cent) of one parent families live in poverty, more than twice the proportion of any other family type including pensioners.
>
> - 42 per cent of all poor children live in one parent families.
> - Over one quarter of lone parents care for a sick or disabled child.
> - One parent families are six times as likely as married couples to have an income of less than £200 per week.
> - Over two thirds (69 per cent) of lone parents receive no maintenance from the other parent.
> - Almost a third of parents leave their job at the time of becoming a lone parent.

In 1998 a scheme called the 'New Deal for Lone Parents' was implemented nationally in order to help and encourage lone parents into employment. The scheme involves an extensive facilitation programme (of which the changes to the tax credits system, noted above, form part). It provides assistance through a Personal Adviser, whom lone parents claiming Income Support must see; and some financial help in the form of a Training Premium of £15 per week for up to 12 months for claimants training for work, and earnings disregard of £20 per week, and help with childcare costs during the first year of employment. An evaluation written in June 2003 for the Department of Work and Pensions by Martin Evans, Jill Eyre, Jane Millar and Sophie Sarre provides the following data:

Figure 1.1 Lone mothers and partnered mothers employment rates 1978–2002

Source: DWP analysis of GHS and LFS

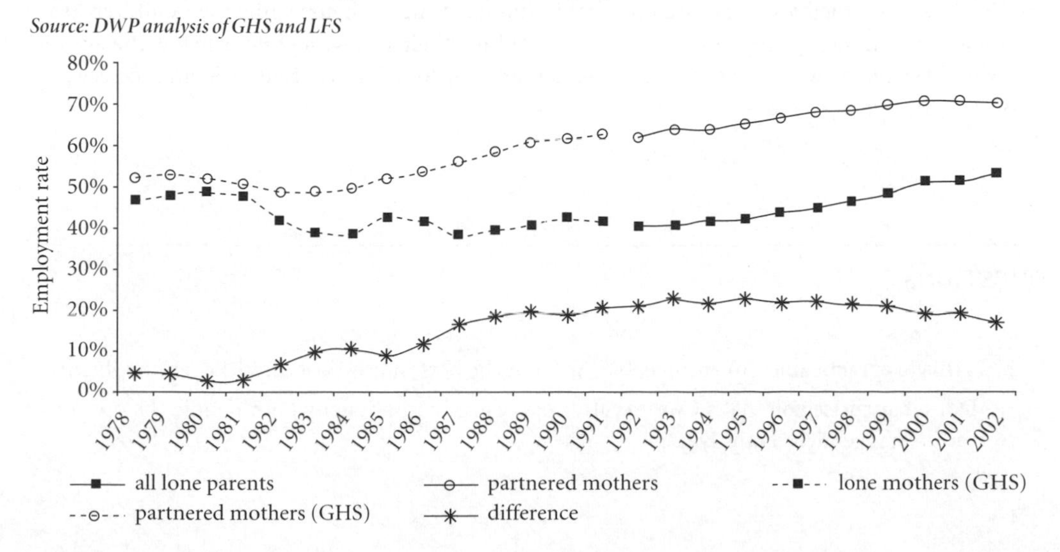

Figure 1.2 Lone parents in receipt of income support, 1991 to 2002

Source: Social Security Statistics 1997 and QSE August 2002

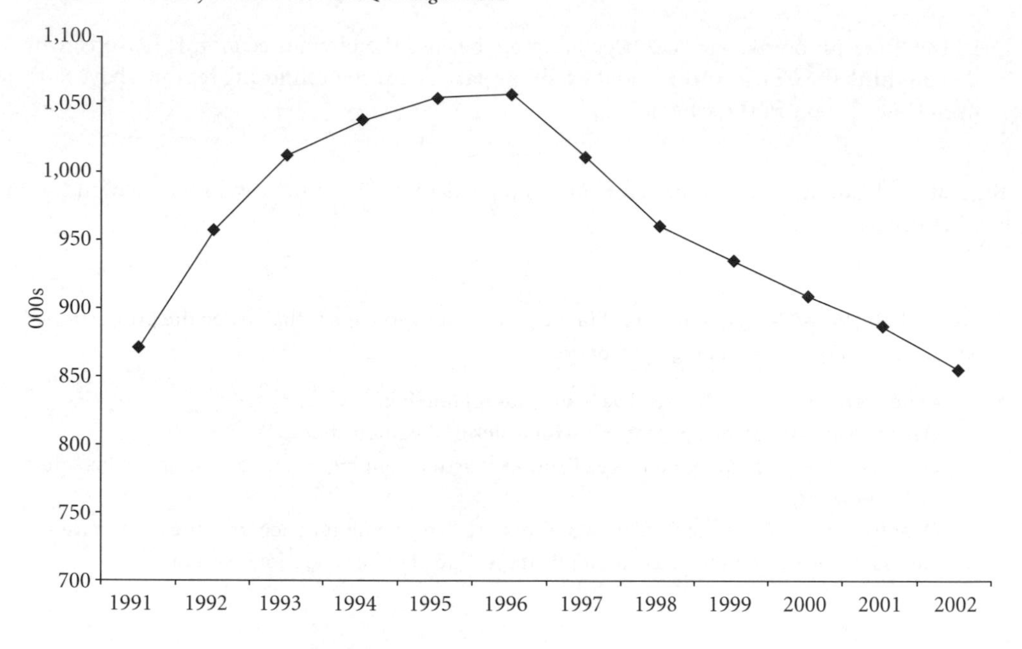

QUESTIONS

i. What are the differences between the objectives of the Finer proposals (see p. 126) and those of the New Deal for Lone Parents?

ii. Which objectives do you prefer, and why?

In *Breakthrough Britain* (2007), a report by the Conservatives' Social Justice Policy Group, *Volume 2, Economic Dependency* it is recommended that 'Lone parents should actively seek, or prepare for, work for 20 hours when their youngest child reaches 5, and full-time (30 hours while their children are of school age) when their youngest child reaches 11. Whilst their youngest child is below the age of 5 they should spend between 5 and 10 hours a week preparing for work.' (Executive Summary; see page 42 of the full report).

QUESTIONS

i. Is this (a) practicable, (b) enforceable, or (c) in the best interests of the children involved?

ii. Does it surprise you that a Conservative party group might deny poor people the option of traditional gendered family life?

A significant note of caution is sounded by Frank Field and Ben Cackett, in *Welfare isn't working* (2007):

> Although the risk of poverty is lower in two parent households, their greater number overall means they represent a larger proportion of all children in poverty: 60 per cent of children in poverty live in two parent families; as compared to 40 per cent in lone parent families. In fact, two parent families in work account for the largest single group of poor children (see chart 5).

Chart 5 Composition of child poverty by household type and work status, 2005/06

Source: Department for Work and Pensions (2007), Households below average income 2005–06. supplementary table E5

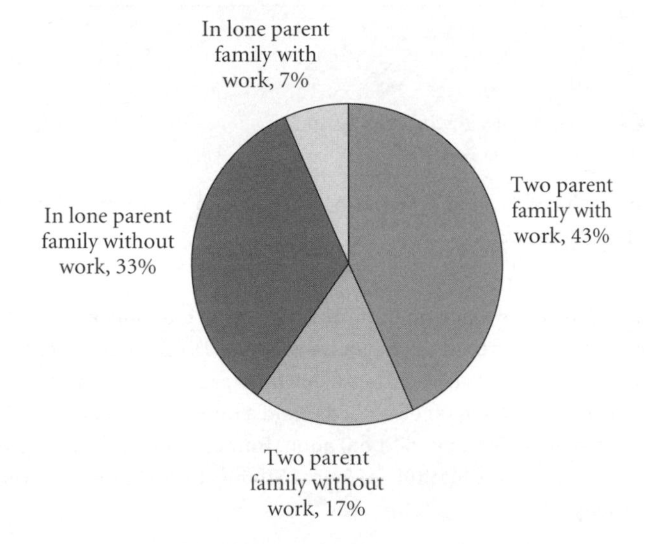

> A significant reason behind the changing risk and composition of child poverty for different households is the Government's tax credit system. Children in working two parent households in poverty are brutally discriminated against.
>
> While it is estimated that two parent households with two children need 30 per cent more income than lone parents to achieve the same standard of living (resulting in a poverty line in 2004–05 for couples with two children of £294 a week, compared with £225 a week for a single parent with two children) the tax credit system does not reflect this. It pays the same amount to a lone parent as to a two parent family (when they have the same number of children and the same gross income).
>
> The result is that two parent households need far greater earnings than lone parent to move past the poverty line. In 2004–05, two parents with two children had to earn £240 a week to have a net income of £295, to lift themselves above the poverty line. By contrast, a lone parent with the same number of children needed to earn just £76 a week to gain a net income of £230, £5 above the poverty line.
>
> And with tax credits not making allowance for the second adult in the household, two parent families needed to work far longer to achieve the same level of income. In 2006, a lone parent with 2 children under 11, working 16 hours a week on the minimum wage, gained a total net income of £487 a week, largely due to tax credits. In order to attain the same weekly income, an equivalent two parent household needed to work 116 hours a week; an extraordinary 100 hours more than the single parent.

The National Council for One Parent Families hit back with a press release (2007) at www.oneparent-families.org.uk/:

> Of course poverty in couple-families must be tackled but far from treating lone parents generously, the UK is particularly bad at protecting them from poverty with the second highest child poverty rate in the EU15 for lone parents. Half of all children living with a lone parent are poor, twice the rate of poverty in couple-families. Forty one per cent of lone parents have gross weekly household incomes under £200, compared to eight per cent of married couple-families and eleven per cent of cohabiting families. Policies need to target increased spending at the poorest families with children, irrespective of their family's shape.

QUESTION

With which of these points of view do you agree?

Breakthrough Britain (volume 1, *Family Breakdown)* draws on the findings of Frank Field and Ben Cackett (see p. 129) and suggests:

> Currently a couple receive the same amount of working tax credit as a lone parent. The basic element paid to everyone who is entitled to receive Working Tax Credit is £1,730. As stated earlier an additional adult in the household receives £1700 on top, but if you are a lone parent you also receive another £1700. So a couple receives £3430 and a lone parent receives £3430. ie. there is, in reality, no allowance made for an additional adult. Rather than suggesting a reduction in the lone parent element we asked the Institute of Fiscal Studies to cost three different ways of reducing the couple penalty.
>
> They told us that if we were to:
> 1. raise the couple (additional adult) element to 2 times the amount currently received by a lone parent, it would cost £5.9 bn and 2.2 million couples with children would gain on average £51.57 per week (this cost includes a £0.2 bn saving on Housing Benefit and Council Tax Benefit because of the way tax credits and benefits interact).
> 2. raise the couple element to 1.5 times the amount currently received by a lone parent, it would cost £2.6bn and 1.8m couples with children would gain on average £28.25 a week.
> 3. raise the couple element so that the ratio of WTC for a couple as compared to a lone parent is the same as under the present income support system, this would cost £3 bn and 1.8m couples with children would gain on average £32.05 a week.
>
> In the interests of consistency with other facets of the benefits system we would recommend option 3. To double the amount of working tax credit (option 1) does not take into account the fact that a couple living together experience economies of scale by virtue of so doing. In other words it overcompensates for the additional adult whereas Option 2 undercompensates or does not sufficiently take a second adult's cost of living into account. The ratio employed by the income support system (where a couple receives around 1.6 times that of a single adult) provides a more realistic figure.

QUESTIONS

i. Do you agree?
ii. Do you think this is practicable?
iii. Is there any way of ensuring that resources are targeted on children, without regard to their families' shape?

It is noteworthy that only a very small proportion of lone-parent families headed by widows or widowers are obliged to rely upon income support. This is because they are entitled to a widowed parent's allowance (under section 36 of the Social Security Contributions and Benefits Act 1992) if the deceased spouse or civil partner has paid the necessary contributions (and the contribution conditions are not very severe). The parent is entitled to a flat-rate benefit and an addition for each child. There is no reduction for earnings, or indeed for any other income, such as a pension from her deceased husband's occupational pension scheme, or from life insurance.

QUESTION

Are there any arguments against extending this benefit to include unmarried, divorced and separated mothers? Or separated fathers?

3.3 FAMILY PROPERTY

We now turn to a different aspect of the family's resources; not what it earns, but what it owns.
Grace Blumberg, in her textbook on matrimonial property in California, *Community Property in California,* (2003) states:

> In the western world, the basic ownership unity has been the conjugal, or husband-wife, dyad. Apparently rooted in Germanic and Visigothic law, community property principles spread all over Europe and many of the areas colonized by Europeans, such as South Africa and Latin America.

But English law does not conform to this pattern of dyadic ownership, as Sir Jocelyn Simon explains in *With all my Worldly Goods* (1964):

> I invite you to accompany me to a village church where a wedding is in progress. The mellifluous cadences of the vicar's voice fall hypnotically on the ear – '... honourable estate... mutual society, help and comfort...comfort her, honour and keep her. ...' Now he has reached the ceremony of the ring. The bridegroom bends a gaze of ineffable tenderness on his bride – '... with this ring...with my body...and with all my worldly goods I thee endow.' I hold my breath,

> aghast. Will the vicar rend his cassock? Will he sprinkle on his head ashes from the ancient coke stove? Will he hurl the bridegroom from the chancel steps with imprecation and anathema? For the man has committed the most horrible blasphemy. In that holy place, at this most solemn moment, actually invoking the names of the Deity, he has made a declaration which is utterly false. He is not endowing the bride with a penny, a stick, a clod. Nor does he intend ever to do so. And yet the service proceeds as if nothing untoward has happened. How does this come about?
>
> The phrase originates in the ancient Use of Sarum, where it is almost unique in liturgy. It reflects a mediaeval custom, the endowment of the bride at the church door, dower *ad ostium ecclesiae* itself a relic, I surmise, of a still more archaic usage, the payment of the brideprice negotiated between the families of bride and bridegroom.

Marriage has no effect upon the property rights of the spouses, save to enable them to register their right to occupy the family home (section 30 Family Law Act 1996). Cohabitation does not even do that. The courts developed the doctrines of informal trusts, particularly during the 1960s and 1970s, as a way of addressing the absence of a formal pool of 'family property' (today those doctrines are relevant particularly to separating cohabitants, and we return to them in chapter 6). Sir Jocelyn Simon made the following observation in his 1964 lecture:

> But men can only earn their incomes and accumulate capital by virtue of the division of labour between themselves and their wives. The wife spends her youth and early middle age in bearing and rearing children and in tending the home; the husband is thus freed for his economic activities. Unless the wife plays her part the husband cannot play his. The cock bird can feather his nest precisely because he is not required to spend most of his time sitting on it.
>
> In such a state of affairs a system of Separation of Goods between married people is singularly ill adapted to do justice. Community of Goods, or at the least community in acquisitions and accumulations, is far more appropriate. And as one leaves the sphere of those who enjoy investment property for that of those whose property largely consists of the home and its contents a regime of Separation is utterly remote from social needs.

Elizabeth Cooke, Anne Barlow and Therese Callus explain what community of property is in their study *Community of Property: a regime for England and Wales* (2006):

> Community of property is one example of a matrimonial régime: that is, the systematic organisation by the law of property rights that result as an automatic consequence of certain relationships – traditionally marriage and more recently registered partnerships. In its most traditional form, community of property provides for the automatic sharing of property and liabilities during the relationship; and all forms of community of property provide for a rule-based sharing of property when the community is dissolved by divorce or death.
>
> ...
>
> In its most basic form, community of property originates in the ideology of the community of persons created through the marriage union. One text on French family law states that it is unthinkable that the union would be of anything other than both persons *and* property. On a more pragmatic level, considerations such as the joint enterprise that marriage represents, the sharing of breadwinner and home-maker roles and the care of children all suggest that marriage is a partnership not only of persons, but also of their contributions to the partnership, be they material or practical. Consequently, where the law deems it necessary to regulate the property rights of the parties by virtue of their formal relationship, community presents itself as a logical default

position. The law provides an empty pot into which the parties will contribute for the benefit of both the union and their own individual interests. Yet the joint enterprise approach is a creature of modern-day thinking and the social desire to see legal recognition not only of the marriage union, but also of a more informal, yet equally committed, relationship for cohabitants. The origins of community lie rather in the legal incapacity of the wife, the desire to keep property within the family (at a time when land was a major source of wealth) and on the basis that marriage was for life. All three elements are far removed from the reality of marriage (and other intimate relationships) at the beginning of the 21st Century.

There are traditionally two ways of perceiving community: (i) within the context of unity of administration which vests all property in one spouse for the benefit of the couple (at least during the marriage); or (ii) as a form of joint ownership and management which recognises property rights of the two spouses over identified communal property (which may range from property acquired only after the marriage (excluding inheritance) to all property held by both spouses, regardless of when it was acquired and including inheritance). The former was the position in England and Wales until the Married Women's Property Act 1882 and translated the incapacity of the women in legal matters and her subservient position to her husband. The 1882 Act however, clearly enshrines the separate nature of property held by each spouse. As a result, the rejection of any community system went hand in hand with the emancipation and proclaimed equality of women with men. This necessarily requires individuals to keep control over their own property. The joint ownership approach, on the other hand, is also compatible with the need for equality between the spouses and also ensures protection for property, such as the family home, which is of importance to the family as a whole. It also entitles the non-earning spouse to some property by virtue of the marriage union. Consequently, the emancipation of women has been translated in some jurisdictions into the reform of community legislation, such as in Sweden and in France. In this context, the equality of the sexes is promoted through the recognition that in the traditional division of roles within a marriage, there may be one breadwinner and one home-maker, but that both activities are of equal value to the marriage union and consequently any property of the union must be held in community for the benefit of both spouses. However, the scope of the community will vary.

The Scope of Community

The extent of the community, whether immediate or deferred, may be vast: at its most basic, it is limited to property acquired during the marriage but excludes inheritance, gifts and personal insurance proceeds even if acquired during the marriage; at its most extensive it includes all property held by either or both spouses from before and during the marriage and includes inheritance. The idea of community means that whatever property falls into the pot will be divided 50:50 between the spouses on the dissolution of the marriage. As we shall see below when we examine some concrete examples, the 50:50 rule may be rigid in some regimes, while in others there may be some flexibility for variation of the shares taking into account certain variables, such as the length of the relationship, or the gains made on property during the relationship. Interestingly (particularly from an English law perspective) immediate community does not only mean community of wealth, it also involves community of debts. There is joint liability for debts relating to the community and the community can also be liable for individual debts. This is a dramatic expression of the 'for better, for worse' of the marriage ceremony! Once again, the extent to which the community will be liable varies according to the régime and also according to the nature of the relationship.

...

Because community of property *stricto sensu* is alien to English law, and because there is in general very little analysis of European matrimonial régimes in English, it is worth examining how different community régimes operate. Consequently, this project examines three European jurisdictions in detail: France, The Netherlands and Sweden.

...

[W]e will begin by looking at the most inclusive form of community as presently operated in the Netherlands, that is universal community. In brief, property owned before the marriage and that acquired during IT will form part of the community pot. Inheritance will also enter into the pot unless the testator has expressly stated that it is to be for the individual benefit of the named spouse. So into the community pot will fall pre- and post marriage property, salaries and, if not expressly bequeathed to one spouse, inheritance. Pension rights do not fall into the community. Universal community is also available in other jurisdictions as a choice of regime. In some areas of France, there was traditionally a high take-up of universal community, and it is often an advisable option for those marrying or changing regime at or near retirement age. There are of course advantages to universal community: not least the fact that it provides an 'easy' and clear solution – there is no calculation to be made of who owns what. However, the Netherlands is almost unique insofar as universal community is the default regime. Elsewhere in Europe, the trend is for a move away from such extensive community and this has also manifested itself in The Netherlands in a proposed Bill to reduce the extent of the community...

Following on from the immediate universal community in the Netherlands, we examined the community of acquests which operates in France. France is perhaps unique in the contractual freedom that couples enjoy to opt out of this default regime, but empirical studies show that over 80% of the population do not contract out and are therefore subject to this regime. Briefly, community reduced to acquests provides, as its name implies, that property acquired after the marriage becomes part of the community. Property acquired before the marriage as well as inheritance and gifts are excluded...

In contrast, Sweden operates a deferred community system which means that during the marriage the spouses maintain their individual property – a concept with which we are familiar in England – but on dissolution a community of marital property is created. The Swedish Marriage Code defines what constitutes personal property, with the remainder being classed as marital property, although the parties are free to contract out of this and make a different arrangement (but are not free to contract into immediate community). All property except inheritance, gifts, life insurance or compensation where it is stated to be for the exclusive benefit of one spouse, will be deemed to be marital property and will thus become part of the community, unless the parties stipulate otherwise. Income from the separate property identified above will become marital property. Moreover, the Swedish Code also allows for what we might term in English 'hidden joint ownership'. This is where one spouse may have purchased property in his own name but with the intention that the other would have a right of ownership.

QUESTION

Given the prevalence of community of property in continental Europe, why do you suppose it was not adopted in this country in 1882?

One aspect of immediate community of property that Sir Jocelyn Simon did not mention was the sharing of liabilities between spouses; where property is owned in community during marriage, as in France and the Netherlands, the whole of the community property can be targeted by creditors to enforce their debts from either spouse. That is why any married person running their own business in a country where immediate community is the default regime is advised to contract out of community, rather than risk all the family assets in the event of business misfortune. This aspect of immediate community would make it difficult seriously to recommend its adoption now. The possibility of a deferred community regime was raised in the English Law Commission Working Paper (1971), and the Commission commented on the results of the consultation in the First Report (1973):

> 47. The proposals relating to such a system of 'deferred community' attracted far more interest and comment than did those relating to legal rights of inheritance. No clear view, however, emerged from the consultation.... On balance, the majority did not support deferred community. Some thought that community would give effect to the partnership element in marriage and create definite property rights without the need to depend upon the exercise of the court's discretion; it was seen as a natural extension of the principle of co-ownership of the home into a wider field. Others thought that community could be unfair if applied arbitrarily without regard to the circumstances and to conduct, that it would be a cause of dissension and that it would be inconsistent with the independence of the spouses....
>
> 49. Very few took the extreme view that fixed principles of deferred community should replace the present discretionary powers exercisable on divorce or in family provision proceedings. The vast majority thought that existing discretionary powers should be retained.
>
> 53. The principle of deferred community should be considered in the light of the conclusions we have already reached in this Report, namely that the principle of co-ownership of the home is a necessary measure which would be widely accepted as better achieving justice than the present law, and that a system of fixed legal rights of inheritance is neither necessary nor desirable. Assuming, for the moment, that the principle of co-ownership of the home will be implemented, is the further step of introducing a system of community needed in order to attain the proper balance of justice?
>
> 54. The Working Paper pointed out that anomalies could arise if a fixed principle of sharing were limited to just one asset. It would apply only where there was a matrimonial home. Further, the spouse who acquired an interest in the matrimonial home under the co-ownership principle might own other assets of similar or greater value which did not have to be shared. It was suggested that a wider principle of sharing might appear fairer. The results of the Social Survey throw some light on both these points. The Survey confirms that spouses who do not own their home seldom have assets of any substantial value. It also indicates that where a home is owned, it represents a substantial proportion of the total value of the spouses' assets. For the majority of home-owners, sharing the home would, in effect, be sharing the most substantial asset of the family. How far is deferred community necessary as a means of eliminating the anomalies in other cases?...
>
> 59. *Our conclusion* is that if the principle of co-ownership of the matrimonial home were introduced into English law much of what is now regarded as unsatisfactory or unfair would be eliminated, and the marriage partnership would be recognised by family property law in this very important context. Having regard to our conclusions regarding co-ownership of the matrimonial home, to the broad interpretation by the court of its powers to order financial provision on divorce, and to our conclusion that the court should have similar powers in family provision proceedings, we do not consider that there is at present any need to introduce a system of deferred community.

However, so far as the matrimonial home was concerned, the Law Commission went further, as the passage above indicates. The Working Paper, *Family Property Law* (1971) discussed the topic in detail, and formed the conclusion that a system of co-ownership should be introduced to meet many of the objections to the present law:

> 0.25 The matrimonial home is often the principal, if not the only, family asset. Where this is the case, if satisfactory provision could be made for sharing the home, the problem of matrimonial property would be largely solved. Under present rules, apart from any question of gift or agreement, ownership is decided on the basis of: (1) the documents of title, and (2) the financial contribution of each spouse. Part 1 of the Paper considers whether there should be alternative ways or additional considerations for determining ownership.
>
> 0.26 One possibility would be to allow the court to decide ownership of the home on discretionary grounds whenever a dispute arose between the spouses, taking into account various factors, including the contribution of each spouse to the family. . . .
>
> 0.27 Another possibility would be to introduce a presumption that the matrimonial home is owned by both spouses equally. . . .
>
> 0.28 A third possibility would be to go further than a presumption, which could be rebutted, and to provide that, subject to any agreement to the contrary, the beneficial interest in the matrimonial home should be shared equally by the spouses. We refer to this as the principle of co-ownership. There are advantages in this solution: it would in the absence of agreement to the contrary apply universally; it would acknowledge the partnership element in marriage by providing that the ownership of the principal family asset should be shared by the spouses; it would provide a large measure of security and certainty for a spouse in case of breakdown of marriage or on the death of the other spouse; and it would help to avoid protracted disputes and litigation.
>
> 0.29. . . The Paper proposes that a new form of matrimonial home trust should apply whenever the beneficial interest in the home is shared between the spouses, in order that they should have a direct interest in the property.

In their First Report on *Family Property – A New Approach* (1973) the Law Commission stated that the principle of co-ownership was widely supported:

> 21. It emerged clearly from the consultation that the principle of co-ownership of the matrimonial home is widely supported both as the best means of reforming the law relating to the home, and as the main principle of family property law. The great majority who supported co-ownership included legal practitioners, academic lawyers, women's organisations and members of the public. Those who opposed co-ownership were those who were opposed to any form of fixed property rights, and they were relatively few in number.
>
> 23. The opinions expressed favouring the co-ownership principle are supported by a change in the pattern of ownership of the matrimonial home in recent years. The Social Survey [Todd and Jones, 1972] analysed the pattern and found that 52% of couples owned their home; among the home owners 52% had their home in joint names. However, when the figures were broken down by the year of purchase of the home it was clear that a marked increase in the rate of joint ownership began in the middle 1960s and is continuing. . . . In cases where the wife had made some financial contribution to the home the proportion of homes put into joint names was higher than in cases where there had been no such contribution. The rate of joint ownership was also very high in cases where the couple had owned more than one home.

Having examined this evidence, the Law Commission arrived at the conclusion that, subject to the proviso that a husband and wife remain free to make any arrangements they choose, the principle of automatic co-ownership of the matrimonial home should be introduced.

The Scottish Law Commission in their Report on *Matrimonial Property* (1984) disagreed with the English proposals:

> (i) Statutory co-ownership of the matrimonial home would not be a good way of giving expression to the idea of marriage as an equal partnership. In some cases it would go too far, particularly if it applied to a home owned before marriage, or acquired by gift or inheritance during the marriage. These are not the results of the spouses' joint efforts. In other cases it would not go far enough and could produce results which were unfair as between one spouse and another. If the wife, say, owned the home and the husband owned other property, he could acquire a half share in the home without having to share any of his property. A spouse with investments worth thousands of pounds could allow the other to buy a home and then claim half of it without contributing a penny. The scheme would also work very unevenly as between different couples. If Mr A had invested all his money in the matrimonial home while his next door neighbour Mr B had mortgaged his home to its full value in order to finance his business, the law would operate very unevenly for the benefit of Mrs A and Mrs B. It would, in short, be a hit or miss way of giving effect to the partnership ideal.
>
> (ii) Statutory co-ownership of the matrimonial home would not be a good way of recognising contributions in unpaid work by a non-earning spouse. It would benefit the undeserving as well as the deserving. Extreme cases can be imagined. A man might marry a wealthy widow, encourage her to buy an expensive house, claim half of her house and leave her. Even in less extreme cases statutory co-ownership would be a poor way of rewarding unpaid work. Most housewives would get nothing from the new law because its effects would be confined to owner-occupiers. Only about 37% of married couples in Scotland live in owner-occupied accommodation. Even where the new law did apply, its effects would be totally arbitrary. Not only would the net value of the home vary enormously from case to case, and from time to time, but so too would the respective values of the spouses' contributions.
>
> (iii) Statutory co-ownership of the matrimonial home would not necessarily bring the law into line with the views of most married people. We know that most married owner-occupiers in Scotland favour voluntary co-ownership of the matrimonial home. We do not know that most married people in Scotland would favour forcing co-ownership on an unwilling owner regardless of the circumstances of the particular case.
>
> (iv) It is not self-evident that property which is used in common should be owned in common. Even if this proposition were accepted, it would lead further than co-ownership between spouses. It would lead to co-ownership between the members of a household, including for example, children and parents.
>
> (v) A scheme for statutory co-ownership of the matrimonial home would be very complex. The scheme we outlined in our consultative memorandum was as simple as we could make it, but even so it raised many difficult questions. Should, for example, co-ownership come about automatically by operation of law (in which case how would third parties, such as people who have bought the house in good faith, be protected) or should it come about only, say, on registration of a notice by the non-owner spouse (in which case would non-owner spouses bother to register before it was too late)? Should co-ownership apply to a house owned by one spouse before the marriage? Should it apply to a home which is part of commercial or agricultural property? Should it apply to a home bought by one spouse after the couple have separated? If not, should it make any difference if the spouses resume cohabitation for a short period? Should the spouses become jointly liable for any debts secured on the home? When should it be possible for one spouse, or both, to opt out of co-ownership and how

should this be done? Should a spouse be able to claim half of the sale proceeds of one home, refuse to contribute to the purchase price of a new home, and then claim half of that one too? If not, how can this be remedied without forcing one spouse to invest in a home he or she does not want to invest in? These are just some of the less technical questions which would have to be answered.

(vi) Statutory co-ownership of the matrimonial home would not benefit many people. ... The majority of... owner-occupier couples already have their home in joint names. Of those owner-occupiers who have their home in the sole name of one spouse, a number will have a good reason for this and would presumably opt out of a statutory scheme. In many cases a co-ownership scheme would confer no long-term benefit on the non-owner spouse because he or she would succeed to the house on the death of the other in any event, or would receive as much by way of financial provision on divorce as he or she would have received if the scheme had applied.

(vii) A scheme for statutory co-ownership of the matrimonial home would have to co-exist with the law on financial provision on divorce. It would make little sense, it might be said, to introduce a complicated scheme for fixed co-ownership rights in the home during the marriage if the whole financial circumstances of the spouses were to be thrown into the melting-pot on divorce. The supposed benefit of fixed rights would be illusory. It would be most useless when most needed.

(viii) Finally, a scheme for forced co-ownership could exacerbate matrimonial disputes. If co-ownership came about only when the non-owner spouse registered a notice, the act of registration might well be seen as a deliberate raising of the level of a domestic dispute. An intimation by one spouse that he or she was opting out of co-ownership would also be unlikely to promote good domestic relations.

QUESTIONS

i. Which if any of these criticisms do you agree with, and why?

ii. Would statutory co-ownership fit better with the Family Law (Scotland) Act 1985 or with the Matrimonial Causes Act 1973?

iii. Why do you think the Law Commission's proposal has not been enacted?

Brenda Hale, in *Family Law Reform: Wither or Whither?* (1995) comments:

The Commission's 1973 proposals for automatic joint ownership of the matrimonial home might have caught the same tide of public opinion which led to the Sex Discrimination Act 1975 and the Domestic Violence and Matrimonial Proceedings Act 1976. But by the time that the Commission's conveyancers had worked out a solution which satisfied them that tide had been missed. The experience of our later proposals on savings and chattels indicates the depth of opposition at official and political level to any alteration of the current rules on the acquisition of property rights, no matter how limited or subject to the contrary intentions of the parties. This seems particularly to occur with proposals [that] are thought to reflect a slightly different balance between the various interests and will be applicable to all couples rather than to those who separate or divorce. ... Continued examination and reform of the discretionary remedies on marital or family breakdown is more likely to bear fruit than attempts to introduce new rules of substantive law which will affect [the] whole population – especially in the property law area where, however misguidedly, this may be seen as benefiting certain (usually less powerful) groups at the expense of others (usually more powerful).

The recent study of views about community of property and joint ownership by Cooke, Barlow and Callus (2006) included some qualitative interview-based research, which indicated considerable support for joint ownership of the family home. But the authors sound a note of caution:

> Most of those who were in favour of statutory joint ownership seemed to refer to the family home rather than to earnings, and many gave one or both of two reasons for their change of view. One common reason was in order to safeguard a home for the children; and the other was to ensure that the children would eventually inherit some or all of the family home. The point to notice is that both these are actually not particularly relevant in assessing whether or not automatic joint ownership is appropriate. Keeping a roof over the children's heads is achieved in our law by other means; and the courts have set their faces against any settlement of property that forces parents to pass on capital assets to the next generation.

(As to that last point, see chapter 6 at p. 263). Any form of automatic joint ownership now seems unlikely. Elizabeth Cooke, in 'Community of property, joint ownership and the family home' (2007), points out the technical problems that would beset any move to automatic joint ownership of the family home, which would probably be the most intuitively popular version of community of property that we might devise.

> It is readily apparent that any proposal of automatic joint ownership involves a choice: should it be legal or equitable? This is not an issue in the civil law jurisdictions, obviously. Here, legal ownership of a registrable estate is not possible without registration; thus our registration system makes automatic legal joint ownership impossible, unless by some computer wizardry it were possible for registration of marriage or of civil partnership to trigger re-registration of any estates in land held by the parties. This can probably be ruled out for the foreseeable future.
>
> The only practicable option is therefore equitable joint ownership. The difficulty faced here is the law's policy – firmly expressed in the 1925 legislation and in case-law throughout the last century – of minimising the powers, and the effect on third parties, of equitable owners who do not also hold the legal estate. The curtain behind which equitable interests are supposed to be hidden is so thick and effective that the proprietary effect of equitable ownership vis-à-vis third parties is minimised.
>
> Thus it is not possible, as things stand, for an equitable joint owner who does not have legal title to restrain or control the legal owner's powers of disposition, unless there is a restriction on the register or, for married persons, a notice recording a right of occupation. Again, the dominance of the register, not only over legal ownership but also as the only source of owner's powers or of restraint of those powers, means that automatic joint ownership without a change in the register is limited in its effect.
>
> Moreover, an equitable joint owner has very little protection against third parties seeking to take the property free of their interest, as buyers or as mortgagees. This is the result of the combination of the fact that trust interests cannot be protected by notice on the register, and the conveyancing practice of seeking waivers from adult occupiers of premises so as to nullify the protection given by paragraph 2 of Schedule 3 of the Land Registration Act 2002. Again, our conceptions of joint ownership, and our concessions to joint occupation, are extremely individualistic, as well as being heavily slanted towards the protection of purchasers. This may need a re-think, unless we are interested in a form of joint ownership that does not affect third parties.

There is another side to this coin too. Not only would joint ownership, in the form available as the law stands, give limited protection to those it is supposed to benefit; it could well be opposed by commercial and financial interests – who would have to have a voice in any consultation about a proposed change to automatic joint ownership. Consider the position of creditors. Secured creditors have been effectively protected by the courts from the risks arising from most instances of unexpected joint ownership (footnoted: *Abbey National BS v Cann* [1991] AC 56, HL; *Bristol & West BS v Hening* [1985] 1 WLR 778, CA; *City of London Building Society v Flegg* [1988] AC 54, HL; etc.). But automatic joint equitable ownership of the matrimonial home would prejudice creditors in two ways:

First, secured creditors are not protected against an unexpected joint owner in the case where the charge secures a loan that is not linked with the acquisition of the property. A mortgagee whose charge secures business debts, and was granted after acquisition and where a co-owning spouse is in occupation, may find itself unexpectedly bound by the spouse's overriding interest. The property which it thought was solely owned is in fact jointly owned and only half the equity is available to meet the debt. [Footnote: This assumes that the waiver system has not worked. The creditor would then have a remedy in misrepresentation against the debtor, which would probably be useless in the circumstances. The waiver system is a horribly imprecise tool. It is therefore used here both as an argument that joint equitable owners have very little protection against third parties (because the system usually works) and that creditors are at risk from unexpected equitable interests (because it sometimes doesn't).]

Second, an unsecured creditor may have relied upon the fact that the debtor was a homeowner, knowing that if the debt was not met it would be able potentially to resort to the value of the house through a charging order. Hidden and automatic joint ownership is a substantial prejudice to such creditors.

The community of property jurisdictions have managed a neat play-off. The system is acceptable to financial interests such as lenders because of the element of joint liability. The housewife spouse who would otherwise be without property gets a credit rating, but the lender gets enhanced protection. English law gives joint owners their severable shares and protects them from each other's creditors; but thereby makes automatic joint ownership rather more controversial, and probably unacceptable to the financial interests who have constituted land law's darlings for the last century or so.

QUESTION

Do you agree that the idea of automatic joint ownership of the family home, for married couples or indeed for other couples, is no longer worth pursuing?

BIBLIOGRAPHY

3.1 The family's income

We quoted from:

H. Barnett, *An Introduction to Feminist Jurisprudence* (1998) London, Cavendish, 54–55.

Equal Opportunities Commission, *The Gender Agenda* (2007).

D. Gittins, *The Family in Question* (1993) Basingstoke, Macmillan, 27, 28.

A. Honoré, *The Quest for Security: Employees, Tenants, Wives* (1982) London, Stevens, 62.

P. Hudson and W.R. Lee, 'Women's Work and the Family Economy in Historical Perspective' in P. Hudson and W.R. Lee (eds.), *Women's Work and the Family Economy in Historical Perspective* (1990) Manchester and New York, Manchester University Press.

J. Pahl, *Money and Marriage* (1990) Basingstoke and London, Macmillan, 94, 108, 178.

Office for National Statistics, *Social Trends 37* (2007) figures 4.2, 4.4, 4.7, 4.18, 5.3, 5.6.

Cabinet Office, Women's Unit, *Briefing: Women's incomes over the lifetime* (2000).

Additional reading

M. Anderson, 'Family, Household and the Industrial Revolution' in M. Anderson (ed.), *Sociology of the Family* (1980) Harmondsworth, Penguin Books.

K. Bellamy and K. Rake, *Money, Money, Money, is it still a rich man's world? An audit of women's economic welfare in Britain today.* (2005) Fawcett, London. Available at www.fawcettsociety.org.uk/documents/£££%20Audit%20full%20report.pdf

S.C. Bolton and D. Muzio, 'Can't Live with'Em: Can't Live without 'Em: Gendered Segmentation in the Legal Profession' (2007) 41(1) *Sociology* 47.

N. Charles, *Gender in Modern Britain* (2002) Oxford, Oxford University Press, chapter 3.

J. Pahl, 'The Allocation of Money Within the Household' in M.D.A. Freeman (ed.), *State, Law and the Family* (1984) London and New York, Tavistock Publications, 36.

K. Rake (ed) *Women's incomes over the lifetime* (2000) Cabinet Office, Women's Unit.

H. Scott, *Working Your Way to the Bottom: the Feminisation of Poverty* (1984) London, Pandora Press.

3.2 State support

We quoted from:

Sir William Beveridge, *Social Insurance and Allied Services* (Cmd. 6404) (1942) London, HMSO, para. 347.

Conservative Party Social Justice Policy Group, *Breakthrough Britain*, volume 1 *Family Breakdown*, 69–70 povertydebate.typepad.com/home/files/economic.pdf and volume 2 *Economic Dependency* povertydebate.typepad.com/home/files/economic.pdf and the Executive Summary of volume 2 at povertydebate.typepad.com/home/files/EcDependency.pdf

M. Evans, J. Eyre, J. Millar, S. Sarre, *New Deal for Lone Parents: Second Synthesis report of the National Evaluation* (Department of Work and Pensions, 2003) www.dwp.gov.uk/jad/2003/163_rep.pdf

F. Field and B. Cackett, *Welfare isn't working* (Reform, 2007) pp 19, 21; www.reform.co.uk/filestore/pdf/070611%20Welfare%20isn't%20working%20-%20child%20poverty.pdf

Report of the Committee on One-Parent Families (Chairman: The Hon Sir Morris Finer) (Cmnd. 5629) (1974) London, HMSO.

J. Haskey, 'One-parent families and their dependant children in Great Britain', *Population Trends 91* (1998).

R. Lister, '*Income Maintenance for Families with Children*' in R. N. Rapoport, M. P. Fogarty and R. Rapoport (eds.), *Families in Britain* (1982) London, Routledge and Kegan Paul, 432.

National Council for One-Parent Families: website www.oneparentfamilies.org.uk/ and press release, 13 June 2007: www.oneparentfamilies.org.uk/1/lx3x1oix9254x1/0/0/190707/0/0// No-bias-in-favour-of-lone-parents.htm Office for National Statistics, *Social Trends 37* (2007) table 2.2.

N. Wikeley, *Child Support* (2006), Oxford, Hart Publishing, 358–9.

Additional reading

J. Bradshaw and J. Millar, *Lone Parent Families in the UK*, Social Security Research Report, no.6, (1991) London, HMSO.

Evaluation of WFTC by Institute for Fiscal Studies: www.hmrc.gov.uk/research/ifs-labour-supply.pdf

S. Osborne et al, '*Welfare Benefits and Tax Credits Handbook*' 8th Ed, (2006), London, Child Poverty Action Group.

For details of working tax credit and child tax credit: www.taxcredits.direct.gov.uk/what.html or www.taxcredits.inlandrevenue.gov.uk/Qualify/WhatAreTaxCredits.aspx

3.3 Family property

We quoted from:

G.G. Blumberg, *Community Property in California* 4th edn., (New York, Aspen, 2004), 1.

E. Cooke, 'Community of property, joint ownership and the family home' in *Contemporary Perspectives on Property, Equity and Trust Law* M Dixon and G Griffiths (eds), (2007) Oxford, Oxford University Press, 39.

E. Cooke, A Barlow, T Callus, *Community of Property: a regime for England and Wales* (2006) Bristol, Nuffield 1, 3–6, 24–25.

B. Hale 'Family Law Reform: Wither or Whither' *Current Legal Problems* 217 (1995), Oxford, Oxford University Press, 228–229.

Law Commission, Working Paper No. 42, *Family Property Law* (1971) London, HMSO, 0.25–0.29.

Law Commission, *First Report on Family Property: A New Approach*, Law Com. No. 52 (1973) London, HMSO, paras. 21–23, 47–59.

Scottish Law Commission, *Family Law: Report on Matrimonial Property* (Scot. Law Com. No. 86HC 467) (1984) Edinburgh, HMSO, para. 3.

Sir J. Simon, *With All My Worldly Goods* (1964) Holdsworth Club, Presidential Address, University of Birmingham.

Additional reading

L. Fox, *Conceptualising Home* (2006), Oxford, Hart Publishing.

4

DIVORCE AND THE DISSOLUTION OF CIVIL PARTNERSHIP

> Divorce is an institution only a few weeks later in origin than marriage.
>
> Voltaire, quoted in A. Alvarez, (1981).

> Le nombre de divorces ne cesse d'augmenter. Le mariage n'est plus considéré comme une institution rigide et indissoluble, mais comme un pacte sui generis renouvelé au jour le jour.
>
> [The divorce rate continues to rise. Marriage is no longer a rigid and indissoluble union, but a unique form of agreement that is renewed from day to day.]
>
> *(From the explanatory material presented to the Belgian parliament in 2006 prior to debate on divorce reform.)*

American psychologist, Gerald Alpern, in *Rights of Passage* (1982), has tried to provide a guide to the emotional realities of divorce:

> Some divorces are simple happenings, a graceful parting in which two people go off in different directions to new lives. Other divorces occur so gradually, over so many years, that the divorce process is not a deeply felt experience. For others, the marriage involved a connection so casual that a legal divorce is but a formality.
>
> However, the majority of divorces are very powerful experiences which, for many, are devastating. For most people, divorce necessitates major revisions in life goals, expectations and personal identities. People involved in divorce find themselves acting in unfamiliar ways. They may behave irrationally, become vicious or promiscuous, or suddenly plan to desert loved children. These unfamiliar actions and feelings are very frightening and cause grave self-doubts which exacerbate the depression so common to divorcing men and women. The most disorienting experience is the wide mood swings which accompany the vacillating positive and negative feelings about the divorce. At one moment the person is high on thoughts of being independent, of being free of a spouse no longer loved. The next moment or day the same person may be crying, longing for the missing spouse and planning an attempt at reconciliation.

John Cleese and Robin Skynner, in *Families and How to Survive Them* (1993), remind us that we are perhaps asking for trouble by entering into the types of marriage expected of us nowadays:

> **John** Let's start with an easy one... Why do people decide to marry each other?
>
> **Robin** Because they're in love.
>
> **John** Oh, come on.
>
> **Robin** No, I'm being serious.

John Well, perhaps, but this falling in love routine is very bizarre. You find perfectly ordinary, rational people like computer programmers and chartered accountants, and there they are, happily computing and chartering away, and suddenly they see someone across a crowded room and think, 'Ah, that person is made for me, so I suppose I'd better spend the rest of my life with them.' It borders on the occult.

Robin Perhaps you'd have preferred it three hundred years ago when parents arranged all the marriages for sensible reasons like land and money and social climbing. They all regarded 'falling in love' as the worst possible basis for marriage – a recipe for disaster.

John Yes, Samuel Johnson said that all marriages should be arranged by the Lord Chancellor without reference to the wishes of the parties involved.

Robin So the point I'm making is that nowadays we are free to marry the person we love, the one who can really make us happy.

John And of course we have the highest divorce rate in history.

Robin Since you and I have both made a contribution to those statistics, we'd better not sound too critical.

John I'm sorry if I did. Actually, I think divorce is underrated. It gives you insights into some of the trickier aspects of marriage, the more delicate nuances as it were, that couples who've been happy together for thirty years wouldn't begin to grasp. But nevertheless, divorced or not, here we are, millions upon millions of us, all blithely pairing off, thinking, 'This is the one for me.' So what's going on, Doctor?

Robin What do you think falling in love is about?

QUESTIONS

i. Do you think that arranged marriages might be less vulnerable to relationship breakdown?
ii. What do you think is the importance, if any, of falling in love?

With that conundrum in mind, we turn our attention first of all to the history of our divorce law up until the major changes of the Divorce Reform Act 1969. Then we look at the current law, to be found in the Matrimonial Causes Act 1973, and we compare the law relating to the dissolution of civil partnerships. We examine the bigger picture, looking at grounds for divorce in Europe and beyond and also at religious divorce. Next we consider the relationship between reform of the law of divorce, and the incidence of divorce; and finally we look to the future for divorce law in this jurisdiction. As we do so, we call to mind the words of Lawrence Stone in *Road to Divorce* (1990). It is his view that there does not exist any single model of change which can explain the history of marital breakdown and divorce in a single country for all periods of time and for all classes of society. He writes:

> Any historian who claims that either the law has always shaped marital practices or that marital practices have always shaped the law, or that the causes of change were at bottom either legal, or economic and social, or cultural and moral, or intellectual, is offering a simplistic solution which is unsupported by the evidence. History is messier than that.

4.1 THE HISTORY OF DIVORCE LAW IN ENGLAND AND WALES

The Gospel according to St Mark lays the foundation for the Christian view of marriage and divorce which has influenced our law for so long:

Chapter 10

. . .

2. And the Pharisees came to him, and asked him, Is it lawful for a man to put away his wife? tempting him.
3. And he answered and said unto them, What did Moses command you?
4. And they said, Moses suffered to write a bill of divorcement, and to put her away.
5. And Jesus answered and said unto them, For the hardness of your heart he wrote you this precept.
6. But from the beginning of the creation God made them male and female.
7. For this cause shall a man leave his father and mother, and cleave to his wife.
8. And they twain shall be one flesh: so then they are no more twain, but one flesh.
9. What therefore God hath joined together, let not man put asunder.
10. And in the house his disciples asked him again of the same matter.
11. And he saith unto them, Whosoever shall put away his wife, and marry another, committeth adultery against her.
12. And if a woman shall put away her husband, and be married to another, she committeth adultery.

An almost identical account appears in St Matthew's Gospel (Chapter 19, verses 3–9), but with the significant addition of the words 'except it be for fornication' in his version of Mark's verse 11.

It is perhaps quite difficult today to imagine the near-impossibility of obtaining a divorce before 1857. The plight of poor Mr Hall (*R v Hall* (1845) 1 Cox CC 231), on trial for bigamy in 1845, recalls how things were:

Maule J:

Prisoner at the bar, you have been convicted before me of what the law regards as a very grave and serious offence: that of going through the marriage ceremony a second time while your wife was still alive. You plead in mitigation of your conduct that she was given to dissipation and drunkenness, that she proved herself a curse to your household while she remained mistress of it, and that she had latterly deserted you; but I am not permitted to recognise any such plea... Another of your irrational excuses is that your wife had committed adultery, and so you thought you were relieved from treating her with any further consideration – but you were mistaken. The law in its wisdom points out a means by which you might rid yourself from further association with a woman who had dishonoured you, but you did not think proper to adopt it. I will tell you what that process is. You ought first to have brought an action against your wife's seducer, if you could have discovered him; that might have cost you money, and you say you are a poor working man, but that is not the fault of the law. You would then be obliged to prove by evidence your wife's criminality in a Court of Justice, and thus obtain a verdict with damages against the defendant, who was not unlikely to turn out pauper. But so jealous is the law (which you ought to be aware is the perfection of reason) of the sanctity of the marriage tie, that in accomplishing all this you would only have fulfilled the lighter portion of your duty. You must then have gone, with your verdict in your hand, and petitioned the House of Lords for a divorce. It would cost you perhaps five or six hundred pounds, and you do not seem to be worth as many pence. But it is the boast of the law that it is impartial, and makes no difference between the rich and the poor. The wealthiest man in the kingdom would have had to pay no less than that sum for the same luxury; so that you would have no reason to complain. You would, of course, have to prove your case over again, and at the end of a year, or possibly two, you might obtain a divorce which would enable you legally to do what you have thought proper to do without it. You have thus wilfully rejected the boon the legislature offered you, and it is my duty to pass upon you such a sentence as I think your offence deserves, and that sentence is, that you be imprisoned for one day; and in as much as the present assizes are three days old, the result is that you will be immediately discharged.

Divorce by Act of Parliament was, of course, far too expensive to be available to more than a very few. Sir Morris Finer and Professor O.R. McGregor explain in *The History of the Obligation to Maintain*, which is Appendix 5 to the *Report of the (Finer) Committee on One-Parent Families* (1974) (the 'Finer Report'):

Parliamentary Divorce

13. As the ecclesiastical courts [the church courts] had no power to dissolve a valid marriage ...and as the secular courts refused to invade the spiritual jurisdiction, only Parliament could break the indissoluble bond of marriage by intervening in particular cases through the procedure of sovereign legislation. The following Table shows the extent of its interference for this purpose by the passing of private Acts of divorce:

[The table] shows how rare parliamentary divorces were before the accession of George I and how their use increased steadily thereafter, so that one quarter of all the private Acts were passed in the twenty years before the system was abolished in 1857. Before the eighteenth century the main reason for Parliament's willingness to grant the privilege of marrying again was to continue the succession to peerages in the male line.

Period	Number	Percentage
Before 1714	10	3
1715–1759	24	8
1760–1779	46	14
1780–1799	53	17
1800–1819	49	15
1820–1839	59	19
1840–1856	76	24
Total	317	100

Source: Adapted from PP 1857, Session 2 (106-I), Volume XLII, page 117.

...

17. This procedure, cumbersome, expensive and intricate as it was, could in practice be utilised only by aggrieved husbands. Only four wives were ever granted Acts and these were all passed in the nineteenth century.... Parliament held...to the principle that adultery without more by the husband was not a sufficient ground for a wife to obtain an Act.

18.... As Lord Chancellor Cranworth explained to the House of Lords:

> 'A wife might, without any loss of caste, and possibly with reference to the interests of her children, or even of her husband, condone an act of adultery on the part of the husband but a husband could not condone a similar act on the part of a wife. No one would venture to suggest that a husband could possibly do so, and for this, among other reasons...that the adultery of the wife might be the means of palming spurious offspring upon the husband, while the adultery of the husband could have no such effect with regard to the wife.'

QUESTIONS

i. So there was one law for the rich and another law for the poor. Could it be that only the rich needed to divorce?

ii. And there was one law for men and one for women. Why?

iii. What social changes in the years leading up to 1857 might have led a wider section of society to seek divorce?

iv. Is there anything exclusively Christian about the idea that divorce should be difficult?

In 1857 the Matrimonial Causes Act created the Court for Divorce and Matrimonial Causes. Judicial separation, scarcely used today, authorised the spouses to live apart. Divorce, under the 1857 Act, was available to a husband on the ground of his wife's adultery; and to a wife, on the ground of adultery aggravated by some other conduct (such as incestuous adultery, adultery coupled with cruelty or with desertion for two years or more) or on the ground of sodomy or bestiality. Only a few hundred decrees of divorce were granted in any year in the nineteenth century; the court was in London; and legal costs were significant. It might be felt that very little had changed.

The story in the twentieth century is one of a gradual opening of the doors to divorce. In 1909 the Second Royal (Gorell) Commission on Divorce proposed 'that the law should be amended so as to place the two sexes on an equal footing as regards the grounds on which divorce may be obtained'. That was done in 1923. It also proposed the broadening of the grounds for divorce, by adding to adultery the offences of desertion for three years and upwards, cruelty, incurable insanity, habitual drunkenness and imprisonment under commuted death sentence. This was put into effect by the Matrimonial Causes Act 1937. Thirdly, the Gorell Report recommended that the High Court should sit and exercise divorce jurisdiction locally, rather than remaining centralised in London. It was not until 1946 that this change was made.

The story since then is taken up in the main body of the Finer Report:

> Lord Buckmaster's Act in 1923 had put husbands and wives on a footing of formal equality in respect of the grounds of divorce, by making it possible for each to petition against the other on the grounds of simple adultery. But it was not until the legal aid scheme of 1949 compensated wives for their lack of income or low earnings that they won practical equality of access to the court.

The Third Royal (Morton) Commission on Marriage and Divorce

4.30 In 1951, Mrs Eirene White proposed, in a private member's bill, to permit divorce to spouses who had lived apart for seven years: that is to say, divorce which depended on the fact of separation over this period, and did not involve the proof, by one spouse against the other, of the commission of a matrimonial offence. ... Mrs White's bill was seen by its opponents as a measure to open the floodgates. Nevertheless, to the alarm of its opponents, and to the surprise of many of the supporters of the bill, it appeared as though the House might respond favourably. At this juncture, the government offered Mrs White a Greek gift in the shape of a Royal Commission. Mrs White accepted.

4.31 The Report of the Morton Commission in 1956, though divided, was decidedly against change. Reformers had urged that the doctrine of the matrimonial offence was out of step with people's actual behaviour and expectations in marriage, that the law was brought into contempt by the perjury thereby encouraged, and that the result was illicit unions and the birth of illegitimate children. The Church of England was the most influential opponent of change in the matrimonial law. ...

Nevertheless, it was a group set up in the 1960s by the Archbishop of Canterbury (under the chairmanship of the Rt. Rev. R.C. Mortimer, Lord Bishop of Exeter) that cleared the way for major reform. Its report was published in 1966, under the title *Putting Asunder – A Divorce Law for Contemporary Society*. It drew three main conclusions.

First, as Jesus himself had accepted the Mosaic law for those whose 'hardness of heart' made them unable to understand the truth of Jesus' own teaching about life-long fidelity, and today's secular society was full of such people:

17. There is therefore nothing to forbid the Church's recognizing fully the validity of a secular divorce law within the secular sphere. It follows that it is right and proper for the Church to co-operate with the State, and for Christians to co-operate with secular humanists and others who are not Christians, in trying to make the divorce law as equitable and as little harmful to society as it can be made. Since ex hypothesi the State's matrimonial law is not meant to be a translation of the teaching of Jesus into legal terms, but [to] allow properly for that 'hardness of heart' of which Jesus himself took account, the standard by which it is to be judged is certainly not the Church's own canon law and pastoral discipline. ...

...

Secondly, having considered the interpretation of the fault-based grounds; the stratagems to which these put couples who were determined on divorce; and the inconsistency of having some fault and some (like incurable insanity and cases of cruelty for which the respondent could not morally be blamed) no-fault grounds:

45(f). ... We are far from being convinced that the present provisions of the law witness to the sanctity of marriage, or uphold its public repute, in any observable way, or that they are irreplaceable as buttresses of morality, either in the narrower field of matrimonial and sexual relationships, or in the wider field which includes considerations of truth, the sacredness of oaths, and the integrity of professional practice. As a piece of social mechanism the present system has not only cut loose from its moral and juridical foundations: it is, quite simply, inept.

Thirdly, the courts should be empowered, after an enquiry into every case, to recognise in law the fact that a marriage had irretrievably broken down.

...

55. ... As we see it, the primary and fundamental question would be: Does the evidence before the court reveal such failure in the matrimonial relationship, or such circumstances adverse to that relationship, that no reasonable probability remains of the spouses again living together as

husband and wife for mutual comfort and support?...The evidence falling to be considered by the court would be all the relevant facts in the history of the marriage, including those acts and circumstances which the existing law treats as grounds for divorce in themselves. The court would then dissolve the marriage if, and only if, having regard to the interests of society as well as of those immediately affected by its decision, it judged it wrong to maintain the legal existence of a relationship that was beyond all probability of existing again in fact.

QUESTION

Why was the doctrine of the matrimonial offence so important?

Immediately following the publication of *Putting Asunder*, the Lord Chancellor referred the matter to the Law Commission. Their report, entitled *Reform of the Grounds of Divorce – The Field of Choice*, was published only five months later. The Divorce Reform Act 1969 came into force on 1 January 1971 and has since been consolidated with other relevant legislation in the Matrimonial Causes Act 1973, which remains the present law on divorce.

4.2 THE PRESENT LAW: THE MATRIMONIAL CAUSES ACT 1973

The statute provides as follows:

1. Divorce on Breakdown of Marriage

(1) Subject to section 3 below, a petition for divorce may be presented to the court by either party to a marriage on the ground that the marriage has broken down irretrievably.

(2) The court hearing a petition for divorce shall not hold the marriage to have broken down irretrievably unless the petitioner satisfies the court of one or more of the following facts, that is to say –

(*a*) that the respondent has committed adultery and the petitioner finds it intolerable to live with the respondent;

(*b*) that the respondent has behaved in such a way that the petitioner cannot reasonably be expected to live with the respondent;

(*c*) that the respondent has deserted the petitioner for a continuous period of at least two years immediately preceding the presentation of the petition;

(*d*) that the parties to the marriage have lived apart for a continuous period of at least two years immediately preceding the presentation of the petition (hereafter in this Act referred to as 'two years' separation') and the respondent consents to a decree being granted;

(*e*) that the parties to the marriage have lived apart for a continuous period of at least five years immediately preceding the presentation of the petition (hereafter in this Act referred to as 'five years' separation').

(3) On a petition for divorce it shall be the duty of the court to inquire, so far as it reasonably can, into the facts alleged by the petitioner and into any facts alleged by the respondent.

(4) If the court is satisfied on the evidence of any such fact as is mentioned in subsection (2) above, then, unless it is satisfied on all the evidence that the marriage has not broken down irretrievably, it shall, subject to sections 3(3) and 5 below, grant a decree of divorce.

...

3. Bar on Petitions for Divorce Within One Year of Marriage

(1) No petition for divorce shall be presented to the court before the expiration of the period of one year from the date of marriage.

(2) Nothing in this section shall prohibit the presentation of a petition based on matters which occurred before the expiration of that period.

...

5. Refusal of Decree in Five Year Separation Cases on Ground of Grave Hardship to Respondent

(1) The respondent to a petition for divorce in which the petitioner alleges five years' separation may oppose the grant of a decree on the ground that the dissolution of the marriage will result in grave financial or other hardship to him and that it would in all the circumstances be wrong to dissolve the marriage.

(2) Where the grant of a decree is opposed by virtue of this section, then—

(*b*) if the court finds that the petitioner is entitled to rely in support of his petition on the fact of five years' separation and makes no such finding as to any other fact mentioned in section 1(2) above, and

(*c*) if apart from this section the court would grant a decree on the petition, the court shall consider all the circumstances, including the conduct of the parties to the marriage and the interests of those parties and of any children or other persons concerned, and if of opinion that the dissolution of the marriage will result in grave financial or other hardship to the respondent and that it would in all the circumstances be wrong to dissolve the marriage it shall dismiss the petition.

QUESTION

Was this what the Archbishop's group had in mind?

In the early years of the Matrimonial Causes Act 1973, analysis of the ground for divorce and the five facts focused on the interpretation of the statute. It was swiftly established that the 'intolerability' referred to in fact (a) does not have to be causally linked to the adultery (*Cleary v Cleary* [1974] 1 WLR 73, [1974] 1 All ER 498); and that the behaviour alleged under fact (b) is to be assessed in terms of what *this* petitioner can be expected to cope with (*Livingstone-Stallard v Livingstone-Stallard* [1974] Fam 47, [1974] 2 All ER 766), and indeed need not be *mis*behaviour at all (*Thurlow v Thurlow* [1976] Fam 32, [1976] 2 All ER 979). The fact that the parties have 'grown apart', fail to communicate, or have nothing in common, however, is not sufficient (*Buffery v Buffery* [1988] 2 FLR 365, [1988] 1 FCR 465). The courts had to examine the meaning of 'living apart' or 'separation', particularly with regard to the cases where one party is unavoidably away from home (for example because he or she is in prison or on military service). They had to ask: is there separation when only one party intends it (in other words, can separation, like desertion, be unilateral)? They concluded, in *Santos v Santos* [1972] Fam 247, [1972] 2 All ER 246, that it can (otherwise there would be no scope for fact (e), separation without consent) and that:

> ...'living apart' referred to in grounds (*d*) and (*e*) is a state of affairs to establish which it is in the vast generality of cases arising under those heads necessary to prove something more than that the husband and wife are physically separated. For the purposes of that vast generality, it is sufficient to say that the relevant state of affairs does not exist whilst both parties recognise the marriage as subsisting.

It became established that 'living with each other in the same household' is as much an abstraction as a physical reality, which can be very helpful to those couples who are still under the same roof (*Fuller (otherwise Penfold) v Fuller* [1973] 1 WLR 730, [1973] 2 All ER 650).

QUESTIONS

i. A long-sentence prisoner petitions for divorce shortly after his release. It seems that his petition should succeed if he made up his mind to do this five years ago but told his wife nothing about it. But if he made up his mind to divorce her just before he was released it seems that the petition should not be successful. Why the difference?

ii. Suppose a woman comes to you and explains that she and her husband have lost interest in each other and have nothing in common. They have had little to do with one another for some time and would now like a divorce, although for convenience they are still living under the same roof. Will you explain the law carefully to her before you seek further and better particulars of their circumstances?

iii. What questions would you then ask?

iv. How do you think all this accords with the concern felt by the Archbishop of Canterbury's group for 'considerations of truth, the sacredness of oaths and the integrity of professional practice'?

v. The husband of the woman in question ii. above does not want a divorce. What would be the purpose of his defending the petition?

Defending a divorce is futile (although it may be tactical); and it is impossible to force people to defend. By 1966, 93 per cent of divorces were undefended. A so-called 'special procedure' was invented for the very simplest of cases and extended to all undefended divorces in 1977. The 'special procedure' is described in Appendix C to the Law Commission's Report, *The Ground for Divorce* (1990):

> 26. ...This requires the [district judge] to scrutinise the petition, supporting affidavit and any other evidence, in order to satisfy himself that the contents of the petition have been proved and that the petitioner is entitled to a decree. Thus the documents are checked both for their procedural regularity and for their sufficiency in substance to prove the petitioner's case. If they

> are found to be lacking in some way, the [district judge] may request further information or evidence. If the [district judge] is satisfied, he will issue a certificate that the petitioner is entitled to a decree and the [county court] judge will pronounce it formally in open court. If the [district judge] is not satisfied, he will remove the case from the special procedure list and require that it be heard before the [circuit] judge.

Appendix C to the Report is a summary of a *Court Record Study* carried out by the Law Commission. One of the major aims of the study was to discover more about the circumstances in which district judges refused their certificates. This is what they reported:

> 31. Procedural or administrative problems fell into the following broad categories: inaccuracies on the face of the documents,... documents, for example the marriage certificate, not filed or the wrong document, for example an acknowledgement of service relating to the wrong fact, filed; disagreement or problems over costs; problems with service; and respondents under a disability for whom a guardian ad litem might have to be appointed...
>
> 32. Substantive problems arose where the [district judge] had questioned the method or sufficiency of proof of the fact asserted in the petition and whether the petitioner was entitled to a decree. These fell into the following broad categories: insufficient evidence of adultery...; failure to name the person with whom the adultery was alleged to have been committed [note that since 1991 this has not been required]...and parties still living at the same address....

And in behaviour cases:

> 44. It might have been thought that assessing behaviour cases would also cause some problems. [District judges] might have been unpersuaded, either that the behaviour complained of had in fact taken place or had the effect alleged, or that however accurately described it was such that it was unreasonable to expect the petitioner to live with the respondent. The files examined did not reveal evidence of this, apart from the problems arising where the couple were still living at the same address. The behaviour itself was generally proved by the assertions made in the petition and subsequently confirmed in the petitioner's affidavit.

The study concludes:

> 51. It is certainly difficult to conclude from the files which we studied that the intervention of the courts, considerable though this may be, has a noticeable impact upon the outcome of cases.

Divorce nowadays is thus largely a matter of paperwork, achieved by a procedure in which neither party need attend court if the petition is undefended (as it is in all but a handful of cases; the Judicial Statistics no longer record numbers for defended divorces). The most widely-used fact is fact (b) ('behaviour'), closely followed by adultery; the grants of divorce by fact proven and by petitioner in 2005 are seen in Figure 2 on p. 153, taken from *Population Trends 2006*.

The Family Law Sub-Committee of the Law Society, in *A Better Way Out* (1979), stated that, in undefended cases, 'the evidence presents little difficulty – after several years of marriage, virtually any spouse can assemble a list of events which, taken out of context, can be presented as unreasonable behaviour [sic] sufficient on which to found a divorce petition'.

Figure 2 Facts proven at divorce and to whom granted, 2005

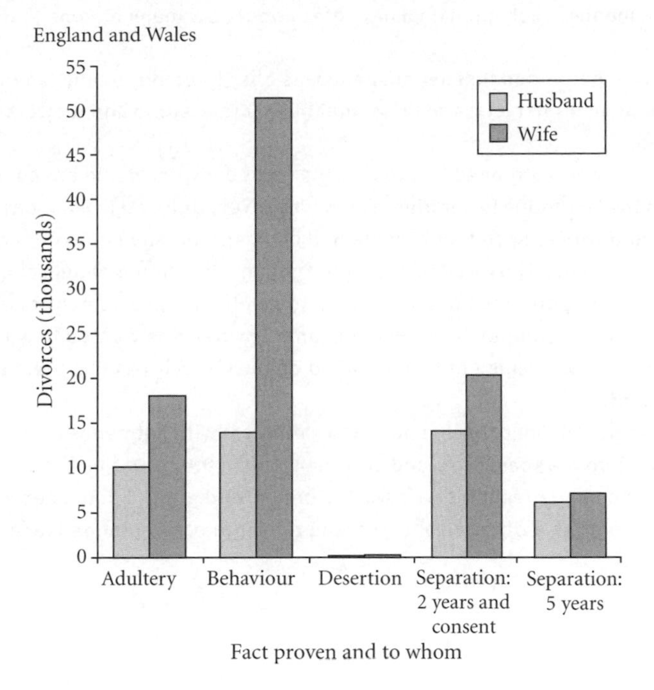

QUESTIONS

i. If you were drafting a petition based upon the other's behaviour, would you be inclined to make it look as bad as possible (lest the court be tempted to probe more deeply) or as little as you think you can get away with (lest the respondent be goaded into defending either the petition itself or ancillary issues)?

ii. How little do you think you can get away with?

The following feature in *The Times*, 19 February 1996, gives some examples of particulars in divorce petitions:

So What's Unreasonable Behaviour?

1. Allegation made by the petitioner – the husband – that his full-time working wife would only ever cook him 'microwave suppers' and not the 'real meals' his mother used to cook.
2. The allegation made by the petitioner – the wife – that her husband was an incompetent do-it-yourself fanatic who spent all his spare time constructing things around the house that would later fall down or – on one occasion – had caused actual structural damage to their home.
3. The wife who petitioned the husband on the ground that he would not speak to her for a year because he had been advised by a medium that he should not do so.

4. The wife who petitioned that her husband would count all the plants in the garden in an obsessive manner each night, making notes about how many blooms there were on each rose bush.
5. The wife who petitioned that her husband was obese and physically repugnant to her. On receiving the petition he was so upset that he lost four stone and they eventually became reconciled.
6. The husband who petitioned that his partner, a housewife, would spend all her evenings talking on the telephone to her friends, recalling every dull detail of her day.
7. The husband who alleged that his wife had claimed that she could not make love to him because she believed he was a reincarnated god and he should remain chaste.
8. The woman who petitioned that her husband would not give up control of the television zapper and would compulsively switch channels when she wanted to watch something. She could cope with this until he installed cable TV. With 24 channels to zap through, she finally left him.
9. The woman who claimed that her husband's problem with flatulence made it necessary for her to move into the spare room and eventually out of the marriage.
10. The man who alleged that his wife was so concerned about being seen without makeup that she never took it off, even at night, and the sight of her clogged face was repugnant to him.

QUESTION

Why not replace the ground for divorce with the single allegation: 'I don't want to be married to you any more'?

What is the role of the 'grave hardship' defence in section 5, given the availability of ancillary relief in response to the needs of either party (see Chapter 5)? Only a handful of cases have been reported, from the early days of the statute, and they offer no encouragement for the use of the defence, whether the hardship is financial or ideological (*Le Marchant v Le Marchant* [1977] 1 WLR 559, 121 Sol Jo 334, CA; *Reiterbund v Reiterbund* [1974] 1 WLR 788, [1974] 2 All ER 455; *Rukat v Rukat* [1975] Fam 63, [1975] 1 All ER 343).

QUESTIONS

i. What do you think was the more radical change: the introduction of irretrievable breakdown as the sole ground of divorce, or the introduction and the extension of the 'special procedure'?

ii. Following the introduction of the special procedure, what do you suppose is now the role of subsections (3) and (4) of section 1 of the Matrimonial Causes Act 1973 (see p. 149, 150)?

iii. Is it necessary or desirable that the termination of the marriage be obtained in a formal or judicial manner?

iv. In some circumstances, we recognise divorces obtained abroad without legal proceedings (Family Law Act 1986, s. 46(2)(*b*)). If we recognise such divorces obtained abroad, why not allow administrative divorces here?

v. Or do we already have that, given that all but a handful of divorces are granted each year under the 'special procedure'?

4.3 THE DISSOLUTION OF CIVIL PARTNERSHIPS

Dissolution of civil partnerships first became possible on 21 December 2006. On 7 December 2006 the news service pinknews.co.uk commented (at http://www.pinknews.co.uk/news/articles/2005-3207.html):

> A group of gay lawyers specialising in same sex relationships, predicts few couples will apply to end a civil partnership when the first opportunity arrives on 21 December. Instead lawyers at QueerPod have seen an increase in gay clients in heterosexual marriages seeking a divorce to form a civil partnership.
>
> ...
>
> QueerPod lawyer, David Allison, said: 'There is no rush to gay divorce as most of the first wave of civil partners are very happily hitched – many waited a long time to have their relationships legally recognised and nothing could be further from their minds on their first anniversary. Traditionally we've had a steady trickle of divorce cases where one of the spouses is gay but since civil partnership was introduced we've seen a noticeable increase in these. One of the greatest positive effects of civil partnership is the cultural change it brought about. People are realising that they don't need to stay in an unhappy marriage and many see the recognition of civil partnership as a signal that gay relationships are equally valid.'

Section 44 of the Civil Partnership Act 2004 contains provisions for the dissolution of a civil partnership in terms almost identical to those of section 1 of the Matrimonial Causes Act 1973. The one difference of substance, rather than of terminology, is that there is no equivalent to section 1(2)(a). Thus there are four facts, and no mention of adultery.

QUESTIONS

i. Why do you think this is so? Look back at Chapter 2 at p. 94.

ii. Do you think a committed relationship has to be, or should be, sexually monogamous?

The Judicial Studies Board's *Equal Treatment Bench Book* (2007, see http://www.jsboard.co.uk) says this:

> It should be stressed...that not all gay and lesbian people regard same-sex couples as the same as heterosexual couples. Many successful gay relationships reject the heterosexual model as unsuitable to the practical, financial, emotional and sexual needs of two men or two women living as a partnership. In many ways, the homosexual partners start life together with a blank sheet of paper, unguided or constrained by precedent, tradition and heterosexual cultural norms, and are therefore required to make their own mutually agreed rules. This flexibility may help sustain gay relationships even if, for example, the definition of fidelity is focused more on emotional and honest behaviour, than on sexual conduct. Judges should be careful not to judge gay relationships according to the principles of heterosexual married life

---

QUESTIONS

i. What are heterosexual cultural norms?

ii. If flexibility might sustain gay relationships, why should it not also sustain heterosexual ones? If it might, should the judges take that into account in divorce?

4.4 DIVORCE: THE INTERNATIONAL PICTURE

The table on pp. 157–158 shows the current grounds for divorce in the Member States of the European Union.

The figures on p. 159 from *Population Statistics 2004* show the rates of marriage and divorce in the EU member states, from 1960 to 2002.

As Mary Anne Glendon explains, in *Abortion and Divorce in Western Law* (1987), the picture we see today follows a period of change:

> Between 1969 and 1985 divorce law in nearly every Western country was profoundly altered. Among the most dramatic changes was the introduction of civil divorce in the predominantly Catholic countries of Italy and Spain, and its extension to Catholic marriages in Portugal. Other countries replaced or amended old, strict divorce laws. The chief common characteristics of all these changes were the recognition or expansion of nonfault grounds for divorce, and the acceptance or simplification of divorce by mutual consent. When California in 1969 became the first Western jurisdiction completely to eliminate fault grounds for divorce, the move was thought by some to prefigure the direction of reforms in other places. But it soon became clear that the purist approach was not to find wide acceptance. That same year England, too, passed a new divorce law which purported to make divorce available only when a marriage had irretrievably broken down. But since the English statute permitted marriage breakdown to be proved by evidence of traditional marital offences as well as by mutual consent or long separation, it did not really repudiate the old fault system. As it turned out, compromise statutes of the English type

Member states' laws on the grounds for divorce

	AUTOMONOUS GROUNDS FOR DIVORCE				
	No ground required	Mutual consent (ground 1)	Irretrievable breakdown of the marriage (ground 2)	Fault (ground 3)	Factual separation (ground 4)
AUSTRIA		YES	YES	YES	No (but a separation of 6 months with consent establishes ground 2. A separation of 5 years is required in the absence of agreement)
BELGIUM		YES		YES	YES (2 years)
CZECH REPUBLIC			YES (sole ground)	NO (but e.g. adultery is a presumption of ground 2)	No (but a separation of 6 months with consent establishes ground 2. A separation of 3 years is required in the absence of agreement)
CYPRUS				YES	YES (5 years)
DENMARK		YES		YES	YES (a separation of 6 months is required if the spouses agree. A separation of 2 years is required in the absence of agreement)
ESTONIA		YES	YES		
FINLAND	No ground is required, but a 6 months consideration period is required in all cases				

(*Continued*)

	AUTOMONOUS GROUNDS FOR DIVORCE				
	No ground required	Mutual consent (ground 1)	Irretrievable breakdown of the marriage (ground 2)	Fault (ground 3)	Factual separation (ground 4)
FRANCE		YES		YES	YES (2 years)
GERMANY		No (but consent and a separation of 1 year establish ground 2)	YES (sole ground)		No (but a separation of 1 year with consent establishes ground 2. A separation of 3 years is required in the absence of agreement)
GREECE		YES	YES	No (but e.g. cruelty establishes ground 2)	No (but a separation of 4 years establishes ground 2)
HUNGARY		No (but consent establishes ground 2)	YES (sole ground)		No (but a separation of 3 years establishes ground 2)
IRELAND					YES (sole ground) 4 years separation is required + no reconciliation
UNITED KINGDOM*			YES (sole ground)	NO (but adultery, unreasonable behaviour and desertion establish ground 2)	NO (but a separation of 2 years with consent establishes ground 2. A separation of 5 years is required in the absence of agreement)
MALTA	DIVORCE NOT ALLOWED				

* Including the separate jurisdictions of England/Wales, Scotland and Northern Ireland.

Marriages in the EU, 1960–2002

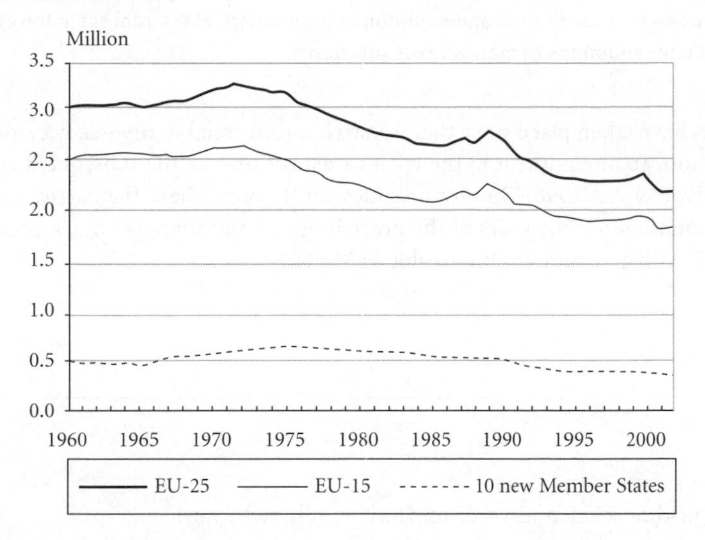

Divorces in the EU, 1960–2002

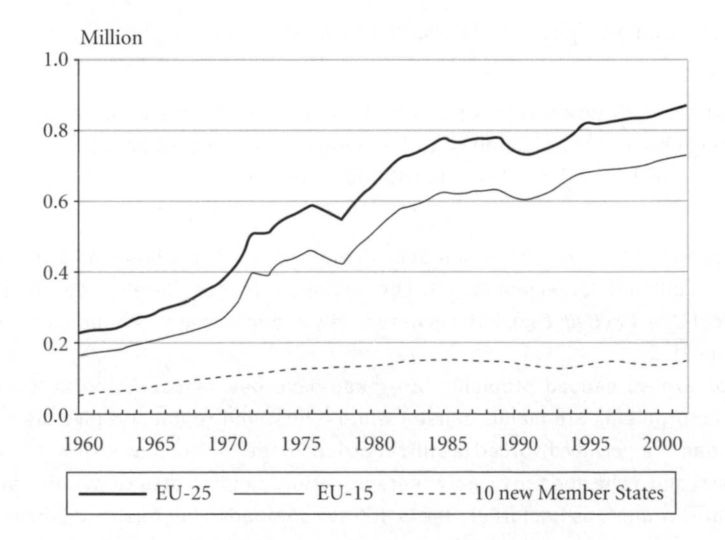

(resembling those already in place in Australia, Canada, and New Zealand) became the prevailing new approach to the grounds of divorce.

...

The changes in divorce law were themselves part of a more general process in which the legal posture of the state with respect to the family was undergoing its most fundamental shift since family law had begun to be secularized at the time of the Protestant Reformation. Beginning in the 1960s, movement in Western family law had been characterized, broadly speaking, and in varying degrees, by a withdrawal of much official regulation of marriage: its formation, its legal effects, and its termination. The removal of many legal obstacles to marriage; the effect of new attitudes of tolerance for diversity combined with older policies of nonintervention in the ongoing marriage; and the transformation of marriage itself from a legal relationship terminable only for serious cause to one increasingly terminable at will, amounted to a dejuridification of marriage. This process of deregulation of the formation and dissolution of marriage, and of

> the relations of the spouses during marriage, was typically accompanied, however – again in varying degrees – by a continued, and sometimes intensified, state interest in the economic and child-related consequences of marriage dissolution.

Further reforms have taken place since that was written. In Ireland, divorce became possible following a referendum, an amendment to the Irish Constitution and the subsequent enactment of the Family Law (Divorce) Act 1996. The Act provides for divorce where the parties have 'lived apart' for a period amounting to four years of the preceding five and there is no 'reasonable prospect' of reconciliation. But divorce remains impossible in Malta.

QUESTIONS

i. Is the 'dejuridification' of divorce inevitable? Why/why not?
ii. Why do you think the Irish legislature opted for separation alone, without alternative grounds?
iii. Is divorce a human right? (See *Johnston and others v Ireland* [1986] ECHR 9697/82.)

For some people, secular divorce is only part of the story; they, and their communities, take the view that their marriage has not been dissolved unless religious formalities have been observed. Michael Freeman's article, 'The Jewish Law of Divorce' (2000) explains:

> According to Jewish law a marriage cannot be dissolved unless the husband gives his wife, and she receives, a bill of divorcement (a *get*). The document is today given under the surveillance of a Rabbinical Court (a *Beth Din*), but it is not strictly a religious act, although it takes place in a religious context...
>
> The *get* has always caused problems but these have been exacerbated in today's secular societies. The problems are mainly caused when a husband refuses to give his wife a *get*. A woman who has been civilly divorced is still regarded, in the eyes of Jewish law, as married. She cannot remarry and if she does so (in a civil ceremony) any children of the new union are *mamzerim* (which tranlates roughly as bastards). She is literally chained to her husband (she is an *agunah*). She is a hostage to a dead marriage and, unfortunately, like other hostages she can be held to ransom. It is not uncommon for women to secure their release by paying sums of money extorted from them by acts little short of blackmail. Nor is it uncommon for the *dayanim* (the judges in the *Beth Din*) to participate in these negotiations...
>
> [T]he consequences of violating Jewish law and remarrying without first complying wth the *get* requirement are much more severe for the wife than for the husband. A 'wife' without a *get* is still 'married' to her husband – despite the civil divorce decree. She cannot remarry, and if she cohabits (or remarries civilly), she and her partner are guilty of adultery. She forfeits (in Jewish law only, of course) her alimony rights, and even if her 'husband' subsequently gives her a *get*, she is barred from marrying her partner. But the husband who is separated from his wife without granting her a *get* is not similarly stigmatised. If he cohabits with another woman – or remarries her in a civil ceremony – he does not commit adultery. He is technically 'guilty' of polygamy. If he has children by his new partner they are not regarded as *mamzerim*. Furthermore, if he subsequently delivers a *get* to his wife, he can marry the woman with whom he has been cohabiting (or has civilly married).

> Jewish law can be reformed by creative and dynamic interpretation. Jewish rabbinical authorities are, however, resistant to reform.

For Muslims, the picture is rather different, and very complex. The *Equal Treatment Bench Book* (2005) gives a summary:

> A Muslim marriage is known as a *nikah* or *aqd* which takes the form of a contract between the bride and groom, which they must enter into freely. The groom has to provide a sum of money for the contract to be valid, and this can be any sum agreed between the parties. This is known as the *mahr* and has sometimes been incorrectly referred to as the dowry. This belongs to the wife who can demand it any time. The contract should be witnessed by two competent witnesses. The contract entails certain rights and obligations for both parties.
>
> Islam has always recognised the possibility of terminating a marriage contract. A husband can do so using various procedures and the divorce is known as *talaq*. In addition a wife has the right to dissolve the marriage contract on her own initiative, in which case she is required to inform a Muslim judge (known as a *Qadi*). This right to divorce could be stipulated in the marriage contract; if it is not so stipulated, the parties can negotiate the wife's release from the marriage contract, and this procedure is known as a *khulla*, whereby the wife must pay a certain amount of money, most often the amount of money (*mahr*) she received from her husband. The marriage can also be dissolved by the wife in certain instances which do not require her to pay anything, but does require the intervention of a Muslim judge; for example, when deserted by her husband, judicial intervention is required to make a formal declaration that the husband is missing, or when the husband is impotent, a formal declaration to that effect is required. The dissolution of the marriage contract is called a *faskh of nikah*, and this can also be declared when the husband causes the wife harm. The category of harm is very broad and includes a husband's refusal to consider the marriage at an end.
>
> To avoid the difficulty faced by Muslim women in the UK who do not have the means to request the intervention of Muslim judges to void their marriage contracts, Muslim community groups have formed organisations comprising individuals trained in Islamic jurisprudence to dissolve their marriages. The oldest and most well-established such organisation is the Muslim Law Shariah Council (based in West London). It has an express policy of not making any decisions which could be seen to conflict with English and Welsh family law, for example with regard to financial or child custody matters.

So what of those who require a religious divorce in order to be free to remarry, but cannot obtain one unilaterally? Or of those who wish to remain married and do *not* want a religious divorce, whatever the secular position? Section 10A of the 1973 Act, added by the Divorce (Religious Marriages) Act 2002, enables the court, on the application of either party where the marriage was of a Jewish or other religious nature, to require the parties to certify that they have fulfilled all the requirements for a religious divorce before the decree absolute is granted.

QUESTIONS

i. What might be the effect of this provision where either party has changed their religious views since the marriage?

ii. What might be its effect upon a Jewish husband who does not want a civil divorce?

iii. If a requirement is imposed under section 10A and the husband refuses to fulfil the requirements of a *get*, what will happen?

iv. Section 10A was enacted with the support of the Rabbinical authorities. Why should the law make special provision for religions that *do* allow divorce on a discriminatory basis, when it is not possible to assist those whose religions do not allow it at all or only on limited grounds?

4.5 THE EFFECT OF DIVORCE REFORM

What is the relationship between law reform and the divorce rate?

The last major change in this country was, of course, in 1971, when the Divorce Reform Act 1969 came into force. The possible impact of that change upon numbers is demonstrated by the figure below, taken from Richard Leete's study of *Changing Patterns of Family Formation and Dissolution 1964–76* (1979):

Divorces, 1966–76 England and Wales

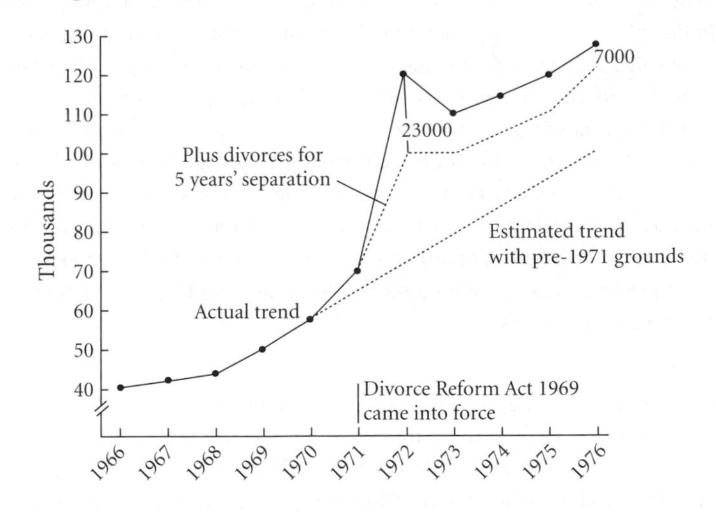

QUESTIONS

i. If in 1976 there were 7,000 more divorces than might have been expected from an extrapolation of the pre-1971 trend together with the five-year cases, how would you account for the increase? Is it (a) that the law was allowing more already broken marriages to be dissolved; or (b) that more marriages were breaking down than even the pre-1971 trend would have suggested; or (c) a bit of both?

ii. If you are inclined to favour explanation (b), does the increase of 7,000 (in a total of 126,000 in 1976) strike you as being large or small?

iii. Bren Neale and Carol Smart (1999) observed that following the divorce reforms of 1970 'the unbreakable marriage was replaced with serial monogamy'. If you think that the law contributes to an attitude of mind, what do you think is the effect of a change in the law? Does the trend in the 1980s and 1990s support this?

iv. How many *other* reasons can you think of for the rise in the divorce rate?

Ira Ellman, in 'Divorce in the United States' (2000), has this to say about the relationship between divorce reform and divorce rates:

> Figure 15.1 shows, for the three states for which we have data, that the divorce rate began climbing long before no-fault divorce was adopted. An increase in the divorce rate followed Arizona's adoption of no-fault, but only for a few years, after which the rate declined. A short-term rate increase is precisely what one would expect from a legal reform that made divorce simpler and quicker to obtain, but which had no fundamental impact on the likelihood of divorce: such a reform would speed up divorces already in the pipeline, leading to a transitory one-time increase, followed by a resumption of the basic trends. This pattern is common, and also appears to be what happened after Utah's more recent adoption of no-fault, not even for the short term. The general pattern shown by these three states is typical – nationally, divorce rates have been stable or declining since 1981 – and is very difficult to reconcile with any claim that no-fault caused any important increase in divorce rates.
>
> *Figure 15.1.* Divorce rates, in divorces per 1,000 population, for three states, 1960 to 1992 (plus partial data from New Mexico, for which other data is missing). For the three states with complete data, the circle marks the date of enactment of a law which added irremediable breakdown as grounds for divorce and adopted property and alimony rules that excluded consideration of fault.

Figure 15.1

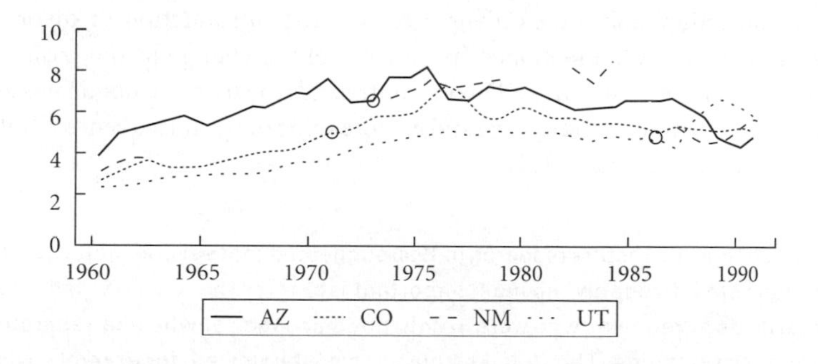

Ellman goes on to suggest that more potent factors in the rising rates may be mobility (he finds a high correlation between the divorce and moving from one state to another) and the employment of wives. On the latter, he comments:

> A second cultural force which most observers believe played an important role in increasing divorce rates is the enormous increase in the participation of married women in the paid labor force. Reviewing the literature, Cherlin concludes that while the evidence that the increase in women's

> participation in the labor force contributed to the 1960–80 rise in divorce rates is necessarily 'circumstantial,...it is stronger and more suggestive than that linking any other concurrent trend with the rise in divorce' [Andrew Cherlin, *Marriage, Divorce, Remarriage* 53 (rev. edn 1992)]. Not mentioned by Cherlin, but supporting his conclusion, is the fact that most divorces today are sought by women. Indeed, the increase in divorce rates between 1950 and 1980 occurred over a period of time during which the proportion of divorces instigated by wives appears to have increased from a minority of the cases to two-thirds of the cases. It thus seems logical to suggest that anyone seeking to explain the increase in divorce rates during this period should look for changes in factors likely to affect the motivation of wives. Their increasing rates of employment is such a factor. Economists suggest simply that such employment, being associated with a decline in marriage role specialization, leads to a decline in the benefits derived by the spouses from their marriage. A more feminist-friendly take on the same phenomenon argues that rising female employment commands a wide consensus in the social science literature, although methodological difficulties have presented some challenge to those seeking empirical support for it. One can perhaps argue that rising divorce rates encouraged women to seek market labor, or that other phenomena caused changes in both women's economic behaviour and their choice to divorce.

QUESTIONS

i. Is it possible, as a matter of social science methodology, to assess whether change in divorce law increases the divorce rate?

ii. Other studies (Haskey, 1992; and see Clarke and Berrington, 1999) have shown that couples who cohabit before they marry are a little more likely to divorce than those who do not. Why do you think this is so? Might it have something to do with the reasons why people marry (see Chapter 2, p. 67).

The one reform that indubitably raises divorce rates is the introduction of divorce when it has previously been impossible. We mentioned (p. 160 above) the change to the Irish constitution in 1996. Jenny Burley and Francis Regan in 'Divorce in Ireland: the fear, the floodgates and the reality' (2002) explain the background to the change and explore some of its consequences. Note that Judicial Separation had been available since 1989.

> The interviews conducted for this research in 1996 suggested that several factors had influenced the way the Irish voted. Probably the most important factor for those who voted 'Yes' was their sympathy for friends or relatives who were in unhappy marriages or who had separated and were living in second relationships. The young single people interviewed, for example, were in favour of change because they had seen the effects of unhappy marriages on their friends or relatives. Paradoxically, however, they also reported that their young married friends voted 'No' because they believed their own marriages were not at risk of failure. Older women, by contrast, were often more conservative but this was less from attachment to a Catholic ethos and more from resentment that men 'could get away with' leaving their families. Legislating for divorce was seen, therefore, as just another ploy by men to escape their spousal and family responsibilities. They did not perceive it as also liberating women from unhappy marriages because, in their view, marriage was for better or for worse as well as for life.

What was clear from this limited number of interviews was that the official Church position against divorce had very little influence on the way these people voted. One reason was that the credibility of bishops, clergy, brothers and nuns alike had been seriously undermined by the revelations of child abuse, paedophilia and the long-term clerical relationships which had borne children. ... This alienation from the Church was confirmed throughout Ireland in the findings of one poll which found that even amongst those voting 'No', 'only seven per cent cited the Church's teaching as the basis of their opposition'.

A further fear was that allowing divorce would open the floodgates to widespread marriage breakdown which, in turn, would have a number of destructive consequences. For example, the Irish people interviewed in 1996 were concerned that if people could get divorced they would not work at overcoming the difficulties which all marriages experience. In other words, it was only when marriage was understood to be life long, as it is in Catholic teaching, that couples would work to preserve their relationship. Many people thought that to allow divorce was to give couples too easy a way out. Such an abandonment of Catholic values would therefore open the floodgates to the secularisation of Irish society which had begun with its membership of the EU and lead to a subsequent drowning of its identity in western culture.

The need for the indissolubility of marriage to remain as part of Irish culture was also strongly connected to fear for the welfare of children of divorced parents. A common response from Irish women in 1996 in particular, regardless of whether they voted 'Yes' or 'No' in the referendum, was the question 'What will happen to the children?'. Anti-divorce campaigns were not slow to pick up on this fear for children's welfare in advertising which stressed themes of families 'broken' by divorce and of children of first marriages missing out on their inheritance. Perhaps the clearest illustration of the fear campaign was the infamous anti-divorce billboard in the last days of the campaign in 1995 which announced 'Hello Divorce, Bye-bye Daddy'.

...

Fears for Ireland's future thus figured prominently in the campaign leading up to the 1995 referendum to remove the constitutional ban on divorce. The power of the anti-divorce campaign can be seen in the polls which sought to measure the strength of support for constitutional change. In May 1995 when the date of the referendum was announced, 69 per cent of the electorate supported divorce but by the time of the poll in November, this support had shrunk to 49 per cent.

A. The Floodgates

When divorce was finally introduced in 1997 there was a general expectation that the courts would be flooded with applications from couples wanting to 'get out' of their marriages. The reality, however, was quite different. According to a report in the *Irish Times* in November 1996, more than 60,000 people appeared to qualify for divorce because they had already been separated for more than four years. However, when the Act came into force in February 1997, Legal Aid, a key provider of legal assistance, had only 1,000 people on the waiting list seeking divorce. During 1997 a further 1,146 applications were received for assistance. In addition, legal advice on divorce was given by Legal Aid to 1,863 persons during 1997 compared to 584 in 1996. This relatively low number of people seeking advice only contradicts the argument of a floodgate. Although this is an increase of over 300 per cent, it does not appear to have translated into grants for aid which in the following year showed less than a 34 per cent increase.

...

Other data also supports the picture not of divorce floodgates opening but of an initial surge followed by a small increase. Statistics from the courts, for example, tell a roughly similar story. From a low 431 divorce applications in the first five months of operation, the number increased to 2,761 in 1998, 3,300 in 1999 and 3,346 in 2000. Meanwhile..., applications for judicial separation dropped in 1997 but have since returned to earlier levels.

...

The numbers of people seeking divorce has therefore stabilised quite quickly at about 3,300 per year....

The most recent trends in divorce numbers in England and Wales are seen in the following figure, published by the Office of National Statistics in August 2007:

Persons divorcing per thousand married population

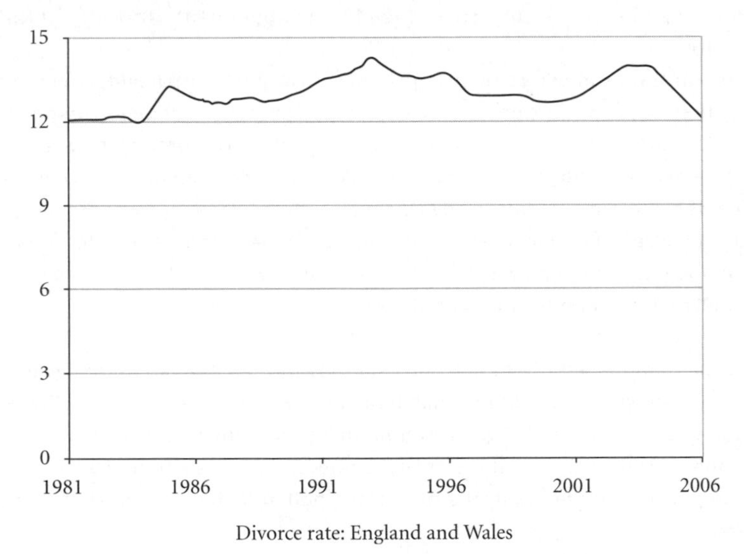

Divorce rate: England and Wales

QUESTION

Why do you suppose the numbers have gone down recently?

4.6 LOOKING BACK AT *LOOKING TO THE FUTURE*: DIVORCE REFORM AND MEDIATION

We have noted that divorce reform has taken place in many jurisdictions in the last few decades, and we have looked at some of the various models in use.

QUESTIONS

i. Look again at the table on p. 153. What do you think is the best way to prove that a marriage (or civil partnership) has broken down irretrievably?

ii. Do you think that there is any need to *prove* this to anyone at all?

iii. Which of the above countries have reached a decision that proof is unnecessary?

In 1990, the Law Commission published their report *Family Law: A Ground for Divorce*. They explained:

1.5 Our inquiries have made three things absolutely plain. First, of the existence of the problem there can be no doubt. The response to *Facing the Future* [the Law Commission's discussion paper, 1988] overwhelmingly endorsed the criticisms of the current law and practice which it contained. The present law is confusing and unjust. It now fulfils neither of its original objectives. These were, first, the support of marriages which have a chance of survival, and secondly, the decent burial with the minimum of embarrassment, humiliation and bitterness of those that are indubitably dead.

1.6 Secondly, it is clear that those basic objectives of a 'good' divorce law, as set out by our predecessors in 1966, still command widespread support, difficult though it may be to achieve them in practice. In 1990, however, any summary would include two further objectives: to encourage so far as possible the amicable resolution of practical issues relating to the couple's home, finances and children and the proper discharge of their responsibilities to one another and their children; and, for many people the paramount objective, to minimise the harm that the children may suffer, both at the time and in the future, and to promote so far as possible the continued sharing of parental responsibility for them.

1.7 Thirdly, there was overwhelming support for the view expressed in *Facing the Future* that irretrievable breakdown of the marriage should remain the fundamental basis of the ground for divorce....

1.8 Our consultations have led us to the firm conclusion that there is one particular model for reform which is to be preferred. It has not only received the support of the great majority of those who responded to *Facing the Future*, but has also been shown by our public opinion survey to be acceptable to a considerable majority of the general population. This was the model described in *Facing the Future* as divorce as a 'process over time' but here described as divorce after a period of consideration and reflection, colloquially a 'cooling-off' period or breathing space. [Our recommendations] constitute in many ways a radical departure from the present law: one designed to retain what are seen as the strengths of the present system while meeting the most serious criticisms.

They identified six criticisms of the present law and practice:

(I) It is Confusing and Misleading

2.8 There is a considerable gap between theory and practice, which can only lead to confusion and lack of respect for the law. Indeed, some would call it *downright dishonest*. There are several aspects to this. First, the law tells couples that the only ground for divorce is irretrievable breakdown, which apparently does not involve fault. But next it provides that this can only be shown by one of five 'facts', three of which apparently do involve fault. There are several recent examples of divorces being refused despite the fact that it was clear to all concerned that the marriage had indeed irretrievably broken down. The hardship and pain involved for both parties can be very great.

2.9 Secondly, the fact which is alleged in order to prove the breakdown need not have any connection with the *real reason* why the marriage broke down. The parties may, for example, have separated because they have both formed different associations, but agree to present a petition based on the behaviour of one of them, because neither wishes their new partner to be publicly named. The sex, class and other differences in the use of the facts make it quite clear that these are chosen for a variety of reasons which need have nothing to do with the reality of the case. This is a major source of confusion, especially for respondents who do not agree with the fact alleged. As has long been said, 'whatever the client's reason for wanting divorce, the lawyer's function is to discover grounds'.

2.10 The behaviour fact is particularly confusing. It is often referred to as 'unreasonable behaviour', which suggests blameworthiness or outright cruelty on the part of the respondent; but this has been called a 'linguistic trap', because the behaviour itself need be neither unreasonable nor blameworthy: rather, its *effect* on the petitioner must be such that it is unreasonable to expect him or her to go on living with the respondent, a significantly different and more flexible concept which is obviously capable of varying from case to case and court to court. Although the test is to be applied by an objective reasonable outsider, the character and personality of the petitioner are particularly relevant in deciding what conduct he or she should be expected to bear.

2.11 Finally, and above all, the present law pretends that the court is conducting an inquiry into the facts of the matter, when in the vast majority of cases it can do no such thing. ... The bogus adultery cases of the past may have all but disappeared, but their modern equivalents are the 'flimsy' behaviour petition or the pretence that the parties have been living apart for a full two years. In that 'wider field which includes considerations of truth, the sacredness of oaths, and the integrity of professional practice', the present law is just as objectionable as the old.

(II) It is Discriminatory and Unjust

2.12 83% of respondents to our public opinion survey thought it a good feature of the present law that couples who do not want to put the blame on either of them do not have to do so, but these couples have to have lived apart for at least two years. This can be extremely difficult to achieve without either substantial resources of one's own, or the co-operation of the other spouse at the outset, or an ouster order from the court. ... It is unjust and discriminatory of the law to provide for a civilised 'no-fault' ground for divorce which, in practice, is denied to a large section of the population. A young mother with children living in a council house is obliged to rely upon fault whether or not she wants to do so and irrespective of the damage it may do.

2.13 The fault-based facts can also be intrinsically unjust. 'Justice' in this context has traditionally been taken to mean the accurate allocation of blameworthiness for the breakdown of the marriage. Desertion is the only fact which still attempts to do this: it requires that one party has brought about their separation without just cause or consent. Desertion, however, is hardly ever used, because its place has been taken by the two year separation fact. A finding of adultery or behaviour certainly need not mean that the respondent is any more to blame than the petitioner for the breakdown of the marriage. If one has committed adultery or behaved intolerably there is usually nothing to stop the other obtaining a divorce based upon it, even though that other may have committed far more adulteries or behaved much more intolerably himself or herself. Nor does the behaviour fact always involve blame: it may well be unreasonable to expect a petitioner to live with a spouse who is mentally ill or disabled or has totally incompatible values or lifestyle. Even when the catalogue of complaints contained in the petition includes violence or other obviously blameworthy behaviour, this might look different if weighed against the behaviour of the other.

...

(III) It Distorts the Parties' Bargaining Positions

2.15 Not only can the law be unjust in itself, it can also lead to unfair distortions in the relative bargaining positions of the parties. When a marriage breaks down there are a great many practical questions to be decided: with whom are the children to live, how much are they going to see of the other parent, who is to have the house, and what are they all going to live on? Respondents to *Facing the Future* told us that the battles which used to be fought through the ground for divorce are now more likely to be fought through the so-called ancillary issues which in practice matter so much more to many people. The policy of the law is to encourage the parties to try and resolve these by agreement if they can, whether through negotiation between solicitors or with the help of a mediation or conciliation service. Questions of the future care of children, distribution of family assets, and financial provision are all governed by their own legal criteria. It is not unjust for negotiations to be affected by the relative merits of the parties' cases on these matters. Yet negotiations may also be distorted by whichever of the parties is in a stronger position in relation to the divorce itself. The strength of that position will depend upon a combination of how anxious or reluctant that party is to be divorced and how easy or difficult he or she will find it to prove or disprove one of the five facts. That might not matter if these represented a coherent set of principles, reflecting the real reasons why the marriage broke down; but as we have already seen, they do not. The potentially arbitrary results can put one party at an unfair disadvantage.

(IV) It Provokes Unnecessary Hostility and Bitterness

2.16 A law which is arbitrary or unjust can exacerbate the feelings of bitterness, distress and humiliation so often experienced at the time of separation and divorce. Even if the couple have agreed that their marriage cannot be saved, it must make matters between them worse if the system encourages one to make allegations against the other. The incidents relied on have to be set out in the petition. Sometimes they are exaggerated, one-sided or even untrue. Allegations of behaviour or adultery can provoke resentment and hostility in a respondent who is unable to put his own side of the story on the record. We are not so naive as to believe that bitterness and hostility could ever be banished from the divorce process. It is not concerned with cold commercial bargains but with the most intimate of human relations. The more we expect of marriage the greater the anger and grief when marriage ends. But there is every reason to believe that the present law adds needlessly to the human misery involved. Our respondents confirmed this.

(V) It Does Nothing to Save the Marriage

2.17 None of this is any help with the law's other objective, of supporting those marriages which have a chance of survival. The law cannot prevent people from separating or forming new relationships, although it may make it difficult for people to get a divorce. The law can also make it difficult for estranged couples to become reconciled. The present law does make it difficult for some couples – in practice a very small proportion – to be divorced, but does so in an arbitrary way depending upon which facts may be proved. It also makes it extremely difficult for couples to become reconciled. A spouse who wishes to be divorced is obliged either to make allegations against the other or to live apart for a lengthy period. If the petitioner brings proceedings based on behaviour, possibly without prior warning, and sometimes while they are still living together, the antagonism caused may destroy any lingering chance of saving the marriage. The alternative of two or five years' separation may encourage them to part in order to be able to obtain a divorce, when their difficulties might have been resolved if they had stayed together. From the very beginning, attention has to be focused on how to prove the ground for divorce. The reality of what it will be like to live apart, to break up the common home, to finance two households where before there was only one, and to have or to lose that day-to-day responsibility for the children which was previously shared, at least to some extent: none of this has to be contemplated in any detail until the decree nisi is obtained. If it had, there might be some petitioners who would think again.

2.18... An undefended decree can be obtained in a matter of weeks. If both parties are contemplating divorce, the system gives them every incentive to obtain a 'quickie' decree based on behaviour or separation, and to think out the practical consequences later.

(VI) It Can Make Things Worse for the Children

2.19 The present system can also make things worse for the children. The children themselves would usually prefer their parents to stay together. But the law cannot force parents to live amicably or prevent them from separating. It is not known whether children suffer more from their parents' separation or from living in a household in conflict where they may be blamed for the couple's inability to part. It is probably impossible to generalise, as there are so many variables which may affect the outcome, including the age and personality of the particular child. But it is known that the children who suffer least from their parents' break-up are usually those who are able to retain a good relationship with them both. Children who suffer most are those whose parents remain in conflict.

2.20 These issues have to be faced by the parents themselves, as they agonise over what to do for the best. However regrettably, there is nothing the law can do to ensure that they stay together, even supposing that this would indeed be better for their children. On the other hand, the present law can, for all the reasons given earlier, make the conflict worse. ... It is often said that couples undergoing marital breakdown are too wrapped up in their own problems to understand their children's needs. There are also couples who, while recognising that their own relationship is at an end, are anxious to do their best for their children. The present system does little to help them to do so.

Conclusion

2.21 These defects alone would amount to a formidable case for reform. The response to Facing the Future very largely endorsed its conclusion that 'Above all, the present law fails to recognise that divorce is not a final product but part of a massive transition for the parties and their children'. It is all too easy to think of divorcing couples in simple stereotypes. In fact they come in many different shapes and sizes. But for most, if not all, the breakdown of their relationship is a painful process, and for some it can be devastating. It affects each party in different ways: one may be far ahead of the other in withdrawing from the relationship before the other even realises that there is a problem. The anger, guilt, bitterness and regret so often felt have little to do with the law, which can seem an irrelevant game to be played by the lawyers. But the law does nothing to give the parties an opportunity to come to terms with what is happening in their lives, to reflect in as calm and sensible a way as possible upon the future, and to re-negotiate their relationship. Both emotionally and financially it is better for them and their children if they can do this by agreement rather than by fighting in the courts. There are always going to be some fights and the courts are there to resolve them. But the courts should be kept to their proper sphere of adjudicating upon practical disputes, ensuring that appropriate steps are properly taken, and enforcing the orders made. They should not be pretending to adjudicate upon matters they cannot decide or in disputes which need never arise.

QUESTIONS

i. Do you accept these criticisms?
ii. What are the strengths of the present law?

The Law Commission rejected the retention of 'fault'; the introduction of a full judicial inquest into the marriage and the possibility of saving it; immediate divorce either unilaterally or by mutual consent; and a divorce after a fixed minimum period of separation. They recommended a divorce after a fixed minimum period for reflection and consideration of the arrangements: the process over time.

The Law Commission's recommendations were:

3.48

(i) that irretrievable breakdown of the marriage should remain the sole ground for divorce; and
(ii) that such breakdown should be established by the expiry of a minimum period of one year for consideration of the practical consequences which would result from a divorce and reflection upon whether the breakdown in the marital relationship is irreparable.

Ruth Deech's response to the Law Commission's work in this area was expressed in the following article in *The Independent* (1990):

Marriage as a Short-term Option

The last time divorce law was reformed, we all still believed that human behaviour was rational and could be shaped by legal rules.

The Law Commission said its 1969 Act, which introduced simpler divorce by separation, would promote marriage stability and reconciliation. It would encourage spouses to omit recriminations from their petitions.

Twenty-one years later, the inaccuracy of the reformers' predictions about the new law's effect on people's lives is striking.

> Cohabiting couples would regularise their unions, they said, the illegitimacy rate would drop as a result of the freedom to remarry, and the divorce rate would not rise. Instead, we find a marked increase in cohabitation and a divorce rate that has trebled to some 190,000 petitions each year.
>
> So why are we about to embark on another reform, and why is the Law Commission... implicitly repeating naive claims that a new law will improve the lot of children?
>
> Liberalised divorce law has not, so far, resulted in a greater sum of human happiness. It has given us over one million unremarried divorcees, many of whom are largely dependent on social security.
>
> ...
>
> The reason for reform is one given several times before: that the law should reflect social reality and the fact that many divorces are undefended and uninvestigated.
>
> On each occasion the law has been brought into line with practice, however, it has simply made divorce easier. Once the rate rises it never drops back to its previous level. The resulting increased faith in divorce as a solution to marital problems leads to increased willingness to use it, which in turn leads to a relaxation of divorce procedure and then a fresh call for further changes to bring the law into line with reality.
>
> That happened in 1937, 1949 and 1969 and is about to happen again. It is a spiralling process that Parliament should not encourage, for the sake of children, if no one else.
>
> ...
>
> The law reformers' argument is that divorce law should bury a dead relationship; it is never conceded that the law itself might have played a part in infecting the couple with a fatal virus.
>
> ...
>
> My own hypothesis is that the most important element in divorce law is the *message* it conveys to the public. We all absorb the prevailing divorce ethos long before we ourselves ever seriously consider ending a marriage, and it is that earlier influence which counts in determining our response....
>
> Everything points to the desirability of leaving the law of divorce unchanged.

Deech makes a further point, about the economic aspects of divorce, in *Divorce Dissent: Dangers in Divorce Reform* (1994):

> We cannot afford serial marriage in our society: poverty is as inevitable as the damage to children from the emotional state of their parents. Yet it seems to be an unspoken political decision that attempts to make divorce more difficult are totally unacceptable. Even while public debate focuses on the plight of single parents and their children, the fact that over half of them are created by divorce and separation is overlooked. It is astonishing that any government should seriously contemplate easing divorce law while simultaneously expressing anxiety about single parents, their children and society's health.

In *Divorce and the Lord Chancellor* (1994) Andrew Bainham commented:

> I must take issue with Ruth Deech who suggests that there is a correlation between divorce reform and the rate of marriage breakdown. Deech confuses the rate of marriage breakdown with the rate of *divorce*. For while it is indisputable that the rate of dissolution is connected to the ease with which the law allows that dissolution to be obtained, it is quite another matter to suggest that divorce law has any significant influence on the *quality* of relationships within marriage – surely the factor most likely to determine whether those relationships end or survive.

QUESTIONS

i. Ruth Deech was concerned about the message the new law would convey to the public. Can you write a short paragraph describing that message? Now write another short paragraph describing the message the Matrimonial Causes Act 1973 conveys to the public.

ii. Do you think it is possible to establish any connection between the divorce rate, the provisions of divorce law, and the rate of relationship breakdown within the European Union?

iii. Can we really use the ground for divorce to stem the tide of relationship breakdown? If so, should we?

The provisions of the Family Law Act 1996 largely followed the Law Commission's proposals. In spite of the simplicity of those proposals, the statute was remarkably complex and difficult to read. The bare bones of the process that it prescribed, greatly over-simplified, were:

1. Attend an information meeting. Wait three months and then:
2. Make a statement under section 5. Wait a fortnight (section 7(3)) and then wait for a period of nine months (in some circumstances fifteen months, sections 7(10)–(13)).
3. Apply for a divorce order.

Section 7(3) stated that the period for consideration and reflection which must elapse between the making of a statement of marital breakdown and the making of the divorce order is nine months. However, the effect of subsections (10)–(13) (the result of a House of Commons amendment) is that the period is extended by a further six months if either party so requests or if there are children of the marriage under sixteen. In these circumstances, it might nevertheless be reduced to one year if there is in force a domestic violence injunction (see Chapter 7, below), or if the court considered that the longer period would be significantly detrimental to the children.

QUESTIONS

i. Do you agree that there should be a longer period for reflection and consideration where there are children of the marriage?

ii. Do you think that the extension of the period to fifteen months increases the chance of reconciliation?

iii. How could a couple with children ensure that they only had to wait nine rather than fifteen months?

Part I of the Family Law Act 1996 consists of a single section, added to the Family Law Bill as a House of Lords amendment:

1. The court and any person, in exercising functions under or in consequence of Parts II and III, shall have regard to the following general principles—

(*a*) that the institution of marriage is to be supported;

(*b*) that the parties to a marriage which may have broken down are to be encouraged to take all practicable steps to save it;

(*c*) that a marriage which has irretrievably broken down and is being brought to an end should be brought to an end—
  (i) with minimum distress to the parties and to the children affected;
  (ii) with questions dealt with in a manner designed to promote as good a continuing relationship between the parties and any children affected as is possible in the circumstances; and
  (iii) without costs being unreasonably incurred in connection with the procedures to be followed in bringing the marriage to an end; and

(*d*) that any risk to one of the parties to a marriage and to any children, of violence from the other party should, so far as reasonably practicable, be removed or diminished.

Part II of the Act is concerned with divorce and separation orders, Part III with Legal Aid for mediation in family matters. Parts I and III have been brought into force but Part II has not.

QUESTIONS

i. Why do you think that happened?
ii. What do you suppose has been the effect of the implementation of Part I?
iii. Who would have gained by the implementation of Part II? Who would have lost?

The title to the Green and the White Papers (1993 and 1995) that preceded the introduction of legislation, *Looking to the Future: Mediation and the Ground for Divorce*, draws attention to the fact that the ground for divorce was not the only concern of the reforms. The Law Commission recommended that the use of mediation be encouraged.

So what is mediation? In *The Ground for Divorce* (1990), the Law Commission tried to summarise the different kinds of processes and their objectives:

Counselling, Conciliation and Mediation

5.29...The umbrella term 'counselling' is used in Australia and New Zealand to encompass a variety of different types of help. All share the characteristic of keeping an open mind about the eventual outcome, while helping the couple or individuals involved to gain a greater understanding of their situation and to reach their own decisions about the future. The focus and method, however, can differ sharply, as can the organisational context in which the service is offered.

5.30 Broadly speaking, there are three different types of activity which may be involved:

(i) Marital counselling is offered, either to a couple or to an individual spouse, with a view to helping the couple to strengthen or maintain their marital relationship. If they are estranged or separated, the aim is to reconcile or reunite them. Historically, attempts at reconciliation were part of the role of 'police court missionaries' who became the probation and divorce court welfare service of today. Generally speaking, however, such services are offered by voluntary organisations, principally Relate Marriage Guidance. Relate counsellors are carefully selected and trained, but do not hold any particular professional qualification and offer their services voluntarily;

(ii) Divorce counselling and other forms of therapy aim to assist individuals, couples, and their children, to come to terms with the fact that their relationship is breaking down, to reduce the sense of personal failure, anger and grief, to disengage from and negotiate a new relationship with the former spouse and with the children, and eventually to move on to new relationships with confidence, avoiding the mistakes of the past. In other words, it seeks to minimise the harm done to either partner and to their children by the breakdown of their marriage. Once again, this is generally offered by voluntary organisations such as Relate, although some probation services offer divorce experience courses, and specialist therapy may be available privately or in some parts of the health service;

(iii) Conciliation or mediation is a way of resolving disputes without resort to traditional adjudication. The aim is to help the couple to reach their own agreements about the future, to improve communication between them, and to help them to co-operate in bringing up their children. Conciliation in this country developed first in the context of resolving disputes about children, often through the efforts of registrars and divorce court welfare officers at the court where a custody or access dispute was to be tried, but also through independent conciliation services, most of which are now affiliated to the National Family Conciliation Council. Conciliators generally hold professional qualifications in social work, undergo specialist training in family conciliation, and are paid for their services. The costs and benefits of various conciliation services have recently been the subject of a major research study conducted by the University of Newcastle. This has revealed that conciliation is indeed effective, both in reducing the areas of conflict and in increasing the parents' well-being and satisfaction with the arrangements made. In general, these benefits are greater when the service is provided away from the courts. The problems with conciliation conducted by or at the court, valuable and effective though it can often be, include the inevitable pressure to reach a settlement quickly, the inevitable authority of the registrar or court welfare officer conducting it, which may unconsciously or consciously dictate the outcome, and the risks of confusing the welfare officer's different roles of reporting to the court and assisting the couple to reach agreement. However, this is a fast-moving field in which developments are taking place all the time. For example, the independent sector is beginning to develop methods of comprehensive mediation, covering property and finance as well as child-related issues.

The Commission concluded that reconciliation attempts should *not* be a mandatory part of the divorce process:

5.33 ... There are several reasons for this. First, there are the views of the organisations at present involved in providing these services. They would of course like there to be a properly funded network of services readily available to all who wish to use them. But such counselling is a two-way process which can only be offered to volunteers, not conscripts. The hostility and bitterness induced by conscription is unlikely to lead to a real and lasting resolution. Secondly, and perhaps more importantly, there are some marriages which it would be wrong in principle to attempt to save. A wife who is regularly subjected to violence or abuse from her husband needs rescuing from her marriage, not pressure to return to it. A system of mandatory reconciliation could not be justified without some attempt to distinguish between marriages, which would only reintroduce the very inquiry into past misbehaviour which it is the object of these proposals to avoid. Thirdly, it would be impossible to justify the enormous public expenditure which would be involved in requiring such attempts in every case, without a better prospect of success than can be demonstrated at present. Finally, it was felt by some respondents that *conciliation* might, paradoxically, be more likely to result in reconciling some couples, by encouraging them to find a way through their difficulties relating to future arrangements while they were still amenable to discussion.

As to mediation, the Law Commission said:

5.34 A more difficult question...is whether conciliation or mediation should be mandatory, if not in all cases at least in those which the court identifies as suitable for it. Once again, however, the majority of our respondents thought it should not. The professionals practising in the field said that mandatory conciliation or mediation was unlikely to be successful and indeed might be counter-productive. The Newcastle research indicated that the greatest benefits came from independent conciliation which was clearly distinguished from the coercive setting of the court. It is also clear that, whatever its benefits in some cases, there are many issues or relationships in which it is quite unsuitable. If so, the aim must be to ensure that adequate services are available to those who wish to use them, and to secure efficient information and referral machinery, rather than coercive sanctions to achieve this. There are also dangers in relying too heavily upon conciliation or mediation instead of more traditional methods of negotiation and adjudication. These include exploitation of the weaker partner by the stronger, which requires considerable skill and professionalism for the conciliator to counteract while remaining true to the neutral role required; considerable potential for delay, which is damaging both to the children and often to the interests of one of the adults involved; and the temptation for the court to postpone deciding some very difficult and painful cases which ought to be decided quickly. It is important that, whatever encouragement is given by the system to alternative methods of dispute resolution, the courts are not deterred from performing their function of determining issues which require to be determined. Where time permits, alternative methods can be explored so as to enable the parties to try and reach their own agreements away from the pressures of the court door. Where, however, an immediate decision is needed in the interests of either party or of their children, the courts should be prepared to give it.

5.35 We therefore *recommend* that undertaking...mediation should be purely voluntary.

5.36 We further *recommend* that opportunities and encouragement to resolve matters amicably should be built into the system where appropriate....

5.37 Furthermore, although participation in conciliation or mediation should be voluntary, we *recommend* that the court should have two additional powers to encourage it. Neither of these powers should be seen as placing any pressure on the parties to participate. They are designed to ensure that the parties are better-informed and to facilitate participation if they wish. They are also designed to some extent to regulate what happens informally at present....

Referral for an Explanation of Conciliation or Mediation

5.38 It is likely that in a number of cases one spouse, or perhaps both spouses, will not appreciate the nature and effectiveness of conciliation or mediation, or even if aware have a totally closed mind on the subject. Many people are confused about the distinctions between counselling, reconciliation and conciliation and are instinctively resistant to reconciliation. We therefore *recommend* that the court should have power, whether on application or of its own motion, to give a direction that the spouses meet a specified conciliator or mediator, in order to discuss the nature and potential benefits of conciliation or mediation in their case....

Adjournment for Participation

5.39 We further *recommend* that, where the parties are in dispute about any issue arising in the context of divorce or separation, the court should have power, whether on application or of its own motion, to adjourn the hearing of that issue, for the purpose of enabling them to participate in conciliation or mediation, or generally with a view to the amicable resolution of the dispute. In deciding to do this, the court should take the interests of any children into account (whether, for example, they will be more helped by the amicable resolution or harmed by the delay). It should, of course, be open to the parties not to participate and if either of them feels unable to do so this should not affect the handling of the case thereafter.

One of the questions raised in the Green Paper was whether mediation should be compulsory; responses to the consultation process indicated that it should not, and this was accepted in the White Paper. At the same time, the Government was encouraged by the positive conclusions of the *Rowntree Report* (*Mediation: the Making and Remaking of Co-operative Relationships* 1994), referred to by the Law Commission (above) as the Newcastle research. Accordingly, the Act contained provision for the court to adjourn proceedings in order for the parties to resolve matters, and to direct that they attend a meeting to have the available mediation facilities explained to them (sections 13 and 14); Part III of the Act amended the Legal Aid Act 1988 so as to make legal aid available for mediation in family matters.

Helen Reece, in *Divorcing responsibly* (2003) comments:

For the first time ever, it is possible to divorce responsibly. Indeed, the White Paper [*Looking to the Future* at 43] informed us that:

> 'The Government is encouraged by recent research which demonstrated that increasing numbers of couples are seeking to dissolve their marriage as responsibly as possible.'

However, in referring to responsible divorce, the legislature was thinking in terms of post-liberal responsibility. It was clear from the language used in the Family Law Act debates to describe responsibility that being responsible was an attitude that existed along a continuum, rather than a quality that the divorcee either had or lacked. Specifically, the divorcee was exhorted to adopt the following approaches to responsibility: have a sense of, address, consider, carefully consider, undertake, take, take into account, take seriously, recognise, acknowledge, face, face up to, face up fully to, have regard to, look to, share, accept, meet, deal with, fulfil and discharge.

We have seen that the ways in which the divorcee is supposed to adopt these approaches to responsibility are by reflecting deeply, taking time and learning his or her lesson. Baroness Scotland aptly summed up the Family Law Act as trying to 'put the emphasis back on conciliation, preparation and thought'.

...

[W]hile people still marry with a sense of commitment, the commitment is no longer to permanence; rather the commitment is the procedural one of *trying to make the marriage work*. The new marriage has its own procedural obligations: a concern for permanence and personal virtue has been replaced by the new virtues of honesty, communication and tolerance.

...

Clearly, the removal of fault from the divorce process both implies and is implied by post-liberal responsibility: if no actions are prescribed or proscribed then there can be no substantive basis for divorce. The emphasis on mediation is also consistent with the new form of responsibility, since mediation requires the adoption of an attitude rather than any particular decision. It is of the essence of mediation that responsibility remains with the parties themselves and that the role of the mediator is simply to assist them.

...Psychological norms have replaced social norms, and therapeutic correctness has become the new standard of good behaviour. This trend is particularly strong when it comes to divorce involving children. While a concern about the effect of divorce upon children is constant, the solution has shifted from preserving the marriage for the sake of the children to instructions about how best to tell the children about divorce.

QUESTIONS

i. What proportion of people think like this, do you suppose?
ii. Do you think divorce is now considered just sad rather than bad?
iii. How would you describe the psychological norms of the good divorce?'

Certainly the idea that divorcing couples have a responsibility at least to consider mediation is embedded in the public funding system. Val Reid, in her 'ADR [alternative dispute resolution] Update from the ASA [Advice Services Alliance]' (2007) reports:

Before 1 October 2007, every client applying for legal aid for representation was required to first attend a meeting with a mediator to discuss whether mediation was appropriate in their case. Solicitors could exempt their clients from that meeting for a number of reasons, in particular if the client had experienced domestic abuse. The NAO [National Audit Office] suggested that solicitors were being rather over-enthusiastic in their use of that exemption and therefore proposed that it should be the mediator rather than the solicitor who decided whether or not domestic abuse made mediation unsuitable. From 1 October 2007, solicitors can only exempt their clients from this meeting with a mediator if it is an emergency application, or if an allegation of domestic abuse has resulted in a police investigation or the issuing of civil proceedings in the last 12 months.

The LSC [Legal Services Commission] claims that the client will not be put in any danger by meeting with the mediator. The first meeting can either be a joint meeting with the ex-partner, or a separate meeting with one client and the mediator on their own. Clients who are nervous about meeting their ex-partner should make sure that they request a separate meeting with the mediator. Mediation itself will remain voluntary – the initial meeting with a mediator is intended to explain how mediation works, but the choice about whether or not to try it is firmly with the two individuals concerned. If one person does not want to mediate, then mediation is deemed unsuitable. If both parties want to go ahead, but there are concerns about being in a room together, family mediators can set up shuttle mediation, where people do not sit in the same room, and arrange staggered start and leave times to provide some degree of protection.

It should be noted that the debate about whether or not mediation is ever suitable where there has been domestic abuse has been going on for many years. Mediators themselves do not all share the same opinion on this. Some believe that the choice should be firmly with the client, and that the victims of abuse should not have their choices reduced even further by the assumption that mediation cannot work for them. Others believe that a significant imbalance of power between the parties, especially where there has been violence, emotional abuse or bullying, means that it is impossible to negotiate a fair solution to any dispute.

Elizabeth Walsh, in *Working in the Family Justice System* (2006) comments:

Many mediators have been trained but few are engaged in full time mediation work. The family justice system has been slow to give mediation a central role. Apart from the compulsory referrals of legally aided persons to mediation for assessment, referrals are relatively few.... [T]he government still resists making mediation assessments compulsory for all, not just for poor people. Opponents argue that compulsory mediation is a contradiction in terms (since the defining principle is empowering participants to reach their own decisions), will be less effective, more likely to disadvantage weaker parties, particularly women, and put victims of domestic violence and their children at risk. However, if there were confidence that adequate screening processes were in place and all mediators skilled at identifying and responding appropriately to domestic violence, then one of the most potent arguments against mandatory mediation assessment would be weakened. There already exists a power for the courts to direct persons to mediation on matters of finance or property but it is seldom used.

QUESTIONS

i. Why do you think that only poor people have to be assessed for their suitability for mediation?

ii. If someone wants to make an agreement with their spouse/partner which gives them less than a court would give them, does it matter?

BIBLIOGRAPHY

Introduction

We quoted from:

G. Alpern, *Rights of Passage* (1982) Aspen, Colorado, Psychological Development Publications, 19.

A. Alvarez, *Life after Marriage: Love in an Age of Divorce* (1981) New York, Simon and Schuster.

Chambre de Représentants de Belgique, *Projet de Loi, réformant le divorce*, Doc51 2341/001, available at http://www.lachambre.be/FLWB/PDF/51/2341/51K2341001.pdf.

J. Cleese and R. Skynner, *Families and How to Survive Them* (1993) London, Cedar, 15, 16.

L. Stone, *Road to Divorce: England 1530–1987* (1990) Oxford, Oxford University Press, 27, 310.

4.1 The history of divorce law in England and Wales

We quoted from:

Sir Morris Finer and O.R. McGregor, 'The History of the Obligation to Maintain' Appendix 5, Report of the Committee on One-Parent Families (Cmnd. 5629–1) (1974), London, HMSO, paras 13, 17, 18.

Report of a Group appointed by the Archbishop of Canterbury (Chairman: The Rt Rev. R.C. Mortimer, Lord Bishop of Exeter), *Putting Asunder – A Divorce Law for Contemporary Society* (1966) London, Society for Promoting Christian Knowledge, paras. 17, 18, 45(f), 55.

Report of the Committee on One-Parent Families (Chairman: The Hon. Sir Morris Finer) (Cmnd. 5629) (1974), London, HMSO, paras 4.29–4.32.

St. Mark, 'Gospel according to St. Mark' Holy Bible Authorised King James version, ch. 10.

Additional reading

Law Commission, Reform of the Grounds of Divorce – The Field of Choice (Cmnd. 3123) (1966), London, HMSO.

Report of the Royal Commission on Divorce and Matrimonial Causes (Chairman: Lord Gorell) (Cmd. 6478) (1912), London, HMSO.

Report of the Royal Commission on Marriage and Divorce (Chairman: Lord Morton of Henryton) (Cmd. 9678) (1956), London, HMSO.

4.2 The present law: the Matrimonial Causes Act 1973

We quoted from:

Law Commission, *Court Record Study* Appendix C to *The Ground for Divorce*, Law Com. No. 192 (1990) London, HMSO, paras 26, 31, 32, 44, 51.

Office for National Statistics, *Population Trends* 125 (2006), Figure 2, 94.

'So What's Unreasonable Behaviour?', *The Times*, 15 February 1996, 15.

Additional reading

Law Society, Family Law Sub-Committee, *A Better Way Out: Suggestions for the Reform of the Law of Divorce and Other Forms of Matrimonial Relief; for the Setting Up of a Family Court; and for its Procedure* (1979) London, The Law Society.

The Scottish Law Commission, *Report on Reform of the Ground for Divorce*, Scot. Law Com. No. 116 (1989) Edinburgh, HMSO.

4.3 The dissolution of civil partnerships

We quoted from:

Judicial Studies Board *Equal Treatment Bench Book* (2007) available at www.jsboard.co.uk.

pinknews.co.uk, 'Civil partners not rushing to divorce' at http://www.pinknews.co.uk/news/articles/2005-3207.html.

Additional reading

S. Clarke, 'Civil Partnership Dissolution' [2006] 36 *Family Law* 604.

4.4 Divorce: the international picture

We quoted from:

European Commission, Green Paper on applicable law and jurisdiction in divorce matters, Table 2, 25.

European Commission, 'Population Statistics' (2004) Luxembourg: Office for Official Publications of the European Communities, p115 epp.eurostat.ec.europa.eu/cache/ITY_OFFPUB/KS-BP-04-001/EN/KS-BP-04-001-EN.PDF

M. Freeman, 'The Jewish Law of Divorce', [2000] *International Family Law* 58, at 58.

M.A. Glendon, *Abortion and Divorce in Western Law* (1987) Cambridge (Mass) and London, Harvard University Press, 63–64, 66–68.

Judicial Studies Board, *Equal Treatment Bench Book* (2005) Chapter 3, Appendix V, available at http://www.jsboard.co.uk.

Additional reading

C. Archbold, P. McKee and C. White, 'Divorce law and divorce culture – the case of Northern Ireland' (1998) 4 *Child and Family Law Quarterly* 377.

S. Bano, '"Standpoint", "Difference" and Feminist Research' in R. Banakar and M. Travers (eds), *Theory and Method in Socio-legal Research* (2005), Oxford, Hart Publishing Ltd.

Bissett-Johnson and C. Barton, 'The similarities and differences in Scottish and English family law in dealing with changing family patterns' (1999) 21(1) *Journal of Social Welfare Law* 1.

H. Conway, 'Divorce and Religion' (1995) *New Law Journal* 1618.

C.L. Eisgruber and M. Zeisberg, 'Religious freedom in Canada and the United States' (2006) *International Journal of Constitutional Law* 244.

J. Haskey, 'Patterns of Marriage, Divorce, and Cohabitation in the Different Countries of Europe' (1992) 69 *Population Trends* 26.

D. Hinchcliffe, 'Divorce in the Muslim World', [2000] *International Family Law* 63.

D. Pearl and W. Menski, *Muslim Family Law*, (1998), (3rd edn), London, Sweet & Maxwell.

J. Rehman, 'The Sharia, Islamic Family Laws and International Human Rights Law' [2007] 21 *International Journal of Law, Policy and the Family* 108.

M. Walls and D. Bergin, *The Law of Divorce in Ireland* (1997) Family Law.

S.A. Warraich and C. Balchin, 'Recognising the un-recognised: Inter-Country Cases and Muslim Marriages and Divorces in Britain, (A policy research by Women Living under Muslim Law)' (2007), Nottingham, available at http://www.wluml.org.

4.5 The effect of divorce reform

We quoted from:

J. Burley and F. Regan, 'The Fear, the Floodgates and the Reality' *International Journal of Law Policy and the Family* (2002) 16, 202.

I. Ellman, 'Divorce in the United States' in S. Katz, J. Eekelaar and M. Maclean, *Cross Currents* (2000) Oxford, Oxford University Press.

R. Leete, *Changing Patterns of Family Formation and Dissolution in England and Wales 1964–1976*, OPCS Studies on Medical and Population Subjects No. 39 (1979) London, HMSO, tables 36, 38, figs. 19, 20.

Office of National Statistics, divorce rates, at http://www.statistics.gov.uk/cci/nugget.asp?id=170.

Additional reading

A.J. Cherlin, *Marriage, Divorce, Remarriage* (Revised and enlarged edition) (1992), Cambridge (Massachusetts), Harvard University Press.

L. Clarke and A. Berrington, *Socio-demographic predictors of divorce* (1999) Lord Chancellor's Departent, Research Paper 2/99, 1999.

I.M. Ellman, 'Divorce Rates, Marriage Rates and the Problematic Persistence of Traditional Marital Roles' (2000) 34 Family Law Quarterly 1. Available at SSRN ssrn.com/abstract=224700 or DOI: 10.2139/ssrn.224700; abstracted at papers.ssrn.com/sol3/papers.cfm?abstract_id=224700.

J. Haskey, 'Social Class and Socio-economic Differentials in Divorce in England and Wales' (1984) *Population Studies* 38.

J. Haskey, 'Recent Trends in Divorce in England and Wales: the Effects of Legislative Changes' (1986) 44 *Population Trends* 9.

J. Haskey, 'Pre-marital Cohabitation and the Probability of Subsequent Divorce' (1992) 68 *Population Trends* 10.

B. Neale and C. Smart, 'In whose interests? Theorising family life following parental separation or divorce' in Day Sclater and Piper (eds) *Undercurrents of Divorce* (1999) Aldershot, Dartmouth, p. 36.

M.P.M. Richards, 'Divorce Research Today' [1991] *Family Law* 70–72.

M.P.M. Richards, 'Private Worlds and Public Intentions – The Role of the State in Divorce' in A. Bainham, D. Pearl and R. Pickford (eds), *Frontiers of Family Law* (1995) Chichester, John Wiley and Sons.

L. Weitzman and R.B. Dixon, 'The Transformation of Marriage through No Fault Divorce – The Case of the United States' in J.M. Eekelaar and S.N. Katz (eds), *Marriage and Cohabitation in Contemporary Societies: Areas of Legal, Social and Ethical Change* (1980) Toronto, Butterworths.

4.6 Looking back at *Looking to the Future*: divorce reform and mediation

We quoted from:

A. Bainham, 'Divorce and the Lord Chancellor: Looking to the Future or Getting Back to Basics?' (1994) 53 *Cambridge Law Journal* 253, 256.

R. Deech, 'Marriage as a Short-term Option' (1990) *The Independent*, 2 November 1990.

R. Deech, *Divorce Dissent: Dangers in Divorce Reform* (1994) London, Centre for Policy Studies, 14, 20–21.

Law Commission, *The Ground for Divorce*, Law Com. No. 192 (1990) London, HMSO, paras. 1.5–1.8; 2.8–2.21; 3.37–3.38; 3.48, 5.29, 5.30–5.39.

H. Reece, *Divorcing Responsibly* (2003) Oxford, Hart Publishing 214–217.
V. Reid, 'ADR Professional: ADR Update from the ASA Alliance' [2007] *Family Law* 1033.
E. Walsh, *Working in the Family Justice System* (2006) Bristol, Jordan Publishing Limited, 79–80.

Additional reading

S. Cretney, 'The Divorce White Paper – Some Reflections' [1995] *Family Law* 302, p. 304.
J. Eekelaar, *Regulating Divorce* (1991) Oxford, Clarendon Press.
J. Eekelaar, 'The Family Law Bill: The Politics of Family Law' [1996] *Family Law* 46.
B. Hale, 'The Family Law Act 1996 – Dead Duck or Golden Goose' in S. Cretney (ed.), *Family Law: Essays for the New Millenium* (2000) Family Law.
Looking to the Future: Mediation and the Ground for Divorce. A consultation paper (Cm. 2424) (1993) London, HMSO, paras 9.28–9.30.
Looking to the Future: Mediation and the Ground for Divorce. The Government's proposals (Cm. 2799) (1995) London, HMSO.
M. Maclean and J. Eekelaar, 'Divorce law and empirical studies – a reply' (1990) 106 *Law Quarterly Review* 621.
J. Walker, P. McCarthy and N. Timms, *Mediation: The Making and Remaking of Co-operative Relationships* (1994) Newcastle upon Tyne, Relate Centre for Family Studies.

5

FINANCIAL PROVISION ON DIVORCE

In this chapter we look at the arrangements which have to be made for the couple's finances and property when a marriage or civil partnership comes to an end. This is mainly dealt with by so-called 'ancillary relief' on divorce or dissolution, which has been going through an exciting period of development in the courts. But first, we must deal with child support, potentially an issue for all couples with children, married or unmarried.

5.1 CHILD SUPPORT

Certain family members have an obligation to support each other. In particular, spouses and civil partners must do so, during the marriage or civil partnership and, to some extent, after it has ended. That duty of support can be enforced through the courts; and both the Matrimonial Causes Act 1973 and the Civil Partnership Act 2004 include provisions for maintenance for children. Cohabitants have no private law obligation to make financial provision for each other. The Children Act 1989, in Schedule 1, expresses the duty of all parents, married or not, to provide for the maintenance and housing of their children. Before we explore the child support legislation, we should ask about the basic assumptions behind that duty of support. Andrew Bainham, in 'Men and Women Behaving Badly: Is Fault Dead in English Family Law?' (2001) has this to say about the basis of liability:

> Is fault at all relevant to the question of financial support of minor children? The existence of a mechanical, mathematical, non-discretionary child support scheme would surely suggest otherwise. But on a closer examination it becomes clear that fault is indeed relevant and, in some cases at least, it is arguably the basis of liability for child support. Liability arises from the fact of being a 'legal parent'. And, with the exception of the minority situations of children conceived by assisted reproduction or adopted children, legal parenthood flows from the genetic link, or at least the presumed genetic link arising from marriage. In other words the legal status of being a parent, the trigger for financial liability, is the result of either intentionally having a child or negligently having a child – as where inadequate precautions are taken with contraception. The issue of liability is very much seen as a matter of personal, individual responsibility, and this is especially argued in the case of men. Perhaps it was a one night stand – but it is a matter of personal responsibility to ensure that children do not result from one night stands, and if they do, those at fault must pay with a lifetime of financial responsibility.
>
> It might be argued that the kind of liability which falls on genetic fathers is in nature more akin to criminal or tortious no-fault or strict liability. The argument would be that liability turns on the responsibility owed to a child. It is the failure to discharge this responsibility voluntarily once a child is born which is the true basis of liability rather than any fault which may or may not have been implicit in the circumstances of conception. There is some force in this argument but, it is submitted, it is necessary to distinguish between those cases in which pregnancy results

from a conscious decision to have a child, in or out of marriage, in the context of a committed relationship and those in which pregnancy results from casual sexual relations. In the case of the former it is reasonable to characterise liability as arising from a voluntary assumption of responsibility for the child which ought to be honoured. In the case of the latter it would be a distortion to describe the father's position as involving any such assumption, or even recognition, of responsibility. The real foundation for the imposition of liability in these cases is, it is argued, a moral judgement about casual sexual relations which manifests itself on the conception and birth of the resulting child. Thus, while it is true that it is not necessary in law to prove fault as such, the reality is that the moral blameworthiness in being responsible for conception is seen as a sufficient justification for imposing an extensive legal obligation. The argument presented here (which is reiterated below in relation to adoption and care proceedings) is that fault operates insidiously, as an unrecognised influence or factor, in the determination of legal issues which ostensibly have nothing at all to do with fault.

Might it be argued that the basis of child support is really welfare? The argument would be that parents are liable because the welfare of children dictates that they be properly provided for financially. And so they should, but this misses the point that in the majority of cases which involve the enforcement of child support liability it is the state which is seeking to recoup from the errant father what it has already paid out in social security benefits for the child. In other words, the social security system exists as the prime safety net to ensure a minimum income for mothers and children and it is this which primarily protects the welfare of those children. The pursuit of the father is not to secure the welfare of the child but to enforce his legal and, what is seen as his moral, responsibility to the child and mother. He is conceptualised as being at fault in not discharging this voluntarily.

QUESTION

Is child support about fault? Or responsibility? Or something else?

The welfare state makes provision for all in times of financial hardship, whether or not that hardship is caused or accompanied by family breakdown. What is the relationship between the duty of individuals, and the provision made by the public purse? In the answer to that difficult question lie the seeds of the child support legislation.

Section 78(6) of the Social Security Administration Act 1992 states:

(*a*) a man shall be liable to maintain his wife or civil partner and any children of whom he is the father, and

(*b*) a woman shall be liable to maintain her husband or civil partner and any children of whom she is the mother.

Section 107 of that Act extends this duty, so that unmarried or divorced parents of children under 16 are 'liable relatives'; that is, they must reimburse the state if it has to pay means-tested benefits to support the other parent and their children. Yet the divorce court has power to absolve parents from that responsibility by *not* awarding maintenance for the benefit of the children of one's former family, if it takes the view that new responsibilities should supercede former commitments. That was what the court did, notoriously, in *Delaney v Delaney* [1991] FCR 161, [1990] 2 FLR 457, where Ward J said:

This court is entitled...to approach the case upon a basis that if, having regard to the reasonable financial commitments undertaken by the husband with due regard to the contribution properly made by the lady with whom he lives, there is insufficient left properly and fully to maintain the former wife and children, then the court may have regard to the fact that in proper cases social security benefits are available to the wife and children of the marriage; that having such regard, the court is enabled to avoid making orders which would be financially crippling to the husband. Benefits are available to this family of which the Judge was not made aware, and I have come to the conclusion that the husband cannot reasonably be expected to contribute at all to the maintenance of his previous family without financially crippling himself. In my judgment, it is far better that the spirit of effecting a clean break and starting with a fresh slate be implemented in this case, not by dismissing the claims of the wife and the children, but by acknowledging that now and, it is likely, in the foreseeable future he will not be able to honour the obligations he has recognised towards his children, and in my judgment the appeal should be allowed and I would substitute a nominal order to each of the children for the order of £10 which each of them is currently ordered to receive.

Appeal allowed; an order of £0.50 per annum per child substituted for the order made by the judge in the court below.

QUESTIONS

i. Do you agree with the proposition that a court should strive to avoid making orders that are financially crippling to the husband?

ii. Can you think of *any* advantages from the point of view of the wife in obtaining an order for nominal maintenance as in *Delaney*?

iii. As a tax payer, can you see any justification for the use of public funding in such a case on behalf of the wife's applications?

iv. Do you see any value at all in sending someone to prison for non-payment of maintenance payments?

v. Does it surprise you that *Delaney* was a major cause of Margaret Thatcher's enthusiasm for the Child Support Act?

A study by Jonathan Bradshaw and Jane Millar, *Lone Parent Families in the UK*, (1991) found that only 30 per cent of lone mothers received regular payments of maintenance. They also found that maintenance formed less than 10 per cent of lone parents' total net income, compared with 45 per cent for income support and 22 per cent for net earnings. *Children Come First* (1990), 'The Government's Proposals on the Maintenance of Children' complained: 'The contribution made by maintenance to the income of lone-parent families therefore remains too low.'
Children Come First explained:

1.3.2 When a lone parent claims Income Support the DSS [the Department of Social Security] tries to ensure that the absent parent pays enough maintenance to remove his dependants' need for Income Support, or as much towards that amount as he can reasonably afford. A separated parent is asked to pay enough to support the claimant and the children fully so that payment of Income Support can stop. Divorced parents and parents who were never married who are not liable to maintain each other are currently asked to pay an amount equal to the personal benefit rates for the children they are liable to maintain plus the family and lone parent premiums payable under Income Support because there are children in the household. The Social Security Act 1990 has provided for courts to be able to include the amount to be recovered from the absent parent in recognition that it is responsibility for the care of the children which prevents the claimant working.

Children Come First proposed a major change in approach both by the courts and the DSS:

2.1 The Government proposes to establish a system of child maintenance which will be equally available to any person seeking maintenance for the benefit of a child and which will:

- ensure that parents honour their legal and moral responsibility to maintain their own children whenever they can afford to do so. It is right that other taxpayers should help to maintain children when the children's own parents, despite their own best efforts, do not have enough resources to do so themselves. That will continue to be the case. But it is not right that taxpayers, who include other families, should shoulder that responsibility instead of parents who are able to do it themselves;
- recognise that where a liable parent has formed a second family and has further natural children, he is liable to maintain all his own children. A fair and reasonable balance has to be struck between the interests of the children of a first family and the children of a second;
- produce consistent and predictable results so that people in similar financial circumstances will pay similar amounts of maintenance, and so that people will know in advance what their maintenance obligations are going to be;
- enable maintenance to be decided in a fair and reasonable way which reduces the scope for its becoming a contest between the parents to the detriment of the interests of the children;
- produce maintenance payments which are realistically related to the costs of caring for a child;
- allow for maintenance payments to be reviewed regularly so that changes in circumstances can be taken into account automatically;
- recognise that both parents have a legal responsibility to maintain their children;
- ensure that parents meet the cost of their children's maintenance whenever they can without removing the parents' own incentives to work, and to go on working;
- enable caring parents who wish to work to do so as soon as they feel ready and able;
- provide an efficient and effective service to the public which ensures that:
  - (a) maintenance is paid regularly and on time so that it provides a reliable income for the caring parent and the children and
  - (b) produces maintenance quickly so that the habit of payment is established early and is not compromised by early arrears;
- avoid the children and their caring parent becoming dependent on Income Support whenever this is possible and, where it is not possible, to minimise the period of dependence.

The proposal, put into effect in the Child Support Act 1991, was for an 'integrated package' involving a formula for the assessment of how much maintenance should be paid, a child support agency with responsibility for tracing absent parents and for the assessment, collection and enforcement of maintenance payments, and changes in the rules of Social Security to encourage parents to go to work. We might say that this was the only instance, during the Thatcher years, of nationalisation of what had previously been a private matter. It marked a major change from the liable relative system, under which the Department of Social Security (as it then was) did not pursue matters very vigorously and would accept (as did the court in *Delaney*) that the liable relative could not afford to pay.

The Child Support Act 1991 in its original form was not a success. Perhaps its most notorious feature was the formula itself, requiring in some cases one hundred items of information for completion. Concerns, and protests, were generated by numerous aspects of the Act's operation, in particular the high levels of assessment generated by the formula, the complete lack of discretion in its operation, the Act's effect in families where a capital settlement had been made in partial satisfaction of child support obligations (see *Crozier v Crozier* [1994] 2 WLR 444, [1994] 2 All ER 362) and the requirement that a person with care in receipt of income support should cooperate with the agency in seeking maintenance from the absent parent.

Nick Wikeley, in 'Child Support reform – throwing the baby out with the bath water' (2008), explains how the law has moved on:

A Tale of Two Schemes

In 1997 New Labour inherited from the Conservatives a failing child support system with a 'legacy of entrenched mistrust and bitterness'. Many commentators took the view that the CSA's well-documented problems 'had put the whole cause back a generation' [Jane Lewis, 2001]. Reform of child support was high on the incoming administration's agenda and came to be seen as one means towards achieving New Labour's goal of abolishing child poverty within a generation. Yet 10 years later, in 2007, as Gordon Brown succeeded Tony Blair, the Government presided over not just one but two failing child support systems – the so-called 'old' and 'new' schemes. How has such a comprehensive failure in public administration come about?

The 'old scheme' (or what we might term for present purposes child support Mark 1) is the child support system that covers most applications for maintenance made between the advent of the CSA in April 1993 and the partial implementation of the new scheme in March 2003. The old scheme is governed by the Child Support Act 1991, as amended by the Child Support Act 1995, and the voluminous secondary legislation. Such child support maintenance assessments are based on the original highly complex formula based on social security rules, under which the incomes of both parents are taken into account but non-resident parents' second families receive scant recognition. The old scheme also operates a relatively high threshold (104 nights a year) before overnight contact visits operate to reduce the non-resident parent's child support liability. Parents with care on income support or income-based jobseeker's allowance who are covered by the old scheme see no financial advantage in the event that child support is paid – every pound received in child support is deducted from the parent with care's benefit entitlement. As a result there is little incentive for either parent to engage with the old child support scheme where the parent with care is on benefit.

The 'new scheme' (or child support Mark 2) is the child support system that governs all applications for child support made to the CSA since 3 March 2003, when the Child Support, Pensions and Social Security Act 2000 amended the Child Support Act 1991. Again, the primary legislation provides no more than the framework – the detail of the new scheme is buried in reams of regulations. Liabilities under the new scheme – 'maintenance calculations', to use the new scheme parlance, rather than 'maintenance assessments' – are based on a much more transparent formula. In the standard case this means that a non-resident parent's child support liability will be 15 per cent of that parent's net income for one child, 20 per cent for two and 25 per cent for three or more children. The new scheme formula is therefore much less complex than its predecessor, but by the same token takes no account of either the parent with care's income or the non-resident parent's housing costs or other special expenditure. The exceptional grounds on which a parent may apply for a variation from the formula are also more restricted than under the old scheme. However, the new scheme recognises the reality of serial partnering at the outset of the calculation by reducing the non-resident parent's net income to reflect responsibility for children in (typically) his second family. The adjustments for overnight contact are also more generous to non-resident parents, with a lower threshold of 52 nights a year. Parents with care on income support or income-based jobseeker's allowance under the new scheme are able to keep the first £10 a week paid in child support – the so-called child maintenance premium – before it affects their benefit entitlement, although there have been major problems in practice in administering this premium.

The Government's original plan was that all separated parents would be subject to the new scheme. Applications made on or after 3 March 2003 (or 'A' Day) would automatically be dealt with under the new rules. Meanwhile, parents on the old scheme would be transferred to the new scheme once the latter was sufficiently robust to cope with the transfer of the existing caseload, on a date known in CSA-speak as 'C Day' ('C' for conversion of old scheme maintenance assessments into new scheme maintenance calculations). However, as the present writer noted in 2000, 'a new scheme means a new computer, and the DSS's recent history with major computerisation projects is less than encouraging'. Indeed, 'C Day' was gradually pushed further and further back as a result of operational difficulties, and especially the CSA's systemic IT problems. According to the Department's Permanent Secretary, the conversion task was, with the benefit of hindsight, 'probably at the edge of being undoable'.

As a result, the Agency currently operates two computer systems as well as two child support schemes, but with some cross-over – about half of the old scheme cases are handled on the original CSCS (child support computer system), whereas all new scheme cases and about half of the old scheme cases are processed on a different IT platform, CS2 (as in the second child support scheme). If CSCS was disastrous, CS2 was worse than disastrous, with the consequence that C Day, and with it the prospect of bulk conversion, has now disappeared over the horizon with no prospect of it ever coming to pass. This has inevitably outraged those (typically non-resident) parents who have been able to work out for themselves the financial advantage to be gained by transferring from the old to the new scheme. However, the Child Support Commissioners have ruled that parents who have been left stranded on the old scheme have no human rights claim against the Secretary of State for the Agency's policy and operational failure to implement full-scale conversion, with their arguments being robustly dismissed as 'self-interest dressed up as discrimination'.

Although there are various ways in which outcomes can be measured, both child support schemes perform poorly whichever indicators are used. The futility of the old scheme is evident in the fact that 49 per cent of the processed caseload has been assessed to have a nil liability. The relevant proportion for the new scheme is much lower (14 per cent), but the new scheme still has 50 per cent of its assessed caseload with a liability calculated at £5 a week or less.

Those figures are presented in the table on p. 190, taken from a *Regulatory Impact Assessment* (2007) carried out by the Department for Work and Pensions for the Child maintenance and Other Payments Bill.

Distribution of weekly liabilities of non-resident parents using the CSA

Source: Child Support Agency administrative data, March 2007

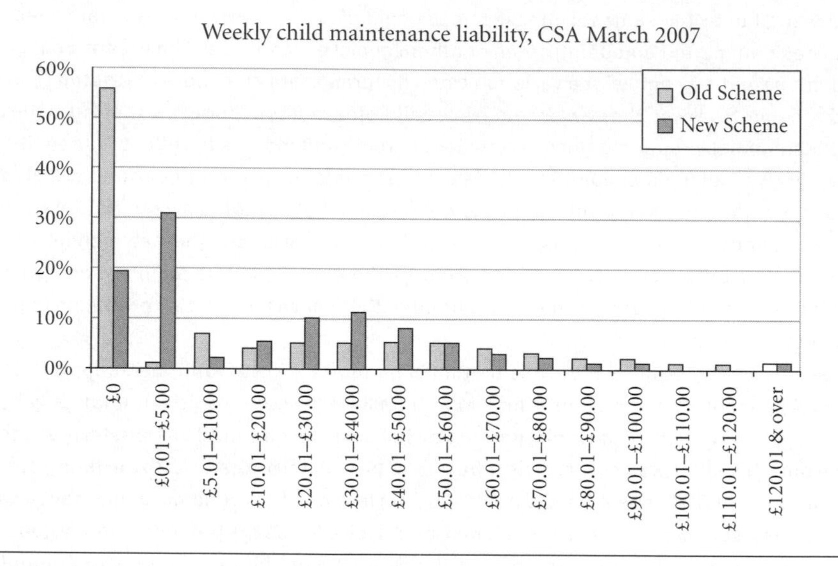

QUESTION

Under the 'new' scheme, the non-resident parent's net income is reduced to allow for the needs of his or her children with a new partner, before calculation of the maintenance payable for children from a former relationship. The reduction is such that the allowance for the children of the 'new' family is greater than that for those of the 'old'. As James Pirrie observed (1999): 'step-children move centre stage for the first time' ('Changes to Child Support – The SFLA View'). Why do you think that change was made?

Wikeley discusses another of the changes in 'child support mark 2' in 'Child Support – the new formula' (2001):

Income

The fundamental point is that under the reformed scheme only the NRP's income is going to be relevant to the formula calculation. The PWC's income will have no effect on the assessment in future. According to Nicholas Mostyn QC (and others), this represents 'gross unfairness' ('The Green Paper on Child Support – Children First: a new approach to child support' [1999] Fam Law 95, at p 99). In practice, however, this makes eminently sound administrative sense: at present some 96% of NRPs with earnings have former partners who earn less than £100 per week. But there remains the very real risk that the general public's perception of the fairness of the new regime may be influenced by a minority of high profile cases in which the NRP's liability is unaffected by the fact that his former partner is earning £100,000 per year herself.

The courts' jurisdiction to order spousal maintenance is, of course, unaffected by all this. However, look back at Chapter 3, and at the evidence for the 'mother gap' (p. 117). Lone parents who are separated or divorced can obtain maintenance from their partners. Lone parents who have not been married to, or a civil partner of, the other parent have no such recourse.

QUESTION

How do you feel about the fact that the Child Support Act formula includes no element of support for the parent with care: 'sound administrative sense', 'gross unfairness', both, or neither?

Under child support Mark 2 there is, as Nick Wikeley (2007) observes, a 52-nights-per-year threshold for staying contact to reduce liability. Jonathan Herring (2007) comments: 'A one-seventh reduction in child support for the cost of a burger and video is a bargain.'

QUESTION

What effect do you think this rule will have had in practice?

More change is in the offing; Nick Wikeley continues the tale in 'Child Support reform – throwing the baby out with the bath water' (2007), and provides a guide to the spate of government publications in 2006 and 2007:

The Road to Redesign

In April 2005 Stephen Geraghty was appointed from outside the civil service as the CSA's new Chief Executive, with part of his brief being to undertake a comprehensive review of the embattled Agency's operations. Ministers, meanwhile, were clearly losing patience. In September 2005, David Blunkett, then Secretary of State for Work and Pensions, described the CSA as a 'complete shambles' and promised an announcement by the end of the year of plans for a 'root and branch' overhaul of the system. In November 2005, however, David Blunkett resigned for the second time from Cabinet, to be replaced by John Hutton, with the Prime Minister asserting that the Agency's combined investigatory, adjudicating and enforcing roles were the root cause of its problems. Hutton dismissed Geraghty's plans for yet further incremental change, and in February 2006 told Parliament that neither the CSA itself nor official child support policy was 'fit for purpose'. A modified and scaled down version of Geraghty's plans was implemented as the Operational Improvement Plan, but Hutton appointed Sir David Henshaw, outgoing chief executive of Liverpool City Council, to undertake a fundamental redesign of child support policy and operations.

The Henshaw Report, published less than six months later in July 2006, recommended a 'fundamental change in the way child support is organised in this country'. In Henshaw's analysis the child support system was failing to deliver as the result of both policy and operational failures. The solution required radical redesign: Government should encourage and support private maintenance arrangements, parents with care on benefit should keep more child support where it is paid, and the CSA should be replaced by a new organisation with stronger enforcement powers as a 'back-up government provided service'. The Government accepted the broad thrust of these proposals in its response published on the same day, agreeing that the Agency's problems were 'profound and structural' and arguing that the Operational Improvement Plan 'does not go to the heart of the current problems'. Both the Henshaw Report and the official response were strong on rhetoric but thin on detail, although rather more information was forthcoming in the December 2006 White Paper [DWP, *A new system of child maintenance*, Cm 6979 (TSO, 2006)], which was followed in turn by a formal consultation process [DWP, *A new system of child maintenance: Summary of responses to the consultation*, Cm 7061 (TSO, 2007)]. The House of Commons Work and Pensions Committee issued a critical report which raised a number of questions about the planned reforms, not all of which were answered satisfactorily by the Department's subsequent reply. The Government's proposals have now been embodied in the Child Maintenance and Other Payments Bill 2007, which received its Second Reading in the House of Commons in July 2007, before being referred to the Public Bill Committee. It is expected to enter the House of Lords in November or December 2007 with Royal Assent anticipated to take place in the Spring of 2008. Some of the powers in the Bill – for example, the repeal of the requirement for parents with care on benefit to engage with the child support system and the new enforcement powers – are expected to come into force in 2008. However, the Government has indicated that it will not be until 2012–2013 that 'all clients will be on a single set of rules managed by a single organisation'.

The Bill includes most, but by no means all, of the measures confirmed in the December 2006 White Paper. Some changes did not require primary legislation (eg, the proposal to increase the level of the disregard for parents with care on benefit) or did not even need secondary legislation (eg, the plan to 'name and shame' those convicted of offences under the child support legislation). The single most controversial reform that was omitted from the Bill was the proposal that both parents' names should be entered on the child's birth certificate unless there is a good reason for not doing so. Henshaw advocated this change principally as a means of reducing the number of untraceable cases, while noting that encouraging fathers' involvement in their children's lives from birth could have a positive effect on compliance in the event of subsequent separation. The idea was taken up enthusiastically, at least by the Department for Work and Pensions and especially by the then Secretary of State. The Department's proposals were explained further in a Green Paper issued just two days before John Hutton was moved as part of Gordon Brown's first cabinet reshuffle [DWP, *Joint birth registration: promoting parental responsibility*, Cm 7160 (TSO, 2007)]. It remains to be seen whether Mr Hutton's successor as Secretary of State, Peter Hain, shares the same enthusiasm for automatic presumption of joint birth registration. The findings of recent research can be read as indicating that there may be serious problems in introducing a statutory requirement of joint registration.

The 'name and shame' plan has been dropped; Wikeley observes that 'the official explanation (in an answer to a Parliamentary Question released on the last day of the session) was that the site was little used after the initial publicity: *Hansard*, HC Debs, vol 463 col 1490W (26 July 2007)'. The government has held a consultation about joint birth registration and we do not yet know the outcome; the response to that consultation of the British Association for Adoption and Fostering (at http://www.baaf.org.uk/res/consultations/consultresponse_jointbirth.pdf) raises important concerns (to some of which we will return in Chapter 9):

The Speed of Change

It is only since the end of 2003 that joint birth registration by two unmarried parents has resulted in the automatic acquisition of parental responsibility by the birth father (although we believe that there was a common misapprehension among the public that before this change naming the father on the birth certificate gave him a stronger legal status than was in fact the case). We note that there is some research ongoing by the National Centre for Social Research concerning motivation for joint registration, and we would suggest that it would be preferable to delay reaching any decision on amending legislation until the outcome of this and, perhaps, other more detailed research is available. The Consultation paper rightly identifies the fact that some single mothers are very vulnerable; the duty to register a birth arises during the time shortly after the birth when they may be particularly so. It is relevant to observe that a mother cannot give a valid consent to adoption during the six weeks after giving birth, and yet she may make a decision about joint registration, committing her to sharing parental responsibility with the father, within a few days of the birth. Given the short period during which this has been so, we believe it would be valuable to allow time to assess whether the change brought about by the Adoption and Children Act 2002 has had any unintended negative consequences.

In addition, as the consultation paper acknowledges, potentially far-reaching changes in respect of legal parenthood following donor conception are likely if the proposals in the draft Human Tissues and Embryos Bill published earlier this year are enacted, and time is needed to consider the implications of these possible changes.

Matters of Detail

There are a number of areas where the consultation paper gives only a very broad outline of the practical consequences of any change that imposed a duty on fathers to register births, subject to the exceptions proposed. It is questionable whether registrars are well placed to assess either the credibility of a mother alleging, say, that the father poses a risk of violence or abuse, or the vulnerability of a mother. While the paper talks of 'adequate safeguards' it is not clear in practice how these could be built into the system. How in practice, for example, would a mother be made aware of her right to object to the father exercising his right to joint registration and assisted to exercise that right? In the case of very young teenage mothers, where the birth appears to be the result of unlawful sexual intercourse, would the father lay himself open to prosecution by acknowledging paternity, and who would have the responsibility of making him aware of such a risk? It would be helpful to consider these matters of detail, as well as the possible additional costs imposed on the registration system, the courts, and counselling and advice services, before making a decision to legislate.

As to the new system for child support, David Burrows, in 'A brave new world' (2007) is pessimistic:

The Child Maintenance and Other Payments Bill...proposes the Child Maintenance and Enforcement Commission (C-MEC) to do the job which the Child Support Agency (CSA) failed to do, and sets out extensive intended amendments to Child Support Act 1991 (CSA 1991). The already derided CSA 1991, with the separate proposed legislation as well, will be doubled in length. And doubtless the excessively cumbersome regulations will be proportionately extended to cover the new provisions in the Bill. Previous efforts at this legislation have gone through Parliament more or less unopposed; and so too, I suspect, will this. Not at all a propitious start...

A Semantic Exercise

The reforming proposals, apart from enforcement, are light. First comes a semantic change with administrative undertones: out goes the CSA – it never had a statutory existence: everything in CSA 1991 was done in the name of the Secretary of State for Work and Pensions – in comes C-MEC. How many of the CSA staff will transfer to C-MEC? Most, we can be sure; and many more, no doubt – mostly bailiffs, ex-policemen and security staff – will be added. This further brave new world of child support – the fourth in 15 years – will require yet more civil servants to run it; and, I fear, they will get it even more wrong.

Benefit Claimants

Second, the compulsion on benefit claimants to authorise the secretary of state to collect child support maintenance goes (CSA 1991, ss 6 and 46). The logic of making this scheme a Department for Work and Pensions (DWP) responsibility therefore goes; though this proposition has probably been overlooked. The original scheme gained most of its impetus from Margaret Thatcher's discovery that the fathers of children whose mothers were receiving income support were getting away without paying maintenance. The taxpayer paid instead. So a scheme was set up which has cost the taxpayer far more than the modest sums paid for children whose fathers paid nothing, or very little; and run by DWP and its predecessors.

Logically, the scheme should be with other child maintenance issues in the new Ministry of Justice (MoJ): child support proceedings are, after all, family proceedings (Supreme Court Act 1981, Sch 1, 3(h)). And perhaps the civil servants in the MoJ would see the absurdity of the variety of court schemes involved with child support.

Calculation

Of the other main proposed amendments, the third is to the basis of calculation of child support maintenance: instead of 15%, 20% and 25% of net earned income for one, two and three or more children, it is proposed that calculation be based on gross income: 12%, 16% and 19% (Sch 4, para 3) – said to be partly as a result of the experiences of Robert Smith in *Smith v Secretary of State for Work and Pensions* [2006] UKHL 35, [2006] 3 All ER 907. Otherwise most of the principles for calculation are much the same as before.

Enforcement

Next comes the main thrust of the Bill: enforcement. To the existing 13 sections on enforcement, 29 more are threaded – rudely thrust might be more appropriate a description of the amendment process – into CSA 1991: clauses 32A–32K will be added. Clauses 39B to 39S come later; and there are copious amendments to existing sections. The present powers remain. New provisions include:

- A liability order alongside all sorts of variants on the deduction from earnings order.
- A lump sum deduction order – which is a third party debt order imposed by administrative fiat.
- A child support form of writ *ne exeat regno* emerges – taking away someone's passport: why for child support but not for other debt?
- A curfew.
- Search orders.

All the paraphernalia of the new police world in which we live under new Labour is there to palliate the politicians who have failed so far to come up with a satisfactory scheme.

Were there any real likelihood of this ensuring more payments it might be tolerable to see the criminal jurisdiction – excluded for civil proceedings since the late 19th century – brought into family law; but I doubt there will be any higher a rate of clearance of arrears than under the existing scheme. Unless C-MEC gets on top of payments from the first day, the rate of arrears will alter hardly at all.

What the Bill Ignores

The present court and tribunal system underpinning child support increases dramatically the cost of collection; but no one knows what this cost is. Nearly £1 is spent to collect each £1 of child support maintenance – the equivalent figure for tax is around 4p to collect £1. This figure does not include – because the data is not available – the cost of the court processes involved with child support. If this cost were added, I suspect the costs of collection would rise to nearer twice the amount collected. The tribunal system and other court processes are a real drain on parent's resources. Appeals can take months, sometimes years, to dispose of; and in the meantime enforcement is frozen.

There are seven separate court and appellate systems involved with child support. The Bill does not add to this – it cannot, for child support draws in all civil jurisdictions as well as the appeal tribunals and the child support commissioners – but it adds to the work envisaged for the tribunals and the magistrates. More aspects of the system, especially as a result of the provisions for the burgeoning enforcement system, require arrangements for appeals. It is proposed that some go to the magistrates, some to the appeal tribunals. Which are the other four court systems involved: county courts, Administrative Court (judicial review), Court of Appeal and House of Lords?

Alec Farley (see *Farley v Secretary of State for Work and Pensions* [2006] UKHL 31, [2006] 3 All ER 935) has tasted six of the seven – and he is still involved with three (appeal tribunal, county court and High Court) nearly five years after 10 years of assessments landed on his doormat in November 2002 telling him he had around £32,000 to pay. Hitherto, he had paid periodical payments under a maintenance agreement. And Smith (*Smith v Secretary of State for Work and Pensions*) has been involved with six as well. Smith has so far avoided the county courts, and Farley the commissioners. Farley is now on his third trip to the Administrative Court: there seems no other way to sort out his particular problem under CSA 1991.

The Bill evinces the continuing ministerial paranoia about the county courts: horrible, because lawyers practise in them. Well, lawyers practise wherever the subject needs protection and assistance; and the present scheme operating outside the county and other civil courts cries out for critical lawyers to help the unfortunates caught up in them. There is a long-standing system of enforcement for all other forms of debt – including all non-child support child and spousal maintenance – in existence. Little would have been needed to graft most of these new enforcement procedures onto the existing county court scheme...

...

Writing Off Debt; But No Claim for the Parent With Care

- The Bill, cl 29, gives the secretary of state power to make regulations to write off child support debt, euphemistically called 'a set off' – which normally implies a *quid pro quo*, for which there is none in evidence in the Bill.

- The current child support debt mountain – incalculable, but probably around £3m – can be cleared; and future arrears can also be 'managed' – another euphemism in the Bill refers to this set off as 'debt management'.
- The one person who truly has an interest in all this – the resident parent – still will have no direct part in the enforcement process.
- Along with the children, one might have thought that the carer parent would be first in line to be able to sue for and to enforce, by any means available, arrears of child support maintenance. But no.
- Mary Kehoe's dismissal by the House of Lords would be the same now as it was then (*see R (Kehoe) v Secretary of State for Work and Pensions* [2005] UKHL 48, [2005] 4 All ER 905). She has, and will continue to have, little recourse – other than judicial review – for compelling a prevaricating government department to enforce arrears.
- It is the DWP only, says the House of Lords, which can enforce child support arrears. The cruel illogic of that position remains with this Bill.

Burrows refers to the following case.

R (on the application of Kehoe) v Secretary of State for Work and Pensions [2005] UKHL 48, [2006] 1 AC 42

Mrs Kehoe had been caring for her four children since her husband left home in 1994. The Child Support Agency's attempts to recover child support from Mr Kehoe were frequently unsuccessful, and substantial arrears built up. She claimed that her inability to enforce his duty to support her children was a breach of Article 6 of the European Convention on Human Rights. The majority in the House of Lords dismissed her appeal from the Court of Appeal's finding that Article 6 was not engaged.

Lord Hope of Craighead sums up the majority view:

> [35] I would conclude that the 1991 Act has deliberately avoided conferring a right on the person with care to enforce a child maintenance assessment against the absent parent. Enforcement is exclusively a matter for the Secretary of State. It follows that the person with care has no right to apply to a court for the enforcement of the assessment.

Does the 1991 Act Create a 'Civil Right' For the Purposes of Article 6?

> [36] Article 6(1) of the Convention provides that in the determination of 'his civil rights and obligations' everyone is entitled to a fair hearing by an independent and impartial tribunal established by law. ... But in order to invoke this principle one must first be able to say that the individual has a claim for the infringement of a 'civil right'.
>
> ...
>
> [41] The key to this case lies in the point of principle that was identified by the Commission in *Pinder v United Kingdom* (1984) 7 EHRR 464, 465, para 5. This is that, while the concept of a 'right' is autonomous to some degree because it does not depend on how the privilege or interest concerned is classified in the domestic system, it is not open to the European Court when it is applying article 6(1) to create a substantive right which has no legal basis in that system at all. Article 6(1), on its own terms, has nothing to say about the content of the individual's civil rights.

> Nor does it impose an obligation on the state party to confer any particular rights in substantive law on the individual....
>
> [42] ... It is not enough to bring article 6(1) into play to assert that, as the whole object of the scheme is that the person with care is the person who will ultimately benefit from the enforcement process, Mrs Kehoe should be allowed at least some say in how that process is conducted. I respectfully agree with Latham LJ that it seems unsatisfactory that she should not have that right, as the agency's priorities are inevitably different from those of the person with care of the child, who may disagree profoundly with the agency as to how the proceedings in which she has such an obvious interest should be conducted: [2004] QB 1378, 1414, para 102. But the fact is that the 1991 Act itself, which is the only source from which it could be derived, does not give her that right. The scheme of the 1991 Act is not designed to allow the person with care to play any part in the enforcement process at all. It is not possible to envisage how that might be done without re-writing the scheme which the Act has laid down. In my opinion this is not even a case where it can be said that the existence of a right to participate in this process is arguable.

Baroness Hale of Richmond delivered a dissenting judgment. She began:

> [49] This is another case which has been presented to us largely as a case about adults' rights when in reality it is a case about children's rights. It concerns the obligation to maintain one's children and the corresponding right of those children to obtain the benefit of that obligation....

Baroness Hale traced the history of the obligation to maintain one's children, and the evolution of the child support legislation. She went on to say:

> [68] It is important to note, however, that neither the private nor the public law obligation, nor the corresponding right of the child to the benefit of that obligation, has been taken away. The public law liabilities, carried over from the old Poor Law, are defined by section 78(6) of the Social Security Administration Act 1992:
>
> '(a) a man shall be liable to maintain his wife and any children of whom he is the father;
> (b) a woman shall be liable to maintain her husband and any children of whom she is the mother.'
>
> It is still an offence persistently to refuse or neglect to perform that obligation, as a result of which income-based benefits are paid in respect of a spouse or child: see s 105(1). And the Secretary of State may still apply for an order against such a liable person: see s 106(1).
>
> [69] The private law liabilities have also been retained in the new scheme. Unlike the father's common law guardianship of his legitimate children, his common law obligation to maintain them has never been abolished, although the wife's agency of necessity was abolished in 1970. Furthermore, the courts' powers to make the full range of orders for the benefit of children remain on the statute book. Despite the general prohibition [on using those powers] in section 8(1) and (3) of the 1991 Act, already referred to, the courts remain able to give effect to the parental obligation in a number of ways:
>
> (i) by making 'top up' orders for periodical payments where the income of the non-resident parent is above a threshold where it may be appropriate for him to pay more than is payable under the formula (s 8(6));
> (ii) by making 'school fees orders' for children who are being educated privately (s 8(7));
> (iii) by making orders to cover expenses attributable to the child's disability (s 8(8));

(iv) by making lump sum and property adjustment orders for the benefit of children under the Matrimonial Causes Act 1973 or the Children Act 1989. Although these are mainly used to make provision for housing or other capital expenditure rather than as a substitute for periodical maintenance, it has been held that they may be used for maintenance purposes if the child support machinery has not been invoked: see *V v V (Child Maintenance)* [2001] 2 FLR 799;

(v) by making and varying consent orders which embody periodical payments for a child (s 8(5) to (11); Child Maintenance (Written Agreements) Order 1993). Unless the parent with care receives relevant social security payments, this precludes any further application for a child support assessment. Thus parents can, in effect, avoid the intervention of the Child Support Agency by agreeing a nominal sum in periodical payments at the outset and then returning to court for it to be varied: see again *V v V*;

(vi) by making an order for spousal maintenance which includes the costs of supporting the children and will be reduced *pro tanto* if and when a maintenance assessment under the 1991 Act is made (a so-called 'Segal order' named after the judge who invented it);

(vii) by enforcing a maintenance agreement made between the parents for the benefit of their children, although such an agreement cannot prevent a person making an application to the Agency for a maintenance assessment, nor does the court have jurisdiction to vary it if the Agency would have jurisdiction to make an assessment (s 9(3), (4) and (5)).

[70] It is obvious, therefore, that the obligation of a parent to maintain his children, and the right of those children to have the benefit of that obligation, is not wholly contained in the 1991 Act. Far from it. The Act left all the previous law intact, merely precluding the courts from using their powers in cases where the Agency was supposed to do it for them.... The Child Support Act 1991 contemplates that, as a minimum, children should have the benefit of the maintenance obligation as defined under the formula; but it does not contemplate that children should be limited to their rights under that Act; in appropriate circumstances, they may be supplemented or replaced in all the ways recounted earlier.

[71] That being the case, it is clear to me that children have a civil right to be maintained by their parents which is such as to engage article 6 of the European Convention on Human Rights. Their rights are not limited to the rights given to the parent with care under the Child Support Act. The provisions of that Act are simply a means of quantifying and enforcing part of their rights.... A civil right to be maintained exists and *prima facie* children are entitled to the benefit of the article 6 rights in the determination and enforcement of that right.

[72] The problem is that this is exactly what the system is trying to do. It is trying to enforce the children's rights. It is sometimes, as this case shows, lamentably inefficient in so doing. It is safe to assume that there are cases, of which this may be one, where the children's carer would be much more efficient in enforcing the children's rights. The children's carer has a direct and personal interest in enforcement which the Agency, however good its intentions, does not. Even in benefit cases, where the state does have a direct interest in enforcement, it is not the sort of interest which stems from needing enough money to feed, clothe and house the children on a day to day basis. Only a parent who is worrying about where the money is to be found for the school dinners, the school trips, the school uniform, sports gear or musical instruments, or to visit the 'absent' parent, not only this week but the next and the next for many years to come, has that sort of interest. A promise that the Agency is doing its best is not enough. Nor is the threat or reality of judicial review. Most people simply do not have access to the Administrative Court in the way that they used to have access to their local magistrates' court. Judicial review may produce some action from the Agency, but what is needed is money from the absent parent. Action from the Agency will not replace the money which has been irretrievably lost as a result of its failure to act in time.

...

[76] But if I am right that the children's civil rights to be properly maintained by their parents are engaged, it follows that the public authority which is charged by Parliament with securing the determination and enforcement of their rights is under a duty to act compatibly with their article 6 right to the speedy determination and effective enforcement of those rights.... It stands to reason that if the state is going to take over the enforcement of a person's civil rights it has a duty to act compliantly with article 6 in doing so. Just as the courts, as public authorities, have to act compliantly with the Convention rights, so does the Agency. The remedies, however, may be different if they do not.

[77] It follows that I have reached the same conclusion, albeit by a slightly different route, as Wall J in the Administrative Court. This comes as no surprise. I would allow this appeal and restore the order that he made.

Mrs Kehoe has pursued her complaint in the European Court of Human Rights.

Clause 3(3) of the Child Maintenance and Other Payments Bill 2007 reads:

> The Commission must exercise its functions effectively and efficiently.

QUESTIONS

i. Do you think that such a provision is likely to be (a) effective or (b) efficient?

ii. If Mrs Kehoe is successful in Strasbourg, what difference do you think that might make to the child support system for the future?

iii. Do you think that the child support system is primarily for the benefit of the state, the child, or the carer?

5.2 ANCILLARY RELIEF: THE HISTORICAL BACKGROUND

At common law the wife acquired the right to be supported by her husband throughout the marriage, albeit how and when the husband chose. When divorce was introduced into English law in 1857, it was thought to be only correct that the wife would have the right to apply to a court to obtain an order for support to substitute for the payments to which she would have been entitled had the marriage continued.

Sir James Wilde (later Lord Penzance) observed, in the Victorian case *Sidney v Sidney* (1865) 4 Sw & Tr 178, 34 LJPM & A 122:

> ...If, it was said, a man can part with his wife at the door of the Divorce Court without any obligation to support her, and with full liberty to form a new connection, his triumph over the sacred permanence of marriage will have been complete. To him marriage will have been a mere temporary arrangement, conterminous with his inclinations, and void of all lasting tie or burden. To such a man the Court may truly say with propriety, 'According to your ability you

> must still support the woman you have first chosen and then discarded. If you are relieved from your matrimonial vows it is for the protection of the woman you have injured, and not for your own sake. And so much of the duty of a husband as consists in the maintenance of his wife may be justly kept alive and enforced upon you in favour of her whom you have driven to relinquish your name and home.'

Further,

> It is the foremost duty of this Court in dispensing the remedy of divorce to uphold the institution of marriage. The possibility of freedom begets the desire to be set free, and the great evil of a marriage dissolved is, that it loosens the bonds of so many others. The powers of this Court will be turned to good account if, while meting out justice to the parties, such order should be taken in the matter as to stay and quench this desire and repress this evil. Those for whom shame has no dread, honourable vows no tie, and violence to the weak no sense of degradation, may still be held in check by an appeal to their love of money; and I wish it to be understood that, so far as the powers conferred by the section go, no man should, in my judgment, be permitted to rid himself of his wife by ill-treatment, and at the same time escape the obligation of supporting her.

Note what Finer and McGregor (1974) say about this case on p. 202.

QUESTION

Do you think that the knowledge that there is no escape from the financial ties and obligations of a marriage would operate today as a deterrent against divorce and a buttress to the institution of marriage?

What of a 'guilty' wife? Historically, a wife who had deserted her husband or committed adultery lost her common law right of maintenance. Although the position was ameliorated to a certain extent, the function of divorce was seen to be that of giving relief where a wrong had been done. This inevitably deprived many women of support after a divorce.

Finer and McGregor describe the position in the following way in 'The History of the Obligation to Maintain' (Appendix 5 to the Finer Report (1974)):

Alimony in the Ecclesiastical Courts

> 26. A right to maintenance in the strict sense – meaning a claim for the payment of money directly enforceable against the husband – was available to the wife only in the ecclesiastical courts, and even there was only ancillary to the power of these courts to pronounce a decree of divorce *a mensa et thoro*. Such a decree, if granted on its own, might have left the wife without the means of survival. The court would therefore at the same time pronounce a decree of alimony, under which the husband would be required to pay his wife an annual sum, calculated as a proportion of his income, or, if the wife had separate estate, a proportion of their joint incomes. It was common to award one third, sometimes less, sometimes – especially where the husband's property had

come substantially from the wife – more. A decree of alimony could not be made separately from a decree of divorce *a mensa et thoro*, from which it followed that a wife who could not establish one of the offences on which such a decree could be granted could not be granted alimony either. Moreover, the means of enforcing an award of alimony were of more theoretical than practical utility. Alimony could not be sued for as a debt in the civil courts. Just as the common law courts refused to award maintenance on the grounds that this would have interfered with the ecclesiastical jurisdiction, so on the same grounds they refused to enforce the awards made in that jurisdiction. Before 1813, the only sanction for non-payment of alimony was excommunication or other ecclesiastical censure. Thereafter, a machinery for the imprisonment of the defaulting husband on a writ of *de contumace capiendo* became available, but there is little evidence to suggest that the threat of punishment here and now proved to be any more effective than the threat of punishment in the hereafter.

Maintenance After Parliamentary Divorce

27. A second species of maintenance attached to divorce by private Act of Parliament. The women who benefited from these awards of maintenance were very few in number. But the parliamentary practice is of cardinal historical importance because it established the principles that were adopted by the legislature as governing the right to maintenance when it established for the first time, in 1857, a system of divorce in the civil courts. The earliest Divorce Acts contained express provisions to ensure that the divorced wife should not be left in a state of destitution. Subsequently, a different practice prevailed:

> 'In the House of Commons there was a functionary called "The Ladies' Friend", an office generally filled by some member interested in the private business of Parliament, who undertook to see that any husband petitioning for divorce made a suitable provision for his wife. No clause to this effect was inserted in the Bill, lest it should be rejected in the other House, but, as a condition of obtaining relief, a husband was made to understand that, before the Bill passed through Committee, he must enter into a bond securing some moderate income to his wife.'

Two features of this practice call for special note. First, unlike the practice in the ecclesiastical court, which granted alimony only to an innocent wife, Parliament deliberately saw to it that a man could not use its process to rid himself of his wife, whatever her matrimonial misconduct might have been, without making some financial provision for her. Secondly, also in contrast with alimony, the provision which had to be made was not for the periodic payment of a sum of money. A husband seeking divorce by Act of Parliament had to make secured provision: that is to say, he had to make property available which, under the terms of an appropriate deed, was permanently set aside to secure whatever gross or annual amount he was to pay.

Finer and McGregor describe the beginning of the divorce court (as to which see Chapter 4, above) and then continue:

Maintenance For Wives Under the New Procedure

32. . . . The new divorce court could grant alimony ancillary to a decree of judicial separation on the same principles as alimony could previously attach to a decree of divorce *a mensa et thoro*. It

could also in granting a decree of divorce dissolving the marriage, insist on the husband making financial provision for the wife of the kind which the Ladies' Friend, under the parliamentary divorce procedure, had previously secured for her benefit. In this connection, the Act provided that on any decree of dissolution of marriage the court might order the husband to secure to the wife such gross sum of money, or such annual sum of money for any term not exceeding her own life, as having regard to her fortune (if any), to the ability of the husband, and to the conduct of the parties, the court should deem reasonable.

33. The use which the divorce court made of its powers of securing maintenance to the wife when dissolving her marriage took rather a curious course. Despite the fact that the distinctive feature of the parliamentary procedure which the court was supposed to have inherited was precisely that it guaranteed provision for the guilty (respondent) wife, the divorce court at first ruled that it would do this only in the rarest of cases. More than that, by 1861 (*Fisher v Fisher* (1861) 2 Sw & Tr 410, 31 LJPM & A 1) Sir Cresswell Cresswell, the first Judge Ordinary of the court, was saying that a wife petitioner should be awarded less by way of maintenance on being granted a decree of divorce than she would have been granted by way of alimony had she sought a judicial separation, for this would tend towards the preservation of the sanctity of marriage. Four years later, this view of the law was rejected by the court (*Sidney v Sidney* (1865) 4 Sw & Tr 178, 34 LJPM & A 122), which indicated in the same case that it would welcome a power, in dissolving a marriage, to make financial provision for the wife by way of an order for periodical payments, as well as by way of a secured sum. This power was granted by the Matrimonial Causes Act 1866, which provided that if a decree for dissolution of marriage were obtained against a husband who had no property on which the payment of a gross or annual sum could be secured, he might be ordered to pay such monthly or weekly amounts to his former wife, during their joint lives, as the court should think reasonable. By about the 1880s, the maintenance jurisdiction in divorce had come to be exercised to the following broad effect: the guilty wife, as under the old parliamentary practice, would have some modicum awarded to her; the innocent wife, as under the old ecclesiastical practice, would be granted a proportion, almost always one third, of the joint income, and, in addition, an amount in respect of any children committed to her custody.

37. In 1873, as part of the general re-organisation of the superior courts which then took place, the jurisdiction of the Court for Divorce and Matrimonial Causes, set up in 1857, was transferred to the High Court of Justice to be exercised in the Probate, Divorce and Admiralty Division of the High Court.

38. ...the court began to state that the rule, borrowed from the ecclesiastical jurisdiction, of awarding one third of the joint income to the innocent wife was not a rule of thumb, and that in awarding maintenance it had to take into account all the circumstances of the particular case. Secondly, signs emerged of a recognition that the moral blame, if there was any, for the breakdown of a marriage might not be coincident with the finding of guilt in the divorce suit. It followed that an adulterous wife might in justice be entitled to a larger award than the sustenance which, following the former Parliamentary practice, the divorce court had conceded to her. As ultimately established, the rule was stated to be:

> 'Nowhere...is there to be found any warrant for the view that a wife who had committed adultery thereby automatically loses her right to maintenance regardless of the other circumstances of the case.... In practice a wife's adultery may or may not disqualify her from succeeding in her application for maintenance and may or may not reduce the amount allotted. At one end of the scale her adultery may indeed disqualify her altogether. It may do so, for example, where it broke up the marriage, where it is continuing and where she is being supported by her paramour. At the other end of the scale, her adultery will not disqualify her and have little, if any, influence on the amount' (*Iverson v Iverson* [1967] P 134, [1966] 1 All ER 258).

Nevertheless, the discretionary nature of the jurisdiction gave ample opportunity to judges so inclined to take an idiosyncratic view on these matters.

The Divorce Reform Act 1969 altered completely the conceptual basis of divorce (see Chapter 4, above). Necessarily, the preconceptions inherent in the legal status of the husband and the wife, especially in relation to the doctrine of unity and the concept of lifelong support obligation unless the wife committed a matrimonial offence – all this could no longer form the underlying philosophy of a marriage. At the same time, there was awareness that in reality, certainly in conventional marriages and perhaps also in dual career marriages a wife's performing the 'domestic chores' *was* a significant contribution in its own right towards the resultant value of the family assets. There was also a view, although perhaps it did not play a major role in the reform, that marriage itself was a substantial impediment to a woman's self-sufficiency in many cases. All this resulted in the enactment of the Matrimonial Proceedings and Property Act 1970. That Act permitted all financial orders to be made in favour of either husband or wife, enabling the court to rearrange all the couple's assets through periodical payments (secured and unsecured), lump sum payments and property adjustment orders.

5.3 THE EVOLUTION OF THE STATUTORY PROVISIONS

The Matrimonial Proceedings and Property Act 1970 was consolidated in the Matrimonial Causes Act 1973. The Act set out detailed guidelines to assist the court in the exercise of its powers. These guidelines were simply that; for the basic philosophy inherent in the Act was to permit a broad discretion within the framework of the legislative target. Section 25 provided that it was the duty of the court to:

> ...exercise those powers [so] as to place the parties, so far as it is practicable and, having regard to their conduct, just to do so, in the financial position in which they would have been if the marriage had not broken down and each had properly discharged his or her financial obligations and responsibilities towards the other.

The Law Commission, in their discussion paper *The Financial Consequences of Divorce: the Basic Policy* (1980), identified four specific complaints about this objective:

(A) Inconsistency With the Modern Law of Divorce

> 24. A fundamental complaint is, we think, that the underlying principle of the law governing the financial consequences of divorce is inconsistent with the modern divorce law. The law (it is said) now permits either party to a marriage to insist on a divorce, possibly against the will of the other party, regardless of the fact that the other party may have honoured every conceivable marital commitment. Why (it is asked), if the status of marriage can be dissolved in this way, should the financial obligations of marriage nevertheless survive – particularly in cases where divorce has been forced on an unwilling partner, or where a wholly innocent partner is required to support one whose conduct has caused the breakdown? Instead (it is argued), divorce ought to provide a 'clean break' with the past in economic terms as well as in terms of status, and, so far as possible, encourage the parties to look to the future rather than to dwell in the past.

(B) Hardship for Divorced Husbands

25. We have been told that the continuing financial obligations imposed by divorce often cause severe economic hardship for those who are ordered to pay, normally of course the husband. It is not uncommon for a man to be ordered to pay as much as one-third of his gross income to his ex-wife until she either remarries or dies, and to be deprived of the matrimonial home (which may well represent his only capital asset) at least during the minority of the children. Unless she remarries this obligation to maintain an ex-wife can put divorced husbands under financial strain not only over a very long period of years but even into retirement. The obligation to maintain an ex-wife is particularly resented if the husband feels that it is his wife who is really responsible for the breakdown of the marriage; and such feelings are further exacerbated where he believes that his ex-wife has either chosen not to contribute toward her maintenance by working, or has elected to cohabit with another man, who might be in a position to support her but whom she has decided not to marry so as not to be deprived of her right to maintenance from her first husband.

(C) Hardship for Second Families

26. ...Particular resentment seems to be felt by men who have remarried after a divorce, and by their second wives. The burden of continuing to provide for a first wife can involve financial deprivation for a man who does not remarry, but the burden may well be acute if he remarries and has a second family. In such cases the impoverishment caused by the first wife's continuing claim upon her husband may well fall on all the members of his new family. ...In particular the effect on a man's second wife is a frequent source of comment. It is claimed that she is invariably forced to accept a reduced standard of living by reason of the fact that part of her husband's income is being diverted to support his first wife; it is also claimed that a second wife may be forced, notwithstanding family commitments, to work, even although her husband's first wife, who possibly has no family commitments, chooses not to do so. Indeed some second wives have told us that they feel that they are being required personally to support their husband's first wife because the courts take a second wife's resources into account when assessing a husband's financial circumstances and his capacity to make periodical payments to a former spouse.

(D) Hardship Suffered by Divorced Wives

27. ...There is no doubt that many divorced wives feel that the law still fails to make adequate provision for them. Not only is the starting point for assessing the provision to be made for a divorced wife only one-third [see *Wachtel v Wachtel* [1973] Fam 72, [1973] 1 All ER 829, CA] (as opposed to one-half) of the parties' joint resources, but in practice divorced wives often face great difficulty in enforcing any order which the court has made. The law, it is true, requires that so far as practicable, the wife should be kept in the position she would have been in had the marriage not broken down, but, as the Finer Committee remarked in 1974, private law is not capable of providing the 'method of extracting more than a pint from a pint pot'. We have seen that economic realities often make it difficult for a husband to provide for his second family. The same economic factors also make it difficult for him to provide for his former wife. ...

One particular aspect of the debate still relevant today is the question of whether married women are justified in looking primarily to their husbands for support if their marriages break down. After all, so the argument goes, emphasis is now placed on equality of opportunity for men and women, and it is indeed a fact that most women are employed outside the home for at least some period during their married lives. The argument was forcefully presented by Ruth Deech over thirty years ago. We quote here from 'The Principles of Maintenance' (1977):

> For some time now there have been available to married women reliable contraception, education and full legal status. Legislation provides for equal opportunities and equal pay: 40% of the working force of employees are female, of whom two-thirds are married and 85% of married women have been in employment at some time during their marriage. But the concept of female dependency on the male continues to permeate the maintenance laws and in addition the comparatively recent state pensions and tax provisions are based on sexual stereotypes of the husband as provider and the wife as full-time housekeeper and child-rearer. This legal supposition of female dependency tends to deny freedom of choice to married and formerly married persons; it is widely considered degrading to women and it perpetuates the common law proprietary relationship of the husband and wife even after divorce. While they express the superiority of the male the maintenance laws are at the same time an irritant to the increasing number of divorced men who have always to be able to provide and who suffer the perpetual drain on their income represented by a former wife. Maintenance awards are emotionally charged with the desire on the part of the wife for retribution and by their nature are unlikely to be readily enforceable because of the hostility surrounding their creation and the fact that the ex-husband is paying money without getting anything in return.

Deech concluded by stating that maintenance should be rehabilitative and a temporary measure confined to spouses who are incapable of work because of infirmity or child care.

QUESTION

Do women have equal opportunities and equal pay (see Chapter 3)?

A different view was presented by Katherine O'Donovan in 'The Principles of Maintenance: An Alternative View' (1978):

> Whilst it cannot be denied that laws based on sexual stereotypes are undesirable and ought to be eliminated what both Deech and Gray (1977) fail to see is that the current organisation of family life is premissed on the assumption that one partner will sacrifice a cash income in order to rear children and manage the home. The dependence of the non-earning spouse on the wage-earner is inevitable under present family arrangements. This leads in turn to inequality of earning power of spouses. Without a major change in social and family structures the Deech or Gray proposals merely serve to perpetuate an already unfair situation and will not ensure equality.
>
> ...
>
> ... The idea of a family wage adequate to support a wife and children with the addition of child benefit has been built into wage structure since the nineteenth century. So the expectation of society is that a wife's work is covered by her husband's wages. On divorce, without maintenance, the housewife will have little or no income from wage-earning and no National Insurance benefits to fall back on. If she does get a job, as already pointed out, her earning ability will be low.

For the majority of couples there will be a period in their marriage when their major asset, other than possible ownership of the matrimonial home, is the earning ability of the husband. This is why the law gives dependants a right of support after [divorce], and not the fact that they are parasites – as suggested by Deech. ...

Ruth Deech's argument is ultimately against marriage itself. If the spouse who undertakes housekeeping and child care should not consider marriage as (in part) an alternative career to one which is economically productive, then the answer is either not to marry, or to engage in paid work during marriage. But society does not seem ready for marriages in which both spouses work full-time. The present provision for nursery and pre-school facilities is inadequate. Children are prone to illness and are naturally dependent. Schools are not open for a full working day. And at present there is high unemployment. Participation in the workforce is not necessarily the answer, where there are young children; at least not without major changes in society, with the provision of communal laundries, cheap family restaurants, full-time nurseries etc. And male work attitudes would have to change to enable fathers to share equally in child care functions. It seems unlikely that this will happen. Deech argues that mothers with children should receive maintenance on divorce, and that it is only those who could earn who should be deprived. But withdrawal from the labour market at any time, current or past, affects earning ability, and it is fair that this diminution in earning ability be shared by both spouses.

Carol Smart, in *The Ties That Bind* (1984), pointed to the difficulty of both positions in the context of a feminist viewpoint:

The question that proponents on either side of this debate have posed is, 'Should individual husbands support their ex-wives after divorce?' This question does not allow for a 'feminist answer' as such because whichever side of the debate a woman supports she does a disservice to feminist arguments. Basically feminists have argued for the financial independence of women, hence dependency on men either during or after marriage is recognised as a major problem. But equally feminists have argued for a recognition of the value of domestic labour which benefits not only the state but also individual men. Hence it can be argued that if domestic labour has a value to both the state and individual men, *both* should recompense the woman who has lost material benefits whilst individual men and the state have been reaping them. If we consider these conflicting principles within the existing framework of family law there is no satisfactory solution. Abolishing maintenance for ex-wives does not give women their financial independence, it just means that even more women have to rely on inadequate supplementary benefit [income support] (assuming they cannot work outside the home or cannot earn a living wage). On the other hand arguing that individual men should pay for their privileges ignores the fact that many simply cannot afford to pay. But in addition this argument has the deleterious effect of containing the 'problem' within the private sphere, with the consequence that women's dependency remains a private issue and a personal conflict, and does not become a matter of public policy. It is an untenable situation for feminists *precisely* because the original question was framed outside feminist priorities.

QUESTIONS

i. O'Donovan argues that Deech's argument is ultimately against marriage itself. Can her argument on maintenance in her 1977 article be reconciled with her views on divorce law reform (see p. 171, above), and if so, how?

ii. Should an able-bodied house-husband be expected to support himself after divorce?
iii. What do you suppose Carol Smart means by the phrase 'feminist priorities'?

What does the divorced person on the Clapham omnibus think about this? Davis, Cretney and Collins, in *Simple Quarrels* (1994), record an interview with one couple which revealed the following disagreement:

> For example, Mrs Merton did not consider that she should be expected to work to support the children post-divorce given that Mr Merton had not wanted her to work whist they were married.... Mr Merton on the other hand made a very clear distinction between his wife's working when they were married and her doing so once they had separated. According to Mr Merton: 'There's no reason, other than her own choice, why she cannot get work and help to support herself. The marriage is over. The children are looked after. I don't see why she should, for the rest of her days, sit down on her bum. I've provided and supported her all these years. She's going to have to support herself now – we're no longer married. And as far as I'm concerned I'm not, morally, legally, or in any other way, obliged to keep her at the level I did when I was responsible for her because I was married to her.'

The authors identify a number of 'folk myths' which make for a gulf between the parties' thinking and the lawyer's assumptions:

- The man's belief that it is his money because he has earned it.
- The presumption of a 50:50 split (the authors comment that this is hardly a myth in Scotland, where it is the principle upon which Scots law is based; and we might add that it is the basis of division of the spousal community of property throughout Europe).
- The man's reluctance to pay maintenance on the basis that his former wife and children are provided for by the state.
- The belief that 'conduct', especially in opting to terminate the marriage, should have a bearing upon the financial resolution.

QUESTIONS

i. Why are these 'folk myths' so prevalent?
ii. Do you think it desirable that the law reflect people's perceptions and expectations in this context?

In Part IV of their discussion paper, *The Financial Consequences of Divorce: the Basic Policy* (1980), the Law Commission described seven models which might form the basis of a law to govern the financial consequences of divorce. These are discussed as separate options, and more briefly in combination. It should be recalled that the Commission was dealing mainly with the parties' finances and only incidentally with reallocation of their property. We summarise below the major characteristics of each model:

Model 1: Retention of Section 25 of the Matrimonial Causes Act 1973

59... Whilst it is true that the failure of the Act to give any indication of the weight to be attached to any particular circumstance, or indeed to 'the circumstances' as a whole, can make it difficult for practitioners to advise clients on how a case is likely to be decided, it is claimed that any such disadvantage is more than outweighed by the advantage to be gained from the court having a discretion which cannot only be adapted to the infinitely varied facts of each case (which can be foreseen neither by a judge nor by the legislature) but also to changing social circumstances. Moreover, in this view it is not only inevitable, but indeed desirable, that it should be left to case law to provide the coherent but evolving guidance on how to deal with such specific problems...

Model 2: Repeal of the Direction to the Court in Section 25 to Seek to Put the Parties in the Financial Position in Which They Would Have Been Had the Marriage Not Broken Down

66... We consider the most fundamental issue raised by the present controversy over section 25 to be whether or not it is desirable to retain the principle of life-long support which that section seems to embody. It might therefore be argued that the simplest solution to the criticisms of the present law would be for Parliament to repeal the specific direction at the end of section 25(1), but otherwise to leave the section intact; the court would simply be directed to make whatever order it considered appropriate in the light of all the circumstances, including the circumstances listed in sub-sections (*a*) to (*g*) of section 25(1). This would enable the courts to adopt a flexible approach, taking into account not only all the relevant individual circumstances of the parties, but also changing economic factors such as the availability of housing and changing attitudes to the proper purpose of financial provision....

Model 3: The Relief of Need

70. Under this model, the economically weaker party would be eligible to receive financial assistance from the economically stronger party if, and so long as, he or she could show that, taking into account his or her particular social and economic conditions, there is actual need of such assistance. The principle adopted would thus be one of individual self-reliance: after a marriage had broken down neither of the parties would have any automatic right to support, but rather only a qualified right insofar as it could be justified by special circumstances....

Model 4: Rehabilitation

73... The concept of rehabilitative financial provision has been explained in a recent American case as:

'sums necessary to assist a divorced person in regaining a useful and constructive role in society through vocational or therapeutic training or retraining, and for the further purpose of preventing financial hardship on society or the individual during the rehabilitative process' *Mertz v Mertz* (1973, 287 So 2d 691 at 692).

The onus is therefore firmly placed on the spouse in receipt of a rehabilitative award to take steps to become self-sufficient, and in this respect we think that such an approach might often result in the wife having to accept a significantly lower standard of living after divorce than that which she enjoyed before. . . .

75. . . The rehabilitative period might be limited by statute, to a maximum of two or three years or to the duration of some course of training, or it might lie in the discretion of the court. . . .

Model 5: The Division of Property – the 'Clean Break'

77. The essence of this model is the analogy of partnership. Where a partnership is dissolved, the partnership property is divided amongst the partners and that is the end of the matter. This, it is said, should also be the case where a marriage is dissolved . . . The principle might be adopted in one of a number of forms. At the one extreme it would involve no continuing financial relationship between ex-spouses: their rights and duties inter se would be resolved at the time of the divorce by dividing the matrimonial property between them. Such division might involve using a fractional approach (e.g. both parties would be entitled to half of the property available for distribution) or it might reflect some other principle such as the 'rehabilitative' or 'needs' models suggested above. Alternatively, the division might be effected solely on the basis of the court's discretion in each individual case. However, other variations on the basic theme that the financial consequences of divorce ought to be resolved by means of a division of the matrimonial property might also be possible. Thus a law based on this model might provide, for instance, for a delay in the division where the matrimonial home is needed to accommodate a growing family, or for additional payments of maintenance on a rehabilitative or needs basis. . . .

Model 6: A Mathematical Approach

80. . . On this approach the spouses' financial rights and duties inter se on divorce would be resolved by reference to fixed mathematical formulae which might then be adjusted to take into account particular factors such as the care of children or the length of the marriage. The result, it is said, would be two-fold. First, the parties and their legal advisers would in most cases be able to save time and money by negotiating a settlement in the knowledge that it accurately reflected current practice. Secondly, adjudicators would be able to decide cases in an entirely consistent fashion. . . .

Model 7: Restoration of the Parties to the Position in Which They Would Have Been had Their Marriage Never Taken Place

84. On this view . . . the court should seek to achieve 'not the position which would have resulted if the marriage had continued, but the position which would have occurred if the marriage had

never taken place at all'. The model is therefore a guiding principle, and might be carried into effect either by imposing an obligation to make periodical payments or by a once and for all division of the parties' capital (or a combination of both) which would be designed to compensate the financially weaker spouse for any loss incurred through marriage. . . .

A Combination of Models

86. . . It might be argued however that many of the problems which could result if a particular model were to be adopted as the sole governing principle might be avoided if the law were to be based on a combination of these models. For instance, elements of the needs or rehabilitative approaches could be used to temper some of the difficulties that might arise if the division of property model were to be adopted by itself. Alternatively it would no doubt be possible, whilst maintaining the main structure of the existing law, to amend the guidelines at present contained in section 25, so as to direct the court's attention more specifically to certain matters, for example the possibility that a wife should be expected to rehabilitate herself after divorce.

In *The Financial Consequences of Divorce* (1980), the Law Commission made the following recommendation:

17. We have come to the conclusion that the duty now imposed by statute to seek to place the parties in the financial position in which they would have been if the marriage had not broken down is not a suitable criterion; and in our view it should be removed from the law.

The Report went on to recommend that the guidelines in section 25(1) should be revised to give greater emphasis: (a) to the provision of adequate financial support for children which should be an overriding priority, and (b) to the importance of each party doing everything possible to become self-sufficient. The latter should be formulated in terms of positive principle and weight should be given to the view that, in appropriate cases, periodical financial provision should be primarily concerned to secure a smooth transition from the status of marriage to the status of independence. Thus, of the models advanced in the discussion paper, the English report argues for the retention of a discretion-based framework.

The proposals were introduced into law by the Matrimonial and Family Proceedings Act 1984 replacing the old section 25 and adding a new section 25A of the Matrimonial Causes Act 1973:

25. Matters to Which Court is to Have Regard in Deciding How to Exercise its Powers Under SS 23, 24 and 24A

(1) It shall be the duty of the court in deciding whether to exercise its powers under section 23, 24, 24A or 24B above and, if so, in what manner, to have regard to all the circumstances of the case, first consideration being given to the welfare while a minor of any child of the family who has not attained the age of eighteen.

(2) As regards the exercise of the powers of the court under section 23(1)(a), (b) or (c), 24, 24A or 24B above in relation to a party to the marriage, the court shall in particular have regard to the following matters—

(a) the income, earning capacity, property and other financial resources which each of the parties to the marriage has or is likely to have in the foreseeable future, including in the case of earning capacity any increase in that capacity in which it would in the opinion of the court be reasonable to expect a party to the marriage to take steps to acquire;
(b) the financial needs, obligations and responsibilities which each of the parties to the marriage has or is likely to have in the foreseeable future;
(c) the standard of living enjoyed by the family before the breakdown of the marriage;
(d) the age of each party to the marriage and the duration of the marriage;
(e) any psychical or mental disability of either of the parties to the marriage;
(f) the contributions which each of the parties has made or is likely in the foreseeable future to make to the welfare of the family, including any contributions by looking after the home or caring for the family;
(g) the conduct of each of the parties, if that conduct is such that it would in the opinion of the court be inequitable to disregard it;
(h) in the case of proceedings for divorce or nullity of marriage, the value to each of the parties to the marriage of any benefit (for example, a pension) which, by reason of the dissolution or annulment of the marriage, that party will lose the chance of acquiring.

...

25A. Exercise of Court's Powers in Favour of Party to Marriage on Decree of Divorce or Nullity of Marriage

(1) Where on or after the grant of a decree of divorce or nullity of marriage the court decides to exercise its powers under section 23(1)(a), (b) or (c), 24, 24A or 24B above in favour of a party to the marriage, it shall be the duty of the court to consider whether it would be appropriate so to exercise those powers that the financial obligations of each party towards the other will be terminated as soon after the grant of the decree as the court considers just and reasonable.

(2) Where the court decides in such a case to make a periodical payments or secured periodical payments order in favour of a party to the marriage, the court shall in particular consider whether it would be appropriate to require those payments to be made or secured only for such term as would in the opinion of the court be sufficient to enable the party in whose favour the order is made to adjust without undue hardship to the termination of his or her financial dependence on the other party.

(3) Where on or after the grant of a decree of divorce or nullity of marriage an application is made by a party to the marriage for a periodical payments or secured periodical payments order in his or her favour, then, if the court considers that no continuing obligation should be imposed on either party to make or secure periodical payments in favour of the other, the court may dismiss the application with a direction that the applicant shall not be entitled to make any future application in relation to that marriage for an order under section 23(1)(a) or (b) above.

One further important step in the evolution of the statute was the addition of the power to make various orders relating to pensions, and in particular pension-sharing.

Until 1995 the courts had no power to divide pensions on divorce; pensions were in effect a 'divorce-proof asset'. True, section 25(2)(h) requires the court to have regard to 'the value to each of the parties to the marriage of any benefit (for example, a pension) which, by reason of the dissolution or annulment of the marriage, that party will lose the chance of acquiring', but without the power to adjust the pension fund itself, that provision was often meaningless. Maggie Rae, in her article 'Pensions and Divorce: Time for Change' (1995), explained:

> This produces unfair results in a significant number of cases. Take for instance the couple who divorce in their early fifties when the children have grown up. The wife may not have worked for a decade or more while the children were young and after that only worked part-time. If she has a pension at all it will only be a small one, and much smaller than her husband's. In happier times both of them looked forward to a secure old age. Divorce changes all of that. Suddenly the wife finds herself unsure of what the future will bring. In the ensuing division of the assets, the family's largest potential asset cannot be the subject of division by the court. Widows' pensions and entitlements to death in service benefits are also affected and also outside the court's jurisdiction.
>
> In this family, as in many others the decision that the wife should stay at home and then only work part-time, was one taken jointly – a family decision. The only fair way to look at this couple's pension provision is as a joint family asset. In some marriages that treatment would not necessarily be right. Nonetheless it ought to be available.

In 1992 the Pensions Management Institute (PMI) set up a working group, in conjunction with the Law Society; its report, *Pensions and Divorce*, was published in May 1993. The report summarised the possible ways of dealing with pensions on divorce as follows:

> We have looked at four ways of reallocating the value of pension rights when divorce takes place before the pension comes into payment:
>
> (*a*) pension rights continue undisturbed but their value is taken into account – any reallocation of resources between the couple is made by adjustment of non-pension assets;
>
> (*b*) earmarking – pension rights continue undisturbed, but a specified amount of whatever benefit eventually becomes payable to or in respect of the scheme member is earmarked for payment direct to the former spouse when the time comes;
>
> (*c*) pension splitting within a scheme – a scheme member's pension rights are reduced by the specified amount mentioned in (*b*), and the resources so released are used to provide, within the scheme, a package of benefit rights for the former spouse as an entirely separate member of the scheme;
>
> (*d*) transfer – a scheme member's pension rights are reduced as in (*c*), and the resources so released are made available to the former spouse in the form of a transfer payment to another pension arrangement.
>
> Method (*a*) is in use at present, particularly in Scotland, but it is effective only if there are adequate non-pension assets, and there are difficulties in comparing the value of pension assets, which enjoy favourable tax treatment, with the value of other assets. Methods (*b*), (*c*) and (*d*) would need changes in the law. We favour method (*d*)....
>
> In addition, the working group favoured the earmarking approach (*b*), coupled with life assurance, in cases where the marriage broke down after retirement.

QUESTIONS

i. Can you see why method (b) is appropriate if divorce takes place once the pension is in payment?

ii. Can you see why changes in the law were required to put methods (b), (c) and (d) into effect?

iii. Which of these methods might you prefer if you were (a) the payer or (b) the payee?

Following amendments in 1995 and 1996, all the above options are now available; option (d) is known as pension sharing. There have now been just a few cases about pension earmarking and pension sharing. As to the former, see *T v T* [1998] 1 FLR 1072, [1998] 2 FCR 364. Inevitably, valuation is complex and difficult; see *Martin-Dye v Martin-Dye* [2006] EWCA Civ 681, [2006] 4 All ER 779.

It is clear that pension splitting and pension earmarking involve very difficult financial considerations and are not for the arithmetically challenged. Equally difficult are the moral/practical problems. At what point is one trying to achieve fairness? At the point of separation? At the time of the hearing? For the foreseeable future? Until death? Until those questions are answered, we suggest, it is not possible to develop a coherent approach to pension earmarking or sharing.

Equally, it may be impossible to get this right until we have taken more seriously the consequences, for women, of child-bearing and divorce. In 'Do divorced women catch up in pension building?' (2002), Jay Ginn and Debbie Pearce argue that even the present legislation does not do enough to compensate women for what they have lost as a result of the termination of the marriage, because divorced and separated women are not able to catch up:

> Despite the general rise in women's employment, mothers' employment rates remain substantially less than for childless women. Over 85% of British women who have ever married have had children, generally restricting their employment while children are young. Despite the Government's national childcare strategy, the constraint on mothers' hours of paid employment remains far more severe in Britain than in those European countries where affordable quality child care services are widely available. In Britain, the net cost of child care for an average income family with two children under the age of three was 28% of their income, compared with 9% in France, 11% in Denmark and 16% in Sweden. The UK system of subsidising child care through tax credits to low income families has fuelled demand for limited services, so that the cost of a nursery place for a child aged under two has rocketed, typically to £120 per week nationally and nearly £150 per week in inner London. For a lone parent, the cost of paying for child care while employed and travelling is generally prohibitive. Many partnered mothers find it impossible to manage full-time employment, but for divorced/separated mothers living alone, the lack of a partner to share the care of the children or to help pay for market child care makes full-time employment even more difficult.
>
> Part-time employment, a common strategy used by partnered mothers, may bring no financial gain to lone mothers, compared with claiming means-tested income support. Moreover, part-time employment is of limited value in pension building. Part-timers are less likely than full-timers to have access to an occupational pension; most part-timers, therefore, lack the advantage of an employer's contribution to their pension. Many part-timers earn below the lower earnings limit for national insurance, so will not be required to contribute to SERPS or a contracted out private pension. Even part-timers who earn above this threshold are unlikely to be able to contribute more than the minimum required. Where part-timers do contribute to an occupational or personal pension, their typically low earnings generate only small pension entitlements. As

a result, their eventual retirement income may be insufficient to exceed the means-tested minimum income guarantee. In this case, their efforts will have been wasted, as they will fall foul of the pensions poverty trap and gain no financial benefit from their investment. Whether this perverse outcome occurs depends, of course, on the duration of part-time employment, the level of earnings and the quality of the pension scheme.

Summary and Conclusions

Women's ability to earn and build... pensions is substantially less than men's and leads to the well-known concentration of poverty among older women. However, divorced/ separated women fare worse than other women in later life, with only a low proportion receiving any income from a private pension and a high likelihood of dependence on means-tested benefits.

...

This research indicates both the need and the scope for pension transfers from ex-husbands to ex-wives through the Pensions and Welfare Act of 1999. However, despite misleading media reports, the Act does not give divorcing women the right to a share of their husband's pension, only the right to argue they should have such a share as part of an overall financial settlement. For owner-occupier couples, past practice has been to allow divorcing mothers to keep the family home while husbands keep their pensions, which are often crudely seen as of comparable value. Since the housing needs of children in the ten years following divorce will remain a priority, the practice of offsetting home against pension may continue, limiting the effectiveness of the legislation in protecting divorced women from poverty-level incomes in retirement.

Even if divorced women with children were routinely awarded half of their husband's pension entitlement at the date of divorce, which would certainly help, substantial disparities in retirement income would remain between ex-spouses. While men are able to earn and accumulate a good pension after the divorce, the constraints on the divorced mother's employment and pension building continue. If the debate about fairness in ancillary relief cases is really about achieving equity between divorcing spouses, then it should encompass the longer-term effects of motherhood in reducing lone mothers' earning capacity, and the fact that a money purchase pension started only in mid-life has insufficient time to mature into a reasonable pension.

QUESTION

Look again at the information given in Chapter 3 (at p. 112) about women in the legal profession. If the typical working patterns of mothers are important to society, how can women be compensated (whether or not they are divorced) for their inadequate pension provision?

5.4 THE SEARCH FOR PRINCIPLE

So there we have it: guidelines in section 25, the possibility of a clean break in section 25A, and the details of what can actually be ordered in sectionc 23, 24, 25B and 25C. Note that what can be *achieved* in the context of a court order is wider than this, because one or both parties may undertake to do something that the court cannot actually order; for example, to make mortgage repayments or to purchase an annuity. An undertaking is enforceable in the same way as an order, ultimately by committal. A package of complex and flexible restructuring of the family's finances can be put together. But to what end are the courts aiming?

Peter Singer QC, as he then was, in his address to the Family Law Bar Association in 1992 (reproduced in 'Sexual Discrimination in Ancillary Relief' (2001)), explained how the courts developed objectives to fill this legislative gap, and asked:

> ... have we misapplied the true legislative intent... in s 25 of the Matrimonial Causes Act 1973? The question may be: what is wrong, in an appropriate case, with equal division as a starting-point? Even though English law has no history or tradition of a regime of community of property.
>
> ... [In section 25 t]here was to be heard for the first time that litany of considerations to which the court was to have specific regard when considering all the circumstances of the case. There was that unattainable objective, since struck from the score, to place the parties as far as practicably and justly could be achieved in the financial position in which they would have been if the marriage had never broken down and each had properly discharged his or her financial obligations and responsibilities towards the other. For all the difficulties it engendered, at least the phrase cumbrously encapsulated an objective to be aimed at, whereas now the amended section could be said to sound aimlessly, purposelessly.

A Wrong Turning?

Of the specific considerations, the two most significant for present purposes are (b) 'financial needs, obligations and responsibilities' and (f) 'contributions'.

The first of these provisions enjoins the court to have regard to: 'the financial needs, obligations and responsibilities which each of the parties to the marriage has or is likely to have in the foreseeable future'. Note please, in particular, how it is the needs of *each of them* to which regard is to be had.

The point at which things may have started to go seriously awry was at [1982] Fam 17, at p 25B, where in the course of his judgment in *Preston v Preston* Ormrod LJ dissected some general propositions out of the specimens he had collected from the meagre body of Court of Appeal authority which then existed on 'big money' cases under the new law.

The second of his propositions related to the word 'needs' in the s 25 phrase quoted above. Ormrod LJ picked up some strands from previous decisions and equated the word 'needs' with the phrase 'reasonable requirements'.

The next stage was for everyone to focus upon that phrase as though it was the wife's reasonable requirements alone which were relevant, and which should be the touchstone of the relief she receives. The syllogism is then completed when the wife is awarded enough for her reasonable needs *and no more*, even though liquidity is not an issue and the husband is left with far more than he reasonably needs.

That is what I suggest may be the first example of unintentional sexual – it is almost rather 'social' – discrimination. The subliminal shift forcing new concepts into old stereotypes, where the expectation was that the former wife would be, as it were, pensioned off with an allotment sufficient to meet her requirements, a dowager put out to graze.

The next of the *Preston* principles, enunciated at p 25, relates to the consideration that:

'the powers of the court ought not to be exercised for the benefit of adult children, by enabling the wife to set up a child in business, *S v S*; or to provide by will for a child who is unlikely to benefit under the husband's will or otherwise, *Page v Page*.'

> I shall be asking you to consider whether that principle is justified by anything in the statute, and whether it may not in any event have been extended in a way for which the statutory language provides no justification whatsoever....
>
> The next of the *Preston* principles I would ask you to analyse critically by reference to the section is this:
>
> 'active participation by the wife either by working in the business or by providing finance, will greatly enhance her contribution to the welfare of the family under paragraph (f) [of s 25(1)], and may lead to a substantial increase over and above her 'reasonable requirements' [that catch-phrase again]. This, in effect, recognises that she has 'earned' a share in the total assets, and should be able to realise and use it *as she chooses*.'
>
> ...Nowhere in the statutory language, if we could read the words afresh and unblinkered by the historical perspective, would we collect the concepts that the court's assessment of the wife's needs would be the limiting factor confining her award, even in a case where liquid assets might be superabundantly available still after both her and the husband's needs, generously assessed, had been met; that the income-producing element of her award should be consumed during her lifetime so as to leave nothing over on her death; but that she might be treated more generously had she contributed financially than if she had not.

Things changed dramatically in October 2000, when the House of Lords gave its judgment in *White v White* [2001] 1 AC 596, [2000] 3 WLR 1571. The Whites were farmers and had carried on business in partnership for many years; but most of the assets were held by Mr White. Of total assets of around £4 million, Mrs White recovered £800,000 at first instance, and £1.5 million by the Court of Appeal (to add to property held in her sole name worth nearly £200,000). Elizabeth Cooke, in '*White v White*: a new yardstick for the marriage partnership' (2002) observes:

> The Court of Appeal's decision rests on the fact of the business partnership between two partners. What of the spouse who is not legally a partner, as Mrs White was, but makes just as much practical contribution to the business? Will the courts be astute to spot that contribution? And what of the wife who has no opportunity to engage in the family business – she has not the skills, or she and her husband have, in happier times, been well content for her to be the homemaker? There seems no room in the Court of Appeal's decision for any value to be given to that contribution so as to take her beyond her 'reasonable requirements'; in such a case the businessman is still left with the lion's share.

The legal profession waited on tenterhooks for the House of Lords' decision in *White*. Negotiations, and lives, were put on hold. There was a feeling that this case was going to be different, partly because of the momentum of concern that had built up over the 'reasonable needs' approach, and partly because this case stood out as one where that approach was unfair. When the House of Lords gave its decision, lawyers hungry for new law were not disappointed, although Mrs White herself probably was. The following is from the judgment of Lord Nicholls of Birkenhead:

> My Lords, Divorce creates many problems. One question always arises. It concerns how the property of the husband and wife should be divided and whether one of them should continue to support the other. Stated in the most general terms, the answer is obvious. Everyone would accept that the outcome on these matters, whether by agreement or court order, should be fair. More realistically, the outcome ought to be as fair as is possible in all the circumstances. But everyone's life is different. Features which are important when assessing fairness differ in

each case. And, sometimes, different minds can reach different conclusions on what fairness requires. Then fairness, like beauty, lies in the eye of the beholder.

So what is the best method of seeking to achieve a generally accepted standard of fairness? Different countries have adopted different solutions. Each solution has its own advantages and disadvantages. One approach is for the legislature to prescribe in detail how property shall be divided, with scope for the exercise of judicial discretion added on. A system along these lines has been preferred by the New Zealand legislature, in the Matrimonial Property Act 1976. Another approach is for the legislature to leave it all to the judges. The courts are given a wide discretion, largely unrestricted by statutory provisions. That is the route followed in this country. The Matrimonial Causes Act 1973 confers wide discretionary powers on the courts over all the property of the husband and the wife. This appeal raises questions about how the courts should exercise these powers in so-called 'big money' cases, where the assets available exceed the parties' financial needs for housing and income. The powers conferred by the 1973 Act have been in operation now for 30 years. This is the first occasion when broad questions about the application of these powers have been considered by this House... It goes without saying that these principles should be identified and spelled out as clearly as possible.

His Lordship summarised the facts, and the decisions below, and went on:

Equality

Self-evidently, fairness requires the court to take into account all the circumstances of the case. Indeed, the statute so provides. It is also self-evident that the circumstances in which the statutory powers have to be exercised vary widely. As Butler-Sloss LJ said in *Dart v Dart* [1997] 1 FCR 21, 38–39, the statutory jurisdiction provides for all applications for ancillary financial relief, from the poverty stricken to the multi-millionaire. But there is one principle of universal application which can be stated with confidence. In seeking to achieve a fair outcome, there is no place for discrimination between husband and wife and their respective roles. Typically, a husband and wife share the activities of earning money, running their home and caring for their children. Traditionally, the husband earned the money, and the wife looked after the home and the children. This traditional division of labour is no longer the order of the day. Frequently both parents work. Sometimes it is the wife who is the money-earner, and the husband runs the home and cares for the children during the day. But whatever the division of labour chosen by the husband and wife, or forced upon them by circumstances, fairness requires that this should not prejudice or advantage either party when considering para (f), relating to the parties' contributions. This is implicit in the very language of para (f):

> '... the contribution which *each* has made or is likely to make to the *welfare of the family*, including any contribution by looking after the home or caring for the family.' (See s 25(2)(f). Emphasis added.)

If, in their different spheres, each contributed equally to the family, then in principle it matters not which of them earned the money and built up the assets. There should be no bias in favour of the money-earner and against the home-maker and the child-carer. There are cases, of which the Court of Appeal decision in *Page v Page* (1981) 2 FLR 198 is perhaps an instance, where the court may have lost sight of this principle. A practical consideration follows from this. Sometimes, having carried out the statutory exercise, the judge's conclusion involves a more or less equal division of the available assets. More often, this is not so. More often, having looked at all the circumstances, the judge's decision means that one party will receive a bigger share than the other. Before reaching a firm conclusion and making an order along these lines, a judge would always be well-advised to check his tentative views against the yardstick of equality of division. As a general guide, equality should be departed from only if, and to the extent that, there is good reason for doing so. The need to consider and articulate reasons for departing from equality would help the parties and the court to focus on the need to ensure the absence of discrimination. This is not to introduce a presumption of equal division under another guise. Generally accepted standards of fairness in a field such as this change and develop, sometimes quite radically, over comparatively short periods of time. The discretionary powers, conferred by Parliament 30 years ago, enable the courts to recognise and respond to developments of this sort. These wide powers enable the courts to make financial provision orders in tune with current perceptions of fairness. Today there is greater awareness of the value of non-financial contributions to the welfare of the family. There is greater awareness of the extent to which one spouse's business success, achieved by much sustained hard work over many years, may have been made possible or enhanced by the family contribution of the other spouse, a contribution which also required much sustained hard work over many years. There is increased recognition that, by being at home and having and looking after young children, a wife may lose for ever the opportunity to acquire and develop her own money-earning qualifications and skills ... In the exercise of these discretions 'the law is a living thing moving with the times and not a creature of dead or moribund ways of thought'. Despite these changes, a presumption of equal division would go beyond the permissible bounds of interpretation of s 25. In this regard s 25 differs from the applicable law in Scotland. Section 10 of the Family Law (Scotland) Act 1985 provides that the net value of matrimonial property shall be taken to be shared fairly between the parties to the marriage when it is shared equally or in such other proportions as are justified by special circumstances. Unlike s 10 of the Family Law (Scotland) Act 1985, s 25 of the 1973 Act makes no mention of an equal sharing of the parties' assets, even their marriage-related assets. A presumption of equal division would be an impermissible judicial gloss on the statutory provision. That would be so, even though the presumption would be rebuttable. Whether there should be such a presumption in England and Wales, and in respect of what assets, is a matter for Parliament. It is largely for this reason that I do not accept Mr Turner's invitation to enunciate a principle that in every case the 'starting point' in relation to a division of the assets of the husband and wife should be equality. He sought to draw a distinction between a presumption and a starting point. But a starting point principle of general application would carry a risk that in practice it would be treated as a legal presumption, with formal consequences regarding the burden of proof. In contrast, it should be possible to use equality as a form of check for the valuable purpose already described without this being treated as a legal presumption of equal division.

QUESTION

What do you understand to be the difference between a principle, a presumption, a starting point and a yardstick? (We are *not* suggesting that there is no difference, but would like you to consider how these different terms may be used.)

Lord Nichols went on to consider another issue:

Inherited Money and Property

I must also mention briefly another problem which has arisen in the present case. It concerns property acquired during the marriage by one spouse by gift or succession or as a beneficiary under a trust. For convenience I will refer to such property as inherited property. Typically, in countries where a detailed statutory code is in place, the legislation distinguishes between two classes of property: inherited property, and property owned before the marriage, on the one hand, and 'matrimonial property' on the other hand. A distinction along these lines exists, for example, in the Family Law (Scotland) Act and the (New Zealand) Matrimonial Property Act 1976. This distinction is a recognition of the view, widely but not universally held, that property owned by one spouse before the marriage, and inherited property whenever acquired, stand on a different footing from what may be loosely called matrimonial property. According to this view, on a breakdown of the marriage these two classes of property should not necessarily be treated in the same way. Property acquired before marriage and inherited property acquired during marriage come from a source wholly external to the marriage. In fairness, where this property still exists, the spouse to whom it was given should be allowed to keep it. Conversely, the other spouse has a weaker claim to such property than he or she may have regarding matrimonial property. Plainly, when present, this factor is one of the circumstances of the case. It represents a contribution made to the welfare of the family by one of the parties to the marriage. The judge should take it into account. He should decide how important it is in the particular case. The nature and value of the property, and the time when and circumstances in which the property was acquired, are among the relevant matters to be considered. However, in the ordinary course, this factor can be expected to carry little weight, if any, in a case where the claimant's financial needs cannot be met without recourse to this property.

Lord Nicholls concluded that the award made in the Court of Appeal was 'well within the ambit of the discretion which the Court of Appeal was exercising afresh'.

QUESTIONS

i. Given Lord Nicholls' reasoning, are you surprised by the result?
ii. How might the 'yardstick of equality' operate where the applicant spouse had contributed (see section 25(2)(f)) neither business activity nor homemaking?
iii. What might be the effect, if any, of *White* in a family where resources are scarce?
iv. Why should inherited property be treated differently?

White thus swept away a lot of the earlier case law, and made something of a fresh start. In doing so it raised lots of new issues; *White* was a relatively uncomplicated case where there were no dependant children and where it was relatively easy to regard the parties as equal partners. What was to be the effect of the new 'yardstick' where there were dependent children? How might it operate in a short marriage? And the Whites were not so rich as some of the couples who come before the higher courts; can the business partner argue that he or she has made so great a contribution that it could not possibly be equated with that of the homemaker?

As to that latter question, the answer evolved in cases such as *Lambert v Lambert* [2002] EWCA Civ 1685, [2003] Fam 103 was 'hardly ever'.

Thorpe LJ explained:

> [45] Having now heard submissions, both full and reasoned, against the concept of special contribution save in the most exceptional and limited circumstance, the danger of gender discrimination resulting from a finding of special financial contribution is plain. If all that is regarded is the scale of the breadwinner's success then discrimination is almost bound to follow since there is no equal opportunity for the homemaker to demonstrate the scale of her comparable success. Examples cited of the mother who cares for a handicapped child seem to me both theoretical and distasteful. Such sacrifices and achievements are the product of love and commitment and are not to be counted in cash. The more driven the breadwinner the less available will he be physically and emotionally both as a husband and a father. There is also some justification in Mr Mostyn's emphasis on the extent to which the homemaker frequently sacrifices her potential to generate assets by undertaking the domestic commitment to husband and children. At the same time she risks the outcome of failure and so earns her entitlement to share in the successful outcome.
> [46] In sum I am much more wary of the issue of special contribution than I was in writing my judgment in *Cowan v Cowan* [2001] EWCA Civ 679, [2002] Fam 97. Perhaps Chief Justice Nicholson, who seems poised to banish the phenomenon, may have found the better path. The circumstances set out in para 43 above allow this court to re-evaluate the whole issue. However for the present, given the infinite variety of fact and circumstance, I propose to mark time on a cautious acknowledgement that special contribution remains a legitimate possibility but only in exceptional circumstances. It would be both futile and dangerous to even attempt to speculate on the boundaries of the exceptional. In the course of argument I suggested that it might more readily be found in the generating force behind the fortune rather than in the mere product itself. A number of hypothetical examples were canvassed ranging from the creative artist via the superstar footballer to the inventive genius who not only creates but also develops some universal aid or prescription. All that seems to me to be more safely left to future case by case exploration.

Discussing both *White* and *Lambert* in 'The Family and the Law – Status or Contract' (2003) Stephen Cretney argues:

> It is thus perhaps not only an exaggeration to describe as 'revolutionary' the way in which the divorce courts exercised their virtually unfettered discretion under the divorce law reformed in 1969, but actually untrue. True, the wife's 'requirement' of housing would be met... (and she would, if it were practicable, get a share of the 'investment' in that housing). True, with the added incentive of legislative prioritising of the 'clean break' on divorce, the courts would often deal with the obligation to meet the wife's needs or requirements by a once-for-all order for the payment of a capital sum. But that sum was (under the, recently unfairly maligned, *Duxbury* principle) calculated by actuaries as being what was necessary to produce an appropriate level of spending power to support the wife's outgoings throughout her life. Crucially, there was to be no nonsense about an equal division of capital, of what our partners in continental Europe call the patrimony. Thus, Lord Denning (who... was – so it is widely believed – a judge of progressive and even radical attitudes) sternly rejected a wife's claim for a share in the £2 million or so proceeds of the take-over of the husband's family business. The wife did not give any active help in the business: 'She did not work in it herself. All she did was what a good wife does do. She gave moral support to her husband by looking after the home. If he was depressed or in difficulty, she

would encourage him to keep going'. That (said Lord Denning bluntly) does not give her any right to a share in the proceeds.

It seemed that if the wife was to get something from the proceeds of such apparently richly rewarding activities as making polystyrene cups or plastic waste sacks or producing 'free' newspapers, she had to show some distinctive 'contribution' *to that activity* – perhaps not as closely related to it as would be required to establish in the Chancery Division the existence of an implied resulting or constructive trust, but certainly something going beyond what we may call a housekeeper role. Far from 'revolutionary' change, the underlying objective had (notwithstanding the efforts, judicial and extra-judicial, of some judges to break away from the 'reasonable requirements' ceiling) remained substantially unchanged virtually throughout the twentieth century. And, as recently as 1996, the Court of Appeal declared that only legislation could displace the 'reasonable requirements' principle.

The Breakthrough – Community of Property by Judicial Decision?

There were some who did not find this outcome either fair or reasonable. After all, if marriage is a partnership, surely the starting point of partnership law – that profits are to be equally divided – should apply. Eventually, in *White v White* the House of Lords tentatively opened the door to a different approach. But the decisive step was taken by the Court of Appeal in *Lambert v Lambert*; deciding when a marriage is ended by divorce the court will (after making provision for the family's housing and other needs – an important qualification entailing, perhaps, the consequence that 'equality' will in practice apply only to the wealthy) divide up the spouses' property so that each has an equal share. Mrs Lambert was thus to have £20 million, rather than the seven and a half awarded at first instance. Of course, there would be exceptional cases. For example, have the assets been acquired by inheritance or gift? What if the marriage is a second or third marriage? And there may be other circumstances in which the matters specified in Matrimonial Causes Act 1973, section 25(2) – the source of the powers which the courts exercise on divorce – may dictate some modification (for example, if the relationship has only been short: see Matrimonial Causes Act 1973, section 25(2)(d)). And there may also be some 'wholly exceptional' cases in which it can legitimately be claimed that the 'fairness', which is the ultimate criterion, requires recognition of one spouse's 'special contribution' to the welfare of the family to be given by allotting less than one half of the family fortune to the homemaker. But the general principle is clear and the change is remarkable. Because in substance (albeit not in form) English law now has, by virtue of judicial decision rather than legislation, a matrimonial regime of community of property (albeit only deferred community) limited to acquisitions.

QUESTION

Look back at Chapter 3 (p. 132). Do we now have community of property, albeit in a deferred form, as practised in Scandinavia for example?

Elizabeth Cooke, in 'Miller/McFarlane: law in search of discrimination' (2007) thinks not:

> The introduction of the yardstick of equality made it inevitable that comparisons would be drawn with community of property systems, where equal division of a defined pot of property is the rule. Community of property is a spectrum; European community systems encompass different ranges of property, they confer differing levels of freedom to contract out of the default regime of an individual's country, and there are varying levels of discretion at the margins. Should we now say that section 25 of the Matrimonial Causes Act 1973 creates a community of property system?
>
> It is suggested that we should not. Some aspects are simply absent: no European community of property system is without a statutory definition of non-matrimonial property; none is without the means for couples to contract out of community. In none is the separate property of the individuals available for division as part of the capital pot. In only a few instances is there a special régime for short marriages, and these are clearly defined. Otherwise it is a matter of degree – none involves a broad discretion for the courts to depart from equality. The system we have is not one which a European lawyer would recognise as a matrimonial régime.

The conjoined appeals in *Miller v Miller; McFarlane v McFarlane* [2006] UKHL 24, [2006] 2 AC 618 concerned two very different couples. The Millers had been married for three years, and the issue was the share Mrs Miller should take from Mr Miller's business fortune of at least £15 million and arguably twice that figure. The McFarlanes were both high earners until Mrs McFarlane gave up her job to look after their children. In the McFarlanes' case there was not sufficient capital to achieve a clean break, and the issue was how much Mrs McFarlane should receive by way of periodical payments. The House of Lords confirmed Mrs Miller's lump sum award of £5 million; and while the Court of Appeal had awarded Mrs McFarlane periodical payments for a limited period of five years, the House of Lords substituted an award of periodical payments until further order. Lord Nicholls of Birkenhead enunciated the principles lying behind section 25 as follows:

> [4] Fairness is an elusive concept. It is an instinctive response to a given set of facts. Ultimately it is grounded in social and moral values. These values, or attitudes, can be stated. But they cannot be justified, or refuted, by any objective process of logical reasoning. Moreover, they change from one generation to the next. It is not surprising therefore that in the present context there can be different views on the requirements of fairness in any particular case.
>
> ...
>
> [8] For many years one principle applied by the courts was to have regard to the reasonable requirements of the Claimant, usually the wife, and treat this as determinative of the extent of the Claimant's award. Fairness lay in enabling the wife to continue to live in the fashion to which she had become accustomed. The glass ceiling thus put in place was shattered by the decision of your Lordships' House in the *White* case. This has accentuated the need for some further judicial enunciation of general principle.
>
> [9] The starting point is surely not controversial. In the search for a fair outcome it is pertinent to have in mind that fairness generates obligations as well as rights. The financial provision made on divorce by one party for the other, still typically the wife, is not in the nature of largesse. It is not a case of 'taking away' from one party and 'giving' to the other property which 'belongs' to the former. The Claimant is not a suppliant. Each party to a marriage is *entitled* to a *fair* share of the available property. The search is always for what are the *requirements* of fairness in the particular case.

[10] What then, in principle, are these requirements? The statute provides that first consideration shall be given to the welfare of the children of the marriage. In the present context nothing further need be said about this primary consideration. Beyond this several elements, or strands, are readily discernible. The first is financial needs. ...

[11] This element of fairness reflects the fact that to greater or lesser extent every relationship of marriage gives rise to a relationship of interdependence. The parties share the roles of money-earner, home-maker and child-carer. Mutual dependence begets mutual obligations of support. When the marriage ends fairness requires that the assets of the parties should be divided primarily so as to make provision for the parties' housing and financial needs, taking into account a wide range of matters such as the parties' ages, their future earning capacity, the family's standard of living, and any disability of either party. Most of these needs will have been generated by the marriage, but not all of them. Needs arising from age or disability are instances of the latter.

[12] In most cases the search for fairness largely begins and ends at this stage. In most cases the available assets are insufficient to provide adequately for the needs of two homes. ...

[13] Another strand, recognised more explicitly now than formerly, is compensation. This is aimed at redressing any significant prospective economic disparity between the parties arising from the way they conducted their marriage. For instance, the parties may have arranged their affairs in a way which has greatly advantaged the husband in terms of his earning capacity but left the wife severely handicapped so far as her own earning capacity is concerned. Then the wife suffers a double loss: a diminution in her earning capacity and the loss of a share in her husband's enhanced income. This is often the case. Although less marked than in the past, women may still suffer a disproportionate financial loss on the breakdown of a marriage because of their traditional role as home-maker and child-carer.

[14] When this is so, fairness requires that this feature should be taken into account by the court when exercising its statutory powers. ...

[15] Compensation and financial needs often overlap in practice, so double-counting has to be avoided. But they are distinct concepts, and they are far from co-terminous. A Claimant wife may be able to earn her own living but she may still be entitled to a measure of compensation.

[16] A third strand is sharing. This 'equal sharing' principle derives from the basic concept of equality permeating a marriage as understood today. Marriage, it is often said, is a partnership of equals. ... This is now recognised widely, if not universally. The parties commit themselves to sharing their lives. They live and work together. When their partnership ends each is entitled to an equal share of the assets of the partnership, unless there is a good reason to the contrary. Fairness requires no less. But I emphasise the qualifying phrase: 'unless there is good reason to the contrary'. The yardstick of equality is to be applied as an aid, not a rule.

[17] This principle is applicable as much to short marriages as to long marriages: see *Foster v Foster* [2003] EWCA Civ 565, [2005] 3 FCR 26, [2003] 2 FLR 299, 305, para 19 per Hale LJ. A short marriage is no less a partnership of equals than a long marriage. The difference is that a short marriage has been less enduring. In the nature of things this will affect the quantum of the financial fruits of the partnership.

... To confine the *White* approach to the 'fruits of a long marital partnership' would be to re-introduce precisely the sort of discrimination the *White* case [2001] 1 AC 596 was intended to negate.

...

[20] For the same reason the courts should be exceedingly slow to introduce, or re-introduce, a distinction between 'family' assets and 'business or investment' assets. ... The rationale underlying the sharing principle is as much applicable to 'business and investment' assets as to 'family' assets.

Matrimonial Property and Non-matrimonial Property

[21] A complication rears its head at this point. I have referred to the financial fruits of the marriage partnership. In some countries the law draws a sharp distinction between assets acquired during a marriage and other assets. In Scotland, for instance, one of the statutorily prescribed principles is that the parties should share the value of the 'matrimonial property' equally or in such proportions as special circumstances may justify. Matrimonial property means the matrimonial home plus property acquired during the marriage otherwise than by gift or inheritance: Family Law (Scotland) Act 1985, ss 9 and 10. In England and Wales the Matrimonial Causes Act 1973 draws no such distinction. By s 25(2)(a) the court is bidden to have regard, quite generally, to the property and financial resources each of the parties to the marriage has or is likely to have in the foreseeable future.

[22] This does not mean that, when exercising his discretion, a judge in this country must treat all property in the same way. The statute requires the court to have regard to all the circumstances of the case. One of the circumstances is that there is a real difference, a difference of source, between (1) property acquired during the marriage otherwise than by inheritance or gift, sometimes called the marital acquest but more usually the matrimonial property, and (2) other property. The former is the financial product of the parties' common endeavour, the latter is not. The parties' matrimonial home, even if this was brought into the marriage at the outset by one of the parties, usually has a central place in any marriage. So it should normally be treated as matrimonial property for this purpose. As already noted, in principle the entitlement of each party to a share of the matrimonial property is the same however long or short the marriage may have been.

[23] The matter stands differently regarding property ('non-matrimonial property') the parties bring with them into the marriage or acquire by inheritance or gift during the marriage. Then the duration of the marriage will be highly relevant. ...

[24] In the case of a short marriage fairness may well require that the Claimant should not be entitled to a share of the other's non-matrimonial property. The source of the asset may be a good reason for departing from equality. This reflects the instinctive feeling that parties will generally have less call upon each other on the breakdown of a short marriage.

[25] With longer marriages the position is not so straightforward. Non-matrimonial property represents a contribution made to the marriage by one of the parties. Sometimes, as the years pass, the weight fairly to be attributed to this contribution will diminish, sometimes it will not. After many years of marriage the continuing weight to be attributed to modest savings introduced by one party at the outset of the marriage may well be different from the weight attributable to a valuable heirloom intended to be retained in specie. Some of the matters to be taken into account in this regard were mentioned in the above citation from the *White* case. To this non-exhaustive list should be added, as a relevant matter, the way the parties organised their financial affairs.

Flexibility

...

[28] I must mention a further matter where flexibility is important. In big money cases, the capital assets are more than sufficient to meet the parties' financial needs and the need for either party to be compensated when one party's earning capacity has been advantaged at the expense of the other party. In these cases, should the parties' financial needs and the requirements of compensation be met first, and the residue of the assets shared? Or should financial needs and compensation simply be subsumed into the equal division of all the assets?

[29] There can be no invariable rule on this. Much will depend upon the amounts involved. Generally a convenient course might be for the court to consider first the requirements of compensation and then to give effect to the sharing entitlement. If this course is followed provision for the parties' financial needs will be subsumed into the sharing entitlement. But there will be cases where this approach would not achieve a fair outcome overall. In some cases provision for the financial needs may be more fairly assessed first along with compensation and the sharing entitlement applied only to the residue of the assets. Needless to say, it all depends upon the circumstances.

Periodical Payments and the Clean Break Principle

[30] So far I have been almost entirely concerned with lump sum payments as distinct from periodical payments. I have therefore made only passing mention of an important principle now embodied in the statute: the clean break principle. This principle is relevant in the McFarlane appeal. Two issues arise in this regard. The first concerns the reach of periodical payments orders. The question is whether periodical payments orders may be made for the purpose of providing compensation as distinct from maintenance.

[31] I see no difficulty on this point. There is nothing in the statutory ancillary relief provisions to suggest Parliament intended periodical payments orders to be limited to payments needed for maintenance. . . .

[32] In particular, I consider a periodical payments order may be made for the purpose of affording compensation to the other party as well as meeting financial needs. It would be extraordinary if this were not so.

. . .

[35] This leads me to the second issue regarding periodical payments orders. It concerns the impact of the clean break principle on periodical payment orders made to provide compensation to a disadvantaged party.

. . .

[38] In one respect the object of s 25A(1) is abundantly clear. The subsection is expressed in general terms. It is apt to refer as much to a periodical payments order made to provide compensation as it is to an order made to meet financial needs. But, expressly, s 25A(1) is not intended to bring about an unfair result. Under s 25A(1) the goal the court is required to have in mind is that the parties' mutual financial obligations should end as soon as the court considers just and reasonable.

[39] Section 25A(2) is . . . concerned with the termination of one party's 'financial dependence' on the other 'without undue hardship'. These references to financial dependence and hardship are apt when applied to a periodical payments order making provision for the payee's financial needs. They are hardly apt when applied to a periodical payments order whose object is to furnish compensation in respect of future economic disparity arising from the division of functions adopted by the parties during their marriage. If the Claimant is owed compensation, and capital assets are not available, it is difficult to see why the social desirability of a clean break should be sufficient reason for depriving the Claimant of that compensation.

Baroness Hale of Richmond (with whom the majority in the House of Lords agreed) said:

[144] Thus far, in common with my noble and learned friend, Lord Nicholls of Birkenhead, I have identified three principles which might guide the court in making an award: need (generously interpreted), compensation, and sharing. I agree that there cannot be a hard and fast rule about

whether one starts with equal sharing and departs if need or compensation supply a reason to do so, or whether one starts with need and compensation and shares the balance. Much will depend upon how far future income is to be shared as well as current assets. In general, it can be assumed that the marital partnership does not stay alive for the purpose of sharing future resources unless this is justified by need or compensation. The ultimate objective is to give each party an equal start on the road to independent living.

QUESTION

Do you agree that this encapsulates the ultimate objective of ancillary relief?

Baroness Hale took a different, and broader, view of the nature of non-matrimonial property:

[149] The question, therefore, is whether in the very big money cases, it is fair to take some account of the source and nature of the assets, in the same way that some account is taken of the source of those assets in inherited or family wealth. Is the 'matrimonial property' to consist of everything acquired during the marriage (which should probably include periods of pre-marital cohabitation and engagement) or might a distinction be drawn between 'family' and other assets?... Prime examples of family assets of a capital nature were the family home and its contents, while the parties' earning capacities were assets of a revenue nature. But also included are other assets which were obviously acquired for the use and benefit of the whole family, such as holiday homes, caravans, furniture, insurance policies and other family savings. To this list should clearly be added family businesses or joint ventures in which they both work. It is easy to see such assets as the fruits of the marital partnership. It is also easy to see each party's efforts as making a real contribution to the acquisition of such assets. Hence it is not at all surprising that Mr and Mrs McFarlane agreed upon the division of their capital assets, which were mostly of this nature, without prejudice to how Mrs McFarlane's future income provision would be quantified.

[150] More difficult are business or investment assets which have been generated solely or mainly by the efforts of one party. The other party has often made some contribution to the business, at least in its early days, and has continued with her agreed contribution to the welfare of the family (as did Mrs Cowan). But in these non-business-partnership, non-family asset cases, the bulk of the property has been generated by one party. Does this provide a reason for departing from the yardstick of equality? On the one hand is the view, already expressed, that commercial and domestic contributions are intrinsically incommensurable. It is easy to count the money or property which one has acquired. It is impossible to count the value which the other has added to their lives together. One is counted in money or money's worth. The other is counted in domestic comfort and happiness. If the law is to avoid discrimination between the gender roles, it should regard all the assets generated in either way during the marriage as family assets to be divided equally between them unless some other good reason is shown to do otherwise.

[151] On the other hand is the view that this is unrealistic. We do not yet have a system of community of property, whether full or deferred. Even modest legislative steps towards this have been strenuously resisted. Ownership and contributions still feature in divorcing couples' own perceptions of a fair result, some drawing a distinction between the home and joint savings accounts,

on the one hand, and pensions, individual savings and debts, on the other...Some of these are not family assets in the way that the home, its contents and the family savings are family assets. Their value may well be speculative or their possession risky. It is not suggested that the domestic partner should share in the risks or potential liabilities, a problem which bedevils many community of property regimes and can give domestic contributions a negative value. It simply cannot be demonstrated that the domestic contribution, important though it has been to the welfare and happiness of the family as a whole, has contributed to their acquisition. If the money maker had not had a wife to look after him, no doubt he would have found others to do it for him. Further, great wealth can be generated in a very short time, as the *Miller* case shows; but domestic contributions by their very nature take time to mature into contributions to the welfare of the family.

[152] My lords, while I do not think that these arguments can be ignored, I think that they are irrelevant in the great majority of cases. In the very small number of cases where they might make a difference, of which *Miller* may be one, the answer is the same as that given in *White v White* [2001] 1 AC 596 in connection with pre-marital property, inheritance and gifts. The source of the assets may be taken into account but its importance will diminish over time. Put the other way round, the court is expressly required to take into account the duration of the marriage: s 25(2)(d). If the assets are not 'family assets', or not generated by the joint efforts of the parties, then the duration of the marriage may justify a departure from the yardstick of equality of division. As we are talking here of a departure from that yardstick, I would prefer to put this in terms of a reduction to reflect the period of time over which the domestic contribution has or will continue (see Bailey-Harris, 'Comment on *GW v RW (Financial Provision: Departure from Equality)*' [2003] Fam Law 386, at p 388) rather than in terms of accrual over time (see Eekelaar, 'Asset Distribution on Divorce – Time and Property' [2003] Fam Law 828). This avoids the complexities of devising a formula for such accruals.

[153] This is simply to recognise that in a matrimonial property regime which still starts with the premise of separate property, there is still some scope for one party to acquire and retain separate property which is not automatically to be shared equally between them. The nature and the source of the property and the way the couple have run their lives may be taken into account in deciding how it should be shared. There may be other examples. Take, for example, a genuine dual career family where each party has worked throughout the marriage and certain assets have been pooled for the benefit of the family but others have not. There may be no relationship-generated needs or other disadvantages for which compensation is warranted. We can assume that the family assets, in the sense discussed earlier, should be divided equally. But it might well be fair to leave undisturbed whatever additional surplus each has accumulated during his or her working life. However, one should be careful not to take this approach too far. What seems fair and sensible at the outset of a relationship may seem much less fair and sensible when it ends. And there could well be a sense of injustice if a dual career spouse who had worked outside as well as inside the home throughout the marriage ended up less well off than one who had only or mainly worked inside the home.

QUESTIONS

i. Do you think that when the House of Lords in *White* introduced the 'yardstick of equality', it did so in the interests of compensating the parties for their equal contributions, or in the interests of the principle of sharing? (See Cooke (2007).)

ii. Would you prefer to see a formula for the accrual over time of one partner's entitlement to the other's wealth? Note John Eekelaar's comments (2003): 'A distinction should be drawn between equal *value* and equal *worth*. Food and water are of equal worth for human sustenance, but a thimbleful of water is not of equal value to a bakery full of bread' so that 'an immediate 50% share of some highly valued after-acquired property could amount to an overvalue of the other spouse's contribution in some circumstances'.

iii. Suppose the assets of a couple amount to £2 million, and the needs of the parties to £200,000 and £800,000 respectively. How is the court to decide whether to meet needs first and then share the surplus, or to share the assets knowing that needs will thereby be met? How, if at all, would your answer differ if the assets were worth £10 million? (Look at what Lord Nicholls says at paragraph [28].)

iv. Would you agree with Nicholas Mostyn QC in *Rossi v Rossi* [2006] 3 FCR 271 at [10] that 'In all cases now a primary function of the court is to identify the matrimonial and non-matrimonial property'?

v. How would you explain to a wealthy client how to identify his non-matrimonial property?

vi. In *Charman v Charman* [2007] EWCA Civ 503 Sir Mark Potter, P, said:

> 'To what property does the sharing principle apply?... We consider...that, subject to the exceptions identified in *Miller* [relating to short marriages]...the principle applies to all the parties' property but, to the extent that the property is non-matrimonial, there is likely to be better reason for departure from equality.'

Is that consistent with what the House of Lords said in *Miller/McFarlane*?

5.5 ANCILLARY RELIEF AT THE GRASS ROOTS

When considering the effect of the legislation upon real families in the throes of reorganising and rebuilding their lives after divorce, we have to bear in mind that in the majority of cases no order is made for financial provision, and that, of the orders made, most are by consent.

In 'The declining number of ancillary financial relief orders' (2000), Chris Barton and Alastair Bissett-Johnson, by an analysis of the judicial statistics, assessed how prevalent the do-it-yourself option had become, and asked:

> [W]hy is it that only a minority of divorces now leads to money and property orders? One suspects many petitions, at least, have ticks in the AFR [Ancillary Financial Relief] application boxes. Yet there are a number of factors which may go some way to explaining the shortfall. They include remarriage, no assets other than local authority housing, and a literal recourse to private ordering. ...But perhaps there are two major factors. The first is the number of short-marriage, child-free divorces involving parties who had not built up much equity in their – anyway equally owned – family home: a young couple with similar salaries where no claim is likely to succeed. Finally, the drop since 1993 may mean that in those cases which previously attracted token spousal PPOs tacked on to child maintenance orders, the financially badly off parent is simply not issuing proceedings (perhaps as an adjunct to DIY divorce).

> Is this declining usage a welcome trend? On the face of it, some spouses are acting like cohabitants in giving up their divorce rights.... What would happen (today) if one of them, not to mention the taxpayer, later regrets her inaction? The Children Act 1989 plus the Child Support Acts 1991–95 would take care of her children and, under s 26 of the Matrimonial Causes Act 1973 she could seek leave to apply for herself. Whilst there are no statistics on the use of s 26, anecdotal evidence suggests that recourse is rare: how many would-be – unremarried – applicants know about it? Whatever the explanation for the falling numbers of ancillary financial relief orders, the decline does not seem to be worrying the parties. Perhaps the essential point of all these figures is the drive towards settlement; positive because of non-adversarial lawyers and mediators and negative because of the prohibitive costs for some people.

It seems, then, that the majority of those for whom the law of ancillary relief is intended manage their financial settlements without recourse to the courts, by choice or by (financial) necessity. The theory is that these people are influenced by what the courts *would* do if the issue were litigated. Equally, in practice, people must be influenced by the sort of folk myths that Davis, Cretney and Collins identified (above, p. 207) and that we have all heard from our friends or read in the newspapers. Anyone who reads section 25 for guidance as to what they should do will, as we have seen, be none the wiser due to the lack of statutory objective. In Chapter 4 we looked at mediation, and we know that differing levels of advice and help are available to those who do not litigate. Even where solicitors are involved, there is evidence that negotiation is a chaotic process. Davis, Cretney and Collins' book *Simple Quarrels* (1994) was researched some time before *White* and many of the bargains they observed would now work differently; but the negotiation process must remain very much the same:

> This was how Mr Daniels's solicitor assessed the situation when we first spoke to him:
>
> > 'Let's just say the equity is £42,000 – it's probably a bit more – as a starting point, two thirds/one-third – automatic starting point. So if we divide that, that comes to about £14,000 for him, taking one third. We know that she can raise £16,000, so I will immediately go to the chap on the other side, and perhaps ask for... I'll ask for £16,000, hoping I'll end up with £14,000, and then I can sell it to Mr Daniels and say: "Look, that's what the court will give you." I may be wrong here, because I think if I were him [the other solicitor] I'd come back and say: "Look, in normal circumstances I can see the approach you're adopting, but here we have [handicapped son] who is different, and this is a complication. We can't say, but [son] could put off somebody wanting to marry my client, [son] could really stop her getting full-time work, [son] may be a liability until he's 25–30, he may need a home for the rest of his life." I've said to Mr Daniels already: "Don't be too sure that you're going to get something."'
>
> Whilst this solicitor could not predict the final outcome (Mr Daniels's barrister agreed a lump sum of £7,500, in fact) and whilst he recognized and to some extent relished the bargaining element in the negotiation, he none the less regarded it as bargaining within narrow limits. The fact that there was an element of uncertainty did not dissuade him from making proposals....
>
> Many solicitors with whom we discussed this point likewise implied, or revealed in their case management, that as far as they were concerned the outcome of ancillary relief proceedings was wholly unpredictable. It was almost as if legal doctrine had no impact upon the actual administration of family law. This was the view of one solicitor, based in Newport:
>
> > 'I suppose it's a terrible reflection of how many things are done on the basis of nothing more than rough horse-trading, with only a very passing shadow of reference to case law.

When one reads the models, the ways in which you should really deal with financial relief, they are so technical and so precise. In 999 cases out of a thousand it's all down to a wing and a prayer and what you can deal with off the back of a truck.'

Those who bargain like this are unlikely to have to worry about stellar contributions or non-matrimonial property. Here we look at some issues that are likely to come to their attention, namely public funding, conduct, housing and the clean break; then we look at patterns of outcomes.

5.5.1 PUBLIC FUNDING

Where the family as a whole has limited resources, it is unlikely that an application will come to trial; still less likely that the case will be reported. In many typical cases the family's only or main asset is the matrimonial home, and we consider later the way the courts deal with this.

In other cases, however, the applicant has limited resources but is seeking a share of his or (usually, still) her spouse's wealth. She may well need help with the cost of legal advice. Public funding is available, subject, as ever, to a means test. Where funding has been granted, we have to consider the application of the statutory charge. Here is an extract from the leaflet, *Paying for your Legal Aid*, produced by the Legal Services Commission, explaining the operation of the charge:

The Statutory Charge

If you had legal aid, and the result of your case is that you kept or gained property or money, you will probably have to pay back some or all of the costs of your case.

The money we spent on your legal costs will therefore act as a loan, and you will have to repay it.

The Commission is under a legal obligation to recover what it has spent on a case where someone has kept or gained property or money. The statutory charge is the name given to how we recover the money we have spent. It is a charge, or claim, on your money or property made by law.

...

4. How You Can Repay Your Legal Aid

If you have gained or kept money, any money you are awarded at the end of the case is normally paid to your solicitor.

When your bill has been assessed, we take what we have spent on your solicitor, and give you what's left. We use any contributions you made to pay towards your solicitor's bill. The example below explains this:

Example

Mr A had legal aid for his divorce. Mr A and his wife each owned half of their house. Although Mr A wanted the house put in his name, his wife did not agree. At the end of the case, the judge decided that Mr A should have ownership of all of the house. Mr A has therefore gained half a house, and according to the rules explained above, he will have to repay the cost of his legal representation.

Damages awarded by the Court: £10,000
Solicitor's Costs: £5,000
Minus contributions paid by you: £2,000
Total Amount you have to pay towards your solicitor's bill: £3,000
You receive: £7,000

If you recover money, and wish to buy a home with this money, we may be able to let you pay back our charge later. We will register a charge on your new property to make sure you repay the money eventually. But we cannot do this if you are able to repay at once without risking losing your home. Please contact your Regional Office for more information.

...

If you cannot repay the whole amount you owe, and ask to delay payment by having a charge on your property, simple interest will accrue on your debt. Simple interest means that the same sum of money is added to your debt each day.

The rate of interest is:
5% to 30 September 2005, then
8% from 1 October 2005.

Once a charge is registered, you will not be able to sell your home or borrow more money against it without first paying us the charge.

...

Methods of Repayment

If we have a charge on your home, you do not necessarily have to make payments towards it. Though in some cases we might ask that you do.

The charge will remain on your house, normally accruing interest, until such time as you sell your house, or you borrow money against your house and pay the outstanding sum owing to the Commission from the money you received through refinancing. You can make regular monthly contributions of £25 or more to reduce your debt. The Land Charge Department will be able to provide you with the necessary information on how to make regular payments.

QUESTIONS

i. Do you think the matrimonial home should be freed from the statutory charge?

ii. Do you think that the new rule that neither side can get costs from the other in ancillary relief cases (see Hatwood, 2007) will work to the advantage or disadvantage of the better or less well-off spouse?

5.5.2 CONDUCT

Section 25(2)(g) of the Matrimonial Causes Act 1973 states that the court shall have regard to the conduct of each of the parties if that conduct is such that it would in the opinion of the court be inequitable to disregard it. Sir George Baker P, in *W v W* [1976] Fam 107, [1975] 3 All ER 970, said that he would be entitled to take account of conduct in a case which would cause an ordinary mortal to throw up his hands and say: 'Surely that woman is not going to be given any money!'

The problem with Sir George Baker's words is that 'ordinary mortals' *are* ordinary mortals, and might throw up their hands in cases where the judges would not. Look, yet again, at the 'folk myths' on p. 207. In particular, Mrs Miller (see above, p. 222) argued that her husband's conduct in bringing the marriage to an end was conduct that it would be inequitable to disregard. The judge at first instance agreed with her, as did the Court of Appeal; yet it seemed that conduct in that sense would not, previously, have been regarded as warranting the raising of judicial hands. The House of Lords restored the mainstream position, as Lord Nicholls of Birkenhead explains in *Miller v Miller; McFarlane v McFarlane* [2006] UKHL 24, [2006] 2 AC 618:

> [59] Next is the question of the parties' conduct. The relevance of the parties' conduct in financial ancillary relief cases is still a vexed issue. For many years now divorce has been based on the neutral fact that the marriage has broken down irretrievably. Some elements of the old concept of fault have been retained but essentially only as evidence of irretrievable breakdown. As already noted, parties are now free to end their marriage and then re-marry.
> [60] Despite this freedom, there remains a widespread feeling in this country that when making orders for financial ancillary relief the judge should know who was to blame for the breakdown of the marriage. The judge should take this into account. If a wife walks out on her wealthy husband after a short marriage it is not 'fair' this should be ignored. Similarly if a rich husband leaves his wife for a younger woman.
> [61] At one level this view is readily understandable. But the difficulties confronting judges if they seek to unravel mutual recriminations about happenings within the marriage, and the undesirability of their attempting to do so, have been rehearsed many times. In *Wachtel v Wachtel*, [1973] 1 All ER 113, [1973] 2 WLR 84, Lord Denning MR led the way by confining relevant misconduct to those cases where the conduct was 'obvious and gross'.

Lord Nicholls considered the history of the statutory provision and continued:

> [64] This history is well known. I have mentioned it only because there are signs that some highly experienced judges are beginning to depart from the criterion laid down by Parliament. In *G v G (Financial Provision: Separation Agreement)* [2004] 1 FLR 1011, 1017, para 34, Thorpe LJ said the judge 'must be free to include within [his discretionary review of all the circumstances] the factors which compelled the wife to terminate the marriage as she did'. This approach was followed by both courts below in the present case. Both the judge and the Court of Appeal had regard to the husband's conduct when, as the judge found, that conduct did not meet the statutory criterion. The husband's conduct did not rank as conduct it would be inequitable to disregard.
> [65] This approach, I have to say, is erroneous. Parliament has drawn the line. It is not for the courts to re-draw the line elsewhere under the guise of having regard to all the circumstances of the case. It is not as though the statutory boundary line gives rise to injustice. In most cases fairness does not require consideration of the parties' conduct. This is because in most cases misconduct is not relevant to the bases on which financial ancillary relief is ordered today. Where, exceptionally, the position is otherwise, so that it would be inequitable to disregard one party's conduct, the statute permits that conduct to be taken into account.

The House of Lords compared the exceptional nature of contributions that would warrant a departure from equality, with the exceptional nature of misconduct severe enough to be reflected in the court's order: Lord Mance said, at paragraph [164]: 'Conduct and contributions are in large measure opposite sides of a coin.'

QUESTIONS

i. Can you see why the courts take a narrow view of misconduct that it would be inequitable to disregard?

ii. Is that the same as the reason why the courts will not normally regard one party as having made a greater contribution than the other?

iii. How relevant do you think conduct should be?

iv. How often do you think that one party is wholly to blame for the break-up of a marriage?

5.5.3 HOUSING

Frequently the most significant problem in ancillary relief is: what is to be done with the matrimonial home? It may be retained, by one or both parties; it may be sold. One of the most flexible solutions is a device distinctive in English property law, in that it controls the use of land over time: it is known as the *Mesher* order:

Mesher v Mesher and Hall
(1973) [1980] 1 All ER 126n, Court of Appeal

The marriage took place in 1956 and the one child of the marriage (aged 9) lived with the mother. The house was in joint names. The judge ordered that the house be transferred to the wife, and the husband appealed.

Davies LJ:

... Counsel for the husband submits that it would be quite wrong to deprive the husband of the substantial asset which his half-interest in the house represents..., one has to take a broad approach to the whole case. What is wanted here is to see that the wife and daughter, together no doubt in the near future with Mr Jones [whom the wife intended to marry], should have a home in which to live rather than that she should have a large sum of available capital. With that end in view, I have come to the conclusion that counsel's submission for the husband is right. It would, in my judgment, be wrong to strip the husband entirely of any interest in the house. I would set aside the judge's order so far as concerns the house and substitute instead an order that the house is held by the parties in equal shares on trust for sale but that it is not to be sold until the child of the marriage reaches a specified age or with the leave of the court.

Harvey v Harvey
[1982] Fam 83, [1982] 1 All ER 693, [1982] 2 WLR 283, 126 Sol Jo 15, Court of Appeal

The parties were married in 1960. They had six children. The marriage broke down in 1979 and it was dissolved in May 1981. The judge made an order in the form used in *Mesher v Mesher*, namely that the home should be held in joint names of husband and wife on trust for sale in equal shares and that the sale of the property should be postponed until the youngest child attained 16 or completed her full-time education, whichever was later, when the wife should be at liberty to purchase the husband's share in the property at a valuation then made. The wife appealed.

Purchas J:

... I am of the opinion that the wife is entitled to live in this house as long as she chooses so to do,... I do that on the basis that was adopted in *Martin v Martin* [1978] Fam 12, [1977] 3 All ER 762, that, had the marriage not broken down, that is precisely what she would have been entitled to do.

I would vary the judge's order, first of all to say that the asset (the matrimonial home) be transferred into the joint names of the wife and the husband on trust for sale in the shares two-thirds to the wife and one-third to the husband; and further that such sale shall be postponed during the lifetime of the wife, or her remarriage, or voluntary removal from the premises, or her becoming dependent on another man. I have in mind that if she begins to cohabit with another man in the premises, then obviously that man ought to take over the responsibility of providing accommodation for her. Until one or other of those events occur, she should be entitled to continue to reside at these premises, but after the mortgage has been paid off, or the youngest child has reached the aged of 18, whichever is the later, she should pay an occupation rent to be assessed by the [district judge].

Ormrod LJ:

I agree. This is another case which illustrates very aptly the proposition which has been stated many times in this court, that the effect of making a *Mesher v Mesher* order is simply to postpone the evil day to avoid facing the facts now.

QUESTIONS

i. What do you think are the advantages and disadvantages of this solution? In *Carson v Carson* [1983] 1 All ER 478, [1983] 1 WLR 285, Ormrod LJ said that the facts of that case, where the judge had made the type of order in *Mesher v Mesher*, were 'a very good example of the chickens coming home to roost'. What exactly does he mean?

ii. Recall the statutory charge (p. 230). Where this is applicable, what difference will it make to the situation when those chickens come home?

iii. What effect do you think the child support legislation will have had upon the prevalence of *Mesher* orders?

iv. What might be the effect of the decisions in the 'big money' cases upon the division of the value of the property at the 'far end' of a *Mesher* order? For some important and disturbing findings see Lucinda Fisher, 'The unexpected impact of *White*' (2002).

v. Where a *Mesher* order is made, is it realistic for sale to be triggered the minute the youngest child leaves university? (See *A v A* in Chapter 6, p. 263, below.)

vi. Why should a new man take over responsibility of providing accommodation for an ex-wife remaining in the former matrimonial home?

vii. Assume the ex-wife is disabled and unable to contemplate moving out of a purpose-built bungalow which is the former matrimonial home. There are no children. Is her disability a sufficient reason by itself to transfer the matrimonial home into her name alone? (Read *Chadwick v Chadwick* [1985] FLR 606, [1985] Fam Law 96, CA.) What if the former spouse is terminally ill? (Consider *M v M (Property Adjustment: Impaired Life Expectancy)* [1993] Fam Law 521.)

There is jurisdiction to order the transfer of a private or council tenancy, if there is security of tenure, from one spouse to the other in a case where the marriage is terminated by divorce or a decree of nullity (Family Law Act 1996, Schedule 7). The court has the power to order the transfer, on granting a decree of divorce, nullity or judicial separation, or, with leave of the court, at any time thereafter. The landlord's consent is not required, but he does have a right to be heard before an order is made.

QUESTIONS

i. Do you think (a) that this provision is an unnecessary interference in the powers and responsibilities of local authorities to determine housing priorities in their area; or (b) that to allow a housing authority to reallocate the home before the judicial decision was made would prejudge the matter and hamper the ousted party's chances of having the children?

ii. There has been evidence that women are sometimes unable to obtain the children without housing and unable to obtain housing without the children. If this is correct, who should break this vicious circle, the court or the housing authority?

iii. What problems may be encountered by a man or woman who has left home because of violence? (Consider the issue of homelessness and intention, Chapter 7, below, p. 338.)

5.5.4 THE CLEAN BREAK

The doctrine of the clean break has emerged as a major target.

Minton v Minton
[1979] AC 593, [1979] 1 All ER 79, [1979] 2 WLR 31, 122 Sol Jo 843, House of Lords

In this case, the House of Lords collectively, and Lord Scarman in particular, stressed the requirement that the parties put the past behind them and begin a new life which is in no way overshadowed by a former relationship:

> ... There are two principles which inform the modern legislation. One is the public interest that spouses, to the extent that their means permit, should provide for themselves and their children. But the other – of equal importance – is the principle of 'the clean break.' The law now encourages spouses to avoid bitterness after family break-down and to settle their money and property

> problems. An object of the modern law is to encourage each to put the past behind them and to begin a new life which is not overshadowed by the relationship which has broken down. It would be inconsistent with this principle if the court could not make, as between the spouses, a genuinely final order unless it was prepared to dismiss the application. The present case is a good illustration. The court having made an order giving effect to a comprehensive settlement of all financial and property issues as between spouses, it would be a strange application of the principle of the clean break if, notwithstanding the order, the court could make a future order on a subsequent application made by the wife after the husband had complied with all his obligations.

QUESTIONS

i. Is Lord Scarman being cruel to be kind?

ii. Is the clean break approach consistent with the interests of the children?

iii. Purchas LJ described a 'clean break' in *Scallon v Scallon* [1990] FCR 911, [1990] 1 FLR 194, CA, as follows:

> Finally, I wish to say a word about 'clean break' which is a phrase which arises since the amendments to the 1973 Act were introduced to ensure that, where there were short-term marriages, one party should not get what is described as 'a meal ticket for life' upon the dissolution of such a marriage. Furthermore, it was to encourage spouses who hitherto had not earned their living to face up to the fact that after the dissolution they should earn their living.

But if the husband insisted that the wife remained at home during the marriage, is it really fair on her that she should now be encouraged to 'face up to the fact...that she should earn her living?' Perhaps it is too late?

Pamela Symes, in 'Indissolubility and the Clean Break' (1985) is sceptical:

> Present divorce is so often merely a readjustment of the former marital relationship. It results in the parties being released from the obligation to share bed and board but they are still saddled with the ongoing financial obligations of the marriage, not unlike judicial separation. Thus the licence to remarry is something of an illusion. In so many ways the parties are *not* free to remarry, as the evidence from numerous pressure groups will testify. Thus divorce, as granted in most cases, is only *a mensa et thoro* simply because most marriages are still indissoluble. True divorce *a vinculo matrimonii* can only be granted when, because the marriage is short, childless or the parties are sufficiently rich, the bond can be truly severed and a clean break imposed – the marriage is, by practical definition, dissoluble. This is because, at the time the reformed divorce law came into operation, we failed to introduce simultaneously the effective means whereby the *vinculum*, the marriage bond could be broken (*i.e.* the necessary changes in the infrastructure). The ongoing marriage tie is reflected in the continuing support obligation which is imposed – admittedly imposed but often not met... If the support obligation is met, there is financial strain where remarriage follows as limited resources are spread between two families; if it is ignored or only partly met, then usually the resort is to subsistence on state benefit for the first family.

This was the inevitable result of attempting the impossible, of trying to introduce divorce for indissoluble marriage. With the passing of the Matrimonial and Family Proceedings Act 1984 the clean break principle now has embryonic statutory form. While it remains unsupported by a reformed social policy it will at best be a non-event, at worst, it will simply open the way to more injustice and suffering. For only when a radical change in the marital relationship takes place, when it becomes a partnership of two economically independent individuals through the abolition of marital dependency and when the corresponding changes in the social infrastructure are brought about, will there be any chance of formulating a coherent, clean break divorce law.

Nevertheless, it seems that the emotional pull of the clean break is such that it may prevent proper consideration of other aspects of the financial situation. In a seminar paper, 'Settling Up: the views and values underpinning financial separation' (2000) Jane Lewis and Sue Arthur make the following points:

There were a number of important factors that shaped people's approach to reaching agreement about financial arrangements. One of the dominant factors was a pragmatic consideration of the financial needs of the two parties and the relative resources available to meet them. Children's needs were generally emphasised over and above the need of either parent. There was a greater emphasis on i) current rather than future need and resources, and ii) capital rather than income provision, for example a greater focus on the provision of a home than on the means to support the home.

There was a reluctance to see income as in any way joint following separation, except in relation to financial support for children, which was generally seen as a moral obligation. Items which had been funded out of the income of one partner also tended to be seen as no longer joint on separation, in the same way as items which had been inherited or acquired prior to the marriage. The clear exception here was the family home, where non-financial contributions (the running of the home, and caring for children) appeared to play a key role in a sense of entitlement. There were mixed views about the role that the assets or needs of new partners should play in a couple's financial division, and again differences in views about income and capital.

Underpinning these views were strong and widely held feelings about equality and a 'clean break'. An equal division was seen as an underlying principle, but one which did not apply in a range of circumstances. Interestingly, the idea of equality of *impact* did not appear to be important in influencing people's approach. The attribution of fault for instigating the break up of the relationship was another key factor underlying people's approaches to financial arrangements.

While some of these factors reflect the legal situation and others do not, it was notable that people's views did not appear to be based strongly in any knowledge or understanding of legal entitlement. Rather they were underpinned by pragmatism, emotional preferences, financial constraints, and moral principles or understandings (such as equal partnerships, or moral obligations to support children). Also interesting was the apparent lack of a systematic approach in applying these factors, for example in assessing needs, or in valuing all assets. ...

Pensions appeared not to have been taken into account in most of the cases involved in this study. They remained with the person in whose name they were held, but this was not seen as part of the arrangements or settlement and there was no compensation, offsetting or other provision for the future for the other party. People were sometimes not aware they had an entitlement to pension rights, or believed the values to be too low to consider, or were resistant to making a claim. The fact that the pension was derived from the husband's earnings appeared to remove any sense of entitlement, even though couples generally had shared access to the husband's earning during the marriage, and to the house which may have largely derived from them. ...

Ultimately, women – and to a lesser extent men with substantial caring responsibilities – traded off housing against income, capital and future provision.

QUESTION

Look back at the observations on pensions made by Jay Ginn and Debbie Pearce (p. 213, above); can you see any way to prevent women making this trade-off?

5.5.5 OUTCOMES

That takes us to a brief consideration of the financial provision that may be ordered or, more usually, negotiated. Clearly 'need', in some form, is a high priority, for the courts or for individuals negotiating. District Judge Roger Bird, in 'Ancillary relief outcomes' (2000), speaks of the 'hierarchy of needs' which the court will try to meet:

> Housing is normally the most important issue; the housing of the parent with care of the children normally takes priority over that of the other parent, although his/her needs must be met wherever possible. Once housing has been disposed of the reasonable needs of the parties should be considered. The clean break should only be imposed where there is no doubt that the parties will be self-sufficient. Attention must be given to pensions. Where the reasonable needs of the parties have been met there is no justification for further adjustment by the court.

That last sentence, of course, no longer holds good following *White*, but of course in so many cases there is no surplus to play with. What are 'reasonable needs'? They have to be placed somewhere between the basic subsistence needs for shelter and food that social security payments are designed to meet, and the standard of living enjoyed during the marriage. Jill Black, Jane Bridge, Tina Bond and Liam Gribbin, in *A Practical Approach to Family Law* (2007) explain:

> Needs and obligations vary from household to household. Invariably, however, spouses will need a roof over their heads and the spouse who has care of the children will have a particularly pressing need for a home for the family. This factor is likely to be of great importance in the court's decision. The court will also look at each party's regular outgoings (fuel bills, rent, council tax, water rates, mortgage, food, hire-purchase debts, payments following a maintenance calculation under the CSA 1991, etc) and take into account such as are reasonable for a person in his circumstances. What is reasonable will obviously vary from case to case – someone travelling a mile to work each day may be expected to use a bicycle or walk if money for the family is tight whereas a person who travels many miles in the course of his job can fairly expect to do so in a relatively comfortable car. The court's approach to each party's regular expenditure will have to be realistic – it may be wholly unreasonable for one party to be purchasing a video recorder on hire-purchase where the other party does not have even enough money for food, but, once the party has entered the commitment, there is very little that can be done about it and continuing obligation to pay will have to be taken into account.

The most large-scale of recent empirical projects was undertaken by a team led by Gwynn Davis at the University of Bristol. He and his colleagues (Julia Pearce, Roger Bird, Hilary Woodward and Chris Wallace) presented their findings in 'Ancillary relief outcomes' (2000); the picture (all of it, of course, pre-*White)* is, to say the least, complex:

Questions for This Study

We undertook this research because we felt we lacked detailed evidence of family financial circumstances matched to outcome in specific cases. We attempted, therefore, to analyse outcomes of ancillary relief applications by reference to specific case characteristics as reflected in the various documents on the court file. We wanted to describe the range of outcomes arrived at in respect of like cases, and to explore the reasons for such differences as emerged. Overall we were seeking to establish whether there was, broadly speaking, congruity of outcome in like circumstances; if not, why not; and whether decisions in leading cases determine settlements and lower court adjudications in the way everyone imagines...

Analysing Family Finances

In was necessary for us, in recording information from the court files, to develop systems of classification in order to try to make sense of what otherwise would have appeared a mass of detail. We divided the family financial information into five categories:

- family type;
- family home;
- other assets;
- husband's income;
- wife's income.

By family type we meant whether the couple had dependent children, and – if there were no dependent children – whether the marriage had been long or short. The breakdown amongst the 285 cases analysed is presented in Table 2 below. We would be the first to admit that this is a very crude (and limited) categorisation. In particular, to group together all those cases which involved dependent children is about as 'broad brush' as one could get – and only justifiable on the basis that the way that courts and lawyers approach these cases is similar to the extent that the children's interests, and in particular their need for a 'roof', will be the first consideration. But of course there is a vast difference between, say, having three children under five and having one teenager on the verge of financial independence (as the parents may fondly hope). Such differences will, of course, be reflected in the ancillary relief orders which are negotiated by lawyers or determined by the court. To that extent it is important to recognise in all that follows that our various categorisations greatly under-represent the complexities which are involved in arriving at a fair – or 'appropriate' – financial outcome in these cases.

As can be seen, 55% of the cases analysed involved dependent children; 22% involved short marriages (less than seven years), not producing children; and the other 23% either involved longer marriages without children, or, if children had resulted, they were no longer dependent.

Our second category of information concerned the family home. Here we distinguished cases in which (as far as we could discern) there was no home to assign, council tenancies; and three categories of private ownership, with the divisions being based on the amount of equity in the property. The breakdown amongst our 285 cases is contained in Table 3 below.

Table 2 Family type

Marriage up to seven years, no children	63	22%
Marriage over seven years, no children	27	9.5%
Marriage with dependent children	157	55%
Marriage with adult children (only)	38	13%
Total	285	

Table 3 Family home

Council tenancy	15	5%
Private (equity up to £5000)	64	22.5%
Private (equity £5000–£20,000)	77	27%
Private (equity over £20,000)	111	39%
No home to assign	18	6%
Total	285	

As can be seen, of the 285 cases, 252 (88.5%) included amongst the assets a privately owned family home. In many of these cases, as previously explained, the home would have been assigned *prior* to a consent application being filed. The three categories of equity were chosen simply on the basis that they generated three roughly equal divisions within the private ownership category. It is perhaps worthy of note that an equity of more than £20,000 was a feature of only 111 cases – which is just 39% of the total sample, or 44% of cases in which there was a privately owned home to assign. It has been observed that following the last Conservative administration's encouragement to local authority tenants to purchase their properties, and especially following house price inflation in the 1980s, many separating couples found themselves 'property rich but income poor'. Most of these divorcing couples were 'income poor', but the majority do not appear 'property rich'.

Our third category was that of 'other assets' – savings in any form, including insurance policies and pension entitlement. As can be seen from Table 4 (below), in over 50% of cases these 'other assets' totalled, as far as we could judge from the file, less than £5000. Just over one-quarter of our sample had assets (other than the family home) in excess of £20,000. Given the inevitable tendency for academic commentators to focus their attention upon cases which reach the higher courts, some of which involve assets running into millions of pounds, it is salutary to note the scale of the assets in the common run of divorce cases.

Table 4 Other assets (including pensions)

Up to £5000	147	51.5%
£5000–£20,000	60	21%
Over £20,000	78	27%
Total	285	

Our final two categories of financial information concerned the incomes of husband and wife respectively. Here again we determined income bands simply on the basis that they created roughly equal divisions within our case sample. Thus we find that the main income band for men was between £9000 and £15,000 (42%), which is significantly below average earnings. Only 8% of these divorced men had an income in excess of £25,000.

One-quarter of the women in the sample had no income other than state benefits. Only 6% had an income in excess of £15,000 and so might be considered, on that simple yardstick, financially independent. It has been pointed out to us that the time at which the parties' incomes were recorded may be critical. A Cardiff University study of parents' financial arrangements in the immediate aftermath of separation found that women's incomes often 'recovered' to some extent in the period following separation. This might explain some aberrant or apparently unfair outcomes.

Table 5 Husband's income

Benefits only	37	13%
Income up to £8000	39	14%
Income £9000–£15,000	119	42%
Income £16,000–£25,000	66	23%
Income over £25,000	24	8%
Total	285	

Table 6 Wife's income

Benefits only	73	25.5%
Income up to £5000	41	14.5%
Income £6000–£10,000	105	37%
Income £11,000–£15,000	49	17%
Income over £15,000	17	6%
Total	285	

Having presented these basic components of family financial information in five categories, we can now move to examine the relationship *between* the various elements. Our first step towards this is contained in Table 7 (below), which gives a breakdown of financial information relating to the home matched against family type.

There are marked differences between the various 'family types' in terms of home ownership – and in terms of the equity in the property. For example, if we take an equity in excess of £20,000 as our yardstick, the position is as given in Table 8 (below).

It is striking, we think, how few divorcing couples with children, in the mid-1990s, had significant equity in the family home. The majority had the bricks and mortar, but for the most part these properties were heavily mortgaged. As we have already said, few of these couples were 'property rich', and this is important in that it allows little room for manoeuvre in assigning the property. On this evidence there can seldom be much scope for selling the home and re-housing the children and their mother in a cheaper property in order to free up capital for the husband...

Table 7 Tabulation of family type by family home

Marriage up to seven years, no children		
Council tenancy	1	0%
Owned – equity to £5000	24	8%
Owned – equity £5000-£20,000	19	6.6%
Owned – equity over £20,000	13	4.5%
No home to assign	6	2%
Marriage over seven years, no children		
Owned – equity to £5000	4	1.4%
Owned – equity £5000-£20,000	11	4%
Owned – equity over £20,000	8	3%
No home to assign	4	1.4%
Marriage with dependent children		
Council tenancy	13	4.5%
Owned – equity to £5000	33	11.5%
Owned – equity £5000-£20,000	43	15%
Owned – equity over £20,000	63	22%
No home to assign	5	1.7%
Adult children		
Council tenancy	1	0%
Owned – equity to £5000	3	1%
Owned – equity £5000-£20,000	4	1.4%
Owned – equity over £20,000	27	9.5%
No home to assign	3	1%
Total	285	

Table 8 Percentage of cases in which the equity in the home exceeded £20,000

Marriage up to seven years, no children	20%
Marriage over seven years, no children	30%
Marriage with dependent children	40%
Adult children only	71%

Our final computing exercise involved bringing together the five components of our analysis, incorporating the breakdowns within each category as previously determined. In the resulting table our 285 cases generated 192 separate case categories – mostly, of course, with a single case in each...

Analysing Outcome

It seemed to us that there were three possible approaches to the task of analysing ancillary relief orders by reference to family financial circumstances as revealed on the court file:

(1) we could start with our case data and try to examine the relationship between case characteristics and outcome, employing whatever categorisations emerge from the data;
(2) we could identify, on the basis of our own experience of these matters, what we believe to be key factors in terms of family relationship, assets/income etc, and then construct a series of categories, each of which should lead to an outcome within a fairly narrow range (in other words, whilst approach (1) would be purely empirical, (2) would involve an element of prior conceptualisation); or
(3) we could forget case classification and focus instead on apparently aberrant outcomes. This would require us to judge cases intuitively, consigning most to a 'non-aberrant' category and then scrutinising the remainder in some depth in order to try to understand the factors which had led to a departure from the norm.

We thought that any of the above was defensible, and would probably lead to similar findings at the end of the day. However, a breakdown of our cases by the five very basic features previously outlined hardly encouraged us to extend this approach to incorporate court orders. Even this very limited set of variables generated 192 distinct categories, rendering comparisons within each case type somewhat impractical. It would obviously have been futile to add more variables, and nor did it seem feasible to superimpose the terms of the court order upon the analysis.

The other difficulty which we faced – and this would have applied whatever approach we took in analysing our data – was that the information available on the file was often insufficient for us to feel confident in judging the appropriateness of the order. The greatest variation in outcome (or the greatest unpredictability of outcome) was in consent applications, with the parties quite often appearing to settle on terms which we doubted a court would have ordered following a trial.

Although we found some variation of order in apparently similar circumstances, commonly, where *additional* information was provided, the order would seem perfectly sensible. What we are saying therefore is that the number of *potentially* relevant factors is enormous, and it would have been impossible for us to incorporate all these factors into our analysis, even if the information had been available...

Our final attempt to solve the conundrum of how to devise a system for matching orders to family finances involved homing in on what appeared – judging these matters intuitively – to be aberrant outcomes. There were in fact quite a few cases which appeared on the face of it to diverge from the norm – either because the children's housing needs were not obviously met, or because there appeared to be inequity between the parties. These comprised perhaps 5% of the case sample – although in each instance the order may not have seemed at all odd had we known the full facts. In what follows we focus on three categories of apparently aberrant outcomes:

(1) apparent inequity between the parties;
(2) possibly inappropriate clean breaks; and
(3) oddities associated with cohabitation.

Apparent Inequality

- Three-year marriage; no children; equity in the home of £2000. Both the home and a life policy to go to the husband; nothing to the wife.
- Short marriage; no children; £7000 equity in the home; husband and wife earning similar amounts. Home to the wife; nothing to the husband.
- Thirty-year marriage; adult children; both cohabiting; £35,000 equity in the home; wife earns £14,000 per annum; husband earns £9000 per annum. Home to the husband; wife to receive £10,000.

- Twenty-eight-year marriage; adult children; £45,000 equity in the home; husband has a pension valued at £225,000; he currently earns over £3000 per month; wife earns £850 per month. Husband to pay £50,000 to the wife; all insurance policies to the husband; home to the husband (in this case the Bill of Costs revealed that the wife went against her solicitor's advice).
- Fourteen-year marriage; three children aged 12, 10 and six – all to live with the wife; £23,000 equity in the home; husband earning £19,000 per annum; wife earning £1200 per annum. Wife to have the home; husband to pay £100 per month per child; wife to have the life policy and a £2000 lump sum.
- Five-year marriage; one child; husband and wife both earning £16,000–17,000; £73,000 equity in the home; neither party cohabiting. Wife to transfer her interest in the home to the husband in return for £20,000; he also to have the life policies, valued at £1400; no reference to where the child is to be housed.
- Husband and wife both earning approximately £16,000 per annum; three teenage children – to live with the wife; equity of £60,000 in the family home. Home to the wife, plus substantial child maintenance; husband to receive £6500.
- Two children aged 16 and 18 to live with the wife; she is disabled and earning £500 per month; husband earns £16,000 per annum (or more – this is disputed) and has other assets valued at £8000, including a life policy; equity of £24,000 in the home. Home to be sold and wife to receive 60% of its value, plus the life policy (valued at £6000); clean break order.

Questionable Clean Breaks

- Twenty-seven-year marriage with adult children; equity of £4000 in the home; husband earns £10,500 per annum, wife on benefits. Wife to have the home; clean break order.
- Sixteen-year marriage; two teenage children; husband earns £400 per month; wife also earns, and receives family credit. Council tenancy transferred to wife; clean break order.
- Six-year marriage; two children aged four and two; husband earns £1400 per month; wife on income support; negative equity in the property. Wife to get the home; not stated whether Child Support Agency involved; clean break order.
- Husband earns £1350 per month; wife on benefits; four-year-old disabled child with mother; husband has 12-year contribution to pension scheme. Home (with £2000 equity) to the wife; clean break order.
- Husband earns £1000 per month; eight-year-old child to live with wife; £26,000 assets in total, including equity in the home. Assets to be split 50/50; husband to pay £30 per week for child; clean break order.

Impact of Cohabitation

- Five-year marriage; four-year-old child to live with wife; equity of £6000 in the home; husband earns £10,000 per annum; wife on incapacity benefit; both parties cohabiting. Wife agrees that she has no interest in the home; life policy divided equally.
- Wife has purchased new property with equity of £11,000; £20,000 equity in former matrimonial home; nine-year-old child living with wife; both parties cohabiting. Former matrimonial home to go to husband; life policy (value not specified) also to go to husband; apparently nothing for the wife, other than new home already purchased.

- Three children aged three, seven and eight all living with the wife; equity in family home £25,000; husband earns £230 per week and has pension valued at £25,000; wife earns £120 per week; wife cohabiting. Husband to have home and life policy (value not stated on file); wife to have £10,000.
- Six-year marriage; no children; husband cohabiting; equity of £9000 in the home; also an insurance policy valued at £1500. Home and insurance policy to the wife; nothing to the husband.
- Eleven-year marriage; no children; both cohabiting; £20,000 equity in the home; wife earns £8500 per annum; husband on Income Support. Husband to have the home; £2000 to the wife.

There were a few other cases which might have been included in these lists, but these were the most obvious ones. As we say, some of them might not appear at all 'odd' were we in possession of the full facts. That aside, it is a difficult policy issue to determine how much leeway the court *ought* to allow in giving its imprimatur to consent applications freely negotiated. Of course one or other party (but usually the wife) may have been subject to a variety of pressures which the court would wish to protect her against. But the possibility of coercion aside, and assuming that the children's interests are safeguarded, it is a moot point how far the court should seek to intervene.

Discussion...

The former Parliamentary Secretary in the Lord Chancellor's Office announced in 1998 that the Government intended to 'deliver a greater sense of certainty for the parties, without preventing the courts from ensuring that the outcome of cases is, as far as possible, fair and just to all concerned'. In keeping with that objective, the Government consultation paper, *Supporting Families*, suggested that – once the children's needs had been met – 'fairness will generally require the value of the assets to be divided equally between the parties'.

This proposal was presumably intended to achieve greater predictability in the determination of these cases. Whether it would promote fairness, or generate a greater sense of satisfaction with the resulting outcomes, is another question. ... In England and Wales we do not at present have an explicitly identified hierarchy of objectives, but it presumably would not hurt were this to be provided, if only as an aid to public understanding. It is not sufficient for experienced practitioners to understand these things: the parties directly concerned need help in penetrating the mysteries. Why should they not be told the basis upon which the finances are meant to be decided? If we really are concerned to provide the separating population with 'information' – and if we mean information, not indoctrination – we might start with a plain man's account of the basis upon which the court expects the financial cake to be apportioned. It is about the most important piece of information people could have – the rest is mainly preaching.

The evidence of the court files, limited as it is, does not encourage us to go further than this. Proposals to achieve greater predictability through, for example, a presumption of equal sharing – perhaps as a kind of 'third tier' principle, following upon those earlier alluded to – would almost certainly be unfair in their effects unless vitiated by yet further 'principles', even the most subtle proposals, such as those contained in Eekelaar's recent article, seem likely to run into definitional problems. If the objective is fairness it is difficult to know precisely when to stop along the road to rendering the whole thing formulaic. It is a paradox of formulae that they generate complexity. It would be our contention, on the evidence of the files, that most of these cases are fairly straightforward – they are simple, but they are idiosyncratic. That calls for individually tailored solutions – but these individual solutions should not require the expenditure of vast amounts of professional time.

What tends to take time is, first, achieving full disclosure, and secondly, an approach to negotiation which rests mostly upon bargaining and attrition. Any steps which limit the scope for bargaining and which place less reliance on attrition are, in principle, to be welcomed, although there are clearly limits to what can be achieved in this regard through the provision of a hierarchy of objectives. When we began this study one of the questions at the forefront of our minds was whether ancillary relief might be rendered more predictable than at present, thereby limiting the scope for unfair pressure of various kinds. As has been seen, our five-way breakdown of family financial information produced nearly 200 separate categories amongst 285 cases. That in itself was not a surprise – any breakdown which employs five variables, each of which has five possible 'values', will generate roughly this number of case categories – it is a statistical inevitability. The problem lies not with the differences which are revealed in our tables, but with all that has been excluded. Our various categories omitted a huge amount that was relevant, for example, cohabitees, debts, mortgage arrears, negative equity, marriage duration, parental support, compensation sums awarded, children from a previous relationship, and so on. The eventual orders – most of which were 'by consent' – could never have been predicted, in all their detail, from the financial pictures in the files. The specific case circumstances were such that whilst the main outlines of the eventual 'solution' were indeed predictable, the precise details were infinitely variable. Most of the bargaining, we presume, is about this detail, rather than about the main themes.

There is also the difficulty that the more we attempt to make ancillary relief formulaic, the more we lock the parties into patterns of division which may not make sense to them and which they would not choose as a reflection of their particular relationship history – or of their residual obligations and financial needs.

QUESTION

i. Do you think that any of the outcomes seen here might have been different after *White*?

ii. Look back at the Law Commission's seven models for ancillary relief. How many of those models do you think we can see in operation here? Which, if any, would you now favour?

What we have not mentioned so far is the financial provision available on the dissolution of a civil partnership. The applicable statutory provisions match those available for spouses; but there are as yet no decisions available to indicate whether they will be operated in the same way.

QUESTION

Having considered, in Chapter 2, the differences between civil partnership and marriage, what differences, if any, do you think there will between the operation of ancillary relief provisions for civil partners and those of the Matrimonial Causes Act 1973? Look again at what Kenneth McK. Norrie has to say in Chapter 2 (p. 94), and look at the comments from the *Equal Treatment Bench Book* in Chapter 4 (p. 156).

5.6 SOLUTION BY AGREEMENT

In 'Private ordering and divorce – how far can we go?' (2003) Stephen Cretney observes:

> The child support legislation will (whatever the parties may wish) have its impact, but broadly speaking there is no reason why a divorcing couple should not make their own arrangements for the future. That, indeed, is what one of the officially sponsored leaflets intended to be used to disseminate information about the divorce process in the approach to the projected implementation of the *Family Law Act 1996* reforms said: you really do not need to trouble the court with these matters. And that is, of course, true – in a sense and up to a point. You may make your agreement; you may, if you wish, seal it with sealing wax (if you have any left). But the law is quite clear: however much your agreement recites that it is intended to mark a final and binding settlement of the financial affairs on the dissolution of the marital partnership, it is open to either party (whether because of changed circumstances or simply because he has had second thoughts) to apply to the court to vary its terms, or revoke it, and make any of the orders it could have made had application been made at the time of the divorce. Of course, lawyers have devised ways of achieving finality: a clean break, as it is often called, can be achieved by the simple expedient of asking the court to make a consent order giving effect to terms agreed by the parties. But the married couple (unlike the unmarried couple) have to submit full details of their affairs to the court and the court has a 'paternal' role (see *Pounds v Pounds* [1994] 1 FLR 775, at p 780, per Waite LJ) in deciding whether or not to approve the terms they have agreed. The principle proclaimed by the House of Lords in 1924 (*Hyman v Hyman* [1929] AC 601, at p 614, per Lord Hailsham LC) that the financial relationship of husband and wife remains a matter of vital public interest, not to be settled by private agreement, remains intact even if the procedures whereby that public interest is asserted have become much more sophisticated.

Edgar v Edgar [1998] 1 WLR 1410, CA, remains authoritative as to the weight the courts will attach to separation agreements. If the parties have had legal advice and have understood the effect of their agreement and have not been pressurised into it, the agreement will stand. But its enforceability remains a matter for the discretion of the court. And *Hyman* (above) remains the starting point for the courts' attitude to agreements made, not at the time of separation or divorce, but before or during the marriage.

Why might such agreements be made? Walter Weyrauch, in 'Metamorphoses of Marriage' (1980), writes:

> The legal device of contract is particularly useful for women from the middle classes and of high educational attainment who are self-assertive and competitive in their relations with men. It is less adequate for parties of the lower classes and those who, because of continued differential treatment of the sexes, lack equal bargaining power. The courts may then fall back on traditional conceptions of marriage as status and emphasize the conjugal obligations of the husband. If there is no marriage, the courts may surreptitiously apply public policy by reading into a supposedly implied contract provisions that never occurred to the parties. A host of legal theories,

> equitable in nature, may also affect the obligations of parties to quasi-marital relationships. Thus, the courts may develop remedies akin to those in modern contract law when dealing with terms that are manifestly unfair and oppressive, and may borrow the reasoning from commercial litigation when deciding marital and quasi-marital disputes. They may refuse to enforce unconscionable terms that have been found to exist between the parties, married or not, and imply a duty of good faith and fair dealing.

The English courts' position on such agreements is explained by Brigitte Clarke in 'Should Greater Prominence Be Given To Pre-Nuptial Contracts In The Law Of Ancillary Relief?' (2004):

> Why in England, unlike most other jurisdictions, is a pre-nuptial contract not prima facie enforceable...? Is this situation tenable? Why should a contract made by two consenting adults to regulate their financial position in the event of a divorce not have a more significant influence? Why are pre-nuptial contracts treated only as a circumstance of the case which the court may consider in division of the assets after divorce, or as part of the conduct of each of the parties, which it would be inequitable to disregard? If such contracts were given binding and enforceable status, what safeguards would be necessary to ensure that there is not an increased risk of injustice, or prejudice to children, particularly in cases of longer marriages?
>
> In response to these questions, it does appear that, although such contracts are prima facie unenforceable in England, the approach of the courts to pre-nuptial agreements is in a developmental phase. A study of the cases indicates that there are various issues that the court will take into consideration in weighing up how much emphasis is to be given to pre-nuptial agreements. These issues include the length of the marriage in question; the contribution that a spouse would make in caring for the child; the source of the wealth of the parties; the standard of provision made for the less wealthy spouse; whether the parties to a pre-nuptial agreement were in an equal bargaining position; and whether there had been a full disclosure of assets, especially by the wealthier party.
>
> Given the current approaches of the courts, there are various ways in which increased recognition could be bestowed upon pre-nuptial contracts. First, pre-nuptial contracts could be specifically mentioned as one of the factors required to be considered by the court, ie by the insertion of a special clause into section 25 of the *Matrimonial Causes Act 1973*. This approach would not really alter the status quo much, apart from formalising in statute the approach which is now taken by the courts. A second approach could be to recognise a contract that dealt only with pre-matrimonial property, leaving the courts' powers otherwise intact. In terms of this approach, the courts would recognise pre-nuptial contracts only insofar as they dealt with assets of the parties that are not to become matrimonial property and thus subject to the court's jurisdiction on divorce. At the moment there is, in general, no such property, although in *White v White* and the 'big money' cases the courts are developing the idea of leaving pre-matrimonial property intact. A third approach would be to have specific legislation to allow for pre-nuptial contracts covering all matrimonial property, subject to certain procedural and substantive safeguards. Just what those safeguards should be is a source of constant debate. Over-extensive safeguards and exceptions might not, in fact, give any credence to private ordering or the value of contractual autonomy.
>
> In some countries, such as Australia, recent evidence indicates that the adoption of such contracts (even when recognised and enforceable in that jurisdiction) has not been widespread. In most European countries and in South Africa, the adoption rate appears to be, in some measure, affected by the popularity and acceptance of the default matrimonial property regime. In South Africa, the percentage of such contracts is very high. However, only 16% of all French couples expressly draw up a marriage contract at the time of marriage, although a further 3%

later adopt a different regime during the marriage. In the USA, only 5% of couples who have never previously married sign such contracts, whereas the number rises significantly for those who have been married before. Pre-marital contracting is much more popular in The Netherlands, where pre-nuptial agreements are signed in a quarter of all marriages. However, the popularity or otherwise of such contracts is not a valid argument against the provision of measures to allow persons the facility for private ordering in their marriage.

Recent cases cited by Clarke and illustrative of the courts' approach include *M v M (Pre-nuptial Agreement)* [2002] 1 FLR 654 and *K v K (Ancillary Relief: Pre-nuptial Agreement)* [2003] 1 FLR 120. Stephen Cretney, in 'The Family and the Law: Status or Contract?' (2003) discusses the change brought about by *White* and the cases that follow it, and looks at the law relating to private ordering in the light of that change:

[W]e have to confront a remarkable anomaly. This is that, while marriage can indeed be described as a partnership, yet that partnership is one of a very special kind. Its distinctive character lies in the fact that English law will not allow husband and wife by contract (whether pre- or post-nuptial) to exercise the right, which it accords virtually all other partners, to make their own agreement as to the terms. As Rayden and Jackson baldly (and accurately) state: 'ante-nuptial contracts by which a man and a woman prior to marriage, seek to regulate their financial liabilities and responsibilities the one towards the other in the event of a divorce are unenforceable in English Law'. Husband and wife are stuck with equality, however inappropriate they may both agree it to be. And you must leave it to the judge who dissolves the partnership (if it should come to that) to decide whether the circumstances – perhaps the fact that you have been a party to other marriages, and have dependants as a result – which led you both to agree that equality was not for you, should determine the outcome or not. No doubt the judge will apply the principle that a formal and freely negotiated agreement made by a couple with full knowledge of the circumstances is not lightly to be set aside. But you cannot make such an agreement *proof* against the exercise of the overriding judicial discretion. On one view, this is to have the worst of all possible worlds. It is almost as if we insisted that every time a business or professional partnership is dissolved, the terms should be approved by the court.

QUESTIONS

i. Why does the development of the idea of non-matrimonial property make the enforceability of pre-nuptial, or post-nuptial, contracts a more pressing concern?

ii. Why might 'the fact that you have been a party to other marriages' be relevant to the question whether your agreement should be enforceable?

As Clarke (2004) observes, in continental Europe and in South Africa the enforceability of such contracts is beyond dispute. In countries that operate a regime of immediate community of property (such as South Africa, France, the Netherlands and others), the ability to contract out of that regime is essential where one of the spouses is in business; the couple will opt (before or during the marriage) for separation of property in order to safeguard the family assets, and in particular the home, from the creditors of the business. Elizabeth Cooke and her colleagues, in *Community of Property: a regime for England and Wales?* (2006) explain:

> [Under regimes of immediate community] it is not only wealth that is shared but also debts. As stated above, community of benefits implies community of liabilities. The union is one for better or for worse. Consequently, in the immediate universal community of the Netherlands, creditors for debts incurred by either spouse, individually or jointly, will be able to satisfy the debts by recourse to the community. In France, again, the community of enrichment is mirrored by a community of debts: creditors may seize communal property for debts incurred for the household or for the children's education by one or both spouses...
>
> It is important to note that the consequence of communal liability means that it is advisable for those running their own business to opt out of an immediate community regime in order to protect the other spouse from business creditors. Indeed, our interviews with notaries in our three jurisdictions revealed that those most likely to seek advice and to adopt a system of separation were those who could be classed as having an 'at risk' financial business status – for example, traditionally farmers in France but extended to all those self-employed.

Such contracts inevitably affect the distribution of property on divorce, because countries that recognise matrimonial regimes (of community or of separation) typically do not have discretionary property adjustment on divorce. But the agreements are made primarily as a means of asset management during the currency of the marriage. It is not unusual for couples who have opted for separate property during their working lives to opt back into community when they retire, partly as a means of tax planning.

However, the availability of enforceable marital property agreements is not limited to jurisdictions that operate community of property regimes. Twenty-seven American states (some of them common law, some community property states) have enacted the Uniform Premarital Agreements Act, which provides as follows:

Section 1. Definitions.

As used in this Act:

(1) 'Premarital agreement' means an agreement between prospective spouses made in contemplation of marriage and to be effective upon marriage.
(2) 'Property' means an interest, present or future, legal or equitable, vested or contingent, in real or personal property, including income and earnings.

Section 2. Formalities.

A premarital agreement must be in writing and signed by both parties. It is enforceable without consideration.

Section 3. Content.

(a) Parties to a premarital agreement may contract with respect to:

(1) the rights and obligations of each of the parties in any of the property of either or both of them whenever and wherever acquired or located;
(2) the right to buy, sell, use, transfer, exchange, abandon, lease, consume, expend, assign, create a security interest in, mortgage, encumber, dispose of, or otherwise manage and control property;
(3) the disposition of property upon separation, marital dissolution, death, or the occurrence or nonoccurrence of any other event;
(4) the modification or elimination of spousal support;
(5) the making of a will, trust, or other arrangement to carry out the provisions of the agreement;
(6) the ownership rights in and disposition of the death benefit from a life insurance policy;
(7) the choice of law governing the construction of the agreement; and
(8) any other matter, including their personal rights and obligations, not in violation of public policy or a statute imposing a criminal penalty.

(b) The right of a child to support may not be adversely affected by a premarital agreement.

Section 4. Effect of Marriage.

A premarital agreement becomes effective upon marriage.

Section 5. Amendment, Revocation.

After marriage, a premarital agreement may be amended or revoked only by a written agreement signed by the parties. The amended agreement or the revocation is enforceable without consideration.

Section 6. Enforcement.

(a) A premarital agreement is not enforceable if the party against whom enforcement is sought proves that:

(1) that party did not execute the agreement voluntarily; or
(2) the agreement was unconscionable when it was executed and, before execution of the agreement, that party:
  (i) was not provided a fair and reasonable disclosure of the property or financial obligations of the other party;
  (ii) did not voluntarily and expressly waive, in writing, any right to disclosure of the property or financial obligations of the other party beyond the disclosure provided; and
  (iii) did not have, or reasonably could not have had, an adequate knowledge of the property or financial obligations of the other party.

(b) If a provision of a premarital agreement modifies or eliminates spousal support and that modification or elimination causes one party to the agreement to be eligible for support under a program of public assistance at the time of separation or marital dissolution, a court, notwithstanding the terms of the agreement, may require the other party to provide support to the extent necessary to avoid that eligibility.

(c) An issue of unconscionability of a premarital agreement shall be decided by the court as a matter of law.

QUESTIONS

i. Say a couple make an agreement as contemplated in this Act, and on the assumption that each will continue with a career. They are determined not to have children. Five years later they change their mind, and one gives up a career to care for their child. Five more years later, they divorce. Their pre-marital agreement states that neither is obliged to make any financial provision for the other. Is it now enforceable?

ii. Is an agreement enforceable under this Act if it unconscionable but made voluntarily, with full disclosure of both parties' assets and financial obligations? If so, should it be? (You might like to think of examples of such agreements.)

Stuart Bridge, in 'Marriage and divorce: the regulation of intimacy' (2001) expresses concern about the effect of private ordering:

> It could well be that widespread adoption of marital contracts could lead to more litigation rather than less. In the United States, where they are common-place, a litigation industry surrounds them, and the lawyers win both ways. They charge for advising upon and drafting the agreement at the inception of the relationship, or whenever the parties consider such an agreement useful. They then charge for unpicking it, for challenging it through the courts, following marital breakdown, either on points of construction or by invoking one of the vitiating factors listed above.

Contrast the view of an American, Jeremy Morley, in 'Enforceable Pre-nuptial Agreements: the World View' (2006), who states:

> Litigation costs in big money divorce cases are enormous. English family lawyers appear to be the current world champions in that arena. Part of the reason is the extreme uncertainty in any such case. Pre-nuptial agreements reduce litigation costs dramatically since there is far less need to litigate property division when the terms have already been agreed.

QUESTIONS

i. How, as social scientists, might we set about discovering whether Bridge or Morley is right?

ii. Of the Whites, the Millers, the McFarlanes or the Charmans, whom might you have advised (with the benefit of hindsight) to enter into a marital property agreement? Bear in mind that the Charmans had been childhood sweethearts from modest backgrounds who married before there was any expectation of riches.

In its consultation paper *Supporting Families* (1998), the Government announced plans for the enforceability of such contracts, on the basis that they would be unenforceable in the following circumstances:

- where there is a child of the family, whether or not that child was alive or a child of the family at the time the agreement was made
- where under the general law of contract the agreement is unenforceable, including if the contract attempted to lay an obligation on a third party who had not agreed in advance
- where one or both of the couple did not receive independent legal advice before entering into the agreement
- where the court considers that the enforcement of the agreement would cause significant injustice (to one or both of the couple or a child of the marriage)
- where one or both of the couple have failed to give full disclosure of assets and property before the agreement was made
- where the agreement is made fewer than 21 days prior to the marriage (this would prevent a nuptial agreement being forced on people shortly before their wedding day, when they may not feel able to resist).

But no steps have been taken to put those plans into effect. In 2004 Resolution (then the Solicitors' Family Law Association) published a report 'A more certain future'. This proposed that:

> ... pre-marital agreements [would] become legally binding subject to an overriding safeguard of significant injustice and be added as a separate section 25 Matrimonial Causes Act 1973 factor. The [Law Reform] Committee [of Resolution] considered the risk of satellite litigation that might flow to define 'significant injustice', but concluded that this was a small price to pay for the certainty of pre-marital agreements.
>
> The amendment to s 25(1), it is proposed, should read:
>
> (a) the first consideration being given to the welfare while a minor of any child of the family who has not attained the age of 18;
>
> (b) any agreement entered into between the parties to the marriage, in contemplation of, or after the marriage, for the purpose of regulating their affairs on the breakdown of their marriage, which shall be considered binding upon them unless to do so will cause significant injustice to either party or to any such minor child of the family.
>
> A parallel amendment would be needed to MCA 1973, s 34 so as to render it subject to the amended provisions of s 25.
>
> ...
>
> The Committee would also propose that there be a Good Practice Guide in relation to the drafting and financial disclosure for such agreements.
>
> This proposal differs from that originally proposed by the Government [in *Supporting Families*]... in that it bolsters the need to consider any pre-marital agreement as a primary factor and in particular would allow the courts to use s.25 discretionary factors to mitigate the need for satellite litigation on 'significant injustice'.

QUESTION

i. How far does Resolution's proposal differ from the terms of the Uniform Pre-Marital Agreements Act (above, p. 250)?

ii. How would you ensure that marital property agreements could safely be enforced, bearing in mind the dangers of pressure and the wide range of changed circumstances?

The position for civil partners may be slightly different. On 7 December 2006 the news service pinknews.co.uk commented, (at http://www.pinknews.co.uk/news/articles/2005-3207.html):

> Most legal advice on civil partnerships for same sex couples has related to pre-partnership agreements (pre-nups). QueerPod lawyer, Haema Sundram, said: 'I did just two pre-nuptial agreements in 13 years and then 7 in the past year. They are more likely to stick for gay couples because, on the face of it, each person will be seen to have equal bargaining power and will know exactly what they are getting into. If they are taken into account in civil partnership breakdown, the courts may then be more likely to take them into account in divorces.'
>
> Gay couples are negotiating agreements using the new collaborative law process which allows them to focus on what's important to them. It also helps avoid the risk of the traditional adversarial approach souring their relationship in advance of their big day.
>
> For those gay couples whose relationships do hit difficulties, collaborative law can provide them with a tailor-made negotiated settlement. This will be especially important as 'gay divorce' is uncharted territory in the courts. It is not yet known how judges will take into account cultural differences between heterosexual married couples and gay couples in a civil partnership.

See also the extract from this comment in Chapter 4 (p. 155).

QUESTION

How do you think the courts will respond to those cultural differences in the context of ancillary relief and of gay pre-nuptial agreements?

BIBLIOGRAPHY

5.1 Child support

We quoted from:

A. Bainham, 'Men and Women Behaving Badly: Is Fault Dead in English Family Law?' (2001) 21 *Oxford Journal of Legal Studies* 219, 229–30.

British Association of Adoption and Fostering, *Consultation on proposals regarding joint birth registration*, available at: http://www.baaf.org.uk/res/consultations/consultresponse_jointbirth.pdf.
D. Burrows, 'A Brave New World' (2007) 157 *New Law Journal* 888.
Children Come First: The Government's Proposals on the Maintenance of Children, (Cm.1264) (1990) London, HMSO, vol. 2, paras 1.3.2, 1.4.
DWP, *Child Maintenance and Other Payments Bill 2007: Regulatory Impact Assessment*, (2007) TSO.
J. Herring, *Family Law* (3rd edn), (2007) Pearson, Harlow, 186.
N. Wikeley, 'Child Support – the new formula' [2000] *Family Law* 820.
N. Wikeley, 'Child Support reform – throwing the baby out with the bath water' [2007] *Child and Family Law Quarterly*.

Additional reading

J. Bradshaw and J. Millar, *Lone Parent Families in the UK*, Social Security Research Report, no.6, (1991) London, HMSO.
DWP, *A fresh start: child support redesign – the Government's response to Sir David Henshaw*, Cm 6895 (TSO, 2006)
DWP, *A new system of child maintenance*, Cm 6979 (2006) TSO.
DWP, *A new system of child maintenance: Summary of responses to the consultation*, Cm 7061 (2007) TSO.
DWP, *Report on the child maintenance White Paper: A new system of child maintenance*, Cm 7062 (2007) TSO.
DWP, *Joint birth registration: promoting parental responsibility*, Cm 7160 (2007) TSO.
J. Graham, C. Creegan, M. Barnard, A. Mowlam and S. McKay, *Sole and joint birth registration: Exploring the circumstances, choices and motivations of unmarried parents*, DWP Research Report No 463 (2007).
House of Commons Work and Pensions Select Committee, *Child Support Reform* (Fourth report of Session 2006–2007), HC 219-I and 219-II (2007).
J. Lewis, 'Women, Men and the Family' in A. Seldon, *The Blair Effect* (2001) London, Little, Brown, ch.22.
N. Mostyn, 'The Green Paper on Child Support – Children First: a new approach to child support' [1999] *Family Law* 95
J. Pirrie, 'Changes to Child Support – The SFLA View' [1999] *Family Law* 838
White Paper, *Improving Child Support* (1995), London, HMSO, Cmnd 2745

5.2 Ancillary relief: the historical background

We quoted from:

Sir Morris Finer and O.R. McGregor, 'The History of the Obligation to Maintain', App. 5, *Report of the Committee on One-Parent Families* (Cmnd. 5629-1) (1974) London, HMSO, paras 26–27, 32–33, 37–38.

Additional reading

M.A. Glendon, *The New Family and the New Property* (1981) Toronto, Butterworths.

5.3 The evolution of the statutory provisions

We quoted from:

G. Davis, S. Cretney, J. Collins, *Simple Quarrels* (1994) Oxford, Clarendon Press, 105–106.

R. Deech, 'The Principles of Maintenance' [1977] *Family Law* 229.

J. Ginn and D. Pearce, 'Can divorced women catch up in pension building?' (2002) 14(2) *Child and Family Law Quarterly* 157, 164.

Independent working group on pensions and divorce appointed by the PMI in agreement with the Law Society, *Pensions and Divorce*, (1993).

Law Commission, *Family Law: The Financial Consequences of Divorce: the basic policy*, (1980) Law Com. No. 103 paras 17, 24 – 27, 59, 66, 70, 73, 75, 77, 80, 84, 86.

K. O'Donovan, 'The Principles of Maintenance: An Alternative View' [1978] *Family Law* 180.

M. Rae, 'Pensions and Divorce: Time for Change' (1995) 145 *New Law Journal* 310.

Carol Smart, *The Ties that Bind: Law, Marriage and the Reproduction of Patriarchal Relations* (1984), Boston, Routledge, pp. 223–8.

Additional reading

K.J. Gray, *The Reallocation of property on Divorce* (1977) Abingdon, Professional Books.

5.4 The search for principle

We quoted from:

E. Cooke, 'A new yardstick for the marriage partnership', [2001] 13 *Child and Family Law Quarterly* 8, 84.

E. Cooke, 'Miller/McFarlane: law in search of discrimination' (2007) 19 *Child and Family Law Quarterly* 98, 110.

S. Cretney, in 'The Family and the Law: Status or Contract?' (2003) 15 *Child and Family Law Quarterly* 403, 411–12.

P. Singer, 'Sexual Discrimination in Ancillary Relief' [2001] *Family Law* 115.

Additional reading

R. Bailey-Harris, 'Comment on *GW v RW (Financial Provision: Departure from Equality)*' (2003) *Family Law* 386.

J. Eekelaar, 'Asset Distribution on Divorce – Time and Property' (2003) *Family Law* 828.

I.M. Ellman, 'Do Americans play football' (2005) 19 *International Journal of Law Policy and the Family* 257.

J. Herring, 'Why Financial Orders on Divorce Should be Unfair' (2005) 19 *International Journal of Law Policy and the Family* 218.

5.5 Ancillary relief at the grass roots

We quoted from:

S. Arthur, J. Lewis, M. Maclean, S. Finch and R. Fitzgerald, *Settling Up: Making financial arrangements after divorce or separa*tion, (2002) National Centre for Social Research.

C. Barton and A. Bissett-Johnson, 'The declining number of ancillary financial relief orders' [2000] *Family Law* 940.

District Judge R. Bird, 'Ancillary Relief Outcomes' [2000] *Family Law* 831.

J. Black, J. Bridge, T. Bond and L. Gribbins, *A Practical Approach to Family Law* (7th edn.) (2007) Oxford, Oxford University Press, 300.

G. Davis, S. Cretney, J. Collins, *Simple Quarrels* (1994) Oxford, Clarendon Press, 105–106.

G. Davis, J. Pearce, R. Bird, H. Woodward, C. Wallace, 'Ancillary Relief Outcomes' (2000) 12 *Child and Family Law Quarterly* 43, 46–63.

Legal Services Commission, LSCIL4E, *Paying for your Legal Aid* (2007), available at http://www.legalservices.gov.uk/docs/cls_main/Paying_for_your_Legal_Aid.pdf.

P. Symes, 'Indissolubility and the Clean Break' (1985) 48(1) *Modern Law Review* 44, 59–60.

Additional reading

Lucinda Fisher, 'The unexpected impact of *White*' [2002] *Family Law* 108.

M. Hatwood, 'Funding Ancillary Relief Cases: the New Costs Rules' [2007] *Family Law* 347.

Home Office, *Supporting Families: A consultation paper* (1998) London, HMSO.

5.6 Solution by agreement

We quoted from:

S. Bridge, 'Marriage and divorce: the regulation of intimacy' in J. Herring (ed.), *Family Law: Issues, Debates, Policy* (2001) Devon, Willan Publishing, 24–29.

B. Clarke, 'Should Greater Prominence Be Given To Pre-Nuptial Contracts In The Law Of Ancillary Relief?' [2004] 16 *Child and Family Law Quarterly* 399.

E. Cooke, A. Barlow, T. Callus, *Community of Property: a regime for England and Wales* (Bristol, Nuffield, 2006), chapter 1.

S. Cretney, 'Private ordering and divorce – how far can we go?' [2003] *Family Law* 399.

J.D. Morley, 'Enforceable Pre-nuptial Agreements: the World View' (2006) *International Family Law Journal* 195.

pinknews.co.uk, 'Civil partners not rushing to divorce' at http://www.pinknews.co.uk/news/articles/2005-3207.html.

SFLA, *A More Certain Future: Recognition of Premarital Agreements in England and Wales* (2004).

Supporting Families (1998) London, Stationery Office, p. 33.

W. Weyrauch, 'Metamorphoses of Marriage' (1980) 13 *Family Law Quarterly* 436.

Additional reading

C. Barton, 'The SFLA And Pre-Marital Agreements: A More Lucrative Future?' [2005] *Family Law* 47.

I. Harris, 'Pre-nuptial Agreements post-*Miller*' [2006] 156 *New Law Journal* 1160.

G. Miller, 'Pre-nuptial Agreements and Financial Provision', in G. Miller (ed), *Frontiers of Family Law* (2003) Ashgate.

F. Wasoff, 'Mutual Consent: Separation Agreements and the Outcomes of Private Ordering in Divorce' (2005) 27:3 *Journal of Social Welfare and Family Law* 237.

6

FINANCIAL PROVISION FOR SEPARATING COHABITANTS

Successive editions of this book have paid increasing attention to cohabitation. Some couples prefer not to marry or form civil partnerships; and it is beyond dispute that many unmarried/non-civil partnered couples found stable and long-lasting families. Certainly financial interdependence is widespread in both contexts, as is a sense of mutual obligation. That interdependence means that when cohabitation comes to an end there is, at the very least, an element of unscrambling to be done and, in many cases, hardship to be faced. How the law should respond to this remains a puzzle, and this chapter explores that puzzle and some possible solutions, paying particular attention to the Law Commission's Report (2007).

6.1 COHABITATION AND INTERDEPENDENCE

John Eekelaar and Mavis Maclean ('Marriage and the Moral Bases of Personal Relationships', 2004) interviewed a small sample of married and unmarried couples; we quote here some of the cohabitants they spoke to:

> Int. Would your partner have any right [against you, now]?
>
> R. I wouldn't have seen it as a right...it sounds almost contractual...I'm trying to search for a softer word than a right...again, obligation is quite a strong word...it's part of being in a relationship.
>
> (Male, 33, cohabitant, White British)
>
> Being together should be mutually supportive...now people provide support in different ways depending on their personality or in their...how they are equipped within the relationship...so a mutual supportive role...otherwise you are just living with a friend...it's a developmental relationship...I don't think I had a right to financial support...emotional support though. ... Ummm...I think you have a right for somebody to support you if you are in a long-term committed relationship.
>
> (Female, 39, cohabiting after previous marriage ended in divorce; White British)
>
> Another respondent, whose partner had a teenage son, when asked whether she had any obligations towards the boy, replied:
>
> We have made a family, the way I want it, there is no 'ought' about taking on [son] I can't see [son] as anything other than part of the relationship with [partner]...we are no different from married...it all depends on the quality of the relationship, not legal status...maybe commitment should contain the length of time together...but that should apply to marriage too...
>
> (Female, 45, cohabitant planning to marry, White British)
>
> Int. Would you help your partner's parents?
>
> R. Yeah.
>
> Int. Why?

> R. To be honest, they're nice people, but more importantly...you should do unto others as you'd have done unto yourself. They've helped me in the past and I would like to reciprocate if it was required.
>
> (Male, 30, cohabitant, White British).
>
> R. The only thing that's ever changed our relationship has been the baby...before the baby came along we were always independent financially, but since the baby came along that just changed instantaneously, and it really became a situation of 'what's mine is hers' and vice versa...I think it's now a very firm bond, I'm one half of a whole, whereas before there was that bit of independence.
>
> (Male, 30, cohabitant, White British).

Rosalind Tennant, Jean Taylor and Jane Lewis carried out qualitative research for the Department for Constitutional Affairs (now the Ministry of Justice) in 2005. In their report *Separating from cohabitation: making arrangements for finances and parenting* (2006) they discuss the patterns of interdependence that they observed:

> It is possible to distinguish four models which broadly describe the ways people held their assets within the cohabitations. They are based around two key dimensions evident in the way ex-cohabitants described their financial arrangements within the cohabitation. The first represents the jointness of the couple's finances and can be represented by a continuum where at one end a couple's finances are completely joint and at the other, quite separate. The second is the equalness of contribution to the couple's finances. Again, this may be represented by a continuum where at one end couples' contributions to their finances are totally equal and at the other, are unequal. Equality in this sense implies either truly equal monetary contributions or contributions deemed equal relative to partners' relative earnings. These dimensions are depicted in figure 2.1. The different financial models have important implications for financial rights and for outcomes when the relationship ends.
>
> The primary elements on which these models are based are home-ownership or tenancies, housing costs and day-to-day living expenses. Secondary elements are earnings and trade-offs with household responsibilities including childcare.
>
> The way that couples held assets within the cohabitation was generally clear, but some participants were more vague about some aspects of their finances. There is therefore sometimes a

Figure 2.1 Key dimensions of cohabiting couples' finances

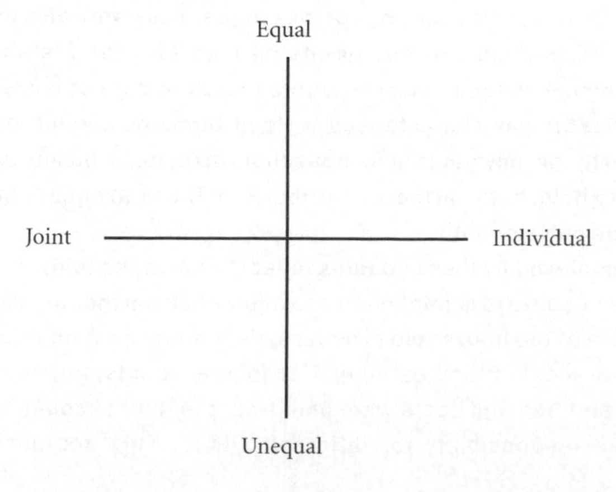

degree of approximation in their assignment to the models. It is also important to emphasise that there is diversity within each model as well.

Joint–Equal

Couples here held their assets jointly, or viewed them as joint, and made equal financial contributions to the relationship. The model was based on the premise that both parties had an equal role in and responsibility for their finances, regardless of relative earnings. It was characterised by joint home ownership, equal contributions to mortgage payments and equal contributions to household expenses. Where a tenancy was held, both partners made an equal contribution to the payment of rent, whether the tenancy was held in one partner's name or both. This model was typically adopted by couples earning similar amounts and who did not have children. . . .

The mechanisms employed to manage finances by the couples who fell into this model provide further evidence of their joint and equal approach to their finances. They had joint current accounts into which some or all of their earnings from work were paid and out of which all home and household expenses were paid, joint savings accounts, and credit cards and household bills in joint names. This approach tended to be formalised in some way, evidenced by the use of Direct Debits from joint accounts to pay bills, or a written record of payments made.

> The participant and his partner were together for two-and-a-half years and cohabited for two of those. They both worked full-time in similar jobs although the man earned slightly more than his partner. They had no children together although the participant's daughter from his previous marriage spent several nights per week at their home. The couple bought a house after about a year together which they owned jointly. They had a joint bills account into which they paid an equal amount every month and out of which was paid the mortgage and all the household bills. They both contributed to an ISA, the money from which was used to pay for family holidays.

Joint–Unequal

In this model, couples held their assets jointly, or viewed them as joint, however they did not contribute equally to the relationship in financial terms. It was typically adopted where there was some difference in the relative earnings of the couple. They were also likely to have children which had affected the working patterns of one partner. Like the first model, this approach was based on the premise of equal financial rights though it did not imply equal nor the same kind of responsibilities. It was characterised by joint home ownership but unequal financial contributions to mortgage payments and household expenses based on relative earnings. Where tenancies were held, both partners contributed to the rent, equally or unequally, whether the tenancy was in one name or both. . . .

The mechanisms employed by these couples reflect those in the joint–equal model, although household bills were not always in joint names to allow each partner to take responsibility for a greater or lesser share of the household expenses, depending on their relative earnings. Some couples directed all or most of their earnings into joint accounts, but in unequal proportions, and household bills and housing costs were paid from the joint account. Others had separate accounts but divided responsibility for different bills. . . . This approach tended not to be formalised in the same way as the joint–equal model but rather was a system based on trust and a partnership approach.

The participant and her partner were together for more than 10 years and cohabited for most of that time. They had two children together. They bought a house together some years into their relationship which they owned in joint names. During the first half of their relationship, both partners worked although the participant's partner earned a considerably higher salary than she did. The couple had a joint account into which both paid all of their earnings and out of which were paid all the bills, including the mortgage. Once their children were born, the couple agreed that the participant would stop work to care for them and that her partner would take responsibility for paying all the household bills and the mortgage.

Individual–Unequal

Here, couples viewed their finances as separate from their partner's and did not make equal contributions to the relationship in financial terms. The individual–unequal model was characterised by home ownership by one party who paid the majority or all of the mortgage costs. The other party either made some contribution to housing costs, sometimes referred to as rent, or made no contribution at all. Responsibilities for payment of other household expenses was often based on home ownership since household bills tended to be in the owner's name. The other partner either paid a contribution to household bills, or took responsibility for other 'non-regular' payments such as food, holidays, and other one-off purchases.

These couples generally did not have joint accounts (although some had a joint savings account that both contributed to). Where one partner earned significantly more than the other, they therefore had unequal financial access.

In general, people within this model did have very different levels of earnings, and sometimes one partner did not work. For some, gender roles were relevant, where the male partner believed it was his responsibility to provide for the woman but there were also cases where it was the woman who earned more and owned the home. The influence of prior relationships was also evident here and both men and women were concerned that past relationships, where they had relinquished some level of financial control, had left them with little money. This led some to retain a greater level of control over their finances and others to ensure they made the biggest financial contribution so that they could be sure they could cope should their partner leave them.

The participant and his partner were together for three-and-a-half years. They had no children together but the participant's three children from his previous marriage spent time at his home. The participant's partner moved into the home he rented six months into their relationship. He later bought the same house but the purchase was in his name only. Both partners worked full-time throughout the relationship though the man earned significantly more. They had no joint accounts and their earnings were paid into individual current accounts. All the household bills were in the participant's name and he paid for these and the mortgage himself. His partner was responsible only for the television and telephone contracts. Both contributed to the food shopping. The participant was keen that his younger partner was able to go out with her friends and do 'women's things' and so did not ask her to make a greater financial contribution.

Individual–Equal

The final model evident in cohabiting couples' accounts is the individual–equal model.

Couples here viewed and held their assets separately but were concerned to make equal financial contributions to the household and housing expenses. In several cases, each partner owned or rented a separate home, whether the couple actually lived in one or both. Parties were responsible for the payment of housing costs and household expenses at their own home but made equal and ad-hoc contributions to any joint expenditure such as food and leisure. The mechanisms for financial management reflected this individualisation of finances and couples were unlikely to have joint accounts (current or savings) or credit cards together.

As in the individual–unequal model above, the influence of past relationships was evident here, especially for older people and those who had been married before.

> The participant and her partner were together for eight years in total and cohabited for more than seven. They lived in the participant's home which she owned in her sole name. Her partner retained his own home throughout the duration of their relationship. The participant described them as 'totally financially independent' and they had no joint bank accounts or credit facilities. Each partner was responsible for paying the mortgage and household bills for the property they owned. Her partner made a small weekly contribution to the cost of food and they shared the cost of holidays and other leisure activities. The participant explained that this approach stemmed from a past relationship in which she had been 'too tied up financially' and found herself in a weak financial situation when it ended. She was keen this did not happen again.

Unsurprisingly, high levels of commitment to the cohabiting relationship were demonstrated by couples whose finances broadly followed the joint–equal model. The other models did not, however, appear to indicate a particular level of commitment. Indeed, within each of the other models, cases with higher and lower levels of commitment were apparent. For example, among couples whose approach to their finances indicated the individual–equal model, there were cases where people were highly committed to the relationship. However, they kept their finances separate to ensure financial security for them or their children. Conversely, others whose finances indicated this model were less certain about the future for the relationship and felt that keeping their finances separate would facilitate an easier separation should the relationship fail.

QUESTIONS

i. Of the models identified by Tennant and her colleagues, which do you think would also be found in married/civil partnered relationships? Which might be found most frequently, and why?

ii. Which model of cohabitant finance do you think would be most difficult to 'unscramble' in the event of separation?

iii. Do you think that any of these models are found in other types of relationship (siblings; friends sharing a home; etc.)?

6.2 THE LAW

The law does not entirely ignore cohabitants, and it certainly does not ignore their children; and we have to start our explanation of the current law with a reminder that the child support legislation applies to all parents within the jurisdiction, whether married, civil partners, former cohabitants, or those who have never lived together at all. All that we said in Chapter 5 about the impact of this legislation applies with equal force to this chapter.

Moreover, where cohabitants have children, the law has provided for property adjustment for the children's benefit. The power to do this originated in the Family Law Reform Act 1987. Paragraph 1(2)(d) and (e) of Schedule 1 to the Children Act 1989 now enables the court to make:

> (*d*) an order requiring a settlement to be made for the benefit of the child, and to the satisfaction of the court, of property—
>
> (i) to which either parent is entitled (either in possession or in reversion); and
>
> (ii) which is specified in the order;
>
> (*e*) an order requiring either or both parents of a child—
>
> (i) to transfer to the applicant, for the benefit of the child; or
>
> (ii) to transfer to the child himself,
>
> such property to which the parent is, or the parents are, entitled (either in possession or in reversion) as may be specified in the order.

These provisions apply to all parents, but married parents and civil partners will not need to use them because of the ancillary relief jurisdiction. Schedule 1 may enable the court to order the transfer of a council tenancy from one parent to the other, as in *K v K* [1992] 1 WLR 530, [1992] 2 FLR 220, or to require one parent to settle a capital sum on a child, as in *H v P (Illegitimate Child: Capital Provision)* [1993] Fam Law 515. Such a settlement will be made so as to last for the child's minority or while he is in full-time education, rather than to make an outright transfer of a capital asset. In *A v A* [1994] 1 FLR 657, [1994] 1 FCR 309, an application had been made for an order for the benefit of a child whose father was immensely wealthy; the settlement made for the child in *A v A* was described by Ward J as follows:

> The terms of the trust, the detail of which can be settled on further argument and if necessary with liberty to apply, should be that the property be conveyed to trustees, preferably... the nominees of the mother and father to hold the same for A for a term which shall terminate 6 months after A has attained the age of 18, or 6 months after she has completed her full-time education, which will include her tertiary education, whichever is latest. I give her that period of 6 months to find her feet and arrange her affairs. The trustees shall permit her to enjoy a reasonable gap between completing her school education and embarking upon her further education. I have regard to para 4(1)(*b*) which requires me to consider the financial needs, obligations and responsibilities of each parent and also subpara (*c*) which requires me to have regard to the financial needs of the child. The mother's obligation is to look after A, and A's financial need is to provide a roof over the head of her caretaker. It is, indeed, the father's obligation to provide the accommodation for the live-in help which A needs. Consequently, it must be a term of the settlement that while A is under the control of her mother and thereafter for so long as A does not object, the mother shall have the right to occupy the property to the exclusion of the father without paying rent therefore for the purpose of providing a home and care and support for A.

QUESTION

What would happen if the young woman decided, later in her teenage years, that she did object to her mother living in the house?

Of course, part of the reason why Schedule 1 to the Children Act 1989 is needed at all is the lack of any obligation upon cohabitants to support each other (let alone upon parents who have never cohabited), and the lack of any regime to adjust the property entitlements of cohabitants. Thus although it is possible for orders to be made under Schedule 1 where the parents are far less extremely wealthy than was the father in *A v A* (above), even so the possibilities are restricted to cases where property can be purchased or transferred free of mortgage: see *T v S* [1994] 1 FCR 743, [1994] 2 FLR 883. Obviously, the availability of these orders for children has an effect upon the housing position, and in some cases the property rights, of unmarried partners. Thus, while the mothers of the children concerned in *A v A* and *T v S* obtained, as a side-effect of the order, the right to live in the child's home until it was eventually disposed of, the mother in *K v K* (above) had the council tenancy transferred to her on a permanent basis. But Schedule 1 was enacted in order to put children of unmarried parents in the same position as children of married parents, and not to provide for the parents.

QUESTION

Where an order is made under Schedule 1 to the Children Act 1989 as in *A v A* or *T v S*, what will the mother do when the house is eventually sold?

In extremely wealthy cases, the courts have been willing to make an order under Schedule 1 for a 'carer's allowance', reasoning that it is in the interests of the child to have his or her carer supported: see *F v G (Child: financial provision)*, [2004] EWHC 1848 (Fam), [2005] 1 FLR 261.

But Schedule 1 would seem to have nothing to offer the children of parents of ordinary means, where the non-resident parent is not able to purchase or transfer a house free of mortgage and of course cannot be obliged to make the mortgage payments as a matter of maintenance for the parent with care. The *Mesher* order (see Chapter 5, p. 233) which, for all its disadvantages, has provided a solution for so many divorcing families, is not available.

Accordingly, for the majority of separating cohabitants, whether or not the parent with whom the children live has a home depends upon his or her own means, and in particular on whether or not that parent is the owner or joint owner of a house. Where that is not the case, rented housing – whether or not in the private sector – will have to be the answer. Note that if the family already lives in rented housing, the Family Law Act 1996 provides for the transfer of tenancies with statutory security of tenure; this means that, say, a woman living in her partner's council house could apply for an order that the tenancy be transferred to her. The court is required to bear a number of considerations in mind, including the housing needs and resources of each party, the health, safety and well-being of the parties and any child living with them, and the nature and length of the parties' relationship. The provisions are to be found in Part IV of the Act (section 53 and Schedule 7), which is concerned both with occupation rights and with mechanisms for protection from domestic violence; but there is no requirement that there need have been any violence or misconduct before such an order can be made.

In some cases, the question whether either or both separating cohabitants has an interest in real property will be in dispute; and the answer is to be found not in family law but in property law, and in the law of resulting and constructive trusts and of proprietary estoppel. The reader is referred to land law and trusts texts. Lord Walker of Gestingthorpe traced its development as follows in *Stack v Dowden* [2007] UKHL 17, [2007] 2 All ER 929:

> [15] It may be worth saying something...about the theoretical underpinning of this area of the law, and its development since those issues were considered by this House in *Pettitt v Pettitt* [1970] AC 777, [1969] 2 All ER 385, [1969] 2 WLR 966; *Gissing v Gissing* [1971] AC 886, [1970] 2 All ER 780, [1970] 3 WLR 255 and *Lloyds Bank v Rosset* [1991] 1 AC 107, [1990] 1 All ER 1111, [1990] 2 WLR 867....
>
> [16] Until the end of the 1960s most of the reported cases are concerned with disputes between married couples, and many of them focus on the issue of whether s 17 of the Married Women's Property Act 1882 was purely procedural, or gave the court a discretion to vary the parties' beneficial interests to accord with the court's view of what was fair.... That s 17 is only procedural, and does not confer any wide discretion, was finally and unanimously settled by this House in *Pettitt v Pettitt* [1970] AC 777, [1969] 2 All ER 385, [1969] 2 WLR 966. The House was also unanimous in the view that the actual disposal of the appeal (absent a wide discretion under s 17) presented few difficulties. It was almost unanimous in rejecting any general doctrine of 'family assets' and in the view that (at least as between husband and wife) the presumption of advancement was no longer appropriate for determining property disputes.
>
> [17] There was however little else on which the House agreed, either in *Pettitt v Pettitt* or in *Gissing v Gissing*. Revisiting these cases with hindsight derived from a further thirty-five years or so of reported decisions, we can discern that of all the questions to be asked about 'common intention' trusts as they emerge from *Pettitt v Pettitt* and *Gissing v Gissing*, the most crucial is whether the court must find a real bargain between the parties, or whether it can (in the absence of any sufficient evidence as to their real intentions) infer or impute a bargain.
>
> [18] In seeking to answer that question we must, I think, focus on the two speeches of Lord Diplock, since these (and especially his later speech in *Gissing v Gissing*) have been hugely influential in the later development of the law. In *Pettitt v Pettitt* [1970] AC 777 Lord Diplock (at p 822E) saw the court's task as being to ascertain the 'common intention' of the parties. He saw this as a task to be carried out, not by reference to the old presumptions of advancement and resulting trust, but by examining the facts and imputing an intention to the parties. He saw this as a 'familiar legal technique', comparable to finding an implied term in a contract. Lord Diplock used the word 'impute' (in various parts of speech) at least eight times in the crucial passage between pp. 822H and 825E.
>
> [19] *Pettitt v Pettitt* was decided in April 1969. It was followed by *Gissing v Gissing* [1971] AC 886, decided in July 1970. Three of the Appellate Committee – Lord Reid, Lord Morris of Borth-y-Gest and Lord Diplock – had sat on *Pettitt v Pettitt*. In his speech Lord Diplock acknowledged (at p 904E-F) that he had been in a minority in *Pettitt v Pettitt* and that 'I must now accept the majority decision that, put in this form at any rate, this is not the law.' But then having in *Pettitt v Pettitt* dismissed the resulting trust as old-fashioned and inappropriate, in *Gissing v Gissing* Lord Diplock apparently equated it (at p 905B-C) to a constructive trust:
>
> > 'A resulting, implied or constructive trust – and it is unnecessary for present purposes to distinguish between these three classes of trust – is created by a transaction between the trustee and the cestui que trust in connection with the acquisition by the trustee of a legal estate in land, whenever the trustee has so conducted himself that it would be inequitable to allow him to deny to the cestui que trust a beneficial interest in the land acquired. And

> he will be held so to have conducted himself if by his words or conduct he has induced the cestui que trust to act to his own detriment in the reasonable belief that by so acting he was acquiring a beneficial interest in the land.'

[20] Lord Diplock then proceeded to explain the circumstances in which the court would find a 'resulting, implied or constructive trust', and in particular when the court would 'infer [the parties'] common intention from their conduct' ([1971] AC 886 at p 906B). The very important passage which follows (pp. 906B-910A) uses the word 'infer' (in various parts of speech) at least 23 times. But for the substitution of the word 'infer' for 'impute' the substance of the reasoning is, it seems to me, essentially the same (although worked out in a good deal more detail) as Lord Diplock's reasoning in *Pettitt v Pettitt*, when he was in the minority.

[21] Since then Lord Diplock's speech in *Gissing v Gissing* has dominated this area of the law. It was seized on with particular enthusiasm by Lord Denning MR (see for instance his observations in *Eves v Eves* [1975] 3 All ER 768, [1975] 1 WLR 1338, 1341: 'Lord Diplock brought it into the world and we have nourished it'). Other judges have been less enthusiastic, being oppressed by the 'air of unreality about the whole exercise' (Griffiths LJ in *Bernard v Josephs* [1982] Ch 391, 404, [1982] 3 All ER 162, [1982] 2 WLR 1052). The whole problem is very helpfully discussed in Ch 10 of Gray & Gray, *Elements of Land Law*, 4th ed (2005), especially (as to the lack of reality of the bargain requirement) paras 10.92 to 10.99. Your Lordships may think that only a judge of Lord Diplock's stature could have achieved such a remarkable reversal of the tidal flow of authority as has followed on his speech in *Gissing v Gissing*. But it might have been better for the long-term development of the law if this House's rejection of 'imputation' in *Pettitt v Pettitt* had been openly departed from (under the statement as to judicial precedent made by the Lord Chancellor in 1966) rather than being circumvented by the rather ambiguous (and perhaps deliberately ambiguous) language of 'inference'.

[22] In *Pettitt* [1970] AC 777 there was a clear majority as to the need for an actual bargain, however imprecisely expressed: see Lord Morris of Borth-y-Gest at 804E-G, Lord Hodson at 810E-F and Lord Upjohn at 817G. Only Lord Reid, as I understand his speech (at 795D and 796D) showed some sympathy for Lord Diplock's views on 'imputation'. In *Gissing* [1971] AC 886 Lord Reid's opinion was again inconclusive, as I understand it but, paradoxically, Lord Reid (at 897F-G) seems to have found 'imputation' a more readily acceptable solution than 'inference' (which is the recurring theme of Lord Diplock's speech). Lord Morris (at 898C) and Viscount Dilhorne (at 900E-F) considered that the court could not construct a bargain for the parties if they had not made one. Lord Pearson (at 902G-H), like Lord Reid, favoured imputation, apparently equating it with inference.

[24] In *Lloyds Bank plc v Rosset* [1991] 1 AC 107 the Appellate Committee (no doubt conscious of the widely differing views expressed in *Pettitt* and *Gissing*) concurred in a single speech by the presiding Law Lord, Lord Bridge of Harwich. The wife claimed (against a bank which was her separated husband's secured creditor) an interest in the matrimonial home (which had been purchased ten years after the marriage and was held in the husband's sole name). She relied on a common understanding or intention arising out of her own efforts in arranging for extensive renovation works and herself carrying out some redecoration (the judge's findings on this are at [1991] 1 AC 107, 129F-131B). At first instance she succeeded on the issue of beneficial interest but failed on a conveyancing issue. She won her appeal ([1989] Ch 350; Purchas and Nicholls, Mustill LJJ dissenting on a conveyancing issue). The House of Lords allowed the bank's appeal on the short ground expressed by Lord Bridge (at 131F):

> 'The judge's view that some of this work was work 'upon which she could not reasonably have been expected to embark unless she was to have an interest in the house' seems to me, with respect, quite untenable.'

> [25] Lord Bridge then asked himself whether it was worthwhile to add any general remarks by way of illumination of the law. He limited himself to drawing attention to one 'critical distinction'. If (at 132E-G) there is to be a finding of an actual 'agreement, arrangement, or understanding' between the parties it must:
>
> > 'be based on evidence of express discussions between the partners, however imperfectly remembered and however imprecise their terms may have been.'
>
> Lord Bridge continued (132H-133B):
>
> > 'In sharp contrast with this situation is the very different one where there is no evidence to support a finding of an agreement or arrangement to share, however reasonable it might have been for the parties to reach such an arrangement if they had applied their minds to the question, and where the court must rely entirely on the conduct of the parties both as to the basis from which to infer a common intention to share the property beneficially and as the conduct relied on to give rise to a constructive trust. In this situation direct contributions to the purchase price by the partner who is not the legal owner, whether initially or by payment of mortgage instalments, will readily justify the inference necessary to the creation of a constructive trust. But, as I read the authorities, it is at least extremely doubtful whether anything less will do.'
>
> In concurring in this passage the House was unanimously, if unostentiously, agreeing that a 'common intention' trust could be inferred even when there was no evidence of an actual agreement. Apart from two bare references to 'a constructive trust or a proprietary estoppel' (at 132G and 133F) Lord Bridge did not refer to the elaborate arguments of counsel (at 110G-125C) addressed to him as to the varieties and interaction of these two concepts.
>
> [26] Lord Bridge's extreme doubt 'whether anything less will do' was certainly consistent with many first-instance and Court of Appeal decisions, but I respectfully doubt whether it took full account of the views (conflicting though they were) expressed in *Gissing* (see especially Lord Reid [1971] AC 886 at 896G–897B and Lord Diplock at 909 D-H). It has attracted some trenchant criticism from scholars as potentially productive of injustice (see Gray & Gray, op cit, paras 10.132 to 10.137, the last paragraph being headed 'A More Optimistic Future'). Whether or not Lord Bridge's observation was justified in 1990, in my opinion the law has moved on, and your Lordships should move it a little more in the same direction, while bearing in mind that the Law Commission may soon come forward with proposals which, if enacted by Parliament, may recast the law in this area.

Stack v Dowden was a case where joint owners had failed to spell out their beneficial interests. Baroness Hale discussed the use of the land registry form TR1 and its potential role in eliminating this problem:

> [52] Form TR1, in use from 1 April 1998, provides a box for the transferees to declare whether they are to hold the property on trust for themselves as joint tenants, or on trust for themselves as tenants in common in equal shares, or on some other trusts which are inserted on the form. . . . If its completion and execution by or on behalf of all joint proprietors were mandatory, the problem we now face would disappear. However, the form might then include an option for those who deliberately preferred not to commit themselves as to the beneficial interests at the outset and to rely on the principles discussed below.

In the absence of a declaration of trust, and against the background of the law and the practical problems we discussed above, Baroness Hale (with whom the majority in the House of Lords agreed) went on to explain the legal principles applicable. Mr Stack was claiming 50 per cent of the net proceeds of sale of the couple's house, while Ms Dowden claimed 65 per cent, on the basis of her contributions to its acquisition:

> [56] Just as the starting point where there is sole legal ownership is sole beneficial ownership, the starting point where there is joint legal ownership is joint beneficial ownership. The onus is upon the person seeking to show that the beneficial ownership is different from the legal ownership. So in sole ownership cases it is upon the non-owner to show that he has any interest at all. In joint ownership cases, it is upon the joint owner who claims to have other than a joint beneficial interest.
>
> ...
>
> [58] The issue as it has been framed before us is whether a conveyance into joint names indicates only that each party is intended to have some beneficial interest but says nothing about the nature and extent of that beneficial interest, or whether a conveyance into joint names establishes a prime facie case of joint and equal beneficial interests until the contrary is shown. For the reasons already stated, at least in the domestic consumer context, a conveyance into joint names indicates both legal and beneficial joint tenancy, unless and until the contrary is proved.
>
> [59] The question is, how, if at all, is the contrary to be proved? Is the starting point the presumption of resulting trust, under which shares are held in proportion to the parties' financial contributions to the acquisition of the property, unless the contributor or contributors can be shown to have had a contrary intention? Or is it that the contrary can be proved by looking at all the relevant circumstances in order to discern the parties' common intention?
>
> [60] The presumption of resulting trust is not a rule of law. According to Lord Diplock in *Pettitt v Pettitt* [1970] AC 777, at 823H, the equitable presumptions of intention are:
>
> > 'no more than a consensus of judicial opinion disclosed by reported cases as to the most likely inference of fact to be drawn in the absence of any evidence to the contrary'.
>
> Equity, being concerned with commercial realities, presumed against gifts and other windfalls (such as survivorship). But even equity was prepared to presume a gift where the recipient was the provider's wife or child. These days, the importance to be attached to who paid for what in a domestic context may be very different from its importance in other contexts or long ago.
>
> There is no need for me to rehearse all the developments in the case law since *Pettitt v Pettitt* and *Gissing v Gissing*, discussed over more than 70 pages following the quoted passage, by Chadwick LJ in *Oxley v Hiscock* [2004] EWCA Civ 546, [2005] Fam 211, and most importantly by my noble and learned friend, Lord Walker of Gestingthorpe in his opinion, which make good that proposition. The law has indeed moved on in response to changing social and economic conditions. The search is to ascertain the parties' shared intentions, actual, inferred or imputed, with respect to the property in the light of their whole course of conduct in relation to it.
>
> [61] *Oxley v Hiscock* was, of course, a different case from this. The property had been conveyed into the sole name of one of the cohabitants. The Claimant had first to surmount the hurdle of showing that she had any beneficial interest at all, before showing exactly what that interest was. The first could readily be inferred from the fact that each party had made some kind of financial contribution towards the purchase. As to the second, Chadwick LJ said this, at para 69:
>
> > '... in many such cases, the answer will be provided by evidence of what they said and did at the time of the acquisition. But, in a case where there is no evidence of any discussion between them as to the amount of the share which each was to have – and even in a case where the evidence is that there was no discussion on that point – the question still

> requires an answer. It must now be accepted that (at least in this court and below) the answer is that *each is entitled to that share which the court considers fair having regard to the whole course of dealing between them in relation to the property.* And in that context, the whole course of dealing between them in relation to the property includes the arrangements which they make from time to time in order to meet the outgoings (for example, mortgage contributions, council tax and utilities, repairs, insurance and housekeeping) which have to be met if they are to live in the property as their home.' (Emphasis supplied)

...The passage quoted is very similar to the view of the Law Commission in *Sharing Homes* (2002,... para 4.27) on the quantification of beneficial entitlement:

> 'If the question really is one of the parties' "common intention", we believe that there is much to be said for adopting what has been called a "holistic approach" to quantification, undertaking a survey of the whole course of dealing between the parties and taking account of all conduct which throws light on the question what shares were intended.'

That may be the preferable way of expressing what is essentially the same thought, for two reasons. First, it emphasises that the search is still for the result which reflects what the parties must, in the light of their conduct, be taken to have intended. Second, therefore, it does not enable the court to abandon that search in favour of the result which the court itself considers fair. For the court to impose its own view of what is fair upon the situation in which the parties find themselves would be to return to the days before *Pettitt v Pettitt* [1970] AC 777 without even the fig leaf of s 17 of the 1882 Act.

[62] Furthermore, although the parties' intentions may change over the course of time, producing what my noble and learned friend, Lord Hoffmann, referred to in the course of argument as an 'ambulatory' constructive trust, at any one time their interests must be the same for all purposes. They cannot at one and the same time intend, for example, a joint tenancy with survivorship should one of them die while they are still together, a tenancy in common in equal shares should they separate on amicable terms after the children have grown up, and a tenancy in common in unequal shares should they separate on acrimonious terms while the children are still with them.

[63] We are not in this case concerned with the first hurdle. There is undoubtedly an argument for saying, as did the Law Commission in *Sharing Homes* (2002, *op cit*, para 4.23) that the observations, which were strictly *obiter dicta*, of Lord Bridge of Harwich in *Lloyd's Bank plc v Rosset* [1991] 1 AC 107 have set that hurdle rather too high in certain respects. But that does not concern us now. It is common ground that a conveyance into joint names is sufficient, at least in the vast majority of cases, to surmount the first hurdle. The question is whether, that hurdle surmounted, the approach to quantification should be the same.

...

[68] The burden will therefore be on the person seeking to show that the parties did intend their beneficial interests to be different from their legal interests, and in what way. This is not a task to be lightly embarked upon. In family disputes, strong feelings are aroused when couples split up. These often lead the parties, honestly but mistakenly, to reinterpret the past in self-exculpatory or vengeful terms. They also lead people to spend far more on the legal battle than is warranted by the sums actually at stake. A full examination of the facts is likely to involve disproportionate costs. In joint names cases it is also unlikely to lead to a different result unless the facts are very unusual. Nor may disputes be confined to the parties themselves. People with an interest in the deceased's estate may well wish to assert that he had a beneficial tenancy in common. It cannot be the case that all the hundreds of thousands, if not millions, of transfers into joint names using the old forms are vulnerable to challenge in the courts simply because it is likely that the owners contributed unequally to their purchase.

[69] In law, 'context is everything' and the domestic context is very different from the commercial world. Each case will turn on its own facts. Many more factors than financial contributions may be relevant to divining the parties' true intentions. These include: any advice or discussions at the time of the transfer which cast light upon their intentions then; the reasons why the home was acquired in their joint names; the reasons why (if it be the case) the survivor was authorised to give a receipt for the capital moneys; the purpose for which the home was acquired; the nature of the parties' relationship; whether they had children for whom they both had responsibility to provide a home; how the purchase was financed, both initially and subsequently; how the parties arranged their finances, whether separately or together or a bit of both; how they discharged the outgoings on the property and their other household expenses. When a couple are joint owners of the home and jointly liable for the mortgage, the inferences to be drawn from who pays for what may be very different from the inferences to be drawn when only one is owner of the home. The arithmetical calculation of how much was paid by each is also likely to be less important. It will be easier to draw the inference that they intended that each should contribute as much to the household as they reasonably could and that they would share the eventual benefit or burden equally. The parties' individual characters and personalities may also be a factor in deciding where their true intentions lay. In the cohabitation context, mercenary considerations may be more to the fore than they would be in marriage, but it should not be assumed that they always take pride of place over natural love and affection. At the end of the day, having taken all this into account, cases in which the joint legal owners are to be taken to have intended that their beneficial interests should be different from their legal interests will be very unusual.

[70] This is not, of course, an exhaustive list. There may also be reason to conclude that, whatever the parties' intentions at the outset, these have now changed. An example might be where one party has financed (or constructed himself) an extension or substantial improvement to the property, so that what they have now is significantly different from what they had then.

...

Applying the Law to the Facts

[89]... The one thing that can clearly be said is that, when Chatsworth Road was bought, both parties knew that Ms Dowden had contributed far more to the cash paid towards it than had Mr Stack. Furthermore, although they planned that Mr Stack would pay the interest on the loan and premiums on the joint policy, they also planned to reduce the loan as quickly as they could. These are certainly factors which could, in context, support the inference of an intention to share otherwise than equally.

[90] The context is supplied by the nature of the parties' conduct and attitudes towards their property and finances. This is not a case in which it can be said that the parties pooled their separate resources, even notionally, for the common good. The only things they ever had in their joint names were Chatsworth Road and the associated endowment policy. Everything else was kept strictly separate. Each made separate savings and investments most of which it was accepted were their own property. It might have been asked, why then did they make an exception for Chatsworth Road? This is the obvious question. The obvious answer, which Ms Dowden has never denied, was that this time it was indeed intended that Mr Stack should have some interest in the property. In the light of all the other evidence, it cannot be conclusive as to what that interest was.

[91] There are other aspects to their financial relationship which tell against joint ownership. Chatsworth Road was, of course, to be a home for the parties and their four children. But they undertook separate responsibility for that part of the expenditure which each had agreed to pay.

The only regular expenditure to which it is clear that Mr Stack committed himself was the interest and premiums on Chatsworth Road. All other regular commitments in both houses were undertaken by Ms Dowden. Had it been clear that he had undertaken to pay for consumables and child minding, it might have been possible to deduce some sort of commitment that each would do what they could. But Mr Stack's evidence did not even go as far as that.

[92] This is, therefore, a very unusual case. There cannot be many unmarried couples who have lived together for as long as this, who have had four children together, and whose affairs have been kept as rigidly separate as this couple's affairs were kept. This is all strongly indicative that they did not intend their shares, even in the property which was put into both their names, to be equal (still less that they intended a beneficial joint tenancy with the right of survivorship should one of them die before it was severed). Before the Court of Appeal, Ms Dowden contended for a 65% share and in my view she has made good her case for that.

QUESTION

In what circumstances might you advise your client to leave it to the courts, as suggested in paragraph [52]?

Lord Neuberger disagreed with the reasoning of Baroness Hale and with the majority in *Stack v Dowden*:

[110] Where the only additional relevant evidence to the fact that the property has been acquired in joint names is the extent of each party's contribution to the purchase price, the beneficial ownership at the time of acquisition will be held, in my view, in the same proportions as the contributions to the purchase price. That is the resulting trust solution. The only realistic alternative in such a case would be to adhere to the joint ownership solution. ...

[111] ... Lord Browne-Wilkinson in *Westdeutsche Landesbank Girozentrale v Islington London Borough Council* [1996] AC 669 at 708A, [1996] 2 All ER 961, [1996] 2 WLR 802 said that the circumstances in which 'a resulting trust arises' included:

> '[W]here A ... pays (wholly or in part) for the purchase of property which is vested ... in the joint names of A and B, there is a presumption that A did not intend to make a gift to B: the ... property is held ... in shares proportionate to their contributions.'

[112] By contrast, while Lord Reid's suggestion in *Gissing* at 897B that the notion that equality is equity is no more than a 'high-sounding brocard' may be a little extreme, the invocation of such a notion as between cohabitants, who have contributed unequally to the acquisition of a home, appears to me to be inconsistent with principle. It is almost a resurrection of the 'family assets' hypothesis disposed of in *Pettitt* – see at 795B, 809H-810H, and 816G-817H. It involves invoking a presumption of advancement between unmarried cohabitants, where such a presumption has never applied, and at a time when, as I have mentioned, the court is increasingly unenthusiastic about the presumption, even in relationships where it does apply.

[113] There are also practical reasons for rejecting equality and supporting the resulting trust solution. The property may be bought in joint names for reasons which cast no light on the parties' intentions with regard to beneficial ownership. It may be the solicitor's decision or

> assumption, the lender's preference for the security of two borrowers, or the happenstance of how the initial contact with the solicitor was made. As the survey mentioned by Baroness Hale in para 45 of her opinion indicates, parties in a loving relationship are often not anxious to discuss how they should divide the beneficial interest in the home they are about to buy. They would have to debate what should happen if their relationship broke down (the most likely circumstance, albeit not the only one, in which the question would arise). While in some cases they may assume equal ownership, in others they may not. ... If they are happy with an equal split at the beginning, one might expect them to say so. The fact that they do not do so may be more consistent with the view that they (or at any rate the bigger contributor) would not be happy with that outcome for the very reason that their contributions differed.

As to the present case, Lord Neuberger said:

> [148] [W]here the resulting trust presumption (or indeed any other basis of apportionment) applies at the date of acquisition, I am unpersuaded that (save perhaps in a most unusual case) anything other than subsequent discussions, statements or actions, which can fairly be said to imply a positive intention to depart from that apportionment, will do to justify a change in the way in which the beneficial interest is owned. To say that factors such as a long relationship, children, a joint bank account, and sharing daily outgoings of themselves are enough, or even of potential central importance, appears to me not merely wrong in principle, but a recipe for uncertainty, subjectivity, and a long and expensive examination of facts. It could also be said to be arbitrary, as, if such factors of themselves justify a departure from the original apportionment, I find it hard to see how it could be to anything other than equality. If a departure from the original apportionment was solely based on such factors, it seems to me that the judge would almost always have to reach an 'all or nothing' decision. Thus, in this case, he would have to ask whether, viewed in the round, the personal and financial characteristics of the relationship between Mr Stack and Ms Dowden, after they acquired the house, justified a change in ownership of the beneficial interest from 35-65 to 50-50, even though nothing they did or said related to the ownership of that interest (save, perhaps, the repayments of the mortgage). In my view, that involves approaching the question in the wrong way. Subject, perhaps, to exceptional cases, whose possibility it would be unrealistic not to acknowledge, an argument for an alteration in the way in which the beneficial interest is held cannot, in my opinion, succeed, unless it can be shown that there was a discussion, statement or action which, viewed in its context, namely the parties' relationship, implied an actual agreement or understanding to effect such an alteration.
> [149] Turning to the present case, I consider that there are no grounds for varying the split of the beneficial ownership, which arose in 1993 on the acquisition of the house, as a result of any events which occurred subsequently, at any rate to an extent more favourable to Mr Stack than the 35% accepted by the Court of Appeal.

Ms Stack and Mr Dowden were, we are told, an extremely unusual case, and it was this that enabled the majority in the House of Lords to go beyond the legal title in determining their entitlement (whereas, as we have seen, Lord Neuberger would have reached the same conclusion by a very different route). Rebecca Probert comments, in 'Cohabitants and Joint Ownership: the Implications of *Stack v Dowden*' (2007):

> There is ... a paradox in the reasoning of both Baroness Hale (with whom Lord Hoffman concurred) and Lord Walker of Gestingthorpe: both stress that it should be difficult to depart from the presumption of equal division, but at the same time both take a wider view of the

financial contributions that may cast light on the parties' intentions and so justify a departure from equality in line with those intentions. ... It is easy to share Lord Walker's hope that there will be a diminishing number of cases in which a detailed examination of the respective contributions of the parties is required (at para [34]), but broadening the range of relevant factors is not necessarily the way to achieve this. A departure from equal division may only be justified in exceptional cases, but until the evidence has been heard, how can it be determined whether any given case is exceptional or not?

QUESTION

i. If you decide – and many of you will, or do, or have done so – to live with your partner, for a long or short period, without getting married or forming a civil partnership, will you keep separate bank accounts? Or a joint account? Or both? Or might you provide your partner with a credit card in her name but with the direct debit to be taken from your sole bank account?

ii. Look again at the financial models identified by Tennant and her colleagues on p. 259; bearing in mind Probert's comments, what sort of financial arrangements might you describe as 'exceptional'?

iii. Charles Harpum, in 'Cohabitation Consultation' (1995), wrote: 'Homesharers are not denizens of some black hole of outlawry. Is it better for the law that regulates their affairs to be developed by legislation after an exhaustive consideration of the issues or should it continue to be left to the chances of litigation?' What is your view?

For separating cohabitants, and even for their solicitors, the law can be a minefield, as Gillian Douglas, Julia Pearce and Hilary Woodward explain in the findings of their research study (2007a):

[W]e found that cohabitation property cases formed only a very small proportion of the caseloads of the practitioners in our study. For the solicitors, a handful of cases per year was not unusual; 12–15 was high. Most solicitors reported that they found it more difficult to explain the relevant law to cohabiting clients than they did to divorcing clients. This difficulty seemed to be because, in the area of cohabitation property disputes, the legal concepts are less comprehensible, the law is generally complex and has developed piecemeal, and there is no 'well-trodden path' to follow, as there is in ancillary relief. Given this, and that solicitors generally handledonly a very few cases, their work could not become routinised. Their approach was therefore more individualised and idiosyncratic, and often a 'learning experience' for them as well as their clients. Not surprisingly, clients struggled to understand what they were told.

Rosalind Tennant, Jean Taylor and Jane Lewis interviewed a number of solicitors as part of their project (2006; see p. 259 above) and noted:

Solicitors approached issues about home ownership from three perspectives: investigating how joint property was held; Schedule 1 of the Children Act; and trust law and proprietary estoppel.

Across the three groups solicitors were generally very familiar with dealing with these issues and spoke confidently about them, and there appeared to be very common understandings and approaches.

Nature of Joint Ownership

Where property was jointly owned, the first consideration was whether it was held as joint tenants or as tenants in common, and whether there was a declaration of trust. Solicitors said that clients are often not familiar with these issues and conveyancing files had to be sought to clarify. If there was no trust deed, the expectation was that jointly owned property would be shared equally, and it was said that this information is not well received by the partner who has contributed most.

Schedule 1 Children Act

There were many references to using Schedule 1 to delay a sale and establish a right for the children and their main carer to remain in the house during the children's minority. ... The solicitors involved in the study saw it as a helpful approach but noted some flaws.

The main problem identified was that it provides a home for the main carer (usually the mother) only until the children have completed full-time education, with resultant uncertainty and potential for hardship when the children leave home.

One solicitor described the law as essentially treating the mother as 'a servant' since her right to occupy derives from her role as the children's carer. There was, as a result, a preference for making claims under [the Trusts of Land and Appointment of Trustees Act] if possible because it provides the mother with immediate capital, certainty and freedom, and potentially a larger share of the equity.

The second problem identified is that Schedule 1 may not provide a solution if the main carer is not in a position to pay the mortgage. It was thought that there is provision under the Children Act to order the father to continue to pay the mortgage, but there was some uncertainty about this. It was also noted that if the children are over 16, a Schedule 1 order could only be expected in exceptional circumstances.

Nevertheless, Schedule 1 was seen as an important protection....

Trust Law

...The discussion of trust law mostly related to constructive trusts. A key problem identified in establishing constructive trusts was the need to produce evidence that the couple intended the house to be jointly owned ... This was seen as an approach which was emotionally unhelpful to the partners, but necessary.

> 'I mean, one of the things I tell my clients to do is go up into the loft and read every single Valentine's card you've got, every single love letter you've got... what he promised you. I want to find that Valentine's card which say, "what's mine is yours, you know, I'll care for you always". I mean that's an horrendous thing to have to tell someone to do when they've just broken up with someone, to go and read their love letters.' (Solicitor)

> They also talked about the difficulty of actually proving intention. Solicitors said that it led to couples accusing each other of lying and a much more confrontational way of dealing with settlements than in divorce cases. It was said to be difficult to establish a constructive trust if the house was bought before the relationship began. Courts were said to be much less sympathetic to trust claims if there are no children in the relationship, and difficulties were presented if the children are over 18.
>
> > 'I mean, she's even more stuffed than she was before [if the children have left home] because at least she can say, "We bought the house together as a home for the children", even though it was in his name. But if they were older and they'd left, tough.' (Solicitors)
>
> Where the home had been bought for the children and they were still under 18, solicitors said that couples could find themselves arguing about who the children should live with as a way of retaining the home. The difficulty of establishing sufficient contributions was also discussed. They said that indirect contributions needed to be substantial and more than just basic outgoings, and direct mortgage payments needed to relate to repayment of equity and not just payment of interest.
>
> As a result, the solicitors said that there is a high degree of uncertainty involved in trust cases.

The answer, as the property law cases tell us, is of course to settle the beneficial ownership of the couple's home long before any dispute arises. But even when this advice is followed, it may give rise to a difficult situation, as Douglas and her colleagues report (2007b):

> [Some] claimed that, though advice may have been given, this had been in circumstances which made it difficult properly to consider or act on it. Rosie, who had not known whether she owned as a joint tenant or tenant in common, told us that she had been present in the solicitor's office when it had been put to her partner, Ewan, that he might want to provide some form of capital protection for the substantial capital sum he was contributing to the purchase price of their home. She acknowledged that this had been his first opportunity to think about this option. He himself told us:
>
> *It was explained to me that I could protect my extra contribution – but she was pregnant, sitting there next to me – you just don't do that.*
>
> Frank had felt similarly constrained:
>
> *It's an embarrassing situation to sit there in front of the financial adviser – when you have to tick the box, when you're with the woman you're engaged to be married to, that you've committed the rest of your life to and say... this is actually all my money and it's going to stay my money just in case we split up.*

When it came to resolving the financial consequences of separation, therefore, some cohabitants found themselves in a predictable situation, which might or might not have been welcome to them. For others, things were not straightforward:

> Pat had owned her own home for several years before her partner moved in. She had only invited him to the property as a temporary measure, as she thought, while he was experiencing financial difficulties. She had no intention of conferring any entitlement in the property and did not have any great commitment to the relationship. When it ended at her behest, her partner refused to leave without payment from her, and then threatened proceedings to establish a share in her property. Perceiving her partner's claim for £24,000 as spurious and nothing more than an underhand attempt to fund the deposit to purchase a property for himself, she commented:
>
> *If he got that, he'd have lived in my house all those years for free.*

6.19 In other cases, the property was owned jointly, but in circumstances where the individual felt it entirely unjust that the partner should take a share in its value. For example, while his fiancée had contributed nothing to the purchase of a home for the two of them, Frank had contributed £90,000 from the proceeds of sale of his previous home, plus a further £26,000 from savings for refurbishments. After nine months, the relationship foundered, but the fiancée refused to co-operate in a sale of the property without payment to herself of half its net proceeds.

...

Four of the individuals in our sample had left a property in which they lived with a partner, and believed strongly that something was due to them as a consequence of their input into the relationship and/or the property, and that they should not be expected simply to walk away without any sort of financial recompense. All the properties involved in this category were in the sole ownership of the other partner. Those in this category may represent the other side of the previous scenario.

6.22 Helen had helped her boyfriend on a major restoration project to a property he had bought in his sole name. As far as she was concerned, this had been a shared enterprise, which took over their lives for a considerable period. As the relationship had developed she had come to perceive it as a quasi-marriage and saw it as grossly unfair that her partner alone should benefit from the fruits of her hard work when they separated. However, he refused to offer any form of financial recompense, or to engage with her at all.

6.23 Martin considered that he had made a substantial financial contribution to his partner Tara's purchase of her council house in her sole name, which she told him would be transferred into their joint names after three years. However, they separated before then and the transfer was never made. The property was subsequently sold for a handsome profit, but Tara refused to pay him anything at all. For her part, she considered that the relationship had been relatively short-term and had not involved a high level of commitment.

She also questioned the sums Martin claimed to have paid, suggesting that he would have to have spent a similar amount for his own living expenditure whether they had been together or not.

QUESTIONS

i. What would you advise Frank and Helen?

ii. Suppose that you have been living with your partner for five years, in your house. Your partner has made the occasional contribution to the domestic bills. The relationship has now broken down and you want your partner to leave, but he or she refuses to do so and claims an interest in the property. You can see what the law is. What are you going to do?

6.3 THE MYTH

We have seen that cohabitants, unlike married couples and civil partners, do not have access to ancillary relief-like provisions to redistribute their property at the end of their relationship. And they are of course under no obligation to maintain each other for the future. Unless Schedule 1 to the Children Act 1989 can be of assistance, they have to resort to the ordinary rules of property law, which are difficult to understand and may generate inappropriate results. A further problem for cohabitants is that many of them have misunderstood the legal effect of their relationship. Anne Barlow and her colleagues explore this in their book *Cohabitation, Marriage and the Law* (2005). They explain:

> [T]here is a widely held belief that heterosexual couples living together 'as man and wife' acquire 'marriage-like' rights and responsibilities through 'common law marriage', at least after a given period of time. This is what we call the common law marriage myth. As family lawyers can testify, this 'myth' often surfaces as a deeply held view with detrimental implications for those who believe. However, the exact scope and depth of this myth have been unclear. The 2000 BSA [British Social Attitudes] survey, which we draw on here, provided the first representative national information about cohabitants' understandings of it.
>
> ...
>
> In the national 2000 BSA survey respondent were asked 'as far as you know do unmarried couples who live together for some time have a "common law marriage" which gives them the same legal rights as married couples?' Only 37 per cent were aware that cohabitants do not have the same legal rights as married couples, while over half of all respondents (56 per cent) believed that cohabitants and married couples are treated equally in law.
>
> Angela ... believed that the law protects her in the same way as it protects married couples – as she put it—
>
> > Oh yes definitely, the same yes ... if it did go wrong I know that half of everything is mine and half my partner's. Oh yes, you've got the same legal rights.
>
> [R]espondents were asked to consider the following scenario:
>
> > I'd like you now to imagine an unmarried couple with no children who have been living together for ten years. Say their relationship ends. Do you think the woman ... does in fact have the same rights as a married woman to claim financial support from the man, or does she have fewer rights?
>
> In the BSA study, over half, 54 per cent, of all respondents correctly thought that a woman in this situation would have fewer rights than a married woman. (38 per cent believed she had the same rights, and eight per cent did not know.) ... For this issue, then, belief in the legal efficacy of a supposed common law marriage was less pervasive, if still widespread.
>
> ...
>
> We asked interviewees about their sources of legal information in the follow-up survey. Generally, the results point to an informal knowledge world where most respondents get the bulk of their information from friends and family.

Rebecca Probert, in 'Why Couples Still Believe in Common-Law Marriage' (2007) adds some further insight into the persistence of the myth:

> It may be argued that an individual only needs to read one article rebutting the common-law marriage myth to be disabused. But conflicting messages from the media may reduce the effect of such information. And individuals may not retain the information unless it is of direct relevance to them. Moreover, not every reader will read every part of the newspaper and may miss the more informative articles in the legal section. By contrast, incidental references to common-law husbands and wives appear in every section of the newspaper: in leaders and columns; in the financial pages and in accounts of sporting heroes; in reviews of books and plays and descriptions of television programmes; in obituaries and in gossip columns; in letters from readers seeking advice on matters of etiquette (see eg J Morgan, 'Modern Manners', *The Times*, 27 March 1999, who advised his correspondent that the cohabiting couple in question were 'to all intents

and purposes... "common-law" husband and wife'); and in humorous pieces (see eg A Coren, 'Seen the digital future? It's 24-hour conkers and yo-yo', *The Times*, 30 September 1998). But by far the most common context for mentions of common-law wives and husbands is crime – with the common-law partner appearing variously as victim, perpetrator, accomplice or partner. Lurid stories of crimes – particularly with headlines such as 'Sex triangle wife to marry lodger' (*The Times*, 22 March 1997) or 'Enslaved ritual killer cut off head of cult's ex-chief' (*The Times*, 21 June 1988) are perhaps more likely to attract readers than the soberly titled articles on legal rights. It is unsurprising, therefore, that the myth persists.

QUESTION

Most people do know that ignorance of the law is no defence. Why do you think that unmarried partners do not take the trouble to inform themselves of the legal consequences of cohabitation?

The government's *Living Together* project has endeavoured to dispel ignorance and put an end to the myth, as well as promoting practical solutions for cohabitants. The project has used a website http://www.advicenow.org.uk/livingtogether and a publicity campaign.

THREE THINGS THAT
DON'T EXIST
1. LOCH NESS
MONSTER
2. CATS' NINE
LIVES
3. COMMON LAW
MARRIAGE

Anne Barlow, Carole Burgoyne and Janet Smithson (2007) have researched the effectiveness of the project, and find as follows:

Actions Taken After Accessing Website

Planning to Get Married

Some of those accessing the website were considering marriage as a way of securing their legal and financial position. Some (the pragmatists) were happy to do this, and were encouraged, after accessing the website, to make plans to get married. One interviewee had got engaged shortly after visiting the website.

Others, who had ideological objections to marriage, were considering marriage for financial and other legal reasons, but very reluctantly.

> 'We might eventually get married, but we're both quite anti-marriage, really. But we might do eventually, which would be for financial reasons, really... There are problems if you've got children and certainly if you've got property together. And so a kind of death bed marriage might come up' (John, partner of Linda, long term cohabitant, 4 children).

Others... were not willing to countenance marriage and lacked what may be described as 'legal rationality' in this context.

Making a Living Together Contract or Will

Some of the respondents had made wills or living together arrangements before accessing the website (both usually informally). Many participants intended after accessing the website to take action such as making wills or living together contracts, or visiting a solicitor.

> 'I found it was like a guide to living together and it had a template of, um, a living together agreement that you could make out, so we've got that and I think we're going to do that.' (Emma, new cohabitant)

Arranging to See a Solicitor

None of the cohabitants interviewed had arranged to see a solicitor after visiting the site, though some thought they might get around to it sometime. In general, the visitors to the website were downloading forms and taking in information but not making any immediate changes.

Reasons for Not Taking Action

Lack of Appropriate Actions

One of the main reasons for not taking action after visiting the website was the perceived lack of suitable actions for cohabitants to take. For the long term, committed cohabitants..., the main reason for not taking actions after accessing the website was the lack of options, short of getting married, for regulating their position in terms of pension and inheritance rights. People also perceived some of the options suggested on the website as not worth following up if they were not necessarily legally binding. For example, people were not sure that in an emergency a hospital would respect the Next of Kin card, even if it was filled out and carried.

Some of the respondents who were ideologically opposed to marriage were considering challenging the legal situation, or waiting for the law to change on these issues.

...

Cost of Actions

Others mentioned the cost of legal action against the likelihood of needing the action at a later stage:

> 'You've got to weigh up the cost of these sort of legal transactions and think, well, you know, is it really worth going into it for, you know, something that's probably not going to happen' (Laura, cohabitant)

Actions Seen as Legally Unenforceable

People generally felt that the cohabitation contract, or living together agreement, suggested on the LTC website, was not very useful as it was not legally binding, and as such not worth filling out.

> 'As I understand it, that stuff [cohabitation contract] is legally unenforceable anyway. So, um... You know, it's like pre-nuptial agreements. Courts don't take them into account.' (Simon, cohabitant with 2 children)
>
> 'I wouldn't feel it [a cohabitation contract] gives me any more security... It... Because these things haven't really been tested enough in court I wouldn't be comfortable with them.' (Claire, cohabiting 7 years, no children)

...

'Getting Round To It'

People talked about the difficulty of getting around to action:

> 'You do think about all these things when you start filling in your forms and going to the solicitor and things, and then when you actually move in it just gets completely forgotten. There's so many other things to do' (Barbara, new cohabitant).

Actions Seen as Too Complex or Confusing

> 'I brought home this thing about filling in a will and it's just kind of sat underneath the table for...two months or so... Well, I was going to do it on my own. That's why I got this pack sent home. But I looked at it and there are so many questions. ...' (Barbara, new cohabitant)

...

Optimism Bias and Risk Assessment

An optimism bias, or not believing the worst will happen, may account for some of the lack of actions taken by cohabitants. ... In general, this group of respondents was very aware that many relationships break down, and did feel that this might be a possibility for their relationship, however most couples felt that if they did split up, both partners would remain reasonable.

...

Difficulty of Talking and Planning for Negative Future Events

Cohabitants talked about the difficulties of thinking ahead, especially about death and splitting up, at a time of moving in together. There was a recurring view that filling out a living together or cohabitation agreement is 'too negative'.

...

'I know when we looked at the cohabitation contract we'd probably been together about 10 years. We just looked at it and just thought, 'This isn't right for us, actually.' It's going to cause more grief to actually specify it all out. Whereas actually if we split up tomorrow, we will find a way of splitting our assets. We know we will.' (Hannah, long term cohabitant)

Difficulties of Persuading Partner of Need For Action

Many of these cohabitants in uneven relationships perceived the main difficulty to be in persuading their partner to agree to an action, either marriage, or making a will, or making a living together agreement. This was particularly the case with older couples with greater assets.

...

'I mentioned once something about [making a will] and he said, 'Oh, well. Do you want me to...?' And I thought, Well, it's a bit rude to say to someone, 'Excuse me, can you just make another will and leave me everything?!' I mean, it does sound like gold-digging then. But it's from a practical point of view, you know.' (Sheila, divorced with adult children, new cohabitant)

Difficulty of Taking Action in Breaking Down or Abusive Relationships

One cohabitant, who had been cohabiting for many years, was concerned about the difficulty of leaving an abusive partner when the house and all assets were in his name. She felt she could not leave the family home without losing any right to a share in it.

'I really would like to see a change in the procedure that says I have to stay in residence to claim any legal rights that I may have. I don't know if this applies to married couples as well, but the strain of having to remain in residence, every day seeing and talking with a partner against whom I will be conducting a court case through the conclusion of the court case and until the sale of the house, is in my opinion a situation which no culture that calls itself civilised should see fit to impose on its members.' (Diane, long term cohabitant)

Deliberately Not Acting as a Way of Retaining Control Over Finances, or Over Partner

Some did not want to get married because they felt they were in a better tax or financial position by remaining unmarried, and others wanted to get married to secure their financial situation. There was some frustration about the perceived arbitrariness of the financial benefits and costs of marrying or cohabiting.

One man talked about how his partner wanted to get married and he didn't, as he wanted to retain control over his finances:

'Essentially it's kind of a way of retaining a bit of balance in the relationship. You know, if she walks away she's going to be poverty stricken. I'll always look after the kids – obviously. Um. But I wouldn't feel particularly inclined to do anything for her' (Simon, cohabitant with 2 children)

Unanticipated Actions by Cohabitants

The legal/government view appears to be that if cohabitants understand the situation fully, they will get married. However, some of the interviewed cohabitants, when they realise the law is not in cohabitants' favour, prefer to try and change the law rather than change their own behaviour by getting married.

QUESTION

Do any of these reasons for not taking action surprise you?

The Living Together Campaign website's booklet on Living Together Agreements says this about enforceability:

> Just like a pre-nup, living together agreements have a slightly odd status in law. The court will not let you sign away the rights that the law gives you but a court will generally follow what you both agreed if:
>
> - It still produces a fair result for both of you
> - You were both honest with each other about your finances at the start.
>
> A court is even *more* likely to uphold the agreement if both of you also had some legal advice about what you were doing.
>
> A second option would be to have it written by a solicitor as a formal legal 'deed'. If you did this it would be legally binding in the same way as any legal contract between two parties is.

QUESTION

Is this advice correct, as a matter of contract law?

At the time of writing this chapter, the data from the 2006 BSA survey are not publicly available, but the Law Commission, in its *Cohabitation* report (see below) was given advance notice of its findings and reports that a majority of those surveyed still believed in the 'common law mariage' myth (at p. 9, n. 30).

QUESTIONS

i. Is the correct response to provide more information, or to change the law?
ii. If the law changes, how can the government ensure that people know it has changed?
iii. Who benefits from the widespread ignorance of the law: mostly men, or mostly women?

6.4 THE REFORM PROPOSALS

In July 2007 the Law Commission published its Report: *Cohabitation: the financial consequences of relationship breakdown*. In the Report they explain how the project was referred to them:

> 1.18 During the passage of the Civil Partnership Bill through Parliament, members of the House of Lords raised questions about the law's treatment of couples and others who live together but who neither marry nor (in the case of same-sex couples) register a civil partnership. Concerns were expressed, amongst other things, about the potential financial hardship suffered by cohabitants on the termination of their relationship owing to the current lack of any coherent legal remedies addressing their financial and property disputes. In a letter of 12 May 2004, Lord Filkin, then Parliamentary Secretary at the Department for Constitutional Affairs with responsibility for family justice, indicated to Peers that he had asked the Law Commission to undertake a review of cohabitation law.

The Report was produced after a project lasting two years, and following a detailed Consultation Paper published in 2006. The Commission addresses in Part 2 of its Report the question whether reform is necessary, at some length. They rehearse the difficulties in the law of implied trusts, and the problems faced by a cohabitant whose contribution to the shared household has been non-financial. They distinguish carefully between the results of their own consultation – non-representative and self-selecting – and the statistically significant results of the BSA survey:

> 2.35 It is difficult to distil an understanding of public opinion on the issue of reform purely on the basis of responses to our consultation. While those who supported and opposed reform clearly felt strongly about the issue, the responses do not form a nationally-representative sample of public opinion. For that, we have to look to the British Social Attitudes survey, most recently carried out in summer 2006, which is conducted on a randomly selected and statistically significant sample and is therefore the best available source of data on the views of the population. Like earlier surveys, the 2006 British Social Attitudes survey reveals a majority in favour of providing financial remedies between cohabitants. The presence of children in a relationship and a long duration both greatly increase the levels of support for making financial relief available on separation. Indeed, majorities of respondents to the survey supported reform that treated spouses and cohabitants in the same way in many situations. As we explain in Part 4, we are not recommending that cohabitants be subject to the current law applicable between spouses and civil partners on dissolution. But this survey evidence forms an important part of the context in which we have to evaluate the responses that we received.

The Commission looked at the problems faced by some cohabitants with children:

> 2.55 Take the position of cohabitants who have children and have been living together for a long time. The mother stays at home to look after the children and has no real prospects of re-entering the job market at a level that would enable her to afford the child-care that her absence from home would require. Her partner is able to provide for the family, but there is not a lot of extra money to go around. In order to obtain any long-term economic security in case of the relationship ending, she would first have to persuade him that he should take steps to protect her position. It may well be that he is quite happy with the status quo, which favours him.

2.56 Even if she were able to overcome this initial hurdle and persuade her partner that something should be done, they would then have to decide what steps were appropriate. It might be thought that the obvious answer is that they should marry. But research suggests that many couples are discouraged from taking this step because of the financial outlay that a wedding is perceived to entail. They are not willing to get married unless they can do it 'properly', and many cohabitants think it wrong to marry purely for legal or financial reasons. The alternative would be for them to declare an express trust over their home or enter into a contract for her benefit. However, such arrangements may be complex and require legal advice. The couple may simply conclude that the issue is not sufficiently pressing to take any further, and that they have other spending priorities. As noted above, research suggests that while individuals may be aware of the potentially vulnerable nature of their position in law, optimism bias persuades many that, in their case, the need for protection will not arise.

2.57 Assume, though, that the woman was unhappy with such a conclusion. She cannot take the required steps without the acquiescence of her partner. The only options are for her to leave the relationship or to stay in it without protection and so to be vulnerable should he later end the relationship. But separation does not solve the problem; it merely causes it to crystallise. And it is in no one's interests for the family to break up, particularly not those of the children.

2.58 As we indicated above, this is not to say that we do not place considerable weight on the importance of steps being taken to improve public understanding of the law: we do. But we consider that information provision cannot be regarded as a satisfactory cure, by itself, for the hardship experienced by many cohabitants and, by extension, their children, on separation.

They also looked at the position of childless couples:

2.76 Consultees were more divided on this issue and a number were undecided. The majority considered that reform is not warranted in such cases. However, most of the legal practitioners, academics and organisations who addressed this question supported reform for cohabitants without children. The majority of respondents to the British Social Attitudes survey also favoured extending financial relief to cohabitants without children, depending on the duration and other circumstances of the relationship, such as contributions that each party made towards the other's wealth and financial sacrifices made for the benefit of the other party.

2.77 There is evidence that cohabitants without children have the same potential to encounter unfairness on separation as cohabitants with children. We note in particular the observations of researchers who have recently been examining outcomes for cohabitants who separate under the current law. Their findings show that injustices currently arise between cohabitants without children who (just like those with children) are subject to the deficiencies of the general law of property and trusts. As we explained earlier, the problems generated by that law are not confined to the effects of caring for children during the relationship. Some consultees specifically observed that the problem of role-allocation within relationships, including care-giving for adult dependants, also occurs between cohabitants without children, creating an economic imbalance between the parties.

QUESTIONS

i. Do you agree with the Law Commission that, in the light of these points, some reform is justified?

ii. Do you think it should apply to all cohabitants, or only to those with children?

iii. It takes two to marry. What advice would you give, as the law stands at present, to a cohabitant whose partner refuses his or her offer of marriage?

Accordingly, the Commission went on to propose the enactment of statutory provision for financial relief for eligible cohabitants: these being cohabitants who have children together, and others who have had a joint household for a minimum qualifying period, which it recommended should be set somewhere between two and five years.

QUESTION

The Commission shied away from recommending a precise minimum period, preferring to leave that issue to Parliament. Do you think that there is any possible rationale for determining what the appropriate minimum duration should be?

If reform is needed, should it be on an opt-in or an opt-out basis? The Commission explains:

> 2.87 We appreciate that, at least in theory, the choice between opt-in and opt-out should make no difference to outcomes. Equipped with the same information, parties ought to reach the same destination (within the scheme or outside it), whether positive action is required in order to come within, or to remain outside, the scope of the scheme. If so, an opt-out scheme would do no better at protecting the vulnerable than an opt-in: the individual who would fail to persuade his or her partner to opt in would equally come under pressure to opt out. However, we consider that such arguments underestimate the practical significance of the default position, combined with the likelihood that many couples who do not actively intend to fall outside the scheme would either not address their minds to the issue or postpone taking action for the sorts of reasons discussed earlier. Only an opt-out scheme would ensure protection in the absence of positive action by the parties; and because of the tendency of people not to get around to things, an opt-in scheme, just like the current law, would leave many unprotected. Moreover, conferring eligibility to apply for financial relief by default may improve the bargaining position of the more vulnerable party where the other party would prefer that the relationship continue on that basis than not continue at all.

QUESTIONS

i. If opt-in legislation were enacted, what proportion of cohabitants do you think might opt in? (Look again at Chapter 2.)

ii. And what should the law do, in that event, for those who choose not to opt in?

Next, if opt-out legislation is required, what model should be followed? For example, could we not simply extend the provisions of the Matrimonial Causes Act 1973 (and the corresponding provisions of the Civil Partnership Act 2004) to separating cohabitants? The Law Commission thinks not:

> 4.6 Some jurisdictions have applied all or part of their divorce regimes to certain cohabiting relationships. Extension of the MCA to cohabitants could be seen as a straightforward option in this jurisdiction because it would simply involve the application of tried and tested principles to a wider range of relationships. Many people, including some district judges who operate the MCA, feel that it works efficiently and predictably in most cases. But many would disagree with that view. Several of our consultees expressed dissatisfaction with the MCA. They pointed in particular to the lack of a statutory objective underpinning the exercise of discretion, the theoretical and practical difficulties in applying its principles to so-called 'big money' cases, and the lack of predictability of outcome.
>
> 4.7 In the CP [the Consultation Paper of 2006] we provisionally rejected the option of extending the MCA to cohabitants. As one consultee observed:
>
> > Some account should be taken of the decision of the parties not to marry: it is one thing to relieve the unequal impact of the relationship, but quite another to treat the parties as if they actually had married.
>
> 4.8 Applying the MCA would impose an equivalence with marriage which many people would find inappropriate, and some consultees suggested that it is unlikely that a scheme which equated cohabitation with marriage in this way would be politically attainable.
>
> 4.9 Recent research [A Park et al, *British Social Attitudes. The 24th Report* (2008)] has indicated that, in particular situations, a majority of the public would like to see couples with children, whether married or unmarried, treated in the same way on separation, whatever that treatment might be. It also seems that a majority would support financial relief being granted between couples without children, at least following a long relationship, and in light of such factors as their contributions to the relationship. However, it is by no means clear that all the members of that majority would support the specific application of the MCA regime to cohabitants with children, let alone to those without. Cohabiting relationships differ widely in terms of duration, commitment and degree of economic interdependence. Case law on the MCA has advocated the treatment of a divorcing couple as a 'partnership of equals' to which the yardstick of equality may be applied. This approach may generate enormous awards even after very short marriages, and we believe that there would be significant public disquiet if cohabitants were to be treated similarly.

QUESTION

What do you think are the advantages and disadvantages of extending the law of ancillary relief to cohabitants?

If, as the Law Commission argues, it is not going to be possible simply to extend existing law, what is needed will be:

> 4.2... a middle ground between, on the one hand, the law that currently applies to cohabitants and, on the other, the law that applies to spouses and civil partners. It follows that there should be a new statutory scheme of specific application to cohabitants on their separation.

4.3 Reform must produce principled outcomes, and must combine some flexibility with certainty and consistency. The law must be capable of being operated by separating cohabitants without litigation, although they may have the help of lawyers and mediators. Results must be predictable, not with mathematical precision but with some degree of confidence.

The principles on which the scheme is to be based are described as follows by the Commission:

4.24 We consider that, while respondents should not have responsibility to meet all categories of need, it is appropriate to recommend a scheme that would respond to needs arising from the parties' contributions to the relationship. However, as we explained in the CP, we consider that such needs are better viewed as a sub-set of a wider principle, focusing on the economic impact of the parties' contributions to the relationship. We have therefore framed our recommended scheme in terms of 'retained benefit' and 'economic disadvantage' rather than 'need'. We use the term economic disadvantage in order to indicate that the loss arising from the relationship may encompass matters that would not usually be described as need. However, given the substantial overlap between needs as a general term and economic disadvantage, we do envisage and intend that awards based on economic disadvantage would often have the practical effect of responding to the applicant's basic needs.

4.25 Accordingly, although we reject need as the guiding principle for financial relief for cohabitants, we do think that it is important to respond to needs arising from the parties' contributions to the relationship. However, we do not think that a scheme defined simply in those terms would go far enough, hence our recommended scheme, to which we now turn.

4.26 In the CP we discussed a scheme based on the economic impact of cohabitation. We argued that hardship following separation often arises because the gains and losses arising from the parties' contributions to the relationship have not been shared fairly. Decisions taken during the relationship about the allocation of the parties' resources or of their respective roles may leave one party in need on separation, or, if not actually in need, at least bearing an unequal share of the costs of the relationship. Equally, one party may be left with an economic gain from the relationship. While there may often be 'need' in consequence, it is likely to be only part of the problem.

...

4.28 The CP provisionally proposed a scheme that would seek to identify the contributions made by each party to the relationship and to assess the economic consequences of those contributions for the parties following their separation. The approach that we now recommend is a development (and, where possible, a simplification) of the scheme discussed in the CP.

4.29 We should emphasise that we are not advocating a scheme whereby contributions are enumerated and their value, once quantified, simply reimbursed. We called that sort of exercise 'global accounting' in the CP and we rejected it because of its evidential complexity and the impossibility of attributing a value to many contributions, in particular those that are not financial. This is why it would not be practicable to recommend a scheme whose single guiding principle was, simply, 'contributions'. Instead, our recommended scheme would examine the lasting economic effect of the parties' contributions to the relationship.

The Commission summarises its recommendations as follows:

4.32 We recommend that financial relief on separation should be granted in accordance with a statutory scheme based upon the economic impact of cohabitation, to the following effect.

4.33 An eligible cohabitant applying for relief following separation ('the applicant') must prove that:

(1) the respondent has a retained benefit; or
(2) the applicant has an economic disadvantage;

as a result of qualifying contributions the applicant has made.

4.34 A qualifying contribution is any contribution arising from the cohabiting relationship which is made to the parties' shared lives or to the welfare of members of their families. Contributions are not limited to financial contributions, and include future contributions, in particular to the care of the parties' children following separation.

4.35 A retained benefit may take the form of capital, income or earning capacity that has been acquired, retained or enhanced.

4.36 An economic disadvantage is a present or future loss. It may include a diminution in current savings as a result of expenditure or of earnings lost during the relationship, lost future earnings, or the future cost of paid child-care.

4.37 The court may make an order to adjust the retained benefit, if any, by reversing it in so far as that is reasonable and practicable having regard to the discretionary factors listed below. If, after the reversal of any retained benefit, the applicant would still bear an economic disadvantage, the court may make an order sharing that loss equally between the parties, in so far as it is reasonable and practicable to do so, having regard to the discretionary factors.

4.38 The discretionary factors are:

(1) the welfare while a minor of any child of both parties who has not attained the age of eighteen;
(2) the financial needs and obligations of both parties;
(3) the extent and nature of the financial resources which each party has or is likely to have in the foreseeable future;
(4) the welfare of any children who live with, or might reasonably be expected to live with, either party; and
(5) the conduct of each party, defined restrictively but so as to include cases where a qualifying contribution can be shown to have been made despite the express disagreement of the other party.

Of these discretionary factors, item (1) above shall be the court's first consideration.

4.39 In making an order to share economic disadvantage, the court shall not place the applicant, for the foreseeable future, in a stronger economic position than the respondent.

4.40 The following range of orders should be available to the court:

(1) lump sums, including payment by instalment, secured lump sums, lump sums paid by way of pensions attachment, and interim payments;
(2) property transfers;
(3) property settlements;
(4) orders for sale; and
(5) pension sharing.

Unlike on divorce, periodical payments should not generally be available.

4.41 In so far as the scheme is engaged, it should apply between the parties to the exclusion of the general law of implied trusts, estoppel and contract.

4.42 Procedural and costs rules must be carefully framed to protect the parties from oppressive litigation and to preserve court time and resources. In particular, the rules must prevent parties who are eligible cohabitants from bringing claims under the general law of implied trusts, estoppel and contract on the basis of facts which constitute qualifying contributions under the scheme.

QUESTIONS

i. Why do you suppose the Commission decided to recommend a scheme which did not require the courts (or the parties) to value each other's contributions to the relationship?

ii. How many examples of qualifying contributions can you think of? (Now look at paragraph 4.44 of the Report.)

iii. Retained benefit is to be reversed, while economic disadvantage is to be shared (subject to the 'economic equality ceiling' of para 4.39). What would be the disadvantages, in terms both of fairness and acceptability, of reversing both forms of economic impact, and thus generating a scheme that required the richer party to bear the entire cost of the relationship?

iv. How is economic disadvantage to be assessed? (Look again at the work of the Women and Equality Unit, Chapter 3, p. 115.)

v. Why do you think the Commission recommended that periodical payments should not be available?

Appendix B of the Law Commission Report sets out a number of scenarios and explains how their recommended scheme would apply in each case. One scenario is as follows:

C and D, both in their thirties, had been living together for three years in C's house when they started a family. C's salary was sufficient to support the family and, as they both wanted the baby (E) to be looked after at home by D, they agreed that D should not return to work after E was born. Their relationship has now foundered and they are separating, after five years together. E, who is now two, is going to live with D.

QUESTIONS

i. How would C and D fare under the Law Commission's scheme? (You can check your response against paragraphs B24 to B36.)

ii. One of the objectives of the Law Commission's scheme is to make possible a greater use of the property adjustment orders available under Schedule 1 to the Children Act 1989. By giving to the parent living with the children an entitlement to financial provision, the scheme would enable that parent to have a stake in the home provided for the children. It would then become possible and worthwhile for her to make contributions to mortgage payments, assuming she has some income available, and so make it practicable for a home to be provided even if it cannot be purchased outright. Can you see how D might be assisted in this way?

Finally, the Law Commission proposed there should be the opportunity to opt out. First, they address in general the issue of the enforceability of cohabitation contracts, already an important feature of the current law:

5.6 Currently, some cohabitants make agreements, commonly referred to as 'cohabitation contracts', to govern their financial arrangements during the cohabitation and in the event of the parties separating. There is some lingering doubt as to whether such contracts might be unenforceable for reasons of public policy. Such doubts may have had substance in the days before cohabitation outside marriage was publicly acceptable, but today they should no longer be warranted.

5.7 We argued in the Consultation Paper (2006) that statute should affirm that cohabitation contracts are no longer unenforceable for that reason. Responses to consultation revealed considerable support for this view.

5.8 We recommend that legislation should provide, for the avoidance of doubt, that, in so far as a contract ('a cohabitation contract') governs the financial arrangements of a cohabiting couple during their cohabitation or following their separation, it should not be regarded as contrary to public policy.

Then they consider specifically the issue of opting out of a new statutory scheme:

Qualifying Criteria

Formalities

5.30 A requirement of writing, signed by both parties, would seem a necessary level of protection, both cautionary and evidential. We therefore consider that the opt-out agreement should be written and signed. By 'writing' we mean a written paper document rather than any other form of writing such as email. An exchange of letters would be sufficient for this purpose.

5.31 Given the protective function of formalities, we do not consider that an agreement that falls short of our qualifying criteria should be of any legal effect. We accept that this means that some genuine agreements between cohabitants which have not been committed to writing should remain unenforceable to the extent that they purport to disapply a new statutory scheme. But if we are to encourage a culture of private ordering, we must encourage a culture that embraces the formalities requirements that we are recommending.

5.32 Nor do we consider that an agreement signed by only one party should be effective to disapply the statute, even if it is signed only by the party against whom it is raised in litigation. We want to encourage parties to engage in a process of discussion in which both participate, and an 'agreement' that amounted only to a unilateral waiver of rights would not meet that objective.

...

Full Financial Disclosure?

5.38 We have considered whether parties to an opt-out agreement should be obliged to make full mutual disclosure of their financial affairs. We take the view that such a requirement would be neither necessary nor desirable. As we have explained, financial relief would be awarded under our recommended scheme in order to address the financial consequences of cohabitation, rather than to redistribute the parties' entire resources. The court would not, therefore, need to know the full extent of the parties' finances. That being the case, cohabitants should be entitled to keep their financial affairs private if they wish.

Mandatory Terms, Model Agreements and Pro Formas

5.39 We have considered whether opt-out agreements should be required to contain particular terms. We explained above that an opt-out agreement is one which disapplied the new statute and would have effect in the event of the parties' separation. We asked in the CP whether such an agreement must in terms disapply the statute (that is, with specific reference to the statute by its title). Of the handful of responses to this question, most thought it should. We accept that it must be clear on the face of the agreement that the parties are aware that they are disapplying a statutory regime and thereby giving up rights. However, we do not think it would be appropriate to insist that any particular form of words, such as a reference to the title of the statute, be used.

5.40 In the CP we invited the views of consultees on the use of model agreements. Responses were very mixed, a majority favouring such agreements being made available. But concern was expressed that comprehensive 'off the shelf' agreements containing a number of model clauses would be inappropriate. We think that this concern is important, and that the adoption of model clauses could lead to arguments that such agreements should be set aside (on the basis that they might not have been properly considered or fully understood).

5.41 However, we think that it would be useful for parties to have the opportunity to use pro forma agreements which did not make any suggestions of alternative financial arrangements. The forms would contain wording to make clear that the parties knew that they were disapplying the statute. Such forms could provide guidance about the scheme of financial relief and about the effect of opting out, suggest those matters the parties might wish to consider in deciding whether to enter into such an agreement, and explain the qualifying criteria. The use of such forms would enable parties (and their legal advisers) to be sure that they had made an effective agreement. We see the use of such a form as worthwhile, in that it might save the parties legal costs and assist couples to create binding opt-out agreements.

5.42 We have also considered whether agreements should be required by law to include 'sunset clauses' to the effect that the agreement would automatically cease to have effect after a certain period of time. But other jurisdictions do not seem to use this mechanism, and they are not imposed upon wills, powers of attorney or any comparable instrument. As consultees did not support the imposition of sunset clauses, we do not consider that there should be any such legal requirement.

...

Effect of an Opt-out Agreement

5.48 We are not offering cast-iron certainty, for the reasons discussed above. Equally, we do not think that it would be satisfactory for the existence of an opt-out agreement, in signed writing, to be simply one of the factors for the court to bear in mind when exercising its discretion. It would be highly undesirable to place the parties in a position whereby their agreement was neither enforceable nor irrelevant. Moreover, the existence of such an agreement would not sit comfortably alongside the other factors pertinent to the court's discretion to grant relief. The other factors would be there to modify the effect of an award under the scheme, whereas the agreement would be relevant to a different question, namely whether or not the statutory scheme should apply at all.

5.49 An alternative is to make an opt-out agreement binding, subject to carefully defined grounds on which the court may set it aside. Potential advantages to making these agreements binding include:

(1) reducing litigation by discouraging challenge; and
(2) putting the onus on the party seeking to challenge the agreement, rather than requiring the other party both to defend the substance of the claim under the scheme and to argue that the agreement should be upheld. If the challenge to the agreement were unsuccessful, there would be no need to invoke the statutory scheme.

5.50 Accordingly, we take the view that where cohabitants had made an opt-out agreement that met the criteria that we recommend for validity, it should be enforceable, subject only to challenge on tightly defined grounds. We discuss what these grounds should be next.

The Grounds for Setting Opt-out Agreements Aside

5.51 We take the view that agreements should not lightly be set aside. Accordingly, we consider that agreements should only be set aside if their enforcement would give rise to manifest unfairness. Manifest unfairness would not be a free-standing criterion but could only be established in the light of certain circumstances, which we discuss below. Equally, the occurrence of those circumstances would not amount to grounds for setting the agreement aside unless it could also be shown that the agreement was manifestly unfair as a result.

5.52 Manifest unfairness might be established having regard to the circumstances at the time the agreement was made. It might be that, although both parties signed the agreement, it could be shown that one of them did not understand its effect. In consequence, those couples who take legal advice would be more likely to have their agreement upheld by the court, as are those who had participated in full mutual disclosure of their financial affairs. It would therefore be in the interests of each party to see that the other had proper information and, where it could be afforded, legal advice.

5.53 Manifest unfairness might also be established where there are circumstances at the time that the agreement is being enforced that were not foreseen at the time that the opt-out agreement was made or in the course of the making of their other contractual arrangements and which, if foreseen, would have had a material effect upon the parties' arrangements. For instance, the birth of a child might be such a circumstance if it appeared that the parties did not contemplate it in making arrangements for what would happen in the event of separation, and if their arrangements are inadequate as a result of the birth. So would unforeseen events such as the bankruptcy of one of the parties, or a large inheritance, a significant change of career or the onset of disability. However, the passage of time would not in itself be sufficient; nor would the mere fact that the agreement yields results different from those that would be generated by the scheme.

QUESTIONS

i. Would it be possible, if the Commission's proposals were enacted, for a rich man who wanted his impecunious girlfriend to come and live with him to ensure that she would have no claim against him if they were later to separate?

ii. You are going to move in with your wealthy partner. How could you ensure, under the Commission's proposals, that you would be entitled to half your partner's house if you later separate? (Look at paragraphs 5.62–5.64 of the Report, available at http://www.lawcom.gov.uk/docs/lc307.pdf.)

iii. Look back at the discussion of property agreements for spouses and civil partners in Chapter 5. Do you think that the policy issues that arise in the context of opt-out agreements for cohabitants are the same, or different?

6.5 THE COMPARATIVE PICTURE

Other jurisdictions legislated long ago. One of the earliest significant legislative interventions came from New South Wales, where the De Facto Relationships Act 1984 was passed to put into effect the recommendations of the New South Wales Law Reform Commission (1983) relating both to property rights and to contractual claims. In 1999 the Act was re-named the Property (Relationships) Act, and now provides for rights of maintenance and property adjustment in a much wider range of relationships than it did originally, including same-sex couples. The basis for the making of property adjustment orders or orders to pay maintenance is as follows:

20. Application for Adjustment

(1) On an application by a party to a domestic relationship for an order under this Part to adjust interests with respect to the property of the parties to the relationship or either of them, a court may make such order adjusting the interests of the parties in the property as to it seems just and equitable having regard to:
   (a) the financial and non-financial contributions made directly or indirectly by or on behalf of the parties to the relationship to the acquisition, conservation or improvement of any of the property of the parties or either of them or to the financial resources of the parties or either of them, and
   (b) the contributions, including any contributions made in the capacity of homemaker or parent, made by either of the parties to the relationship to the welfare of the other party to the relationship or to the welfare of the family constituted by the parties and one or more of the following, namely:
      (i) a child of the parties,
      (ii) a child accepted by the parties or either of them into the household of the parties, whether or not the child is a child of either of the parties.

(2) A court may make an order under subsection (1) in respect of property whether or not it has declared the title or rights of a party to a domestic relationship in respect of the property.

...

26. No General Right to Maintenance Between Parties to Relationship

A party to a domestic relationship is not liable to maintain the other party to the relationship, and neither party is entitled to claim maintenance from the other, except as provided in this Division.

27. Orders for Maintenance

(1) On an application by a party to a domestic relationship for an order under this Part for maintenance, a court may make an order for maintenance (whether for periodic maintenance or otherwise) where the court is satisfied as to either or both of the following:

(a) that the applicant is unable to support himself or herself adequately by reason of having the care and control of a child of the parties to the relationship or a child of the respondent, being, in either case, a child who is, on the day on which the application is made:

(i) except in the case of a child referred to in subparagraph (ii) under the age of 12 years, or

(ii) in the case of a physically handicapped child or mentally handicapped child under the age of 16 years,

(b) that the applicant is unable to support himself or herself adequately because the applicant's earning capacity has been adversely affected by the circumstances of the relationship and, in the opinion of the court:

(i) an order for maintenance would increase the applicant's earning capacity by enabling the applicant to undertake a course or programme of training or education, and

(ii) it is, having regard to all the circumstances of the case, reasonable to make the order.

Sections 45–52 provide, moreover, for the ability of any two persons to make a domestic relationship agreement (what we would call a cohabitation contract; see p. 290, above), which will be enforced by the court save where circumstances have changed so that enforcement would lead to serious injustice, and, of course, without prejudice to the courts' powers to make orders in respect of children.

A similar process has been seen in New Zealand, where the De Facto Relationships Act 1976 has been renamed the Property (Relationships) Act 1976, from February 2002, and definitions have been amended to cover a range of relationships including same-sex couples. The statutory provisions for financial relief on separation are, as in New South Wales, identical across the range of relationships; but in the New Zealand statute they are based on definitions of 'relationship property' and 'separate property' (sections 8 and 9). Relationship property includes the family home and chattels, all jointly owned property, anything acquired after the beginning of the relationship, and anything acquired immediately before it commenced and in contemplation of its commencement. The core provisions then read as follows:

11 Division of Relationship Property

(1) On the division of relationship property under this Act, each of the spouses or [partners] is entitled to share equally in –

(a) the family home; and

(b) the family chattels; and

(c) any other relationship property.

...

13 Exception to Equal Sharing

(1) If the Court considers that there are extraordinary circumstances that make equal sharing of property or money under section 11 or section 11A or section 11B or section 12 repugnant to justice, the share of each spouse or... partner in that property or money is to be determined in accordance with the contribution of each spouse to the marriage [or of each civil union partner to the civil union] or of each de facto partner to the de facto relationship.

...

15 Court May Award Lump Sum Payments or Order Transfer of Property

(1) This section applies if, on the division of relationship property, the Court is satisfied that, after the marriage[, civil union,] or de facto relationship ends, the income and living standards of 1 spouse or [partner] (party B) are likely to be significantly higher than the other spouse or [partner] (party A) because of the effects of the division of functions within the marriage [, civil union,] or de facto relationship while the parties were living together.

(2) In determining whether or not to make an order under this section, the Court may have regard to –
 (a) the likely earning capacity of each spouse or [partner]
 [(b) the responsibilities of each spouse or partner for the ongoing daily care of any minor or dependent children of the marriage, civil union, or de facto relationship;]
 (c) any other relevant circumstances.

(3) If this section applies, the Court, if it considers it just, may, for the purpose of compensating party A, –
 (a) order party B to pay party A a sum of money out of party B's relationship property:
 (b) order party B to transfer to party A any other property out of party B's relationship property.

Compare and contrast the following provisions of the Family Law (Scotland) Act 2006:

28 Financial Provision Where Cohabitation Ends Otherwise Than by Death

(1) Subsection (2) applies where cohabitants cease to cohabit otherwise than by reason of the death of one (or both) of them.

(2) On the application of a cohabitant (the 'applicant'), the appropriate court may, after having regard to the matters mentioned in subsection (3) –
 (a) make an order requiring the other cohabitant (the 'defender') to pay a capital sum of an amount specified in the order to the applicant;
 (b) make an order requiring the defender to pay such amount as may be specified in the order in respect of any economic burden of caring, after the end of the cohabitation, for a child of whom the cohabitants are the parents;
 (c) make such interim order as it thinks fit.

(3) Those matters are—
  (a) whether (and, if so, to what extent) the defender has derived economic advantage from contributions made by the applicant; and
  (b) whether (and, if so, to what extent) the applicant has suffered economic disadvantage in the interests of—
    (i) the defender; or
    (ii) any relevant child.
(4) In considering whether to make an order under subsection (2)(a), the appropriate court shall have regard to the matters mentioned in subsections (5) and (6).
(5) The first matter is the extent to which any economic advantage derived by the defender from contributions made by the applicant is offset by any economic disadvantage suffered by the defender in the interests of—
  (a) the applicant; or
  (b) any relevant child.
(6) The second matter is the extent to which any economic disadvantage suffered by the applicant in the interests of—
  (a) the defender; or
  (b) any relevant child,

is offset by any economic advantage the applicant has derived from contributions made by the defender.

...

(9) In this section—

...

'contributions' includes indirect and non-financial contributions (and, in particular, any such contribution made by looking after any relevant child or any house in which they cohabited); and

'economic advantage' includes gains in–
  (a) capital;
  (b) income; and
  (c) earning capacity;

and 'economic disadvantage' shall be construed accordingly.

(10) For the purposes of this section, a child is 'relevant' if the child is–
  (a) a child of whom the cohabitants are the parents;
  (b) a child who is or was accepted by the cohabitants as a child of the family.

QUESTIONS

i. There is a fundamental difference in approach between the New South Wales statute and the New Zealand legislation. What is it?

ii. Which of these two models does the Scottish legislation resemble?

iii. How far is the Scottish legislation, with its reference to economic advantage and disadvantage, different from the English Law Commission's proposals?

iv. Which model do you like best? Or does it not matter, so long as some legislative provision is made?

v. Or might the issue be: do you prefer certainty or discretion, and why?

BIBLIOGRAPHY

6.1 Cohabitation and interdependence

We quoted from:

J. Eekelaar and M. Maclean, 'Marriage and the Moral Bases of Personal Relationships', (2004) 31 *Journal of Law and Society* 510.

R. Tennant, J. Taylor and J. Lewis, *Separating from cohabitation: making arrangements for finances and parenting*, (2006) DCA Research Series 7/06, 31-36, available at http://www.dca.gov.uk/research/2006/07_2006.htm.

Additional reading

A. Arthur, J. Lewis, M. Maclean, S. Finch, R. Fitzgerald, *Settling Up: making financial arrangements after divorce or separation* (2002) London: National Centre for Social Research

C. Burgoyne, V. Clarke, J. Reibstein and A. Edmunds, '"All my worldly goods I share with you?" Managing money at thc transitiun to heterosexual marriage' (2006) 54(4) *The Sociological Review* 619.

J. Haskey, 'New estimates and projections of the population cohabiting in England and Wales' (1999) *Population Trends* 13.

M. Maclean and J. Eekelaar, 'Taking the plunge: perceptions of risk-taking associated with formal and informal partner relationships' (2005) 17 *Child and Family Law Quarterly* 247.

J. Pahl, 'Individualisation in Couple Finances: Who Pays for the Children' (2005) 4:4 *Social Policy and Society* 381.

6.2 The law

We quoted from:

G. Douglas, J. Pearce, H. Woodward, 'Dealing with property issues on cohabitation breakdown' [2007] *Family Law* 36 (2007a).

G. Douglas, J. Pearce, H. Woodward, *A Failure of Trust: Resolving Property Disputes on Cohabitation Breakdown* (Cardiff, Cardiff Law School, 2007), 56-7, 73-4, available at http://www.law.cf.ac.uk/researchpapers/papers/1.pdf (2007b).

C. Harpurn, 'Cohabitation Consultation' [1995] *Family Law* 657.

R. Probert, 'Cohabitants and Joint Ownership: the Implications of *Stack v Dowden*' [2007] *Family Law* 924.

R. Tennant, J. Taylor and J. Lewis, *Separating from cohabitation: making arrangements for finances and parenting*, (2006) DCA Research Series 7/06, 55-7, available at http://www.dca.gov.uk/research/2006/07_2006.htm.

Additional reading

K. Gray and S.F. Gray, *Elements of Land Law* (4th edn) (2005), Oxford, Oxford University Press.

The Law Commission, *Sharing Homes: a discussion paper* Law Comm No 278 (2002).

6.3 The myth

We quoted from:

A. Barlow, C. Burgoyne, J. Smithson, *The Living Together Campaign: An investigation of its impact on legally aware cohabitants* Ministry of Justice Research Series 5/07, July 2007, 32-36, http://www.justice.gov.uk/docs/living-together-research-report.pdf.

A. Barlow, S. Duncan, G. James and A. Park, *Cohabitation, Marriage and the Law* (2005) Oxford, Hart Publishing Ltd, 27-8, 30, 39.

The 'Living Together' website: http://www.advicenow.org.uk/livingtogether.

The LTC's Li*ving Together Agreements* leaflet, at http://www.advicenow.org.uk/fileLibrary/pdf/Living_Together_Agreements.pdf.

R. Probert, 'Why Couples Still Believe in Common-Law Marriage' [2007] *Family Law* 403.

Additional reading

S. Duncan, A. Barlow, G. James, 'Why don't they marry? Cohabitation, commitment and DIY marriage' (2005) 17 *Child and Family Law Quarterly* 383.

The 'Living Together' agreement: http://www.advicenow.org.uk/fileLibrary/pdf/Living_Together_Agreements.pdf.

6.4 The reform proposals

We quoted from:

The Law Commission, *Cohabitation: the financial consequences of relationship breakdown* Consultation Paper No 179 (2006)

The Law Commission, *Cohabitation: the financial consequences of relationship breakdown* Law Comm No 307 (2007), 1.18, 2.35, 2.55-2.58, 2.76-2.77, 2.87, 4.2-4.3, 4.6-4.9, 4.24-4.29, 4.32-4.42, 5.6-5.8, 5.30-5.53, Appendix B

Additional reading

D. Allison, 'All Change?' (2007) 157 *New Law Journal* 386.

The Law Commission, *Sharing Homes: a discussion paper* Law Comm No 278 (2002).

A. Park, J. Curtis, K. Thomson, M. Phillips, M. Johnson, L. Clery, *British Social Attitudes. The 24th Report* (2008).

6.5 The comparative picture

Additional reading

J. Miles, 'Financial Provision and property Division on Relationship Breakdown: a Theoretical Analysis of the New Zealand Legislation' (2004) 21 *New Zealand Universities Law Review* 268.

7

DANGEROUS FAMILIES

Home is generally regarded as a place of safety, but in this chapter we examine some of the dangers which can face family members. We shall look first at the different kinds of abuse and ill-treatment which can be suffered, and then at some of the research into explanations, before turning to the remedies in criminal and civil law.

Domestic violence has many causes, and its effects are complex. An examination of the civil remedies can portray it as a two-party problem, usually between a man and a woman. But of course it goes much further than that. The abuse of children may lead to the involvement of local authority social services departments, or the NSPCC, exercising 'public law' powers under the Children Act 1989, which we consider in Chapter 11. Even if that does not happen, when children are the victims of violence or have to watch a parent being victimised, their relationships with other family members are profoundly affected, and we have to keep this in mind when we look at what happens when parents part, in Chapter 10.

7.1 WHAT ARE THE DANGERS?

Cathy Humphries and Ravi Thiara, in 'Neither justice nor protection: women's experiences of post-separation violence', quote some of the women who participated in their research study (2003):

> My ex-partner asked a friend of his to come to my home and beat me up because I had left him. I did not know this man. I opened the door to a knock one night, a man asked my name. I told him and basically he kicked and punched the hell out of me. He got hold of my three-year-old son and literally threw him into the glass door, which smashed. My son needed his head injuries glued at hospital. I had a fractured skull and extensive bruising to my body and a couple of broken ribs. I had to get immediate hospital attention for both of us... the police were a waste of time ... they never even questioned my ex-husband... I moved about six times in all.
>
> (Rose)

> I did call the police. After that, he got locked up for two nights; it was the weekend. He got arrested on the Saturday, stayed there the whole day Sunday and then Monday, half a day. I feel that sort of made him think, then he stopped completely and he hasn't, even to this day, harassed me.
>
> (Razia)

> They took him to the end of the estate where I lived and dropped him off. He came straight back and because he had had to walk back he was angrier than what he was before he went and he beat me for ringing the police. I didn't bother then to re-ring. They weren't doing anything anyway, just dropping him at the end of the estate... a favourite of the police is to say, 'She'll take him back'. And they say that in front of you to their colleague. So they're basically just reinforcing what my husband used to say all the time we were together ... that I was weak... you know if they'd given

me some support or made injunctions work, or made conditional bail work I don't think the final violence incident would have happened. (Elaine, who has five children and wanted to stay in her own home. The violent harassment continued for 3 years until he was charged with grievous bodily harm and sentenced to 9 months in prison. He served 4 months and moved to another area from which he harasses her intermittently.)

Figure 1.2, again from the findings of the British Crime Survey 2004–05, indicates something of the range of behaviour that the survey asked about:

Figure 1.2 Prevalence of intimate violence in last year, 2004/05 BCS

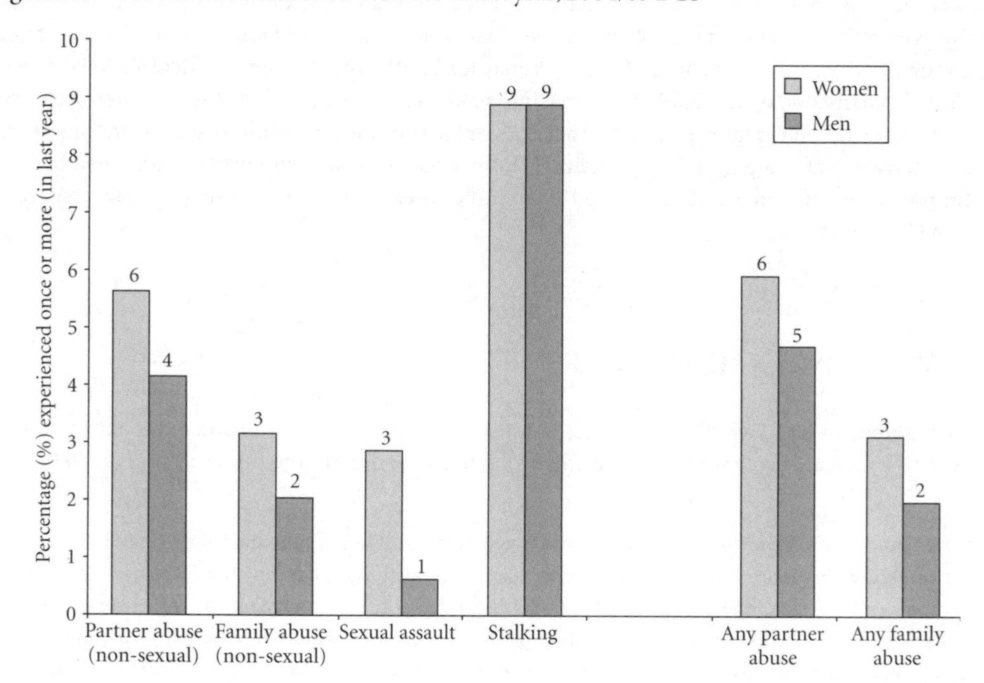

The following are listed as key points on the findings of the British Crime Survey 2004–05:

- Long term trends in violent crime as measured by the BCS, have shown a significant decline since their peak in 1995, in particular there have been large falls in both domestic and acquaintance violence. Between 1995 and 2004/05, domestic violence has fallen by 59 per cent and acquaintance violence has fallen by 54 per cent.
- Women were more likely than men to report having had experienced intimate violence across all four forms since the age of 16. The differences in relation to experience in the last year were less marked.
- Partner abuse (non-sexual) was more likely to have been experienced since the age of 16 by women (28%) and men (18%) than other forms.
- In the last 12 months, however, stalking was more likely to have been experienced by both women (9%) and men (9%) than any other form. A half of women (50%) and a third of men (35%) who had experienced intimate violence since the age of 16 had experienced more than one type of intimate violence in that time.

- Among intimate violence victims, two in five women (40%) and almost a third of men (31%) had experienced some form of intimate abuse by offenders of more than one relationship type.
- Among victims of less serious sexual assault, almost two-thirds of women (62%) reported that the offender was a stranger. Men were more likely to report the offender as someone known to them in some way, rather than a stranger.
- Offenders of serious sexual assault against both men and women were more likely to have been reported as being known to the victim than as being a stranger.
- Marital status (especially being unmarried), being young and having a limiting disability or illness were found to be independently associated with intimate violence across the forms for men and women (it should be noted that association does not however prove causation).

QUESTIONS

i. Why do you think women are more likely than men to report having experienced intimate violence?

ii. Is 'intimate violence' the same as 'domestic violence'? If not, is it a larger or a smaller category?

It is widely agreed that domestic violence goes beyond physical assault. CAFCASS (on which see Chapter 10) defines domestic violence as follows:

> Patterns of behaviour characterised by the misuse of power and control by one person over another who are or have been in an intimate relationship. . . . It may be physical, emotional and/or psychological. The latter may include intimidation, harassment, damage to property, threats and financial abuse.

The Crown Prosecution Service's *Policy for Prosecuting Cases Of Domestic Violence* (2005) states:

> The Government's definition of domestic violence was agreed in 2004 and is:
>
> > 'any incident of threatening behaviour, violence or abuse [psychological, physical, sexual, financial or emotional] between adults who are or have been intimate partners or family members, regardless of gender or sexuality'.

Women from ethnic minorities may face particular difficulties. *Unlocking the secret: Women Open the Door on Domestic Violence* (Women's National Commission, 2003) reports on interviews with many women survivors, including these:

> Women from black and minority ethnic (BME) groups told us how difficult it is to go outside the community for help, and asked for training for their own community leaders and workers. Asian women told us that women are expected to take responsibility for making the marriage work, regardless of family violence; the woman herself would usually be blamed for provoking this. Leaving home is not an option in these circumstances, as they have nowhere to go. Orthodox Jewish women told us they face ostracism or even murder for speaking outside the community.

Specialist refuge provision is needed to provide these women with safe havens, together with a programme to train and fund work within the communities.

'I am a Moslem, and I have heard our so-called leaders are perpetrators of domestic violence themselves. So they will not support women who go to them with this problem. Even the police are scared to go to the leadership because they will be afraid it will turn into a racist issue. Something should be done about that. It is very difficult for a women to go to a community leader because woman are considered the homemakers and home-breakers. Women are told that they have to accept their situation, and by the time the kids come along, it is too late.'

'I know a Somali woman who complained to the community leaders and they told her to put up with it. But it happened again and she had difficulty with English. Her husband, who was Dutch and white, told the police she was disturbed.'

'I'm from Pakistan. I came here eight months ago. A lot of Asian people get offended that I talk about domestic violence in the Asian Community. They think it portrays us to the outside world in a negative way. But the Asians themselves are the biggest block to improving things. Although they have been in this country for 30 years, they do not want to face reality. But the Government might be called racist if it interferes. When it comes to training and awareness, an effort should be made by each community to understand each other's issues.'

'A lot of times husbands blackmail their wives by saying that if the women report anything, the Government will kick them out of the country.'

In Chapter 2 we looked at the problem of forced marriage (pp. 84–91). Introducing to Parliament the Bill that became the Forced Marriages (Civil Protection) Act 2007 in Parliament, Lord Lester said (emphasis supplied):

The serious social evil which the Bill seeks to combat and remedy is the forcing of children and young adults to marry against their will. It gives rise to gross abuses of human rights especially affecting children and young people of either sex within our British Asian communities and elsewhere. It involves inhuman and degrading treatment and punishment of those who resist coercion, even their murder. *It is a form of domestic violence* and there is a direct link between forced marriages and honour killings...

In *Comparing Domestic Abuse in Same-Sex and Heterosexual Relationships* (2005), Catherine Donovan and her colleagues report on the findings of their empirical project. They comment:

Sexuality can be used in different ways to exert control over a partner's behaviour and access to support/friendship networks: by accusations that a survivor is not a real lesbian or gay man; by the abusive partner asserting their inability to be out; by their denigration of the scene; and by using jealousy as a way of keeping their partners from the scene. Women were more likely to have sexuality used against them in these ways.

Previous literature on domestic abuse in same sex relationships highlights the ways in which sexuality can be used as a way of controlling a partner's behaviour: by threatening to out partners to child care agencies of the parent or to employers, friends and family if they are not out. However what we found in interviews was not that abusive partners used their partner's sexuality to control them but that they used their own issue with sexuality (either that they were not out or did not want other people to know about the relationship) or the scene (that it presented a threat to their relationship in some way) as a way of controlling their partner's social life and friendship networks.

Section 3 of the New Zealand Domestic Violence Act 1995 states:

(1) In this Act, domestic violence, in relation to any person, means violence against that person by any other person with whom that person is, or has been, in a domestic relationship.
(2) In this section, violence means–
 (a) Physical abuse:
 (b) Sexual abuse:
 (c) Psychological abuse, including, but not limited to,–
  (i) Intimidation:
  (ii) Harassment:
  (iii) Damage to property
  (iv) Threats of physical abuse, sexual abuse, or psychological abuse:
  (v) In relation to a child, abuse of the kind set out in subsection (3) of this section.
(3) Without limiting subsection (2)(c) of this section, a person psychologically abuses a child if that person–
 (a) Causes or allows the child to see or hear the physical, sexual, or psychological abuse of a person with whom the child has a domestic relationship; or
 (b) Puts the child, or allows the child to be put, at real risk of seeing or hearing that abuse occurring;–

 but the person who suffers that abuse is not regarded, for the purposes of this subsection, as having caused or allowed the child to see or hear the abuse, or, as the case may be, as having put the child, or allowed the child to be put, at risk of seeing or hearing the abuse.
(4) Without limiting subsection (2) of this section–
 (a) A single act may amount to abuse for the purposes of that subsection:
 (b) A number of acts that form part of a pattern of behaviour may amount to abuse for that purpose, even though some or all of those acts, when viewed in isolation, may appear to be minor or trivial.
(5) Behaviour may be psychological abuse for the purposes of subsection (2)(c) of this section which does not involve actual or threatened physical or sexual abuse.

QUESTION

Do you think that any difficulties or adverse consequences could arise if the definition of domestic violence is drawn too widely?

Sylvia Walby's study, *The cost of domestic violence* (2004), calculates that:

Domestic violence costs the state around £3.1 billion and employers around £1.3 billion. The cost of human and emotional suffering is estimated to be around £17 billion. The total cost [per year] is estimated at around £23 billion.

Walby's Tables S.1 and S.2 break down these totals:

Table S.1 Summary estimates of the cost of domestic violence

Type of cost	Cost (£billions)
Criminal Justice System	1.017
Of which police	(.49)
Health care	1.396
Of which physical	(1.22)
Of which mental health	(.176)
Social services	.228
Emergency housing	.158
Civil legal	.312
All services	3.111
Economic output	2.672
Sub-total	5,783
Human and emotional	17.086
Total	22.869

Note: Costs are estimated for one year for England and Wales and are centred on 2001.

Table S.2 Who bears the cost?

Type of cost	State	Individual victim	Employers	Total cost (£billions)
Criminal Justice System	1,017			1,017
Health care Physical	1,206	15		1,220
Mental health	176			176
Social services	228			228
Housing and refuges	130	28		158
Civil legal costs	159	152		312
All services	2,916	195		3,111
Employment		1,336	1,336	2,672
Sub-total	2,916	1,531	1,336	5,783
Human costs		17.082		17.086
Total	2,916	18,613	1,336	22.869

Note: Costs are estimated for one year for England and Wales and are centred on 2001.

Before we consider the responses of the criminal justice system and the family justice system, we will briefly consider some of the possible explanations for domestic violence.

7.2 THE SEARCH FOR EXPLANATIONS

In *Domestic Violence: Action for Change* (1993), Gill Hague and Ellen Malos review some of the different types of explanation which have been developed:

Individual Pathological Models of Explanation

This kind of explanation is based on the idea that the individual using violence suffers from a pathological condition which leads to deviance from a non-violent norm. In practice it might only be quite extreme forms of violence or repeated violence that would be included in this kind of diagnosis. A certain kind of 'low-level' aggression might be seen as 'normal' at least in some families. Pathological deviance, however, might be thought to be based on either psychiatric illness or faults of temperament of one or both partners. Often it has been regarded as a sign of inadequacy, of an inarticulate person who had not learned to assert himself in non-violent ways.

When violence within families began to be perceived as a major problem in the early 1970s, it was in the context of medical evidence of the physical abuse of children in the United States. Initial explanations of violence within families at that time arose from concern about child abuse and focused on 'abusive families'. Women, as mothers, were viewed as colluding in the abuse of their children and also colluding in, or provoking, violence against themselves. The early research into 'family violence' in the United States in particular, where most of the large-scale studies have been carried out, was often based on this kind of assumption.

Such ideas are still current in psychiatry and psychology. They also persist in certain kinds of therapeutic social work, most notably in family therapy, where individualistic explanations shade over into theories of group pathology in which those who experience the violence are themselves often seen as helping to cause it. Certain kinds of psychotherapy too involve the idea that violence arises from 'issues' which the individuals concerned have not 'worked through' in their relationship. In recent years, some researchers with such views have been moving towards other types of explanation as they have asked more sophisticated questions.

Cycles of Violence

The 'cycle of violence' theory suggests that there is a direct transmission of violence down the generations by learned behaviour, creating a cycle in which the violence continuously reproduces itself. This theory has a variant in which it is argued that the behaviour is learned by children who either witness or experience violence within an individual family. There is also a 'sub-cultural model' in which the use of violence is learned as part of a wider way of life, either in neighbourhoods in criminal sub-cultures or gangs, or in certain professions such as the police and the army.

There is certainly some evidence that violence can be learned, but these theories cannot explain why some individuals who observe such behaviour or live in such environments are not violent, or why some people are violent who do not live in this kind of family or social setting. Nor can they explain why, according to a rather indiscriminate lumping together of different kinds of learned behaviour, it ends up that boys both observing and experiencing violence should, according to the theory, become perpetrators of violence whereas girls apparently learn to choose violent partners and 'enjoy', or passively put up with, violent assault.

The theory rests ultimately on assumptions about the natural aggressiveness of boys and men, and the passivity of girls and women. This kind of explanation also loses force if violence, and violence against women in particular, is both very common and often accepted in the whole society, as suggested by Elisabeth Wilson in *What's to be Done about Violence Against Women*? (1983):

> 'If you are one of only 500 [abused] women in a population of 50 million then you have certainly been more than unlucky and there may perhaps be something very peculiar about your husband, or unusual about your circumstances, or about you; on the other hand, if you are one of 500,000 women then that suggests something very different – that there is something wrong not with a few individual men, or women, or marriages, but with the situation in which many women and children regularly get assaulted – that situation being home and the family.'

Yet, as we will see in later chapters, the cycle of violence is still a very popular kind of explanation. One possible reason for its popularity is that it seems to suggest that those men who attack their wives or partners, and those women who experience violence, are not 'people like us' – but rather belong to a special deviant group of 'violent families', who are completely different from the rest of us. Even if the violence happens more often than we would like to think and is much worse than we ever imagined, it has been explained. And, using the theory, it can be dealt with, perhaps by removing children from the violent family or violent sub-culture – and thus 'breaking the cycle'.

As to the adults, it might be too late to change the ingrained pattern. Perhaps all you can do is to recognize that, or perhaps you can help the women and children to get away. Perhaps you prosecute the man, or break the cycle by re-educating the parents or the perpetrator (in more optimistic variants of the theory which think it is actually possible to change what happens). Ultimately, though, if you believe that this is why domestic violence takes place, all you can probably hope to do is to minimize the transmission of violence, because it is all a result of some unexplainable situation in the violent past. It is not about the present situation of many families, as Elisabeth Wilson suggests. Some people are 'just like that', even if there are a large number of them.

...

Social-Structural Explanations

This is another kind of explanation of 'family violence'. It bases itself on the stress caused by lack of access to money, housing and education common to both men and women in the family. This view was expressed very succinctly in a discussion document drawn up by the British Association of Social Workers in 1975:

> 'Economic conditions, low wages, bad housing, and isolation; unfavourable and frustrating work conditions for the man; lack of job opportunities for adolescent school leavers, and lack of facilities such as day care (e.g. nurseries), adequate transport, pleasant environment and play space and recreational facilities, for mother and children were considered to cause personal desperation that might cause violence in the home.'

This kind of explanation usually assumes that violence occurs mainly in working-class and poor families. There is a 'middle-class' version in terms of financial pressures and stressful careers, but more commonly in this view the greater resources of middle-class families or, in some cases, the ability of middle-class men to maintain dominance without resorting to violence are thought to explain what is believed to be the relative lack of violence in these families.

However, as Michael Freeman (1987) and others point out, it is likely that violence in middle-class families can more easily remain hidden from neighbours and public agencies like the police and social services. Borkowski, Murch and Walker found in their study *Marital Violence* (1983) that the more significant class differential was not in whether violence occurred but in the kind of agencies consulted, the middle class being more likely to use lawyers and the divorce courts than the police, social services or women's refuges. Although it seems very likely that the pressures of poverty might increase the occurrence of violence or make it worse, this type of analysis fails adequately to account for the predominant direction of serious violence from men towards women or the fact that it occurs in all social classes.

...

Feminist Explanations

...In the feminist view, domestic violence arises out of men's power over women in the family. This male power has been built into family life historically, through laws which assume that men have the right to authority over both women and children within families, where this does not conflict with public policy and the interests of the state. Rebecca and Russell Dobash in *Violence Against Wives* (1980), for example, describe the inferior historical position of women in British and North American society and in marriage, which arose from laws and customs which excluded women from public life and placed them under the authority of their husband or their father within the private sphere of the family.

...

Many feminists would use the kind of explanation which stresses the need to examine the historical position of women in particular societies and the way in which it was, and still is, embodied in law and custom. However, some forms of feminist explanation, basing themselves on the male-dominated nature of most known forms of society, come close to arguing that inherent biological differences between men and women are at the core of male violence and female non-violence. Others argue that there can be no such definite, undifferentiated categories as 'men' and 'women', but that we live among conflicting or intersecting sets of inequalities and differences in power.

Most feminist accounts draw attention to the economic position of women. They point to the way in which the responsibility that society assigns to women for looking after children often places them in a position of enforced financial dependency on their partners or ex-partners, a situation which will be reinforced in Britain by the new Child Support Act. It is also used as an excuse for paying women low wages or minimal state income support. Some feminists would also want to argue that class and racial oppression, and social stresses such as unemployment, bad housing and poverty, are likely to increase violence and make it harder to escape. Yet they would point out that this does not explain why it is that it is predominantly men who become violent in these circumstances, or why so much of the violence is directed towards women whom the men would profess to love.

Unlocking the Secret (Women's National Commission, 2003) looked at some of the reasons why people stay in violent relationships:

Women spoke of their fear of having their children taken away if they reported abuse and of the many competing reasons to stay. Most just wanted the violence to stop and lived in the constant hope that it would. None wanted their lives and, more importantly for them, those of their children to be disrupted if there was a chance the violence would stop. Some felt they would not be believed and be blamed for breaking the family up. Some women chose not to leave because the refuges in their areas could not accept children above a certain age. Often women didn't know where or who to go to: they just had no information. Women spoke of the enormity of taking this step and how they knew that they faced great danger at the point of leaving. They also spoke of how physically and emotionally worn down they were by this point.

> 'The authorities said to me that I could have left. But it was not that easy. With children, some women put up with a bit more.'
>
> 'In some cases, Social Services fight to remove children who need help. They say to the women, 'it is your fault because you did not leave the man'. Social Services need education in how hard it is to break away and how hard it is to keep the man away.'
>
> 'A lot of women drop charges because they are threatened with the kids being taken into care.'
>
> 'Once you have called for help it makes it worse, because you have broken the rule about keeping it behind closed doors. The minute you have done that you are upping the ante. There is no incentive to do that. You can get an alarm and a mobile phone if you are being followed, but things should be in place to stop him coming around. All the onus is on the women to get an injunction and everything. It should be up to the police; the women are running around everywhere and trying to find out who can help. Someone else needs to take the responsibility for your safety.'
>
> 'Women are having to go from decent homes to squalor. That is why women are not leaving relationships. They are lucky to get into B&Bs if refuges are full.'
>
> 'Asylum seekers have an image of the police connected with rape and torture [formed in their own countries]. It brings back those memories, so they never call the police.'

QUESTION

Do you think that the law's response to domestic violence should be influenced in any way by its causes? If so, how?

7.3 THE TROUBLE WITH THE CRIMINAL LAW . . .

Violence, and threats of violence, are criminal offences. Erin Pizzey's book *Scream Quietly or the Neighbours will Hear* (1974) alerted the public to the modern realities of domestic violence and to the trouble with the criminal law:

> The police attitude to wife-battering reveals an understandable but unacceptable schizophrenia in their approach to violence. Imagine that Constable Upright is on his beat one night and finds Mr Batter mugging a woman in the street. Mr Batter has already inflicted heavy bruises to the woman's face and is just putting the boot in when Constable Upright comes on . . . the scene. The

constable knows his duty and does it. He arrests Mr Batter, who is charged with causing grievous bodily harm and goes to prison for ten years.

Ten years later Constable Upright is on his beat when he is sent to investigate screaming which neighbours have reported coming from the home of the newly released Mr Batter. Mr Batter is mugging his wife. He's thrown boiling water at her, broken her nose, and now he's trying for her toes with a claw hammer. When Constable Upright arrives what does he do? Does he make an arrest? Of course not.

He knocks on the door and Mr Batter tells him to 'sod off'. He tells Mr Batter that the neighbours are complaining and he wishes to see his wife. Mr Batter says they have been having a minor row and he gets his wife who is looking bruised round the face and crying. The policeman will not arrest. In one case the husband even assaulted his wife in front of a policeman but still there was no arrest. All that he did was to advise her to go to the local magistrates' court the next morning and take out a summons against her husband, but he knew that she was unlikely to do this because she would have to live in the same house as her husband while she was taking him to court.

QUESTIONS

i. What powers does Constable Upright have, if told to 'sod off' by a man who is apparently beating his wife inside the matrimonial home? (Consult *R v Thornley* (1980) 72 Cr App Rep 302, and also the Police and Criminal Evidence Act 1984, section 17(1)(e) and (6).)

ii. If Mr Batter breaks his wife's nose in the pub, what might Constable Upright do? (Consider, for example, section 1 of the Crime and Disorder Act 1998.)

Perhaps the courts have not been above reproach; see *Foulkes v Chief Constable of Merseyside* [1998] 3 All ER 705, [1998] 2 FLR 789, in which the police responded to a call from a husband who had been locked out of the house by his wife and adult children. The officers established that the wife did not want to allow the husband into the house, and suggested that the husband should go for a cup of tea until tempers had cooled. When the husband continued his attempts to re-enter the house, he was arrested. He was released the next morning when his wife decided that she did not want him to be taken before a magistrate to be bound over to keep the peace. The Court of Appeal found that the husband's arrest had been unlawful. Thorpe LJ said that the wife's exclusion of the husband was wrongful in the light of his statutory rights of occupation (under what is now section 30 of the Famly Law Act 1996; see p. 327), and that the police should have pointed out to the wife that she was not entitled to resolve the dispute by a lock out. He said:

> It is only in the most extreme cases that conflict between spouses results in imprisonment, absent some criminal act. The imprisonment of a spouse has a profound effect on the future family dynamics. In my experience the invariable response of the police if called to a domestic dispute in a family uncontrolled by orders made in the family justice system is to decline involvement in the absence of a criminal act or the apprehension of a criminal act. I find it hard to envisage a situation in which the power of arrest for an apprehended breach of the peace would be an appropriate management of a dispute between husband and wife within the matrimonial home.

QUESTIONS

i. If a husband and wife are engaged in a heated argument but there has not yet been any violence, is it sensible to attempt to resolve the situation by explaining the husband's statutory rights of occupation to the wife?

ii. Should the police response differ where the parties are not married, and therefore have no statutory rights of occupation?

iii. How should the police decide which situations are likely to escalate into violence? What should they do if they believe that violence is likely to occur?

Mildred Dow identified one difficulty in 'Police Involvement', her contribution to *Violence in the Family* (1976):

> ...it has become obvious to the writer, through years of police experience...that however often one says to a wife, 'Your rights are...' she will invariably be re-influenced by her husband and refuse to give the necessary evidence. Whether this is basically due to personal fear or to an essentially sexual attraction and influence or to fear for the children of the union, it is difficult to determine. I only know how frustrating it is for a police officer who has taken much care and trouble in the preparation of the presentation of the case at court to be let down because his principal witness has had 'second thoughts'... From a practical viewpoint it would appear better to charge the husband and keep him in custody, rather than to follow the practice in some few police areas where the husband is reported for summons, thus giving him time to influence his wife. If some aggressive husbands are, by these means, kept away from the matrimonial home, more wives may be prepared to give the relevant evidence.

In contrast to its view in 1975, the Association of Chief Police Officers' evidence to the Home Affairs Committee (1993) said that, during the late 1980s, 'the Police Service changed its focus from one of conciliation to intervention'. A major change was marked by the Home Office Circular to police officers (60/1990) on *Domestic Violence:*

Nature and Extent of Problem

2. Chief officers will be aware of the wide range of abuse which is covered by the term 'domestic violence'. It encompasses all aspects of physical, sexual and emotional abuse, ranging from threatening behaviour and minor assaults which lead to cuts and bruises to serious injury, and sometimes even death. (In about 44% of homicide cases where the victim is a female the suspect is or was married to or lived with her.)...

...

4. Domestic violence is not simply a challenge for the criminal justice system. Victims will often need assistance which is beyond the capacity of the police to provide, requiring close cooperation with medical, social work and housing authorities and with victim support groups. Domestic violence is, however, a crime and it is important that the police should play an active and positive role in protecting the victim and that their response to calls for help is speedy and effective.

...

Force Policy Statements

11. The Home Secretary recommends that chief officers should consider issuing a force policy statement about their response to domestic violence. ... Central features of the force policy statement should be:

- the overriding duty to protect victims, and children, from further attack;
- the need to treat domestic violence as seriously as other forms of violence;
- the use and value of powers of arrest;
- the dangers of seeking conciliation between assailant and victim;
- the importance of comprehensive record-keeping to allow the chief officer to monitor the effectiveness of the policy in practice.

The circular went on to give advice about the police response at the scene of the crime and about prosecution. Did it change things? A Home Office Research Study, *Policing Domestic Violence in the 1990s* (1995) by Sharon Grace, addressed this issue:

The General Police Response

Virtually all forces have developed policies on domestic violence which closely adhere to the recommendations in Home Office Circular 60/1990. However, the findings in this report suggest that the translation of this policy into practice has been limited. Just over half of the forces had a specialist unit with *some* responsibility for domestic violence but only five forces had domestic violence units dedicated solely to this offence. While there was a general awareness among officers about how domestic violence *should* be policed, this awareness was not always reflected in the way they dealt with such cases. It appeared that managers were overly optimistic about how effective they had been in getting the message across to their operational colleagues and were somewhat out of touch about what was happening at ground level.

Most officers felt that the policing of domestic violence had improved and that such incidents were now being taken more seriously with more positive intervention and more support and advice available for victims. There was evidence that officers had increased their awareness of domestic violence issues and showed a greater understanding and sympathy for victims. However, a third of operational officers had not heard of Circular 60/1990 at all and over half said that they had not received any new guidelines on domestic violence – despite their managers' confidence that the guidance had been successfully disseminated.

...

Although most officers were aware that arrest should be a priority in domestic violence cases, almost half of them put it below all other considerations (e.g. the safety of the victim and any children) when asked to prioritise their actions at a domestic violence scene. Their decision to arrest appeared to be heavily influenced by whether a complainant would support any police action. However, the use of informal responses to domestic violence incidents appeared from interviews to be unsatisfactory both for officers – who will usually have to return to that address at a later date – and for victims – who feel the police have not taken their plight seriously enough. If they are to follow the guidance in Circular 60/1990, officers need to consider arrest more often in domestic violence cases.

QUESTIONS

i. Are you surprised that operational police officers are more concerned about the safety of women and children than about making arrests?
ii. Are these objectives incompatible?

In view of Grace's findings it is perhaps unsurprising that the stories of survivors, quoted in *Unlocking the Secret* (2003), give mixed messages about the police:

> Women had particularly bad experiences of policing in rural areas:
>
> > 'I'm 15 miles away from a police station. I had to wait for 45 minutes for the police to arrive. 45 minutes with a man who was being violent.'
> >
> > 'I called the police when my husband hit me over the head with a brass candlestick. He went to get the shotgun. We lived on a farm so I ran out in the dark. It was the middle of winter. I stayed in the fields for over three hours. I had head injuries and was covered in blood. I went to a call box and dialled 999. I was taken to the hospital and stitched up. Then the police came to take me home and I said that I did not want to go. But they said he was sorry; he was depressed because he had lost his business. The police accepted that and said there was no more that they were going to do.'
>
> Women also spoke of how invaluable the police had been.
>
> > 'The police response to me was very good. The officers I got were brilliant. They let me know what was going on and were at the end of a phone, but it all fell apart when I got to court.'
> >
> > 'In my case the police took him out and gave me time to pack for myself and the baby. They were sympathetic and gave me good advice on where to go.'
> >
> > 'If you've got a domestic violence officer with you, you feel safe. I felt better because I had her with me.'

A revised edition of the 1990 Home Office Circular – again with an uncompromising message – was issued to the police in 2000. Moreover, the Domestic Violence, Crime and Victims Act 2004 created the new offence of Causing or Allowing the Death of a Child or Vulnerable Adult (in section 5). Home Office Circular 9/2005, explains:

> 3. The new offence and procedural changes form a package of measures which are intended to solve the problem that arises when a child or vulnerable adult suffers an unlawful death and it can be proved that one or more of a small group of people living in the same household as the victim caused the death, but not which of them. In such circumstances there may be no case to answer against any member of the household for murder/manslaughter. Until now this loophole in the law has enabled those co-accused of the death of a child or vulnerable adult to escape justice by remaining silent or by blaming each other.
>
> ...
>
> 12. The offence is contained in section 5 of the DVCV Act. A summary of the offence is given above. The offence will only apply to a person who, because they were members of the household

who had frequent contact with the victim, had a duty to protect the victim from harm. It is reasonable that a person in those circumstances should be expected to take some action if this is possible, not simply stand by and do nothing. It is also reasonable that such a person should be expected to account to the court for the circumstances of the victim's death. It is expressly mentioned within the offence that it is not necessary for the prosecution to prove whether the defendant caused the death or allowed the death to occur. This is to enable a prosecution to be brought against both defendants even where they remain silent about what happened or blame each other.

...

14. The offence applies to members of the household who have frequent contact with the victim. This may include family members or carers, but is not confined to that group. This is different from other offences such as those in the Children and Young Person's Act 1933, which are based on cruelty or negligence by a carer. This is for a number of reasons. One is that the offence encompasses vulnerable adults, who often do not have an identifiable 'carer'. The other is that it is a frequent scenario that a child is placed at risk when a new member of the household arrives, such as when a parent strikes up a relationship with a new partner after splitting up with a previous one. The new partner might legitimately claim that he or she has no caring role for the child. But the new offence makes clear that if he or she is in the position of a household member who has frequent contact with a child or vulnerable person, he does have a responsibility to protect that child or vulnerable person from harm.

15. The term 'household' will be given its ordinary English meaning by the courts. This means it is not likely to include care homes or, for example, nurseries where a child is looked after with a number of others. A child or vulnerable person who is being cared for in this situation will be covered by professional safeguards and standards and professional duties of care....

16. The offence also allows for the fact that, with modern lifestyles and increasingly flexible family arrangements, a person may be a member of more than one household at any one time. But if this is so, the offence will only apply to members of the household where the victim was living at the time of the act which caused their death.

...

18. In order to prove the offence, it will be necessary to show that the defendant either caused the death of the victim or failed to take reasonable steps to protect the victim from a foreseeable risk of serious physical harm. What will constitute those 'reasonable steps' will depend on the circumstances of the person and their relationship to the victim, and will vary from case to case. The court will need to take all the circumstances into account. For example, if the defendant is a foster-child of 16, the steps which he or she could be expected to take to protect a younger member of the household might be limited. If one of the defendants has themselves been the victim of domestic violence, the steps that defendant could have reasonably taken may be more limited than someone not suffering that violence. Depending on the facts of the particular case the court may find that the defendant may have been too frightened to take some of the steps which in other circumstances might have been available to them.

Jonathan Herring, in 'Familial homicide, failure to protect and domestic violence: who's the victim?' (2007) gives some examples where that last point seems to have been overlooked, such as the following:

In May 2005 Rebecca Lewis, aged 21, was sentenced for failing to prevent the murder of her baby, Aaron Gilbert, at the hands of her partner, Andrew Lloyd, with whom she had lived for six weeks. She was sentenced to six years in prison. Lloyd was sentenced to 24 years in prison for murder. The court was told that Lewis was largely absent during Lloyd's attacks and was not present when he killed the baby. However, she knew that Lloyd had flicked Aaron's ears and feet when he cried; had picked him up by his ears and ankles; and had thrown him onto a bed. The jury must have found that these acts indicated a risk of death or serious harm. In sentencing her the judge said:

> 'You put your own interests first, above and beyond that of your vulnerable child. You could have stopped the violence that Lloyd was subjecting Aaron to. You could so easily have got the authorities to stop it.'

At the trial Lewis had explained that she did not summon help because Lloyd had said he would kill her if she left. For 'putting her interests first' she was given a sentence only a little shorter than the average given for rape. In fact the local social services had been warned about the child by Lewis' cousin. They responded to these concerns by writing a letter seeking to make an appointment, but it was sent to the wrong address. It is noticeable that for Lewis' failure to protect her child due to threats to her life she received a lengthy prison sentence. For the authorities who failed to protect the same child, but who faced no such threat, no legal responsibility has been attached.

QUESTIONS

i. What light does this new offence shed upon the nature of *domestic* violence?
ii. What should be expected of domestic violence victims in Rebecca Lewis's position?

The current policy of the Crown Prosecution Service is described in their *Policy for Prosecuting Cases Of Domestic Violence* (2005). It includes the following paragraph:

> 5.5 Sometimes victims will ask the police not to proceed any further with the case and say that they no longer wish to give evidence. This does *not* mean that the case will automatically be stopped. As a general rule, we will prosecute cases where there is sufficient evidence and it is in the public interest to do so.

Evidence, of course, may be a problem.

> 5.16 In cases where it is necessary to call victims against their wishes, an experienced prosecutor will only make that decision after consultation with the police and with the safety of the victim and any child or vulnerable person as a prime consideration...
>
> 5.17 The law allows us to use the victim's statement in court without calling the victim, but only in very limited circumstances, for example, where the victim cannot be found. The court ultimately makes the decision whether to allow such a statement to be used in this manner and only if it is convinced that it is in the public interest to do so. If the victim is the only witness to the offence it maybe very difficult to satisfy the court that justice is being served when the defence cannot cross-examine the only witness against them.

But should the criminal law go further, where the victim does not wish to proceed with a prosecution? Louise Ellison, in *Prosecuting domestic violence without victim participation* (2002) discusses an approach pioneered in America:

> Complainant withdrawal presents prosecutors in England and Wales with formidable challenges in domestic violence cases. In one recent study as many as 46 per cent of victims withdrew their support for a prosecution following an initial complaint. Others estimate a significantly higher withdrawal rate. In England and Wales, complainant withdrawal in the context of domestic violence appears to have an almost singular effect; namely, discontinuance.

Ellison refers to Carolyn Hoyle's findings (1998)

> ... For example, one officer asked whether a suspect had confessed explained: 'Most of the time in these cases we don't waste much time interviewing the bloke because she's [the victim is] bound to withdraw and then it'll go nowhere.' Another added: 'They [the arresting officers] don't go flat out for confessions in these cases because they know the women will withdraw and once she pulls out the CPS won't want to know'.

Ellison goes on to explain 'victimless' prosecution:

> A decisive development in the prosecution of domestic violence in the United States has been a shift from so-called 'victim-based' policing towards what may be described as 'evidence-based' policing and the adoption of specific evidence-gathering techniques. San Diego has been at the forefront of developments and has provided a model for the police departments of other counties...
>
> Officers are specifically advised to investigate domestic violence crime with the assumption that the victim will be unable to participate in any subsequent trial. Recognising that the initial investigation at the scene of an alleged incident will be crucial in all instances, investigating officers are encouraged to make a case as strong as possible by using the first golden hour' to gather evidence. As part of this strategy officers are advised in all cases to conduct separate interviews with the alleged victim and suspect on arrival at the scene and to identify and interview any possible witnesses including children and neighbours. Specific advice is provided on the most appropriate interrogative techniques when questioning a domestic violence suspect following arrest. The overarching aim is to obtain a confession or at least to elicit and record any damaging admissions for future use in criminal proceedings. At the scene officers are directed to take photographs of the victim, suspect, the setting and any weapon used as a matter of routine and impound evidence such as bloody clothing and damaged property. ... The standard reporting form used by the San Diego police department... prompts officers to describe the physical and emotional condition of the alleged victims. The form contains diagrams of two human bodies, one female, one male, and officers are required to indicate the location of any injuries...
>
> The adoption, *inter alia*, of 'evidence-based' police investigation in domestic violence cases has reportedly led to the successful prosecution of increased numbers of offenders in San Diego. Casey Gwynn estimates that nearly 70 per cent of filed cases involve uncooperative or absent victims and that convictions are obtained in nearly 90 per cent of cases...

Introduction of Evidential Rules

> To compensate for the absence of a complainant's live testimony in domestic violence trials a number of US states have... introduced evidential rules that allow for the admission of evidence traditionally excluded in criminal proceedings. Most controversially, some state legislatures have introduced rules that authorise the admission of evidence of prior domestic violence against other alleged victims to show propensity. When [these rules are] applied previous partners of the defendant have been permitted to testify to prior acts of abuse in support of an instant allegation of domestic violence where the complainant has been unable or unwilling to appear in court. Other states have introduced new exceptions to the hearsay rule to admit into evidence the prior out of court statements of an absent complainant.

Ellison goes on to explain that some police forces in England and Wales are taking steps to enhance the gathering of evidence in domestic violence cases, in particular by taking photographs of injuries.

QUESTIONS

i. What do you think are the advantages and disadvantages of prosecuting without the victim's cooperation?

ii. Is it safe to change the rules of evidence in this way? Consider whether it might be safe for the alleged offender and/or for the victim. Note that section 116 of the Criminal Justice Act 2003 provides that '[i]n criminal proceedings a statement not made in oral evidence in the proceedings is admissible as evidence of any matter stated if... through fear the relevant person does not give (or does not continue to give) oral evidence in the proceedings, either at all or in connection with the subject matter of the statement, and the court gives leave for the statement to be given in evidence.'

7.4 DEVELOPING CIVIL LAW REMEDIES FOR MOLESTATION AND HARASSMENT

It is clear that policing policy and practice have undergone a change in the period from 1990 onwards. But that change has been a gradual one. Against the background of an unsatisfactory (albeit changing) criminal law, the civil law has endeavoured to provide effective remedies.

In its evidence to the Home Affairs Committee (1993), the Women's Aid Federation England pointed out some of the reasons why victims of domestic violence might prefer to use civil remedies, rather than the criminal law:

> From the point of view of the woman experiencing the abuse, it may seem preferable to apply for protection in the civil courts rather than to give evidence in a criminal prosecution of her partner. Firstly, the process seems to be more under her control: she instructs the solicitor, who will represent her in court, or will instruct a barrister on her behalf. Secondly, in most cases

> the hearing will be in a closed court or in the Judge's chambers, and there will be no publicity. Thirdly, her partner will not acquire a criminal record, which could hamper his employment prospects and hence indirectly affect the economic situation of the woman and her children. For all these reasons it is important that the process of obtaining injunctions or personal protection orders should be as straightforward as possible, and that the orders, once obtained should be effective and if breached, should be strictly enforced.

The victim's control over the process is a strength of the civil law, but it may also be a limitation – as we saw when we looked at the difficulties experienced in the context of criminal prosecution. As John Stuart Mill pointed out in 1869, 'it is contrary to reason and experience to suppose that there can be any real check to brutality, consistent with leaving the victim still in the power of the executioner'. The first step had therefore to be to improve and extend the procedures for releasing wives from their lifelong promise and legal duty to live with their husbands. But it is one thing to be told that you need no longer live with your husband, and another thing to pluck up the courage to live through the interim before the divorce and to find somewhere to live both then and thereafter. The civil law has endeavoured to ease this process by providing 'tailor-made' injunctions, traditionally known as non-molestation and ouster orders (the latter are now known as occupation orders) with a view to providing quick and straightforward safety measures.

By the mid-1990s domestic violence injunctions were available to both married and unmarried couples (the latter since enactment of the Domestic Violence and Matrimonial Proceedings Act 1976), from a variety of statutory and non-statutory sources. In *Domestic Violence and the Occupation of the Family Home* (1992) the Law Commission examined the various remedies which had been developed, and concluded:

> 2.24 The fact that different remedies are available to different applicants on different criteria in different courts with different enforcement procedures has resulted in a vastly complicated system, made even more confusing by the complex inter-relationship between the statutory remedies and the general principles of property and tort law.

The Family Homes and Domestic Violence Bill 1995 was based upon the Law Commission's recommendations. However, these proved unexpectedly controversial, particularly in relation to the availability of orders to unmarried applicants. The Bill was withdrawn, but an amended version of its provisions eventually became Part IV of the Family Law Act 1996.

Under the Family Law Act 1996, a non-molestation order may be made for a specified period or until further order (section 42(7)) and may be 'expressed so as to refer to molestation in general, to particular acts of molestation, or to both' (section 42(6)). As the Law Commission pointed out in their Report (1992):

> 2.3 Domestic violence can take many forms. The term 'violence' itself is often used in two senses. In its narrower meaning it describes the use or threat of physical force against a victim in the form of an assault or battery. But in the context of the family, there is also a wider meaning which extends to abuse beyond the more typical instances of physical assaults to include any form of physical, sexual or psychological molestation or harassment which has a serious detrimental effect upon the health and well-being of the victim, albeit that there is no 'violence' involved in the sense of physical force. Examples of such 'non-violent' harassment or molestation cover a very wide range of behaviour [*Vaughan v Vaughan* [1973] 1 WLR 1159]. Common instances include persistent pestering and intimidation through shouting, denigration, threats or argument, nuisance telephone calls, damaging property, following the applicant about and repeatedly calling at her home or place of work. Installing a mistress into the matrimonial home with a wife and three

children [*Adams v Adams* (1965) 109 Sol Jo 899], filling car locks with superglue, writing anonymous letters and pressing one's face against a window whilst brandishing papers [*Smith v Smith* [1988] 1 FLR 179] have all been held to amount to molestation. The degree of severity of such behaviour depends less upon its intrinsic nature than upon it being part of a pattern and upon its effect on the victim. Acts of molestation often follow upon previous behaviour which has been violent or otherwise offensive. Calling at the applicant's house on one occasion may not be objectionable. Calling frequently and unexpectedly at unsocial hours when the victim is known to be afraid certainly is. Such forms of abuse may in some circumstances be just as harmful, vicious and distressing as physical injuries.

The next development was the Protection from Harassment Act 1997, enacted largely as a result of the difficulty of finding a 'tort of harassment' within the general law; victims of 'stalking' had no civil remedy, not least because they were not among the categories of 'associated person' in the Family Law Act 1996 (on which see below, at p. 321). Emily Finch, in *Stalking the Perfect Stalking Law* (2002) explains:

It is clear that the behaviour that is common in stalking cases is varied in nature; it may be inherently unpleasant or apparently innocuous, it may be entirely lawful or amount to a substantive criminal offence. Stalking has a nebulous quality that renders the formulation of a precise legal definition somewhat problematic. Disciplines other than the law have not found it difficult to formulate definitions of stalking. For example, stalking has been described as 'a constellation of behaviours involving repeated and persistent attempts to impose on another person unwanted communication and/or contact' and as a situation in which 'one person causes another a degree of fear or trepidation by behaviour which is on the surface innocent but which, when taken in context, assumes a more threatening significance'. Such definitions encapsulate the central characteristics of stalking but do not readily translate into a workable legal definition.

The Scope of The Protection from Harassment Act 1997

The Protection from Harassment Act 1997 created two new criminal offences and a statutory tort of harassment. The basic offence of harassment is a summary offence that carries a maximum penalty of six months' imprisonment whilst the more serious offence of causing fear of violence is triable either way with a maximum penalty of five years' imprisonment. In addition to these offences, the Act also facilitates the imposition of indirect criminal liability on a defendant who contravenes either of the orders that may be made following civil or criminal proceedings. Section 3 provides for criminal proceedings to be taken for breach of civil injunction as an alternative to the more usual contempt proceedings whilst section 5 introduces the concept of restraining orders. Restraining orders can be attached to any other penalty that is imposed upon conviction and prohibit the defendant from engaging in specific conduct that is deemed likely to amount to further harassment. These provisions indicate the combined aims of the Protection from Harassment Act, which is to punish harassment that has already occurred whilst seeking to prevent any further incidents from taking place.

The combination of civil and criminal proceedings ensures that a victim of harassment has a choice between initiating civil proceedings or invoking the protection of the criminal justice system.

Civil or criminal liability under the Act requires a 'course of conduct'. The meaning of this phrase was considered in *R v Patel* [2004] EWCA Crim 3284, [2005] 1 FLR 803. Maurice Kay LJ explained:

> [7] In a nutshell, the prosecution case was that between October 1, 2002 and July 23, 2003 the appellant had subjected his wife to regular episodes of domestic violence. His case was that the allegation was untrue; he had never used or threatened violence. He asserted that his wife had fabricated the allegation in order to secure indefinite leave to remain in the United Kingdom as a victim of domestic violence.
>
> ...
>
> [36] ...[I]f, as we consider must have been the case, the jury took a very selective view of Mrs Patel's evidence, then the question arises as to whether they had received appropriate assistance from the Judge in relation to the 'course of conduct'. In dealing with s. 4 [of the Protection from Harassment Act 1996] the Judge told the jury, correctly, that a course of conduct must involve conduct on at least two occasions. He added this:
>
> > 'First of all, members of the jury, before you can convict you have to be satisfied that there was a course of conduct and, as I have said to you, as far as a course of conduct is concerned, it must involve conduct on at least two occasions, and it is not therefore good enough, if one were to take a hypothetical example, if you came to the conclusion that there was merely one incident which you were satisfied so that you were sure about. The course of conduct has to be at least two occasions. Members of the jury, that is the first point that you have to bear in mind.'
>
> The Judge then went on to give appropriate directions as to how the course of conduct must cause the other person to fear on at least two occasions that violence will be used.
>
> [37] He revisited the subject briefly when he came to define the s. 2 offence for the jury. Having set out the requirements that have to be proved for that offence, he added in that context:
>
> > 'A course of conduct is exactly the same in this section as in the other one, namely that it must involve conduct on at least two occasions.'
>
> [38] Mr Kay [for Mr Patel] submits that those directions were inadequate if, as appears to have been the case, the jury was considering conviction on the basis of findings of fact falling significantly short of Mrs Patel's account, and particularly if the findings of fact were limited to a small number of incidents (maybe no more than two or three), which may have been separated by some period of time. In this regard he referred us to a number of recent authorities. It is necessary to mention two of them. In *Lau v Director of Public Prosecutions* [2000] 1 FLR 799 the Divisional Court was concerned with a situation in which magistrates trying a defendant had accepted the evidence of the complainant on only two of five alleged incidents. Those two incidents occurred in November 1998 and March 1999. Schiemann LJ, giving the lead judgment in the Divisional Court, said at pp. 801–802:
>
> > 'I fully accept that the incidents which need to be proved in relation to harassment need not exceed two incidents, but, as it seems to me, the fewer the occasions and the wider they are spread the less likely it would be that a finding of harassment can reasonably be made. One can conceive of circumstances where incidents, as far apart as a year, could constitute a course of conduct and harassment. In argument [counsel] put the context of racial harassment taking place outside a synagogue on a religious holiday, such as the day of atonement, and being repeated each year as the day of atonement came round. Another example might be a threat to do something once a year on a person's birthday. None the less the broad position must be that if one is left with only two incidents you have to see whether what happened on those two occasions can be described as a course of conduct.'

[39] The second authority is another decision of the Divisional Court, *Pratt v. Director of Public Prosecutions* [2001] EWHC Admin 483, (2001) 165 JP 800, in which the magistrates found proved two incidents, one on December 25, 1999, and one on March 17, 2000. Giving the lead judgment Latham LJ set out the passage from *Lau* to which we have just referred and then said:

> '10. In my view these propositions accurately set out the law and the cautious approach that any court should adopt where the allegation of harassment is based upon either two incidents or any other series of incidents, if few in number and widely spaced in time. The issue for the court is whether or not the incidents, however many they may be, can properly be said to be so connected in type and in context as to justify the conclusion that they can amount to a course of conduct.'

[40] It is... apparent from what we have already said when considering the first ground of appeal that in our judgment it is probable that the jury convicted the appellant by reference to two or perhaps three incidents that were more separated in time than the totality of incidents which had been recounted by Mrs Patel, but in our judgment in all probability to a significant extent rejected by the jury. If the jury found themselves considering conviction by reference to a much reduced number of incidents – and we consider that that must have been the case then the assistance which they had received by way of the summing up was, in our judgment, deficient. In essence that assistance came to little more than a direction that there must be at least two or more incidents. Adopting the approach of the Divisional Court, we conclude that if there is any possibility (seen prospectively or retrospectively) that the jury has convicted on the sort of basis to which we have referred, then assistance of the kind prescribed by the Divisional Court is in our judgment essential. It is not just a matter of counting the incidents and saying, 'We have two, that is enough'. It is necessary for the jury to be given some guidance so that they address the question of whether the incidents give rise to a nexus sufficient for there to be a 'course of conduct'. As Latham LJ said in *Pratt*, the issue is whether or not the incidents, however many there may be, can properly be said to be so connected in type and in context as to justify the conclusion that they can amount to a course of conduct.

[41] Applying those principles to this case, we repeat, it seems to us that there is a risk that the jury convicted the appellant by reference to two or three incidents separated (although not enormously so) in time and place and to some extent in context, having regard to the fact that the final incident on July 22, was not wholly domestic in its location or implication.

[42] For that reason we have come to the conclusion that the verdict is unsafe. Accordingly, we allow the appeal and quash the conviction.

Finch (2002) comments on alternatives to the 'course of conduct' requirement:

> Some insight may be provided by an examination of the approach taken in stalking legislation in the United States where an association between the incidents comprising a course of conduct is required. For example, section 646.9(e) of the Californian Penal Code defines a course of conduct as 'a pattern of conduct composed of a series of acts over a period of time, however short, evidencing a continuity of purpose'. It is clear from this definition that the nexus between the incidents is provided by the motivation of the stalker in engaging in the conduct hence the elusive factor would appear to be continuity of purpose. The notion that the purpose underlying the conduct may provide the requisite nexus has received some support in English law. For example, in *Baron v Crown Prosecution Service* (Divisional Court, July 27, 1998, unreported), it was held that the defendant's ulterior purpose in sending two letters four months' apart would provide the necessary link between what would otherwise be regarded as two separate incidents. An alternative method of establishing a nexus between what is often wholly disparate conduct can be seen in

Australia. State legislation defines stalking by reference to a list of prima facie lawful conduct when it is undertaken for a particular prohibited purpose, such as an intention to intimidate or intention to cause apprehension or fear of serious harm.

QUESTIONS

i. Which of the following might amount to molestation, and which might constitute harassment actionable under the 1997 statute?

   a. Telephoning the victim's mother-in-law to complain about her.
   b. Telephoning the victim's employer to make allegations.
   c. Sitting outside the victim's home on the garden wall, doing nothing.
   d. Attending the victim's church.
   e. Texting the victim. (How often?)
   f. Continuing to shop in the local Tesco's where the victim also shops.

ii. Which of the above would amount to a criminal assault?

iii. Would it be possible to obtain a 'restraining order' under section 5 of the Protection from Harassment Act after a single incident of domestic violence? Is there a 'course of conduct' or an 'anticipated' course of conduct in such circumstances?

iv. Look at *Singh v Bhakar and Bhakar* [2007] 1 FLR 880. Was this the sort of harassment that the legislature had in mind? If not, does that matter?

v. Part IV of the Family Law Act 1996 was intended to reduce confusion by providing a single set of remedies for domestic violence under a single statute. Is there a danger that similar confusion could develop as a result of the use of the Protection of Harassment Act in domestic violence cases?

Non-molestation orders are available, under the Family Law Act 1996, only against someone who is an 'associated person' vis-à-vis the victim; and the availability of occupation orders is similarly limited. Following the amendments made by the 2004 statute, the list of associated persons is as follows:

62 (3) For the purposes of this Part, a person is associated with another person if –

(a) they are or have been married to each other;
[(aa) they are or have been civil partners of each other;]
(b) they are cohabitants or former cohabitants;
(c) they live or have lived in the same household, otherwise than merely by reason of one of them being the other's employee, tenant, lodger or boarder;
(d) they are relatives;
(e) they have agreed to marry one another (whether or not that agreement has been terminated);
[(eza) they have entered into a civil partnership agreement (as defined by section 73 of the Civil Partnership Act 2004) (whether or not that agreement has been terminated);]
[(ea) they have or have had an intimate personal relationship with each other which is or was of significant duration;]

(f) in relation to any child, they are both persons falling within subsection (4); or

(g) they are parties to the same family proceedings (other than proceedings under this Part).

(4) A person falls within this subsection in relation to a child if–

(a) he is a parent of the child; or

(b) he has or has had parental responsibility for the child.

QUESTION

Why should a victim of violence, harassment or molestation have to demonstrate that he or she is 'associated' with the perpetrator of the molestation before he or she can seek a remedy?

In its Report (1992), the Law Commission considered the possibility of allowing anyone to seek a non-molestation order, but decided against this:

> 3.19...We do not think it is appropriate that this jurisdiction should be available to resolve issues such as disputes between neighbours, harassment of tenants by landlords or cases of sexual harassment in the workplace. Here there is no domestic or family relationship to justify special remedies or procedures and resort should properly be had to the remedies provided under property or employment law. Family relationships can, however, be appropriately distinguished from other forms of association. In practice, many of the same considerations apply to them as to married or cohabiting couples. Thus the proximity of the parties often gives unique opportunities for molestation and abuse to continue; the heightened emotions of all concerned give rise to a particular need for sensitivity and flexibility in the law; there is frequently a possibility that their relationship will carry on for the foreseeable future; and there is in most cases the likelihood that they will share a common budget, making financial remedies inappropriate.

Helen Reece, in *The End of Domestic Violence* (2006) is unhappy with the broad range of the category of associated persons. She argues that domestic violence arises in relationships characterised by 'proximity coupled with isolation, controlled emotions within unequal power structure, barriers to ending relationship and financial dependence' and goes on to say:

> Undoubtedly, some types of associated persons could share all these relevant features; for example, an elderly relative who was being abused in the family home might be more isolated, less able to end the relationship, more financially dependant and might have less power than most battered wives. However, in the aggregate 'there is nothing unique in relationship terms about the people in the Law Commission's list, despite the fact that the Commission would have us believe that the listed relationships have special attributes and merit particular attention' (Hayes, 1996).
>
> There are two aspects to this lack of uniqueness. First, associated persons are generally no more likely, and on occasions will be less likely, than people who are not associated to

exhibit the features identified as relevant: an aunt is less likely to be isolated than a nanny, an ex-flatmate less likely to be trapped in the relationship than a neighbour, a sister-in-law less likely to be financially dependant than an employee and a father less likely to be powerless than a tenant.

Secondly, the aggregate of associated persons are far less likely than wives and female heterosexual cohabitants to exhibit the requisite features.... The mis-match [between the nature of the included relationships and the nature of domestic violence legislation] has only been exacerbated by another amendment that the Domestic Violence, Crime and Victims Act makes to the Family Law Act 1996: it will no longer be necessary to attach a power of arrest to a non-molestation order, because section 1 of the 2004 Act turns breach of a non-molestation order into a criminal offence in itself. As domestic violence law becomes tougher, it becomes even less suited to general family or household disputes.

...The debate that accompanied the creation of the category of associated person contained nuggets of a new rationale. This debate treated 'associated person' as synonymous with 'member of the family' and the boundaries of the concept of the family as being set by the boundaries of the category of associated persons. There was no opposition to speak of to the creation of the category of associated person; however, limitations to the category were proposed partly out of concern to contain our understanding of the family, while both the category itself and extension to the category were welcomed partly as a means of expanding our conception of the family.

A concrete illustration of this is the debate in the House of Lords Special Public Committee over whether 'associated persons' should extend as far as people in a sexual relationship. One of the main objections expressed was that sexual partners were not members of the same family. It was suggested that sexual partners did not necessarily have either 'the same family connections' or 'the same domestic link' as other associated persons. It was claimed that they had not 'entered membership of a family'; had no 'nexus of some kind of family relationship', no 'sensible family nexus'. One witness...explained succinctly that sexual partners should be excluded 'because this is essentially a Family Bill'.

The counter-argument followed suit: the definition of associated person should be wide because our definition of the family should be wide.

...In the lead-up to the Domestic Violence, Crime and Victims Act 2004, one of the arguments in favour of the two additions to the category [sections 62(3) (eza) and (ea)] was again that this would further widen our understanding of the concept of the family. Interestingly, this discussion was different from that which preceded the Family Law Act 1996 in that, this time, there was no opposition to the idea that it was desirable to expand the concept of the family. According to Baroness Anelay for example, 'family life – indeed the very definition 'family' – has evolved. We need to take account of that.

In many contexts, there are progressive aspects to expanding our understanding of the concept of the family but if the boundaries of the family are also treated as the boundaries for enhanced protection against domestic violence then in this context expanding the boundaries of the family is regressive, because expansion endangers the specificity of the category of domestic violence. ... Intimacy is replacing inequality as the touchstone of domestic violence law.

...Feminist commentators have commonly interpreted the state's *apparent* concern to protect women from domestic violence as motivated by a *real* concern to preserve the status of the traditional nuclear family. They have suggested that the state achieves this by minimising domestic violence in various connected ways. The claim that domestic violence occurs in every kind of relationship seems to be the reverse of minimising domestic violence, but in fact it is another method, because if domestic violence occurs in every type of relationship then domestic violence occurs nowhere.

QUESTIONS

i. If inequality is the touchstone of domestic violence law, how do we explain battered husbands?

ii. Are injunctions under the Protection from Harassment Act available to people who are 'associated' under the Family Law Act 1996? Can you think of any reasons why an associated person might choose to use the 1997 Act instead of seeking a non-molestation order under the Family Law Act? Or vice versa?

iii. What, if anything, is the benefit of a law that relates specifically to *domestic* violence over a more general provision such as the Protection from Harrassment Act 1997?

The Domestic Violence, Crime and Victims Act 2004 strengthened the civil procedures and brought the criminal law and civil law closer together, in particular by making it a criminal offence to breach a civil injunction (see section 42A of the Family Law Act 1996).

QUESTIONS

i. What messages are conveyed by this change in the law?

ii. What might be the disadvantages of mingling the civil and criminal law in this way?

7.5 OCCUPATION ORDERS

The Law Commission (1992) recognised the importance of occupation orders in cases of domestic violence:

> 4.6... where the parties live together, an occupation order ousting the respondent from the home will often be the only way of supporting a non-molestation order and giving the applicant effective protection.

However, the Law Commission's Report (1992) also drew attention to the effect of such orders on the other party:

> 2.48 In principle, there must be a distinction between an order not to be violent towards or molest another family member, which can be obeyed without prejudice to the interests of the person concerned, and an order to leave or stay away from the home (or part of it), which obviously does prejudice those interests, however temporarily or justifiably.

The following story by Frances Gibb, Legal Correspondent, in *The Times* (1997), illustrates the impact of an occupation order:

Husband Who Snapped Told to Leave Home

A deputy headmaster who temporarily lost control and pushed his wife against a door after she confessed to an affair with one of his 'best friends' was ordered yesterday to give up his home to her. Despite expressing sympathy for the man's plight, two Court of Appeal judges yesterday refused to overturn an earlier ruling ordering the husband out of the family home, although they said that his estranged wife had 'created the situation'. The husband, from the Portsmouth area, had vowed not to harm his wife again and had offered to sleep in a separate room and stay out of the main part of the house.

After dismissing his appeal Lady Justice Butler-Sloss and Lord Justice Phillips gave him until noon on September 6 to leave so that his wife and their three children, aged nine, seven and five, and who are currently living in a women's refuge, can move back in. In June this year the wife confessed that she had had a brief affair with a family friend. Her husband later admitted that he had reacted badly over the following three or four days, pushing her against the door once and gripping her wrists hard enough to leave a mark on two other occasions. But he was stunned when his wife took the children and fled, claiming she was too frightened to return while he was in their home. In July she won a ruling from Portsmouth County Court that her husband should leave the house by August 8 despite his promise not to harm her. But the order was stayed when the husband applied for leave to appeal against the decision.

Lady Justice Butler-Sloss said: 'Members of the public might be forgiven for thinking that when a man finds his wife has committed adultery with one of his best friends and she tells it to him his reaction is likely to be uncontrolled.' But to have been violent on three occasions had been 'over the top' and although she had no doubt that the husband's promise not to harm his wife was genuine, to allow them to live under the same roof would create a situation 'fraught with emotional turmoil' leading to the risk of further violence.

Before the Family Law Act 1996, the criteria for 'ouster orders' were settled by the House of Lords in *Richards v Richards* [1984] AC 174, [1983] 2 All ER 807. When the Law Commission reviewed the law in 1992, they outlined the criticism of these criteria:

4.23... They do not give priority to the applicant's personal protection, but require this to be balanced against all other factors, including hardship to the respondent. Thus the level of protection provided for an applicant suffering from violence may not be adequate. Also a requirement to decide upon occupation of the family home on the basis (at least in part) of fault, thus encouraging parties to make allegations about behaviour, sits uneasily with the general trend in matrimonial law towards reducing the need for recrimination and fault-finding, and enabling the courts to deal with problems of family breakdown without allocating blame, with a view to enhancing the possibility of agreement or even reconciliation between the parties. The test is also thought to give insufficient weight to the interests of children as the balancing exercise throws the children into the scales along with all the other factors and gives no priority to their welfare.

However, the Law Commission stopped short of recommending that the welfare of children should be the paramount consideration. Instead, they recommended a 'balance of harm' test should apply, so that a court should have a duty to make an order if it appears likely that the applicant or any relevant child will suffer significant harm if an order is not made and that such harm will be greater than the harm which the respondent or any relevant child will suffer if the order is made. They said:

> 4.34...It is likely that a respondent threatened with ouster on account of his violence would be able to establish a degree of hardship (perhaps in terms of difficulty in finding or unsuitability of alternative accommodation or problems in getting to work). But he is unlikely to suffer significant harm, whereas his wife and children who are being subjected to his violence or abuse may very easily suffer harm if he remains in the house. In this way the court will be treating violence or other forms of abuse as deserving immediate relief, and will be directed to make an order where a risk of significant harm exists. However, by placing an emphasis on the need for a remedy rather than on the conduct which gave rise to that need, the criteria will not actually put a premium on allegations of violence and thus may avoid the problems which would be generated by a scheme which focuses on it.

QUESTION

Why was the Law Commission concerned not to put a premium on allegations of violence?

An amended version of the 'balance of harm' test appears in section 33 of the Family Law Act 1996:

> **33.** –...(3) An order under this section may –
>
> (*a*) enforce the applicant's entitlement to remain in occupation as against the other person ('the respondent');
> (*b*) require the respondent to permit the applicant to enter and remain in the dwelling-house or part of the dwelling-house;
> (*c*) regulate the occupation of the dwelling-house by either or both parties;
> (*d*) if the respondent is entitled [to occupy the dwelling-house by virtue of a beneficial estate or interest or contract or by virtue of any enactment giving him the right to remain in occupation], prohibit, suspend or restrict the exercise by him of his right to occupy the dwelling-house;
> (*e*) if the respondent has matrimonial home rights in relation to the dwelling-house and the applicant is the other spouse, restrict or terminate those rights;
> (*f*) require the respondent to leave the dwelling-house or part of the dwelling-house; or
> (*g*) exclude the respondent from a defined area in which the dwelling house is included.
>
> ...
>
> (6) In deciding whether to exercise its powers under subsection (3) and (if so) in what manner, the court shall have regard to all the circumstances including –
>
> (*a*) the housing needs and housing resources of each of the parties and of any relevant child;
> (*b*) the financial resources of each of the parties;

(*c*) the likely effect of any order, or of any decision by the court not to exercise its powers under subsection (3), on the health, safety or well-being of the parties and of any relevant child; and

(*d*) the conduct of the parties in relation to each other and otherwise.

(7) If it appears to the court that the applicant or any relevant child is likely to suffer significant harm attributable to conduct of the respondent if an order under this section containing one or more of the provisions mentioned in subsection (3) is not made, the court shall make the order unless it appears to it that –

(*a*) the respondent or any relevant child is likely to suffer significant harm if the order is made; and

(*b*) the harm likely to be suffered by the respondent or child in that event is as great as, or greater than, the harm attributable to conduct of the respondent which is likely to be suffered by the applicant or child if the order is not made.

...

'Harm' is defined in section 63 of the Act to mean ill-treatment or the impairment of physical or mental health, and (in the case of children) impairment of development.

QUESTION

Why does section 33(7) require that the harm likely to be suffered is 'attributable to the conduct of the respondent'?

An application under section 33 of the Family Law Act 1996 is only possible where the applicant is entitled to occupy the home by virtue of a legal or beneficial estate or interest or a contractual or statutory right. Section 33 will, therefore, always be available between spouses and civil partners since in the absence of any other right, they will have a statutory right of occupation under section 30 of the Family Law Act 1996. Occupation orders will be available between unmarried people, provided that they are 'associated' in the same way as for non-molestation orders, but only if the applicant can establish that he or she has some entitlement to occupy the property in question (section 33(1)) (as to non-entitled applicants, see below at p. 333).

An application for an occupation order by an unmarried 'entitled' applicant was considered by the Court of Appeal in *Chalmers v Johns* [1999] 1 FLR 392; [1999] 2 FCR 110. Thorpe LJ had this to say about section 33:

...[Section] 33 of the Family Law Act 1996... applies to those cases where the applicant has an estate or interest in the family home. It is common ground that these two are joint tenants. In those circumstances the court may, under sub-s (3) order the prohibition, suspension or restriction of the exercise by the respondent of his right to occupy the residence. Equally under that subsection the court may require the respondent to leave the dwelling house.

Now the exercise of that power is ordinarily governed by sub-s (6). Subsection (6) is in these terms:

'In deciding whether to exercise its powers under subsection (3) and (if so) in what manner, the court shall have regard to all the circumstances including – (a) the housing needs

> and housing resources of each of the parties and of any relevant child; (b) the financial resources of each of the parties; (c) the likely effect of any order, or of any decision by the court not to exercise its powers under subsection (3), on the health, safety or well-being of the parties and of any relevant child; and (d) the conduct of the parties in relation to each other and otherwise.'

However, the following subsection, sub-s (7), is designed to cater for an altogether more extreme situation, where it appears to the court that any applicant or any relevant child is likely to suffer significant harm attributable to conduct of the respondent if an order under this section containing one or more of the provisions mentioned in sub-s (3) is not made. In that more extreme circumstance, the court's discretion is much confined. The statute says that in such a situation –

> 'the court shall make the order unless it appears to the court that – (a) the respondent or any relevant child is likely to suffer significant harm if the order is made; and (b) the harm likely to be suffered by the respondent or the child in that event is as great as, or greater than, the harm attributable to conduct of the respondent which is likely to be suffered by the applicant or child if the order is not made.'

So it seems to me that in approaching its function under this section, the court has first to consider whether the evidence establishes that the applicant or any relevant child is likely to suffer significant harm attributable to the conduct of the respondent if an order is not made. If the court answers that question in the affirmative, then it knows that it must make the order unless balancing one harm against the other, the harm to the respondent or the child is likely to be as great. If, however, the court answers the question in the negative, then it enters the discretionary regime provided by sub-s (6) and must exercise a broad discretion having regard to all the circumstances of the case, particularly those factors set out in the statutory check list within paras (a)–(d) inclusive. ...

...The gravity of an order requiring a respondent to vacate a family home, an order overriding proprietary rights, was recognised in cases under the Domestic Violence and Matrimonial Proceedings Act 1976 and a string of authorities in this court emphasise the draconian nature of such an order, and that it should be restricted to exceptional cases. I do not myself think that the wider statutory provisions contained in the Family Law Act 1996 obliterate that authority. The order remains draconian, particularly in the perception of the respondent. It remains an order that overrides proprietary rights and it seems to me that it is an order that is only justified in exceptional circumstances. ...

QUESTION

Can this approach be reconciled with the Law Commission's desire to give greater weight to the need to protect victims of violence and children, rather than to the 'draconian' effect of the order? Why do you think that the courts persist in an approach which is narrower than the words of the statute? Whose approach do you prefer?

The interests of a child had a dramatic impact in the following case.

B v B (Occupation Order), [1999]
2 FCR 251, [1999] 1 FLR 715, Court of Appeal

Butler-Sloss LJ:

...

The essential facts are not in dispute, and can be stated quite shortly. Mr and Mrs B were married on 30 May 1996. From a previous relationship, Mr B has a son, MB born on 21 December 1992 and so now six. When Mr and Mrs B began their relationship in 1996, and indeed up to the time of his marriage to Mrs B, Mr B was living with MB, and MB's mother, Ms M. However, it appears that immediately after the marriage, Mr and Mrs B set up home together with MB as part of their household.

On 17 June 1996 Mr and Mrs B were given the tenancy of two-bedroomed council accommodation (the property) which became the matrimonial home. On 4 October 1997 their daughter, YB, was born.

The parties separated when Mrs B left the property on 21 July 1998, taking YB (then aged nine months) with her, but leaving MB in the care Mr B. Mrs B's case, accepted by the judge, was that Mr B had treated her with violence.

On 22 or 23 July the local authority rehoused Mrs B and YB in temporary bed and breakfast accommodation. On 1 September Mrs B applied to the county court for an ex parte non-molestation order and for an occupation order against Mr B. On 9 September Mr B gave an undertaking not to molest Mrs B and the latter, who originates from Ghana, gave an undertaking not to remove YB from the jurisdiction. On 21 September the question of Mr B's contact to YB was resolved by agreement.

The Hearing Before the Judge

The hearing of Mrs B's application for an occupation order under s 33 of the 1996 Act took two days, concluding late in the day on 10 November 1998. As already indicated, the judge made the order sought by Mrs B, and refused leave to appeal.

The judge first of all dealt with Mrs B's application for an injunction. This involved a resolution of the factual issues between the parties on the subject of domestic violence and Mrs B's reasons for leaving the matrimonial home. The judge made a number of adverse findings against Mr B, and concluded:

> 'It seems to me that this is a situation where there has been substantial violence, and it is clearly apprehended that in the absence of some form of injunction that is likely to happen again.'

...

As the judge recognised, the critical subsections of s 33 for the purposes of this case are sub-ss (6) and (7). Both MB and YB are relevant children within s 33(6)(a) and (c) – see s 62(2)(a) of the 1996 Act which defines 'relevant child' as 'any child who is living with or might reasonably be expected to live with either party to the proceedings'. The judge also found, correctly, that on the facts of the instant case the reference in s 33(7) to 'harm' did not mean ill-treatment, but did mean 'impairment of health or development' within s 63(1) of the Act.

...

In our judgment, ... the judge's analysis of the 'housing needs and housing resources of each of the parties and of any relevant child' under s 33(6) led him into error. The respective housing needs of the parties are, in one sense, equal. Each needs two bedroom accommodation provided by the local authority; but the 'housing resources', using that term to include the duty owed to each by the local authority, were quite different. Unsatisfactory as Mrs B's current temporary accommodation is, there is every prospect that in the reasonably foreseeable future she and YB will be rehoused by the local authority in suitable two-bedroomed accommodation. There is no such prospect for Mr B and MB if the occupation order stands.

In our judgment the judge's mistaken analysis of the housing position is sufficient to vitiate the exercise of his discretion in making an occupation order. There is, however, in our view, an additional point which flows from it, and which reaffirms our conclusion that the order made by the judge was plainly wrong.

... Applying the terms of s 33(7) to the facts of this case, the judge was plainly entitled to find that Mrs B and YB were likely to suffer significant harm attributable to Mr B's conduct if an occupation order was not made. The judge thus had to make an occupation order unless Mr B or MB were likely to suffer significant harm if the order was made, and that the harm likely to be suffered by Mr B or MB was as great or greater than the harm attributable to Mr B's conduct likely to be suffered by Mrs B or YB.

In this context it seems to us, with great respect to the judge, that he paid no attention to the fact that if an accommodation order [*sic*] was made, MB would not only have the disruption of leaving home, but would also have to leave his school, at which he was doing well. The judge's statement that MB would at least have 'the respite during term-time of being off at school with his friends' takes no account of this fact.

In our judgment, and whilst in no sense under-estimating the difficulties and frustrations of living with and caring for a toddler in bed and breakfast accommodation, the essential security for a child of YB's age is being where her mother is. Furthermore, of course, on the evidence, Mrs B's residence in bed and breakfast accommodation is likely to be temporary.

For MB the position is much more complex. His security depends not just on being in the care of his father, but on his other day-to-day support systems, of which his home and his school are plainly the most important.

... In our judgment, if, on the facts of this case, the respective likelihoods of harm are weighed so far as the two children are concerned, the balance comes down clearly in favour of MB suffering the greater harm if an occupation order is made.

... This case turns on its own very special facts. We have no sympathy for Mr B. He has behaved towards his wife in a manner which the judge found to be disgraceful. He treated her with serious domestic violence. Such conduct is unacceptable, and plainly falls to be considered within s 33(6)(d). Thus, were it not for the fact that he is caring for MB, and that MB has particular needs which at present outweigh those of YB, an accommodation order would undoubtedly have been made.

The message of this case is emphatically *not* that fathers who treat their partners with domestic violence and cause them to leave home can expect to remain in occupation of the previously shared accommodation. Equally, such fathers should not think that an application for a residence order in relation to a child or children of the relationship will prevent accommodation orders being made against them.

Part IV of the 1996 Act is designed to protect cohabitants from domestic violence and to secure their safe occupation of previously shared property. Nothing in this judgment should be read as weakening that objective.

Each case will, of course, turn on its facts. The critical, and highly unusual facts in this case are (1) that MB is not a child of the parties; (2) that there is no question of MB being cared for by Mrs B or anyone other than Mr B; (3) that Mr B is thus the full-time carer of a child who is likely to suffer greater harm than the harm which will be suffered by Mrs B and YB if an occupation order is made. It is the position of MB alone which, in our judgment, makes it inappropriate for an occupation order to be made on the facts of this case.

The injunction against Mr B will remain in force, and he should not think that, by setting aside the occupation order made by the judge, this court has vindicated him or in any way condoned his behaviour.

QUESTION

Apart from the difference in age between the two children, the availability of local authority housing appears to have been a significant factor in this case. How significant do you think this factor should be when deciding whether to grant occupation orders?

The facts of *B v B* are unusual, but what about the more commonplace situation where a relationship breaks down, and the parties find it impossible to continue living together. Are occupation orders available to resolve the situation?

In *Re Y (children) (occupation order)* [2000] 2 FCR 470, Court of Appeal, Civil Division, the facts, briefly, were that the wife began divorce proceedings in 1998 and continued to live in the matrimonial home with the husband and the two youngest children, R, who was sixteen years old and pregnant, and J, who was thirteen years old. It was a dysfunctional family with R and the mother allied against J and the father, and living in separate quarters. R and the father had a very bad relationship and there were frequent rows and fights between them. On 29 October 1999 the husband applied, *inter alia*, for an order restraining the wife from molesting him and an occupation order. On 14 December cross-undertakings were given by each of the parents not to molest the other. On 9 February 2000 the recorder observed that the family 'was a family divided among itself and at war with itself, with people taking sides', and that there had been violence. He concluded that harm was likely to be caused if both parties continued to live in the house and he applied section 33(7) of the Family Law Act 1996. He then referred to the matters to be taken into account in the exercise of his discretion under section 33(6) of the 1996 Act, and he observed that, according to the father's solicitors, the local authority's view was that were they to become involved they might more easily accommodate the mother and R, rather than the father and J. He ordered the mother to vacate the matrimonial home on the ground that he was satisfied under section 33 that on balance greater harm would be caused by not making the order, given the existing antagonism and the children taking sides. The mother appealed.

Ward LJ:

...

[26] ...the question turns on s 33(6). The housing needs and housing resources of each of the parties is a relevant matter. Here the matrimonial home could reasonably be divided to meet the housing needs of each of them. They had established their separate camps and there was no real reason, apart from the atmosphere that prevailed, why they could not share the house until the court could resolve matters under the ancillary relief jurisdiction. The financial resources of each were relevant. The judge made no finding about this, but there is nothing to suggest that the wife's modest earnings put her in such a strong position that she was able to go into the private housing market and rent accommodation. There was certainly no finding to that effect. The likely effect of the order on the health, safety and well-being of the parties and of any relevant child may in the judge's view have tipped the balance in favour of the husband because of his health. But upon analysis it seems difficult to see what misconduct by the wife leads to the deterioration of his health. His unhappiness stems, if anything, from his inability to establish a good and proper working relationship with his daughter. On the conduct of the parties in relation to each other, they are perhaps one as bad as the other. The actual finding of violence, as I have said, is against the husband and not specifically against the wife.

[27] But the problem about the exercise of discretion under s 33(6) is that the eviction of a co-owner of a matrimonial home is a Draconian remedy. It is a last resort and is not an order lightly to be made. That was the position before the 1996 Act and it remains the position now,

as this court has confirmed in the matter of *Chalmers v Johns* [1999] 2 FCR 110. I give it emphasis again. Reading the judgment as a whole, one cannot but infer that the recorder was unduly swayed by the atmosphere in the house. He described it variously as 'hatred in the house', 'constant fighting', 'an armed ... truce', 'a family divided amongst itself and at war with itself'. Reading between the lines, it is plain the recorder took the view that, no progress having been made with the ancillary relief proceedings, the situation had to end sooner rather than later; and better sooner than later. But that too is an impermissible approach to an exercise of discretion under s 33(6).

[28] In my judgment the most salient facts emerging from this unhappy dispute are (a) each of the parties and the children in their camp can be satisfactorily accommodated in the matrimonial home and (b) the undertakings given not to molest each other were effective, as the judge himself recognised. In my judgment he misdirected himself on the application of s 33(7). It falls to us, therefore, to exercise the discretion under s 33(6). I am quite satisfied that we have the evidence available to us to conclude, despite Miss Meachin's very attractive submissions, that the right order here is to dismiss the application for the requested order on the basis that the neutral undertakings against molestation will continue. I would allow the appeal accordingly.

Sedley LJ:

...

[30] The purpose of an occupation order, however large its grounds may potentially be, is not to break matrimonial deadlocks by evicting one of the parties, much less to do so at the expense of a dependent, and in this case a heavily pregnant, child. Nor is it to use publicly-funded emergency housing as a solution for domestic strife – see *Warwick v Warwick* [1982] 3 FLR 393.

[31] There is no finding, and no evidential basis for any finding, that J was likely to suffer significant harm attributable to his mother's conduct. For this reason alone, s 33(7) of the Family Law Act 1996 could never come into play. If it were to do so, it is clear that the consequent harm to R, who is a relevant child just like J, would be at least as great as to J. There is now, of course, a yet further relevant child, R's new baby. As to the harm which will result if no order is made, I agree with all Ward LJ has said of the significance of the father's health and the absence of any evidence that the mother will be a source of harm if she stays.

[32] The more general power under s 33(6) is not at large, especially where the court is asked to deploy it to the Draconian end sought here. It is there to afford necessary protection which can be afforded in no better way.

...

[39] The nearest one can come to finding the recorder's reason for his decision is in this passage in the judgment:

> '... it is clear that harm is likely to be caused if both parties continue to live in the house ... Making any order requiring one parent to leave the home inevitably causes some harm and some distress, certainly in the short term; but, in the long term, hopefully peace will break out.'

[40] There is no finding, and in my view none was possible, as to who it was caused the supposed harm and to whom. In my view no occupation order should even have been contemplated in this situation, much less made. Indeed, I take leave to doubt whether it was responsible (presumably on legal aid) to seek it in the circumstances disclosed by the judgment.

[41] To use the occupation order as a weapon in domestic warfare is wholly inappropriate. Parliament has made provision for it as a last resort in an intolerable situation, not as a move in a game of matrimonial chess. ...

QUESTION

Remember that occupation orders were meant to deal with the deadlock which can occur between spouses with equal rights of occupation in the matrimonial home irrespective of any violence or misconduct between them. What should happen in these cases (*pace* Sedley LJ)?

So far we have been considering applications for occupation orders by 'entitled applicants'. Of course, a person with no right to occupy the home may be just as much in need of protection, but under the Family Law Act 1996 such a person may only apply for an occupation order against a former spouse, cohabitant or former cohabitant, and there are different criteria for such applications. Sections 37 and 38 of the 1996 Act provide for occupation orders where neither of the parties has a right of occupation. A more common situation will be where a non-entitled applicant is seeking an occupation order against a former spouse, cohabitant or former cohabitant who is entitled to occupy the property. These applications are governed by section 35 (for former spouses) and section 36 (for cohabitants and former cohabitants); see *S v F Occupation Order)* [2000] 1 FLR 255, [2000] 3 FCR 365. The Law Commission (1992) explained why it was, nevertheless, thought necessary to distinguish between 'entitled' and 'non-entitled' applicants:

> 4.7...the grant of an occupation order can severely restrict the enjoyment of property rights, and its potential consequences to a respondent are therefore more serious than those of a non-molestation order which generally only prohibits conduct which is already illegal or at least, anti-social. Such consequences may be acceptable when both parties are entitled to occupy, but they are more difficult to justify when the applicant has no such right. ... In the case of non-entitled applicants, particularly when the respondent is also entitled, an occupation has a purpose beyond short term protection, namely to regulate the occupation of the home until its medium or short term destiny has been decided, or in some cases, indefinitely. ... In the case of non-entitled applicants, an occupation order is essentially a short term measure of protection intended to give them time to find alternative accommodation, or, at most, to await the outcome of an application for a property law remedy.

Under sections 35 and 36, there is a two-stage approach to non-entitled applicants. Under both sections, an applicant must first obtain an order under sub-sections (3) or (4) which gives the applicant the right to enter the home (if not already in occupation), and to remain there without being evicted or excluded by the respondent.

Before making such an order, the court is required to have regard to:

> (6)...all the circumstances including –
>
> (a) the housing needs and housing resources of each of the parties and of any relevant child;
> (b) the financial resources of each of the parties;
> (c) the likely effect of any order, or of any decision by the court not to exercise its powers under subsection (3) or (4) on the health, safety or well-being of the parties and of any relevant child; and
> (d) the conduct of the parties in relation to each other and otherwise.

This checklist occurs in identical form in sections 35(6) and 36(6). However, the remainder of each subsection is different. In cases involving former spouses the court must also consider:

> **35.** –... (6)...
> (e) the length of time that has elapsed since the parties ceased to live together;
> (f) the length of time that has elapsed since the marriage was dissolved or annulled; and
> (g) the existence of any pending proceedings between the parties –
> (i) for an order under section 23A or 24 of the Matrimonial Causes Act 1973 (property adjustment orders in connection with divorce proceedings etc.);
> (ii) for an order under paragraph 1(2)(*d*) or (*e*) of Schedule 1 to the Children Act 1989 (orders for financial relief against parents); or
> (iii) relating to the legal or beneficial ownership of the dwelling-house.

In cases involving cohabitants or former cohabitants the court must consider:

> **36** –... (6)...
> (e) the nature of the parties' relationship;
> (f) the length of time during which they have lived together as husband and wife;
> (g) whether there are or have been any children who are children of both parties or for whom both parties have or have had parental responsibility;
> (h) the length of time that has elapsed since the parties ceased to live together; and
> (j) the existence of any pending proceedings between the parties –
> ...
> (ii) for an order under paragraph 1(2)(*d*) or (*e*) of Schedule 1 to the Children Act 1989 (orders for financial relief against parents); or
> (iii) relating to the legal or beneficial ownership of the dwelling-house.

If a non-entitled applicant obtains an order under subsections (3) or (4), the court may then consider whether to include a provision under subsection (5) to:

> (a) regulate the occupation of the dwelling-house by either or both of the parties;
> (b) prohibit, suspend or restrict the exercise by the respondent of his right to occupy the dwelling-house;
> (c) require the respondent to leave the dwelling-house or part of the dwelling-house; or
> (d) exclude the respondent from a defined area in which the dwelling-house is included.

In deciding whether to include such a provision, the court is once more required to consider the basic criteria in subsections (6)(*a*)–(*d*) (see p. 326 above). However, there are further additional criteria at this stage, which differ according to whether the non-entitled applicant is a former spouse (applying under section 35) or a cohabitant or former cohabitant (applying under section 36).

In the case of former spouses, section 35(7) requires the court to consider the length of time that has elapsed since the parties ceased to live together. In addition, the 'balance of harm' test (see p. 326, above) applies at this stage.

In the cases of a non-entitled cohabitant or former cohabitant, the court is required by sections 36(7) and (8) to consider:

(a) whether the applicant or any relevant child is likely to suffer significant harm attributable to conduct of the respondent if the subsection (5) provision is not included in the order; and
(b) whether the harm likely to be suffered by the respondent or child if the provision is included is as great or greater than the harm attributable to conduct of the respondent which is likely to be suffered by the applicant or child if the provision is not included.

QUESTIONS

i. Why, contrary to the recommendations of the Law Commission (1992), does the balance of harm test not apply to applications by non-entitled cohabitants or former cohabitants?
ii. Many of the complexities in the criteria for occupation orders for different types of non-entitled applicants were introduced after the failure of the Family Homes and Domestic Violence Bill in 1995. Is the complexity of the provisions necessary or justifiable?

Fairness to the respondent requires that he be given a chance to hear the applicant's case, and respond to it. However, in some cases, the risk to the victim will be such that she should be able to seek an immediate remedy, either without informing the respondent at all, or without giving him as much notice of the application as would usually be required. Section 45 of the Family Law Act 1996 sets out the criteria for without notice non-molestation or occupation orders. In deciding whether to make such orders, the court must have regard to all the circumstances including:

(a) any risk of significant harm to the applicant or a relevant child, attributable to conduct of the respondent, if the order is not made immediately;
(b) whether it is likely that the applicant will be deterred or prevented from pursuing the application if an order is not made immediately; and
(c) whether there is reason to believe that the respondent is aware of the proceedings but is deliberately evading service and that the applicant or a relevant child will be seriously prejudiced by the delay involved–
  (i) where the court is a magistrates' court, in effecting service of proceedings; or
  (ii) in any other case, in effecting substituted service.

QUESTION

Which is the more unjust: making an alleged batterer leave the home for a short while before he has an opportunity of defending himself against the allegations, or making the alleged victim leave for a short while before she has an opportunity of putting her case before a court?

7.6 PLACES OF SAFETY: COURTS, REFUGES AND COMMUNITIES

Much of the material in this chapter has focused on the courts and the police. The criminal law and civil law are joining hands in this area of the law; but the courts have been central to both. Erin Pizzey said in 1974 that 'going to court can be quite an ordeal', and of course it still is. But steps have been taken to try to make the court experience less traumatic. The government's *Multi-Agency Guidance for Addressing Domestic Violence*, issued in 2000, says:

> Those involved in the practical management of domestic violence cases should ensure that the best use is made of the available accommodation in terms of reducing stress for the witnesses. There are separate waiting areas for witnesses in most Crown Court Centres, and this is a requirement in the design of new court buildings. The Court Service is also currently developing a model layout for all new courts. This will include provision for a segregated hearing suite and a dedicated area for children. In the older buildings where it is not possible to provide separate areas, the prosecution or defence can ask the court administration if special arrangements can be made. Child witnesses must be brought into court through an entrance which is not used by the general public and must be kept away from them while waiting to go into court.
>
> In the civil courts, if the applicant (survivor) informs court staff of concerns about coming into contact with an alleged abuser, the staff should do everything they practically can to make sure the parties do not come into contact. Great care must be given to protecting applicants, particularly for example, where proceedings might otherwise disclose the address of the victim and so put them in danger. Similarly, if notice is given and accommodation at the court allows, courts should seek to provide separate children's waiting rooms. (Such provision will usually be the case, though some courts are at present unable to provide supervision for this accommodation.)
>
> Women who come to court to seek an order against a domestic violence perpetrator, or as witnesses in criminal proceedings, should be able to do so without their experience at court adding to their worries. The Courts Charter recognises the needs of those who may feel vulnerable or apprehensive about appearing in court. The special booklet that has been prepared for witnesses in the Crown Court (*Witness in Court*) should be made readily available, and the important role that the Victim Support Witness Service has here in offering support to those who need it, as well as other voluntary sector organisations, should be recognised and facilitated.

Discussion of court layout and personnel highlights again the problems arising from the interplay of the civil and criminal law in this context. Mandy Burton, in *Coherent and effective remedies for victims of domestic violence – time for an integrated domestic violence court?* (2004), comments:

> A crucial limitation of the specialist domestic violence courts in England and Wales is that they currently operate only in the criminal setting, usually adopting the method of clustering cases to a single session in the magistrates' court once a week. There is only so much this model of a domestic violence court can do to overcome the limitations of multiple legal interventions in different justice systems. While specially trained personnel in a criminal specialist domestic violence court are more aware of the need to take into account what might be happening in the civil and family courts, the mechanisms for ensuring exchange of that information are weak. The police and the CPS do not always have information about concurrent civil/family proceedings and the main source of information may be the victim's advocate or the defendant's lawyer. ... Information provided by the victim may not be fully accurate either but access to information that can be verified by the police or CPS does assist the court. In this way victim advocates, who may be supporting victims in a range of different legal contexts, can perform an invaluable role in

informing the criminal justice agencies about concurrent proceedings as well as acting as a conduit of the victim's views where relevant to the case. The recent overview of five specialist domestic violence courts did find some examples of courts trying to overcome the weak mechanisms for ensuring the criminal courts are aware of orders by the civil court. For example, the specialist court in West London keeps a running log of civil protective orders from the Inner London Family Proceedings Court.

Interviews with key informants from both the criminal justice agencies and voluntary support sector in the specialist court study revealed that they felt that specialist domestic violence criminal courts had taken important steps towards the goals of bringing more perpetrators of domestic violence to justice and increasing victim satisfaction and safety. However, most also acknowledged that there was more that still could be done. For some the next logical step was the development of an integrated domestic violence court. Although detailed empirical studies of integrated courts in the US are as yet scarce, the research that exists does appear to suggest that the combined criminal/civil model of a domestic violence court has a number of advantages over the criminal-only model.

Some courts in the US have looked at the criminal model and deliberately avoided it, preferring to set up integrated domestic violence courts from scratch. An example of this is the Clark County Domestic Violence Court in Vancouver, Washington. Other domestic violence courts have started life operating in a single justice system only and decided to progress to an integrated court model. ... Westchester county domestic violence court in New York started as a criminal court but moved to a combined criminal/civil model where the same judge hears the criminal domestic violence matters and related family matters but does so on different days. The separation of civil and criminal matters to different lists aims to mitigate one of the possible disadvantages of integration: a modified form of plea-bargaining whereby criminal law matters and family law matters may be traded against each other. One of the key advantages of this integrated court is the ability to ensure that the judge has a complete understanding of the issues facing each family and to avoid inconsistent orders being made. However, the separation of criminal and civil matters to different days arguably involves a significant disadvantage in that the victim may be required to attend court on two occasions when the matter could have been dealt with on one.

The District of Columbia integrated domestic violence court has different judges hearing criminal and family related matters but has a single intake centre, the courtrooms are in close proximity and each judge has ready access to related files. This reduces the burden on the victim when attending court. The evaluators of this court assert that the one-stop-shop facility 'improves the likelihood that the victim will stay engaged with the justice process'. The US experience demonstrates that combining the criminal and civil justice systems in an integrated domestic violence court requires difficult practical and legal decisions to be taken about the organisation of work and allocation of judges, however it appears to be a worthwhile exercise.

However, the courts may not be able to fix things. Gill Hague and Ellen Malos discuss the difficulties in 'Children, Domestic Violence and Housing', in the collection *Children Living with Domestic Violence* (1994):

For very large numbers of women and children escaping domestic violence, the only way to achieve a safe and secure life is to leave the violent perpetrator completely and begin again somewhere else.

In our study [Malos and Hague (1993)], however, we collected evidence that women and children attempting to escape violence and seeking rehousing in various local authorities were refused any assistance from the council once they had obtained a legal order against the violent

> perpetrator.... But, for women and children to be safe and secure in this situation, there will need to be an as yet unachieved level of effective legal protection and enforcement, accompanied by multi-layered support within the community and community intolerance of domestic violence. At the moment, this is not the situation in this country, and many women and children escaping violence in the home do not wish, under any circumstances, to return to their former home.

The availability of alternative housing will be crucial in these circumstances. The Working Group of the Women's National Commission discussed the possibilities in *Violence Against Women, Report of an Ad Hoc Working Group* (1985):

> 115. ... An alternative to restraining the man is to remove the woman to a place of safety where she can begin a new separate existence if she wishes.... Women's Aid refuges serve a number of purposes admirably, and are an exceedingly welcome development which needs supporting. But women often return to violent husbands because of concern about the quality of their own and their children's lives in refuges, which are often overcrowded. This underlines the importance of the Housing (Homeless Persons) Act 1977, which defines women victims of domestic violence as in 'priority need' and obliges a local authority to find permanent accommodation for them. Women's Aid groups normally find that the existence of the Act now enables them to negotiate some permanent local authority accommodation for women living in their refuges. But local authorities tend to strictly ration what is available. The assumption sometimes made that a very high proportion of women in refuges return permanently to their violent partners is not true. One research study undertaken by Jan Pahl (1985) found that:
>
>> 'Out of the 42 women, 20 (48%) never lived with their husbands again after leaving the refuge, while only two lived with their husbands continuously from the time they left the refuge until the time of the second interview (about two years later). The remaining 20 of the women (48%) made between one and nine attempts at reconciliation.... Of these only nine couples were still together at the second interview....'
>
> Lack of a housing offer amongst other factors has forced large numbers of women to try again with their husbands and to suffer further violence. The Working Group therefore urge Housing Authorities to accept their responsibilities in relation to battered wives. It has been suggested that if Housing Authorities had a policy of seeking to find some accommodation (temporary or permanent) for violent husbands they would enable battered wives and children to remain in the family home in family sized accommodation which would be under-utilised by the man himself. To effect this kind of sensible solution probably requires multi-agency working groups to be set up on which police, personal social services, housing authority, and women's organisations representatives could serve.

QUESTIONS

i. Section 177(1) of the Housing Act 1996 states: 'It is not reasonable for a person to continue to occupy accommodation if it is probable that this will lead to domestic violence against him'; coupled with the definition of homelessness in section 191(1), this means that a victim who leaves in circumstances covered by section 177(1) cannot be treated as intentionally homeless. Given that, would you be more or less inclined to grant an order ousting her husband from the matrimonial council house?

ii. Will the court be able to transfer the tenancy into her name (Family Law Act 1996, Schedule 7)? What if the couple are not married?

iii. As the House of Commons Select Committee on Violence in Marriage (1975) asked during its proceedings, why do we not create hostels to receive the battering men?

Part of the inspiration for the *Multi-Agency Guidance* (2000) is the realisation that no one agency can provide a complete response to domestic violence. The umbrella linking the various facets of the new multi-disciplinary approach is the 'co-ordinated community response model'. The figures below reproduce this in diagram form – although no reproduction can quite capture the dynamism of the original on the internet at http://www.crimereduction.gov.uk/dv/dv014a.ppt.

QUESTION

What single agency do you think might be the most effective in tackling domestic violence?

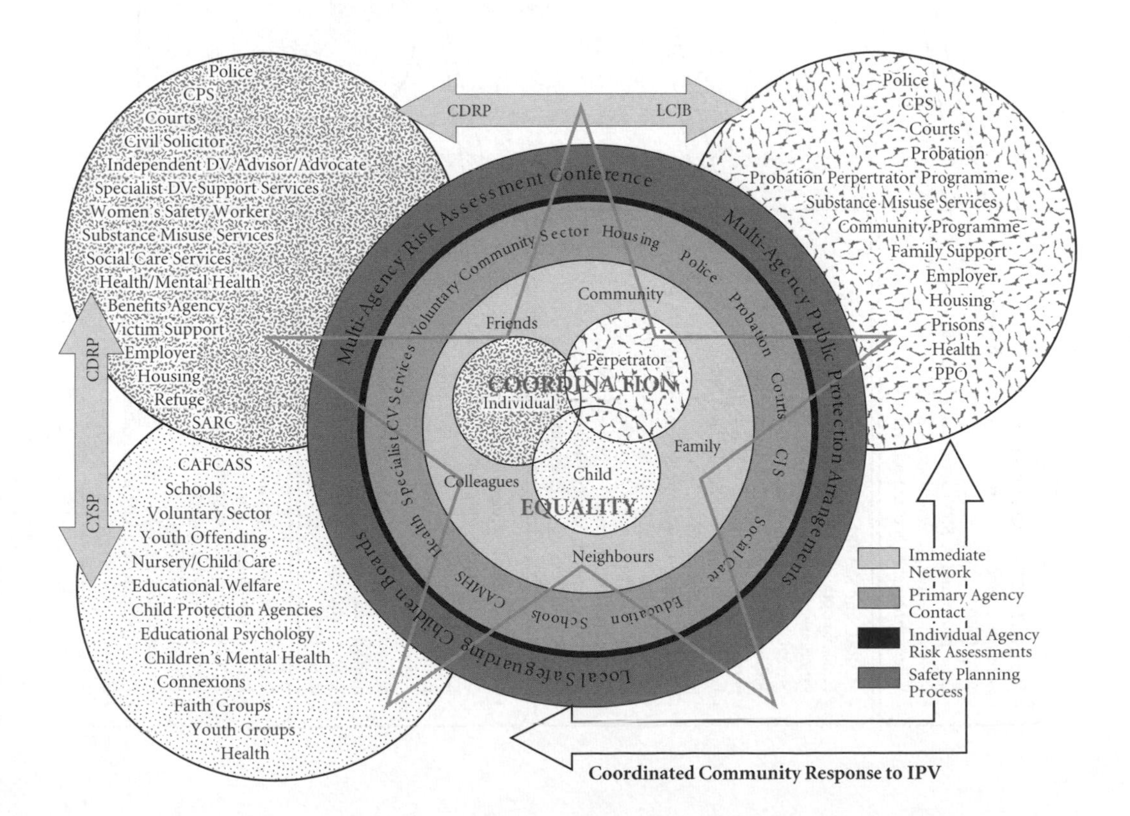

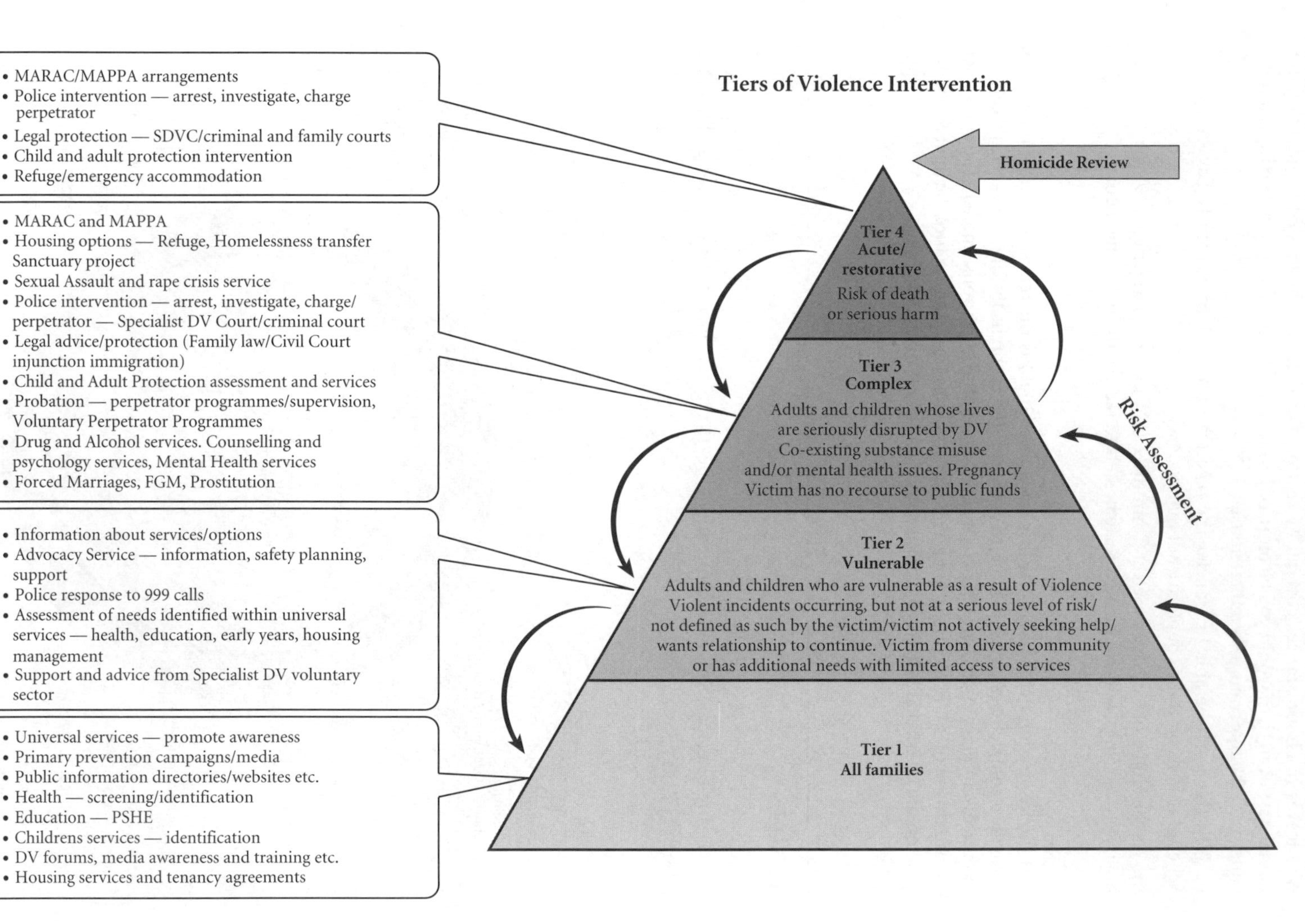
Tiers of Violence Intervention
Homicide Review
Risk Assessment
Tier 4
Acute/
restorative
Risk of death
or serious harm
Tier 3
Complex
Adults and children whose lives
are seriously disrupted by DV
Co-existing substance misuse
and/or mental health issues. Pregnancy
Victim has no recourse to public funds
Tier 2
Vulnerable
Adults and children who are vulnerable as a result of Violence
Violent incidents occurring, but not at a serious level of risk/
not defined as such by the victim/victim not actively seeking help/
wants relationship to continue. Victim from diverse community
or has additional needs with limited access to services
Tier 1
All families
• MARAC/MAPPA arrangements
• Police intervention — arrest, investigate, charge perpetrator
• Legal protection — SDVC/criminal and family courts
• Child and adult protection intervention
• Refuge/emergency accommodation
• MARAC and MAPPA
• Housing options — Refuge, Homelessness transfer Sanctuary project
• Sexual Assault and rape crisis service
• Police intervention — arrest, investigate, charge/ perpetrator — Specialist DV Court/criminal court
• Legal advice/protection (Family law/Civil Court injunction immigration)
• Child and Adult Protection assessment and services
• Probation — perpetrator programmes/supervision, Voluntary Perpetrator Programmes
• Drug and Alcohol services. Counselling and psychology services, Mental Health services
• Forced Marriages, FGM, Prostitution
• Information about services/options
• Advocacy Service — information, safety planning, support
• Police response to 999 calls
• Assessment of needs identified within universal services — health, education, early years, housing management
• Support and advice from Specialist DV voluntary sector
• Universal services — promote awareness
• Primary prevention campaigns/media
• Public information directories/websites etc.
• Health — screening/identification
• Education — PSHE
• Childrens services — identification
• DV forums, media awareness and training etc.
• Housing services and tenancy agreements

BIBLIOGRAPHY

7.1 What are the dangers?

We quoted from:

CAFCASS Domestic Violence Assessment Policy, available at http://www.cafcass.gov.uk/English/Publications/consultation/04DecDV%20Policy.pdf.

Crown Prosecution Service, *Policy on Prosecuting Cases of Domestic Violence 2005*, available at http://www.cps.gov.uk/publications/docs/DomesticViolencePolicy.pdf.

C. Donovan, M. Hester, J. Holmes and M. McCarry, *Comparing Domestic Abuse in Same-Sex and Heterosexual Relationships*, (2006), available at http://www.bristol.ac.uk/sps/downloads/FPCW/cohsarfinalreport.pdf.

Home Office, Domestic violence, sexual assault and stalking: findings from the 2004/05 British Crime Survey available at http://www.homeoffice.gov.uk/rds/pdfs06/rdsolr1206.pdf.

House of Lords Hansard, 26 Jan 2007: Column 1319: http://www.publications.parliament.uk/pa/ld200607/ldhansrd/text/70126-0001.htm#07012689000004.

C. Humphreys and R.K. Thiara, 'Neither justice nor protection: women's experiences of post-separation violence' (2003) 25.3 *Journal of Social Welfare and Family Law*, 195, 201–206.

S. Walby, *The Cost of Domestic Violence* (2004; Women and Equality Unit), available at http://www.womenandequalityunit.gov.uk/research/cost_of_dv_Report_sept04.pdf.

The Women's National Commission, *'Unlocking the Secret: Women Open the Door on Domestic Violence, Findings from Consultations with Survivors'* 2003, 39, at http://www.thewnc.org.uk/pubs/unlockingthesecret.pdf.

Additional reading

C. Donovan, J. Holmes, M. Hester and M. McCarry, 'Research update: comparing domestic abuse in same sex and heterosexual relationships', (2007) *Safe: The Domestic Abuse Quarterly*, 21.

H. Reece, 'UK Women's groups' child contact campaign: "so long as it is safe"' (2006) 18 *Child and Family Law Quarterly* 538.

7.2 The search for explanations

We quoted from:

G. Hague and E. Malos, *Domestic Violence: Action for Change* (1993) Cheltenham, New Clarion Press, 54–56, 58, 61–62.

The Women's National Commission, *'Unlocking the Secret: Women Open the Door on Domestic Violence, Findings from Consultations with Survivors'* 2003, 27, 28, http://www.thewnc.org.uk/pubs/unlockingthesecret.pdf.

Additional reading

M. Borkowski, M. Murch and V. Walker, *Marital Violence: The Community Response* (1983) London, Tavistock.

British Association of Social Workers (1975) 'A code of ethics for Social Work', Social Work Today, 6, October 30.

R.E. Dobash and R.P. Dobash, *Violence Against Wives: A Case Against the Patriarchy* (1980) London, Open Books.

M.D.A. Freeman, *Dealing with Domestic Violence* (1987) Oxford, CCH.

L.F Lowenstein, 'Domestic Violence: Recent Research' (2005) *Justice of the Peace* 715.

J. Pahl (ed.) *Private Violence and Public Policy. The needs of battered women and the response of the public services* (1985) London, Routledge and Kegan Paul.

L. Smith, *Domestic Violence: an overview of the literature*, Home Office Research Study 107 (1989) London, HMSO, pp. 27–29.

L.E. Walker, *The Battered Woman Syndrome* (1984) New York, Springer.

E. Wilson, *What is to be Done about Violence against Women? Crisis in the Eighties* (1983) Penguin Books.

7.3 The trouble with the criminal law...

We quoted from:

Crown Prosection Service, *Policy on Prosecuting Cases of Domestic Violence 2005*, available at http://www.cps.gov.uk/publications/docs/DomesticViolencePolicy.pdf.

M. Dow, 'Police Involvement' in M. Borland (ed.), *Violence in the Family* (1976) Manchester, Manchester University Press, 132–133.

L. Ellison, 'Prosecuting domestic violence without victim participation' (2002) 65 *Modern Law Review* 834.

S. Grace, *Policing Domestic Violence in the 1990s*, Home Office Research Study 139 (1995) London, HMSO, 53–54, 56.

J. Herring, 'Familial homicide, failure to protect and domestic violence: who's the victim?' [2007] *Criminal Law Review* 923, 926–7.

Home Office Circular (60/90), *Domestic Violence* (1990) London, Home Office, paras. 2, 4, 11.

Home Office Circular (9/2005) *The Domestic Violence, Crime and Victims Act 2004. The New Offence Of Causing the Death Of A Child Or Vulnerable Adult* available at http://www.knowledgenetwork.gov.uk/HO/circular.nsf/79755433dd36a66980256d4f004d1514/72c8d698fde27b5380256faf003565bf?OpenDocument.

House of Commons Home Affairs Committee, *Domestic Violence, Evidence and Appendices* HC 245–11 (1992–93) (1993), 26, 104.

House of Commons Select Committee on Violence in Marriage, Report, Minutes of Evidence and Appendices, HC 553–11 (1974–75) (1975) London, HMSO.

E. Pizzey, *Scream Quietly or the Neighbours Will Hear* (1974) Harmondsworth, Penguin Books, 98.

The Women's National Commission, 'Unlocking the Secret: Women Open the Door on Domestic Violence, Findings from Consultations with Survivors' 2003 available at http://www.thewnc.org.uk/pubs/unlockingthesecret.pdf.

Additional reading

R.E. Dobash and R.P. Dobash, *Women, Violence and Social Change* (1992) London, Routledge.
E. Finch, *The Criminalisation of Stalking* (2001) London, Cavendish.
C. Hoyle, *Negotiating Domestic Violence: Police, Criminal Justice and Victims* (1998) Oxford, Oxford University Press.
F. Wasoff, 'Legal Protection from Wife Beating: The Processing of Domestic Assaults by Scottish Prosecutors and Criminal Courts' (1982) 10 *International Journal of the Sociology of Law* 187.

7.4 Developing civil law remedies for molestation and harassment

We quoted from:

E. Finch, 'Stalking the perfect stalking law' [2002] *Criminal Law Review* 703.
House of Commons Home Affairs Committee, *Domestic Violence, Evidence and Appendices*, HC 245–11 (1992–93) (1993), 87 88.
Law Commission, *Domestic Violence and the Occupation of the Family Home* Law Com. No. 207 (1992) London, HMSO, paras 2.24, 2.3, 3.19, 4.6.
J.S. Mill, *The Subjection of Women* (1869); reprinted in Everyman's Library (1929) London, Dent.
H. Reece, 'The End of Domestic Violence' (2006) 69(5) *Modern Law Review* 770.

Additional reading

C. Bessant, 'Enforcing Non-Molestation Orders in the Civil and Criminal Courts', [2005] *Family Law* 640.
S. Choudry and J. Herring, 'Domestic Violence and the Human Rights Act 1998: a new means of legal intervention?' [2006] *Public Law* 752.
M. Hayes, 'Non-molestation Protection: Only Associated persons Need Apply' [1996] *Family Law* 134.

7.5 Occupation orders

We quoted from:

F. Gibb, 'Husband who snapped told to leave home' (1997) *The Times*, 28 August.
Law Commission, *Domestic Violence and the Occupation of the Family Home* Law Com. No. 207 (1992) London, HMSO, paras 2.48, 4.6, 4.23, 4.34, 4.7.

7.6 Places of safety: courts, refuges and communities

We quoted from:

M. Burton, 'Coherent and effective remedies for victims of domestic violence – time for an integrated domestic violence court?' (2004) 16 *Child and Family Law Quarterly* 317.

The Government's *Multi-Agency Guidance for Addressing Domestic Violence* at http://www.crimereduction.gov.uk/dv/dv08d.htm#1.2.

G. Hague and E. Malos, 'Children, Domestic Violence and Housing' in R. Morley and A. Mullender (eds), *Children Living with Domestic Violence* (1994) London, Whiting and Birch, 131–132.

Home Office, Domestic Violence Mini-Site, 'Co-ordinated Community response Model', available at http://www.crimereduction.gov.uk/dv/dv014a.ppt.

E. Pizzey, *Scream Quietly or the Neighbours Will Hear* (1974) Harmondsworth, Penguin Books, 120–121.

Womens National Commission (1985), *Violence Against Women, Report of an Ad Hoc Working Group*, Cabinet Office, London, para. 115.

Additional reading

Communities and Local Government, '*Options for Setting up a Sanctuary Scheme*' 2006, available at http://www.communities.gov.uk/pub/297/OptionsforSettingupaSanctuaryScheme_id1505297.pdf.

D. Cook, M. Burton. M. Robinson, C. Vallely, *Evaluation of Specialist Domestic Violence courts/Fast Track Systems,* available at http://www.cps.gov.uk/publications/docs/specialistdvcourts.pdf.

Home Office, *Safety and Justice: The Government's Proposals on Domestic Violence* Cm 5847, (2003), available at http://www.archive2.official-documents.co.uk/document/cm58/5847/5847.pdf.

Home Office Research Study 290, Marianne Hester and Nicole Westmarland, 'Tackling Domestic Violence: effective interventions and approaches', 2005, available at http://www.homeoffice.gov.uk/rds/pdfs05/hors290.pdf.

8

PARENTS, CHILDREN AND FAMILY LIFE

Relying on parents to bring up their children is seen as an essential feature of Western democratic society. But is this for the parents', the children's, or society's sake? Parents and children alike are entitled to respect for their private and family life under the Human Rights Act 1998, and the Children Act 1989 focuses on the responsibility of parents and the welfare of children. We begin this chapter with an examination of the differing demands of parental rights and children's welfare; we then look at the arguments for and against parental autonomy. Next we consider the children's rights, and the United Nations Convention on the Rights of the Child. Finally, we look at parental responsibility, in preparation for our consideration of parental status in Chapter 9.

8.1 PARENTAL RIGHTS AND CHILDREN'S WELFARE

The concept of parental 'rights' achieved its greatest legal prominence in the nineteenth century. An example of eighteenth-century thinking is provided by Sir William Blackstone in the first volume of his *Commentaries on the Laws of England* (1765):

> 1. And, first, the duties of parents to legitimate children: which principally consist in three particulars; their maintenance, their protection, and their education.
>
> The duty of parents to provide for the *maintenance* of their children is a principle of natural law; an obligation, says Puffendorf, laid on them not only by nature herself, but by their own proper act, in bringing them into the world: for they would be in the highest manner injurious to their issue, if they only gave the children life, that they might afterwards see them perish. By begetting them therefore they have entered into a voluntary obligation, to endeavour, as far as in them lies, that the life which they have bestowed shall be supported and preserved. And thus the children will have a perfect *right* of receiving maintenance from their parents....
>
> 2. The *power* of parents over their children is derived from the former consideration, their duty; this authority being given them, partly to enable the parent more effectually to perform his duty, and partly as a recompence for his care and trouble in the faithful discharge of it. And upon this score the municipal laws of some nations have given a much larger authority to the parents, than others. The ancient Roman laws gave the father a power of life and death over his children; upon this principle, that he who gave had also the power of taking away....
>
> The power of a parent by our English laws is much more moderate; but still sufficient to keep the child in order and obedience. He may lawfully correct his child, being under age, in a reasonable manner; for this is for the benefit of his education. The consent or concurrence of the parent to the marriage of his child under age, was also *directed* by our ancient law to be obtained: but now it is absolutely *necessary*; for without it the contract is void. And this also is another means, which the law has put into the parent's hands, in order the better to discharge his duty; first, of protecting his children from the snares of artful and designing persons; and, next of settling them properly in life, by preventing the ill consequences of too early and precipitate marriages. A father has no other power over his son's *estate*, than as his trustee or guardian; for, though he may receive the profits during the child's minority, yet he must account for them when he comes

of age. He may indeed have the benefit of his children's labour while they live with him, and are maintained by him: but this is no more than he is entitled to from his apprentices or servants. The legal power of a father (for a mother, as such, is entitled to no power, but only to reverence and respect) the power of a father, I say, over the persons of his children ceases at the age of twenty one: for they are then enfranchised by arriving at years of discretion, or that point which the law has established (as some must necessarily be established) when the empire of the father, or other guardian, gives place to the empire of reason. Yet, till that age arrives, this empire of the father continues even after his death; for he may by his will appoint a guardian to his children. ...

3. The *duties* of children to their parents arise from a principle of natural justice and retribution. For to those, who gave us existence, we naturally owe subjection and obedience during our minority, and honour and reverence ever after; they, who protected the weakness of our infancy, are entitled to our protection in the infirmity of their age; they who by sustenance and education have enabled their offspring to prosper, ought in return to be supported by that offspring, in case they stand in need of assistance. Upon this principle proceed all the duties of children to their parents, which are enjoined by positive laws.

QUESTION

To what extent do you think Blackstone's rationale underlying parental power is applicable today?

The following case represents the 'highwater mark of common law bias in favour of fathers' (Freeman, 2000).

Re Agar-Ellis, Agar-Ellis v Lascelles (1883)
24 Ch D 317, 53LJ Ch 10, Court of Appeal

A Protestant father agreed on marriage that the children would be brought up Roman Catholics. Having changed his mind he took the children away from their mother. In 1883, a daughter, aged sixteen, and her mother asked the court to allow them a holiday together and free correspondence and access. They failed.

Brett MR:

... The rights of a father are sacred rights because his duties are sacred duties. ...

Cotton LJ:

... It is for the general interest of children, and really for the interest of the particular infant, that the court should not except in very extreme cases, interfere with the discretion of the father but leave him to the responsibility of exercising that power which nature has given him by the birth of the child.

Bowen LJ:

... Judicial machinery is quite inadequate to the task of educating children in this country. It can correct abuses and it can interfere to redress the parental caprice, and it does interfere when the natural guardian of the child ceases to be the natural guardian, and shews by his conduct that he has become an unnatural guardian, but to interfere further would be to ignore the one principle which is the most fundamental of all in the history of mankind, and owing to the full play of which man has become what he is. ... If that were not so we might be interfering all day and with every family. I have no doubt that there are very few families in the country in which fathers do not, at some time or other, make mistakes, and there are very few families in which a wiser person than the father might not do something better for that child than is being done by the father, who however has an authority which never ought to be slighted.

QUESTION

Take out the sex discrimination and apply these arguments to a couple's decision: (a) that their child shall not go on the school trip to France; (b) that their child shall go to Sunday school every week. When do you think the law should interfere?

The status of the father was radically changed by judicial development of what has become known as the 'paramountcy principle'. This was later enacted in the Guardianship of Infants Act 1925, consolidated in the Guardianship of Minors Act 1971 and subsequently replaced by the Children Act 1989 as follows:

1.—(1) When a court determines any question with respect to—

(a) the upbringing of a child; or

(b) the administration of a child's property or the application of any income arising from it,

the child's welfare shall be the court's paramount consideration.

We discuss how this works in disputes between parents in Chapter 10. It also applies to disputes between parents and non-parents. *J v C* [1970] AC 668, [1969] 1 All ER 788 concerned a nine-year-old Spanish boy who had lived for all but eighteen months of his life with English foster parents. When his parents asked for him back, the court held that the paramountcy principle meant that there was no presumption in favour of even the 'unimpeachable' natural parents of the child, although their relationship with the child will often carry great weight as they 'can be capable of ministering to the total welfare of the child in a special way'. Lord MacDermott, commenting on the expression 'first and paramount consideration' in the 1925 statute, observed that it:

...must mean more than that the child's welfare is to be treated as the top item in a list of items relevant to the matter in question. I think they connote a process whereby, when all the relevant facts, relationships, claims and wishes of parents, risks, choices, and other circumstances are taken into account and weighed, the course to be followed will be that which is most in the interests of the child's welfare.

One consequence of the introduction of the principle, some argue the reason for its introduction, was that by challenging the rights of the father it protected the interests of mothers. However, one of the criticisms frequently made of the principle is its indeterminacy: as people disagree about what is best for children the principle enables judges to use their own prejudices to determine cases (see, e.g. Reece, 1996, Eekelaar, 2002).

Jonathan Herring in 'Farewell Welfare?' (2005) defends the paramountcy principle:

> ... indeterminacy reflects the fact that a judge is assessing the facts of each case carefully. ... while principles of certainty are important where people carry out activities that rely on legal structures (contract law might be an example), this is of less importance in areas of law, such as family law, where people do not live their lives on the basis of the law.

More generally he argues that:

> ... the welfare principle sends out an important symbolic message. It recognises the value, the importance and vulnerability of children.

QUESTIONS

i. Do you agree with the paramountcy principle?
ii. Do you think it should apply to all issues relating to children?

Compare *J v C* with *Re M (Child's Upbringing)* [1996] 2 FCR 473, [1996] 2 FLR 441. Sifiso, a ten-year-old Zulu boy, was looked after by his mother's employer and brought to England with her consent. He had been living in England for four years, when his mother decided that she wanted him returned to her in South Africa. In the Court of Appeal Neill LJ stated that there was a 'strong supposition' that it was in the child's interests to be brought up with his natural parent. Sifiso was sent back to South Africa even though he wanted to stay here. However, he was unable to settle in South Africa, and eventually returned to England. In a later case, Thorpe LJ stated that 'subsequent developments in the life of the Zulu boy demonstrate that the endeavour to override his deep-seated attachment to his psychological mother proved disastrous in outcome.' (See *Re B* [1998] 1 FLR 520.)

QUESTION

Do you think that the decision to send Sifiso home was flawed: (a) because the court gave too much weight to the need for children to be brought up by their natural parents; or (b) because it gave too little weight to Sifiso's own wishes and feelings; or (c) because it gave too much weight to the view that Sifiso's development 'must be, in the last resort and profoundly, Zulu development and not Afrikaans or English development'?

The significance of a child's cultural background was also an issue in the next case.

Re P (a child) (residence order: child's welfare)
[2000] Fam 15, [1999] 3 All ER 734, Court of Appeal

The child, N, was born in 1990, and she was diagnosed with Down's syndrome and serious respiratory problems. Her parents were orthodox Jews, and her father was a rabbi. The parents asked the local authority to accommodate the child, because they could not meet all of her needs. The child was placed with foster parents who were non-practising Roman Catholics. In 1994, the parents sought the child's return, but a residence order was made in favour of the foster parents, with reasonable contact to the parents. In 1998 the parents again applied for the child to be returned to their care. They argued that the child had a presumptive right to be brought up by her own parents and in her own religion and that the judge had failed to give sufficient weight to the child's religious and cultural heritage.

Butler-Sloss LJ:

... The undoubted importance for an orthodox Jew of his religion which provides in itself a way of life which permeates all activities, is a factor to be put in the balancing exercise, particularly in considering the welfare of the daughter of a rabbi. But N's religious and cultural heritage cannot be the overwhelming factor in this case for the reasons set out by the judge nor can it displace other weighty welfare factors.

Ward LJ:

[who referred to Articles 14, 3 and 9 of the United Nations Convention on the Rights of the Child (see pp. 383, 384)]:

That children have rights is acknowledged in international conventions ratified by the United Kingdom. They may not have the force of law but, as international treaties, they command and receive our respect.

Those articles were considered by the European Court of Human Rights in *Hoffmann v Austria* [1994] 1 FCR 193 at 205–206, [1994] 17 EHRR 293, a case concerning the Jehovah's Witnesses. The majority of the European Court held:

> 'In assessing the interests of the children, the Supreme Court (of Austria) considered the possible effects on their social life of being associated with a particular religious minority and the hazards attaching to applicant's total rejection of blood transfusions not only for herself but – in the absence of a court order – for her children as well; that is, possible negative effects of her membership of the religious community of Jehovah's Witnesses. It weighed them against the possibility that transferring the children to the care of their father might cause them physiological stress, which in its opinion had to be accepted in their own interests. This court does not deny that, depending on the circumstances of the case, the factors relied on by the Austrian Supreme Court in support of its decision may in themselves be capable of tipping the scales in favour of one parent rather than the other. However, the Supreme Court also introduced a new element, namely the Federal Act on the Religious Education of Children. This factor was clearly decisive of the Supreme Court. The European Court therefore accepts that there has been a difference in treatment and that the difference was on the ground of religion; this conclusion is supported by the tone and phrasing of the Supreme Court's consideration regarding the practical consequences of the applicant's religion. Such a difference in treatment is discriminatory in the absence of an "objective and reasonable justification" that is, if it is not justified by a "legitimate aim" and if there is no reasonable relationship of proportionality between the means employed and the aim sought to be realised. The aim pursued by the judgment of the Supreme Court was a legitimate one, namely the protection of the health and rights of the children ...'

In other words, in the jurisprudence of human rights, the right to practise one's religion is subservient to the need in a democratic society to put welfare first.

QUESTIONS

i. In *Hoffmann v Austria* (1993) 17 EHRR 293 the European Court of Human Rights decided that the Austrian Supreme Court should not have denied the mother custody on the basis of her religion (although they could take account of the impact of her religious practices on the child). Is a prohibition on discrimination between parents on the basis of religion the same as saying that 'the right to practise one's religion is subservient to the need in a democratic society to put welfare first'?

ii. Is it possible to consider a child's welfare without taking account of issues of culture or religion? Should we take account of these factors even if the child is unable to appreciate their significance? Are we doing this for the sake of the child, or the parents, or in the interests of social pluralism and nondiscrimination? (See Scolnicov at p. 358.)

It is one thing to decide between competing sets of parents, one 'natural' and the other 'social', but what about interfering in a particular upbringing decision made by otherwise 'unimpeachable' parents?

In cases where parents refuse life-saving treatment for religious reasons, the courts have consistently acted to override the parental decision (for example, *Re R (a minor) (blood transfusion)* [1993] 2 FLR 757). However, some life-saving problems are harder than others.

Re A (children) (conjoined twins: surgical separation)
[2001] Fam 147, [2000] 4 All ER 961, [2001] 2 WLR 480, [2000] 3 FCR 577, (2000) 57 BMLR 1, Court of Appeal

Jodie and Mary were born 'conjoined', linked together and sharing vital organs. The medical evidence was that an operation to separate them would cause the death of Mary within a very short time, but that Jodie might live a relatively normal life after separation. Without the operation, both girls would die, since Jodie's organs were too weak to sustain them both. The parents were opposed to the operation, at least partly for religious reasons. Ward LJ confirmed that the paramountcy principle enabled the court to override the wishes of the parents – even where those wishes were reasonable.

Ward LJ:

...Is the court reviewing the parental decision as it reviews an administrative decision or does the court look at the matter afresh, in the round, with due weight given to the parental wish? If there was doubt about that, it has been resolved in favour of the latter approach by the decision of this court in *In Re T (Wardship: Medical Treatment)* [1997] 1 W.L.R. 242. That was an agonising decision for the court to take. The baby, a year old, had a life threatening liver defect. An operation when he was 3½ weeks old was unsuccessful. The unanimous medical opinion was that without a liver transplant he would not live beyond the age of 2½ years. His parents refused to consent to that operation. Their wish eventually prevailed. On this particular point Butler-Sloss LJ said at p. 250 F:-

> '... The first argument of Mr Francis that the court should not interfere with the reasonable decision of a parent is not one that we are able to entertain even if we wish to do so. His suggestion that the decision of this mother came within that band of reasonable decisions

within which a court would not interfere would import into this jurisdiction the test applied in adoption to the refusal of a parent to consent to adoption. It is wholly inapposite to the welfare test and is incompatible with the decision in *In Re Z (A Minor) (Identification: Restrictions on Publication)* [1997] Fam 1.' Waite LJ said at 254 C:-

'An appraisal of parental reasonableness may be appropriate in other areas of family law (in adoption, for example where it is enjoined by statute) but when it comes to an assessment of the demands of the child patient's welfare, the starting point – and the finishing point too – must always be the judge's own independent assessment of the balance of advantage or disadvantage of the particular medical step under consideration. In striking that balance, the court will of course take into account as a relevant, often highly relevant, factor the attitude taken by the natural parent, and that may require examination of his or her motives. But the result of such an enquiry must never be allowed to prove determinative. It is a mistake to view the issue as one in which the clinical advice of doctors is placed in one scale and the reasonableness of the parent's view in the other.

...

It can only be said safely that there is a scale, at one end of which lies the clear case where parental opposition to medical intervention is prompted by scruple or dogma of a kind which is patently irreconcilable with principles of child health and welfare widely accepted by the generality of mankind; and that at the other end lie highly problematic cases where there is genuine scope for a difference of view between the parent and the judge. In both situations it is the duty of the judge to allow the court's own opinion to prevail in the perceived paramount interest of the child concerned, but in cases at the latter end of the scale, there must be a likelihood (though never of course a certainty) that the greater the scope for genuine debate between one view and another the stronger will be that inclination of the court to be influenced by a reflection that in the last analysis the best interests of every child include an expectation that difficult decisions affecting the length and quality of its life will be taken for it by the parent to whom its care has been entrusted by nature.'...

Conclusion on the Family Law Aspect of This Case

I would grant permission for the operation to take place provided, however, what is proposed to be done can be lawfully done. That requires a consideration of the criminal law to which I now turn.

After consideration of difficult issues of the criminal law, the Court of Appeal authorised the operation. Mary died shortly after the separation, but Jodie was reported to be doing well.

QUESTIONS

i. If you were the judge, would you have authorised the operation? If so, is this because you think Jodie's interests should be given more weight than Mary's? Why?

ii. Should parental decisions about life-saving treatment be respected if the decision falls within a band of 'reasonable' decisions, or should the courts always have the final say if parents and doctors are unable to agree?

iii. Can you think of any other situations in family law where two children have competing interests? In such situations, do you think that the interests of both children should be given equal weight, or do you think that it should depend upon which child is the subject of the litigation? (See, for example, *Birmingham City Council v H (A Minor)* [1994] 2 AC 212; and *Re T and E (Children's Proceedings: Conflicting Interests)* [1995] 3 FCR 260.)

iv. How, if at all, would you have reconciled this decision with the right to life in Art 2 of the European Convention on Human Rights (see *NHS Trust v M; NHS Trust v H* (2001) 2 FLR 367)?

v. Are there some parental decisions which should always be approved by a court? If so, would you include the sterilisation of (a) a female child or (b) a male child? (See *Re B (a minor) (wardship: sterilization)* [1988] AC 199, [1987] 2 All ER 206.)

In *Re A*, Johnson J at first instance, and Robert Walker LJ in the Court of Appeal, considered that the interests of the twins might not be in conflict, since the operation would bring Mary's pain and suffering to an end. However, the majority in the Court of Appeal (Ward and Brooke LJJ) concluded that the operation was *against* Mary's interests, but should be performed because of the potential benefit to Jodie.

Nevertheless, there are cases in which the courts have decided that it is *not* in a child's interests to be kept alive.

Re J (a minor) (wardship: medical treatment)
[1991] Fam 33, [1990] 3 All ER 930, Court of Appeal

J was born very prematurely and suffered severe and permanent brain damage at birth. He was epileptic, likely to be quadriplegic, blind, deaf and very severely mentally disabled, but able to feel pain like a normal baby. He could survive for a few years. The judge ordered that he should be given antibiotics if he developed a chest infection but not reventilated if he stopped breathing unless the doctors thought it appropriate. The Official Solicitor appealed on his behalf:

Taylor LJ:

The plight of baby J is appalling and the problem facing the court in the exercise of its wardship jurisdiction is of the greatest difficulty. When should the court rule against the giving of treatment aimed at prolonging life?

Three preliminary principles are not in dispute. First, it is settled law that the court's prime and paramount consideration must be the best interests of the child. That is easily said but not easily applied. What it does involve is that the views of the parents, although they should be heeded and weighed, cannot prevail over the court's view of the ward's best interests. In the present case the parents, finding themselves in a hideous dilemma, have not taken a strong view so that no conflict arises.

Second, the court's high respect for the sanctity of human life imposes a strong presumption in favour of taking all steps capable of preserving it, save in exceptional circumstances. The problem is to define those circumstances.

Third, and as a corollary to the second principle, it cannot be too strongly emphasised that the court never sanctions steps to terminate life. That would be unlawful. There is no question of approving, even in a case of the most horrendous disability, a course aimed at terminating life or accelerating death. The court is concerned only with the circumstances in which steps should not be taken to prolong life....

I consider that the correct approach is for the court to judge the quality of life the child would have to endure if given the treatment and decide whether in all the circumstances such a life would be so afflicted as to be intolerable to that child. I say 'to that child' because the test should not be whether the life would be tolerable to the decider. The test must be whether the child in question, if capable of exercising sound judgment, would consider the life tolerable. This is the approach adopted by McKenzie J in *Re Superintendent of Family and Child Service and Dawson* (1983) 145 DLR (3d) 610 at 620–621. ... It takes account of the strong instinct to preserve one's life even in circumstances which an outsider, not himself at risk of death, might consider unacceptable. The circumstances to be considered would, in appropriate cases, include the degree of existing disability and any additional suffering or aggravation of the disability which the treatment itself would superimpose. In an accident case, as opposed to one involving disablement from birth, the child's pre-accident quality of life and its perception of what has been lost may also be factors relevant to whether the residual life would be intolerable to that child. ...

Appeal dismissed.

QUESTIONS

i. Guidance on the withdrawal of life-sustaining medical treatment issued by the Royal College of Paediatrics and Child Health (2004) suggests that 'legal intervention should only be considered when disputes between the Health Care Team, the child, parents and carers cannot be resolved by attempts to achieve consensus'. Should the doctors be able to withhold life-saving treatment without parental agreement, or court approval? (See *R v Portsmouth Hospital NHS Trust, ex p Glass* [1999] 2 FLR 905, [1999] 3 FCR 145; *Re C (Medical Treatment)* [1998] 1 FLR 384; *NHS Trust v M* [2001] 2 FLR 367.) (We look at the child's rights at pp. 370, 371.)

ii. Money can also be a factor. In *R v Cambridge Health Authority, ex p B* [1995] 2 All ER 129, Laws J in judicial review proceedings had quashed the authority's decision not to fund further chemotherapy and a second bone marrow transplant for a child with leukaemia. Allowing the appeal, Sir Thomas Bingham MR said:

> I have no doubt that in a perfect world any treatment which a patient, or a patient's family, sought would be provided if the doctors were willing to give it, no matter how much it cost, particularly when a life was potentially at stake. It would however, in my view, be shutting one's eyes to the real world if the court were to proceed on the basis that we do live in such a world. ... Difficult and agonising judgments have to be made as to how a limited budget is best allocated to the maximum advantage of the maximum number of patients. That is not a judgment that the court can make.

Do you agree with this decision? What should the role of the judiciary be here?

iii. Do you agree that the test of 'best interests' in matters of life and death should be what the child himself would have wanted? Or should the court adopt the 'same attitude as a responsible parent... in the case of his or her own child' (per Balcombe LJ in *Re J (a minor) (wardship: medical treatment)* [1991] Fam 33, [1990] 3 All ER 930)? What difference would it make?

iv. The Royal College of Paediatrics and Child Health guidance (2004) states that 'A severe/intolerable disability is indefinable'. Do cases like *Re J*, and the outcome of *Re A* itself, suggest to you that disabled children have an equal right to life with other children?

8.2 PARENTAL AUTONOMY AND THE HUMAN RIGHTS ACT 1998

In this section we look at conflicts between parents and the state and the role of the Human Rights Act 1998 in resolving them.

The following anonymous discussion of the 'Mental Hospitalisation of Children and the Limits of Parental Authority' (1978) provides a summary of the arguments for and against parental autonomy. While written from a US perspective the references to the Constitution can equally apply to the European Convention on Human Rights:

> Five justifications are most often advanced to support parental authority. They may for convenience be termed *social pluralism, social order, parental privilege, family autonomy* and *child's welfare.*

A. Social Pluralism

> It is a 'fixed star in our constitutional constellation,' especially with respect to the education of children, that the state shall not impose an orthodoxy 'in politics, nationalism, religion, or other matters of opinion.' And, especially in matters that relate to families and childrearing, the Constitution also disfavors state practices that threaten to impose on all a single conception of a worthwhile way of life. The institution of parental authority, by fragmenting decisions about the goals and methods of childrearing, serves to militate against such an orthodoxy. This, historically, has been part of its rationale and is today one reason for treating parental authority, when asserted against the state, as a constitutional right. It is therefore not surprising that the Supreme Court has acted more readily to protect parental authority against state intrusion when the threat to social pluralism has been acute.
>
> Compare *Wisconsin v Yoder* 406 US 205 (1972) (invalidating state compulsory education law as applied to Amish children) and *Pierce v Society of Sisters* 268 US 510 (1925) (invalidating state law requiring parents to send their children only to public schools) with *Prince v Massachusetts* 321 US 158 (1944) (upholding statute prohibiting street solicitation by children as applied to Jehovah's Witnesses distributing religious literature)....

B. Social Order

> Historically, the law recognized society's interest in having children reared so that as adults they would be economically self-sufficient and would conform their conduct to society's norms. Parents, according to one court, were ordinarily entrusted with this task 'because it [could] seldom be put into better hands,' but they were subject to state supersession if they failed. Parents are still, to some extent, viewed as child-socialization agents of the state. ...

C. Parental Privilege

> It is not uncommon for parents to seek to express their own personalities through their children. This interest of parents may serve as the basis for the claim they advance to have 'the power to dictate their [children's] training, prescribe their education and form their religious opinions.' To

the extent that the law protects this claim of parents, it creates a *parental privilege* – that is, a prerogative of a parent to rear his child to be a person whose conduct, character, and belief conform to standards of the parent's choosing. There can be no doubt that this interest of parents, when asserted against the state, is within the scope of liberty protected by the Constitution. ...

It is regarded by many as unjust for one adult to impose his conception of the good life on another and as demeaning to another's dignity not to respect his choice of his own life plan. Psychological studies show that at adolescence, children of normal intellect are in this respect substantially like adults: they have the basic cognitive capacities to choose intelligently among competing values and to formulate their own life plans. So, as applied to adolescents, parental privilege – the prerogative of parents to impose on their children values and styles of life that best express the *parents'* personalities – is especially hard to justify on moral grounds. ...

D. Family Autonomy

The state's interest in preserving the family unit is often cited to justify state sanction of parental authority. But protecting the family from outside interference is quite distinct from fortifying the family's power over one of its members. ...

When a parent, in his role of family governor, exercises authority over the child, his action has a moral basis that the exercise of bare parental privilege lacks. But there are other criteria for the moral assessment of social institutions – whether an institution that makes claims against some provides some reciprocal benefit for each of those whose liberty it restricts, or whether it makes an equal relative contribution to the good life of each of its participants. Although family life may often require that some good of one individual be foregone for the well-being of the family as a whole, a family that excessively derogates the interests of one for the sake of the others undermines its own moral basis.

These moral considerations suggest a legal norm. The state need not intervene in every family dispute, but if it does, it must treat each family member affected as having a distinguishable interest, which is equally entitled to the protection of the state. ...

E. Child's Welfare

The last of the proffered justifications of parental authority is that it serves the child's welfare. It has been suggested that allowing parents to be the supreme arbiters of their child's fate is justified because it is conducive to the child's long term psychological health. More commonly, parental authority is defended on the ground that someone must choose for children since they lack the capacity to choose for themselves; parents are assigned this role because they are presumed to be better able to perform the task than anyone else.

Frances Olsen in 'The Myth of State Intervention in the Family' (1984) argues that 'neither "intervention" nor "nonintervention" is an accurate description of any particular set of policies, and the terms obscure rather than clarify the policy choices that society makes'. Using economic policies as a comparison, she argues that 'the free market could not exist independently of the state. The enforcement of property, tort, and contract law requires constant political choices that may benefit one economic actor, usually at the expense of another'. Consequently,

> [A]lthough the state defines and reinforces specific roles and particular hierarchies within the family, these policies are often considered nonintervention; indeed, a refusal to bolster family hierarchy has sometimes been considered state intervention in the family. The idea that the state can intervene or not intervene in the family, and particularly that the state practices a policy of nonintervention when it bolsters family hierarchy, would seem to depend upon the belief that a natural family exists separate from legal regulations, and that the hierarchy the state enforces is a natural hierarchy, created by God or by nature, not by law.

QUESTION

Is there anything natural about parental power?

As the US cases referred to above (p. 354) indicate, it is in conflicts about education that the tensions between the different justifications of parental autonomy frequently come to the fore. One reason for this is that education is a civil and political right and, at the same time, a social and economic right.

Home education is a growing phenomenon, but it is also an important test case as it represents the realisation of complete parental authority over the educational environment of children. In Germany, home education is prohibited. The legitimacy of this was considered by the European Court of Human Rights.

Konrad and Others v Germany (2006) ECHR Application No 35504/03

> The applicant parents alleged that the refusal of permission to educate their children at home violated their right to ensure an education for their children in conformity with their own religious convictions as guaranteed by Article 2 of Protocol No. 1, which provides:
>
> > 'No person shall be denied the right to education. In the exercise of any functions which it assumes in relation to education and to teaching, the State shall respect the right of parents to ensure such education and teaching in conformity with their own religious and philosophical convictions.'
>
> The applicant parents submitted that it was their duty to educate their children in accordance with the Bible and Christian values. They inferred from numerous quotations from the Bible that their children's education was an obligation on them which could not easily be transferred to third persons. They submitted that, by teaching their children at home, they were obeying a divine order. Their children's attendance of a primary school would inevitably lead to grave conflicts with their personal beliefs as far as syllabus and teaching methods were concerned. Compulsory school attendance would therefore severely endanger their children's religious education, especially regarding sex education and concentration training (as provided in some schools), which in their view amounted to esoteric exercises. The State's obligation of religious neutrality would render it impossible to educate their children in a State school in accordance with the applicant parents' beliefs... Moreover, the applicants pointed out that home education was permitted in the United States, Canada, Switzerland, Austria and Norway. Countries such as Denmark, Finland and Ireland provided for home education in their constitution.

In the present case, the Court notes that the German authorities and courts have carefully reasoned their decisions and mainly stressed the fact that not only the acquisition of knowledge but also integration into and first experiences of society are important goals in primary-school education. The German courts found that those objectives could not be met to the same extent by home education, even if it allowed children to acquire the same standard of knowledge as provided by primary-school education. The Court considers that this presumption is not erroneous and falls within the Contracting States' margin of appreciation in setting up and interpreting rules for their education systems. The Federal Constitutional Court stressed the general interest of society in avoiding the emergence of parallel societies based on separate philosophical convictions and the importance of integrating minorities into society. The Court regards this as being in accordance with its own case-law on the importance of pluralism for democracy (see, *mutatis mutandis*, *Refah Partisi (the Welfare Party) and Others v Turkey* [GC], nos. 41340/98, 41342/98, 41343/98 and 41344/98, § 89, ECHR 2003-II).

Moreover, the German courts pointed to the fact that the applicant parents were free to educate their children after school and at weekends. Therefore, the parents' right to education in conformity with their religious convictions is not restricted in a disproportionate manner. Compulsory primary-school attendance does not deprive the applicant parents of their right to 'exercise with regard to their children natural parental functions as educators, or to guide their children on a path in line with the parents' own religious or philosophical convictions' (see, *mutatis mutandis*, *Kjeldsen, Busk Madsen and Pedersen*, cited above, pp. 27–28, § 54, and *Efstratiou v Greece*, judgment of 27 November 1996, *Reports of Judgments and Decisions* 1996-VI, p. 2359, § 32).

It follows that this complaint must be rejected as manifestly ill-founded, in accordance with Article 35 §§ 3 and 4 of the Convention.

The applicants also complained that the refusal to allow the applicant parents to educate their children in accordance with their religious beliefs amounted to a violation of their respect to private life under Article 8. ...

Moreover, the applicants complained of a violation of their freedom of thought, conscience and religion, as guaranteed by Article 9 of the Convention, which provides:

> '1. Everyone has the right to freedom of thought, conscience and religion; this right includes freedom to change his religion or belief and freedom, either alone or in community with others and in public or private, to manifest his religion or belief, in worship, teaching, practice and observance.
>
> 2. Freedom to manifest one's religion or beliefs shall be subject only to such limitations as are prescribed by law and are necessary in a democratic society in the interests of public safety, for the protection of public order, health or morals, or for the protection of the rights and freedoms of others.'

The Court finds that any interference with the applicants' rights under either of these provisions would, for the reasons stated above, be justified under Article 8 § 2 and Article 9 § 2 respectively as being provided for by law and necessary in a democratic society in view of the public interest in ensuring the children's education.

Andrew Bainham (2005) argues that 'To deprive a child of the experience of school life would, in itself, be a denial of children's rights and a failure to discharge parental responsibility'. However, the UK distinguishes the right to education from the right to school life, and parents have the right to home educate, as long as they provide 'sufficient education' (Education Act 1996, section 9). In *R v Secretary of State for Education and Science, ex p Talmud Torah Machzikei Hadass School Trust* (*The Times*, 12 April 1985, CO/422/84) the court was required to consider the adequacy of the curriculum of an independent religious Jewish school. In his judgment, Woolf J defined a 'suitable' education as one that:

> ... primarily equips a child for life within the community of which he is a member, rather than the way of life in the country as a whole, as long as it does not foreclose the child's options in later years to adopt some other form of life if he wishes to do so.

QUESTIONS

i. A number of German families have moved to the UK in order to home educate. They consider themselves 'political refugees'. Do you think the ECHR is right in permitting such a wide margin of appreciation to individual states? Which approach do you agree with?

ii. Hans Magnus Enzensberger in *Political Crumbs* (1990) argues that 'The state school has always been the domain of a distant administration ... a single glance tells one that, like madhouses and reformatories, they have been erected for the custody and disciplining of people'. What are the state's interests in education? Are they always the same as the interests of the child? Do you think children should have the right to decide themselves whether they attend school?

iii. In *Konrad* the court referred to 'the general interest of society in avoiding the emergence of parallel societies based on separate philosophical convictions and the importance of integrating minorities into society'. With this in mind can you distinguish home education from faith schools and private schools?

iv. Is the court in *Konrad* right when it suggests that integration and pluralism are the same thing?

v. In *Kjeldsen v Denmark* (1976) 1 EHRR 711 the ECHR upheld the legality of compulsory sex education in state schools. However, in the UK, parents have the right to remove their children from sex education classes (Education Act 1996, section 405). Do you agree with this 'opt out' provision?

vi. Do you think it acceptable to impose a national curriculum, including evolution within its compulsory science teaching, upon children of a family who believe in the literal truth of the book of Genesis? Should private and/or maintained schools be permitted to teach 'creationism' or 'intelligent design' as scientific fact?

Anat Scolnicov (2007) in 'The Child's Right to Religious Freedom and Formation of Identity' considers the religious identity of children and in doing so highlights a tension faced by liberal democratic states:

> There is a problem in defining neutrality in education. There can be two definitions: education which fosters a neutral religious identity, or education which imparts a lack of prejudice against any religious viewpoint. Is it possible to impart the second kind of neutrality rather that the first? It can be argued that such a negative capability can be taught, but not at a very young age. In order to grow up as full individuals, according to this argument, children should first

be given an affiliation, whether national or religious. It is not advisable, or even possible, to raise a child with no sense of identity. Similarly, it would seem impossible to instill in a child a completely neutral gender identity, lacking in any gender role. But this does not mean that we cannot teach children not to accept stereotypical gender roles and to accept different sexual orientations. The argument against a neutral education can be understood by reference to Nagel's general claim that liberal theory is non-neutral, because it discounts conceptions that depend on inter-personal relations. Indeed, the family and particularly the parental bond constitute such relations, ignored by the call for religiously-neutral education. It can be argued that the family as a group has rights. O'Neill (1994) has commented on the tension between children's rights and family rights. He sees the individualistic approach to rights as unsatisfactory when it comes to the intrafamily relationship and suggests instead a mode of family covenant. O'Neill does not deal with the role of religion in the family covenant. However, it seems that religious cohesion might play an important part in this covenant. ... A judgment must be made whether the value of this bond is enough to overcome the individualistic conception of rights... international human rights law has prevaricated between two approaches, one protecting the family bond and the other protecting the individual right of the child.

QUESTION

Can you distinguish family (or group) rights from the rights of parents?

The Human Rights Act 1998 renewed long-standing questions about the compatibility of the paramountcy principle with Article 8 of the European Convention on Human Rights. An example of this is *Payne v Payne* [2001] EWCA Civ 166, [2001] 1 FLR 1051 (to which we shall return in Chapter 10):

Butler-Sloss P:
All those immediately affected by the proceedings, that is to say the mother, the father and the child, have rights under article 8(1). Those rights, inevitably in a case such as the present appeal, are in conflict and, under article 8(2), have to be balanced against the rights of the others. In addition and of the greatest significance is the welfare of the child which, according to European jurisprudence, is of crucial importance and, where in conflict with a parent, is overriding: see *Johansen v Norway* (1996) 23 EHRR 33, 67, 72. Article 8(2) recognises that a public authority, in this case the court, may interfere with the right to family life where it does so in accordance with the law, and where it is necessary in a democratic society for, inter alia, the protection of the rights and freedoms of others and the decision is proportionate to the need demonstrated. That position appears to me to be similar to that which arises in all child-based family disputes and the European case law on children is in line with the principles set out in the Children Act 1989. I do not, for my part, consider that the Convention has affected the principles the courts should apply in dealing with these difficult issues.

But is considering child welfare the same as addressing their rights? According to Jane Fortin in 'Accommodating Children's Rights in a Post Human Rights Act Era' (2006):

The domestic courts have responded to the demands of the HRA in an extraordinarily haphazard manner when dealing with children's cases. ...[I]n many areas of law involving children, there has been little attempt to articulate children's interests as rights. ... Parents are entitled to use the HRA to complain over the state's interference with their upbringing of their children. Unfortunately, however, the phrasing of some of the Convention's articles, particularly that of article 8, implicitly encourages parents to see their grievances from an entirely adult standpoint. When they do so, both parents and court appear to lose sight of the fact that the children, who are the focus of the dispute, may have rights and interests of their own which need proper assessment and deliberation.

R (on the application of Williamson) v Secretary of State for Education and Employment [2005] UKHL 15, [2005] AC 246

Parents and teachers at independent Christian schools complained that the ban on corporal punishment in all schools violated their right under Article 9 of the ECHR to manifest their religious beliefs. The High Court and Court of Appeal found that it did not interfere with these beliefs. Only in the House of Lords was serious consideration given to whether it was justified to protect the rights of children:

Baroness Hale of Richmond:

[71] My Lords, this is, and has always been, a case about children, their rights and the rights of their parents and teachers. Yet there has been no one here or in the courts below to speak on behalf of the children. No litigation friend has been appointed to consider the rights of the pupils involved separately from those of the adults. No non-governmental organisation, such as the Children's Rights Alliance, has intervened to argue a case on behalf of children as a whole. The battle has been fought on ground selected by the adults.

[77] Some people believe so strongly that all corporal punishment of children is wrong that they may find it hard to accept that a belief that it is right can in any circumstances be worthy of respect in a democratic society or compatible with the human dignity of either the punished or the punisher. That must sometimes be so. The sort of punishment in which Victoria Climbie's murderers apparently believed is not worthy of any respect at all [see p. ?? below]. But in this case we are concerned with carefully controlled, mild and loving discipline administered in the context of a clear moral code. Many people in this country still believe that it is right. The rightness or wrongness of either belief is not a scientifically provable fact. Nor does either necessarily depend upon the practical efficacy of corporal punishment in developing character and behaviour. Many would believe it to be wrong even if it was proven to work. Both are essentially moral beliefs, although they may be underpinned with other beliefs about what works best in bringing up children. Both are entitled to respect. A free and plural society must expect to tolerate all sorts of views which many, even most, find completely unacceptable.

[78] Respect is one thing. Allowing them to be practised is another. I am prepared to accept that the practice of corporal punishment in these schools is a manifestation of the parents' and teachers' beliefs: a belief that as a last resort children may need physical correction as part of their education can only be manifested by correcting them in that way. I find it difficult to understand how a ban on that practice is anything other than a limitation of the right to manifest that belief: the belief in question is not only a belief that parents should be able to punish their children but that such punishment is an essential part of the sort of Christian education in which these parents and teachers believe. I am deeply troubled by the solution adopted in the Court of Appeal, which depended upon the parents' continued right to punish the children themselves. The real question is whether any limits set by the state can be justified under art 9(2).

[80] There can be no doubt that the ban on corporal punishment in schools pursues the legitimate aim of protecting the rights and freedoms of children. It has long been held that these are

not limited to their rights under the convention. The appellants were anxious to stress that the corporal punishment in which they believe would not breach the child's rights under either art 3 or art 8. But it can still be legitimate for the state to prohibit it for the sake of the child. A child has the same right as anyone else not to be assaulted; the defence of lawful chastisement is an exception to that right. It has long been held in the context of art 8 that the rights and freedoms of the child include his interests: see *Hendriks v Netherlands* (1982) 5 EHRR 223; *Andersson v Sweden* [1992] ECHR 12963/87; *Johansen v Norway* [1996] ECHR 17383/90. ...

Above all, the state is entitled to give children the protection they are given by an international instrument to which the United Kingdom is a party, the United Nations Convention on the Rights of the Child 1989 [see p. 383 below]. ...

More significantly in the present context, art 19(1) provides:

> 'States parties shall take all appropriate legislative, administrative, social and educational measures to protect the child from all forms of physical or mental violence, injury or abuse, neglect or negligent treatment, maltreatment or exploitation, including sexual abuse, while in the care of parent(s), legal guardian(s) or any other person who has the care of the child.'

This is reinforced by art 28(2):

> 'States Parties shall take all appropriate measures to ensure that school discipline is administered in a manner consistent with the child's human dignity and in conformity with the present Convention.'

[82] The United Nations Committee on the Rights of the Child commented, in its consideration of the United Kingdom's first report on its compliance with the convention (see *Concluding Observations of the Committee on the Rights of the Child: United Kingdom* (1995)) that it was—

> 'worried about the national legal provisions dealing with reasonable chastisement within the family. The imprecise nature of the expression of reasonable chastisement as contained in these legal provisions may pave the way for it to be interpreted in a subjective and arbitrary manner. Thus, the Committee is concerned that legislative and other measures relating to the physical integrity of children do not appear to be compatible with the provisions and principles of the Convention, including those of its articles 3, 19 and 37. The Committee is equally concerned that privately funded and managed schools are still permitted to administer corporal punishment to children in attendance there which does not appear to be compatible with the provisions of the Convention, including those of its article 28, paragraph 2.' (See para 16.)

The committee went on to recommend that physical punishment of children in families be prohibited 'in the light of the provisions set out in articles 3 and 19 of the Convention' (para 31); further 'legislative measures are recommended to prohibit the use of corporal punishment in privately funded and managed schools' (para 32).

[83] At its second review in October 2002, the committee welcomed the abolition of corporal punishment in all schools in England, Wales and Scotland following its 1995 recommendations (see *Concluding Observations: United Kingdom of Great Britain and Northern Ireland* (2002), para 35). It went on (para 38):

> 'The Committee recommends that the State party:
> (a) with urgency adopt legislation throughout the State party to remove the "reasonable chastisement" defence and prohibit all corporal punishment in the family and in any other contexts not covered by existing legislation;...'

[84] We are not in this case concerned with physical punishment within the family. This raises more complex questions than does corporal punishment in institutional settings. ...But in

relation to corporal punishment in schools they have been quite unequivocal. ... How can it not be a legitimate and proportionate limitation on the practice of parents' religious beliefs to heed such a recommendation from the bodies charged with monitoring our compliance with the obligations which we have undertaken to respect the dignity of the individual and the rights of children?

[86] With such an array of international and professional support, it is quite impossible to say that Parliament was not entitled to limit the practice of corporal punishment in all schools in order to protect the rights and freedoms of all children. Furthermore, the state has a positive obligation to protect children from inhuman or degrading punishment which violates their rights under art 3. But prohibiting only such punishment as would violate their rights under art 3 (or possibly art 8) would bring difficult problems of definition, demarcation and enforcement. It would not meet the authoritative international view of what the UN convention requires. The appellants' solution is that they and other schools which share their views should be exempted from the ban. But this would raise exactly the same problems. How could it be justified in terms of the rights and protection of the child to allow some schools to inflict corporal punishment while prohibiting the rest from doing so? If a child has a right to be brought up without institutional violence, as he does, that right should be respected whether or not his parents and teachers believe otherwise.

Corporal punishment is now banned in virtually all officially regulated situations where children are looked after away from home. But what about parents? Decisions of the European Court of Human Rights have led to reform. In *A v UK* [1998] EHLR 82 the Court held that the repeated beating of a boy by his stepfather with a garden cane was a breach of the child's rights under Article 3 and that the common law defence of 'reasonable chastisement' failed to provide adequate protection to children. A government consultation followed and further clarification was given in *R v H* [2001] 2 FLR 431. However it was a private member's amendment, supported by pressure from children's groups, that led to section 58 of the Children Act 2004. This does not ban corporal punishment, but limits the availability of the defence of reasonable chastisement to the extent that parents must stop short of causing actual bodily harm.

QUESTIONS

i. Hammarberg (1995) argues that:

> It would be seen as strange to propose that some violence against a wife should be possible, only the beatings should not be too severe or leave any marks. Why should there be any difference in the approach to children?

Wald (1979) however argues that:

> ...the concept of total independence is just unrealistic unless we are prepared to place an outside monitor in every home to eliminate the authority parents have stemming from their greater strength and economic power.

Do you think Parliament should have banned corporal punishment by parents? Why do you think it chose not to?

ii. Is section 58 of the Children Act 2004 compatible with the Convention of the Rights of the Child?

iii. The government has argued that section 58 seeks to protect children and provide greater legal certainty by clarifying the legal framework protecting children from parental violence and abuse. What do you think?

iv. In *Re D (Care: Threshold Criteria: Significant Harm)* [1998] *Fam Law* 656 the court addressed the issue of corporal punishment within a Jamaican family.

Wilson J:

> 'We are not a collection of ghettos, but one society . . . governed by one set of laws. It would concern me if the same event could give rise to in one case to a finding of significant harm and in another to a finding of the contrary. On the other hand if the child can say . . . "my brothers, sisters and friends are all treated in this way from time to time: it seems to be part of life", that child may suffer less emotional harm than a child who perceives him or herself to be a unique victim'.

Julia Brophy (2003) rejects the argument for cultural relativism but argues that:

> . . . questions remain about how to resolve issues of over-representation of black children in care populations, and whether Euro-centric models of parenting are inappropriately imposed on parents who do not share the lifestyles and belief systems broadly associated with white parents.

Do you think a child's cultural background is a relevant consideration in relation to corporal punishment? (For an international review, see http://www.endcorporalpunishment.org.)

v. The Secure Training Centre (Amendment) Rules 2007, SI 2007/1709 extend the circumstances in which physical restraint can be used beyond where it is necessary to prevent harm to a person or to property to circumstances where it is necessary to ensure good order and discipline. When does physical restraint become corporal punishment? Are these rules compatible with the international human right standards referred to in *Williamson*? (See NSPCC/CARE, 'The Use of Restraint in Secure Training Centres', 2007.)

vi. In *It hurts you inside – children talking about smacking* Carolyne Willow and Tina Hyder surveyed the views of young children on smacking. The exercise produced ten major messages:

> Children defined smacking as hitting; most of them described a smack as a hard or very hard hit.
>
> Children said smacking hurts.
>
> The children we listened to said children are the main people who dislike smacking followed by parents, friends and grandparents.
>
> The vast majority of the children who took part thought smacking was wrong.
>
> The children said children respond negatively to being smacked, and adults regret smacking.
>
> The children said parents and other grown ups are the people that mostly smack children.
>
> The children said they usually get smacked indoors and on the bottom, arm or head.
>
> The children said the main reasons children are smacked include: they have been violent themselves; they have been naughty or mischievous; they have broken or spoiled things; or because they have disobeyed or failed to listen to their parents.

The children we listened to said children do not smack adults because they are scared they will be hit again; adults do not smack each other because they are big and know better and because they love and care about each other.

Half the children involved in this consultation exercise said they will not smack children when they are adults; five-year-olds most often said they will not smack children when they are big.

How relevant do you think the views of children should be in determining what the law should be?

8.3 CHILDREN'S RIGHTS

The last question raises the possibility of children defining their own understanding of welfare – independently of both their parents and the state. But before we consider the extent to which law respects their views, we consider the role of the concept of 'childhood' and the different meanings of 'children's rights'.

Valerie Walkerdine, 'Developmental psychology and the study of childhood' (2004):

Childhood is always produced as an object in relation to power. Thus, there can no timeless truth, sociological or psychological, about childhood. There can rather be understandings of how childhood is produced at any one time and place and an imperative to understand what kinds of childhoods we want to produce, if indeed we want childhood at all. For example, developmental psychology understands children's thinking as becoming more and more like adults. It figures therefore that children's thinking is assumed to be different from adult thinking and that this difference is understood as a deficiency, a natural deficiency that will be put right as the child grows up. This position is described by James and Prout (1997) as seeing children as 'human becomings' rather than human beings. However, Lee (2001) understands this position as in some ways 'throwing the baby out with the bath water' in the sense that children are in need of supplementation. Lee asks 'how does the "being" child change if that change is not thought of as the supplementation of lack? What could "growing up" mean once we have distanced ourselves from the dominant frameworks' account of socialization and development?' (Lee 2001: 54). Of course, we can also argue that supplementation and lack define aspects of that so-called stable state of adulthood. After all, old people (for example) often need supplementation as they get older. Indeed, we can understand the definition of adulthood as a stable state of being, and indeed equally as a definition of childhood as unstable, as a product of power. That is, liberal government is dependent on a notion of rights and responsibilities carried out by rational, stable beings. Any instability is often described as childlike and as developmentally regressive. Whereas, we could understand adulthood as an unstable state too, with a fictional stability produced in the practices in which adulthood is defined and accomplished.

The other important issue to remember is that childhood as defined in terms of economic dependency on adults, access to schooling etc., is in fact, still the norm for only a minority of the world's children. Children in many countries routinely work, and as we know, multinationals like Nike are very dependent upon inexpensive child labour. In that sense, the modern western conception of the child exists, as Castenada (2002) argues, in circuits of exchange between the First World and the Third. In that case, for example, the situation of prosperity for adults and children in the West is directly produced by the exploitation of children in the Third World. There is no figure of the child that stands outside such circuits of exchange. In that case, the story of the developing child does something more than universalize human becomingness. It also means that we can only see the relation of exploitation between the First World and the Third as one in which Third-World children are being denied a childhood or are underdeveloped. If the first World child exists, in a sense, at the expense of the Third, the complex economic relationality is being lost in the development explanation.

However, in relation to the western present, arguments have been made that globalization and neo-liberalism have produced a situation which has extended education and therefore childhood dependence well into the twenties, a period which would previously have been considered adult. Similarly, low pay and casual work have produced a situation in which people are not able to afford to leave the parental home until they are into their twenties and thirties. Lee (2001) understands this historical shift in the West as blurring the lines between adulthood and childhood and therefore presenting childhood as a shifting state.

QUESTIONS

i. What practices do you think define adulthood?

ii. The criminal law provides that a child cannot give lawful consent to sex until the age of sixteen but can be convicted of rape at the age of eleven. Can you explain this distinction?

Hillary Rodham Clinton (1973) described children's rights as 'a slogan in search of a definition'. John Eekelaar in 'The Emergence of Children's Rights' (1986) discusses the concept and distinguishes three different kinds of interest they may have:

> We may accept that the *social perception* that an individual or class of individuals has certain interests is a precondition to the conceptualization of rights. But these interests must be capable of isolation from the interests of others. I might believe that it is in my infant daughter's interests that I (and not she) take decisions concerning her medical welfare. This may even be supportable by objective evidence. But my interest, or right, to take such decisions is not identical with her interests. I might make stupid or even malicious decisions. Her interest is that I should make the best decisions for her. I am no more than the agent for fulfilling her interests. Hence we should be careful to understand that when we talk about rights as protecting interests, we conceive as interests only those benefits which the subject himself or herself might plausibly claim in themselves. This point is of great importance in the context of modern assertions of the right to parental autonomy. This has been advanced as a fuller enhancement of children's rights. Goldstein, Freud and Solnit construct the concept of 'family integrity' which is a combination of 'the three liberty interests of direct concern to children, parental autonomy, the right to autonomous parents and privacy'. But can we say the children might plausibly claim any of these things in themselves? If they are claimed (which they may be) it will be because they are believed to advance other desirable ends (perhaps material and emotional stability) which are the true objects of the claims. Observe that the formulation refers to claims children might plausibly make. Not, be it noted, what they actually claim. We here meet the problem that children often lack the information or ability to appreciate what will serve them best. It is necessary therefore to make some kind of imaginative leap and guess what a child might retrospectively have wanted once it reaches a position of maturity. In doing this, values of the adult world and of individual adults will inevitably enter. This is not to be deplored, but openly accepted. It encourages debate about these values. There are, however,

some broad propositions which might reasonably be advanced as forming the foundation of any child's (retrospective) claims. General physical, emotional and intellectual care within the social capabilities of his or her immediate caregivers would seem a minimal expectation. We may call this the 'basic' interest. What a child should expect from the wider community must be stated more tentatively. I have elsewhere [Eekelaar, 1984] suggested the formulation that, within certain overriding constraints, created by the economic and social structure of society (whose extent must be open to debate), all children should have an equal opportunity to maximize the resources available to them during their childhood (including their own inherent abilities) so as to minimize the degree to which they enter adult life affected by avoidable prejudices incurred during childhood. In short, their capacities are to be developed to their best advantage. We may call this the 'developmental' interest. The concept requires some elaboration.

It seems plausible that a child may expect society at large, no less than his parents, to ensure that he is no worse off than most other children in his opportunities to realize his life-chances. Could a child also plausibly claim that he should be given a *better* chance than other children, for example, by exploitation of his superior talents or a favoured social position? As an expectation addressed to the child's parents, such a claim might have some weight. A child of rich parents might retrospectively feel aggrieved if those resources were not used to provide him with a better chance in life than other children. On the other hand, such an expectation is less plausibly addressed to society at large, except perhaps with respect to the cultivation of singular talents. But from the point of view of a theory of rights, it does not much matter whether we decide that a privileged child has an interest in inequality favourable to himself. For, if the interest is to become a right, it must be acknowledged in the public domain as demanding protection for its own sake. As far as the 'developmental' interest is concerned, therefore, societies may choose to actualize it in harmony with their overall social goals, which may (but not necessarily) involve creating equality of opportunity and reducing socially determined inequalities, but encouraging diversity of achievement related to individual talent.

There is a third type of interest which children may, retrospectively, claim. A child may argue for the freedom to choose his own lifestyle and to enter social relations according to his own inclinations uncontrolled by the authority of the adult world, whether parents or institutions. Claims of this kind have been put forward on behalf of children by Holt (1975) and by Farson (1978). We may call them the 'autonomy' interest. Freeman (1983) has argued that such interests might be abridged insofar as children also have a right to be protected against their own inclinations if their satisfaction would rob them of the opportunity 'to mature to a rationally autonomous adulthood... capable of deciding on [their] own system of ends as free and rational beings'. This may be no more than a version of the developmental interest defined earlier. The problem is that a child's autonomy interest may conflict with the developmental interest and even the basic interest. While it is possible that some adults retrospectively approve that they were, when children, allowed the exercise of their autonomy at the price of putting them at a disadvantage as against other children in realizing their life-chances in adulthood, it seems improbable that this would be a common view. We may therefore rank the autonomy interests subordinate to the basic and the developmental interests. However, where they may be exercised without threatening these two interests, the claim for their satisfaction must be high.

QUESTION

Provide examples of children's basic, developmental and autonomy interests. Are they compatible? How can they be enforced? (See Chapter 11.)

Gillick v West Norfolk and Wisbech Area Health Authority [1986] AC 112, [1985] 3 All ER 402

This decision of the House of Lords was a landmark in children's rights. The plaintiff, a mother of five daughters under the age of sixteen, sought a declaration that the guidance issued by the Department of Health and Social Security, to the effect that in exceptional circumstances a doctor might give contraceptive advice and treatment to a girl under sixteen without her parents' consent, was unlawful. She failed at first instance, but succeeded in the Court of Appeal. On appeal to the House of Lords:

Lord Fraser of Tullybelton:

... Three strands of argument are raised by the appeal. These are: (1) whether a girl under the age of 16 has the legal capacity to give valid consent to contraceptive advice and treatment including medical examination; (2) whether giving such advice and treatment to a girl under 16 without her parents' consent infringes the parents' rights; and (3) whether a doctor who gives such advice or treatment to a girl under 16 without her parents' consent incurs criminal liability. I shall consider these strands in order.

1. The Legal Capacity of a Girl Under 16 to Consent to Contraceptive Advice, Examination and Treatment

There are some indications in statutory provisions to which we were referred that a girl under 16 years of age in England and Wales does not have the capacity to give valid consent to contraceptive advice and treatment. If she does not have the capacity, then any physical examination or touching of her body without her parents' consent would be an assault by the examiner. One of those provisions is s. 8 of the Family Law Reform Act 1969, which is in the following terms:

> '(1) The consent of a minor who has attained the age of sixteen years to any surgical, medical or dental treatment which, in the absence of consent, would constitute a trespass to his person, shall be as effective as it would be if he were of full age; and where a minor has by virtue of this section given an effective consent to any treatment it shall not be necessary to obtain any consent for it from his parent or guardian.
>
> ...
>
> (3) Nothing in this section shall be construed as making ineffective any consent which would have been effective if this section had not been enacted.'

The contention on behalf of Mrs Gillick was that sub-s (1) of s. 8 shows that, apart from the subsection, the consent of a minor to such treatment would not be effective. But I do not accept that contention because sub-s (3) leaves open the question whether consent by a minor under the age of 16 would have been effective if the section had not been enacted. That question is not answered by the section, and sub-s (1) is, in my opinion, merely for the avoidance of doubt. ...

... It seems to me verging on the absurd to suggest that a girl or a boy aged 15 could not effectively consent, for example, to have a medical examination of some trivial injury to his body or even to have a broken arm set. Of course the consent of the parents should normally be asked, but they may not be immediately available. Provided the patient, whether a boy or a girl, is capable of understanding what is proposed, and of expressing his or her own wishes, I see no good reason for holding that he or she lacks the capacity to express them validly and effectively and to authorise the medical man to make the examination or give the treatment which he advises. After all, a minor under the age of 16 can, within certain limits, enter into a contract. He or she can also sue and be sued, and can give evidence on oath. Moreover, a girl under 16 can give sufficiently effective consent to sexual intercourse to lead to the legal result that the man involved does not commit the crime of rape: see *R v Howard* [1965] 3 All ER 684 at 685, [1966] 1 WLR 13 at 15, ...

Accordingly, I am not disposed to hold now, for the first time, that a girl aged less than 16 lacks the power to give valid consent to contraceptive advice or treatment, merely on account of her age.

2. The Parents' Rights and Duties in Respect of Medical Treatment of Their Child

... It was, I think, accepted both by Mrs Gillick and by the DHSS, and in any event I hold, that parental rights to control a child do not exist for the benefit of the parent. They exist for the benefit of the child and they are justified only in so far as they enable the parent to perform his duties towards the child, and towards other children in the family. If necessary, this proposition can be supported by reference to *Blackstone's Commentaries* (1 Bl Com (17th edn, 1830) 452) [see p. 345 above].

...

From the parents' right and duty of custody flows their right and duty of control of the child, but the fact that custody is its origin throws but little light on the question of the legal extent of control at any particular age. ...

It is my view, contrary to the ordinary experience of mankind, at least in Western Europe in the present century, to say that a child or a young person remains in fact under the complete control of his parents until he attains the definite age of majority, now 18 in the United Kingdom, and that on attaining that age he suddenly acquires independence. In practice most wise parents relax their control gradually as the child develops and encourage him or her to become increasingly independent. Moreover, the degree of parental control actually exercised over a particular child does in practice vary considerably according to his understanding and intelligence and it would, in my opinion, be unrealistic for the courts not to recognise these facts. Social customs change, and the law ought to, and does in fact, have regard to such changes when they are of major importance. ...

Once the rule of the parents' absolute authority over minor children is abandoned, the solution to the problem in this appeal can no longer be found by referring to rigid parental rights at any particular age. The solution depends on a judgment of what is best for the welfare of the particular child. Nobody doubts, certainly I do not doubt, that in the overwhelming majority of cases the best judges of a child's welfare are his or her parents. Nor do I doubt that any important medical treatment of a child under 16 would normally only be carried out with the parents' approval. That is why it would and should be 'most unusual' for a doctor to advise a child without the knowledge and consent of the parents on contraceptive matters. But, as I have already pointed out, Mrs Gillick has to go further if she is to obtain the first declaration that she seeks. She has to justify the absolute right of veto in a parent. But there may be circumstances in which a doctor is a better judge of the medical advice and treatment which will conduce to a girl's welfare than her parents. ...

The only practicable course is, in my opinion, to entrust the doctor with a discretion to act in accordance with his view of what is best in the interests of the girl who is his patient. He should, of course, always seek to persuade her to tell her parents that she is seeking contraceptive advice, and the nature of the advice that she receives. At least he should seek to persuade her to agree to the doctor's informing the parents. But there may well be cases, and I think there will be some cases, where the girl refuses either to tell the parents herself or to permit the doctor to do so and in such cases the doctor will, in my opinion, be justified in proceeding without the parents' consent or even knowledge provided he is satisfied on the following matters: (1) that the girl (although under 16 years of age) will understand his advice; (2) that he cannot persuade her to inform her parents or to allow him to inform the parents that she is seeking contraceptive advice; (3) that she is very likely to begin or to continue having sexual intercourse with or without contraceptive treatment; (4) that unless she receives contraceptive advice or treatment her physical or mental health or both are likely to suffer; (5) that her best interests require him to give her contraceptive advice, treatment or both without the parental consent. ...

Lord Scarman:

...Parental rights clearly do exist, and they do not wholly disappear until the age of majority. Parental rights relate to both the person and the property of the child: custody, care and control of the person and guardianship of the property of the child. But the common law has never treated such rights as sovereign or beyond review and control. Nor has our law ever treated the child as other than a person with capacities and rights recognised by law. The principle of the law, as I shall endeavour to show, is that parental rights are derived from parental duty and exist only so long as they are needed for the protection of the person and property of the child. The principle has been subjected to certain age limits set by statute for certain purposes; and in some cases the courts have declared an age of discretion at which a child acquires before the age of majority the right to make his (or her) own decision. But these limitations in no way undermine the principle of the law, and should not be allowed to obscure it. ...

...The underlying principle of the law was exposed by Blackstone and can be seen to have been acknowledged in the case law. It is that parental right yields to the child's right to make his own decisions when he reaches a sufficient understanding and intelligence to be capable of making up his own mind on the matter requiring decision. Lord Denning MR captured the spirit and principle of the law when he said in *Hewer v Bryant* [1970]1 QB 357 at 369, [1969] 3 All ER 578 at 582:

> 'I would get rid of the rule in *Re Agar-Ellis* (1883) 24 Ch D 317 and of the suggested exceptions to it. That case was decided in the year 1883. It reflects the attitude of a Victorian parent towards his children. He expected unquestioning obedience to his commands. If a son disobeyed, his father would cut him off with a shilling. If a daughter had an illegitimate child, he would turn her out of the house. His power only ceased when the child became 21. I decline to accept a view so much out of date. The common law can, and should, keep pace with the times. It should declare, in conformity with the recent report of the Committee on the Age of Majority [Cmnd. 3342, 1967], that the legal right of a parent to the custody of a child ends at the eighteenth birthday; and even up till then, it is a dwindling right which the courts will hesitate to enforce against the wishes of the child, the older he is. It starts with a right of control and ends with little more than advice.'

But his is by no means a solitary voice. It is consistent with the opinion expressed by the House in *J v C* [1970] AC 668, [1969] 1 All ER 788, where their Lordships clearly recognised as out of place the assertion in the *Agar-Ellis* cases (1878) 10 Ch D 49; (1883) 24 Ch D 317 of a father's power bordering on 'patria potestas'. It is consistent with the view of Lord Parker CJ in *R v Howard* [1965] 3 All ER 684 at 685, [1966] 1 WLR 13 at 15, where he ruled that in the case of a prosecution charging rape of a girl under 16 the Crown must *prove* either lack of her consent or that she was not in a position to decide whether to consent or resist and added the comment that 'there are many girls who know full well what it is all about and can properly consent'. And it is consistent with the views of the House in the recent criminal case where a father was accused of kidnapping his own child, *R v D* [1984] AC 778, [1984] 2 All ER 449. ...

In the light of the foregoing I would hold that as a matter of law the parental right to determine whether or not their minor child below the age of 16 will have medical treatment terminates if and when the child achieves a sufficient understanding and intelligence to enable him or her to understand fully what is proposed. It will be a question of fact whether a child seeking advice has sufficient understanding of what is involved to give a consent valid in law. Until the child achieves the capacity to consent, the parental right to make the decision continues save only in exceptional circumstances. Emergency, parental neglect, abandonment of the child or inability to find the parent are examples of exceptional situations justifying the doctor proceeding to treat the child without parental knowledge and consent; but there will arise, no doubt, other exceptional situations in which it will be reasonable for the doctor to proceed without the parent's consent.

Lord Templeman:

... I accept also that a doctor may lawfully carry out some forms of treatment with the consent of an infant patient and against the opposition of a parent based on religious or any other grounds. The effect of the consent of the infant depends on the nature of the treatment and the age and understanding of the infant. For example, a doctor with the consent of an intelligent boy or girl of 15 could in my opinion safely remove tonsils or a troublesome appendix. But any decision on the part of a girl to practise sex and contraception requires not only knowledge of the facts of life and of the dangers of pregnancy and disease but also an understanding of the emotional and other consequences to her family, her male partner and to herself. I doubt whether a girl under the age of 16 is capable of a balanced judgment to embark on frequent, regular or casual sexual intercourse fortified by the illusion that medical science can protect her in mind and body and ignoring the danger of leaping from childhood to adulthood without the difficult formative transitional experiences of adolescence. There are many things which a girl under 16 needs to practise but sex is not one of them. ...

Appeal allowed.

QUESTION

Are all three of their Lordships saying the same thing? Does the parental right yield to the child's autonomy? Or does the child's autonomy allow a third party to take over the decision of what will be best?

John Eekelaar (1986) discusses the autonomy interest in the light of *Gillick*:

... Of the nine judges who gave a decision in this litigation, five were in favour of the plaintiff. This perhaps illustrates the ambiguity in current perceptions of the proper scope of children's autonomy interests. But the majority decision of the House of Lords has implications which extend beyond the parent-child relationship and into the scope of state power over the lives of children themselves. ...

The significance of Lord Scarman's opinion with respect to children's autonomy interests cannot be over-rated. It follows from his reasoning that, where a child has reached capacity, there is no room for a parent to impose a contrary view, *even if this is more in accord with the child's best interests*. For its legal superiority to the child's decision can rest only on its status as a parental right. But this is extinguished when the child reaches full capacity. ...

This recognition of the autonomy interests of children can be reconciled with their basic and developmental interests only through the empirical application of the concept of the acquisition of full capacity. This, as Lord Scarman made clear, may be no simple matter. The child must not only understand the nature of the transaction, but be able to evaluate its implications.

Intellectual understanding must be supplemented by emotional maturity. It is easy to see how adults can conclude that a child's decision which seems, to the adult, to be contrary to his interests, is lacking in sufficient maturity. In this respect, the provision of the simple test of age to provide an upper limit to the scope of a supervisory, paternalistic power has advantages. We cannot know for certain whether, retrospectively, a person may not regret that some control was not exercised over his immature judgment by persons with greater experience. But could we not say that it is on balance better to subject all persons to this potential inhibition up to a defined age, in case the failure to exercise the restraint unduly prejudices a person's basic or developmental interests? It avoids judgments in which questions of fact and value will be impenetrably mixed. But the decision, it seems, has been taken. Children will now have, in wider measure than ever before, that most dangerous but most precious of rights: the right to make their own mistakes.

Michael Freeman in 'Rethinking *Gillick*' (2005) argues that while *Gillick* 'seemed to usher in a new age ... the courts in England, starting in 1992, have beat a hasty retreat'.

In *Re R (a minor) (wardship: medical treatment)* [1992] Fam 11, [1991] 4 All ER 177, it was held that the court could authorise the administration of anti-psychotic drugs to a 15-year-old girl despite her refusal. Lord Donaldson MR went further: adopting a keyholder analogy, he stated that the consent of either the parents or a competent child could unlock the door to treatment. In response to *Gillick* he argued that 'I do not understand Lord Scarman to be saying that , if a child was Gillick competent ... the parents have ceased to have an independent right of veto of consent as contrasted with ceasing to have a right of determination, ie a veto'.

In the next case he took a different metaphor but with a similar result.

Re W (a minor) (medical treatment: court's jurisdiction) [1993] Fam 64, [1992] 4 All ER 627, Court of Appeal

W was a 16-year-old girl in local authority care who suffered from anorexia nervosa. She was admitted to an adolescent psychiatric unit but her physical condition had deteriorated so much that it was proposed to move her to a hospital specialising in eating disorders. She did not wish to go. The local authority asked the court, in the exercise of its inherent jurisdiction, to authorise this. Thorpe J held that she was competent to make the decision but that the court could make the order sought. She appealed, arguing that the Family Law Reform Act, section 8 gave her the exclusive right to consent and therefore an absolute right to refuse treatment.

Lord Donaldson of Lymington MR:

... On reflection I regret my use in *In re R (A Minor) (Wardship: Consent to Treatment)* [1992] Fam 11, 22, of the keyholder analogy because keys can lock as well as unlock. I now prefer the analogy of the legal 'flak jacket' which protects the doctor from claims by the litigious whether he acquires it from his patient who may be a minor over the age of 16, or a '*Gillick* competent' child under that age or from another person having parental responsibilities which include a right to consent to treatment of the minor. Anyone who gives him a flak jacket (that is, consent) may take it back, but the doctor only needs one and so long as he continues to have one he has the legal right to proceed. ...

Hair-raising possibilities were canvassed of abortions being carried out by doctors in reliance upon the consent of parents and despite the refusal of consent by 16- and 17-year-olds. Whilst this may be possible as a matter of law, I do not see any likelihood taking account of medical ethics, unless the abortion was truly in the best interests of the child. This is not to say that it could not happen. This is clear from the facts of *In re D (A Minor) (Wardship: Sterilisation)* [1976] Fam 185.

...

...I have no doubt that the wishes of a 16- or 17-year-old child or indeed of a younger child who is '*Gillick* competent' are of the greatest importance both legally and clinically, but I do doubt whether Thorpe J was right to conclude that W. was of sufficient understanding to make an informed decision. ...

There is ample authority for the proposition that the inherent powers of the court under its parens patriae jurisdiction are theoretically limitless and that they certainly extend beyond the powers of a natural parent: see for example *In re R (A Minor) (Wardship: Consent to Treatment)* [1992] Fam 11, 25B, 28G. There can therefore be no doubt that it has power to override the refusal of a minor, whether over the age of 16 or under that age but '*Gillick* competent'. It does not do so by ordering the doctors to treat which, even if within the court's powers, would be an abuse of them or by ordering the minor to accept treatment, but by authorising the doctors to treat the minor in accordance with their clinical judgment, subject to any restrictions which the court may impose.

...This is not, however, to say that the wishes of 16- and 17-year-olds are to be treated as no different from those of 14- and 15-year-olds. Far from it. Adolescence is a period of progressive transition from childhood to adulthood and as experience of life is acquired and intelligence and understanding grow, so will the scope of the decision-making which should be left to the minor, for it is only by making decisions and experiencing the consequences that decision-making skills will be acquired. ...

Balcombe LJ delivered a judgment agreeing with Lord Donaldson. Nolan LJ was more cautious both about the parents' rights to override the child's wishes and the role of the court.

Nolan LJ:

...I am very far from asserting any general rule that the court should prefer its own view as to what is in the best interests of the child to those of the child itself. In considering the welfare of the child, the court must not only recognise but if necessary defend the right of the child, having sufficient understanding to take an informed decision, to make his or her own choice. In most areas of life it would be not only wrong in principle but also futile and counter-productive for the court to adopt any different approach. In the area of medical treatment, however, the court can and sometimes must intervene.

...One must, I think, start from the general premise that the protection of the child's welfare implies at least the protection of the child's life. I state this only as a general and not as an invariable premise because of the possibility of cases in which the court would not authorise treatment of a distressing nature which offered only a small hope of preserving life. In general terms, however, the present state of the law is that an individual who has reached the age of 18 is free to do with his life what he wishes, but it is the duty of the court to ensure so far as it can that children survive to attain that age.

To take it a stage further, if the child's welfare is threatened by a serious and imminent risk that the child will suffer grave and irreversible mental or physical harm, then once again the court when called upon has a duty to intervene. It makes no difference whether the risk arises from the action or inaction of others, or from the action or inaction of the child. Due weight must be given to the child's wishes, but the court is not bound by them. ...

Appeal dismissed.

QUESTIONS

i. Given what Lord Donaldson says about the girl's competence, how much of the rest of what he says is *ratio decidendi*?

ii. What would you advise a doctor to do if a mother insists that her pregnant daughter (a) of seventeen or (b) of thirteen should have an abortion which she does not want?

iii. In *Re P* [2004] 2 FLR 1117 a hospital was seeking leave to administer blood to a Jehovah's Witness aged seventeen who objected on the grounds of his religious belief. Johnson J granted the order:

> there may be cases as a child approaches the age of 18 when his refusal would be determinative. A court will have to consider whether to override the wishes of a child approaching the age of maturity when the likelihood is that all that will have been achieved will have been deferment of an inevitable death and for a matter of months.

However, he agreed with Nolan LJ's argument in *Re W* that it was the duty of the court to ensure that children survive to that age. If P had been 18 he would have had the right to refuse treatment, even if he would die as a result (see *Re C* [1994] 1 FLR 31). Do you agree with his decision?

iv. To what extent do you think the judgments in *Gillick*, *Re W*, *Re R* and *Re P* are influenced by the views of the medical profession?

v. Michael Freeman in 'Why It Remains Important to Take Children's Rights Seriously' (2007) comments that there:

> ... needs to be less emphasis on what these young persons know – less talk in other words of knowledge and understanding – and more on how the decision they have reached furthers their goals and coheres with their system of values. ... Merely imposing treatment on them, as had happened all-too-frequently, by itself achieves nothing in the long term. And we have to look at these decisions not just in terms of what impact they have on the young person in question, but with an understanding of what they say about our concept of childhood.

What do you think the decisions of the courts tell us about the concept of childhood?

vi. How might recognising the child's 'autonomy interest' itself be a means of recognising 'basic' and 'developmental' interests? (See, for example, Adler and Dearling (1986).)

vii. John Eekelaar (see p. 365 above) acknowledges the political implications of society recognising the developmental interests of children: how far is it possible to go, in a democracy?

The following case concerned similar facts to those in *Gillick*.

R (on the application of Axon) v Secretary of State for Health
[2006] EWHC 37 (Admin), [2006] 1 FCR 175

Silber J:

> ... there is nothing in this judgment, which is intended to encourage young people to seek or to obtain advice or treatment on any sexual matters without first informing their parents and discussing matters with them. Indeed, everybody must hope that all young people will discuss these sexual matters with their parents at the earliest opportunity. After all, the best judges of a young person's welfare are almost invariably his or her parents. ...

> ... the right of young people to make decisions about their own lives by themselves at the expense of the views of their parents has now become an increasingly important and accepted feature of family life. ... as a matter of principle, it is difficult to see why a parent should still retain an art 8 right to parental authority relating to a medical decision where the young person concerned *understands* the advice provided by the medical professional and its implications. ... Nevertheless, if I am wrong. ... I must still consider whether the Secretary of State can invoke the provisions of art 8(2).

In deciding that he can, Silber J referred to the high rates of teenage pregnancy in the UK, the 'clear evidence that confidentiality increases the use of contraceptive and abortion services for those under the age of sixteen' and 'the disturbing consequences of the young people being deterred from obtaining advice and treatment on sexual matters'.

QUESTIONS

i. Do you agree that parents are the best judges of a young person's welfare in sexual matters?

ii. Rachel Taylor (2007) argues that:

> The decision suggests that we are entering a period of respect for the rights and autonomy of teenagers ... but it is not clear whether the autonomy of teenagers will be given more respect where their choices conflict with the courts view of their welfare.

Where does the child's 'autonomy interest' now stand in the light of the above decisions. Is Silber J wrong about the Article 8 rights of parents?

In the cases above there is a conflict between the child's views and judicial, parental or medical assessments of the child's best interests. But a child's view may also conflict with the interests of other children.

R (on the application of Begum) v Headteacher and Governors of Denbigh High School [2006] UKHL 15, [2006] 2 WLR 719

Sabina Begum wanted to wear a jilbab (a garment that covers the entire body, except for hands, feet, face, and head). This was contrary to the school uniform policy and she declined to come to school rather than comply with the policy. She claimed that this was an unjustifiable interference with her right to manifest her religion under Article 9 (see p. 357 above). In determining the uniform policy, the school governors had consulted parents, students, staff and the Imams of the three local mosques. There was no objection to the shalwar kameeze (a smock-like dress with loose trousers) or the hijab (Islamic headscarf). The majority in the House of Lords, referring to employment law cases and the margin of appreciation permitted by the European Court of Human Rights over this issue, held that the school's decision did not interfere with her Article 9 right, but that if it did it was justified.

> **Lord Hoffman:**
> [50] ... Shabina's discovery that her religion did not allow her to wear the uniform she had been wearing for the past two years created a problem for her. Her family had chosen that school for her with knowledge of its uniform requirements. She could have sought the help of the school

and the local education authority in solving the problem. They would no doubt have advised her that if she was firm in her belief, she should change schools. ... Instead, she and her brother decided that it was the school's problem. They sought a confrontation and claimed that she had a right to attend the school of her own choosing in the clothes she chose to wear.

...

[64] In my opinion a domestic court should accept the decision of Parliament to allow individual schools to make their own decisions about uniforms. The decision does not have to be made at a national level and national differences between Turkey and the United Kingdom are irrelevant. In applying the principles of *Şahin v Turkey* [App No 44774/98] the justification must be sought at the local level and it is there that an area of judgment, comparable to the margin of appreciation, must be allowed to the school. ...

[65] In criticizing the school's decision, Miss Booth QC (who appeared for Shabina) said that the uniform policy was undermined by Muslim girls being allowed to wear headscarves. That identified them as Muslims and it would therefore make no difference if they could wear jilbabs. But that takes no account of the school's wish to avoid clothes which were perceived by some Muslims (rightly or wrongly) as signifying adherence to an extremist version of the Muslim religion and to protect girls against external pressures. These are matters which the school itself was in the best position to weigh and consider.

The minority (Baroness Hale of Richmond and Lord Nicholls of Birkenhead) held that it was an interference but that it was justified.

Baroness Hale of Richmond:

[92]... Most of your lordships take the view that Shabina Begum's right to manifest her religion was not infringed... It was she who had changed her mind about what her religion required of her, rather than the school which had changed its policy. I am uneasy about this. The reality is that the choice of secondary school is usually made by parents or guardians rather than by the child herself. The child is on the brink of, but has not yet reached, adolescence. She may have views but they are unlikely to be decisive. More importantly, she has not yet reached the critical stage in her development where this particular choice may matter to her.

[93] Important physical, cognitive and psychological developments take place during adolescence. Adolescence begins with the onset of puberty; from puberty to adulthood, the 'capacity to acquire and utilise knowledge reaches its peak efficiency'; and the capacity for formal operational thought is the forerunner to developing the capacity to make autonomous moral judgments. Obviously, these developments happen at different times and at different rates for different people. But it is not at all surprising to find adolescents making different moral judgments from those of their parents. It is part of growing up. The fact that they are not yet fully adult may help to justify interference with the choices they have made. It cannot be assumed, as it can with adults, that these choices are the product of a fully developed individual autonomy. But it may still count as an interference. I am therefore inclined to agree with my noble and learned friend, Lord Nicholls of Birkenhead, that there was an interference with Shabina Begum's right to manifest her religion.

[94] However, I am in no doubt that that interference was justified. It had the legitimate aim of protecting the rights and freedoms of others. The question is whether it was proportionate to that aim. This is a more difficult and delicate question in this case than it would be in the case of many similar manifestations of religious belief. If a Sikh man wears a turban or a Jewish man a yamoulka, we can readily assume that it was his free choice to adopt the dress dictated by the teachings of his religion. I would make the same assumption about an adult Muslim woman who

chooses to wear the Islamic headscarf. There are many reasons why she might wish to do this. As Yasmin Alibhai-Brown (*WHO do WE THINK we ARE?,* (2000), p 246) explains:

> 'What critics of Islam fail to understand is that when they see a young woman in a hijab she may have chosen the garment as a mark of her defiant political identity and also as a way of regaining control over her body.'

Bhikhu Parekh makes the same point (in 'A Varied Moral World, A Response to Susan Okin's "Is Multiculturalism Bad for Women"', *Boston Review*, October/November 1997):

> 'In France and the Netherlands several Muslim girls freely wore the hijab (headscarf), partly to reassure their conservative parents that they would not be corrupted by the public culture of the school, and partly to reshape the latter by indicating to white boys how they wished to be treated. The hijab in their case was a highly complex autonomous act intended to use the resources of the tradition both to change and to preserve it.'

...

[95] But it must be the woman's choice, not something imposed upon her by others. It is quite clear from the evidence in this case that there are different views in different communities about what is required of a Muslim woman who leaves the privacy of her home and family and goes out into the public world. There is also a view that the more extreme requirements are imposed as much for political and social as for religious reasons. If this is so, it is not a uniquely Muslim phenomenon. The Parekh Report on *The Future of Multi-Ethnic Britain* (Runnymede Trust 2000, at pp. 236–237, para 17.3), for example, points out that:

> 'In all traditions, religious claims and rituals may be used to legitimise power structures rather than to promote ethical principles, and may foster bigotry, sectarianism and fundamentalism. Notoriously, religion often accepts and gives its blessing to gender inequalities.'

Gita Saghal and Nira Yuval-Davis, discussing 'Fundamentalism, Multiculturalism and Women in Britain' (in *Refusing Holy Orders, Women and Fundamentalism in Britain*, (2000), p 14) argue that the effect of and on women is:

> '... central to the project of fundamentalism, which attempts to impose its own unitary religious definition on the grouping and its symbolic order. The "proper" behaviour of women is used to signify the difference between those who belong and those who do not; women are also seen as the "cultural carriers" of the grouping, who transmit group culture to the future generation; and proper control in terms of marriage and divorce ensures that children who are born to those women are within the boundaries of the collectivity, not only biologically but also symbolically.'

According to this view, strict dress codes may be imposed upon women, not for their own sake but to serve the ends of others. Hence they may be denied equal freedom to choose for themselves. They may also be denied equal treatment. A dress code which requires women to conceal all but their face and hands, while leaving men much freer to decide what they will wear, does not treat them equally. Although a different issue from seclusion, the assumption may be that women will play their part in the private domestic sphere while men will play theirs in the public world. Of course, from a woman's point of view, this may be a safer and more comfortable place to be....

[96] If a woman freely chooses to adopt a way of life for herself, it is not for others, including other women who have chosen differently, to criticise or prevent her. Judge Tulkens, in *Sahin v Turkey*, at p 46, draws the analogy with freedom of speech. The European Court of Human Rights has never accepted that interference with the right of freedom of expression is justified by the fact that the ideas expressed may offend someone. Likewise, the sight of a woman in full purdah may offend some people, and especially those western feminists who believe that it is a symbol of her oppression, but that could not be a good reason for prohibiting her from wearing it.

[97] But schools are different. Their task is to educate the young from all the many and diverse families and communities in this country in accordance with the national curriculum. Their task is to help all of their pupils achieve their full potential. This includes growing up to play whatever part they choose in the society in which they are living. The school's task is also to promote the ability of people of diverse races, religions and cultures to live together in harmony. Fostering a sense of community and cohesion within the school is an important part of that. A uniform dress code can play its role in smoothing over ethnic, religious and social divisions. But it does more than that. Like it or not, this is a society committed, in principle and in law, to equal freedom for men and women to choose how they will lead their lives within the law. Young girls from ethnic, cultural or religious minorities growing up here face particularly difficult choices: how far to adopt or to distance themselves from the dominant culture. A good school will enable and support them. This particular school is a good school: that, it appears, is one reason why Shabina Begum wanted to stay there. It is also a mixed school. That was what led to the difficulty. It would not have arisen in a girls' school with an all-female staff.
[98] In deciding how far to go in accommodating religious requirements within its dress code, such a school has to accommodate some complex considerations. These are helpfully explained by Professor Frances Radnay in 'Culture, Religion and Gender' [2003] 1 International Journal of Constitutional Law 663:

> '... A mandatory policy that rejects veiling in state educational institutions may provide a crucial opportunity for girls to choose the feminist freedom of state education over the patriarchal dominance of their families. Also, for the families, such a policy may send a clear message that the benefits of state education are tied to the obligation to respect women's and girls' rights to equality and freedom...On the other hand, a prohibition of veiling risks violating the liberal principle of respect for individual autonomy and cultural diversity for parents as well as students. It may also result in traditionalist families not sending their children to the state educational institutions. In this educational context, implementation of the right to equality is a complex matter, and the determination of the way it should be achieved depends upon the balance between these two conflicting policy priorities in a specific social environment.'

It seems to me that that was exactly what this school was trying to do when it devised the school uniform policy to suit the social conditions in that school, in that town, and at that time. Its requirements are clearly set out by my noble and learned friend, Lord Scott of Foscote, in para 76 of his opinion. Social cohesion is promoted by the uniform elements of shirt, tie and jumper, and the requirement that all outer garments be in the school colour. But cultural and religious diversity is respected by allowing girls to wear either a skirt, trousers, or the shalwar kameez, and by allowing those who wished to do so to wear the hijab. This was indeed a thoughtful and proportionate response to reconciling the complexities of the situation. This is demonstrated by the fact that girls have subsequently expressed their concern that if the jilbab were to be allowed they would face pressure to adopt it even though they do not wish to do so. Here is the evidence to support the justification which Judge Tulkens found lacking in the *Şahin* case.

QUESTIONS

i. Is this a case of judicial paternalism or, as Edwards in 'Imaging Islam ... of meaning and metaphor symbolizing the jilbab' (2007) argues, 'A disconcerting trend of religious intolerance dressed up as a benign state secularism justified in the name of harmony and the protection of the rights of others'? How else might you describe the decision?

ii. In *R (on the application of Lydia Playfoot (A Child) v Millais School Governing Body* [2007] EWHC 1698 (Admin), [2007] ELR 484, the decision of a school to refuse to permit a pupil to wear a purity ring as an expression of her Christian faith and sign of her belief in celibacy before marriage was held not to breach her rights under Article 9. The court held that the uniform policy was prescribed by law and served a number of important functions.

How would you balance the rights of the school, society and individual school pupils?

iii. In *Re (S) (A Child) (identification: Restrictions on Publication)* [2004] UKHL 47 the court held that a boy's right to privacy under Article 8 did not outweigh the rights of the press to report freely the details of his mother's trial for murder of his older brother. Lord Steyn commented that: 'Full contemporaneous reporting of criminal trials in progress promotes public confidence in the administration of justice. It promotes the values of the rule of law'. In the Court of Appeal Hale LJ observed that the trial judge:

> stated that he would have reached the same conclusion even if the child's welfare had been the paramount consideration. With the greatest of respect to him, I cannot understand this. If the child's welfare is the paramount consideration, then when everything else has been taken into account and weighed, it rules on or determines the issue before the court. It is the trump card.

Why did the paramountcy principle in section 1 of the Children Act 1989 not apply to this case? Do you think the rights of the child should always be balanced against the rights of others?

iv. Contrast *Re S* with the decision in *Re Roddy (a child) (identification: restriction on publication) Torbay Borough Council v News Group Newspapers* [2003] EWHC 2927 (Fam) [2004] 2 FLR 949. Here a 16-year-old mother wanted to tell to the press the story of the circumstances of her pregnancy at the age of thirteen, and, in particular, the role of the Roman Catholic Church, which had paid her not to have an abortion. Balancing the respective rights the court upheld an injunction in the interests of her child and the child's father. In what circumstances would you restrict the press reporting information about a child?

Re K (a child) (secure accommodation order: right to liberty) [2001] Fam 377, [2001] 2 All ER 719

The child was a 15-year-old boy, who had been showing disturbed behaviour since the age of two. Assessments suggested that he had learning difficulties, but that he was not mentally ill. In view of his aggressive and sexualised behaviour, he was considered to be extremely dangerous to other children, and also to staff involved in his care.

Thorpe LJ:

The first issue is... whether K has been deprived of his right to liberty guaranteed by art 5(1).

... As a matter of first impression the answer must be yes. Secure accommodation is defined in the section itself (Children Act 1989 s 25) as 'accommodation provided for the purpose of restricting liberty'. However the order authorising the restriction of K's liberty was made on the ground that, if kept in any other accommodation, he was likely to injure himself or other persons.

Thus the primary purpose of the restriction was protective, both of K and of others. ... Plainly not all restrictions placed on the liberty of children constitute deprivation. Obviously parents have a right and a responsibility to restrict the liberty of their children, not only for protective and corrective purposes, but also sometimes for a punitive purpose. So acting they only risk breaching a child's art 5(1) rights if they exceed reasonable bounds. The order...did not breach K's art 5 rights since the deprivation of liberty was a necessary consequence of an exercise of parental responsibility for the protection and promotion of his welfare.

QUESTIONS

i. What restrictions on a child's liberty would you consider to be within 'normal parental authority'?

ii. Should a father be able to prevent his daughter leaving the house, in order to stop her from meeting her boyfriend, or if he is concerned that she is taking drugs, or if he wants her to finish her homework? Practically, how could he prevent her leaving? Would your answers differ if she was eleven, fifteen or seventeen years old? Is it reasonable to expect a father to obtain a court order if he wants to restrict his child's liberty?

At the end of her judgment in *Re K* [2001], Dame Elizabeth Butler-Sloss P commented on the way in which the child had been given an opportunity to take part in the proceedings:

Having been assessed as having a mental age of eight, one might raise an eyebrow at his ability to give instructions and his separate representation at various proceedings including before this court. But there is no doubt that it has been very beneficial for him to be allowed to play a part, and to have some understanding of the legal procedures which have the effect of depriving him of his liberty. I should like to commend the local authority for its careful, conscientious and sensitive approach to this very difficult case and to ensuring that K has been able to play such a full part in it.

Does this suggest that there are other rights at stake when courts make decisions about a child? For example, is it necessary to consider whether the child has a right to participate by virtue of Article 6 of the European Convention (right to a fair trial) or Article 12 of the United Nations Convention on the Rights of the Child (see p. 383, below)? Are there any risks involved in allowing children to participate in legal proceedings?

Here we look at the extent to which the law treats children as adults in proceedings. (In Chapter 10 we look at the how the courts take into account their wishes and feelings in disputes between parents.)

The Children Act 1989 allows the child to make applications about his own care and upbringing. Usually he or she must first have leave.

Re SC (a minor) (leave to seek residence order)
[1994] 1 FLR 96, [1993] Fam Law 618

S was a 14-year-old girl who had been in the care of a local authority under a care order for eight years. She was living in a children's home and wanted to apply for an order that she should live with a friend's family who were willing to provide her with a home. The local authority did not know whether they would oppose the eventual application but did not oppose letting her apply; her mother opposed the application for leave.

Booth J:

... Mr Petrou, the solicitor instructed by S ... submitted that the first test which must be satisfied is that contained in s. 10(8) of the Act:

> 'Where the person applying for leave to make an application for a section 8 order is the child concerned, the court may only grant leave if it is satisfied that he has sufficient understanding to make the proposed application for the section 8 order.'

S approached Mr Petrou of her own initiative in February 1993. She has given him clear instructions and he assesses her to have a good understanding of the situation. She does not suffer from any psychiatric or mental disability. The issues to which the substantive application would give rise are not complex, and the mother does not contend that S could not properly deal with them.

In the circumstances I am satisfied that the child does have sufficient understanding to enable the court to grant her leave to make the application. It does not, however, follow that the court is bound to grant leave once the test of s. 10(8) is satisfied. The court still has a discretion whether or not to do so. Where the application is made by a child, no guidance is to be found in the Act or in the rules as to the matters which should be taken into account in the exercise of this discretion. Where the person applying for leave is not the child, s. 10(9) lists the matters to which the court must have particular regard. No equivalent check-list exists in the case of an application by the child.

... In my judgment it is right for the court to have regard to the likelihood of success of the proposed application and to be satisfied that the child is not embarking upon proceedings which are doomed to failure.

... Mr Petrou submits that the application for leave made by a child gives rise to a question with respect to the upbringing of the child and accordingly s. 1 of the Act applies.

That submission I am unable to accept. In *Re A (Minors) (Residence Order: Leave to Apply)* [1992] Fam 182, [1992] 2 FLR 154. ... Balcombe LJ said (at pp. 191G and 160D respectively):

> 'In granting or refusing an application for leave to apply for a s. 8 order, the court is not determining a question with respect to the upbringing of the child concerned. That question only arises when the court hears the substantive application. The reasoning of this court in *F v S (Adoption: Ward)* [1973] Fam 203, CA supports this conclusion.'

... In my judgment the court should not fetter the statutory ability of the child to seek any s. 8 order, including a residence order, if it is appropriate for such an application to be made. Although the court will undoubtedly consider why it is that the person in whose favour a proposed residence order would be made is not applying, it would in my opinion be wrong to import into the Act any requirement that only he or she should make the application.

QUESTION

Do you think the judge should hear the child before granting leave?

These are not the only circumstances in which a child may become a party to proceedings. A child may be given leave to make an application about herself or about another child; or become a respondent to proceedings brought by others; or, unusually, be made a party to the adults' disputes. A child party to family proceedings may sometimes be allowed to act for himself without a guardian or litigation friend. Mainly because of the last situation, rule 9.2A of the Family Proceedings Rules 1991, makes an exception to the usual rules about child parties to litigation.

Mabon v Mabon and others
[2005] EWCA Civ 634, [2005] 2 FLR 1011

This case concerned a residence dispute between the parents of three boys, aged respectively seventeen, fifteen and thirteen. The boys had sought to instruct solicitors to represent them. This was refused on the initial hearing.

His Honour Judge Dixon:

... I ask myself what advantages are to be gained from independent representation? I see none, save perhaps for the more articulate and elegant expression of what I already know. I ask myself what disadvantages will there be from independent representation? I see several. Delay from the prolongation of the proceedings, unquantifiable emotional damage from contact with the material in this case, and exposure to the harshness of the litigation process.

On appeal:

Thorpe LJ:

...

[25]... In our system we have traditionally adopted the tandem model for the representation of children who are parties to family proceedings, whether public or private. First the court appoints a guardian-ad-litem who will almost invariably have a social work qualification and very wide experience of family proceedings. He then instructs a specialist family solicitor who, in turn, usually instructs a specialist family barrister. This is a Rolls Royce model and is the envy of many other jurisdictions. However its overall approach is essentially paternalistic. The guardian's first priority is to advocate the welfare of the child he represents. His second priority is to put before the court the child's wishes and feelings. Those priorities can in some cases conflict. In extreme cases the conflict is unmanageable. That reality is recognised by the terms of r 9.2A. The direction set by r 9.2A(6) is a mandatory grant of the application provided that the court considers 'that the minor concerned has sufficient understanding to participate as a party in the proceedings concerned.' Thus the focus is upon the sufficiency of the child's understanding in the context of the remaining proceedings.

[26] In my judgment the rule is sufficiently widely framed to meet our obligations to comply with both art 12 of the United Nations Convention and art 8 of the ECHR, providing that judges correctly focus on the sufficiency of the child's understanding and, in measuring that sufficiency, reflect the extent to which, in the 21st Century, there is a keener appreciation of the autonomy of the child and the child's consequential right to participate in decision making processes that fundamentally affect his family life.

....

[28] The guidance given by this court in *Re S* [1993] Fam 263 on the construction of r 9.2A is now 12 years old. Much has happened in that time. Although the United Kingdom had ratified the UN

Convention some 15 months earlier, it did not have much impact initially and it is hardly surprising that it was not mentioned by this court. Although the tandem model has many strengths and virtues, at its heart lies the conflict between advancing the welfare of the child and upholding the child's freedom of expression and participation. Unless we in this jurisdiction are to fall out of step with similar societies as they safeguard art 12 rights, we must, in the case of articulate teenagers, accept that the right to freedom of expression and participation outweighs the paternalistic judgment of welfare.

[29] In testing the sufficiency of a child's understanding I would not say that welfare has no place. If direct participation would pose an obvious risk of harm to the child arising out of the nature of the continuing proceedings and, if the child is incapable of comprehending that risk, then the judge is entitled to find that sufficient understanding has not been demonstrated. But judges have to be equally alive to the risk of emotional harm that might arise from denying the child knowledge of and participation in the continuing proceedings.

...

[32] In conclusion this case provides a timely opportunity to recognise the growing acknowledgement of the autonomy and consequential rights of children, both nationally and internationally. The Rules are sufficiently robustly drawn to accommodate that shift. In individual cases trial judges must equally acknowledge the shift when they make in individual cases a proportionate judgment of the sufficiency of the child's understanding.

Wall LJ:

...

[37] In a paper entitled The Voice of the Child in Private Family Law proceedings in England and Wales... Professor Mervyn Murch, identified neatly the difficulties which the English legal system puts in the way of children's participation in the family law process. He said:

> '... notwithstanding the entrenchment of the welfare principle, traditionally under English law, children's futures have been decided on the views of adults, that is the parents and the professionals. ... The common law adversarial mode of trial which still forms the basis of our civil family proceedings, although modified and in continuous development, makes it difficult for all but the most confident and competent children to participate effectively.'

[38] An example of this difficulty, and one which perplexes our colleagues on the continent of Europe, is the reluctance of the English judge to talk to children in private. This reluctance has several origins, but one of them is undoubtedly rooted in the rules of evidence and the adversarial mode of trial. What is said in private by the child to the judge cannot be tested in evidence or in cross-examination. As a consequence, a judge in England and Wales cannot promise a child that any conversation with the child will be entirely confidential. That fact may inhibit children from expressing their true wishes and feelings to the judge in such circumstances – see, for example, *B v B (Minors) (Interviews and Listing Arrangements)* [1994] 2 FLR 489, [1994] 2 FCR 667.

...

[44] In these circumstances, I do not agree with the judge that the only advantage from independent representation was 'perhaps the more articulate and elegant expression of what I already know'. That analysis overlooks, in my judgment, the need for the boys on the facts of this particular case to emerge from the proceedings (whatever the result) with the knowledge that their position had been independently represented and their perspective fully advanced to the judge.

Appeal allowed.

QUESTIONS

i. Is the understanding required to make an application about yourself the same as the understanding required to conduct the proceedings by yourself?

ii. What legal advice would you give to (a) an 11-year-old boy who wanted to instruct his own lawyer in a bitterly contested dispute between his parents (b) a 12-year-old girl who had run away from home after an argument with her mother and wanted to live with her boy-friend's parents?

iii. If a brother and sister are living in separate households, and the sister is seeking contact with her brother, whose welfare would be paramount: the applicant, the child who is the subject of the application, or should the court be required to balance their interests? (See *Re S (Contact: Application by Sibling)* [1998] 2 FLR 897.)

iv. If a child is conducting the proceedings himself, should he be in court like any other party?

v. If the judge cannot promise the child confidentiality, can the CAFCASS officer do so? (See p. 501 below.)

vi. Section 122 of the Adoption and Children Act 2002 amended the Children Act 1989 to allow children to be separately represented in all private law cases (in line with public law proceedings). In *Separate Representation of Children* (DCA, 2006) the government suggests that such provision is only relevant for a small proportion of children. (For a critique of this, see Lord Justice Wall, 2007.)

To what extent do you think public resources should be made available to represent children? What criteria would you use?

8.4 THE UN CONVENTION ON THE RIGHTS OF THE CHILD

The courts increasingly refer to the UN Convention on the Rights of the Child. (For example, see *Williamson, Axon and Mabon* above.) It has three overriding themes: the child's best interests; respect for the child's evolving capacities; and protection against all forms of discrimination. The UK Government ratified the Convention in December 1991. It made reservations, as we shall see.

Philip Alston and Stephen Parker in their introductory essay to *Children, Rights and the Law* (1992) point to the extraordinary commitment to the convention:

> No other treaty, particularly in the human rights field, has been ratified by so many states in such an extraordinarily short period of time. The Convention has thus generated an unprecedented degree of formal commitment on the part of Governments and the task confronting children's rights advocates will be to ensure that this commitment is matched by action.

The following are the most important of its fifty-four articles:

> Article 3
>
> 1. In all actions concerning children, whether undertaken by public or private social welfare institutions, courts of law, administrative authorities or legislative bodies, the best interests of the child shall be a primary consideration.

Article 9

1. States Parties shall ensure that a child shall not be separated from his or her parents against their will, except when competent authorities subject to judicial review determine, in accordance with applicable law and procedures, that such separation is necessary for the best interests of the child. ...

Article 12

1. States Parties shall assure to the child who is capable of forming his or her own views the right to express those views freely in all matters affecting the child, the views of the child being given due weight in accordance with the age and maturity of the child.

Article 18

1. States Parties shall use their best efforts to ensure recognition of the principle that both parents have common responsibilities for the upbringing and development of the child. Parents or, as the case may be, legal guardians, have the primary responsibility for the upbringing and development of the child. The best interests of the child will be their basic concern.

QUESTIONS

i. Keep these articles in mind as we look at the provisions and implementation of the Children Act 1989, especially in Chapters 11 and 12. Do you think that English law falls short of or goes beyond the principles laid down in these articles?

ii. Boyden in 'Childhood and the Policy Makers' (1997) discusses a study by UNICEF about proposed legislation in the US that would ban importing of products from companies that employed children under the age of fifteen:

> The industry was found to be an important income source of for the families of child employees. ... The mere threat of the Bill lead to many thousands of children being removed from the garment sector. The study showed a sample of former garment children to be worse off than children still in the industry. ... None were attending school and many were involved in activities such as brick chipping and rickshaw pulling which are more hazardous than garment work. Children outside the industry suffered both acute and chronic illnesses at rates four times those of the children inside and ate less food which was of poorer quality.

Do you think concerns about child labour are just a western imposition?

iii. Bettina Cass in 'The Limits of the Public/Private Dichotomy' (1992) states that the Convention disaggregates the rights of children from the rights of 'families', to constitute children as independent actors with rights vis-à-vis their parents and vis-à-vis the state. She goes on to say that 'the very crux of the conservative ideology of family as unified, private and inviolate is exposed' by the Convention. Is that your view of a conservative ideology of the family? Is the Convention undermining any such ideology?

iv. Why do you think the United States of America has not ratified the Convention? (See Kilbourne, 1998).

There is a growing literature about the Convention. Frances Olsen (1992) discusses four different feminist approaches:

Reformist Approaches

Most of the legal reforms that have improved the role and status of women have taken place within a broad liberal legal reformist perspective. ...From such a perspective, rights for children, and specifically the United Nations Convention on the Rights of the Child, can be seen to have both positive and negative potentials.

Rights for women and children are usually seen as complementary, not as a zero sum game. The patriarchal family is generally understood to have denied rights to both women and children.

The legal and social treatment of women and of children during much of the past two or three centuries has been criticized as 'feudal'. Thus, the extension of rights to children is in one sense simply a more or less logical next step after the extension of rights to women.

Yet there are also less positive evaluations of the Convention on the Rights of the Child to be made from a feminist liberal reform perspective. One of the most significant of these concerns is whether the Convention may be used to control and confine women. Children, and the expressed interest in their welfare (expressed often by people who show no other interest in children) have often been used to control women...

Although the provisions making *both* parents responsible for children would seem to be generally beneficial to women, who otherwise too often wind up solely responsible for children, the provisions may also work against the interests of women as a group. It may well be that the obligations placed 'equally' upon fathers will turn out to be unenforceable as a practical matter, but that the provisions can be used by 'father's rights' groups, composed often of recently-divorced, angry and misogynistic men, to harass the women who are taking care of 'their' children. ...

Law as Patriarchy

... Cultural feminists criticize legal reformist demands for women's equality with men as settling for too little. Men do not represent an adequate aspiration. The greatest problem with society is not just the suppression of women, but the suppression of the values associated with women. Indeed, the effort to achieve legal and social equality could even contribute to the devaluation and suppression of those values.

... The primary evil of 'paternalistic' behaviour toward adults is really not that it treats an adult with the kind of care and concern that would be proper toward a child. As Onora O'Neill (1992) recognizes, the claim of fatherly concern by those exercising illegitimate power over women, minorities, colonial peoples, or other oppressed groups is generally not made in good faith but is 'highly political rhetoric'. The same kind of negative, bad faith 'paternalism' that oppresses adults is just as oppressive to children.

Feminist Critical legal Theory

A... dimension of the public/private distinction is the dichotomy between the 'private' family or domestic world, and the 'public' commercial world. A critical examination of this distinction allows us to 'denaturalize' the family, and to recognize the contingent character of family life. The Convention on the Rights of the Child is striking in its ability to bridge over different family forms found throughout the world. Someone whose only knowledge of life on earth came from a careful reading of the Convention would be puzzled by the occasional references to 'traditional practices' and 'those responsible for children' other than parents. Throughout most of the document, one would assume that all children were born into two-parent families that look a lot like the family of my first grade reader – Dick, Jane and Baby Sally, Mom baking cookies at home, Daddy coming home from the office in a nice suit and playing with the children.... The family is the private haven to which Dick and Jane return from the public world of school and Daddy from the public world of work. Baby Sally and Mom stay at home, non-productive. If Sally helps bake the cookies, we all know that this is not child labour.

Post-Modern Feminism

...The concerns of post-modern feminism that bear most closely on the Convention on the Rights of the Child include the whole notion of a universal document to deal with all children, throughout the world; the concern that such an effort will almost inevitably result in a western-oriented document that merely purports to be universal; and, more positively, the question of the category 'child' and the status of that category.

Universal standards have serious problems, however. One such problem is that they seem to overlook particular social meanings. The social meaning of a law forbidding abortion for sex selection, for example, is very different in India than in the United States. In the United States where there is no history of gender-specific abortion nor a realistic danger of the practice, such a law serves the purpose of chipping away at the woman's right to abortion by entitling the State to harass a woman with questions regarding why she is choosing to have an abortion. At some point, it may serve to drive women to overseas or back-alley abortions. In India, the meaning is different. There amniocentesis has been used specifically to determine the sex of a foetus and if the sex is female, the pregnancy is in most instances terminated. Moreover, in India the abortion decision is all too often forced upon women by their families.

In contrast to Olsen, Geraldine Van Bueren (1996) is supportive of the Convention:

The Convention... has been criticised because it appears to place duties directly on individuals, thereby confusing the nature of duties and international law. However, such criticism fails to understand that... family responsibilities and rights are interconnected like a double helix.

She continues:

By incorporating a reference to 'all matters affecting the child' there is no longer a traditional area of exclusive parental or family decision-making. Similarly by referring to two criteria of equal value, the age and maturity of the child, States Parties do not have an unfettered discretion as to when to consider and when to ignore the views of children when children disagree with the traditional family decision-makers. Hence the participation rights of children, which are essential to child empowerment, are consistent with the ideological basis of the Convention on the Rights of the Child which is based upon the principle that children have rights which 'transcend those of the family of which they are part.'

Despite being in force less than five years articles 12 and 13 of the Convention on the Rights of the Child have already had a significant impact on domestic family legislative policies.

A third approach is taken by Michael King (1994). He suggests that both the detractors and the supporters concentrate their minds on policy and the philosophical aspects of rights for children. He offers a different analysis, drawing on 'autopoietic theory':

Among all the prevailing images of 'the child', it is the child-as-victim which dominates the Convention. As we move from the national to the international stage, however, it is not evil individuals who are seen as the instigators and perpetuators of crimes against children, but the generalised scourges of injustice, intolerance, inequality and failure to respect fundamental human rights and dignity. The preamble to the Convention asks us to 'bear in mind' that 'the child by reason of his physical and mental immaturity, needs special safeguards and care, including appropriate legal protection' and recognise that 'in all countries of the world there are children living in difficult conditions and such children need special consideration.' It recognises also 'the importance of international cooperation for improving the living conditions in every country, in particular in developing countries.'

... The phenomenon of the campaign by adults for children's rights may seem, at first sight, a strange one. On a rather simplistic psychological level, it may be explainable by the fact that many adults who have suffered as children wish to prevent future generations from having similar experiences. More sophisticated sociological explanations have pointed to the relatively recent social construction of the parent-child relationship as a combination of strong emotional bonds with due recognition of the child's autonomy. This autonomy is sustained and given a public form through the notion of children's rights. As a philosophical and political phenomenon, the rights perspective owes much to Kantian rationality, social hygienics and liberal theories of justice. It proceeds as if children represent an oppressed group, who are likely to suffer hardship, exploitation and lack of respect for their dignity as human beings and of their capacity for self-determination. Children are, in other words, denied those rights which would, if granted, reduce their suffering and enhance their dignity and allow them to seize some control over their own lives. They have no way of achieving these objectives unless rights are granted to them. As Onora O'Neill (1992) points out, however, the logic that is relevant to the provision of rights for oppressed *adult* groups – that the notion of rights provides the necessary capacity and rhetoric for such groups to exert the necessary 'pressure from below' and so improve their situation – does not apply or applies only to a limited degree to children. 'Childhood,' she explains, is a stage of life from which children normally emerge and are helped and urged to emerge by those who have power over them. Those with power over children's lives usually have some interest in ending childish dependence. Oppressors usually have an interest in maintaining the oppression of social groups. ... The introduction into international law of the 'manifesto rights' or 'dignified statements' about interests of and 'pious hopes' for children is clearly seen by the promoters of the Convention as the first stage in a process of taking children's rights seriously. It is certainly true that the Convention is likely to have the effect of drawing the attention of governments and the mass media of post-industrial Western societies to the needs of children as a weak, vulnerable and sensitive group and to the harms that they may suffer if those needs are not met.

It is no startling conclusion to suggest that at the level of international law the mechanisms do not exist to force governments to comply with the demands which may involve the massive redeployment of resources and major changes in policy. Nor is it particularly surprising if we find that, at the level of individual states, campaigns for substantive rights for children may become obstructed by government inertia, poverty or indifference. What autopoietic theory is able to add, however, is the image of demands for substantive rights for children being reconstructed as legal communications which governments are then able to respond to and operate upon within the closed system of law and so avoid the complexities and, at times, embarrassment that these demands generate.

Reconstructing children's rights as law has the additional advantage for governments and the United Nations of giving the impression that something is being done for the children of the world. In its communications, the legal system provides society with an image of law as capable of providing order and structure in an unruly and disordered world. The United Nations in its Convention on the Rights of the Child offers us a vision of a three-tiered hierarchy consisting of international law at the top, state law in the middle, and those national institutions, agencies and organisations concerned with child protection and welfare at the bottom. In the exhortations to national governments to 'assure,' 'promote,' 'encourage,' 'undertake,' 'provide,' 'respect,' 'use their best efforts' and 'take all appropriate legislative, social and educational measures,' and in the impressive tally of countries that have ratified the Convention, the impression is conveyed of a direct line of command (or at least strong influence), from the United Nations to nation-state to citizen. As we have seen, this impression bears little relation to any realities except those created by law.

Any false hopes generated by the Convention are nobody's fault. One cannot blame those advocates of children's rights, stirred into action by the spectacle of widespread child suffering and the powerlessness of children in the face of adult tyranny, insensitivity or indifference, for being carried away on the magic carpet of excessive optimism. It was not they who misled us into believing that the law was capable of improving children's lives by the imposition of legal order, but law itself. They were themselves misled. Their hopes arose from a genuine misreading of the nature of law and legal operations. To enter into and operate within the communicative world of law is to talk and think like a lawyer, that is to commit oneself increasingly to a belief in law's version of the social universe where political, economic and moral statements are all represented as amenable to direct legal transformation and to enforcement by law. At times when people are reeling from the uncertainties and insecurities created by global political and economic upheavals of enormous proportions law's vision of itself and of society may prove particularly attractive. To see children, the hope for the future, as protected and respected for their human attributes by an all-embracing legal order, which offers them rights, is to give the impression that the rational control of that future is within our grasp, if only we were to take seriously children's rights, now reconstructed by law, by believing in them and their magic.

QUESTIONS

i. Which if any of these various approaches do you support? Are they inconsistent with each other?

ii. How does O'Neill's argument that children 'grow up' limit the use of rights. What is the difference between children's rights and human rights?

In their 2007 report to the UN, the Children's Rights Alliance for England made the following summary:

> The UK has the fourth richest economy in the world. We should be a world leader in implementing the UNCRC. But there are still far too many areas where insufficient or no progress has been made. With the UN Committee's next examination of the UK now less than a year away, we focus in this report on some of the worst aspects of children's human rights in England today.
>
> ### Resistance to a Rights-Based Approach
>
> CRAE very much welcomed the appointment in this year of Ed Balls as the first Children's Secretary, and the establishment of new government machinery working for children. However, just five days before the government submitted its children's rights report to the UN Committee, Ed Balls announced the development of a Children's Plan without any mention of the UNCRC. Why are Ministers still silent on children's human rights? How can a government that has put children centre stage be so insulated from the commitment and change that children's rights bring? ... Where children uniquely experience unfair treatment – in schools, for example, where they still have no legal rights to be consulted and no independent right to appeal exclusions or to opt in or out of religious or sex education – it is hard to convince Ministers of the need to act.
>
> We believe that the failure to take a rights-based approach is a fatal flaw, making it impossible for Government to tackle entrenched inequalities. There remain several key areas where the UK continues to badly fail children.
>
> ### Children in Conflict With the Law
>
> We are the biggest child incarcerators in Western Europe: this year the Youth Justice Board (YJB) admitted even its paltry target to reduce the child custody population by 10 per cent by 2008 is unachievable. Why?
>
> In the very same month that Ministers sent their report to the UN in Geneva, they approved regulations that permit staff in privately run child prisons to use painful nose, rib and thumb 'distraction' techniques to achieve good order and discipline. This effectively introduces corporal punishment into secure training centres – places of detention for children as young as 12. ...
>
> ### Failure to Abolish 'Reasonable Punishment' Defence
>
> ... Seventeen European countries have already given children full legal protection. We were the last country in Europe to ban teachers from using corporal punishment; we should not be the last to fully protect children in the home.
>
> ### Failure to Protect Asylum Seeking Children
>
> This year the chasm between two different groups of children in care grew wider. ... Asylum seeking families still receive much less in the way of benefits than other destitute families, and the

healthy start scheme introduced this year – providing fruit and vegetables to young children – is withheld from asylum seeking families.

Growing Inequality – A Rights Issue

The NCRC covers the full breadth of human rights, going beyond the civil and political rights contained in the European Convention on Human Rights ... it demands that States Parties use the maximum resources available to improve the well being of all children. The consensus is that about £4 billion a year more is needed to reach Labour's 2010 target of halving child poverty. We can afford this....

A baby boy born in Manchester has a life average expectancy of 72.8 years compared with the 82.8 years that a baby boy born in Kensington and Chelsea can expect to enjoy – a difference of 10 years (for girls the difference is 8.3 years between Liverpool and Kensington and Chelsea).

Time to Turn Things Around

... In 2002, world leaders gathered in New York to pledge to make a world fit for children, based on the UNCRC provisions. Gordon Brown urged a global 'partnership for children so wide, so powerful and so determined that no obstacle should be allowed to impede its path or progress'. CRAE is part of this global partnership and we demand much more for the children and young people of this country.

Jane Fortin (2002) says this about the difficulties of enforcement of the UN Convention:

It was hoped that the obligation on ratifying countries to produce periodic reports to the UN Committee and the knowledge that they would be subjected to criticisms would encourage states to implement the UNCRC effectively. Countries are expected to be candid over any difficulties they have in reaching the standards required. Unfortunately, the overall impression created by the UK's first and second reports to the Committee on the Rights of the Child is that the Government is relatively untroubled by fear of criticism by the UN Committee. A cynic might argue that a casual approach to the UNCRC will continue until there are improved enforcement procedures. Its lack of teeth means that, in reality, it is legally unenforceable. Its impact would be strengthened significantly were enforcement procedures to be grafted on to it. This would bring the UNCRC in line with the African Charter on the Rights and Welfare of the Child, which incorporates the right of individual petition for all children.

QUESTIONS

i. What are the areas of family law, other than those where there are reservations, which in your opinion most fall short of the principles of the Convention?

ii. Articles 10, 22 and 40 of the Convention concern immigration, refugee children, and juvenile justice. Does it surprise you to be told that the UK Government has entered reservations to all three of the above articles? Why do you think it has done so?

iii. What happens if the UK Government fails to live up to its obligations under the Convention?

iv. Do you think that the lack of effective enforcement might be one of the reasons why so many countries were prepared to sign up for the convention in the first place?

v. After much resistance Children's Commissioners have been established for Wales (2001), Northern Ireland (2003), Scotland (2004) and England (2005). In England the general function of the Commissioner is to promote 'awareness of the views and *interests* of children' (Children Act 2004 section 2(1)) whereas the other commissioners are required to promote and safeguard their *rights*. What is the difference, and does it matter?

vi. Clucas (2005) argues that powers of the Commissioner are so limited that what ought to have been a 'a cause for celebratory fireworks ... more nearly resembles a damp squid'. Take a look at the Commissioners' website: http://www.childrenscommissioner.org.uk/index.html. What do you think?

8.5 PARENTAL RESPONSIBILITY

The Children Act 1989 introduced the concept of 'parental responsibility', defining it as follows:

> **3.**—(1) In this Act 'parental responsibility' means all the rights, duties, powers, responsibilities and authority which by law a parent of a child has in relation to the child and his property...

The reasons for what might be thought a purely cosmetic change appear in the Law Commission's Report on *Guardianship and Custody* (1988):

Parental Responsibility

> 2.4 Scattered through the statute book at present are such terms as 'parental rights and duties' or the 'powers and duties', or the 'rights and authority' of a parent. However, in our first Report on Illegitimacy we expressed the view that 'to talk of parental 'rights' is not only inaccurate as a matter of juristic analysis but also a misleading use of ordinary language.' The House of Lords, in *Gillick* [see p. 367 above]...has held that the powers which parents have to control or make decisions for their children are simply the necessary concomitant of their parental duties. To refer to the concept of 'right' in the relationship between parent and child is therefore likely to produce confusion, as that case itself demonstrated. As against third parties, parents clearly have a prior claim to look after or have contact with their child but, as the House of Lords has recently pointed out in *Re KD (A Minor) (Ward: Termination of Access)* [1988] AC 806, [1988] 1 All ER 577, HL, that claim will always be displaced if the interests of the child indicate to the contrary. The parental claim can be recognised in the rules governing the allocation of parental responsibilities, but the content of their status would be more accurately reflected if a new concept of 'parental responsibility' were to replace the ambiguous and confusing terms used at present. Such a change would make little difference in substance but it would reflect the everyday reality of being a parent and emphasise the responsibilities of all who are in that position. ...

2.5 One further advantage is that the same concept could then be employed to define the status of local authorities when children have been compulsorily committed to their care. The reports of the inquiries into the deaths of Jasmine Beckford and Tyra Henry indicate how helpful this would be in emphasising the continuing parental responsibility of the local authority even if the child has been allowed to live at home.

QUESTIONS

i. What do you think the Commission meant when they argued that the concept of parental 'responsibility' would 'reflect the everyday reality of being a parent'?
ii. Provide examples of a parental 'duty', 'right', 'power' and 'responsibility'.

In 'Parental Responsibility: State of Nature or Nature of the State?' (1991) John Eekelaar pointed out that the concept of parental responsibility can be used in two rather different senses:

It was...in the context of appreciation that parental 'rights' needed to be exercised for the benefit of the child that the Law Commission (1982) first suggested that it might be more appropriate to talk about parental responsibilities than parental rights. ... The shift in terminology reflects...the conception of 'parental responsibilities' recommended by the Committee of Ministers of the Council of Europe in 1984 (Recommendation No. R(84)4, February 28, 1984), which states that 'parental responsibilities are a collection of duties and powers which aim at ensuring the moral and material welfare of the child, in particular by taking care of the person of the child, by maintaining personal relationships with him and by providing for his education, maintenance, his legal representation and the administration of his property.' I shall refer to this sense of 'responsibility' as *responsibility (1)*.

However, also in paragraph 1.11 of its 1985 Working Paper, the Commission introduced a different concept of responsibility. 'Further,' they wrote, 'to the extent that the law enables parents to decide how to bring up their children without interference from others or from the state, it does so principally because this is a necessary part of the parents' responsibility for that upbringing and in order thus to promote the welfare of their children'. 'Responsibility' does not here refer to the way in which a parent behaves *towards* his child (as is reflected in the references to duties and supervision over parental conduct made earlier) but rather to a role which is to be exercised by the parent rather than some other entity. Of course, the assumption of responsibility for a child in this sense is not necessarily inconsistent with the presence of duties towards the child (as we shall see, it is sometimes thought that it encourages their performance). But the focus is not upon those duties but rather upon the distance between the parent and others in making provision for the child; indeed, on the degree of *freedom* given to parents in bringing up their children. And the more scope that is given to parental autonomy, the less room there is for external supervision over the way duties (under *responsibility (1)*) towards children are discharged. This will be referred to as *responsibility (2)*.

QUESTIONS

i. As various provisions of the Children Act 1989 appear, try to identify whether they owe more to responsibility (1) or responsibility (2).

ii. The Children (Scotland) Act 1995, section 1(1) provides a fuller list of parental responsibilities:

> (a) to safeguard and promote the child's health, development and welfare;
> (b) to provide in a manner appropriate to the child's stage of development, direction and guidance to the child;
> (c) if not living with the child, to maintain personal relations and direct contact with the child on a regular basis. . . .

Furthermore, section 2(1) of the Act provides that, in order to meet their responsibilities, parents have the *right* to have the child living with them, or otherwise to regulate the child's residence, to control, direct or guide in a manner appropriate to the stage of development of the child, the child's upbringing.
Do you prefer the English or the Scottish approach?
iii. Is parental responsibility primarily a 'status' or an 'activity'?

The Anti-Social Behaviour Act 2003 makes parents more responsible for their children's crimes and misdemeanours. This Act builds on the Crime and Disorder Act 1998 which introduced parenting orders. These compel parents to attend counselling or guidance programmes and, as a result of the 2003 Act, these can now take the form of a residential course.

Kathryn Hollingsworth comments on these developments in 'Responsibility and Rights: Children and their Parents in the Youth Justice System' (2007):

> A large amount of criticism has been directed towards the Labour Government's attempts to increase parental responsibility within the youth justice context. ... They highlight the inappropriateness of using criminal law mechanisms to coerce 'good parenting', the increased likelihood of family conflict, the targeting of particular social groups for increased social control, the displacement of the state's responsibility towards children, and the (mis)use of the law as part of a normative project to re-moralize the family and mould images of 'good' parenting.
>
> However, criticism is also due on a conceptual level ... it should be recognized that where parents are held accountable in an evaluative and explanatory sense this is not a form of criminal legal liability, but a way of enforcing the parent's role responsibility *to their child.* Parental responsibility should not be used as a mask to control and police the activities of children but to support them. As such, it is inappropriate to use the criminal justice sphere to coerce or encourage certain types of parenting. But as long as the current scheme is in place, then greater consideration must be given to the impact this has on parental and child autonomy rights and on the Article 6 ECHR rights of the parent and child.

QUESTIONS

i. In *Barnfather v London Borough of Islington Education Authority and the Secretary of State for Education and Skills* [2003] ELR 263 the court, with some reluctance, held that the strict liability nature of the offence under section 444 of the Education Act 1996 of failing to secure that a child attendance at school did not infringe the parents' right to a fair trial under Article 6 of the European Convention. However, Elias J held that:

> [T]here is nonetheless a real stigma attached to being found guilty of a criminal offence of this nature. It suggests either a indifference to one's children, or incompetence at parenting, which in the case of the blameless parent will be unwarranted ... justice is not served by prosecuting the innocent (para 57).

To what extent should a parent be held responsible for a child's behaviour? Is holding a parent responsible for the behaviour of a teenager compatible with the decision in *Gillick* that the 'parental right yields to the child's right to make his own decisions when he reaches a sufficient understanding and intelligence'.

ii. Helen Reece in 'From Parental Responsibility to Parenting Responsibly' (2006) argues that:

> Parental responsibility as authority was clear-cut: either the responsible parent fulfilled his or her responsibility or in extreme cases the responsibility was removed. But now that responsibility has become an attitude for which the parent is held to account,... The shift in the meaning of parental responsibility enables the law to be uniquely intrusive and judgmental, because every parent, on being held up to scrutiny, is found lacking.

Has the introduction of parenting orders changed the legal meaning of parental responsibility?

Section 2 of the Children Act 1989 makes clear that 'more than one person may have parental responsibility for the same child at the same time' (section 2(5)) and that 'where more than one person has parental responsibility for a child, each of them may act alone and without the other (or others) in meeting that responsibility' (section 2(7)).

These provisions are explained in the Law Commission's Report (1988):

(B) The Power to Act Independently

2.10... We believe it important to preserve the equal status of parents and their power to act independently of one another unless and until a court orders otherwise. This should be seen as part of the general aim of encouraging both parents to feel concerned and responsible for the welfare of their children. A few respondents suggested that they should have a legal duty to consult one another on major matters in their children's lives, arguing that this would increase parental co-operation and involvement after separation or divorce. This is an objective which we all share. However, whether or not the parents are living together, a legal duty of consultation seems both unworkable and undesirable. The person looking after the child has to be able to take decisions in the child's best interests as and when they arise. Some may have to be taken very quickly. In reality... it is that person who will have to put those decisions into effect and that person who has the degree of practical control over the child to be able to do so. The child may well suffer if that parent is prevented by the other's disapproval and thus has to go to court to resolve the matter, still more if the parent is inhibited by the fear that the other may disapprove or by the difficulties of contacting him or of deciding whether what is proposed is or is not a major matter requiring consultation. In practice, where the parents disagree about a matter of upbringing the burden should be on the one seeking to prevent a step which the other is proposing, or to impose a course of action which only the other can put into effect, to take the matter to court. ...

(C) The Effect of Court Orders

2.11 Allied to this is the principle that parents should not lose their parental responsibility even though its exercise may have to be modified or curtailed in certain respects, for example if it is necessary to determine where a child will live after his parents separate. Obviously, a court order to that effect will put many matters outside the control of the parent who does not have the child with him. However, parents should not be regarded as losing their position, and their ability to take decisions about their children, simply because they are separated or in dispute with one another about a particular matter. Hence they should only be prevented from acting in ways which would be incompatible with an order made about the child's upbringing. If, for example, the child has to live with one parent and go to a school near home, it would be incompatible with that order for the other parent to arrange for him to have his hair done in a way which will exclude him from the school. It would not, however, be incompatible for that parent to take him to a particular sporting occasion over the weekend, no matter how much the parent with whom the child lived might disapprove. These principles form part of our general aim of 'lowering the stakes' in cases of parental separation and divorce, and emphasising the continued responsibility of both parents. ...

QUESTIONS

i. Does section 2(7) of the Children Act 1989 mean that one parent can change the child's school without consulting the other parent? To what extent should the views of the resident parent with responsibility for ensuring the child's day-to-day attendance at school take precedence? Contrast *Re A (children) (specific issue order: parental dispute)* [2001] 1 FLR 210 with *Re W (children) (education: choice of school)* [2002] EWCA Civ 1411.

ii. In *Re J (child's religious upbringing and circumcision)* [2000] 1 FCR 307, Dame Elizabeth Butler-Sloss P said:

> There is, in my view, a small group of important decisions made on behalf of a child which, in the absence of agreement of those with parental responsibility, ought not to be carried out or arranged by a one-parent carer although she has parental responsibility under s 2(7) of the Children Act 1989. Such a decision ought not to be made without the specific approval of the court. Sterilisation is one example. The change of a child's surname is another. Some of the examples, including the change of a child's surname, are based upon statute (see s 13(1) of the 1989 Act).
>
> The issue of circumcision has not, to my knowledge, previously been considered by this court, but in my view it comes within that group. The decision to circumcise a child on grounds other than medical necessity is a very important one; the operation is irreversible, and should only be carried out where the parents together approve of it or, in the absence of parental agreement, where a court decides that the operation is in the best interests of the child. This requirement for a determination by the court should also apply to a local authority with parental responsibility under a care order.

Does sterilisation require court approval only where there is no parental agreement, or is court approval required in all cases? What do male circumcision and changing the child's surname have in common, apart from being in this special category? Would you include anything else in this category?

iii. In *Re S (specific issue order: religion: circumcision)* [2004] EWHC 1282 (Fam) [2005] 1 FLR 236 a mother applied for permission for her children to become practising members of the Islamic faith and for her son to be circumcised. The mother was concerned that if the children were not raised as Muslims she, and possibly her entire family, would be expelled from the religious community. The father, who was Hindu, objected and expressed concern that if the children were raised as Muslims he would lose contact with them and they would lose their freedom of choice.

The court rejected the application and the judge commented that children of mixed heritage should be able to decide for themselves.

Should the views of the children only be relevant when parents disagree?

iv. In *Re C (welfare of child: immunisation)* [2003] 2 FLR 1054 the father applied to the court to ensure that his children received the MMR immunisation against the wishes of the mother, who alleged that the father's application was motivated solely by a desire to exert control over her. After a lengthy consideration of the expert medical evidence Sumner J ordered the immunisation.

Do you think parents should have the right not to immunise their children? Where the matter is, as Sumner J accepted in this case, 'a subject of genuine debate', should the decision be left to the parent with day-to-day care? What is the relevance of the mother's rights under Article 8 of the European Convention of Human Rights?

v. The radical children's rights liberationist John Holt (1975) argued that children are often little more than a 'super-pet'. Do you believe that parents are for children, rather than children for parents? Do you consider that the law, as it now is, supports your belief?

BIBLIOGRAPHY

8.1 Parental rights and children's welfare

We quoted from:

W. Blackstone, *Commentaries on the Laws of England* (1st edn, 1765) Oxford, Clarendon Press, book 1, 434–435, 440–441.

M. Freeman, 'Feminism and Child Law', in J. Bridgeman and D. Monk (eds), *Feminist Perspectives on Child Law* (Cavendish, 2000) 27.

J. Herring. 'Farewell Welfare?' (2005) 27(2) *Journal of Social Welfare and Family Law* 159–171.

Royal College of Paediatrics and Child Health, 'Withholding or Withdrawing Life Saving Treatment in Children: A Framework for Practice' (2004), paras 2.3.2.13 and 2.7.3.

Additional reading

C. Bridge, 'Religion, culture and conviction – the medical treatment of young children' (1999) 11 *Child and Family Law Quarterly* 1.

J. Eekelaar, 'Beyond the Welfare Principle' (2002) 14(3) *Child and Family Law Quarterly* 237.

H. Reece, 'Paramountcy Principle: Consensus or Construct?' (1996) 49 *Current Legal Problems* 267.

S. Sheldon and S. Wilkinson (2001) 'On the sharpest horns of dilemma: *Re A (Conjoined Twins)*' 9 *Medical Law Review* 201–207.

8.2 Parental autonomy and the Human Rights Act 1998

We quoted from:

Anon., 'Mental Hospitalisation of Children and the Limits of Parental Authority' (1978) 88 *Yale Law Journal* 186, 194–208.

A. Bainham, 'Children: the modern law' [2005] 3rd edn *Family Law* at 694.

J. Brophy, 'Diversity and Child Protection', [2003] *Family Law* at 674.

H.M. Enzensberger *Political Crumbs* (1990), London, Verso at 100.

J. Fortin, 'Accommodating Children's Rights in a Post Human Rights Act Era' (2006) *Modern Law Review* 69(3): 299–326, at 300.

T. Hammerberg, 'Child Offenders: UK and International Practice' (1995) *The Howard League* 21.

NSPCC/CARE, 'The Use of Restraint in Secure Training Centres: Written Evidence to the Parliamentary Joint Committee on Human Rights' (2007) http://www.nspcc.org.uk/Inform/policyandpublicaffairs/Westminster/nspcc_crae_jchrresponse_sirestraint_wdf51360.pdf.

F. Olsen, 'The Myth of State Intervention in the Family' (1984) *University of Michigan Journal of Law Reform* 835, at 837, 846.

A. Scolnicov 'The Child's Right to Religious Freedom and Formation of Identity' (2007) 15 *International Journal of Children's Rights* 251–267 at 259–260.

M. Wald, 'Children's Rights: A Framework for Analysis', (1979) 12 *University of California Davis Law Review* 225, at 272.

J. Williams, 'Incorporating children's rights: the divergence in law and policy' (2007) 27(2) *Legal Studies* 261–287, at 270.

C. Willow and T. Hyder, *It hurts you inside — children talking about smacking* (1998) Save the Children UK/NCB.

Additional reading

J. Fortin, 'Children's rights and the use of physical force' (2001) 13 *Child and Family Law Quarterly* 243.

J. Masson, 'Securing human rights for children and young people in secure accommodation' (2002) *Child and Family Law Quarterly* 77: 14.

D. Monk, 'Problematising Home Education: Challenging "parental rights" and "socialization"' (2004) 24(4) *Legal Studies* 568–598.

J. O'Neill, *The Missing Child in Liberal Theory* (1994) Toronto University Press, Toronto.

8.3 Children's rights

We quoted from:

J. Eekelaar, 'The Emergence of Children's Rights' (1986) 6 *Oxford Journal of Legal Studies* 161, 169–174, 176, 180–182.

S. Edwards, 'Imaging Islam ... of meaning and metaphor symbolizing the jilbab' (2007) *Child and Family Law Quarterly*, 19(2): 247–268, at 268.

M. Freeman, 'Rethinking *Gillick*' (2005) 27(2) *Journal of Social Welfare and Family Law* 159–171, at 160.
M. Freeman, 'Why It Remains Important to Take Children's Rights Seriously' (2007) 15 *International Journal of Children's Rights* 5–23.
H. Rodham, 'Children under the law' (1973) 43(4) *Harvard Educational Review* 487.
R. Taylor, 'Reversing the retreat from *Gillick?*' (2007) 19(1) *Child and Family Law Quarterly* 81–97.
V. Walkerdine, 'Developmental psychology and the study of childhood' in Mary Jane Kehily (ed.), *An Introduction to Childhood Studies*, (2004) Open University Press, 101–102.
Lord Justice Wall, 'Separate Representation of Children' (2007) *Family Law* 124–129.

Additional reading

R. Adler and A. Dearling, 'Children's Rights: A Scottish Perspective' in B. Franklin (ed.), *The Rights of Children* (1986) Oxford, Basil Blackwell.
P. Alderson, J. Hawthorne, and M. Killen, 'The Participation Rights of Premature Babies' (2005) 13 *International Journal of Children's Rights*, 31–50.
D. Archard, *Children: Rights and Childhood* (2004) Routledge.
G. Douglas, M. Murch, C. Miles and L. Scanlan, *Research into the Operation of Rule 9.5 of the Family Proceedings Rules 1991* (DCA, 2006).
H. Fenwick, 'Clashing Rights, the Welfare of the Child and the Human Rights Act' (2004) *Modern Law Review* 67(6): 889–927.
B. Franklin (ed.) *The New Handbook of Children's Rights* (2001) Routledge.
M. Idriss '*Laicite* and the Banning of the "*hijab*" in France' 25(2) *Legal Studies* (2005) 260–295.
A. James and A. Prout (eds.), *Constructing and Reconstructing Childhood* (2nd edn.) (1997) London, Falmer.
N. Lee, *Childhood and Society* (2001) Buckingham, Open University Press.
D. Monk, 'Children's rights in education: making sense of contradictions' (2002) 14(1) *Child and Family Law Quarterly* 45–56.
M. Murch, 'The Voice of the Child in Private Law Proceedings in England and Wales' [2005] *International Family Law* 8.

8.4 The UN Convention on the Rights of the Child

We quoted from:

P. Alston and S. Parker, 'Introduction' in P. Alston, S. Parker and J. Seymour (eds), *Children, Rights and the Law* (1992) Oxford, Clarendon Press, p. viii.
J. Boyden, 'Childhood and the Policy Makers: A Comparative Study on the Globalization of Childhood', in A. James and A. Prout (eds) *Constructing and Reconstructing Childhood* (2nd edn.) (1997) London, Falmer, at 221–222.
B. Cass, 'The Limits of the Public/Private Dichotomy: A Comment on Coady & Coady' in P. Alston, S. Parker and J. Seymour (eds), *Children, Rights and the Law* (1992) Oxford, Clarendon Press, p. 140.
Children's Rights Alliance for England (2007), *State of Children's Rights in England* (Number 5) at 9–10 (see http://www.crae.org.uk).
B. Clucas, 'The Children's Commissioner for England: The Way Forward?' [2005] *Family Law* 290 at 293.

J. Fortin, 'Children's Rights and the Impact of Two International Conventions' in Thorpe LJ and C. Cowton (eds), (2002) *Delight and Dole*, Family Law.

M. King, 'Children's Rights as Communication: Reflections on Autopoietic Theory and the United Nations Convention' (1994) 57 *Modern Law Review* 385, at 388–389, 392, 400–401.

F. Olsen, 'Children's Rights: Some Feminist Approaches to the United Nations Convention on the Rights of the Child' in P. Alston, S. Parker and J. Seymour (eds), *Children, Rights and the Law* (1992) Oxford, Clarendon Press, pp. 195–216.

G. Van Bueren, 'The Challenges for the International Protection of Family Members' Rights as the 21st Century Approaches' in N. Lowe and G. Douglas (eds), *Frontiers of Family Law* (1996) The Hague, Martinus Nijhoff Publishers.

Additional reading

D. Buss, '"How the UN stole Childhood?": the Christian Right and the International Rights of the Child', in J. Bridgeman and D. Monk (eds) *Feminist Perspectives on Child Law* (2000) London, Cavendish.

K. Green and H. Lim, 'What is this thing about female circumcision? Legal Education and Human Rights' (1998) 7(3) *Social and Legal Studies* 365.

S. Kilbourne, 'The wayward Americans – why the USA has not ratified the UN Convention on the Rights of the Child' (1998) 10 *Child and Family Law Quarterly* 243.

U. Kilkelly and L. Lundy, 'Children's rights in action: using the UN Convention on the rights of the Child as an auditing tool' (2006) 18(3) *Child and Family Law Quarterly* 331.

C. Lyon, 'Interrogating the Concentration on the UNCRC Instead of the ECHR in the Development of Children's Rights in England' (2007) 21 *Children and Society* 147–153.

O. O'Neill, 'Children's Rights and Children's Lives' in P. Alston, S. Parker and J. Seymour (eds), *Children, Rights and the Law* (1992) Oxford, Clarendon Press, 24–42, 37–39.

C. Sawyer, 'Not Every Child Matters: the UK's Expulsion of British Citizens' (2006) *The International Journal of Children's Rights,* 14: 157–185.

8.5 Parental responsibility

We quoted from:

J. Eekelaar, 'Parental Responsibility: State of Nature or Nature of the State?' (1991) *Journal of Social Welfare and Family Law* 37, at 38–39.

K. Hollingsworth, 'Responsibility and Rights: Children and their Parents in the Youth Justice System' (2007) 21(2) *International Journal of Law, Policy and the Family* 190–219.

J. Holt, *Escape from Childhood* (1974) Penguin, at 15.

Law Commission, Report on Guardianship and Custody, Law Com. No. 172 (1988) London, HMSO, paras 2.4–2.16.

H. Reece, 'From Parental Responsibility to Parenting Responsibly' (2006) *Current Legal Issues* 459–483.

Additional reading

R. Arthur, 'Punishing parents for the crimes of their children', (2005) 44 *The Howard Journal of Criminal Justice* 233.

S. Day Sclater, and C. Piper, 'Re-moralising the family?: Family policy, family law and youth justice' (2000) 12 *Child and Family Law Quarterly* 135.

B.M. Dickens, 'The Modern Function and Limits of Parental Rights' (1981) 97 *Law Quarterly Review* 462.

L. Gelsthorpe, 'Youth Crime and Parental Responsibility', in A. Bainham, S. Day Sclater and M. Richards (eds) (1999) *What is a Parent? A Socio-Legal Analysis*, Oxford and Portland, Oregon, 231.

B. Goldson and J. Jamieson, 'Youth crime, the "parenting deficit" and state intervention: A contextual critique', (2002) 2 *Youth Justice* 82.

N. V. Lowe, 'The Meaning and Allocation of Parental Responsibility – A Common Lawyer's Perspective' (1997) 11 *International Journal of Law, Policy and the Family* 192.

K. Standing, 'Reasserting father's rights? Parental responsibility and involvement in education and lone mothers families in the UK' (1999) 7 *Feminist Legal Studies* 33–46.

9

BECOMING A PARENT

Identifying who is a child's parent is not as simple as it might seem, and medical and cultural developments have made it more complex. As we will see, legal parentage can be determined by genetic, gestational and social factors and much still depends on the marital status of the adults. One of the major policy questions is: is truth always the best policy?

9.1 HOW TO BECOME A FATHER

Until the advent of DNA tests, proving paternity had always been thought to be a problem. Somehow it is easier to remember the first part of Lancelot's speech to Old Gobbo – 'It's a wise father, that knows his own child' – than the second – 'Truth will come to light; murder cannot be hid long, a man's son may; but in the end, truth will out'. Hence there is a long-standing presumption in law that any child born to a married woman is her husband's child.

This used to be extremely difficult to rebut as it had to be established 'beyond reasonable doubt' that the husband could not be the father. There was also a procedure for conclusively determining a person's legitimacy. Both are illustrated by the *Ampthill Peerage Case* [1977] AC 547, [1976] 2 All ER 411, House of Lords' Committee of Privileges.

In 1921, Christobel, wife of the man who was later to become the third Baron Ampthill, gave birth to Geoffrey, who had been conceived by external fertilisation while his mother was still a virgin. Her husband petitioned for divorce, alleging that this was the result of Christobel's adultery. At the trial, the husband gave evidence that he had had no sexual intimacy of any kind with his wife at the probable date of conception and was granted a decree. On appeal, the House of Lords decided that evidence of non-access by a husband or a wife was inadmissible both in legitimacy proceedings and in divorce proceedings (*Russell v Russell* [1924] AC 687, 93 LJP 97: the rule was subsequently reversed in the Law Reform (Miscellaneous Provisions) Act 1949, s. 7(1)). The divorce decree was rescinded. In 1925, the High Court made a declaration that Geoffrey was the legitimate child of Christobel and her husband. Under the Legitimacy Declaration Act 1858, such declarations were binding... but could not prejudice anyone who had not been given notice or made a party... or if obtained by fraud or collusion. The marriage was eventually dissolved in 1937. In 1950, a son John was born of the third Baron's third marriage. The third Baron died in 1973 and both Geoffrey and John claimed to succeed him. Geoffrey relied upon the declaration, but John alleged that this was not binding, inter alia, because it had been procured by fraud. Blood samples were available from Christobel and the third Baron, but not from Geoffrey.

Lord Simon of Glaisdale:

...There is one status for which Parliament, in the wisdom of experience, has made special provision. This is the status of legitimacy ... it is the condition of belonging to a class in society the members of which are regarded as having been begotten in lawful matrimony by the men whom the law regards as their fathers. Motherhood, although also a legal relationship, is based on a fact, being proved demonstrably by parturition. Fatherhood, by contrast, is a presumption. A woman can have sexual intercourse with a number of men any of whom may be the father of her child; though it is true that modern serology can sometimes enable the presumption to be rebutted as regards some of these men. The status of legitimacy gives the child certain rights both against the man whom the law regards as his father and generally in society. ...

It was probably for two reasons that Parliament made special provision for judgment as to the status of legitimacy. First, no doubt, because, since fatherhood is not factually demonstrable by parturition, it is questionable; and it is generally in the interest of society that open questions should be finally closed. Second, no doubt, because since the legitimate child, by virtue of his legal relationship with the man whom the law regards as his father, is entitled to certain rights both as against the father and generally in society, it is desirable that the legal relationship between father and child should be decisively concluded.

His Lordship then reviews the law and the evidence, and concludes that the decree was not obtained by fraud or collusion, not least because, as the law stood in 1925, Geoffrey was entitled to the benefit of the presumption even if his mother had confessed to committing adultery at the relevant time.

QUESTIONS

i. This case demonstrates the strength of the courts' traditional reluctance to question the presumption of and their respect for the status of legitimacy. Now that almost half of children are born outside marriage and most of the legal distinctions between birth in and outside marriage have been removed, is there any longer a need for this presumption?

ii. Why is it in 'the interest of society that open questions should be finally closed'? Are the interests of society here the same as those of children?

The presumption of legitimacy was made easier to rebut by the Family Law Reform Act 1969, which provided that it could be rebutted by evidence showing that it is more probable than not that the child is illegitimate (section 26). The leading case was decided shortly afterwards.

S v S; W v Official Solicitor
[1972] AC 24, [1970] 3 All ER 107, House of Lords

Both were divorce cases in which the husband denied paternity of a child to whom the presumption of legitimacy applied. They raised the question whether or not the court should direct the use of blood tests to determine a child's paternity (as to which, see the extracts quoted in *Re H (a minor) (blood tests: parental rights)* at p. 404 below). On the presumption of legitimacy:

Lord Reid:

...The law as to the onus of proof is now set out in s 26 of the Family Law Reform Act 1969...

That means that the presumption of legitimacy now merely determines the onus of proof. Once evidence has been led it must be weighed without using the presumption as a make-weight in the scale for legitimacy. So even weak evidence against legitimacy must prevail if there is not other evidence to counterbalance it. The presumption will only come in at that stage in the very rare case of the evidence being so evenly balanced that the court is unable to reach a decision on it.

I cannot recollect ever having seen or heard of a case of any kind where the court could not reach a decision on the evidence before it. ...

QUESTIONS

i. Do you think that the approach of the House of Lords to the standard of proof in care proceedings (see *Re H (minors) (sexual abuse: standard of proof)* [1996] AC 563, [1996] 1 All ER 1, [1996] 2 WLR 8, HL, p. 566, below) has, or should have, any relevance here?

ii. Do you think that the standard of proof of paternity should be the same: (a) if the mother is applying for financial provision or a property settlement for her child, or (b) if the father is applying for a contact, residence or parental responsibility order, or (c) if the child is applying for a declaration of parentage?

The whole debate has now been overtaken by the scientific development known as 'DNA profiling' or 'genetic fingerprinting', to the extent that the courts have held that the inference from a refusal to participate in such scientific testing outweighs the presumption of legitimacy (see *Secretary of State for Work and Pensions v Jones* [2003] EWHC 2163 (Fam), [2004] 1 FLR 282). The process is explained by Alec Jeffreys in 'Genetic fingerprinting: applications and misapplications' (1993):

What is DNA Fingerprinting?

While most of our DNA shows little variation, regions called 'minisatellites' scattered along our chromosomes can show extreme levels of variability. These minisatellites consist of 'stuttered' regions of DNA, in which a short chemical sequence of bases is repeated over and over again. ...

In 1984, we showed that the repeat units (DE in the above example) of different minisatellites tend to share a similar sequence motif, which seems to predispose DNA towards this stuttering. Discovering of this shared motif allowed us to design a method for highlighting many of these minisatellite regions simultaneously in human DNA, thus producing the first DNA or genetic 'fingerprint'.

DNA fingerprinting is a complex process, taking perhaps a week to proceed from biological sample to final result. ... The end result of this process is a pattern of 30 or so bands or stripes on X-ray film, resembling to some extent the bar code used on supermarket goods. These film patterns... have three critical properties:

(1) The degree of pattern variation between individuals, even if they are closely related, is so extraordinary that we can legitimately refer to these patterns as DNA fingerprints, a unique biological identifier. Extensive comparisons of different people's patterns have shown that the odds against two people (other than identical twins) having the same pattern is remote in the extreme, to the extent to that it would be very unlikely that *any* two people on earth would by chance share the same pattern.

(2) Despite this extraordinary variation, an individual's DNA fingerprint is essentially constant, irrespective of the source of DNA (blood, semen). Thus DNA fingerprinting can be applied to any appropriate source of DNA.

(3) DNA fingerprints show a simple pattern of inheritance, a child receiving approximately one-half of its bands from the mother and the remainder from the father.

There may be some concerns over quality control in the forensic context, but there is no doubt as to the reliability of the technique in the family law context. Tests are often undertaken by agreement, but the Family Law Reform Act 1969 provides that a court can *direct* that scientific tests can be used to ascertain parentage in civil proceedings (section 20). As the consent of the individual is explicitly required (section 21) the court cannot *order* the tests to be undertaken. (The only exceptions to this are in relation to children under the age of 16, if it is considered to be in their best interests, and persons suffering from a mental disorder, as long as it is not prejudicial to their proper care and treatment (section 21(3), (4)). If a person fails to give effect to a direction, the court can draw such inferences as appear proper; if such a person is relying on the presumption of legitimacy, the court can dismiss his claim without further evidence to rebut the presumption.

A typical case is where the child's mother has had an affair with a third party but is now reconciled to her husband; she may not know the truth, but she does not want the presumption of legitimacy, the status quo, and indeed the beliefs of her family members to be disturbed.

Re H (a minor) (blood tests: parental rights)
[1996] 2 FLR 65, [1996] 4 All ER 28, Court of Appeal

The mother's husband, Mr H, had a vasectomy in 1990. The mother became pregnant in March 1994. At the time she was having a sexual relationship with both her husband and the applicant, Mr B. The understanding then was that the husband would leave and the applicant move into the matrimonial home. The husband left in May 1994 but the mother changed her mind and ended the affair in July. A year later the mother and her husband were reconciled. The applicant applied for a blood test direction but the mother adamantly refused to agree that either herself or the child, Haydon, should be tested. The judge granted the application and the mother appealed.

Ward LJ:

...The mother is ... totally convinced that blood testing is likely to be detrimental to Haydon's welfare which she believes depends, for the foreseeable future, on his settled relationship in a happy family unit, the stability of which may be disturbed by a blood test and the pursuit of litigation by Mr B. which is doomed to fail. She saw no advantage in establishing the truth by science because, as she said:

> 'Haydon has a father, it is Mr H...'
>
> 'Even if a blood test or a DNA test were to show that B. is the father, I will never allow contact...'
>
> 'Even if H. died I would not let B. have any contact with Haydon....'
>
> 'Haydon will never know the truth. My husband's name is on the birth certificate as the father. He is Haydon's father...'

The following issues arise in this appeal:

1. Is refusal to undergo blood testing determinative of the application for a direction under section 20(1) of the Family Law Reform Act 1969?
2. Can an inference adverse to the refusing party be drawn only if the refusal is made after the court has directed the use of blood testing?
3. How does the child's welfare influence the decision?
4. How do the prospects of success in the proceedings influence the decision?
5. What are this child's best interests?

Issue 1 has now been resolved since this case was decided. Following the cases of *Re R (Blood test: constraint)* [1998] 2 WLR 796, [1998] 1 FLR 745 and *Re O and J (Paternity: blood tests)* [2000] 2 All ER 29, [2000] 1 FLR 418, the law was amended to make clear that a parent does not have the right to veto the necessary sample being taken from a child (Family Law Reform Act 1969, section 21(3)).

Ward LJ continued:

2. Can an Inference be Drawn Only if the Refusal to Give Blood Samples is Made After the Court's Direction?

Mr Blair QC supports the judge's conclusion that, 'because of the existence of the statutory provision it must be only in the circumstances in which an adverse inference may be drawn as laid down in the Act that any such inference can be drawn and this cannot happen outside the Act'. ...

The question seems to me to be not so much whether the court is entitled to draw an adverse inference but what, if any, inference can be drawn from a refusal. ... It seems to me that a refusal to comply after the solemnity of the court's decision is more eloquent testimony of an attempt at hiding a truth than intransigent objection made as a forensic tactic. Science has now advanced. The whole truth can now be known ... Common sense seems to me to dictate that if the truth can be established with certainty, a refusal to produce the certainty justifies some inference that the refusal is made to hide the truth, even if the inference is not as strong as when the Court's direction is flouted.

3. How do Considerations of the Child's Welfare Influence the Decision?

The judge correctly directed himself that he should 'refuse the test if satisfied it would be against the child's interests to order it'. This is wholly in accordance with *S v McC*. ... [1972] AC 25 Lord Hodson said at p.58G:

> 'The court in ordering a blood test in the case of an infant has, of course, a discretion and may make or refuse an order for a test in the exercise of its discretion, but the interests of the other persons than the infant are involved in ordinary litigation. The infant needs protection but that is no justification for making his rights superior to those of others.'

It is clear, therefore, that whereas welfare is the paramount consideration in deciding the applications for parental responsibility and contact orders, welfare does not dominate this decision.

4. How do the Prospects of Success in the Proceedings Influence the Decision? ...

1. The paternity issue must be judged as a free standing application entitled to consideration on its own.
2. The outcome of the proceedings in which the paternity issue has been raised, insofar as it bears on the welfare of child, must be taken into account.

3. Any gain to the child from preventing any disturbance to his security must be balanced against the loss to him of the certainty of knowing who he is.
4. The terms of section 10(4) of the Children Act 1989 are explicit in giving parent a right to apply for contact. ...

There is no statutory justification for transforming the paternity issue into a disguised application for leave to apply and judging the paternity issue by the criteria set out in section 10(9).

5. Accordingly, whilst the outcome of the section 8 proceedings and the risk of disruption to the child's life both by the continuance of the paternity issue as well as the pursuit of the section 8 order are obviously factors which impinge on the child's welfare, they are not, in my judgment, determinative of the blood testing question.

In this case the judge's conclusion was that 'it would be rather unlikely that the court would make an order for contact'. That is a conclusion he was plainly entitled to reach, and one which I would support. He did not, however, expressly deal with the parental responsibility order. ...

5. What are the Child's Best Interests?

The mother submits that 'pursuing contact would be to destabilise her own marriage which has only recently been put together again to the disadvantage of the child'. Miss Scotland QC submits accordingly that the case is indistinguishable from *Re F*.

I do not agree. ... The material facts of the case under appeal before us include these features which may or may not have applied in *Re F*:

1. As the judge found, Mr B. has a substantial case for his claim to be this child's father. That can be seen from:
   a. The mother's clear belief, at least until she set eyes on her baby, that the child was born of her adulterous relationship. She now closes her mind even to the possibility that might be so.
   b. The fact that Mr H. has had a vasectomy. He admitted thinking that it was 'unlikely that I would be the father'.
2. If Mr and Mrs H. were reconciled in that state of mind, having their worst fears realised is unlikely of itself to be the cause for the breakdown of a fragile reconciliation. ...
3. It may well be correct, as Miss Scotland submits, that denial of the truth is essential to this mother for the restoration of her self-esteem and for the expiation of her guilt. That creates a danger in putting her welfare to the forefront, not the child's. ...
4. This secret cannot be hidden forever. Mr H. knows the substantial difficulty of his position. Moreover, and most importantly, 14 year old Christopher knows, because his mother told him, that his father may not be Haydon's father. It is unrealistic to pretend that the time will not come when Haydon has to face these doubts about his paternity. If his peace of mind is likely to be threatened, and if he has a right to know, the question then becomes one of when it is best he should learn the truth.
5. In my judgment every child has a right to know the truth unless his welfare clearly justifies the cover up. The right to know is acknowledged in the United Nations Convention on the Rights of the Child (Treaty Series No 44 of 1992) (Cm. 1976) which has been ratified by the United Kingdom and in particular Article 7 which provides 'that a child has, as far as possible, the right to know and be cared for by his or her parents'. ...
6. ... The Houghton Committee reporting in 1972 called for greater openness in adoption. That call was heeded. Section 51 of the Adoption Act 1976 now enables adopted persons to obtain access to their birth records. The Inter-departmental Review of Adoption Law in 1992

expressed the opinion that 'it is fundamental to the welfare of the child that he or she is told (when of sufficient age and understanding) about his or her adoptive status'. It is a recognition that the child's shock at discovering the truth about his origins at a later stage in childhood will be increased by the realisation that his adopted parents have, to date, allowed him to believe in a falsehood that he was their child.

7. Section 56 of the Family Law Act 1986 gives Haydon the right to apply for a declaration—
   '(a) that a person named in the application is or was his parent: or
   (b) that he is the legitimate child of his parents.'
8. Given the real risk bordering on inevitability that Haydon will at some time question his paternity, then I do not see how this case is not concluded by the unassailable wisdom expressed Lord Hodson at p. 57H:

> 'The interests of justice in the abstract are best served by the ascertainment of the truth and there must be few cases where the interests of children can be shown to be best served by the suppression of truth.'

If, as she should, this mother is to bring up her children to believe in and to act by the maxim, which is her duty to teach them at her knee, that honesty is the best policy, then she should not sabotage that lesson by living a lie.

9. If the child has the right to know, then the sooner it is told the better. The issue of biological parentage should be divorced from psychological parentage. Acknowledging Mr B.'s parental responsibility should not dent Mr H.'s social responsibility for a child whom he is so admirably prepared to care for and love irrespective of whether or not he is the father. If the cracks in the H. marriage are so wide that they will be rent asunder by the truth then the piece of paper which dismisses the application hardly seems adhesive enough to bind them together.
10. If Haydon grows up knowing the truth, that will not undermine his attachment to his father figure and he will cope with knowing he has two fathers. Better that than a time-bomb ticking away.

Conclusions

The judge concluded that it was not within his power to prevent this father pursuing his application. I agree. ...

Appeal dismissed. Order below varied to direct rather than to order taking of blood samples from applicant, mother and child.

QUESTIONS

i. What would your answer have been if (a) it had been the applicant who had had the vasectomy, and/or (b) there was a strong physical resemblance between the child and the mother's husband?

ii. If everyone has the right to know who their biological parents are, does this apply (a) to all adopted people, (b) to all people born of donated sperm, or (c) to all people born of donated eggs? (See p. 438 below.)

Re H and A (Children)
[2002] EWCA Civ 383, [2002] All ER (D) 331

The trial judge had rejected an application for an order that blood samples be taken from the children whose paternity was challenged, on the basis that it would have a disastrous effect upon the family as the respondent's husband would leave the family and that 'if no test is ordered there is a fundamental unlikelihood of the matter ever becoming a real talking point to the degree that there is a danger that the children themselves will get to know of it'.

Thorpe LJ:

[20] First I cannot accept the validity of the judge's assessment that the issue was and would remain a family secret. There was clear evidence that Mr B's possible paternity of the twins had been the subject of gossip at Mrs R's place of work. Second Mr B had obviously made his convictions known amongst his family and friends. Third the issue had been the subject of proceedings in the local county court already on foot for three years and by no means completed...

[21]...it is necessary to introduce into the balance the advantages of establishing scientific fact, which allows for planned management, against the risks of perpetuating a state of uncertainty that breeds gossip and rumour, with its risk that at some unpredictable future date the twins might be exposed to either a malicious taunt or an unintended indiscretion with shocking consequence.

[22] Second I am in no doubt that the judge fell into error in his seeming acceptance of the estimation of Mr and Mrs R that the real chance of Mr B having fathered the twins was minimal or 1%.

....

[24] Third and perhaps of the greatest significance are my misgivings over the judge's strongly expressed assessment that to order the test would be to drive Mr R from the family.... The judge himself cast a question mark over the status of his findings when he said:

> 'I stress that as far as all these matters that I am considering now are concerned, I am not making formal findings of fact but giving the impression which I currently hold, as I must, as a background to the considerations which will apply to the question of whether or not blood tests should be ordered.'

[25] Beyond that a distinction must be drawn between a finding of fact as to a past happening and a judicial assessment of the probability of a future happening. Such an assessment must rest upon a sound evaluation of the relevant present facts and circumstances. The judge proceeded on the basis that the marriage between Mr and Mrs R was sound at the date of trial. Thus the children's loss of the father and primary carer from such a family would be the greatest deprivation. His assumption is expressed in this passage:

> 'The marriage of Mr and Mrs R has lasted 26 years. I have no doubt that it has had its hard knocks, somewhat harder than either Mrs R or Mr R were prepared to acknowledge to this court. But it has survived and I find at the moment that it has all the appearances of being a warm and loving relationship.'

[26] That does seem to me too simplistic a starting point. Mrs R had grossly deceived her husband both as to her relationship with Mr B and also in concealing from her husband both the proceedings and the contact between the twins and Mr B both before and after the commencement of the proceedings. Her continuing lack of candour is illustrated by Mr R's statement of March 2001. Even at the trial the judge held 'There was, and I believe there still is, active concealment of many vital facts on the part of Mrs R as far as Mr R is concerned...'
[27] Thus whatever might have been the appearances, surely the reality was that Mr R was on an uncompleted journey of discovery of the truth. Major adjustments still had to be made. There was much with which he had yet to come to terms, including a more realistic acknowledgement of the chances that Mr B was the father of the twins. Mr and Mrs R had much to reconcile if their marriage was to endure. The complex processes which would have to continue post judgment might equally well be assisted by certainty, which may bring relief or which may alternatively at least excise doubt and suspicion. Unpalatable truth can be easier to live with than uncertainty.
[28] In addition to my misgivings as to whether the necessary balancing exercise was correctly performed, I doubt whether the judge gave sufficient weight to the importance of certainty. ...
[30] The judge made it plain that in the absence of scientific evidence then the issue was to be decided on the application of 'a very important, well established principle. ... that is, the presumption of the legitimacy of children born during the currency of the marriage'. He went on to refer to the case of *Serio v Serio* [1983] 4 FLR 756, 13 Fam Law 255. Twenty years on I question the relevance of the presumption or the justification for its application. In the nineteenth century, when science had nothing to offer and illegitimacy was a social stigma as well as a depriver of rights, the presumption was a necessary tool, the use of which required no justification.... But as science has hastened on and as more and more children are born out of marriage it seems to me that the paternity of any child is to be established by science and not by legal presumption or inference. ...

Appeal allowed and case remitted for re-trial.

QUESTIONS

i. To what extent do you think the ability keep the matter secret and the quality of the relationship between the mother and her husband should be relevant factors?

ii. Suppose, for example, that Miss B is brutally raped by Mr X, who is a very rich man, and a child Y results; 20 years later X is killed in a road accident having left no will. Should he have been registered as Y's father when his application for contact with the baby was refused?

iii. Most of these cases concern babies or very young children, but in *Re D (Paternity)* [2006] EWCA 3545 (Fam); [2007] 2 FLR 26 the child concerned was ten years old and strongly opposed tests being carried out. He had also lived most of his life with the person whom he believed to be his paternal grandmother. The court held that tests should be carried out on the man alleging paternity and that the results be held in a file with social services. The court refused however to order tests on the child against his will. However, if the child agreed at a later date to provide a sample Hedley J stated that that 'I would regard it as an obligation either of the social worker or the guardian to inform' the applicant of the results. Do you think this approach should be adopted in all cases, regardless of the child's age or wishes?

Do you think it should be left to the child to decide whether to inform the person claiming to be his father of the results of a later test?

iv. While in *Re F (Children)* [2007] EWCA 873, [2007] All ER (D) 389, CA the court confirmed that it had the power to order that a child be informed of the truth of his or her paternity against the wishes of the parent with care, in *J v C* [2006] EWHC 2837, [2006] All ER (D) 147 the court accepted the mother's arguments that disclosure of the truth should wait until her children reached the age of sixteen. What factors do you think the court should consider when making these decisions?

v. In *Birmingham City Council v S* [2006] EWHC 3065 (Fam), [2007] 1 FLR 1223 an unmarried father wished to prevent his traditional Muslim parents being told of the existence of his child. However, the court held that: 'To deprive a significant member of the wider family of the information that the child exists who might otherwise be adopted, is a fundamental step that can only be justified on cogent and compelling grounds' (paragraph 73). Should a parent have the right not to tell his or her parents about the existence of their grandchild?

The Lord Chancellor's Department's Consultation Paper, *Procedures for the Determination of Paternity and on The Law on Parental Responsibility for Unmarried Fathers* (1998) helpfully summarises the contexts in which a determination of paternity may be needed:

> 6. a. A person may need to prove that he or she is a child of a specified person, for example in order to amend his birth certificate, to establish his or her right to inherit property, or to acquire nationality or citizenship (which may be relevant for immigration purposes).
>
> b. A father may need to prove his relationship with his child, for example in order to seek a parental responsibility order, or an order for residence or contact, under the Children Act 1989.
>
> c. The child's mother, or the Child Support Agency, may need to establish paternity so that the father can be required to contribute to the child's maintenance.
>
> 7. At present there is no single procedure, covering all these circumstances, for obtaining a determination of parentage from the court. Paternity may be established in one of three ways:
>
> a. by a declaration of parentage under section 56 of the Family Law Act 1986, which is binding for all purposes but is available only on the application of the 'child' in question; or
>
> b. by a declaration under section 27 of the Child Support Act 1991, which is effective only for child support purposes and is available on the application of the person with care of the child or the Secretary of State; or
>
> c. by a direction from the court for blood tests under section 20 of the Family Law Reform Act 1969; this is only available when the court has to resolve a dispute about paternity in the course of existing civil proceedings, and no freestanding application can be made under section 20.

Section 56(1) of the Family Law Act 1986 allows a child to apply for a declaration: (a) that a person named in the application is or was his parent; or (b) that he is the legitimate child of his parents. Section 56(2) allows him to apply for a declaration that he has or has not become a legitimated person.

QUESTIONS

i. Why should only the child himself be able to apply? Why not a grandchild? Why not a father? Why not a mother?

ii. If you know who your parents are, in what circumstances might you also have to know whether you were legitimate or legitimated?

iii. Do you think that a mother should be obliged to name a child's father for the purpose of claiming benefits (so that steps can be taken to recover a contribution from him)?

9.2 MOTHERHOOD: A FACT OR A CHOICE?

Lord Simon in the *Ampthill Peerage* case stated that 'Motherhood ... is based on a fact, being proved demonstrably by parturition'. Developments in reproductive technology have made the question of who is a child's mother not always so obvious, and we look at these situations later. Moreover, even before these developments, cases have arisen where motherhood has been disputed; see, for example, *Slingsby v A-G* (1916) 33 TLR 120, HL where a wife attempted to pass a child off as her own.

But what if the mother wishes to conceal the birth? In *Re AB (Care Proceedings)* [2003] EWCA Civ 1842, [2003] All ER (D) 129, the mother had managed to conceal the pregnancy from her husband of twenty years, who had had a vasectomy, and with whom she had had two children. She claimed that the pregnancy was a result of a rape by an unknown man, and that she did not want the child after the birth. The local authority issued an application for a care order and the mother requested that the court exercise its discretion to exclude her husband from any knowledge of the proceedings. The judge found that the mother could only succeed if her evidence was of such cogency that, even if the husband was informed of the proceedings, it was more probable than not that the mother would establish that the child was not his. The court held that the mother was not a credible witness and her application failed. The Court of Appeal upheld the decision of the trial judge on the basis that such an application should only be granted in the most extreme circumstances.

Thorpe LJ:

There is a human tendency, which we all recognize, to escape the consequences of our errors and shames. The mental search for an escape route is necessarily egocentric and often inspired by fantasies. The appellant's success in giving birth to her daughter without the knowledge of her husband and her other children is surprising, leaving aside any comments on her responsibility and candour (at para 19)

Katherine O'Donovan and Jill Marshall in 'After Birth: Decisions about becoming a Mother' (2006) comment on this case and contrast it with the legal position in France.

The concealment of the care and adoption proceedings, as wished for by the birthgiver, 'was never a realistic conception', according to the appeal judge who supported this observation with a reference to 'the responsibilities of public authority, the rights of the child, the rights of the husband and the rights of other children' (para 19). There was no reference to the rights of the woman herself. She is depicted as a fantasist, who has failed to encounter reality and truth. The outcome was that the husband 'must be served with the proceedings'. Realistic or not, the option of confidentiality, or 'concealment', is recognised in other jurisdictions of the European Union, a point which will be developed below. ...

Giving birth is positioned in the United Kingdom as a public act. A new person enters the world, her arrival must be documented in a birth certificate, showing the name of the woman who gave birth, who is the legal mother, regardless of whether she is the genetic parent. (Registration of Births Act 1953 s 2; Human Fertilisation and Embryology Act 1990 s 27). The only recourse of a birthgiver who does not want to be identified is to give birth in secret and to abandon the child, committing at least one crime. Estimates of the frequency of such actions in England and Wales vary, but an educated guess is about one hundred a year. Concealment of parturition from a husband or family does not necessarily involve concealment of identity from the child, who, if adopted will have access to her original birth certificate at the age of 18. However, an abandoned child whose birthgiver disappears will not have the mother's name on the birth certificate. Most of the debate on abandonment has taken place around the question of the child's identity rights, with little focus on the birthgiver, for the obvious reason that her identity is unknown.

France, Luxembourg and Italy continue an ancient tradition whereby a woman can enter a hospital; give her name as X, indicating that she does not wish to reveal her identity; give birth; and leave her child in the hands of the authorities. In *Odievre v France,* (2004) EHRR 43, [2003] 1 FCR 621, the European Court of Human Rights, by a majority of ten to seven, upheld the provisions of the French Civil Code which enable anonymous birthing. Although the issue in that case is presented in terms of a right of access to information about one's origins, it can be represented as a case concerned with the autonomy of the birthgiver. It is estimated that a current 400,000 French persons were born to anonymous mothers. Pressure groups exist to change the French legislation, but, whilst it has been modified, the woman's right has been maintained. The history of the French legislation has been documented elsewhere (see paras 15 and 16 of the judgment in *Odievre v France*). The focus here is on the construction of this right in the language of autonomy.

One approach to autonomy might argue that a woman who carries a child to full term and gives birth is not autonomous, for she is encumbered, confined, and analogous to the person portrayed in communitarian classics. Even if this argument is acknowledged, it does not preclude the recovery of autonomy once confinement is over. In the French discourse of *accouchement sous X,* giving birth anonymously is positioned as a woman's right. This position was upheld by the European Court of Human Rights, although the rationale for the decision was in terms of welfare than autonomy.

In the judgment of the majority of the Court, various interests had to be weighed. Article 8 of the European Convention on Human Rights has been interpreted to cover identity rights. The interests of the applicant, now an adult, in knowing her origins and the identity of her biological mother are placed against the interests of the birthgiver, 'in remaining anonymous in order to protect her health by giving birth in appropriate medical conditions'. Further considerations are the general interest of protection of health of both child and birthgiver and the avoidance of abandonment of a child at birth. These interests are presented as the right to life under Article 2 of the Convention. The Court observed that the competing interests between applicant and her biological mother 'do not concern an adult and a child, but two adults, each endowed with her own free will'. This is the only suggestion of autonomy. It is noteworthy that, in justifying the decision, the right to life is trump, with welfare and health as the best suit.

Criticisms of the judgment are based on the identity rights of the child, recognised by international conventions, and come largely from France. Other jurisdictions, such as Belgium and Hungary, provide a way for mothers to give birth *discreetly.* Some German Lander have already instituted baby boxes, where babies can be left anonymously, and legislation allowing anonymous births is under active consideration. The language of justification in these jurisdictions is of protection of the life and development of the child. Thus, despite a growing trend in giving birth *discreetly,* it is only in France, Italy and Luxembourg that the political justification for anonymous birthing is couched in terms of women's rights. Steiner (2003, p 430) comments on this: 'One has to place the French legislation relating to anonymous birth in the wider context of parenthood, a concept in French family law at the heart of which has always existed an adult-centred individualistic philosophy of freedom of choice.' To a degree, the concept of parenthood in French law is a question of volition.

Examination of the French discourse surrounding *accouchement sous X* reveals a variety of arguments. Although the antiquity of the woman's right involved goes back to the French Revolution, utilitarian arguments based on welfare and vulnerability and the characteristics of the women concerned are also used. Against the child's identity rights, the right to life is positioned as trumps. Yet beneath these arguments lie legal and cultural attitudes to the mother-child dyad.

Could it be that becoming a mother in the new century requires a different form of self-abnegation from that of the past? This is the thesis that is advanced in popular literature from the United States:

> 'Central to the new momism, in fact, is the feminist insistence that women have choices, that they have autonomy. But here's where the distortion of feminism occurs. The only truly enlightened choice to make as a woman, the one that proves, first, that you are a "real woman", and second that you are a decent worthy one, is to become a "mom". Thus the new momism is deeply contradictory. It both draws from and repudiates feminism'. (Nedelsky, 1989, p 221).

QUESTION

'As feminists, we can fight against specific events, such as rape or abuse and against structural conditions in the economy and social provisions that lead a woman to give up her child. But do we want to deny her the choice to do so?' (O'Donovan and Marshall).

What do you think? Why do you think the UK has not introduced 'baby boxes'? Do you think they should?

9.3 HOW TO ADOPT A CHILD

Another way of becoming a parent is to adopt a child. Adoption means a great many different things. In Chapter 10 we look at adoption by stepparents, and in Chapter 12 adoption as a care resource, often by way of compulsory adoption.

For a summary of the extraordinary diversity of the institution, we may turn to Barbara Tizard's account, *Adoption: A Second Chance* (1977):

> The essence of adoption is that a child not born to you is incorporated into your family as though he were your own. This practice can be found in some form in most cultures – one of the best-known early adoptions was that of Moses. But just as the family, although a constant feature of all societies, has assumed many different forms and functions, so the characteristics of adoption

have varied enormously during history. Today most people think of adoption as a process in which a young child, usually an infant, is permanently incorporated into a family into which he was not born. Typically, the adoptive parents and the biological parents are strangers, and the adoption is arranged through an agency or other third party. Great stress is laid on keeping the two sets of parents from meeting or even knowing each others' identity. All links between the adopted child and his natural parents are severed, and the adopted child has all the rights, and is treated in the same way, as a natural child of his new family. The primary purpose of the adoption is seen to be the satisfaction of the desire of a married couple to rear a child; at the same time, a home is provided for a child whose natural parents are unable to rear it....

Perhaps the greatest contrast is with the custom of child exchange, or kinship fostering, formerly prevalent in Polynesia and parts of Africa. In these societies children were often not reared by their biological parents but sent to be raised by relatives, sometimes after weaning, sometimes from the age of 6 or 7. The exchange of children was arranged by the parents, who continued to maintain some contact with their biological child. It was believed that aunts, uncles and grandparents would bring children up and train them more effectively than their parents. This custom of child exchange seems to have been part of a system of mutual kinship obligations.

Adoption played a very different role in such ancient civilisations as the Babylonian, Chinese and Roman. There, its function was primarily to ensure the continuity of wealthy families by providing for the inheritance of property and the performance of ancestral worship. Roman law, for example, permitted adoption only in order to provide an heir to the childless, and laid down that the adopters must be past child-bearing age and the adoptee must be an adult. Until recently, the adoption laws of many European countries were influenced by Roman law; often adoptive parents had to be childless and over the age of 50.

Hindu law also recognised adoption as a method of securing an heir, both for religious purposes and for the inheritance of property. It specified, however, that the adopted child should be if possible a blood relative, and that the transaction must take place directly between the two sets of parents. For this reason, orphans could not be adopted. In most ancient civilisations adoption was only one among several possible ways of providing an heir, and often not the preferred one. In Islam, for example, divorce and remarriage, polygamy, and the legitimisation of children by maidservants were common practices, while adoption was not permitted.

In all these societies adoption was essentially concerned with preserving the property and the religious observances of the families of the ruling class. It was very much a service for the rich, and for men; it was men who wanted heirs, and for this purpose they wanted boys. The emotional needs of childless wives were not recognised; indeed if they did not produce an heir they were likely to be divorced or otherwise replaced. Nor was it a service for homeless children; the adoptees were often adult, or, if children, they were given to the adoptive parents by their biological parents in order to better their social status.

Tizard adds that 'It is only relatively recently that adoption has become a recognised practice in Western society'. Certainly in England there was no legal form of adoption until the 1920s. In 1921, the Hopkinson Committee reported in favour of providing for legal adoption, but its recommendations proved so controversial that a second Committee was appointed, under the chairmanship of Mr Justice Tomlin. The Report of the Child Adoption Committee in 1925 was far from enthusiastic:

4. ... There have no doubt always been some people who desire to bring up as their own the children of others but we have been unable to satisfy ourselves as to the extent of the effective

demand for a legal system of adoption by persons who themselves have adopted children or who desire to do so. It may be doubted whether any such persons have been or would be deterred from adopting children by the absence of any recognition by the law of the status of adoption. The war led to an increase in the number of de facto adoptions but that increase has not been wholly maintained. The people wishing to get rid of children are far more numerous than those wishing to receive them and partly on this account the activities in recent years of societies arranging systematically for the adoption of children would appear to have given to adoption a prominence which is somewhat artificial and may not be in all respects wholesome. The problem of the unwanted child is a serious one; it may well be a question whether a legal system of adoption will do much to assist the solution of it.

...

9. [Nevertheless]...we think that there is a measure of genuine apprehension on the part of those who have in fact adopted other people's children, based on the possibility of interference at some future time by the natural parent. It may be that this apprehension has but a slight basis in fact notwithstanding the incapacity of the legal parent to divest himself of his parental rights and duties. The Courts have long recognised that any application by the natural parent to recover the custody of his child will be determined by reference to the child's welfare and by that consideration alone. The apprehension, therefore, in most cases has a theoretical rather than a practical basis. There is also a sentiment which deserves sympathy and respect, that the relation between adopter and adopted should be given some recognition by the community. We think, therefore, that a case is made out for an alteration in the law. ...

Having reluctantly reached that conclusion, the Committee went on to consider how adoption should take place, and to what effect. Some of their arguments cast an interesting light upon more recent debates:

11. ...some form of judicial sanction should be required. ...

...

15. ...Whichever be the tribunal selected it is important that the judicial sanction, which will necessarily carry great weight, should be a real adjudication and should not become a mere method of registering the will of the parties respectively seeking to part with and take over the child. To avoid this result we think that in every case there should be appointed...some body or person to act as guardian ad litem of the child with the duty of protecting the interests of the child before the tribunal.

...

18. ...No system of adoption, seeking as it does to reproduce artificially a natural relation, can hope to produce precisely the same result or to be otherwise than in many respects illogical, and this is made apparent in the diversity of provisions in relation to succession and marriage which appear in the adoption laws of other countries.

19. We think that in introducing into English law a new system it would be well to proceed with a measure of caution and at any rate in the first instance not to interfere with the law of succession...it does not require any profound knowledge of the law of succession to bring home to an enquirer (1) the impracticality of putting an adopted child in precisely the same position as a natural child in regard to succession, and (2) the grave difficulties which would arise if any alteration were to be made in the law of succession for the purpose of giving an adopted child more limited rights...but...the tribunal which sanctions the adoption should have power if it thinks fit, to require that some provision be made by the adopting parent for the child.

QUESTIONS

i. What, if anything, was so different about the system of succession in classical Roman law that the complete absorption of a person into his new family presented none of the difficulties apparently so obvious to English lawyers in 1925?

ii. Why is it, do you think, that even now an adopted person cannot succeed to a peerage or hereditary title in his adoptive family?

If these passages in the Tomlin report betray (although they do not confess to) deep-seated attitudes about 'natural' and 'artificial' relationships, there is one point upon which the Committee's views have a decidedly modern ring:

> 28. ...Certain of the Adoption Societies make this feature an essential part of their policy. They deliberately seek to fix a gulf between the child's past and future. This notion of secrecy has its origin partly in a fear (which a legalised system of adoption should go far to dispel) that the natural parents will seek to interfere with the adopter and partly in the belief that if the eyes can be closed to facts the facts themselves will cease to exist so that it will be an advantage to an illegitimate child who has been adopted if in fact his origin cannot be traced. Apart from the question whether it is desirable or even admissible deliberately to eliminate or obscure the traces of a child's origin...we think that this system of secrecy would be wholly unnecessary and objectionable in connection with a legalised system of adoption.

The first cautious steps were taken in the Adoption of Children Act 1926; the issue of succession was resolved following the Houghton Report (1972) so that, since 1975, there have been only three important exceptions to the principle that an adopted child is the same as a child born to married parents:

1. he cannot succeed to peerages and similar dignities;
2. the rules prohibiting marriages with certain relatives in his birth family remain and he is only debarred from marriage with his adoptive parent in the new family;
3. and if he is adopted abroad he will not gain the same rights under nationality and immigration laws as would a child born abroad to United Kingdom parents or adopted here.

That last point has disappeared for most overseas adoptions, following section 7 of the Adoption (Intercountry Aspects) Act 1999.

The Adoption Act 1976 was the principal Act for a generation; now the law is to be found in the Adoption and Children Act 2002. Sections 95 and 96 of the 2002 Act preserves one principle which has been taken for granted from the start:

95. Prohibition of Certain Payments

(1) This section applies to any payment (other than an excepted payment) which is made for or in consideration of—

(a) the adoption of a child,

(b) giving any consent required in connection with the adoption of a child,

(c) removing from the United Kingdom a child who is a Commonwealth citizen, or is habitually resident in the United Kingdom, to a place outside the British Islands for the purpose of adoption,
(d) a person (who is neither an adoption agency nor acting in pursuance of an order of the High Court) taking any step mentioned in section 92(2),
(e) preparing, causing to be prepared or submitting a report the preparation of which contravenes section 94(1).

(2) In this section and section 94, removing a child from the United Kingdom has the same meaning as in section 85.

(3) Any person who—
(a) makes any payment to which this section applies,
(b) agrees or offers to make any such payment, or
(c) receives or agrees to receive or attempts to obtain any such payment, is guilty of an offence.

(4) A person guilty of an offence under this section is liable on summary conviction to imprisonment for a term not exceeding six months, or a fine not exceeding £10,000, or both.

96. Excepted Payments

(1) A payment is an excepted payment if it is made by virtue of, or in accordance with provision made by or under, this Act, the Adoption (Scotland) Act 1978 or the Adoption (Northern Ireland) Order 1987.

(2) A payment is an excepted payment if it is made to a registered adoption society by—
(a) a parent or guardian of a child, or
(b) a person who adopts or proposes to adopt a child,
in respect of expenses reasonably incurred by the society in connection with the adoption or proposed adoption of the child.

(3) A payment is an excepted payment if it is made in respect of any legal or medical expenses incurred or to be incurred by any person in connection with an application to a court which he has made or proposes to make for an adoption order, a placement order, or an order under section 26 or 84.

...

QUESTIONS

i. What is so wrong about paying an unmarried mother to let you have her baby?

ii. Can it be distinguished from paying a doctor to inseminate you with the semen of an unknown donor?

iii. Or paying a woman to bear your child? (See p. 442, below.)

iv. Wait a moment – is not that what husbands do?

At first, however, while payment was prohibited, adoptions could be arranged either by adoption societies, or by individual third parties (such as doctors or lawyers) or by the mother herself. Regulation of adoption societies was introduced in 1939 and improved in 1950. The increasing professionalism of adoption societies led to an increasing concern about the private placement of children for adoption, discussed in the *Report of the Departmental Committee on the Adoption of Children* (the Houghton Report) in 1972:

> The decision to place a child with a particular couple is the most important stage in the adoption process. Adoption law must give assurance of adequate safeguards for the welfare of the child at this stage, otherwise it is ineffective. This assurance rests mainly upon the skilled work of the adoption services, which includes preparation for adoptive parenthood. An independent adoption is one in which this assurance is lacking. We therefore suggested in our working paper that independent placements with non-relatives should no longer be allowed.

Section 92 of the Adoption and Children Act 2002 provides:

92. Restriction on Arranging Adoptions, etc.

(1) A person who is neither an adoption agency nor acting in pursuance of an order of the High Court must not take any of the steps mentioned in subsection (2).

(2) The steps are—

(a) asking a person other than an adoption agency to provide a child for adoption,

(b) asking a person other than an adoption agency to provide prospective adopters for a child,

(c) offering to find a child for adoption,

(d) offering a child for adoption to a person other than an adoption agency,

(e) handing over a child to any person other than an adoption agency with a view to the child's adoption by that or another person,

(f) receiving a child handed over to him in contravention of paragraph (e),

(g) entering into an agreement with any person for the adoption of a child, or for the purpose of facilitating the adoption of a child, where no adoption agency is acting on behalf of the child in the adoption,

(h) initiating or taking part in negotiations of which the purpose is the conclusion of an agreement within paragraph (g),

(i) causing another person to take any of the steps mentioned in paragraphs (a) to (h).

(3) Subsection (1) does not apply to a person taking any of the steps mentioned in paragraphs (d), (e), (g), (h) and (i) of subsection (2) if the following condition is met.

(4) The condition is that—

(a) the prospective adopters are parents, relatives or guardians of the child (or one of them is), or

(b) the prospective adopter is the partner of a parent of the child.

...

By section 93, contravening this section, or receiving a child placed in contravention of it, or taking part in the management of a body which exists to arrange adoptions but is not an approved adoption agency, is an offence.

QUESTIONS

i. Now that so few babies are offered for adoption here, many more couples are going abroad, often to South America or China, to adopt: what can we do to insist that restrictions on arrangements and payments are obeyed?

ii. If a couple succeed in finding a child and bring him back here, should we allow them to adopt?

iii. What can we do (a) to stop them or (b) to protect the children?

Some of the many possible answers to that last question may be found in the Adoption (Intercountry Aspects) Act 1999 and in the Children and Adoption Act 2006 (look particularly at section 9).

The fluctuating fortunes of adoption over the years are shown in Figure 9.1, taken from Nigel Lowe's 'English Adoption Law, Past, Present and Future' (2000):

Figure 9.1 The total number of adoptions in England and Wales

Source: 1927–71: Houghton Committee Report – Appendix B. 1975–98: 1997 Marriage, Divorce and Adoption Statistics.

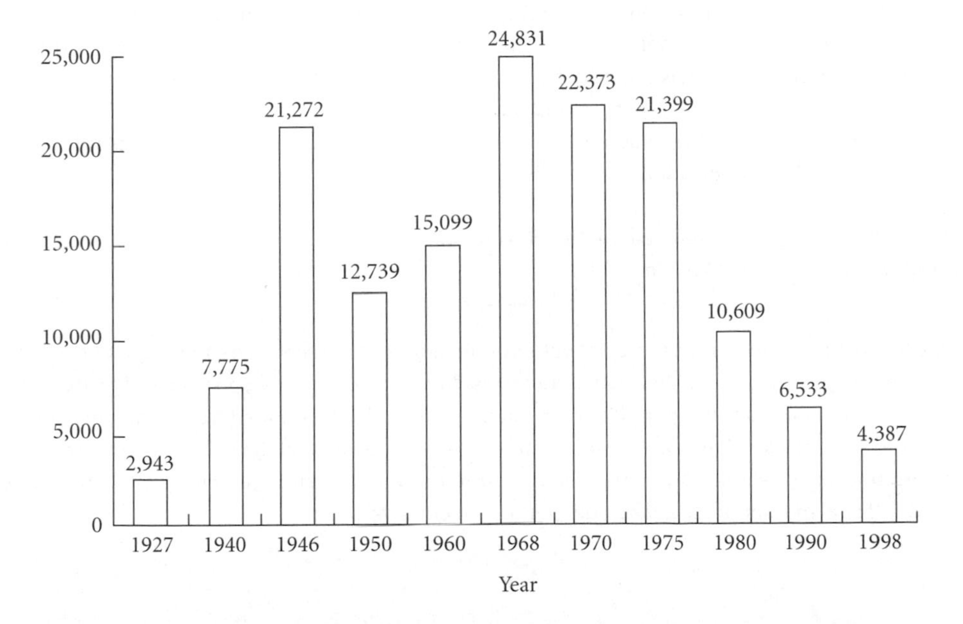

In 2005 there were 5,600 adoptions in England and Wales. Between 1994 and 2006 there was a decrease in the number of children aged five to fourteen who were adopted and a marked increase in the proportion adopted who were aged one to four.

The British Association for Adoption and Fostering reports (2007) that, in 2006:

- The average age at adoption was 4 years 1 month
- 5% (190) of children adopted during the year ending 31st March 2006 were under 1 year old
- 64% (2,300) were aged between 1 and 4 years old

- 26% (900) were aged between 5 and 9 years old
- 5% (180) were aged between 10 and 15 years old
- 0% (20) were aged 16 and over

Nigel Lowe, in 'The changing face of adoption – the gift/donation model versus the contract/services model' (1997), comments:

> ...the 'mind set' which is, rightly or wrongly associated with the adoption of babies, still permeates thinking not only behind the law and, possibly to a lesser extent, practice, but also the attitudes of adopters themselves. Under this 'mind set'... adoption is seen very much as the last and irrevocable act in a process in which the birth parent – normally, of course, the mother – has 'given away' her baby via the adoption agency to the adopters, who are then left to their own devices and resources to bring up the child as their own. Associated with this model is the 'exclusive' view of adoption, ie that the child is both *de jure* and *de facto* transplanted *exclusively* to the adoptive family, with no further contact or relationship with the birth family. This model, however, sits uneasily with the adoption of older children, and it will be my contention that in these instances, at least, a different model is needed in which it is recognised that adoption is not the end of the process, but merely part of an ongoing and often complex process of family development.

Thus three quite different kinds of adoption have emerged: the voluntary, if deeply painful, surrender of a baby or young child to complete strangers; the adoption of a child by a step-parent or other member of his existing family network; and the compulsory removal from one family to another of a child who usually already has a family history of his own. We shall here concentrate on the first, dealing with the others in Chapters 10 and 12. Here we ask: in the once typical but now unusual 'baby adoption', who should be able to adopt? And is it right to continue the 'total transplant' model of adoption – what about 'open adoption'?

Eligibility to adopt is discussed in the *Review of Adoption Law – Report to Ministers of an Interdepartmental Working Group* (1992):

> 26.4 We recommend that agencies should not be allowed to operate absolute rules governing people's eligibility for consideration as adopters. In other words, a person who meets the statutory criteria for an adoptive parent should not automatically be excluded from consideration on account, say, of his or her age. An agency may, however, decide that, having regard to the needs of the children for whom adoptive families are required and to agency guidelines on suitability, it would not be appropriate to accept that person for consideration.
>
> ...

Upper Age Limits

> 26.7 Agencies may not impose strict age limits on adopters, as there is no provision for this in legislation, but they do operate their own age guidelines in relation to people who want to adopt healthy infants. These vary from the early to late thirties, and few agencies will accept applicants over 40 for consideration as adopters for healthy infants. The guidelines reflect the view that it is better for very young children to be placed with adopters who are not older by too wide a margin than most couples starting a family.

26.8 We do not consider it appropriate to set down requirements or guidelines in relation to an upper age for adopters, or a maximum interval between the ages of adopter and child. Some children may benefit from having adoptive parents who do not differ greatly in terms of age from their birth parents or from the parents of their peers. But there may be circumstances where older applicants, by virtue of their maturity, experience, or other special qualities, are particularly well-qualified to provide a home for a child. Agencies should always be satisfied, however, that adopters have a reasonable expectation of retaining health and vigour to care for a child until he or she is grown up; age is one of a number of factors which should be taken into account in determining whether an applicant meets this criterion.

Marital Status

26.9 At present, an adoption order may be made on the application of a married couple. A single person may also apply for an adoption order. However, a married person may only adopt alone if the court is satisfied that the spouse cannot be found or is incapable of applying by reason of physical or mental ill-health; or that the couple have separated and are living apart, and the separation is likely to be permanent.

26.10 In practice, some agencies assess and prepare unmarried couples together, although only one partner may apply for the order and become the child's legal parent. It has been asked whether an unmarried couple should be allowed to adopt jointly. Family structures are changing and more children are born to parents who are not married but are living in stable unions. Under section 4 of the Children Act 1989, an unmarried father may acquire the same parental status as one who is married. On the other hand, unmarried parents do not have the same legal obligations to one another as a married couple have. Should the relationship break down, the caring parent may therefore be less financially secure than if they were married. Furthermore, one of the special features of adoption is that it transfers a child from one family to another and gives the child a legal relationship with all members of the new family, including grandparents, aunts and uncles. However great the commitment of unmarried adoptive parents to a child might be, it is open to question how far their wider families would be willing to accept that child as part of their family.

26.11 It is also important to bear in mind Article 6(1) of the European Adoption Convention which prohibits adoption by unmarried couples. [European Convention on the Adoption of Children, CETS No 058, 1967] Although some unmarried couples might be suitable adoptive parents for a child, we feel that the security and stability which adopted children need are still more likely to be provided by parents who have made a publicly recognized commitment to their relationship and who have legal responsibilities towards each other. Taking into account also the United Kingdom's international obligations, we consider that it would not be appropriate to allow two unmarried people to adopt jointly.

26.12 The fact that two people are married to each other is not of course in itself a sufficient guide to the likely stability of their relationship. Agencies generally expect applicants to have been married for at least three years, although some are prepared to take into account periods of co-habitation preceding marriage, where there is evidence of it available. We consider that agencies should have flexibility to operate their own criteria in forming views on the likely stability of a marriage, and that this should be the subject of guidance.

26.13 We do not propose any changes to the law relating to single applicants, including lesbians and gay men. There are examples of extremely successful adoptions, particularly of older children and children with disabilities, by single adopters. Some children are only able to settle in single-parent households, as a result of experiences in their early lives.

26.14 Some agencies may place a child with a single applicant who is living with a partner. As a matter of practice, to safeguard the child, they also assess the suitability of the partner. We have suggested above that an unmarried couple should not be allowed to adopt jointly, ie that it should not be possible for them to have the same legal relationship towards a child which they would have if they were a married couple adopting together. We do not feel that this is necessarily incompatible with allowing a single person who has a partner to adopt. We recommend that, where assessing a single applicant, agencies should have a duty to assess any other person who is likely to act in a parental capacity towards the adopted child.

Health

26.15 There are no statutory requirements in respect of the health of adopters. Adoption agencies are required to obtain a report on the prospective adopters' health, covering matters such as personal and family health history and current state of health, and consumption of tobacco, alcohol and other habit-forming drugs.

26.16 Professionals, agencies and courts can face difficult decisions in relation to the extent to which health factors may influence a prospective adopter's suitability. Agencies appear to employ a variety of approaches, particularly in relation to smoking. Central guidelines on general principles might help to achieve a greater sense of fairness among prospective adopters and assist agencies in making difficult decisions.

In *Adoption – a new approach*, the White Paper published by the Department of Health in 2000, the issue of eligibility is addressed again. It is said that there is:

> ... little evidence of agencies using arbitrary criteria for assessment, [but] if these are used, children are the losers. There have been cases where potential adopters have been told they cannot adopt solely because they are too old or because they smoke. Blanket bans of this kind are unjust and unacceptable. Each case should be judged on its merits and the needs of children considered – the important thing is to ensure that adopters can offer children a safe, stable and loving home through childhood and beyond.

QUESTIONS

i. Who do you think would be more suitable to bring up a little girl of two, recently released for adoption by her mother, who had found it impossible to cater for either her physical or her psychological needs: (a) a childless couple in their thirties, who have turned to adoption in desperation after unsuccessful attempts to cure the wife's infertility, or (b) a couple in their forties whose own three children are now aged eighteen, fifteen and ten and who have been acting as short-term foster parents but would prefer a permanent placement?

ii. Would you say the same if the child were of mixed race and couple (a) were white and couple (b) were black?

In 2003 Brenda Hale (in the foreword to Bridge and Swindells, 2003) was able to write:

> Who would have thought it? In 1995 a very modest proposal to improve the procedures for deciding property disputes between unmarried couples proved so controversial...that the whole Family Homes and Domestic Violence Bill had to be withdrawn for a rethink. Now only 7 years later we have on the statute book a law permitting unmarried couples to adopt...

The enactment of that dramatic change in eligibility, in the Adoption and Children Act 2002, is described by Caroline Bridge and Heather Swindells in *Adoption: The Modern Law* (2003):

> 3.30 The scope for change in the new law was great. Previous legislation and practice had privileged the traditional private, heterosexual, married family, headed by a man... The point has been made that this particular family form was portrayed as powerful and protective, offering the greatest chance of stability and permanence and was the model of family life sought by social workers and adoption panels. ... At the same time, the 2000 White Paper's call for an increase in adoption and the consequent need for more adoptive families required, in philosophical as well as in legal and practical terms, a rethinking of family forms and an acceptance of social change. Did the marriage relationship still warrant the exclusivity granted by the White Paper?
>
> 3.31 It became increasingly obvious that demography, changing social perceptions, acceptance of cohabitation and the well-recognised willingness of many unmarried fathers to shoulder financial and parental responsibility for a child would inevitably lead to the conclusion that a search for a stable and permanent family must extend to the unmarried cohabiting couple. However, the Adoption and Children Bill, even when introduced for the second time in 2001, did not take up that challenge but went instead to the Special Standing Committee in November of that year retaining the same restrictions on joint applications as the AA 1976 had enacted. Despite evidence brought to the Committee in November 2001 by the Department of Health that 'married couples, given the publicly recognised commitment that they had given... were more likely to provide the child with the stability and security that it needed' and that such a restriction was, on balance, compatible with the European Convention on Human Rights, other witnesses endorsed the view that Parliament should grasp the opportunity for amending the law. British Agencies for Adoption and Fostering (BAAF), in particular, took the view that the exclusion (the 'blanket ban') of some suitable, albeit non-married, couples as prospective adopters was to be condemned, and argued that the relationship between the two adults would always be a critical factor in the assessment process, that a court would always have the final say, and that at a time when debate was ongoing about the possibility of some sort of registration for relationships outside marriage it would be regrettable to omit such changes from the Bill. The arguments for change were compelling, but the Minister of State for Health still concluded that it was the Government's belief that 'the security and stability that is needed for joint adoption is more likely to be provided by a suitably assessed married couple.'
>
> ...
>
> 3.32 When the Bill thus returned from the Special Standing Committee there was no change. It was only later that the fundamental shift was mooted and a group of amendments tabled to the effect that a 'couple' would mean a married couple or two people living as partners in an enduring family relationship, whether they were of different sexes or the same sex. Argument for the amendments focused on modernity and keeping pace with changes in society, coupled with welfare and good assessment of suitability. The views of BAAF, in contrast to their reception in the Special Standing Committee, were frequently endorsed by the Government. In the twenty-first century, it was claimed, 40 per cent of children were born outside marriage, and children, after all, 'must grow up in the real world'. In total contrast to earlier statements by Government

members in Committee, it was stressed that 'in this real world, loving stable families... come in all shapes and sizes' and that children do not grow up in an idealised world that never was. The welfare argument stressed the enhanced hope of adoption that unmarried couples could bring to children in care, and the Government appeared convinced that there were many such couples just waiting to adopt, who would otherwise be deterred. The point that it was in a child's interests to have two legal parents, rather than being adopted by a single parent only, albeit with a residence order to the other, added to the welfare perspective. Rigorous assessment was to be made on a case-by-case basis so that there was 'no justification for disqualifying a couple from adopting jointly simply because they do not possess a marriage certificate, if they clearly possess all the characteristics that the agencies would otherwise expect from suitable adoptive parents'. Opposition argument centred on the attributes of marriage *per se* – in particular, its greater financial security and its greater apparent stability – but in the end the Government's claim that its amendments were about welfare rather than marriage or the promotion of alternative lifestyles won the day. The U-turn was complete, and those who remained supportive of the Government's original stance and the maintenance of the status quo were accused of attempting to 'spoil the life chance of so many young people'. On 16 May 2002, the House of Commons voted overwhelmingly to extend eligibility to make adoption applications to both unmarried and same-sex couples. The prospective pool of adopters was widened and all talk of 'social engineering' and the 'politically correct social worker brigade' was quashed.

3.33 In the event, as noted in Chapter 2, the particular provisions of the Bill were voted down by the House of Lords, returned to the House of Commons, and finally passed by the Lords at the last minute on 5 November 2002.

...

Single and Homosexual Families

3.43 [T]he extension of joint application rights to same-sex couples was bound to follow the shift in thinking on the purpose of adoption and the widening of the adoption pool. As the focus of parliamentary debate moved almost exclusively to the characteristics of adopters during the latter stages of the passage through Parliament of the Adoption and Children Bill 2002, same-sex couples were tagged on to the coat tails of unmarried couples more generally. Having only been introduced at the Report Stage, the issues had not been subject to any wider public discussion and instead became primarily subsumed into the debate on marriage. As a result, the term 'unmarried couple' was effectively construed as including both heterosexual and homosexual couples, albeit some rather more focused debate occurred in the closing stages of the Bill. Three major reasons were put forward for extending joint application rights to same-sex couples: first, the legal disadvantages to a child of having only one parent with a full legal relationship with him; secondly, the potential adopters who were deterred from applying to adopt because of the legal restrictions, and, thirdly, the need to end discrimination as between unmarried and same-sex couples. The first and second reasons applied with equal force to unmarried couples. Their focus was essentially on the provision of a greater number of adopters and the enhanced legal benefits for the child after adoption. Only the human rights argument based on discrimination was of direct relevance and, even then, the supporters of the amendment were in an uncertain position. ... Even the... Government's legal advisers confirmed that the stance of the AA 1976, as reproduced in the Adoption and Children Bill as first introduced, was compatible with the European Convention on Human Rights. Subsequently, when the Bill was amended by the House of Commons to allow joint applications from unmarried couples but was further amended by the

House of Lords so as to return to the original position, the opinion of the same Joint Committee on Human Rights was to the opposite effect. That original stance was confirmed as incompatible with Convention rights.

3.44... In the House of Lords, however, perhaps the most sanguine and common-sense view was that expressed by the Bishop of Oxford. In supporting the rights of same-sex couples to apply jointly to adopt a child, the Bishop emphasised the welfare of the child. He stated that the issue was, in reality, a simple one — that, as a homosexual single person could already adopt a child, the extension of that right so as to give legal responsibility to both parents, if it were in the child's best interests to do so, was a positive step. Unlike much of the debate, the Bishop's view was an informed one based on research. He noted that existing research findings suggested that a mother's sexual orientation was, among other things, of less importance for a child's psychological adjustment than 'warm supportive relationships with parents in a positive family environment' and that it was not clear that children who were brought up in such relationships would be more confused about their sexual identity than children adopted by married or single people....

3.45 In practice, same-sex couples who have been rigorously assessed as suitable parents are likely to fill the family void for some children, albeit these children may be very difficult and hard to place. While such people may not necessarily be placed at the top of the list of prospective adopters – it is likely that a hierarchy will develop – it must surely be right in principle for suitable couples of whatever sexual orientation to have the right to apply jointly, in the best interests of a child.

QUESTIONS

i. Can you see that hierarchy changing in the future? If so, over what sort of time-scale?

ii. *McClintock v Department for Constitutional Affairs*, (2007) Appeal No UKEAT/0223/07/CEA concerned a magistrate who asked to be relieved from hearing cases in which he might be required to place a child with a same-sex couple. His request was refused and consequently he resigned from the Family Panel and complained to the employment tribunal that the refusal was discrimination and harassment contrary to the Employment Equality (Religion or Belief) Regulations 2003. His case was rejected by the Tribunal and the Employment Appeal Tribunal on the grounds that there was no evidence of any discrimination for religious or philosophical reasons and, moreover, that even if there was, it was justified and that the respondent was entitled to require him to carry out the full duties of the office in accordance with his judicial oath.

Do you agree with this decision? (Note also that religious adoption agencies are not exempt from the Equality Act (Sexual Orientation) Regulations 2007, SI 2007/1263, although they have been given until December 2008 to adapt their services.)

Bridge and Swindells (2003) conclude:

But in all the millions of words spoken about adoption law reform there was never any question raised about the desirability of adoption *per se*. ... Widening the pool of adopters by extending eligibility to apply to couples of all persuasions became the perceived *modus operandi* for achieving the Government's 'more adoption' target.

But what should adoption mean? Is it simply a way of providing a home for a child who needs one, or is it a total transfer from one family to another? And can that transfer ever be quite complete? In fact this raises two issues. First, how far is adoption incompatible with a continuing relationship with the birth family, and the appropriateness of 'open adoption'; second, the question of access to birth records. (We look at the question of contact with the birth family in more detail in the context of compulsory adoption in Chapter 12.)

Open adoption is an issue because, despite the reservations expressed by the Tomlin committee (pp. 414, 415, above), secrecy has long been a feature of adoption. Nigel Lowe in 'The changing face of adoption – the gift/donation model versus the contract/services model' (1997) comments:

> Today, the practice of so-called 'open adoption' is very much a fact of adoption life. Of the respondents to our family questionnaire we found that about half had met the birth mother, and 21 per cent the father. There were also a substantial number who had had some form of contact with other birth relatives, and nearly as many had ongoing contact after the adoption order. Indeed, considerable post-adoption work is involved with various forms of contact, whether it is direct or indirect – and, if the latter, through letter-box and telephone schemes. Reflecting this *de facto* growth in post-adoption contact and evident change of policy is the change of recruiting practice. As one social worker told to us:
>
> > 'The whole issue of contact, letter-boxes, post-adoption work and that sort of thing has just come into our practice. It is also a standard feature of our assessment. There is a line in our agreement with prospective adopters which says Mr and Mrs Smith would be very happy for you to exchange information [ref to letter-box contact scheme]. That's just par for the course now. In fact if Mr and Mrs Smith weren't happy with that then we would wonder whether we should be approving them as adopters.'
>
> This last point was echoed by another comment, 'Our agency has a policy of only recruiting prospective adopters who understand what openness means and are prepared to actively work with it'. This is not to say that we did not find consumer resistance to this; indeed, one adoptive couple questioned the whole rationale for contact and whether it is really helpful to a child's development, especially as the child has to hold in mind and understand so many relationships. When the couple sought to explain this to adoption agency staff they were told in no uncertain terms that their views were 'old fashioned' and unacceptable in the light of the agency's policy on open adoption and supporting contact. They had, therefore, in their own words 'to soft peddle' and keep their mouths shut. But, in fact, the couple accept letter-box contact with their adoptive daughter's half-brother and a great aunt in her eighties.

But in many cases, particularly baby adoption, there is no contact with the birth family. The effect of the transplant is an important issue, not only for many children today, but for many of today's adults who were adopted years ago. A total legal transplant does not mean a total physical or psychological transplant, as shown by these quotations from adopted adults who had sought their original birth certificates, as then permitted by Scottish but not English law, in John Triseliotis' study *In Search of Origins* (1973):

> 'You look at yourself in the mirror and you can't compare it with anybody. You're a stranger because you don't know what your real mother looks like or what your father looks like. ...'

'All through my life I had the feeling of unreality about myself; a feeling of not being real, something like an imitation antique... I have been told that I was born in the Poor House and that my birth mother was a bad lot. This has been haunting me. I tried desperately to avoid being like her but then who am I like? I feel I have nothing to pass on to my children. ...'

'My parents were kind people but very isolated. We had few relatives calling and we had no habit of calling on others. My parents' relatives meant nothing to me and I must have meant nothing to them. ... When I was 15 or 16 I was very curious to know "who I was" and especially to know about my natural parents and their families. With your adoptive family you can only go as far back as they are and not beyond. But with your natural ones you feel you want to go further back. ...'

Since 1975, adopted children have had the right to gain access to their birth certificates on reaching the age of eighteen. The Adoption Contact Register, set up under section 51A of the Adoption Act 1976, enables adopted persons and their birth families to register a willingness to be contacted; and many adoption agencies are willing to assist adopted people in tracing their origins. David Howe and Julia Feast's book, *Adoption, Search and Reunion* (2000) presents the results of a study carried out from 1997 by The Children's Society of adopted people's experience of search and reunion. They report:

Why do Adopted People Search?

Explanations for the desire to search are broadly captured by two models – the normative and the pathological. The normative model sees searching as a natural outcome of adoption and not as a negative response to an adverse adoptive situation. This model stresses the fluidity of identity, and sees searching as an attempt to integrate one's roots and to develop a fuller understanding of who one is. The act of searching adds to, rather than replaces, one's existing identity. Adopted people's desire to know their roots is a universal phenomenon and is part of normal personality development. For adopted people, finding out who one is and where one comes from just happens to be a more complex process.

The pathological model suggests that the desire to search arises out of a dissatisfaction or difficulty with one's adoption. The adopted person is seeking a new, or reclaiming some lost, original identity. The model predicts that those with mental health or personality problems are more likely to search to fulfil a need. It is suggested that knowledge of one's origins is essential for mental health and identity formation. Triseliotis (1973) interviewed 70 people in Scotland who had sought further information about their parents. He found evidence of mental health problems and/or disturbed family relationship, concluding that the need to seek genealogical information and search for birth parents was activated by some deeply felt psychological need and rarely related to a matter-of-fact attitude.

The idea that adopted people have trouble with their identity is prevalent in the literature. Sorosky *et al.* (1974) believed that many adopted people cannot realise their full identity until they have information about their birth parents. 'For some, the existing block to the past may create the feeling that there is a block to the future as well'. The authors describe feelings of 'genealogical bewilderment' caused by a lack of biological connection. The term genealogical bewilderment was first used by Sants (1964) to describe an adopted person not having access to information about their ancestry. Feeling a lack of connectedness is not necessarily caused by an unhappy adoption experience; it is simply a lack of knowledge about one's past that interferes with identity formation...

Supporters of the normative model argue that since adoption is essentially a social construct, and that adoption is constructed through interactions within a social environment, it is not useful to talk about adopted people being psychologically impaired. Being adopted marks people out *socially* as being either different and special; or different, disadvantaged, and in a sense not 'normal'. Searching, then, is seen as an attempt to account for this difference and establish a more complete social identity.

March (1995) formulated the idea that searching was associated with adopted people's feelings of stigma. In order to gain social acceptance, adopted people must neutralise their stigma. This they do by searching: normalising themselves by identifying a past that is theirs. In the study by March, adopted people's 'search and reunion activities were not symptomatic of adoption breakdown. They represented an attempt to neutralise the stigma trait by placing self within a biosocial context valued by their community.' In a similar vein, Haimes and Timms (1985) describe adopted people who search as trying to place themselves in a narrative framework. For adopted people, parts of their narrative are missing and by searching for birth relatives they seek to fill in the gaps.

Searching, therefore, can either be seen as a normal part of development or as an adverse response to adoption. Adopted people who search can be viewed as either psychologically impaired or mentally healthy, fully exploring their pasts in a positive manner. Searching for identity involves either trying to connect with one's biological past or seeking to place oneself in a social context. Adopted people also search to neutralise feelings of loss, cancel out the past, or connect the past to the future. Summing up her research of people who had sought access to their Barnardo's childcare record, Pugh (1999) identified three motivations to search: the wish to understand the meaning and significance of one's roots, the need to know about one's history, and the need to make sense of one's past.

Who is Sought?

To some extent, who is sought appears to affect the outcome of the search and reunion process. The emotional agenda with birth parents, particularly birth mothers, is complex and often highly charged. In terms of issues of loss and rejection, meeting birth siblings is likely to be more neutral. In practice, most adopted people set out initially to search for their birth mother. However, Humphrey and Humphrey (1989) suggest that it is easier to build a more comfortable relationship with siblings than with birth parents. McMillan and Irving (1994) echo this, saying 'starting from a position of loss without the responsibility for the loss, siblings are freer for their relationship to develop in a more normal way, on the basis of relatedness and compatibility' (see also Sachdev, 1992).

Sachdev (1992) reports that few of his respondents expressed a desire to meet their biological father. Only 10% said they ever thought about their biological father.

It is not always the adoptive person who searches for the birth relative. Sometimes the birth relative decides to search for the adopted person. The Children's Society has been providing an intermediary service for birth relatives since 1991. They found that search and reunion for this group was, in many ways, more complicated. Feast and Smith (1993, 1995) reported that contacts initiated by birth relatives had a number of positive effects for both adopted adults and birth parents in terms of identity fulfilment and reassurance about lost relatives.

Why do Some Adopted People Not Search?

Gaining research access to adopted people who do not search for their birth parents has proved difficult and many studies of the search and reunion process have omitted this group from their investigations. However, a small number of studies have looked at why some adopted people delay or forestall their search. The speculation is that the reasons for some adopted people stopping their search might be similar to the reasons that non-searchers choose not to search at all.

Gonyo and Watson (1988) suggest that a decision to search is inhibited by three things: (i) a hesitancy to intrude on the life of the unknown party; (ii) fear of failure, discovering unforeseen problems, or upsetting the adoptive parents; and (iii) guilt or feeling disloyal to the adoptive family.

Howe and Feast record the accounts of Susie, who searched:

Searcher Susie

It was four or five years ago and I was discussing it with my partner, Les, and he said to me 'Have you ever thought of trying to find your blood mother?' And I think that everybody who is adopted, it always crosses their mind: 'I wonder if this bit's like her, or I wonder if that bit's like her?' I was about five or six months when I was adopted and I wanted to know what happened in that part of my life that nobody knew. Or just to ask the question, 'Why did you have me adopted? Why didn't she struggle?' Especially once I had my daughter, I thought, 'I couldn't give my daughter up. How could she give her child away?' And then my mum had a major clear out of her attic and she came across my adoption papers and she kept asking me if I wanted them and I said 'Yes' but then I conveniently kept forgetting to take them with me... I kept leaving it because I think I didn't really want to know... while I didn't have them I could accept my life the way it's been. Once I'd got them, you've got to read them... It didn't really bother me until later on in life when I'd had my children and the oldest one had left home and so, as I say, she gave me the adoption papers and I came home and read them and that's when my partner said, 'Why don't we go and look – ask your mum to make sure she doesn't mind – and we'll see what we can find.'

And of Jessica, who did not:

Non-Searcher Jessica

When I was 18 I took that opportunity then to start trying to trace my natural mother. At the time you had to go through a social worker so that's what I did... On the second meeting with him he actually had a piece of paper with the details surrounding the circumstances of my adoption. I always remember it was rather impersonal and upsetting at the time. It just basically said my mother was 5ft 5ins, brown hair, brown eyes, an art student – the purportive father was blonde, 6ft – and that they regretted having to give me up for adoption but they did. And there was also a note about my mother, at the time when she was carrying me, that she had actually attempted to commit suicide – and it all sounded really quite traumatic and sad...

I decided then that it was just too big a thing for me to take on board and especially as the circumstances seemed quite traumatic for my natural mother. I started thinking, 'Maybe it's not right for me just to turn up in her life so many years later' – so I thought I'd just leave it.

Contact can be a wonderful experience; but it may be unwelcome. The way in which it is initiated may be crucial (consider the disastrous history related in *Buchanan v Milton* [1999] 2 FLR 844, 53 BMLR 176).

QUESTIONS

i. Is access to birth records a question of psychological welfare or of human rights (see p. 427 above)?

ii. Recall Triseliotis' interviewee (pp. 426, 427, above) who looked in the mirror and had no one to compare. Now imagine looking, for the first time in your life, at the face of someone to whom you are physically related. How might you feel about this?

9.4 ASSISTED REPRODUCTION

Assisted reproduction technologies enable people to become parents in ways previously unimaginable. However they sometimes result in more than two people having a genetic, gestational or social link with the child, and so the challenge for law is to decide who should be the legal parents or, indeed, if they need two at all. More generally, as Sally Sheldon comments in 'Fragmenting Fatherhood: The Regulation of Reproductive Technologies' (2005), assisted reproduction is a 'resource through which we can trace the values and assumptions which underpin our views regarding fathers and their role in the family'. The Human Fertilisation and Embryology Authority (HFEA, 2005) provides the following background information:

> In the UK today, 1 in 7 couples have some problems in conceiving naturally. It may be twenty-seven years since the first IVF birth in this country but the issue remains at the forefront of public health. Infertility is the single biggest reason for women aged 20–45 going to see their GP, apart from pregnancy itself. Doctors predict that health and social changes could lead to a rapid increase in demand and fertility treatment in the coming years, due to the trend for putting off pregnancy until later in life; an increase in obesity and the higher rate of sexually transmitted infections. Professor Bill Ledger from the Centre for Reproductive Medicine in Sheffield has said the UK will experience a 'fertility time bomb' within ten years. ... The HFEA's role is to ensure safe and appropriate treatment in the 85 licensed clinics in the UK. We have no role in scrutinising the level of provision of treatment. Even though assisted reproduction has been in existence for many decades and steps are being taken by Government to improve NHS availability, the provision of treatment on the NHS remains limited: roughly 20% is carried out by the public sector, with 80% in the private sector.
>
> The HFEA recognises that the public are cautious over the long term consequences of IVF treatment and the ethics of embryo research. ... For science to progress, it must stay in step with the mainstream of public opinion.

QUESTIONS

i. Does IVF using both parents' gametes actually raise any moral or ethical issues at all? If so, what? And how are they different from the issues raised by any use of donated eggs or sperm?

ii. Emily Jackson (2001) comments that:

> Hostility to public funding for assisted conception services derives in part from the common perception that infertility treatment is a 'luxury' that should not be paid for with scarce NHS funds. According to these critics, infertility is best understood not as a disease but as an incapacity, in which case infertile individuals are not ill and needing treatment to restore their health, but instead are simply unable to perform a socially desirable function.

Do you think assisted reproduction should receive more public funding? Is there such a thing as a right to a child? (see *R v Sheffield AHA, ex p Seale* [1994] 25 BMLR 1 where a decision to refuse treatment to women over thirty-five was upheld). What about single people or same-sex couples?

Assisted reproduction takes many different forms (see http://www.hfea.gov.uk/ for more details). The four most well known methods are: artificial or intrauterine insemination, first employed over 100 years ago, where a partner's or donated sperm is inserted into the womb; IVF (in vitro fertilisation), first used in 1984, where a woman's or donated eggs are collected and fertilised with her partner's or donated sperm in a laboratory and are then put into her womb; GIFT (Gamete Intra-Fallopian Transfer), similar to IVF but the eggs and sperm are injected into the woman's fallopian tube so that fertilisation occurs in vivo; and surrogacy, either 'full', where an embryo is created by IVF using the egg and sperm of the commissioning couple or 'partial', where the surrogate mother is inseminated with the commissioning man or donor's sperm.

It is only when the treatment involves the donation of eggs, sperm or embryos or in a case of surrogacy that the issue of legal parenthood is complicated. The Human Fertilisation and Embryology Act 1990 provides the current rules regarding parental status and was much influenced by the Warnock Report (1984). However, significant reforms have been proposed by the Human Fertilisation and Embryology Bill 2007.

The 1990 Act rules relating to fatherhood are summarised by Collier and Sheldon in *Fragmenting Fatherhood* (2008):

> Where a child results from Assisted Reproduction techniques regulated by the 1990 Act, the woman's husband will be the father unless it can be shown that he did not consent to the treatment (section 28(2)). In the absence of consent there is, nonetheless, a rebuttable presumption that the husband is the father (section 28(5)) saving the common law presumption of paternity. Marriage retains a similarly privileged place as the preferred way of attributing paternity in the 2007 Bill, which retains this provision (cl 35). If no father exists by virtue of marriage then, under the 1990 Act, an unmarried man will be deemed the legal father where treatment services were provided for him and the women together (section 28(3)). ... While significantly rewriting these provisions the 2007 Bill remains true to their spirit. The proposed reform abandons reference to 'treatment together' in favour of setting out a list of 'agreed fatherhood conditions' which will apply in cases where no father is designated by virtue of marriage.

The agreed fatherhood conditions (clause 37) are met if: both the man and the woman being treated under licence give written notice that they consent to the man being treated as the father of any child resulting from treatment; neither of them have since then withdrawn their consent; the woman has not since her initial consent provided a further notice that she consents to another man being treated as the father of any resulting child; and, that the woman and the man are not within prohibited degrees of relationship to each other.

> Unmarried male partners can thus gain the same parental rights as married men, though without the presumption of consent that occurs in marriage. Where someone is treated as a father by virtue of one of these provisions, no other man is to be treated as the father of the child. Where sperm is obtained through a licensed clinic, a sperm donor is not to be treated as the legal father. As such, where treatment services are provided for a single women or a woman in a same sex relationship, the resulting child will be legally fatherless. That legally fatherless children can only be created where sperm is obtained through a licensed clinic and a doctor oversees the process might suggest that he, in some way, operates as a kind of surrogate or 'coital' father (see M Johnson, 1999 at 54).

The rules regarding motherhood are more straightforward. Section 27(1) of the 1990 Act makes clear that only the birth mother – the women who is carrying or has carried the child – is to be treated as the mother. Thus, in cases of egg or embryo donation it is the gestational rather than the genetic link that is taken to be the significant indicator of motherhood and this rule applies equally to surrogacy arrangements – full or partial (see pp. 442–443 below). The 2007 Bill, if enacted, will not alter this, but it provides that a lesbian partner of a birth mother can be legally recognised as a 'female parent' and, as a result, will be treated in the same way as a husband, if they are civil partners, or, if not, as an unmarried father (clauses 42–44). (For a case concerning lesbian co-parents under the present law, see p. 483, below.) However where a woman donates an egg to her lesbian partner, she will not be treated as a second mother (clause 47), the general rule remaining unchanged.

QUESTIONS

i. How many arguments can you think of for making (a) the carrying mother, or (b) the genetic mother the legal mother? A man can become the legal father even when another man's sperm is used, but a lesbian partner who donates her egg to her partner cannot become a mother. Why is that?

ii. Are the arguments for recognising 'social' rather than 'genetic' fatherhood stronger or weaker?

iii. Does the widespread availability of unlicensed donor insemination, whether by artificial or more conventional methods, on a 'do-it-yourself' basis, affect matters?

iv. Why should not the same provisions apply when a husband accepts his wife's naturally born child by another man? (See p. 404 above.)

v. As licensed donors can never be fathers, what do you think of the re-introduction of a class of children who are inevitably 'fatherless by law'?

vi. Do you think the rules are in the best interests of the children?

A number of high-profile cases have focused on the requirement of consent and the meaning of being 'treated together'.

Re R (A Child) (IVF: Paternity of Child)
[2005] UKHL 33, [2005] AC 621

Mr B and the mother, Ms D, who were not married, sought IVF treatment involving the removal of eggs from D and their fertilisation by sperm provided by an anonymous donor. D signed a consent form for the treatment, and the form was countersigned by B, acknowledging that he would become the legal father of any resulting child. The treatment was initially unsuccessful, and by the time D returned to have a further set of embryos implanted she and B had separated and B was in a new relationship with Mr S. She continued with the treatment without B's knowledge and without informing the clinic of her new situation. The implantation of the second set of embryos was successful, and D gave birth to R.

On B's application, Hedley J declared that under section 28(3) of the Human Fertilisation and Embryology Act 1990, B was R's legal father. This decision was overruled by both the Court of Appeal and the House of Lords.

Lord Walker of Gestingthorpe:

Hedley J's judgment laid emphasis on the need for clarity and certainty on an issue which might attain practical importance only after the lapse of many years. If a male partner changed his mind about treatment services he could withdraw his acknowledgment, and a clinic, if informed of a change of circumstances, should reconsider the position. But in the absence of the partner expressly withdrawing his acknowledgment or a review by the clinic:

> then in my judgment the original course of treatment continues as treatment services provided to both of them together and, if a child is conceived in the course of that, the man will be the father. This approach affords clarity, simplicity and certainty.

[39] The Court of Appeal...took a different view. Hale LJ agreed with the submission of Mr Jackson:

> that section 28(3) is an unusual provision, conferring the relationship of parent and child on people who are related neither by blood nor by marriage. Conferring such relationships is a serious matter, involving as it does not only the relationship between father and child but also between the whole of the father's family and the child. The rule should only apply to those cases which clearly fall within the footprint of the statutory language.

She analysed the structure of section 28(2) and (3) and found an indication that both referred to the same time as critical for legal paternity, that is, when the embryo or the sperm and eggs (which eventually result in the birth of a child) are placed in the woman. She noted that 'treatment services' are widely defined, and are not limited to a particular cycle or course of treatment. She concluded:

> There must be a point in time when the question has to be judged. The simple answer is that the embryo must be placed in the mother at a time when treatment services are being provided for the woman and the man together.

[40] Hale LJ considered that this conclusion supported rather than undermined the legislative purpose of regulating treatment services in a way that takes account of the welfare of any child who may be born. She observed:

> The Act requires that consideration be given to the welfare of the child and that counselling be offered to the prospective parents. If the circumstances which were taken into account when the couple were together change dramatically, it would better serve the purposes of the Act if the matter had to be reconsidered and fresh counselling offered before a further attempt at implantation is offered. That can only be beneficial to the children born as a result. [Counsel then appearing for B] accepted that had the mother not misled the centre, the treatment would have had to stop and a fresh assessment be made. She stopped short of accepting that had the clinic gone ahead regardless of the

changed situation the subsection would not have applied. But that must be the inescapable result.

[41] My Lords, I consider that the Court of Appeal was right to allow the appeal. ... I would add three observations... important though legal certainty is, it is even more important that the very significant legal relationship of parenthood should not be based on a fiction (especially if the fiction involves a measure of deception by the mother). Infertility treatment may be very protracted and a general rule of 'once together, always together' (absent express withdrawal of his acknowledgment by the male partner, or review by the clinic) could produce some very undesirable and unjust consequences.

...

[43] Second, my last paragraph does not imply the view that no weight should be given to the perspective (or perception) of medical staff at the clinic. ... But they cannot be the decisive element if they are based partly on deception, and if the rest of the evidence shows that at the material time there is no longer any 'joint enterprise' between the woman and her ex-partner.

[44] Third, in common with the Court of Appeal I do not think that the appellant can get any assistance from article 8 of the European Convention for the Protection of Human Rights and Fundamental Freedoms. The assertion that B has a right to family life with R (when he is neither her social father nor her biological father) really assumes that which has to be established.

Appeal dismissed.

QUESTIONS

i. Despite the fact that there is a genetic father (the sperm donor), a potentially social father (S) and another man (the applicant D) fighting to establish paternity, the decision results in R being legally fatherless. Do you agree with this outcome? What does it tell us about the purpose and meaning of fatherhood?

ii. D was granted indirect contact with R in *Re D (Contact: Human Fertilisation and Embryology Act 1990)* [2001] EWCA Civ 230, [2001] 1 FLR 972. If the 2007 Bill is enacted under the 'agreed fatherhood conditions', D would be the legal father. Which approach do you prefer?

Leeds Teaching Hospital NHS Trust v A and others
[2003] EWHC 259, [2003] All ER (D) 374

Mr and Mrs A, both white, and Mr and Mrs B, both black, underwent fertility treatment using their own genetic material. When Mrs A gave birth to twins it emerged that Mr B's sperm had been injected into the eggs of Mrs A. Although it was agreed by all parties that Mr and Mrs A would raise the twins, the court held that Mr B was the legal father as Mr A could not be said to have consented to the treatment.

Butler-Sloss P [referring to art 8 of the ECHR]:

[55] The twins unquestionably have rights. ... They are clearly entitled to respect for their family life with their mother, Mrs A, and with Mr A whom they regard as their father. ... Through no fault of theirs, they have been born children of mixed race by a mistake which cannot be rectified.

> Their biological mother and their biological father are not married and cannot marry. They may not be able during their childhood to form any relationship with their biological father. They have inherited two cultures but, in reality, can only gain real benefit from one during their childhood.... If section 28 applies they would have a complete sense of belonging to Mr A. If section 28 is found not to apply then there is a period of uncertainty which is to their detriment.... I agree that it is imperative that their rights and their welfare are secured and protected. In Children Act proceedings their welfare would be the paramount consideration and, similarly, in adoption proceedings the duty of the court would be to promote their welfare throughout their childhood.
>
> [56] In my judgment the twins' rights to respect for their family life with their mother and Mr A can be met by appropriate family or adoption orders and those orders would be proportionate to the infringements of their rights. The effect of the decision of the court that sections 28 and 29 do not apply to their case does not create any greater difficulty for the twins than the unfortunate circumstances surrounding their conception and birth. Although they lose the immediate certainty of the irrebuttable presumption that Mr A is their legal father, they will remain within a loving, stable and secure home. They also retain the great advantage of preserving the reality of their paternal identity.

QUESTIONS

i. Sally Sheldon (2005) argues that 'there seems to be a troubling implication that to be born mixed race is a misfortune, which the children have suffered "through no fault of theirs"... the idea that the twins "have inherited two cultures" might not have been compelling had all four "parents" shared a common ethnic background.' Had the twins not been mixed race, do you think the court would have decided this case in the same way?

ii. Do you think the paramountcy principle should be applied in order to determine who should be the legal father? Why do you think it is not? If it were, who do you think should be the legal father?

iii. Under the 2007 Bill would Mr B be considered the legal father under the 'agreed fatherhood conditions' in clause 37 (see p. 431 above)?

The consent to treatment provisions have also been central to cases where sperm or embryos have been frozen and the courts have had to make difficult decisions as to whether treatment should be permitted to continue.

In *R v Human Fertilisation and Embryology Authority, ex p Blood* [1997] 2 WLR 806, [1997] 2 All ER 687 the Court of Appeal granted Diane Blood the right to travel to Belgium for fertility treatment using the sperm of her dead husband that had been collected by electro-ejaculation before he died but after he had lapsed into a coma. Her case hinged on the right to obtain medical services in other member states under European Community law, and not the 1990 Act under which the husband's consent to use of his sperm was essential. The law was subsequently amended by the Human Fertilisation and Embryology Authority (Deceased Fathers) Act 2003 which provides that where a man's sperm or an embryo using his sperm is used after his death, he may be considered the legal father, for the symbolic purposes of birth registration only, if certain conditions are met. It also applies to embryos where the donor sperm was used as part of treatment that the dead man had entered into together with the mother. The 2007 Bill extends these provisions to lesbian couples (clauses 42, 43).

QUESTIONS

i. Diane Blood's position was treated with much sympathy by the media, the courts and Parliament. Sir Stephen Brown in the High Court commented that: 'My heart goes out to this applicant who wishes to preserve an essential part of her late husband. The refusal to permit her so to do is for her in the nature of a double bereavement' ([1996] 3 WLR 1176, at 1191). However, the Chair of the HFEA at the time, Ruth Deech in 'Assisted Reproductive Techniques and the Law' (2001) described it as 'the most famous case of infertility treatment for convenience'. Do you think widows have a greater 'right to a child' then single woman or lesbian couples?

ii. Mary Warnock while supporting the 2003 reforms recalled in a House of Lords debate that:

> the committee of inquiry was fairly strongly opposed to the use of assisted conception to bring about the birth of a posthumous child largely on the grounds of the possible psychological damage that might be caused if, for example, a widow who had remarried and had other children decided to use her first husband's sperm and to have a child by that husband after all (HL Debs Vol 650 Col 1151 (4 July 2003)).

Sally Sheldon (2005) comments that the change in law reflects the fact that now: 'it is accepted that a child can have a legally recognised link to more than one "father", with this construed as a benefit rather than a potentially harmful, disruptive and confusing state of affairs.' Do you think the reforms are in the best interests of the child?

What should happen if the husband or partner consented to in vitro fertilisation of the woman's egg by his sperm and the resulting embryo was frozen for some years before implantation and he subsequently changes his mind? This situation was considered in the next case.

Evans v Amicus Health Care
[2004] EWCA (Civ) 727, [2004] All ER (D) 309

The situation was complicated by the fact that the ovaries of the woman in question had been removed due to cancer. Consequently, in contrast to *Blood*, using the frozen embryos was her only chance to have a child that she was genetically connected to. The Court of Appeal held that the embryos should be destroyed and this decision was upheld by the European Court of Human Rights (Application no 6339/05; [2006] 1 FCR 843).

Thorpe LJ:

[19] In our domestic law it has been repeatedly held that a foetus prior to the moment of birth does not have independent rights or interests: see *Re F (In Utero)* [1998] 2 All ER 193 and *Re MB (Medical Treatment)* (1997) 2 FLR 426. Thus even more clearly can there be no independent rights or interests in stored embryos. In this respect our law is not inconsistent with the decisions of the ECHR. Article 2 protects the right to life. No Convention jurisprudence extends the right to an embryo, much less to one which at the material point of time is non-viable.

Arden LJ:

[89]...the court asked Mr Johnston, the genetic father in this case, whether he would consent to the storage of the embryos in question in case Miss Evans met another partner who would

become the legal father of any child resulting from implantation of the embryos. Mr Johnston in that event would not have legal responsibility for such a child. ... Mr Johnston did not agree to this on the grounds of principle. He does not want to know there is a child of his growing up in some other town. So the wider issue arises whether in a world in which many people have come to accept a woman's right of choice as to whether she should have a child or not the genetic father should have the equivalent right – a right greater than that conferred by nature. Should there be a continuing requirement for consent when there is no link between mere biological parenthood and legal responsibility? Is it to be supposed that, if a father in this situation some years after the birth of the child met the child, in whom the spark of human life had by then been kindled by his ex-partner, he would be bound to say 'I wish you had never been'? These are difficult questions.

[90] Ms Evans wants the freedom to have the embryos containing her genetic material transferred to her. She wants to exercise her reproductive liberty in this way. The courts respect freedoms for many reasons, not least because to do so demonstrates respect for the dignity of each individual as a human being. The difficulty for Ms Evans is that the genetic material is now not simply hers alone. If the 1990 Act contained no restriction, or if there had been no Act, the courts might well say that the father had given his consent.

[91] A feature of modern society is that conditions are changing very rapidly. Only in 1978 was it possible for a child to be conceived by IVF and for the hope of parenthood to be given by technology. Parenthood is one of the great privileges and joys of life. Not all adults want it, but for those who do want it, it is, and I repeat, one of the privileges and joys of life. Moreover, many women feel parenthood gives them an assurance of their position in society. Parenthood is a very important matter to women, even today.

...

[97] The requirement for treatment together appears to reflect an expectation that, if two persons are jointly involved in the creation of an embryo and its transfer to the woman, both will be responsible for the upbringing of the child when born. As I have sought to show, this aim is not necessarily achieved simply by a requirement for two people to be involved together at that stage. It may one day be possible for a child to have only one genetic parent. Even now, there is no need for a child to be brought up by two persons and very often these days this does not happen. However, the appellant has not argued that the word 'together' must be given a contemporary meaning to reflect this change in social conditions and accordingly this is not an argument on which it would be appropriate for me to express a view in this case.

...

[110] Like Thorpe and Sedley LJJ, I consider that the imposition of an invariable and ongoing requirement for consent in the 1990 Act in the present type of situation satisfies art 8(2) of the Convention. The requirement is supported by ... the argument based on the primacy of consent. As this is a sensitive area of ethical judgment, the balance to be struck between the parties must primarily be a matter for Parliament ... Parliament has taken the view that no-one should have power to override the need for a genetic parent's consent. The wisdom of not having such a power is, in my judgment, illustrated by the facts of this case. The personal circumstances of the parties are different from what they were at the outset of treatment, and it would be difficult for a court to judge whether the effect of Mr Johnston's withdrawal of his consent on Ms Evans is greater than the effect that the invalidation of that withdrawal of consent would have on Mr Johnston. The court has no point of reference by which to make that sort of evaluation. The fact is that each person has a right to be protected against interference with their private life. That is an aspect of the principle of self-determination or personal autonomy. It cannot be said that the interference with Mr Johnston's right is justified on the ground that interference is necessary to protect Ms Evans' right, because her right is likewise qualified in the same way by his right. They must have equivalent rights, even though the exact extent of their rights under art 8 has not been identified.

[111] The interference with Ms Evans' private life is also justified under art 8(2) because, if Ms Evans' argument succeeded, it would amount to interference with the genetic father's right to decide not to become a parent. Motherhood could surely not be forced on Ms Evans and likewise fatherhood cannot be forced on Mr Johnston, especially as in the present case it will probably involve financial responsibility in law for the child as well.

QUESTIONS

i. Do you agree with the decision? (Note, that the 2007 Bill suggests that while a man may withdraw his consent to be treated as the legal father, the woman may still be able to proceed with the treatment without his involvement (clause 21(3)(6C).)

ii. If a women becomes pregnant through sexual intercourse the man cannot require her to have an abortion. Should men and women always be treated as equal partners in matters of reproduction? (See Chapter 12 and the need, or otherwise, to obtain consent from the father in a situation where the mother consents to adoption.)

iii. Go back to the discussion of *Odievre v France* at p. 412. Is Arden LJ right that 'motherhood could surely not be forced on Ms Evans'?

A further issue is the question whether a child conceived by means of sperm donation should have the right to know the identity of his or her genetic parents. The Warnock Committee's Report (1984) considered this issue and concluded that:

4.22 We were agreed that there is a need to maintain the absolute anonymity of the donor, though we recognise that in privately arranged donation, for example between brothers, a different situation would of course apply; such domestic arrangements, however, fall outside any general regulation. Anonymity would give legal protection to the donor but it would also have the effect of minimising the invasion of the third party into the family. Without anonymity, men would, it is argued, be less likely to become donors... We recognise that one consequence of this provision would be that AID children, even if informed about the circumstances of their conception would never be entitled to know the identity of their genetic fathers.

The 1990 Act adopted a compromise and provided that only non-identifying information about the donor could be made available to the child, and only when he/she reaches the age of eighteen (section 31). However, since then the idea that there is a right to know one's genetic identity has attracted more support. Mary Warnock's position has changed and she now argues that 'all such deception is an evil' (2006). Similarly, John Eekelaar in *Family Law and Personal Life* (2006) argues that:

Children have an interest in having knowledge of the physical truth because it provides an underlying certainty about the world they have come into, incapable of manipulation by the adults. ... Fictitious fatherhood in cases of parenthood by donor insemination sustains a perception of shame of infertility, and the deviant nature of artificial reproduction. ... If society provides the means of artificial reproduction. ... it presumably believes they are morally acceptable practices. Let it then shout it from the rooftops. As for the rest let us confront the world, as our children do when they come into it, as we have made it.

In *R (on the application of Rose and another) v Secretary of State for Health and another* [2002] EWHC 1593 (Admin), [2002] All ER 398 the court held that the right to obtain both identifying and non-identifying information about a biological parent engaged the right to respect for private and family life in Article 8:

Scott Baker J:

It is to my mind entirely understandable that A.I.D. children should wish to know about their origins and in particular to learn what they can about their biological father or, in the case of egg donation, their biological mother. ... I do not find this at all surprising bearing in mind the lessons that have been learnt from adoption. A human being is a human being whatever the circumstances of his conception and an A.I.D. child is entitled to establish a picture of his identity as much as anyone else. We live in a much more open society than even 20 years ago. Secrecy nowadays has to be justified where previously it did not.

Following this decision in 2004 the law was changed and people born as a result of sperm, eggs or embryos donated after April 2005 now have the right to know their donor's identity, but, again, only once they reach the age of eighteen (Human Fertilisation and Embryology Authority (Disclosure of Donor Information) Regulations 2004.

QUESTIONS

i. Despite the change in the law there is no obligation on parents to tell their children of their mode of conception. Do you think information about a child's method of conception should be included on a child's birth certificate?

ii. Emily Jackson (2001) reminds us that:

> [A] significant proportion of the population, perhaps as many as 10 per cent, are in fact biologically unrelated to their presumed fathers. Infidelity may then be a statistically greater threat to accurate knowledge of our biological origins than the relatively small number of DI births.

Is 'truth' always the best policy? Is it always in the best interest of the child? (See *Re J (Paternity: Welfare of the Child)* [2006] EWHC 2837 (Fam), [2007] 1 FLR 1064.) What about the rights of a mother who fears a violent reaction from her husband if the truth was to be known?

iii. HFEA advises that 'Demand for donors has always outstripped supply and this is still true today.... We do not know what the effect of the change in law will have, but we suspect that, in the short term at least, it may lead to a dip in the number of donors.' If you were considering donation, would you be more put off by (a) the change in the anonymity rules, or (b) the banning of payment?

iv. How relevant is the comparison made by Scott Baker J in *Rose* with adoption? (see p. 427).

v. Do the 2004 reforms comply with a child's right to an identity under Articles 7 and 8 of the UN Convention on the Rights of the Child 1989?

vi. How much information about donors should potential parents be entitled to when undergoing treatment? Should a white woman be able to ask for sperm from a black man?

The concern here is with the long-term welfare and interests of a person who has been born as a result of licensed treatment. But what about the welfare of children who may be born if treatment is given? Section 13(5) of the 1990 Act provides that:

> A woman shall not be provided with treatment services unless account has been taken of the welfare of any child who may be born as a result of the treatment (including the need of that child for a father), and of any other child who may be affected by the birth.

The then Lord Chancellor (Lord Falconer) explained what this meant to the House of Lords (*Hansard* (HL), vol. 516, c. 1097) thus:

> I think everyone would agree that it is important that children are born into a stable and loving environment and that the family is a concept whose health is fundamental to the health of society in general. A fundamental principle to our law about children, including the legislation which this House considered in such detail last Session and which became the Children Act 1989, is that the welfare of children is of paramount consideration. I think that it is, for these general reasons, entirely right that the Bill should be amended to add that concept...
>
> Among the factors which clinicians should take into account will be the material circumstances in which the child is likely to be brought up and also the stability and love which he or she is likely to enjoy. Such stability is clearly linked to the marital position of the woman and in particular whether a husband or long-term partner can play a full part in providing the child with a permanent family setting in the fullest sense of that term, including financial provision.
>
> The House does not need to be reminded of the plight of childless people and the very strong and deeply felt emotions which those in that position experience. We may on the one hand pay the tribute which is due to the importance of ensuring that children are born into the family environment by specifically excluding from treatment women who are not married or have no stable partner to be involved in the decision about treatment and in counselling beforehand, but I wonder what will happen if we do that. Surely there is a risk that such women, driven by the very strong desire for a child, may turn elsewhere for treatment. I am advised that it is a relatively easy matter for AID to be carried out in clinically unsupervised conditions. It may be that the result of the amendment would be to encourage those few single woman who are infertile to seek unsuitable donors if we were to introduce such a restriction. Any children who may be born as a result of uncontrolled treatment are at risk of serious disease, including HIV infection.
>
> On the other hand, if the law recognises that in a very small number of cases single women will come forward for treatment, it may be better to encourage them to seek clinical advice. With the child and welfare amendments we have just discussed there is a likelihood that through counselling and discussion with those responsible for licensed treatment they may be dissuaded from having children once they have fully considered the implications of the environment into which their child would be born for its future welfare.

However, the 2007 Bill proposes to delete the phrase 'including the need of that child for a father'. Collier and Sheldon (2008) argue that:

> This can be seen as a reflection of shifting attitudes towards the family, and specifically, the criticism that the provision discriminates against single women and lesbian couples. ... A House of Commons Select Committee specifically recommended reform of s 13(5) on the basis that:

> the requirement to consider whether a child born as a result of assisted reproduction needs a father is too open to interpretation and unjustifiably offensive to many. It is wrong for legislation to imply that unjustified discrimination against 'unconventional families' is acceptable (Recommendation 21, HC Science and Technology Committee Human Reproductive Technologies and the Law (Fifth Report of Session, 2004–5, HC 701) at para 101.)

More recently, however... the Joint Parliamentary Committee charged with scrutinizing the draft legislation has recommended retention of this provision, albeit in a form which makes it clear that the provision should be understood as requiring consideration of the need for a second parent who can either be a father or a second 'female patient'. Intriguingly, the Committee states:

> In making this recommendation, we do not seek to discriminate against single women seeking treatment and we recommend that in such circumstances...the requirement to consider the need of a child for a second parent should, as now, not be a barrier to treatment

How it is possible to prefer a two parent model while not so discriminating receives no further attention.

QUESTION

Do you think the reference to the 'need for a father' should be kept, revised or deleted?

Guidance on the welfare of the child is given by the Human Fertilisation and Embryology Authority in its *Code of Practice* (2007):

> G.3.2.1 Where the child will not be raised by the carrying mother (i.e. in a surrogacy arrangement) the centre should carry out an assessment both in relation to those commissioning the surrogacy arrangement and the surrogate (and her partner, if she has one).
>
> G 3.2.2 The centre should carry out a risk assessment in relation to each patient and their partner (if applicable) before any treatment is provided. The assessment should be carried out in a non-discriminatory way. In particular, patients should not be unfairly discriminated against on grounds of gender, race, disability, sexual orientation, religious belief or age.
>
> ...
>
> G 3.3.2 Those seeking treatment are entitled to a fair assessment. The centre is expected to conduct the assessment with skill and care, and have regard to the wishes of all those involved. In order to take into account the welfare of the child, the centre should consider factors which are likely to cause serious physical, psychological or medical harm, either to the child to be born or to any existing child of the family. These factors include:
>
> (a) any aspect of the patient's (or, where applicable, their partner's) past or current circumstances which means that either the child to be born or any existing child of the family is likely to experience serious physical or psychological harm or neglect. Such aspects might include:
>
> (i) previous convictions relating to harming children, or

(ii) child protection measures taken regarding existing children, or
(iii) serious violence or discord within the family environment;

(b) any aspect of the patient's (or, where applicable, their partner's) past or current circumstances which is likely to lead to an inability to care for the child to be born throughout its childhood or which are already seriously impairing the care of any existing child of the family. Such aspects might include:
(i) mental or physical conditions, or
(ii) drug or alcohol abuse;

(c) any aspect of the patient's (or, where applicable, their partner's) medical history which means that the child to be born is likely to suffer from a serious medical condition;

(d) any other aspects of the patient's (or, where applicable, their partner's) circumstances which treatment centres consider to be likely to cause serious harm to the child to be born or any existing child of the family.

G 3.3.3 Where the child will have no legal father, the centre should assess the prospective mother's ability to meet the child's/children's needs and the ability of other persons within the family or social circle willing to share responsibility for those needs.

QUESTIONS

i. Can you improve upon this? Would it also be useful in adoption placements?

ii. What is the case for imposing these requirements upon couples who need IVF or other assistance but can use their own eggs and sperm?

iii. Should it be available to a woman who is HIV positive?

iv. What difference, if any, does it make that treatment is more readily available for people who can pay for it? How rigorously do you think that the Code will be applied (a) in an NHS hospital and (b) in a private clinic?

v. Blyth in 'Assisted reproduction: what's in it for the children?' (1990) points out that: 'the extent to which welfare principles might apply to children in the field of AR is questionable... Firstly, it is hardly valid to claim that anyone would have been better off not having been born in the first place. Secondly, the implication that alternatives exist from which a choice may be made does not hold.' Do you agree?

Finally, we turn to surrogacy, a practice that arouses strong views and has received much media attention (see, e.g., the 'Baby Cotton' case: *Re C (A Minor) (Wardship: Surrogacy)* [1985] FLR 846, [1985] Fam Law 191; and, more recently, when a gay male couple had twins using an egg donated by one woman and their own sperm and carried by a US surrogate: Woodward (1999)).

The Warnock Committee's Report (1984) summarised the arguments like this:

Arguments Against Surrogacy

8.10 There are strongly held objections to the concept of surrogacy, and it seems from the evidence submitted to us that the weight of public opinion is against the practice. The objections turn essentially on the view that to introduce a third party into the process of procreation which should be confined to the loving partnership between two people, is an attack on the value of the marital relationship. Further, the intrusion is worse than in the case of AID, since the contribution of the carrying mother is greater, more intimate and personal, than the contribution of a semen donor. It is also argued that it is inconsistent with human dignity that a woman should use her uterus for financial profit and treat it as an incubator for someone else's child. The objection is not diminished, indeed it is strengthened, where the woman entered an agreement to conceive a child, with the sole purpose of handing the child over to the commissioning couple after birth.

8.11 Again, it is argued that the relationship between mother and child is itself distorted by surrogacy. For in such an arrangement a woman deliberately allows herself to become pregnant with the intention of giving up the child to which she will give birth, and this is the wrong way to approach pregnancy. It is also potentially damaging to the child, whose bonds with the carrying mother, regardless of genetic connections, are held to be strong, and whose welfare must be considered to be of paramount importance. Further it is felt that a surrogacy agreement is degrading to the child who is to be the outcome of it, since, for all practical purposes, the child will have been bought for money.

8.12 It is also argued that since there are some risks attached to pregnancy, no woman ought to be asked to undertake pregnancy for another, in order to earn money. Nor, it is argued should a woman be forced by legal sanctions to part with a child, to which she has recently given birth, against her will.

Arguments For Surrogacy

8.13 If infertility is a condition which should, where possible, be remedied it is argued that surrogacy must not be ruled out, since it offers to some couples their only chance of having a child genetically related to one or both of them. In particular, it may well be the only way that the husband of an infertile woman can have a child. Moreover, the bearing of a child for another can be seen, not as an undertaking that trivialises or commercialises pregnancy, but, on the contrary, as a deliberate and thoughtful act of generosity on the part of one woman to another. If there are risks attached to pregnancy, then the generosity is all the greater.

8.14 There is no reason, it is argued, to suppose that carrying mothers will enter into agreements lightly, and they have a perfect right to enter into such agreements if they so wish, just as they have a right to use their own bodies in other ways, according to their own decision. Where agreements are genuinely voluntary, there can be no question of exploitation, nor does the fact that surrogates will be paid for their pregnancy of itself entail exploitation of either party to the agreement.

8.15 As for intrusion into the marriage relationship, it is argued that those who feel strongly about this need not seek such treatment, but they should not seek to prevent others from having access to it.

8.16 On the question of bonding, it is argued that as very little is actually known about the extent to which bonding occurs when the child is in utero, no great claims should be made in this respect. In any case the breaking of such bonds, even if less than ideal, is not held to be an overriding argument against placing a child for adoption, where the mother wants this.

The Committee were divided between those who wanted an almost complete ban on the practice, and those who wanted only profit-making agencies banned. The Surrogacy Arrangements Act 1985 banned commercial agencies and advertising of and for surrogacy services. The Human Fertilisation and Embryology Act 1990 inserted a further provision making all surrogacy arrangements unenforceable; however, it allows the commissioning parents to take over if: the child is in the care of the couple; the surrogate mother and the legal father give full, voluntary, informed and unconditional consent; the child is genetically related to at least one of the commissioning couple; one or both of the commissioning parents is domiciled in the UK; the application is made within six months of the birth; and, no money other than reasonable expenses are paid (section 30). The 2007 Bill extends these provisions to same-sex couples (clause 54).

In 1998 the Brazier Committee found that 'incomplete implementation of the recommendations of either the majority or the minority of the Warnock Committee created a policy vacuum within which surrogacy has developed in a haphazard fashion'. They recommended the registration of non-profit-making agencies, who would have to abide by a Code of Practice, the continued banning of commercial agencies, statutory limitations so that surrogate mothers could only be paid genuine expenses, and the tightening of the section 30 process, with no power retrospectively to authorise illegal payments. The 2007 Bill adopts some of the recommendations, exempting not-for-profit agencies from the prohibitions in the current rules from adverting their services and from receiving money for them (clause 66). Emily Jackson (2001) argues for a greater acceptance of surrogacy:

> Hostility to facilitative regulation is based upon two principal misconceptions. First.... there is little evidence to support the twin assumptions that surrogacy exploits women and harms children. Second, making it difficult to engage lawfully in surrogacy arrangements is unlikely to lead people who cannot have children in any other way to simply resign themselves to their childlessness. Rather restrictive regulation may be the catalyst for them to travel abroad to find a surrogate mother, or to make unlawful contracts in a regulatory vacuum.
>
> There are several ways in which the law relating to surrogacy could be reformed so it more accurately reflected the intentions of the parties. Much depends upon the status provisions because if intention governs the determination of parenthood, then the commissioning couple are the child's parents, and there is no need for any rules governing the transfer of legal parenthood. Although this solution would have an appealing simplicity, it might also lack clarity and certainty, and would require some default position in the event of a dispute. A second possibility might be to make surrogacy contracts enforceable, provided that they satisfied various conditions. So contracts which had been made in circumstances of undue influence, or which were oppressive or unconscionable would be unenforceable. The surrogate mother would continue to be considered the child's legal mother at the moment of birth, and if she chose not to perform her side of the bargain by carrying the pregnancy to term and handing the child over, she would be in breach of contract. If this is characterised as a contract for services, it would not be specifically enforceable and she would instead be liable in damages. Although there would be the usual objections to the commercialization of something as sacred as childbearing, it might be important to recognize that the real danger posed by surrogacy is the creation of a legal framework which encourages would-be surrogates and would-be commissioning couples to have children without the safeguards that can exist within an effective regulatory scheme.

In relation to assisted reproduction more generally Jackson argues that:

> A commitment to liberty and moral pluralism should lead us to restrict an individual's reproductive autonomy only where the risk of harm to another person outweighs her undeniably compelling interest in deciding for herself whether and how to reproduce.

QUESTIONS

i. In *A v C* [1985] FLR 445, Ormrod LJ referred to a surrogacy arrangement (from which the mother had withdrawn) as a 'quite bizarre and unnatural arrangement' and Cumming-Bruce J called it a 'kind of baby-farming operation of a wholly distasteful and lamentable kind': do you agree? What if the commissioning parents can offer the child far better opportunities? (See *Re S (Surrogacy: Residence)* December [2007] Family Law 1135.)

ii. How much of the law relating to adoption would you apply to the procedure under section 30?

iii. (a) In 1987, Mrs Pat Anthony gave birth to triplets. Doctors in South Africa had implanted into her eggs from her daughter Karen which had been fertilised by Karen's husband's sperm. Mrs Anthony therefore became the world's first surrogate grandmother (see Reid, 1988). Should treatment be provided in such a case? (b) In 1989, an English husband, infertile as a result of mumps, was told that it was 'ethically impossible' for his wife to be artificially inseminated with his brother's sperm. Can you think what the ethical objection might be?

iv. Do you think the distinction made by the Brazier Committee and the 2007 Bill between commercial and not-for-profit agencies is valid?

v. Why do you think the 1990 Act requires one or both of the commissioning parents to be domiciled in the UK before a parental order under section 30 can be applied for? (See *Re G (Surrogacy: Foreign Domicile)* [2007] EWHC 2814 (Fam).)

vi. Why do you think family law is so reluctant to accept the principles and practice of contract law? (Contrast this issue with the agreements discussed in Chapter 5 (p. 247) and Chapter 6 (p. 281.)

vii. Why does public policy not allow the carrying mother to decide what she finds 'inconsistent with [her] human dignity'?

9.5 ILLEGITIMATE CHILDREN OR ILLEGITIMATE PARENTS?

As we have seen above, in determining who is a child's legal father, the marital status of the parents is a significant factor. This might seem surprising when we consider the proportion of children born outside of marriage. The trend is summarised below in *Social Trends 37* (2007):

> Although most children are born to married couples, there has been a substantial rise in the proportion of births occurring outside marriage [see Figure 2.18]. With the exception of the periods immediately after the two World Wars, few births occurred outside marriage during the first 60 years of the 20th century. During the 1960s and 1970s such births became more common and by 1980, 12 per cent of all births in the UK were outside marriage. By 2005 this had increased to 43 per cent. Most births outside marriage were registered by both parents rather than only one parent, indicating an increase in cohabiting parents. In 2005, 84 per cent of births outside marriage in England and Wales were jointly registered by both parents. Three in four of jointly registered births were to parents living at the same address.

The proportions of births outside marriage vary across the UK. More than one-half of all births in Wales in 2005 were outside marriage (52 per cent). This compared with 47 per cent of births in Scotland, 42 per cent in England and 36 per cent of births in Northern Ireland. Within England, the North East region had the highest proportion of births outside marriage (55 per cent), followed by the North West (49 per cent), and Yorkshire and the Humber (47 per cent). The lowest proportions of births outside marriage in England were in London and the South East (35 per cent and 38 per cent respectively). In 2005 the UK had one of the highest levels of births outside marriage in the EU-25 (42 per cent), together with Estonia (58 per cent), Sweden (55 per cent), France (47 per cent), Denmark, Latvia and Slovenia (each 45 per cent) and Finland (41 per cent). The lowest proportion was in Cyprus at 3 per cent.

Figure 2.18 Births outside marriage[1]

Source: Office for National Statistics; General Register Office for Scotland; Northern Ireland Statistics and Research Agency

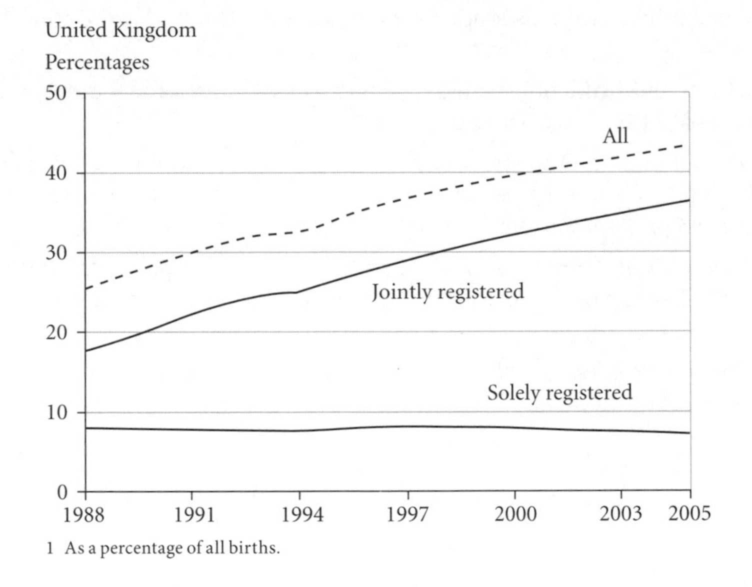

1 As a percentage of all births.

QUESTIONS

i. Do these figures surprise or concern you? How would you explain the trend?

ii. Do you think the laws relating to husbands and legal fatherhood are still appropriate or necessary?

iii. The Law Commission's working paper on *Illegitimacy* (1979, paragraph 2.10) concluded that 'It may be that the biggest discrimination suffered by a person born out of wedlock is the legal characterisation of him as "illegitimate"'. Do you think there are any negative connotations or prejudices attached to the label of illegitimacy?

iv. For centuries, law tried to deter parents from having children outside wedlock (see Laslett, 1971) Do you think this is a legitimate or possible role for law?

Reforms introduced by the Family Law Reform Acts 1969 and 1987 removed most of the distinctions between children born inside and outside marriage. In keeping with this trend most recently the Nationality Immigration and Asylum Act 2002 and British Nationality (Proof of Paternity) Regulations 2006 provided that children born outside of the UK are now entitled to British citizenship through an unmarried father. Two distinctions, however, still exist: unlike on divorce, when unmarried parents separate there is no scrutiny of the arrangements for the children (see p. 150), and children born outside marriage cannot inherit titles of honour.

QUESTIONS

i. Do you think these remaining distinctions are justified? Is there any way in which the arrangements made by unmarried parents when they separate could be scrutinised?

ii. The Human Fertilisation and Embryology Act 1990 also provides that the rules relating to legal parenthood by donor or sperm donation do not apply to the inheritance of titles (section 29(4)). Brazier (2000) argues that this provision represents a 'characteristically British obsession with heredity'. Do you think the inheritance of titles should have been exempted from legal reforms?

The most controversial aspect of the retention of the distinction concerns not so much the child but the status of the unmarried father. As the Law Commission (1979, paragraphs 2.11; 3.16) explained:

> From a strictly legal point of view, the father of an illegitimate child is today probably at a greater disadvantage than the child himself.

In their Report on *Illegitimacy* (1982), the Law Commission concluded that:

> 4.44...Some commentators expressed the view...that it would be perfectly possible to abolish the status of illegitimacy whilst preserving the existing rules whereby parental rights vest automatically only in married parents. We do not accept this view. The argument for 'abolishing illegitimacy' (rather than merely removing such legal consequences of that status as are adverse to the child) is essentially that the abolition of any legal distinction based on the parents' marital status would itself have an influence on opinion. The marital status of the child's parents would cease to be legally relevant, and thus the need to refer to the child's distinctive legal status would (in this view) disappear. This consequence could not follow if a distinction – albeit relating only to entitlement to parental rights – were to be preserved between children which would be based solely on their parents' status.

Under the Children Act 1989, as amended by the Adoption and Children Act 2002, an unmarried father can now obtain parental responsibility by becoming registered as the child's father on or after 3 December 2003 (section 4(1)(a)), by agreement with the mother (section 4(1)(b)), by order of the court (section 4(1)(c)), or if the court makes a residence order in his favour (section 12(1)). Thus, an increasing number of unmarried fathers now have parental responsibility. The 2002 Act change has not led to a decrease in joint registrations as some had predicted, though we do not know why parents do not co-register.

In 2007 the Secretary of State for Work and Pensions published a consultation paper that proposes that joint registration be the legal default position. This would:

> 3. ... help develop a culture in which the welfare of children is paramount and people are clear that fatherhood, as well as motherhood, always comes with both rights and responsibilities.

However it also recommended the following safeguards:

> 56. We understand that ... it is essential that women are protected from having to name a father if there is good cause for them not to do so. ...
> 57. With this in mind, joint registration will not be required where the:
>   - mother does not know, or is not clear about, who is the father of her child
>   - mother does not know where the father of the child is; or
>   - father is deceased.
> 58. In addition, we believe that certain cases should be exempt from joint registration where the:
>   - mother alleges that a father is, or could become violent or abusive;
>   - mother alleges that the child is conceived as a result of rape or non-consensual sex;
>   - mother alleges that the child was conceived as a result of incest;
>   - man alleges that he is not the father of the child;
>   - mother alleges that the man claiming paternity is not the father of the child.
> 59. In these cases, if ether parent wants to continue to pursue joint registration, the matter should be decided by the courts rather than by the registration service.
>
> ...
>
> 62. ... Where the father has not come forward to register, a mother should be required to pass on those details which would enable him to be traced and invited to register, unless she gives reasons that fall within one of the exempt categories. ... A father who acknowledges paternity but refuses to register will be subject to the current penalty regime, which is a fine, that exists for failure to register a birth.

QUESTIONS

i. In *B v UK* (Application No. 39076/97) [2000] 1 FLR 1 (decided before the 2002 reforms) the European Court of Human Rights held that there was no violation of Article 14 in conjunction with Article 8:

> ... the relationship between unmarried fathers and their children varies from ignorance and indifference to a close stable relationship indistinguishable from the conventional family based unit. For this reason the court has held that there exists an objective and reasonable justification for the difference in treatment between married and unmarried fathers with regard to the automatic acquisition of parental rights.

Do you think the 2002 reforms adequately protect women? Do you agree with the 2007 proposals that further reform is needed?

ii. The 2007 Green Paper states that 'Mothers who register solely are likely to be younger and poorer, with lower levels of educational attainment than those who jointly register' (paragraph 2). Why do you think these woman are less likely to co-register? Do you think the proposals will improve the lives of their children? (See the response to the proposals from the British Association for Adoption and Fostering in Chapter 5, p. 192.)

The vast majority of the applications for Parental Responsibility Orders under the Children Act 1989 are successful: in 2004 only 2 per cent were refused and in 2005 just under 3 per cent (*Judicial Statistics* 2004, 2005, Table 5.3). The approach of the courts is conveniently summarised in the following case.

Re S (Parental Responsibility)
[1995] 3 FCR 225, [1995] 2 FLR 648, Court of Appeal

The parents lived together from 1985 and the child was born in January 1988. The parents separated when she was eighteen months old. The father regularly paid the mother £500 per month. In 1990 he was convicted of possessing obscene literature. The mother stopped contact for a while, but resumed it because of the child's distress. It developed into staying contact. The father applied for a parental responsibility order but was refused. He appealed.

Ward LJ:

The first important case on this subject... is *Re H (Minors) (Local Authority: Parental Rights) (No 3)* [1991] Fam 151, [1991] 1 FLR 214. Balcombe LJ... suggested, and most helpfully, this test

> 'In considering whether to make an order under s.4 of the 1987 Family Law Reform Act, the court will have to take into account a number of factors of which the following will undoubtedly be material (although there may well be others, as the list is not intended to be exhaustive):
>
> (1) the degree of commitment which the father has shown towards the child;
> (2) the degree of attachment which exists between the father and the child; and
> (3) the reasons of the father for applying for the order.'

...

[I]t is my increasing concern, both from the very fact that there are so many reported cases on this topic and from my experience when dealing with the innumerable appeals from justices to the Family Division, that applications under s. 4 have become one of these little growth industries born of misunderstanding. Misunderstanding arises from a failure to appreciate that, in essence, the granting of a parental responsibility order is the granting of status. It is unfortunate that the notion of 'parental responsibility' has still to be defined by s. 3 of the Children Act to mean '...all the rights, duties, powers, responsibilities and authority which by law a parent...has in relation to the child and his property', which gives outmoded pre-eminence to the 'rights' which are conferred. That it is unfortunate is demonstrated by the very fact that, when pressed in this case to define the nature and effect of the order which was so vigorously opposed, counsel for the mother was driven to say that her rooted objection was to the rights to which it would entitle the father and the power that it would give him. That is a most unfortunate failure to appreciate the significant change that the Act has brought about where the emphasis is to move away from rights and to concentrate on responsibilities. She did not doubt that if by unhappy chance this child fell ill whilst she was abroad, her father, if then enjoying contact, would not deal responsibly with her welfare. ...

Butler-Sloss LJ:

I also agree ... It is important for parents and it is important, indeed, for these parents to remember the emphasis placed by Parliament on the order which is applied for. It is that of duties and responsibilities as well as rights and powers. Indeed, the order itself is entitled 'parental responsibility'. A father who has shown real commitment to the child concerned and to whom there is a positive attachment, as well as a genuine bona fide reason for the application, ought, in a case such as the present, to assume the weight of those duties and cement that commitment and attachment by sharing the responsibilities for the child with the mother. This father is asking to assume that burden as well as that pleasure of looking after his child, a burden not lightly to be undertaken.

Appeal allowed.

QUESTIONS

i. Is Ward LJ right that, 'in essence, the granting of a parental responsibility order is the granting of status'? Contrast this approach with the decision in *Re M (handicapped child: parental responsibility)* [2001] All ER (D) 449, [2001] 3 FCR 454 where parental responsibility was refused as the court considered that the father would be likely to use it to cause the mother stress and undermine her ability to care properly for the child. Should fathers be able to acquire parental responsibility for their children without undertaking any responsibility towards the children's mothers?

ii. Look at *Re B (a minor) (adoption: natural parent)* [2001] UKHL 70, [2002] 1 FLR 196, HL. Would the result have been the same if the mother had applied to adopt?

iii. The new section 4 (2A) of the Children Act 1989 refers to the loss of parental responsibility. What do you think might be the criteria for its removal? Why should it be possible to remove parental responsibility from fathers and not from mothers? How does this compare with the law on adoption?

iv. It will still be possible to remove parental responsibility from unmarried fathers, but not from married fathers nor from mothers, married or unmarried. (a) Can this discrimination be justified? (b) In what circumstances do you think this can or should be done?

v. If a father is granted a residence order, section 12(1) insists that a parental responsibility order must also be made; why do you think there is no corresponding requirement for when a contact order is made?

vi. In *Re H (minors) (local authority: parental rights) (No 3)* [1991] 2 All ER 185, [1991] Fam 151, the Court of Appeal held that a father should be granted parental responsibility, so that his agreement to the child's adoption was required, but then that this could be dispensed with on the ground that it was unreasonably withheld: what good did this do for either the father or the child?

vii. What now are the advantages, from the child's point of view, of his mother being married to his father?

BIBLIOGRAPHY

9.1 How to become a father

We quoted from:

A. Jeffreys, 'Genetic fingerprinting: applications and misapplications' in B. Holland and C. Kyriakou (eds), *Genetics and Society* (1993) London, Addison-Wesley, 51–53.

Lord Chancellor's Department, *Procedures for the Determination of Paternity and on The Law on Parental Responsibility for Unmarried Fathers* (1998), 5.

Additional reading

A. Bainham, 'Parentage, Parenthood and Parental Responsibility: Subtle, Elusive Yet Important Distinctions', in A. Bainham, S. Day Sclater and M. Richards (eds), *What is a Parent?* (1999) Oxford, Hart.

E. Jackson (2006) 'What is a Parent?' in A. Diduck and K. O'Donovan (eds), *Feminist Perspectives on Family Law* (2006) London, Routledge-Cavendish.

9.2 Motherhood: a fact or a choice?

We quoted from:

K. O'Donovan and J. Marshall, 'After Birth: Decisions about becoming a Mother', in A. Diduck and K. O'Donovan (eds) *Feminist Perspectives on Family Law* (2006) London, Routledge-Cavendish, 115–118.

Additional reading

J. Nedlesky, 'Preconceiving autonomy: sources, thoughts and possibilities' in A. Hutchinson and L. Green (eds), *Law and the Community: The End of Individualism?* (1989) Toronto, Carswell.

E. Steiner (2003) '*Odievere v France* – desperately seeking mother – anonymous births in the European Court of Human Rights' 15 *Child and Family Law Quarterly*, 425.

9.3 How to adopt a child

We quoted from:

C. Bridge and H. Swindells, *Adoption, The Modern Law* (2003), Bodmin, Family Law, 40–49.

British Association for Adoption and Fostering website: http://www.baaf.org.uk/info/stats/england.shtml.

Department of Health, White Paper, *Adoption – a new approach* (2000) London, HMSO.

B. Hale, foreword to Bridge and Swindells (see above).

D. Howe and J. Feast, *Adoption, Search and Reunion* (2000) London, The Children's Society, 16–18, 38, 58.

N. Lowe, 'The changing face of adoption – the gift/donation model versus the contract/services model' (1997) 9 *Child and Family Law Quarterly*, 371.

N. Lowe, 'English Adoption Law, Past, Present and Future' in S. Katz, J. Eekelaar, and M. Maclean (eds), *Cross Currents* (2000) Oxford, Oxford University Press, 314.

Report (first) of the Child Adoption Committee (Chairman: Mr Justice Tomlin) (Cmd. 2401) (1925) London, HMSO, 4, 9, 11, 15, 18, 19, 28.

Report of the Departmental Committee on the Adoption of Children (Chairman: Sir William Houghton, later Judge F.A. Stickdale) (Cmnd. 5107) (1972) London, HMSO, 83.

Review of Adoption Law – Report to Ministers of an Interdepartmental Working Group (1992) London, Department of Health and Welsh Office, 26.4, 26.7–26.16.

B. Tizard, *Adoption: A Second Chance* (1977) London, Open Books, 1, 3–8.

J. Triseliotis, *In Search of Origins: The Experiences of Adopted People* (1973) London, Routledge and Kegan Paul, 84, 85, 101.

Additional reading

J. Feast and J. Smith, 'Working on behalf of birth families – The Children's Society experience' (1997) 21 *Adoption and Fostering* 8.

B. Gonyo and K.W. Watson, 'Searching in adoption' (1988) *Public Welfare* (Winter), 14.

E. Haimes and N. Timms, *Adoption, Identity and Social Policy: The Search for Distant Relatives* (1997) Aldershot, Gower.

M. Humphrey and H. Humphrey, 'Damaged identity and the search for kinship in adult adoptees' (1989) 62 *British Journal of Medical Psychology*, 301.

R. McMillan and G. Irving, *Heart of Reunion: Some Experiences of Reunion in Scotland* (1994) Essex, Barnardo's.

K. March, 'Perception of adoption as a social stigma: Motivation for search and reunion' (1995) 57 *Journal of Marriage and the Family*, 653.

G. Pugh, *Unlocking the Past: The Impact of Access to Barnardo's Childcare Records* (1999) Aldershot, Gower.

P. Sachdev, 'Adoption reunion and after: a study of the search process and experience of adoptees' (1992) 71 *Child Welfare*, 53.

H.J. Sants, 'Genealogical bewilderment in children with substitute parents' (1964) 37 *British Journal of Medical Psychology*, 133.

A. Sorosky, A. Baran, R. Pannpr, 'The reunion of adoptees and birth relatives' (1974) 3 *Journal of Youth and Adolescence*, 195.

F. Tasker, 'Reviewing Lesbian and Gay Adoption and Foster Care: the Developmental Outcomes for Children' [2007] *Family Law*, 524.

9.4 Assisted reproduction

We quoted from:

E. Blyth, 'Assisted reproduction: what's in it for the children?' (1990) 4 *Children and Society*, 167, 174–177.

R. Collier and S. Sheldon, *Fragmenting Fatherhood*, (2008) Oxford, Hart, Chapter 3.

R. Deech (2001) 'Assisted Reproductive Techniques and the Law' 69 *Medico-Legal Journal*, 13, 18.

J. Eekelaar (2006) *Family Law and Personal Life*, Oxford, OUP, 75–76.

HFEA, Parliamentary briefing, Issue 2 December 2005.

Human Fertilisation and Embryology Authority, *Code of Practice* (2007), G.3.2.2-G.3.3.3

E. Jackson, *Regulating Reproduction* (2001) Oxford, Hart, 199, 213–214, 315–316, 323.

Report of the Committee of Inquiry into Human Fertilisation and Embryology (Chairman: Dame Mary Warnock) (Cmnd. 9314) (1984) London, HMSO, paras. 4.22, 8.10–8.16.

S. Sheldon 'Fragmenting Fatherhood: The Regulation of Reproductive Technologies' (2005) 68(4) *Modern Law Review*, 523–553, 540, 545.

M. Warnock, *Making Babies: Is there a Right to Have Children?* (2006) Oxford, OUP, 66.

Additional reading

H. Biggs 'Madona Minus Child Or : Wanted: Dead or Alive! The Right to have a Dead Partner's Child' (1997) 5 *Feminist Legal Studies*, 225.

E. Blyth, 'Secrets and lies; barriers to the exchange of genetic origins information following donor assisted conception' (1999) 23 *Adoption and Fostering*, 49.

Brazier: *Surrogacy, Review for Health Ministers of Current Arrangements for Payments and Regulations*, Report of the Review Team, 1998 (Cm 4068).

T. Callus, 'First "designer babies", now *à la carte* parents!' [2008] *Family Law*, 143.

DHSS, *Legislation on Human Infertility Services and Embryo Research, A Consultation Paper* (1986) (Cm. 46) London, HMSO, paras 8–13.

M. Johnson (1990) 'A Biomedical Perspective on Parenthood', in A. Bainham, S. Day Sclater and M. Richards (eds), *What is a Parent?* (1999) Oxford, Hart.

D. Langridge and E. Blyth, 'Regulation of assisted conception services in Europe: Implications of the new reproductive technologies for "the family"' (2001) 23 *Journal of Social Welfare and Family Law*, 45.

C. Lind, 'Unmarried paternity under the Human Fertilisation and Embryology Act 1990' (2003) 15 *Child and Family Law Quarterly*, 327.

C. Lind, '*Evans v UK* – judgments of Solomon: power, gender and procreation' (2006) 18 *Child and Family Law Quarterly*, 576.

S. Millns, 'Reproducing inequalities: assisted conception and the challenge of legal pluralism' (2002) 24 *Journal of Social Welfare and Family Law* 19.

S. Reid, *Labour of Love: Story of the World's first Surrogate Grandmother* (1988) Oxford, Bodley Head.

D. Roberts 'The Genetic Tie' (1995) 62 *University of Chicago Law Review* 209.

J. Wallbank 'Reconstructing the HFEA 1990: is blood really thicker than water?' (2004) 16 *Child and Family Law Quarterly*, 387.

W. Woodward, 'Gay couple celebrate birth of twins Aspen and Saffron', *The Guardian*, 13th. December, 1999, 6.

9.5 Illegitimate children or illegitimate parents?

We quoted from:

M. Brazier 'Reproductive Rights: Feminism or Patriarchy?' in J. Harris and S. Holm (eds), *The Future of Human Reproduction* (2000) Oxford, OUP, 67.

Law Commission, Working Paper No. 74, *Illegitimacy* (1979) London, HMSO, 2.10–2.12, 3.2–3.5, 3.8, 3.9, 3.14–3.16.

Law Commission, *Report on Illegitimacy*, Law Com. No. 118 (1982) London, HMSO, 4.44.

The Office for National Statistics, *Social Trends 37* (2007) 22.

Secretary of State for Work and Pensions (2007) *Joint Birth Registration: Promoting Responsibility* (Cm 7160, June 2007).

Additional reading

H. Elisofon, 'A Historical and Comparative Study of Bastardy' (1973) 2 *Anglo-American Law Review* 306, 318.

P. Laslett, *The World We Have Lost* (2nd edn) (1971) London, Methuen, 137, 140–141.

Law Commission, *Report on Guardianship and Custody*, Law Com. No. 172 (1988) London, HMSO, 2.18–2.20.

The Lord Chancellor's Department's Consultation Paper, *Procedures for the Determination of Paternity and on the Law of Parental Responsibility for Unmarried Fathers* (1998) London, HMSO.

N. Lowe 'The Family Reform Act 1987 – Useful Reform but an Unhappy Compromise? (1988) *Denning Law Journal* 77.

R. Pickford, 'Fathers, marriage and the law' (1999) Family Policy Studies Centre (summarised by the Joseph Rowntree Foundation at http://www.jrf.org.uk/knowledge/findings/socialpolicy/989.asp).

S. Sheldon, 'Unmarried fathers and British citizenship: Nationality Immigration and Asylum Act 2002 and British Nationality (Proof of Paternity) Regulations 2006', (2007) 19 *Child and Family Law Quarterly* 1.

10

WHEN PARENTS PART

Two lone parents, and others, talked about their lives to Catherine Itzin for her book *Splitting Up: Single Parent Liberation* (1980):

> *Doreen*: I feel very angry sometimes, that a man can literally decide that he wants to be free, free of responsibilities that somebody must take. Somebody needs to when children are involved. But men can just walk off. I think because they know that the woman is going to be the strong one, that she will not... walk away.
>
> *Michael*: The effects on my career have hurt.... The company begins to assess you a bit lower perhaps because your mind has family welfare as a higher priority than it should be.... I took Anne down to junior church as I always have done... but I'd never brushed her hair before or tied ribbons, and this was actually impossible to me.

A child's view comes from a primary school reading book, *Ugly Mug* by Annie Dalton (1994):

> Mum didn't want to stay married to Dad. She'd told them one terrible bedtime months ago. Dad didn't want to say married to her, either. She'd explained it very calmly. As if a family was some bit of old knitting people could unpick without hurting anyone.
>
> Then, Ned and Rose had had to go and brush their teeth as usual. That didn't seem right to Ned. There should have been a smoking hole in the middle of Osborne Street. There should have been screams, ambulances, flashing lights. Not this careful niceness that left Ned feeling crazy inside.
>
> The trouble was that Mum wanted Ned to treat Dad the same as before. Even though they lived in different streets and had to arrange to meet like strangers. Even though Ned woke every morning to a new scared feeling in his stomach.
>
> But Ned would never be the same again. And it just wasn't fair of Mum to try to make him.

This chapter deals with how it is decided what should happen to the children when their parents part. We shall look first at the debates about what children need; then at the present law and the reasons for it; then at how the child's point of view is, or is not, considered; and finally we look at starting afresh – repartnering and relocating.

10.1 WHAT CHILDREN NEED

The proportion of households with dependent children and only one parent has more than doubled over the past thirty-five years, from 3 per cent in 1971 to 7 per cent in 2006. Twenty-four per cent of children in Great Britain currently live in one-parent households. The following tables taken from *Social Trends 37* (2007), show how the types of family in which children are living have changed:

Table 2.5 Dependent children:[1] by family type

Great Britain					Percentages
	1972	1981	1997[2]	2001[2]	2006[2]
Couple families					
1 child	*16*	*18*	*17*	*17*	*18*
2 children	*35*	*41*	*37*	*37*	*36*
3 or more children	*41*	*29*	*25*	*24*	*22*
Lone mother families					
1 child	*2*	*3*	*6*	*6*	*7*
2 children	*2*	*4*	*7*	*8*	*9*
3 or more children	*2*	*3*	*6*	*6*	*6*
Lone father families					
1 child	..	*1*	*1*	*1*	*1*
2 or more children	*1*	*1*	*1*	*1*	*1*
All children[3]	*100*	*100*	*100*	*100*	*100*

1 See Appendix, Part 2: Multi-sourced tables, Households, and Families.
2 Data are at Q2 each year. See Appendix, Part 4: Labour Force Survey.
3 Excludes cases where the dependent child is a family unit, for example, a foster child.
Source: General Household Survey, Census, Labour Force Survey, Office for National Statistics

Figure 3.1 Frequency of direct contact

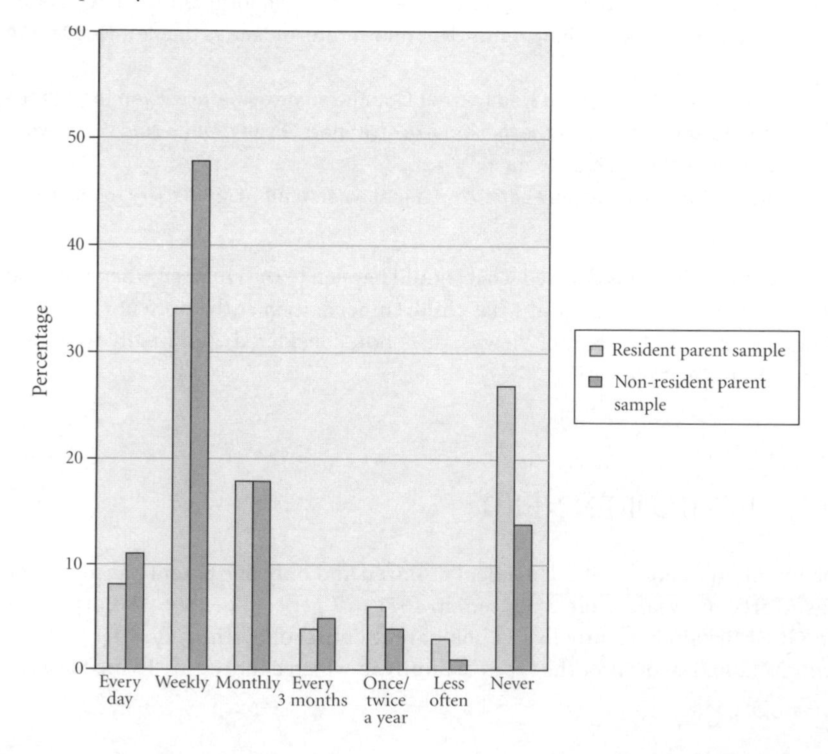

But more than 10 per cent of families with dependent children in 2005 were step-families: 86 per cent with children from the woman's previous relationship, 11 per cent with children from the man's previous relationship, and 3 per cent with children from both partners' previous relationships. Whether by consent, default or court-based decision, the great majority of children end up living with their mothers. For most children, therefore, the vital question is not where, or with whom, they will live, but how much, if anything, they will see of the other parent. The Office for National Statistics survey of *Non-Resident Parental Contact* (2003) found quite high levels of direct contact (though resident and non-resident parents differed in their estimates), shown in Figure 3.1 on the previous page. They also found quite high levels of satisfaction with the arrangements, shown in Figure 3.2 below.

Figure 3.2 Satisfaction with contact arrangements

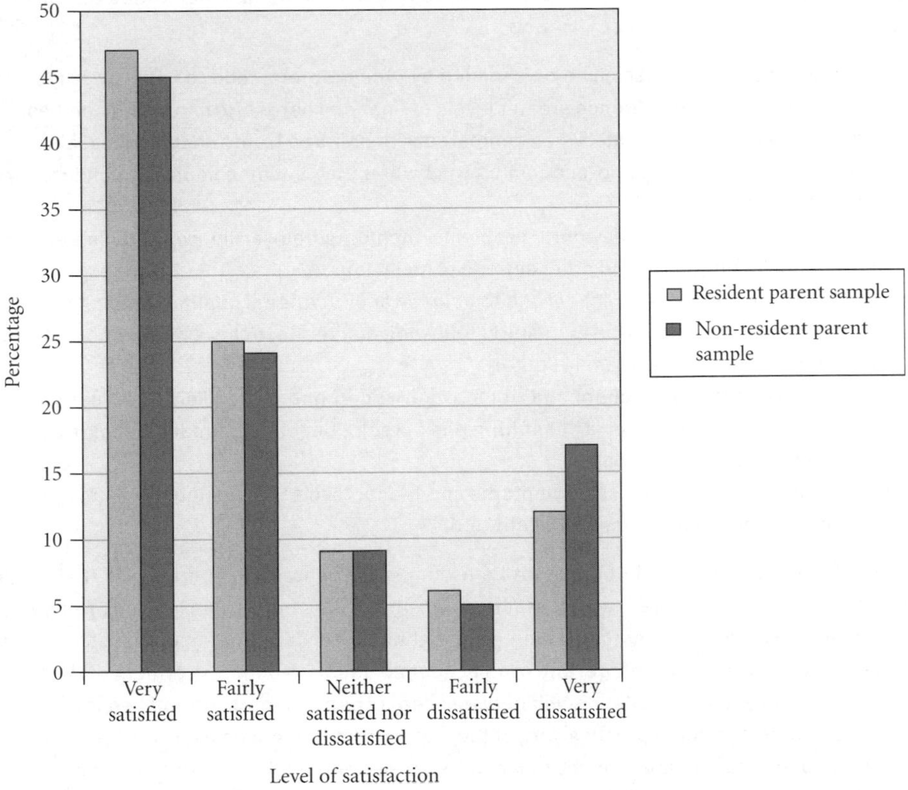

QUESTIONS

i. Why, do you think, has the proportion of lone-parent families headed by fathers gone up since 1971 but now seems to have levelled off?

ii. Why, do you think, do we talk about 'lone-parent' rather than 'one-parent' families these days?

iii. Why, do you think, do some parents never see their children?

There is much debate and a large research literature about the effects of family disruption upon the children. Bryan Rodgers and Jan Pryor, in *Divorce and Separation: The outcomes for children* (1998) sum up:

Disadvantages Among Children of Separated Families

Typically, the areas of disadvantage identified by research only apply to a minority of those whose parents have separated during childhood. There is no simple or direct relationship between parental separation and children's adjustment, and poor outcomes are far from inevitable. As a rule of thumb many adverse outcomes are roughly twice as prevalent among children of divorced families compared with children from intact families. However, the disadvantages identified by research typically apply only to a minority of those whose parents have separated during childhood ...

- Separated families, especially those headed by lone mothers, tend to have lower incomes, poorer housing and experience greater levels of financial hardship than intact families.

Children whose parents separate, when compared with children from intact families, also:

- tend to achieve less in socio-economic terms when they become adult than children from intact families;
- are at increased risk of behavioural problems, including bedwetting, withdrawn behaviour, aggression, delinquency and other antisocial behaviour;
- tend to perform less well in school and to gain fewer educational qualifications;
- are more likely to be admitted to hospital following accidents, to have more reported health problems and to visit their family doctor;
- are more likely to leave school and home when young and more likely at an early age to: become sexually active; form a cohabiting partnership; become pregnant; become a parent; and give birth outside marriage;
- tend to report more depressive symptoms and higher levels of smoking, drinking and other drug use during adolescence and adulthood.

These differences are clear but it cannot be assumed that parental separation is their underlying cause. The complexity of factors that impinge on families before, during and after separation indicates a *process*, rather than a single *event*, that merits careful examination. Much of the confusion seen in media coverage, and even academic debate, about 'the effects of divorce on children' reflects a failure to distinguish between separation as a process and separation as an event. An understanding of process, and of the factors that influence this, is crucial if ways are to be found of optimising the chances that children experiencing the separation of their parents will emerge relatively unharmed.

Step-Families and Lone-Parent Families

There are many adjustments that children whose parents separate may have to make, most obviously that of no longer living with both parents. If their parents subsequently form new partnerships, they may experience a further transition into a household comprising one natural parent, another adult and, sometimes, step-siblings. Research findings for children from step-families suggest a number of ways in which they do not fare as well as those from intact families – and, in some instances, not as well as those from lone-parent families. The risk of adverse outcomes for young people in step-families compared with those in lone-parent families appears higher for older children, especially in areas of educational achievement, family relationships and sexual activity, partnership formation and parenthood at a relatively young age. Young children in step-families seem to fare better, possibly because it is easier to adapt to a new family structure at an age when they have had a relatively short period of living with either both or just one biological parent.

So what can be done to optimise the chances of the children emerging unharmed? CAFCASS, in *Parenting Plans – Putting Your Children First: A Guide for Separated Parents* (2007) is quite clear about what children need:

Key Facts About Children's Best Interests

Children are entitled to a relationship with both their parents, whether or not they live together. Research shows that it is normally in the child's best interests if:

- Children are raised by both parents whether or not they live together, as long as it is safe.
- Each parent supports their children to enjoy a positive relationship with the other parent.
- Children are clear about the arrangements for spending time with each parent.
- Children should not be exposed to sudden changes in arrangements unless it is unavoidable.
- Children should not be exposed to continuing conflict as it can harm them.
- Parents support children to keep in touch with important people in their lives, such as wider family members and close family friends.
- New partners support the arrangements and have a good relationship with your child. They can really help to make things work without replacing you as a parent.

The message is clear but not uncontroversial. In *Beyond the Best Interests of the Child* (1973), Joseph Goldstein, Anna Freud and Albert J. Solnit (respectively a lawyer, a psychoanalyst and a psychiatrist) attempted to use 'psychoanalytic theory to develop generally applicable guidelines to child placement'. They develop three basic concepts. The first is the relationship between a 'psychological parent' and a 'wanted child', whom they later define as follows:

A wanted child is one who receives affection and nourishment on a continuing basis from at least one adult and who feels that he or she is and continues to be valued by those who take care of him or her.

A psychological parent is one who, on a continuing, day-to-day basis, through interaction, companionship, interplay, and mutuality, fulfills the child's psychological needs for a parent, as well as the child's physical needs. The psychological parent may be a biological..., adoptive, foster, or common law... parent, or any other person. There is no presumption in favor of any of these after the initial assignment at birth....

Secondly, they stress the need for continuity in this relationship:

Continuity of relationships, surroundings, and environmental influence are essential for a child's normal development. Since they do not play the same role in later life, their importance is often underrated by the adult world.

Physical, emotional, intellectual, social, and moral growth does not happen without causing the child inevitable internal difficulties. The instability of all mental processes during the period of development needs to be offset by stability and uninterrupted support from external sources. Smooth growth is arrested or disrupted when upheavals and changes in the external world are added to the internal ones.

Disruptions of continuity have different consequences for different ages:

In *infancy*, from birth to approximately 18 months, any change in routine leads to food refusals, digestive upsets, sleeping difficulties, and crying. Such reactions occur even if the infant's care is divided merely between mother and baby-sitter. They are all the more massive where the infant's day is divided between home and day care center; or where infants are displaced from the mother to an institution; from institutional to foster care; or from fostering to adoption. Every step of this kind inevitably brings with it changes in the ways the infant is handled, fed, put to bed, and comforted. Such moves from the familiar to the unfamiliar cause discomfort, distress, and delays in the infant's orientation and adaptation within his surroundings.

Change of the caretaking person for *infants and toddlers* further affects the course of their emotional development. Their attachments, at these ages, are as thoroughly upset by separations as they are effectively promoted by the constant, uninterrupted presence and attention of a familiar adult. When infants and young children find themselves abandoned by the parent, they not only suffer separation distress and anxiety but also setbacks in the quality of their next attachments, which will be less trustful. Where continuity of such relationships is interrupted more than once, as happens due to multiple placements in the early years, the children's emotional attachments become increasingly shallow and indiscriminate. They tend to grow up as persons who lack warmth in their contacts with fellow beings.

For *young children* under the age of 5 years, every disruption of continuity also affects those achievements which are rooted and develop in the intimate interchange with a stable parent figure, who is in the process of becoming the psychological parent. The more recently the achievement has been acquired, the easier it is for the child to lose it. Examples of this are cleanliness and speech. After separation from the familiar mother, young children are known to have breakdowns in toilet training and to lose or lessen their ability to communicate verbally.

For *school-age children*, the breaks in their relationships with their psychological parents affect above all those achievements which are based on identification with the parents' demands, prohibitions, and social ideals. Such identifications develop only where attachments are stable and tend to be abandoned by the child if he feels abandoned by the adults in question. Thus, where children are made to wander from one environment to another, they may cease to identify with any set of substitute parents. Resentment toward the adults who have disappointed them in the past makes them adopt the attitude of not caring for anybody; or of making the new parent the scapegoat for the shortcomings of the former one. In any case, multiple placement at these ages puts many children beyond the reach of educational influence, and becomes the direct cause of behavior which the schools experience as disrupting and the courts label as dissocial, delinquent, or even criminal.

With *adolescents*, the superficial observation of their behavior may convey the idea that what they desire is discontinuation of parental relationships rather than their preservation and stability. Nevertheless, this impression is misleading in this simple form. It is true that their revolt against any parental authority is normal developmentally since it is the adolescent's way toward establishing his own independent adult identity. But for a successful outcome it is important that the breaks and disruptions of attachment should come exclusively from his side and not be imposed on him by any form of abandonment or rejection on the psychological parents' part.

Adults who as children suffered from disruptions of continuity may themselves, in 'identifying' with their many 'parents,' treat their children as they themselves were treated – continuing a cycle costly for both a new generation of children as well as for society itself.

Thus, continuity is a guideline because emotional attachments are tenuous and vulnerable in early life and need stability of external arrangements for their development.

Thirdly, they discuss the child's sense of time:

> A child's sense of time, as an integral part of the continuity concept, requires independent consideration. That interval of separation between parent and child which would constitute a break in continuity for an infant, for example, would be of no or little significance to a school-age youngster. The time it takes to break an old or to form a new attachment will depend upon the different meanings time has for children at each stage of their development.
>
> Unlike adults, who have learned to anticipate the future and thus to manage delay, children have a built-in time sense based on the urgency of their instinctual and emotional needs. As an infant's memory begins to incorporate the way in which parents satisfy wishes and needs, as well as the experience of the reappearance of parents after their disappearance, a child gradually develops the capacity to delay gratification and to anticipate and plan for the future.
>
> Emotionally and intellectually an infant and toddler cannot stretch his waiting more than a few days without feeling overwhelmed by the absence of parents. He cannot take care of himself physically, and his emotional and intellectual memory is not sufficiently matured to enable him to use thinking to hold on to the parent he has lost. During such an absence for the child under two years of age, the new adult who cares for the child's physical needs is latched onto 'quickly' as the potential psychological parent. The replacement, however ideal, may not be able to heal completely, without emotional scarring, the injury sustained by the loss.
>
> For most children under the age of five years, an absence of parents for more than two months is equally beyond comprehension. For the younger school-age child, an absence of six months or more may be similarly experienced. More than one year of being without parents and without evidence that there are parental concerns and expectations is not likely to be understood by the older school-aged child and will carry with it the detrimental implications of the breaches in continuity we have already described. After adolescence is fully launched an individual's sense of time closely approaches that of most adults.

Finally, they point to the limits of the law's ability to supervise personal relationships and of knowledge to predict long-range outcomes:

> While the law may claim to establish relationships, it can in fact do little more than give them recognition and provide an opportunity for them to develop. The law, so far as specific individual relationships are concerned, is a relatively crude instrument. It may be able to destroy human relationships; but it does not have the power to compel them to develop. It neither has the sensitivity nor the resources to maintain or supervise the ongoing day-to-day happenings between parent and child – and these are essential to meeting ever-changing demands and needs. Nor does it have the capacity to predict future events and needs,... [However] placement decisions can be based on certain generally applicable and useful predictions. We can, for example, identify who, among *presently available adults*, is or has the capacity to become a psychological parent and thus will enable a child to feel wanted. We can predict that the adult most likely suited for this role is the one, if there be one, with whom the child has already had and continues to have an affectionate bond rather than one of otherwise equal potential who is not yet in a primary relationship with the child. Further, we can predict that the younger the child and the more extended the period of uncertainty or separation, the more detrimental it will be to the child's well-being and the more urgent it becomes even without perfect knowledge to place the child permanently.
>
> Beyond these, our capacity to predict is limited.

These concepts lead the authors to propose the following guidelines for all child placement decisions:

> As an overall guideline for child placement we propose, instead of the 'in-the-best-interests-of the-child' standard, 'the least detrimental available alternative for safeguarding the child's growth and development.' The new standard has as its major components the three guidelines which we have already described. The least detrimental alternative, then, is that specific placement and procedure for placement which maximizes, in accord with the child's sense of time and on the basis of short-term predictions given the limitations of knowledge, his or her opportunity for being wanted and for maintaining on a continuous basis a relationship with at least one adult who is or will become his psychological parent.

However, the reasoning behind this proposal also reveals how unhelpful it is in the normal dispute between parents:

> The concept of 'available alternatives' should press into focus how limited is the capacity of decisionmakers to make valid predictions and how limited are the choices generally open to them for helping a child in trouble. If the choice, as it may often be in separation and divorce proceedings, is between two psychological parents and if each parent is equally suitable in terms of the child's most immediate predictable developmental needs, the least detrimental standard would dictate a quick, final, and unconditional disposition to either of the competing parents.

QUESTION

Goldstein, Freud and Solnit's footnote to the last passage quoted suggests that 'a judicially supervised drawing of lots between two equally acceptable psychological parents might be the most rational and least offensive process for resolving the hard choice'. Do you agree?

Their arguments, however, did lead to some firm and highly controversial conclusions on post-separation contact:

> Children have difficulty in relating positively to, profiting from, and maintaining the contact with two psychological parents who are not in positive contact with each other. Loyalty conflicts are common and normal under such conditions and may have devastating consequences by destroying the child's positive relationships to both parents. A 'visiting' or 'visited' parent has little chance to serve as a true object for love, trust, and identification, since this role is based on his being available on an uninterrupted day-to-day basis.
>
> Once it is determined who will be the custodial parent, it is that parent, not the court, who must decide under what conditions he or she wishes to raise the child. Thus, the noncustodial parent should have no legally enforceable right to visit the child, and the custodial parent should have the right to decide whether it is desirable for the child to have such visits. What we have said is designed to protect the security of an ongoing relationship – that between the child and the custodial parent. At the same time the state neither makes nor breaks the psychological relationship

between the child and the noncustodial parent, which the adults involved may have jeopardized. It leaves to them what only they can ultimately resolve.

Another psychologist, Martin Richards, in *Post Divorce Arrangements for Children: A Psychological Perspective* (1982), on the other hand, argues that continued contact is so much in the interests of the child that the system should encourage it:

A continued relationship with the non-custodial parent would appear to offer many psychological advantages for children. One of the most obvious is that it offers a wider variety of experience; the experience of a relationship with a second parent. A child is not denied a close and continuing relationship with a parent of each gender. This may be of special value in the development of his or her own gender identity (which has been shown to be disturbed in some studies of children of divorce). With two parents a child is given the opportunity of learning how to move from one relationship to another. Often this is seen in a rather negative sense as something a child must learn to cope with. But I think we should see it much more positively as a very necessary skill for adult life that allows us to live within a whole network of relationships of differing kinds and qualities. It might be argued that these aspects of development should be satisfied equally by any two (or more) adults, not just a child's parents. To some extent this may be true, but there are many indications that parental relations are usually very special and cannot be replaced by other adults in any easy way. To say this is not to evoke any concept of a blood tie but one of a psychological parent. The potency of a psychological parent lies in the continuity of the relationship with their child and their symbolic position as a parent. A separation that does not involve the loss of one parent is likely to be much less disturbing of a child's social connections outside the immediate family. Friends and relatives of the noncustodial parent are not lost to the child. The child has a much better chance of maintaining links with both sets of grandparents.

At a separation, it is usual that among the many feelings a child is likely to experience is anger. This anger is associated with the wish or fantasy that the parents will come back together again and it is generally expressed towards the parent who spends most time looking after the child regardless of their role in the separation. If a child is able to maintain a relationship with both parents this anger gradually dissipates as the child begins to feel confident in the new kind of relationship that develops with both parents. The separation of the parents gradually ceases to be the total threat to the child's life it once had seemed. In a case where the child does not have contact with the non-custodial parent the resolution of the anger at the parents' separation may be much more complex and prolonged. The absent parent, just because he or she is absent, may be built up into a totally idealised figure while the custodial parent's role is seen as that of the person who has driven out the 'ideal' parent. Everything that goes wrong or frustrates the child may be laid at the door of the custodial parent. Under this emotional pressure even the strongest of parents begins to react so that the child may feel signs of rejection or anger in return. This in turn increases the child's anger and insecurity. Of course, not all children of divorce react in this way, but those who do are probably those who have lost contact with one parent.

It has been suggested that a continued relationship with both parents makes the acceptance of a step-parent much more difficult for a child. There is no evidence to support this idea, which is improbable in view of our understanding of a child's parental relations. The unlikely assumption here is that a child has the capacity for two parental relations and if both spaces are filled there will be no space for anybody else. In fact there is great variation in number and kind of relations that a child can maintain. It seems much more likely that if children feel confident that they are going to lose neither of their parents despite the marital separation, that they will accept a new adult more easily. Certainly, we need to move beyond the simplistic notion of very fixed parental roles which can be occupied by anybody that a parent or a court chooses to place in that position.

At the social level there are several very powerful arguments that can be given for the maintenance of ties with both parents.

For many, if not most children, a marital separation is followed by a permanent or temporary period in a single-parent family. We have abundant evidence that these families suffer from many disadvantages. Among these are the effects of a single person providing for all the children's needs day in and day out and the low incomes typical of such families. Both of these are likely to be reduced by continuing [contact] with the non-custodial parent. Such a parent not only provides the child with an alternative home but is also a relief for the custodial parent. These breaks allow the custodial parent to recharge emotional batteries and indulge in some adult life uninterrupted by the demands of childcare.

In principle, there is no connection between access and the payment of maintenance by non-custodial parents. However, this is not the way it is always seen by those involved. Parents who have regular contact with their children and maintain a close relationship are much more likely to want to pay maintenance and feel that it is fair and reasonable to do so. If the contact is maintained the needs of the children including financial ones will be more obvious and are likely to be more freely met.

One can also see the non-custodial parent as a kind of insurance policy for children. Lives of custodial parents cannot be predicted with certainty; changes may occur which make it very difficult or impossible for them to cope with children. If there is a disaster a second parent who is in close touch can often take the children and so avoid another major upheaval.

... Part of our ambivalence about access is expressed in the common attitude that, though access is desirable, it can easily be overdone and so it is necessary to limit visits in terms of both their duration and frequency. Over-long or frequent visits are held to lead to confusions of loyalty for the children and to undermine their security in their main home. Clearly, if two parents are determined to continue their battles via their children, heavy pressures can be brought to bear which, if long-lasting, could make life a misery for children. However, such battles are usually relatively short-lived. As the separated parents begin to rebuild their lives and acquire new concerns and interests the old battles begin to lose their fire. Also children are surprisingly resourceful in avoiding situations which cause them pain.

One of the feelings that most concerns children at a parental separation is the fear of loss of both parents. If one parent has chosen to leave home and live elsewhere, why should not the other one make the same decision at a future date? The only way in which these fears can be countered is by a demonstration that there is continuity in the new arrangements. But it is not always understood that a child's fears are best countered if continuity is demonstrated in both parental relationships. Part of the mistaken fear that access visits are disturbing rests on the assumption that they may unsettle the relationship with the custodial parent. However, unless the child has a reasonable amount of time with the non-custodial parent there is no chance to regain confidence in that relationship.

Perhaps the most common cause of difficulties in access is that visits are too brief. We are well-used to descriptions of the Sunday afternoon access visit spent in the park and cafe. Only a moment's reflection is required to see how difficult or impossible it would be to recreate a normal parental relationship on that kind of basis. What children and adults need is the chance to share some of the very ordinary and routine aspects of life. Access visits must be long enough to remove the sense that they are a special occasion. Excessive gifts and the provision of 'treats' are sure signs that an ordinary relationship has not been recreated. The matter was summed up very clearly by a man I interviewed who told me that it was only after he had first got angry with his children during a visit that he began to feel that they were getting back to a reasonable relationship....

Sometimes it is felt important that things like rules about bedtimes should be as similar as possible in the two homes. Children often make comparisons and talk about any differences they have noted. In general, I would take the ability to talk openly about such differences as evidence that they were coming to terms with the separateness of their parents. Children will, of course, also try to exploit differences between the homes, supposed and real, to get what they want from a parent. But it is simple enough to make it clear to them that rules between the homes may differ and the fact that they are allowed to do X in the other house is no reason why they should do it here. Far from seeing differences in rules and routines in the two homes as confusing for children, I think there are good reasons for viewing them as advantages. They are ways of seeing something of variety in life and learning that there is not always a single answer to a problem. If different activities are possible in the two homes, just as the two relationships with the two parents will each have its own characteristics, so much the better for the children.

In *Private Worlds and Public Intentions – The Role of the State in Divorce* (1993), Richards goes further and suggests that the need for contact should dictate where the children are to live:

The principle of the primacy of the welfare of the children should still obtain in such situations but I suggest it should be given a single simple definition, that the children should reside with whichever parent is able to convince the court that they are the parent most likely to foster and maintain the children's links with the other parent. Such a criterion has a long history (Solomon, 1 Kings 3.16–28) and should ensure that attention is focused on the welfare of the children rather than the supposed moral worth of each parent. Here my argument directly contradicts that of those feminists who have argued for a system based exclusively on who was the primary caretaker within marriage (Smart and Sevenhuijsen, 1989). While such a system is attractive in its simplicity, it fails to take account of the changes in living arrangements and employment that divorce may bring and seems likely to reinforce further the expectation that child care should remain a mother's duty.

This is how sociologist Carol Smart put her argument in *The Legal and Moral Ordering of Child Custody* (1990):

We are now in a position to recognise the complexity of the concept of 'care' and to appreciate that it is not simply a natural outpouring of instinctual love but a moral practice...[T]here is a distinction to be made between 'caring about' and 'caring for'. Typically we have taken 'caring about' to be a moral position. Hence caring about what happens to people is regarded as taking a moral stance. But 'caring for' has not been regarded as a moral stance, merely a maternal activity which arises from instinct which is, if anything, amoral.

Herein lies an important distinction between the moral claims that women and men make in relation to children. In relation to fathers it is common to hear the sort of statement that takes the form, 'He is their father after all'. What is meant by this and how does it compare with how both men and women typically talk about mothers' relationships to children?

'He is their father after all.'

This statement carries two quite contradictory meanings. The first is an assertion of a right arising from biological fatherhood. This is a statement which implies a legal or moral right arising out of a procreative act. But why isn't it sufficient to say 'He is their father' or 'I am their father'? Why is the 'after all' added? What does this add or take away? This 'after all', which men add as often as women, is a form of apology. It means 'I may not have done much but I am still their father'. It means 'I may not occupy the same moral terrain in terms of what I should claim, but I shall claim it anyway because of my biological status'.

Consider the following statement.

Maureen: He said he hadn't been a bad father and he didn't see why any judge would say to him that he couldn't have joint custody. I thought he had quite a good point really because he hadn't been a bad father. He had left them, but before that he wasn't cruel or vindictive and we didn't go short of anything so really I couldn't say that he had abused the children in any way.

In this construction it is enough for this mother that her husband has not done any harm for her to acknowledge his legal rights. But consider her reaction when asked how she might have felt if her husband had tried to gain care and control of their sons.

Maureen: I would have fought tooth and nail that he couldn't have them. There is no way he would have taken the children off me because I am a good mother and I love my children. ... Yes, I think mothers and fathers feel differently about their children and a mother's love is a strong deep love and even though they are boys, and boys are supposed to be closer to their father, I think in a stable background I would give them the best stability and love in their lives until they are old enough to go on their own.

Now, we can dismiss this as special pleading based on an outdated ideology of motherhood and mother love. It might even be that she is mistaken and that she can't give her sons what they most need and so on. But this is not the point. She was making a moral claim which had its foundations in the years of care she had given to her sons. If we say this is nothing, or that it counts for little, we are adopting a position which affirms that the act of 'caring for' has no (moral) value in our culture. We continue to place 'caring about' above 'caring for' and turn the moral content of acts of caring into self-interest.

In her statement Maureen is obviously associating the moral claim that arises out of caring with gender identity. That is to say she does use the language of the ideology of motherhood which is held as suspect in many quarters. Indeed one of the main claims of fathers' rights groups is that there is nothing intrinsic to being a woman/mother which means you can love deeply and care well. But this is not the end of the story as it is so often presumed. We can accept that there is nothing intrinsically caring about being a woman, but that does not mean we should reject the meanings that arise from providing care and nurture. Indeed, this research has indicated quite clearly that as soon as men begin to 'care for' children dramatic changes can occur. They become, metaphorically, 'born again'.

Smart also has something to say about the practical problems of sharing parenthood after separation:

...Maureen had been devastated when her husband left her and she remained extraordinarily sad at the turn of events she had endured. Notwithstanding her pain she was able to see how hard it was for her husband to (re)form and sustain his relationship to their sons and she was working hard to make this possible even though she was not prepared to include the 'other' woman in her efforts. ...

What comes as a shock to many parents who have had little involvement in 'caring for' children during a marriage is the emotional work that is required to sustain relationships after divorce. The parents who were successfully sharing parenting shared this work. That is to say they took on an extra dimension of planning and negotiating in order to make it work. This was arduous but regarded as essential. The parents who had 'cared about' but had done little 'caring for' often seemed angry at the emotional work that was required. One father remarked that he could not see why things could not be just like they were during their marriage. He did not want to do the emotional work that was necessary to keep things going. In other cases the mothers merely took on the work of keeping access going. They prepared the children emotionally for their fathers, they consoled the children when their fathers left, they kept up the flow of information and so on. The work of 'caring for' merely extended beyond the boundaries of divorce and dealing with access and sustaining their former husbands as adequate fathers became an additional task in the repertoire of care giving.

It is interesting that when mothers refuse to take on this extra work they become identified as bad or vindictive mothers. The work of sustaining access is like housework, it is only visible when it is not done. When it is done it is expected to be its own reward, but when it is not done the mother becomes blameworthy.

QUESTIONS

i. Do you agree with Andrew Bainham (1998) that Smart (with her co-authors) 'is pushing a feminist agenda and that it is the interests of mothers, and not those of children, which preoccupy the authors. They are in reality crudely equating the interests of women and children and setting them up in opposition to those of men.'?

ii. How would you define (a) a 'good father', and (b) a 'good mother'? And in each case (a) while they were living together, and (b) after they had separated?

iii. Do you think there should be any connection between supporting and seeing your child? If so what?

iv. Do you believe that children mainly live with their mothers because it is better for them, or because their mothers have earned the right to go on looking after them by doing so in the past?

v. Do you believe that children should go on seeing their fathers because it is better for them, or because their fathers have a right to go on seeing them?

vi. Do you agree with Martin Richards' suggestion (see further *Making Contact Work*, p. 493, below)?

vii. What reasons can you think of *not* to encourage or order contact?

Child psychiatrists Claire Sturge and Danya Glaser were asked by the Official Solicitor to write a report for the Court of Appeal which was considering four cases about the relevance of domestic violence to contact decisions (see *Re L*, p. 490 below). In *Contact and Domestic Violence – the Experts' Report* (2000), they discuss the core principles that should guide decisions whatever the nature of the case.

(i) We see the centrality of the child as all important. There will be tensions around the child because, in disputed cases, the parents will hold differing positions. The needs of the adult positions obscure and overwhelm the needs of the child but promoting the child's mental health remains the central issue.

Decisions about contact must be child-centred and relate to the specific child in his or her specific situation, now. Every child has different needs and these also alter with the different needs at different stages of development. The eventual plan for the child must be the one that best approximates to these needs.

(ii) To consider contact questions the purpose of any proposed contact must be overt and abundantly clear.

Contact can only be an issue where it has the potential for benefiting the child in some way. Defining in what way this might be will help guide decisions about whether there should be contact and also its nature, duration and frequency.

The different purposes of contact include:

- the sharing of information and knowledge; curiosity is healthy; sense of origin and roots contribute to the sense of identity which is also important as part of self-esteem;

- maintaining meaningful and beneficial relationships (or forming and building up relationships which have the potential for benefiting the child; this may be particularly relevant to infants);
- experiences that can be the foundations for healthy emotional growth and development; children benefit from being the special focus of love, attention and concern and of loving and being concerned;
- reparation of broken or problematic relationships;
- opportunities for reality testing for the child; children need to balance reality versus fantasy and idealisation versus denigration;
- facilitating the assessment of the quality of the relationship or contact – most relevant where a return to a particular parent is being considered;
- severing relationships, for example, goodbye meetings.

(iii) Decisions must involve a process of balancing different factors and the advantages and disadvantages of each. This includes contact versus no contact and whether to accept or go against the wishes of a child.

Fathers

Contact with fathers, as opposed to other family members or people with whom the child has a significant relationship, brings the following, in particular, to bear, although the general principles remain the same:

- the father's unique role in the creation of the child;
- the sharing of 50% of his or her genetic material;
- the history of his or her conception and the parental relationships;
- the consequent importance of the father in the child's sense of identity and value;
- the role of modelling a father can provide of the father's and male contribution to parenting and the rearing of children which will have relevance to the child's concepts of parental role models and his or her own choices about choosing partners and the sort of family life he or she aims to create.

They then go on to answer some specific questions which the court had posed for them:

(2) (I) What are the Benefits of (a) Direct and (b) Indirect Contact With the Non-Residential Parent?

Benefits of Contact

... In summary, the benefits include the meeting of his or her needs for:

- warmth, approval, feeling unique and special to a parent;
- extending experiences and developing (or maintaining) meaningful relationships;
- information and knowledge;
- reparation of distorted relationships or perceptions.

... Direct contact can meet one or more or all of these needs. ...

Indirect contact can only meet a much more limited number of needs, amongst these in particular, are:

(i) experience of the continued interest of the absent parent which, in a very partial way, will meet the need to feel valued and wanted, ie not rejected, by that parent;
(ii) knowledge and information about the absent parent;
(iii) the keeping open of the possibility of the development of the relationship, for example, when the child is older or has some specific need of that parent;
(iv) there may be some opportunity, through letters or phone calls, for reparation. Much depends, particularly with small children, on the manner in which the indirect contact is managed by the resident parent. ...

(2) (II) What are the Risks of (a) Direct and (b) Indirect Contact With the Non-Residential Parent?

Direct Contact

The overall risk is that of failing to meet and actually undermining the child's developmental needs or even causing emotional abuse and damage – directly through the contact or as a consequence of the contact.

Specifically, this includes:

(i) Escalating the climate of conflict around the child which will:
  (a) undermine her or his general stability and sense of emotional well-being;
  (b) inevitably result in tugs of loyalty and a sense of responsibility for the conflict (except in the smallest of babies);
  (c) affect relationships between the child and the resident and the non-resident parent. It may, for example, result in extreme polarisation with enmeshment with the resident parent and rejection of the non-resident parent as a result of the child's efforts to reduce the conflictual situation.
(ii) Direct experiences within the contact:
  (a) Abuse: physical or sexual, or emotional, see below; neglect; dangerous situations include those in which the parent has delusional beliefs at the time of contact, ie is acutely mentally ill or is under the influence of alcohol or drugs.
  (b) Emotional abuse through the denigration of the child directly or the child's resident carer, through using the contact as a means of continuing or escalating the 'war' with the resident parent, for example, seeking derogatory information, engendering secrets, making derogatory remarks in an attempt to undermine the resident parent. ...
  (c) Continuation of unhealthy relationships, for example, inappropriately dominant or bullying relationships, controlling relationships through subtly or blatantly maintaining (or initiating) fear or through other means (for example bribes, emotional blackmail). ...
  (d) Undermining the child's sense of stability and continuity by deliberately or inadvertently setting different moral standards or standards of behaviour. Rules for the child may be very different with the contact parent and the child may be allowed to do quite different things which are normally forbidden. This can affect his or her understanding of right and wrong and/or give him or her the means to then challenge or defy the resident parent. ...

(e) Experiences lacking in endorsement of the child as a valued and individual person, for example, where little or no interest is shown in the child himself or herself. Contact where the contact parent is unable to consistently sustain the prioritisation of the child's needs.

(f) Unstimulating experiences which are lacking in interest, fun or in extending the child and his or her experiences.

(iii) Other:

(a) Continuation of unresolved situations, for example, where the child has a memory or belief about a negative aspect of the contact parent, for example, abuse, and where this is just left as if unimportant. . . .

(b) Unreliable contact in which the child is frequently let down or feels rejected, unwanted and of little importance to the failing parent. This also undermines a child's need for predictability and stability. . . .

(c) The child is continuing to attend contact against his or her ongoing wishes such that the child feels undermined as someone in his or her own right whose feelings are considered and heeded.

(d) All significantly difficult contact situations for the child where there is little potential and prospect for change, for example, wholly implacable situations, contact which is failing to prioritise the child's needs.

(e) The stress on the child, on his or her resident carer and on the situation as a whole of ongoing proceedings or frequently re-initiated proceedings, of periods of contact and then no contact on and off also need taking into account. . . .

Indirect Contact

The above apply only inasmuch as the non-resident parent is able to convey undermining and distorting messages through whatever indirect contact medium is agreed. Obviously, there is greatest scope for harm in telephone contact and least in vetted contact such as letters.

Other risks are that of the non-resident parent, in abduction risk situations, using the child's communications to establish details about the child that could lead to identifying the child's home address, school or routines, or as ammunition in legal proceedings or simply in undermining the resident parent.

In summary: in contested contact cases it is unlikely that the best contact situation for the child can be established – one which both parents support and in which the child's needs are consistently met. Hence the balancing act between the potential benefit versus detriment of contact.

(3) What Weight is to be Placed Upon the Following Factors in Children Contact Cases?

(I) Where there is a history of significant intra-familial violence and the child has had a negative experience of the non-residential parent, for example, witnessing an incident of intra-familial violence or threats to the mother

. . . Domestic violence is relevant in the following ways with regard to contact (and all relate to the general principles already set out).

(a) There may be a continuing sense of fear of the violent parent by the child.
(b) The child may have post-traumatic anxieties or symptoms which the proximity of the non-resident violent parent may re-arouse or perpetuate.
(c) There may be a continuing awareness of the fear the violent parent arouses in the child's main carer.
(d) There are likely to be all or many of the issues referred to under 'risks of direct contact', some of which may not be directly the responsibility of the violent parent, for example, the mother's or resident parent's reaction and post-traumatic symptoms in relation to the past violence.
(e) There is the important, but largely neglected area, of the effects of such situations on children's own attitudes to violence, to forming 'parenting' relationships and to the role of fathers in such relationships and in caring for and protecting their children...
(f) Direct physical abuse: parents who are violent to each other are more likely to be violent to their children. The same review mentioned above, taking the research together, puts the risks as between three and nine times greater than in non-violent families.

We are not in these questions asked to address the issue of the mother's part in any domestic violence which complicates the picture but less so if the decision that she is to be the main carer is already taken and if she has successively extricated herself from that and other violent relationships.

(II) Where the child is adamant that he/she does not wish to see the parent or contemplate contact

... The following need to be accepted:

(i) the child must be listened to and taken seriously;
(ii) the age and understanding of the child are highly relevant;
(iii) the child, and the younger and the more dependent, either for developmental or emotional reasons, if in a positive relationship with the resident parent will inevitably be influenced by:
  - that parent's views;
  - their wish to maintain her or his sense of security and stability within that household.
(iv) Going against the child's wishes must involve the following.
  - Indications that there are prospects of the child changing his or her view as a result of preparation work or the contact itself; for example, there is a history of meaningful attachment and a good relationship; the non-resident parent has child-centred plans as to how to help the child overcome his or her resistance; there are some indications of ambivalence such as an adamant statement of not wanting to see that parent accompanied by lots of positive memories and affect when talking of that parent.
  - Consideration of the effects on the child of making a decision that appears to disregard their feelings/wishes. It is damaging to a child to feel he or she is forced to do something against his or her will and against his or her judgment if the child cannot see the sense of it.
(v) Unreliable contact: see (2)(iii)(b) above.

(III) Where there is an absence of a bond between the child and the parent with whom he or she does not live

The following need to be taken into account.

(i) The age and developmental level of the child: infants invoke and promote parenting behaviour towards them by their own behaviour and interactions. The interactions and experience of the carer of the infant and the infant of the carer are necessary to the formation of attachment and bonds (positive and significant relationships in either direction) between them. The lack of attachment or bonds in a small baby should not therefore in itself be seen as a reason for not promoting contact.

Toddlers and older children remain capable of forming bonds and attachments although these will be of different quality and type according to the situation. A strong bond for years with a single carer is likely to result in a greater resource for forming future strong bonds and relationships. However, if they remain with the longstanding 'attachment' parent new bonds are unlikely to become as strong or meaningful as the basic one.

In adolescence, other significant developmental issues come into the situation. In relation to an absent bond with the non-residential parent, the seeking of a clear and separate identity may lead to greater interest in a little-known biological parent. The introduction of contact may, at the same time, because of the adolescent's seeking of independence, add complications which undermine the 'main' placement (for example expressing a wish or leaving to live with the non-resident parent as an act of defiance towards the resident parent and his or her controls).

(ii) The question, perhaps, needs to be looked at the other way around. If there is a strong relationship, bond or attachment that is a good reason to continue and promote contact as failure to do so will be an emotional loss for the child and much more likely to be experienced as an abandonment or rejection.

Lack of such a bond means there is not that argument for furthering contact but it is not, in itself, a reason not to try to build a new relationship.

In this last situation, other considerations may come into play, such as other emotional investments of the child, for example, in a step-parent and what specifically the new relationship might add to the child's life and well-being.

In the event that there is no meaningful relationship between the child and non-residential parent and an established history of domestic violence with or without opposition to contact by the resident parent, there would need to be very good reason to embark on a plan of introducing direct contact and building up a relationship when the main evidence is of that non-residential parent's capacity for violence within relationships.

They also discuss a concept which has become common currency in the United States, labelling resistance to contact as a mental disorder:

(IV) Where there is a case of Parental Alienation Syndrome

Parental Alienation Syndrome does not exist in the sense that it is:

- not recognised in either the American classification of mental disorders (DSMIV) or the international classification of disorders (ICD10);
- not generally recognised in our or allied child mental health specialities.

We do not consider it to be a helpful concept and consider that the sort of problems that the title of this disorder is trying to address is better thought of as implacable hostility. The essential and important difference is that the Parental Alienation Syndrome assumes a cause (seen as misguided or malign on the part of the resident parent) which leads to a prescribed intervention whereas the concept (which no one claims to be a 'syndrome') is simply a statement aimed at the understanding of particular situations but for which there is no single and prescribed solution, this depending on the nature and individuality of each case...

The possible reasons for a resident parent taking a position of implacable hostility (by implication to the ex-partner as much as to contact) are as follows:

(a) A fully justified fear of harm or abduction resulting from any direct contact with the non-resident parent.
(b) A fear of violence or other threat and menace to herself if the non-resident parent has indirect contact to her through the child, ie it could lead to direct contact.
(c) Post-traumatic symptoms in the custodial parent which are acutely exacerbated by the prospect or the fact of contact.
(d) The aftermath of a relationship in which there was a marked imbalance in the power exercised by the two parents and where the mother fears she will be wholly undermined and become helpless and totally inadequate again if there is any channel of contact between herself and the ex-partner, even when that only involves the child. The child can be used as a weapon in such a bid to continue to hold power over the mother. As in (a), (b), and (c) above this can be a sequelae of domestic violence.
(e) Wholly biased hostility which is not based on real events or experience. This may be conscious and malign or perceived to be true. The latter encompass the full continuum from misperceptions and misunderstandings through overvalued ideas to delusional states. The former may result from a simple wish to wipe the slate clean and start again and can be seen after relationships that were initially highly romantic or idealised and for the breakdown of which the woman can only account for by vilifying the partner in order to avoid facing the possibility that the breakdown in the relationship was her failure and amounts to rejection.

It is in this last situation (e), in which there are often sexual abuse allegations emanating mainly from the resident carer, which particularly exercise experts and the courts as the fathers may be well-functioning, well-meaning and represent a real potential for a good relationship with the child. . . .

(4) In What Circumstances Should the Court Give Consideration to a Child Having no Direct Contact With the Non-Residential Parent?

The Core Question

. . . From all that is written above, it will be clear that we consider that there should be no automatic assumption that contact to a previously or currently violent parent is in the child's interests; if anything the assumption should be in the opposite direction and the case of the non-residential parent one of proving why he can offer something of such benefit not only to the child but to the child's situation (ie act in a way that is supportive to the child's situation with his or her resident parent and able to be sensitive to and respond appropriately to the child's needs), that contact should be considered. . . .

Without the following we would see the balance of advantage and disadvantage as tipping against contact:

(a) some (preferably full) acknowledgement of the violence;
(b) some acceptance (preferably full if appropriate, ie the sole instigator of violence) of responsibility for that violence;
(c) full acceptance of the inappropriateness of the violence particularly in respect of the domestic and parenting context and of the likely ill-effects on the child;

(d) a genuine interest in the child's welfare and full commitment to the child, ie a wish for contact in which he is not making the conditions;
(e) a wish to make reparation to the child and work towards the child recognising the inappropriateness of the violence and the attitude to and treatment of the mother and helping the child to develop appropriate values and attitudes;
(f) an expression of regret and the showing of some understanding of the impact of their behaviour on their ex-partner in the past and currently;
(g) indications that the parent seeking contact can reliably sustain contact in all senses.

What about the children themselves? Carol Smart's research, reported in *Objects of concern? – children and divorce* (1999), found that children had strong views about how contact might be organised and agreed. For these children at least, contact was immensely important (but bear in mind that they were living in shared care arrangements and so their views may be untypical).

One of the ironies of [the] exclusion of children from open discussions about divorce and changes in family life is that they are a fount of knowledge and information themselves on what it is like, on how to cope, on how to intervene (even in limited ways) and what it all feels like. They may even have a very different perspective on the process when compared to parents, and they may even have solutions to some of the typical problems thrown up by parenting across households. We may have a lot to learn about divorce from children if we suspend the presumption that they are damaged goods in need of protection.

Here are some of the conversations Smart relates:

Q: 'Is there anything that you might like to change?'
Rosie (9): 'Yes. For there to be *eight* days in the week. That's the only thing.'
Q: 'What difference would that make?'
Rosie: 'Four days with both people.'

In the quotation above Rosie is performing a modern day version of the Judgment of Solomon. However, rather than envisaging an emotional and grim scenario of splitting a child into two, she seeks a more prosaic solution, namely to split the week equally into two halves to ensure fairness between parents. . . .

Claudia, who was 12 years old, could sometimes feel like a referee in just the same way that many parents can:

Claudia: '[T]hey always say I can say something but then, like, it's a bit hard you see because both of them want different things and if you agree with one, then the other one will feel a bit upset. I mean they won't say that to you, but you can sense it so it's a bit annoying. So even if you didn't want to do that, if you wanted to do something completely different, it's better to say [that] you want to do something completely different 'cos then neither of them wins, then they'll just find an argument about something else.'

. . .

Nick (14): 'It's almost made it easier though, our mum and dad not living together, because before there was arguments and things like that and it was really difficult really to live. But now that they've moved apart they're both much happier and much more relaxed. Like my mum, she comes in tense from work just 'cos her work's like that, but she comes home and she'll relax rather than before she would have come home and there would probably have been an argument about something.'

Emma (10): 'I think it works quite well for [my mother] because she likes to have a rest, so on a Friday night, well once every fortnight on a Friday night, she just has herself and she just sort of goes to sleep and enjoys having no children I think.' (co-parented, ESRC)

These children appreciate their parents as separate individuals with needs and interests – and even tastes:

Beth (14): 'It works for my mum 'cos she's got time with Ian, where they can have fish and stuff, 'cos I hate the smell of fish, and it gives her a break from like worrying about me all the time.'

QUESTIONS

i. How might (a) parents and (b) the law tap into the resources of children's wisdom?

ii. The judgment of Solomon is related in the *New English Bible* I Kings 3, vs. 22–27:

So they went on arguing in the king's presence.... Then he said, 'Fetch me a sword.' They brought in a sword and the king gave the order: 'Cut the living child in two and give half to one and half to the other.' At this the woman who was the mother of the living child, moved with love for her child, said to the king, 'Oh! sir, let her have the baby; whatever you do, do not kill it.' The other said, 'Let neither of us have it; cut it in two.' Thereupon the king gave judgment: 'Give the living baby to the first woman; do not kill it. She is its mother.'

How can the modern law reflect the wisdom of Solomon?

10.2 THE LAW

10.2.1 THE ORDERS AVAILABLE

The Children Act 1989 provides four kinds of order:

8.—(1) In this Act—

'a contact order' means an order requiring the person with whom a child lives, or is to live, to allow the child to visit or stay with the person named in the order, or for that person and the child otherwise to have contact with each other;

'a prohibited steps order' means an order that no step which could be taken by a parent in meeting his parental responsibility for a child, and which is of a kind specified in the order, shall be taken by any person without the consent of the court;

'a residence order' means an order settling the arrangements to be made as to the person with whom a child is to live; and

'a specific issue order' means an order giving directions for the purpose of determining a specific question which has arisen, or which may arise, in connection with any aspect of parental responsibility for a child.

(2) In this Act 'a section 8 order' means any of the orders mentioned in subsection (1) and any order varying or discharging such an order.

Either parent (married or unmarried) is entitled to apply for any section 8 order; the court may also make an order of its own motion in any family proceedings (section 10(1), (2)(a), (4)). Supplementary provisions (see also p. 495, below) include:

11.—(4) Where a residence order is made in favour of two or more persons who do not themselves all live together, the order may specify the periods during which the child is to live in the different households concerned.

...

(7) A section 8 order may—

(a) contain directions about how it is to be carried into effect:
(b) impose conditions which must be complied with by any person—
  (i) in whose favour the order is made;
  (ii) who is a parent of the child concerned;
  (iii) who is not a parent of his but who has parental responsibility for him; or
  (iv) with whom the child is living, and to whom the conditions are expressed to apply;
(c) be made to have effect for a specified period, or contain provisions which are to have effect for a specified period;
(d) make such incidental, supplemental or consequential provision as the court thinks fit.

...

13.—(1) Where a residence order is in force with respect to a child, no person may—

(a) cause the child to be known by a new surname; or
(b) remove him from the United Kingdom;

without either the written consent of every person who has parental responsibility for the child or the leave of the court.

(2) Subsection (1)(b) does not prevent the removal of a child, for a period of less than one month, by the person in whose favour the residence order is made.

(3) In making a residence order with respect to a child the court may grant the leave required by subsection (1)(b), either generally or for specified purposes.

The thinking was explained in the Law Commission's Report on *Guardianship and Custody* (1988):

Orders Between Parents

...

4.5 In framing a scheme of orders to replace the present law, we have had in mind throughout the clear evidence that the children who fare best after their parents separate or divorce are those who are able to maintain a good relationship with them both. The law may not be able to achieve this – indeed we are only too well aware of the limits of the law in altering human relationships – but at least it should not stand in their way. Our respondents were generally agreed on three points. Where the parents are already able to co-operate in bringing up their children, the law should interfere as little as possible. Where they may be having difficulty, it should try to 'lower the stakes' so that the issue is not one in which 'winner takes all' or more importantly 'loser loses all'. In either case, the orders made should reduce rather than increase the opportunities for conflict and litigation in the future.

4.8 ... It is 'a mistake to see custody, care and control and access as differently-sized bundles of powers and responsibilities in a descending hierarchy of importance'. Most parental responsibilities can only be exercised while the parent has the child, for only then can the parent put into effect the decisions taken. Equally, however, it is then that the parent must be in a position to meet his responsibilities as the circumstances and needs of the child dictate. Parental responsibilities, therefore, largely 'run with the child'. Clearly, in most cases, one parent carries a much heavier burden of that responsibility than does the other. The present system of orders, by concentrating on the allocation of 'rights', appears more concerned with whether one parent can control what the other parent does while the child is with the other, than with ensuring that each parent properly meets his responsibilities while the child is with him. The practical question in most cases is where the child is to live and how much he is to see of the other parent.

....

(A) Residence Orders

4.12 Apart from the effect upon the other parent,...the main difference between a residence order and a custody order is that the new order should be flexible enough to accommodate a much wider range of situations. In some cases, the child may live with both parents even though they do not share the same household. It was never our intention to suggest that children should share their time more or less equally between their parents. Such arrangements will rarely be practicable, let alone for the children's benefit. However, the evidence from the United States is that where they are practicable they can work well and we see no reason why they should be actively discouraged. None of our respondents shared the view expressed in a recent case [*Riley v Riley* [1986] 2 FLR 429] that such an arrangement, which had been working well for some years, should never have been made. More commonly, however, the child will live with both parents but spend more time with one than the other. Examples might be where he spends term time with one and holidays with the other, or two out of three holidays from boarding school with one and the third with the other. It is a far more realistic description of the responsibilities involved in that sort of arrangement to make a residence order covering both parents rather than a residence order for one and a contact order for the other. ...

4.14 The effect of a residence order is simply to settle where the child is to live. If any other conditions are needed they must usually be specified. However, the Matrimonial Causes Rules 1977 at present specify two conditions which must be included in divorce court custody orders unless the court otherwise directs. First, the parent with custody must not change the child's surname without the written consent of the other parent or the leave of a judge. The child's surname is an important symbol of his identity and his relationship with his parents. While it may well be in his interests for it to be changed, it is clearly not a matter on which the parent with whom he lives should be able to take unilateral action. ...

4.15 Secondly, a divorce court order for custody or care and control must provide for the child not to be removed from England and Wales without leave of the court except on such terms as the court may specify in the order. This means that, unless the court makes an exception at the outset, the child cannot be taken on holiday abroad (or even to Scotland), even if the other parent agrees, without the trouble and expense of an application for leave. This is clearly quite unrealistic these days and we suspect that the requirement is often ignored. ... However, taking the child abroad indefinitely can obviously have a serious effect upon his relationship with the other parent and it may be important to remind the residential parent of this, and of the steps to be taken if she wishes to do so. A simple, clear general rule seems most likely to be remembered and observed.

...

(B) Contact Orders

4.17 Where the child is to spend much more time with one parent than the other, the more realistic order will probably be for him to live with one parent and to visit the other. There are important differences between this and the present form of access order. It will not provide for the 'non-custodial' parent to have access to the child. It will provide for the child to visit and in many cases stay with the parent. While the child is with that parent, the parent may exercise all his parental responsibilities. He must not do something which is incompatible with the order about where the child is to live. The court may also attach other conditions if there are particular anxieties or bones of contention but these should rarely be required. If visiting is not practicable, the court may nevertheless order some other form of contact with the child, including letters or telephone calls or visits to the child. We would expect, however, that the normal order would be for reasonable contact, which would encompass all types....

(C) Specific Issue Orders

4.18 Specific issue orders may be made in conjunction with residence or contact orders or on their own.... As with conditions attached to other orders, the object is not to give one parent or the other the 'right' to determine a particular point. Rather, it is to enable either parent to submit a particular dispute to the court for resolution in accordance with what is best for the child. A court can determine in the light of the evidence what decision will be best for the child at the time. It may equally be content for decisions to be taken by each parent as they arise in the course of everyday life in the future. It may even attach a condition to a residence or contact order that certain decisions may not be taken without informing the other or giving the other an opportunity to object. But to give one parent in advance the right to take a decision which the other parent will have to put into effect is contrary to the whole tenor of the modern law. A court can scarcely be expected to know in advance that the first parent's decision will be the best for the child.

4.19 However, a specific issue order is not intended as a substitute for a residence or contact order. There is obviously a slight risk that they might be used, particularly in uncontested cases, to achieve much the same practical results but without the same legal effects. We recommend, therefore, that it should be made clear that a specific issue order cannot be made with a view to achieving a result which could be achieved by a residence or contact order.

(D) Prohibited Steps Orders

4.20 Prohibited steps orders are also modelled on the wardship jurisdiction. The automatic effect of making a child a ward of court is that no important step may be taken without the court's leave. An important aim of our recommendations is to incorporate the most valuable features of wardship into the statutory jurisdictions. It is on occasions necessary for the court to play a continuing parental role in relation to the child, although we would not expect those occasions to be common. If this is in the best interests of the child, it should be made clear exactly what the limitations on the exercise of parental responsibility are. Hence, instead of the vague requirement in wardship, that no 'important step' may be taken, the court should spell out these matters which will have to be referred back to the court. We would expect such orders to be few and far between,... As with specific issue orders, however, we recommend that these orders should not be capable of being made with a view to achieving a result which could be achieved by a residence or contact order.

The Law Commission clearly contemplated that children might divide their time between two homes, in what became known as a 'shared residence order', but it took a little time to catch on.

Re D (children) (shared residence orders)
[2001] 1 FLR 495, [2001] 1 FCR 147, Court of Appeal

A father and mother married in 1986. They had three children aged thirteen, eleven and nine years. The marriage broke down in 1995. The pattern was quickly established of the children living with the mother, under sole residence orders, but having very substantial contact with their father. There was an exceptionally high level of animosity between the parents. The father complained that he had difficulty in gaining information about the children's education and medical treatment. He applied to determine the contact schedule for 2000/01, for shared residence, and for an order prohibiting the mother from causing third parties to withhold information about the children from him. The judge found that the mother was using the sole residence order as a weapon in the war with the father. He ordered shared residence in order to reduce the conflict between the parties. The mother appealed.

Hale LJ:

....

[21] It may be helpful to go back to basics. Before the Children Act 1989 there was a Court of Appeal authority in *Riley v Riley* [1986] 2 FLR 429, to the effect that a shared residence order, which had been made and worked comparatively well in that case for five years, should never have been made at all. It is clear, as the court appreciated in the later cases, that the intent of the Act was to change that decision.

Hale LJ then referred to the Law Commission's Working Paper No. 96 on Custody, Law Com No. 172, paragraph 4.12, the Children Act 1989, sections 8(1) and 11(4), above, and *Re H* [1993] 1 FCR 671:

[29] The matter next came before the Court of Appeal on 3 February 1994, in *A v A (minors)*; Butler-Sloss LJ (as she then was) said:

> 'Miss Moulder, representing the father, accepts that the conventional order still is that there would be residence to one parent with contact to the other parent. It must be demonstrated that there is positive benefit to the child concerned for a s. 11(4) order to be made, and such positive benefit must be demonstrated in the light of the s.1 checklist. The usual order that would be made in any case where it is necessary to make an order is that there will be residence to one parent and a contact order to the other parent. Consequently, it will be unusual to make a shared residence order. But the decision whether to make such a shared residence order is always in the discretion of the Judge on the special facts of the individual case. [I suspect that when My Lady used the word "special" she meant "particular".] It is for him alone to make that decision. However, a shared residence order would, in my view, be unlikely to be made if there were concrete issues still arising between the parties which had not been resolved, such as the amount of contact, whether it should be staying or visiting contact or another issue such as education, which were muddying the waters and which were creating difficulties between the parties which reflected the way in which the children were moving from one parent to the other in the contact period.' (See [1995] 1 FCR 91 at 100.)

[30] She went on to say:

> 'If a child, on the other hand, has a settled home with one parent and substantial staying contact with the other parent, which has been settled, long-standing and working well, or

> if there are future plans for sharing the time of the children between two parents where all the parties agree and where there is no possibility of confusion in the mind of the child as to where the child will be and the circumstances of the child at any time, this may be, bearing in mind all the other circumstances, a possible basis for a shared residence order, if it can be demonstrated that there is a positive benefit to the child.'

[31] It is quite clear that in those words my Lady was moving matters on from any suggestion, which is not in the legislation, that these orders require exceptional circumstances. She was also recognising that it stands to reason that if it has not yet been determined where the children are to live, how much contact there is to be, or whether or not there is to be staying contact with the parent with whom they are not spending most of their time, then there could not be a shared residence order, because that would be an order that the children were to live with both parents.

[32] If, on the other hand, it is either planned or has turned out that the children are spending substantial amounts of their time with each of their parents then, as both the Law Commission and my Lady indicated . . . it may be an entirely appropriate order to make. For my part, I would not add any gloss on the legislative provisions, which are always subject to the paramount consideration of what is best for the children concerned.

[33] This case is one in which, as the judge said, the arrangements have been settled for some considerable time. The children are, in effect, living with both of their parents. They have homes with each of them. They appear to be coping extremely well with that. I accept entirely what we have been told by the mother today, that she would never seek to turn the children against their father, because she herself so loves her own father that she could not possibly do that. It is greatly to her credit that her children have been able to maintain such a very strong and good relationship with both of their parents. Of course, it is to the father's credit as well that he has remained as dedicated to their interests as he has.

[34] In those circumstances it seems to me that there is indeed a positive benefit to these children in those facts being recognised in the order that the court makes. There is no detriment or disrespect to either parent in that order. It simply reflects the reality of these children's lives. It was entirely appropriate for the judge to make it in this case and neither party should feel that they have won or lost as a result. I would, therefore, dismiss the appeal.

QUESTIONS

i. What do you think is the difference between (a) a shared residence order specifying that a child is to live with the mother during the week and with the father at the weekend, and (b) a residence order in favour of the mother together with a contact order stating that the child is to have staying contact with the father at the weekend? Does it matter?

ii. Some fathers' groups have been pressing for a norm of 50/50 shared parenting. The House of Commons Constitutional Affairs Committee, in its report on *Family Justice: the operation of the family courts* (2005), commented:

> 60. . . . The welfare of the individual child should be the paramount consideration in every case. . . . An arbitrary template imposed on all families, whatever the needs of the child, would relegate the welfare of individual children to a secondary position.
>
> 61. There are significant practical objections to an automatic sharing of the time which children spend with one parent or another. In particular, an arbitrary apportionment of

time does not take into account the views of children. The amount of contact a child will want with its parents will depend upon a number of factors and is likely to change over the course of its childhood...

Do you agree?

10.2.2 THE WELFARE PRINCIPLE

The Children Act 1989 restates the welfare principle like this:

1.—(1) When a court determines any question with respect to—

(a) the upbringing of a child; or
(b) the administration of a child's property or the application of any income arising from it,
the child's welfare shall be the court's paramount consideration.

...

(3) In the circumstances mentioned in subsection (4), a court shall have regard in particular to—

(a) the ascertainable wishes and feelings of the child concerned (considered in the light of his age and understanding);
(b) his physical, emotional and educational needs;
(c) the likely effect on him of any change in his circumstances;
(d) his age, sex, background and any characteristics of his which the court considers relevant;
(e) any harm which he has suffered or is at risk of suffering;
(f) how capable each of his parents, and any other person in relation to whom the court considers the question to be relevant, is of meeting his needs;
(g) the range of powers available to the court under this Act in the proceedings in question.

(4) The circumstances are that—

(a) the court is considering whether to make, vary or discharge a section 8 order, and the making, variation or discharge of the order is opposed by any party to the proceedings; or
(b) the court is considering whether to make, vary or discharge an order under Part IV [see Chapter 11].

105.—(1) In this Act—
... 'harm' has the same meaning as in section 31(9). ...
31.—(9) In this section—
...'harm' means ill-treatment or the impairment of health or development including, for example, impairment suffered from seeing or hearing the ill-treatment of another.

QUESTIONS

i. The Law Commission had recommended (paragraph 3.14) that the interests of any child likely to be affected by the decision should be the court's 'only concern'. Is there a difference between a 'paramount' and an 'only' consideration?

ii. If other considerations can be taken into account, should they include, for example, (a) the 'justice' of the matrimonial dispute, (b) the need to minimise public expenditure, or (c) the wishes and feelings of any of the adults involved?

iii. What would an economist or utilitarian think of a law which, in theory, required that a small gain to the child's welfare, in living with the marginally more suitable parent, should outweigh a much greater detriment to the welfare of a parent who would be devastated by the loss of his or her child?

iv. The words 'including, for example, impairment suffered from seeing or hearing the ill-treatment of another' were added to section 31(9) by the Adoption and Children Act 2002. Why?

The Human Rights Act 1998 has added a new question: is the paramountcy principle compatible with Article 8 of the European Convention on Human Rights? We have already raised this issue in Chapter 8 (see p. 359 above and Eekelaar, 2002) and will return to it at the end of this chapter.

The Law Commission (1988) explained the 'checklist' in section 1(3) like this:

3.18 The 'checklist' received a large majority of support from those who considered the matter. It was perceived as a means of providing a greater consistency and clarity in the law and was welcomed as a major step towards a more systematic approach to decisions concerning children. Respondents pointed out that it would help to ensure that the same basic factors were being used to implement the welfare criterion by the wide range of professionals involved, including judges, magistrates, registrars, welfare officers, and legal advisers. One respondent, for example, who is a magistrates' clerk, thought that the list would be particularly useful when advising magistrates in making decisions in contested custody cases and in formulating reasons in the event of an appeal. It would also provide a practical tool for those lacking experience and confidence in this area. Perhaps most important of all, we were told that such a list could assist both parents and children in endeavouring to understand how judicial decisions are made. At present, there is a tendency for advisers and their clients (and possibly even courts) to rely on 'rules of thumb' as to what the court is likely to think best in any given circumstances. A checklist would make it clear to all what, as a minimum, would be considered by the court. At the very least, it would enable the parties to prepare and give relevant evidence at the outset, thereby avoiding the delay and expense of prolonged hearings or adjournments for further information. Moreover, we were informed that solicitors find the checklist applicable to financial matters most useful in focusing their clients' minds on the real issues and therefore in promoting settlements. Anything which is likely to promote the settlement of disputes about children is even more to be welcomed. We recommend, therefore, that a statutory checklist similar to that provided for financial matters be provided for decisions relating to children.

QUESTIONS

i. The list deliberately steers clear of statements like 'young children need their mothers', or 'boys need a masculine influence', or 'brothers and sisters need to stay together': is this a good thing?

ii. The House of Commons Constitutional Affairs Committee (2005) proposed 'the insertion of a statement in s. 1(3) of the Children Act 1989 (the welfare checklist) indicating that the courts should have regard to the importance of sustaining a relationship between the children and a non-residential parent'. Why, do you suppose, was this not taken up in the Children and Adoption Act 2006 (cf. p. 495, below)?

Re G (Children) (Residence: Same-sex Partner) [2006] UKHL 43; [2006] 1 WLR 2305, House of Lords

G and W lived together in a lesbian relationship from 1995 to 2002. Wanting to have a family together, they arranged for G to be artificially inseminated, using sperm from an anonymous donor. She gave birth to two children, born in 1999 and 2001. In 2002 the relationship broke down, and the parties entered into relationships with new partners. In September 2003 W applied for an order for contact and a shared residence order, and an order was made for alternate weekend and holiday contact. The judge prohibited G from moving without W's consent or the court's leave, but rejected W's proposal for a shared residence order, largely because of hostility between the parties. The Court of Appeal allowed W's appeal against that refusal. Shortly afterwards, G moved secretly with her new partner and the children to Cornwall. W, who lived in Shropshire, applied for the children's primary home to be with her. The judge, who said that she had no confidence that if the children remained in Cornwall G would promote their essential close relationship with W and her family, ordered that the children should have their primary home with W. The Court of Appeal dismissed G's appeal, and she appealed to the House of Lords.

Baroness Hale of Richmond:

...

[30] My Lords, the 1989 Act brought together the Government's proposals in relation to child care law and the Law Commission's recommendations in relation to the private law. In its Working Paper No 96, *Family Law: Review of Child Law: Custody* (1986), at para 6.22, having discussed whether there should be some form of presumption in favour of natural parents, the Law Commission said:

> 'We conclude, therefore, that the welfare of each child in the family should continue to be the paramount consideration whenever their custody or upbringing is in question between private individuals. The welfare test itself is well able to encompass any special contribution which natural parents can make to the emotional needs of their child, in particular to his sense of identity and self-esteem, as well as the added commitment which knowledge of their parenthood may bring. We have already said that the indications are that the priority given to the welfare of the child needs to be strengthened rather than undermined. We could not contemplate making any recommendation which might have the effect of weakening the protection given to children under the present law.'

Nor should we. The statutory position is plain: the welfare of the child is the paramount consideration. As Lord MacDermott explained in *J v C* [1970] AC 668 , 711, this means that it 'rules upon or determines the course to be followed'. There is no question of a parental right. As the Law Commission explained, 'the welfare test itself is well able to encompass any special contribution which natural parents can make to the emotional needs of their child' or, as Lord MacDermott put it, the claims and wishes of parents 'can be capable of ministering to the total welfare of the child in a special way'.

[31] None of this means that the fact of parentage is irrelevant. The position in English law is akin to that in Australian law, as explained by Lindenmayer J, at p 80, 343, in *Hodak v Newman* (1993) FLC 92–421 , and subsequently approved by the Full Court of the Family Court of Australia in *Rice v Miller* (1993) FLC 92–415 and *In re Evelyn* (1998) FLC 92- 807 :

> 'I am of the opinion that *the fact of parenthood is to be regarded as an important and significant factor in considering which proposals better advance the welfare of the child.* Such fact does not, however, establish a presumption in favour of the natural parent, nor generate a preferential position in favour of the natural parent from which the Court commences its decision-making process... Each case should be determined upon an examination of its own merits and of the individuals there involved.' (Emphasis supplied.)

[32] So what is the significance of the fact of parenthood? It is worthwhile picking apart what we mean by 'natural parent' in this context. There is a difference between natural and legal parents. Thus, the father of a child born to unmarried parents was not legally a 'parent' until the Family Law Reform Act 1987 but he was always a natural parent. The anonymous donor who donates his sperm or her egg under the terms of the Human Fertilisation and Embryology Act 1990 is the natural progenitor of the child but not his legal parent: see the 1990 Act, sections 27 and 28 . The husband or unmarried partner of a mother who gives birth as a result of donor insemination in a licensed clinic in this country is for virtually all purposes a legal parent, but may not be any kind of natural parent: see the 1990 Act, section 28 . To be the legal parent of a child gives a person legal standing to bring and defend proceedings about the child and makes the child a member of that person's family, but it does not necessarily tell us much about the importance of that person to the child's welfare.

[33] There are at least three ways in which a person may be or become a natural parent of a child, each of which may be a very significant factor in the child's welfare, depending upon the circumstances of the particular case. The first is genetic parenthood: the provision of the gametes which produce the child. This can be of deep significance on many levels. For the parent, perhaps particularly for a father, the knowledge that this is 'his' child can bring a very special sense of love for and commitment to that child which will be of great benefit to the child: see, for example, the psychiatric evidence in *In re C (MA) (An Infant)* [1966] 1 WLR 646. For the child, he reaps the benefit not only of that love and commitment, but also of knowing his own origins and lineage, which is an important component in finding an individual sense of self as one grows up. The knowledge of that genetic link may also be an important (although certainly not an essential) component in the love and commitment felt by the wider family, perhaps especially grandparents, from which the child has so much to gain.

[34] The second is gestational parenthood: the conceiving and bearing of the child. The mother who bears the child is legally the child's mother, whereas the mother who provided the egg is not: the 1990 Act, section 27 . While this may be partly for reasons of certainty and convenience, it also recognises a deeper truth: that the process of carrying a child and giving him birth (which may well be followed by breast-feeding for some months) brings with it, in the vast majority of cases, a very special relationship between mother and child, a relationship which is different from any other.

[35] The third is social and psychological parenthood: the relationship which develops through the child demanding and the parent providing for the child's needs, initially at the most basic level of feeding, nurturing, comforting and loving, and later at the more sophisticated level of guiding, socialising, educating and protecting. The phrase 'psychological parent' gained most currency from the influential work of *Goldstein, Freud & Solnit, Beyond the Best Interests of the Child* (1973).

36. Of course, in the great majority of cases, the natural mother combines all three. She is the genetic, gestational and psychological parent. Her contribution to the welfare of the child is unique. The natural father combines genetic and psychological parenthood. His contribution is

also unique. In these days when more parents share the tasks of child rearing and breadwinning, his contribution is often much closer to that of the mother than it used to be; but there are still families which divide their tasks on more traditional lines, in which case his contribution will be different and its importance will often increase with the age of the child.

[37] But there are also parents who are neither genetic nor gestational, but who have become the psychological parents of the child and thus have an important contribution to make to their welfare. Adoptive parents are the most obvious example, but there are many others. This is the position of CW in this case. Whatever may have been the mother's stance in the past, Mr Jackson on her behalf has not in any way sought to diminish the importance of CW's place in these children's lives or to challenge the legal arrangements put in place as a result of the first proceedings. Indeed, he asks us to restore those orders.

[38] What Mr Jackson challenges is the reversal in the parties' positions in response to the mother's removal of the children to Cornwall. He points out that, with one exception at the beginning of Bracewell J's judgment, there was no reference to the important fact that CG is these children's mother. While CW is their psychological parent, CG is, as Hallett LJ pointed out, both their biological and their psychological parent. In the overall welfare judgment, that must count for something in the vast majority of cases. Its significance must be considered and assessed. Furthermore, the evidence shows that it clearly did count for something in this case. These children were happy and doing very well in their mother's home. That should not have been changed without a very good reason.

[39] Mr Jackson argues that there was not a very good reason to change the children's primary home. The judge over-emphasised what she saw as the 'crux' of the case at the expense of the overall picture of what would be best for these children. Although she twice referred to the 'checklist' of relevant factors in section 1(3) of the 1989 Act, had she gone through the evidence relating to each of those factors systematically, giving proper weight to the children's relationship with their mother, she could not have reached the conclusion which she did. In particular, when concluding that she had no confidence that the mother would not seek to marginalise CW in the future, she gave no weight to the fact that regular and good quality contact had been continuing since it was re-established after the move.

...

[41] Making contact happen and, even more importantly, making contact work is one of the most difficult and contentious challenges in the whole of family law. It has recently received a great deal of public attention. Courts understandably regard the conventional methods of enforcing court orders as a last resort: fining the primary carer will only mean that she has even less to spend upon the children; sending her to prison will deprive them of their primary carer and give them a reason to resent the other parent who invited this. Nor does punishment address the real sources of the problem, which may range from a simple failure to understand what the children need, to more complex fears resulting from the parents' own relationship. That is why the assistance of a professional such as Mr Martin in this case can be so valuable. It is also why more constructive measures are to be introduced under the Children and Adoption Act 2006. The court will be able to direct either parent to engage in activities which will help them to understand and work through the difficulties. The range of penalties for breach of court orders will include an order to engage in unpaid work, thus reducing the risk that punishing the parent will also punish the child.

[42] However, at least as long ago as *V-P v V-P (Access to Child)* (1978) 1 FLR 336 , it was realised that a more potent encouragement to comply with court orders may be to contemplate changing the child's living arrangements. Ormrod LJ put it very directly, pp. 339–340:

> '... I do not wish to issue threats, but the mother should, I think, realise this: the father has a home with the half brother in it, he is unemployed, he is available to look after both these children full time. The mother is fully occupied, so that the grandmother is playing a very

> important part in this child's life... That being so, it would be a mistake on the part of the mother, in my judgment, to assume that the order for custody in her favour is inevitable; it is not and if the situation goes on as it is at present then it may be necessary to reconsider the question of custody.'

It is, I believe, becoming more common for family judges not only to issue such warnings but also to implement them. However, the object is to ensure that the arrangements which the court has made in the best interests of the child are actually observed. Only if this is not happening will the court conclude that other arrangements will be better for the child.

[43] In this particular case, the mother had behaved very badly. She, together with MG, had deliberately disobeyed the court's order. This had required considerable planning and the deception of her own solicitor. More importantly, it had been a terrible thing to do to the children. The aim had been to frustrate the contact arrangements ordered by the court. However, once she had been located and contact arrangements reinstated, she had abided by them. Had this been the usual case of a similar dispute between mother and father, I find it impossible to believe that a court would have contemplated changing the children's primary home and schooling while contact was continuing in accordance with the court's order. Of course, were the contact itself to be further frustrated, that would be a different matter.

[44] My Lords, I am driven to the conclusion that the courts below have allowed the unusual context of this case to distract them from principles which are of universal application. First, the fact that CG is the natural mother of these children in every sense of that term, while raising no presumption in her favour, is undoubtedly an important and significant factor in determining what will be best for them now and in the future. Yet nowhere is that factor explored in the judgment below. Secondly, while it may well be in the best interests of children to change their living arrangements if one of their parents is frustrating their relationship with the other parent who is able to offer them a good and loving home, this is unlikely to be in their best interests while that relationship is in fact being maintained in accordance with the court's order.

[45] I would therefore allow the appeal and make the order which Mr Jackson invites us to make. This is simply to reverse the names in the current allocation of time between the two households. I would also make a fresh family assistance order so that Mr Martin may continue his excellent work with this family for a further six months from today's date. That order may, of course, be repeated in due course and Mr Martin may refer the case back to court if the arrangements are not working: see the 1989 Act, section 16(6) . I am very conscious, as was Dr Sturge, the child psychiatrist who gave evidence in *In re D (Contact and Parental Responsibility: Lesbian Mothers and Known Father)* [2006] 1 FCR 556, of the vulnerability of someone in CW's position. Her importance in these children's lives has been stressed by both the professionals and all the judges who have decided this case. The mother should now be in no doubt about that or about the possible consequences should she not adhere to the arrangements which we have ordered....

Appeal allowed.

QUESTIONS

i. All the other judges agreed with Lady Hale: would either Goldstein, Freud and Solnit or Martin Richards (see pp. 459 and 463, above) have done so? Do you?

ii. Lord Scott added this:

> Mothers are special and, even after account is taken of CG's breach of the 'residence' order (the justification for which I, for my part, doubt) and her reprehensible attitude towards the important relationship between the girls and CW, their other parent, CG was, on the evidence, a good and loving mother. I find myself unable to accept that the circumstances of this case came even close to justifying the judge's and the Court of Appeal's conclusion that the welfare of the girls required their primary home to be changed from that of their mother to that of CW.

Do you agree (a) that 'mothers are special' (and by implication that one can only have one mother, see p. 432, above), or (b) that the order prohibiting relocation should never have been made (see p. 514, below)?

iii. Lord Nicholls added this:

> In reaching its decision the court should always have in mind that in the ordinary way the rearing of a child by his or her biological parent can be expected to be in the child's best interests, both in the short term and also, and importantly, in the longer term. I decry any tendency to diminish the significance of this factor. A child should not be removed from the primary care of his or her biological parents without compelling reason. Where such a reason exists the judge should spell this out explicitly.

(a) What did he mean by a 'biological' parent? Does it include a 'psychological parent' (see Johnson, 1999)? (b) Is there a difference between him and Lady Hale?

iv. Do you think that the same sex context should have made a difference? If so, what?

v. What difference would it have made if the 2007 Human Fertilisation and Embryology Bill (see p. 432, above) had become law (a) before either child was born, or (b) before this case was decided?

vi. Would this have been a case for a shared residence order if this had not been necessary in order to give CW parental responsibility?

10.2.3 CONTACT IN PRACTICE

Re O (contact: imposition of conditions)
[1995] 2 FLR 124, [1995] Fam Law 541, Court of Appeal

The parents lived together for three and a half years, separating in July 1992. Their son was born in November 1992. The father undertook not to pester or molest the mother, and was punished for breaking that undertaking. Early on, the father made clear his wish to have contact with his son and the mother made clear her intention to resist this. There were orders for contact at a contact centre, but the child became upset. The court welfare officer's view was that contact would only work if the mother was prepared to take part until the boy became acquainted with his father. An order was made for indirect contact with conditions that the mother send photographs every three months, inform the father if the child began at nursery or playgroup and send copies of all reports on his progress, inform the father of any significant illness and send copies of all medical reports, accept delivery of cards and presents from the father, read and show them to the child and give him any present. The mother objected to these conditions, because she was not prepared to have any contact with the father.

Sir Thomas Bingham MR:

. . . It may perhaps be worth stating in a reasonably compendious way some very familiar but none the less fundamental principles. First of all, and overriding all else as provided in s. 1(1) of the 1989 Act, the welfare of the child is the paramount consideration of any court concerned to make an order relating to the upbringing of a child. It cannot be emphasised too strongly that the court is concerned with the interests of the mother and the father only insofar as they bear on the welfare of the child.

Secondly, where parents of a child are separated and the child is in the day-to-day care of one of them, it is almost always in the interests of the child that he or she should have contact with the other parent. The reason for this scarcely needs spelling out. It is, of course, that the separation of parents involves a loss to the child, and it is desirable that that loss should so far as possible be made good by contact with the non-custodial parent, that is the parent in whose day-to-day care the child is not. . . .

Thirdly, the court has power to enforce orders for contact, which it should not hesitate to exercise where it judges that it will overall promote the welfare of the child to do so. I refer in this context to the judgment of the President of the Family Division in *Re W (A Minor)(Contact)* [1994] 2 FLR 441 at p. 447H, where the President said:

> 'However, I am quite clear that a court cannot allow a mother, in such circumstances, simply to defy the order of the court which was, and is, in force, that is to say that there should be reasonable contact with the father. That was indeed made by consent as I have already observed. Some constructive step must be taken to permit and encourage the boy to resume contact with his father.'
>
> . . .

Fourthly, cases do, unhappily and infrequently but occasionally, arise in which a court is compelled to conclude that in existing circumstances an order for immediate direct contact should not be ordered, because so to order would injure the welfare of the child. In *Re D (A Minor) (Contact: Mother's Hostility)* [1993] 2 FLR 1 at p.7G, Waite LJ said:

> 'It is now well settled that the implacable hostility of a mother towards access or contact is a factor which is capable, according to the circumstances of each particular case, of supplying a cogent reason for departing from the general principle that a child should grow up in the knowledge of both his parents. I see no reason to think that the judge fell into any error of principle in deciding, as he clearly did on the plain interpretation of his judgment, that the mother's present attitude towards contact puts D at serious risk of major emotional harm if she were to be compelled to accept a degree of contact to the natural father against her will.'

I simply draw attention to the judge's reference to a serious risk of major emotional harm. The courts should not at all readily accept that the child's welfare will be injured by direct contact. Judging that question the court should take a medium-term and long-term view of the child's development and not accord excessive weight to what appear likely to be short-term or transient problems. Neither parent should be encouraged or permitted to think that the more intransigent, the more unreasonable, the more obdurate and the more uncooperative they are, the more likely they are to get their own way. Courts should remember that in these cases they are dealing with parents who are adults, who must be treated as rational adults, who must be assumed to have the welfare of the child at heart, and who have once been close enough to each other to have produced the child. It would be as well if parents also were to bear these points in mind.

Fifthly, in cases in which, for whatever reason, direct contact cannot for the time being be ordered, it is ordinarily highly desirable that there should be indirect contact so that the child grows up knowing of the love and interest of the absent parent with whom, in due course, direct contact should be established. This calls for a measure of restraint, common sense and unselfishness on the part of both parents. If the absent parent deluges the child with presents or writes long and obsessive screeds to the child, or if he or she uses his or her right to correspond to criticise or insult the other parent, then inevitably those rights will be curtailed. The object of indirect contact is to build up a relationship between the absent parent and the child, not to enable the absent parent to pursue a feud with the caring parent in a manner not conducive to the welfare of the child.

The caring parent also has reciprocal obligations. If the caring parent puts difficulties in the way of indirect contact by withholding presents or letters or failing to read letters to a child who cannot read, then such parent must understand that the court can compel compliance with its orders; it has sanctions available and no residence order is to be regarded as irrevocable. It is entirely reasonable that the parent with the care of the child should be obliged to report on the progress of the child to the absent parent, for the obvious reason that an absent parent cannot correspond in a meaningful way if unaware of the child's concerns, or of where the child goes to school, or what it does when it gets there, or what games it plays, and so on. Of course judges must not impose duties which parents cannot realistically be expected to perform, and it would accordingly be absurd to expect, in a case where this was the case, a semi-literate parent to write monthly reports. But some means of communication, directly or indirectly, is essential if indirect contact is to be meaningful, and if the welfare of the child is not to suffer.

...

The court has ample power to compel the mother to send photographs, medical reports and school reports in order to promote meaningful contact between the father and the child, which would almost certainly wither and die if the father received no information about the child's progress. It is in my view plain that the court does have power under these sections as a necessary means of facilitating contact. ...

Appeal dismissed.

QUESTION

In what circumstances, if any, would you consider that a parent's 'implacable hostility' to contact was justified?

By the late 1990s considerable concern had been voiced about cases where contact had been ordered in the face, not so much of hostility, as of well-founded fear. Felicity Kaganas and Shelley Day Sclater sum up the concerns in *Contact and Domestic Violence – the Winds of Change?* (2000):

In recent years there has been growing concern about the ways in which contact disputes are managed by *professionals* and decided by courts in cases involving domestic violence. This concern has developed as a result of an accumulating body of social scientific research about violence to mothers and children. In particular, researchers have suggested that separation and divorce may lead to an escalation of violence. Also, there is research drawing links between woman abuse and child abuse. Two major research studies by the research team led by Marianne Hester and Lorraine Radford highlighted the plight of those mothers and children who were expected to participate in contact arrangements despite the violence or abuse perpetrated by non-resident fathers [Hester and Radford, 1996], and pointed to a number of deficiencies in professional practice in dealing with such cases [Hester, Pearson and Radford, 1997]. Both the legal process and mediation have been criticised as, at best, failing to meet the safety needs of women and children and, at worst, as perpetuating the abuse....

The leading case is now generally referred to as '*Re L*'.

Re L (a child) (contact: domestic violence); Re V (a child) (contact: domestic violence); Re M (a child) (contact: domestic violence); Re H (children) (contact: domestic violence)
[2001] Fam 268, [2000] 4 All ER 609, Court of Appeal

Dame Elizabeth Butler-Sloss P:
These four appeals on issues arising out of contact applications have certain features in common. In each case a father's application for direct contact has been refused by the circuit judge against a background of domestic violence between the spouses or partners....

The Report

The report by the Children Act Sub-Committee [Advisory Board on Family Law Children Act Sub-Committee: A Report to the Lord Chancellor on the Question of Parental Contact in Cases where there is Domestic Violence (12 April 2000)] underlined the importance of the question of domestic violence in the context of parental contact to children. Domestic violence takes many forms and should be broadly defined. The perpetrator may be female as well as male. Involvement may be indirect as well as direct. There needs to be greater awareness of the effect of domestic violence on children, both short-term and long-term, as witnesses as well as victims and also the impact on the residential parent. An outstanding concern of the court should be the nature and extent of the risk to the child and to the residential parent and that proper arrangements should be put in place to safeguard the child and the residential parent from risk of further physical or emotional harm. In cases where domestic violence is raised as a reason for refusing or limiting contact, the report makes it clear that the allegations ought to be addressed by the court at the earliest opportunity and findings of fact made so as to establish the truth or otherwise of those allegations and decide upon the likely effect, if any, those findings could have on the court's decision on contact....

The Psychiatric Report

Drs Sturge and Glaser in their joint report to this court had the opportunity to see the responses to the Sub-Committee consultation paper and to read the report and recommendations. Their psychiatric report was read and approved by a number of other consultant child psychiatrists and incorporates the views of a distinguished group of consultants....

General Comments

There are however a number of general comments I wish to make on the advice given to us. The family judges and magistrates need to have a heightened awareness of the existence of and consequences (some long-term) on children of exposure to domestic violence between their parents or other partners. There has, perhaps, been a tendency in the past for courts not to tackle allegations of violence and to leave them in the background on the premise that they were matters affecting the adults and not relevant to issues regarding the children. The general principle that contact with the non-resident parent is in the interests of the child may sometimes have discouraged sufficient attention being paid to the adverse effects on children living in the household where violence has occurred. It may not necessarily be widely appreciated that violence to a partner involves a significant failure in parenting – failure to protect the child's carer and failure to protect the child emotionally.

In a contact or other section 8 application, where allegations of domestic violence are made which might have an effect on the outcome, those allegations must be adjudicated upon and found proved or not proved. It will be necessary to scrutinise such allegations which may not always be true or may be grossly exaggerated. If however there is a firm basis for finding that violence has occurred, the psychiatric advice becomes very important. There is not, however, nor should there be, any presumption that, on proof of domestic violence, the offending parent has to surmount a prima facie barrier of no contact. As a matter of principle, domestic violence of itself cannot constitute a bar to contact. It is one factor in the difficult and delicate balancing exercise of discretion. The court deals with the facts of a specific case in which the degree of violence and the seriousness of the impact on the child and on the resident parent have to be taken into account. In cases of proved domestic violence, as in cases of other proved harm or risk of harm to the child, the court has the task of weighing in the balance the seriousness of the domestic violence, the risks involved and the impact on the child against the positive factors, if any, of contact between the parent found to have been violent and the child. In this context, the ability of the offending parent to recognise his past conduct, be aware of the need to change and make genuine efforts to do so, will be likely to be an important consideration. Wall J in *Re M (minors) (contact: violent parent)* [1999] 2 FCR 56 at 68–69 suggested that often in cases where domestic violence had been found, too little weight had been given to the need for the father to change. He suggested that the father should demonstrate that he was a fit person to exercise contact and should show a track record of proper behaviour. Assertions, without evidence to back it up, may well not be sufficient.

In expressing these views I recognise the danger of the pendulum swinging too far against contact where domestic violence has been proved. It is trite but true to say that no two child cases are exactly the same. The court always has the duty to apply s 1 of the Children Act 1989 that the welfare of the child is paramount and, in considering that welfare, to take into account all the relevant circumstances, including the advice of the medical experts as far as it is relevant and proportionate to the decision in that case. It will also be relevant in due course to take into account the impact of art 8 of the Convention for the Protection of Human Rights and Fundamental Freedoms (the European Convention on Human Rights) (Rome, 4 November 1950; TS 71 (1953); Cmd 8969) on a decision to refuse direct contact. …

The President went on to consider the first appeal:

Appeal in Re L (a Child) (Contact: Domestic Violence)

The child T is a little girl born on 29 June 1998 and is still under two years old. She lives with her mother. The parents did not marry or cohabit. The father was and remains married with a child by that marriage. T was registered in the father's name but is now known by her mother's name. There is no issue on the change of name. Contact ceased soon after the birth of the child. The father applied for a parental responsibility order and contact to the child. The applications came before Judge Allweis on 29 September 1999. He heard evidence of violence alleged by the mother both before and during the latter part of her pregnancy which included slapping, hitting her with an umbrella and trying to strangle her which caused bruising to her neck. An incident occurred when the baby was four weeks old. She was sitting naked on the bed feeding the child. The father pulled her hair and using foul language threatened to cut it off with scissors he was holding. He then cut off her pubic hair with the scissors. She was in tears and felt shaken, scared and degraded. She decided to leave him and did so three weeks later. On that occasion he collected her from her mother's home. She told him she wanted to stay with her mother because the child had colic. She locked herself into the bathroom and he kicked the door open and grabbed her and the baby in her baby seat so she felt she had to go with him. The next day she went to the police. She then received threatening telephone calls including threats to remove T. The police went to the mother's home on 19 August 1998 which they found had been vandalised and rendered uninhabitable. The father completely denied the violence and the vandalism of the mother's home. He continued to deny the violence at the contact hearing and on appeal. The judge gave judgment on 4 October 1999 and said that the allegations amounted to a catalogue of sadistic violence. He found the mother's account of violence to be true. He said:

> '... this is a man who has mood swings and a temper... I would add this: that a father who systematically went through and damaged his partner's home, as he did, has a very real anger and control problem. It indicates a cruel streak, which suggests a significant psychological problem ...'

He then considered the mother's opposition to contact:

> 'I conclude that the mother's opposition to contact is implacable but reasonable. Her fear is genuine and based on rational grounds, namely actual violence and a genuine fear of him, and that [T] will in time witness violence. I believe that direct contact, if ordered, would trigger enormous anxiety which would affect the mother... The mother's attitude towards contact would put [T] at serious risk of major emotional harm if she were to be compelled to accept a degree of contact to the father against her will, and indeed in time that heightened anxiety would be conveyed to the child ...'

He made a residence order to the mother. He ordered indirect contact and made a family assistance order to help set up the indirect contact and dismissed the father's application for a parental responsibility order and granted permission to appeal. The father appeals to this court on both issues and raises arts 8 and 14 of the European Convention on Human Rights.

On the issue of contact, the judge found the mother's opposition to contact to be reasonable and that her fear of him was genuine and based on actual violence and that T would in time witness violence....

The risks to the child were obvious and the father, in refusing to face up to them, was clearly unable to reduce those risks. In her able submissions to the court, Miss de Haas QC, on behalf of the father, made the point that the mother was white and the father was black and, since the child was of mixed race, she needed to understand her roots and establish her identity, which would best be achieved by direct contact. In the circumstances of this case, in my view, it would certainly be possible to achieve that important objective by indirect contact. The judge applied the proper principles and the decision to which he came was not only well within his exercise of discretion, but on the facts of this case, clearly right.

Although a decision on the point is not yet strictly relevant, there was no failure, in my view, by the judge, under art 8(1), to have proper respect for family life.... The observation by the Court in *Johansen v Norway* (1996) 23 EHRR 33 is particularly apposite to this appeal. The Court said:

'In particular...the parent cannot be entitled under Article 8 of the Convention to have such measures taken as would harm the child's health and development.'

In the present appeal, there are very real risks of emotional harm that require the court to protect the child. I would dismiss the appeal on the issue of contact.

QUESTION

But are there other reasons than violence to refuse contact? What, for example, if the child does not wish to see the other parent? (See *Re S (Contact: Children's Views)* [2002] 1 FLR 1156, and look back at Sturge and Glaser, p. 467, above.)

If an order for contact is made, how can it be enforced? Court orders are normally enforced by committal to prison; but will that be more damaging to the child than the failure to enforce the order? The Children Act Sub-Committee of the Advisory Board on Family Law, in *Making Contact Work, a report to the Lord Chancellor* (2002) reported on the results of its survey of individuals and organisations:

What alternative to committal to prison do you think there should be in a case where the court finds that contact is in the best interests of the child but is being irrationally frustrated by the residential parent? Should the court be given broader powers to deal with recalcitrant residential parents – for example to require them to attend parenting classes?

14.21 This is, we think, the most important question in this part of the Consultation Paper, and it was the question which produced a substantial number of suggestions. There was widespread support for the proposition that the Court should be given the power to impose a range of alternative options.

14.22 In our view the most constructive suggestions were those which proposed either community penalties, or the attendance by the person in contempt at parenting classes or meetings designed to persuade that person that the order should be obeyed. Professor Walker summed up a number of responses here when she said:

> Parenting education would be an obvious option here. Yes – courts should be given broader powers to refer parents to such classes. The general rule ought to be to find 'therapeutic' approaches to the problem and to support parents to work through difficulties, hostilities, etc. The more rigid and punitive the responses/court orders, the more likely that contact will fail.

14.23 In this respect, many respondents were attracted, as were we by the thinking behind the Australian model, in which a three stage process is proposed as follows:-

> The first stage is preventative. It requires the court to include in its orders a clause which sets out the obligations the order creates and the consequences which follow should the order not be observed. The Court is also required to provide the parties with information about parenting programmes to assist the parties in meeting their new parenting responsibilities as well as information about the use of location and recovery orders. These

measures are intended to improve the knowledge and understanding of parents leading to an increased rate of compliance.

The second stage provides the court with a range of powers where a breach of the order first occurs. The court will have the power to order one or both parties to a programme termed a 'post separation parenting programme'. The aim of such referral is to enable the parties to explore the real or underlying reason for the breach so that as the parties come to terms with their new parenting responsibilities after separation, they are able to obtain professional assistance. Some of the parenting programmes are anger management programmes. In addition, the court will be able to order compensatory contact.

The third stage arises where there has been a second or subsequent breach of the order. This stage provides the court with a range of sanctions extending from community service order, bond or fine, but in the most serious case, imprisonment. This third stage provides the court with discretion to return to stage 2 where further parenting program attendance may be warranted, such as where the first and second breaches were of a trivial nature and the more punitive sanctions are not warranted.

14.24 We were also very attracted by response on this point by CAFCASS, which summed up its approach by saying:-

What is proposed is an approach that gives practitioners more time to work with parents and children within a vision of a range of services such as supervised Contact Centres, child *counselling*, perpetrator programmes, information giving meetings, conciliation meetings prior to initial directions and psychological assessments. There will be cases where even this level of intervention will fail to bring about change in a situation. In such cases attempting to facilitate some form of indirect contact is more appropriate than resorting to fines or imprisonment.

14.25 For courts in England and Wales to be given these powers would require legislation. Equally, there would be no point in giving the courts wider powers, if programmes of the type envisaged were not to be available. We are, however, convinced that this is the way forward.

Transfer of Residence to the Other Parent

14.26 This was discussed in a number of responses. It was, however, clear that such a transfer would have to be in the interests of the children concerned, since such a course clearly fell within section 1 of the Children Act and when determining that question the welfare of the children concerned was paramount. In the large majority of cases, therefore, a transfer of residence is unlikely to be the appropriate response to a committal summons without a substantial degree of further investigation. Judge Richard Jenkins, we thought, described the dilemma well:-

The dilemma is increased because a transfer of residence will very rarely be appropriate. On the advice of the Official Solicitor and a consultant psychiatrist I have had success in ordering a transfer of residence where contact was unreasonably being refused. An extensive investigation and lengthy evidence persuaded me that a change of residence would have been appropriate in any event. The mother of a seven-year-old boy had placed herself in a socially isolated position with the child and was thoroughly over-protective of him. He was sensible enough to realise as soon as transfer had taken place where his best interests lay. That was an isolated case and I disparage the use of a residence application as a tactical weapon.

14.27 We wholly endorse Judge Jenkins' disapproval of the use or threat of a residence application as a means of achieving contact. It is a legitimate complaint by Women's Groups that

> abused women are sometimes induced to agree to unsuitable and unsafe contact with violent fathers by their belief in unfounded threats that their children will either be transferred to the father or taken into care. At the same time there will be cases in which a refusal of contact will be sufficiently damaging to a child as to outweigh the trauma caused by removing the child from the care of the residential parent. Judge Jenkins gives one example. Others are where children are being brought up in the false belief that they have been sexually abused by the absent parent, or where children of mixed race are being brought up in the belief that the race to which the absent parent belongs consists of people who are dangerous and/or bad.

The Children and Adoption Act 2006 adds several new sections to the Children Act 1989: principally, sections 11A and 11B provide for a court considering whether to make, vary or discharge a contact order to make a 'contact activity direction requiring an individual who is a party to the proceedings to take part in an activity that promotes contact with the child concerned'. Sections 11C and 11D provide for 'contact activity conditions' requiring the person with whom the child lives or is to live, the person whose contact with the child concerned is provided for in the order, or a person upon whom the order imposes a condition under section 11(7)(b) (see p. 476, above) 'to take part in an activity that promotes contact with the child concerned'. Section 11H gives the court power to ask a CAFCASS officer to monitor and report back on compliance with a contact order. Section 11J allows a court which is satisfied beyond reasonable doubt that a person has failed to comply with a contact order to impose upon that person an 'unpaid work requirement' (unless that person can prove that she had a reasonable excuse). Section 16A requires CAFCASS officers exercising any of their functions under the Act to carry out a risk assessment if 'given cause to suspect that the child concerned is at risk of harm'.

QUESTIONS

i. Residence orders can be enforced by the High Court tipstaff or a police officer physically delivering the child to the person with whom he is to live: why not enforce contact in the same way?

ii. Applications for unpaid work requirements can be made by the person with whom the child lives, and by the child, as well as by the person whose contact with the child is provided for in the order. Look back at the definition of a contact order in section 8 (p. 475, above). In what circumstances could the person whose contact with the child is provided for in the order fail to comply with the order?

iii. What, if any, should be the sanctions against a parent who (a) fails to turn up for contact as arranged; (b) turns up drunk; or (c) fails to return the child at the time agreed?

In *Divorce and the Reluctant Father* (1980), Anne Heath-Jones gives a vivid account of this last problem and her solution to it:

> When my husband and I separated 12 years ago, we had two children who were then one and three years of age with long years of childhood ahead of them....
>
> James was never a doting father, which had been one of the problems of the marriage. In effect I had always been a single parent. The boys were very young and their awareness of, and attachment to, their remote father was slight. James was all set to vanish from our lives completely.

> But somehow in all the mess, in all my own grief and loneliness, and in spite of all the bitterness I harboured against him, I knew that if I had strength to fight for anything it should be to maintain contact between the children and their father. . . .
>
> In those early years the fact that he saw them at all was due to every imaginable ploy. Persuasion, appeal, anger and tears. I met him more than half-way on any arrangement that he was prepared to concede. I would deliver them to his flat and collect them. If he refused to have them to stay overnight then I settled for one day – or half a day. I felt anything was better than that they should lose touch and become strangers.
>
> Meanwhile, I kept James informed of progress at nursery and later primary school. I made sure the boys remembered his birthday; I showed him school reports. I begged him (swallowing large hunks of indigestible pride) to attend school open days, birthday parties and Guy Fawkes parties. Most important of all I kept his image intact for his children. They never heard from me any criticism of his character, or knew of my deep hurt and resentment that their father needed so much coercion to see them or be involved in their lives.
>
> For many years all the initiative for contact came from us. He never 'phoned or wrote or asked to see them. Then slowly, very slowly, the years of effort began to pay off. The boys and I moved from London into the country. James came down occasionally for the weekend and I would clear off and leave the cottage to them. After he re-married a more or less regular arrangement was worked out for the school holidays.
>
> We were lucky in his choice of a new wife. She was friendly and accepted her two step-sons, and in time they formed an easy relationship with her. Christmases were now peopled with a whole new branch of extended family. Instead of moping alone with me (and some Christmases were very mopey) they had a welcome at their father's and his relations and even at the big family gatherings of his new wife. . . .
>
> Now, 1967 seems a long time ago and their childhood is nearly over. The relationship with their father now is mutually warm, positive and spontaneous. At times the price to pay for nurturing that relationship has been high. If you idealise the absent parent you must be prepared for the consequences.
>
> When life got tough for us, when the boys were unhappy with school or friends, or when they sobbed for the father whose contact I had so carefully preserved, the cry was 'I want to live with Dad.' It hurt of course because I had provided the years of love and security, it hurt because I knew their father wouldn't want them and it hurt because that was the last thing in the world that I could explain to the crying child.
>
> In spite of the upheavals of those early years we have all survived. They now have a father they can respect and admire, a man they can talk to and learn from, and a model to emulate when they become husbands and fathers themselves.

But while it can be hard for the parent with whom the children are living, it can also be hard for the other one, as an anonymous mother explained in *Saturday Parent* (1980):

> One morning nine years ago, when she was seven years old, I watched my youngest daughter walk across the school yard, knowing that it would not be me who collected her at the end of school that day. I do not care to describe the pain of that moment, nor the many pains that followed in the years to come. The decision had been made in court the day before – henceforward she was to live with her father, my ex-husband, and his new wife and her two adopted children. From that day on I have been a 'Saturday Parent' – the one who has access – that part-time travesty of parenting that is shared by an increasing number of separated parents in our present society. For years I could not see the problems with any kind of objectivity – I merely experienced them. . . .

It is this vexed question of management which I wish to highlight – by-passing all the aggravation of actually settling on mutually convenient times and places – a most flourishing battle ground for embittered ex-spouses. I would like to enumerate some of the areas of difficulty personally experienced.

Firstly, there is the passage of time. Access is usually fixed at one hearing at a given point in time when the child is of a certain age. Obviously times and frequency of contact negotiated then frequently become obsolete, a child passes rapidly from toddler, to schoolchild, to independent teenager, and unless there is good-will – a scarce commodity in the devastation of a broken marriage – the poor youngster is stuck with every second Saturday from 9 a.m. to 7 p.m. whether it will or no. Access is for the benefit of children. The law acknowledges this; many parents do not.

Then there is the vexed question of discipline and training – something which was an everyday part of living, suddenly becomes a major issue. There is no time to confront, disagree, sulk and make-up when all you have is a truncated week-end. One vacillates between turning a 'blind eye' to everything and jumping on the poor kid at every turn. Related to this is one's attitude to the 'other' set of parents – the real (?) parents – does one share their values, opinions, standards? It is all too easy to fall into the role of permissive Aunty who lets the kid go to parties and stay out late, only to find that a 10 p.m. ban is standard at home. (No one bothered to tell you, though – unless something goes wrong!)

Matters of loyalty to ex-spouses, towards whom one's feelings are, to say the least, ambivalent, arise continually. 'So-and-so (in my case, step-mother) would not let me do so-and-so, isn't she unfair?' 'Well no, actually. If you were with me all the time, I too would'...etc.

One had to fight an overwhelming desire to put all one's frustrated love into the small parcel of time allowed – a present on the bed, a cake specially baked – one yearns to be perceived as loving and lavishing, for after all one has also to cope with one's own feeling of guilt about letting the child go. However it happened, and whatever your reasons, you did it. Recounting the story of Solomon's wise judgment to a colleague, he remarked sadly: 'Trouble is, there's no one around with Solomon's wisdom or his knowledge.' Too true. Judges have to make life decisions for people they hardly know and who are not likely to be presenting themselves in the best light anyway.

QUESTIONS

i. Helen Reece, in *UK women's groups' child contact campaign: 'so long as it is safe'* (2006) argues:

> ... that women's groups' contribution to the child contact debate drew on feminist understandings of domestic violence as well as feminist research into the connection between child contact and domestic violence, to the exclusion of autonomy-based feminist critiques of child contact. The author has argued that this focus damaged mothers' interests by creating two mutually exclusive categories of mother, the unreasonable mother and the domestic violence victim. The focus of the campaign can be partly explained by women's groups' quest for consensus; nevertheless, there is a tension between the demand for domestic violence to be taken more seriously in child contact disputes and the demand for a feminist interpretation of domestic violence. If women's groups believe that post-separation child contact arrangements currently allow fathers to exercise too much power and control over mothers then they need to make an argument that is explicitly autonomy-based,

> not violence-based. Using safety as a stand-in for autonomy has benefited neither mothers who are nor mothers who are not domestic violence victims.

Why, do you think, did the women's groups concentrate on 'so long as it is safe' rather than the analyses of Smart (p. 465, above) and others?

ii. Why, do you think, does this chapter contain so many references, from different sources, to the judgment of Solomon?

10.2.4 ISN'T THERE A BETTER WAY?

Section 1 of the Children Act 1989 contains another important, but novel, principle:

> **1.** — (5) Where a court is considering whether or not to make one or more orders under this Act with respect to a child, it shall not make the order or any of the orders unless it considers that doing so would be better for the child than making no order at all.

Carol Smart, in *The Legal and Moral Ordering of Child Custody* (1990), exposes this provision to a feminist critique:

> The Law Commission report espoused a policy of non-intervention by the courts into matters of child care arrangements on the basis that parents are the best people to decide what is right for their children. This exalted principle was wisely underscored by the recognition that even if parents were not, there is not a great deal of evidence to suggest that judges or local authority social workers are much better equipped for the job (except in cases of actual harm or abuse). The legislation therefore seeks to allow parents to make their own decisions. In practice this is what happens in the vast majority of cases anyway and the courts merely legitimate arrangements which have occurred elsewhere (even though these agreements take place in the shadow of the law). On the face of it the Act simply acknowledges this, but at the same time it goes further and promotes a 'hands off' approach as the ideal....
>
> The criticism which has been made of non-interventionist family law in general, and this provision in particular, is that non-intervention is really intervention by another name. In other words to stand outside the 'fray' and do nothing is to be just as influential as doing something. The classic examples are, of course, domestic violence and child abuse where critics of non-intervention have shown that 'inaction' is not a position which is somehow morally superior to intervention. Non-intervention is therefore not automatically good but, by the same token, research in both of these fields has also shown that some caution must be applied to rushing to embrace intervention as if it must be better. Olsen suggests that we really should abandon such terms as indications of political orientation rather than as objective statements of how the law operates in relation to the family and there is some merit in this.
>
> There is, however, another side to this argument (and it is one which was reflected in the interviews for this research). Murch, as long ago as 1980, pointed to the resentment caused to parents by the experience of state intervention into their lives at the point of marriage breakdown. It is also often remarked upon that if we allow parents to raise children according to their own values whilst a relationship is ongoing, there is no reason to assume that they become especially incapacitated in this respect just because the relationship ends. ...[We] do not require a judge to be satisfied with arrangements made for a child when a spouse dies or simply leaves. In other words there is no reason to draw the line between intervention and

non-intervention at the point of divorce although we may still wish to draw it where violence occurs for example.

But how is non-intervention working in practice? Rebecca Bailey-Harris, Gwynn Davis, Jacqueline Barron and Julia Pearce, in *Settlement culture and the use of the 'no order' principle under the Children Act 1989* (1999) report:

Our study showed that section 1(5) receives a very mixed response in practice at county court level. These variations may simply reflect the width of discretion afforded to judges in children proceedings under the Act. Nevertheless, the evidence from our study could be interpreted as suggesting two themes. First, the 'no order principle' is invoked by judges to reinforce the concept of parental autonomy and the vigorous promotion of agreement; this results in the court declining or refusing to make an order even when parties have sought one. It is highly questionable whether this use of the principle accords with the original intention of the legislature, and we found that it could be productive of acute dissatisfaction on the part of parents who were expecting an adjudicated outcome. Secondly, and in complete contrast, the principle is very commonly breached or not observed by judges, particularly when legal practitioners press for resolution by consent order. There are various forms of outcome in which the principle can be reflected. The court can refuse or dismiss an application, or give leave for it to be withdrawn, or adjourn it not to be restored under certain conditions. Sometimes the court makes a formal 'order of no order'. Our file survey showed that, overall, a substantive order was made in 67 per cent of cases, no substantive order in 27 per cent, and an order of 'no order' in 5 per cent. The extent of non-observance of the principle by the courts we sampled is thus immediately apparent.

To pursue the first theme: it is possible to argue from the evidence of our study that in practice the courts are using the 'no order principle' in cases to which it was never intended to apply. In many cases where there is originally real conflict between parents who have invoked the court's jurisdiction specifically to resolve their dispute, the principle is invoked by judges to reinforce the promotion of parental autonomy and agreement as the preferred mode of resolution: the court asserts that no order is needed where parents can eventually agree, even though their preferred original intention was to obtain an order.

Our study reveals many examples of judges using the rhetoric of parental autonomy to justify the refusal to make an order, even in proceedings where there is real dispute and where proceedings are protracted. The judicial message delivered ranges through 'parents know better for their children than the court can' to 'your agreement is more likely to "stick" than a court order'. Examples abounded in each of the four courts we observed. In one, a particular district judge was notable for his strong messages regularly delivered to parties during the course of family days that the policy of the Children Act 1989 is that the court is not there to tell parents how to bring up their children; parental co-operation is everything, parental agreement is the preferred option and that the court's role is to make a decision only when parents cannot agree. ... In another court... a district judge frequently told parties on family days that anything he ordered would be strictly second best to anything the parties could decide themselves since they know their children far better than the court could. He commented to us in general discussion that 'The object of directions appointments is to get as much as possible solved without a contest – if parties get to a stage where they agree, it is more likely to stick'. ...

There is considerable evidence of the dissatisfaction of parents with the outcome of 'no order' when they consider that they have invoked the court's jurisdiction precisely for the exercise of its authority in a matter which they find difficult to resolve themselves. ...

QUESTIONS

i. Why, do you think, are some judges so reluctant to decide these disputes?

ii. We have already discussed in-court conciliation and out-of-court mediation (see p. 174, above). Are you surprised that a recent follow-up study (L. Trinder and J. Kellett, 2007) concludes that in-court conciliation is an effective way of reaching agreements and restoring contact over the short term but is often followed by further litigation and has very limited impact on making contact actually work well for children?

iii. Can the practice of letting (or making) the parents decide be reconciled with the following requirements in Article 12 of the United Nations Convention on the Rights of the Child?

> 1. States Parties shall assure to the child who is capable of forming his or her own views the right to express those views freely in all matters affecting the child, the views of the child being given due weight in accordance with the age and maturity of the child.
> 2. For this purpose, the child shall in particular be provided the opportunity to be heard in any judicial and administrative proceedings affecting the child, either directly, or through a representative or an appointed body, in a manner consistent with the procedural rules of national law.

It is to the child's perspective that we now turn.

10.3 THE CHILD'S EYE VIEW

10.3.1 WISHES AND FEELINGS

The Law Commission (1988) dealt with the 'wishes and feelings' of the child himself (item (a) in the Children Act checklist, p. 481, above) in this way:

> 3.23 The opinion of our respondents was almost unanimously in favour of the proposal to give statutory recognition to the child's views. Obviously there are dangers in giving them too much recognition. Children's views have to be discovered in such a way as to avoid embroiling them in their parents' disputes, forcing them to 'choose' between their parents, or making them feel responsible for the eventual decision. This is usually best done through the medium of a welfare officer's report, although most agreed that courts should retain their present powers to see children in private. Similarly, for a variety of reasons the child's views may not be reliable, so that the court should only have to take due account of them in the light of his age and understanding. Nevertheless, experience has shown that it is pointless to ignore the clearly expressed wishes of older children [*M v M (transfer of custody: appeal)* [1987] 1 WLR 404, [1987] 2 FLR 146]. Finally, however, if the parents have agreed on where the child will live and made their arrangements accordingly, it is no more practicable to try to alter these to accord with the child's views than it is to impose the views of the court. After all, united parents will no doubt take account of the views of their children in deciding upon moves of house or employment but the children cannot expect their wishes to prevail.

3.24 These considerations all point towards including the child's views as part of a statutory checklist, which in practice will be limited to contested cases, rather than as a separate consideration in their own right. This solution was generally favoured by our respondents and we so recommend....

QUESTIONS

i. Is it right to limit the obligation to take into account the child's wishes and feelings to contested cases?

ii. If not, how might parents be encouraged or obliged to consult their children when making their own arrangements?

iii. How should the child's views be discovered in contested cases: (a) through a court welfare officer or other professional; (b) by the judge interviewing the child in private or in the course of the case; or (c) by appointing a guardian and lawyer to represent the child?

If the child is making his own application, or there is some other good reason, he may be made a party and even, if old and mature enough, instruct his lawyer directly rather than through an adult guardian (see Chapter 8, p. 379, above). The usual practice, however, is to obtain a report from a professional, formerly known as a court welfare officer, and now a children and family reporter from the Children and Family Court Advisory and Support Service (CAFCASS). Vanessa May and Carol Smart, in *Silence in court? Hearing children in residence and contact disputes* (2004), report on their study of court files:

... Because of the pressures put on parents to settle their disputes before they get to court, many children are never seen by a representative of the court, and even fewer are seen alone without their parents present. Sawyer [2000] found that court welfare officers in her study believed their job to be to conciliate between the parents – or 'bang their heads together' – and to make parents understand that contact was the child's right. Because their efforts were often deemed to be successful, the court welfare officers rarely saw the children. The time restraints placed on the preparation of welfare reports may also contribute to the relatively low number of children being consulted. Piper [1999] has noted that despite the apparent focus on children's welfare, there is an undercurrent of non-engagement when it comes to children, as evidenced by the fact that only a minority of children are actually heard.

... Forty-seven per cent of our 430 cases had a court welfare, or social services, report on file and in one half of these children had been consulted. This means that children had been consulted in only one quarter of the cases we examined. Our impression was that, where children were not directly consulted, the most usual reason was related to the age of the child (usually under 5 years) or the fact that the parents managed to come to an agreement....

We found a continuum of children's involvement in these cases. At one end of the continuum children were not interviewed at all and thus appear to have had no influence on the outcome of the case. Further along the continuum there were cases where the children were interviewed extensively and appear to have had an influence on the final outcome. Then, at the furthest end there were cases where the children decided the outcome of the case themselves, going against the wishes of the court welfare officer by 'voting with their feet'. These children simply went to live with the parent of their choice or restricted contact according to their own wishes.

We found that three factors were central to children's involvement in a case:

The Child's Age

Not surprisingly, the older the children were, the more likely they were to be seen by a representative of the court and to have their wishes and feelings considered in detail. The desire that children have to exercise some control over their own destinies often becomes more apparent as they grow older. Previous studies [Smart and others, 2001] have shown that sometimes parents are unwilling to allow children to alter arrangements even when the children become adolescents and wish to spend more time with friends, on hobbies or even on school commitments. In these sorts of cases the court welfare officer appeared to have an important role in mediating between the children and a parent who seemed incapable of hearing what his or her children were saying....

... It is also sometimes hard for parents to appreciate that different children in a family may want different arrangements for contact and residence. One child may be happy to stay overnight with a parent, while another might not be. One child might be frightened of a parent and the other might not be. We found cases in our sample where the courts demonstrated that they were able to understand these differences and were willing to make different orders for siblings if the report recommended it....

... It was not always the case that children's stated wishes resulted in the outcome they appeared to want. Younger children (especially children under seven) were less likely to be influential in terms of outcomes, particularly if their accounts did not have some form of corroboration. Davis and Pearce [1999] identified that one of the tests used by the courts is that only children over a certain age can be deemed to have valid opinions (although this age often varies from one representative of the court to another). Consequently, what younger children say is irrelevant to the final outcome of a court case. We did not find that court welfare officers or judges directly dismissed the opinions of younger children. Rather we found that court welfare officers appeared to take the view that young children were not speaking for themselves, or they tended to come to the conclusion that these children could not adequately weigh up the advantages and disadvantages of their preferences. In other words, the children were not seen as fully competent....

The Level of Conflict Between the Parents

It would seem that children's views became central to a case either when there was a high degree of hostility between the parents (often involving violence) or where parents offered different accounts of what the children wanted. Where the parents could not reach an agreement and continued to present differing versions of events and circumstances, it was not unusual for court welfare officers to turn to older children in order to gauge which account was 'true'.

... The following case, however, reflects the tendency of the courts to prefer a parental agreement to an order imposed by the court on the basis that 'parents know their children best'. In the example, the children had clearly stated to the court welfare officer that they were too frightened of their father to go on contact visits, yet when the parents reached an agreement over contact, the court granted the father a contact order.

The Court Welfare Officer's Assessment

... There were cases in our sample where the outcome contradicted the expressed wishes and feelings of the children involved. Either the court welfare officer considered these not to be in the child's best interests, or the parents reached an agreement that was not in line with what the children had said they wanted.

... James et al [2003] have found that: 'practitioners attach greater importance to their judgements about the welfare of the child than to the child's wishes and feelings. When in practice these principles come into conflict with each other, the welfare principle has to predominate'. Our findings substantiate this conclusion but we do not suggest that this means that the recommendation of the court welfare officer was 'wrong'. Rather we would suggest that it may be these cases that most need ongoing support so that children have access to independent assistance should their view of the situation prove to be confirmed.

How do families, and particularly children, perceive the welfare inquiry process? Ann Buchanan, Joan Hunt, Harriet Bretherton and Victoria Bream summarised their research findings in *Families in Conflict – perspectives of children and parents on the family court welfare service* (2001):

Key Findings

- Parents were highly distressed (84% were above the threshold of the General Health Questionnaire (GHQ)). Distress was, in part, related to the court case and, to some extent, was alleviated once proceedings were over.
- Children were also highly distressed (46% had significant levels of emotional and behavioural difficulties). Levels for children who were interviewed were comparable with those reported for children subject to child protection proceedings and nearly twice the level expected in the general child population. Distress in children was linked to distress in the resident parent and to domestic violence. For boys, it did not alleviate once proceedings were over and it also remained high for girls.
- Most children believed that the family court welfare officer (FCWO) had listened to them and understood what they were saying. However, half did not feel that their voices had been heard, either by the court process or by their parents.
- Parents' perceptions of the preparation of the welfare report varied, but more than half were dissatisfied, voicing strong criticisms of the assessment process. The main criticism was that the investigation was not thorough enough. The best predictors of satisfaction were outcome and initial expectations.
- While satisfaction with welfare reporting was principally linked to outcome and initial expectations, some parents were particularly dissatisfied.
- Almost all parents, irrespective of outcome, were dissatisfied with the court process. Their reported experiences paralleled those of parents involved in care proceedings.
- Parents whose cases were settled before the court hearing were more likely to be satisfied with both the process and the outcome, and contact was more likely to progress over the next 12 months.
- Many parents were critical of a system that each gender saw as favouring the other, ignoring their own perspectives and needs.
- Comprehensive services are needed to prevent and alleviate the negative effects of conflict associated with parental separation. Some families where parents cannot agree on

arrangements may have particularly complex social and emotional needs and require therapeutic, rather than primarily investigative services, to safeguard children's well-being.

...

The Parents' Experiences of Welfare Reporting

Many parents were highly anxious about the first meeting with the FCWO, which was often critical in that it altered their attitude to the process. The main criticism was that the investigation was not thorough enough, either in the amount of time spent, or the number of professionals and other family members who were contacted. Reading a 'negative' report was a very distressing experience.

Differing Perspectives

A total of 56 per cent of parents were dissatisfied or mainly dissatisfied with the process of welfare reporting. Gender, ethnicity and experience of domestic violence did not go far to explain different perceptions. The best predictors of satisfaction were negative expectations at the outset and positive reactions to the outcome. Both mothers and fathers (primarily those who were dissatisfied with the process) were critical of a system that each gender saw as favouring the parent of the opposite sex and ignoring their own perspectives and needs. Black parents' accounts of the FCWO's sensitivity to issues of ethnicity, culture and religion were mixed. Four out of the 20 interviewed believed that their race, culture or religion had counted against them.

Seven of the 11 mothers for whom domestic violence was an issue in the proceedings were dissatisfied with the process. However, in their view, violence was not the key factor in making a decision about the arrangements for their child. Many parents believed that their concerns about how the other parent looked after their child were discounted by the FCWO. ...

Children's Voices

Most of the children who were interviewed said that they knew why they were seeing the FCWO and what he did. They liked the FCWO and thought they had been taken seriously by him, but this was not the same as feeling that their voices had been heard. Some children were worried that their parents would learn about what they had said to the FCWO.

Less than half the children thought they had been involved in the decision-making process. A total of 83 per cent would have liked to have been involved, and half thought children should be allowed to go to court. Up to half would have liked another family member or a friend involved.

Children described positive relationships with both parents. However, half were aware that their parents disagreed about contact arrangements and one-third had witnessed their parents pushing or shoving in an argument. Just under one-third of children said they would rather not see the parent they did not live with if this meant an end to the arguments.

Gillian Douglas, Mervyn Murch, Margaret Robinson, Lesley Scanlan and Ian Butler also write about children's views in their report of their research into *Children's perspectives and experience of the divorce process* (2001):

Children's Feelings About Involvement in the Divorce Process

Although the legal side aroused rather little interest, the question of involvement in critical decisions was of vital concern to the children. Like Libby (13), many of them reported feeling excluded from the changes that were occurring in their family:

> 'It was like, "Oh well, it's not really your problem, you're just not going to be affected by it. You don't have to go through all the divorce things." But, no one seemed to realise I was sort of THERE. They were all concerned with what they were doing.'

Fewer than half of the children (45%) had been asked whom they wanted to live with; more (55%) said they wished that they had been asked. The children were strong in their belief, expressed in terms of rights and fairness, that their opinion was important and should be considered when decisions were being made concerning their future. As Louise (12) explained:

> 'It would have been well... not nice, but a GOOD thing to be ASKED. Because if they'd asked my parents I know my Dad would be saying "They've got to live with me" and my Mum would be saying "They've got to live with me". So I knew if I was ASKED I'd say my Mum. Still, I'd feel that I said it and they didn't MAKE me live with one of them.'

QUESTIONS

i. How can the Government's plan to refocus CAFCASS' efforts away from report writing and 'towards a more active, problem-solving approach' (DfES, 2004, 2005) be reconciled with listening to the child?

ii. Should the children see the judge? Would it help them? Would it help the judge? Which is more important?

iii. Who should tell the children what the judge has decided, and how?

10.3.2 THE CHILD'S SENSE OF TIME

There is one value judgment in the Children Act 1989 about what is good for children:

> **1.** — (2) In any proceedings in which any question with respect to the upbringing of a child arises, the court shall have regard to the general principle that any delay in determining the question is likely to prejudice the welfare of the child.

Again, Bailey-Harris and her colleagues (1999) show how the reality can be very different:

> Our study suggests that cases fall into two categories: those which achieve early settlement and those which fail to do so. The former are disposed of with considerable rapidity, the latter tend to be drawn out through a large number of directions hearings.
>
> The court process undoubtedly starts with considerable momentum. Initial appointments generally take place within a short time of the filing of the application. Our file study showed that a quarter came to court on the day of the application, and three-quarters were in court within one

month. A large number of cases are normally heard during the family day by the district judge in each of the county courts which we observed; 12 to 20 was the norm – a remarkable figure when one observes that most family day hearings are primarily concentrated in the morning. The momentum of the initial stages of the legal process results in rapid disposition of those cases which are capable of early agreement. Our file survey conducted across the four courts showed that 24 per cent of cases settled with only one appointment and a further 26 per cent with two; furthermore, 26 per cent of cases were resolved within one month and a further 20 per cent between one and three months... However, we found that the initial momentum drops off rapidly if cases fail to settle at an early stage. The file study showed that 27 per cent of cases took between three and six months and 19 per cent from six months to one year....

In the more protracted cases the parties frequently expressed their frustration at the delays in the legal process. For example, to quote Mr Rose, a divorced father seeking contact: 'It's taken too long, basically. It's taken miles too long'. Similar were the sentiments of Mrs Miles involved in a prolonged dispute over the details of holiday contact: 'I thought (the legal process) would be a lot faster'. In the Twine's case we first interviewed the father, who was seeking contact with his daughter, in May 1996:

> 'I've tried to read up on the Children Act... I agree delay is bad. It's really bad in my case. The welfare bloke admitted on the phone that the quicker (my daughter) and I start seeing each other the better. I think it is being dragged out... I think the law needs a real shakeup because I don't think I'm getting a very fair deal... it's being dragged out. This has gone on now since last July. I made the application to court just after Christmas.'

... One obvious cause of delay is the time required for the welfare report – 12 to 16 weeks was normal in the courts we observed – which poses dilemmas for district judges. The file survey showed that in 26 per cent of cases the welfare report took up to three months to submit, and between three and six months in 13 per cent of cases. While the report obviously provides a unique opportunity for exploration of considerations in the 'welfare checklist' (section 1(3)), including the child's wishes, some district judges are understandably reluctant to order a welfare report because of the inevitable delays which will result, and try instead to manage the case judicially in an attempt to give maximum opportunity to parents to reach agreement, without the case being 'tracked' down the report route. The file survey showed that welfare reports were ordered in 49 per cent of cases. The problem of delay here is essentially one of under-resourcing of the service.

QUESTIONS

i. Do you agree with the value judgment in section 1(2)?
ii. Which would you put first, the child's need to be heard or the child's sense of time?

10.4 STARTING AFRESH

We have seen how many children are now living in step-families. These 'new' step-families are very different from the stereotype of fairy tales. In *Making a Go of It* (1984), sociologists Jacqueline Burgoyne and David Clark construct a typology to reflect the different ways in which the step-families they studied saw themselves.

Table 6.1 A typology of stepfamilies

1	*'Not really a stepfamily'* The stepchildren of the family were young at the time of divorce and remarriage; within a short time they were able to think of themselves as an 'ordinary' family. Children of new marriage confirm this.
2	*'Looking forward to the departure of the children'* Older couples with teenage children await departure of dependent children so that they can enjoy their new partnership more fully. Too old for children in new marriage.
3	*The 'progressive' stepfamily* Prototype 'new' stepfamily in which conflicts with ex-partners have been resolved. They stress the advantages of their circumstances. Few barriers to additional children of new marriage.
4	*The successful conscious pursuit of an 'ordinary' family life together* Stepparent becomes full 'social' parent transferring allegiance to stepchildren. Their initial problems are solved or successfully ignored. Children of new marriage symbolise 'normality' of their family life.
5	*The conscious pursuit of 'ordinary' family life frustrated* The legacy of their past marriage(s) frustrates their attempts to build an ordinary family life together. Children of new marriage are unlikely because of continuing problems.

The largest recent study is by Marjorie Smith, *New stepfamilies – a descriptive study of a largely unseen group* (2003):

Identification as a Stepfamily

Most parents, step-parents and children currently in stepfamilies did not identify themselves as being in a 'stepfamily'. When asked directly, over three quarters of parents (N = 121, 78%) said they never identified as being in a 'stepfamily', while nine parents (6%) said that they only occasionally did. Less than one fifth (N = 24, 16%) said that they usually or always thought of their families as 'stepfamilies'.

Identification as a stepfamily did not appear to be associated with the length of time that the stepfamily had been in existence, nor with marital status. However, those in simple stepfamilies were more likely to identify as stepfamilies, and those with new 'shared' children (the 'simple plus' stepfamilies) less likely to do so... For those who did not identify as being in a stepfamily, the most common reason given was that they felt like a 'normal family'. Over three quarters of parents who did not view their families as stepfamilies (N = 97, 80%) gave an explanation along these lines. For example, one mother said in response to the question, 'No, it feels like a proper family. Her natural father is out of the way and it feels like a normal mummy, daddy, child-type family'. Another mother said, 'I've never considered it. We're just a normal family'.

Children's Views of Their Family

Children tended to have inclusive views of families. When asked about who were the members of their family, nearly two thirds of children (N = 112, 64%) included their non-resident parent as part of their family, and this figure rose to 85% in the children who had had some contact with their non-resident parent in the previous year. At the same time, nearly four fifths of the children (N = 140, 79%) also included their step-parent as part of their family, and the majority of those who did not were those from the recently separated stepfamilies. Of those currently in stepfamilies, 86% included the step-parent as family.

It was most usual for children to call their step-parent by their first name–three quarters of children (N = 128, 75%) did so. When asked to explain the relatedness to the child, of the individuals who had been identified by name, the largest group of children (38%) described the step-parent in terms of their relatedness only to the parent (for example, as, 'he's my Mum's boyfriend'). Only slightly fewer children (32%) described them as step-parents, but one fifth of the children, mostly younger children, described them as if they were biological parents (for example, 'he's my dad').

. . .

Step-Parents' Views of Their Role

Step-parents were asked a more direct question about whether they considered themselves to be a stepfather (or stepmother) to their partner's children. Although nearly one quarter (N = 28, 24%) said that they did, it was notable that almost one half (N = 57, 48%) definitely did not. The remainder were qualified in their identification with the role of step-parent, for example, saying, 'not really, but I suppose I am'. Those who did not feel like step-parents or were dubious about the role, were most likely to give explanations in terms of feeling that this was 'a normal family'. Although one third of step-parents said that they did not feel like a father (mother) to their partner's children, two thirds (N = 75, 66%) either definitely did, or did to some extent.

. . .

Outcomes for Children and Children's Well-being

A more systematic assessment of the children's well-being was made,...

There was no association between any of the variables relating to contact with the non–resident parent and child well-being. There was no statistically significant association between child well-being and whether the child had contact with the non-resident parent or not (regular contact, irregular contact, or no contact in the last year). Nor, for those children who had seen their non-resident parent in the past year, was there any relationship between their well-being and the frequency of contact. Similarly, there was no association between children's accounts of their well-being and whether they regularly stayed with the non-resident parent, or not.

There was, however, some evidence that the nature of the relationship with the non-resident parent was important. Children who viewed their relationship with their non-resident father as the same as before (and him as just like a father) had significantly lower symptom scores (indicating greater well-being) than children who felt that their relationship with their non–resident parent had changed in some way. ... Similarly, children who reported that they enjoyed contact with their non-resident father also had higher levels of well–being (demonstrated by lower symptom scores) than those who had mixed feelings about contact, or did not enjoy it. ...

Strongly associated with child well-being, however, was the quality of relationships within the household. This applied to the quality of the parent/child relationship, the quality of the adults' marital or cohabiting relationship and, to a slightly lesser extent, to the quality of the step-parent/child relationship. Where these were good, children in stepfamilies showed considerably higher levels of well-being than when they were poor.

Stepfamily Adoption

... Out of the 184 families and 233 children in the study, only one child had been adopted. A few parents said that they did not know about stepfamily adoptions (N = 8, 5%, excluding past stepfamilies) but many more said that they had not thought about it (N = 87, 56%). While this may partly reflect the fact that this was a sample of fairly recently constituted stepfamilies, of those who had considered adoption (N = 61, 39%) the majority had rejected it (N = 39, 25%), two as a result of taking legal advice. In 20 families (13%), none of whom had yet taken legal advice, the decision was still being considered. In one other family, legal advice had been sought and there were definite plans to proceed with the adoption.

Where adoption had been considered and discussed, it was sometimes rejected when the parent discovered some of the peculiarities of the legislation, which requires the parent to adopt their own child. More commonly, however, their reasons for rejecting the idea related to problems (or perceived problems) with the non-resident parent. A mother said, 'We've discussed it but we can't do it while [the non-resident parent] is alive because he wouldn't allow it'. In another family, a stepfather said, 'we can't do it as we need his (child's) father's permission. We don't want any contact as we're worried about [child's] safety. At the practical level it doesn't make any difference'.

In 2005, 800 (20 per cent) of the 3,867 adoption orders made in England and Wales were to step-parents. The court can always make a residence order instead, although this also seems uncommon. The *Review of Adoption Law – Report to Ministers of an Interdepartmental Working Group* (1992) discussed other ways of giving a step-parent legal status:

19.2 Adoption by a step-parent and parent severs the legal links between a child and the other side of his or her birth family. There may be circumstances in which this is appropriate, for instance where the other parent has never acted in a parental capacity and the child has never really known any member of that side of the birth family. But where the child has some relationship with the parent, or with his or her relatives, it is unlikely to be in the child's interests for their legal relationship to be extinguished. A parent may agree to adoption simply because he has no interest in the child, or even where he has such an interest and is keen to retain it but wishes to end the payment of maintenance. Where the other parent has died or is no longer in the picture, the possible benefits to the child of retaining a legal relationship with grandparents or other relatives may be overlooked. Of course, the adoption order need not mean severance of practical links. But where the prime motivation behind an adoption application is the wish to cement the family unit and put away the past, this may be confusing and lead to identity problems for the child, especially if (as is statistically not unlikely) the new marriage breaks down. It is also possible that the step-parent's family has little or no involvement or interest in the adopted child, so that the child loses one family without really gaining another. As divorce has become more common, it is less necessary for families to pursue step-parent adoption in order to avoid embarrassment and difficult explanations. We do not consider it appropriate to prevent step-parent adoptions; but there may be ways in which the law can help to discourage inappropriate applications.

Step-Parent Adoption Orders

19.3 Where adoption by a step-parent is in a child's interests, we consider it anomalous that the parent who is caring for the child should also become an adoptive parent. It can be disturbing for a birth parent and child to have the birth certificate replaced by an adoption certificate on which the birth parent is shown as an adoptive parent. We therefore recommend that there should be a new type of adoption order, available only to step-parents, which does not make the birth parent (ie the step-parent's spouse) an adoptive parent but in almost all other respects resembles a normal adoption order. Application for the order would be by the step-parent with the agreement of his or her spouse. The order could not be made unless the child's other parent (if he or she had parental responsibility) – and the child (if 12 or over) – agreed to the adoption, or the court dispensed with agreement on one of the specified grounds [see p. 630, below]. The child's legal links with the other birth parent and family would be severed. Consideration would have to be given to an appropriate way of amending the adoption certificate and of recording the adoption on the Adopted Children Register. The order should only be open to a step-parent, not to an unmarried partner.

19.4 We are concerned by the relative incidence of breakdown of second and subsequent marriages. Where a step-parent who has adopted a child subsequently becomes divorced from the child's birth parent, it is possible that the parent and child may wish to have restored their legal relationship with the other side of the child's birth family. We therefore recommend that there should be provision for a step-parent adoption order to be undone where the marriage ends by divorce or death and the child is under the age of 18. Application would be by the birth parent whose parental responsibility had been extinguished by the adoption order. Agreement to the revocation of the order would be required from the step-parent, the parent who retained parental responsibility and the child if aged 12 or over. If any of these people did not agree to the revocation of the order, it would stand unless their agreement could be dispensed with. ... Consideration should also be given to whether, and if so in what circumstances, a child who has reached the age of 18 should be able to apply for the revocation of an order.

Alternative Orders

19.5 We have already made clear our concern that some applications by step-parents appear to be made without full consideration of the needs of the child. It is likely that in many circumstances a residence order would be a better way of confirming a step-parent's responsibility for a child, because it does not alter a child's legal relationship with his or her parents and family. ...

19.6 ... we do not feel it would be advisable to have a ... legislative presumption in favour of residence orders for step-parents. We have already recommended (see above, paragraph 6.3) that the court should have a duty to consider alternative orders, including residence orders. It is even more important that any step-parent who is considering applying for an adoption order should be encouraged to explore alternative orders before the application comes to court. ...

...

Acquisition of Parental Responsibility by Step-Parents

19.8 Inappropriate applications might also less frequently be made if step-parents were able to acquire parental responsibility without a court order by making an agreement with the birth parent, in the same way that unmarried fathers may now acquire parental responsibility under section 4 of the Children Act 1989. A person with parental responsibility has all the rights, duties, powers, responsibilities and authority which by law a parent of a child has in relation to the child and the child's property. A person with a residence order has parental responsibility but only while the residence order remains in force. ... It would therefore be a significant step to allow step-parents to acquire parental responsibility, but one which we feel is justified in view of the public relationship which the step-parent has with the child's parent and their entitlement to apply for an adoption order, which is likely to be far less appropriate. We therefore propose that a step-parent should acquire parental responsibility for a child if at any time he and both parents make an agreement to share parental responsibility (in a form prescribed under regulations made by the Lord Chancellor). We propose also that a court should have the power to make a parental responsibility order in favour of a step-parent. Where the other parent does not agree to the step-parent's acquisition of parental responsibility, the step-parent could apply for such an order. It would also be one of the alternatives available to a court (and which the court would have a duty to consider) when considering an application for a step-parent adoption order.

19.9 It should not be possible, under this system, for an unmarried co-habitant to acquire parental responsibility in respect of his or her partner's child, or for the court to grant it.

The Adoption and Children Act 2002 made two changes. First, under section 51(2), an adoption order may be made on the application of one person who is the partner of a parent of the person to be adopted. Under section 67(2) the child is then the legitimate child of the adopter and is to be treated as the child of the couple's relationship and under section 67(3) not as the child of anyone other than the adopter and the other one of the couple. Secondly, a new section 4A is added to the Children Act 1989:

4A—(1) Where a child's parent ('parent A') who has parental responsibility for the child is married to a person who is not the child's parent ('the step-parent')—

(a) parent A or, if the other parent of the child also has parental responsibility for the child, both parents may by agreement with the step-parent provide for the step-parent to have parental responsibility for the child; or
(b) the court may, on the application of the step-parent, order that the step-parent shall have parental responsibility for the child.

(2) An agreement under subsection (1)(a) is also a 'parental responsibility agreement', and section 4(2) applies in relation to such agreements as it applies in relation to parental responsibility agreements under section 4.

(3) A parental responsibility agreement under subsection (1)(a), or an order under subsection (1)(b), may only be brought to an end by an order of the court made on the application—

(a) of any person who has parental responsibility for the child; or
(b) with the leave of the court, of the child himself.

(4) The court may only grant leave under subsection (3) (b) if it is satisfied that the child has sufficient understanding to make the proposed application.

QUESTIONS

i. Why can a step-parent who is in an unmarried relationship with a parent adopt under section 51(2) of the 2002 Act (see Chapter 9, p. 423, above) but not acquire parental responsibility by agreement or court order under section 4A of the 1989 Act?

ii. Suppose you were adopted by your stepfather, then your mother died and your stepfather could not look after you, but your birth father now wanted to do so: should it be possible for the adoption order to be revoked? (See *Re M (minors) (adoption)* [1990] FCR 993, [1991] 1 FLR 458, CA, and *Re B (adoption: jurisdiction to set aside)* [1995] Fam 239, [1995] 2 FLR 1, CA.)

Two important issues for reconstituted families can be change of surname and relocation (especially abroad). These questions can arise whether or not the parent with whom the children are living remarries, but the courts tend to be more sympathetic when she has re-partnered than when she simply wants to go back home. Change of name may be less important in practice than appears from the law reports. Marjory Smith (2003) tabulated the names actually used by the children in her study.

Table 6 Who child shared a family name with (N = 233)

	N	%
Resident parent only	59	25.3
Resident parent and step-parent	19	8.1
Parent and non-resident parent	59	25.3
Non-resident parent only	88	37.8
Other/variable	8	3.4

Re W (A Child) (Illegitimate Child: Change of Surname); Re A (A Child); Re B (Children)
[2001] Fam 1, [1999] 2 FLR 930, Court of Appeal

In the first of these three cases, the mother registered her illegitimate child, J, with her surname. She subsequently married the father and had another child who was registered with his surname. The parents applied to re-register J's name following their marriage, but by the time the registrar contacted them the marriage had failed. The mother reverted to her original surname. The father applied to change J's surname to his own. The judge refused the application and the father appealed.

Butler-Sloss LJ:

[1] These three appeals have one issue in common, the circumstances in which a child registered at birth in one surname may have that name changed by deed poll by one parent against the wishes of the other parent. Before turning to the individual facts and issues which arise on each appeal, following the decision of the House of Lords in *Dawson v Wearmouth* [1999] 2 AC 308 it may be helpful to set out what appears to be the present position on change of name applications.

...

[9] The present position, in summary, would appear to be as follows. (a) If parents are married they both have the power and the duty to register their child's names. (b) If they are not married the mother has the sole duty and power to do so. (c) After registration of the child's names, the grant of a residence order obliges any person wishing to change the surname to obtain the leave of the court or the written consent of all those who have parental responsibility. (d) In the

absence of a residence order, the person wishing to change the surname from the registered name ought to obtain the relevant written consent or the leave of the court by making an application for a specific issue order. (e) On any application the welfare of the child is paramount, and the judge must have regard to the section 1(3) criteria. (f) Among the factors to which the court should have regard is the registered surname of the child and the reasons for the registration, for instance recognition of the biological link with the child's father. Registration is always a relevant and an important consideration but it is not in itself decisive. The weight to be given to it by the court will depend upon the other relevant factors or valid countervailing reasons which may tip the balance the other way. (g) The relevant considerations should include factors which may arise in the future as well as the present situation. (h) Reasons given for changing or seeking to change a child's name based on the fact that the child's name is or is not the same as the parent making the application do not generally carry much weight. (i) The reasons for an earlier unilateral decision to change a child's name may be relevant (j) Any changes of circumstances of the child since the original registration may be relevant. (k) In the case of a child whose parents were married to each other, the fact of the marriage is important and I would suggest that there would have to be strong reasons to change the name from the father's surname if the child was so registered. (l) Where the child's parents were not married to each other, the mother has control over registration. Consequently on an application to change the surname of the child, the degree of commitment of the father to the child, the quality of contact, if it occurs, between father and child, the existence or absence of parental responsibility are all relevant factors to take into account.
[10] I cannot stress too strongly that these are only guidelines which do not purport to be exhaustive. Each case has to be decided on its own facts with the welfare of the child the paramount consideration and all the relevant factors weighed in the balance by the court at the time of the hearing. I turn now to the three appeals. The issue in the first appeal concerns the amendment of the register in relation to a child legitimated by the subsequent marriage of the parents. . . .

. . .

[14] In this case there has been no unilateral change of name so the child has always been called by her registered name of W. The judge directed himself that the approach was what is in the best interests of the child now. There had to be good and cogent reasons shown to allow a change. In applying the section 1(3) welfare checklist the likely effect of any change of circumstances (section 1(3)(c)), her present name should not be changed without good reason. . . . He concluded:

> 'When I come back to this case and consider the reasons advanced; first the maintenance of the link with the father and the question of the two girls attending the same school and having the same name. The maintenance of a link is not a matter of a name but a matter of contact, how the father gets on [with it] and treats and cares for the girls. . . . Change of name takes away from the family unit. In general those considerations balance out and favour no change. When I look to see good and cogent reasons I can find none. In this case I see no reason to disturb the little girl's name, state of mind or knowledge.'

. . .

Appeal dismissed.

QUESTIONS

i. What weight should be given to the views of the children on this question?

ii. Are the arguments against allowing a change of name any less strong in cases which do not need a court order – for example, if the father consents or is dead?

iii. What do you think the answer would be if a divorced mother reverted to her maiden name and wanted her children to use it too?

iv. If both parents have parental responsibility but use different surnames, which name should they choose?

What about relocation? When should a parent be allowed to go back home or to start afresh somewhere else?

Payne v Payne
[2001] EWCA Civ 166, [2001] Fam 473, Court of Appeal

The mother of a four-year-old child was originally from New Zealand but had met and married the father in England. She was not happy in England and the parties had discussed relocating to New Zealand. The father accepted employment in Kuala Lumpur, and whilst he was there the mother and the child resided in New Zealand. The parties separated and the mother applied in New Zealand for custody and an order that the father be prevented from removing the child from that jurisdiction, arguing that the move to New Zealand was intended as a permanent relocation of the family. The judge did not find the mother a convincing witness and ordered that the child be returned to the United Kingdom, which was done. On arrival the mother disappeared with the child but was discovered within a few days by the father with the help of the police. The mother applied for residence and to remove the child from the country permanently. She succeeded in the county court and the father appealed, relying on the increased importance attached to maintaining contact and on Article 8 of the European Convention on Human Rights.

Thorpe LJ:

...

[16] The modern law regulating applications for the emigration of children begins with the decision of this court in *P (LM) (otherwise E) v P (GE)* [1970] 3 All ER 659; sub nom *Poel v Poel* [1970] 1 WLR 1469. I doubt that the judges deciding the case recognised how influential it would prove to be. Whilst emphasising that the court should have regard primarily to the welfare of the child, both Sachs LJ and Winn LJ emphasised the importance of recognising and supporting the function of the primary carer. That consideration was most clearly expressed by Sachs LJ when he said:

> 'When a marriage breaks up, then a situation normally arises when the child of that marriage, instead of being in the joint custody of both parents, must of necessity become one who is in the custody of a single parent. Once that position has arisen and the custody is working well, this court should not lightly interfere with such reasonable way of life as is selected by that parent to whom custody has been rightly given. Any such interference may, as Winn LJ has pointed out, produce considerable strains which would be unfair not only to the parent whose way of life is interfered with but also to any new marriage of that parent. In that way it might well in due course reflect on the welfare of the child. The way in which the parent who properly has custody of a child may choose in a reasonable manner to order his or her way of life is one of those things which the parent who has not been given custody may well have to bear, even though one has every sympathy with the latter on some of the results.'

...

[26] In summary a review of the decisions of this court over the course of the last 30 years demonstrates that relocation cases have been consistently decided upon the application of the following two propositions: (a) the welfare of the child is the paramount consideration; and (b) refusing the primary carer's reasonable proposals for the relocation of her family life is likely to impact detrimentally on the welfare of her dependent children. Therefore her application to relocate will be granted unless the court concludes that it is incompatible with the welfare of the children.

...

[31] Logically and as a matter of experience the child cannot draw emotional and psychological security and stability from the dependency unless the primary carer herself is emotionally and psychologically stable and secure. The parent cannot give what she herself lacks. Although fathers as well as mothers provide primary care I have never myself encountered a relocation application brought by a father and for the purposes of this judgment I assume that relocation applications are only brought by maternal primary carers. The disintegration of a family unit is invariably emotionally and psychologically turbulent. The mother who emerges with the responsibility of making the home for the children may recover her sense of well-being simply by coping over a passage of time. But often the mother may be in need of external support, whether financial, emotional or social. Such support may be provided by a new partner who becomes stepfather to the child. The creation of a new family obviously draws the child into its quest for material and other fulfilment. Such cases have given rise to the strongest statements of the guidelines. Alternatively the disintegration of the family unit may leave the mother in a society to which she was carried by the impetus of family life before its failure. Commonly in that event she may feel isolated and driven to seek the support she lacks by returning to her homeland, her family and her friends. In the remarriage cases the motivation for relocation may well be to meet the stepfather's career needs or opportunities. In those cases refusal is likely to destabilise the new family emotionally as well as to penalise it financially. In the case of the isolated mother, to deny her the support of her family and a return to her roots may have an even greater psychological detriment and she may have no one who might share her distress or alleviate her depression....

[32] Thus in most relocation cases the most crucial assessment and finding for the judge is likely to be the effect of the refusal of the application on the mother's future psychological and emotional stability.

...

[34] However with the commencement of the Human Rights Act 1998 on 2 October 2000 it was not hard to foresee that a father responding to a relocation application would submit that the emigration of his child to a distant land constituted a breach of his right to family life under art 8....

[35] I am in broad agreement with the views expressed by Ward LJ to the effect that the advent of the Convention within our domestic law does not necessitate a revision of the fundamental approach to relocation applications formulated by this court and consistently applied over so many years

...

[38] The acknowledgement of child welfare as paramount must be common to most if not all judicial systems within the Council of Europe. It is of course enshrined in Art 3(1) of the United Nations Declaration of the Rights of the Child 1959 [sic]. Accordingly the jurisprudence of the European Court of Human Rights inevitably recognises the paramountcy principle, albeit not expressed in the language of our domestic statute.

[39] In *Johansen v Norway* (1996) 23 EHRR 33, the Court held that 'particular weight should be attached to the best interests of the child... which may override those of the parent ...'. In *L v Finland (Case 25651/94)* [2000] 2 FLR 118 the Court stressed that the consideration of what is in the best interests of the child is of crucial importance. In *Scott v UK* [2000] 1 FLR 958, a case concerned with whether the mother's Art 8 rights had been breached by a local authority who

had applied to free her child for adoption, the court once again stated that the best interests of the child is always of crucial importance. As early as 1988, the House of Lords stated that the European Convention in no way conflicted with the requirements in English law that in all matters concerning the upbringing of a child, welfare was paramount (*Re KD (a minor) (ward: termination of access)* [1988] FCR 657, [1988] AC 806)....

[40] However there is a danger that if the regard which the court pays to the reasonable proposals of the primary carer were elevated into a legal presumption then there would be an obvious risk of the breach of the respondent's rights not only under art 8 but also his rights under art 6 to a fair trial. To guard against the risk of too perfunctory an investigation resulting from too ready an assumption that the mother's proposals are necessarily compatible with the child's welfare I would suggest the following discipline as a prelude to conclusion. (a) Pose the question: is the mother's application genuine in the sense that it is not motivated by some selfish desire to exclude the father from the child's life? Then ask is the mother's application realistic, by which I mean founded on practical proposals both well researched and investigated? If the application fails either of these tests refusal will inevitably follow. (b) If however the application passes these tests then there must be a careful appraisal of the father's opposition: is it motivated by genuine concern for the future of the child's welfare or is it driven by some ulterior motive? What would be the extent of the detriment to him and his future relationship with the child were the application granted? To what extent would that be offset by extension of the child's relationships with the maternal family and homeland? (c) What would be the impact on the mother, either as the single parent or as a new wife, of a refusal of her realistic proposal? (d) The outcome of the second and third appraisals must then be brought into an overriding review of the child's welfare as the paramount consideration, directed by the statutory checklist in so far as appropriate.

[41] In suggesting such a discipline I would not wish to be thought to have diminished the importance that this court has consistently attached to the emotional and psychological well-being of the primary carer. In any evaluation of the welfare of the child as the paramount consideration great weight must be given to this factor....

...

Appeal dismissed.

QUESTIONS

i. Why do you suppose that all the relocation cases Thorpe LJ has met (paragraph 31, above) have been brought by mothers?

ii. Suppose the child's mother wishes to relocate from, say, Tyneside, where she has lived with the father, to Cornwall. What application could the father make to challenge that decision and what would be his prospects of success (read *Re E* [1997] 2 FLR 638 and see pp. 483, 487, above)?

iii. Do you think that the approach adopted by Thorpe LJ is compatible with the father's Convention rights?

In *Relocating Relocation* (2006), Jonathan Herring and Rachel Taylor take issue with Thorpe LJ's view that the Human Rights Act 'requires no re-evaluation of the judge's primary task to evaluate and uphold the welfare of the child as the paramount consideration, despite its inevitable conflict with adult rights':

The Payne Approach to Human Rights

Respectfully we do not agree with this understanding of the jurisprudence of the European Court of Human Rights. ... The actual words of the judgment in *Johansen* give a very different impression to the paraphrased quotation given by Thorpe LJ:

> 'a fair balance has to be struck between the interests of the child in remaining in public care and those of the parent in being reunited with the child. *In carrying out this balancing exercise,* the Court will attach particular importance to the best interests of the child, which, *depending on their nature and seriousness*, may override those of the parent.' (1997) 23 EHRR 33, para 78 (emphasis added)

When seen in its context, the approach of the European Court of Human Rights is very different from the welfare principle indicated by Thorpe LJ. There are two key differences between the welfare principle and the approach in *Johansen*. First, the European Court of Human Rights clearly states that it is engaged in a balancing exercise between the interests of the parties. The welfare principle, on the other hand, does not admit such a balancing exercise; indeed the interests of the parents are strictly irrelevant to the decision unless they affect the welfare of the child. Secondly, the *Johansen* approach implies that the interests of the child will not always override those of the parent but that this will depend on the 'nature and seriousness' of those interests. Again, this contrasts with the welfare principle which demands that the welfare of the child prevails over the rights of the parents without regard to its nature and seriousness.

Although Thorpe LJ uses a quotation from *Johansen*, the European Court of Human Rights has not used consistent language in stating the test to be used when analysing a clash of rights between parents and children. The *Johansen* test is the most commonly used test, although occasionally the court has appeared to give more weight to the rights of children by stating that they will be of 'crucial importance' within the balancing test[cases cited in *Payne*, paragraph 39]. There is, however, one case that appears to give overriding importance to the rights of children. In *Yousef v Netherlands* the European Court of Human Rights stated that:

> 'The court reiterates that in judicial decisions where the rights under art 8 of parents and those of a child are at stake, the child's rights *must be the paramount consideration.* If any balancing of interests is necessary, the interests of the child *must always prevail.*' [2003] 1 FLR 210, para 73 (emphasis added)

On first reading this test appears to be very close to the test advocated by Thorpe LJ in *Payne*, as it seems to suggest that the interests of children will automatically outweigh any competing parental right. A closer reading, however, suggests that the Court did not intend to make such a radical departure from its previous approach. As Shazia Choudhry [2003] notes, the court's use of the word 'reiterates' suggests that it did not intend to create a new principle. Indeed the cases that the court cites in support of this proposition adopt the conventional balancing test. Later cases in the European Court of Human Rights have not adopted this test and have returned to the *Johansen* test.

It seems, then, that the welfare approach adopted by the Court of Appeal in *Payne* does not give adequate consideration to rights protected by the HRA. Although the European Court of Human Rights recognises that children's rights should be given additional weight when balanced against the rights of their parents, the children's rights are not automatically overriding. While the parent may not use Article 8 to justify serious harm to the rights of the child, the rights of the child do not remove the need to consider the rights of the parent.

Reconciling Welfare and the HRA

If the welfare approach is incompatible with the HRA, the question remains what should be done. The courts are obliged by statute to apply the principle and such a statutory obligation takes precedence over their role under section 6 of the HRA. Nevertheless, section 3 of the HRA obliges the court to interpret the welfare principle, as far as possible, to be compatible with the parties' Convention rights. As Shazia Choudhry and Helen Fenwick [2005] point out, one way in which the welfare principle can be interpreted compatibly with Convention rights is to interpret 'paramount' to mean 'most important'. In other words, the interests of the child will be the most important consideration for the court but will not inevitably determine the outcome, particularly where there are weighty countervailing interests. On this interpretation, the welfare principle can be read compatibly with the approach of the European Court of Human Rights, to require a 'parallel analysis' balancing exercise between all of the rights involved, but with particular importance given to the rights and interests of the child within that analysis.

They go on to develop their own model of a rights based approach:

It therefore seems clear that the balancing exercise demands careful attention to the underlying values raised in each particular case. While the answer will vary between cases, it is possible to identify the values that are most commonly raised in relocation cases.

Strasbourg jurisprudence shows that notions of personal autonomy lie at the heart of Article 8 and its interpretation. At the heart of the right to autonomy is the right to develop one's vision of the good life free from improper interference from either the State or other people. This gives us some assistance in considering competing rights under Article 8: the right to autonomy. The closer the desired act is to the individual's vision of their life and their self, the stronger the claim is and the greater the justification required to interfere with it. The more marginal the claim is to the individual's vision of their life the less strong the right and the less that needs to be demonstrated to justify an interference. So, just because two parties can claim competing Article 8 rights does not mean that their claims are equal. Not all interferences with autonomy are equal. Some are major setbacks in plans for life; others are minor interruptions.

Therefore, when dealing with a clash between the rights of the mother and father in a relocation case, the court should consider which interference will constitute a greater blight on the vision of the good life that each had. In developing a vision of the good life, it is likely that most parents would place great value both on their freedom of movement and consequent freedom to develop new relationships and opportunities, and on their relationship with their children. In most relocation cases the question will be how far the court's decision will *interfere* with that vision. For example, if refusal prevents a mother from pursuing a new relationship, it is more likely to have a serious impact on her ability to live her chosen vision of the 'good life' than a father having substantial but less frequent contact with his child. Where the mother has no particular reason to relocate and the relocation will effectively bring to an end a strong father–child relationship, it would, no doubt, be found that permitting the relocation would be a greater interference with the father's autonomy than denying it would be for the mother.

More problematic on this model are the rights of children. A child may not yet have developed her own vision of autonomy and will not, therefore, have a vision of a good life that we can use to assess the severity of interference with autonomy. However, use can be made of the extensive literature on children's rights, which emphasises the importance of a child growing up with an 'open future'. As John Eekelaar [1994] puts it we should aim 'to bring a child to the threshold of adulthood with the maximum opportunities to form and pursue life-goals which reflect as closely as possible an autonomous choice'. This then would provide some kind of benchmark against which to measure competing rights of the child. Which interference in a child's rights will constitute a greater hindrance in the goal of providing the child with the opportunity of developing her own vision of the 'good life'? Where the child is an adolescent she will have already have begun to formulate what this vision might be and so less weight need be attached to the idea of preserving an 'open future'.

We do not suggest that this approach provides for easy answers. Relocation cases are truly difficult and any approach which did provide a ready answer should be treated with a great deal of suspicion. However, we suggest that it provides a principled way of weighing up the competing interests and rights of the parties while fully realising the implications of the HRA.

QUESTION

Have they cracked the problem? Could the same approach be applied to all competing claims to respect for family life?

BIBLIOGRAPHY

We quoted from:

A. Dalton, *Ugly Mug*, (1994) Harmondsworth, Puffin.
C. Itzin, *Splitting Up: Single Parent Liberation* (1980) London, Virago, 130, 138.

10.1 What children need

We quoted from:

A. Bainham, 'Changing families and changing concepts – reforming the language of family law' (1998) 10 *Child and Family Law Quarterly* 1, 6.
CAFCASS, *Parenting Plans – Putting your children first: A guide for separating parents* (2007) London, Department for Education and Skills, 4.
J. Goldstein, A. Freud and A.J. Solnit, *Beyond the Best Interests of the Child* (1973) London, Collier Macmillan, 31–34, 37, 40–41, 49–50, 51, 53, 62–63.
New English Bible (1972) The Bible Societies, I Kings 3, vs. 22–27.
Office for National Statistics, *Social Trends 37* (2007) London, TSO, table 2.5.
Office for National Statistics, Alison Blackwell and Fiona Dawe, *Non-Resident Parental Contact, Final Report* (2003) London, Office for National Statistics figures 3.1, 3.2.
M. Richards, 'Post Divorce Arrangements for Children: A Psychological Perspective' [1982] *Journal of Social Welfare Law* 133, 142–149.
M. Richards, 'Private Worlds and Public Intentions – The Role of the State at Divorce' in A. Bainham and D. Pearl (eds), *Frontiers of Family Law* (1993) London, Chancery Law Publishing, 26–27.
B. Rodgers and J. Pryor, *Divorce and Separation: The outcomes for children* (1998) York, Joseph Rowntree Foundation, 4–6.

C. Smart, 'The Legal and Moral Ordering of Child Custody' (1990) University of Warwick, Department of Sociology, pp. 9–12, 82–85, 91–92; also published in (1991) 8 *Journal of Law and Society* 485.

C. Smart, 'Objects of concern? – children and divorce' (1999) 11 *Child and Family Law Quarterly* 365, 366–370.

C. Sturge and D. Glaser, 'Contact and Domestic Violence – the Experts' Report' [2000] *Family Law* 615.

Additional reading

J. Bradshaw and J. Millar, *Lone Parent Families in the UK, Department of Social Security Research Report No. 6* (1991) London, HMSO.

Department for Education and Skills, *Evidence from Research about Parental Separation* (2004), http://www.dfes.gsi.gov.uk/childrensneeds/docs/supplementary.

K. Faller, 'The Parental Alienation Syndrome: What is it and What Data Support It' (1998) 3(2) *Child Maltreatment* 100.

J. Pryor and B. Rodgers, *Children in Changing Families* (2002) Oxford, Blackwell.

C. Smart and S. Sevenhuijsen (eds), *Child Custody and the Politics of Gender* (1989) London, Routledge.

10.2 The law

We quoted from:

Anon., 'Saturday Parent' (1980) 144 *Justice of the Peace* 353.

R. Bailey-Harris, G. Davis, J. Barron, J. Pearce, 'Settlement culture and the use of the no order principle under the Children Act 1989' (1999) 11 *Child and Family Law Quarterly* 53, 57–60.

Children Act Sub-Committee of the Advisory Board on Family Law, *Making Contact Work* (2002) Lord Chancellor's Department, paragraphs 14.21–14.27.

A. Heath-Jones, 'Divorce and the Reluctant Father' (1980) 10 *Family Law* 75, 75.

House of Commons Constitutional Affairs Committee, *Family Justice: the operation of the family courts, Fourth Report of Session 2004–05* (2005) London, TSO, paragraphs 47, 60, 61.

F. Kaganas and S. Day Sclater, 'Contact and Domestic Violence – the Winds of Change? [2000] *Family Law* 630.

Law Commission, *Report on Guardianship and Custody*, Law Com. No. 172 (1988) London, HMSO, paragraphs 3.18, 4.5–4.20.

H. Reece, 'UK Women's Groups' child contact campaign: so long as it is safe' [2006] *Child and Family Law Quarterly* 538, 561.

C. Smart, *The Legal and Moral Ordering of Child Custody* (1990), *op cit*, 82–85, 91–92.

Additional reading

R. Bailey-Harris, G. Davis, J. Barron, J. Pearce, *Monitoring Private Law Applications under the Children Act* (1998) London, The Nuffield Foundation.

Children Act Sub-Committee of the Advisory Board on Family Law, *Contact Between Children and Violent Parents: the Question of Parental Contact in Cases where there is Domestic Violence* (1999) London, Lord Chancellor's Department.

F. Collier, 'Fathers4Justice, Law and the New Politics of Fatherhood' (2005) 17 *Child and Family Law Quarterly* 511.

J. Eekelaar, 'Beyond the welfare principle' (2002) 14 *Child and Family Law Quarterly* 237.

J. Eekelaar and M. Maclean, *The Parental Obligation* (1997) Oxford, Hart.

S. Gilmore, 'Court decision-making in shared residence order cases: a critical examination' (2006) 18 *Child and Family Law Quarterly* 478.

M. Hester, C. Pearson and L. Radford, *Domestic Violence: A national survey of court welfare and voluntary sector mediation practice* (1997) Bristol, Polity Press.

M. Hester and L. Radford, *Domestic Violence and Child Contact Arrangements in England and Denmark* (1996) Bristol, Polity Press.

M. Johnson, 'A Biomedical Perspective on Parenthood' in A. Bainham, S. Day Sclater and M. Richards (eds) *What is a Parent?* (1999) Oxford, Hart.

Law Commission, Working Paper No. 96, *Review of Child Law: Custody* (1986) London, HMSO.

J. Masson, 'Thinking about contact – a social or a legal problem?' (2000) 12 *Child and Family Law Quarterly* 15.

B. Neale and C. Smart 'Good and Bad Lawyers? Struggling in the Shadow of the New Law' (1997) 19 *Journal of Social Welfare and Family Law* 377.

C. Piper, 'Assumptions About Children's Best Interests' (2000) 22 *Journal of Social Welfare and Family Law* 261.

C. Piper and F. Kaganas, 'Divorce and Domestic Violence' in S. Day Sclater and C. Piper (eds) *Undercurrents of Divorce* (1999) Aldershot, Ashgate.

J.A. Priest and J.C. Whybrow, *Custody Law in Practice in the Divorce and Domestic Courts, Supplement to Law Commission W.P. No. 96, Review of Child Law: Custody* (1986) London, HMSO.

M. Richards and M. Dyson, *Separation, Divorce and the Development of Children: A Review* (1982) Child Care and Development Group, University of Cambridge.

C. Smart and B. Neale, 'Arguments Against Virtue – Must Contact Be Enforced?' [1997] *Family Law* 332.

L. Trinder and J. Kellett, *The longer-term outcomes of in-court conciliation*, Ministry of Justice Research Series 15/07, (2007) Ministry of Justice.

J. Wallbank, 'Getting tough on mothers: regulating contact and residence' (2007) 15 *Feminist Legal Studies* 189.

10.3 The child's eye view

We quoted from:

A. Buchanan, J. Hunt, H. Bretherton and V. Bream, 'Families in Conflict – perspectives of children and parents on the family court welfare service' [2001] *Family Law* 900, 900–902.

G. Douglas, M. Murch, M. Robinson, L. Scanlan and I. Butler, 'Children's perspectives and experience of the divorce process' [2001] *Family Law* 373, 375–377.

Law Commission, *Report on Guardianship and Custody*, Law Com. No. 172 (1988), *op cit*, paras 3.23–3.24.

V. May and C. Smart, 'Silence in Court? – hearing children in residence and contact disputes' (2004) 16 *Child and Family Law Quarterly* 305, 306, 308–309, 311, 312–314.

Additional reading

G. Davis and J. Pearce, 'The welfare principle in action' [1999] *Family Law* 237.

Department for Education and Skills, *Parental Separation: Children's Needs and Parents' Responsibilities* (2004), Cm 6273, London, TSO.

Department for Education and Skills, *Parental Separation: Children's Needs and Parents' Responsibilities. Next Steps* (2005) Cm 6452, London, TSO.

A.L. James, A. James and S. McNamee, 'Constructing children's welfare in family proceedings' [2003] *Family Law* 889.

C. Piper, 'The wishes and feelings of the child', in S.D. Sclater and C. Piper (eds), *Undercurrents of Divorce* (1999) Aldershot, Ashgate.

C. Sawyer, 'An inside story: Ascertaining the child's wishes and feelings' [2000] *Family Law* 170.

C. Smart, B. Neale and A. Wade, *The changing experience of childhood: Families and divorce* (2001) Bristol, Polity Press.

J. Timms, S. Bailey and J. Thoburn, *You shout too! A survey of the views of children and young people involved in court proceedings when their parents divorce or separate* (2007) London, NSPCC publications.

10.4 Starting afresh

We quoted from:

J. Burgoyne and D. Clark, *Making a Go of It – A study of stepfamilies in Sheffield* (1984) London, Routledge and Kegan Paul, table 6.1.

J. Herring and R. Taylor, 'Relocating relocation' (2006) 18 *Child and Family Law Quarterly* 517, 528–529, 531.

Review of Adoption Law – Report to Ministers of an Interdepartmental Working Group (1992) London, Department of Health, paragraphs 19.2–19.9.

M. Smith, 'New stepfamilies – a descriptive study of a largely unseen group' (2003) 15 *Child and Family Law Quarterly* 185, 189–190, 194–195, 196.

Additional reading

S. Choudry, 'The Adoption and Children Act 2002, the welfare principle and the Human Rights Act 1998 – a missed opportunity' (2003) 15 *Child and Family Law Quarterly* 119.

S. Choudry and H. Fenwick, 'Taking the rights of children and parents seriously: Confronting the welfare principle under the Human Rights Act' (2005) 25 *Oxford Journal of Legal Studies* 453.

J. Eekelaar, 'The interests of the child and the child's wishes: the role of dynamic self-determination' (1994) 8 *International Journal of Law, Policy and the Family* 42.

J. Herring, 'The Human Rights Act and the Welfare Principle in Family Law – Conflicting or Complementary?' (1999) 11 *Child and Family Law Quarterly* 223.

J. Masson, D. Norbury and S. Chatterton, *Mine, Yours or Ours? A study of stepparent adoption* (1984) London, HMSO, 84, 103–105.

C. Webber and D. Delvin, at http://www.netdoctor.co.uk/sex_relationships/facts/stepfamilies.

11

SOCIAL SERVICES FOR CHILDREN AND FAMILIES

In this chapter we shall consider the legal mechanisms that are available to local authority social services departments to meet the needs of children and their families. We shall consider the range of needs which must be met, and the influences which have shaped the law in this area. It is necessary to distinguish between (i) children in need, (ii) looked-after children and (iii) children subject to a care order. Children in need are those that have particular needs which must be addressed by the public authorities, for these children to achieve or maintain a reasonable standard of health or development, or to prevent their development being impaired. They, and possibly also their families, may need, or benefit from, a range of extra support and services. Many children in need will be 'looked-after children' (sometimes referred to, confusingly, as being 'children in care'). Local authorities have a duty to provide accommodation for a child in need who requires it. The third category relates to children compulsorily in care; a local authority may seek a care order under section 31 Children Act 1989 if it considers it appropriate in relation to a child in need. Thus a 'looked-after child' may be either one who is accommodated by the local authority under section 20 Children Act 1989 or accommodated under a care order under section 31 Children Act 1989. More on this later.

11.1 SOME STATISTICS

Figures reported by Local Authority Social Services' Children and Families Teams for a survey week in February 2005 (*Issue No vweb-02-2006*) suggest that in that week there was a total of 385,000 children in need.

The Department for Children, Schools and Families has provided statistics on looked-after children, that is of children both voluntarily being accommodated and those who are the subject of a care order (*SFR 27/2007*), shown in Table A3.

Table A3 Children looked after at 31 March by placement, 2003–2007

England										numbers and percentages
	numbers					percentages				
Placement at 31 March	2003[4]	2004[5]	2005[5]	2006[5]	2007[5]	2003[4]	2004[5]	2005[5]	2006[5]	2007[5]
All children looked after at 31 March[1,2]	61,200	61,200	61,000	60,300	60,000	100	100	100	100	100
Foster placements	41,000	41,200	41,300	41,700	42,300	67	67	68	69	71
Foster placement inside Council boundary										
With relative or friend	5,800	5,800	5,600	5,300	5,100	9	9	9	9	8
With other foster carer										
provided by Council	21,900	21,000	20,400	20,000	20,200	36	34	33	33	34
arranged through agency	1,100	1,400	1,600	2,000	2,400	2	2	3	3	4
Foster placement outside Council boundary										
With relative or friend	1,900	2,000	2,000	2,000	1,900	3	3	3	3	3
With other foster carer										
provided by Council	4,900	5,100	5,200	5,400	5,300	8	8	9	9	9
arranged through agency	5,300	6,100	6,500	7,000	7,400	9	10	11	12	12
Placed for adoption[6]	3,800	3,600	3,400	3,000	2,500	6	6	6	5	4
Placed for adoption with consent with current foster carer (under S19 AA 2002)			360	330	130					0
Placed for adoption with placement order with current foster carer (under S21 AA 2002)	3,800	3,600			150	6	6	1	1	0
Placed for adoption with consent not with current foster carer (under S19 AA 2002)					640			5	4	1
Placed for adoption with placement order not with current foster carer (under			3,100	2,700	1,600					3

Table A3 *Continued*

England										numbers and percentages
	numbers					percentages				
Placement at 31 March	2003[4]	2004[5]	2005[5]	2006[5]	2007[5]	2003[4]	2004[5]	2005[5]	2006[5]	2007[5]
Placement with parents	6,300	5,900	5,800	5,400	5,100	10	10	9	9	9
Other placement in the community										
Living independently	1,300	1,500	1,500	1,600	1,600	2	2	3	3	3
Residential employment	1,200	1,500	1,500	1,600	1,600	2	2	2	3	3
	–	10	10	–	–	–	0	0	–	–
Secure units, children's homes and hostels	6,800	7,000	7,000	6,600	6,500	11	11	11	11	11
Secure unit inside Council boundary	40	30	30	20	30	0	0	0	0	0
Secure unit outside Council boundary[7]	210	210	220	170	170	0	0	0	0	0
Homes and hostels subject to Children's Homes regulations										
inside Council boundary	3,300	3,200	3,000	3,000	2,900	5	5	5	5	5
outside Council boundary	2,700	2,600	2,600	2,300	2,300	4	4	4	4	4
Homes and hostels *not* subject to Children's Homes regulations	530	910	1,100	1,100	1,100	1	1	2	2	2
Other residential settings	600	560	560	570	610	1	1	1	1	1
Residential care homes	220	200	210	230	230	0	0	0	0	0
NHS Trust providing medical/ nursing care	90	80	90	80	70	0	0	0	0	0
Family centre or mother and baby unit	170	130	150	120	150	0	0	0	0	0
Young offenders institution or prison	110	140	110	140	160	0	0	0	0	0

Table A3 *Continued*

England										numbers and percentages
	numbers					percentages				
Placement at 31 March	2003[4]	2004[5]	2005[5]	2006[5]	2007[5]	2003[4]	2004[5]	2005[5]	2006[5]	2007[5]
Residential schools	1,300	1,200	1,100	1,100	1,100	2	2	2	2	2
Missing – absent for more than 24 hours from agreed placement	120	120	140	140	160	0	0	0	0	0
In refuge (section 51 of Children Act, 1989)	–	0	0	–	–	–	0	0	–	–
Whereabouts known (not in refuge)	40	40	20	20	30	0	0	0	0	0
Whereabouts unknown	80	90	120	120	120	0	0	0	0	0
Other placement	100	110	100	120	120	0	0	0	0	0

1. Source: SSDA903 return on children looked after.
2. Figures exclude children looked after under an agreed series of short term placements.
3. Historical data may differ from rider publications. This is mainly due to the implementation of amendments and corrections sent by some local authorities after the publication date of previous materials.
4. Figures are derived from the SSDA903 one third sample survey.
5. Figures are taken from the SSDA903 return which, since 2003–04 has covered all children looked after.
6. Since 2004–05 placed for adoption has been disaggregated by whether the placement is or is not with current foster carer. In 2006–07 placement also disaggregated according to whether consent was given or a placement order sought.
7. There are currently only 19 secure units operating in England therefore most placements will inevitably be outside the council boundary.

At the extreme end of children in need are those who are subjected to abuse, and who will be (or should be) the subject of a care order:

> I burned him later with the iron; I did it deliberately. I'd look at him, and think, oh you little bastard, you know? I just got hold of him and burned him on the back of the hand. I was so fed up! He'd been grizzling; he was tired out in the daytime because he didn't sleep at night. And of course I was tired too, and he wouldn't stop grizzling. I was ironing on the floor in the lounge because it was just something quick I wanted – I was kneeling down and he was sitting over by the window. I just got hold of his hand and I said, that'll make you sleep! It was all done in such a quick second, you know, that I didn't... it wasn't sort of premeditated; I just looked at him, had the iron in my hand, and did it.
>
> Jasmine Beckford died at the age of four and a half, in Kensal Rise, North-West London, at the home of Mr Morris Beckford (her step-father) and Miss Beverley Lorrington (her mother) of cerebral contusions and subdural haemorrhage as a direct result of severe manual blows inflicted on the child's head shortly before death. At the time of her death, and for some months (if not years) before, Jasmine was a very thin little girl, emaciated as a result of chronic undernourishment. When she was discharged from hospital after being taken into care she weighed 18 lbs, 14 ozs. Seven months later, when she was reunited with her parents after being fostered, she weighed 25 lbs, 5 oz. She died, 27 months later, weighing 23 lbs. Apart from her stunted development, she had been subjected to parental battering over a protracted period, multiple old scars appearing both to the pathologist who conducted the post-mortem and to the consultant orthopaedic surgeon who gave evidence to us, as being consistent with repeated episodes of physical abuse, to say nothing of the psychological battering she must have undergone.
>
> Samantha's mother died when she was very young and her father brought up her younger brother and herself single-handed. He began to abuse her when she was 4. When she was little he covered her head and top half with a blanket and interfered with her vagina. By the age of 10 it was regular sexual intercourse and thereafter it included buggery and oral intercourse. 'He made me say that I enjoyed it, that I wanted it. He wouldn't like any disagreement.' As she got older she began to realise that this did not happen to other girls. She said that: 'it got to the stage that if I wanted a favour, to go out with a friend, or buy a new pair of shoes, I had to let him do it first.'
>
> She had no-one to confide in, no-one to turn to: 'I thought any adult would not believe me – they would think I was making up a story. ... I didn't know what might happen. For my brother's sake I didn't want my family split up... I loved my father so much. I respected him as a father. But I was confused, didn't understand. I wanted it to stop. I hated that part of it so much.'

So said, respectively, the mother who told her story to Jean Renvoize for her investigation into *Children in Danger* (1974), the report of the panel of inquiry into the circumstances surrounding the death of Jasmine Beckford, *A Child in Trust* (1985), and 'Samantha', whose history is told in the Report of the *Inquiry into Child Abuse in Cleveland 1987* (1988). There were some eighteen reports of child abuse inquiries between 1973 and 1980 (see DHSS, 1982), beginning with Maria Colwell (1973) and including Susan Auckland (1975) and Wayne Brewer (1977). Between 1980 and 1989 there were at least nineteen more (see DH, 1991), including Jasmine Beckford (1985), Heidi Koseda (1986), Tyra Henry (1987) and Kimberley Carlile (1987). One of the more recent inquiries, the report by Lord Laming into the death of Victoria Climbie (*The Victoria Climbie Inquiry* 2003), illustrates that the lessons from the earlier reports have been unable to prevent further tragic abuse. Victoria spent much of her last days in the winter of 1999–2000 'living and sleeping in a bath in an unheated bathroom, bound hand and foot inside a bin bag, lying in her own urine and faeces.' (Laming Report 1.4.)

Understandably, tragic cases like these receive a great deal of professional and public attention. However, local authority social services departments are concerned with a much wider range of problems. Three broad types of children were identified by Jean Packman, John Randall and Nicola Jacques, in *Who Needs Care?* (1986):

...Admission to care is not a unitary concept: it clearly has several purposes, and is a response to a wide range of different problems and situations, as this study has underlined. At its simplest, there are at least three distinct sorts of public child care on offer. One is for families who are beset by difficulties or handicaps which interrupt or interfere with their capacity to look after their children. Their problems may be acute or chronic, one-dimensional or, more usually, multifaceted and interconnected, and they are likely to be short on supportive networks of relatives or friends to help out, and without the means to pay for child-care services outside these networks. For such families the local authority can provide – and, indeed, is legally obliged to provide (under the old 1948 Act and its [successors]) – a child-care service. Provided that it is judged to be in the interests of the child's welfare, no limits are set on the circumstances in which an admission can take place, nor (apart from an upper age limit) to the time the child may spend in care. Parents can and do request such admissions (more properly, 'receptions' into care), though they can also be effected in their absence. In the words of one commentator, it 'does not imply any criticism of parents who may seek care for their child as a solution to a crisis. It can be a very constructive move by the parents.' [Holden, 1980] It is therefore a type of admission that responds to parents as unfortunate rather than blameworthy, and casts the local authority in the role of the child's caretaker, acting on the parents' behalf. As such, it can be seen to be at one end of a continuum of services which includes domiciliary help and day care for children. It therefore forms, in our view, part of a range of child-care services for families and not, as the narrower interpretations of 'care' and 'prevention' would imply, a stark alternative to such services....

A second type of admission provides a protection and rescue service for children who are thought to be in danger, whether it be physical, sexual, moral, emotional or developmental. Here the emphasis is on parental faults and failings and on the child as a victim of inadequate or inappropriate parenting. The local authority intervenes on the child's behalf, and, more often than not, if an admission is arranged (and even if it is requested by the parents) the local authority itself takes over parental rights as well as duties. In essence, the child-care service offered is protection for very vulnerable children.

The third type of admission relates to the child whose own behaviour is causing problems. Children whose behaviour troubles no one but their own families, or who behave in ways which adults too easily overlook – depressed and withdrawn children, for example – are unlikely candidates for care. But children whose disruptive and antisocial behaviour spreads beyond the family, and is visible to schools, police, neighbours and strangers, may well be so. For them, admission to care has a more ambiguous meaning. The intentions of the 1969 Children and Young Persons Act were to cast admitted 'villains' in the role of 'victims' of another sort – vulnerable youngsters from difficult backgrounds who had succumbed to family, neighbourhood and societal pressures, and were in need of care or control not otherwise available to them. In practice, familiar elements of punishment, containment and deterrence are also in the minds of decision-makers and, it must be said, the parents themselves. In the event, the child-care service offered to this group is as much a retributive and protective service for the public as it is a 'care' service for the young people themselves.

Tables C. 3 and C. 4 portray the primary reason why children are being accommodated by local authorities, together with the age of these children and the race/ethnicity of children, so as to provide more detailed information of the categories as identified by Packman *et al.* These statistics were published in *Care matters: Transforming the Lives of Children and Young People in Care* (Cm 6932, October 2006).

Table C.3 Children in care are a diverse group and the two charts below illustrate the age and race of children in care

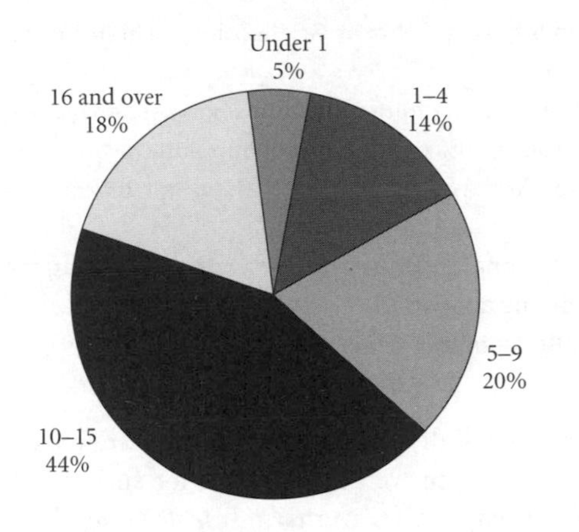

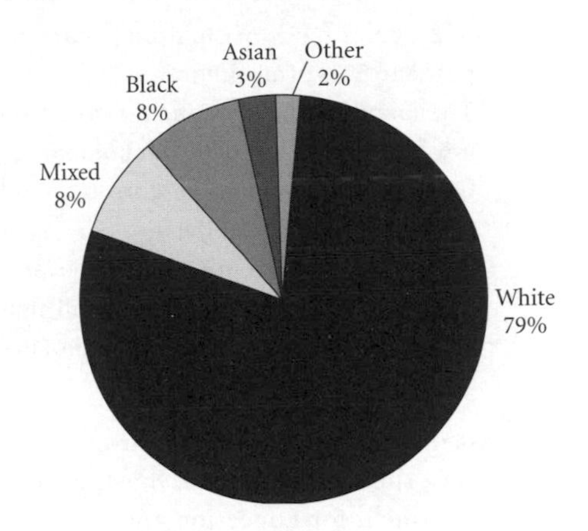

Table C.4 Local authorities record the primary reason for a child coming into care - 63% come into care because of abuse or neglect

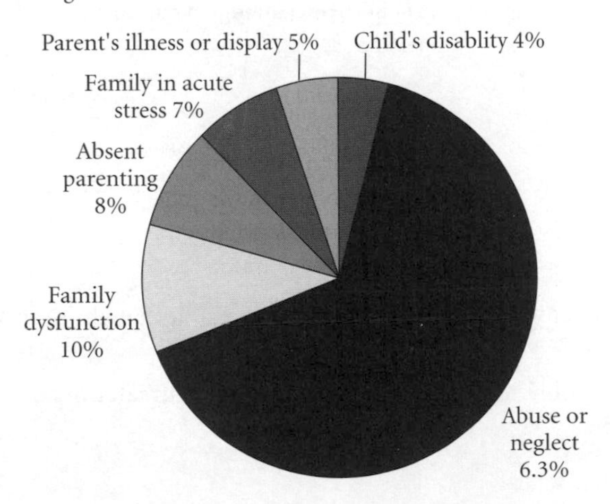

Accommodating children either by way of a care order or on a voluntary basis has not stopped the problem of abuse and neglect, as Sir Robert Waterhouse found when considering the alleged abuse of children in children's homes in the former county council areas of Gwynedd and Clwyd since 1974, *'Lost in Care'* (2000). The tribunal of inquiry found that there was widespread sexual abuse of boys in children's residential establishments in Clwyd between 1974 and 1990. It found also that physical abuse, in the sense of unacceptable use of force in disciplining and excessive force in restraining residents, occurred in most of the residential establishments that the inquiry examined. It concluded that the quality of care provided in all the local authority homes and private residential establishments examined was below an acceptable standard throughout the period under review, and in most cases far below the required standard.

But even if there is no abuse or neglect in care, whether it be at a children's home or in a foster home, much of the evidence suggests that looked-after children have poor education outcomes, and are more likely to receive a warning, reprimand or conviction than other young people. These concerns are developed in the White Paper, *Care Matters: Time for Change* (DFES, 2007):

> - In 2006, only 12% of children in care achieved 5 A*-C grades at GCSE (or equivalent) compared to 59% of all children;
> - Their health is poorer than that of other children. 45% of children in care are assessed as having a mental health disorder compared with around 10% of the general population;
> - Over 50% of children in care responding to *Care Matters* said that they had difficulties accessing positive activities;
> - 9.6% of children in care aged 10 or over, were cautioned or convicted for an offence during the year – almost 3 times the rate for all children of this age; and
> - 30% of care leavers aged 19 were not in education, employment or training

The cost involved for providing for children in need generally and looked-after children specifically is very substantial indeed. But this doesn't seem to improve the outcomes for such children. The Department for Education and Skills in its Green Paper *Care Matters: Transforming the Lives of Children and Young People in Care* (Cm 6932, 2006) acknowledges that the situation is very troublesome:

> 1.13 Despite all of [the] investment and reform and despite the work and commitment of local authorities, carers and social workers, the life chances of many children in care remain bleak. Especially in the light of the scale of investment in supporting children in care, it is unacceptable that their outcomes remain so poor.

QUESTIONS

i. Given what you have read so far, do you think that children should be kept out of care at all costs?

ii. Is it possible to support families in a non-threatening way, and also protect children effectively?

11.2 HOW THE LEGISLATION DEVELOPED

The starting point for us when examining the legal mechanisms that are available to provide public support (the phrase often used is 'corporate parenting') for children and their families must be the implementation of the Children Act 1948. Prior to that date, the care of deprived children was based to a very large extent on the Poor Law, which had its origins as long ago as the Poor Relief Act 1601. The Children Act 1948 established new local government departments and gave them, among other things, the duty to care for orphaned, abandoned or deprived children, the power to assume parental rights over children in their care who had no parents, or parents who were in some way incapable or unfit to look after them, and the duty to act as a fit parent for children compulsorily removed from home by a court.

John Eekelaar, Robert Dingwall and Topsy Murray in 'Victims or Threats? Children in Care Proceedings' (1982) explain how the next major legislative development; section 1 of the Children and Young Persons Act 1969, came about:

The Ingleby Committee (1960) and the 1969 Act

...In dealing with the general issue of the circumstances in which the state may properly intervene in proceedings against parents for child neglect, the Committee states that 'difficulty has not arisen for several years over the reasonable requirements for nutrition, housing, clothing and schooling' although there had been some cases where parents had refused to give their children proper medical attention. No mention is made at all by the Committee of child abuse cases and the Committee proceeds, throughout the rest of the chapter, to consider the issue solely in terms of delinquency cases. By 1960, then, our society had become blind to potential conflicts between family autonomy and child protection. Apart from a few troublesome cases involving unconventional religious sects, the resolution of welfarist child protection and family autonomy was considered simple and unproblematic. In fact, it had been obscured by the overwhelming preoccupation with delinquency....

The two Government White Papers, The Child, the Family and the Young Offender and Children in Trouble (Home Office, 1965 and 1968) were, as their titles indicate, wholly concerned with the problem of juvenile delinquents. They set the basis for the policy of the 1969 Act. One cornerstone of that policy was that children should progressively cease to be prosecuted for offences and should, instead, be made subject to care proceedings under the Act. Accordingly, the grounds for bringing care proceedings were to be extended to include a ground that the child had committed an offence (excluding homicide). Child offenders were now to be treated under (almost) exactly the same process as troublesome children who were not offenders. And, as we have seen, child victims had by now been assimilated into this category. The logic of this assimilation compelled the abandonment, for all categories of these children, of any reference to parental inadequacy among the conditions precedent to bringing care proceedings. For, as the Home Office observed in its official guide to the Act, such a provision 'meant that proceedings inevitably appeared to cast blame for the child's situation or behaviour directly into his parents or those looking after him' a fact which was quite irrelevant for the delinquent child... The Act, therefore, took the line originally proposed by the Ingleby Report and simply required that it be shown that the child was in need of 'care of control' which he would not receive if an order was not made.

Implementation of the 1969 Act, which tried to cater for the villains and the victims by the same process, coincided with the Local Authority Social Services Act 1970, which amalgamated the children's services with those provided for the old, the mentally disordered or handicapped, and the disabled, into new all-purpose social services departments.

Jean Packman in the *The Child's Generation* (1981) explains the development, after the 1948 Act, of the concept of 'prevention':

Research studies of the period [principally Bowlby (1953)] stressed the importance of the mother-child relationship and the damaging effects on a child's mental, emotional and even physical development, if the relationship were inadequate, disturbed or broken. Most studies examined the latter – deprivation by separation – the phenomenon in its most readily observable form. The emphasis therefore tended to rest on the temporary, or even irreversible damage caused to children by removing them from home. To these studies were added the observations of the child care workers themselves. Seeing, at first hand, the unhappiness and distress of many children in care, they were naturally spurred to seek ways of avoiding admissions. Depressingly, too, they saw that many deprived children themselves grew up to be inadequate parents whose children were, in turn, deprived. A 'cycle of deprivation' was acknowledged long before it became a political catchphrase.

To this central concern to avoid separating children from their parents, was added the complicating factor that some families were clearly incapable of providing even a minimum of physical or emotional care and stability for their children. Social workers were therefore faced with decisions about whether or not the deprivations suffered by a child within his family were worse and more hazardous than those he would suffer by removal from home. Such decisions were also affected by estimates of their own skills and the resources available to them, to intervene and improve the family situation, to the child's benefit; and by the standards of substitute care that might offset and compensate the child for the effects of separation.

Prevention thus came to be a two-pronged concept; prevention of admission to care; and prevention of neglect and cruelty in the family. A variety of methods of working towards each of these ends can be seen emerging, in response to the differing circumstances of the families concerned. With some families the work was clearly directed to their weaknesses, whether these were problems of poor home management and low standards of hygiene, or of disturbed and volatile relationships....

In other situations more stress was laid on family and community strengths. Child care workers were aware that many children came into care at a time of family crisis, for lack of any alternative. It was their task to explore and encourage links with kin or with neighbours who could offer care for the children in a familiar environment....

A third dimension to preventive work grew from the knowledge that some families collapsed through external pressures which were beyond their control, yet were within the power of children's departments to influence. A prime example lies in the field of housing. As early as 1951 concern was expressed at the effects on children, separated from their parents because of homelessness....

The *Review of Child Care Law* (1985) and the Government's White Paper on *The Law on Child Care and Family Services* (1987), which led to the 1989 Act, emphasised the importance of preventative services:

18. It is proposed to give local authorities a broad 'umbrella' power to provide services to promote the care and upbringing of children, and to help prevent the breakdown of family relationships which might eventually lead to a court order committing the child to the local authority's care. Within this power the local authority will be able to provide services to a child at home, for example a family aide to assist within the home; at a day centre, for example a day nursery for preschool children, an after school scheme for school age children or placement with a childminder; or residential facilities allowing a child to stay for short or long periods away from home, say with a foster family or in a children's home. The local authority will also be able to offer financial assistance in exceptional circumstances.

...

20. Local authorities have a duty under current legislation to receive children into their care in special circumstances, generally where there is a need to care for the child away from home because of the absence or incapacity of parents. This duty will be maintained broadly as at present. So will the duty to return the child to his family where this is consistent with his welfare.

21. The Government wish to emphasise, however, that the provision of a service by the local authority to enable a child who is not under a care order to be cared for away from home should be seen in a wider context and as part of the range of services a local authority can offer to parents and families in need of help with the care of their children. Such a service should, in appropriate circumstances, be seen as a positive response to the needs of families and not as a mark of failure either on the part of the family or those professionals and others working to support them. An essential characteristic of this service should be its voluntary character, that is it should be based clearly on continuing parental agreement and operate as far as possible on a basis of partnership and co-operation between the local authority and parents.

Hence the abolition of the power to assume parental rights by administrative resolution and the insistence (in s. 20(8), (9) and (10)) that any person who is entitled to have the child living with him may remove the child from local authority accommodation at any time.

The major themes of the Children Act (1989) can be illustrated by the following extracts. The Department of Health's guide, *Working Together* (1991), emphasised the importance of working in 'partnership' with parents:

1.4. Local authorities have, under the Children Act 1989, a general duty to safeguard and promote the welfare of children within their area who are in need and so far as is consistent with that duty to promote the upbringing of such children by their families. As parental responsibility for children is retained notwithstanding any court orders short of adoption, local authorities must work in partnership with parents, seeking court orders when compulsory action is indicated in the interests of the child but only when this is better for the child than working with the parents under voluntary arrangements.

The 2006 edition of *Working Together* puts the same point in this way:

1.3. Patterns of family life vary and there is no one, perfect way to bring up children. Good parenting involves caring for children's basic needs, keeping them safe, showing them warmth and love, and providing the stimulation needed for their development and to help them achieve their potential, within a stable environment where they experience consistent guidance and boundaries.

1.4. Parenting can be challenging. Parents themselves require and deserve support. Asking for help should be seen as a sign of responsibility rather than as a parenting failure.

1.5. A wide range of services and professionals provide support to families in bringing up children. In the great majority of cases, it should be the decision of parents when to ask for help and advice on their children's care and upbringing. However, professionals do also need to engage parents early when to do so may prevent problems or difficulties becoming worse. Only in exceptional cases should there be compulsory intervention in family life – e.g. where this is necessary to safeguard a child from significant harm. Such intervention should – provided this is consistent with the safety and welfare of the child – support families in making their own plans for the welfare and protection of their children.

And a similar point is made in *Care Matters: Time for Change* (2007):

9. Every child requires love, care and stability when they are growing up, but not all children are fortunate enough to have a loving family which is capable of providing this support. Children in

care are frequently in greater need, but paradoxically less likely to receive the help they require. Many of them suffer terrible abuse and neglect before entering into a State care system that can seem cold and aloof.

Wherever possible we should support children within their own families. This requires a focus on support for parents and the provision of evidence-based parenting programmes and short breaks for families with more complex needs. For those children and young people who need to be cared for outside their immediate family, we should, at all relevant stages of the care planning process, explore the potential for enabling children to live with or be supported by wider family and friends.

The key provisions of the Children Act 1989 are these:

17.—(1) It shall be the general duty of every local authority (in addition to the other duties imposed on them by this Part)—

(a) to safeguard and promote the welfare of children within their area who are in need; and

(b) so far as is consistent with that duty, to promote the upbringing of such children by their families,

by providing a range and level of services appropriate to those children's needs.

(2) For the purpose principally of facilitating the discharge of their general duty under this section, every local authority shall have the specific duties and powers set out in Part I of Schedule 2.

(3) Any service provided by an authority in the exercise of functions conferred on them by this section may be provided for the family of a particular child in need or for any member of his family, if it is provided with a view to safeguarding or promoting the child's welfare.

...

(4A) Before determining what (if any) services to provide for a particular child in need in the exercise of functions conferred on them by this section, a local authority shall, so far as is reasonably practicable and consistent with the child's welfare–

(a) ascertain the child's wishes and feelings regarding the provision of those services; and

(b) give due consideration (having regard to his age and understanding) to such wishes and feelings of the child as they have been able to ascertain.

...

(10) For the purposes of this Part a child shall be taken to be in need if–

(a) he is unlikely to achieve or maintain, or to have the opportunity of achieving or maintaining, a reasonable standard of health or development without the provision for him of services by a local authority under this Part;

(b) his health or development is likely to be significantly impaired, or further impaired, without the provision for him of such services; or

(c) he is disabled,

and 'family', in relation to such a child, includes any person who has parental responsibility for the child and any other person with whom he has been living.

(11) For the purposes of this Part, a child is disabled if he is blind, deaf or dumb or suffers from mental disorder of any kind or is substantially and permanently handicapped by illness, injury or congenital deformity or such other disability as may be prescribed; and in this Part–

'development' means physical, intellectual, emotional, social or behavioural development; and

'health' means physical or mental health.

QUESTIONS

i. Consider the following situation. A mother has three children, two of whom are autistic and require constant supervision. Her own health has started to deteriorate. Do you believe that an assessment under section 17 gives rise to an enforceable *duty* or alternatively *empowers* the local authority to provide accommodation in these circumstances? (Read *R(G) v Barnet London Borough Council; R(W) v Lambeth London Borough Council; R(A) v Lambeth London Borough Council* [2004] 1 FLR 454, HL.)

ii. What rights, if any, do (i) children, (ii) their families, have under section 17? (Read *Re J (Specific Issue Order: Leave to Apply)* [1995] 1 FLR 669.)

Part I of Schedule 2 lists many specific services for children living at home or elsewhere.

Section 20 deals with the provision of accommodation:

20.—(1) Every local authority shall provide accommodation for any child in need within their area who appears to them to require accommodation as a result of—

(a) there being no person who has parental responsibility for him;
(aa) who is a special guardian of the child; or
(b) his being lost or having been abandoned; or
(c) the person who has been caring for him being prevented (whether or not permanently, and for whatever reason) from providing him with suitable accommodation or care.

(2) Where a local authority provide accommodation under subsection (1) for a child who is ordinarily resident in the area of another local authority, that other local authority may take over the provision of accommodation for the child within—

(a) three months of being notified in writing that the child is being provided with accommodation; or
(b) such other longer period as may be prescribed.

(3) Every local authority shall provide accommodation for any child in need within their area who has reached the age of sixteen and whose welfare the authority consider is likely to be seriously prejudiced if they do not provide him with accommodation.

(4) A local authority may provide accommodation for any child within their area (even though a person who has parental responsibility for him is able to provide him with accommodation) if they consider that to do so would safeguard or promote the child's welfare.

(5) A local authority may provide accommodation for any person who has reached the age of sixteen but is under twenty-one in any community home which takes children who have reached the age of sixteen if they consider that to do so would safeguard or promote his welfare.

(6) Before providing accommodation under this section, a local authority shall, so far as is reasonably practicable and consistent with the child's welfare—

(a) ascertain the child's wishes and feelings regarding the provision of accommodation; and
(b) give due consideration (having regard to his age and understanding) to such wishes and feelings of the child as they have been able to ascertain.

(7) A local authority may not provide accommodation under this section for any child if any person who—

(a) has parental responsibility for him; and
(b) is willing and able to—

(i) provide accommodation for him; or
(ii) arrange for accommodation to be provided for him, objects.

(8) Any person who has parental responsibility for a child may at any time remove the child from accommodation provided by or on behalf of the local authority under this section.

(9) Subsections (7) and (8) do not apply while any person—

(a) in whose favour a residence order is in force with respect to the child;
(aa) who is a special guardian of the child; or
(b) who has care of the child by virtue of an order made in the exercise of the High Court's inherent jurisdiction with respect to children,

agrees to the child being looked after in accommodation provided by or on behalf of the local authority.

(10) Where there is more than one such person as is mentioned in subsection (9), all of them must agree.

(11) Subsections (7) and (8) do not apply where a child who has reached the age of sixteen agrees to being provided with accommodation under this section.

Consider the following comments from a High Court judge, Stanley Burnton J, sitting in the Administrative Court to hear the case of *R (on the application of J) v The London Borough of Sutton* [2007] EWHC 1196(Admin). The applicant was a 17-year-old girl who had been sentenced by a criminal court to a Detention and Training Order. Prior to sentencing, she had stayed with a friend. During her detention, the local authority decided that as she did not wish to live within their authority, but to be near her father in another local authority area, she should be treated as a homeless person rather than as a person requiring accommodation under section 20. She sought a judicial review of this decision and a declaration and order requiring the local authority to provide an assessment of her needs. Her application succeeded.

Stanley Burnton J:

[59] I have to say that I consider [counsel's] criticisms to be well-founded. . . . the basis for the conclusion that J could be suitably accommodated by the Homeless Persons team is wholly unclear, and the conclusion difficult to understand in any event. In relation to her development needs and strengths, the Core Assessment referred to her wish to attend college and pursue a career working with children, but made no comment on the practicality of that ambition . . . Nothing was said as to any plan to assist her to manage in the community. . . . The Core Assessment stated: 'The overall aim of the plan is for J to receive appropriate support and guidance from the Youth Offending Team. The Team will arrange for the accommodation officer to meet J at the point of her release and take her to appropriate Homeless Persons Team for accommodation . . .'

This was vague and unsubstantiated. I do not find in the Assessment 'a realistic plan of action (including services to be provided), detailing who has responsibility for action, a timetable and a process for review)'.

QUESTIONS

i. Can you think of any situation where a child abandons his or her 'right' to be treated as a child in need?

ii. In *R (W) v Lambeth LBC* [2002] EWCA Civ 613, [2002] 2 All ER 901, when in the Court of Appeal, that Court decided that in cases where a family with dependent children was not entitled to help from the local housing authority, section 17 of the 1989 Act gave the local authority social services a power to assist the family with the provision of accommodation, but that the exercise of that power was a matter of discretion for the local authority, and the latter could, if it saw fit, reserve it to extreme cases. Do you think that the applicant in the above case is an extreme case, and if so, what is the difference between section 17 and section 20?

A clear distinction should be drawn between children 'in care', who are the subject of care orders (see p. 561, below), and other children who are simply provided with accommodation by the authority. A sharp eye, however, is needed to recognise the differences in the sections of the 1989 Act dealing with all children being 'looked after':

22.—(1) In this Act, any reference to a child who is looked after by a local authority is a reference to a child who is—

(a) in their care, or
(b) provided with accommodation by the authority in the exercise of any functions (in particular those under this Act) which are social services functions within the meaning of the Local Authority Social Services Act 1970, apart from functions under sections 17, 23B and 24B.

(2) In subsection (1) 'accommodation' means accommodation which is provided for a continuous period of more than 24 hours.

(3) It shall be the duty of a local authority looking after any child—

(a) to safeguard and promote his welfare; and
(b) to make such use of services available for children cared for by their own parents as appears to the authority reasonable in his case.

(3A) The duty of a local authority under subsection 3(a) to safeguard and promote the welfare of a child looked after by them includes in particular a duty to promote the child's educational achievement.

(4) Before making any decision with respect to a child whom they are looking after, or proposing to look after, a local authority shall, so far as is reasonably practicable, ascertain the wishes and feelings of—

(a) the child;
(b) his parents;
(c) any person who is not a parent of his but who has parental responsibility for him; and
(d) any other person whose wishes and feelings the authority consider to be relevant, regarding the matter to be decided.

(5) In making any such decisions a local authority shall give due consideration—

(a) having regarded to his age and understanding, to such wishes and feelings of the child as they have been able to ascertain;
(b) to such wishes and feelings of any person mentioned in subsection (4)(b) to (d) as they have been able to ascertain; and
(c) to the child's religious persuasion, racial origin and cultural and linguistic background.

(6) If it appears to a local authority that it is necessary, for the purpose of protecting members of the public from serious injury, to exercise their powers with respect to a child whom they are looking after in a manner which may not be consistent with their duties under this section, they may do so.

(7) If the Secretary of State considers it necessary, for the purpose of protecting members of the public from serious injury, to give directions to a local authority with respect to the exercise of their powers with respect to a child whom they are looking after, he may give such directions to the authority.

(8) Where any such directions are given to an authority they shall comply with them even though doing so is inconsistent with their duties under this section.

QUESTIONS

i. Section 22(3A) was introduced by the Children Act 2004. How would you define 'educational achievement'?

ii. The local authority is looking after Mary, a seven-year-old child, under section 20. The father is a Schedule 1 offender currently in prison, and the mother has recently been sentenced to a community order for an offence connected with prostitution. The local authority places the child in a foster placement that breaks down. The local authority has found another foster placement, but because the allocated social worker is concerned about Mary's behaviour, therapy sessions are recommended. Does the local authority need to inform the parents (i) that it is considering moving Mary to another foster placement; (ii) that it is considering therapeutic sessions for Mary? (Read *Re P (Children Act 1989, ss 22 and 26: Local Authority Compliance)* [2000] 2 FLR 910; and *Re C (Care: Consultation with Parents not in Child's Best Interests)* [2006] 2 FLR 787.)

A 'local authority foster parent' is defined in section 23(3):

23.—(1) It shall be the duty of any local authority looking after a child—

(a) when he is in their care, to provide accommodation for him; and
(b) to maintain him in other respects apart from providing accommodation for him.

(2) A local authority shall provide accommodation and maintenance for any child whom they are looking after by—

(a) placing him (subject to subsection (5) and any regulations made by the Secretary of State) with—
(i) a family;
(ii) a relative of his; or
(iii) any other suitable person,

on such terms as to payment by the authority and otherwise as the authority may determine subject to section 49 of the Children Act 2004;

(aa) maintaining him in an appropriate children's home; or
(b) making such other arrangements as—
(i) seem appropriate to them; and
(ii) comply with any regulations made by the Secretary of State.

(2A) Where under subsection (2)(aa) a local authority maintains a child in a home provided, equipped and maintained by the Secretary of State under section 82(5), it shall do so on such terms as the Secretary of State may from time to time determine.

(3) Any person with whom a child has been placed under subsection (2)(*a*) is referred to in this Act as a local authority foster parent unless he falls within subsection (4).

(4) A person falls within this subsection if he is—

(a) a parent of the child;

(b) a person who is not a parent of the child but who has parental responsibility for him; or

(c) where the child is in care and there was a residence order in force with respect to him immediately before the care order was made, a person in whose favour the residence order was made.

(5) Where a child is in the care of a local authority, the authority may only allow him to live with a person who falls within subsection (4) in accordance with regulations made by the Secretary of State.

(5A) For the purposes of subsection (5) a child shall be regarded as living with a person if he stays with that person for a continuous period of more than 24 hours.

(6) Subject to any regulations made by the Secretary of State for the purposes of this subsection, any local authority looking after a child shall make arrangements to enable him to live with—

(a) a person falling within subsection (4); or

(b) a relative, friend or other person connected with him,

unless that would not be reasonably practicable or consistent with his welfare.

(7) Where a local authority provide accommodation for a child whom they are looking after, they shall, subject to the provisions of this Part and so far as is reasonably practicable and consistent with his welfare, secure that—

(a) the accommodation is near his home; and

(b) where the authority are also providing accommodation for a sibling of his, they are accommodated together.

(8) Where a local authority provide accommodation for a child whom they are looking after and who is disabled, they shall, so far as is reasonably practicable, secure that the accommodation is not unsuitable to his particular needs.

(9) Part II of Schedule 2 shall have effect for the purposes of making further provision as to children looked after by local authorities and in particular as to the regulations that may be made under subsections (2)(a) and (f) and (5).

(10) In this Act—

'appropriate children's home' means a children's home in respect of which a person is registered under Part II of the Care Standards Act 2000; and 'children's home' has the same meaning as in that Act.

QUESTION

What if a 13-year-old girl accommodated in a local authority children's home under section 20 has a boyfriend (a) to whom the allocated social worker objects but the parents do not, or (b) to whom the parents object but the social worker does not? What legal advice can you provide to the local authority?

The Children's Rights Director at OFSTED produced a report entitled *Children and Safeguarding* (January 2007, available at http://www.rights4me.org) which provides the views of children about staying safe from harm, from children who are living away from home or getting help from social care services. Here is a summary of some of the comments:

- Two young people told us how they had been moved out of a city into a country area where they were the only black people in the school. They had been the subject of racist bullying, and then got into trouble for fighting back. They blamed social services for putting them at risk of harm from bullying and racism.
- One group said that staff in their children's home often spent a lot of their time in the staff office rather than with the children and young people.
- Even for children living away from home, parents are by far the most likely people to tell if someone else is harming them.

QUESTIONS

i. You are a child aged fifteen being looked after by Wessex County Council in a small residential home. You like this because it is near to your school and friends. Visits to or from your family are easy. Wessex then decides to privatise its provision of residential care and to close the home. You are likely to be sent to a similar home 50 miles away. What can you do?

ii. Your 16-year-old sister thinks you have a lovely life in the home and would like to join you. What can she do?

iii. Your 21-year-old boyfriend would like to visit you in the home, but the home's rules prohibit such visits. What can he do?

iv. What should the two young people quoted from the survey above do about the bullying?

v. Suppose that you are twelve, and you have been accommodated with local authority foster parents under section 20 for several years. Wessex Social Services thinks that returning you to your family at this crucial stage in your education and development will not be for the best. If your mother decides to take you away from them, what can Wessex do? What can your foster parents do?

Some children of course are a risk to themselves. The Children Act 1989 places limits in which children may be placed in 'secure accommodation':

25.—(1) Subject to the following provisions of this section, a child who is being looked after by a local authority may not be placed, and, if placed, may not be kept, in accommodation provided for the purpose of restricting liberty ('secure accommodation') unless it appears—

(a) that—

(i) he has a history of absconding and is likely to abscond from any other description of accommodation; and

(ii) if he absconds, he is likely to suffer significant harm; or

(b) that if he is kept in any other description of accommodation he is likely to injure himself or other persons.

(2) The Secretary of State may by regulations—

(a) specify a maximum period—

(i) beyond which a child may not be kept in secure accommodation without the authority of the court; and

(ii) for which the court may authorize a child to be kept in secure accommodation;

(b) empower the court from time to time to authorize a child to be kept in secure accommodation for such further period as the regulations may specify; and

(c) provide that applications to the court under this section shall be made only by local authorities.

QUESTIONS

i. Why is this not restricted to 'children in care'?

ii. Should the welfare of the child be the paramount consideration when a court is asked to authorise the use of secure accommodation? (See *Re M (secure accommodation order)* [1995] Fam 108, [1995] 3 All ER 407, [1995] 2 WLR 302, [1995] 1 FLR 418, CA).

iii. Do you think that Article 5 of the EConHR has any bearing on section 25? (Recall that in *Re K (a child) (secure accommodation order: right to liberty)* [2001] Fam 377, [2001] 2 All ER 719, CA Butler-Sloss P said that a secure accommodation order is a deprivation of liberty.)

iv. Jane is a 16-year-old girl who has been living with a foster parent for some six months. She had previously been looked after by her father, but he had sought the local authority's help after he had realised that he was unable to care for her needs. She has a history of absconding from the foster home and there are concerns that she is spending time as a prostitute. Can section 25 be used in this case, and if not, why not?

v. Section 51 of the Act allows the Secretary of State to exempt from criminal liability for harbouring or assisting runaways specified voluntary organisations and others who provide refuges for children 'at risk': is this a better solution?

vi. Should we tolerate a public care system from which children want to run away?

11.3 CHILD PROTECTION INQUIRIES

In *Working Together* (2006) the Department of Health defines child abuse thus:

1.29 Abuse and neglect are forms of maltreatment of a child. Somebody may abuse or neglect a child by inflicting harm, or by failing to act to prevent harm. Children may be abused in a family or in an institutional or community setting, by those known to them or, more rarely, by a stranger. They may be abused by an adult or adults, or another child or children.

Physical Abuse

1.30 Physical abuse may involve hitting, shaking, throwing, poisoning, burning or scalding, drowning, suffocating, or otherwise causing physical harm to a child. Physical harm may also be caused when a parent or carer fabricates the symptoms of, or deliberately induces, illness in a child.

Emotional Abuse

1.31 Emotional abuse is the persistent emotional maltreatment of a child such as to cause severe and persistent adverse effects on the child's emotional development. It may involve conveying to children that they are worthless or unloved, inadequate, or valued only insofar as they meet the needs of another person. It may feature age or developmentally inappropriate expectations being imposed on children. These may include interactions that are beyond the child's developmental capability, as well as overprotection and limitation of exploration and learning, or preventing the child participating in normal social interaction. It may involve seeing or hearing the ill-treatment of another. It may involve serious bullying, causing children frequently to feel frightened or in danger, or the exploitation or corruption of children. Some level of emotional abuse is involved in all types of maltreatment of a child, though it may occur alone.

Sexual Abuse

1.32 Sexual abuse involves forcing or enticing a child or young person to take part in sexual activities, including prostitution, whether or not the child is aware of what is happening. The activities may involve physical contact, including penetrative (e.g. rape, buggery or oral sex) or non-penetrative acts. They may include non-contact activities, such as involving children in looking at, or in the production of, sexual online images, watching sexual activities, or encouraging children to behave in sexually inappropriate ways.

Neglect

1.33 Neglect is the persistent failure to meet a child's basic physical and/or psychological needs, likely to result in the serious impairment of the child's health or development. Neglect may occur during pregnancy as a result of maternal substance abuse. Once a child is born, neglect may involve a parent or carer failing to:

i. provide adequate food, clothing and shelter (including exclusion from home or abandonment)
ii. protect a child from physical and emotional harm or danger
iii. ensure adequate supervision (including the use of inadequate care-givers)
iv. ensure access to appropriate medical care or treatment.

It may also include neglect of, or unresponsiveness to, a child's basic emotional needs.

The Department of Health's *Child Protection – Messages from Research* (1995) outlines some of the difficulties involved in defining what is 'abusive':

> A look at changes over the last century would suggest that the threshold beyond which child abuse is considered to occur is gradually being lowered. This is happening for a variety of reasons, including an emphasis on the rights of children as individuals, ease of disclosures, the influence of feminist social theories about victimisation and public expectation that the state should intervene in the privacy of family life. Society continually reconstructs definitions of maltreatment which sanction intervention; in 1871 the concern was abuse by adoptive parents; in 1885 it was teenage prostitution; in 1923 incest; then, later, neglect, physical abuse, sexual and emotional abuse. The state remains selective in its concerns and there is a difference between behaviour known to be harmful to children and behaviour which attracts the attention of child protection practitioners. For example, professionals' interest in school bullying is perhaps not as great as parents and children would wish it to be and domestic violence is only just beginning to achieve salience as a cause of concern. Jane Gibbons helpfully summarises the situation when she says that 'as a phenomenon, child maltreatment is more like pornography than whooping cough. It is a socially constructed phenomenon which reflects values and opinions of a particular culture at a particular time'.

QUESTIONS

i. Can you think of any cultures in which it would not be considered abusive to deliberately inflict injury upon a child, or for an adult to have sexual intercourse with a child?
ii. Is corporal punishment of a child abusive, or is 'moderate chastisement' an aspect of parental responsibility?
iii. Would you expect there to be widespread agreement about what is emotional abuse or neglect? (See above, Chapter 8.)

Working Together (2006) describes the process of referral:

> 5.16 If somebody believes that a child may be suffering, or be at risk of suffering, significant harm, then they should always refer their concerns to LA children's social care. In addition to social care, the police and the NSPCC have powers to intervene in these circumstances. Sometimes concerns will arise within LA children's social care itself, as new information comes to light about a child and family with whom staff are already in contact. While professionals should seek, in general, to discuss any concerns with the family and, where possible, seek their agreement to make referrals to LA children's social care, this should only be done where such discussion and agreement-seeking will not place a child at increased risk of significant harm.
>
> ...
>
> 5.19 Sharing of information in cases of concern about children's welfare enables professionals to consider jointly how to proceed in the best interests of the child and to safeguard children more generally.
>
> 5.20 In dealing with alleged offences involving a child victim, the police should normally work in partnership with children's social care and/or other agencies. While the responsibility to

instigate a criminal investigation rests with the police, they should consider the views expressed by other agencies. There will be less serious cases where, after discussion, it is agreed that the best interests of the child are served by a children's social care led intervention rather than a full police investigation.

5.21 In deciding whether there is a need to share information, professionals need to consider their legal obligations, including whether they have a duty of confidentiality to the child. Where there is such a duty, the professional may lawfully share information if the child consents or if there is a public interest of sufficient force. This must be judged by the professional on the facts of each case. Where there is a clear risk of significant harm to a child, or serious harm to adults, the public interest test will almost certainly be satisfied. However, there will be other cases where practitioners will be justified in sharing some confidential information in order to make decisions on sharing further information or taking action – the information shared should be proportionate.

5.22 The child's best interests must be the overriding consideration in making any such decision, including in the cases of underage sexual activity . . . The cross-Government guidance, *Information sharing: Practitioners' guide*, provides advice on these issues – see www.everychildmatters.gov.uk.

For health professionals, the normal rules of confidentiality may well be overridden. The General Medical Council advice appears in *GMC Confidentiality: Protecting and Providing Information* (2004) (http://www.gmc-uk.org/guidance/current/library/confidentiality):

Disclosures Where a Patient May be a Victim of Neglect or Abuse

29. If you believe a patient to be a victim of neglect or physical, sexual or emotional abuse and that the patient cannot give or withhold consent to disclosure, you must give information promptly to an appropriate responsible person or statutory agency, where you believe that the disclosure is in the patient's best interests. If, for any reason, you believe that disclosure of information is not in the best interests of an abused or neglected patient, you should discuss the issues with an experienced colleague. If you decide not to disclose information, you must be prepared to justify your decision.

The framework for children's services is set out in the Children Act 2004, which establishes a structure for the management, inspection and improvement of services for children. There is a Director of Children's Services and an elected 'lead member' for children's services in each local authority area, and a Local Safeguarding Children's Board (LSCB). A major aspect to their work is provided by section 47 of the Children Act 1989 which imposes extensive obligations upon local authorities to investigate cases of suspected child abuse and take action where necessary, and upon other agencies to assist them.

QUESTION

If everything goes dreadfully wrong, should there be a right of action against the local authority or any other body available to (i) the child who has been injured by the parent;

(ii) the parent who cried out for support from the Social Services but did not receive it; (iii) the wrongly accused parent whose child has been removed or placed on a protection register as a result of a diagnosis that is incorrect; and (iv) the social worker who was criticised in a subsequent report but who did not receive sufficient training? (See *JD & ors v East Berkshire Community Health* [2003] EWCA Civ 1151 (CA); *JD (FC) v East Berkshire Community Health NHS Trust & ors* [2005] UKHL 23 (HL), and don't forget to re-read Article 6 of the EConHR.)

There is Government guidance in *Working Together* (most recently, 2006) (http://www.everychildmatters.gov.uk). The 'Every Child Matters' website makes clear that the framework is not just about stopping children and young people from being harmed by adults. It is about 'doing all kinds of things to help every child and young person to be safe, healthy, happy and successful.' Co-operation between health, education and social services, and the police, is seen as the key to effective protection by the 'Every Child Matters' team at the Department for Children, Schools and Families (DCSF).

The reasons for co-operation appeared as long ago as the White Paper, *The Law on Child Care and Family Services* (1987):

> 42. Under existing legislation the local authority have a duty to investigate cases where information is received which suggests that there are grounds for care proceedings. The Review proposed that this should be replaced by a more active duty to investigate in any case where it is suspected that the child is suffering harm or is likely to do so. The Government endorse that proposal and accept that the enquiries made should be such as are necessary to enable the local authority to decide what action, if any, to take.
>
> 43. The Jasmine Beckford Report declared that there were powerful reasons why the duty on local authorities or health authorities to co-operate under section 22 of the NHS Act 1977 should in the context of child abuse be made more specific, to include the duty to consult and the duty to assist by advice and the supply of information so as to help in the management of such cases. Such a duty would, it was argued, operate as a positive and practical step to promote multidisciplinary working in this area, which is important not only at the stage of identification of abuse but also in subsequent follow-up action. The Government accept this view, and therefore intend to make legal provision for co-operation between statutory and voluntary agencies in the investigation of harm and protection of children at risk.

The importance of co-operation is emphasised in *Every Child Matters: Cross-Government Working with local partners to achieve better outcomes for children and young people* (DCSF, 2007):

> It has often proved difficult to establish the exact impact of multi-agency working, mainly because of the difficulty of isolating why and how a particular outcome has been achieved. This is changing as major programmes are evaluated... School staff working with child and adolescent mental health services (CAMHS) identified that the joint work has led to an increase in children's happiness and well-being. They identified a measurable improvement in children's behaviour in two areas of the services reviewed, and better peer relationships were identified by workers... In its first two-years of operation the Darnell and Tinsley On Track service reported a 50% reduction in levels of crime among 10-12 year olds and a 50% reduction in the number of referrals to social services of children and young people aged 0 to 17, against a city wide backdrop of just over 25%... Practitioners with backgrounds in single, traditional agencies report high levels of satisfaction with multi-agency working. In particular, they feel liberated from the narrow bureaucratic

and cultural constraints of their parent organization . . . and many value the opportunity to take a more holistic approach to the needs of children.

After referral, the local authority (or NSPCC) must call an initial Child Protection Conference. We summarise below the persons that *Working Together* (2006) suggests may be invited to attend:

(i) family members (including in some cases the wider family);
(ii) social services staff who have undertaken assessment of the child and family;
(iii) former and current foster carers, in appropriate cases;
(iv) professionals who are or have been involved with the child;
(v) professionals who are or have been involved with the parents;
(vi) police officers who have been involved in inquiries;
(vii) a representative of the local authority legal services;
(viii) NSPCC or other voluntary organisation.

There should be a written report that summarises the information. *Working Together* (2006) states that the Report should contain information on the following five matters:

(i) a chronology;
(ii) information regarding the health and development of the child;
(iii) information regarding the capacity of the parents and other family members to protect the child from harm and to promote the child's development;
(iv) the wishes and feelings of the child and other family members;
(v) analysis of the implications of the information obtained for the child's future welfare.

One possible result of a Conference is for a decision to be made to register the child on the Child Protection Register under one or more of the following headings: physical, emotional or sexual abuse; or neglect.

QUESTIONS

i. A study of forty serious case reviews, half of them conducted before and half after the introduction of the guidance in *Working Together* (1999), found that professionals were being helped to focus on the issues, but that the wide variation of characteristics and circumstances of the children meant that findings in one review were of little help in predicting child abuse (R. Sinclair and R. Bullock, *Learning from past experience: a review of serious case reviews* (2002)). So what is the point of all these reviews?

ii. In *Local Safeguarding Children Boards: A Review of Progress* (2007), it is reported that the review team did not come across much evidence about the engagement or otherwise of parents and carers with the LSCBs, and that LSCBs were finding it difficult to engage with children in any meaningful way. Do you think that it matters, and if it does matter, can you suggest any ways by which the LSCBs can improve their contact with parents and children?

iii. Can you see any risks in the model of a multi-agency working in the area of suspected child abuse, and if so to whom would they apply?

iv. John is reported as arriving at school without having had any breakfast, and in clothes that are too small for him and worn out. The mother informs the Child Protection Conference that she has no money. Should the Conference place John on the child protection register?

Let us now look at two of the leading cases:

D v National Society for Prevention of Cruelty to Children
[1978] AC 171, [1977] 1 All ER 589, House of Lords

Lord Diplock:

...The uncontradicted evidence of the director of the NSPCC is that the work of the society is dependent upon its receiving prompt information of suspected child abuse and that, as might be expected, the principal sources of such information are neighbours of the child's family or doctors, school-teachers, health visitors and the like who will continue to be neighbours or to maintain the same relationship with the suspected person after the matter has been investigated and dealt with by the NSPCC. The evidence of the director is that without an effective promise of confidentiality neighbours and others would be very hesitant to pass on to the society information about suspected child abuse. There is an understandable reluctance to 'get involved' in something that is likely to arouse the resentment of the person whose suspected neglect or ill-treatment of a child has been reported....

The fact that information has been communicated by one person to another in confidence, however, is not of itself a sufficient ground from protecting from disclosure in a court of law the nature of the information or the identity of the informant if either of these matters would assist the court to ascertain facts which are relevant to an issue on which it is adjudicating.... The private promise of confidentiality must yield to the general public interest that in the administration of justice truth will out, unless by reason of the character of the information or the relationship of the recipient...to the informant, a more important public interest is served by protecting the information or the identity of the informant from disclosure in a court of law. The public interest which the NSPCC relies on as obliging it to withhold from the respondent and from the court itself material that could disclose the identity of the society's informant is analagous to the public interest that is protected by the well-established rule of law that the identity of police informers may not be disclosed in a civil action, whether by the process of discovery or by oral evidence at the trial (*Marks v Beyfus* (1890) 25 QBD 494; 59 LJQB 479)...in *Rogers v Home Secretary* [1973] AC 388, [1972] 2 All ER 1057 this House did not hesitate to extend to persons from whom the Gaming Board received information for the purposes of the exercise of their statutory functions, under the Gaming Act 1968, immunity from disclosure of their identity analogous to that which the law had previously accorded to police informers. Your Lordships' sense of values might well be open to reproach if this House were to treat the confidentiality of information given to those who are authorised by statute to institute proceedings for the protection of neglected or ill-treated children as entitled to less favourable treatment in a court of law than information given to the Gaming Board so that gaming may be kept clean.

QUESTIONS

i. Should busy-bodies be encouraged or discouraged?

ii. At 31 March 2006, there were more boys subject to a child protection plan than girls, and this has been the position for a decade or more. The position some twenty years ago was the reverse. Can you think of any reason for this?

iii. Thirteen per cent of the children registered during 2006/07 had previously been registered. What does this tell us?

R v Harrow London Borough Council, ex p D [1990] Fam 133
[1990] 3 All ER 12, [1989] 3 WLR 1239, Court of Appeal

Following divorce proceedings, the mother was granted custody of three children, with fortnightly access to the father and a supervision order to the local authority. Access to the two elder children had been a cause of continuing litigation between the parents and there was a dispute over the paternity of the youngest child. In May 1986, following the father's allegations that the children were victims of physical abuse by the mother, the eldest child was examined by a paediatrician, who found serious bruising and formed the view that the injuries were non-accidental. The child accused the mother of inflicting the injuries. A place of safety order was obtained and the two elder children were detained overnight in hospital where they were examined by a consultant paediatrician the following day. The youngest child was never removed from home. The paediatrician found injuries to the eldest child, that were incompatible with the mother's account. In June 1986 a case conference was convened, attended by the two paediatricians and the headmistress of the children's school. The mother's request to attend was refused but she was allowed to and did make written representations. As a result of the conference, the names of the children and the mother were placed on the 'at risk' register. The two children were then returned home. The mother applied for judicial review of the local authority's decision, on the basis that the conclusion of the case conference and the subsequent placing of the mother's and children's names on the register were unfair and unreasonable and contrary to natural justice. The judge dismissed the application and the mother appealed. The local authority contended, *inter alia*, that judicial review did not lie in respect of a decision to place a name on the register.

Butler-Sloss LJ:

...Before the judge it was argued that the mother should have been permitted to attend the case conference and to have been heard. That suggestion is not pursued before this court. Rather, it is urged upon us that the lowest degree of fairness to the mother, the opportunity to know about and to be allowed to meet the material allegations made against her, was not afforded to her. It is said that the decision was unfair, and the decision-making process was defective on *Wednesbury* principles.

[Counsel], for the appellant mother, made a number of points. The effect of entry on the register, even if the names of the children are subsequently removed, is to leave a stigma on the character of the mother. He asserts that the inclusion of the name of the mother in the register was the equivalent of a 'finding of guilt', that she had physically abused J. The record of J reads:

> '3. Nature of injury and by whom inflicted, whether child abuse has been substantiated: bruise on back and forehead, graze on side of nose, near eye (black eye), inflicted by mother. Child abuse substantiated.'

That finding had to be on the basis of suitable evidence which she was entitled to know about and to have an opportunity to answer. He accepts that not all the minutiae require to be disclosed, but asserts that relevant and important matters were taken into account without prior disclosure.

The case conference was given background information about the family, which included the information that the child J had previously been on the register shortly after birth in 1979 for about 2 years. The mother says that she was unaware of that fact, and the accuracy of that statement was not explored. There were other matters relating to why J did not attend swimming lessons, why the children did not drink milk at school, the failure of the mother to take the youngest for medical check-ups, the explanation for an earlier accident to D and the failure of the social workers to ask the mother for an explanation of the injuries to J.

In the context of these facts, the earlier registration was of peripheral relevance.

What was critical was whether the mother was responsible for J's injuries. What the mother required was an opportunity of giving her account as to how these injuries could have occurred, and this was given to her by the consultant paediatrician. She took advantage of the opportunity to give her account, both orally and in written representations.

The child J was clearly on the register as a result of the findings and conclusions of the consultant paediatrician, together with the allegations of the child J and the unsatisfactory explanations of the mother. The failure of a social worker to elicit an explanation from the mother was not only understandable but, in my view, probably wise. In allegations of physical injury, the most appropriate person to be given the account of the parent is likely to be the paediatrician who is often specially qualified to assess its probability in the light of the type, place, severity and other aspects of the injuries which have occurred.

Although the mother's request to attend, be represented and speak at the case conference was refused, [counsel for the mother] does not submit that the case conference erred in that respect. She was permitted to make written representations, both from herself and a friend. The representations were placed before the case conference. The decision to place the name of J on the register cannot, in my view, be faulted. [Counsel for the mother] accepts that if J's name was properly there, the inclusion of the other children was reasonable since they would be at risk.

I am satisfied that the procedure and the result did not in any way offend the *Wednesbury* principles. The conclusion of the judge was that the appellant failed 'to show that the decision was in any way unfair, unreasonable, or contrary to natural justice' (see [1989] 2 FLR 51, at p.55F).

I agree with him.

That would be sufficient to dispose of this matter, but it has been contended by the respondent council that judicial review does not lie in respect of a decision to place a name upon the child abuse register. [Counsel for the local authority] also submits that the decision of Waite J to grant judicial review of such a decision in *R v Norfolk County Council, ex p X* [1989] 2 FLR 120 was wrong. The facts in the Norfolk case were very different, of a plumber working in a house where a teenage girl made allegations of sexual abuse by him. She had twice previously been the victim of sexual abuse, and a few days later made similar allegations against another man. The plumber's name was entered in the child abuse register as an abuser, after a case conference. His employers were informed and suspended him, pending an internal inquiry. The first knowledge the plumber had of the allegations was the letter informing him of the decision to place his name on the register. He was not told that his employers had been informed. Although the contents of the register are confidential, a significant number of people inevitably have to be aware of the information contained in it. As the Norfolk case demonstrates, the effect upon outsiders may be dramatic. If the decision to register can be shown to be utterly unreasonable, in principle I cannot see why an application to review the decision cannot lie. In coming to its decision, the local authority is exercising a most important public function which can have serious consequences for the child and the alleged abuser. I respectfully agree with the decision of Waite J.

It would also seem that recourse to judicial review is likely to be, and undoubtedly ought to be rare. Local authorities have laid on them by Parliament the specific duty of protection of children in their area. The case conference has a duty to make an assessment as to abuse and the abuser, if sufficient information is available. Of its nature, the mechanism of the case conference leading to the decision to place names on the register, and the decision-making process, is unstructured and informal.

It is accepted by [Counsel for the mother] that it is not a judicial process. It is part of a protection package for a child believed to have been the victim of abuse.

In balancing adequate protection to the child and fairness to an adult, the interest of an adult may have to be placed second to the needs of the child. All concerned in this difficult and delicate area should be allowed to perform their task without looking over their shoulder all the time for the possible intervention of the court.

Appeal dismissed.

QUESTIONS

i. Do you agree that it was 'probably wise' of the social worker not to 'elicit an explanation' from the mother?

ii. What are the objections to parental attendance at case conferences? What are the advantages?

iii. What are the objections to a more structured and formal procedure at case conferences? What are the advantages (a) to the child, (b) to the parents or carers, or (c) to third parties?

The Safeguarding Vulnerable Groups Act 2006 creates the Independent Safeguarding Agency that bars people from working with children and/or vulnerable adults.

QUESTIONS

i. Suppose that a local authority is convinced that a man, trained as a teacher, has downloaded indecent images of children on to his home computer, but there has never been a successful prosecution. Suppose also that the Independent Safeguarding Authority place his name on the list of those considered as unsuitable to work with children on the grounds of harm to a child (Safeguarding Vulnerable Groups Act 2006 Schedule 3 Part 1 paragraph 4(2)(a)). If he moves into a household with a single mother and two small children, should the local authority warn her that he has been placed on the Children's Safeguarding List?

ii. What can the man above do to have his name removed from the list? (See section 4 of the Safeguarding Vulnerable Groups Act 2006.)

An important part of the investigation, particularly when sexual abuse is suspected, is to 'interview' the child. Any interview which does not follow the guidance given in the report of the *Inquiry into Child Abuse in Cleveland 1987* (1988) will certainly attract judicial criticism.

12.1 An essential part of the investigation of an allegation or a complaint of sexual abuse will be an interview with the child if he or she is old enough to say what did or did not happen to them. The child telling of abuse was often referred to as 'in disclosure' and assisting the child to talk of it as 'disclosure work'. The use and potential abuse of 'disclosure work' was the subject of a considerable amount of evidence to the Inquiry. Dr David Jones defined 'disclosure' as: 'a clinically useful concept to describe the process by which a child who has been sexually abused within the family gradually comes to inform the outside world of his/her plight'. He defined 'disclosure work' as: the 'process by which professionals attempt to encourage or hasten the natural process of disclosure by a sexually abused child'.

12.2 The young child may speak innocently of behaviour which an adult recognises as abuse; an older child may wish to unburden and tell of abuse to anyone they may trust and that may occur informally to, for instance, a parent, school teacher, paediatrician on a medical examination or foster mother. Dr Zeitlin told us that: 'There is evidence that material produced spontaneously without prompting is undoubtedly the most reliable form of statements that children make, and often these have been made before disclosure interviews to various people.' However as a step in the inter-disciplinary investigation of sexual abuse there needs to be the formal process of interviewing the child.

12.3 During the Inquiry the question as to whether any child involved was or was not telling the truth was not an issue. The problems related to the interpretation by professionals of the comments of children who were not making clear allegations against their parents. Nevertheless, the question of whether or not to believe the child where there is concern about sexual abuse is important and evidence was given to the Inquiry about it.

12.4 What should an adult do when a child speaks of abuse? According to Dr Bentovim, until a few years ago, it was the practice for professionals to disbelieve the child. He said: 'If a child described a sexual experience, you first of all disbelieved and it had to be proven to you, rather than you first of all taking it seriously and saying he is entitled to belief and then obviously investigating it properly and thoroughly.'

12.10 When the possibility of sexual abuse is raised the formal interview with a child of sufficient age and understanding is a necessary step in the investigation. Different types of interview must be distinguished and the purposes for which the interview is being held must be clear.

...

Disclosure Work

12.18 The problem arises when there is reason to believe there may be abuse and the child may need help to tell, or where the assessment to that date is inconclusive and then a somewhat different type of interview may take place. This is a second or so-called facilitative stage which needs further consideration. The interviewer at this time may be trying a more indirect approach, with the use of hypothetical or leading questions, or taking cue from the child's play or drawings. According to Dr Bentovim, it should be used sparingly by experts, who may include suitably trained social workers....

12.19 There is a danger, which should be recognised and avoided from the experience in Cleveland, that this facilitative second stage may be seen as a routine part of the general interview, instead of a useful tool to be used sparingly by experts in special cases. In the first stage the child tells the interviewer. The second stage is a process whereby the professional attempts to encourage the child who may be reluctant to tell the story.

...

Agreement of the Professionals

12.34 All those who provided evidence to the Inquiry were agreed on the following points to be observed conducting all interviews. We endorse their views:

1. The undesirability of calling them 'disclosure' interviews, which precluded the notion that sexual abuse might not have occurred.
2. All interviews should be undertaken only by those with some training, experience and aptitude for talking with children.
3. The need to approach each interview with an open mind.
4. The style of the interview should be open-ended questions to support and encourage the child in free recall.
5. There should be where possible only one and not more than two interviews for the purpose of evaluation, and the interview should not be too long.
6. The interview should go at the pace of the child and not of the adult.
7. The setting for the interview must be suitable and sympathetic.
8. It must be accepted that at the end of the interview the child may have given no information to support the suspicion of sexual abuse and position will remain unclear.
9. There must be careful recording of the interview and what the child says, whether or not there is a video recording.
10. It must be recognised that the use of facilitative techniques may create difficulties in subsequent court proceedings.
11. The great importance of adequate training for all those engaged in this work.
12. In certain circumstances it may be appropriate to use the special skills of a 'facilitated' interview. That type of interview should be treated as a second stage. The interviewer must be conscious of the limitations and strengths of the techniques employed. In such cases the interview should only be conducted by those with special skills and specific training.

Parents at Interviews

12.35 The professionals who gave evidence to the Inquiry were unanimous about the unsuitability of having a parent present at an interview held because of the suspicion of sexual abuse. Dr Bentovim said the presence of parents made the interview very difficult, but the presence of a person familiar to the child, such as teacher or social worker, may be helpful to the child. However he/she must not take part in the interview.

QUESTION

What difficulties can you think of that the use of the 'facilitative technique' might cause in any subsequent court hearing?

11.4 ASSESSMENT AND PROTECTION ORDERS

The *Cleveland Report* (1988) described something remarkably like abuse:

Place of Safety Orders

10.6 The initial route to the Juvenile Court was by way of place of safety orders. Between 1st January and 31st July 1987, 276 place of safety orders were applied for by social workers under the powers granted in s.28 of the Children and Young Persons Act 1969. ... All but one application appears to have been made ex parte, that is to say without the parent present, and none appears to have been refused.

...

10.7 The Social Services Department operated a highly interventionist policy in the use of place of safety orders. The effect of their general approach to the use of these orders was accentuated by the memorandum of the 29th May issued by Mr Bishop, directing social workers to apply for them on receiving a diagnosis of child sexual abuse from a paediatrician. Further a trend away from applications for the maximum 28 days to periods not exceeding 7 days as advocated in their manual was not maintained in 1987 and was specifically reversed in early June. ...

10.8 Before the crisis period of May/June and before the 29th May memorandum a number of place of safety orders in cases of diagnosis of sexual abuse were applied for and granted for 28 days. The reason for the longer order was not so much the need to protect the child as the need perceived by social workers to have sufficient time to engage in 'disclosure work' with the child.

10.9 Of the 276 orders 227 were applied for out of hours by the Emergency Duty Team. The majority of the orders were likely to have been granted during the day. We learnt however that of those 227, 174 were heard by a single magistrate at home, during the hours of court sittings, despite a clear understanding between the Clerk to the Justices and the Social Services Department that social workers would make these applications in the first instance to the full court. ...

Interim Care Orders

10.10 During early June the numbers of interim care orders applied for dramatically increased. On Monday 8th June there were 45 applications for interim care orders waiting to be heard. This increase in the workload led the Clerk to the Justices, Mr Cooke, to talk to one of the Court Liaison Officers, Mr Morris to discuss the implications for resources and to ask for a meeting with the Director of Social Services. In the evidence to the Inquiry there was some difference of recollection as to what was said between Mr Cooke and Mr Morris. Mr Morris went away with the impression that Mr Cooke was suggesting that Social Services should apply for 28 day orders to ease the strain on the courts, and he then advised the Emergency Duty Team to apply for 28 day orders. ...

Level of Concern

10.13 Mr Davies said that there were three matters of special concern to magistrates receiving the applications.

1. The effect on the courts of applications which were increasing in volume and complexity. There was great concern about the backlog of cases and the delay to the regular work of the courts.
2. Prior to 1987 it was not the practice of the Social Services Department to refuse access to parents on the obtaining of a place of safety order and this approach was known to the Bench. Mr Morris told us that in the past access was almost invariably granted and

denial was a marked change of policy. The requirement of separation of child from parents during 'disclosure work', which might take weeks or months was a new development. Mr Davies said that the denial of access on a place of safety order or on an interim care order was recognised by the magistrates as a most serious deprivation for parents and children and knowledge that it was now a common practice was a matter of deep concern. The reason for denying access in particular circumstances was known to the magistrates but there was unease that access might be denied too readily.

3. The conflict of medical evidence was also of great concern. Mr Davies told us that: 'It was the first time in my experience that Teesside magistrates had been invited to assess the quality of conflicting medical evidence provided by experts in child abuse.' Mr Cooke said that his magistrates were not used to dealing with that sort of thing....

QUESTIONS

i. What level of concern do you think might justify removing a child and keeping him away from his parents for weeks in order to undertake disclosure work?

ii. Look back to the discussion of *without notice* orders in domestic violence cases on p. 316. Why do you think that well-meaning social workers prefer to remove the child before telling the parents that they are bringing proceedings?

As for the law, the Cleveland Report supported the proposals, made in the *Review of Child Care Law* (1985) and the White Paper (1987), to replace place of safety orders with a new 'emergency protection order'.

The grounds for an order are these:

44.—(1) Where any person ('the applicant') applies to the court for an order to be made under this section with respect to a child, the court may make the order if, but only if it is satisfied that—

(a) there is reasonable cause to believe that the child is likely to suffer significant harm if—
  (i) he is not removed to accommodation provided by or on behalf of the applicant; or
  (ii) he does not remain in the place in which he is then being accommodated;

(b) in the case of an application made by a local authority—
  (i) the enquiries are being made with respect to the child under section 47(1)(b); and
  (ii) those enquiries are being frustrated by access to the child being unreasonably refused to a person authorised to seek access and that the applicant has a reasonable cause to believe that access to the child is required as a matter of urgency; or

(c) in the case of an application made by an authorised person—
  (i) the applicant has reasonable cause to suspect that a child is suffering, or is likely to suffer, significant harm;
  (ii) the applicant is making enquiries with respect to the child's welfare; and
  (iii) those enquiries are being frustrated by access to the child being unreasonably refused to a person authorised to seek access and the applicant has reasonable cause to believe that access to the child is required as a matter of urgency.

As the Department of Health *Guidance* (1991) observes:

> 4.44 As with all orders under the Act, even where the above conditions apply the court will not automatically make an emergency protection order. It must still consider the welfare principle and the presumption of no order [see pp. 481 and 498, above]. In most cases it is unlikely that the parents will be present at the hearing. With only one side of the case before it the court will want to examine very carefully the information it is given, especially where the basis of the application is likelihood of future harm or inability to see the child. It may be that the initial order will be made for a very short time such as the next available hearing date so that an extension to the order will be on notice to parents and others.

Sadly, the approach as set out above is sometimes ignored, both by social workers and by the Family Proceedings Court, as McFarlane J found out in *Re X: Emergency Protection Orders* [2006] EWHC 510 (Fam) High Court, Family Division.

Prior to the commencement of the proceedings, X had always lived at home, the father suffered from a schizo-affective disorder and there was some suggestion that the mother suffered from the condition known as 'fabricated or induced illness invented by the mother' sometimes referred to as Munchausen's Syndrome by Proxy. After concern about X's behaviour at home and at school, her name was entered on the Child Protection Register in the category of 'emotional abuse'. At a subsequent case conference, the social worker received information from a nurse that the mother was at the hospital requesting that X be seen by a doctor for stomach pain, despite the fact that the triage nurse had assessed her and considered that there was no problem. An application for an Emergency Protection Order was made immediately, without notice to the parents, and granted that afternoon. The social workers attended the hospital with four uniformed police officers and removed X from her mother's care. X was placed in emergency foster placement.

The trial judge takes up the story:

McFarlane J:

Care proceedings were then commenced. At that time the local authority asserted that the child was being emotionally abused. The social services' stated concerns for the child's wellbeing were wide ranging and included:

a) Possible sexual abuse;
b) Unhealthy beliefs within the family regarding spirits and ghosts;
c) Symptoms of illness being fabricated or induced in the child;
d) The mother's anxiety about the child being bullied at school, where the school have found no evidence of this; and
e) The father's history of mental ill-health.

[17] A central plank of the social services case was that this was a case of fabricated or induced illness (previously referred to a Munchausen's Syndrome by Proxy). This was clearly the factor that was uppermost in the minds of the social workers when, having heard that the mother was at the hospital, they determined that the child needed to be immediately removed from her parents' care. X had indeed received medical attention in the previous months and years. However no doctor had ever raised any question relating to induced or fabricated illness. Despite the fact that the social workers had entertained the view for some weeks that this was such a case, at no time did they seek any medical advice. Moreover, once the care proceedings began and the local authority lawyers set out that the case was based on an allegation of induced or fabricated illness, even at that stage the local authority made no attempt to obtain a medical opinion on the

point. In the course of the guidance that follows, I will give specific attention to cases of alleged induced or fabricated illness.

[18] Finally, by way of background, it should be recorded that one year after X was taken into care, and only after receipt of all of the expert assessments that were prepared for these proceedings, the local authority abandoned its reliance upon any allegation of sexual abuse or induced/fabricated illness. The case thus proceeded on the basis solely of allegations of emotional abuse to X. At the conclusion of the hearing I found that the threshold criteria of 'significant harm' under CA 1989, s 31 were not established. With the agreement of all parties, I made X a ward of the High Court for a short period in order facilitate the child's return home and the provision for support to the family as they began to rebuild their life together.

[19] The local authority's actions on the 23rd November 2004 in applying for and obtaining the EPO based on the social worker's uninformed opinion that this was a case of fabricated illness were described by counsel for the mother as 'outrageous' and 'inexcusable' leading, as it did, to 'the destruction of this family's ordinary life'; such descriptions do not, in my view, overstate the quality of what took place on that day.

[20] The child protection system depends upon the skill, insight and sheer hard work of front line social workers. Underlying those key features, there is a need for social workers to feel supported and valued by the courts, the state and the general populace to a far greater degree than is normally the case. Working in overstretched teams with limited resources, social workers frequently have to make crucial decisions, with important implications, on issues of child protection; often of necessity these decisions must be based upon the available information which may be inchoate or partial. There are often risks to a child flowing from every available option (risk of harm if the child stays at home, risk of emotional harm at least if the child is removed). It is said that in these situations, social workers are 'damned if they do, and damned if they don't' take action. Despite these difficulties, it is my experience that very frequently social workers 'get it right' and take the right action, for the right reasons, based upon a professional and wise evaluation of the available information. Such cases sadly do not hit the headlines, or warrant lengthy scrutiny in a High Court judgment. I say 'sadly' because there is a need for successful social work, of which there are many daily examples, to be applauded and made known to the public at large.

[21] I wish to record without hesitation that I have found no evidence of any malevolent or unprofessional motive featuring in the actions of any of the individual social workers who have been involved in the case. They had, I am sure, only a desire to meet X's needs (as they perceived them to be) as their motive. The only exception to this generalised observation might have been with respect to team manager's actions in giving the evidence that she gave at the EPO hearing, but, as she was not in a position to be asked directly about this (because the material to challenge her was only available after she had given evidence) I am not able to express a concluded view on her motives.

[22] Against the background that I have described in the previous paragraph, it gives me absolutely no pleasure to have to record the multiple failings of the local authority in this case in its involvement in the life of this family. To do so was necessary not only in order to come to a conclusion on the issues in this case, but also in order that lessons may be learned for the future in other cases.

The judge said that where the need, correctly perceived by the case conference and the social workers, was for expert assessment, then the proper course if indeed there had been a failure by the parents to cooperate in the assessment process, was for an application for a Child Assessment Order under section 43, or issuing section 31 proceedings for an interim care order and seeking the court's directions under section 38(6) for assessment.

The purpose of the section 43 Assessment Order is explained in the Departmental of Health *Guidance* (1991) as follows:

4.6 The child assessment order, established by section 43, had no parallel in previous legislation. It deals with the single issue of enabling an assessment of the child to be made where significant harm is suspected but the child is not thought to be at immediate risk (requiring his removal, or keeping him in hospital), the local authority or authorised person considers that an assessment is required, and the parents or other persons responsible for him have refused to co-operate. Its purpose is to allow the local authority or authorised person to ascertain enough about the state of the child's health or development or the way in which he has been treated to decide what further action, if any, is required. It is less interventionist than the emergency protection order, interim care order and interim supervision order and should not be used where the circumstances of the case suggest that one of these orders would be more appropriate.

...

4.9 A child assessment order will usually be most appropriate where the harm to the child is long-term and cumulative rather than sudden and severe. The circumstances may be nagging concern about a child who appears to be failing to thrive; or the parents are ignorant of or unwilling to face up to possible harm to their child because of the state of his health or development; or it appears that the child may be subject to wilful neglect or abuse but not to such an extent as to place him at serious immediate risk. Sexual abuse, which covers a wide range of behaviour, can fall in this category. The harm to the child can be long-term rather than immediate and it does not necessarily require emergency action. However, emergency action should not be avoided where disclosure of the abuse is itself likely to put the child at immediate risk of significant harm and/or where there is an urgent need to gather particular forensic evidence which would not otherwise be forthcoming in relation to the likelihood of significant harm.

...

4.12 The court can allow up to 7 days for the assessment. The order must specify the date which the assessment is to begin. The applicant should make the necessary arrangements in advance of the application, so that it would usually be possible to complete within such a period an initial multidisciplinary assessment of the child's medical, intellectual, emotional, social and behavioural needs.

...

4.15 Section 43(9) provides for keeping the child away from home for the purposes of the assessment. This is intended to be a reserve provision, and if used the number of overnight stays should be kept as low as possible. The assessment should be conducted with as little trauma for the child and parents as possible. It is important that the child assessment order is not regarded as a variant of the emergency protection order with its removal power. The purposes of the two orders are quite different. The child may only be kept away from home in the circumstances specified, namely:

(a) the court is satisfied that it is necessary for the purposes of the assessment;
(b) it is done in accordance with directions specified in the order; and it is limited to such period or periods (which need not be the full period of the order) specified in the order.

QUESTIONS

i. Do you think it is an 'emergency' if the social worker has just found out about the situation?

ii. Research conducted by Masson, Oakley and Pick (2004) suggests that emergency protection orders invariably lead on to care proceedings. Is this of concern to you or does it reassure you that the approach of the social workers and the Family Proceedings Court in *Re X: (Emergency Protection Orders)* may have been unusual?

iii. Are you convinced by the arguments in the Department of Health *Guidance* (1991) of the need for a child assessment order?

iv. Why is it thought less drastic than an emergency protection order?

v. Can a section 38(6) Order be made, to enable treatment and therapy to be provided? (See *Re G* [HL] [2006] UKHL 43.)

vi. The child can be kept away from home during all or part of the assessment in certain circumstances. Are you worried about Article 8 of the EConHR?

Despite the provision of section 1(2) of the Children Act 1989 (see p. 505 above), care proceedings can be a very lengthy process. In *Re X: (Emergency Protection Orders)* it took fourteen months from the initial Emergency Protection Order made by the Family Proceedings Court and the removal of the child from its parents before the matter was dealt with by McFarlane J. According to the Lord Chancellor's Department in *Scoping Study on Delay in Children Act Cases* (2002), when the Children Act 1989 was implemented it was anticipated that it would take an average of twelve weeks for care cases to be resolved. This has rarely been realised in practice. By 1996, care cases were in fact taking 46.1 weeks from the time they started to the time of a final decision. By the end of 2000, this figure had risen again to an average of 50.3 weeks. It reduced slightly in 2001 to 47.1 weeks, but it had increased again to almost a year by October 2005, four times as long as the original projection.

In a Report for the Lord Chancellor's Department published in 1996, Dame Margaret Booth had identified the need for:

- adequate resourcing;
- effective administration;
- more effective procedures for the transfer of cases;
- firm judicial case management;
- more certain timetabling and listing of cases;
- better partnership working.

There have been many attempts to put these principles into practice and to reduce the delay in care cases. A case management protocol, designed to enable the holding of the final hearing within forty weeks of the initial application was first issued in June 2003, and has been revised in the light of experience, two reviews, and a detailed consultation process. The new scheme, the Public Law Outline, came into general application in April 2008, and reduces the court processes to four; namely the Issue and First Appointment, the Case Management Conference, the Issues Resolution Hearing, and the Final Hearing. Emphasis is given to preparation pre-proceedings. There have been attempts to appoint Specific Case Progression Officers to address the cause of delay, help improve case management and case progression between hearings. The Progression Officer is expected to take on a proactive role in ensuring that all court directions and court orders are followed in a timely manner. There have been moves to provide a more flexible use of judges and court facilities, and in particular recorders and district judges have been enabled to take on this work.

QUESTIONS

i. Do you think that it is acceptable for child protection cases to take so long to be completed? Are there any advantages? (See *C v Solihull Metropolitan Borough Council* [1993] 1 FLR 290.)

ii. How can the child be protected during this period? (See Children Act 1989, section 38.)

iii. Lynn Davis in 'Protecting Children in an Emergency - Getting the Balance Right' in *Family Law* vol. 37 (2007) at p. 727 concludes her article as follows: 'Perhaps the resources we are prepared as a society to dedicate to the emergency protection of children are a measure of how much we really care about children in crisis.' Given the resources which have been devoted to the topic as outlined above, do you think that we do care about children in crisis?

It may be better, in some cases, for the child to stay at home while the decision is being made, provided that he can be adequately protected. The Department of Health *Guidance* (1991) talks about removing the alleged abuser rather than the child:

> 4.31 Where the need for emergency action centres on alleged abuse of the child the local authority will always want to explore the possibility of providing services to and/or accommodation for the alleged abuser as an alternative to the removal of the child. This could be on a voluntary basis backed up by the provisions of schedule 2 paragraph 5 which gives authorities the discretion to provide assistance with finding alternative housing or assistance to the person who leaves the family home. Such practical assistance may be crucial in persuading the alleged abuser to co-operate in this way. Existing legislation makes no public law provision empowering a court to order an alleged abuser out of the family home. However, in certain circumstances private law remedies may be used to achieve the same effect, and the local authority should explore these where it is in the child's best interest to do so. The non-abusing parent may agree to apply [for an occupation order], forcing the alleged abuser out of the home. This may be particularly appropriate in sexual abuse cases where the non-abusing parent has no wish to protect or shield the alleged abuser and where immediate removal of the child is not always in the child's best interests.

Occupation orders under the Family Law Act 1996 are considered in Chapter 7, above, but the 1996 Act also amends the Children Act 1989, so that an 'exclusion requirement' may be added to an emergency protection order:

> **44A.**—(1) Where—
>
> (a) on being satisfied as mentioned in section 44(1)(a), (b) or (c), the court makes an emergency protection order with respect to a child, and
>
> (b) the conditions mentioned in subsection (2) are satisfied, the court may include an exclusion requirement in the emergency protection order.
>
> (2) The conditions are—
>
> (a) that there is reasonable cause to believe that, if a person ('the relevant person') is excluded from a dwelling-house in which the child lives, then—

(i) in the case of an order made on the ground mentioned in section 44(1)(a), the child will not be likely to suffer significant harm, even though the child is not removed as mentioned in section 44(1)(a)(i) or does not remain as mentioned in section 44(1)(a)(ii), or

(ii) in the case of an order made on the ground mentioned in paragraph (b) or (c) of section 44(1), the enquiries referred to in that paragraph will cease to be frustrated, and

(b) that another person living in the dwelling-house (whether a parent of the child or some other person)—

(i) is able and willing to give to the child the care which it would be reasonable to expect a parent to give him, and

(ii) consents to the inclusion of the exclusion requirement.

(3) For the purposes of this section an exclusion requirement is any one or more of the following—

(a) a provision requiring the relevant person to leave a dwelling-house in which he is living with the child,

(b) a provision prohibiting the relevant person from entering a dwelling-house in which the child lives, and

(c) a provision excluding the relevant person from a defined area in which a dwelling-house in which the child lives is situated.

(4) The court may provide that the exclusion requirement is to have effect for a shorter period than the other provisions of the order.

(5) Where the court makes an emergency protection order containing an exclusion requirement, the court may attach a power of arrest to the exclusion requirement.

(6) Where the court attaches a power of arrest to an exclusion requirement of an emergency protection order, it may provide that the power of arrest is to have effect for a shorter period than the exclusion requirement.

(7) Any period specified for the purposes of subsection (4) or (6) may be extended by the court (on one or more occasions) on an application to vary or discharge the emergency protection order.

(8) Where a power of arrest is attached to an exclusion requirement of an emergency protection order by virtue of subsection (5), a constable may arrest without warrant any person whom he has reasonable cause to believe to be in breach of the requirement.

(9) Sections 47(7), (11) and (12) and 48 of, and Schedule 5 to, the Family Law Act 1996 shall have effect in relation to a person arrested under subsection (8) of this section as they have effect in relation to a person arrested under section 47(6) of that Act.

(10) If, while an emergency protection order containing an exclusion requirement is in force, the applicant has removed the child from the dwelling-house from which the relevant person is excluded to other accommodation for a continuous period of more than 24 hours, the order shall cease to have effect in so far as it imposes the exclusion requirement.

An exclusion requirement can also be attached to an interim care order under section 38A, which may be renewed as many times as necessary up to the final hearing of the local authority's application.

QUESTIONS

i. Can you think of any reasons why the person mentioned in subs (2)(b) would not apply for an occupation order under the Family Law Act 1996?

ii. Why is it necessary for the local authority to have an emergency protection order, or interim care order, as well as the exclusion requirement?

iii. Should local authorities be able to apply for an order excluding someone from the child's home indefinitely?

Under section 46, where a police officer has reasonable cause to believe that a child would otherwise be likely to suffer significant harm, he may take the child into police protection for up to seventy-two hours.

QUESTION

Why should such a power be thought necessary, and do you see any issues relating to Article 5 of the EConHR?

11.5 THE THRESHOLD TEST

Care proceedings are designed solely for cases where the parents' shortcomings are such that the local authority should assume parental responsibility for the child. The *Review of Child Care Law* (1985) recommended that the criteria for care and supervision orders should focus upon the condition of the child, the shortcomings of the home and the comparative advantages of local authority intervention:

> 15.12 In our view the primary justification for the state to initiate proceedings seeking compulsory powers is actual or likely harm to the child....
>
> ...
>
> 15.14 We consider that newly drafted grounds should make it clear that 'harm' consists of a deficit in or detriment to the standard of health, development and well-being which can reasonably be expected for the particular child. By 'development' we mean not only his physical progress but also his intellectual, emotional and social or behavioural development, so that it is clear that a child who is failing to learn to control his anti-social behaviour as others do is included. We refer to the standard expected for the particular child because some children have characteristics or handicaps which mean that they cannot be expected to be as healthy or well-developed as others, but equally it must be clear that if the child needs special care or attention (perhaps, for example, because he is unusually difficult to control) then this is to be expected for him. However, the standard should only be that which is reasonable to expect, rather than the best that could possibly be achieved, for each particular child. To apply the 'best' standard would be to introduce by other means the risk that a child could be removed from home simply because some other arrangements could cater better for his needs than care by his parents.
>
> 15.15 We consider that, having set an acceptable standard of upbringing for the child, it should be necessary to show some substantial deficit in that standard. Minor short-comings in the health care provided or minor deficits in physical, psychological or social development should

not give rise to compulsory intervention unless they are having, or are likely to have, serious and lasting effects upon the child. The courts are used to assessing degrees of harm, for example in the context of prosecution for assaults, and we consider that they could also do so here.

15.16 The inclusion of 'well-being' in the standard to be expected is intended to cover those deficits which cannot necessarily be described in terms of health or development but which may equally amount to 'harm' to a child. Principal amongst these is ill-treatment. A child who has suffered non-accidental injury may not have suffered any lasting impairment in his health and the resulting emotional damage may be difficult to prove. The same may be said of older children who suffer sexual abuse. We consider that the concept of substantial detriment to their well-being will cover such cases and adequately distinguish between cases of real harm to the child and cases of acceptable variation in parenting standards.

...

15.18 In our view, a requirement that the harm be 'likely' will place a burden of proof upon local authorities which will be sufficiently difficult for them to discharge, especially in relation to mental or emotional harm, and this will prevent unwarranted intervention. A substantial or serious likelihood would be much more difficult to assess than substantial or serious harm and is not recommended. We have also considered whether anticipatory harm should be restricted by reference to specific circumstances from which risk could be inferred. ... However, a list would inevitably leave gaps unless the categories of risk were themselves very broadly expressed. Such broad expression would defeat the purpose of having express reasons for apprehended harm. In any event, it would perpetuate the arbitrariness and unfairness complained of by the Select Committee, would be complex and unwieldy, and would amount to a consolidation of the existing conditions rather than a genuine simplification in the law.

...

15.20 As regards more specific free-standing conditions,... we do not consider them desirable. Their operation can be arbitrary or unfair and we doubt the traditional claim that specific preconditions of that sort operate to protect parents and children against unwarranted interference by the state. Rather we consider that such specific preconditions in practice may have the opposite effect and operate as magnets for drawing children within the sphere of compulsory care. ...Overall, there is a danger that very specific preconditions lead to a generalised view that once the conditions are satisfied an order follows unless there is some special reason for refusing one. What is more, the section 3 grounds, by focusing on parental unfitness, may have a stigmatising effect which may itself provoke unnecessary conflict and be detrimental to all concerned by unnecessarily prolonging proceedings and adding to their traumatic effects. We therefore, recommend that the sole primary ground should be actual or likely harm.

...

15.23 In our view the ground should also require that the source of the harm is the absence of a reasonable degree of parental care. Put another way, the court should be expressly required to find that the care available to the child is not merely wanting, but falls below an objectively acceptable level or that he is beyond parental control so that he cannot benefit from the care on offer. At present, the use of words such as 'prevented or neglected' or 'avoidably impaired', together with the care or control test in section 1(2), carry with them the flavour of lack of parental care. They fail, however, to express it clearly and more importantly give no indication of how great that failure must be....

15.24 We also consider that the grounds should in future make a clear reference to the likely effectiveness of an order. At present in section 1(2) there is the requirement that the child's need for care or control is unlikely to be met unless the court makes an order. Our impression is that the test is often satisfied by proof that his needs will not be met outside care, rather than by positive proof that a care order or supervision order will result in his needs being met or at least better catered for, and further that intervention will not do more overall harm than good. In our view the matter should be put beyond doubt. We consider that this might be achieved best by linking the idea of effectiveness with the child's best interests, that being the ultimate purpose of an order and in our view itself a matter which needs to be drawn expressly to the court's attention. Accordingly, we think there is a strong case in future for requiring the court to be satisfied before it makes an order that it is the most effective means available to it (including refusing an order) of safeguarding and promoting the child's welfare.

The Children Act 1989 provides as follows:

31.—(1) On the application of any local authority or authorised person, the court may make an order—

(a) placing the child with respect to whom the application is made in the care of a designated local authority; or
(b) putting him under the supervision of a designated local authority or of a probation officer.

(2) A court may only make a care order or supervision order if it is satisfied—

(a) that the child concerned is suffering, or is likely to suffer, significant harm; and
(b) that the harm, or likelihood of harm, is attributable to—
(i) the care given to the child, or likely to be given to him if the order were not made, not being what it would be reasonable to expect a parent to give to him; or
(ii) the child's being beyond parental control.

(3) No care order or supervision order may be made with respect to a child who has reached the age of seventeen (or sixteen, in the case of a child who is married).

(4) An application under this section may be made on its own or in any other family proceedings.

(5) The court may—

(a) on an application for a care order, make a supervision order;
(b) on an application for a supervision order, make a care order.

(6) Where an authorised person proposes to make an application under this section he shall—

(a) if it is reasonably practicable to do so; and
(b) before making the application, consult the local authority appearing to him to be the authority in whose area the child concerned is ordinarily resident.

(7) An application made by an authorised person shall not be entertained by the court if, at the time when it is made, the child concerned is—

(a) the subject of an earlier application for a care order, or supervision order, which has not been disposed of; or
(b) subject to—
(i) a care order or supervision order;
(ii) an order under section 7(7)(b) of the Children and Young Persons Act 1969; or
(iii) a supervision requirement within the meaning of the Social Work (Scotland) Act 1968.

(8) The local authority designated in a care order must be—

(a) the authority within whose area the child is ordinarily resident; or
(b) where the child does not reside in the area of a local authority, the authority within whose area any circumstances arose in consequence of which the order is being made.

(9) In this section—

'authorised person' means—

(a) the National Society for the Prevention of Cruelty to Children and any of its officers; and
(b) any person authorised by order by the Secretary of State to bring proceedings under this section and any officer of a body which is so authorised;

'harm' means ill-treatment or the impairment of health or development [including, for example, impairment suffered from seeing or hearing the ill-treatment of another];

'development' means physical, intellectual, emotional, social or behavioural development;

'health' means physical or mental health; and

'ill-treatment' includes sexual abuse and forms of ill-treatment which are not physical.

(10) Where the question of whether harm suffered by the child is significant turns on the child's health or development, his health or development shall be compared with that which could reasonably be expected of a similar child.

(11) In this Act—

'a care order' means (subject to section 105(1)) an order under subsection (1)(a) and (except where express provision to the contrary is made) includes an interim care order made under section 38; and

'a supervision order' means an order under subsection (1)(b) and (except where express provision to the contrary is made) includes an interim supervision order made under section 38.

31A Care Orders: Care Plans

(1) Where an application is made on which a care order might be made with respect to a child, the appropriate local authority must, within such time as the Court may direct, prepare a plan ('a care plan') for the future care of the child.
(2) While the application is pending, the authority must keep any care plan prepared by them under review and, if they are of the opinion some change is required, revise the plan, or make a new plan, accordingly.
(3) A care plan must give any prescribed information and do so in the prescribed manner.

QUESTIONS

i. Does the idea of a 'similar' child in section 31(10) mean a child (a) with similar physical or psychological characteristics, or (b) of a similar racial, ethnic or religious background?

ii. Do you think that the definition of harm to include 'impairment suffered from seeing or hearing ill-treatment of another' can be capable of objective proof?

iii. When a court assesses whether 'harm' is 'significant', is a court entitled to find that the harm is significant in the case of the particular child?

iv. Is it the responsibility of the local authority to spare children all the consequences of defective parenting? (*See Re L (Care: Threshold criteria)* [2007] Fam Law 297, and *A Local Authority v N, Y and K* [2005] EWHC 2956 (Fam).)

The use of the present tense in the first limb of section 31(2)(a) – 'is suffering' – has caused some difficulty. In *Re M (a minor) (care order: threshold conditions)* [1994] 2AC 424, [1994] 3 All ER 298, HL, when the child, G, was four months old, his mother was murdered by his father. He went to live with foster parents, and his older siblings and half-siblings were looked after by the mother's cousin, Mrs W. The father was sentenced to life imprisonment, with a recommendation that he be deported on release. At first Mrs W did not feel able to care for G, and the local authority applied for a care order. Later Mrs W decided to seek a residence order for G, and the local authority supported this application. However, the child's guardian, and the child's father, argued that G should be adopted. Bracewell J decided that the section 31 threshold test was satisfied because of the harm that the child had suffered when he was deprived of the love and care of his mother. A care order was made. The Court of Appeal, allowing Mrs W's appeal, held that a court must decide whether the child is suffering or is likely to suffer significant harm at the time of the hearing. Since G was being adequately cared for by foster parents at the time of the final hearing, it was not possible to say that he was suffering harm. The father appealed to the House of Lords.

Lord Mackay LC:

...In my opinion the opening words of s. 31 link the making of an order by the court very closely with the application to the court by a local authority or authorised person. Section 31(2) then goes on to specify the conditions which are necessary to be satisfied before the court can make a care order or supervision order, but it is plain from this and the statute as a whole that even if these conditions are satisfied the court is not bound to make an order but must go through the full procedure particularly set out in s.1 of the statute. It is also clear that Parliament expected these cases to proceed with reasonable expedition and in particular I refer to s. 32 in which the hearing by the court is not regarded only as taking place at the time when the applications are disposed of. Indeed, I think there is much to be said for the view that the hearing that Parliament contemplated was one which extended from the time the jurisdiction of the court is first invoked until the case is disposed of and that was required to be done in the light of the general principle that any delay in determining the question is likely to prejudice the welfare of the child. There is nothing in s. 31(2) which in my opinion requires that the conditions to be satisfied are disassociated from the time of the making of the application by the local authority. I would conclude that the natural construction of the conditions in s. 31(2) is that where, at the time the application is to be disposed of, there are in place arrangements for the protection of the child by the local authority on an interim basis which protection has been continuously in place for some time, the relevant date with respect to which the court must be satisfied is the date at which the local authority initiated the procedure for protection under the Act from which these arrangements followed. If after a local authority had initiated protective arrangements the need for these had terminated, because the child's welfare had been satisfactorily provided for otherwise, in any subsequent proceedings it would not be possible to found jurisdiction on the situation at the time of initiation of these arrangements. It is permissible only to look back from the date of disposal to the date of initiation of protection as a result of which local authority arrangements had been continuously in place thereafter to the date of disposal. It has to be borne in mind that this in no way precludes the court from taking account at the date of the hearing of all relevant circumstances. The conditions in sub-s. (2) are in the nature of conditions conferring jurisdiction upon the court to consider whether or not a care order or supervision order should be made. Conditions of that kind would in my view normally have to be satisfied at the date on which the order was first applied for. It would in my opinion be odd if the jurisdiction of the court to make an order depended on how long the court took before it finally disposed of the case....

...In my opinion the provisions of s. 31(2) must be considered before the question of any competing order under the provisions of Pt II of the Act are decided upon. The scheme of

s. 1(3) and (4) and in particular s. 1(3)(g) appears to me to require that the court decide whether or not it has power available to it to make a care order or a supervision order before it decides whether or not to make an order at all and in particular whether or not to consider a s. 8 order. ... It remains to consider what should now be done in the present case. As I said, the information available to your Lordships at the hearing before your Lordships suggests that G's stay with Mrs W has been very satisfactory to date. In the light of the options available, and the provisions of s. 1 of the Children Act 1989, I am of opinion that the choice is between a residence order in favour of Mrs W or a care order as asked for by the appellant father. I am clearly of the view that it would be quite wrong at present to disturb the arrangements presently existing for G's residence and that whether or not a care order is made, the local authority would be perfectly right to continue the present arrangements for G making his home with Mrs W. However, we cannot foresee the future and the learned judge who heard all the evidence did foresee the possibility in the longer term of difficulties. Although I hope that no difficulties will materialise I think it best in the difficult circumstances of this child that your Lordships should restore the care order which will enable the local authority to monitor the progress of the child ...

QUESTIONS

i. If a local authority initially responds to a situation by providing services under section 17, but later decides to seek a care order, can it argue that 'protective arrangements' have been continuously in place?

ii. An 18-month-old boy has been accommodated by the local authority since birth. His mother was homeless and immature, but she now has a decent home to offer. Can the local authority apply for a care order on the grounds that the child 'is suffering' significant harm, based on the facts at the date when accommodation was first provided? Alternatively, could they argue that the child would be likely to suffer significant harm if he was removed from the only parents he knows?

The House of Lords has also considered the second limb of section 31(2)(a) – 'likelihood' of significant harm in *Re H (minors) (sexual abuse: standard of proof)* [1996] AC 563, [1996] 1 All ER 1, HL. The case concerned four girls (referred to as D1, D2, D3 and D4). When she was fifteen, the eldest girl (D1) complained that she had been sexually abused by her stepfather, who was the father of D3 and D4. He was charged with rape, but acquitted. D1 was no longer living in the household, but the local authority were concerned that the younger children were at risk of abuse. They sought care orders arguing that, although sexual abuse could not be proved to the standard required for a criminal conviction, there was sufficient evidence to satisfy the civil standard of proof in care proceedings. The judge dismissed the applications because he said that he could not be sure 'to the requisite high standard of proof' that D1's allegations were true. He said: 'This is far from saying that I am satisfied the child's complaints are untrue. ... I am, at the least, more than a little suspicious that [the stepfather] has abused her as she says. If it were relevant, I would be prepared to hold that there is a real possibility that her statement and her evidence are true.' By a majority, the Court of Appeal dismissed the local authority's appeal, and an appeal to the House of Lords was also dismissed by a majority of three to two. Lord Nicholls gave the leading speech, with which Lord Goff and Lord Mustill agreed:

Lord Nicholls:

...

'Likely' to Suffer Harm

I shall consider first the meaning of 'likely' in the expression 'likely to suffer significant harm' in s. 31. ... In everyday usage one meaning of the word likely, perhaps its primary meaning, is probable, in the sense of more likely than not. This is not its only meaning. If I am going walking on Kinder Scout and ask whether it is likely to rain, I am using likely in a different sense. I am inquiring whether there is a real risk of rain, a risk that ought not to be ignored. In which sense is likely being used in this subsection? In s. 31(2) Parliament has stated the prerequisites which must exist before the court has power to make a care order. These prerequisites mark the boundary line drawn by Parliament between the differing interests. On one side are the interests of parents in caring for their own child, a course which prima facie is also in the interests of the child. On the other side there will be circumstances in which the interests of the child may dictate a need for his care to be entrusted to others. In s. 31(2) Parliament has stated the minimum conditions which must be present before the court can look more widely at all the circumstances and decide whether the child's welfare requires that a local authority shall receive the child into their care and have parental responsibility for him. The court must be satisfied that the child is already suffering significant harm. Or the court must be satisfied that, looking ahead, although the child may not yet be suffering such harm, he or she is likely to do so in the future. The court may make a care order if, but only if it is satisfied in one or other of these respects. In this context Parliament cannot have been using likely in the sense of more likely than not. If the word likely were given this meaning, it would have the effect of leaving outside the scope of care and supervision orders cases where the court is satisfied there is a real possibility of significant harm to the child in the future but that possibility falls short of being more likely than not. Strictly, if this were the correct reading of the Act, a care or supervision order would not be available even in a case where the risk of significant harm is as likely as not. Nothing would suffice short of proof that the child will probably suffer significant harm. The difficulty with this interpretation of s. 31(2)(a) is that it would draw the boundary line at an altogether inapposite point. What is in issue is the prospect, or risk, of the child suffering significant harm. When exposed to this risk a child may need protection just as much when the risk is considered to be less than fifty-fifty as when the risk is of a higher order. Conversely, so far as the parents are concerned, there is no particular magic in a threshold test based on a probability of significant harm as distinct from a real possibility. It is otherwise if there is no real possibility. It is eminently understandable that Parliament should provide that where there is no real possibility of significant harm, parental responsibility should remain solely with the parents. That makes sense as a threshold in the interests of the parents and the child in a way that a higher threshold, based on probability, would not. In my view, therefore, the context shows that in s. 31(2)(a) likely is being used in the sense of a real possibility, a possibility that cannot sensibly be ignored having regard to the nature and gravity of the feared harm in the particular case. By parity of reasoning, the expression likely to suffer significant harm bears the same meaning elsewhere in the Act; for instance, in ss. 43, 44 and 46. Likely also bears a similar meaning, for a similar reason, in the requirement in s. 31(2)(b) that the harm or likelihood of harm must be attributable to the care given to the child or 'likely' to be given to him if the order were not made.

The Burden of Proof

The power of the court to make a care or supervision order only arises if the court is 'satisfied' that the criteria stated in s. 31(2) exist. The expression 'if the court is satisfied', here and elsewhere in the Act, envisages that the court must be judicially satisfied on proper material. . . . The legal burden of establishing the existence of these conditions rests on the applicant for a care order. . . .

The Standard of Proof

Where the matters in issue are facts the standard of proof required in non-criminal proceedings is the preponderance of probability, usually referred to as the balance of probability. This is the established general principle. There are exceptions such as contempt of court applications, but I can see no reason for thinking that family proceedings are, or should be, an exception. By family proceedings I mean proceedings so described in the 1989 Act, ss. 105 and 8(3). Despite their special features, family proceedings remain essentially a form of civil proceedings. Family proceedings often raise very serious issues, but so do other forms of civil proceedings. The balance of probability standard means that a court is satisfied an event occurred if the court considers that, on the evidence, the occurrence of the event was more likely than not. When assessing the probabilities the court will have in mind as a factor, to whatever extent is appropriate in the particular case, that the more serious the allegation the less likely it is that the event occurred and, hence, the stronger should be the evidence before the court concludes that the allegation is established on the balance of probability. Fraud is usually less likely than negligence. Deliberate physical injury is usually less likely than accidental physical injury. A step-father is usually less likely to have repeatedly raped and had non-consensual oral sex with his under-age step-daughter than on some occasion to have lost his temper and slapped her. Built into the preponderance of probability standard is a serious degree of flexibility in respect of the seriousness of the allegation. Although the result is much the same, this does not mean that where a serious allegation is in issue the standard of proof required is higher. It means only that the inherent probability or improbability of an event is itself a matter to be taken into account when weighing the probabilities and deciding whether, on balance, the event occurred. The more improbable the event, the stronger must be the evidence that it did occur before, on the balance of probability, its occurrence will be established. Ungoed-Thomas J expressed this neatly in *Re Dellow's Will Trusts, Lloyd's Bank v Institute of Cancer Research* [1964] 1 WLR 451 at p. 455:

> 'The more serious the allegation the more cogent is the evidence required to overcome the unlikelihood of what is alleged and thus to prove it.'

. . .

The Threshold Conditions

There is no difficulty, in applying this standard to the threshold conditions. The first limb of s. 31(2)(a) predicates an existing state of affairs: that the child is suffering significant harm. The relevant time for this purpose is the date of the care order application or, if temporary protective arrangements have been continuously in place from an earlier date, the date when those arrangements were initiated. This was decided by your Lordships' House in *Re M (A Minor) (Care Order: Threshold Conditions)* [1994] 2 AC 424, [1994] 2 FLR 577. Whether at that time the child was suffering significant harm is an issue to be decided by the court on the basis of the facts admitted or proved before it. The balance of probability standard applies to proof of the facts. The same approach applies to the second limb of s. 31(2)(a). This is concerned with evaluating the risk of something happening in the future: aye or no, is there a real possibility that the child will suffer significant harm? Having heard and considered the evidence and decided any disputed questions of relevant fact upon the balance of probability, the court must reach a decision on how highly it evaluates the risk of significant harm befalling the child, always remembering upon whom the burden of proof rests.

...

A Conclusion Based on Facts

The starting-point here is that courts act on evidence. They reach their decisions on the basis of the evidence before them. When considering whether an applicant for a care order has shown that the child is suffering harm or is likely to do so, a court will have regard to the undisputed evidence. The judge will attach to that evidence such weight, or importance, as he considers appropriate. Likewise with regard to disputed evidence which the judge accepts as reliable. None of that is controversial. But the rejection of a disputed allegation as not proved on the balance of probability leaves scope for the possibility that the non-proven allegation may be true after all. There remains room for the judge to have doubts and suspicions on this score. This is the area of controversy. In my view these unresolved judicial doubts and suspicions can no more form the basis of a conclusion that the second threshold condition in s.31(2)(a) has been established than they can form the basis of a conclusion that the first has been established. ...

Thus far I have concentrated on explaining that a court's conclusion that the threshold conditions are satisfied must have a factual base, and that an alleged but unproved fact, serious or trivial, is not a fact for this purpose. Nor is judicial suspicion, because that is no more than a judicial state of uncertainty about whether or not an event happened.

I must now put this into perspective by noting, and emphasising, the width of the range of facts which may be relevant when the court is considering the threshold conditions. The range of facts which may properly be taken into account is infinite. Facts include the history of members of the family, the state of relationships within a family, proposed changes within the membership of a family, parental attitudes, and omissions which might not reasonably have been expected, just as much as actual physical assaults. They include threats, and abnormal behaviour by a child, and unsatisfactory parental responses to complaints or allegations. And facts, which are minor or even trivial if considered in isolation, when taken together may suffice to satisfy the court of the likelihood of future harm. The court will attach to all the relevant facts the appropriate weight when coming to an overall conclusion on the crucial issue. I must emphasise a further point. I have indicated that unproved allegations of maltreatment cannot form the basis for a finding by the court that either limb of s. 31(2)(a) is established. It is, of course, open to a court to conclude there is a real possibility that the child will suffer harm in the future although harm in the past has not been established. There will be cases where, although the alleged maltreatment itself is not proved, the evidence does establish a combination of profoundly worrying features affecting the care of the child within the family. In such cases it would be open to a court in appropriate circumstances to find that, although not satisfied the child is yet suffering significant harm, on the basis of such facts as are proved there is a likelihood that he will do so in the future. That is not the present case. The three younger girls are not at risk unless D1 was abused by Mr R in the past. If she was not abused, there is no reason for thinking the others may be. This is not a case where Mr R has a history of abuse. Thus the one and only relevant fact is whether D1 was abused by Mr R as she says. The other surrounding facts, such as the fact that D1 made a complaint and the fact that her mother responded unsatisfactorily, lead nowhere relevant in this case if they do not lead to the conclusion that D1 was abused. To decide that the others are at risk because there is a possibility that D1 was abused would be to base the decision, not on fact, but on suspicion:

the suspicion that D1 may have been abused. That would be to lower the threshold prescribed by Parliament.

Conclusion

I am very conscious of the difficulties confronting social workers and others in obtaining hard evidence, which will stand up when challenged in court, of the maltreatment meted out to children behind closed doors. Cruelty and physical abuse are notoriously difficult to prove. The task of social workers is usually anxious and often thankless. They are criticised for not having taken action in response to warning signs which are obvious enough when seen in the clear light of hindsight. Or they are criticised for making applications based on serious allegations which, in the event, are not established in court. Sometimes, whatever they do, they cannot do right. I am also conscious of the difficulties facing judges when there is conflicting testimony on serious allegations. On some occasions judges are left deeply anxious at the end of a case. There may be an understandable inclination to 'play safe' in the interests of the child. Sometimes judges wish to safeguard a child whom they fear may be at risk without at the same time having to fasten a label of very serious misconduct onto one of the parents. These are among the difficulties and considerations Parliament addressed in the Children Act when deciding how, to use the fashionable terminology, the balance should be struck between the various interests. As I read the Act Parliament decided that the threshold for a care order should be that the child is suffering significant harm, or there is a real possibility that he will do so. In the latter regard the threshold is comparatively low. Therein lies the protection for children. But, as I read the Act, Parliament also decided that proof of the relevant facts is needed if this threshold is to be surmounted. Before the s.1 welfare test and the welfare 'checklist' can be applied, the threshold has to be crossed. Therein lies the protection for parents. They are not to be at risk of having their child taken from them and removed into the care of the local authority on the basis only of suspicions, whether of the judge or of the local authority or anyone else. A conclusion that the child is suffering or is likely to suffer harm must be based on facts, not just suspicion.

QUESTIONS

i. When the *Review of Child Care Law* (p. 561, above) recommended that harm must be 'likely', do you think that they intended to exclude only cases where there was 'no real risk' of harm?

ii. Horrendous sexual abuse is, hopefully, less common than relatively trivial failures of parental care, but is a child who claims to have been repeatedly raped more likely to be lying than a child who claims to have been slapped once?

iii. Lord Nicholls pointed out that the case was unusual because everything turned on one allegation. He said that there would be some cases where alleged maltreatment could not be proved, but other proven facts would demonstrate a likelihood of future harm. What sort of facts would demonstrate that someone is likely to harm a child, without demonstrating that he or she has already done so?

iv. Is it possible for the threshold to be satisfied in a situation where neither parent is proved to be responsible for any harm which the child has suffered? (See *Lancashire County Council v B* [2000] 2 AC 147.)

v. How should you draft the threshold document when there are three possible perpetrators: mother, father and mother's boyfriend, but you do not consider that a court would be able to identify the perpetrator? (See *Re O and N, Re B (A Minor)* [2003] UKHL 18.)

vi. Let us assume that in the above case, all three adults concede that abuse has occurred but all three deny that they are the perpetrator of this abuse. Should the court identify the perpetrator of the abuse on the balance of probabilities?

In many cases, medical evidence will be required to establish whether the threshold test is met. In *Re AB (child abuse: expert witness)* [1995] 1 FCR 280, [1995] 1 FLR 181, High Court, Family Division, a baby of ten weeks was found to have multiple fractures and some brain damage. Several expert witnesses gave evidence that the injuries were non-accidental. However, the parents called an expert who gave evidence that the child's injuries were due to 'temporary brittle bone disease'. Wall J found that the injuries were non-accidental, and gave guidance on the role of expert witnesses in cases of alleged child abuse:

Wall J:

...

The Duties of Experts in Children's Cases

...

In my judgment it is of critical importance in discussing the role of the expert witness in children's cases to bear in mind throughout the respective functions of expert and judge. The expert forms an assessment and expresses his opinion within the particular area of his expertise. The judge decides particular issues in individual cases. It is therefore not for the judge to become involved in medical controversy except in the extremely rare case where such a controversy is itself an issue in the case and a judicial assessment of it becomes necessary for the proper resolution of the proceedings.... The judge's task is difficult enough as it is in sensitive child cases. To have, in addition, to resolve a subtle and complex medical disagreement or to make assessments of the reliability of expert witnesses not only adds immeasurably to the judge's task but, given his fallibility and lack of medical training, may help to lead him to a false conclusion. It is partly for this reason that the current practice of the courts in children's cases is to require disclosure of all medical reports and to invite the experts to confer pre-trial. By these means the ambit of agreement and disagreement can be defined....

...there are sometimes cases in which there is a genuine disagreement on a scientific or medical issue, or where it is necessary for a party to advance a particular hypothesis to explain a given set of facts. Where that occurs, the judge will have to resolve the issue which is raised. Two points must be made. In my view, the expert who advances such a hypothesis owes a very heavy duty to explain to the court that what he is advancing is a hypothesis, that it is controversial (if it is) and to place before the court all the material which contradicts the hypothesis. Secondly, he must make all his material available to the other experts in the case....

In another case, *Oldham MBC and GW and PW and KPW (a child) and Dr W St C Forbes* [2007] EWHC 136 (Fam), High Court Family Division, the judge set out some general principles on the use of experts:

Ryder J:

[100] It may be that in due course the opportunities that exist in family proceedings for case management, issue identification and dispute resolution hearings can be developed to further enhance the scrutiny of experts' evidence by the court prior to the ultimate resolution of the issues in a case at a full hearing. For example, there may be merit in considering the approach of the courts in the United States of America as derived from *Daubert v. Merrell Dow Pharmaceuticals Inc* (1993) 509 US 579. But at the end of the day whether it be during case management, issues resolution or at a contested hearing the court must engage in the process described by Stuart-Smith LJ in *Loveday v Renton* [1990] 1 Med LR 117 at 125:

> 'In reaching my decision a number of processes have to be undertaken. The mere expression of opinion or belief by a witness, however eminent, ... does not suffice. The court has to evaluate the witness and soundness of his opinion. Most importantly this involves an examination of the reasons given for his opinions and the extent to which they are supported by the evidence. The judge also has to decide what weight to attach to a witness's opinion by examining the internal consistency and logic of his evidence; his precision and accuracy of thought as demonstrated by his answers; how he responds to searching and informed cross-examination and in particular the extent to which a witness faces up to and accepts the logic and proposition put in cross-examination or is prepared to concede points that are seen to be correct; the extent to which a witness has conceived an opinion and is reluctant to re-examine it in light of later evidence, or demonstrates a flexibility of mind which may involve changing or modifying opinions previously held; whether or not a witness is biased or lacks independence.'

QUESTION

You may know that the criminal courts have overturned convictions for murder in child deaths where it has subsequently been found that the medical evidence upon which the convictions were based was faulty (see for example *R v Cannings* [2004] 2 Cr App R 63). Do you think it likely that care orders have been made on similar faulty medical evidence?

We turn finally in this section to the impact of the European Convention on Human Rights.

In *P, C and S v UK* [2002] All ER (D) 239 (July), European Court of Human Rights, P, born in 1958, was a citizen of the United States of America; C, the husband of P, was born in 1962 and was a United Kingdom citizen; S, their daughter was born in 1998 and was a United Kingdom and American citizen. They were all resident in the United Kingdom. In January 1976 P, then living in the United States of America, gave birth to a son A, shortly before her eighteenth birthday. In 1980 P married her first husband, and had a second son, B, in February 1985. In 1992 she and her husband separated. Both parents contested custody of B. Between December 1990 and January 1994 B was referred to his general practitioner for some forty-seven complaints, and the mother was convicted of various criminal offences. On 23 August 1994 a Californian court ordered that B live with his father. During 1996 P met her present husband, C.

P and C were married in September 1997 in the United Kingdom. P discovered shortly afterwards that she was pregnant. The local authority was informed of the pregnancy by P's doctor and commenced an investigation. On 7 May 1998, S was born. The local authority applied for an emergency protection order on that day, and subsequently commenced care proceedings. At a hearing, which began on 2 February 1999 and ended on 1 March 1999, the High Court heard the local authority's application for a care order in respect of S. The local authority informed the judge that there were nine families available and wanting to adopt S. P and C were parties, as were S's paternal grandparents, while S was represented by a professional guardian *ad litem*, solicitors and both senior and junior counsel.

The proceedings in court followed this route, as described in the Judgment of the European Court:

> [58] On 4 February 1999 C applied for leave to withdraw from the proceedings, on the ground that he saw no prospect of success in obtaining custody of S. and that the stress of the proceedings was likely to lead to a breakdown in his health. On 5 February 1999 the judge granted him leave to withdraw. C's parents also withdrew from the proceedings.
> [59] On the same date P's legal representatives (leading counsel and solicitors) withdrew from the case, informing the judge that her legal aid had been withdrawn. It was later stated by the judge that they had withdrawn because P was asking them to conduct the case unreasonably. In fact, her legal aid had not been withdrawn, as the judge made clear in his judgment. The legal-aid certificate could not be formally discharged until P had been given the opportunity to show why that should not happen.
> [60] P asked for an adjournment until 9 February 1999, which was granted. On that date P asked for a further adjournment in order to apply for the reinstatement of her legal-aid certificate.
> [61] The judge refused the adjournment. As a result of this decision, P conducted her own case, assisted by a 'McKenzie friend', Mrs H. The applicant stated that she found conducting her own case immensely difficult. At one stage, she told the judge that she simply could not continue because she was so distressed. That was after cross-examining her own husband C, which she found very painful. However, the judge said that she should carry on. The solicitor for the guardian *ad litem* and a social worker visited P that evening to persuade her to carry on.
> [62] In his judgment, the judge explained his refusal of an adjournment:
>
>> 'In the first place I was satisfied that the mother had a very clear grasp of the voluminous documentation, at least as good and if not better a grasp than the lawyers in the case. Secondly, it was clear to me from the documents that the mother, who is an intelligent woman, was fully able to put her case in a clear and coherent way, an assessment that has been amply borne out by the hearing itself.
>>
>> Thirdly, I was confident that the Bar, in the form of leading and junior counsel for the local authority and the guardian *ad litem*, would not only treat the mother fairly but in the tradition of the Bar would assist her in the presentation of any points she wished to advance, in so far as it would be professionally proper for them to do so. Once again that assessment has been fully justified by the conduct of counsel during the hearing. As examples, the local authority both facilitated and paid for the attendance of Dr Toseland, consultant toxicologist, to attend as part of the mother's case. Junior counsel for the local authority ... struggled manfully to ensure that the mother had a complete set of the ever growing documentation. There were other examples.
>>
>> Fourthly, the outcome of the case seemed to me to hinge or be likely to hinge substantially on the mother's cross-examination, an area of the case in which the ability of lawyers to protect her was limited.

> Finally, and most importantly, I was concerned about the prejudice to [S] of what would have had to have been a very lengthy adjournment. Section 1(2) of the Children Act expresses the general principle that delay in resolving a child's future is prejudicial to that child's welfare. In this particular case intensive preparation for the hearing had been going on effectively since [S's] birth in May 1998 and up until the outset of the hearing before me the mother had had the benefit of advice from her lawyers, latterly of course from leading counsel. An adjournment would have involved a very substantial delay in resolving [S's] future.
>
> The hearing was estimated to last, and did indeed, last something in the order of twenty working days. A fresh legal team, assuming legal aid was restored, would have needed a substantial amount of time to master the voluminous documentation and to take instructions. Twenty days of court time simply cannot be conjured out of thin air.
>
> Furthermore the evidence of Dr Bentovim, the consultant child psychiatrist jointly instructed to advise me, amongst other things, on [S's] placement, was that a decision on her long-term future needed to be both made and if possible implemented before her first birthday.
>
> ...
>
> If the mother had been represented by counsel her case would, I think, have been conducted differently, but I am entirely satisfied that the result would have been the same. As so often happens the mother was given a latitude which would not be given to a litigant who was legally represented. For example, I allowed her to call a witness, Professor Robinson, who had not provided a statement prior to the hearing. I was also prepared for her to call a consultant psychologist who had given evidence in the American proceedings, Dr [P], who in the event was unable to attend. I also allowed the mother to cross-examine witnesses twice ... I have throughout the hearing endeavoured to ensure that the mother was treated fairly. ...
>
> It is my judgment that the mother's case has been fully heard and that the hearing has been fair ... I reject any suggestion that had the mother been legally represented the result would have been different.'

> [63] On 8 March 1999 the judge made a care order. In reaching his decision, he did not consider himself bound by the American conviction and reached his own findings of fact on the available material ...
>
> [64] While the judge accepted that P had not put S at risk during her pregnancy and that the parents' treatment of S during contact sessions had been exemplary, he found that P suffered from a personality disorder, and that such people were very difficult to treat and did not change easily. He considered that P was in a state of deep denial about what had happened to her son B and the potential risk that she posed to her daughter S.

The European Court then considered issues relating to Article 6:

> [88] There is no automatic right under the Convention for legal aid or legal representation to be available for an applicant who is involved in proceedings which determine his or her civil rights. Nonetheless, Article 6 may be engaged under two interrelated aspects.
>
> [89] Firstly, Article 6 § 1 of the Convention embodies the right of access to a court for the determination of civil rights and obligations (see *Golder v. the United Kingdom*, judgment of 21 February 1975, Series A no. 18, p. 18, § 36). Failure to provide an applicant with the assistance of a lawyer may breach this provision where such assistance is indispensable for effective access to court, either because legal representation is rendered compulsory as is the case in certain Contracting

States for various types of litigation, or by reason of the complexity of the procedure or the type of case (see *Airey v. Ireland*, judgment of 9 October 1979, Series A no. 32, pp. 14-16, §§ 26-28, where the applicant was unable to obtain the assistance of a lawyer in judicial separation proceedings). Factors identified as relevant in *Airey* in determining whether the applicant would have been able to present her case properly and satisfactorily without the assistance of a lawyer included the complexity of the procedure, the necessity to address complicated points of law or to establish facts, involving expert evidence and the examination of witnesses, and the fact that the subject matter of the marital dispute entailed an emotional involvement that was scarcely compatible with the degree of objectivity required by advocacy in court. In such circumstances, the Court found it unrealistic to suppose that the applicant could effectively conduct her own case, despite the assistance afforded by the judge to parties acting in person.

[90] It may be noted that the right of access to a court is not absolute and may be subject to legitimate restrictions. Where an individual's access is limited either by operation of law or in fact, the restriction will not be incompatible with Article 6 where the limitation did not impair the very essence of the right and where it pursued a legitimate aim, and there was a reasonable relationship of proportionality between the means employed and the aim sought to be achieved (see *Ashingdane v. the United Kingdom*, judgment of 28 May 1985, Series A no. 93, pp. 24-25, § 57). Thus, although the pursuit of proceedings as a litigant in person may on occasion not be an easy matter, the limited public funds available for civil actions renders a procedure of selection a necessary feature of the system of administration of justice, and the manner in which it functions in particular cases may be shown not to have been arbitrary or disproportionate, or to have impinged on the essence of the right of access to a court (see *Del Sol v. France*, no. 46800/99, ECHR 2002-II, and *Ivison v. the United Kingdom* (dec.), no. 39030/97, 16 April 2002). It may be the case that other factors concerning the administration of justice (such as the necessity for expedition or the rights of others) also play a limiting role as regards the provision of assistance in a particular case, although such restriction would also have to satisfy the tests set out above.

[91] Secondly, the key principle governing the application of Article 6 is fairness. In cases where an applicant appears in court notwithstanding lack of assistance by a lawyer and manages to conduct his or her case in the teeth of all the difficulties, the question may nonetheless arise as to whether this procedure was fair (see, for example, *McVicar v. the United Kingdom*, no. 46311/99, §§ 50-51, ECHR 2002-III). There is the importance of ensuring the appearance of the fair administration of justice and a party in civil proceedings must be able to participate effectively, *inter alia*, by being able to put forward the matters in support of his or her claims. Here, as in other aspects of Article 6, the seriousness of what is at stake for the applicant will be of relevance to assessing the adequacy and fairness of the procedures.

2. Application to the Present Case

[92] The Court observes that the applicant P was awarded legal aid for representation by a lawyer in the proceedings brought by the local authority in applying for a care order and a freeing for adoption order in respect of her daughter S. This reflected the position in the domestic legal system that in such proceedings as a general rule the interests of justice require a parent to be given legal assistance. Initially, therefore, P was represented by senior and junior counsel and solicitors, who prepared her case and advised her up until the hearing of the application for a care order which commenced on 2 February 1999. However, on 5 February 1999, her lawyers applied to the judge to withdraw from the proceedings, alleging that P was asking them to conduct the case in an unreasonable manner. The judge allowed them to withdraw. He allowed P an adjournment of four days until 9 February 1999, at which point he refused any further adjournment, giving

detailed reasons for that decision which obliged the applicant to conduct her own case over the bulk of the trial. After making the care order on 8 March 1999, the judge fixed the hearing of the application for the freeing of S for adoption for one week later on 15 March 1999. On that date, he refused the application of P for the proceedings to be deferred to allow her to obtain legal representation. He then proceeded after the hearing of the application to issue an order freeing S for adoption without any provision for continued direct contact. There can be no doubt therefore of the seriousness of the outcome of the proceedings for P and C, which deprived them of the possibility of bringing S up in their family and of any future contact with her and which severed their legal relationship with her.

[93] The applicants' complaints about the lack of legal assistance during these proceedings were met by the Government's arguments largely based on the reasoning given by the judge for the procedural decisions which he took. In the care proceedings, the judge considered that P was well able, and had shown herself able, to present her own case, with assistance from counsel representing other parties in court and with considerable leeway given by himself. He gave great weight to the opinion given by Dr Bentovim (the expert) that the future of S should be settled by her first birthday and considered that any adjournment would inevitably jeopardise her welfare due to the delay factor. The Government have emphasised the difficulties which would have been attached to re-listing a trial of this length.

[94] The Court has paid careful attention to the reasons given by the trial judge in this case, whose long judgment received merited praise in the Court of Appeal for the thoroughness of his analysis and who had first-hand experience of the events and participants. It also notes that the Court of Appeal considered that the proceedings had been fair, an opinion shared by counsel for the guardian *ad litem*, who represented S.

[95] Nonetheless, P was required as a parent to represent herself in proceedings which, as the Court of Appeal observed, were of exceptional complexity, extending over a period of twenty days, in which the documentation was voluminous and which required a review of highly complex expert evidence relating to the applicants P and C's fitness to parent their daughter. Her alleged disposition to harm her own children, together with her personality traits, were at the heart of the case, as was her relationship with her husband. The complexity of the case, along with the importance of what was at stake and the highly emotive nature of the subject matter, lead this Court to conclude that the principles of effective access to a court and fairness required that P receive the assistance of a lawyer. Even if P was acquainted with the vast documentation in the case, the Court is not persuaded that she should have been expected to take up the burden of conducting her own case. It notes that at one point in the proceedings, which were conducted at the same time as she was coping with the distress of the removal of S at birth, P broke down in the courtroom and the judge, counsel for the guardian *ad litem* and a social worker, had to encourage her to continue ...

[96] The Court notes that the judge himself commented that if P had been represented by a lawyer her case would have been conducted differently. Although he went on in his judgment to give the opinion that this would not have affected the outcome of the proceedings, this element is not decisive as regards the fairness of the proceedings. Otherwise, a requirement to show actual prejudice from a lack of legal representation would deprive the guarantees of Article 6 of their substance (see *Artico v. Italy*, judgment of 13 May 1980, Series A no. 37, pp. 17-18, § 35). Similarly, while the judge considered that the case would turn on the cross-examination of P, where a lawyer would have been able to give only limited assistance, that assistance would nonetheless have furnished P with some safeguards and support.

[98] Nor is the Court convinced that the importance of proceeding with expedition, which attaches generally to child-care cases, necessitated the draconian action of proceeding to a full and complex hearing, followed within one week by the freeing for adoption application, both without legal assistance being provided to the applicants. Although it was doubtless desirable

for S's future to be settled as soon as possible, the Court considers that the imposition of one year from birth as the deadline appears a somewhat inflexible and blanket approach, applied without particular consideration for the facts of this individual case. S was, according to the care plan, to be placed for adoption and it was not envisaged that there would be any difficulty in finding a suitable adoptive family (eight couples were already identified by 2 February 1999). Yet, although S was freed for adoption by the court on 15 March 1999, she was not in fact placed with a family until 2 September 1999, a gap of over five months for which no explanation has been given, while the adoption order which finalised matters on a legal basis was not issued until 27 March 2000, that is, more than a year later. S's placement was therefore not achieved by her first birthday in May in any event. It is not possible to speculate at this time as to how long the adjournment would have lasted had it been granted in order to allow the applicant P to be represented at the care proceedings, or for both parent applicants to be represented at the freeing for adoption proceedings. It would have been entirely possible for the judge to place strict time-limits on any lawyers instructed, and for instructions to be given for re-listing the matter with due regard to priorities. As the applicants have pointed out, S was herself in a successful foster placement and unaffected by the ongoing proceedings. The Court does not find that the possibility of some months' delay in reaching a final conclusion in those proceedings was so prejudicial to her interests as to justify what the trial judge himself regarded as a procedure which gave an appearance of 'railroading' her parents.

[99] Recognising that the courts in this matter were endeavouring in good faith to strike a balance between the interests of the parents and the welfare of S, the Court is nevertheless of the opinion that the procedures adopted not only gave the appearance of unfairness but prevented the applicants from putting forward their case in a proper and effective manner on the issues which were important to them. For example, the Court notes that the judge's decision to free S for adoption gave no explanation of why direct contact was not to be continued or why an open adoption with continued direct contact was not possible, matters which the applicants apparently did not realise could, or should, have been raised at that stage. The assistance afforded to P by counsel for other parties and the latitude granted by the judge to P in presenting her case was no substitute, in a case such as the present one, for competent representation by a lawyer instructed to protect the applicants' rights.

[100] The Court concludes that the assistance of a lawyer during the hearing of these two applications which had such crucial consequences for the applicants' relationship with their daughter was an indispensable requirement. Consequently, the parents did not have fair and effective access to a court as required by Article 6 § 1 of the Convention. There has, therefore, been a breach of this provision as regards the applicant parents, P and C.

So far as Article 8 is concerned, the Court said:

[117] Following any removal into care, a stricter scrutiny is called for in respect of any further limitations by the authorities, for example on parental rights of access, as such further restrictions entail the danger that the family relations between the parents and a young child are effectively curtailed (see *Johansen 17383/90* [1996] ECHR 31; *Kutzner no 46544/99* [2002] ECHR 160). The taking into care of a child should normally be regarded as a temporary measure to be discontinued as soon as circumstances permit, and any measures of implementation of temporary care should be consistent with the ultimate aim of reuniting the natural parent and child (see *Olsson (no. 1)* 10465/83 [1988] ECHR 2, cited above, pp. 36-37, § 81; *Johansen*, cited above, pp. 1008-09, § 78; and *E.P. v. Italy,* no. 31127/96, § 69, 16 November 1999). In this regard a fair balance has to be struck between the interests of the child remaining in care and those of the parent in being reunited with the child (see *Olsson (no. 2)*, 13441/87 [1992] ECHR 75, pp. 35-36, § 90, and *Hokkanen*, cited

above, p. 20, § 55). In carrying out this balancing exercise, the Court will attach particular importance to the best interests of the child which, depending on their nature and seriousness, may override those of the parent (see *Johansen*, cited above, pp. 1008-09, § 78).
[118] As regards the extreme step of severing all parental links with a child, the Court has taken the view that such a measure would cut a child from its roots and could only be justified in exceptional circumstances or by the overriding requirement of the child's best interests (see *Johansen*, cited above, p. 1010, § 84, and *Gnahoré v. France*, no. 40031/98, § 59, ECHR 2000-IX). That approach, however, may not apply in all contexts, depending on the nature of the parent-child relationship (see *Söderbäck v. Sweden*, judgment of 28 October 1998, *Reports* 1998-VII, pp. 3095-96, §§ 31-34, where the severance of links between a child and father, who had never had care and custody of the child, was found to fall within the margin of appreciation of the courts which had made the assessment of the child's best interests).
[119] The Court further reiterates that, whilst Article 8 contains no explicit procedural requirements, the decision-making process involved in measures of interference must be fair and such as to afford due respect to the interests safeguarded by that Article:

> '[W]hat ... has to be determined is whether, having regard to the particular circumstances of the case and notably the serious nature of the decisions to be taken, the parents have been involved in the decision-making process, seen as a whole, to a degree sufficient to provide them with the requisite protection of their interests. If they have not, there will have been a failure to respect their family life and the interference resulting from the decision will not be capable of being regarded as "necessary" within the meaning of Article 8.' (See *W. v. the United Kingdom*, judgment of 8 July 1987, Series A no. 121, pp. 28-29, §§ 62 and 64.)

[120] It is essential that a parent be placed in a position where he or she may obtain access to information which is relied on by the authorities in taking measures of protective care or in taking decisions relevant to the care and custody of a child. Otherwise the parent will be unable to participate effectively in the decision-making process or to put forward in a fair or adequate manner those matters militating in favour of his or her ability to provide the child with proper care and protection (see *McMichael v. the United Kingdom*, judgment of 24 February 1995, Series A no. 307-B, p. 57, § 92, where the authorities did not disclose to the applicant parents reports relating to their child, and *T.P. and K.M. v. the United Kingdom* [GC], no. 28945/95, ECHR 2001-V, where the applicant mother was not afforded an early opportunity to view a video of an interview of her daughter, crucial to the assessment of abuse in the case; see also *Buchberger v. Austria*, no. 32899/96, 20 December 2001).
[128] Questions of emergency care are, by their nature, decided on a highly provisional basis and on an assessment of risk to the child reached on the basis of the information, inevitably incomplete, available at the time. The Court considers that it was within the proper role of the local authority in its child-protection function to take steps to obtain an emergency protection order. It finds that there were relevant and sufficient reasons for this measure, in particular the fact that P had been convicted for harming her son B and had been found by an expert in those proceedings to suffer from a syndrome which manifested itself in exaggerating and fabricating illness in a child, with consequent significant physical and psychological damage to the child.
[130] In the circumstances, the Court considers that the decision to apply for the emergency protection order after S's birth may be regarded as having been necessary in a democratic society to safeguard the health and rights of the child. The local authority had to be able to take appropriate steps to ensure that no harm came to the baby and, at the very least, to obtain the legal power to prevent C or any other relative from removing the baby with a view to foiling the local authority's actions, and thereby placing the baby at risk.
[131] It has nonetheless given consideration to the manner of implementation of the order, namely, the steps taken under the authority of the order ... [T]he removal of a baby from its mother at birth

requires exceptional justification. It is a step which is traumatic for the mother and places her own physical and mental health under a strain, and it deprives the new-born baby of close contact with its natural mother and, as pointed out by the applicants, of the advantages of breast-feeding. The removal also deprived the father, C, of being close to his daughter after the birth.
[133] The Court concludes that the draconian step of removing S from her mother shortly after birth was not supported by relevant and sufficient reasons and that it cannot be regarded as having been necessary in a democratic society for the purpose of safeguarding S. There has therefore been, in that respect, a breach of the applicant parents' rights under Article 8 of the Convention.
[137] The lack of legal representation of P during the care proceedings and of P and C during the freeing for adoption proceedings, together with the lack of any real lapse of time between the two procedures, has been found above to have deprived the applicants of a fair and effective hearing in court. Having regard to the seriousness of what was at stake, the Court finds that it also prevented them from being involved in the decision-making process, seen as a whole, to a degree sufficient to provide them with the requisite protection of their interests under Article 8 of the Convention. Emotionally involved in the case as they were, the applicant parents were placed at a serious disadvantage by these elements, and it cannot be excluded that this might have had an effect on the decisions reached and eventual outcome for the family as a whole.
[138] In the circumstances of this case, the Court concludes that there has been in this regard a breach of P, C and S's rights under Article 8 of the Convention.

QUESTIONS

i. Does the European Convention on Human Rights require: (a) that parent should always be able to obtain expert evidence to challenge a local authority's case; (b) that parents should always be entitled to the assistance of a lawyer during court hearings?
ii. What about the issue of delay?

11.6 THE CHOICE OF FINAL ORDER

If the section 31 threshold criteria are established, the court must go on to apply the welfare test in the light of the 'checklist' (p. 481, above) and the 'non-intervention principle' (p. 498, above). Expert evidence may also be important at this stage, and the court will also consider the recommendations of the child's guardian (see section 41). The principal options are: a care order, a supervision order, a section 8 order, or no order at all.

Before the Children Act 1989, supervision orders were not widely used. The Department of Health and Social Security's *Review of Child Care Law* (1985) suggested:

18.5 The Select Committee were concerned about the small number of cases in which supervision orders were made (in 1983 there were about 1,400 supervision orders made in care proceedings as compared with about 3,000 care orders). They suggested that the reason was the perceived ineffectiveness of supervision orders and that these might be used more widely if the supervisor were given greater powers not only over the child but over the parents as well. In particular supervision might be used instead of a care order where the local authority intended to place the child at home on trial if a care order was obtained.

Imposing Requirements on Parents

18.6 One way forward would be to enable the court to impose conditions on the parent or whoever has the actual custody of the child provided that the actual custodian has had an opportunity to be heard. . . .

18.7 Whether the requirements under a supervision order are met may depend on the parent rather than the child, especially where the child is young. At present orders may be frustrated, for example simply by the parent refusing the supervisor access to the child. Refusal to allow a supervised child to be visited or medically examined is now automatically reasonable cause for suspicion so that a warrant to search for and remove the child may be obtained. Nevertheless, where the object of the supervision is in fact to impose requirements on the parents for the protection of the child we consider that the court should have express power to do so.

. . .

18.9 As to what requirements precisely the court should be able to impose on adults the following list has occurred to us:

a. to keep the supervisor informed of his address and that of the child;
b. to allow the supervisor access to the child in the home and to assess the child's welfare, needs and condition;
c. to allow the child to be medically examined;
d. to comply with the supervisor's direction to attend with the child at a specified place (such as a clinic or day centre) for the purpose of medical examination, medical or psychiatric treatment, or participation in specified activities;
e. to permit the child to receive medical or psychiatric treatment; and
f. to comply with the supervisor's directions on matters relating to the child's education.

. . .

18.15 The power to require the child to live with a named individual will in our view be largely overtaken by our recommendation that the court in care proceedings should have power to grant legal custody to another person for example a relative or friend and should therefore be abolished. This will have the advantage of clarifying the legal status of the other person and enabling him to combine both the powers and responsibilities of a parent. The order could be coupled with a supervision order if required.

The Children Act 1989 implemented these recommendations in section 15 and Schedule 2, Parts I and II.

Some of the reasons why care orders are often preferred are shown by the case of *Re D (a minor) (care or supervision order)* [1993] 2 FCR 88, [1993] 2 FLR 423, High Court, Family Division.

While in the father's care, a child aged four had been injured, and a baby aged two months had died from a fractured skull and many other injuries. The father had been convicted of wilful cruelty, but was acquitted of murder. The case concerned a baby, R, who was born after the father was released from prison. The local authority applied for a care or supervision order, and the judge found that the section 31 threshold test was satisfied because there was a serious risk of violence from the father towards the child. The local authority argued that a care order would undermine the co-operation which they were receiving from the child's parents. The guardian *ad litem* argued that a care order was necessary to protect the child.

Ewbank J:

... At first sight it would appear that a supervision order should be made if the child is living with the parents, a care order if the child is not living with the parents. But the statute is more flexible than that. ... it is open under a care order for the child to live with the parents, as in this case.

A supervision order can only be made in the first instance for one year, as provided by Sch. 3, para. 6(1) to the Children Act. Paragraphs 6(3) and (4) allow an extension for a further 2 years. Schedule 3, paras 2, 3 and 4 provide for directions to be given on a supervision order. ... It is suggested that these paragraphs and the powers given to the supervising officer would enable the child's welfare to be monitored by regular medical examinations, by attendance at a children's centre, and directions as to where the child should live, and any other directions which seem appropriate.

If there is a breach of a supervision order the supervising officer, under s.35(1)(c), has to consider whether to apply to the court for a variation of the supervision order or the discharge of the order. There is no direct way of enforcing the directions made under a supervision order.

...

If a care order were made then, under s.33(3)(a), the local authority would have parental responsibility for R and they would have the power to limit the parental responsibility of the mother and father if they thought it was necessary under s.33(3)(b). Under reg. 9 of the Placement of Children with Parents Etc Regulations 1991 the local authority have to satisfy themselves of the welfare of a child who has been placed by them and might visit the child in any event at intervals of not more than 6 weeks during the first year of the placement and thereafter at intervals of not more than 3 months. The advantage of a care order as opposed to a supervision order, in the submission of the guardian *ad litem*, is that a care order is unlimited in time and can only be revoked by an application to the court and even when revoked the court can substitute a supervision order. That is under s.39 of the Children Act. The local authority feel that a care order is too strong an order to be made in the circumstances of this case. They feel that they are working well together with the parents and that a care order would undermine that. But in my judgment that approach misses the real point in the case. The point in the case is the protection of R. ...

... The life of this family is harmonious. The child is thriving and much loved by his mother and father. But the protection of the child, in my judgment, is the most important aspect of this case and the decisive point in coming to a decision whether there should be a supervision order or a care order is that, in my judgment, if there is to be a lifting of the safeguards surrounding this child that lifting ought to be done by the court on consideration of the evidence and the lifting of the safeguards ought not to be left to the responsibility of individuals. So, in my judgment, a care order should be made in this case, despite the views of the local authority. ...

The balancing act that has to be achieved when deciding on a supervision order rather than a care order is set out by Hale LJ in *Re O (Supervision Order)* [2001] EWCA Civ 16, [2001] 1 FCR 289, [2001] 1 FLR 923, CA. In this case, a mother had had four previous children taken into care following allegations of sexual abuse by the father. The mother had failed to protect the children and had neglected them. The proceedings concerned a fifth child, aged fifteen months at the time of the hearing in the

Court of Appeal. A new partner had fathered him. The mother suffered from mental health difficulties. The local authority did not seek to remove the child but sought a care order. The trial judge concluded that the appropriate order was a supervision order rather than a care order, and the local authority appealed.

Hale LJ:

[24] A care order is very different from a supervision order. There are 3 main points. First, it gives the local authority power to remove the child without recourse even to a family proceedings court for an emergency protection order. The parents' only means of challenging that removal is by an application to discharge the care order, which usually takes some time to be heard, especially if, as in this case, it would have to be transferred to a higher court. Given the judge's findings as to the nature of risk, the slowness of any deterioration, the level of protection available from other sources including the father, it is very difficult to say that the local authority need to have this power. The care plan itself, as I have already indicated, does not suggest that they do.

[25] Secondly, it gives the local authority parental responsibility for the child coupled with the power to control the parents' exercise of that responsibility. Again, the care plan does not suggest that the local authority wish to exercise parental responsibility or control the parents' exercise of it ...

[26] The third difference is one of timing. Mr Forbes in particular has argued that it might be difficult to achieve a further order in three years' time, but of course that difficulty would only arise if by then the risk of harm had disappeared or almost disappeared, or the need for an order had disappeared or almost disappeared. If that were not the case, the local authority would have to investigate and take any action which was thought appropriate to protect the child.

[27] ... Each case is an exercise of discretion on its own particular facts and earlier case law may be of limited help in this context. In any event, it has to be considered in the light of the Human Rights Act 1998 and Art 8 of the European Convention for the Protection of Human Rights and Fundamental Freedoms 1950. As I said in the case of *Re C + B (Care Order: Future Harm)* [2001] 1 FLR 611, paras (33)–(34) at 620–621:

> 'I do note that under Art 8 of the Convention both the children and the parents have the right to respect for their family and private life. If the state is to interfere with that there are three requirements: first, that it be in accordance with the law; secondly, that it be for a legitimate aim (in this case the protection of the welfare and interest of the children); and thirdly, that it be "necessary in a democratic society".'

There is a long line of European Court of Human Rights jurisprudence on that third requirement, which emphasises that the intervention has to be proportionate to the legitimate aims.

[28] Proportionality, therefore, is the key. It will be the duty of everyone to ensure that, in those cases where a supervision order is proportionate as a response to the risk presented, a supervision order can be made to work, as indeed the framers of the Children Act 1989 always hoped that it would be made to work. The local authorities must deliver the services that are needed and must ensure that other agencies, including the health service, also play their part, and the parents must co-operate fully.

QUESTIONS

i. Are you surprised that the local authority placed so much weight on the need to maintain the co-operation of the parents?

ii. Could the court have made a care order against the wishes of the local authority, if the local authority had not originally applied for a care or supervision order?

Another possibility, introduced by the Children Act 1989, is for the court to make section 8 orders (see p. 474, above). Local authorities are prohibited from applying for residence or contact orders by section 9(2) of the Children Act 1989. However, they can invite the court to make an order of its own motion under section 10(1)(b), or support an application by another person. If the parents have separated, a residence order in favour of one parent may be appropriate where the risk to the child comes from the other parent, or there may be a member of the extended family who is able to care for the child adequately. However, as in *Re M* (p. 565, above), a care order may still be appropriate in such cases.

In *Re K (care order or residence order)* [1996] 1 FCR 365, [1995] 1 FLR 675, High Court, Family Division, the local authority applied for care orders in relation to two children, aged five and six. One of them had suffered an injury while in the care of their mother, who was schizophrenic. The children went to live with their grandparents under interim care orders. They were diagnosed as suffering from an incurable muscle-wasting disease which would confine them to wheelchairs by the age of ten. The local authority asked the court to make a supervision order and a residence order in favour of the grandparents. The grandparents' position was that a care order would give them greater support, and they did not want the responsibility of a residence order. The mother supported the making of a care order because that would require the local authority to promote contact between her and the children (section 34). The local authority eventually withdrew its opposition to a care order.

Stuart-White J:

...First, I find it rather difficult to conceive of circumstances in which it would not be wrong in principle to oblige an individual who has not applied for and does not desire a residence order, with its concomitant parental responsibility, to accept such an order and such responsibility. I accept that the power to make such an order does exist under s. 10(1)(b) of the Act, but it seems to me that the cases in which it would be right to exercise that power in the circumstances which I have mentioned, must be wholly exceptional, and this is not a wholly exceptional case of that kind.

The second principle which seems to me to emerge is this: that if I do not exercise the power to impose a residence order and parental responsibility on individuals who do not want it, then the only persons with parental responsibility will be the mother and the father. It is not suggested, as I understand it, that there exist any practicable means of preventing their exercising that parental responsibility with potentially harmful and possibly disastrous effects on the children, save by the making of a public law order: see *Nottinghamshire County Council v P* [1993] 1 FLR 514, and the Court of Appeal decision in the same case at [1994] Fam 18, [1993] 2 FLR 134. Thus, in the absence of a residence order, it seems to me that the argument that there are no child protection concerns could not be and cannot be maintained.

The third point of principle is this: I accept that in ordinary circumstances the court should be slow indeed to make a care order to a local authority which has applied for it but ultimately decides that it does not want it. The court will plainly, it seems to me, only make such an order under what may be unusual circumstances. The power to do so of course not only exists, it is in a sense emphasised by the Family Proceedings Rules 1991 (SI 1991/1247), r. 4.5, which provides that any application may only be withdrawn with leave. ...If the court concludes that the threshold criteria are satisfied and the welfare of the child demands it, a conclusion of course which would only be reached after considering the matters set out in s. 1(3) of the Act, then in my judgment the court should not shrink from making such a care order, even if the local authority which has applied for it should change its mind. Similarly, where the application is for a supervision order, the court should not in like circumstances shrink from exercising its powers under s. 31(5)(b) of the Act to make a care order.

Thirdly, whereas it will often be unnecessary and inappropriate to make a care order within the context of a family placement, I am not prepared to go so far as to say that it is only in exceptional circumstances that such an order should be made in that context. There may very well be circumstances where the making of a care order is the only way to protect children placed with members of their extended families from significant harm.

Fourthly, whilst it would be wholly inappropriate to make a care order solely for the purpose of conferring a financial benefit on the carers, the fact that such a financial benefit if it accrues will materially contribute to the welfare of the child, is in my judgment a factor which can properly be regarded as relevant in the balancing exercise which in any case like this is demanded. There is a complex interrelation between the general duties owed by all local authorities to children in need in their areas and the specific duties owed to children in care, as set out in ss. 21, 22, 23 and 24 of the Act, and in the relevant regulations, including the Review of Children's Cases Regulations 1991 (SI 1991/895) and the Foster Placement (Children) Regulations 1991 (SI 1991/910), to the details of which I have helpfully had my attention drawn.

...

Now bearing in mind these general principles as I have endeavoured no doubt inadequately to enunciate them, and on the overwhelming weight of the evidence in this unusual and in many ways tragic case, I have no hesitation in holding that the welfare of these children demands that a care order be made. That will provide them with security and protection during their minorities. I am quite sure that the applicant local authority has shown both good sense and, as one would expect, a true concern for these children in making the concession that it has made. I therefore make care orders in each case.

The restrictions of the High Court's inherent (wardship) jurisdiction are contained in section 100 of the Children Act 1989:

Restrictions on Use of Wardship Jurisdiction

100.—(1) Section 7 of the Family Law Reform Act 1969 (which gives the High Court power to place a ward of court in the care, or under the supervision, of a local authority) shall cease to have effect.

(2) No court shall exercise the High Court's inherent jurisdiction with respect to children—

(a) so as to require a child to be placed in the care, or put under the supervision, of a local authority;

(b) so as to require a child to be accommodated by or on behalf of a local authority;

(c) so as to make a child who is the subject of a care order a ward of court; or

(d) for the purpose of conferring on any local authority power to determine any question which has arisen, or which may arise, in connection with any aspect of parental responsibility for a child.

(3) No application for any exercise of the court's inherent jurisdiction with respect to children may be made by a local authority unless the authority have obtained the leave of the court.

(4) The court may only grant leave if it is satisfied that—

(a) the result which the authority wish to achieve could not be achieved through the making of any order of a kind to which subsection (5) applies; and

(b) there is reasonable cause to believe that if the court's inherent jurisdiction is not exercised with respect to the child he is likely to suffer significant harm.

(5) This subsection applies to any order—

(a) made otherwise than in the exercise of the court's inherent jurisdiction; and
(b) which the local authority is entitled to apply for (assuming, in the case of any application which may only be made with leave, that leave is granted).

These provisions mean that local authorities can only invoke the inherent jurisdiction in order to achieve a result which cannot be achieved under another provision of the Children Act 1989, and only then if there is reasonable cause to believe that the child is otherwise likely to suffer significant harm.

A major area of concern that has exercised all those working in the field has been the ability of the courts to control the exercise of the powers of the local authorities. Concern often relates to the inability to supervise the local authority after a care order has been made.

These issues were considered by the House of Lords in the two cases:

Re S (Children: Care Plan), Re W (Children: Care Plan)
[2002] UKHL 10, [2002] 2 AC 291, [2002] 2 All ER 192, House of Lords

In the Court of Appeal, the Court had decided, in a case concerning Bedfordshire County Council, that a court should have a wider discretion to make an interim rather than a final care order where the care plan was inchoate or there were uncertainties that were capable of resolution. The Court of Appeal had held in relation to the second matter, from Torbay District Council, that essential milestones in the care plan should be assessed and 'starred'. The Court of Appeal had decided further that any failure to achieve a starred milestone within a reasonable time of a prescribed date should reactivate the interdisciplinary process. In those circumstances the guardian or the local authority should have the right to apply to the court for further directions.

In the House of Lords, Lord Nicholls of Birkenhead described the two innovations fashioned by the Court of Appeal in the following way. First the Court enunciated guidelines intended to give trial judges a wider discretion to make an interim care order rather than a final order. The second innovation was more radical. It concerns the position after the court has made a final order. The Court of Appeal propounded a new procedure, by which at the trial the essential milestones of a care plan would be identified and elevated to a 'starred status'.

This is Lord Nicholls' view of the 'starred status' idea:

[23]...[A] cardinal principle of the Children Act is that when the court makes a care order it becomes the duty of the local authority designated by the order to receive the child into its care while the order remains in force. So long as the care order is in force the authority has parental responsibility for the child. The authority also has power to decide the extent to which a parent of the child may meet his responsibility for him: section 33. An authority might, for instance, not permit parents to change the school of a child living at home. While a care order is in force the court's powers, under its inherent jurisdiction, are expressly excluded: section 100(2)(c) and (d). Further, the court may not make a contact order, a prohibited steps order or a specific issue order: section 9(1).

[24] There are limited exceptions to this principle of non-intervention by the court in the authority's discharge of its parental responsibility for a child in its care under a care order. The court retains jurisdiction to decide disputes about contact with children in care: section 34. The court

may discharge a care order, either on an application made for the purpose under section 39 or as a consequence of making a residence order (sections 9(1) and 91(1)). The High Court's judicial review jurisdiction also remains available.

[25] These exceptions do not detract significantly from the basic principle. The Act delineated the boundary of responsibility with complete clarity. Where a care order is made the responsibility for the child's care is with the authority rather than the court. The court retains no supervisory role, monitoring the authority's discharge of its responsibilities. That was the intention of Parliament.

...

[28] The Children Act, embodying what I have described as a cardinal principle, represents the assessment made by Parliament of the division of responsibility which would best promote the interests of children within the overall care system. The court operates as the gateway into care, and makes the necessary care order when the threshold conditions are satisfied and the court considers a care order would be in the best interests of the child. That is the responsibility of the court. Thereafter the court has no continuing role in relation to the care order. Then it is the responsibility of the local authority to decide how the child should be cared for.

...

[33] The jurisprudential route by which the Court of Appeal found itself able to bring about this development was primarily by recourse to section 3 of the Human Rights Act. Hale LJ said, at paragraphs 79-80:

> 'Where elements of the care plan are so fundamental that there is a real risk of a breach of Convention rights if they are not fulfilled, and where there is some reason to fear that they may not be fulfilled, it must be justifiable to read into the Children Act a power in the court to require a report on progress. ...the court would require a report, either to the court or to CAFCASS ...who could then decide whether it was appropriate to return the case to court. ...[W]hen making a care order, the court is being asked to interfere in family life. If it perceives that the consequence of doing so will be to put at risk the Convention rights of either the parents or the child, the court should be able to impose this very limited requirement as a condition of its own interference.'

Section 3 of the Human Rights Act

[34] The judgments in the Court of Appeal are a clear and forceful statement of the continuing existence of serious problems in this field. In the nature of things, courts are likely to see more of the cases which go wrong. But the view, widespread among family judges, is that all too often local authorities' discharge of their parental responsibilities falls short of an acceptable standard. A disturbing instance can be found in the recent case of *F v London Borough of Lambeth* (28 September 2001, unreported). Munby J said, in paragraph 38 of his judgment, that the 'blunt truth is that in this case the state has failed these parents and these boys'.

[35] It is entirely understandable that the Court of Appeal should seek some means to alleviate these problems: some means by which the courts may assist children where care orders have been made but subsequently, for whatever reason, care plans have not been implemented as envisaged and, as a result, the welfare of the children is being prejudiced. This is entirely understandable. The courts, notably through their wardship jurisdiction, have long discharged an invaluable role in safeguarding the interests of children. But the question before the House is much more confined. The question is whether the courts have power to introduce into the working of the Children Act a range of rights and liabilities not sanctioned by Parliament.

> [36] On this I have to say at once, respectfully but emphatically, that I part company with the Court of Appeal. I am unable to agree that the court's introduction of a 'starring system' can be justified as a legitimate exercise in interpretation of the Children Act in accordance with section 3 of the Human Rights Act...

Lord Nicholls went on state that the starring system was judicial innovation that passed 'well beyond the boundary of interpretation'. He could see no provision in the 1989 Act which lends itself to the interpretation that Parliament was conferring a supervisory function on the court after a care order had been made. He said that the Court of Appeal's approach constituted an amendment to the 1989 Act, not its interpretation. After considering the important issues of sections 7 and 8 of the Human Rights Act 1998 and any possible incompatibility with Article 8(2) and Article 6 of the European Convention on Human Rights (which he rejected), he turned his attention to interim care orders:

> ### Interim Care Orders
>
> [89] I turn to the other 'reversionary application' of the Children Act adumbrated by the Court of Appeal. This concerns the extended use of interim care orders. The source of the court's power to make a interim care order is section 38. The power exists when an application for a care order or a supervision order is adjourned (section 38(1)(a)) or the court has given a direction to a local authority under section 37 to undertake an investigation of a child's circumstances (section 38(1)(b)). Section 38 contains tight limits on the period for which an interim care order has effect: eight weeks initially, thereafter four weeks. The circumstances in which an interim care order ceases to have effect include also the disposal of the application for a care order or a supervision order, in both section 38(1)(a) and section 38(1)(b) cases.
>
> [90] From a reading of section 38 as a whole it is abundantly clear that the purpose of an interim care order, so far as presently material, is to enable the court to safeguard the welfare of a child until such time as the court is in a position to decide whether or not it is in the best interest of the child to make a care order. When that time arrives depends on the circumstances of the case and is a matter for the judgment of the trial judge. That is the general, guiding principle. The corollary to this principle is that an interim care order is not intended to be used as a means by which the court may continue to exercise a supervisory role over the local authority in cases where it is in the best interests of a child that a care order should be made.
>
> [91] An interim care order, thus, is a temporary 'holding' measure. Inevitably, time is needed before an application for a care order is ready for decision. Several parties are usually involved: parents, the child's guardian, the local authority, perhaps others. Evidence has to be prepared, parents and other people interviewed, investigations may be required, assessments made, and the local authority circular LAC(99)29. Although the Children Act itself makes no mention of a care plan, in practice this is a document of key importance. It enables the court and everyone else to know, and consider, the local authority's plans for the future of the child if a care order is made.
>
> [92] When a local authority formulates a care plan in connection with an application for a care order, there are bound to be uncertainties. Even the basic shape of the future life of the child may be far from clear. Over the last ten years problems have arisen about how far courts should go in attempting to resolve these uncertainties before making a care order and passing responsibility to the local authority. Once a final care order is made, the resolution of the uncertainties will be a matter for the authority, not the court.

[93] In terms of legal principle one type of uncertainty is straightforward. This is the case where the uncertainty needs to be resolved before the court can decide whether it is in the best interests of the child to make a care order at all. In *C v Solihull Metropolitan Borough Council* [1993] 1 FLR 290 the court could not decide whether a care order was in the best interests of a child, there a 'battered baby', without knowing the result of a parental assessment. Ward J made an appropriate interim order. In such a case the court should finally dispose of the matter only when the material facts are as clearly known as can be hoped. Booth J adopted a similar approach, for a similar reason, in *Hounslow London Borough Council v A* [1993] 1 FLR 702.
[94] More difficult, as a matter of legal principle, are cases where it is obvious that a care order is in the best interests of the child but the immediate way ahead thereafter is unsatisfactorily obscure. These cases exemplify a problem, or a 'tension', inherent in the scheme of the Children Act. What should the judge do when a care order is clearly in the best interests of the child but the judge does not approve of the care plan? This judicial dilemma was descried by Balcombe LJ in *In re S and D (Children: Powers of Court)* [1995] 2 FLR 456, 464, perhaps rather too bleakly, as the judge having to choose between 'the lesser of two evils'.
[95] In this context there are sometimes uncertainties whose nature is such that they are suitable for immediate resolution, in whole or in part, by the court in the course of disposing of the care order application. The uncertainty may be of such a character that it can, and should, be resolved so far as possible before the court proceeds to make the care order. Then, a limited period of 'planned and purposeful' delay can readily be justified as the sensible and practical way to deal with an existing problem.
[96] An instance of this occurred in *In re C H (Care or Interim Care Order)* [1998] 1 FLR 402. In that case the mother had pleaded guilty to causing grievous bodily harm to the child. The judge was intensely worried by the sharp divergence of professional view on placement. The local authority cautiously favoured rehabilitation. The child's guardian *ad litem* believed adoption was the realistic way to promote the child's future welfare. The judge made the care order without hearing any expert evidence on the disputed issue. The local authority would itself obtain expert advice, and then reconsider the question of placement. The Court of Appeal (Kennedy and Thorpe LJJ) held that the fact that a care order was the inevitable outcome should not have deflected the judge from hearing expert evidence on this issue. Even if the issue could not be finally resolved before a care order was made, it was obviously sensible and desirable that, in the circumstances of the case, the local authority should have the benefit of the judge's observations on the point.
[97] Frequently the case is on the other side of this somewhat imprecise line. Frequently the uncertainties involved in a care plan will have to be worked out after a care order has been made and while the plan is being implemented. This was so in the case which is the locus classicus on this subject: *In re J (Minors) (Care: Care Plan)* [1994] 1 FLR 253. There the care plan envisaged placing the children in short-term foster placements for up to a year. Then a final decision would be made on whether to place the children permanently away from the mother. Rehabilitation was not ruled out if the mother showed herself amenable to treatment. Wall J said, at page 265:

> 'there are cases (of which this is one) in which the action which requires to be taken in the interests of children necessarily involves steps into the unknown ... provided the court is satisfied that the local authority is alert to the difficulties which may arise in the execution of the care plan, the function of the court is not to seek to oversee the plan but to entrust its execution to the local authority.'

In that case the uncertain outcome of the treatment was a matter to be worked out after a care order was made, not before. The Court of Appeal decision in *In re L (Sexual Abuse: Standard of Proof)* [1996] 1 FLR 116 was another case of this type: see Butler-Sloss LJ, at page 125E-H. So also was the decision of the Court of Appeal in *In re R (Care Proceedings: Adjournment)* [1998] 2 FLR 390.

[98] These are all instances of cases where important issues of uncertainty were known to exist before a care order was made. Quite apart from known uncertainties, an element of future uncertainty is necessarily inherent in the very nature of a care plan. The best laid plans 'gang aft a-gley'. These are matters for decisions by the local authority, if and when they arise. A local authority must always respond appropriately to changes, of varying degrees of predictability, which from time to time are bound to occur after a care order has been made and while the care plan is being implemented. No care plan can ever be regarded as set out in stone.

[99] Despite all the inevitable uncertainties, when deciding whether to make a care order the court should normally have before it a care plan which is sufficiently firm and particularised for all concerned to have a reasonably clear picture of the likely way ahead for the child for the foreseeable future. The degree of firmness to be expected, as well as the amount of detail in the plan, will vary from case to case depending on how far the local authority can foresee what will be best for the child at that time. This is necessarily so. But making a care order is always a serious interference in the lives of the child and his parents. Although article 8 contains no explicit procedural requirements, the decision making process leading to a care order must be fair and such as to afford due respect to the interests safeguarded by article 8: see *TP and KM v United Kingdom* [2001] 2 FLR 549, 569, paragraph 72. If the parents and the child's guardian are to have a fair and adequate opportunity to make representations to the court on whether a care order should be made, the care plan must be appropriately specific.

[100] Cases vary so widely that it is impossible to be more precise about the test to be applied by a court when deciding whether to continue interim relief rather than proceed to make a care order. It would be foolish to attempt to be more precise. One further general point may be noted. When postponing a decision on whether to make a care order a court will need to have in mind the general statutory principle that any delay in determining issues relating to a child's upbringing is likely to prejudice the child's welfare: section 1(2) of the Children Act.

[101] In the Court of Appeal Thorpe LJ, at paragraph 29, expressed the view that in certain circumstances the judge at the trial should have a 'wider discretion' to make an interim care order: 'where the care plan seems inchoate or where the passage of a relatively brief period seems bound to see the fulfilment of some event or process vital to planning and deciding the future'. In an appropriate case, a judge must be free to defer making a care order until he is satisfied that the way ahead 'is no longer obscured by an uncertainty that is neither inevitable nor chronic'.

[102] As I see it, the analysis I have set out above adheres faithfully to the scheme of the Children Act and conforms to the procedural requirements of article 8 of the Convention. At the same time it affords trial judges the degree of flexibility Thorpe LJ is rightly concerned they should have. Whether this represents a small shift in emphasis from the existing case law may be a moot point. What is more important is that, in the words of Wall J in *Re J*, the court must always maintain a proper balance between the need to satisfy itself about the appropriateness of the care plan and the avoidance of 'over-zealous investigation into matters which are properly within the administrative discretion of the local authority'. This balance is a matter for the good sense of the tribunal, assisted by the advocates appearing before it: see [1994] 1 FLR 253, 262.

QUESTIONS

i. Where does all of this leave dissatisfied parents (and children) when confronted by a local authority that is unwilling, or possibly unable, to implement its plan?

ii. If there is 'drift', can you think of any existing mechanisms that can be prayed in aid? (Look at sections 22 (p. 537 above) and 26 of the Children Act 1989 and sections 7 and 8 of the Human Rights Act 1998.

iii. How can the court decide whether a care order is in a child's interests, if it cannot be sure whether the child will be rehabilitated with the parents, or placed in a children's home, with a succession of short-term foster-parents, or with a long-term substitute family?

The court and the local authority have a shared objective to achieve a result that is in the best interests of the child. Sadly, local authorities sometimes have to be reminded, as shown in *Cheshire County Council v S (Children) and W (A Child)* [2007] EWCA Civ 232, CA.

SW (the mother) and DS (the father) had three children. All three children were the subjects of care proceedings instituted by the local authority. The threshold criteria under section 31 of the 1989 Act were plainly satisfied, and there was no question of any of the children living with either of their parents, who had separated but remained in contact. The local authority's original care plans were that each child should be placed separately for adoption outside the natural family. Those care plans were supported in each case by the children's guardian in the proceedings. The children had, for a short time, lived with their maternal grandparents. The latter had been unable to cope, and the children had moved into foster care. The local authority's fostering panel recommended that the children's maternal great aunt and uncle should be approved as kinship foster carers for the middle child (CO). This caused the local authority to revise its care plan for that child, which became placement with the great aunt and uncle under a care order. However, the knock-on effect of the change of plan was that the maternal grandparents then sought to intervene in the proceedings, and to seek orders that the other two children, CH and L, should live with them.

Wall LJ:

Some Basic Propositions

[25] Before turning to examine the local authority's decision making processes in these proceedings, we regret to say that we think it necessary to set out what we had previously thought to be some elementary principles of family law and practice as they affect the relationship between a judge hearing proceedings under Part IV of the 1989 Act, and the local authority which brings them.

...

[27] Parliament has placed the responsibility for making care orders on the court, not on the local authority which brings the proceedings. Before a care order can be made, the local authority has to satisfy the court that the threshold criteria under section 31 of the 1989 Act are satisfied, and the court also has to be satisfied that a care order is in the best interests of the child concerned. To the latter end, the court is under a duty rigorously to scrutinise the care plan advanced by the local authority, and if the court does not think that it meets the needs of the child concerned, the court can refuse to make a care order. So much is elementary.

[28] The significance of local authority care plans was, we think, both recognised and reinforced by Parliament in the enactment of section 31A of the 1989 Act through the medium of section 121(2) of the 2002 Act. There is now a mandatory duty on local authorities to prepare a care plan for each child who is the subject of care proceedings, to keep that care plan under review and if some change is required, to revise the care plan or to make a new plan accordingly – see section 31A(1) and (2) of the 1989 Act. This case, it seems to us, is about both the merits of the

local authority's late changes of plan on the facts, and the methodology of its decision making processes.

[29] What, however, is equally elementary is that once the court has made a final care order, responsibility for its implementation passes to the local authority, and save for the powers identified by the House of Lords in the case of *Re S (Children: Care Plan); Re W (Children: Care Plan)* [2002 UKHL 10, [2002] 2 AC 291 (hereinafter *Re S; Re W*), neither the court nor the children's guardian has any further role in the children's lives.

[30] What appears not to be understood, however, and thus needs to be clearly repeated, is that not only does the court have the duty rigorously to scrutinise the care plan and to refuse to make a care order if it does not think the plan in the child's best interests; the court also has the right to invite the local authority to reconsider the care plan if the court comes to the conclusion that the plan – or any change in the plan - involves a course of action which the court believes is contrary to the interests of the child, and which would be likely to lead the court to refuse to make a care order if the local authority were to adhere to the care plan it has proposed.

[31] In the instant case, the local authority's second ground of appeal begins with the following sentence:

> It is submitted that the learned judge when faced with a cohate [*sic*] care plan ***cannot*** [emphasis supplied] adjourn the matter in order that the Director of Social Services shall reconsider the plan.

[32] In our judgment, that submission is simply and plainly wrong. We express surprise that it was advanced. To be fair to counsel instructed on behalf of the local authority, she acknowledged in oral argument that the judge did have the power to invite the local authority to reconsider the care plan: her complaint was that he should not have exercised it on the facts of this case, or exercised it differently. That, of course, is a quite separate argument.

[33] However, the grounds of appeal advanced by the local authority contain a second, equally fallacious submission. This was:-

> It is submitted that in asking the appellant authority to reconsider its position the learned judge did not adopt the 'lesser of two evils' test. It is submitted that the options available to the learned judge in this case were the making of no order or approving the care plan.

[34] Once again, in oral argument, counsel agreed that the second sentence of this ground of appeal should be struck through as erroneous. However, in our judgment, the first sentence is also plainly wrong ...

[35] It is, we think, worthwhile pausing for a moment to reflect on why a court is entitled to exercise a discretionary jurisdiction to adjourn in order to invite a local authority to reconsider. The answer, we think, is, like much of what we have already said, self-evident. Care proceedings are only quasi-adversarial. There is a powerful inquisitorial element. But above all, they are proceedings in which the court and the local authority should both be striving to achieve an order which is in the best interests of the child. There needs to be mutual respect and understanding for the different role and perspective which each has in the process. We repeat: the shared objective should be to achieve a result which is in the best interests of the child.

...

[38] Two members of this court sat for many years hearing care proceedings ... Neither can recall a case in which a local authority behaved as this authority has done. In the overwhelming majority of cases in which there is a disagreement between the local authority and the court over a child's care plan, that disagreement is resolved by careful reconsideration on both sides. In our experience, as a consequence, such disagreements are extremely rare. That is as it should be. It is patently not in the interests of the already disadvantaged children involved

in care proceedings for there to be a stand-off between the court and the local authority, the result of which, as here, is still further delay in resolving the children's future placements.

...

[42] In *Re S and D* [1995] IFCR 626, Balcombe LJ made the following well-known statement: 'It is an unhappy position, where there is a dispute between all those whose professional duty it is to have the best interests of the children at heart, if they cannot reach agreement. But in those particular circumstances, as I see it, the Judge really has no alternative. He has to choose what he believes to be the lesser of two evils. That may be making a care order with the knowledge that the care plan is one which he does not approve, or it may be making no order with the consequences to which I have already adverted.'

...

[47] In our judgment, nothing done by the judge in the instant case comes anywhere near ... 'overzealous investigation'... : nor were the matters about which the judge was concerned 'properly within the administrative discretion of the local authority'. They went to the heart of the case, and the critical decision about CO's welfare which it was the function of the judge to make.

[48] The judge is also criticised for making an interim care order in relation to CO pending the return of the case to his list after reconsideration of the care plan by the local authority. This is a criticism we simply do not understand. What other order was the judge to make? If he had made a care order he would have abnegated his responsibility for CO's welfare and the local authority would have placed him with Mr and Mrs W. If he had made no order, the outcome would have been in the manifestly inappropriate hands of CO's parents. A further interim order was the only order the judge could make in these circumstances.

[49] Finally on this topic, we are equally bewildered by the fact that both the local authority and Mr and Mrs W assert that the judge was either invoking or intending to invoke section 38(6) of the 1989 Act. The judge was doing nothing of the kind. In particular, he was not directing a further assessment of CO: he was simply inviting the local authority to reconsider its care plan. Section 38(6) is irrelevant in this context.

[50] Now that the care proceedings are to be re-heard, it will be for the judge re-hearing them to decide what directions should be given as to the evidence to be filed for the purposes of the re-hearing. Inevitably, the children must now be subject to interim care orders under section 38 of the 1989 Act. ... We hope, however, that the local authority will not be so foolish as to think that, because interim orders are being made to hold the ring until such time as final decisions are made, it is entitled to implement whatever placements it thinks appropriate pending the re-hearing. The children must plainly remain where they are until the matter is re-heard. Any attempt to implement the changed care plans without the express approval of the court would, in our view, not only be unprincipled in the context of the relationship between the court and local authorities: it would also be irrational, and likely to be struck down by a court exercising the power of judicial review. ...

[51] We have to say that [we] find a discussion in the terms of the preceding paragraph highly distasteful. As the authorities we have cited demonstrate, both the court and the local authority should be engaged in cooperation, not confrontation. Our response has been provoked by the behaviour of the local authority. We remain, however, of the hope that the re-hearing will be conducted differently. We think the local authority should take heed of the wise words of the judge when he said in paragraph 12 of his judgment:

> 'I remind myself that it is particularly important, in circumstances such as these, for the court to be mindful that neither sympathy with relatives, nor exasperation with the local authority is the court's prime concern. The court's prime concern is the welfare of these children. It is the court's duty to scrutinise the local authority care plan with this

principle in mind. The court is not bound to approve any decision of a panel convened by the local authority to make recommendations to it. It is pertinent, in my judgment, to remind the local authority that the director of Social Services is equally not bound to accept a recommendation of panel if he or she considers it to be contrary to the welfare of the child'.

[52] In our judgment, that is an accurate statement of the law.

QUESTION

This case illustrates a very sad state of affairs. Do you think that such occurrences could be prevented if the 'starred status' approach were to be introduced (see above p. 585)?

BIBLIOGRAPHY

11.1 Some statistics

We quoted from:

Brent Council, *A Child in Trust – The Report of the Panel of Inquiry into the Circumstances surrounding the Death of Jasmine Beckford* (Chairman: L. Blom-Cooper QC) (1985) London, London Borough of Brent.

Department for Children, Schools and Families, *Statistical First Release 27/2007* Table A3.

Department for Education and Skills, *Care Matters: Transforming the Lives of Children and Young People in Care* (2006) (Cm 6932), para 1.13; Tables C. 3; C.4.

Department for Education and Skills, *Care Matters: Time for Change*, (2007) executive summary, para. 3.

J. Packman, with J. Randall and N. Jacques, *Who Needs Care? Social-Work Decisions about Children* (1986) Oxford, Basil Blackwell, 194–197.

J. Renvoize, *Children in Danger* (1974) London, Routledge and Kegan Paul; (1975) Harmondsworth, Penguin Books, 20, 24.

Report of the Inquiry into Child Abuse in Cleveland 1987 (Chairman: The Hon Mrs Justice Butler-Sloss DBE) (Cm. 412) (1988) London, HMSO, 4.

Additional reading

Department of Health, Report of an Inquiry by Lord Laming *The Victoria Climbie Inquiry* (2003) (Cm 5730) London, Department of Health.

Report of the Tribunal of Inquiry into the abuse of children in care in the former county council areas of Gwynedd and Clwyd since 1974 *Lost in Care* (Chairman: Sir Ronald Waterhouse), HC 201 (2000) London, The Stationery Office.

11.2 How the legislation developed

We quoted from:

Department for Education and Skills, *Care Matters: Time for Change* (2007), para 9.

Department of Health, *Working Together to Safeguard Children* (1991) London, HMSO 1.4.

Department of Health, *Working Together – A guide to arrangements for inter agency co-operation for the protection of children from abuse* (2006) London, HMSO, paras 1.3–1.5.

DHSS and others, *The Law on Child Care and Family Services* (Cm. 62) (1987) London, HMSO, paras 18, 20, 21.

J.M. Eekelaar, R. Dingwall and T. Murray, 'Victims or Threats? Children in Care Proceedings' [1982] *Journal of Social Welfare Law* 67, 71–78.

J. Packman, *The Child's Generation: Child Care Policy in Britain* (2nd edn, 1981) Oxford, Basil Blackwell, 57–59, 156, 161.

Additional reading

The Children's Rights Director, OFSTED *Children and safeguarding* (2007), available at http://www.rights4me.org.

J. Masson, 'From Curtis to Waterhouse: State Care and Child Protection in the UK 1945–2000' in S.N. Katz, J. Eekelaar and M. Maclean, *Cross Currents* (2000), Oxford, Oxford University Press, 565–587.

W. Utting, *People Like Us* (1997) London, The Stationery Office.

11.3 Child protection inquiries

We quoted from:

Department for Children, Schools and Families *Every Child matters: Cross-Government Working with local partners to achieve better outcomes for children and young people* (2007) London.

Department of Health, *Child Protection – Messages from Research* (1995) London, HMSO, pp. 15, 25–29, 32, 54–55.

Department of Health, *Working Together – A guide to arrangements for inter agency co-operation for the protection of children from abuse* (2006) London, HMSO, paras 1.29–1.33; 5.16; 5.19–5.22; 5.89

DHSS and others, *The Law on Child Care and Family Services* (Cm. 62) (1987) London, HMSO, paras 42–43.

General Medical Council, *GMC Confidentiality: Protecting and Providing Information* (2004), para. 29, available at http://www.gmc-uk.org/guidance/current/library/confidentiality.asp#29.

Report of the Inquiry into Child Abuse in Cleveland 1987 (Chairman: The Hon Mrs Justice Butler-Sloss DBE) (Cm. 412) (1988) London, HMSO, paras 12.1–12.4; 12.10; 12.18–12.19; 12.34–12.35.

Additional reading

D. Archard 'Can child abuse be defined?' in *Moral Agendas for Children's Welfare*, by M. King (ed.) (1999) Routledge.

Department of Education and Skills, *Local Safeguarding Children Boards: A Review of Progress* (2007) London, HMSO.

Department of Health and others, *Child Protection – Medical Responsibilities* (1994) London, Department of Health.

Department of Health *Working together to safeguard children* (2006) London, The Stationery Office.

DHSS, *Review of Child Care Law – Report to Ministers of an Interdepartmental Working Party* (1985) London, HMSO.

Michael Freeman 'The Sexual Abuse of Children' in *Sexuality Repositioned* by B. Brooks-Gordon, L. Gelsthorpe, M. Johnson and A. Bainham (eds) (2004) Oxford, Hart Publishing, 317–338.

A. Levy (ed.), *Refocus on Child Abuse* (1994) London, Hawksmere.

J. Packman, *The Child's Generation: Child Care Policy in Britain* (2nd edn, 1981) Oxford, Basil Blackwell.

Nigel Parton, *The Politics of Child Abuse* (1985) Macmillan.

R. Sinclair and R. Bullock, *Learning from Past Experience: A Review of Serious Case Reviews* (2000) London, Department of Health.

The Children's Rights Director, OFSTED *Children and Safeguarding* (2007), available at http://www.rights4me.org.

The Pindown Experience and the Protection of Children: The Report of the Staffordshire Child Care Enquiry (Allan Levy QC and Barbara Kahan) (1991) London, HMSO.

H. Ward, *Looking after Children: Research into Practice* (1995) London, HMSO.

11.4 Assessment and protection orders

We quoted from:

Department of Health, *Guidance and Regulations on the Children Act 1989*, vol. 1, *Court Orders* (1991) London, HMSO, paras 4.44, 4.6, 4.12, 4.15, 4.31.

Report of the Inquiry into Child Abuse in Cleveland 1987 (Chairman: The Hon Mrs Justice Butler-Sloss DBE) (Cm. 412) (1988) London, HMSO, paras 10.6–10.10, 10.13.

Additional reading

Dame Margaret Booth, *Report on the Delays in Children Act Proceedings* (1996) London, Lord Chancellor's Department.

L. Davis, 'Protecting Children in an Emergency – Getting the balance right' [2007] *Family Law* 727.

Department of Health, *Framework for the Assessment of Children in Need and their Families* (2000) London, Department of Health.

Lord Chancellor's Department, *Scoping Study on Delay in Children Act Cases* (2002) London, Lord Chancellor's Department.

J. Masson, M. Winn Oakley and K. Pick *Emergency Protection Orders, Court Orders for Child Protection Cases*, Research funded by NSPCC and Nuffield, (2004) School of Law, University of Warwick.

11.5 The threshold test

We quoted from:

DHSS, *Review of Child Care Law – Report to Ministers of an Interdepartmental Working Party* (1985) London, HMSO, paras 15.12, 15.14–15.16, 15.18, 15.20, 15.23, 15.24.

Additional reading

Dame Margaret Booth, *Report on the Delays in Children Act Proceedings* (1996) London, Lord Chancellor's Department.
M. Hayes 'Re O and N; Re B – Uncertain evidence and risk taking in Child protection cases' (2004) 16 *Child and Family Law Quarterly* 63.
J. Herring 'The Suffering Children of Blameless Parents' (2000) 116 *Law Quarterly Review* 116.
Sir William Utting, *People Like Us* (1997) London, The Stationery Office.

11.6 The choice of final order

We quoted from:

DHSS, Review of Child Care Law – Report to Ministers of an Interdepartmental Working Party (1985) London, HMSO, paras 18.5–18.7, 18.9.

Additional reading

Department of Health, *Children's Safeguards Review: Choosing with Care*, HSC 1998/212 (1998) London, Department of Health.
Department of Health, *Quality Protects*, (1998) Circular LAC (98) (28).
M. Thorpe and E. Clarke, *Divided Duties* (1998) Bristol, Family Law.
R. White 'Planning for Children in Care' in S. Cretney (ed.), *Family Law Essays for the new Millennium* (2000) Bristol, Family Law, 143–148.

12

THE 'PERMANENCY' PRINCIPLE: WHO ARE MY FAMILY?

TWO STORIES

> *Former foster child D*: I must have been 7 when I went to live with my foster parents. They were the second family I went to. The first family went abroad after promising to take me with them. They didn't and it broke my heart at the time. ... The [foster parents] had two of their own and another foster child. Somehow I never felt I belonged there. We foster children did not fit in very well. I cannot say that I developed much attachment to them. My foster mother often threatened to send me back to the Corporation. Sometimes she would ring them but they would make her change her mind. I suppose I was difficult too, and I would hark back or argue. She would then smack me and send me to bed... I could be nasty and so could my foster mother... I left at 17 when our quarrels became worse, and I went to live in a hostel.

John Triseliotis, 'Growing Up in Foster Care and After' (1980).

> *Clair:* I was put into care at 13. The reason being that I was considered to be a threat to my family because I kept starting fires in the house. I was also self harming, but a difficult set of circumstances within my family had affected me deeply and my attempts at damaging my home and myself were really a cry for help... Eventually I revealed to a social worker what had actually happened to me within my family and I was immediately taken to a place of safety. I went to an emergency placement for the night but... I just wanted to go home. My mother had always used putting me in care as a threat so I thought it was something to be frightened of, but at the same time I felt relieved... In foster care I settled down and was able to behave like a normal teenager... I honestly think that if I hadn't been put into care I would now be dead. Suddenly I had a whole network of people to support me. It was like one big family.

http://www.bbc.co.uk/threecounties for 30 September 2007.

In 2004, the Children's Rights Director, now attached to OFSTED and then an official within the Commission for Social Care Inspection, sent questionnaires to 1,096 children in foster care. These children would have been placed by a local authority under section 20 of the Children Act 1989 (see above p. 535), placed by a voluntary organisation under section 59(1)(a) Children Act 1989, or subject to compulsory care by a section 31 care order (see above p. 563). It is not likely that any of the children would have been fostered privately. Four hundred and ten of the children (37 per cent) returned completed questionnaires. They had lots of positive things to say about foster care, and a good deal of sound advice, summarised in *Being Fostered* (2005). The Commission for Social Care Inspection incorporated some of the key messages in its Report *The Right People For Me* (2004) as follows:

> Two out of three children in the survey had been in at least one foster home before the one they were living in when they completed the survey. There were things that children liked about foster

> care. They liked the care and support that many were given. They liked being part of a family and valued the opportunities that fostering gave. However, amongst the things they did not like were: two thirds of these children said they had no choice at all when they moved into their present foster home. This may be the result of a lack of potential placements to choose from, or the child feeling that his or her opinions are not counted. One third of the children said they had not been given enough information about their present foster family before they moved in.
>
> One in five said they had wanted more reassurance about their future foster homes before they moved in. One third of children said they no longer had any contact with their birth parents. One in eight had some contact, but it was 'hardly ever'. Just under one third had contact most weeks. Coming into foster care had stopped one in ten children from doing a sport or activity they had done before. Children said the worst things about being fostered were missing your birth family and past friends, the rules and punishments in your foster home, and feeling you are the odd one out because you are in care. The ideal foster carer, according to children, is friendly, kind, cheerful, fun, caring – and easy to talk to. But however friendly, kind and caring the foster carer, the stress inherent in joining a new family remains something every child has to negotiate. For those whose placements 'work', there is much to celebrate. Those who, for whatever reasons, are repeatedly moved may find the odds increasingly stacked against them. They may come to expect change, and even rejection, as normal, and lose any sense of control.

The foster parent's position is no easier, as this quotation from a study by Gillian Schofield and others of *Growing Up in Foster Care* (2000) shows:

> We've got a lot closer relationship, especially since we've known she's staying here permanently. Because I always held something back because I thought she was going. And I also didn't want Roxanne to get too close to me so that she had to go away to someone else because that would have been another break in her life. Not just for my own sake but for Roxanne's sake. I kept a little bit of distance with her. Now I know she's staying permanently we don't need to do that anymore because there's not going to be a move.

Whenever children have to be looked after away from home for any length of time, for whatever reasons, three questions arise. First, is the ultimate plan that they should go back home eventually, as most children do, or is it that they should stay away permanently? Secondly, if they are to stay away, what should be the legal basis on which they do so – fostering, adoption or something in between, now known as special guardianship? Thirdly, what in any event should be their links with their family of origin?

12.1 THE LAW ON MAINTAINING FAMILY LINKS

Among other things, Schedule 2 to the Children Act 1989 contains this duty towards all children who are looked after by local authorities:

> **15.**—(1) Where a child is being looked after by a local authority, the authority shall, unless it is not reasonably practicable or consistent with his welfare, endeavour to promote contact between the child and–
>
> (a) his parents;
>
> (b) any person who is not a parent of his but who has parental responsibility for him; and

(c) any relative, friend or other person connected with him.

(2) Where a child is being looked after by a local authority–

(a) the authority shall take such steps as are reasonably practicable to secure that–
  (i) his parents; and
  (ii) any person who is not a parent of his but who has parental responsibility for him, are kept informed of where he is being accommodated; and
(b) every such person shall secure that the local authority are kept informed of his or her address.

If the child is subject to a care order (see above p. 563), and so cannot simply go home, this duty is reinforced with the powers of the courts:

34.—(1) Where a child is in the care of a local authority, the authority shall (subject to the provisions of this section) allow the child reasonable contact with–

(a) his parents;
(b) any guardian or special guardian of his;
(ba) any person who by virtue of section 4A has parental responsibility for him;
(c) where there was a residence order in force with respect to the child immediately before the care order was made, the person in whose favour the order was made; and
(d) where, immediately before the care order was made, a person had care of the child by virtue of an order made in the exercise of the High Court's inherent jurisdiction with respect to children, that person.

(2) On an application made by the authority or the child, the court may make such order as it considers appropriate with respect to the contact which is to be allowed between the child and any named person.

(3) On an application made by–

(a) any person mentioned in paragraphs (a) to (d) of subsection (1); or
(b) any person who has obtained the leave of the court to make the application; the court may make such order as it considers appropriate with respect to the contact which is to be allowed between the child and that person.

(4) On an application made by the authority or the child, the court may make an order authorising the authority to refuse to allow contact between the child and any person who is mentioned in paragraphs (a) to (d) of subsection (1) and named in the order.

(5) When making a care order with respect to a child, or in any family proceedings in connection with a child who is in the care of a local authority, the court may make an order under this section, even though no application for such an order has been made with respect to the child, if it considers that the order should be made.

(6) An authority may refuse to allow the contact that would otherwise be required by virtue of subsection (1) or an order under this section if–

(a) they are satisfied that it is necessary to do so in order to safeguard or promote the child's welfare; and
(b) the refusal–
  (i) is decided upon as a matter of urgency; and
  (ii) does not last for more than seven days.

(7) An order under this section may impose such conditions as the court considers appropriate.

(8) The Secretary of State may by regulations make provision as to–

(a) the steps to be taken by a local authority who have exercised their powers under subsection (6);
(b) the circumstances in which, and conditions subject to which, the terms of any order under this section may be departed from by agreement between the local authority and the person in relation to whom the order is made;
(c) notification by a local authority of any variation or suspension of arrangements made (otherwise than under an order under this section) with a view to affording any person contact with a child to whom this section applies.

(9) The court may vary or discharge any order made under this section on the application of the authority, the child concerned or the person named in the order.

(10) An order under this section may be made either at the same time as the care order itself or later.

(11) Before making a care order with respect to any child the court shall–

(a) consider the arrangements which the authority have made, or propose to make, for affording any person contact with a child to whom this section applies; and
(b) invite the parties to the proceedings to comment on those arrangements.

The way in which section 34 operates was explored by the Court of Appeal in the following cases:

Re H (children) (termination of contact) [2005] EWCA (Civ) 318, Court of Appeal

The judge in this case had to consider the future of two children, aged five and three. There was a care order in favour of the local authority in respect of the five-year-old. The parents sought the discharge of that order, and the local authority sought an order in respect of the younger child. The trial judge decided that both children should be committed into care with a care plan that provided for adoption. The judge said that there should be a plan for post-adoption contact with the birth parents, and refused the application by the local authority for an order under section 34(4). He said that were he to make a section 34(4), order he would be sending the wrong signals to all presently engaged with the case and also to prospective adopters, and this would be something contrary to the interests of the children. The local authority appealed.

Thorpe LJ:

[Counsel for the local authority] says that the judge fell into fundamental error because he did not sufficiently recognise that to refuse them the order sought was to jeopardise an adoptive placement, or to make it more difficult for the local authority to achieve, or to delay its achievement. For, she said, having identified an adoptive family, the local authority would be obliged to return to the court to seek the section 34(4) order all over again with consequential litigation delay which would impact upon a successful placement. It certainly cannot be said that the judge ignored that factor. He said . . . 'I know the Local Authority may find it easier, and will find it easier, to find adopters if they have a s 34(4) order. I am sorry about that . . .' . . . The function of the judge in upholding the Parliamentary intention of section 34 and in granting section 34(4) orders restrictively and stringently is an important one . . .

Sedley LJ:

Lord Atkin once remarked that justice and convenience are frequently not on speaking terms. [The trial judge] was plainly alive to this. He was rightly concerned that leaving contact in the hands of the local authority might allow the best interests of the children to take second place to the practicalities of finding adopters with the minimum of impediment...[The] practical convenience of the local authority matters, but only to the extent that to impede it would be contrary to the best interests of the children. On [the trial judge's] findings this was not such a case. It was a case in which the children needed as much continued contact with their natural parents as was compatible with the long-term plan for them. The section 34(4) order would not have prevented this, but it would have transferred the discretion to the local authority. It is not surprising that the judge preferred to ensure that the lifeline of parental contact should not for the time being be placed at risk of severance.

Appeal dismissed.

Re E (a minor) (care order: contact)
[1994] 1 FCR 584, [1994] 1 FLR 146, Court of Appeal

The parents of two little boys, aged five and a half and nearly four at the date of the hearing, had personality problems which made it difficult for them to look after the children. Over a period of some twenty-two months leading up to the hearing, the boys had been first looked after by family friends, then accommodated by the local authority, and then the subject of care proceedings. Everyone agreed that there should be a care order. But the local authority also applied for an order under section 34(4) because the care plan was adoption. The judge adopted the approach that he could not order contact which was incompatible with the care plan unless this could be attacked as capricious or invalid in judicial review terms. He granted the application and the parents and children's guardian appealed.

Simon Brown LJ:

...even when the s.31 criteria are satisfied, contact may well be of singular importance to the long-term welfare of the child: first, in giving the child the security of knowing that his parents love him and are interested in his welfare; secondly, by avoiding any damaging sense of loss to the child in seeing himself abandoned by his parents; thirdly, by enabling the child to commit himself to the substitute family with the seal of approval of the natural parents; and, fourthly, by giving the child the necessary sense of family and personal identity. Contact, if maintained, is capable of reinforcing and increasing the chances of success of a permanent placement, whether on a long-term fostering basis or by adoption.

There is, I appreciate, an ongoing debate regarding the merits of open or closed adoption and it is not one that I propose to enter. But whatever be the arguments, there will undoubtedly be cases, and this I believe to be one, in which some continuing face-to-face contact is clearly desirable and which call, accordingly, at the very least for some positive efforts on the local authority's part to find, if at all possible, prospective open adopters; here, it seems to me, there have been none.

Even, therefore, were the appeal to be decided without reference to further evidence, I myself would have been inclined to allow it. For good measure, however, there is now before the court further evidence indicating at the very least this: that the admirable short-term foster-mother in whose care over the last 17 months these children have continued to thrive has indicated a wish to be considered, together with her husband, as a long-term foster-parent for these children, a placement which would allow continuing face-to-face contact.

> For that reason too it seems to me highly desirable that this matter be considered afresh... by a judge who will have the advantage of hearing from the local authority, both (a) what upon further investigation appears to be the up-to-date prospects of open adoption, and (b) their considered views upon the merits or otherwise of long-term fostering by the foster-parents.
>
> Those advantages, in my judgment, clearly outweigh the disadvantages of delaying yet further a final decision upon the long-term placement of these children.
>
> *Order accordingly.*

Taking children into public care is, of course, an interference with their own and their families' right to respect for their family life under Article 8(1) of the European Convention on Human Rights. As such it must be justified under Article 8(2) as proportionate to the legitimate aim of protecting the child (see p. 30, above). The courts have stated that the Children Act 1989 is compliant with the Human Rights Act 1998 and the European Convention. Attempts to argue otherwise have been singularly unsuccessful.

In *Re V (Care Proceedings: Human Rights Claims)* [2004] EWCA 54, CA, the parents were disadvantaged people from deprived and abusive backgrounds. The father had been convicted of a serious sexual offence; indeed he had sexually abused the mother when she was fourteen years old. In 2001, care proceedings were instituted only days after the birth of the parents' first child. During the care proceedings, the parents underwent a number of assessments. The predominant view of the experts regarding the father was that he posed a very serious risk towards vulnerable young females, and the risk of reoffending was high. The final hearing of the proceedings came to an end when the mother revealed for the first time that she was expecting a second child. The parents withdrew their opposition to the making of the care order and the first child was put up for adoption. Four days after the birth of the second child, the local authority again instituted proceedings. On the first day of the final hearing regarding the second child, the parents made an application for an adjournment on the basis of a discrete point under the Human Rights Act 1998. The judge granted an adjournment and the local authority and the guardian appealed. The appeal was allowed, the Court of Appeal stating that the issues raised by the parents were manifestly capable of being dealt with by the judge in the county court proceedings, and that the application for an adjournment was misconceived and should never have been made.

Counsel for the mother in this case had attempted to persuade the trial judge that the local authority had failed to meet its duty to take positive steps to reunite the family. She relied on the decision of the European Court of Human Rights in *K and T v Finland* [2001] 2 FLR 707 (as discussed above in Chapter 1 in respect of the European Court's approach to 'family life'), where the Grand Chamber had held that the authorities had taken insufficient steps in that case to try to reunite the family. The Grand Chamber had set out its thinking in this way:

3. 'Necessary in a Democratic Society'

> [154] In determining whether the impugned measures were 'necessary in a democratic society', the Court will consider whether, in the light of the case as a whole, the reasons adduced to justify these measures were relevant and sufficient for the purpose of art 8(2) of the Convention (see, inter alia, *Olsson v Sweden (no 1)* (1988) 11 EHRR 259 at 285 (para 68)).
>
> In so doing, the Court will have regard to the fact that perceptions as to the appropriateness of intervention by public authorities in the care of children vary from one contracting state to another, depending on such factors as traditions relating to the role of the family and to state intervention in family affairs and the availability of resources for public measures in this particular area. However, consideration of what is in the best interests of the child is in every case of crucial importance. Moreover, it must be borne in mind that the national authorities have the

benefit of direct contact with all the persons concerned (see *Olsson v Sweden (no 2)* (1992) 17 EHRR 134 at 181 (para 90)), often at the very stage when care measures are being envisaged or immediately after their implementation. It follows from these considerations that the Court's task is not to substitute itself for the domestic authorities in the exercise of their responsibilities for the regulation of the public care of children and the rights of parents whose children have been taken into care, but rather to review under the Convention the decisions taken by those authorities in the exercise of their power of appreciation (see, for instance, *Hokkanen v Finland* [1995] 2 FCR 320 at 330 (para 55); *Johanssen v Norway* (1996) 23 EHRR 33 at 67 (para 64)).
[155] The margin of appreciation so to be accorded to the competent national authorities will vary in the light of the nature of the issues and the seriousness of the interests at stake, such as, on the one hand, the importance of protecting a child in a situation which is assessed to seriously threaten his or her health or development and, on the other hand, the aim to reunite the family as soon as circumstances permit. After a considerable period of time has passed since the child was originally taken into public care, the interest of a child not to have his or her de facto family situation changed again may override the interests of the parents to have their family reunited. The Court thus recognises that the authorities enjoy a wide margin of appreciation in assessing the necessity of taking a child into care. However, a stricter scrutiny is called for in respect of any further limitations, such as restrictions placed by those authorities on parental rights of access, and of any legal safeguards designed to secure an effective protection of the right of parents and children to respect for their family life. Such further limitations entail the danger that the family relations between the parents and a young child are effectively curtailed (the above-mentioned *Johansen v Norway* (1996) 23 EHRR 33 at 67 (para 64)).

It is against this background that the Court will examine whether the measures constituting the interferences with the applicants' exercise of their right to family life could be regarded as 'necessary'.

Then it applied the underlying principles to the facts of this case:

[178] The Grand Chamber, like the Chamber, would first recall the guiding principle whereby a care order should in principle be regarded as a temporary measure, to be discontinued as soon as circumstances permit, and that any measures implementing temporary care should be consistent with the ultimate aim of reuniting the natural parents and the child (see, in particular, the above-mentioned *Olsson v Sweden (no 1)* (1988) 11 EHRR 259 at 290 (para 81). The positive duty to take measures to facilitate family reunification as soon as reasonably feasible will begin to weigh on the responsible authorities with progressively increasing force as from the commencement of the period of care, subject always to its being balanced against the duty to consider the best interests of the child.
[179] As to the particular circumstances, the Court notes that some inquiries were carried out in order to ascertain whether the applicants would be able to bond with the children ... They did not, however, amount to a serious or sustained effort directed towards facilitating family reunification such as could reasonably be expected for the purposes of art 8(2) – especially since they constituted the sole effort on the authorities' part to that effect in the seven years during which the children have been in care. The minimum to be expected of the authorities is to examine the situation anew from time to time to see whether there has been any improvement in the family's situation. The possibilities of reunification will be progressively diminished and eventually destroyed if the biological parents and the children are not allowed to meet each other at all, or only so rarely that no natural bonding between them is likely to occur. The restrictions and prohibitions imposed on the applicants' access to their children, far from preparing a possible reunification of the family, rather contributed to hindering it. What is striking in the present case is the exceptionally firm negative attitude of the authorities.

> Consequently, the Grand Chamber of the Court agrees with the Chamber that there has been a violation of art 8 of the Convention as a result of the authorities' failure to take sufficient steps directed towards a possible reunification of the applicants' family regardless of any evidence of positive improvement in the applicants' situation.

Wall LJ in *Re V* was not impressed with counsel's submissions in the case before him. He stated that the positive duty to take measures to facilitate family reunion is not, and cannot, be an absolute duty and is always to be balanced against the duty to consider the best interests of the child.

QUESTIONS

i. Do you think that Wall LJ has correctly interpreted paragraph 178 of the *K and T* judgment?
ii. The issue in *Re V* was returned to the trial judge for him to decide. We do not know his decision. If you were the trial judge, what decision would you take?

The parents in *Re K (a minor) (wardship: adoption)* [1991] FCR 142, [1991] 1 FLR 57, CA, had two older children and, despite some social services involvement with the family, there was no question of removing them. The marriage was a stormy one, the father was addicted to gambling and had a criminal record, and the mother was receiving treatment for heroin addiction. The mother became unexpectedly pregnant with child N during a particularly difficult time. A private arrangement was made to hand over the child to foster parents, as the foster parents thought permanently. This was done when the child was six weeks old, but less than three months later the mother wanted her back. The foster parents made the child a ward of court and obtained interim care and control. When the child was seven and a half months old, the judge gave them care and control with a view to adoption and terminated the mother's access. The mother, father and local authority all appealed.

Butler-Sloss LJ:

> ... This is a very sad case in which the little girl was handed over by the mother at a time of great stress and financial difficulty within 6 weeks of the birth of the child to a much older couple who are childless and have for some years hoped to care for a child on a long-term basis. The mother and the father have repented of their decision to hand over N and wish to reintroduce her into the family with her elder brother and sister. She has, however, settled into a warm and loving family who are currently caring for her admirably and wish to continue to do so. If she moves there will be inevitable upheaval and upset for the child. If she goes back to her natural family there are question marks as to their suitability. There are also question marks as to the long-term suitability of the family with whom she is at present.
>
> ...
>
> Once the judge found that this mother genuinely wanted her child back and was a mother who cared properly for the other two children, not to give her at least an opportunity to try to rehabilitate the family was to deprive the child of any chance of her own family. I recognise that the placement of the child back with the natural family poses considerable risks and requires careful consideration from the local authority concerned. But, backed as it is by all the professionals who gave evidence, it cannot be said to be wholly unreasonable. One attempt at rehabilitation

with a young baby and a mother capable of loving her children would have been likely to have been attempted if this private arrangement had not been entered into...

There is a second matter raised in the arguments of the local authorities. ...the position of the plaintiffs as permanent caretakers presents its own problems and would have done so even if the natural family had been entirely unsuitable. ...

Appeal allowed.

QUESTION

Can Butler-Sloss LJ's comment in *Re K (A Minor) (Custody)* in the penultimate paragraph quoted above be reconciled with *J v C* (see above p. 347), or should different considerations apply in public law proceedings?

Local authorities are now enjoined to develop 'concurrent planning'. This is explained in *Care matters: Time for Change* (2007) as follows:

3.52 Concurrent planning can provide a way in which young children can achieve permanence with the minimum of placement moves. In concurrent planning arrangements, a child in care is placed with approved foster carers who, as well as providing temporary care for the child, bring him/her to regular supervised contact sessions with his/her birth parents and other relatives. The carers are also approved as prospective adopters so that if the birth parents' rehabilitation plan is not successful, the child does not need to move when the care plan changes and can remain in the same placement while his/her adoption plan is developed and implemented.

3.53 Concurrent planning has the potential to benefit those children in care for whom reunification with their birth parents does not look promising but where it cannot yet be ruled out and who will need an adoptive family if reunification is not successful. Its purpose is to prevent children from drifting in care and becoming harder to place because they have suffered placement breakdown and disrupted attachments.

3.54 Concurrent planning is not the right option for all children and we should not overestimate its potential. It needs to be seen in the wider context of care planning, as one of a number of options for achieving permanence. However, it can offer significant benefits for a small group of children.

...

3.56 The Government is committed to promoting and enabling greater use of concurrent planning, including by raising awareness of its benefits and limitations, the availability of existing services and the learning from these projects

QUESTIONS

i. Can you see risks, and if so, what are they?

ii. Do you think that the problem highlighted by *Re K* could have been ameliorated if the local authority had applied for a care order and then had been able to achieve permanence by concurrent planning?

12.2 LEGAL OPTIONS FOR RELATIVES AND OTHER CARERS

We have already seen how, in *J v C* [1970] AC 668, [1969] 1 All ER 788 (p. 347, above), the House of Lords decided that there was no presumption of law in favour of parents in private law disputes with non-parents. We have also seen how the Children Act 1989 deliberately endorses the paramountcy of the child's welfare.

However, parents and non-parents do not have equal rights of access to the courts. The Children Act 1975 allowed non-parents to apply for 'custodianship' once they had looked after the child for some time. Even this was not implemented until 1988, and it was little used. Emma Bullard and Ellen Malos in their study of *Custodianship* (1990) looked into the reasons for *not* applying for custodianship:

> 9.39... Most of the responses received were from unrelated foster carers. 14% of the respondents had not heard of custodianship until receiving our letter and questionnaire. The great majority (90%) of non-users described it as an advantage that, under a custodianship order, the child in their care could not be moved to another placement by a social worker. Nevertheless they had not wanted to apply for custodianship, and gave a variety of reasons for their decision.
>
> 9.40 Apart from the people who had not heard of custodianship, there was a group who had heard of it but had found the available information confusing and inadequate. Some carers had decided that adoption was preferable, while others said simply that they could see no advantages to be gained by applying for custodianship. Financial considerations were mentioned by some carers who were caring for a child with special needs or who were dependent on state benefits. A number of respondents felt that they needed continued social work support for a variety of reasons such as making access arrangements, the child's special needs, or behaviour problems in adolescence.

The Law Commission discussed non-parent applicants in their Working Paper on *Custody* (1986):

> 5.37 The simplest way of removing the arbitrariness, gaps and inconsistencies in the present law is to allow non-parents the same rights to apply for custody as have parents. They already have the right to apply for care and control in wardship proceedings, so that no new principle is involved in extending the statutory procedures to them. Given the large numbers of children who have experienced divorce, after which in theory any person can intervene to seek custody (or indeed access), it might not be such a radical step in practice as it at first sight appears.
>
> ...
>
> 5.39 It may therefore be that a requirement of leave, which currently applies to most interventions in divorce suits, would be a sufficient deterrent against unwarranted applications and would allow the court to judge whether the applicant stood a reasonable prospect of success in the light of all the circumstances of the case.

Special considerations applied, however, to children in care:

> 5.42 The unqualified right in foster parents to apply for custody could... be seen as an unprecedented interference in the child care responsibilities of the local authority... If foster parents were able to challenge their placement decisions in the courts, there would clearly be even greater pressure to allow parents to do so.
>
> ...

5.46... The security and stability which might be gained from a custodianship order must be set against the difficulties which premature applications might cause in the making and realisation of the local authority's plans, particularly for children who have been compulsorily removed from inadequate homes. Current child care practice places great emphasis upon planning a secure and permanent home for children who might otherwise have to grow up in care. This may be achieved either through making strenuous efforts to solve the family's problems and reach a position where parents and child may be reunited or through finding an alternative family which can provide the sort of care which is best suited to the child's needs. Such plans may obviously take some time to formulate and put into effect.

The end result, in the Children Act 1989, was a modified 'open door' that has been widened over the years. We have already seen (p. 476, above) how section 10(1) and (2) provide for the court to make any section 8 order, either in any family proceedings or on free-standing application, and that applications can be made either by people entitled to do so or by anyone with the court's leave. The section continues:

10.—(5) The following persons are entitled to apply for a residence or contact order with respect to a child–

(a) any party to a marriage (whether or not subsisting) in relation to whom the child is a child of the family;
(aa) any civil partner in a civil partnership (whether or not subsisting) in relation to whom the child is a child of the family
(b) any person with whom the child has lived for a period of at least three years;
(c) any person who–
  (i) in any case where a residence order is in force with respect to the child, has the consent of each of the persons in whose favour the order was made;
  (ii) in any case where the child is in the care of a local authority, has the consent of that authority; or
  (iii) in any other case, has the consent of each of those (if any) who have parental responsibility for the child.

(5A) A local authority foster parent is entitled to apply for a residence order with respect to a child if the child has lived with him for a period of at least one year immediately preceding the application.

(8) Where the person applying for leave to make an application for a section 8 order is the child concerned, the court may only grant leave if it is satisfied that he has sufficient understanding to make the proposed application for the section 8 order.

(9) Where the person applying for leave to make an application for a section 8 order is not the child concerned, the court shall, in deciding whether or not to grant leave, have particular regard to–

(a) the nature of the proposed application for the section 8 order;
(b) the applicant's connection with the child;
(c) any risk there might be of that proposed application disrupting the child's life to such an extent that he would be harmed by it; and
(d) where the child is being looked after by a local authority–
  (i) the authority's plans for the child's future; and
  (ii) the wishes and feelings of the child's parents.

(10) The period of three years mentioned in subsection (5)(b) need not be continuous but must not have begun more than five years before, or ended more than three months before, the making of the application.

A case that sets the scene is:

Re M (care: contact: grandmother's application for leave)
[1995] 2 FLR 86, [1995] Fam Law 540, Court of Appeal

Two boys, aged twelve and a half and nine, had been in care since 1987, a period of some seven and a half years, because of their mother's psychiatric illness. They still had contact with both their mother and their grandmother, even after they had been made wards of court and the court had endorsed the plan that they be placed for adoption, but the contact caused difficulties and was suspended in 1991. Shortly after that the older boy ran away to his grandmother, and she returned him to care. The boys were not placed with prospective adopters until 1993. In 1994, the grandmother sought leave to apply for contact. The judge had no information on the children's views or those of the prospective adopter. He refused leave and the grandmother appealed.

Ward LJ:

...Section 34(3) [See above p. 599] gives the court a wide and unfettered discretion in dealing with such applications. This can be contrasted with s. 10(9) which deals with leave to apply for s.8 orders.

...If the court were faced with an application by a grandparent for leave to apply for a residence order, alternatively a contact order, it would be anomalous, in my judgment, were the court not to take into account for the exercise of the s. 34(3) discretion the criteria specifically laid out for consideration in s. 10(9). Those particular factors seem to me to be also apposite for s. 34(3). The court must, of course, have regard to all the circumstances of the case, for each case is different, but in my judgment the court should always have particular regard at least to the following:

(a) The nature of the contact which is being sought. Contact to children in care varies infinitely from that which is frequent, to that which takes place two, three or four times a year to keep memory alive. It varies from contact which is face-to-face, to contact which is indirectly maintained through the exchange of letters, cards, photographs and gifts.

(b) The connection of the applicant to the child. The more meaningful and important the connection is to the child, the greater is the weight to be given to this factor. Grandparents ought to have a special place in any child's affection worthy of being maintained by contact but it is easy to envisage family circumstances, very much like those before us in this case where, however loving the grandparent may be, life's wheel of misfortune has diminished the importance to the child of that blood tie and may, for example, have strengthened the claims for contact by former foster-parents who have forged close attachment to the child. The fact is that Parliament has refused to place grandparents in a special category or to accord them special treatment. Nevertheless, by virtue of Sch. 2, para. 15 [p. 598, above], contact between a child and his or her family will be assumed to be beneficial and the local authority will need to file evidence to justify why they have considered that it is not reasonably practicable or consistent with the child's welfare to promote that contact.

(c) Disruption. This seems to me to be the factor of crucial significance, a fortiori when the child is in care. The child will only have come into care if life had already been so thoroughly disrupted that such intervention was judged to be necessary. The need then for stability and security is

usually vital. The breakdown of the foster placement may be so harmful that it should not be placed at risk. All that is obvious. It is, none the less, significant and appropriate that the risk of disruption which is primarily contemplated in s.10(9)(*c*) is the risk 'there might be of that *proposed application* [for a s.8 order] disrupting the child's life to such an extent that he would be *harmed* by it'. I add the emphasis to make two points. The harm envisaged is harm which, through s.105(1), is defined by s.31(9) to mean impairment of health or development as those words are there defined. A child's upset, unhappiness, confusion or anxiety, needs to be sufficiently severe before it can amount to an impairment of emotional, social or behavioural development. Secondly, the risk must arise from the proposed application. The very knowledge that litigation is pending can be sufficiently unsettling to be harmful; if leave is given, the process of investigating the merits of the application can be sufficiently disruptive if it involves the children in more interviews, psychiatric investigations and so forth. The stressfulness of litigation may impair the ability of those who have care of the child properly to discharge their responsibility to the child's detriment. Questions of that sort are the narrow focus of the court's attention in weighing this factor. That is not to say that the court shuts its eyes to what prospects of eventual success the application has, and if the making of a contact order would be so manifestly disruptive as to be totally inimical to the child's welfare, then such an obviously unsustainable claim will not be permitted to get off the starting-blocks. Except in the most obvious case, it is incumbent on the respondent to the application to produce some evidence to establish disruption.

(d) The wishes of the parents and the local authority. They are very material, though not determinative. That the parents' wishes are relevant is consistent with the whole underlying philosophy of the Act, a cornerstone of which is the protection of the integrity and independence of the family. When a care order is made, the local authority acquires parental responsibility. Their exercise of that responsibility commands equal protection from unwarranted interference. ...

I have attempted to identify the main factors which will be material for the court considering any application for leave. The list is not, however, intended to be exhaustive. I turn next to the question of what test the court must apply to decide whether or not to grant leave.

...

In my judgment the approach should be this:

(1) If the application is frivolous or vexatious or otherwise an abuse of the process of the court, of course it will fail.

(2) If the application for leave fails to disclose that there is any eventual real prospect of success, if those prospects of success are remote so that the application is obviously unsustainable, then it must also be dismissed:...

(3) The applicant must satisfy the court that there is a serious issue to try and must present a good arguable case. 'A good arguable case' has acquired a distinct meaning: see the long line of authorities setting out this as the convenient approach for the grant of leave to commence proceedings and serve out of the jurisdiction under RSC Ord. 11. One should avoid unprofitable inquiry into what precisely these turns of phrase mean. Their sense is well enough known – is there a real issue which the applicant may reasonably ask the court to try and has he a case which is better than merely arguable yet not necessarily one which is shown to have a better-than-even chance, a fair chance, of success? One should avoid over-analysis of these 'tests' and one should approach the matter in the loosest way possible, looking at the matter in the round because only by such imprecision can one reinforce the importance of leaving the exercise of discretion unfettered. ...

It would be equally unwise to circumscribe rigidly the manner of the exercise of discretion. Each case is different and the weight to be given to the various factors will accordingly vary from case to case. The weight to be given to those factors is the very essence of the exercise of discretion.

Appeal allowed and case remitted to the High Court. Official Solicitor to act as guardian ad litem. Contact application to be heard on same day and immediately preceding adoption application.

QUESTIONS

i. Do you think that Ward LJ's approach needs reconsideration in the light of the Human Rights Act 1998?

ii. How would you weigh the comparative entitlements of grandparents (or other close relatives), who have a good relationship with the child but are not currently looking after him, with those of his current local authority foster parents?

iii. How many reasons can you think of why (a) the applicants, (b) the child, (c) the parents, or (d) the local authority might prefer (1) an adoption, (2) long-term fostering, or (3) a residence order?

iv. In *Care Matters: Time for Change* (2007) the Department for Education and Skills state that it intends to put in place a 'gateway approach' to family and friends to make sure that care by family and/or friends is considered as an option at the first and every subsequent stage of decision making. It intends to introduce a requirement that relatives and friends are, as far as possible, considered in all cases as potential carers as part of the care plan lodged with the court at the outset of care proceedings. Does this approach mean that a section 10(9) application will not be necessary?

v. Perhaps the answer is to remove leave requirement for grandparents. Do you agree? (Read Felicity Kaganas, 'Grandparents' rights and Grandparents campaigns' (2007) 19 *Child and Family Law Quarterly* 17.)

vi. Mary and John have two children. John has never really had much time for his in-laws. Mary recently died, and John has a new partner. They are bringing up the children, and John makes it difficult for the maternal grandparents to see their grandchildren. What can the grandparents do? If, sadly, John has also died, and the children are taken into care, what then can the grandparents do to ensure that they have good contact with their grandchildren? (See *Anon*, 'Judicial Inconsistency and the Family Court System' (2007) *Family Law*.)

The Department of Health's *Review of Adoption Law* (1992) favoured residence orders over adoption for relatives and other long-term carers, and looked for ways of making the former more attractive:

> 6.2 Where a child is living away from his parents and it is unlikely that he will be able to return home, he and his carers – be they relatives, foster-parents, or people with a residence order – may wish to enhance the security and stability of their relationship. Unless the child no longer feels part of his parents' family and would prefer to look on his present carers as his parents, his needs are more likely to be met by a residence order under the Children Act 1989 than by an adoption order. A residence order confers parental responsibility upon the child's carers without interfering with the child's identity and family relationships. Although it can be revoked, in practice a residence order will generally provide the necessary permanence for the family concerned, as once a child is settled the courts are reluctant to disturb the status quo and are most unlikely to discharge the order in favour of another party. Extra security may be gained by applying for a prohibited steps order restraining the parent from meeting aspects of parental responsibility without the permission of the court. The court may also prohibit any named person from applying for an order under the Act without the court's leave: this power could be used to prevent a parent disturbing the status quo by applying for a residence or contact order.
>
> 6.3 We are concerned that a number of adoption applications, particularly by relatives and step-parents, are made without giving proper consideration to the needs of the child and the effect of being cut off from his or her birth family. Adoption is too often regarded as the only way of

securing permanence, in part no doubt because it is more familiar than other orders and because its long-term implications are not always fully understood. We therefore recommend that the court should have a duty when deciding whether or not to make a placement order or an adoption order to consider the alternative orders available under the 1989 Act or adoption legislation. . . .

6.4 Responses to the review revealed a wide degree of concern that residence orders are not perceived as being likely to offer a sufficient sense of permanence for a child and his carers. It is hoped that in time residence orders will grow in familiarity and acceptance. One must nonetheless recognise the importance of the public perception of an order of this kind: some potential applicants may be deterred by the possible difficulty of explaining to other people what their relationship with the child is and by the relative attractiveness of an order which enables them to be regarded as the child's parents. It may therefore be beneficial to enhance the attractiveness of residence orders in certain circumstances.

6.5 We propose that, where a court makes a residence order in favour of a person other than a parent or step-parent and considers that that person will be responsible for the child's upbringing until he grows up, the court should have a further power to appoint, where appropriate, that person as the child's inter vivos guardian. Such a guardian would have parental responsibility until the child reached the age of 18, even though the residence order would normally come to an end at the age of 16. The guardian would have all the rights, duties and powers of a guardian under section 5 of the Children Act 1989 except for the right to agree or withhold agreement to the adoption of the child and the power to change the child's surname except with leave of the court. The appointment could of course be ended in the usual way by the court. An inter vivos guardian would be able to appoint a person to be the child's guardian after his or her death. Any guardian so appointed would have the right to agree or refuse to agree to the adoption of the child.

The Government's White Paper, *Adoption – a new approach* (2000), although generally enthusiastic about adoption for children in care, also favoured something along these lines:

Adoption

5.5 Adoption can offer children who are unable to return to their birth families a legally permanent new family, which they will belong to all their lives. Children say that this security, and a sense of 'belonging', is important to them (see box). Adoption is therefore a key means of providing a permanent family for these children.

> What children have said about adoption
> 'In adoption you have a real mum and dad'
> 'You cannot be taken away'
> 'I can call them mum and dad'
> 'I felt like my life was starting again'

5.6 Some looked after children, especially if they have developed a strong attachment to their foster carers, may want to be adopted by them. Some foster carers want to adopt the children in their care. Where this is in the child's best interests, it should be encouraged, as, like permanence with wider family, it allows the children to keep important attachments.

5.7 The new Standards specify that where a foster carer wants to adopt the child in their care, and that adoption would be in the interests of the child, the foster carer's application to adopt should be viewed positively and processed in three months – faster than adoptive parents who are not currently foster carers.

'Special Guardianship'

5.8 Adoption is not always appropriate for children who cannot return to their birth parents. Some older children do not wish to be legally separated from their birth families. Adoption may not be best for some children being cared for on a permanent basis by members of their wider birth family. Some minority ethnic communities have religious and cultural difficulties with adoption as it is set out in law. Unaccompanied asylum-seeking children may also need secure, permanent homes, but have strong attachments to their families abroad. All these children deserve the same chance as any other to enjoy the benefits of a legally secure, stable permanent placement that promotes a supportive, lifelong relationship with their carers, where the court decides that is in their best interests.

5.9 In order to meet the needs of these children where adoption is not appropriate, and to modernise the law so it reflects the religious and cultural diversity of our country today, the Government believes there is a case to develop a new legislative option to provide permanence short of the legal separation involved in adoption.

The White paper gave an 'illustrative case study' based on a study by Julie Selwyn and Wendy Sturgess 'Achieving permanency: Proposals for UK policy' (2000). It reads as follows:

J (13) and S (9) have been in the care of the same foster carers for some time. They came into care as the result of J disclosing sexual abuse, and are unable to return home. The foster carers and the children would like to remain together but J does not want to be adopted. She wants to keep her birth name, have contact with some members of her birth family but live with her foster cares. 'Special Guardianship' would provide her and her sister with a permanent home within their foster family.

The Adoption and Children Act 2002 provides for the new status of 'special guardianship' by inserting sections 14A-F in the Children Act 1989. In addition to those entitled to apply for an order as of right, and those who require the court's leave to apply, section 14A(6) provides for the court to make an order of its own motion. A special guardian is in the same position as a guardian after death: thus his consent, along with that of any parent with parental responsibility, will be required for the child to be adopted and he is able to appoint a guardian to act after his own death. The remaining consequences are spelled out in sections 14C and 14D:

Special Guardianship Orders: Effect

14C—(1) The effect of a special guardianship order is that while the order remains in force—

(a) a special guardian appointed by the order has parental responsibility for the child in respect of whom it is made; and

(b) subject to any other order in force with respect to the child under this Act, a special guardian is entitled to exercise parental responsibility to the exclusion of any other person with parental responsibility for the child (apart from another special guardian).

(2) Subsection (1) does not affect—

(a) the operation of any enactment or rule of law which requires the consent of more than one person with parental responsibility in a matter affecting the child; or

(b) any rights which a parent of the child has in relation to the child's adoption or placement for adoption.

(3) While a special guardianship order is in force with respect to a child, no person may—

(a) cause the child to be known by a new surname; or
(b) remove him from the United Kingdom,

without either the written consent of every person who has parental responsibility for the child or the leave of the court.

(4) Subsection (3)(b) does not prevent the removal of a child, for a period of less than three months, by a special guardian of his.

(5) If the child with respect to whom a special guardianship order is in force dies, his special guardian must take reasonable steps to give notice of that fact to –

(a) each parent of the child with parental responsibility; and
(b) each guardian of the child;

but if the child has more than one special guardian, and one of them has taken such steps in relation to a particular parent or guardian, any other special guardian need not do so as respects that parent or guardian.

(6) . . .

Special Guardianship Orders: Variation and Discharge

14D—(1) The court may vary or discharge a special guardianship order on the application of—

(a) the special guardian (or any of them, if there are more than one);
(b) any parent or guardian of the child concerned;
(c) any individual in whose favour a residence order is in force with respect to the child;
(d) any individual not falling within any of paragraphs (1) to (c) who has, or immediately before the making of the special guardianship order had, parental responsibility for the child;
(e) the child himself; or
(f) a local authority designated in a care order with respect to the child.

(2) In any family proceedings in which a question arises with respect to the welfare of a child with respect to whom a special guardianship order is in force, the court may also vary or discharge the special guardianship order if it considers that the order should be varied or discharged, even though no application has been made under subsection (1).

(3) The following must obtain the leave of the court before making an application under subsection (1)—

(a) the child;
(b) any parent or guardian of his;
(c) any step-parent of his who has acquired, and has not lost, parental responsibility for him by virtue of section 4A;
(d) any individual falling within subsection (1)(d) who immediately before the making of the special guardianship order had, but no longer has, parental responsibility for him.

(4) Where the person applying for leave to make an application under subsection (1) is the child, the court may only grant leave if it is satisfied that he has sufficient understanding to make the proposed application under subsection (1).

(5) The court may not grant leave to a person falling within subsection (3)(b)(c) or (d) unless it is satisfied that there has been a significant change in circumstances since the making of the special guardianship order.

A further consequence is set out in s 10(7A):

10 (7A) If a special guardianship order is in force with respect to a child, an application for a residence order may only be made with respect to him, if apart from this subsection the leave of the court is not required, with such leave.

QUESTIONS

i. *Care Matters: Time for Change* (2007) at 3.47 states: 'It is expected that foster carers and children in long-term foster placements, minority ethnic communities with religious and cultural difficulties with adoption, carers who are relatives and older children who do not want to sever legal ties with their birth family, will benefit particularly from special guardianship.' Do you think that the Government is over-optimistic in its assessment?

ii. If you were either a grandparent who had looked after grandchildren from infancy or a local authority foster parent, would you be attracted or put off by (a) the requirement, in section 14A(7)–(11) to notify the local social services authority, which must then make a report to the court before any order can be made; or (b) the prospect of special guardianship support services (including financial support), under section 14F?

iii. Do you agree with the proposition that 'it is important that adoption is not seen as the only or best means of providing a child with a permanent home'? If so, why, and if not, why not?

Three important Court of Appeal cases consider the advantages and disadvantages of special guardianship over adoption: *S (A Child) (No 1)* [2007] EWCA 54, *AJ (A Child)* [2007] EWCA Civ 55 and *MJ (A Child)* [2007] EWCA 56.

In *S (A Child)(No 1)*, the court was concerned with a child who was placed with a foster mother when she was three years old. The trial judge rejected the submission that there be an adoption order and made a special guardianship order. The judge said that a special guardianship order would provide a legal expression for S's loyalty to both the foster parent and her mother. The Court of Appeal dismissed the appeal.

In contrast, in *AJ (A Child)*, the trial judge dispensed with the consent of the parents of AJ (a child of five) to his adoption by his paternal aunt and uncle, who had looked after him since he was six months old. This was a case under the Adoption Act 1976 and the judge dispensed with the mother's consent on the basis that it was being unreasonably withheld. (See *Re W (an Infant)* [1971] AC 682.) Wall LJ dismissed the appeal, stating that AJ had been with his paternal aunt and uncle since the age of six months, and both he and his carers plainly needed the assurance that the security of that placement could not be disturbed. He said that that security could not be provided by a special guardianship order but could be provided by adoption.

In *MJ (A Child)*, the mother sought to appeal the order of the judge that MJ (aged three) be adopted by the mother's maternal half-sister, with whom MJ had been placed pursuant to a care order. The mother acknowledged that she was not in a position to care for MJ but argued that MJ should remain with the half-sister under a special guardianship order. The trial judge asked herself this question: How important in the context of MJ's welfare is the additional element of certainty and clarity for all provided by adoption? She answered the question by concluding that no lesser order than adoption would meet MJ's welfare, and that adoption is a proportionate order. She dispensed with the mother's consent, applying the test in section 52(1)(b) of the Adoption and Children Act 2002 on the basis that the welfare of the child requires the consent to be dispensed with (see pp. 631–2 below). The appeal was dismissed.

The differences between adoption and special guardianship orders is set out as an appendix to *AJ (A Child)*:

	SCHEDULE OF MAIN DIFFERENCES BETWEEN SPECIAL GUARDIANSHIP ORDERS & ADOPTION	
	SPECIAL GUARDIANSHIP	ADOPTION
1. STATUS OF CARER	Special Guardian: If related to child retains existing relative status	Parent for all purposes: If related to child existing relative status changes
2. STATUS OF CHILD	A child living with relatives/carers who remains the child of birth parent	The child of the adoptive parent as if born as a child of the marriage and not the child of any other person therefore adoption includes a vesting of 'parenthood'. Section 39(1)&(2)A A 1976/ Section 67 ACA 2002
3. DURATION OF ORDER	Ceases automatically on reaching 18 if not revoked by court earlier ?whether also ceases on death The legal relationship created is therefore time limited and not lifelong Section 91(13)CA 1989	Permanent The legal relationship is lifelong Section 39(1) AA 1976/ Section 67 ACA 2002
4. EFFECT ON BIRTH PARENT PR	PR retained by birth parent SG can impose limitations in use (see 6 below) Section 14C(1)&(2) CA 1989	Birth Parent PR extinguished Section 39(2) AA 1976/ Section 46 ACA 2002

	SPECIAL GUARDIANSHIP	ADOPTION
5. CARER'S PR	PR vests in special guardian/s Section 14C(1)&(2) CA 1989 Subject to limitations (see 6 below)	PR vested in adopter/s Section 39(1) AA 1976/ Section 49 ACA 2002/ Section 2 CA 1989 No limitations (but see joint operation* below)
6. LIMITATION/ RESTRICTION OF PR (a) removal from jurisdiction	(a) up to three months without leave, thereafter only with written consent of all PR holders or leave of court unless court gave general leave on making SG order Sections 14C(3)(b)&14C(4)/14B(2)(b) CA 1989	(a) No restriction
(b) change of name	(b) can not change surname without written consent of all PR holders or order of the court Sections 14C(3)(a)/14B(2)(a)	(b) No restriction name change may take place at time of making adoption order or thereafter
(c) consent to adoption	(c) consent required from birth parents and special guardians or court must dispense with consent of birth parents and special guardians Sections 19,20,52 & 144 ACA 2002/ Section 14C(2)(b)CA 1989	(c) consent required from adopters only or court must dispense with consent of adopters only
(d) medical treatment	(d) may be difficulties where each special guardian agrees but birth parents do not in the following circumstances: Sterilisation of a child This is the example given in the government guidance to SGO in 'Every Child Matters' in Relation to effect of section 14C(2)(a) – no authority is cited Ritual Circumcision See *Re J* [2000] 1 FLR 571 Suggests that like sterilisation the consent of all PR holders would be required for this procedure	(d) no restrictions where each adoptive parent agrees (subject to age/*Gillick* competence of child) on giving consent for medical treatment *However where adoptive parents themselves disagree in these scenarios a court order may be required (see below)

	SPECIAL GUARDIANSHIP	ADOPTION
	Immunisation See *Re C* [2003] 2FLR 1095 This added contested immunisations to the small group of important decisions where the consent of both parents was required Life prolonging/Life shortening If the above scenarios require consent of all with PR surely it must then extend to issues of whether treatment should be given or withheld in terminal cases Section 14C(1)(b) with (2)(a) Section1 does not effect the operation of any enactment or rule of law which requires the consent of more than one person with PR in a matter effecting the child If consent of all PR holders is required for these type of decisions does this then impose a duty upon SG to consult with birth parents in advance and to bring the matter back to court for determination if birth parents indicate an objection?	*Section 2(7) CA 1989 Where more than one person has PR for a child each may act alone and without the other but nothing in this part shall be taken to affect the operation of any enactment which requires the consent of more than one person in a matter affecting the child
(e) voluntary accommodation	(e) If SG objects LA cannot accommodate child unless court order If all SGs consent but birth parents object would appear that LA cannot accommodate child unless court order if birth parent willing and able to provide accommodation or arrange for accommodation to be provided This is not the case if there is in force a residence order and the residence order holder consents nor if there is a care and control	(e) where adoptive parents agree they can accommodate voluntarily

	SPECIAL GUARDIANSHIP	ADOPTION
	order pursuant to wardship or inherent jurisdiction and the person in whose favour the order is made consents.	
(f) removal from voluntary accommodation	(f) Any person may remove from voluntary accommodation at any time This is not the case if residence order holder of carer under wardship/inherent jurisdiction agrees to the voluntary accommodation How is the 'exclusive' nature of the SG's PR intended to operate in these circumstances? It appears that the statute requires the consent of all PR holders therefore if SGs consent to accommodation but parents do not the parents can simply remove the child. Sections 20 (7)(8) &(9) CA 1989	(f) adoptive parents can remove from voluntary accommodation
(g) consent to marriage under 18	(g) if all SG agree no restriction the Marriage Act 1949 has been amended to enable SGs to give valid consent where SGO in force (unless also care order in force) Sections 3(1), (1A)(a)&(b)	(g) if all agree no restriction
7. DEATH OF CHILD	Special guardian must notify parents with PR Section 14C(5) CA 1989 Special guardians may not be able to arrange for burial/cremation in circumstances where parents wish to undertake such a task if the SGO ends on death. See by way of analogy *R-v-Gwynedd CC ex p B* [1991] 2FLR 365	No requirements for notification The rights and duties of legal parents do not end on death therefore would be no such conflict
8. REVOCATION OF ORDER	Specific statutory provision for birth parents to apply for discharge of SGO with leave of the court, leave not to be granted unless there has been a significant change of circumstances	No statutory provision for revocation in wholly exceptional circumstances court may set aside adoption order, normally limited to where has been a fundamental breach of natural justice.

	SPECIAL GUARDIANSHIP	ADOPTION
	Specific statutory provision for court to discharge of its own motion even where no application in any 'family proceedings' Section 14D CA 1989	See for example Re K Adoption & Wardship [1997] 2FLR 221
9. FUTURE APPLICATIONS BY PARENTS (a) Residence (b) Contact (c) Prohibited Steps (d) Specific Issue	(a) Leave required (b) no automatic restriction (c) no automatic restriction (d) no automatic restriction Sections 10(4), (7A)&(9) CA 1989 A parent is entitled to apply for any section 8 order except residence where is SGO	leave required leave required leave required leave required Section 10(2)(b), (4), (9)
10. RESPONDENTS TO FUTURE LEGAL PROCEEDINGS RE CHILD	Birth parents would be respondents in addition to the SGs to any applications in relation to the child for Section 8 orders, EPOs, Care/Supervision Orders, Secure accommodation etc	Only Adopters would be automatic respondents
11. MAINTENANCE	Does not operate to extinguish any duty on birth parents to maintain the child	Operates to extinguish any duty on birth parents to maintain the child Section 12(3)(b) AA1976/Section 46(2)(d)ACA 2002
12. INTESTACY	Child placed under SGO will not benefit from the rules relating to intestacy if the SGs die intestate	Adopted Child will have rights of intestate succession

Wall LJ set out the underlying principles to be applied in making a Special Guardianship Order rather than an Adoption Order in *S (A child) No 1* [2007] EWCA Civ 54, CA:

Wall LJ:

General Comments

[41] The *White Paper* contains a helpful summary of the main features of the special guardianship regime, as being to:

- give the carer clear responsibility for all aspects of caring for the child or young person, and for making the decisions to do with their upbringing.

- provide a firm foundation on which to build a lifelong permanent relationship between the carer and the child or young person;
- preserve the legal link between the child or young person and their birth family;
- allow proper access to a full range of support services including, where appropriate, financial support.

[42] It also gives some helpful illustrations of some circumstances in which guardianship may be appropriate:

(i) Older children who do not wish to be legally separated from their birth families.
(ii) Children being cared for on a permanent basis by members of their wider birth family.
(iii) Children in some minority ethnic communities, who have religious and cultural difficulties with adoption as it is set out in law.
(iv) Unaccompanied asylum-seeking children who need secure, permanent homes, but have strong attachments to their families abroad.

...

[44] It is important to note also that the statutory provisions draw strong and clear distinctions between the status of children who are adopted, and those who are subject to lesser orders, including special guardianship. ...

[45] Thus, although section 14C(1) of the 1989 Act gives special guardians exclusive parental authority, this entitlement is subject of a number of limitations...

[46] ... in addition to the fundamental difference in status between adopted children and those subject to special guardianship orders, there are equally fundamental differences between the status and powers of adopters and special guardians. These, we think, need to be borne in mind when the court is applying the welfare checklist under both section 1(3) of the 1989 Act and section 1 of the 2002 Act.

[47] Certain other points arise from the statutory scheme:–

(i) The carefully constructed statutory regime (notice to the local authority, leave requirements in certain cases, the role of the court, and the report from the local authority – even where the order is made by the court of its own motion) demonstrates the care which is required before making a special guardianship order, and that it is only appropriate if, in the particular circumstances of the particular case, it is best fitted to meet the needs of the child or children concerned.
(ii) There is nothing in the statutory provisions themselves which limits the making of a special guardianship order or an adoption order to any given set of circumstances. The statute itself is silent on the circumstances in which a special guardianship order is likely to be appropriate, and there is no presumption contained within the statute that a special guardianship order is preferable to an adoption order in any particular category of case. Each case must be decided on its particular facts; and each case will involve the careful application of a judicial discretion to those facts.
(iii) The key question which the court will be obliged to ask itself in every case in which the question of adoption as opposed to special guardianship arises will be: which order will better serve the welfare of this particular child?

[48] We would add, however, that, although the 'no order' principle as such is unlikely to be relevant, it is a material feature of the special guardianship regime that it is 'less intrusive' than adoption. In other words, it involves a less fundamental interference with existing legal relationships. The court will need to bear Article 8 of ECHR in mind, and to be satisfied that its order is a proportionate response to the problem, having regard to the interference with family life which is involved. In choosing between adoption and special guardianship, in most cases Article 8 is

unlikely to add anything to the considerations contained in the respective welfare checklists. Under both statutes the welfare of the child is the court's paramount consideration, and the balancing exercise required by the statutes will be no different to that required by Article 8. However, in some cases, the fact that the welfare objective can be achieved with less disruption of existing family relationships can properly be regarded as helping to tip the balance.

...

Special Guardianship Orders Within Pre-existing Family Relationships

[50] It is clear from the *White Paper* that special guardianship was introduced at least in part to deal with the potential problems arising from the use of adoption in the case of placements within the wider family.

[51] A particular concern is that an adoption order has, as a matter of law, the effect of making the adopted child the child of the adopters for all purposes. Accordingly, where a child is adopted by a member of his wider family, the familial relationships are inevitably changed. This is frequently referred to as the 'skewing' or 'distorting' effect of adoption, and is a factor which the court must take into account when considering whether or not to make an adoption order in such a case. This is not least because the checklist under section 1 of the 2002 Act requires it to do so: – see section 1(4)(f) ('the relationship which the child has with relatives.'). However, the weight to be given to this factor will inevitably depend on the facts of the particular case, and it will be only one factor in the overall welfare equation.

...

[64] ...under a special guardianship order, the only section 8 application for which a parent requires the leave of the court is one for a residence order. This seems to be implicit in section 10(7A). There is a specific requirement for leave for an application for a residence order. It seems to follow that leave is not required to make an application for any other section 8 order.

[65] The absence of a general requirement for leave may seem surprising. Special guardianship orders are designed to produce finality, and there is, accordingly, logic in the proposition that a parent requires the leave of the court to reopen the issue of the order itself or of the child's residence. But, if so, one might expect similar considerations to apply to other forms of order under section 8. An essential component of the advantages produced by an adoption order for both adopters and children is that they are in most cases then free from the threat of future litigation. If the same protection is not available in respect of special guardianship orders, this may be a substantial derogation from the security provided.

...

It is true that the court may invoke section 91(14) to place a filter on further applications by parents for other section 8 orders (including contact, and specific issue orders such as schooling).

...

[67] In a statutory structure designed to achieve permanence and security for children and their carers outside adoption, it may seem an anomaly that the natural parent, whose parental responsibility is effectively and largely neutered, should nonetheless have an automatic right to apply to the court for section 8 relief (other than a change of residence). The very nature of such an application may be to interfere with the exercise of parental responsibility by the special guardian which is meant to be exclusive. The need to invoke section 91(14) to protect special guardians and children from the anxiety imposed by the prospect of future litigation is a possible weakness in the scheme.

[68] In any event, anomalous or not, it is plain to us that the statutory scheme for making special guardianship orders was designed generally to allow unfettered access to the court thereafter by parents in relation to all section 8 orders apart from residence. In this respect it must be

accepted that special guardianship does not always provide the same permanency of protection as adoption. In our judgment, this is a factor, which in a finely balanced case, could well tip the scales in favour of adoption.

...

In What Circumstances (if Any) Should the Court Impose A Special Guardianship Order on Unwilling Parties?

[73] There is no doubt, as section 14A(6)(b) of the 1989 Act makes clear, that the court has power to make a special guardianship order of its own motion, where the welfare of the child is in issue in any family proceedings,...

QUESTIONS

i. Do you think there has been a consistent policy to discourage adoption where the child is being cared for by members of the wider family?

ii. Is the approach of the judges in these three cases that which the policy makers and the legislature intended?

iii. Do you think that a child's relationship within his wider family is often 'skewed' by an adoption order, and if so, so what?

iv. Assuming a special guardianship order is not made, what advantages would there be to (a) the foster parents and (b) the child, if the court decide that the child should remain with the foster parents under a care order rather than a special guardianship order.

v. Looking at the differences set out above (see pp. 615–19 above), do you think there will be more, fewer, or about the same number of (a) local authority foster parents, (b) grandparents who have looked after their grandchildren from infancy, who apply for special guardianship orders as applied for custodianship orders?

12.3 ADOPTION AS A CHILD CARE RESOURCE

In *Adoption Now–Messages from Research* (1999), a report prepared by Professor Roy Parker with the help of an advisory group and the support of the Department of Heath, the context is set as follows:

The last 25 years have seen a dramatic change in the character of adoption. Its most significant feature has been the sharp reduction, from the early 1970s onwards, in the number of babies of unmarried mothers being given up for adoption. There were several reasons for this.

First, there was the 'contraception revolution', accelerated by the increasing use of the 'pill' from the early 1960s. Then, in 1967, the Abortion Act extended the grounds upon which a legal abortion could be obtained. ...

Gradually, the stigma associated with illegitimacy diminished, a trend reflected in the Family Law Reform Act 1987. It had been this sense of stigma which had persuaded many unmarried mothers to give up their babies for adoption. ...

In addition to these changes the status of unmarried motherhood came to be absorbed into the rapidly growing number of 'lone mothers' which followed the relaxation of the grounds for divorce introduced in the Divorce Law Reform Act 1969. ...

Another factor which contributed to the reduction in the number of babies of unmarried mothers who were given up for adoption was the shift in attitudes to sexual morality and to the institution of marriage. ...

There were, finally, various changes in housing and social security policies, especially in the 1970s, that eased (although they by no means eliminated) some of the practical problems of bringing up a child single-handedly. ...

Thus, as a result of these converging trends, the character of unmarried motherhood underwent a radical transformation, starting in the 1960s. Over much the same period, however, changes were also occurring in the way in which the well-being of vulnerable children was being perceived.

First, there was a growing conviction, which has continued to be supported by experience and research, that children should not be separated from their parents and family if at all possible. This encouraged efforts to restore to their families children who had been separated from them, a principle codified in the Children Act 1948 but only gradually put into practice. This was followed somewhat later by the official encouragement of preventive work which was aimed at avoiding the need for such separation in the first place, a development that was given legal endorsement in the Children Act 1963 but which, again, took time to gather momentum.

To the extent that these two policies – of restoration and prevention – were successful, the circumstances of the children coming into and remaining in local authority care became more problematic than those of the children who had preceded them. Of course, neither policy was pursued with equal vigour in all areas; but their cumulative effect, certainly after 1978 with the downturn in the number of children in care, was to increase the proportion who were considered to have 'special needs'. These children tended to be older and to have had more chequered and damaging childhoods. Furthermore, the emphasis upon rehabilitation also meant that social workers were expected to persevere in their efforts to secure the safe return of children to their families, thereby delaying the point at which any other plan was made for their future if that became necessary.

However, the 1970s saw a growing concern that steps should be taken to ensure that children like these had a stable home, reliable relationships and committed and enduring care. In 1973 Rowe and Lambert published *Children Who Wait* which showed that many children were indeed languishing in care for want of effective planning. Some, it was argued, could have rejoined their families; others required a long-term alternative. At much the same time the notion of 'permanency planning' was arriving in Britain from the United States. This, in particular, was thought to advocate adoption as the best permanent solution for separated children who could not, within a reasonable time, be rehabilitated with their families.

These ideas found expression in the Children Act 1975 and then in the Adoption Act 1976. In essence this made it easier for children who were in the care of local authorities to be adopted where that was appropriate. It also required each local authority to ensure that an adoption service was provided in their area. However, the legislation was not implemented until 1988, although by then most authorities had such a service as it was then understood to be.

Nevertheless, there was no substantial increase in the *number* of adoptions from care until after 1988. A peak of 2700 was reached in 1992, falling back thereafter to 1900 in 1996, although rising again slightly to 2000 in 1998. This fall, it has been claimed, was attributable to the effect of the Children Act 1989 which was implemented in October, 1991. It was reported that local authorities then became more hesitant to recommend adoption, believing that the court would now only be prepared to grant an order if there was indisputable evidence that a child's rehabilitation with their family was impossible or unwise.

However, adoptions from care came to account for an increasingly large *proportion* of all adoptions: from just 7% in 1975 to around 40% during the 1990s with most of the others being adoptions by step-parents or relatives.

Although there were fewer babies being relinquished for adoption, by the second half of the 1970s social services departments were being encouraged to consider adoption for more of the children in their care, more of whom were older and regarded as having special needs. The characteristics of the children who could be considered for adoption therefore had changed in a far-reaching fashion. Rather than children being 'available' for adoption, the emphasis shifted to finding families for those children who needed a permanent home. Adoption came to be acknowledged in official and professional circles primarily as a means of meeting the needs of certain children rather than as a solution to the problem of unmarried motherhood or to the needs of infertile couples.

For all these reasons it is plain that the institution of adoption has undergone profound changes, changes that have brought with them new challenges. Many more adoptions are now contested; the selection of adopters and their suitability for particular children with particular needs demands more exacting assessment; once adopted, more children continue to have some form of contact with their birth families; and the need for adoptive parents and their children to be offered support after the order has been granted places special demands upon social and other services. In the past it has been assumed that having adopted a baby or infant with the agreement of the birth parents, and with all contact having been discontinued and secrecy preserved, the adopters could be left to raise the child as they would a child born to them; that is, without any special services needing to be provided. Such an assumption is no longer tenable.

The law as laid down in section 1 of the Adoption and Children Act 2002 makes welfare the paramount consideration, aligning adoption with the Children Act 1989.

Considerations Applicable to the Exercise of Powers

1.—(1) This section applies whenever a court or adoption agency is coming to a decision relating to the adoption of a child.

(2) The paramount consideration of the court or adoption agency must be the child's welfare, throughout his life.

(3) The court or adoption agency must at all times bear in mind that any delay in coming to the decision is likely to prejudice the child's welfare.

(4) The court or adoption agency must have regard to the following matters (among others)—

(a) the child's ascertainable wishes and feelings regarding the decision (considered in the light of the child's age and understanding),
(b) the child's particular needs,
(c) the likely effect on the child (throughout his life) of having ceased to be a member of the original family and become an adopted person,
(d) the child's age, sex, background and any of the child's characteristics which the court or agency considers relevant,
(e) any harm (within the meaning of the Children Act 1989) which the child has suffered or is at risk of suffering, and

(f) the relationship which the child has with relatives, and with any other person in relation to whom the court or agency considers the question to be relevant, including—
    (i) the likelihood of any such relationship continuing and the value to the child of its doing so,
    (ii) the ability and willingness of any of the child's relatives, or of any such person, to provide the child with a secure environment in which the child can develop, and otherwise to meet the child's needs,
    (iii) the wishes and feelings of any of the child's relatives, or of any such person, regarding the child.

(5) In placing the child for adoption, the adoption agency must give due consideration to the child's religious persuasion, racial origin and cultural and linguistic background.

(6) The court or adoption agency must always consider the whole range of powers available to it in the child's case (whether under this Act or the Children Act 1989); and the court must not make any order under this Act unless it considers that making the order would be better for the child than not doing so.

(7) In this section, 'coming to a decision relating to the adoption of a child', in relation to a court, includes—

(a) coming to a decision in any proceedings where the orders that might be made by the court include an adoption order (or the revocation of such an order), a placement order (or the revocation of such an order), or an order under section 26 (or the revocation of such an order),
(b) coming to a decision about granting leave in respect of any action (other than the initiation of proceedings in any court) which may be taken by an adoption agency or individual under this Act,

but does not include coming to a decision about granting leave in any other circumstances.

(8) For the purposes of this section—

(a) references to relationships are not confined to legal relationships,
(b) references to a relative, in relation to a child, include the child's mother and father.

Some of the issues surrounding this section were considered by the Court of Appeal in the following case.

Re C (A Child) and XYZ County Council and EC
[2007] EWCA Civ 1206

The case concerned a child of a young unmarried mother. The mother had placed the child for adoption immediately after its birth, and the question was whether the local authority should make enquiries to see if any of the child's birth family would be suitable carers. The mother was against making any enquiries. She had not told her family about her pregnancy or the birth. Her only relationship with the baby's father had been a 'one-night stand'. Thus, the particular features of the case were: (i) a young unmarried mother; (ii) a child born as a result of a sexual encounter on one occasion with someone with whom the mother had no other relationship; (iii) a clear view by the mother that she wished the child to be placed for adoption; and (iv) the mother had never cared for the child. The question before the court was whether there was a duty to make enquiries about the father, and to disclose the existence of the child to the maternal extended family, so as to give the father (if identified) and the maternal extended family a wider role in the future of the child. The trial judge said that the local authority were under a duty to inform themselves of as much information about the background of the extended family as they were able to. This approach was reversed on appeal:

Lady Justice Arden (Thorpe LJ and Lawrence Collins LJ were the other two judges): The 2002 Act puts the interests of the child at the forefront of decision-making about a child who is to be adopted, and it sets out a '"welfare checklist"' which any court or adoption agency making a decision about a child adoption must work through. This welfare checklist is modelled on the welfare checklist in the Children Act 1989 ('"the 1989 Act"'), but it is adapted to the particular circumstances of adoption...

[9] If the parents and the guardian give their consent, a local authority may place a child with prospective adopters under s 19 without making an application to the court: s 19 of the 2002 Act. They may, at the same time, give consent to the making of an adoption order. A reporting officer must verify that the consent is valid. Where ss 19 and 20 apply, there is a 'fast track adoption', which takes less time than an adoption where the court is involved. The consent of a parent who does not have parental responsibility is not required: s 52 of the 2002 Act. E's father has not been named on her birth certificate and he does not have parental responsibility for her. If he were hereafter to obtain parental responsibility, and by then the agency had placed E for adoption under section 19, he would be treated as having given consent when the mother gave consent: s 52(9) and (10). Where a parent with parental responsibility does not consent but the court has power to make an order of its own initiative, the court may decide not to give notice of its intention to make an order to the parent who does not consent: reg 13 of the Family Procedure (Adoption) Rules 2005 ('the 2005 Rules'). The court may dispense with the consent of a parent who cannot be found where it is in the interests of the child that the consent should be dispensed with: reg 27 of the 2005 Rules.

...

The Issues for Decision

[13] There are two issues for decision. The first issue is whether the 2002 Act imposed a duty on the local authority to make enquiries about long-term care for E with her mother's family and, if those enquiries did not yield a long-term carer for E, with E's father, if identified, and his family. I have already indicated that in my judgment there was no such duty unless the interests of the child so require. The second issue is how the court's discretion to give directions about contacting the extended family or father of a child in case of this kind should be exercised.

Issue (1): Where a mother places her child for adoption, does S 1 of the 2002 Act impose a duty on the local authority to make enquiries of a child's extended family or father about the possibility of their providing long-term care?

[14] This is a question of statutory interpretation. It is necessary to go back to s 1... In my judgment, the governing provision is subs (2), because it lays down a 'paramount' or overarching consideration, and not surprisingly that paramount consideration is the child's welfare. Parliament has added that the reference to welfare is to welfare throughout a child's life and not simply in the short term future or the child's childhood. All the other provisions of s 1 about decision-making take effect subject to this provision.

[15] The result is that s1 is child-centred. It is not 'mother-centred'. The emphasis is on the interests of the child and not those of the mother. As the European Court of Human Rights ('the

Strasbourg court') expressed it in one case, adoption means 'giving a family to a child and not the child to a family' (Fretté v France (2004) 38 EHRR 21 at [42]). The interests of the child will include the child's interest in retaining its identity, and this is likely to be important to the child in adulthood. But identity is only one factor in the balance that has to be struck. S 1 does not privilege the birth family over adoptive parents simply because they are the birth family. This is underscored by s 1(6), which requires the court or adoption agency to consider the whole range of powers available to it in the child's case.

[16] S 1 then lists a number of matters that the court or adoption agency must have in mind when it makes any decision about adoption. Importantly, those matters include delay (subs (3)). Then subs (4) lists a large number of matters. These are not matters on which the court must necessarily act but it must certainly 'have regard' to them.

[17] There are a number of important points to note about the structure of s1. The list of matters is not exhaustive. The court is required to have regard to the specified matters 'among others'. It is not therefore an exclusive list. Moreover, s 1 still leaves a great deal to the discretion of the court since it does not prescribe the weight which the court or adoption agency must give to any particular matter. That will depend on what is required to fulfil the paramount consideration. S 1 stipulates that particular matters are to be taken into account, but does not provide any express machinery for ascertaining those matters. The means of ascertaining those matters is left to the inherent powers of the court or statutory powers of the adoption agency. The legislation is not prescriptive, and it has been left to the exercise of discretion as to whether any means available as a matter of inherent jurisdiction or under statutory powers is actually employed. Finally, with one exception, s 1 does not establish any preference for any particular result or prescribe any particular conclusion...The one exception is delay. Delay is always to be regarded as in some degree likely to prejudice the child's welfare: see subs (3). Parliament has here made a value judgement about the likely impact of delay and it is not open to the court or the adoption agency to quarrel with that basic value judgement.

[18] In this particular case, subs (4) (c) and (f) are particularly important...Subs (4) (c) explicates the extended meaning of the child's welfare, and requires the court to look at the likely effect on the child throughout the child's life of having ceased to be a member of the original family and having become a member of his or her adoptive family. This means that the court will have to take into account the importance to a child of their identity, and accordingly, I will have to deal with this matter when I consider how the discretion should be exercised.

[19] Subs (4) (f) requires the court to have regard to the relationship 'which the child has' with relatives. Relatives are not confined to legal relationships or close relations (see subs (8)). They would therefore include de facto relationships. This provision is wide enough to cover relationships that have potential for development in the future. E has no relationship with her father at the present time, other than the blood relationship and the potential social relationship were they ever to be in contact with each other. Their relationship is therefore a matter to be considered under subs (4) (f). Likewise the potential relationship that E has with her grandparents is a matter to be considered under that provision. There is nothing to confine subs (4) (f) to relatives who happen to know of the child's birth.

[20] Subs (4) (f) requires the court to have regard to the wishes and feelings of a child's relatives and their ability and willingness to provide the child with long-term care. However, that assumes that information is reasonably available about these matters. If the information is not readily available, the court or adoption agency may want to obtain it. But in the light of subs (2) they are only required to do so, if that is required for the purposes of the child's welfare and if they consider it right to take those steps notwithstanding that any delay is likely to prejudice the child's welfare.

[21] It can be seen from this analysis that when a decision requires to be made about the long-term care of the child, whom a mother wishes to be adopted, there is no duty to make enquiries

of an absolute kind. There is only a duty to make enquiries, if it is in the interests of the child to make those enquiries. In the present case, the judge considered that in adult life the child would benefit from more information about the child's father. But in the context of the decision-making with which the judge was concerned, I do not consider that that fact could of itself animate indeed the exercise of discretion. The immediate question with which the guardian and local authority were concerned was who would look after the child on a long-term basis. The enquiries had to be focused on that result. That meant looking at the evidence about the prospective carers within the mother's family. It was not enough simply to say that it would be in the child's interests to be placed with her birth family. I will have to consider the evidence on that when I come to consider discretion. Finding out more about the child's background for E's information in the future was secondary to that objective, and it would inevitably lead to delay. In the circumstances, I consider that the judge misdirected himself about what enquiries s 1 required in the instant case.

[22] It is convenient at this point to deal with another argument relevant to the interpretation of s 1. E is a looked after child, that is a child provided with accommodation by the local authority in exercise of its functions referred to in s 22 (1) of the 1989 Act. The guardian points out that before a local authority makes any decision with respect to a child whom they are looking after, they must ascertain the wishes and feelings of persons such as the child's parents: s 22(4) of the 1989 Act. Moreover, under s 23 of the 1989 Act, the local authority must provide accommodation for a looked after child by placing him with a family, or a relative of his. The guardian submits that the 1989 Act places heavy emphasis on consulting widely within a child's immediate and wider family in order to plan for the child's future. In my judgment, those provisions cannot apply where special provision is made by the 2002 Act. Decisions as to E's long-term care, in circumstances where the mother has given her up for adoption, fall within the 2002 Act. There is no reason to give the care proceedings initiated by the local authority precedence over adoption. The only active proposal for long-term care for E is via adoption...

[23] The guardian accepts that there can be no absolute obligation under section 1 to approach the father or the wider family of the child. But she submits that the circumstances in which this should not occur would be limited to cases such as those where the life of the child would be at risk. The guardian relies on the societal shift towards greater involvement of natural father in the upbringing of children. The guardian accepts that each case must turn on its facts, and that a balancing act has to be conducted in each case. But she rejects the mother's contention that the judge was plainly wrong. She submits that the effect of s 1(4) (c) and (f) is that there is now an expectation of disclosure and that the courts should require compelling reasons to prevent it taking place, certainly to a natural father and probably too to close members of the wider family. ... In many cases disclosure will be in the interests of the child, but it cannot be assumed that it will always be so. Moreover, disclosure has to be directed to an end that furthers the making of the decisions which require to be made. That requirement was not met in the present case.

[24] The logical consequence of my interpretation of s 1 is that exceptional situations can arise in which relatives, or even a father, of a child remain in ignorance about the child at the time of its adoption. But this result is consistent with other provisions of the 2002 Act. There are situations when the court does not require the consent of the father. For example, the consent of the father without parental responsibility is not required for a placement under ss 19 or 20, and, even if E were to be placed for adoption with her mother's consent but her father later obtained parental responsibility, he would be deemed to have consented to the placing of E for adoption (see above).

...

[26] There will be situations in which it is impossible to ascertain who the father is without the mother's co-operation. That situation may not be this case.

The Right to Respect for Family Life

...

[30] Self-evidently, if a person has a right to respect for their family life with a child proposed to be adopted, the adoption of that child will constitute an interference with the right. That interference will have to be justified under art 8(2). Likewise, the disclosure of confidential information about the child could violate the mother's right to respect for her private life, so that too must be capable of justification under article 8 (2). That requirement is likely to be met where the disclosure will promote the interests of the child in a relevant respect.

[31] The Strasbourg jurisprudence appears to establish that near relatives, particularly grandparents, automatically have a family life with a child even if the child has never lived with them: see *Marckx v Belgium* (1979–1980) 2 EHRR 330 at [45]. But, in other situations at least, it all depends on the facts. It includes a potential relationship, that is, a relationship which may develop. However, family life as between a father and a child born out of wedlock is not automatic. The father must have had some relationship with the mother and expressed his commitment to the child in some way, even if there was no cohabitation: *Nylund v Finland* Application No 27110/95, 29.12.99; cf J.R.M. v Netherlands [Application No. 16944/90]... Moreover, intended family life may, in some circumstances, be enough to establish a right to respect for one's family life: *Pini v Romania* (2005) 40 EHRR 13.

[32] It follows from the authorities given above that the father of E would as matters stand, have no right to respect for his family life with E because he has no family life with her. He has never lived with her mother or expressed any commitment to E. He could not have done so because he does not know of her existence. But it is not a violation of a Convention right to deprive him of the possibility of obtaining a right to respect family life with E. He has therefore no Convention right under art 8(1) and accordingly it is unnecessary to ask whether art 8(2) would apply in his case.

...

[35] The guardian submits that E has her own Convention right to be brought up by her natural father; in other words, that while he may not have a right to respect for his family life with her, she may have a right to respect for her potential family life with him... But, if she does have that right, there would be no interference if the court's decision on her adoption fulfilled the requirements of art 8(2). That matter can only be determined when the application for an adoption order is made. There is no reason in principle why an appropriate order should not comply with that provision. Her potential right would not afford a justification for disclosing material to the extended family or the father at this stage.

...

Issue (2): Factors relevant to exercising the discretion in this situation

[40] I propose to start with a few general observations. There will inevitably be a wide variety of cases where there arises the question whether a newborn child should be adopted. Every case has to be determined on its particular facts. The fact that the father or a relative has no right to respect for family life in the particular case does not mean that their position should not be considered: s 1(4)(f) of the 2002 Act applies irrespective of art 8 rights. However, the position of a person would command more importance if they were entitled to that right.

[41] I accept the submission of the local authority that the court or adoption agency cannot simply act on what the mother says. It has to examine what she says critically. It is a question of judgement whether what the mother says needs to be checked or corroborated.

[42] The local authority goes on to say that the ordinary rule should be that the near family and father should be identified and informed unless the court is satisfied that such enquiries would be inappropriate. The local authority submits that there is a growing trend towards involving the natural family and the father in such cases. It is no doubt true to say that there are a substantial number of cases where a child who would otherwise be placed for adoption is offered long term care by a member of the family.

...

[44] I now turn to this case. The mother has given information about her family. There is no reason to think that it is materially inaccurate. She considers that neither her siblings nor her parents could offer E long-term care. She points out, for instance, that her father has retired and remarried. His new wife has three children from a previous relationship all of whom are teenagers. She has moreover had a bad relationship with her mother and her father and there is nothing to suggest those difficulties would be magically resolved by introducing E into the wider family. On the contrary, those difficulties may well be exacerbated. The local authority takes the view that the concerns that the mother had about her parents have not materialised.

[45] In my judgment, while it is correct that the mother's parents have written a letter to the local authority, they have not explained, whether and if so, how they could assist. In my judgment, it would not be right to delay the placing of E for adoption on such thin evidence. Given the passage of time that has already taken place, I take the view that the grandparents would have to have a better than evens chance to justify the making of an assessment of them as long-term carers. The material provided so far does not support that assessment. A strict view needs to be taken of the situation because E is already four months old, and starting to form relationships. If more time had been available, the court might have been (but would not necessarily have been) more willing to order disclosure in their favour. Moreover, in view of my conclusion that the local authority should not have informed the mother's parents about E, it would be unfair to the mother if they were placed in a better position than they would have been in if the local authority had not told them about E simply because of the mistake that has occurred. The mother had no part in that. Furthermore, the mother's parents are not shut out from making their own application to have long-term care of E, if they wish to do so. They can take out an application under the 1989 Act. Nothing said in this judgment expresses any view on any such application, which would be decided on the evidence then before the court.

[46] That leaves the position of the father. He was only a one-night stand, and has no family life with E or the mother, entitling him to the guarantee of respect for that family life under article 8. There is no basis for supposing that he could provide a home for E. Steps would have to be taken to identify who he is. It is possible that he is in fact fully employed and in a long-term relationship with someone else. There is no suggestion that he already has a family that E could join. The prospects of his being a long-term carer are too intangible to justify a delay in making a placement for E.

QUESTIONS

i. Would you advise a woman proposing to place her newborn baby for adoption without the consent of the child's father, that this may not be possible as a matter of law?

ii. In *F and H (children)* [2007] EWCA Civ 880, Wall LJ said:

> In my view the Applicant's arguments under ECHR Article 8 are misconceived. Everyone, including the children in this case, has a respect for their family life. Every case under

the Children Act involves a balance between the respective ECHR Article 8 rights of all the participants. The judge's task is to select an outcome which, in the judge's view, best serves the interests of the children. The judge was fully entitled to take the view that the best interests of the children required them to be adopted. The ECHR Article 8 rights of the adults are, in this sense, subservient to those of the children. The welfare of the children is paramount: that is to say more important than anything else.

Can you think of any situation where Article 8 rights of a relative will prevent the making of an adoption order where all the professionals involved recommend the making of such an order?

This leads us to the vital subject of parental consent. The Tomlin Committee (p. 414, above) treated adoption as a consensual 'transaction' between birth and adoptive parents, in which the court's task was to ensure that their agreement did not prejudice the welfare of the child. The agreement of each parent with parental responsibility is still required, although it can be dispensed with on defined grounds. Over the years, the circumstances in which the court may be empowered to dispense with the parent's consent have expanded. The Adoption Act 1996 section 16 empowered the court to dispense with the parent's consent, amongst other grounds, when he or she was withholding his or her agreement unreasonably. In *Re W (an infant)* 1971 AC 682, Lord Hailsham LC said: '... although welfare *per se* is not the test, the fact that a reasonable parent does pay regard to the welfare of his child must enter into the question of reasonableness as a relevant factor.'

The present list of such grounds is set out in section 52 of the Adoption and Children Act 2002:

Parental etc. Consent

52.—(1) The court cannot dispense with the consent of any parent or guardian of a child to the child being placed for adoption or to the making of an adoption order in respect of the child unless the court is satisfied that–

(a) the parent or guardian cannot be found or lacks capacity (within the meaning of the Mental Capacity Act 2005) to give consent, or

(b) the welfare of the child requires the consent to be dispensed with.

QUESTIONS

i. Do you think that section 52(1)(b) takes the law further than *Re W (an infant)*?

ii. Do you think that section 52(1)(b) adds anything to the principles as set out in the checklist in section 1?

iii. Will the court inevitably make an adoption order if it forms the view that adoption would be better for the child than any other available option?

iv. If you believe that this is the situation, can it be reconciled with the EConvHR jurisprudence that we have discussed throughout the book, some of which was cited by Arden LJ in *Re C (A Child) and XYZ County Council and EC*?

v. Has social engineering gone too far?

There are two routes for placing a child for adoption. Each parent may consent to the child being placed for adoption (section 19), or the local authority may secure a placement order from the court authorising it to place a child with adopters (section 21). The system contained in the Adoption and Children Act 2002 is similar to that outlined in *Adoption – A Service for Children, Adoption Bill – A Consultative Document* (1996):

Placement Orders

4.8 Arrangements for placing a child for adoption introduce a new provision – placement orders. Where the parent or guardian does not consent to the placement for adoption and the adoption agency has considered all available options and is satisfied that adoption is in the child's best interests, the matter is to be put to the court at an early stage to enable the court to make realistic decisions about the child's future. The purpose of a placement order is to enable the court to be involved at an early stage in those cases where the agency considers that adoption is in the child's best interests but the parent or guardian is not prepared to give his consent to placement and while other available options for the child's future can also be considered.

4.9 A placement order authorises the adoption agency to place the child for adoption with suitable prospective adopters. An order will not restrict a placement to named prospective adopters even where they are known to the agency; this is to avoid the agency having to go back to court for a new placement order in the event of the first placement breaking down.

4.10 Once a placement order has been made, parental responsibility is given while the child is placed with prospective adopters, to them. Regulations will provide for the names of the prospective adopters to be notified to the court by the adoption agency. Where the child is removed from that placement and subsequently placed with another set of adopters, the court is to be notified of the change. Parental responsibility reverts to the agency when the child is removed and in due course is given to new prospective adopters.

Placement of Children Under a Care Order

4.11 A placement order will be required for a child who is the subject of a care order; once the placement order is made it is to have the effect of suspending the care order for the duration of the placement order. Where a local authority applies to the court for a care order most courts already require them to provide a care plan for the child. Where the recommendation in the care plan is that the child should be adopted, the authority must also apply for a placement order at the same time as they apply for a care order. Should the placement order be revoked, the care order will automatically revive. This means that where placement for adoption turns out not to be the best solution there is no obstacle to revoking the placement order because the child will remain protected.

4.12 Where the care plan did not originally contain a recommendation that the child be placed for adoption but is revised at a later stage to make such a recommendation, an application for a placement order must be made at this stage. This will usually be heard by the same court which made the care order.

Placement Generally

4.13 Once a child is placed with prospective adopters whether with the parent's consent or under a placement order, he ceases to be a 'looked after' child under the Children Act. Where the local authority may place a child for adoption, the authority may provide accommodation for him at any time when he is not so placed and during that period he will be a 'looked after' child under that Act.

Removal Provisions

4.14 Where placement is by consent, the parent may withdraw that consent and require the return of the child (subject to set procedures) at any time up to the time when an application to adopt is made. After that, leave of the court is required. Where a child is placed under a placement order, the parent will not be able to have the child back unless the placement order is revoked. An application to revoke the order by the parent may only be made where the child is not placed with prospective adopters, at least a year has elapsed since the order was made and the court gives leave, being satisfied that there has been a change in circumstances.

The major provisions of the Act are as follows:

Placing Children with Parental Consent

19(1) Where an adoption agency is satisfied that each parent or guardian of a child has consented to the child–

(a) being placed for adoption with prospective adopters identified in the consent, or
(b) being placed for adoption with any prospective adopters who may be chosen by the agency,

and has not withdrawn the consent, the agency is authorised to place the child for adoption accordingly.

(2) Consent to a child being placed for adoption with prospective adopters identified in the consent may be combined with consent to the child subsequently being placed for adoption with any prospective adopters who may be chosen by the agency in circumstances where the child is removed from or returned by the identified prospective adopters.

(3) Subsection (1) does not apply where–

(a) an application has been made on which a care order might be made and the application has not been disposed of, or
(b) a care order or placement order has been made after the consent was given.

(4) References in this Act to a child placed for adoption under this section include a child who was placed under this section with prospective adopters and continues to be placed with them, whether or not consent to the placement has been withdrawn.

(5) This section is subject to section 52 (parental etc. consent).

Advance Consent to Adoption

20(1) A parent or guardian of a child who consents to the child being placed for adoption by an adoption agency under section 19 may, at the same or any subsequent time, consent to the making of a future adoption order.

(2) Consent under this section–

(a) where the parent or guardian has consented to the child being placed for adoption with prospective adopters identified in the consent, may be consent to adoption by them, or
(b) may be consent to adoption by any prospective adopters who may be chosen by the agency.

(3) A person may withdraw any consent given under this section.
(4) A person who gives consent under this section may, at the same or any subsequent time, by notice given to the adoption agency–

(a) state that he does not wish to be informed of any application for an adoption order, or
(b) withdraw such a statement.

(5) A notice under subsection (4) has effect from the time when it is received by the adoption agency but has no effect if the person concerned has withdrawn his consent.
(6) This section is subject to section 52 (parental etc. consent).

Placement Orders

21(1) A placement order is an order made by the court authorising a local authority to place a child for adoption with any prospective adopters who may be chosen by the authority.
(2) The court may not make a placement order in respect of a child unless–

(a) the child is subject to a care order,
(b) the court is satisfied that the conditions in section 31(2) of the 1989 Act (conditions for making a care order) are met, or
(c) the child has no parent or guardian.

(3) The court may only make a placement order if, in the case of each parent or guardian of the child, the court is satisfied–

(a) that the parent or guardian has consented to the child being placed for adoption with any prospective adopters who may be chosen by the local authority and has not withdrawn the consent, or
(b) that the parent's or guardian's consent should be dispensed with.

This subsection is subject to section 52 (parental etc. consent).
(4) A placement order continues in force until–

(a) it is revoked under section 24,
(b) an adoption order is made in respect of the child, or
(c) the child marries, forms a civil partnership or attains the age of 18 years.

QUESTIONS

i. James is a four-year-old who has been living with foster parents for some six months because the mother is unable to provide for his needs. The father has recently been sentenced to a lengthy period of imprisonment. The assessment of the mother makes clear that she has a borderline verbal learning disability, and that she will be unable to improve her parenting skills within a realistic timeframe. The local authority seeks a placement order and the mother refuses her consent. What argument could be presented to the court in favour of the mother? (Read section 52 and the European Court of Human Rights cases again.)

ii. Assume in the above factual situation that the mother gives advance consent under section 20, and nine months later, having attended parenting classes, therapy and counselling, withdraws her consent (section 20(4)(b)). What arguments could now be presented to the court in favour of the mother who is opposed to the adoption of James by the foster parents?

iii. In (ii) above, leave is required by the court for the mother to oppose the making of the adoption order (section 47). Can you think of any reason why a court should grant leave to a mother to seek to oppose the making of the adoption order? (See *Re P(A Child)* [2007] EWCA Civ 616.)

iv. Do you think that section 52 read with section 20 and sections 1(2) and 1(3) is compatible with either the child's or the birth family's right to respect for their family life, protected by Article 8 of the European Convention on Human Rights (see p. 30 above)?

v. Section 25 states that either consent to placement or a placement order gives parental responsibility to the adoption agency, shared with the parents and with any prospective adopter once the child is placed, but with the power to restrict their exercise of that responsibility. Is it acceptable for a state agency to acquire control over parental responsibility without a court order? Is it acceptable for a state agency to have the right to restrict the exercise of parental responsibility without a court order?

12.4 ADOPTION: AN OPEN OR SHUT CASE?

The Tomlin Committee (see above, Chapter 9 at p. 414) had disapproved of secrecy in adoption, yet over the years since then the complete segregation of birth and adoptive families became the norm. But there were exceptions, particularly for older children adopted by foster parents. In *Re B (MF) (an infant), Re D (SL) (an infant)* [1972] 1 All ER 898, [1972] 1 WLR 102, Salmon LJ said this:

> As a rule, it is highly undesirable that after an adoption order is made there should be any contact between the child or children and their natural parents. This is the view which has been taken, and rightly taken, by adoption societies and local authorities as it has been by the courts in dealing with questions of adoption. There is, however, no hard and fast rule that if there is an adoption it can only be on the terms that there should be a complete divorce of the children from their natural parents. ... Although the courts will pay great attention to the general principle to which I have referred, namely, that it is desirable in normal circumstances for there to be a complete break, each case has to be considered on its own particular facts.

The changing face of adoption has contributed to a more flexible attitude, although it is essential to note that section 26 of the Adoption and Children Act 2002 states:

> ### Contact
>
> 26(1) On an adoption agency being authorised to place a child for adoption, or placing a child for adoption who is less than six weeks old, any provision for contact under the 1989 Act

ceases to have effect and any contact activity direction relating to contact with the child is discharged.

(2) While an adoption agency is so authorised or a child is placed for adoption–

(a) no application may be made for any provision for contact under that Act, but
(b) the court may make an order under this section requiring the person with whom the child lives, or is to live, to allow the child to visit or stay with the person named in the order, or for the person named in the order and the child otherwise to have contact with each other.

The court can make a contact order under section 8 at the final adoption hearing (section 26(5)). This is not new, as this case illustrates.

Re C (a minor) (adoption: conditions) [1989] AC 1, [1988] 1 All ER 705, [1988] 2WLR 474, House of Lords

C was taken into care, together with her two older brothers, at a very early age. C became very attached to her brother M during the next seven years, spent mainly in children's homes, and remained in touch with him after her placement with the prospective adopters. C wanted to be adopted, but her mother withheld agreement in case adoption might weaken her relationship with M. The judge thought this should be preserved at all costs. Both the judge and the Court of Appeal refused to dispense with the mother's agreement, being doubtful of the power to make continued contact a condition of the adoption order. The prospective adopters appealed.

Lord Ackner:

...It seems to me essential that, in order to safeguard and promote the welfare of the child throughout his childhood, the court should retain the maximum flexibility given to it by the Act and that unnecessary fetters should not be placed on the exercise of the discretion entrusted to it by Parliament. The cases to which I have referred illustrate circumstances in which it was clearly in the best interests of the child to allow access to a member of the child's natural family. The cases rightly stress that in normal circumstances it is desirable that there should be a complete break, but that each case has to be considered on its own particular facts. No doubt the court will not, except in the most exceptional case, impose terms or conditions as to access to members of the child's natural family to which the adopting parents do not agree. To do so would be to create a potentially frictional situation which would be hardly likely to safeguard or promote the welfare of the child. Where no agreement is forthcoming the court will, with very rare exceptions, have to choose between making an adoption order without terms or conditions as to access, or to refuse to make such an order and seek to safeguard access through some other machinery, such as wardship. To do otherwise would be merely inviting future and almost immediate litigation.

The cases in the Court of Appeal have essentially been concerned with the question of whether provision can properly be made in an adoption order for access to a natural parent or parents. Although it is one of degree, a distinction can properly be drawn between access to natural parents on the one hand and other natural relatives on the other. Other relatives and, in particular, brothers and sisters have no parental rights which by the adoption order are being extinguished and then vested in the adopters. The Court of Appeal was, in my judgment, correct in paying no regard to the suggestions made by the judge that if C were told that M was no longer her brother, she would be bitterly and desperately hurt. Fresh evidence put before the Court of Appeal established that C, when interviewed a little over a year ago, had made it clear that she wanted to be adopted, that to her adoption meant that 'she would then know that no one could ever take her away from her mum and dad' (the appellants). She said she could not see how it would affect her relationship with M or how she felt for him and he for her. Even without this additional evidence, it seems to me that the judge's evaluation of C's reaction to learning that technically M was no longer her *legal* brother was quite unreal.

...

The order which the judge made sacrificed the benefits of adoption in order to provide for an event which might never eventuate, namely the failure of the adopters properly to co-operate in maintaining access between C and M. The fresh evidence put before the Court of Appeal established that there continued to be no obstacles put by the appellants in the way of such access and none were anticipated by M. Indeed, your Lordships have been informed, without objection, that the appellants took C to London twice last year so that she could visit M, and had invited M to come to see his sister in Norfolk. Contact had continued by phone and letter. Moreover, the judge failed to appreciate that, were it to become necessary to enforce access between C and M, to do so through the machinery of wardship was no easier and, indeed, might be more complex, then by seeking to enforce a term or condition of the adoption order.

Appeal allowed.

QUESTIONS

i. But what if the local authority had been unable to find prospective adopters who could recognise and respect the child's relationship with her brother?
ii. Does the distinction drawn between birth parents and other relatives make sense?

The *Family Rights Group Advice Sheet for Families* (2006) provides the following summary of the research findings about open adoption:

What does research say about open adoption? Can contact with birth relatives help adopted children?

Here is a summary of some of the main messages from research about the different ways in which contact with birth relatives can help adopted children.

Maintaining established relationships. Most children who know and remember their birth family feel very unhappy about losing these relationships. They would prefer to stay in touch with these important people, especially people with whom they have had a good relationship.

Staying in touch with important people from the past can help children settle in their new families. Some adopted children worry about what is happening to members of their birth family, especially their siblings and parents, and keeping in contact can reassure children that their birth relatives are managing OK.

Helping children understand their roots. For both older adopted children who remember their birth family, and children adopted very young who have no memories, contact with birth relatives can help children to understand their own history and roots. This is important because most adopted people ask questions such as 'who am I?', 'where do I come from?' and 'why was I adopted?' If birth relatives can provide the adopted child and/or the adoptive parents with information about their past and current lives this helps adopted children to answer these important questions, giving them a better sense of identity.

Contact with birth relatives can help children feel that although their birth family couldn't care for them, they still care about them. This is very important, as some adopted children can feel rejected or unloved.

Helping children feel positive about their background. It is important for adopted children's feelings about themselves, that they have a balanced and realistic view of their birth family. When adoptive parents and the adopted child don't have much information about the birth family, or when they are only given a one sided view, sometimes they can get a negative picture in their minds. Having contact with birth family members can help both adopted children and adoptive parents know the birth family as real people with a positive side.

Helping adoptive parents. Adopted children have to manage issues of loss and identity and it is important that adoptive parents understand and can support children with these issues. Contact with birth family members:

1. can help adoptive parents support the child in a number of ways.
2. can help adopters to understand and empathise with the birth family, enabling them to answer children's questions sensitively;
3. help them to feel OK about taking over the parenting role and reduce their feelings of anxiety about the birth family;
4. give them access to important information about the child's development, including the family medical history; and
5. can help them to keep an open communication with their child about adoption.

The *Family Rights Group* then goes on to talk about the Research findings:

Research findings about whether or not contact is good for adopted children are mixed. Contact will only benefit children in the ways described above if it is good quality contact.

What Are the Factors Associated With Contact That Works?

Adoptive parents' attitudes. Contact works best when adoptive parents have an open and respectful view of the birth family, and a commitment to maintaining contact.

Birth relatives' attitudes. Contact works best when birth relatives accept and support the child's place in the adoptive family (even if they didn't want or agree to the adoption), accept the adoptive parents as the child's new parents, and can work co-operatively with adoptive parents. It is important for the child that birth relatives let them know that they still care about them but that they are OK about them having and loving a new family, otherwise children can feel very torn and unable to settle.

Adults working together. Post-adoption contact is most likely to be a positive experience for the child when adult parties can work together with give and take and when conflict between people is low. Research has highlighted the importance of flexibility, as the needs of all parties change as time goes by.

Keeping up contact over time. Post-adoption contact plans are not always kept up over time and when contact stops this can be very upsetting for children, birth relatives and adopters. Some people, especially birth relatives, may need help to be able to keep up contact as it can be a painful as well as a good experience.

A safe and pleasant experience for the child. Several studies have found that contact can be a mixed experience for children because their relationships with birth relatives can be tense or difficult. It is important that children feel, and are, safe during contact meetings and in some cases this means they will need their adoptive parents or another adult that they know and trust to stay with them. Birth relatives may need help to be able to get on better with their child.

It is indeed the case that the researchers' views have been hotly debated. An enthusiastic promoter of post-adoption contact is Murray Ryburn (echoing perhaps similar conclusions by Sturge and Glasyer in the different context of contact with a non-resident parent, see Chapter 10, p. 468) in, for example, 'In whose best interests? – post-adoption contact with the birth family' (1998):

Extent of Post-Adoption Contact Today

Despite growing adversarialism in adoption, since the beginning of the 1990s there has been a significant trend in practice to more post-adoption contact, although the extent of this at a national level cannot, with any precision, be established. This trend began in the 1980s, and was helped by the voice of consumer and advocacy groups. In particular, the movement to greater openness received an impetus from the Children Act 1989 with its research-based emphasis on the importance of contact for 'looked after' children.

Although the national picture on contact is not completely clear, we can glean a fair amount from two recent studies, one a Social Services Inspectorate (SSI) report which set out to establish the extent of post-adoption contact in the North of England, the other a study which sought to establish the level of post-adoption contact where adoption had been opposed to the point of the final hearing. In the SSI study, researchers approached 51 agencies, 37 social services departments and 14 voluntary adoption agencies, and received responses, although not to each question, from a total of 44. In the year commencing April 1993 30 agencies identified 371 children placed during that year for adoption. In 14 per cent of cases there was continuing direct contact between the parties, in 41 per cent of cases there was indirect contact, in 13 per cent of cases there was both direct and indirect contact, and in only 31 per cent of cases was there either no contact or no knowledge of this contact....

In my own survey involving 74 placements, all made after contested final hearings in 42 per cent of cases, there was some form of post-adoption contact. Usually this was indirect, and often, but not always, involved the services of an agency as a mailbox. Typically, it involved the exchange of letters and photographs and the giving of presents at birthdays and Christmas. In 14 per cent of cases contact was direct, ranging from infrequent to very regular contact, including, in addition to meetings, a good deal of telephone contact. ...

What are the Broad Findings?

The research is clear that there can be advantages to all parties as a result of the maintenance of post-adoption contact. It indicates that, in general, if there is freedom for parties to set their own levels, contact tends to move from limited and indirect contact to more open contact, and to change, sometimes significantly, over time. It further indicates that greater advantages can accrue from more open forms of contact. A recent public attitudes survey on open adoption found that of a random sample of 136 adults, 66 per cent supported the practice of post-adoption contact, whilst 74 per cent believed that adoptees would want to search for birth parents, with most other responses in the 'do not know' category. Further, 90 per cent of the sample supported the idea of adoptive parents initiating contact for their children if their children wanted it. As the first public opinion survey on adoption in this country the results are particularly interesting, both as a common sense view and because they would appear to confirm a trend away from any climate of secrecy. ...

Advantages of Contact for Children

The research studies suggest that with indirect contact children's information needs begin to be met, but that with direct contact their questions are more likely to be met at a level that is satisfying. One of the key advantages of any contact is that facts can more readily replace difficult aspects of their past lives – aspects that might otherwise be a source of difficulty for them. Thus in the study on contact following contested adoption an adopter indicated how important it was for her daughter to have contact, including direct contact, with her mother, who suffered a mental illness. This contact had helped her to locate this illness realistically in context, and otherwise, her adopters believed, it might have remained as a continuing source of worry and anxiety, especially in relation to her fears of inheriting it herself.

Children also appear to gain a sense of reassurance as a consequence of contact, particularly direct contact, with their birth relatives. In particular, it gives them a clear message that the placement is supported by their original family since otherwise they would not be visiting, and it is a visible symbol that their adoptive parents feel positively about their original family or contact would not be permitted. The largest survey of adoption and permanent foster care placements ever undertaken in the UK, involving 1165 placements, also found that birth family contact was the single factor which could be identified as enhancing the stability of placements. Finally, contact, in particular direct contact, appears to strengthen children's sense of attachment to their adoptive parents. Thus Dominick in her study of 156 adopters found that only two believed that contact diminished the strength of attachment between them and their child, three-quarters believed that contact enhanced feelings of attachment, and the remainder felt that the influence was neutral.

This was in response to a more cautious review by D. Quinton, A. Rushton, C. Dance and D. Mayes, 'Contact between children placed away from home and their birth parents: research issues and evidence' (1997). Their conclusions are summarised in 'Contact with birth parents in adoption – a response to Ryburn' (1998):

Conclusions From Our Review

In our review we dealt separately with the evidence on adoptions made in infancy and adoptions made later in childhood because of the different psychological implications of placement at different ages as well as the different family experiences of early and late placed children. Our conclusions can be summarised quite briefly.

Adoptions Made in Infancy

Research on infant adoptions could safely be taken to show: that continuing information about their children is important to many birth mothers; that direct contact can be acceptable to all parties in some cases; and that some birth and adoptive parents see this as bringing benefits. Our caveats were first that the majority of studies were of small self-selected samples or samples with high refusal rates (which made them self-selected as well), and secondly, that no studies had yet compared the outcomes of adoption with contact to adoption without it. For this reason we observed that it was not possible to conclude that infant adoptions with contact are either superior or inferior to those without, nor what proportion of placements have difficulties directly related to openness. Finally, we pointed out that existing research concerned adoptive parents' reactions to openness when the children were still in early or mid-childhood and that it could not be assumed that the story would be the same as the children passed through adolescence.

As Ryburn pointed out we did not deal with some recent papers from the study by Grotevant and his colleagues that do contain the appropriate comparisons and throw further light on these issues. We review these below to see whether they alter our conclusions.

Adoption of Older Children

With respect to the permanent placement of older children we first pointed out that the arguments put forward in favour of contact had much in common with earlier arguments against it, but in neither case had these arguments been systematically tested against each other in research. However, we concluded that research had shown that open adoption with contact can work amicably and that there was no evidence that contact made placements less stable and some evidence that it made them more so. At the time we were writing no studies of infant or later adoptions had systematic data on the intellectual or psychosocial development of the children in closed and open adoptions, despite the fact that benefits are sometimes claimed in these areas.

Our overall summary located the current state of knowledge on contact in a stage model of research that begins with the identification of an issue, proceeds through small-scale practitioner studies, is followed by larger scale, sometimes epidemiological, research and finally leads to the testing of specific hypotheses. As far as studies of adoption were concerned we observed that these were still predominantly in the second stage with some third-stage investigations but none in which specific hypotheses had been tested using representative samples and comparative designs. We outlined testable hypotheses that could be derived from beliefs about the advantages of contact and concluded:

> 'In our present state of knowledge it is seriously misleading to think that what we know about contact is at a level of sophistication to allow us to make confident assertions about the benefits to be gained from it, *regardless of family circumstances and relationships* (italics added). At least in the case of permanent placements the social experiment that is currently underway needs to be recognised as an experiment, not as an example of the development of evidence-based practice. It is important that the effects of this experiment are properly evaluated.'

Methodological Issues

These summary conclusions were arrived at following a discussion of the methodological problems that were common in much of the research in this field. ... We discussed four problems: the adequacy of sampling; the measurement of contact; failure to account for individual adjustment as a predictor; and analytic weaknesses. We presented tables summarising the studies we reviewed so that the reader could see whether these problems applied to them or not. ...

Re-examination of Missing Studies

It is now necessary to deal in a little more detail with the recent data from the major investigation that we did not review: the comparative study of the correlates of openness in infant adoptions by Grotevant and his colleague. ... We now review this and two subsequent papers to see whether this research alters our conclusions. This study is important because it included planned comparisons of children with and without contact. One hundred and ninety families who adopted children prior to one year-of-age were studied; the children were aged between four and 12 at the time of the research. They had been relinquished by their birth parents primarily because the mothers were young and poor rather than because of major mental health or parenting problems. The adoptions were not transracial, inter-country or 'special needs'. The sample was stratified according to the degree of openness and the study is exceptional in having data from a very high proportion of birth parents as well as adopted children. The research is methodologically sophisticated and the data are well analysed but, by definition, it cannot be used to draw conclusions about the effects of contact on children adopted later in life and/or following marked maltreatment.

Two major analyses have been presented. The first examined the associations between the level of openness in the adoptions and a number of issues. These included: the adoptive parents' communication with the child about adoption; their empathy with the need for connection with the past; empathy with the birth parents over their decision; recognition of the special nature of adoptive parenting; acknowledgment of the child's need for information; satisfaction with control over birth parent involvement; fear of reclaiming; perception of the strength of their relationship with the child; entitlement to act as a 'full' parent; and the coherence of their account of adoption.

The authors concluded first that what stood out was the similarity across the levels of openness on these measures, with the majority of ratings on all dimensions falling within a 'moderate range' for all levels of openness. Most parents felt secure in their roles and were not worried about permanence, regardless of whether the adoptions were confidential or fully disclosed. It was notable that parents in fully disclosed adoptions felt as much in control of birth parents' involvement as those in confidential ones and also that they showed a higher degree of empathy about adoption and talked more to the children about it; however, it was not possible to tell whether this was a consequence of prior parental characteristics or an effect of openness itself.

We agree with the authors' conclusion that 'the results of this study are not compatible with the hypothesis that openness necessarily produces undesirable outcomes for adoptive families'. In addition we would agree with their observation that the design makes it impossible to make causal statements about the effects of different levels of openness. Their conclusions are a model of appropriate caution. It is striking that Ryburn omits to mention their remarks on what the research can and cannot say about the associations between family patterns and the level of openness.

A second paper examined differences in the children's views depending on the level of openness. The interview with them revealed interesting but predominantly subtle effects. The level of openness was not related to the children's satisfaction with openness, to their understanding of adoption, to their self-worth, or to their curiosity about their birth parents, although most were curious, and girls more curious than boys. Parental withholding of information did not make children more curious but there was reasonable speculation that withholding would create more problems as adolescent identity issues arose.

There were two further interesting findings. Although the level of curiosity about birth parents did not differ according to the level of openness, the more curious children were about their origins the lower their self-worth, especially boys. Curiosity was negatively related to the level of satisfaction with their circumstances, except for the children in fully disclosed adoptions. This suggests a complex of responses that linked unhappiness with their situation, for whatever reasons, to their feelings of self-worth and to greater curiosity about their origins. On the other hand, the study does not link this complex of feelings to the level of openness in a consistent way, nor is it possible to determine whether the feelings are primarily a consequence of the quality of family relationships rather than the information the children had, although there is some suggestion that the way information is handled was important.

The general conclusion from both papers is the same. The study provides no evidence that openness is harmful to these early adopted children, an important conclusion. Neither does it provide evidence for obvious benefits to psychosocial development in the years leading up to adolescence. A follow-up of all the children through the teenage years, where identity issues become central, would be illuminating.

Summary

In summary the studies we omitted from our review do not alter overall conclusions that continuing information about their children is important to many birth mothers; that direct contact can be acceptable to all parties in some cases; and that some birth and adoptive parents see this as bringing benefits.

QUESTIONS

i. If you had to decide what to do in an individual case, which would you find more helpful: (a) the views of a clinician who had interviewed all concerned, or (b) the results of the research studies discussed?

ii. How would you go about being 'open' with a child whose birth parent had seriously abused or neglected him?

iii. Would you consider openness more or less important in trans-racial or trans-cultural placements?

iv. How much do you think prospective adopters should be told about their prospective children's past?

v. Is there a duty of care owed by adoption agencies to prospective adopters in adoption placements?

12.5 THE CROSS-CULTURAL DIMENSION

We have seen in Chapter 11 (p. 529, above) that disproportionate numbers of children looked after by local authorities come from certain ethnic minorities. How, then, are local authorities to place them appropriately, when the resources available to them are unlikely to match all the children's needs? The issue is discussed in *Adoption Now – Messages from Research* (1999):

Ethnicity

Several important points concerning the linking of children from minority ethnic groups with adopters or foster carers emerged from the Thoburn team's study (2000). Both the children and their new parents in 'same-race' placements believed that this policy should be followed if at all possible. Some of the children who had been placed trans-racially also argued strongly for a policy of ethnically matched placements, although most also acknowledged that they had learned much from their white parents. Children of mixed parentage appeared to feel less strongly about the issue. Of course, all these arrangements had been made in the early 1980s when the placement of black children with white families was more common. ...

Nonetheless, the Thoburn results provide a benchmark, as well as indicating some of the characteristics of trans-racial placements. First, they were more likely to have involved foster carers than adopters. Secondly, it was more common for younger children to be placed trans-racially. Thirdly, this was also the case for children of mixed parentage, 88% of whom had been placed with new parents who were white compared with 63% of those whose birth parents were both black. However, as Thoburn and her colleagues point out, the idea of 'ethnic matching' can suggest a closer similarity between the child and the new family than is in fact the case. For instance, although some of the children of direct African origin had been placed with black parents, in no instance were they both also from a direct African background. Children of south Asian parents were the most likely to have been placed with those of a similar background, perhaps because of religious considerations. The importance of such findings lies in what they suggest about the assumptions which lie behind decisions concerning the 'matching' of children and new parents. In this case the clearest of these was a greater willingness to placed mixed-parentage than black children with white families and the belief that colour was a more significant consideration than race, ethnicity or culture, except possibly with respect to religion.

Some of the complexities of 'ethnic matching' are also exposed in the Quinton and Rushton research (1998), although only one in six of the children in that sample had minority ethnic backgrounds. Half of them were 'ethnically matched'; but it was the descriptions of those who were not which illustrated some of the dilemmas faced by social workers. All except one were of mixed parentage, and all of these were more than one generation removed from their minority ethnic origins. The one African-Caribbean child who was placed trans-racially was placed together with a white sibling. Furthermore, many of these children had been born to white mothers and had grown up in a predominantly white culture.

A third of the children in the Owen study were black or of mixed parentage. All had been placed with black adopters except one whom the white adopter had known beforehand through family connections. The research suggested that the priority attached to racial or cultural matching by the three voluntary agencies concerned seemed to favour the choice of a single parent in some cases because a single black woman was seen as preferable to a white couple (although not necessarily to a black couple) and because such applicants were seen as having a high level of acceptability within the black community.

Almost all the agencies that replied to the Lowe and Murch postal questionnaire explained that ethnic or cultural matching was the preferred option but some two-fifths said that various circumstances could lead to a departure from that policy. It was notable, however, that the voluntary agencies were more likely than the local authorities to pursue unwavering 'same-race' policies (52% of them compared with 24% of the statutory bodies). Where second or third best options had to be found preferences tended to follow an order of diminishing connection with minority ethnic status; for example, from families where one of the adopters was black to those where the couple were of mixed parentage; then on to families where one of the partners had a mixed background, and finally to a white family, but one living in a multi-cultural community.

This last option draws attention to the extent to which efforts are or are not made to place minority ethnic children in areas where they will have the opportunity to mix with others of a similar background, at school, in clubs or simply in the neighbourhood. The importance of this was stressed by the black children in the Owen study and by those in the Thoburn research. However, the extent to which such considerations affected the selection of a particular family for a child was not explored in any of the studies, nor was the question of whether this only became a serious consideration if an 'ideal' ethnic 'match' proved impossible to achieve.

Re N (a minor) (adoption)
[1990] FCR 241, [1990] 1 FLR 58

In this case, the child, N, was born in 1984 of Nigerian parents who were not married. The mother placed her with white foster parents, the Ps, two weeks after birth and went to the USA. The father lived there but they did not live together. The father took an interest in the child and sought consistently to have care for her, but there were visa difficulties. In 1987, the foster parents applied to adopt and then to dispense with the mother's agreement. The father, with the mother's support, applied for care and control. He proposed a gradual transition, through a relative or bridging placement.

Bush J:

... The most important question to decide is where does N's future lie. We are all of us parents or potential parents and it is very difficult and sad for us to say that a child should be brought up by someone other than the natural parents. It should of course always be borne in mind that in English law N is a person in her own right and not just an appendage of her parents.

...

Not only does the court in this case have to cope with practical difficulties involved in a transfer of N from the Ps to the father in a foreign land where the father will have to work long hours, and Miss F too has to work long hours, but I have also been bombarded by a host of theories and opinions by experts who derive their being from the political approach to race relations in America in the 1960s and 1970s. The British Agencies for Fostering and Adoption forcefully expressed the view that black children should never be placed with white foster parents. That that part of the approach was politically inspired seems clear from reading the summary to a practice note, the date of which is not clear. Nevertheless, it is an approach which due to the zeal of its authors has persuaded most local authorities not to place black children with white foster parents. The summary note reads as follows:

> 'Over and above all these basic needs, children need to develop a positive identity, including a positive racial identity. This is of fundamental importance since ethnicity is a significant component of identity. Ideally such needs are met within the setting of the child's birth family. Historically black people have been victims of racism for centuries. This has manifested and continues to manifest itself in many forms. Racism permeates all areas of British society and is perpetuated through a range of interests and influences, including the media, education and social service policies and practices. Negative and stereotypical images and actions can have a major impact on black children through the internalisation

> of these images, resulting in self-hate and identity confusion. Black children therefore require the survival skills necessary to develop a positive racial identity. This will enable them to deal with the racism within our predominantly white society.'

As Dr B, an eminent and experienced child psychiatrist... pointed out... there seems little real evidence, save anecdotal, to suggest that black-white fosterings are harmful. Indeed, Dr B says that her experience... indicates to the contrary namely, that the placement of black children with white foster parents works just as well as black foster children with black foster parents, and the real problem, of course, is that black foster parents are in short supply in this country.

...

In my view – and I have no wish to enter into what is clearly a political field – the emphasis on colour rather than cultural upbringing can be mischievous and highly dangerous when you are dealing in practical terms with the welfare of children. Also, the fact remains that this child has been placed with white foster parents and they have been the only real family she has ever known. I do not for one moment think that the father subscribes to this dogma. He does not have to be condescended to because he is black; he has made his way and his children will make their own way in the world because of intelligence and flair. To suggest that he and his children need special help because they are black is, in human terms an insult to them and their abilities. Yet it is to this principle that a whole social work philosophy has been dedicated. I do not need persuading that if at all possible, the parents being suitable, a child should be brought up by its natural parents. Nor do I need persuading that experience tells us that particularly during teenage years there is a desire in children who have not been brought up by their natural parents, or who have not been having a regular access to them, to seek them out and that, if the whole of their placement has not been handled responsibly and delicately throughout their childhood, and sometimes even then, there may be psychological problems. There are of course serious psychological problems likely to arise when an effort is made to part a 4 and a half-year-old child from the only carers she has ever known. ...

...

There is, of course, a very important question which relates not so much to colour as to national origins. The father and mother are Nigerian. The father is under some pressure from his father, who will be disgraced if it appears that even an illegitimate child has been abandoned. The father is a Roman Catholic, and I accept that he has a genuine desire to bring up his own child. An older illegitimate child of his, a boy, lives with a different mother in Nigeria and visits his father at regular intervals.

The evidence of Mrs B, a consultant social worker, as to Nigerian practice is of use. ... She said there is no concept of adoption in Nigerian society. It is the normal cultural pattern for children to be brought up by others, often for most of their minority, and to be aware of their birth parents. Adoption rather than fostering of a West African child has particular difficulties. Adoption is to transfer a child from one family into another permanently and although the adoptive parents strive to inform the child about its origins in adoption it is clear the child is as if it were born to the adopters. In fostering, even long-term carers and the child are aware this is another and different family from a true family. If the child is moved from a white foster home to Nigerian culture, with his foster parents not wanting the child to go, this can be devastating. Growing up with a set of values, a way of looking at family life, is constant in the same culture. However, to move from a British family with a closeness, autonomy and freedom to express what you want and to do what you want to a place where you cannot can be very distressing long-term. The damage of losing the people you trust at the same time as the trauma can be life-long. ...

... I am satisfied, as are the local authority and the guardian ad litem that N could not be moved without immense harm to her psychological development and her psychiatric health, both now and in the future. The later harm that may arise in her teens when she wished to seek out her cultural roots can best be dealt with by sympathetic understanding and education, upon which the

Ps have already embarked, and it can also hopefully be met by the father continuing his interest and having access to N. It can only be helped if the father accepts the situation and enjoys access not on the basis of an expected rehabilitation but on the basis of a contact access designed to keep N in touch with her origins. If the father cannot accept this, then it may be that for N's security access would have to cease.

The Ps want adoption with an access order. The local authority and the guardian ad litem oppose adoption on the ground: (i) that the father has a useful and important part to play in the child's life in the future, particularly when she is nearing adulthood; (ii) that access to which the Ps are to some extent agreeable might very well be imperilled, the fact being that an adoption would result in the father and the whole of his family losing face. The father told me, and I have no reason to disbelieve, in the course of his argument that in his culture adoption is viewed as a restoration of slavery, which would be a deep and hurtful blow to him and his family. The question one has to ask oneself is whether the security that adoption would give to both the Ps and to N is offset by the fact that it clearly would not be in N's interests for her father to feel the shame and distress that in his culture an adoption order would bring. ...

I know all the arguments, I have heard them many times, about the security that an adoption could give and in the main I accept the arguments and have in the past acted upon them, but in the particular circumstances of this case I would not think it right to make an adoption order. Circumstances of course may change in the future. The guardian ad litem is most concerned, as we all are, that what has really become open warfare between the Ps and the father should cease. It is in the interests of N that it should so cease. I accept that the father is bitterly hurt and distressed and feels utterly betrayed by the Ps, and no doubt my decision has distressed him even more. However, the future of N throughout her childhood lies with the Ps and the father is intelligent enough and dedicated enough to his daughter to appreciate that changes of attitude on his part must come about. ...

Accordingly, the order that I make is that the wardship shall continue, that there be care and control to Mr and Mrs P, that there be reasonable access to the father to be agreed. In default of agreement it should be access once a week over a period of one year to begin with and that access to take place in England.

QUESTIONS

i. Would you have made an adoption order if the facts in *Re N* occurred today bearing in mind section 1(4) of the Adoption and Children Act 2002?

ii. Does it surprise you to learn that Nigel Lowe and Mervyn Murch, in their study of *The plan for the child, Adoption or long-term fostering* (2002), found that, along with age and level of contact with the birth family, an ethnic minority background tended to militate against planning for adoption rather than long-term fostering?

iii. Should white families be allowed to foster or adopt black children? What is 'black' for this purpose? Should black families be allowed to foster or adopt white children?

iv. Should a Christian family be allowed to adopt a Jewish child? (Read *Re P (a child) (residence order: child's welfare)* [2000] Fam 15, [1999] 3 All ER 734, CA.)

v. There are Christian and Jewish adoption agencies, but there is no Muslim adoption agency. Do you know why not?

BIBLIOGRAPHY

Introduction

We quoted from:

Commission for Social Care Inspection, *The Right People for Me* (2004).

G. Schofield, M. Beek and K. Sargent with J. Thoburn, *Growing Up in Foster Care* (2000) London, BAAF, 291.

J. Triseliotis, 'Growing Up in Foster Care and After' in J. Triseliotis (ed.), *New Developments in Foster Care and Adoption* (1980) London, Routledge and Kegan Paul, 138 and 148.

Additional reading

Children's Rights Director *Being Fostered: A National Survey of the Views of Foster Children, Foster Carers, and Birth Parents about Foster Care* (2005) London, Commission for Social Care Inspection (available at: http://www.rights4me.org.uk).

Social Care Institute for Excellence (2004) Practice Guide 3: *Fostering.*

12.1 The law on maintaining family links

We quoted from:

Department for Education and Skills, *Care matters: Time for Change* (2007) Cm 7137.

Additional reading

H. Cleaver, 'Fostering Family Contact: A Study of Children, Parents and Foster Carers', in J. Aldgate and J. Statham (eds), *The Children Act Now: Messages from Research*, prepared for the Department of Health (2001) London, The Stationery Office, 178–181.

D. Cullen 'Adoption – a (fairly) new approach' (2005) 17 *Child and Family Quarterly*, 511.

D. Howe, 'Assessing adoptions in difficulty' (1992) 22 *British Journal of Social Work* 1.

B. Maugham and A. Pickles, 'Adopted and Illegitimate Children Growing Up,' in L.N. Robbins and M. Rutter (eds), *Straight and Devious Pathways from Childhood to Adulthood* (1990) Cambridge, Cambridge University Press.

A. Rushton, J. Treseder and D. Quinton, 'Sibling Groups in Permanent Placements' (1989) 13(4) *Adoption and Fostering*, 5.

J. Stone, *Making Positive Moves – Developing Short-Term Fostering Services* (1995) London, BAAF, 52–61.

J. Thoburn, *Success and Failure in Permanent Family Placement* (1990) Avebury, Gower.

J. Thoburn, 'Survey Findings and Conclusions', in J. Fratter, J. Rowe, D. Sapsford and J. Thoburn (eds), *Permanent Family Placement – a decade of experience* (1991) London, BAAF, 37, 51–56.

P. Wedge and H. Mantle, *Sibling Groups and Social Work* (1991) Avebury, Gower.

12.2 Legal options for relatives and other carers

We quoted from:

E. Bullard and E. Malos, with R.A. Parker, *Custodianship – A report to the Department of Health on the Implementation of Part II of the Children Act 1975 in England and Wales from*

December 1985 to December 1988 (1990) Bristol, Department of Social Policy and Social Planning, University of Bristol, 9.39–9.40.
Law Commission, Working Paper No. 96, *Review of Child Law – Custody* (1986) London, HMSO, 5.37–5.39, 5.42, 5.46.
Review of Adoption Law, Report to Ministers of an Interdepartmental Working Group. A Consultation Document (1992) London, Department of Health and Welsh Office, 6.2–6.5.
White Paper, Adoption – a new approach (Cm. 5017) (2000) London, HMSO, 5.5–5.9.

Additional reading

F. Kagaras, 'Grandparents' rights and grandparents' campaigns' (2007) 19 *Child and Family Law Quarterly*, 17.

12.3 Adoption as a child care resource

We quoted from:

Department of Health and Welsh Office, Adoption – *A Service for Children, Adoption Bill – A Consultative Document* (1996) London, Department of Health and Welsh Office, 4.4–4.14.
R. Parker, for the Department of Health, Social Services Inspectorate, *Adoption Now – Messages from Research* (1999) Chichester, Wiley, 1–6.

Additional reading

E.J. Cooke, 'Dispensing with parental consent to adoption – a choice of welfare tests' (1997) 9 *Child and Family Law Quarterly*, 259.
Department of Health, *White Paper, Adoption: The Future* (Cm. 2288) (1993) London, HMSO.
Department of Health, *White Paper, Adoption – a new approach* (Cm. 5017) (2000) London, HMSO, 2.1–2.6.
Department of Health and Social Services, *Report of the Departmental Committee on the Adoption of Children* (Chairman: Sir William Houghton, later Judge F.A. Stockdale) (Cmnd. 5107) (1972).
Department of Health and Welsh Office, *Review of Adoption Law, Report to Ministers of an Interdepartmental Working Group. A Consultation Document* (1992) London, 7.1, 7.2, 12.4–12.6, 14.1–14.5, 20.4–22.1.
N. Lowe, 'Freeing for Adoption – the Experience of the 1980s' (1990) *Journal of Social Welfare Law*, 220.
P. Presdee and S. Miller 'Parental opposition to adoption: The two-stage test' (2007) *Family Law* 1004.
G. Prosner 'Section 47 of the 2002 Act: has Somebody lost the plot' (2007) *Family Law* 940.
J. Selwyn, W. Sturgess, D. Quinton and C. Baxter, 'Costs and outcomes of non-infant adoptions' (2006) London, BAAF.

12.4 Adoption: an open or shut case?

We quoted from:

Family Rights Group Advice Sheet for Families (2006), available at http://www.frg.org.uk/pdfs/Open%20Adoption.pdf.

D. Quinton, A. Rushton, C. Dance and D. Mayes, 'Contact with birth parents in adoption – a response to Ryburn' (1998) 10 *Child and Family Law Quarterly*, 349, 349–150, 355–357.

M. Ryburn, 'In whose best interests? – post adoption contact with the birth family' (1998) 10 *Child and Family Law Quarterly*, 536.

Additional reading

J. Fratter, *Adoption with Contact: Implications for Policy and Practice* (1996) London, BAAF.

H. D. Grotevant, R.G. McRoy, C. Elde and D.L. Fravel, 'Adoptive family system dynamics – variations by level of openness in the adoption' (1994) 33:2 *Family Process* 125.

J. Logan, 'Exchanging information post adoption: Views of adoptive parents and birth parents' (1999) 23(3) *Adoption and Fostering*, 27–37.

N. Lowe, M. Murch, M., Borkowski, A. Weaver, V. Beckford, and C.Thomas, (1999) *Supporting Adoption Reframing the Approach*. London, BAAF.

E. Neil, 'Contact after Adoption: A Research Review' in A. Bainham, B. Lindley, M. Richards, and L. Trinder (eds), *Children and their families: Contact, rights and welfare* (2003) London and Oxford, Hart.

D. Quinton and J. Selwyn, 'Adoption: research, policy and practice' (2006) 18(4) *Child and Family Law Quarterly*, 459.

D. Quinton and J. Selwyn, A. Rushton and C. Dance, 'Contact between children placed away from home and their birth parents: Ryburn's "Reanalysis" Analysed' (1999) 4:4 *Clinical Child Psychology and Psychiatry*, 519.

J. Thoburn, 'Post-placement contact between birth parents and older children: the evidence from a longitudinal study of ethnic minority children', in E. Neil and D. Howe (eds), *Contact in adoption and permanent foster care: research, theory and practice* (2004) London, BAAF.

J. Triseliotis, J. Feast and F. Kyle, *The adoption triangle revisited: a study of adoption, search and reunion* (2005) London, BAAF.

J. Young, and E. Neil, 'The "Contact after Adoption" study: The perspective of birth relatives after non-voluntary adoption', in E. Neil and D. Howe (eds), *Contact in adoption and permanent foster care: research, theory and practice* (2004) London, BAAF.

12.5 The cross-cultural dimension

We quoted from:

R. Parker, for the Department of Health, Social Services Inspectorate, *Adoption Now – Messages from Research* (1999) Chichester, Wiley, 42–44.

Additional reading

P. Harris, *In search of belonging: reflections by transracially adopted people* (2006) London, BAAF.

N. Lowe and M. Murch, *The plan for the child, Adoption or long-term fostering* (2002) London, BAAF.

P. Moffar and J. Thoburn, 'Outcomes of permanent family placement for children of minority ethnic origin' (2001) 6 *Child and Family Social Work*, 13.

M. Owen, 'Single-person adoption: For and Against' (1994) 8 *Children and Society*, 151.

T. Patel, C. Williams and P. Marsh, 'Identity, race, religion an adoption: the public and legal view' (2004) 28 *Adoption and Fostering*, 8.

D. Quinton, A. Rushton, C. Dance and D. Mayes, *Joining New Families: A Study of Adoption and Fostering in Middle Childhood* (1998) Chichester, Wiley.

J. Thoburn, L. Norford and S. Rashid, *Permanent Family Placement for Children of Minority Ethnic Origin* (2000) London, Jessica Kingsley.

INDEX

Page references to Figures or Tables are in *italic* print. References to publications beginning with 'A' or 'The' will be filed under the first significant word.

D

H